Environmental Law

Emmanuel Onyeabor

Environmental Law

International and Regional African Perspectives on Law and Management

Springer

Emmanuel Onyeabor
Department of International and Comparative Law, Faculty of Law
University of Nigeria
Nsukka, Nigeria

ISBN 978-3-031-68958-1 ISBN 978-3-031-68956-7 (eBook)
https://doi.org/10.1007/978-3-031-68956-7

This Springer imprint is published by the registered company Springer Nature Switzerland AG
The registered company address is: Gewerbestrasse 11, 6330 Cham, Switzerland

Dedication
To my children—Ifechukwu, Ebubechukwu and Adaeze—for all their love, support and inspiration

Preface

There is a growing need for text materials on environmental law that integrate environmental issues, principles and policies in one text for the benefit of an array of practitioners in the field of environmental studies, in general, and environmental law, in particular. The text is on law and the environment with reference to legislation, as well as on environmental management. The book is a one-stop shop, in that it discusses various principles, theories and liabilities for damage to various environmental media as well as legislative provisions for the protection of the environmental media. The book also discusses various control and remedial approaches to pollution and the degradation of the environment.

By way of introducing the subject matter, the book firstly discusses the understanding of environmental law in Part I, touching on such issues as the concept of environment, the factors threatening the environment, the need to protect the environment and the concept and scope of environmental law. Also discussed as aspects of Part I are sources of environmental law, both domestic and international. Theories and concepts in environmental legislation zeroing on such issues like free-market environmentalism, the Coase theorem, environmental Kuznets theory, command and control, emission trading and environmental legislation, the concept of sustainability and economic development, market-based concepts in environmental legislation and the concept of strict and absolute liability are also discussed as part of the introductory aspect of the book.

Various environmental media are also discussed. Emphasis is on international law principles establishing standards in environmental legislation, the tenets of environmental rights and waste management strategies. Where an environmental damage has occurred, what remedies are available to the victims? The discussion on this centred on the nature of liabilities for environmental damage under international and national legal regimes and remedies for redressing environmental damage.

Finally, the nature and extent of the marine environment, the control of pollution and damage to the marine environment as well as liability and compensation for pollution damage to the marine environment are also discussed. The main idea behind the book is to set out, in one volume, a text on environmental law that will serve as a reference guide to practitioners, teachers, the judiciary and students who are interested in trending issues in both environmental law and environmental management.

The book, it is hoped, will serve a wide range of users: practitioners in the field of environmental studies, particularly practitioners in the field of environmental law; corporate bodies; policymakers; judges as well as students in the field of environmental studies and law; and all others who may be interested in environmental issues, principles, policies and law.

Nsukka, Nigeria
23 September 2023

Emmanuel Onyeabor

Acknowledgements

I am indebted to my family, friends, colleagues and students at the Faculty of Law, University of Nigeria, Enugu Campus. Without their help and encouragement, the publication of this book would not have been possible.

I appreciate the kind motivation and support of Professors Ifeoma Enemo, Edith Nwosu, Joy Ezeilo, Miriam Anozie, Obiajlu Nnamuchi and Edwin Ezike. I am also indebted in various ways to Rev. Fr. Anthony Nnaji, Ndubuisi, Uchenna, Judith, Chinenye and Ifeoma. I am eternally grateful to others, who are too numerous to mention. I would also like to thank all those who proofread the manuscripts at various stages for their useful ideas and input.

Most importantly, my thanks and appreciation to God the Almighty for His guidance and for the successful publication of this book.

Contents

Part II Management and Control of Pollution of the Environmental Media

Part IV Pollution Damage and the Marine Environment

About the Author

Emmanuel Onyeabor is currently a lecturer in the Department of International and Comparative Law at the Faculty of Law, University of Nigeria, where he teaches Planning Law, Environmental Law and Climate Change Law and Policy. He holds the following academic qualifications: B.Ed (Hons.) in Geography (UNIPORT), M. Sc (Development Planning) (UNIPORT), M.Sc (Environmental Management) (ESUT), LL.B (Hons.) (Nig), LL.M (Environmental Rights) (Nig) and Ph.D (Environmental Law and Policy (Nig), BL.

Abbreviations

ACE	Affordable Clean Energy
AfCLR	African Commission Law Report
AML	Anti-Money Laundering Laws and Regulations
ARA	African Refiners and Distributors Association
BOPC	International Convention on Civil Liability for Bunker Oil Pollution Damage (the Bunker Oil Convention)
BP	British Petroleum
BSER	Best system of emission reduction
CAP	Chapter
CAT	Climate change tracker
CITES	Convention on International Trade on Endangered Species
CLC	International Convention on Civil Liability for Oil Pollution Damage
CRAMRA	Convention on the Regulation of Antarctic Mineral Resource Activities
CWA	Clean Water Act of USA 1977
DDT	Dichlorodiphenyltrichloroethane
DOJ	US Department of Justice
DPR	Department of Petroleum Resources
EEZ	Exclusive economic zone
EIA	Environmental impact assessment
EIA	Environmental Investigation Agency
ELNI	Environmental Law Network International
EPA	US Environmental Protection Agency
ERGP	Economic Recovery and Growth Plan
ESP	Economic Sustainability Plan
EFT	Enhanced Transparency Framework
Euro (€)	Euro (currency of the European Union)
FAO	Food and Agriculture Organization

FFr	French francs (French currency)
FREL	Forest reference emission level
GESAMP	Joint Group of Experts on the Scientific Aspects of Marine Environmental Protection
GHGs	Greenhouse gases
GI WACAF	Global Initiative for West, Central and Southern Africa
GPA	Global Programme of Action for the Protection of the Marine Environment from Land-Based Activities
GST	Global stocktake
GT	Gross tonnage
HFO	Higher fuel oil
HNS	International Convention on Liability and Compensation for Damage in Connection with the Carriage of Hazardous and Noxious Substances by Sea
HWSCPA	Harmful Wastes (Special Criminal Provisions etc) Act
IAEA	International Atomic Energy Agency
ICJ	International Court of Justice
IFO	Intermediate fuel oil
ILC	International Law Commission
ILS	Israeli shekel (Israeli currency)
IMO	International Maritime Organization
INDC	Intended nationally determined contribution
IOPC	International Oil Pollution Compensation Funds
IPIECA	International Petroleum Industry Environmental Conservation Association
ISA	International Seabed Authority
ITMO	International Transferred Mitigation Outcomes
ITOPF	International Tanker Owners Pollution Federation Limited
IUCN	International Union for Conservation of Nature
KES	Kenyan shilling
KRW	Korean won (Korean currency)
LFN	Laws of the Federation of Nigeria
LLMC	Convention on Limitation of Liability for Maritime Claims, 1976, as modified by the 1996 Protocol
LPFO	Low pour fuel oil
LTV	Nigeria's Long-Term Vision
LULUCF	Land use, land-use change and forestry
MAIB	Marine Accident Investigation Branch
MARPOL	International Convention for Prevention of Pollution from Ships
MDO	Marine diesel oil
MGO	Marine gas oil
MTNDP	Medium-Term National Development Plan
NAAQS	National Ambient Air Quality Standards
NAS	National Academy of Science

NASPACCN	National Adaptation Strategy and Plan of Action on Climate Change for Nigeria
NCCC	National Council on Climate Change
NCCP	National Climate Change Policy
NCCP-RS	National Climate Change Policy and Response Strategy
NDC	Nationally determined contribution
NESREA	National Environmental Standards and Regulations Enforcement Agency
NFWF	National Fish and Wildlife Foundation
NGN (₦)	Nigerian naira (Nigerian currency)
NIIMP	National Integrated Infrastructure Master Plan
NIMASA	Nigerian Maritime Administration and Safety Agency
NNPC	Nigerian National Petroleum Corporation
NOSDRA	National Oil Spill Detection and Response Agency
NURPA	Nigerian Urban and Regional Planning Act
OECD	Organisation for Economic Co-operation and Development
ONWA	Oil in Navigable Waters Act
OPRC	International Convention on Oil Pollution Preparedness, Response and Cooperation
OSTI	US Department of Energy Office of Scientific and Technical Information
P&I clubs	Protection and indemnity associations
PAHs	Polycyclic aromatic hydrocarbons
PCBs	Polychlorinated biphenyls
PCIJ	Permanent Court of International Justice
PPMC	Pipelines and Product Marketing Company
PSIA	Post-spill impact assessment
Pts	Pesetas (Spanish currency)
RECIEL	Review of European Community and International Law
REDD	Mitigation measures related to 'Reducing Emissions from Deforestation and forest Degradation'
REDD+	Conservation, Sustainable Management of Forests and Enhancement of Forest Carbon Stocks
RUB	Russian rouble (Russian currency)
SDC	Seabed Disputes Chamber
SDR(s)	Special drawing right(s)
SOLAS	International Convention for the Safety of Life at Sea
STOPIA	Small Tanker Oil Pollution Indemnification Agreement
TAPAA	Trans-Alaska Pipeline Authorization Act
TBT	Tributylin
TOPIA	Tanker Oil Pollution Indemnification Agreement
TTC	Total Transport Corporation
TZHC	Tanzanian High Court
UK	United Kingdom

UN	United Nations
UNCAC	United Nations Convention Against Corruption
UNCC	United Nations Compensation Commission
UNCED	United Nations Conference on Environment and Development
UNCLOS	United Nations Convention on Law of the Sea
UNDP	United Nations Development Programme
UNECE	United Nations Economic Commission for Europe
UNEP	United Nations Environment Programme
UNESCO	United Nations Education, Scientific and Cultural Organisation
UNFCCC	United Nations Framework Convention on Climate Change
UNODC	United Nations Office on Drugs and Crime
UN-REDD	United Nations collaborative initiative on Reducing Emissions from Deforestation and forest Degradation (REDD) in developing countries
UNRIAA	United Nations Reports of International Arbitral Award
UNTOC	United Nations Against Transnational Organised Crime
US$/USD	United States dollar
WIM	Warsaw International Mechanism
WHO	World Health Organisation
WMO	World Meteorological Organization

List of Tables

Part I
Understanding Environmental Law

Chapter 1
Introduction

Abstract Man is both creature and moulders of his environment, which gives him physical sustenance and affords him the opportunity for intellectual, moral, social and spiritual growth. In the long and tortuous evolution of the human race on this planet a stage has been reached when, through the rapid acceleration of science and technology, man has acquired the power to transform his environment in countless ways and on an unprecedented scale. Both aspects of man's environment, the natural and the man-made, are essential to his well-being and to the enjoyment of basic human rights the right to life itself (Stockholm Declaration (1972), Preamble, para 1). This chapter focuses generally on the concept and scope of environment, discusses factors threatening the environment, the need to protect the environment as well as the concept of pollution. The chapter also discusses the concept and scope of environmental law. These are basic concepts that lay the foundation to the issues that are discussed in subsequent chapters

1.1 Concept and Scope of the Environment

1.1.1 Concept of Environment

"Environment" is a very comprehensive term. It includes within its ambit a wide variety of phenomena. It is a dynamic term that may be used to describe a limited area on one hand, and the entire planet on the other. The term environment may be perceived with different connotations. There are numerous definitions of the term as provided by different national and international legal instruments. Generally, environment includes the external conditions, resources, stimuli, etc. with which an organism interacts.[1]

The English-language term "environment" is borrowed from an ancient French word "environner," meaning to encircle; surround.[2] Most languages had to borrow

[1] Wilkinson (2002), p. 33.

[2] The Free Dictionary (2020).

E. Onyeabor, *Environmental Law*, https://doi.org/10.1007/978-3-031-68956-7_1

or invent new terms when concern emerged about the potential destruction of natural resources and processes on which life depended. The word "environment" has been defined variously.

Environment literally means surrounding and everything that affects an organism during its lifetime is collectively known as its environment.[3] In other words "Environment is sum total of water, air and land interrelationships among themselves and also with the human being, other living organisms and property."[4] It includes all the physical and biological surrounding and their interactions.[5]

A programme of the United Nations Education, Scientific and Cultural Organisation (UNESCO)[6] uses the term "biosphere" to designate the part of the universe where, according to present knowledge, all life is concentrated.[7] Webster's Dictionary[8] begins with a general definition of the environment, reflecting the original French meaning: "the circumstances, objects, or conditions by which one is surrounded." It continues with a more precise meaning: "the complex of physical, chemical, and biotic factors (such as climate, soil, and living things) that act upon an organism or an ecological community and ultimately determine its form and survival" to which it adds "the aggregate of social and cultural conditions that influence the life of an individual or community."[9] This last definition is very broad and brings problems such as traffic congestion, crime, and noise within the field of environmental protection.

"Environment" therefore means different things to different groups. This assertion, in the words of Olawuyi,[10] "reflects age-long contentions amongst scholars and practitioners on the appropriate aim, boundaries and operating parameters of environmental protection." According to him, generally, there are two different schools of thought on environment and environmental protection.

> While some scholars view the environment from an ecocentric and nature standpoint, others assign an anthropocentric/human-related connotation to the term environment. From an anthropocentric or human point of view, the environment has been defined as the relationship of human beings with water, air, land and all biological forms; the combination of elements whose inter-relationships make up the settings, surroundings, and conditions of life of the individuals and the society. From the eco-centric or nature standpoint, the environment is defined as the sum of all external conditions affecting the life, development and survival of an organism. It has also been described as the metaphor of life that provides ecological support for all organisms on earth. This means the source, support and the ingenious life-giving matrix for all living organisms.

[3] World Press (2020).

[4] Ibid.

[5] Ibid.

[6] Brabyn and Hadley (1988), p. 10.

[7] Ibid.

[8] Webster's Dictionary (2020).

[9] Ibid.

[10] Olawuyi (2015), p. 8.

Despite the different views expressed above, Olawuyi[11] posits that:

> an all-encompassing view of the environment, which includes both human and non-human elements. Both aspects have long lasting effects and desire equal attention, just as humans may find the earth unlivable if we have to live without the ecosystem; plants, human interests cannot also be sidelined in providing for nature since humans are inevitably in a better position to care for the environment.

1.1.2 *Scope of the Environment*

A legal definition of the word "environment" is important to delineate the scope of the subject matter, determine the application of legal rules and establish the extent of liability when harm occurs.

International legal instruments generally define "environment" broadly. Under a text of the European Community "environment" includes: "water, air and land and their interrelationship as well as relationships between them and any living organism."[12] To this end, the European Convention on Civil Liability for Damage Resulting from Activities Dangerous to the Environment (European Convention on Civil Liability)[13] contains comprehensive definitions. It provides as follows: For this Convention ... "Environment" includes:

(i) natural resources both abiotic and biotic, such as air, water, soil, fauna and flora and the interaction between the same factors;
(ii) property which forms part of the cultural heritage; and
(iii) the characteristic aspects of the landscape.[14]

The International Court of Justice[15] defines the environment to include a social dimension, stating that "the environment is not an abstraction, but represents the living space, the quality of life, and the very health of human beings, including generations unborn."

According to the Environment Act of New Zealand 1986,[16] environment includes:

(a) the ecosystems and their constituent parts including people and communities;
(b) all natural and physical resources;

---

[11] Ibid.

[12] European Union (2020).

[13] European Convention on Civil Liability (Council of Europe-ETS No. 150), Art. 2 (10).

[14] Ibid.

[15] Legality of the Threat or Use of Nuclear Weapons, Advisory Opinion, ICJ Report 1996, 241–242, para 29.

[16] New Zealand Environment Act of 1986, Public Act 1986 No. 127, s. 2.

(c) those physical qualities and characteristics of an area that contribute to people's appreciation of its pleasantness, aesthetic coherence, and cultural and recreational attributes; and
(d) the social, economic, aesthetic, and cultural conditions which affect the matters stated in paragraphs (a) to (c) or which are affected by those matters.

The Environment Protection Act of the United Kingdom 1990,[17] defines the "environment" as consisting "of all, or any, of the [media] the air, water and land; and the medium of air includes the air within buildings and the air within other natural or man-made structures above or below ground."

According to the International Law Institute (ILI), the environment must be considered as an indivisible whole, comprising the "biotic and abiotic natural resources, notably air, water, land, fauna and flora and the interaction between these same factors."[18] Thus, the environment is essential to every human being. The quality of human life depends on the quality of the environment.[19]

At the domestic level, under the National Environmental Standards and Regulations Enforcement Agency (Establishment) (NESREA) Act 2007,[20] the word "environment" "includes water, air, land and all plants and human beings or animals living therein and the inter-relationship which exists among these or any of them."[21] To the Environmental Impact Assessment Act (EIA Act)[22] "environment" means the components of the Earth, and includes:

(a) land, water and air, including all layers of the atmosphere;
(b) all organic and inorganic matter and living organisms; and
(c) the interacting natural systems that include components referred to in paragraphs (a) and (b).[23]

Again, according to the provisions of the Water Resources Act of Nigeria 1993[24] "environment" includes all aspects of the surroundings of man whether affecting him as an individual or in his social and aesthetic factors of those surroundings.[25]

The term "environment" therefore could be said to cover "all those elements which in their complex inter-relationships form the framework, setting and living

[17] Ibid., s. 1(2).

[18] International Law Institute, Resolution of 4 September 1997, Art. 1.

[19] SERAP v. Federal Republic of Nigeria (2012), Judgment No. ECW/CCJ/JUD/18/12, ECOWAS (14 Dec. 2012) at 25, para 100.

[20] Enacted in 2007 vide Government Notice No. 61, Act No. 25, 2007, Federal Republic of Nigeria Official Gazette No. 92, Vol. 94, 31 July 2007 and amended in 2018 vide Government Notice No. 106, Act No. 26 2018, Federal Republic of Nigeria Official Gazette No. 146, Vol. 105, 14 November 2018.

[21] NESREA Act 2007, s. 37.

[22] Cap E12 Laws of the Federation of Nigeria (LFN) 2004.

[23] Ibid., s. 61.

[24] Cap W2 LFN 2004.

[25] Ibid., s. 20.

conditions for mankind, by their very existence or by virtue of their impact."[26] It therefore refers to a limited area or encompassing the entire planet, including the atmosphere and stratosphere.

Thus, a more expansive view is that the scope of the word "environment" includes all the elements of the physical and biological world (including humans), and the interactions between them. These elements may be categorised as ecosystem goods and services. Goods, meaning the actual natural resources themselves (flora, fauna, soil mineral, air, water); while services, include the harvestable products (crops, timber), processes essential to sustain the provision of these resources (nutrient cycles, climate patterns, flooding control) and aesthetic and cultural benefits of ecosystems (recreation).[27]

From the above discussions, although scholars and environmentalists have defined the word "environment" from different perspectives, in all one thing is clear, the environment is made up of different component parts that interact with one and another that must work harmoniously together.

1.2 Factors Threatening the Environment

The environment is humanity's life support system. It supplies us with air, water and food for our bodily survival and with raw materials and energy for housing, drugs, transportation and manufactured goods. Over the years, factors that threatened, and continue to threaten the environment are epochal in nature. From the pre-historic era to the era of increased population and proliferation of industrial processes up to modern times, various human activities and developmental strides have in one way or another threatened the environment.

1.2.1 Man and His Environment in the Pre-historic Era

Over the years man has had some effects upon the natural environment since the Palaeolithic era during which the ability to generate fire was acquired. In the Iron Age, the use of tooling led to the practice of metal grinding on a small scale and resulted in minor accumulations of discarded material probably easily dispersed without too much impact. Human wastes would have polluted rivers or water sources to some degree. However, these effects as could be expected were predominantly dwarfed by the natural world and the Earth's ability for self-purification as its carrying capacity had not been exceeded. Thus, for thousands of years man had

[26] Larsson and Assia (2019).

[27] Olawuyi (2018), pp. 272–273.

altered his environment through hunting, the use of fire and agriculture, but most of the changes had been gradual, reversible and highly localised.[28]

The first advanced civilisations of China, Egypt, Persia, Greece and Rome increased the use of water for primitive industrial processes. Over time, there was an increase in the use of forged metals[29] and the use of wood and peat for fire.[30] These activities had some impacts on the environment. Still, at this time the scale of higher activity did not disrupt ecosystems or greatly alter air or water quality, or cause a high degree of land degradation. The Dark Ages and early Middle Ages were a great boon for the environment, in that industrial activity fell, and population levels did not grow rapidly. Towards the end of the Middle Ages populations grew and concentrated more within cities, creating pockets of readily evident contamination. In certain places, air pollution levels were recognisable as health issues, and pollution in population centres was a serious medium for disease transmission from untreated human waste.[31]

Since travel and widespread information were less common, there did not exist a more general context than that of local consequences in which to consider pollution. Foul air would have been considered a nuisance and wood, or eventually, coal burning produced smoke, which in sufficient concentrations could be a health hazard in proximity to living quarters. Septic contamination or poisoning of a clean drinking water source was very easily fatal to those who depended on it, especially if such a resource was rare. Superstitions predominated and the extent of such concerns would probably have been little more than a sense of moderation and an avoidance of obvious extremes.[32]

1.2.2 Era of Increased Population and Proliferation of Industrial Processes

The gradual increase in populations and the proliferation of basic industrial processes saw the emergence of a civilisation that began to have a much greater collective impact on its surroundings. It was to be expected that the beginnings of environmental awareness would occur in the more developed cultures, particularly in the densest urban centres. The first medium warranting official policy measures in the emerging Western world would be the most basic: the air we breathe.[33] Thus, King Edward 1 of England banned the burning of sea coal by proclamation in London in 1272, after its smoke had become a problem. However, the fuel was so

[28] Strahler and Strahler (1977), p. 45.

[29] For forging of hunting and farming implements as well as for implements for war.

[30] For bathing and heating as well as for other purposes.

[31] Strahler and Strahler (1977), p. 35.

[32] Ibid., 36.

[33] Ibid.

common in England that this earliest of names for it was acquired because it could be carted away from some shores by the wheelbarrow. Air pollution would continue to be a problem there, especially later during the Industrial Revolution, and extending into the recent past with the Great Smog of 1952. This same city also recorded one of the earlier extreme cases of water quality problems with the Great Stink on the Thames of 1858, which led to the construction of the London sewerage system soon afterward.[34]

It was the industrial revolution that gave birth to environmental pollution, as we know it today. The emergence of great factories and the consumption of immense quantities of coal and other fossil fuels gave rise to unprecedented air pollution and the large volume of industrial chemical discharges added to the growing load of untreated human waste. Heavy metals such as lead, and mercury have a role in geochemical cycles and they occur naturally. These metals may also be mined and, depending on their processing, may be released disruptively in large concentrations into an environment they had previously been absent from. Just as the effect of the anthropogenic release of these metals into the environment may be considered "polluting," similar environmental impacts could also occur in some areas due to either autochthonous or historically "natural" geochemical activity.[35]

1.2.3 *Era from the Industrial Revolution*

Public awareness that the environment could not absorb limitless amounts of waste, therefore, came with the Industrial Revolution. By the latter part of the nineteenth century, many industrial areas were experiencing severe air pollution caused by the burning of coal to run mills and machinery. The quantities of fly ash, smoke, carbon and sulphur gases, and other wastes had become too great for local environments – like those of London and Pittsburgh –to disperse rapidly. Similarly, industrial effluents and sewage were polluting river systems. Not until after World War II, however, was pollution generally viewed as more than a nuisance that blackened buildings and sullied streams, i.e., as a pervasive threat to human health.[36]

By the 1960s the threat had become great enough, many believed, to challenge the integrity of the ecosystem and the survival of numerous organisms including humans. Population explosion, industrial expansion, and burgeoning truck and automobile use were producing wastes in such gigantic quantities that natural dispersing and recycling processes could not keep pace. Exacerbating the problem was the appearance of new substances that degraded with extreme slowness or not at all: plastics, synthetic fibres, detergents, synthetic fertilisers, synthetic organic pesticides such as DDT, synthetic industrial chemicals such as polychlorinated

[34] Enger and Smith (2002).

[35] Ibid. p. 19.

[36] Strahler and Strahler (1977), p. 37.

biphenyls (PCBs) and wastes from their manufacture. Thus, waterways and dumps festered with disease-breeding garbage. Industrial wastes created corrosive smog and, with municipal wastes, polluted inland and marine waters, including drinking supplies. Automobile emissions choked urban and suburban communities.[37] Pesticides and PCBs poisoned fish and birds. These conditions, persisting into the 1970s as year-by-year waste output increased, evoked demand in many nations, and on the part of the United Nations, for worldwide pollution abatement.[38]

1.2.4 Era of Nuclear Science and Industrial Disasters

The development of nuclear science introduced a new form of pollution, radioactive contamination, which can remain lethally radioactive for hundreds of thousands of years. Lake Karachay, named by the Worldwatch Institute[39] as the "most polluted spot" on Earth, served as a disposal site for the then Union of Soviet Socialist Republics (USSR or the Soviet Union) throughout the 1950s and 1960s. Nuclear weapons continued to be tested in the Cold War, sometimes near inhabited areas, especially in the earlier stages of their development. The toll on the worst affected populations and the growth since then in understanding about the critical threat to human health posed by radioactivity has also been a prohibitive complication associated with nuclear power. Although extreme care is practiced in that industry, the potential for disaster suggested by incidents such as those at Three Mile Island in 1979 and Chernobyl in 1986 poses a lingering spectre of public mistrust. One legacy of nuclear testing before most forms were banned had significantly raised levels of background radiation.[40]

International catastrophes such as the wreck of the Amoco Cadiz oil tanker off the coast of Brittany in 1978 and the Bhopal industrial disaster in 1984 have demonstrated the universality of such events and the scale on which efforts to address them needed to engage. The borderless nature of the atmosphere and oceans inevitably resulted in the implication of pollution on a planetary level with the issue of global warming. Most recently, the term persistent organic pollutant (POP) has come to describe a group of chemicals such as PBDEs and PFCs among others which, though their effects remain somewhat less well understood owing to a lack of experimental data, have been detected in various ecological habitats far removed from industrial activity such as the arctic, demonstrating bioaccumulation after only a relatively brief period of widespread use.[41]

---

[37] Adinna (2001), p. 27.

[38] Hamblin (2008).

[39] Worldwatch Institute (2020).

[40] Carson (2002).

[41] Enger and Smith (2002), p. 23.

Again, bad bouts of local pollution helped increase consciousness. For instance, pollution began to draw major public attention in the United States between the mid-1950s and early 1970s. The National Environmental Policy Act in 1969 and the establishment of the Environmental Protection Agency the following year was a turning point in federal regulatory policy. Since then, Congress has also passed the Clean Air Act (1970), the Clean Water Act (1972), the Noise Control Act (1979), and the Comprehensive Environmental Response, Compensation, and Liability Act (1980), more commonly known as the Superfund Act, which created a fund to clean up hazardous waste sites. The dumping of PCB in the Hudson River resulted in a ban by the Environmental Protection Agency on the consumption of its fish in 1974. Long-term dioxin contamination at Love Canal starting in 1947 became a national news story in 1978 and led to the Superfund legislation of 1980. Legal proceedings in the 1990s helped bring to light Chromium-6 releases in California.[42]

In Nigeria, it was not until the "infamous" Koko dump of toxic wastes in 1988 that galvanised the government of Nigeria to enact two legislations on environmental protection.[43] This also led to the establishment of the Federal Environmental Protection Agency in 1988, and subsequently, the Federal Ministry of Environment in 1999.

1.3 Need to Protect the Environment

We see around us growing evidence of man-made harm in many regions of the Earth: dangerous levels of pollution in water, air, earth and living beings; major and undesirable disturbances to the ecological balance of the biosphere; destruction and depletion of irreplaceable resources; and gross deficiencies, harmful to the physical, mental and social health of man, in the man-made environment, particularly in the living and working environment.[44]

The growing evidence of global and local pollution and an increasingly informed public over time have given rise to environmentalism and the environmental movement, which generally seek to limit human impact on the environment. Industry and concerned citizens have battled for decades over the significance of various forms of pollution. Salient parameters of these disputes were whether:

i) a given pollutant affects all people or is simply a genetically vulnerable set.
ii) an effect is only specific to certain species.

---

[42] Beck (2020).

[43] In 1988, a shipload of substances, later identified as containing toxic and hazardous substances, were dumped at Koko Port in Delta State, Nigeria. Although the public was outraged by this, there was no law under which the perpetrators would have been tried. This led to the promulgation of the Harmful Wastes (Special Criminal Provisions) Act and the Federal Environmental Protection Agency (Establishment) Act, all in 1988 by the then Military Government of Nigeria.

[44] Stockholm Declaration 1972, Preamble, para 3.

iii) the effect is simple, or whether it causes linked secondary and tertiary effects, especially on biodiversity.
iv) an effect will only be apparent in the future and is presently negligible.
v) the threshold for harm is present.
vi) the pollutant is of direct harm or is a precursor.
vii) employment or economic prosperity will suffer if the pollutant is abated.[45]

Under natural conditions processes including photosynthesis and respiration, nitrogen fixation and denitrification, evaporation and precipitation, and diffusion by wind and water action continually recycle organic and certain inorganic materials in the biosphere. However, the introduction of massive quantities of waste matter at any point in the bio-system may "overload" it, disrupting the natural recycling mechanisms, and thus resulting in a disturbance in natural processes. Disturbances of natural processes are clearly shown when you look at human interference in matter cycles, such as the hydrological cycle, phosphorus cycle, nitrogen cycle, sulphur cycle and carbon cycle, which have caused various environmental problems that are important issues today.[46] An understanding of how interference creates environmental problems is a pathway to deciding robust ways of tackling the environmental problems so created.

1.3.1 Human's Interference with the Hydrological Cycle

There are three ways in which humans cause environmental problems by interfering with the hydrological cycle. First, we remove large quantities of freshwater from rivers, lakes and groundwater supplies. In areas where great amounts of people use the water from groundwater supplies, groundwater may be fully depleted. This effect is enhanced by vegetation removal to create new farmland or underground mines, or to build roads. Second, because of vegetation removal, rainwater washes away and no longer infiltrates, so the groundwater supplies are not restored. In many cases, groundwater supplies will then be filled up with salt water from rivers and lakes. When groundwater is salinated, the entire area is influenced. Other effects also occur because of the removal of vegetation: the risk of flooding is enhanced, and soil erosion and land sliding increase. Finally, people change the quality of water, by adding nutrients and contaminants. This causes the ecological processes that usually purify the water to be disturbed.[47]

[45] Goudie (2013), p. 7.

[46] Allaby (2000), pp. 3–6.

[47] Allaby (2000), pp. 3–6.

1.3.2 Human's Interference with the Phosphorus Cycle

Humans also cause environmental problems by interfering with the phosphorus cycle. We remove phosphates in certain locations, to apply them on farmland as fertilisers. In these locations the phosphate supply is moving, causing phosphate levels of surrounding land-soils and groundwater to become too high. On farmland where phosphates are applied as fertilisers, plants do not absorb all phosphate. The phosphates end up in water and stream towards lakes and reservoirs, where they cause a phenomenon called eutrophication. Eutrophication means that the water is so rich in nutrients that it causes certain water plants, such as green algae, to grow extensively causing algae bloom. As a result, the oxygen supply in the water depletes, causing fish and other oxygen-dependent organisms to die and bacteria that are not oxygen-dependent to take over.[48]

Again, when people practice extensive wood chopping in forest areas, such as the tropical rain forest, phosphate supplies deplete, because most of the phosphate can be found in the ground under the trees in such areas. When the trees are removed the rain washes phosphates away, causing the ground to become unproductive. Phosphate supplies are restored very slowly because most phosphate in soils and water comes from weathering rocks and oceanic sediments.[49]

1.3.3 Human's Interference with the Nitrogen Cycle

Humans also cause environmental problems by interfering with the nitrogen cycle in several ways. During fuel combustion, various compounds are released, among which nitrogen oxides (NO_x). Nitrogen oxides react with oxygen in the air so that nitrous oxide gas (N_2O) is formed. Nitrous oxide is a greenhouse gas, which enhances the Earth's temperature when it is present in the atmosphere too extensively. It can also react with ozone in the atmosphere, so that the ozone layer is broken down. The ozone layer is a kind of shell around the Earth that consists entirely of ozone. This layer protects the Earth and all its life from damaging UV radiation. When the ozone layer is broken down, humans and animals can experience serious sunburns and skin cancer. Nitrogen dioxide may also react with hydrogen in the atmosphere, to form nitric acid (HNO_3). Nitric acid causes acid deposition, which can damage trees and marine ecosystems, due to increases in the pH of soil and water.[50]

Human activities are also responsible for shortages of nitrogen in certain locations. The shortages happen when humans remove nitrogen, to create fertilisers to apply on farmland. As a result, farmland becomes too rich in nutrients and other

[48] Pretty (2008), p. 3.

[49] Ibid.

[50] Adinna (2001), p. 32.

areas will suffer nitrogen shortages. Vegetation in these areas depletes. When people want to create new farmland, they often burn parts of forests, because the ground underneath these forests is very fertile. While the wood is burned more nitrogen dioxide escapes into the air and nutrients are removed from the ground.[51]

Today, human beings are responsible for the consistency of 90% of the sulphur salts that are found on Earth. These salts are mainly formed during industrial processes, such as coal combustion processes, petroleum refining processes and melting processes. Sulphur compounds, such as sulphuric acid, sulphur dioxide and hydrogen sulphide can cause acid deposition in water and soil. This phenomenon causes the pH of water and soil to fall, which can influence life in the soil and water and disturb natural processes.[52]

1.3.4 Human's Interference with the Carbon Cycle

In respect of the carbon cycle, human activities cause environmental problems by influencing the carbon cycle in two ways. First, the removal of forests has caused depletion in plants and trees that absorb carbon dioxide. Humans cause great carbon emissions to the atmosphere, which take place during industrial processes, such as coal and oil combustion. These processes serve the generation of energy. As a result of these effects, the carbon dioxide levels in the atmosphere have greatly increased. Between 1870 and 1990, carbon dioxide emissions into air have increased by 25%. The carbon dioxide levels in the air are now so high, that the uptake by plants and oceans is not fast enough.[53]

Carbon dioxide is a greenhouse gas. This means that increasing carbon dioxide levels in the air supports the greenhouse effect. The greenhouse effect is a term that is used for climate change on Earth, caused by greenhouse gases in the atmosphere. Too much carbon dioxide in the atmosphere can cause the Earth to warm up. This will in time cause all kinds of negative effects, such as melting ice from the Arctic causing floods on other continents, among other impacts.[54]

Furthermore, during the industrial revolution human beings used fossil fuels extensively, and are still using the same to date, for the generation of energy, as had been mentioned before. Since fossil fuels consist of dead organic matter it takes a very long time to restore the supplies. As a result of man's actions in the use of fossil fuel over the past decades fossil fuel supplies are in danger of being exhausted. These have made the need to protect the environment from pollution a serious issue.[55]

---

[51] Ibid., 32.

[52] Ehrlich and Holden (1974), p. 282.

[53] Ibid.

[54] Goudie (2013), p. 216.

[55] Ibid.

1.4 Concept of Pollution and Its Sources

1.4.1 *Concept of Pollution*

What is Pollution one may be tempted to ask. The term "pollution," can be defined as a chemical or physical agent in an inappropriate location or concentration.[56] It is an unfavourable alteration of our surroundings, wholly or partly, as a result of man's actions through direct or indirect effects of changes in energy patterns, radiation levels, chemical constitution and abundance of organisms.[57]

"Pollution" means: "the release (into any environmental medium) from any process of substances which are capable of causing harm to man or any other living organisms supported by the environment."[58] In a report submitted in 1966 to the Federal Council for Science and Technology[59] environmental pollution was defined as:

> an undesirable change in physical, chemical or biological character of our air, land and water so that they may or will harmfully affect human life or that of other desirable species, our industrial process, living condition and cultural assets, or that may or will waste, deteriorate or completely damage our raw material resources.

The Royal Commission on Environment Pollution in the United Kingdom in its third report gave the following definition of the term "Pollution," namely: "The introduction by man into the environment of substances or energy liable to cause hazards to human health, harm to living resources and ecological systems, damage to structure or amenity or interference with legitimate uses of the environment."[60]

A working definition of pollution therefore would be "any material introduced into the environment above its normal 'background' levels as a result of human activity."[61] Therefore, pollution occurs when an amount of any substance or any form of energy is put into the environment at a rate faster than it can be dispersed or safely stored. The term "*pollution*" can refer to both artificial and natural materials that are created, consumed, and discarded in an unsustainable manner.[62]

Under the provisions of the National Environmental Standards Regulation and Enforcement Agency (Establishment) (NESREA Act 2007[63] "pollution" means

---

[56] Encyclopedia of Public Health (2006).

[57] Allaby (2000), pp. 3–6.

[58] Environment Protection Act of United Kingdom (1990), s. 1(3).

[59] Federal Council for Science and Technology (1966).

[60] Appannagari (2017).

[61] McShaffrey (2019).

[62] Britannica (2020).

[63] Enacted in 2007 vide Government Notice No. 61, Act No. 25 2007, Federal Republic of Nigeria Official Gazette No. 92, Vol. 94, 31 July 2007 and amended in 2018 vide Government Notice No. 106, Act No. 26 2018, Federal Republic of Nigeria Official Gazette No. 146, Vol. 105, 14 November 2018.

man-made or man-aided alteration or chemical, physical, or biological quality of the environment beyond acceptable limits. . . .[64]

These definitions imply that pollution injects into the environment pollutants that are of dire consequences to both the natural and human environment. Pollutants can be natural, such as volcanic ash. They can also be created by various aspects of human activities. Pollutants damage the quality of air, water, and land.[65] The problems associated with pollutants from activities are multifarious. For instance, pollutants from the activities in the oil industry may cause flooding and coastal erosion, sedimentation and siltation, degradation and depletion of water and coastal resources, land degradation, pollution of the air, land subsidence, biodiversity depletion, noise and light pollution, low agricultural production, health problems and socio-economic problems.[66]

Again, pollution may create muddy landscapes, poison soils and waterways, or kill plants and animals. Humans are also regularly harmed by pollution. Long-term exposure to air pollution, for example, can lead to chronic respiratory disease, lung cancer and other diseases. Toxic chemicals that accumulate on top predators can make some species unsafe to eat. More than one billion people lack access to clean water and 2.4 billion do not have adequate sanitation, putting them at risk of contracting deadly diseases.[67]

Perhaps because of all these and many more, the Stockholm Declaration 1972 enjoins that "States shall take all possible steps to prevent pollution of the seas by substances that are liable to create hazards to human health, to harm living resources and marine life, to damage amenities or to interfere with other legitimate uses of the sea."[68]

1.4.2 Sources of Pollution

The sources of pollution are varied. Natural sources include those that are not directly under human control, such as volcanoes, which spew forth sulphur oxides and particles; and those sources that people could avoid: such as groundwater with naturally high levels of arsenic, which had caused poisoning in Bangladesh and Taiwan. All human activities have the potential to pollute the environment by contaminating air, water, food, or soil, The earliest human pollution-control efforts dealt with the avoidance of diseases caused by contamination of water and food by human excreta and with the control of smoke from fires used for cooking and heating. Sanitary engineering to manage human wastes remains a central public

[64] NESREA Act 2007, s. 37.

[65] National Geographic (2020).

[66] Human Rights Watch (1999), p. 59.

[67] World Wildlife (2020).

[68] Stockholm Declaration 1972, Principle 7.

health need. Indoor air pollution due to the use of wood and fossil fuels in poorly ventilated residences also remains a major source of exposure to pollutants and a cause of respiratory disease in much of the world.[69]

Sources of pollution can be considered under the heading of the four major human activity sectors: industry, energy, transportation, and agriculture. With the marked increase in human population and the industrialisation of much of the globe has come a whole new set of pollutants. Scientific advances based upon the understanding of the chemical and physical forces underlying nature have led to new processes and new products that have transformed society and have had a major positive impact on human health. However, these industrial activities also result in air and water emissions and contamination of the soil and food as by-products of the processes involved in manufacture. The products themselves may be the means by which pollutants are distributed to the general population, such as lead poisoning through the use of lead in house paints.[70]

Understanding the effects of pollutants requires understanding how pollutants change following their release from a source, and how they can have an effect many kilometres from their sources. For example, there are no significant direct emitters of air pollutant ozone. Rather, this major component of oxidant smog is formed in the air through the action of sunlight on a mixture of nitrogen oxides and hydrocarbons coming from many different sources, primarily automobiles.[71] The precursors may have been emitted hundreds of kilometres upwind of where the ozone is eventually formed. Similarly, acid rain and other forms of particulate air pollution can be derived from atmospheric reactions of gaseous sulphur dioxide and nitrogen oxide precursors occurring many hundreds of miles downwind.

Agents released into the water can also undergo significant changes. For example, methylmercury, which is far more toxic than elemental mercury, is formed in water through the action of bacteria and makes its way into the food chain.[72] The dumping of inorganic mercury from a single chloralkali plant in Minamata Bay, Japan, led to the contamination of fish with methyl mercury and to over a hundred deaths and thousands of people being affected by what is known as Minamata disease. In Minamata Bay, Japan mercury waste from Chisso Corporation, a plastic manufacturing company in 1966 afflicted 397 persons with mercury poison, resulting in 60 deaths, $3.8 million was paid as compensation to 45 survivors and the company Executives charged with "Professional negligence resulting in death."[73]

There is also a global air circulation of metals, such as mercury, and of persistent organic pollutants, such as PCBs, which tends to carry these agents toward the Arctic where they often bioaccumulation.[74]

---

[69] Appannagari (2017).

[70] Ehrlich and Holden (1974), p. 282.

[71] Adinna (2001), p. 35.

[72] Travnikov and Rozovskya (2014), pp. 1047–1063.

[73] The History and the Present of Minamata Disease (2020).

[74] Travnikov and Rozovskya (2014), pp. 1047–1063.

A transition is occurring in our understanding of the health effects of pollutants. It is now recognised that there are subtle health effects of environmental pollutants, such as endocrine disruption and neurobehavioral changes, for which newer toxicological paradigms are being developed. The unravelling of the human genome may provide a better understanding of the role of genetic susceptibility factors in response to pollution.[75]

Understanding the effects of pollutants on human health requires not only an understanding of the intrinsic hazard of the chemical or physical agent, but also the extent of human exposure. Local pathways within a community often determine exposure, such as whether drinking water comes from wells or surface sources or whether individuals consume vegetables grown in their backyards or brought to market from far away communities. Individual activities can also alter pollutant intake; exercise, for example, increases respiratory uptake of air pollutants. Health effects due to pollutants are heavily dependent upon susceptibility factors, including age, gender, and genetic predisposition.

All these environmental problems gave rise to the need to control human activities that impair the environment. This gave birth to environmental law.

1.5 Concept and Scope of Environmental Law

1.5.1 Concept of Environmental Law

Environmental law arose to strike a balance between encouraging investments and growth and the need to protect the environment from abuse, neglect and degradation and to preserve it for present and future generations.

Hitherto man's interest in harnessing nature for his development was seen largely in terms of its wealth-producing possibilities. Little, if any, thought was given to the longer terms of environmental implications of his wealth-creating activities. It is no longer acceptable to create wealth from the environment without consideration of the immediate and long-term effects that such activities may have on the environment. To tackle environmental problems so created man developed technical solutions to remediate his past actions and, hopefully, prevent and control future environmental degradation. To harness man's technical capabilities appropriately, and apply them decisively, a strong legal framework is necessary. This legal framework is called environmental law.

While the environment is defined as the conditions and influences of the place in which an organism lives, the concept of environmental law refers to the integrated rules and principles, that is, legal norms, the purpose of which is to achieve environmental conservation.[76]

[75] Pothirat et al. (2019).

[76] Crystal (2019).

Environmental law, therefore, is a body of law, which is a system of complex and interlocking statutes, common law, treaties, conventions, regulations and policies which seek to protect the natural environment which may be affected, impacted or endangered by human activities. Some environmental laws regulate the quantity and nature of impacts of human activities: for example, setting allowable levels of pollution or requiring permits for potentially harmful activities. Other environmental laws are preventive in nature and seek to assess the possible impacts before human activities can occur.[77] It is therefore part of the law discipline that can be seen as a system of statutes, regulations, guidelines, factual conclusions and case-specific judicial and administrative interpretations which relate one to another.[78]

1.5.2 *Scope of Environmental Law*

Environmental law is regarded as an organised way of using all the laws in our legal system such as the Constitution, Statutes, Regulations, Rules of Evidence and Procedures, Judicial interpretations and Common Law Tort, International Treaties, Conventions and obligations and all other laws which are being applied towards achieving environmental ends,[79] to minimise, prevent, punish and remedy the consequences of actions which damage or threaten the environment, public health and public safety.

With the advent of environmental law, it became necessary to harness various statutes, regulations, guidelines and standards to develop new approaches, new concerns and new awareness aimed at controlling, reducing, preventing, remediation and, at times, punishing environmental degradation. This gave birth to environmental laws. They consist of Statutes, Regulations, Standards, Guidelines, Institutions and Administrative procedures adapted to control or prevent and punish activities damaging to the environment within an entity. They, therefore, form part of the mechanisms adapted to control and prevent environmental problems.

Broad definitions and the fact that all human activities have an impact on the environment make it difficult to establish the limits of environmental law as an independent legal field; indeed, they imply the integration of environmental protection into all areas of law and policy.

Environmental law thus sprang from the understanding that the environment determines the form and survival of each organism and community; thus, national, regional, and international efforts must be taken to ensure the continued viability of the planet and the sustainability of its myriad species, through holistic approaches such as integrated or ecosystem protection. Thus, "in order to achieve a more rational

[77] Vidyavihar (2022).

[78] Sullivan (1999), p. 95.

[79] Environmental ends means the creation of a benign, friendly, aesthetically pleasing and undegraded environment.

management of resources and thus to improve the environment, States should adopt an integrated and coordinated approach to their development planning so as to ensure that development is compatible with the need to protect and improve the environment for the benefit of their population."[80]

The whole idea of environmental law is that "man has the fundamental right to freedom, equality and adequate conditions of life, in an environment of a quality that permits a life of dignity and well being and he bears a solemn responsibility to protect and improve the environment for present and the future generation."[81] This position re-echoed in 1984 in a report by World Commission on Environment,[82] where the principle of sustainable development was enunciated. In that Report sustainable development was defined as "development that meets the needs of the present without compromising the ability of the future generations to meet their own needs."[83] This concept, "sustainable development," has become a buzz upon which environmental protection revolves around. The concept was reiterated under the Rio Declaration on Environment and Development 1992 (Rio Declaration 1992)[84] where it was stated that "the right to development must be fulfilled so as to equitably meet developmental and environmental needs of present and future generations."[85]

"This concept of living within environmental constraints underpins the International Union for Conservation of Nature (IUCN), United Nations Environment Programme (UNEP) and World Wide Fund for Nature (WWF) definition of sustainability: improving the quality of human life while living within the carrying capacity of supporting eco-systems."[86] The Earth Charter[87] goes beyond defining what sustainability is, and seeks to establish the values and direction needed to achieve it. It posits as follows:

> We must join together to bring forth a sustainable global society founded on respect for nature, universal human rights, economic justice, and a culture of peace. Towards this end, it is imperative that we, the peoples of Earth, declare our responsibility to one another, to the greater community of life, and to future generations.

[80] Stockholm Declaration (1972), Principle 13.

[81] Stockholm Declaration (1972), Principle 1.

[82] World Commission on the Environment and Development (WCED) (1987).

[83] Ibid.

[84] United Nations (1992).

[85] Rio Declaration (1992), Principle 3.

[86] The H C Coombs Policy Forum (2020).

[87] Earth Charter (2000).

1.6 Summary

The environment is humanity's life support system. It supplies us with air, water and food for our bodily survival and with raw materials and energy for housing, drugs, transportation and manufactured goods. Over the years, factors that threatened, and continuc to threaten the environment are epochal in nature. Right from the beginning of increased population growth to the proliferation of industrial processes and technological processes ushered in from the era of the Industrial Revolution humans had interfered with nature's hydrological cycle, the phosphorus cycle, the nitrogen cycle and even the carbon cycle creating pollution problems with its attendant consequences. An understanding of the nature of the environment and its relationship with humans is the first step in fashioning out how best to protect it, especially through the instrumentality of the law: environmental law.

Overall, environmental law is a complex and interlocking body of treaties, conventions, statutes, regulations, and common law that, very broadly, operate to regulate the interaction of humanity and the rest of the biophysical or natural environment, toward the purpose of reducing the impacts of human activity, both on the natural environment and on humanity itself.[88] Therefore, the purpose of environmental law is to prevent, minimise, remedy and punish actions that threaten or damage the environment and those that live in it.[89]

References

Adinna EN (2001) Environmental hazard and management. Snaaps, Enugu

Allaby M (2000) Basic of environmental science, 2nd edn. Routledge, London

Appannagari RR (2017) Environmental pollution causes and consequences: a study. North Asian Int Res J Soc Sci Humanit 3(8). ISSN: 2454-9827. https://www.nairjc.com. Accessed on 13 May 2023

Beck EC (2020) The love Canal Tragedy. https://www.archive.epa.gov/epa/aboutepa/love-canal. Accessed on 19 May 2023

Brabyn H, Hadley M (1988) Man belongs to the earth: international cooperation in environmental research, United Nations Education, Scientific and Cultural Organisation's (UNESCO) Man and the Biosphere Programme, 92-3-102547-3, 92-9089-007-x (spa), 7-200-01021-9 (chi). https://unesdoc.unesco.org/ark:/48223/pf0000080638. Accessed on 25 June 2023

Britannica (2020) Science. https://www.britannica.com/science. Accessed on 25 June 2023

Carson R (2002) In Enger and Smith: environmental science, a study of interrelationships, 8th edn. McGraw Hill, Boston

Crystal D (2019) Cambridge encyclopedia of English language, 3rd edn. Cambridge University, Cambridge. https://www.Cambridge.org. ISBN 978-1-108-42359-8. https://doi.org/10.1017/9781108528931

Duke University School of Law (2023) Environmental law research guides. https://www.law.duke.edu-libry/sites/env.pdf. Accessed on 6 May 2023

[88] Duke University School of Law (2023).

[89] Lumen Learning (2021).

Earth Charter (2000). http://www.earthcharterinaction.org/2000/10/the_earth_charter.html. Accessed on 30 June 2023. https://www.un.org/en/development/A/CONF.151/26 (Vol. I) Rio Declaration.pdf. Accessed on 14 May 2023
Ehrlich PR, Holden JP (1974) Human population and the global environment. Am Sci 62(3):282
Encyclopedia of Public Health (2006) Definitions, synonyms and much more. Answer. com HTML Document, 11 September 2006. Accessed on 20 July 2023
Enger ED, Smith BF (2002) Environmental science, a study of interrelationships, 8th edn. McGraw Hill, Boston
European Union (2020). http://www.eu.org/env. Accessed on 28 June 2023
Federal Council for Science and Technology (1966) Report on Nature of the Environment, Federal Council for Science and Technology, USA, 1966. https://books.google.com.ng/books/about/Waste_Management_and_Control.html?id=ImgrAAAAYAAJ&redir_esc=y. Accessed on 26 May 2023
Goudie A (2013) The human impact on the natural environment: past, present and future, 7th edn. Wiley-Blackwell, Oxford. ISBN 978-1-118-57657-1 (cloth) – ISBN 978-1-118-57658-8 (pbk.)
Hamblin JD (2008) Poison in the well: radioactive waste in the oceans at the dawn of the nuclear age. Rutgers University, New York
Human Rights Watch (1999) The price of oil: corporate responsibilities and human rights violations in Nigeria's oil producing communities. Human Rights Watch, New York
Larsson M, Assia (2019) Legal definitions of the environment and of environmental damage. October 2019. https://www.researchgate.net/publication/336315959_Legal_Definitions_of_the_Environment_and_of_Environmental_Damage. Accessed on 13 June 2023
Lumen Learning (2021) Environmental laws and regulations. https://www.lumenlearning.com. Accessed on 6 June 2023
McShaffrey D (2019) Leaders in environmental activism- pollution. Leadership 333, Adobe Acrobat Document, 19 October 2019
National Geographic (2020) Encyclopedia-pollution. https://www.nationalgeographic.org-encyclopedia-pollution. Accessed on 25 June 2023
Olawuyi DS (2015) Principles of Nigerian environmental law. Afe Babalola University, Ado Ekiti. ISBN 978-1-026832-30-2
Olawuyi DS (2018) Extractives industry law in Africa. Springer Nature, Switzerland. ISBN 978-3-319-97663-1 ISBN 978-3-319-97664-8 (eBook). https://doi.org/10.1007/978-3-319-97664-8
Pothirat C et al. (2019) Acute effects of air pollutants on daily mortality and hospitalizations due to cardiovascular and respiratory diseases. J Thoracic Dis 11(7). https://jtd.amegroups.com/article/view/30220/21811. Accessed on 18 May 2023
Pretty J (ed) (2008) Sustainable agriculture and food, Vol II Agriculture and Environment, Earthscan Reference Collection 2008, 3. ISBN 13.978-1-84407-408-2
Stockholm Declaration (1972) Declaration of the United Nations Conference on the Human Environment, preamble, para 1, UN Document A/CONF.48/14/Rev.1. https://www.un.org/en/conferences/environment/stockholm1972. Accessed on 14 May 2023
Strahler AH, Strahler AN (1977) Geography and Man's environment. John Wiley and Sons, New York
Sullivan TF (ed) (1999) Environmental law hand book, 15th edn. Government Institute, Rockville, Maryland
The Free Dictionary (2020) Environing-Definition of Environing. http://www.thefreedictionary.com. Accessed on 25 June 2023
The H C Coombs Policy Forum (2020) ANU College of Asia and the Pacific. http://coombs.anu.edu.au/~vern/caring/caring.html. Accessed on 30 June 2023
The History and the Present of Minamata Disease (2020). https://www.med.or.jp/englis/pdf/2006_03/112_118.pdf. Accessed on 28 June 2023
Travnikov BN, Rozovskya O (2014) Chemical and LLK physical transformations of mercury in the ocean: a review. Ocean Sci 10:1047–1063
United Nations (1992) Report of the United Nations Conference on Environment and Development

Vidyavihar S (2022) Introduction to environmental law and policy. https://cdem.somaiya.edu/media/pdf/Env. Accessed on 19 July 2023
Webster's Dictionary (2020). http://www.webster-dictionary.org. Accessed on 25 Jan 2020
Wilkinson D (2002) Environment and law. Routledge, London. eBook ISBN 9780203994443. https://doi.org/10.4324/9780203994443
World Commission on the Environment and Development (WCED) (1987) Our common future. Oxford University, Oxford
World Press (2020) Definition of environment. https://sudarshan800.files.wordpress.com/2016/03/our-environment.pdf. Accessed on 13 June 2023
World Wildlife (2020). https://www.worldwildlife.org/threats/pollution. Accessed on 25 June 2023
Worldwatch Institute (2020). https://www.worldwatch.org/env-policy. Accessed on 26 June 2023

Chapter 2
Sources of Environmental Law

Abstract Nations have to grapple with environmental pollution abatement within the context of their national laws, and at times within the context of international environmental agreements. The need for these laws arose on the realisation that the environment is the most formidable source of national and international development and should be protected from damage, destruction and annihilation in order to enthrone a decent, benign, disease free and aesthetically pleasing environment. This chapter focuses on the international law as a source of environmental law with other sources at the national levels in fashioning out national legislation on environmental protection. Nigeria is used as the main jurisdiction on the applicability of international law and other sources that can readily blend in enacting laws on environmental protection, The choice of Nigeria is on the premise that environmental legislation in most African countries take the same part of a blend of international law and some principles and concepts inherited from their colonial past.

2.1 International Law as a Source of Environmental Law

2.1.1 Introduction

From the field of international law sprang international environmental law which has formed a veritable source of national environmental law. International environmental law has rapidly expanded in recent decades to encompass many issues of fundamental concern to international law scholars and practitioners, environmental lawyers, public officials and civil society. International environmental law aims to protect the biosphere from major deterioration that could endanger its present or future functioning.

International environmental law is complex and vast, comprising hundreds of global and regional norms that aim to protect the earth's living and non-living elements and its ecological processes. This relatively recent body of law emerged from growing public awareness, informed by scientists' warnings, that our planet is endangered by the activities of an ever-increasing number of humans, invasive technology, and rapid consumption of the Earth's resources. Environmental

E. Onyeabor, *Environmental Law*, https://doi.org/10.1007/978-3-031-68956-7_2

degradation is evident in the pollution of rivers and lakes, black tides along the coasts, and poisonous fog and smog in the cities of nearly all countries. Other problems stem from endemic poverty, including desertification and the creation of immense urban areas.[1] Sources of environmental law from international law perspectives are:

2.1.2 *International Conventions*

The first source of international environmental law is "conventional norms," which now number more than one thousand in this field, although many agreements contain only a few provisions concerning the environment.[2] Article 21(a) of the Vienna Convention on the Law of Treaties 1969[3] defines a "treaty" as "an international agreement concluded between States in written form and governed by international law, whether embodied in a single instrument or in two or more related instruments and whatever its particular designation." This definition omits all international agreements to which intergovernmental or non-governmental organisations are parties as well as agreements concluded by internal agencies not entitled to bind the state, for example, port authorities or customs offices. Yet, all these entities increasingly enter into agreements intending to cooperate under agreed norms for environmental protection.

For our purpose, therefore, a treaty (environmental treaty) includes not only international agreements between states but also all international environmental agreements[4] to which intergovernmental or non-governmental organisations are parties as well as agreements concluded by internal agencies that are ordinarily not entitled to bind a state.

The geographic coverage of environmental treaties varies widely. In fact, a broad global framework of international law has been established for the four "traditional" sectors of the environment: water, soil, atmosphere and biological diversity. Some instruments contain norms regulating the entire international community in these four broad areas.

---

[1] Sands (2003), p. 251.

[2] The Outer Space Treaty 1967, for example, contains only one relevant provision, Article IX, which relates to protecting the Earth against pollution from outer space and, in turn, protecting outer space from Earth source contamination: "... States Parties to the Treaty shall pursue studies of outer space, including the moon and other celestial bodies, and conduct exploration of them so as to avoid their harmful contamination and also adverse changes in the environment of the Earth resulting from the introduction of extraterrestrial matter and, where necessary, shall adopt appropriate measures for this purpose." Article IX, Treaty on Principles Governing the Activities of States in the Exploration and Use of Outer Space.

[3] Vienna Convention on the Law of Treaties (1969), Art. 21(a).

[4] Whether multi-lateral or bi-lateral.

For instance, Article 35(3) of Protocol I to the Geneva Conventions Relative to Protecting Victims of International Armed Conflicts 1949, prohibits all states in such conflicts from employing methods or means of warfare that are intended or may be expected to cause widespread, long-term and severe damage to the natural environment. The Convention on Wetlands of International Importance especially for Waterfowl Habitat 1971 (Ramsar Convention) is targeted towards the protection of the wetland. The London Conventions of 1972 and 1973 concerning pollution of the high seas.

Other conventions that had been put in place to combat the pollution of the marine environment include: the International Convention for the Prevention of Oil Pollution 1969; the International Convention for the Prevention of Pollution from Ships 1973 as modified by the Protocol of 1978 (MARPOL 73/78); International Convention for the Safety of Life at Sea (SOLAS) 1974; United Nations Convention on Law of the Sea (UNCLOS) 1982; International Convention on Oil Pollution Preparedness, Response and Cooperation (OPRC) 1990; and the Convention on International Trade on Endangered Species (CITES) 1973 regulations of trade in endangered species similarly address global problems.

There are also conventions for the protection of the atmosphere that contain norms regulating the entire international community. They include: the Vienna Convention for the Protection of the Ozone Layer 1985 and its Protocols, the United Nations Framework Convention on Climate Change 1992, the Kyoto Protocol 1997 and the Paris Agreement on Climate Change 2015. In the same vein Conventions such as the Stockholm Declaration 1972, the Rio Declaration on Environment and Development 1992, the Convention on Biological Diversity 1992, AGENDA 21 also contain norms regulating the entire international community.

It should be noted that each international environmental agreement contains legally binding rules, although such engagements may differ considerably from most traditional norms, for in many treaties there are few precise duties created. Instead, the provisions indicate areas of cooperation, and, in some cases, the means states parties should adopt to achieve the goals of the treaty.[5] This is on the assumption that the principles and norms adopted for the whole community of nations often are more effective when implemented and enforced regionally, as has been experienced in the field of human rights. To this end, some of these conventions had been ratified and domesticated by Nigeria.

2.1.3 *Customary International Law*

Besides treaties and conventions, customary international law forms another source of environmental law under international law. Although treaties are the most frequently used form of international environmental lawmaking, customary

[5] Sands (2003), p. 251.

international law remains important. The burdensome procedures of treaty ratification are absent, and customary rules may more easily acquire universal application since acquiescence will often be enough to ensure that "the inactive are carried along by the active," a particular advantage in environmental matters.[6]

Customary international law is an aspect of international law involving the principle of custom. Along with general principles of law and treaties, custom is considered by the International Court of Justice, jurists, the United Nations, and its member states to be among the primary sources of international law. Many governments accept in principle the existence of customary international law, although there are differing opinions as to what rules are contained in it.[7]

Customary international law "consists of rules of law derived from the consistent conduct of States acting out of the belief that the law required them to act that way."[8] It follows that customary international law can be discerned by a "widespread repetition by States of similar international acts over time (State practice); Acts must occur out of sense of obligation (*opinio juris*); Acts must be taken by a significant number of States and not be rejected by a significant number of States."[9] A marker of customary international law is consensus among states exhibited both by widespread conduct and a discernible sense of obligation.[10]

The Statute of the International Court of Justice (ICJ) defines customary international law in Article 38(1)(b) as "a general practice accepted as law."[11] This is generally determined through two factors: the general practice of states and what states have accepted as law.[12] The Statute of the International Court of Justice acknowledges the existence of customary international law in Article 38(1)(b), incorporated into the United Nations Charter by Article 92: "the Court, whose function is to decide in accordance with international law such as disputes that are submitted to it, shall apply . . . international custom, as evidence of a general practice accepted as law."[13]

Against this background, several practices by the international community in the protection of the environment against environmental harm have over the years coalesced into acceptable norms. For instance, in the *Trail Smelter* case,[14] the tribunal held that:

> under the principles of International Law. . .no state has the right to use or permit the use of territory in such a manner as to cause injury by fumes in or to the territory of another, the

---

[6]Birnie et al. (2009), p. 22.

[7]Dinstein (2005), p. 5.

[8]Rosenne (1984), p. 55.

[9]International Law (2020).

[10]Rosenne (1984), p. 55.

[11]See "Statute of the International Court of Justice."

[12]Dinstein (2005), p. 5.

[13]See Statute of the International Court of Justice (1945).

[14]Trail Smelter Arbitration Case (United States v. Canada) 1941 U.N. Rep. Int'l Arb. Awards 1905 (1949).

> properties or persons therein, when the case is of serious consequence and the injury is established by clear and convincing evidence.[15]

In that case, the dispute arose out of damage done to crops, pasture land, trees and agriculture in the United States of America (USA) from a smelting plant at the Consolidated Mining and Smelting Company of Canada at Trail, in British Columbia. It was damage caused by one State to the environment of the other that triggered the legal claim. The dispute arose out of damage done to crops, pasture land, trees and agriculture in the USA from a smelting plant at the Consolidated Mining and Smelting Company of Canada at Trail, in British Columbia. The Columbia River rises in Canada and flows past a lead and zinc smelter located at Trail, in British Columbia (Canada). The smelter company was alleged to cause damage to trees, crops and land in the American State of Washington. The climate from beyond Trail on the United States boundary is dry, but not arid.[16]

The smelter was built under the auspices of the USA but had been taken over. In 1906, the Consolidated Mining and Smelting Company of Canada, Limited acquired the smelter plant at Trail. Since that time, the Canadian company, without interruption, had operated the Smelter, and from time to time had greatly added to the plant until it became one of the best and largest equipped smelting plants on the American continent. In 1925 and 1927, stacks, 409 feet high, were erected and the smelter increased its output, resulting in more sulphur dioxide fumes. The higher stacks increased the area of damage in the United States. From 1925 to 1931, the damage had been caused in the State of Washington by the sulphur dioxide coming from the Trail Smelter, and the International Joint Commission recommended payment of $350,000 in respect of damage to 1 January 1932.[17]

The United States informed Canada that the conditions were still unsatisfactory and an Arbitral Tribunal was set up to "finally decide" whether further damage had been caused in Washington and the indemnity due, whether the smelter should be required to cease operation; the measures to be adopted to this end; and compensation due. The Tribunal was directed to apply the law and practice of the United States as well as international law and practice. The United States Government, on 17 February 1933, represented to the Canadian Government that the existing conditions were entirely unsatisfactory and that damage was still occurring and diplomatic negotiations were entered into, which resulted in the signing of the present convention.[18]

The Court held Canada responsible for the conduct of the Trail Smelter and enjoined it to pay compensation to the United States. The court also provided for

[15] Trail Smelter Arbitration Case (United States v. Canada) 1941 U.N. Rep. Int'l Arb. Awards 1905 (1949).

[16] Ibid.

[17] Ibid.

[18] Convention for Settlement of Difficulties Arising from Operation of Smelter at Trail, B.C. U.S. Treaty Series No. 89.

future monitoring of the effects of the factory's activities on the environment, to prevent possible future damages to the United States environment.[19]

The *Trail Smelter* case came up with the issue of "duty" of states to "prevent trans-boundary harm." For the first time, an international tribunal propounded the principle that a state may not use, or allow its nationals to use, its own territory in such a manner as to cause injury to a neighbouring country.[20]

From a large body of international agreements and other acts and domestic applications and practices, it is possible to discern general rules and principles that have broad, if not necessarily universal, support and are frequently endorsed in practice and applied in environmental protection agreements.

For instance, one of the derivatives of the dictum in the *Trail Smelter* case is the principle of good neighbourliness under the Charter of the United Nations Organisation (UN).[21] Article 74 of the Charter reflects the agreement of the UN members that "their policy in their metropolitan areas must be based on the general principle of good neighbourliness" and must take account of "the interests and well-being of the rest of the world, in social, economic and commercial matters." The principle of good-neighbourliness underlies the dicta of the ICJ in the *Corfu Channel* case.[22] In that case on 22 October 1946, damage was caused to Her Majesty's Ships, *Saumarez* and *Volage*, which resulted in the death and injuries of 44 and injuries to 42 British officers and men by a minefield of anchored automatic mines in international waters of Corfu strait in an area South-west of Bay of Saranda by or with the connivance or knowledge of the Albanian government.[23] The court stated in that case that the principle of sovereignty embodies "the obligation of every state not to allow its territory to be used for acts contrary to the rights of other state."[24]

The principle of good neighbourliness was applied in the *Lake Lanoux Arbitration*.[25] The arbitration concerned the use of the waters of Lake Lanoux, in the Pyrenees. Briefly, the French Government proposed to carry out certain works for the utilisation of the waters of the lake and the Spanish Government feared that these works would adversely affect Spanish rights and interests, contrary to the Treaty of Bayonne of 26 May 1866, between France and Spain and the Additional Act of the same date. In any event, it was claimed that, under the treaty, such works could not be undertaken without the previous agreement of both parties. The arbitral tribunal affirmed that a state has an obligation not to exercise its rights to the extent of ignoring the rights of another when it stated as follows: "France [the upstream state] is entitled to exercise her rights; she cannot ignore the Spanish interests. Spain [the

---

[19] Trail Smelter Arbitration Case (United States v. Canada) 1941.

[20] Bratspies and Miller (2006), p. 347.

[21] Although the UN Charter does not expressly address environmental issues.

[22] United Kingdom v. Albania; *Merits*, International Court of Justice (ICJ) (1949) ICJ Reports 4 at 22, 9 April 1949.

[23] Ibid.

[24] Ibid.

[25] France v. Spain (1957) 12 R.I.A.A. 281; 24 I.L.R. 101, Arbitral Tribunal, 16 November 1957.

downstream state] is entitled to demand that her rights be respected and that her interests be taken into consideration."[26]

By 1972, shortly before the Stockholm Conference in 1972, the United Nations General Assembly Resolution (UNGA) was able to direct that the Conference must "respectfully the exercise of permanent sovereignty over natural resources, as well as the right of each country to exploit its own resources in accordance with its own priorities and needs and in such a manner as to avoid producing harmful effects on other countries."[27] This resolution was aptly captured in Principle 21 of the Stockholm Declaration 1972.[28] It provides that:

> States, have, in accordance with the Charter of the United Nations and the principles of international law, the sovereign right to exploit their own resources pursuant to their own environmental policies, and the responsibility to ensure that activities within their jurisdiction or control do not cause damage to the environment of other States or of areas beyond the limits of national jurisdiction.

Shortly after the Stockholm Conference, Principle 21 of the Stockholm Declaration, above cited, alongside Principle 22, provides that: "States shall cooperate to develop further the international law regarding liability and compensation for the victims of pollution and other environmental damage caused by activities within the jurisdiction or control of such States to areas beyond their jurisdiction," echoed in the UNGA Resolution 2996[29] to lay down the basic rules governing the international responsibility of states in regard to the environment and formed the basis of Article 30 of the United Nations Charter of Economic Rights and Duties of States in 1974. The said article provides that:

> The protection, preservation and enhancement of the environment for the present and future generations is the responsibility of all States. All States shall endeavour to establish their own environment and development policies in conformity with such responsibility. The environmental policies of all States should enhance and not adversely affect the present and future development potential of developing countries. All States have the responsibility to ensure that activities within their jurisdiction or control do not cause damage to the environment of other States or of areas beyond the limits of national jurisdiction. All States should co-operate in evolving international norms and regulations in the field of the environment.[30]

In other words, all states have the responsibility to ensure that activities within their jurisdiction or control do not cause damage to the environment of other states or areas beyond the limits of national jurisdiction.

From thence, the responsibility of states not to cause environmental damage in areas outside their jurisdiction has found application in a number of international

[26] Ibid., 101.

[27] United Nations General Assembly (UNGA) (1972a) Resolution 2849 (XXVI).

[28] Declaration of the United Nations Conference on the Human Environment (Stockholm Declaration) (1972).

[29] UNGA (1972b) Resolution 2996.

[30] United Nations Charter of Economic Rights and Duties of States in 1974, Art. 30.

conventions. For instance, Principle 3 of the United Nations Environment Programme (UNEP) Draft Principles 1978 requires states to ensure that "activities within their jurisdiction or control do not cause damage to the natural systems located within other states or in areas beyond the limits of national jurisdiction." The World Charter for Nature 1982, in the same vein declares the need to "ensure that activities within their jurisdictions or control do not cause damage to the natural systems located within other States or in the areas beyond the limits of national jurisdiction."[31] Akin to that, the Charter further emphasised that:

> Activities which are likely to pose a significant risk to nature shall be preceded by an exhaustive examination; their proponents shall demonstrate that expected benefits outweigh potential damage to nature, and where potential adverse effects are not fully understood, the activities should not proceed.[32]

Thus, "activities which may disturb nature shall be preceded by assessment of their consequences, and environmental impact studies of development projects shall be conducted sufficiently in advance, and if they are to be undertaken, such activities shall be planned and carried out so as to minimize potential adverse effects."[33]

Again, under the United Nations Convention on Law of the Sea (UNCLOS) 1982,[34] states have the sovereign right to exploit their natural resources pursuant to their environmental policies and in accordance with their duty to protect and preserve the marine environment. UNCLOS shifts the emphasis from a negative obligation to prevent harm to a positive commitment to preserve and protect the environment. To that end, Article 194 (2),[35] however, does provide that:

> States shall take all measures necessary to ensure that activities under their jurisdiction or control are so conducted as not to cause damage by pollution to other states and their environment, and that pollution arising from incidents or activities under their jurisdiction or control does not spread beyond the areas where they exercise sovereign rights in accordance with (the) Convention.

In 1992, after the World Conference on Environment and Development,[36] the Rio Declaration on Environment and Development (Rio Declaration) 1992, re-instated the provisions of Principle 21 of the Stockholm Declaration 1972.[37] Principle 2, Rio Declaration 1992 provides that:

> States have, in accordance with the Charter of the United Nations and the principles of international law, the sovereign right to exploit their own resources pursuant to their own environmental and developmental policies, and the responsibility to ensure that activities

---

[31] World Charter for Nature (1982), Art. 21(d).

[32] Ibid., Art. 11(b).

[33] Ibid., Art. 11 (c).

[34] United Nations Convention on Law of the Sea (UNCLOS) (1982), Art. 193.

[35] Ibid., s. 194(2).

[36] Held between 3–14 June 1992 at Rio de Janeiro, Brazil.

[37] Declaration of the United Nations Conference on the Human Environment (Stockholm Declaration) (1972).

within their jurisdiction or control do not cause damage to the environment of other States or of areas beyond the limits of national jurisdiction.

The principle of preventive action is reflected in state practice concerning a broad range of environmental objectives. Broadly stated, it prohibits activity that causes or may cause damage to the environment in violation of the standards established under the rules of international law. It has been described by Kramer[38] as being of "overriding importance in every effective environmental policy, since it allows action to be taken to protect the environment at an earlier stage. It is no longer primarily a question of repairing damage after it has occurred." The preventive principle is supported by an extensive body of domestic environmental protection legislation which establishes authorisation procedures, as well as the adoption of international and national commitments on environmental standards, access to environmental information, and the need to carry out environmental impact assessments on the conduct of certain proposed activities. The preventive principle may, therefore, take a number of forms, including the use of penalties and the application of liability rules.[39]

The preventive approach has been endorsed, directly or indirectly by some Multilateral Environmental Agreements.[40] Principle 11 of the Rio Declaration[41] requires states to enact "effective environmental legislation;" while Principle 14 calls on states "to prevent the relocation and transfer to other states of hazardous activities or substances" and Principle 15 specifically provides for a precautionary approach by states in environmental matters. More significant for its development as an international legal principle is the fact that the principle has been relied upon or endorsed in many treaties dealing with environmental media or activities.

For example, the preventive principle has been specifically incorporated into treaties of more general application. For example, the Lome IV Convention 1995[42] in Article 35 provides for parties to agree to "a preventive approach aimed at avoiding harmful effects on the environment as a result of any programme or operation."

Again, the preventive principle is implicitly supported in relation to transboundary resources by the awards in the *Trial Smelter* case[43] and *Lake Lanoux Arbitration*.[44] It was supported in the pleadings of Australia in the *Nuclear tests* case

[38] Kramer (1990), p. 61.

[39] Kramer (1990), p. 61.

[40] Stockholm Declaration (1972), Principles 6,7,15,18 and 24, UNEP Draft Principles 1978, Principle 1 and the World Charter for Nature (1982).

[41] Rio Declaration on Environment and Development (Rio Declaration) (1992), Principle 11.

[42] The Lomé Convention is a trade and aid agreement between the European Economic Community (EEC) and 71 African, Caribbean, and Pacific (ACP) countries, first signed in February 1975 in Lomé, Togo but had gone through a series of amendments. The Lome IV is an Agreement amending the Fourth ACP-EC Convention of Lomé and was signed in Mauritius on 4 November 1995.

[43] Trail Smelter Arbitration Case (United States v. Canada) (1941).

[44] France v. Spain (1957).

and in the claim by Nature that Australia had breached its legal obligation to administer the territory of Nauru in such a way as to not bring about changes in the territory which would cause irreparable damage to, or substantially prejudice, Nauru's legal interests in respect of that territory in the case *Concerning Certain Phosphate Lands*.[45]

In that case, on 19 May 1989, the Republic of Nauru filed in the Registry of the ICJ an Application instituting proceedings against the Commonwealth of Australia in respect of a dispute concerning the rehabilitation of certain phosphate lands mined under Australian administration before Nauruan independence. In its Application, Nauru claimed that Australia had breached the trusteeship obligations it had accepted under Article 76 of the Charter of the United Nations and under the Trusteeship Agreement for Nauru of 1 November 1947. Nauru further claimed that Australia had breached certain obligations towards Nauru under general international law, more particularly on the implementation of the principle of self-determination and permanent sovereignty over natural wealth and resources. Australia was said to have incurred an international legal responsibility and to be bound to make restitution or other appropriate reparation to Nauru for the damage and prejudice suffered. Within the time limit fixed for the filing of its Counter-Memorial, Australia raised certain preliminary objections relating to the admissibility of the Application and the jurisdiction of the Court.[46]

A Counter-Memorial of Australia on the merits was subsequently filed and the Court fixed the dates for the filing of a Reply by the Applicant and a Rejoinder by the Respondent. However, before those two pleadings were filed, the two Parties, by a joint notification deposited on 9 September 1993, informed the Court that they had, in consequence of having reached a settlement, agreed to discontinue the proceedings.[47]

Furthermore, the preventive principle may also be discerned in Hungary's Original Application to the ICJ in the case concerning the *Gabcikovo-Nagymaros Project*.[48] In that case, Hungary, as the plaintiff claimed that Czechoslovakia as the defendant violated the provisions of a treaty[49] when it appropriated the waters of the Danube River to construct a dam. The fact of the case was that in 1977, Hungary and Czechoslovakia signed a treaty for the construction of dams and other projects along the Danube River that bordered both nations. Former Czechoslovakia began work on damming the river in its territory when Hungary stopped working on the project and negotiation could not resolve the matter which led Hungary to terminate the treaty. Hungary based its action on the fact that the damming of the river had been agreed to only on the ground of a joint operation and sharing of benefits

[45] Nauru v. Australia (1992) ICJ Reports 240 at 244, 80.

[46] Nauru v. Australia (1992).

[47] Ibid.

[48] Hungary v. Slovakia (1997) ICJ Reports 7 at 78, para 140.

[49] That watercourse states shall participate in the use, development and protection of an international watercourse in an equitable and reasonable manner.

associated with the project, to which Czechoslovakia had unlawfully unilaterally assumed control of a shared resource.[50]

The issue for determination based on the treaty was: Shall watercourse states participate in the use, development and protection of an international watercourse in an equitable and reasonable manner?[51]

The ICJ held that watercourse states shall participate in the use, development and protection of an international watercourse in an equitable and reasonable manner. Hungary was deprived of its rights to an equitable and reasonable share of the natural resources of the Danube by the then Czechoslovakia and failed to respect the proportionality that is required by international law. Cooperative administration must be reestablished by the parties of what remains of the project.[52] The Court decided that the joint regime must be restored. To achieve most of the treaty's objectives, common utilisation of shared water resources was necessary. Hence, the defendant was not authorised to proceed without the plaintiff's consent.[53]

Besides being relied upon or endorsed in a large number of treaties dealing with particular environmental media or activities, the preventive approach is endorsed by a large number of international environmental treaties, aiming to prevent inter alia: the spread of hazardous waste and substances,[54] degradation of the natural environment; significant adverse environmental impacts and trans-boundary impacts generally;[55] and damage to health and the environment from chemicals and persistent organic pollutants.[56]

Akin to the principle of preventive action is the principle of co-operation. The principle of "good neighbourliness" enunciated in Article 74 of the United Nations (UN) Charter on social, economic and commercial matters has been translated into the development and application of rules promoting international environmental co-operation. This is traditionally considered by reference to the application of the maxim *utere tuo ut alienum non laedas*. In the context of inter-state relations this maxim *utere tuo ut alienum non laedas*, meaning, use your own property in such a manner as not to injure that of another, stands for the proposition that one state's sovereign right to use its territory is circumscribed by an obligation not to cause injury to, or within, another....[57] The maxim was invoked, for example, as a fundamental rule by Hungary in its Original Application in the

---

[50] Hungary v. Slovakia (1997), para 140.

[51] Hungary v. Slovakia (1997), para 140.

[52] Ibid.

[53] Ibid.

[54] International Convention for the Prevention of Pollution from Ships 1973 as modified by the Protocol of 1978 (MARPOL 73/78), Art. 1 (1).

[55] Convention on Environmental Impact Assessment in a Transboundary Context (Espoo Convention) 1991, preamble.

[56] Stockholm Convention on Persistent Organic Pollutant Convention (2001), Art. 1.

[57] Oxford Public Law (2018).

Gabcikovo-Nagymaros Project case[58] citing in support of the maxim of the decision in the *Corfu Channel* case,[59] the *Trail Smelter* arbitration case.[60] Also relied upon in the *Gabcikovo-Nagymaros Project* case are the provisions of the Stockholm Declaration 1972,[61] the World Charter for Nature 1982 and the Rio Declaration 1992.[62]

The principle is reflected in many treaties and other international acts, and is also supported by state practice, particularly in relation to hazardous activities and emergencies. For instance, Principle 24 of the Stockholm Declaration reflects a general political commitment to international co-operation in matters concerning the protection of the environment, and Principle 27 of the Rio Declaration states rather more succinctly that "States and people shall co-operate in good faith and in a spirit of partnership in the fulfilment of the principles embodied in this Declaration and in the further development of international law in the field of sustainable development."

The importance attached to the principle of co-operation, and its practical significance, is reflected in many international instruments, such as the Preamble to the Industrial Accident Convention 1992, which underlined in support of the convention's specific commitments, "the principles of international law and custom, in particular the principles of good-neighbourliness, reciprocity, non-discrimination and good faith; and the procedural rules reflected in the Watercourses Convention, 1997."[63] The obligation to co-operate is affirmed in virtually all international environmental agreements of bilateral and regional application, and global instruments. For instance, the provisions of Articles 123 and 197 of UNCLOS 1982, Article 2(2) of the Vienna Convention and Article 5 of the Convention on Biological Diversity (Biodiversity Convention 1992). The principle also underscores the ICJ's reminder of the need to establish suitable common regimes.[64]

The general obligation to co-operate has also been translated into more specific commitments through techniques designed to ensure information sharing and participation in decision-making.[65] These include: rules on environmental impact assessment; rules ensuring that neighbouring states receive necessary information requiring information exchange, consultation and notification; the provision of emergency information; and transboundary enforcement of environmental standards. The extent to which these commitments are interrelated is reflected in Principle 7 of the United Nations Environment Programme (UNEP) Draft Principles 1978 which states that the: "Exchange of information, notification, consultation and

---

58 Hungary v. Slovakia (1997), 147.

59 Corfu Channel Case (United Kingdom v. Albania) (1949).

60 Trail Smelter Arbitration Case (United States v. Canada) (1941).

61 Stockholm Declaration (1972), Principle 24.

62 Rio Declaration (1992), Principle 27.

63 Sands (2003), p. 251.

64 Ibid.

65 Information sharing and participation in decision-making are part of two main pillars guiding tenets in the implementation of environmental rights.

other forms of co-operation regarding shared natural resources are carried out on the basis of the principle of good faith and in the spirit of good neighbourliness."

A similar commitment is expressed in Article 4 of the International Law Commission's (ILC) Draft Articles on Prevention of Trans-boundary Harm from Hazardous Activities (2001). State practice supporting good neighbourliness and international co-operation is reflected in decisions and awards of international courts and tribunals.[66] The nature and extent of the obligation to co-operate is being invoked in international disputes. It was a central issue in the dispute between Hungary and Slovakia in the *Gabcikovo-Nagymaros Project* case,[67] at least as originally formulated by Hungary claiming that Czechoslovakia and then Slovakia had not co-operated in good faith in the implementation of principles affecting transboundary resources, including the obligation to negotiate in good faith and in a spirit of co-operation, to prevent disputes, to provide timely notification of plans to carry out or permit activities which may entail a trans-boundary interference or a significant risk thereof and to engage in good faith consultations to arrive at an equitable resolution of the situation.

The ICJ did not address in any detail what the obligation to co-operate entailed, beyond recalling what it had said earlier in the *North Sea Continental Shelf* cases,[68] as well as the principle of good faith which obliged the parties to apply their 1977 treaty "in a reasonable way and in such a manner that its purpose can be realized."[69]

The *North Sea Continental Shelf* case involved the delimitation of the continental shelf areas in the North Sea between Germany and Denmark and Germany and the Netherlands beyond the partial boundaries previously agreed upon by these states. The parties requested the Court to decide the principles and rules of international law that are applicable to the above delimitation because the parties disagreed on the applicable principles or rules of delimitation.[70]

Netherlands and Denmark relied on the principle of equidistance (the method of determining the boundaries in such a way that every point in the boundary is equidistant from the nearest points of the baselines from which the breath of the territorial sea of each state is measured). Germany sought to get a decision in favour of the notion that the delimitation of the relevant continental shelf was governed by the principle that each coastal state is entitled to a just and equitable share (hereinafter called just and equitable principle/method). Contrary to Denmark and the Netherlands, Germany argued that the principle of equidistance was neither a mandatory rule in the delimitation of the continental shelf nor a rule of customary international law that was binding on Germany. The Court was not asked to delimit because the parties had already agreed to delimit the continental shelf between their

---

[66] Such as in the Lake Lanoux Arbitration Case (France v. Spain) (1957).

[67] Hungary v. Slovakia (1997).

[68] North Sea Continental Shelf cases (1997) ICJ Reports 78–9, paras 141–142.

[69] Ibid.

[70] Ibid.

countries, by agreement, after the determination of the Court on the applicable principles.[71]

The jurisprudence of the *North Sea Continental Shelf* cases sets out the dual requirement for the formation of customary international law: (1) State practice (the objective element) and (2) *opinio juris* (the subjective element). In these cases, the Court explained the criteria necessary to establish state practice – widespread and representative participation. It highlighted that the practices of those states whose interests were especially affected by the custom were especially relevant in the formation of customary law. It also held that uniform and consistent practice was necessary to demonstrate *opinio juris* – *opinio juris* is the belief that state practice amounts to a legal obligation. The *North Sea Continental Self* cases also dispelled the myth that the duration of the practice (i.e., the number of years) was an essential factor in forming customary international law.[72]

The requirements of the obligation to co-operate are at the heart of the *MOX Plant* case.[73] The MOX plant was located in Sellafield, Cumbria in the Irish Sea. Its objective was to reprocess spent nuclear fuel, containing a mixture of plutonium dioxide and uranium dioxide, into a new fuel which is known as mixed oxide fuel (MOX).[74] After the power plant was installed and began operating, Ireland quickly became concerned with the safety and protection of their territory. Distribution of radioactive materials and the pollution of their sea led the Irish government to file on 9 November 2001 a formal complaint with the International Tribunal on Law of the Sea (ITLOS) Tribunal on the following grounds:

(i) that the United Kingdom immediately ensure that there are no movement into or out of the waters over which it has sovereignty or exercises sovereign rights of any radioactive substances or materials or wastes which are associated with the operation of, or activities preparatory to the operation of the MOX plant;
(ii) that the United Kingdom ensure that no action of any kind is taken that might aggravate, extend or render more difficult of solution the dispute submitted to the Annex VII tribunal; and
(iii) that the United Kingdom ensure that no action is taken which might prejudice the rights of Ireland in respect of the carrying out of any decisions on the merits of the Annex VII tribunal may render.[75]

In her application instituted under the UNCLOS 1982, Ireland claimed that the United Kingdom had failed to co-operate as required by Articles 123 and 197 of UNCLOS, for example by failing to reply to communications and request for information in a timely manner or at all, by withholding environmental information

[71] Gunaratne (2014).

[72] Ibid.

[73] Ireland v. United Kingdom (2001) ITLOS Documents, 25 October 2001.

[74] Global issue laws of the sea (2020).

[75] Ireland v. United Kingdom (2001).

requested by Ireland, and by refusing to prepare a supplementary environmental statement.[76]

During the hearings, Ireland pointed out that the operation of the plant would contribute to the pollution of the Irish Sea and underline the potential risks involved in the transportation of radioactive material to and from the plant.[77]

On 3 December 2001, the Tribunal delivered its order to both parties involved. The court "noted and placed on record the assurances given by the United Kingdom that there will be no additional marine transports of radioactive material either to or from Sellafield as a result of the commissioning of the MOX plant until summer of 2002."[78] In its Provisional Measures Order, the ITLOS affirmed that:

> the duty to co-operate is a fundamental principle in the prevention of pollution of the marine environment under Part XII of the Convention and general international law and that rights arise therefrom which the Tribunal may consider appropriate to preserve under Article 290 of the Convention.[79]

Due to the complexity of the justice system, the Tribunal prescribed several provisional measures that both sides were legally bound to follow. These measures stated that Ireland and the United Kingdom shall cooperate and shall, for this purpose, enter into consultations forthwith to:

(i) exchange further information on possible consequences for the Irish Sea arising out of the commissioning of the MOX plant;
(ii) monitor risks or the effects of the operation of the MOX plant for the Irish Sea; and
(iii) devise, as appropriate, measures to prevent pollution of the marine environment which might result from the operation of the MOX plant.[80]

The basis of the decision of the ITLOS in the *MOX Plant* case was that UNCLOS 1982 had adopted during the long process of its elaboration by states of the world, a certain number of existing rules were codified and there also arose a consensus on several new norms. From this consensus, an international practice formed, even before the adoption of the treaty. This was particularly the case with the creation of the "exclusive economic zone," now codified in Part V of the Convention.[81] During the negotiations, it was clearly recognised that coastal states have sovereign rights for the purpose of conserving and managing living and non-living natural resources and have jurisdiction to preserve the marine environment.[82] It also became accepted that coastal state jurisdiction to legislate regarding ships in innocent passage through the territorial sea includes measures to conserve marine biological resources and

[76] Ibid.

[77] Global issue laws of the sea (2020).

[78] Ireland v. United Kingdom (2001).

[79] Ibid.

[80] Ireland v. United Kingdom (2001).

[81] UNCLOS (1982), Arts. 55–75.

[82] Ibid., Art. 56(a).

preserve the marine environment and to prevent, reduce and control marine pollution.[83]

Other rules of customary international law can be observed emerging and at different stages in their evolution. The formulation of non-binding principles undoubtedly plays an important role in this process. Another factor is the repetition of specific rules in numerous international texts. Third, the process of formulating a rule that may or may not have been applied by different states may create a rather rapid consensus which leads to general acceptance of the rule in state practice. The follow-up to the nuclear accident at Chernobyl illustrates this development.

Although the then Soviet government evacuated nearly 50,000 persons in the days immediately following the incident, it failed to inform other states until much later and did not give a complete explanation of the event until a specially organised meeting of the International Atomic Energy Agency took place between 25 and 29 August 1986.

One of the general principles that had emerged from repeated conventional requirements was the duty of a state to urgently notify other states at risk of having their environment adversely affected by any situation or any event. The non-application of this principle by the former Union of the Soviet Socialist Republic (USSR) after Chernobyl made it necessary to formulate the norm in more detail, based on the parallel conventional provisions. Thus, fifty-eight states signed an agreement in Vienna on early notification of a nuclear accident and the treaty entered into force with unusual speed one month later.[84] As its title indicates, it requires states to give notification without delay of any nuclear accident which will or might lead to radioactive consequences for another state.[85] The information to be transmitted is specified in the convention.[86] The speed of codification of this rule can only be explained by the circumstances and by the recognition of a prior international duty to notify.

Other principles may be cited that form the core of an international common law of the environment. In sum, it is possible to speak of a body of customary international environmental law composed of fundamental principles underlying the entire system and applicable to all environmental subjects. The number of treaties and other international instruments reproducing the same legal norms concerning the environment continues to grow. United Nations Conference on Environment and Development (UNCED) contributed greatly to this evolution. The work of the International Law Commission shows that the repetition of the same norms in numerous international instruments can be considered as giving birth to new customary rules.

In this regard, it is worth noting that several international instruments have declared that Part XII of UNCLOS, relating to the protection of the marine

[83] Ibid., Art. 21.

[84] Convention on Early Notification of Nuclear Accidents 1986.

[85] Ibid., Art. 1.

[86] Ibid., Art. 5.

environment, is part of customary international law, even before the entry into force of the convention in 1994.[87]

2.1.4 General Principles of Law

The third source of environmental law under international law is general principles of law. The underlying concept seeks to identify those principles that are common to the major legal systems of the world, if not to all of them. This is because laws and policies adopted at the global, regional, and national levels influence each other. Initiatives begun at one level of governance often lead to similar approaches being adopted in other legal orders. A few examples demonstrate this widespread practice.

The 1941 arbitral decision resolving a long-standing dispute between the United States and Canada over air pollution originating in a Canadian smelter found no applicable international law on the topic and turned to norms articulated in the case law of federal states, the USA and Switzerland, in particular, to establish the principle that states have a duty not to cause significant trans-boundary air pollution.[88] It should be noted that after the *Trail Smelter* case, Principle 21 of the Stockholm Declaration in 1972 made this duty not to cause transboundary air pollution a general obligation. The Rio Declaration in 1992 reiterated the duty and it has been incorporated since then into numerous environmental treaties and other texts.

International norms similarly can formulate new principles that pass into regional and national laws. Most states traditionally had few rules protecting wildlife, which was freely available for capture, killing, or other use. From hunting safaris in Africa to whaling on the open seas and plant collectors in Latin America, unregulated access was the general rule.[89] Many of the norms that now protect wildlife developed first in international agreements to protect migratory species and resources of the commons.

For example, the Convention on International Trade Endangered Species (CITES) 1973. CITES is a multilateral treaty to protect endangered plants and animals. It was drafted as a result of a resolution adopted in 1963 at a meeting of members of the International Union for Conservation of Nature. The convention was opened for signature in 1973 and entered into force on 1 July 1975.[90] Another example is the Convention on Biological Diversity 1992. The convention had been integrated into national laws by some countries. For instance, Nigeria has made bold efforts towards biodiversity conservation. These steps relate to the strengthening of

[87] Sands (2003), p. 332.

[88] Trail Smelter Arbitration Case (United States v. Canada) (1941).

[89] Birnie et al. (2009), p. 37.

[90] United Nations Environment Program (UNEP), https://cites.org/eng/disc/text.php (accessed on 14 July 2019).

policy, legislative and institutional frameworks and the implementation of intervention measures aimed at the conservation of biological diversity, the sustainable utilisation of its components and equitable sharing of benefits.[91]

Another aspect is the environmental impact assessment procedure (EIA). EIA was first introduced in the USA at the end of the 1960s in the State of Michigan. Its aim was and remains to ensure that adequate and early information is obtained on the likely environmental consequences of development projects and on possible alternatives and measures to mitigate harm. United States legislation adopted the EIA as national law in 1969, following which it was introduced into the laws of many other countries, for instance, Nigeria. Nigeria adopted the EIA procedures as a requirement for the commencement of certain development projects through the promulgation of the Environmental Impact Assessment Decree in 1992[92]

Another example showing the effects international law and policy can have on national environmental law is the provisions of the Rio Declaration on Environment and Development (Rio Declaration) 1992. Principle 15 of the Rio Declaration 1992 formulated the precautionary approach, according to which lack of full scientific certainty shall not be used as a reason for postponing measures to prevent environmental degradation where there are threats of serious or irreversible damage. During the same period, the precautionary principle appeared in regional texts as well. For example, the Bamako Convention on the Ban of Import into Africa and the Control of Trans-boundary Movement and Management of Hazardous Wastes within Africa (Bamako Convention) 1991, contain such text on the precautionary principle. In addition, there are certain principles,[93] techniques and practices that are or could be extended from one level to others providing dynamic and creative solutions to environmental problems.

2.1.5 *Judicial Decisions and Doctrines*

Although the Statute of the International Court of Justice refers to jurisprudence as a subsidiary source for determining rules of law, judgments and advisory opinions of the World Court and arbitral or other international tribunals are quite important in fact. These decisions often are considered as the affirmation or the revelation of customary international rules. The arbitral judgment of 11 March 1941 in the *Trail Smelter* arbitration case (*US v. Canada*)[94] is considered to have laid the foundations

[91] These have found expression in the National Environmental (Access to Genetic Resources and Benefit Sharing) Regulations 2009, discussed in 16.2.5.4 of Chap. 16 of this book.

[92] Now retained as Act 1992, Cap E 12 LFN 2004. This law was discussed in 16.2.3.2 of Chap. 16 of this book.

[93] Such as the principle of "No Harm Rule," principle of sustainable development, the precautionary principle, the polluter-pays principle, the principle of strict and absolute liability, among others.

[94] Trail Smelter Arbitration Case (United States v. Canada) (1941).

of international environmental law, at least regarding trans-frontier pollution. Confirmed by a more general principle enunciated in the *Corfu Channel* case (*UK v. Albania*)[95] and referred to in the 1956 *Lake Lanoux* arbitration (*France v. Spain*)[96] in the context of trans-frontier water pollution, where it was held that "No state may utilize its territory contrary to the rights of other States."[97] These announced rules undoubtedly form part not only of positive international law today but also affect the development of national environmental law.

2.1.6 Resolutions and Decisions of International Organisations

One of the principal characteristics of international organisations is that very few have the power to adopt legally binding texts. Only three have such power among all the organisations which are concerned with matters of environmental protection. Thus, since their beginning in the nineteenth century, international organisations have adopted non-binding resolutions addressed to member states. This procedure has taken on increased importance over the years, particularly for new fields of international regulation such as environmental protection.[98] Recommendations and declarations of principles of conferences such as those held in Stockholm, Rio de Janeiro, United Nations Convention on Climate Change Conference of Parties (UNFCCC) (CoP) or meetings of the United Nations Environmental Programme[99] have had a great impact on the evolution of international environmental law and these have impacted greatly on national environmental law.[100]

The Security Council of the United Nations, under its peace-keeping functions and other roles conferred on it, is one of the few organisations that can adopt binding decisions. Its actions regarding environmental destruction in the Persian Gulf in the aftermath of the Iraqi invasion of Kuwait indicate a heightened concern for environmental protection during armed conflict. In addition, according to Article 5 of the Convention on the Prohibition of Military or Any Other Hostile Use of Environmental Modification Techniques,[101] each state party that has reason to believe another state party is violating its obligations can file a complaint with the Security

[95] UK v. Albania (1949).

[96] France v. Spain (1957).

[97] Ibid.

[98] Sands (2003), p. 339.

[99] For instance, Vancouver 1976, Mar del Plate 1977, Nairobi 1978, Rio de Janeiro 1992, etc.

[100] For instance, the Environmental Impact Assessment Act 1992 Cap E12 Laws of the Federation of Nigeria (LFN) 2004 was influenced by the outcome of the Rio de Janeiro Conference of 1992. Also, the Climate Change Act 2021 of Nigeria was influenced by the outcome of CoP to the UNFCCC in France which led to the signing of the Paris Agreement on Climate Change in 2015.

[101] Geneva, 10 December 1976.

Council. The latter may undertake an inquiry with the power to decide that the state bringing the complaint has been or might be harmed due to a violation of the convention. No doubt they would include the application of Articles 36 and 37 of the United Nations Charter, which recommend dispute-settlement procedures.[102]

Resolutions issued from conferences or international organisations are often in the form of directive recommendations or declarations of principles. Directive recommendations form the bulk of acts by which intergovernmental organisations address themselves to member states. The importance of such recommendations derives from the law of international organisations.[103]

Directive recommendations concerning environmental protection have played an important role in the activities of most intergovernmental organisations and the general development of international environmental law. The UN General Assembly has adopted resolutions on global climate change, Antarctica, driftnet fishing, sustainable development, and, indeed, nearly all the subjects of international concern.[104]

Another function of principles is to set forth a fundamental societal consensus on the underlying rationale for a body of law. In this respect, principles serve one of the fundamental objectives of any legal system, which is to recognise and formulate the emergency of new social values recognised as essential within the society. At this international level, this can be achieved through declarations adopted and proclaimed by global organisations or international conferences.[105]

2.1.7 *Decisions of Conference of Parties (CoPs)/Meeting of Parties (MoPs)*

The Vienna Convention on the Law of Treaties 1969 makes it clear that the states parties to international agreements may interpret the agreement or define its terms through subsequent state practice.[106] The policy-making conferences or meetings of the parties that are created by Multilateral Environmental Agreements (MEAs) are increasingly adopting interpretive decisions, recommendations and guidelines for action. The decisions and recommendations can have considerable juridical value when they express the common understanding of the state parties concerning the norms and obligations contained in the agreement.

[102] Birnie et al. (2009), p. 37.

[103] Sands (2003), p. 338.

[104] Ibid.

[105] Ibid.

[106] Vienna Convention 1969, Art. 31.

For example, the Ramsar Convention 1971,[107] Convention on Biological Diversity 1992[108] and Convention on International Trade on Endangered Species (CITES) 1973 meetings have produced numerous and lengthy guidelines, recommendations, and decisions, such as the Bonn Guidelines on Access to Genetic Resources and Fair and Equitable Sharing of the Benefits Arising out of their Utilization adopted by the sixth conference of the parties to the Convention on Biological Diversity. Also, decisions of the CoP on the United Nations Framework Convention on Climate Change (UNFCCC) in 1997[109] and 2015[110] produced guidelines on carbon emissions reduction as steps towards curbing global warming and climate change.

Taken together, an increasing number of concepts, principles and norms appear repeatedly in national, regional, and global instruments, usually following an initial formulation in a non-binding instrument. Principles such as public participation, EIA, notification of environmental emergencies, prevention, precaution, and polluter pays are examples of principles that have been incorporated into treaties and given greater specificity. In many cases, this can result in greater agreed specification, such as when the same definition of a term appears from one treaty to another. In some instances, however, the effort to detail obligations leads to divergences from one instrument or region to another. For example, the duty not to cause transboundary harm has been variously qualified under various international legal instruments as "significant," "measurable," "serious" or "appreciable" harm.

2.2 Received English Laws as Source of Environmental Law

2.2.1 Introduction

The history of the inception of English law into the traditional society of Nigeria dates back to 1863, through the introduction of English law into the colony of Lagos. The introduction of English law came with the introduction of the English court, where a court was empowered to administer the received law, provisions relating to its certification by the court as contained in the enactment creating the court and subsidiary legislation made under such enactment. Thus, received English laws are laws that were originally enacted and were in operation in England and due to the reception of English law were co-opted into our laws as part of the colonial legacy of Great Britain and they become applicable in Nigeria. The major reception Act in

[107] Ramsar Convention (1971).

[108] United Nations, Convention on Biological Diversity 1992, Art. 3.

[109] Kyoto Protocol on Climate Change 1997.

[110] Paris Agreement on Climate Change 2015.

Nigeria is the Interpretation Act. The Interpretation Act[111] receives English law in section 32(1). It provides as follows:

> Subject to the provisions of this section and except in so far as other provision is made by any Federal law, the common law of England and the doctrines of equity, together with the statutes of general application that were in force in England on the 1st day of January, 1900, shall, in so far as they relate to any matter within the legislative competence of the Federal legislature, be in force in Nigeria

However, the application of the received English laws is limited as they are subject to Nigerian jurisdiction as provided under the Interpretation Act thus: "Such Imperial laws shall be in force so far only as the limits of the local jurisdiction and local circumstances shall permit and subject to any Federal law."[112] This was seen in the case of *Labinjoh v. Abake*[113] where the application of the Infant Relief Act was rejected because there was already local legislation that covered that area.

The received English laws are made up of rules of common law, doctrines of equity and statutes of general application. Of interest to us as sources of environmental law are:

1) Rules of Common Law
2) Doctrines of Equity

2.2.2 *Rules of Common Law*

Although the modern trend in environmental protection is for regulatory agencies to control and protect the environment under authority derived from statutes, common law may also be used to control damages to the environment. This is so because common law tort can be used to impose certain restrictions on land use and elicit a certain level of environmental compliance on a developer or occupier of land. Tort is the word used to denote common law civil wrong for which a court will provide a remedy. It arises from the existence of a generalised legal duty to avoid causing harm to others, through acts of omission, as well as commission.[114] Flowing from the above tortuous liability therefore "arises from the breach of duty primarily fixed by law towards persons generally and the redressal for which is bringing of an action for unliquidated damage."[115] In today's environmental protection efforts common law tortuous liabilities are used to control environment damage as they impose certain restrictions in land use through the application of the following tort principles:

[111] Interpretation Act Cap I 23 LFN 2004.

[112] Interpretation Act Cap I 23 LFN 2004, s. 32(2).

[113] (1924) 5 NLR 33.

[114] Sullivan (1999), p. 7.

[115] Winfield and Jolowicz (2006), p. 50.

a) Tort of Nuisance
b) Rules in *Rylands v. Fletcher*
c) Tort of Negligence

2.2.2.1 Tort of Nuisance

The common law principle of nuisance, which is defined as "an unreasonable interference by one party with another's enjoyment of his or her land,"[116] serves to preserve the character of neighbourhoods through the elimination of non-conforming uses of land, activities or acts. For instance, the operation of a company may result in air or noise pollution, diminishing the value of a neighbouring parcel of land. If the neighbour takes the offending company to court, the result might be an injunction of the offending activity or monetary compensation to the neighbouring property owner. The nuisance complained of may be private or public nuisance or statutory.

A nuisance is private if it does not cause damage or inconvenience to the public at large, but does interfere with a person's use or enjoyment of land or some right connected with land in his possession.[117] To this end, private nuisance may be caused by a person, who though he is lawfully doing acts on his land, his lawful acts produce consequences that are not confined to his own land but extend to the land of his neighbour, by causing encroachment on his neighbour's land, or building, or unduly interferes with his neighbour in the comfort and convenient enjoyment of his land.[118] Therefore, liabilities in private nuisance may arise by incursions onto the plaintiff's property, or interference with his enjoyment of that property by water, smoke, smell, fumes, gas, noise, heat, vibrations, electricity, animals and vegetation.[119]

Arising from the above, the law of private nuisance protects a person's freedom to use land. This is so because long before planning and environmental legislation placed limits on this freedom, it was recognised that the very exercise of a freedom to enjoy land creates, as its corollary, an obligation of non-interference with the freedoms enjoyed by owners of neighbouring land. In order words, the freedom to use land can never be absolute but must be exercised so that it does not unreasonably prevent a neighbouring landowner from enjoying his freedom.

Therefore, in an action for private nuisance, the court strives to strike an appropriate balance between the rights of particular landowners and the rights of their neighbours. It is therefore necessary for a claimant who wishes to bring an action in

---

[116] Enemo (2007), p. 123.

[117] Enugu State of Nigeria Tort Law, Laws of Enugu State 2004, s. 235.

[118] See Akpata J.C.A. in Abdullah v. Governor of Lagos State (1989) 3 NWLR (pt 97) 358 and applied in the case of Ojo Eholor v. Idemudia Idahosa (1992) 2 NWLR (pt 223) 327. See, also, the case of Ige v. Taylor Woodrow Nig. Ltd. (1963) LLR, 140.

[119] Per Viscount Maugham in Sedleigh-Denfield v. O'Callaghan [1940] A.C. 880 at 888.

private nuisance to show that he has an existing interest in the land affected by the nuisance, either as owner of the land in question or as an occupier. In the same vein, a potential defendant in an action for nuisance includes the creator of the nuisance and the person who, being an occupier of land on which a nuisance has arisen, fails to take reasonable steps to remedy the state of affairs giving rise to the nuisance. As was noted by Veale J, in *Halsey v. Esso Petroleum Company Ltd*[120] there appears to be no requirement that the acts complained of must emanate from land belonging to the defendant.

Again, there is no precise test for deciding whether the defendant's use of his land is unreasonable, the matter being dependent on the facts of each particular case. However, the extent and nature of the harm alleged,[121] the duration of the nuisance,[122] the utility of the defendant's activities,[123] the abnormal sensitivity of the claimant,[124] malice on the part of the defendant,[125] and the character of the neighbourhood in which the activity is carried on,[126] have all been identified as relevant considerations. Taken together, the basis for liability in private nuisance will arise where:

(i) An act which causes unreasonable interference with a person's enjoyment of his land, for example, ingress onto the land of fumes, smoke, or noise.
(ii) An act which causes physical damage to a person's land.

In the first situation, the plaintiff must show that the defendant's activities constituted an unreasonable use of his land. Here the plaintiff need not prove physical damage to his property, all he needs to prove is that there was substantial interference with his use or enjoyment of his land. Thus, in *Abiola v. Ijeoma*,[127] the parties occupied adjoining premises in Surulere Lagos. The plaintiff complained that excessive noise made by the defendant's chickens in the early morning hours disturbed his sleep and that nauseating smells emanating from the pens interfered with his comfort. The court found that the plaintiff had suffered more than a trifling inconvenience than an ordinary person living in that part of Surulere. The injunction sought was granted, although the plaintiff suffered no physical damage.

However, in arriving at its conclusion when no physical damage is shown, the court must consider the locality in question to establish the standard for the particular locality to which the land is situated. The defendant will be liable only if his conduct or the nuisance created by him falls short of the standard of that locality. This is because the court does not consider the nuisance merely "according to elegant and

[120] [1961] 1 W.L.R. 683.
[121] As in the case of St Helen's Smelting Company v. Tipping (1865).
[122] As in the case of Cunard v. Antifyre Ltd (1933).
[123] As in the case of Bellew v. Cement Company Ltd (1948).
[124] As in the case of Robinson v. Kilvert (1884) 88.
[125] As in the case of Hollywood Silver Fox Farm Ltd v Emmett [1936] 468.
[126] M.K.O. Abiola v. Felix Ijeoma (1970) 569.
[127] Ibid.

dainty attitudes and habits of living, but according to plain and sober and simple notions obtaining among the members of the community."[128]

Therefore, the inconvenience suffered must be substantial and substantial interference is given an objective construction. In *Tebite v. Nigeria Marine and Trading Co. Ltd.*,[129] the plaintiff, a Legal Practitioner with office at 11 Robert Road Warri (a mixed-use zone) succeeded in an action in nuisance against the defendant with a workshop for boat building and repairing at 9 Robert Road, Warri. The defendants by operating their machines continuously for several hours a day persistently caused to emit from their workshop loud and excessive noise and noxious fumes, which diffused to the plaintiff's premises and caused him much discomfort and inconvenience. The court held that the noise was completely out of character with that ordinarily produced by ordinary people in any neighbourhood in the country.

The basis for the above decision, and other decisions, is that a just balance must be struck between the rights of the defendant and that of the plaintiff to the undisturbed enjoyment of his property, it is a compromise that borders on social co-existence. It follows that a trivial interference with the enjoyment of land cannot be a nuisance. Thus, in the case of *Southwark BC v. Mills,*[130] where the claimant complained about noise from adjoining flats, the court held that ordinary use of residential premises was not capable of amounting to an actionable nuisance.[131]

Furthermore, in the light of the provisions of planning legislation, a grant of a planning permit may change the character of the neighbourhood, and thereby permit certain activities which, prior to that change, would have been actionable nuisances. In the case of *Gillingham B.C v. Medway (Chatham) Dock Company Ltd,*[132] the defendants were granted planning permission by the Planning Authority to change a little-used naval dock into a commercial port, with the result that levels of noise and disturbance to local residents increased dramatically. The local council, on behalf of the local residents, brought an action in nuisance and sought an injunction to restrict the movement of vehicles at night. The court in refusing the relief sought held that the grant of planning permission had changed the character of the neighbourhood so that 24-hour access to the dock was permissible. The reasoning of the court is predicated on the fact that the planning permission in question is strategic and designed to promote the regeneration of a large area, which had in practical terms extinguished the resident's claims of private nuisance.

In the second situation, an act which causes physical damage to a person's land can also result in an actionable nuisance. In the case of *Ojo Eholor v. Idemudia*

[128] Moore v. Nnado (1967) FNLR 156.

[129] (1971) UILR, 432.

[130] [1999] 4 All E R 449.

[131] It is hoped that in the present situation where power generating sets are found in virtually every residential accommodation in Nigeria in the face of power outage an action on nuisance arising from noise may be decided in the same way.

[132] [1993] Q B 343.

Idahosa,[133] the respondent/plaintiff built his house in line with the building regulations. When, however, the appellant/defendant built his, the building was high and overdeveloped by building wall to wall causing rainwater from his roof to drip on the roof and into the premises of the respondent's house causing deterioration and a considerable reduction in the value of the house. The lower court awarded =N=56,429 and =N=43,671 as special and general damages respectively, because the appellant/defendant action constituted a nuisance. On appeal, the appeal was dismissed by the Court of Appeal and upheld the judgment of the trial court.

It should be noted it is now immaterial that the plaintiff brought himself to the nuisance, that is, that the act complained of was in existence before the plaintiff commenced his occupation of the land. What is important is that the plaintiff had suffered some physical damage to his property. Thus, in the case of *St. Helen's Smelting Co. v. Tipping*,[134] the defendant's plea that the locality in question was devoted to industries was rejected and the plaintiff recovered damages.

Again, the fact that the act of the defendant is usually in the locality or is beneficial or useful to the community will not in itself act as a bar or deny the plaintiff the claims sought. To this end, in *Rushmer v. Polsue and Alfieri Ltd*,[135] the court granted a plaintiff's claim for injunction to restrain the use of the defendants' printing presses at night, even though the premises were in the printing area of London. Furthermore, in the case of *Bellew v. Cement Co. Ltd*,[136] the court was unmoved by the defendants' argument that their cement production was vital to the public interest at a time when building was an urgent public necessity. While granting the injunction sought,[137] the court held that the plaintiff should put up with harm because it is beneficial to the community as a whole is unacceptable, for that would amount to requiring him to carry the burden alone of an activity for which many others benefit.

A public nuisance, on the other hand, is an unlawful act or omission to discharge a legal duty which act or omission endangers the lives, safety, health, property or comfort of the public. According to Karibi-Whyte, J.S.C. (as he then was) in the case of *Adediran and Ors v. Interland Transport Ltd*,[138] a public nuisance is one which inflicts damage, injury or inconvenience to the generality of the population or upon all of a class who come within its ambit.

In an action under public nuisance, a private individual must establish that he sustained particular damage other than and beyond the general inconvenience and injury suffered by the public and that the particular damage is direct and substantial. Failure to show this will mean that the action will be dismissed by the court. In the

---

[133] (1992) 2 NWLR (pt 223) 327.

[134] (1865) 11 E R 1483.

[135] (1906) 1 Ch 234, (1907) AC 121.

[136] (1948) E R 61.

[137] Closure of the Factory for 3 months.

[138] (1991) 9 NWLR (pt 214) 164.

case of *A.S. Amos and Ors v. Shell Petroleum Development Company*,[139] the plaintiff claimed general and special damages from the defendant for "unlawful damages caused by the defendants by deliberately and negligently blocking for about three months the Kolo Creek new water way." The Supreme Court dismissed the action, inter alia, because the plaintiff failed to prove they suffered damage over and above that suffered by the general public.[140]

However, in the case of *Ejowhomu v. Edok-Eter Mandilas Ltd*,[141] the plaintiff who sued the defendant for blocking a public road, which consequently barred access to his poultry farm and caused him some loss, recovered. The court found that the plaintiff's injury was "beyond the general inconvenience and injury suffered by the public." Also, in the case of *Anthony Savage v. Akinrinade*,[142] the defendant caused a public nuisance by blocking a public highway. The plaintiff's action was based on the fact that the blockage interfered particularly with the access of the staff, parents and pupils to his school. The court held that this amounts to particular damage to the plaintiff over and above that suffered by other users of the highway.

2.2.2.2 The Rule in *Rylands v. Fletcher*

Another means through which environmental protection is achieved is through the application of the rule in *Rylands v. Fletcher*.[143] Under this rule, a defendant, who in the course of non-natural use of his land accumulates thereon for his own purpose anything likely to do mischief if it escapes, is liable for all the direct damage or interference with the use of the land of another which results from the escape of the thing from his land.[144] Things likely to do mischief on escape include not only inherently dangerous materials such as explosives, gas, petrol, fire or petroleum chemicals, but also reasonably safe things which only become dangerous when accumulated in large quantities, such as water, crude oil, sewage, and slag heaps.

For the rule to apply, the question is whether the thing was dangerous in the circumstances of the particular case, and not whether the thing was dangerous per se. In the case of *Oladehin v. Continental Textile Mills Ltd*,[145] industrial waste accumulated by the defendant escaped from its factory premises into the uncompleted house of the plaintiff, flooding it. It was found that the factory was in the habit of storing large quantities of water on the premises to facilitate its job. This was deemed to be a special use of the premises. The defendants were held liable

[139] (1977) 6 SC. 109.

[140] The same reason was applied by the Supreme Court to dismiss the claims in Adediran & Ors v. Interland Transport Ltd (1991) 9 NWLR (pt 214).

[141] (1986) 5 NWLR (pt 39) 1 or (1986) 9 SC. 41 at 107–108.

[142] (1964) All NLR 238.

[143] (1868) LR H L 330.

[144] Ibid.

[145] (1977) 2 SC 23.

under the rule in *Rylands v. Fletcher.* Also, in the case of *Machine Umudje v. Shell B.P. Petroleum Development Company,*[146] oil escaped from the defendants' premises destroying the plaintiff's fish and fishpond. The oil was crude oil waste previously accumulated in a pit burrowed by, and in control of, the defendants. The rule was applied to hold the defendants liable.

Besides accumulation of dangerous substances, for the rule to apply the plaintiff must also show that the defendant engaged in a non-natural use of the land. "Non-natural user" was classically defined in the case of *Rickards v. Lothian*[147] as follows, "a non-natural user must be some special use bringing with it increased danger to others and must not merely be ordinary use of the land or such a use as is proper for the general benefit of the community."

To this end, in the case of *San Ikpede v. Shell B.P Development Company Ltd,*[148] where the plaintiffs suffered damage because of the escape of crude oil from the pipelines of the defendant, the court held that to lay pipelines carrying crude oil through swamp land is a non-natural user of land. There is no objective universal test for determining "non-natural" use as it varies from place to place and from time to time. Therefore, the court, in so determining, must look not only at the thing or activity in isolation, but also at the place and manner in which it is maintained and its relation to its surroundings. This preposition was applied in the case of *Rainham Chemical Works Ltd v. Belvedere Fish Guano Co.*[149] In that case, the court took the view that the defendants manufacturing explosives, in peacetime, constituted a non-natural use of land.

But, in the case of *Read v. Lyons & Co Ltd,*[150] the court expressed the view that manufacturing explosives in times of war to defeat the King's enemies was not a non-natural use of the land. It must be borne in mind that a defendant may escape liability by proving that:

(i) it has statutory authority, provided that the public authority kept or accumulated the substance in their efforts to provide public service; but can be found to be negligent if not properly kept.[151]
(ii) the escape was caused by a deliberate act of a third party or stranger which could not reasonably have been anticipated by the defendant.[152]
(iii) the escape was caused by an act of God in circumstances which no human foresight can provide against and of which human prudence is not bound to recognise the possibility.

[146] (1975) 9–11 SC. 155.

[147] (1913) A.C. 263 at 280.

[148] (1973) MWSJ 61.

[149] (1921) 12 AC 465.

[150] (1947) AC 156 at 168.

[151] As in Green v. Chelsea Waterwork Co (1894) 70 LF, 547.

[152] As in Shell Petroleum Development Company of Nigeria Ltd v. Graham Otoko and Ors (1990) 6 NWLR (pt 159) 693, where defendant/appellant successfully raised the defence that the act of a third party caused the spillage.

However, in claiming that the escape was caused by a deliberate act of a third party or stranger which could not reasonably have been anticipated by the defendant, this defence may fail in situations where he failed to take appropriate steps to guard against actions of trespassers and other third parties, equipment failure or natural events, the defence of deliberate act of a third party or stranger, or break in the chain of events, shall not avail him.

In the case of *Empress Cars (Arbertillery) Ltd v. National Rivers Authority*,[153] the defendants maintained an oil storage tank on their site. A bund wall protected the tank. Standing outside the bund was a much smaller oil drum which was connected to the oil tank by a rubber hose. The open/close valve on the tank was not lockable and the site security was poor. A trespasser entered the site and opened the valve on the oil tank. Oil flowed from the tank to the drum which rapidly filled up and overflowed. The escaped oil found its way into the surface water drains and from there entered the river. The defendants argued that it had not caused the oil pollution but had merely created circumstances whereby a trespasser could enter the site, and turned on the oil storage tank that caused the pollution. The defendant further submitted that the act of the trespasser broke the chain of causation linking the defendant to the pollution and absolved it of liability. The court rejected this defence and found the defendant liable.

Again, where the nature of an intervening act of a third party is clearly foreseeable, the defendant will not escape liability by relying on an act of a third party. In the case of *National Rivers Authority v. Yorkshire Water Service Ltd*,[154] the defendants were responsible for a sewer into which an unidentified industrial customer of theirs had discharged solvents. It was held that there was sufficient evidence on which the court could conclude that the defendants were *prima facie* guilty of causing the pollution.

2.2.2.3 Tort of Negligence

Negligence is another tort that is usually applied to elicit compliance with environmental protection. Here the plaintiff maintains that the defendant owed him a duty of care and that duty had been breached either through negligent performance of the duty or omission to perform such duty. To sustain an action in negligence, it must be shown that the negligence found by the court is the proximate cause of the damage, and where the proximate cause is the malicious act of a third person, against which precautions would have been in operative, the defendant is not liable in the absence of a finding either that he instigated it or that he ought to have foreseen and provided against it.[155] In the case of *Chief G.B.A. Tiebo VII and Ors v. Shell Petroleum*

---

[153] [1998] Env L R 369.

[154] [1995] 1 All E R 225.

[155] Shell Petroleum Development Company of Nigeria Ltd v. Graham Otoko and Ors (1990) 6 NWLR (pt 159), 725.

Development Company Ltd,[156] the plaintiffs succeeded in proving negligence against the defendant when the defendant's act caused the spill of crude oil into the Peremabiri Creek in Yenogoa causing damages. The court awarded the sum of =N=6 million as damages.

Where it is impossible to prove negligence, the plaintiff can rely on the doctrine of *res ipsa locquitor*. This doctrine applies to actions for injury by negligence where no proof of such negligence is required beyond the accident itself.[157]

It should however be noted that a plaintiff can institute action on one head of common law tort and another head in the alternative. This is because a single act may give rise to liability under the rule in *Ryland v. Fletcher* and in negligence. Under this situation, if things within the defendant's control are dangerous things and likely to escape and do damage, any resulting damage constitutes liability in negligence on the part of the owner.[158] Also, an action may be commenced under nuisance and in alternative under negligence.[159]

2.2.3 Doctrine of Equity

The doctrine of equity that is of relevance as a source of environmental law is the doctrine of restrictive covenant. It applies to environmental protection through land use control and development. Restrictive covenants are mechanisms for private land use control that supplement or even replace zoning regulations. They are often employed in new housing developments as a means of providing property value protection for adjacent landowners by placing restrictions on the use of property.[160] Thus, when a person purchases a piece of property, he or she agrees to certain restrictions in terms of what can be done with that property. The restrictive covenants may provide more stringent requirements than those imposed by the zoning restrictions. For example, covenants might place limitations on the density (e.g., only single-family detached units in a zone allowing attached housing) or they might increase the building setback lines beyond the zoning limits.

Covenants may also be included to enhance property value protection requirements. For example, they may specify minimum building square footage requirements, limitations in terms of acceptable construction materials, or specifications on architectural styles. In other words, the restrictions may affect the use of the land

---

[156] (1996) 4 NWLR (pt 445), 657.

[157] Per Obaseki (JSC as he then was) in Management Enterprises v. Otusanya (1987), 181.

[158] Shell Petroleum Development Company Ltd v. Otoko and Ors (1990), 724.

[159] Ibid. See, also, Shell Petroleum Development Company of Nigeria Ltd v. HRH Chief G.B.A. Tiebo VII and 4 Ors (1996), 657.

[160] Duxbury (1999), p. 96.

and/or preserve the amenities within the area.[161] Restrictive covenants may also be used to address environmental protection issues, relating to amounts of grading allowed, digging of wells and septic requirements, vehicle, storage, etc.

Restrictive covenants as instruments for land use control was an attempt by common law to come to grips with the uncontrolled development of land. The term restrictive covenant is used to describe a special obligation that imposes restrictions on the use or enjoyment of land for the benefit of other lands within the area in question. The doctrine was enunciated in the case of *Tulks v. Moxhay*[162] where the conditions for the applicability of the doctrine were laid. The conditions to be met for the doctrine to apply are as follows:

(i) The covenant in question must be negative in nature or restrictive in nature. The test is whether the observance of the covenant will involve expenditure on the part of the covenantor.
(ii) The covenantee must own land which will benefit from the covenant. In other words, the land owned must be of a nature of dominant tenement.
(iii) The covenant must touch and concern the land.

These conditions have been applied in several cases. In the case of *LEDB v. Raji*,[163] a clause contained in the lease agreement provides that the land is to be used for "residential purpose only." The building was later used for prayers for church programmes. The court held that this act amounted to a breach of the covenant. The reason is predicated on the fact that for the restrictive covenant to apply, its observance by the covenantor will not require any expenditure from him. However, in the case of *Zaid v. Saliba*,[164] the plaintiff sought an injunction to restrain the defendant from using the leased premises as a club claiming that the business of running a proprietary club did not come within the meaning of trading purposes in the sub-lease. The injunction sought was refused by the court on the grounds that the words "trade" or "business" were applicable to a proprietary club.

Restrictive covenant as an instrument for land use control has some flaws. One major limitation of restrictive covenants is that they must be diligently overseen to be effectively enforceable. The reason is that they require self-policing by the members of the community to whom the deed restrictions apply as well as by the planning authority that imposed them in the first instance. It is because of these limitations in the application of common law nuisance and restrictive covenants that it became necessary to control land use and development, and therefore protect the environment, through statutory regulations. The reason being that as Lord Goff pointed out

---

[161]These are common practices in housing development schemes, for instance at Trans-Ekulu layout Enugu, Nigeria, the Enugu State Housing Development Authority imposes such restrictions as to set-backs, set-offs, building heights, etc., on land developers and this is also a common practice by various Urban Planning Authority across the country.

[162](1848) 2 Ph 774.

[163](1939) 5 WACA 137.

[164](1962) 1 All NLR 73.

in the case of *Cambridge Water Company v. Eastern Counties Leather Co. plc*,[165] "public bodies, both national and international, are taking significant steps towards the establishment of legislation which will promote the protection of the environment… given that so much well informed and carefully structured legislation is now being put in place for this purpose, there is less need for the courts to develop a common law principle to achieve the same end and indeed it may well be undesirable that they should do so."

To this end, these rules of common law and doctrine of equity have in no small measure contributed as a source of environmental law and as such form part of the mechanisms for environmental protection and control not minding their limitations in being applied for that purpose.

2.3 National Legislation as a Source of Environmental Law

Over the years, Nigeria has passed pieces of environmental laws to not only protect the environment but also control and manage it for human survival. National legislation on the environment can be found under the following heads:[166]

i) Framework Legislation
ii) Sectoral Legislation
iii) Incidental Legislation

2.3.1 *Framework Legislation*

Framework legislation comprises laws that were enacted with overall environmental protection in mind. They target the protection of every aspect of the environment in Nigeria. They are comprehensive in nature in that their provisions target the protection of every segment of the environmental media. These laws are:

a) The Harmful Wastes (Special Criminal Provisions etc.) Act 1988[167]
b) The Environmental Impact Assessment Act 1992[168]
c) The Nigerian Urban and Regional Planning Act 1992[169]

[165] [1994] 1 All E R 53 at 76.
[166] These laws mentioned here were discussed in Chap. 16 of this book.
[167] Cap H1 Laws of the Federation of Nigeria (LFN) 2004.
[168] Cap E12 LFN 2004.
[169] Cap N138 LFN 2004.

d) The National Environmental Standards and Regulations Enforcement Agency (Establishment) Act) 2007[170] and Regulations thereto
e) Climate Change Act 2021

2.3.2 Sectoral Legislation

The next set of environmental legislation in Nigeria are set of laws referred to as sectoral legislation. These are laws enacted for the protection of a segment or sector of the environment like land, water or the atmosphere. The legislations within this category are:

a) Oil in Navigable Waters Act 1969[171]
b) Oil Pipelines Act 1965[172]
c) National Oil Spill Detection and Response Agency (NOSDRA) Act 2006[173]
d) Nigerian Maritime Administration and Safety Agency (NIMASA) Act 2007[174]

2.3.3 Incidental Legislation

These are laws whose mischiefs are not directly on environmental protection but have a section or more that can be applied to achieve an environmental end. Some of these laws are:

a) Agricultural (Control of Importation) Act[175]
b) Animal Diseases (Control) Act[176]
c) Bees (Impact Control and Management) Act[177]
d) Civil Aviation (Repeal and Re-enactment) Act[178]
e) Constitution of the Federal Republic of Nigeria 1999, as amended[179]

---

[170] Enacted in 2007 vide Government Notice No. 61, Act No. 25 2007, Federal Republic of Nigeria Official Gazette No. 92, Vol. 94, 31 July 2007 and amended in 2018 vide Government Notice No. 106, Act No. 26 2018, Federal Republic of Nigeria Official Gazette No. 146, Vol. 105, 14 November 2018.

[171] Cap 06 LFN 2004.

[172] Cap 07 LFN 2004.

[173] Act No. 15 2006 as amended by National Oil Spill Detection and Response Agency (Establishment, etc.) (Amendment) Act 2008.

[174] Act No. 17 2007.

[175] Cap A13 LFN 2004.

[176] Cap A17 LFN 2004.

[177] Cap B6 LFN 2004.

[178] Cap C13 LFN 2004.

[179] Cap C23 LFN 2004.

f) Criminal Code[180]
g) Endangered Species (Control of International Trade and Traffic) Act[181]
h) Factories Act[182]
i) Hides and Skins Act[183]
j) Land Use Act[184]
k) National Parks Service Act[185]
l) Niger-Delta Development Commission (Establishment, etc) (NDDC) Act[186]
m) Nigerian Minerals and Mining Act 2007[187]
n) Nigerian Mining Corporation Act[188]
o) Nuclear Safety and Radiation Protection Act[189]
p) Pest Control of Produce (Special Powers) Act[190]
q) Petroleum Act and Regulations[191]
r) Petroleum Industry Act 2021[192]
s) Quarantine Act 1926[193]
t) River Basins Development Authority Act[194]
u) Sea Fisheries Act[195]
v) Water Resources Act[196]

2.4 Customary Law as a Source of Environmental Law

2.4.1 Introduction

Before the advent of Statutes on planning and environmental pollution abatement and control, the Nigerian rural environment had enjoyed mutual environmental

[180] Cap C38 LFN 2004.
[181] Cap E9 LFN 2004.
[182] Cap F1 LFN 2004.
[183] Cap H3 LFN 2004.
[184] Cap L4 LFN 2004.
[185] Cap N65 LFN 2004.
[186] Cap N86 LFN 2004.
[187] Act No. 20 2007.
[188] Cap N120 LFN 2004.
[189] Cap N142 LFN 2004.
[190] Cap P 9 LFN 2004.
[191] Cap P10 LFN 2004.
[192] Act No. 6 2021.
[193] Cap Q2 LFN 2004.
[194] Cap R9 LFN 2004.
[195] Cap S4 LFN 2004.
[196] Cap W2 LFN 2004.

protection through customary physical planning principles and environmental pollution abatement practices. Although not in any written form, such practices existed, and still exist, in our rural communities as a collection of obligatory practices for environmental pollution abatement, dynamic in nature and preserved in the memories of elders and community leaders who through oral tradition passed them down from generation to generation. Although the impacts of modern planning and environmental laws are yet to be fully felt in our rural communities, it is without doubt that physical planning and environmental pollution abatement mechanisms were not unknown in traditional rural communities of Nigeria. These practices can be regarded as veritable tools for environmental pollution abatement and control. Perhaps the following customary practices shall buttress the above assertions.

2.4.2 *Theory of Corporate Ownership of Land*

This theory while recognising the right of individual land ownership vested predominant land ownership either in the community or family. Members of the corporate group enjoyed equal rights to such land. The community or family head allocated land to members or strangers for cultivation, housing or grazing. The standard condition for such a grant of land was that the grantee's family or individual must put the land to beneficial use. According to T. O. Elias:[197]

> This overriding postulate of valid occupancy accounts for the restriction which local customary law places on the acquisition of land by any individual beyond his immediate needs or what he can usefully cultivate and that it measures fairness of land distribution which is so vital to social policy and economic well-being.

Thus, development control of land use through zoning was being effectively practiced in traditional Nigeria. Any non-conforming use of land for an unauthorised purpose could lead to forfeiture of the grant and even ostracism.[198] To this end, where a grantee of purely agricultural land converted it to a residential accommodation the court ordered a forfeiture.[199] Individual land use as well as communal decisions was subject to this customary development control. This rudimentary form of development control perhaps, had laid the foundation for the complex land use pattern provided under the Nigerian Urban and Regional Planning Act (NURPA) 1992.[200]

---

197 Elias (1951), p. 115.

198 Elias (1951), p. 115.

199 Taiwo v. Akinwumi (1975) 1 ALL NLR (pt 1) 222.

200 Cap N138 LFN 2004. This law was discussed in Chap. 8 of this book.

2.4.3 *Doctrine of Eminent Domain*

This doctrine postulates that positive land use planning and control involves the compulsory acquisition of land for public use. The practice of eminent domain ensures that the state can reassert either temporarily or permanently its dominion over any portion of the soil of the state for the public good. It has been suggested that the origin, meaning and effects of this practice depict our traditional concept of zoning of land among various traditional uses, such as markets, housing, agriculture, roads, public shrines, playgrounds, etc.[201]

The expropriated individual or family is usually resettled where practicable, otherwise cash payment may be made. In recent years the native inhabitants of Mokwa, Abuja Federal Capital Territory and Ajaokuta were resettled in new towns before the government could affect its development and new planning schemes. This customary planning control practice is almost on all fours with some of the provisions of the NURPA 1992 on revocation of development permits,[202] acquisition of land and compensation.[203]

2.4.4 *Customary Farming and Land Use Pattern*

Farming rights in some communities are granted by the family head and in others by the community head. Before the arrival of received English law and local statutes, the planning law device of development control had been extensively practiced in our traditional society. Our land use control devices are based on the principle of corporate ownership and the doctrine of eminent domain. Also, before the present era of land fragmentation arising from unbridled population growth, our rural community practiced shifting cultivation and crop rotation. By these farming practices, the fertility of the farmland is allowed to regenerate without resorting to the new practice of application of fertiliser.

2.4.5 *Customary Law and Forest Protection*

Apart from hunting, certain forests are reserved in rural Nigeria for various purposes such as preservation of animal species, ritual worship, and conservation of pharmaceutical raw materials, or as instant refugee camps in war times. The Afi Forest, Mbe Mountains, Obudu Cattle Ranch, all in Cross River State, the Okomu Forest Reserve in Edo State and the Omo Forest Reserve in Ogun State had their origin in these

[201] Alder (1979), p. 10.

[202] Revocation of Permit, see NURPA (1992), s.39.

[203] NURPA (1992), ss. 75 and 76.

customary practices. Any contravention of these customary laws and practices is visited with immediate sanction. In *Bale of Idona v. Abuodun Kova*[204] the defendant was alleged to have entered a sacred grove in the community and cut down some trees. The native court held that although the defendant's farmland was adjacent to and in fact part of the grove, he was ordered to vacate the whole land. In a similar Ijebu-Ode case, *Disu Omisanya v. Adeshina Gabriel*,[205] the defendant was allowed by the court to remain on the land. In some parts of the Eastern and Western States of Nigeria firewood, fruit and vegetable collection from certain forests is prohibited, in other parts; it can only be collected on certain days.

In many communities, for instance, it is prohibited to cut down certain trees,[206] kill certain species of snakes (such as pythons worshiped in such communities with the belief that the python was part of their departed ancestors.), and kill reptiles such as crocodiles. All these have some religious connotations to such communities.

These customary practices helped to conserve the ecosystem from environmental abuse. The implication of the above discussions is that although there were no specific written regulations on planning control or control of development, environmental protection, "was historically based on native law and custom and legal since customary law is law."[207] Thus, the various customary law devices discussed above clearly show that before the advent of modern environmental and planning law, the customary practices that existed and still exist today in our rural communities, have the protection of the environment as one of its main objectives.

2.5 Summary

The environment is the most formidable source of national and international development and should be protected from damage, destruction and annihilation to enthrone a decent, benign, disease-free and aesthetically pleasing environment. In this respect, environmental law comes into play to achieve these. There is an intermingling of international law, common law, and national legislation as well as extracts from customary law that have formed the basic sources of environmental law. Over the years on the realisation of the importance of protection of the environment through legislation, the international community through bi-lateral and multi-lateral treaties has served as a beacon in the direction that national laws should follow in their quest to create an environment free from abuse and

[204] Itugun Native Court, 85/1956 – The case was later transferred to Ijebu-Ode Native Court.

[205] Ijebu Ode Native Court 1033/1955.

[206] Such trees include Igi Ajura, Igi Akoko, Igi Safsaf, Igi Oro, Igi Maghu, Igi Mango and Igfi Keafi: A similar situation exists at Okpa-Inyi Forest of Igbanaro Oyi L.G.A. Anambra State. See, also, ENAV Aliar Ake Native Court Grade "A" Abeokuta of 10/12/23. See NURPA (1992), ss. 73 and 74.

[207] Ola (1977), p. 5.

dislocation, showing the interconnectedness of environmental problems and the need for uniformity, or near it, in the fight against environmental pollution and degradation.

References

Alder J (1979) Development control, modern legal studies. Sweet and Maxwell, London
Birnie P et al (2009) International law and the environment, 3rd edn. Oxford University, Oxford
Bratspies RM, Miller RA (eds) (2006) Transboundary harm in international law: lessons from the Trail Smelter Arbitration. Cambridge University, New York
"Customary International Law," https://www.internationallaw.uslegal.com/source-of-international-law. Accessed on 12 June 2023
Dinstein Y (2005) The conduct of hostilities under the law of international armed conflict. Cambridge University, Cambridge
Duxbury RMC (1999) Telling and Duxbury's planning law and procedure, 11th edn. Butterworths, London
Elias TO (1951) Nigerian. Land law and custom. Rutledge & Kegan Paul, London
Enemo IP (2007) The law of tort. Chenglo, Enugu
Global issue laws of the sea (2020). https://globalissuelawsofthesea.weebly.com/mox-plant-case.html. Accessed on 10 June 2023
Gunaratne R (2014). https://ruwanthikagunaratne.wordpress.com/2014/02/28/north-sea-continental-shelf-cases-summary. Accessed on 12 June 2020
Kramer L (1990) EEC treaty and environmental protection. Sweet and Maxwell, London. ISBN 13: 9780421432901
Ola CS (1977) Town & country planning law in Nigeria. Oxford University, Ibadan
Oxford Public Law (2018). https://opil.ouplaw.com/view. Accessed 19 on June 2023
Rosenne S (1984) New practice and methods of international law. Oceana, New York
Sands P (2003) Principles of international environmental law, 2nd edn. Cambridge University, Cambridge
Statute of the International Court of Justice (1945). https://www.icj-cij.org/documents/index.php. Accessed on 12 June 2023
Sullivan T (1999) Fundamentals of environmental law. In: Sullivan T (ed) Environmental law handbook, 15th edn. Government Institutes, Rockville, Maryland
United Nations (1972) Declaration of the United Nations Conference on the Human Environment (Stockholm Declaration) (1973), UN Document A/CONF.48/14/Rev.1
United Nations (1992) Rio Declaration on Environment and Development, UN Doc A/Conf.151/26 (14 June 1992) https://www.un.org/en/development/A/CONF.151/26 (Vol. I).pdf. Accessed 14 on May 2023
United Nations Environment Programme (1992) Rio Declaration on Environment and Development, Rio de Janeiro, UN Doc A/Conf.151/26 (14 June 1992)
United Nations Environment Programme (UNEP) (2023). https://cites.org/eng/disc/text.php. Accessed on 14 July 2023
United Nations General Assembly (UNGA) (1972a) Resolution 2849 (XXVI) (1972)
United Nations General Assembly (UNGA) (1972b) Resolution 2996 (1972) Resolutions and Decisions, 19 September – 19 December 1972
Winfield R, Jolowicz (2006) Winfield and Jolowicz on Tort, 17th edn. Sweet and Maxwell, London

Chapter 3
Theories and Concepts in Environmental Legislation

Abstract Some assumptions have been postulated over the years on why environmental pollution persists and on how best to limit, and where possible, control it. This preposition is predicated on the fact that stopping environmental pollution is an impossible task. Once developmental activities take place, there is bound to be environmental pollution. The pollution becomes a problem when by its nature, and by an aggregate of it, the environmental medium's carrying capacity is exceeded hampering its self-purification processes. Some of these theories and concepts and how they have influenced environmental legislation in recent years are: theory of free-market environmentalism, the Coase theorem, environmental Kuznets theory, theory of command and control, theory of emission trading and environmental legislation, concept of sustainability and economic development, market-based concepts in environmental legislation, and the concept of strict and absolute liability. This chapter discusses these theories and concepts.

3.1 Introduction

Understanding environmental legislation is better appreciated by examining the various theories and concepts found inroads in the enactment of environmental laws. Theory has been defined as an assumption or system of assumptions, accepted principles, and rules of procedure based on limited information or knowledge, devised to analyse, predict, or otherwise explain the nature or behaviour of a specified set of phenomena.[1] Concepts on the other hand are defined as abstract ideas or general notions that occur in the mind, in speech, or in thought. They are understood to be the fundamental building blocks of thought and belief.[2] Both theories and concepts are forms of abstract reasoning. They therefore play an important role in all aspects of cognition and in legislating on environmental matters.

---

[1] Redmond (2009).

[2] Carey (1991), pp. 257–291.

E. Onyeabor, *Environmental Law*, https://doi.org/10.1007/978-3-031-68956-7_3

3.2 Theory of Free-Market Environmentalism

3.2.1 Introduction

Free-market environmentalism is a position that argues that the free market, property rights, and tort law provide the best tools to preserve the health and sustainability of the natural environment.[3]

Under the economics of environmental destruction theory, it is believed that environmental problems arise from market failures because laws governing property rights have failed to adequately protect or define those rights.[4] Again, laws governing class or individual tort claims provide polluters with immunity from tort claims, or interfere with those claims in such a way as to make it difficult to legally sustain them.[5] Thus, the best way to protect the environment is to change laws governing property rights[6] and tort claims[7] so that those laws no longer suffer from the defects they believe give individuals and corporations perverse incentives not to guard the environment. This process results in negative externalities of industrial production and excessive depletion of non-renewable resources.

In this view, firms receive the full benefit of creating their products in a way that generates pollutants but do not bear the full social costs of the increased pollution.[8] These firms, especially multinational corporations (MNCs), therefore have no economic incentive to create products in a way that minimises pollution because it would be profitable for them to over pollute, while letting others absorb the costs of its effects and clean up.[9] Regarded this way, the solution to the problem of pollution is that market mechanisms left to their own devices contain built-in incentives for environmental degradation.[10]

---

[3] Newton and Cantarello (2014), p. 125.

[4] Newton and Cantarello (2014), p. 125.

[5] Ibid., 126.

[6] For instance, under the provisions of the Constitution of the Federal Republic of Nigeria 1999 (CFRN 1999) as amended, s. 43 and Petroleum Industry Act 20211, s. 1, once oil is discovered in any land, the land automatically becomes the property of the Federal Government, and the rights of the indigenous land owners are expropriated.

[7] Under the tort law, various obstacles lie in wait for prospective litigants. For instance, a litigant must prove that the tort complained affected him over and above other persons within the vicinity, whether the litigant is the owner of the land or occupier.

[8] Daly and Farley (2004), p. 54.

[9] As is the case in the oil and gas industry where oil companies are comfortable paying for gas flaring rather than embarking on gas re-injection projects.

[10] Daly and Farley (2004), p. 54.

3.2.2 How Free-Market Environmentalism Works

Hahnel,[11] an ecological economist, had enumerated what he termed the four basic effects of a market economy with respect to the environment. According to him, these four basic defects are: overexploitation of common property resources; over-pollution; too little pollution clean-up; and over-consumption.

It is believed that overexploitation occurs to the extent of the lack of ownership incentives to care for the property, and that this communalisation effect occurs to the extent of multiplicity of ownership.[12] Overexploitation reduces the intrinsic and retail value of the property, the effect of which is most clearly felt by individual owners or through limited co-ownership.[13] Thus, pollution occurs where and to the extent that victims are prevented or hindered from seeking tort restitution for such aggression.[14] The reason is not farfetched. Legislative and judicial authorities have tended to favour heavy industries over individual or class action in favour of "public property" and the "common good."

Several judicial decisions in Nigeria reflect the above assertion. This attitude is aptly illustrated in the case of *Allar Irou v. Shell B.P.*[15] where the judge refused to grant an injunction in favour of the plaintiff whose land and fishpond had been polluted by the defendant's operations. The refusal of the judge was based on social and economic reasons. The judge intoned that if such an injunction is granted, "it could stop the defendant's trade and render many unemployed and even affect the country's revenue since oil was, and still remains, the main income generator of the country."[16]

Again, in the case of *Godpower Nweke v. Nigerian Agip Oil Company Ltd,*[17] the issue before the court was compensation for economic trees, fish, ponds, lakes, juju shrines, damaged fishing creeks and lands belonging to the plaintiff. These damages were caused by the defendant's oil operations. After going through administrative procedures for compensation, the plaintiff brought this action because the compensation advanced by the defendant was inadequate. The Supreme Court of Nigeria queried the approach of the lower court in not dismissing the case since the defendant had offered an amount to the plaintiff and entered judgment for the plaintiff in the amount earlier agreed upon. In this case, the judiciary succumbed

---

[11] Hahnel (2005), pp. 66–72.

[12] Ibid.

[13] Hahnel (2005), pp. 66–72.

[14] A case in point is the high level of environmental degradation in the oil- producing communities in Nigeria and their quest for restitution hindered by the government's economic interest through stultifying bureaucracy and unending judicial processes.

[15] Suit No. WW/89/71 (Unreported), delivered by Ovie Whiskey (J), Warri High Court on 6 November 1972.

[16] Allar Irou v. Shell B.P., ibid.

[17] (1976) 9 & 10 S. C. 107.

to the dictates of the power of the influential defendant,[18] and felt more comfortable with awarding the amount dictated by the environmental polluter. The basis for this is that the polluters should be protected since the revenue derived from their activity is the economic life wire of the country.

As a result of all these and many more, free-market enterprises create negative externalities in industrial production and encourage excessive depletion of non-renewable resources.[19] The prevalence of these externalities normally has serious implications for the environment. If negative externalities are unaccounted for, it would imply that market prices will not accurately reflect true social opportunity costs, leading to misallocations of goods.[20]

To this end, when a firm pollutes a river, it uses some of society's resources just as surely as when it uses fossil fuels as a source of energy during production. Therefore, if the firm pays for the source of energy used during production but not for the use of clean water, it is expected that management will be economical in its use of the energy source and wasteful in its use of water.

In the long run, the standard approach to addressing negative externalities is governmental regulation proscribing polluting activities.[21] But this approach has been criticised by free-market economists and others as being inefficient and ineffective.[22] For instance, multinational corporations operating in the oil industry in Nigeria prefer to flare gas and pay the penalty under Regulation 13 of the Flare Gas (Prevention of Waste and Pollution) Regulations 2018.[23] To curb the excesses of polluters it is suggested that full accountability as dictated by courts that respect the rights of property owners in absolute terms should be pursued.

Again, in other to overcome the problems inherent in free-market enterprises, it is advocated that consequences of production be internalised through the establishment of a property right over some phenomenon formerly in the public domain, a sophisticated variant of the "polluter-pays" principle.[24] Through this means environmental pollution can be controlled. It works this way:

> If industries internalized the costs of negative externalities they would face an incentive to reduce them, perhaps even becoming enthusiastic about taking advantage of opportunities to improve profitability through lower costs. This would lead to the optimal balance between

[18] Nigerian Agip Oil Company Ltd, a multinational oil company.

[19] Such as land and water.

[20] Russo (1999), p. 98.

[21] The Nigerian government through the National Environmental Standards Regulation and Enforcement Agency (NESREA) established in 2007 had put in place about 33 regulations for such purpose. Efforts by NESREA to protect the Nigerian environment were discussed in Chap. 6 of this book.

[22] Such as Richard L Stroup, and Murray Rothbard, among others.

[23] Among the reasons adduced by the oil companies was that the terrain where oil is produced in Nigeria is too swampy thus affecting the cost of gas re-injection. They therefore prefer to flare the associated gas and pay a fine.

[24] This principle was discussed in detail in Chap. 4 of this book.

the marginal benefits of pursuing an activity and the marginal cost of its environmental consequences.[25]

Overall, if the environmental costs, such as pollution taxes, and corporate social responsibility practices, among others, are internalised by the oil companies operating in Nigeria, being the heaviest polluters in Nigeria, it may go a long way in addressing the environmental problems prevalent in the oil-producing communities in Nigeria.

3.2.3 *Arguments Against the Theory of Free-Market Environmentalism*

Although the discussions above highlighted the main thrusts of free-market environmentalism, however, there are several arguments against the theory.

First, not all aspects of the public domain are easily "privatisable" in practice. According to Barbier,[26] it may be impossible to establish property rights on things like air and water that circulate the globe, so stopping air pollution or global warming would be very difficult. Thus, the Coase theorem[27] environmentalists often support carbon trading schemes advocated by other environmentalist movements as a way out. However, economists such as Rothbard[28] rejected carbon trading schemes viewing it as government-imposed emissions trading schemata. He instead maintained that pollution is by definition a matter of property rights being violated, and hence should be handled as a subject of individual or class action tort, as any other invasion of property. That as long as there is an aggressor and a victim, there is a tort.

Second, the conservation of endangered species is not necessarily achievable using the free market, especially where there is little economic value in the species in question. For example: there might be only limited profit to be made from a piece of land by maintaining it as the habitat of a rare beetle, whereas alternative economic uses for that land (which might be deleterious to the welfare of the beetle) – such as building a parking lot on it – might yield a greater profit.[29] Regardless of the broader ecological importance of the beetle, it is much more likely that the landowner will prioritise short-term profits to be gained from development, rather than a long-term benefit which may be of comparably little (perhaps even imperceptible on the surface) benefit to himself.[30] Thus, threatened or endangered species could be lost by relying on the willingness of individual landowners to take a loss in order to

---

[25] United States Environmental Protection Agency (USEPA) (1999), p. 125.

[26] Barbier (2014), p. 234.

[27] Discussed in sect. 3.3 below.

[28] Rothbard (1982).

[29] Westra and Vilela (2014), p. 178.

[30] Ibid.

protect them. However, this view does not account for non-profit organisations which exist solely to preserve rare species.

Third, a related philosophical objection is that free-market environmentalism is entirely anthropocentric and ignores the "innate" value of nature outside of human perception. But even in politics, someone must place a value on the environment in question.[31]

Fourth, the principle of limited liability protects investors from the costs of the activities from which they benefit. In the US, there have been recent suggestions that, while limited liability towards creditors is socially beneficial in facilitating investment, the privilege ought not to extend to liability in tort for environmental disasters or personal injury. In fact, most free-market environmentalists oppose limited liability in torts as a form of corporate welfare and a limitation of full property rights.[32]

Lastly, countering the tragedy of the commons claim, Ostrom[33] had studied a large number of empirical cases where common property resources have been managed successfully. Her work emphasises neither private property/market arrangements nor government regulation but the successes of "communities" consciously designing institutional arrangements in response to particular common property dilemmas. The stress is on democratic institutions that allow the users of the common to govern the commons.[34]

3.3 The Coase Theorem

3.3.1 Introduction

The theorem was propounded by Nobel Laureate Ronald Coase, Professor Emeritus of Law and Economics at the University of Chicago. He was interested in the "efficiency" of tort rules, that is, in the rules' tendency to bring about an "efficient" outcome, defined as one in which the net sum of social wealth (a proxy for social happiness, but more easily measured) is maximised.[35] Recognising that safety has costs, Coase and his followers think of an efficient rule as one that minimises the sum of accident costs and prevention costs, because such a rule will, given other assumptions, subtract the least from social wealth. Note that "efficiency" in this sense does not require that costs be allocated justly between people. To him and his protagonists, justice is a separate ideal, from the economists' perspective.[36]

[31] Adams (1999), p. 136.

[32] Hansmann and Kraakman (1991), p. 1879.

[33] Elinor (2019).

[34] Ibid.

[35] Coase (1960), p. 10.

[36] Ibid.

3.3.2 Main Theses of Coase Theorem

Coase developed his theory when considering the regulation of radio frequencies, analogous to competing industries and their bids to protect the environment. According to him, competing radio stations could use the same frequencies and would therefore interfere with each other's broadcasts.[37] The problem faced by regulators was how to eliminate interference and allocate frequencies to radio stations efficiently. And that as long as property rights in these frequencies were well defined, it ultimately did not matter if adjacent radio stations interfered with each other by broadcasting in the same frequency band. Furthermore, it did not matter to whom the property rights were granted. He reasoned that the station able to reap the higher economic gain from broadcasting would have the incentive to pay the other station not to interfere. In the absence of transaction costs, both stations would strike a mutually advantageous deal. It would not matter whether one or the other station had the initial right to broadcast; eventually, the right to broadcast would end up with the party that was able to put it to the most highly valued use.[38]

Coase's main point was that transaction costs, however, could not be neglected, and therefore, the initial allocation of property rights often mattered.[39] As a result, one normative conclusion sometimes drawn from the Coase theorem is that property rights should initially be assigned to the actors gaining the most utility from them. The problem in real life is that nobody knows *ex ante* the most valued use of a resource and that there exist costs involving the reallocation of resources by the government.[40] Another, more refined normative conclusion also often discussed in law and economics is that government should create institutions that minimise transaction costs, to allow misallocations of resources to be corrected as cheaply as possible.[41]

3.3.3 Application of the Coase Theorem

The Coase theorem has been used by jurists and legal scholars in the analysis and resolution of disputes involving both contract law and tort law. In contract law, Coase is often used as a method to evaluate the relative power of the parties during the negotiation and acceptance of a traditional or classical bargained-for contract. In modern tort law, the application of economic analysis to assign liability for damages was popularised by Judge Hand of the United States of America's 2nd Circuit Court

[37] Ibid.

[38] Coase (1960).

[39] Ibid.

[40] Burdon (2014), p. 96.

[41] Ibid.

of Appeals in his decision in the case of *United States v. Carroll Towing Co.*[42] Judge Hand's holding resolved simply that liability could be determined by applying the formula:

$$\mathbf{B} < \mathbf{PL}$$

where:

B = the burden (economic or otherwise) of adequate protection against foreseeable damages
P = the probability of damage (or loss) occurring
L = the gravity of the resulting injury (loss)

In resultant scholarship using economic models of analysis, prominently including the Coase theorem, theoretical models demonstrated that when transaction costs are minimised or non-existent, the legal appropriation of liability diminishes in importance or disappears completely. In other words, parties will arrive at an economically efficient solution that may ignore the legal framework in place. For example, two property owners own land on a mountainside. Property Owner No. 1's land is upstream from Property Owner No. 2 and there is significant, damaging run-off from Owner No. 1's land to Owner No. 2's land.[43]

Four scenarios are considered:[44]

(i) If a cause of action exists (i.e., Owner No. 2 could sue Owner No. 1 for damages and win) and the property damage equals =N=100,000 while the cost of building a wall to stop the run-off equals =N=50,000, the wall will probably exist. Owner No. 1 will build the wall, rather than pay Owner No. 2 between =N=100,000 and =N=50,000 to tolerate the run-off.
(ii) If a cause of action exists and the damage equals =N=50,000 while the cost of a wall is =N=100,000 the wall will not exist. Owner No. 2 may sue, win the case and the court will order Owner No. 1 to pay Owner No. 2 =N=50,000. This is cheaper than actually building the wall.[45]
(iii) If a cause of action does not exist, and the damage equals =N=100,000 while the cost of the wall equals =N=50,000, the wall will exist. Even though Owner No. 2 cannot win the lawsuit, he or she will still pay Owner No. 1 some amount between =N=51,000 and =N=99,000 to build the wall.
(iv) If a cause of action does not exist, and the damage equals =N=50,000 while the wall will cost =N=100,000 the wall will not exist. Owner No. 2 cannot win the lawsuit and the economic realities of trying to get the wall built are prohibitive.

---

[42] 159 F.2d 169 (2d. Cir. 1947).

[43] Coase (1960).

[44] Adopted from Coase (1960).

[45] This is the case in the oil industry where oil companies prefer to flare associated gas and pay penalty because it is cheaper rather than engage in gas re-injection projects, which are more costly.

The Coase theorem considers all four of these outcomes logical because economic incentives will be stronger than legal incentives. Pure or traditional legal analysis will expect that the wall will exist in both scenarios where No. 2 has a cause of action and that the wall will never exist if No. 2 has no cause of action.

3.3.4 Criticisms of the Coase Theorem

The theorem is not without criticisms. The main criticism often targeted at the Coase theorem is that transaction costs are almost always too high for efficient bargaining to happen. For instance, economist Meade[46] argued that even in a simple case of a beekeeper's bees dusting a nearby farmer's crops, Coasean bargaining is inefficient.[47] Ronald Coase[48] himself asserts that it would be unrealistic to assume there were no costs in the conduction of market transactions, and that these costs are "often extremely costly, sufficiently costly at any rate to prevent many transactions that would be carried out in a world in which the pricing system worked without cost." On the other hand, this is not really a criticism of the theorem itself, since the theorem considers only those situations in which there are no transaction costs. Instead, it is a criticism of applications of the theorem that neglect this crucial assumption.

Another strain of criticism often points out other problems often associated with public goods which manifest in Coasean bargaining. In many cases of externalities, the bargaining does not happen between two economic factors, but instead, the parties might be a single large factory versus a thousand landowners nearby. In such situations, say the critics, not only do transaction costs rise extraordinarily high, but bargaining is hindered by what is termed basic prisoner's dilemma problems.[49] For instance, property rights might say the landowners must pay the factory to stop polluting; certain landowners might downplay the harm of pollution on them, trying to freeride on the other landowners' wallets.

3.4 Environmental Kuznets Curve (EKC) Theory

3.4.1 Introduction

Kuznets curve is the graphical representation of Simon Kuznet's theory that economic inequality increases over time while a country is developing, then after a

[46]Meade (2007), as cited by Halpin (2007), p. 327.

[47]Halpin (2007), p. 327.

[48]Coase (1960), p. 43.

[49]Halpin (2007).

critical average income is attained, begins to decrease.[50] One theory as to why this happens is that states in the early stages of development, when investment in physical capital is the main mechanism of economic growth, inequality encourages growth by allocating resources towards those who save and invest the most. Whereas in mature economies human capital accrual, or an estimate of cost that has been incurred but not yet paid, takes the place of physical capital accrual as the main source of growth, and inequality slows growth by lowering education standards because poor people lack finance for their education in imperfect credit markets.[51]

3.4.2 Application of the Kuznets Curve

Although the theory was developed purely in an economic scenario, the Kuznets curve has applications in environmental protection.[52] The relevance of the environmental Kuznet's curve is based on the following argument. In a developing industrial economy, little weight is given to environmental concerns, raising environmental pollution by-products. After attaining a certain standard of living from the industrial production system and when environmental pollution is at its greatest, the focus changes from self-interest to social interest. The interests give greater weight to a clean environment by reducing and reversing the environmental pollution trend from industrialisation.[53] For instance, from the 1970s there was an upsurge in legislating against environmental problems by the federal government of the USA. According to Carlarne:[54]

> The changing role of the Federal Government in the 1970 can be attributed to a variety of factors. First, US society was more affluent and more educated than at any point in its history and, as a result, had time and resources to focus on improving its quality of life, which was increasingly seen as intricately tied to environmental factors. Consequently, the public demanded that the federal government take action to preserve and improve the environment in ways that would contribute to the quality of life.

This trend also occurred in Nigeria. Before 1988, environmental legislation in Nigeria was piece-meals, non-comprehensive and without a fully functional and independent coordinating Agency. However, with the Koko toxic dump of 1988, there was a twist occasioned by the level of enlightenment of the Nigerian populace. In a screening headline in June 1988, many Nigerian daily newspapers alerted the country of the shipment of tonnes of toxic waste from factories in Italy and dumped in the sleeping Koko port in the then Bendel State. Without adequate knowledge of

---

[50] Anderson (2014), p. 145.

[51] Anderson (2014), p. 145.

[52] Many environmental health indicators, such as water and air pollution, show the inverted U-shaped curve.

[53] McManus (2009), p. 57.

[54] Carlarne (2010), p. 26.

the impact of such waste, nothing would have been done. Noting her vulnerability to a future occurrence of the Koko saga the Federal government of Nigeria promulgated two laws and set up an environmental protection agency.[55]

The following illustration buttresses the applicability of Kuznets's curve in environmental matters, especially in environmental health concerns, such as air pollution. Many of the problems associated with increased energy usage are due to the use of fossil fuels and this follows the economic growth of the country. Thus, carbon dioxide appears to follow a Kuznets curve, and its emissions appear to peak at a higher per capita gross domestic product (GDP).[56]

Again, the problem of deforestation also appears to follow a Kuznets curve. Among countries with a per capita GDP of at least $4600, net deforestation has ceased to exist. Furthermore, rich countries can afford desalination to provide their populations with clean, safe water. For instance, Israel desalinizes water for a cost of 53 cents per cubic metre; Singapore desalinizes water for 49 cents per cubic metre.[57] Even people who live far away from the ocean are benefiting from the technology. For instance, after being desalinised at Jubail, in Saudi Arabia, water is pumped about 320 kilometres inland through a pipeline to the capital city of Riyadh.[58] In summary, the main kernels of the theory are as follows:

(i) Environmental pressure increases up to a point as income goes up.
(ii) After the turning point, environmental quality improves as income rises.
(iii) Developing economies over time move from clean agrarian economies to polluting industrial economies.
(iv) Developed economies with improved levels of efficient infrastructure transfer cleaner technology.

3.4.3 *Shortfalls of the Kuznets Curve Theory*

A difficulty with this model is that it lacks predictive power because it is highly uncertain how the next phase of economic development will be characterised. Wealthy nations have a trend of exporting the activities that create the most pollution, like manufacturing of clothing and furniture, to poorer nations that are still in the process of industrial development. This means that as the world's poor nations develop, they will have no place to export their pollution.[59] Thus, this

[55] These laws were Harmful Waste Act (Special Criminal Provision Act 1988 (currently retained as CAP H1 LFN 2004) and the Federal Environmental Protection Agency (Establishment) Act 1988 (FEPA Act). This Act established the Federal Environmental Protection Agency (FEPA). However, the FEPA Act was repealed in 2007 by the National Environmental Standards Regulations and Enforcement (Establishment) Act (NESREA) 2007.

[56] Tisdell (2001), p. 190.

[57] Ibid., 195.

[58] Ibid.

[59] Ibid.

progression of environmental clean-up occurring in conjunction with economic growth cannot be replicated indefinitely because there will be nowhere to export waste and pollution-intensive processes.[60]

3.5 Theory of Command and Control

3.5.1 Introduction

Command and control can be defined as "the direct regulation of an industry or activity by legislation that states what is permitted and what is illegal."[61] In this respect, "command" is the presentation of quality standards/targets by a government authority that must be complied with, while "control" on the other hand signifies the negative sanctions that may result from non-compliance.[62]

In command and control, there is a perception of a problem, and the solution for its control is developed and subsequently implemented. It encompasses a variety of methods that could elicit the required compliance with regulations on environmental pollution abatement. According to Holling and Meffe,[63] such methods include: laws, incentives, contracts and agreements. For our purpose, we have limited ourselves to the theory of command and control with specific reference to environmental criminal law. The reason is that the principles that inform criminal legislation can be used to elicit environmental pollution abatement compliance.

To begin with, do we have environmental crimes? "What social harms are these crimes addressing, and what interests will be vindicated through use of the criminal sanctions?"[64] The answers to these questions are not found in traditional criminal law principles. This is because environmental interests and values do not enjoy absolute protection in environmental law. Unlike theft or homicide, for example, which may cause personal benefits only to the criminal, most polluting activities generate substantial societal benefits as well as environmental costs. However, environmental criminal law is aimed largely at an administrative control of pollution, usually through licensing and permitting systems. Environmental criminal statutes largely function to help ensure that control. Thus, environmental criminal law focuses on punishing the lack of a permit or the violation of a permit or other regulatory requirements and conditions.

---

[60] One of the most serious environmental concerns at present is the issue of transboundary movement of wastes, especially hazardous waste from developed economies to developing economies.

[61] McManus (2009), p. 98.

[62] Baldwin and Lodge (2011), p. 34.

[63] Holling and Meffe (1996), p. 328.

[64] Mandiberg and Faure (1995), p. 448.

However, if the role of the environmental criminal law is restricted to defining the conditions of an administrative permit, and the authorities at the same time determine the conditions of criminal liability, this may point to the fact that more direct environmental protection by the criminal law, such as those that exist for traditional crimes, will be more difficult to reach in environmental law, thus the need to institutionalise environmental crimes under command-and-control approach. It is in this regard that we can now find in some environmental laws provisions that prohibit acts that may have serious consequences of causing death, serious injury, or a significant risk of death or serious injury.[65] In this regard, criminal liability may arise irrespective of a violation of administrative obligations. An example to which this preposition referred to can be found in the provisions of Nigeria's Harmful Waste (Special Criminal Provisions, etc.) Act (HWSCP Act).[66]

The HWSCP Act prohibits all activities relating to the purchase, sale, importation, transit, transportation, deposit, and storage of harmful wastes.[67] Thus, under Section 1(2):[68]

> Any person who, without lawful authority carries, deposits, dumps or causes to be carried, deposited or dumped, or is in possession for the purpose of carrying, depositing or dumping, any harmful waste on any land or in any territorial waters or contiguous zone or Exclusive Economic Zone of Nigeria or its inland water ways shall be guilty of an offence.

It is also an offence "to transport, or causes to be transported or is in possession of transporting; imports, or causes to be imported or negotiates for the purposes of importing; or sells, offers for sale, buys or otherwise deal in any harmful waste."[69] The reason for this is the deleterious effect that harmful waste may have on the environment and human health.

In the HWSCP Act 1988,[70] harmful waste is defined to include "semi-solid, liquid or solid substance as well as any injurious, poisonous toxic or noxious substance... which can subject any person to the risk of death, fatal injury or incurable impairment of physical and mental health...."[71] It therefore means that actual harm to the environment, and the threat of such harm, is more serious than mere administrative disobedience. It then follows that when the government can prove that a person has both acted unlawfully and caused or threatened such harm, an effective system should have criminal sanctions in place to address the situation.[72] But this must be done after determining both the act element and the mental-state element of the polluter. The act element of a criminal statute articulates the social harm at which the crime is directed. The mental-state element articulates the attitude

---

[65] For instance, Harmful Waste (Special Criminal Provisions, etc.) Act (HWSCP Act) (1988), s. 12.

[66] Cap H1 Laws of the Federation of Nigeria (LFN), 2004.

[67] HWSCP Act (1988), s. 1(1).

[68] Ibid.

[69] Ibid., s. 1(2) (b)–(d).

[70] Ibid.

[71] Ibid., s. 15.

[72] Ibid., ss. 6 and 7 provide for criminal sanctions against the offenders.

a defendant must have had toward the social harm to be criminally culpable. Although the mental state is a crucial element in determining criminal liability, however, determining culpability in environmental crimes should focus exclusively on the act element of the crime.

Every framework legislation,[73] and some sectoral legislation[74] in Nigeria, establish some form of provisions for criminal sanction against violators. Under these statutes, violators are subject to charges that vary from simple negligence to injury or death. Various concepts have been developed in criminalising environmental harm, collectively referred to as concepts of environmental crimes. These concepts are categorised as:[75]

a) Abstract endangerment crimes
b) Concrete endangerment crimes
c) Concept of concrete harm
d) Concept of serious environmental pollution

3.5.2 *Abstract Endangerment Crimes*

When an environmental law is used to punish actions in violation of a permit condition that does not involve a discharge or any other possible effect on the environment the act fits within the abstract endangerment crimes. The basic characteristic of environmental crimes under this concept is that punishment does not relate to the actual causing of specific or certain environmental harm, rather this theory criminalises disobedience to administrative rules and requirements per se. They do not punish environmental pollution. Instead, the role of abstract endangerment crimes is to enforce prior administrative decisions, and so they punish the failure of a regulated entity to adhere to administrative dictates concerning environmental regulations.[76]

---

[73]Framework legislation are those laws that are comprehensive in nature in that their provisions target the protection of every segment of the environmental media and are enacted with the overall protection of the Nigerian environment in mind. They include laws such as: Harmful Wastes (Special Criminal Provisions, etc.) Act (n66), Environmental Impact Assessment Act 1992 Cap E12 LFN, 2004, National Environmental Standards and Regulations Enforcement (Establishment) Agency Act 2007 (NESREA Act 2007) Act No. 25 2007 Government Notice No. 61, Federal Republic of Nigeria Official Gazette No. 92, Vol. 94, 31 July 2007.

[74]These are laws enacted for the protection of a segment or sector of the environment such as land, water or the atmosphere. They include: Oil in Navigable Waters Act 1969 Cap 06 Laws of the Federation of Nigeria (LFN) 2004, Oil Pipelines Act 1965 Cap 07 Laws of the Federation of Nigeria (LFN) 2004, National Oil Spill Detection and Response Agency (NOSDRA) Act 2006 Act No. 15 2006 as amended by National Oil Spill Detection and Response Agency (Establishment, etc.) (Amendment) Act, 2008, Nigerian Maritime Administration and Safety Agency (NIMASA) Act 2007 Act No. 17 2007, etc.

[75]Mandiberg and Faure (1995), p. 448.

[76]Ibid.

The criminal aspect of such laws normally contains a general statement such as: "anyone who violates the provisions of the act, or the regulations, licenses, or permits issued to implement it," will be punished with a specific sanction. For example, the National Environmental (Ozone Layer Protection) Regulations 2009,[77] provides that "with effect from 1st January 2010, a person shall not possess halon that is, or has been, for use in halon-based equipment unless he is a holder of a halon special permit. . . ."[78] In this case, possessing a halon without a special halon permit, although does not harm the environment per se, is regarded as an offence under Regulation 22 (1).[79] This regulation provides that "any person who violates the provisions of these Regulations commits an offence. . . ." Here it is immaterial that no harm was done to the environment. The bottom line therefore is that adherence to the regulatory scheme is the most effective way to prevent serious environmental harm. In essence, the abstract endangerment crimes merely add criminal law to the enforcement mechanisms available to ensure compliance with monitoring, paperwork, licensing, and other rules meant to regulate pollution-producing activities.

Conversely, an entity that demonstrates regulatory adherence by obtaining and complying with a permit is sometimes rewarded with a "permit shield" that protects it from criminal and other enforcement actions. For example, under the National Environmental (Textile, Wearing Apparel, Leather and Footwear Industry) Regulations 2009[80] several incentives for environmental leadership have been put in place. Regulation 52(1)[81] provides that:

> Each facility and organisation that demonstrates environmental leadership, adopt environmentally responsible practices, demonstrate commitment to environmental quality and maintain exemplary environmental compliance records shall be recognized and encouraged by the Agency.

Some statutes criminalise discharging a pollutant in the absence of a required permit to do so. If the amount of the discharge is small, it is possible to argue that the social harm is primarily the flaunting of administrative requirements. For instance, Section 6 (1) of the Harmful Wastes Act 1988[82] punishes operating a storage facility without a permit, even though no actual pollution is involved in doing so.[83] Thus, criminal sanctions under the concept of abstract endangerment crimes support

---

[77] Government Notice No. 283, S.I. No. 32. Federal Republic of Nigeria Official Gazette No. 64, Vol. 96, 13 October 2009.

[78] National Environmental (Ozone Layer Protection) Regulations (2009), Regulation 18.

[79] Ibid.

[80] Government Notice No. 287, S.I. No. 34. Federal Republic of Nigeria Official Gazette No. 66 Vol. 96, 16 October 2009.

[81] National Environmental (Textile, Wearing Apparel, Leather and Footwear Industry) Regulations (2009).

[82] HWSCP Act (1988).

[83] This is so because among the acts prohibited under Section 1 of the HWSCP Act 1988 is the issue of storage of hazardous substances.

regulations that allow environmental protection agencies to ensure that their environmental protection scheme is functioning properly. For example, environmental statutes incorporate many duties that force the licensee to retain data and provide information to administrative authorities. For example, Regulation 10(1) of the National Environmental (Chemical, Pharmaceutical, Soap and Detergent Manufacturing Industries) Regulations 2009[84] provides that "every facility shall submit to the nearest office of the Agency[85] the following items:

(a) a list of the chemicals used in the manufacture of its products including their Material Safety Data Sheet (MSDS);
(b) details of stored chemicals and storage conditions;
(c) list of where chemicals are bought, sold or obtained, the name of secondary buyer;
(d) list of obsolete or abandoned chemicals and the proposed plan for environmental sound management."

Failure to comply with this directive amounts to an offence under Regulation 46 (b) of the Regulations.[86] An offence is also committed where the facility in purported compliance with the requirements of an enforcement notice or a closure notice makes a statement that is known to be false or misleading.[87] Although these provisions may not directly protect the environment, the requirements make transparent the licensee's ways of dealing with pollutants. The environmental protection agency can then use this information to control whether the licensee is complying with statutes that more directly protect the environment.

Although abstract endangerment crimes focus on vindicating administrative values, punishing the administrative violation indirectly furthers ecological values in two ways. First, an entity that obtains required permits and adheres to paperwork, monitoring, and inspection requirements displays a willingness to follow administrative rules; such an entity is also likely to follow the rules more closely connected to preventing environmental harm. Second, and more to the point, if administrative rules are followed, the regulatory agency can monitor the entity's operations to ensure that harm is less likely to occur.

In summary, crimes that fit the abstract endangerment crimes can be organised into three categories, namely:

---

[84] Government Notice No. 289, S.I. No. 36. Federal Republic of Nigeria Official Gazette No. 68 Vol. 96, 10 October 2009. Such provisions are also provided under the National Environmental Regulations 2009 (n80), Regulation 9, and the National Environmental (Food, Beverages and Tobacco Sector) Regulations 2009, Regulation 9.

[85] National Environmental Standards and Regulations Enforcement Agency.

[86] National Environmental (Chemical, Pharmaceutical, Soap and Detergent Manufacturing Industries) Regulations (2009).

[87] Ibid., Regulation 47(1) (a) similar provisions are also provided under the National Environmental (Textile, Wearing Apparel, Leather and Footwear Industry) Regulations (2009), Regulation 46(1) (a) and National Environmental (Food, Beverages and Tobacco Sector) Regulations (2009), Regulation 46(1) (a).

i) Operating without a required license or permit. For example, the National Environmental (Ozone Layer Protection) Regulations 2009,[88] provides that "with effect from the phase-out date for the different substances as specified in Schedule 6,[89] 'no person shall handle or deal in Ozone Depleting Substances (ODS) refrigerants unless such a person holds an ODS refrigerant handling permit'." Similar provisions can be found in Regulation 18 (a)[90] as it affects the handling of halon. Under HWSCP Act 1988,[91] all activities relating to the purchase, sale, importation, transit, transportation, deposit, and storage of harmful wastes are prohibited. An offence is deemed to have been committed where "any person who, **without lawful authority**, carries, deposits, dumps or causes to be carried, deposited or dumped, or is in possession for the purpose of carrying, depositing or dumping, any harmful waste on any land or in any territorial waters or contiguous zone or Exclusive Economic Zone of Nigeria or its inland water ways."[92]

ii) Violating paperwork, monitoring, or inspection requirements. For instance, it shall be an offence under Regulation 46(1) (d),[93] if a facility fails to furnish all information to an inspector. Under Section 31 of National Environmental Standards and Regulations Enforcement (Establishment) Agency Act 2007 (NESREA Act 2007):[94]

> A person who obstructs an officer of the Agency in the performance of his duties under section 3 of the Act[95] commits an offence and is liable on conviction to a fine of not less than =N= 200,000 for an individual or to imprisonment for a term not exceeding one year or to both such fine and imprisonment, and an additional fine of =N=20,000 for each day the offence subsist and in the case of a body corporate, it shall be liable for a fine of =N=2,000,000, on conviction and an additional fine of =N=200,000 for every day the offence subsist.

It is also an offence under Regulation 46(2)(b)[96] to knowingly obstruct the inspectors from performing their duties.

iii) Other regulatory violations that do not involve harm or threat of harm to the environment. For instance, under the Environmental Impact Assessment Act (EIA Act) 1992.[97] non-adherence to the provisions of the mandatory

[88] National Environmental (Ozone Layer Protection) Regulations (2009), Regulation 16(1).

[89] Ibid.

[90] Ibid.

[91] HWSCP Act (1988), s 1(1).

[92] Ibid., s. 1(2) (a).

[93] National Environmental (Textile, Wearing Apparel, Leather and Footwear Industry) Regulations (2009).

[94] Act No. 25 2007 Government Notice No. 61, Federal Republic of Nigeria Official Gazette No. 92, Vol. 94, 31 July 2007.

[95] NESREA Act (2007).

[96] National Environmental (Textile, Wearing Apparel, Leather and Footwear Industry) Regulations (2009).

[97] Cap E12 Laws of the Federation of Nigeria (LFN) 2004.

environmental impact statement before the commencement of any project to which an environmental impact assessment is compulsory[98] or where through screening a project is identified as having potential significant environmental impact,[99] amounts to an offence under Section 60 of the EIA Act 1992. Similarly, the HWSCP Act 1988[100] prohibits and punishes various acts relating to "unauthorized" dealings with toxic waste. Punishment for these acts, that is, dealing variously with harmful waste without authorisation is provided under Section 6 of the Act.[101]

3.5.3 *Concrete Endangerment Crimes*

The second concept is the concrete endangerment crimes. Concrete endangerment crimes involve behaviour that both violates regulatory law and poses a threat of harm to the environment. Here, the violations complained of in terms of causing environmental harm are certain and specific. As with the first concept (the abstract endangerment crimes), the activity in question must take place in an unlawful way: either without a required permit or in violation of terms and conditions contained in a statute, regulation, or permit. The characteristic of this concept is the unlawfulness of the act complained of. To this end, violating regulatory law is a requisite element. However, proof of unauthorised activity amounts to a defence. For example, Section 27(1) of the NESREA Act 2007[102] provides that "the discharge in such harmful quantities of any hazardous substance into the air or upon the land and the waters of Nigeria or at the adjoining shorelines is prohibited, except where such discharge is permitted or authorized under any law in force in Nigeria."

According to Clifford,[103] concrete endangerment crimes differ from crimes under the first concept (the abstract endangerment crimes) in that they either presume or require proof that the unlawful activity involved a threat of harm to the environment but do not require proof that harm to the environment did, in fact, occur. While all concrete endangerment crimes involve a threat of harm to the environment, the concept has two variations. The first variation is termed "presumed endangerment," and the second category, "demonstrated endangerment." These two variations represent different approaches to vindicating environmental values.

[98] Ibid., s. 12.

[99] Ibid., s. 18.

[100] HWSCP Act (1988), s. 1(2) (a)–(d).

[101] Ibid.

[102] NESREA Act (2007).

[103] Clifford (1998), p. 139.

3.5.3.1 Presumed Endangerment

Statutes in this category criminalise, per se, the unlawful contact of some quantity of polluting materials with the environment on the assumption that such contact necessarily causes at least some threat of harm to the environment. Presumed endangerment crimes are easiest to prove and thus allow earlier and more frequent intervention by environmental protection agencies. However, any situation in which the agency can prove an actual threat of environmental harm arguably represents a far more serious violation.

From one perspective, presumed endangerment statutes provide the greatest protection for ecological values because the agency can obtain a conviction with the least amount of proof.[104] In this situation, all that the agency needs to show is that an unpermitted emission occurred; either that the facility had no permit at all, or that it allowed polluting materials to come into direct contact with air, water, or that discharging or emitting a pollutant without a permit was involved[105] or that discharging or emitting polluting materials violates permit limits,[106] or that an amount greater than that allowed was discharged,[107] or that the emission standards in the existing license or operating permit were involved.[108] One thing is clear in all these provisions: such discharges or emissions threaten the natural environment or the human environment.

Presumed endangerment crimes also exist in our Criminal Code of Nigeria.[109] Under Section 245 of the Code:

> Any person who corrupts or fouls water of any spring, stream, well, reservoir so as to render it less fit for the purpose for which it is ordinarily used, is guilty of a misdemeanour and is liable to imprisonment for six months.

What this provision envisages is that the offender's act must be detrimental to the ordinary use of the water in question and that his act caused changes to the water quality. Thus, as soon as the water is no longer in its natural or improved condition, the act is interpreted to mean an endangerment of water quality which should lead to criminal liability. Arising from the above, the provision of Section 245 of the Criminal Code can be classified as a "presumed endangerment" offence. Conviction under this section does not require actual proof of harm but relies on contact alone.

---

[104] Clifford (1998), p. 139.

[105] HWSCP Act (1988), s. 1.

[106] As is the case in the provisions of the National Environmental (Food, Beverages and Tobacco Sector) Regulations (2009), Regulation 15(2) (a) Government Notice No. 286, S.I. No. 33. Federal Republic of Nigeria Official Gazette No. 65 Vol. 96, 14 October 2009.

[107] As is the case in the provisions of the National Environmental (Chemical, Pharmaceutical, Soap and Detergent Manufacturing Industries) Regulations (2009), Regulation 17.

[108] As is the case in the provisions of the National Environmental (Noise Standards and Control) Regulations (2009), Regulation 3, Government Notice No. 288, S.I. No. 35. Federal Republic of Nigeria Official Gazette No. 67 Vol. 96, 19 October 2009.

[109] Cap C38 Laws of the Federation of Nigeria (LFN) 2004.

Furthermore, Section 247 of the same law proscribes noxious acts. It provides that, any person who:

i) vitiates the atmosphere in any place so as to make it noxious to the health of persons in general dwelling or carrying on business in the neighbourhood or passing along a public way; or
ii) does any act which is, and which he knows or has reason to believe to be likely to spread the infection of any disease dangerous to life whether human or animal is guilty of a misdemeanour and is liable to imprisonment for six months.

In the above provisions, actual harm is not needed. What is needed is that the offender engaged in a prohibited act which may be presumed to endanger not only the environment but also human life.

Presumed endangerment crimes therefore are important in that they provide the basis for prosecuting crimes under the NESREA Act 2007[110] even when the Agency cannot prove that the violator actually caused environmental harm. The reason is that any kind of discharge, release, or emission of substances into the environment is regarded as a more serious harm than other environmental crimes. This is so because any discharge into the environment that causes contamination of the environment is regarded as being equivalent to actual harm to the environment, and this may be detrimental to both the natural and human environment. For instance, under Section 20(1)[111] "the Agency may make regulations setting specifications and standards to protect and enhance the quality of Nigeria's air resources, so as to promote the public health or welfare and the natural development and productive capacity of the nations' human, animal, marine or plant life."[112]

A person who violates the regulations made thereto commits an offence and shall on conviction, in the case of an individual, be liable to a fine not **less than** =N=200,000 or to imprisonment for a term not **less than six months** or to both such fine and imprisonment and an additional fine of =N=20,000 for every day the offence subsists.[113] And where a body corporate contravenes the regulations made thereto, it commits an offence and is liable on conviction to a fine not **less than** =N=2,000,000 and an additional fine of =N=50,000 for every day the offence subsists.[114] Note, all the words in bold such as **"less than"** and **"less the six months,"** etc. were inserted into the NESREA Act 2007 pursuant to the National

[110] NESREA Act (2007).

[111] Ibid.

[112] Similar provisions can the found in NESREA Act (2007), s. 22(1)(3)(4) (for air resources), s. 23 (1)(3)(4) (for water quality), s. 24 (1)(3(4) (for effluent limitation), s. 25(1)(2) (for environmental sanitation), s. 26(1)(3)(4) (for land resources) and s. 27 (1)(2)(3) (for hazardous substances).

[113] NESREA Act (2007), s. 20(3).

[114] Ibid., s. 20(4).

Environmental Standards and Regulations Enforcement Agency (Establishment) Amendment) (Amendment Act) 2018 (NESREA Amendment Act 2018).[115]

3.5.3.2 Demonstrated Endangerment

Demonstrated endangerment is the second variant of the concrete endangerment crimes. Here, statutes require affirmative proof of a threat to the environment beyond the mere fact of an unlawful emission or release. It is this requirement of affirmative proof that distinguishes crimes in this category from the first variant of the concrete endangerment crimes (the presumed endangerment crimes) as offences under this variant are harder to prove than those under the presumed endangerment crimes.

Some conceptual problems exist in articulating demonstrated endangerment crimes. Certainly, to know what endangers the environment, it is necessary at some level to know what is meant by "environmental harm."[116] In addition, demonstrated endangerment crimes raise the issue of how imminent the harm must be for the environment to be in danger. After all, mere failure to follow regulatory paperwork requirements could "endanger" the environment in some attenuated way. In this sense, statutes punishing situations that stop short of actual environmental harm are inchoate in nature and raise issues similar to those raised by the crime of attempt. According to Clifford,[117] should the statute allow official intervention as soon as authorities identify an actor who intends harm, or should it delay intervention until the social harm at issue is about to be realised?

In environmental cases, it makes a great deal of sense to refer to the objective dangerousness of the situation. Thus, posits Adams:[118] "the subjective state of mind of an actor in an environmental case is often difficult to judge: was it the actor's purpose to harm the environment, or was the actor merely indifferent to the consequences of the actions?"

Irrespective of the foregoing, what is material under the demonstrated endangerment crimes is that once the statute provides that "if any person causes or knowingly permits any poisonous, noxious or polluting matter or solid waste matter to enter any controlled water" or any person who "causes or knowingly permits any effluent or sewage be discharged (a) into any controlled waters; or (b) from land in, through a pipe, into the sea outside the seaward limits of controlled waters," then the offence under demonstrated endangerment is complete. It does not require the regulatory agency to prove a regulatory violation.[119] Why this is so is that the courts presume that discharges of wastewater result in pollution and that "polluting" requires a

---

[115]NESREA (Amendment Act) 2018, ss. 7 and 8, Government Notice No. 106, Act No. 26 2018, Federal Republic of Nigeria Official Gazette No. 146, Vol. 105, 14 November 2018.

[116]This term is better explained than defined as can be seen subsequently.

[117]Clifford (1998), p. 139.

[118]Adams (1999), p. 55.

[119]Adams (1999), p. 55.

likelihood or capability of causing harm to animals, plants, or those who use the water, but does not require actual harm.[120]

This preposition has been applied in several cases. One of such cases is the case of *Alphacell Ltd v. Woodward.*[121] Here, the defendant, a paper manufacturing company, was charged with causing polluting matter to enter a river. Settling tanks in the paper factory overflowed, when vegetation clogged up the pumps which maintained the level of effluent in the tanks. The tanks filled up and overflowed causing polluting matter to enter the river. An overflow channel led directly from the tanks to the river. The defendant claimed it did not cause polluting matter to enter the river, rather the presence of vegetation in the settling tank was the real cause of the incident. The court held that the act of constructing and operating the effluent tank was a positive and deliberate act which led to the overflow which caused the pollution. According to Lord Wilberforce, "…the appellants abstract water, pass it through their works where it becomes polluted, conduct it to a settling tank communicating directly with the stream, into which the polluted will inevitably flow if the level rises over the flowing point."[122]

Again, in the case of *CPC (UK) Ltd v. National Rivers Authority,*[123] a factory operator was held to have caused polluting matter to enter a stream when a pipe carrying cleaning fluid fractured, allowing the fluid to flow into a river via a storm drain. Although the cause of the fracture was defective work carried out by sub-contractors for the previous owner, which was not exposed by environmental audit, the court still held the current owners liable. The reason is that they were actively operating the storm drain at the time of the polluting incident.

However, in the case of *Price v. Cromack,*[124] a farmer had a contract permitting an animal firm to discharge waste into lagoons on his land. One lagoon wall failed and the resulting escape severely polluted a river. The farmer was charged with polluting the river. He was acquitted on the grounds that he only permitted the accumulation and had not caused the pollution.

But, in the case of *Wychavon District Council v. National Rivers Authority,*[125] raw sewage escaped from a sewer under the control of the appellant Council acting as an agent of the water company in maintaining and repairing the sewerage system. The immediate cause of the escape was a blockage in the sewer. The court held that the Council was not guilty of causing the pollution since it had mainly remained inactive.

---

[120] Bell and McGillivray (2001), pp. 588–589.

[121] (1972) AC 824. See, also, the case of *FJH Wrothwell v. Yorkshire Water Authority* [1984] Criminal Law Report, 43.

[122] Alphacell Ltd v. Woodward (1972), 824.

[123] [1995] Environmental Law Report, 131.

[124] [1975] 1WLR, 988.

[125] [1993] 1WLR, 125; see, also, the case of National Rivers Authority v. Welsh Development Agency [1993] Env LR, 407.

Furthermore, in the case of *United States v. Borowski*,[126] workers discharged spent nickel-plating and nitrous-acid baths directly into sinks without any pre-treatment. The sinks drained directly into underground pipes that fed into the municipal sewer system and then into a publicly owned treatment works (POTW). Discharging the untreated liquid into a POTW violated the Clean Water Act. The court indicated that a "knowing endangerment" charge might be valid if the discharge threatened workers at the POTW. However, between the time the liquid was poured into the sink and the time the discharge reached the POTW, it would never have been outside of the pipes.

In all these cases, although no violation of the provisions of the law was shown, the courts still applied the demonstrated endangerment crimes concept to elicit environmental protection compliance.

3.5.4 Concept of Concrete Harm Crimes

The concrete harm crimes, the third concept of typology of criminal sanctions in environmental crimes, punish very serious environmental harm even if the activity at issue was not otherwise unlawful. They appear to be aimed at preventing or punishing only harm to the environment itself. Statutes fitting this theory are similar to concrete endangerment crimes in that they require proof that the actor violated an administrative rule. However, these crimes go beyond threats and require proof of actual environmental harm. The identification of crimes fitting this concept can be tricky, as successful prosecution will depend upon determining (a) what act amounts to "environmental harm," and (b) the issue of "causation." These issues are discussed below.

3.5.4.1 Defining Environmental Harm

It is difficult to define what is meant by "harm" to the environment. Clifford[127] posits the following questions:

i) If mere contact between the environment and a pollutant amounts to a "threat" of harm, where is the threshold at which actual harm begins?
ii) How do we measure or describe it?
iii) Should all harm be treated equally, or should statutes provide different sanctions for unlawful emissions that result in different degrees of environmental harm?

Some environmental harm focuses on the environment directly while others focus on man. However, the difference between the two is merely academic. This is

[126] 977 F.2d 27 (1st Cir. 1992).
[127] Clifford (1998), p. 139.

because emissions or releases that threaten or harm human health, safety, or other interests must of necessity also harm the environment.

However, a traditional way of measuring environmental harm is to look through the lens of harm to human beings instead of examining the effect on the environment itself. The reason for this, according to Clifford,[128] is that "our ethical heritage largely attaches values and rights to persons, and if non-personal realms enter, they enter only as tributary to the personal." Thus, many discharges and effluent limitations are set with human health and welfare in mind. For example, regulations made under the NESREA Act 2007[129] set their provisions with a view of protecting the human environment. In this respect some of the regulations set permissible limits for noise,[130] permissible levels for effluent discharges into the water bodies,[131] and emission standards for facilities.[132]

Again, the purpose of the environmental impact assessment requirements under the EIA Act 1992[133] is to predict the likely impact of a proposed project on the environment to protect human health and safety.

For instance, under the EIA Act 1992,[134] the objectives of any environmental impact assessment shall be to establish, before a decision is taken by any person, authority, corporate body or unincorporated body, including the Government of the Federation, State or local government intending to undertake or authorise the undertaking of any activity, those matters that may likely or to a significant extent affect the environment or have an environmental effect on those activities and which shall first be taken into account.

Furthermore, under Section 2(2) of the EIA Act 1992,[135] where the extent, nature or location of a proposed project or activity is such that it is likely to significantly affect the environment, its environmental impact assessment shall be undertaken under the provisions of this Act.

A final way to look through the lens of harm to human beings is to measure financial costs other than damage to property itself. For example, some of the regulations on environmental standards have provisions for the application of the

---

[128] Ibid.

[129] NESREA Act (2007).

[130] National Environmental (Noise Standards and Control) Regulations (2009), Regulation 2. Under Regulation 10 any person may complain to the Agency in writing if such a person considers that the noise levels being emitted, or likely to be emitted may be higher than the permissible noise levels set out under Regulation 2.

[131] National Environmental (Food, Beverages and Tobacco Sector) Regulations (2009), Regulation 16 (1).

[132] National Environmental (Chemical, Pharmaceutical, Soap and Detergent Manufacturing Industries) Regulations (2009), Regulation 20 (1).

[133] EIA Act (1992).

[134] Ibid., s. 1(a).

[135] Ibid.

polluter-pays principle.[136] Under these provisions in the event of pollution resulting in an impact on the environment whether socio-economically or health-wise, the facility that caused the polluting act shall be responsible for: the cost of clean-up; remediation; reclamation; compensation to all affected parties; and cost of damage assessment and control.

Although not mentioning harm to the environment per se by statutes may lead to a conclusion that statutes are only interested in the protection of humans, this may not be correct as these statutes are part of an environmental protection scheme. To this end, one may say that harm to humans is used as a surrogate measure for harm to the environment. The premise is that if the pollution is extreme enough to threaten human interests, the environment must of necessity also be threatened. As can be seen under the above provisions on the polluter-pays principle for any polluting activity that results in an impact on the environment, the polluter shall bear the cost of clean-up, remediation and reclamation of the environment. These remediating acts are targeted towards the rehabilitation of the environment. In other words, under the existing scheme of polluter-pays principle, protection of both the human environment and the environment per se is envisaged. This preposition was brought to the fore in the British Petroleum (BP) Deepwater Horizon oil spill in the Gulf of Mexico in the USA on 20 April 2010.[137]

As a result of the existence of these problems, it is advocated that a legislature that wants to address a full spectrum of environmental harm must articulate a standard that reflects purely environmental values. The statute must require proof of something more than mere contact between a pollutant and the environment; otherwise, it would be functionally no different from the "presumed endangerment" variety of the concept of concrete endangerment crimes discussed earlier. The legislature should therefore go beyond an anthropocentric focus.

To this end, it is suggested that an alternative approach to focusing on the regulatory standards might be to define "environmental harm" in the criminal provision itself. A legislature might, for example, vary the seriousness of the criminal sanction based on the toxicity of the substance at issue; the risk versus fact of contact with air or water; the risk versus fact of an effect on flora, fauna, or human populations; and the magnitude of the violation. Thus, sanctions in terms of environmental "harm" or "damage" or authorised differences in sanctions may be based on degrees of "harm," proof of "pollution," and negative changes to the existing environment, among other considerations. For instance, while Regulation 8(2) of the National Environmental (Wetlands, River Banks and Lake Shores)

---

[136] National Environmental (Mining and Process of Coal, Ores and Industrial Minerals) Regulations (2009) Regulation 13(2) Government Notice No. 284, S.I. No. 28. Federal Republic of Nigeria Official Gazette No. 63 Vol. 96, 12 October 2009. Similar provisions can be found in the National Environmental (Textile, Wearing Apparel, Leather and Footwear Industry) Regulations (2009), Regulation 5 as well as National Environmental (Food, Beverages and Tobacco Sector) Regulations (2009), Regulation 5.

[137] BP paid out about $65 billion in compensation, legal fees and clean-up costs, which included billions paid to affected states.

Regulations 2009[138] permits traditional use of wetland resources, Regulation 14(1)[139] enjoins every land owner, occupier or user of property contiguous to a wetland to prevent the degradation or destruction of the wetland and such a person shall maintain the values of the wetland.

However, Regulation 14(2)[140] makes it an offence for any person who fails, neglects or refuses to protect a wetland, and further offence is committed under Regulation 30(d) where any person deposits in, on, or under any wetland a substance in a manner that has or is likely to have an adverse effect on the wetland. Punishment is provided under Regulation 31 of the Regulations.[141]

3.5.4.2 Issue of Causation

Concrete harm crimes require the prosecutor to prove that the defendant's behaviour caused environmental harm, however defined. Proving causation is not particularly difficult in the case of a single polluting event that immediately results in clear damage instantly. However, the requirement could present a challenge to prosecutors in other situations. For example, causation problems are likely to be difficult for a prosecutor where the effects of a polluting event may not be clear for a great many years.

Another problem is that a defendant may be able to show that one or more additional actors independently emitted pollutants into the same water, soil, or air, either previously, simultaneously, or subsequently to the defendant's own actions. To this end, proving causation could be daunting in many environmental cases. The question therefore is whether there is really a need to undertake the task of developing a body of causation law in the context of environmental crimes.

As a result of the peculiarities of environmental cases, and the nature of the impact, relying on causation as proof of environmental harm may jeopardise effective environmental protection. To this end, it is suggested that the use of abstract endangerment and concrete endangerment crimes, which do not require proof that the defendant caused a concrete result is preferable. In the alternative, actual harm need not be proved as is now provided under Regulation 10(2) of the National Environmental (Noise Standards and Control) Regulations 2009.[142] Under the regulation where any person had complained to the Agency[143] in writing that the noise being emitted is higher than the permissible levels, the complainant does not

[138]Government Notice No. 279, S.I. No. 26. Federal Republic of Nigeria Official Gazette No. 58 Vol. 96, 2 October 2009.

[139]National Environmental (Wetlands, River Banks and Lake Shores) Regulations (2009).

[140]Ibid.

[141]Ibid.

[142]National Environmental (Noise Standards and Control) Regulations (2009).

[143]National Environmental Standards, Regulations and Enforcement Agency (NESREA).

need to show or prove personal loss, injury or discomfort caused by the emission of the alleged noise.

3.5.5 *Concept of Serious Environmental Pollution*

This concept, "serious environmental pollution," aims at punishing very serious pollution regardless of whether there is any underlying regulatory violation. In fact, statutes following this concept impose criminal sanctions despite the defendant having obeyed license or permit conditions or other regulatory laws. For instance, under Regulation 12(2) (a) of National Environmental (Textile, Wearing Apparel, Leather and Footwear Industry) Regulations 2009,[144] "no facility shall discharge or cause to be discharged any effluent, or oil in any form into water system, public drains, or underground injection and land without a permit."

However, under Regulation 17(1) of the same Regulations, "no facility shall discharge effluent on land, into a water body unless the facility ensures that the parameters of the effluent do not exceed the permissible limits specified under the Regulations." Non-compliance with the conditions set out in the regulations amounts to a violation of the terms and conditions contained in the permit. It shall therefore be an offence if a facility fails to comply with or contravenes a condition of a permit.[145] In this respect, the concept of serious environmental pollution concept differs from the third concept, the concrete harm crimes, in that it severs the connection between criminal law and existing administrative decisions. Crimes fitting this concept of serious environmental pollution are independent in the sense that traditional criminal law can intervene irrespective of administrative law.[146]

To this end, the administrative link is broken. The administrative link is broken for a reason: crimes following the concept of serious environmental pollution are based on the assumption that the environmental harm in issue is of a magnitude beyond that contemplated by the administrative rules with which the entity complied. The assumption is that the administrative regulation never actually allowed the risks or harms in issue. This means that the effects of the released emission, discharge effluents or other problems arising thereto should be extreme in nature and the statute must make that clear for a variety of reasons. For example, more extreme harm is a prerequisite for more severe punishment. For another, some regulatory schemes anticipate that accidents will happen and provide some margin of safety for entities responding appropriately.

---

[144] National Environmental (Textile, Wearing Apparel, Leather and Footwear Industry) Regulations (2009).

[145] Ibid., Regulation 46(a).

[146] For instance, effluent discharges amount to fouling of the water body which is an offence on its own under the Criminal Code Act Cap C38 LFN 2004, s. 245.

It should be noted that environmental crimes following the "concept of serious environmental pollution" approach are relatively rare. However, applying this concept in addressing what may be considered "serious environmental pollution" will involve eliminating the administrative rules by doing away with the "permit shield" or the "unlawfulness" element from the crime's definition. The concept can also be applied by the adoption of traditional crimes, as opposed to specifically environmental criminal provisions in the prosecution of the offenders. These approaches are discussed below.

3.5.5.1 Eliminating the "Permit Shield"

One way to sever the link with administrative rules is to provide that compliance with such rules is not a defence. For example, a defendant who relied on a building permit to construct his house, but the permit is subsequently attacked, for instance, for violating essential procedural requirements or statutory provisions or violation of terms and conditions contained in the permit. Under the Nigerian Urban and Regional Planning Act 1992 (NURP Act),[147] "no development of land shall be commenced unless such developer had applied for and granted a permit to develop such land."[148] Once the permit is granted, the Development Control Department[149] shall enforce all terms and conditions contained in the permit against the developer.[150] Failure to comply with any of the terms and conditions amounts to an offence and this could lead to the revocation of the permit.[151] Where the permit is revoked under this head the developer shall not be entitled to payment of compensation.[152]

3.5.5.2 Eliminating the "Unlawfulness" Element from the Environmental Crime

Another way to eliminate the administrative link is to define an environmental crime without the element of "unlawfulness." If the legislature takes this approach, criminal law can be applied irrespective of whether there is compliance with a permit or any other regulatory rule.

This approach is prevalent in the HWSCP Act 1988.[153] Under the Act, it is an offence "to transport, or cause to be transported or be in possession of transporting;

[147] Cap N138 LFN 2004.

[148] Ibid., s. 28.

[149] Set up under NURPA (1992), s. 27.

[150] Ibid., s. 35.

[151] Ibid., s. 39.

[152] Ibid., s. 43.

[153] HWSCP Act (1988).

import, or cause to be imported or negotiate for the purposes of importing; or sell, offer for sale, buy or otherwise deal in any harmful waste."[154]

A person shall be deemed to have committed the offence if he actually does the act or makes the omission which constitutes the crime; or does or omits to do any act for the purpose of enabling or aiding another person to commit the crime; or aids another person in committing the crime; or counsels or procures any person to commit the crime, in which case he may himself be charged with committing the crime or with counselling or procuring the commission of the crime.[155]

3.5.5.3 Using Traditional Crimes to Address Serious Environmental Pollution

Another approach in the application of the concept of serious environmental pollution is to move outside the context of environmental crimes themselves and into the context of traditional crimes. That is, when a release, emission, or other polluting activity causes serious actual damage to property or harm to people, a prosecutor might charge the responsible parties with assault, homicide, property destruction, or some other traditional crime, away from the environmental crime as provided in the environmental law or regulations. For instance, assuming, in a situation in which an entity violates statutes regarding water pollution, and people drink the polluted water and death occurs as a result, charging the polluter under Section 27 of NESREA Act 2007[156] for discharging or depositing hazardous substance may suffice.

However, better environmental justice may be achieved if such a person is charged under the traditional criminal law such as homicide.[157] The reason is that the death of the victim was a violation of his fundamental right as protected under Section 33 of the Constitution of the Federal Republic of Nigeria 1999 (CFRN), as amended.[158] Under that section, "every person has a right to life, and no one shall be deprived intentionally of his life, save in execution of the sentence of a court in respect of a criminal offence of which he has been found guilty in Nigeria."

Although cases of this nature are rare or non-existent in Nigeria,[159] perhaps its application in other jurisdictions may ginger our courts into adopting this approach, especially in cases where the action of the offender is capable of causing harm to life

[154] Ibid., s. 1(2) (b)–(d).

[155] Ibid., s. 2.

[156] NESREA Act (2007).

[157] The reason for this is that while liability under the NESREA Act carries imprisonment for five years and/or a fine, the death penalty, or at least life imprisonment, may be invoked under the traditional criminal law of homicide.

[158] Cap C3 LFN 2004.

[159] Except where common tort principles such as nuisance, negligence, trespass, or the rule in *Rylands v. Fletcher* are applied.

and limb.[160] Some of the cases in other jurisdictions, especially in the USA and Europe, to which this approach had been applied, may suffice.

The case of *People v. Polvino*[161] shows that the manslaughter prosecution can be applied if the prosecution presents sufficient evidence to the court. In that case, the defendant knew the proper way to dispose of corrosive and hazardous chemicals that were on his property. Evidence showed, however, that the defendant did not follow such procedures; instead, he hired another man to haul the barrels away in a trailer. The contents spilled, and the hauler died at the scene of the spill from resulting lung damage. The court found that evidence of foreseeability was sufficient to allow the case to continue.[162]

Again, in the case of *People v. Thoro Products Co.*,[163] the defendant company stored and disposed of hazardous waste without a permit. A quantity of the substance leaked, causing contamination to the soil of down-gradient property owners. Even after learning of the problem, the company did nothing to clean up its property or stop the contamination. The statute of limitations barred prosecution for environmental crimes, as the actual leaks occurred decades earlier. However, the court affirmed the company's conviction for criminal mischief, a generally applicable felony. The statute of limitations problem did not prevent this prosecution because the defendant's act, failure to clean up the contamination, was ongoing.[164]

Another example of the use of traditional homicide law was found in the case of *People v. Roth.*[165] In that case, an employee who was cleaning a truck trailer died when petroleum vapours exploded.[166] The defendants, charged with manslaughter and negligent homicide, were a petroleum transport company, its district manager, and the operations manager of the facility where the deceased worked. The state's theory was that the defendants were responsible for the unsafe conditions and improper practices that led to the explosion. The court affirmed the dismissal of the charges, finding that the evidence presented to the Grand Jury was insufficient to show foreseeability that death would occur in the manner it did, a requirement of New York's causation law. Although the evidence was insufficient for the homicide counts, the court allowed a general reckless endangerment prosecution to continue. Under the reckless endangerment, the prosecution did not have to prove injury, and so the defendant's inability to foresee how the injury occurred was immaterial.

---

[160] For instance, discharging oil or oily substances into a water body, for example under Oil in Navigable Waters Act (ONWA) Cap 06 LFN 2004, ss. 1(1) and 3(1)(2). See Chap. 16 of this book.

[161] 580 N.Y.S. 2d 616 (1991).

[162] People v. Polvino (1991), 617.

[163] 70 P.3d 1188 (Colo. 2003).

[164] The prosecution was based on the defendant's "knowing failure to remediate or clean up its own property so as to stop the process by which the solvent-laden soils contaminated the property of down-gradient owners."

[165] 604 N.E. 2d 92 (N.Y. 1992).

[166] Petroleum vapours contain, for example, benzene and toluene, both of which are hazardous air pollutants under the Clean Air Act of the USA.

Similarly, in the case of *People v. Macellaro*,[167] the court allowed a reckless endangerment prosecution where evidence showed that the defendant dumped two 35-gallon drums on the side of a roadway. One drum was leaking, and when the defendant attempted to remove the "hazardous" warning label by burning it with a lighter, the substance ignited.

In November 2012, British Petroleum was criminally charged, including felony and manslaughter, as a result of an explosion on 20 April 2010 in the BP Deepwater Horizon oil rig operated by it in the Gulf of Mexico, off the Southern coast of the USA. The explosion killed 11 people and spilled hundreds of millions of gallons of crude oil into the Gulf of Mexico in the four months it took to cap the well. The company pleaded guilty and agreed to pay a record $4.5 billion in criminal fines.[168]

In addition to the adoption of the above decisions by courts, it is also suggested that the legislature, in the case of serious environmental harm, should borrow a leaf from the French and Belgium Penal Codes. The French Penal Code provides for what is termed the crime of "ecological terrorism." By Articles 421–422 of the Code:

> The introduction into the atmosphere, on the ground, in the soil, in foodstuff or its ingredients, or in waters, including territorial waters, of any substance liable to imperil human or animal health or the natural environment is an act of terrorism where it is committed intentionally in connection with an individual or collective undertaking whose aim is to seriously disturb public order through intimidation or terror.

In the case of the Belgium Penal Code, where traditional crimes apply to pollution-related harms, Articles 418–20 of the Belgian Penal Code authorise punishment of anyone who negligently causes harm to another.

3.5.6 *Applying Concepts of Environmental Crimes in Environmental Legislation*

Environmental criminal law can serve a variety of interests: administrative and human as well as purely environmental. In fact, as we have seen, purely environmental interests are served only indirectly when crimes are defined in terms of disobedience to administrative rules and when harm is viewed through the lens of human health, safety, and property. To vindicate all the relevant interests, and especially to address environmental harm that is not extreme or dramatic, a legislature can promulgate a variety of different environmental crimes. The four concepts discussed above, along with the variants within each concept, suggest the sorts of sanctions that might be adopted.

The examples provided in the discussions for each concept demonstrate that the legislature can adopt a variety of environmental criminal statutes to not only protect the environment, but also form the basis for compensating pollution victims. For

---

167 516 N.Y.S. 2d 950 (N.Y. App. Div. 1987).

168 Eboh (2013).

instance, the USA in February 2013 had proposed a $16 billion settlement to British Petroleum, BP, over the 2010 oil spill in the Gulf of Mexico. The settlement covered fines BP owes under the Clean Water Act, a federal water pollution law, as well as payments under the Natural Resources Damage Assessment Act, an environmental evaluation law.[169]

The legislature should, however, make efforts to differentiate among the various crimes according to the seriousness of the offence. One reason for doing this is to satisfy the demands of the proportionality principle. Environmental crimes certainly do vary in seriousness, and the authorised punishments ought to reflect this reality. However, another reason (and one that is perhaps more compelling to legislators), is that a graduated system of crimes is arguably more effective than a flat or incoherent system. The existence of crimes that truly reflect degrees of seriousness saves prosecutors from the burden of overcharging or undercharging defendants in specific cases, and it allows the court to convict guilty defendants of a crime that matches their behaviour.[170]

One way to achieve a graduated punishment system is to focus on mental state; an actor who knowingly violated an administrative rule, for example, is more culpable than the one who was not aware that the rule existed but who ought to have known of their existence. However, it is also possible to differentiate crimes according to their act elements, that is, according to the type of social harm involved in the offence. We therefore advocate the act-oriented and integrated approach.[171]

Under this approach, crimes should be differentiated according to the social harm at issue. It is therefore necessary to agree on some hierarchy of affected interests. For example, most people would agree that the interest in protecting human life is more compelling than the interest in protecting property (and thus harm to the former is more serious than harm to the latter). However, before discussing such a hierarchy for the interests implicated by environmental crimes, it is useful to remember why we use criminal sanctions at all. What does it mean to say that a criminal statute serves or vindicates a certain interest, for example, the interest in avoiding environmental harm? The answer is related to punishment goals or justifications generally. Punishment goals are traditionally seen as being either utilitarian or deontological.[172]

Utilitarian goals include deterrence (scaring the actor into refraining from the activity),[173] rehabilitation (changing the actor into one who no longer wishes to

[169] Eboh (2013).

[170] Onyeabor and Nnaji (2020), p. 75.

[171] Ibid.

[172] Relating to philosophical theories that state that the moral content of an action is not wholly dependent on its consequences.

[173] Commentators like Susan F Mandiberg and Michael G Faure distinguish between specific and general deterrence. Specific deterrence focuses on the defendant being prosecuted and sentenced; general deterrence focuses on the effect of that defendant, as an example, on others who might be tempted to violate the law.

engage in the activity), and incapacitation (putting the actor in a situation where the activity cannot occur).

The deontological goal is retribution, correcting the moral imbalance caused by the activity in question. The interest in avoiding environmental harm, then, is served when the application of a criminal statute deters the defendant or other actors from harming the environment in the future, changes the actor into one who no longer wishes to harm the environment, creates a situation in which the defendant can no longer harm the environment, or inflicts just desserts on the defendant for having harmed the environment in the past. Of course, the interest is served even more when a sentence accomplishes more than one of these goals. Retribution is implicated only when it is immoral to violate administrative rules. If the agency must prove the defendant's awareness of violating the administrative rule, some retributive value exists in punishing the knowing violation of a law. However, when these factors are missing retribution is not involved. When these goals of punishment are factored into the equation, that is vindicating only administrative values, then the abstract endangerment crimes theory may be used. This is because an abstract endangerment crime may only accomplish utilitarian punishment goals.

In contrast to the abstract endangerment crimes, crimes fitting the other three theories implicate both utilitarian and deontological goals of punishment. Similarly to the first concept, abstract endangerment crimes, the existence of meaningful punishment serves as a deterrent, and, perhaps, other utilitarian goals. However, unlike the first concept, retribution also comes into play in the other three concepts. This is surely true when environmental harm is defined in terms of danger or harm to human health, safety, or property.

In addition, as ethical values develop with regard to the environment, people increasingly feel a moral obligation to prevent even environmental harm that does not directly affect human beings.[174] For example, Pope Benedict XVI[175] declared that "the wonder of God's creation reminds us of the need to protect the environment and to exercise responsible stewardship of the goods of the earth." Still, most people seem to feel more concerned about the damage that affects human interests than they do about the damage that affects only the environment.

Taken together, contrasting the interests implicated by environmental crimes in terms of the goals of punishment suggests how we might place our four concepts along a continuum that represents the seriousness of the offence and the severity of the authorised punishment. First, it makes sense to place abstract endangerment crimes at the lowest end of the continuum. These crimes vindicate only administrative interests, and they mainly achieve only utilitarian punishment goals. This does

[174] A survey found that "73 percent deem it our 'moral obligation' and 'duty as Americans' to reduce global warming pollution"; support for this position "cuts across party lines, county lines, and income and education levels." Moral Obligation, Patriotic Duty, *GRIST*, 17 June 2008, http://www.grist.org/article/moral-obligation-patriotic-duty (accessed on 25 January 2019).

[175] Pope Benedict (2008).

not mean, necessarily, that punishment should be a slap on the wrist or a mere cost of doing business.

Meaningful sanctions must exist if utilitarian goals are to be met. In addition, abstract endangerment crimes often do vindicate environmental and, perhaps, human interests indirectly by providing a mechanism for government intervention before these values are actually harmed. In sum, it is desirable to have abstract endangerment crimes in the mix with meaningful sanctions attached. The fact that these crimes allow early intervention and are easy to prosecute means that they may end up serving environmental values effectively, and in a more widespread manner than the other concepts as the concept adopts proactive inhibition on environmental protection.[176] Nevertheless, they should be punished with milder sanctions than crimes in the other three concepts, which vindicate more important interests and serve an additional punishment goal.

So where do the other three types of environmental crimes (concrete endangerment crimes, concrete harm crimes and serious environmental pollution crimes) fit along the continuum, one may be tempted to ask? It is easy to conclude that the concrete endangerment concept and the concrete harm concept are both more serious than abstract endangerment crimes, the first concept. The administrative predicate ensures that these crimes vindicate administrative interests.

However, unlike the first concept, the other concepts vindicate one or two other interests as well. They require proof that the environment was threatened, as required under the second concept, or actually harmed, as in the third concept, and thus implicate environmental interests. In addition, anthropocentric interests are implicated if "harm" is defined in terms of human health, safety, or property. As to the goals of punishment, some people become morally outraged when the environment is harmed, and most people do so when human health, safety, or property is harmed. Thus, unlike abstract endangerment crimes, crimes fitting these concepts clearly serve both utilitarian and retributive goals.[177]

It is also easy to conclude that concrete harm crimes, the third concept, are more serious than concrete endangerment crimes, the second concept. This ordering reflects the notion that realised harm is more serious than the threat of harm. In addition, it is often difficult to prove that harm actually occurred and that the actor in question caused it; when the environmental protection agency can make such proof, it is likely that the behaviour at issue was egregious. All these factors add up to an argument that concrete arm crimes should carry more severe punishments than those authorised for concrete endangerment crimes.

This leaves us with the task of positioning crimes in the serious environmental harm, the fourth concept, which requires proof of serious environmental harm, but not a violation of administrative rules. Comparing this concept with concrete harm, the third concept, is tricky. Both require proof of harm to the environment. Serious

---

[176]We should note that this theory applies the no-harm rule as the crimes are committed for non-compliance to administrative directives and not for actual harm to the environment.

[177]Onyeabor and Nnaji (2020), p. 75.

environmental harm requires that the harm be extreme, which suggests that these crimes are more serious than those in concrete harm crimes. On the other hand, as there is no administrative predicate, serious environmental harm crimes implicate one less interest than those in concrete harm crimes.

Another approach to providing sanctions against environmental harm is further subdividing the concepts. This is not an unusual approach: it is common for modern statutory schemes to subdivide a single crime into degrees of seriousness based on nuances in the social harm at issue.[178] Each degree is defined to be slightly more serious than the next lower degree, and the increasing seriousness of the degrees of crime is reflected in the punishments authorised. Where these concepts are articulated by the legislature in environmental protection legislation, it is hoped it will go a long way in the protection and management of our environment. It is believed that where these theories and concepts are internalised in our environmental laws and policies it will go a long way in controlling environmental pollution.

3.6 Theory of Emission Trading and Environmental Legislation

3.6.1 Introduction

Pollution is a prime example of a market externality. An externality is an effect of some activity on an entity (such as a person) that is not party to a market transaction related to that activity. Emission trading is a market-based approach to address pollution. The overall goal of an emission trading plan is to minimise the cost of meeting a set emissions target.[179] In an emission trading system, the government sets an overall limit on emissions, and defines permits (also called allowances), or limited authorisations to emit, up to the level of the overall limit. The government may sell the permits, but in many existing schemes, it gives permits to participants (regulated polluters) equal to each participant's baseline emissions.

The baseline is determined by reference to the participant's historical emissions. To demonstrate compliance, a participant must hold permits at least equal to the quantity of pollution it actually emitted during the period. If every participant complies, the total pollution emitted will be at most equal to the sum of individual limits.[180]

Since permits can be bought and sold, a participant can choose either to use its permits exactly (by reducing its own emissions); or to emit less than its permits, and perhaps sell the excess permits; or to emit more than its permits, and buy permits

[178] For instance, in the case of homicide which may be murder or manslaughter, as the case may be.

[179] Center for American Progress (2008).

[180] Boswall and Lee (2002), pp. 62–66.

from other participants. In effect, the buyer pays a charge for polluting, while the seller gains a reward for having reduced emissions.

In many schemes, organisations that do not pollute (and therefore have no obligations) may also trade permits and financial derivatives of permits.[181] In some schemes, participants can bank allowances to use in future periods.[182] In some schemes, a proportion of all traded permits must be retired periodically, causing a net reduction in emissions over time. Thus, environmental groups may buy and retire permits, driving up the price of the remaining permits according to the law of demand.[183] In most schemes, permit owners can donate permits to a nonprofit entity and receive a tax deduction. Usually, the government lowers the overall limit over time, with an aim towards a national emissions reduction target.[184]

According to the Environmental Defense Fund,[185] cap-and-trade is the most environmentally and economically sensible approach to controlling greenhouse gas emissions, the primary cause of global warming, because it sets a limit on emissions, and the trading encourages companies to innovate in order to emit less.

Thus, the overall goal of an emission trading plan is to reduce emissions of greenhouse gases (GHGs)[186] into the atmosphere. This provides economic incentives for achieving reductions in the emissions of pollutants. It is sometimes called "cap and trade." In this system a portion of all traded credits must be retired, causing a net reduction in emissions each time a trade occurs. In many cap-and-trade systems, organisations that do not pollute may also participate, thus environmental groups can purchase and retire allowances or credits and hence drive up the price of the remainder according to the law of demand. Corporations can also prematurely retire allowances by donating them to a non-profit entity and then be eligible for a tax deduction.[187]

Since emission trading uses markets to determine how to deal with the problem of pollution, it is often touted as an example of effective free-market environmentalism. While the cap is usually set by a political process, individual companies are free to choose how or if they will reduce their emissions. In theory, firms will choose the least-costly way to comply with the pollution regulation, creating incentives that reduce the cost of achieving a pollution reduction goal.

---

[181] Parliament of Australia (2013).

[182] United States Environmental Protection Agency (USEPA) (2019).

[183] O'Sullivan and Sheffrin (2003).

[184] Center for American Progress (2008).

[185] Environmental Defense Fund (2019).

[186] GHGs include: carbon dioxide, methane, nitrous oxide, hydrofluorocarbons, perfluorocarbons, and sulphur hexafluoride.

[187] Freestone and Streck (2009), p. 15.

3.6.2 Workings of Emission Trading Work

A central authority, usually a government, government agency or international body, sets a limit or "cap" on the amount of a pollutant that can be emitted. Companies or other groups are issued emission permits and are required to hold an equivalent number of "allowances" or "carbon credits" which represent the right to emit a specific amount of carbon. The total amount of allowances and credits cannot exceed the cap, limiting total emissions to that level. Companies that need to increase their emission allowance must buy credits from those who pollute less. The transfer of allowances is referred to as a "trade." In effect, the buyer is paying a charge for polluting, while the seller is being rewarded for having reduced emissions by more than it needed. Thus, in theory, those that can easily reduce emissions most cheaply will do so, achieving pollution reduction at the lowest possible cost to society.[188]

3.6.3 History of Emission Trading

The international community began the long process of building effective international and domestic measures to tackle GHG emissions in response to the increasing assertions that global warming is happening due to man-made emissions and the uncertainty over its likely consequences. That process began in Rio de Janeiro in 1992 when 160 countries agreed on the United Nations Framework Convention on Climate Change (UNFCCC).[189]

The efficiency of what later was to be called the "cap-and-trade" approach to air pollution abatement was first demonstrated in a series of micro-economic computer simulation studies between 1967 and 1970 for the National Air Pollution Control Administration (predecessor to the United States Environmental Protection Agency's Office of Air and Radiation) by Ellison Burton and William Sanjour.[190]

These studies used mathematical models of several cities and their emission sources to compare the cost and effectiveness of various control strategies. Each abatement strategy was compared with the "least-cost solution" produced by a computer optimisation program to identify the least-costly combination of source reductions to achieve a given abatement goal. In each case, it was found that the least-cost solution was dramatically less costly than the same amount of pollution reduction produced by any conventional abatement strategy.[191] Burton and later Sanjour along with Pechan[192] continued improving and advancing these computer models at the newly created United States Environmental Protection Agency

[188] Montgomery (1972), pp. 395–418.

[189] United States Environmental Protection Agency (USEPA) (2019).

[190] Burton and Sanjour (1967), p. 17.

[191] Burton and Sanjour (1969), pp. 412–415.

[192] Burton et al. (1969), pp. 412–415.

(USEPA). The Agency introduced the concept of computer modelling with least-cost abatement strategies (i.e., emissions trading) in its 1972 annual report to Congress on the cost of clean air. This led to the concept of "cap and trade" as a means of achieving the "least-cost solution" for a given level of abatement.[193]

In the United States of America (USA), the acid rain-related emission trading system was principally conceived by C. Boyden Gray, who worked with the Environmental Defense Fund (EDF) and the USEPA to write the bill that became law as part of the Clean Air Act of 1990.[194]

In 1997, the Conference of Parties (CoP) to the UNFCCC agreed, in what has been described as a watershed in international environmental treaty-making, the Kyoto Protocol, where 38 developed countries (Annex 1 countries) committed themselves to targets and timetables for the reduction of GHGs. These targets for developed countries are often referred to as Assigned Amounts.[195]

The resulting inflexible limitations on GHG growth could entail substantial costs, perhaps running into many trillions of dollars globally if countries have to solely rely on their own domestic measures – one important economic reality recognised by many of the countries that signed the Kyoto Protocol. As a result, international mechanisms that would allow developed countries flexibility to meet their targets were included in the Kyoto Protocol. The purpose of these mechanisms is to allow the parties to find the most economical ways to achieve their targets.[196]

3.6.4 Theories of Emissions Trading

Several emissions trading theories have been developed. However, in applying the theories, the nature of the pollutant plays a very important role when policymakers decide which framework should be used to control pollution and therefore be included in statutes on the environment. For instance, carbon dioxide acts globally, but its impact on the environment is generally similar wherever it is released in the globe. So, the location of the originator of the emissions does not really matter from an environmental standpoint.[197] Thus, the policy framework should be different for regional pollutants because the impact exerted by these pollutants may not be the same in all locations. The same amount of a regional pollutant can exert a very high impact in some locations and a low impact in other locations, so it does actually matter where the pollutant is released. This is known as the "Hot Spot" problem.[198]

[193] USEPA (2019).

[194] Ibid.

[195] Grimeaud (2001), p. 39.

[196] Boswall and Lee (2002).

[197] Giorgi (2008), p. 338.

[198] Ibid.

One of the theories of emissions trading is the Euler-Lagrange equation.[199] This is commonly used to determine the least cost of achieving an objective, in this case, the total reduction in emissions required in a year. In some cases, it is possible to use the Lagrange optimisation framework to determine the required reductions for each country so that the total cost of reduction is minimised. In such a scenario, the Lagrange multiplier represents the market allowance price (P) of a pollutant, such as the current market allowance price of emissions in Europe. All countries face the market allowance price as existent in the market that day, so they can make individual decisions that would maximise their profit while at the same time achieving regulatory compliance. This is also another version of the Equi-Marginal Principle, commonly used in economics to choose the most economically efficient decision.

Another type of theory is the "prices versus quantities" theory. Under this theory, a "quantity" is an emission cap and permit trading system. This is an instrument that fixes the overall emission level (quantity) and allows the price to vary. In contrast, a "price" is the instrument that fixes the price, for instance, an emission tax, for the emission level allowed in accordance with the economic activity in issue. One problem of this theory is the uncertainty of the cost of compliance as the price of a permit is not known in advance and will vary over time according to market conditions. Another drawback of the theory is that the environmental outcome or a limit on the amount of emissions, to fix a price (e.g., emission tax), is not guaranteed. To overcome this however, it is advocated that the best choice depends on the sensitivity of the costs of emission reduction, compared to the sensitivity of the benefits (i.e., climate damages avoided by a reduction) when the level of emission control is varied.

The third theory is the "safety and valve" theory. This is a hybrid of the price and quantity theory. The system is essentially an emission cap and tradable permit system, but the maximum (or minimum) permit price is capped. Emitters have the choice of either obtaining permits in the marketplace or purchasing them from the government at a specified trigger price (which could be adjusted over time). This system is sometimes recommended as a way of overcoming the fundamental disadvantages of earlier theories discussed above. The reason is that the government is given the flexibility to adjust the system as new information comes to light. In, as Jacoby and Ellerman[200] pointed out, setting the trigger price high enough, or the number of permits low enough, the safety valve can be used to mimic either a pure quantity or pure price mechanism.

These theories now form a veritable tool for emissions reduction to curb environmental problems associated with climate change. For this purpose, an international legal instrument has been developed: the Kyoto Protocol. The Kyoto Protocol, a 1997 international treaty that came into force in 2005, binds most developed

[199] Ibid.

[200] Jacoby and Ellerman (2004), p. 481.

nations to a cap-and-trade system for the six major greenhouse gases.[201] Emission quotas were agreed upon by each participating country to reduce their overall emissions by 5.2% of their 1990 levels by the end of 2012 (although this was not realised and it gave impetus to the Paris Agreement on Climate Change in 2015).

Under the Kyoto Protocol, for the five-year compliance period from 2008 until 2012, nations that emitted less than their quota were required to sell carbon credit to nations that exceeded their quota. Under this system, it was possible for developed countries within the trading scheme to sponsor carbon projects that provide a reduction in greenhouse gas emissions in other countries, as a way of generating tradable carbon credits. The Protocol allowed this through Clean Development Mechanism (CDM) and Joint Implementation (JI) projects, in order to provide flexible mechanisms to aid regulated entities in meeting their compliance with their caps.

The United Nations Framework Convention on Climate Change Office (UNFCCC) validates all CDM projects to ensure they create genuine additional savings and that there is no "carbon leakage." The Intergovernmental Panel on Climate Change (IPCC) has projected that the financial effect of compliance through trading within the Kyoto commitment period will be "limited" at between 0.1–1.1% of GDP among trading countries.[202]

Carbon emission trading has been steadily increasing in recent years. According to the World Bank's Carbon Finance Unit, 374 million metric tonnes of carbon dioxide equivalent were exchanged through projects in 2005, a 240% increase relative to 2004. In terms of dollars, the World Bank has estimated that the size of the carbon market was 11 billion USD in 2005, and 30 billion USD in 2006.[203]

Carbon emission trading therefore comes with financial incentives and benefits to the participants. With the creation of a market for mandatory trading of carbon dioxide emissions within the Kyoto Protocol, the City of London financial marketplace which has established itself as the centre of the carbon finance market grew into a market valued at $60 billion in 2007. The voluntary offset market, by comparison, grew to about $4 billion in 2010. The European Union, UK, USA, Australia, Denmark, and Canada have all set up emission trading markets. Kenya has set in motion machineries to launch a Climate Change Exchange Platform to facilitate the trading of carbon credits.

It should be noted that all three theories are not mutually exclusive as they are now being used as policy instruments to control greenhouse gas emissions in different parts of the World. For instance, the European Union Emissions Trading System (EU-ETS) is a "quantity" system using the cap and trading system to meet targets set by National Allocation Plans, the United Kingdom's Climate Change

[201] The United States is the only industrialised nation under the United Nations Framework Convention on Climate Change Annex I countries that did not ratify the Kyoto Protocol and therefore are not bound by it.

[202] Intergovernmental Panel on Climate Change (IPCC) (2007) Item 25, 33.

[203] Carbon Finance (2019).

Levy is a "price" system using a direct carbon tax, while China uses the Carbon (CO_2) market price for funding of its Clean Development Mechanism projects, but imposes a "safety valve" of a minimum price per tonne of CO_2.

3.6.5 *Shortfalls of Emission Trading*

It should be noted that despite the laudable nature of emissions trading theory in pollution control meaningful emission reductions within a trading system can only occur if they can be measured at the level of operator or installation and reported to a regulator. For greenhouse gases all trading countries maintain an inventory of emissions at national and installation level; in addition, the trading groups within North America maintain inventories at the state level through The Climate Registry. For trading between regions, these inventories must be consistent, with equivalent units and measurement techniques. In some industrial processes emissions can be physically measured by inserting sensors and flowmeters in chimneys and stacks, but many types of activity rely on theoretical calculations for measurement. Depending on local legislation, these measurements may require additional checks and verification by a government or third-party auditor, prior to or post submission to the local regulator.[204]

Another critical problem associated with the use of emissions reduction in environmental pollution control is that of enforcement. Without effective measurement, reporting and verification (MRV) and enforcement, the value of allowances is diminished. Enforcement can be done using several means, including fines or sanctioning those that have exceeded their allowances. Concerns include the cost of MRV and enforcement and the risk that facilities may be tempted to mislead rather than make real reductions or make up their shortfall by purchasing allowances or offsets from another entity. The net effect of a corrupt reporting system or poorly managed or financed regulator may be a discount on emission costs, and a (hidden) increase in actual emissions.[205]

Practitioners of carbon trade have also been criticised for the practice of "grandfathering," where polluters are given free allowances by governments, instead of being made to pay for them. Critics instead advocate for auctioning the credits. The proceeds could be used for research and development of sustainable technology.[206] This system of grandfathering it is also argued, places disproportionate emphasis on individual lifestyles and carbon footprints, distracting attention from the wider, systemic changes and collective political action that needs to be taken to tackle climate change.[207]

---

[204] Jacoby and Ellerman (2004), p. 481.

[205] Carbon Finance (2019).

[206] Carbon Trade Watch (2019).

[207] Ibid.

3.7 Concept of Sustainability and Economic Development

3.7.1 Introduction

The problem of environmental pollution is attributable to man's quest for economic development and as such feel that a balance has to be struck between our quest to develop and the need to protect the environment. This has given rise to the concept of sustainability. Sustainability, in general terms, is the ability to maintain the balance of a certain process or state in any system. It is now most frequently used in connection with biological and human systems. In an ecological context, sustainability can be defined as the ability of an ecosystem to maintain ecological processes, functions, biodiversity, and productivity into the future.[208]

The concept of environmental sustainability is about the natural environment and how it remains productive and resilient to support human life. Environmental sustainability relates to ecosystem integrity and the carrying capacity of the natural environment.[209] It requires that natural capital be sustainably used as a source of economic inputs and as a sink for waste. The implication is that natural resources must be harvested no faster than they can be regenerated while waste must be emitted no faster than they can be assimilated by the environment. This is because the Earth systems have limits or boundaries within which equilibrium is maintained.[210]

Sustainability has become a complex term that can be applied to almost every system on Earth: to many different levels of biological organisation, such as wetlands, prairies and forests;[211] to human organisation concepts, such as eco-municipalities and sustainable cities; and human activities and disciplines, such as sustainable agriculture, sustainable architecture and renewable energy.[212] For humans to live sustainably, the Earth's resources must be used at a rate at which they can be replenished.[213]

However, there is now clear scientific evidence that humanity is living unsustainably, and that an unprecedented collective effort is needed to return human use of natural resources within sustainable limits.[214]

---

[208] Definition of ecological sustainability, http://www.reo.gov/general/definitions_r-s.htm (accessed on 30 January 2019).

[209] Mensah (2019), p. 75.

[210] Ibid.

[211] Ausubel and Harpignies (2004), p. 98.

[212] Berkeley Library Web (2019).

[213] That is, not exceeding the Earth's carrying capacity and its ability for self-regeneration.

[214] Millennium Assessment (2019).

3.7.2 *Defining Sustainability*

Since the 1980s, the idea of human sustainability has become increasingly associated with the integration of economic, social and environmental spheres. In 1987, the Brundtland Commission (World Commission on Environment and Development) articulated what has now become a widely accepted definition of sustainability: "to meet the needs of the present without compromising the ability of future generations to meet their own needs."[215] In addition to the definition given by the Brundtland Commission definitions of sustainability may also be expressed as statements of fact, intent, or value with sustainability treated as either a "journey" or "destination,"[216] "where we are now, where we need to be going, and how we are to get there,"[217] as a result of all these the term has been described as a "dialogue of values" that "defies consensual definition."[218]

The idea of sustainable development is sometimes viewed as an oxymoron[219] because development inevitably depletes and degrades the environment. Be it as may be, for our purpose the term "sustainability" is viewed within the context of its dimensions. The dimensions of sustainability are often taken to be: the natural environment, social environment and economic environment, known as the "three pillars." These can be depicted as three overlapping circles (or ellipses), to show that they are not mutually exclusive and can be mutually reinforcing. Thus, posits Porritt,[220]

> the economy is, in the first instance, a subsystem of human society ... which is itself, in the second instance, a subsystem of the totality of life on Earth (the biosphere). And no subsystem can expand beyond the capacity of the total system of which it is a part.

For this reason, it is argued that the economy is a component of society, both bounded by, and dependent upon, the environment. As the American ecological economist Herman Daly famously asked, "what use is a sawmill without a forest?"[221]

This concept of living within environmental constraints underpins the International Union for Conservation of Nature (IUCN), United Nations Environment Programme (UNEP) and World Wide Fund for Nature (WWF) definition of sustainability: "improving the quality of human life while living within the carrying

[215] United Nations General Assembly (1987).

[216] Commonwealth of Australia (2019).

[217] USA Congress House Standing Committee on Environment and Heritage (2009), Chapter 2.

[218] Ratner (2004), pp. 50–52.

[219] An expression with contradictory words: a phrase in which two words of contradictory meaning are used together for special effect, e.g., "wise fool" or "legal murder."

[220] Porritt (2006), p. 46.

[221] Australian House Committee (2019).

capacity of supporting eco-systems."[222] The Earth Charter[223] goes beyond defining what sustainability is but seeks to establish the values and direction needed to achieve it. It posits as follows:

> We must join together to bring forth a sustainable global society founded on respect for nature, universal human rights, economic justice, and a culture of peace. Towards this end, it is imperative that we, the peoples of Earth, declare our responsibility to one another, to the greater community of life, and to future generations.

3.7.3 History and Evolution of Sustainability

The concept of sustainability is not of recent origin. It is as old as antiquity and dates to the history of human civilisation. In early human history, the energy and natural resource demands of nomadic hunter-gatherers were small. The use of fire and the desire for specific foods may have altered the natural composition of plant and animal communities. Agrarian communities like the ancient civilisations of Sumer in southern Mesopotamia (now Iraq) and Egypt, both dating from around 3000 BC, depended largely on their natural environment and the creation of a structure of permanence. Societies outgrowing their local food supply or depleting critical resources either moved on or faced collapse.[224]

The emergence of industrial societies, the steam engine, fuelled primarily by coal propelled the Industrial Revolution in the United Kingdom and the world's technological advances over several millennia gave humans increasing control over the environment. It was the Industrial Revolution of the seventeenth to nineteenth centuries that tapped into the vast growth potential of energy in fossil fuels, especially coal. Coal was used to power ever more efficient engines and later to generate electricity. At that time modern sanitation systems and advances in medicine protected large populations from disease. Such conditions led to a human population explosion and unprecedented industrial, technological, and scientific growth that has continued to this day. This marked the commencement of a period of global human influence known as the Anthropocene. And from 1650 to 1850 the global population doubled from around 500 million to 1 billion people.[225]

At the turn of the twentieth century, the Industrial Revolution had led to an exponential increase in the human consumption of resources. The increase in health, wealth and population was perceived as a simple path of progress. However, in the 1930s, economists began developing models of non-renewable resource management and the sustainability of welfare in an economy that uses non-renewable resources. Ecology has now gained general acceptance as a scientific discipline,

[222] The H C Coombs Policy Forum (2019).

[223] Earth Charter (2019).

[224] Earth Charter (2019).

[225] Goudie (2013), p. 89.

and many concepts vital to sustainability are being explored. These included: the interconnectedness of all living systems in a single living planetary system, the biosphere; the importance of biogeochemical cycles (of water, nutrients and other chemicals, materials, waste); and the passage of energy through trophic levels of living systems.[226]

By the late twentieth century, increasingly environmental problems were viewed as global in scale. The 1973 and 1979 energy crises demonstrated the extent to which the global community had become dependent on non-renewable energy resources. While the developed world was considering the problems of unchecked development, the developing countries, faced with continued poverty and deprivation, regarded development as essential to raise the living standards of their people. In 1980 the International Union for Conservation of Nature (IUCN) published its "World Conservation Strategy," followed in 1982 by its "World Charter for Nature." They drew attention to the decline of the world's ecosystems. It was in this respect that in 1983 the UN General Assembly set up the World Commission on Environment and Development,[227] chaired by the then Norwegian Prime Minister, Dr. Gro Harlem Brundtland. It had three objectives:

(i) To examine critical environment and development issues and formulate realistic proposals for dealing with them.
(ii) To propose new forms of international cooperation on these issues that would influence policies and events in the direction of needed changes.
(iii) To raise levels of understanding and commitment to action of individuals, voluntary organisations, businesses, institutions and governments.[228]

The Commission published its report in 1987 entitled *Our Common Future*.[229] The Report, although a strictly non-legal text, was pivotal in changing the direction of international environmental law and environmental protection, as it signalled changes in the way we look at the world. It provided support for expanding the role of sustainable development in environmental management and proposed a United Nations Organisation (UN) programme on sustainable development.[230] The programme identified the central legal and institutional issues such as the increasing globalisation of various crises: environmental development, energy, etc., and a marked increase in the incidence of environmental crises of a "global nature," such as drought in Africa, which put some 35 million people at risk and killed perhaps a million. According to the report:

> Until recently, the planet was a large world in which human activities and their effects were neatly compartmentalized within nations, within sectors and within broad areas of concern.

---

[226] Goudie (2013), p. 89.

[227] The Commission was set up as an independent body linked to, but outside the control of the government and the United Nations system.

[228] United Nations General Assembly (1987).

[229] The report is also known as the Brundtland Report.

[230] A United Nations Conference on Sustainable Development was eventually held in 2002.

> These compartments have begun to dissolve. This applies in particular to the global 'crises' that have seized public concern, particularly over the last decade. These are not separate crises: an environmental crisis, a development crisis, an energy crisis. They are all one.[231]

On policy matters, the Report focused attention on population, food security, the loss of species and genetic resources, energy, industry and human settlements recognising that they are connected and cannot be treated in isolation from each other. It concluded that if natural resources continued to be used at the current rate, if the plight of the poor was ignored, and if pollution and wasting of resources continued, a decline was to be expected in the quality of the world's population.[232]

On the issue of sustainable development, the report defined it as "a dynamic process designed to meet today's need without compromising the ability of future generations to meet their own needs."[233] According to the Report,[234] sustainable development not only requires societies to meet human needs by increasing productivity potential but ensuring equitable economic, social and political opportunities for all both today and tomorrow but also sees it as a process of change in which resource use, economic policies, technological development, population growth, poverty and institutional structures are in harmony and enhance current and future potentials for human progress.

To this end, the main thrust of sustainable development is that the atmosphere, water, soil and all components of the ecosystem that support life on Earth must not be endangered. Therefore, society today should satisfy its needs from the available resources without jeopardising the quality of life and resources for the future generation. Moreso, each generation has a moral responsibility that future inhabitants of our Earth will inherit an undiminished stock of the Earth's natural resources. To this end, the Commission posits that development is acceptable but must be done to meet the needs of the poor, but not worsen environmental problems.[235]

Two key concepts are contained within this report: the concept of needs, in particular the essential needs of the present generation, and the idea of limitations imposed by the state of technology and social organisation on the environment's ability to meet present and future needs. To this end, the report identified critical objectives for environmental and development policies reflected in the concept of sustainable development thus:

(i) Reviving growth and changing its quality
(ii) Meeting essential needs for jobs, food, energy water and sanitation
(iii) Ensuring a sustainable level of population
(iv) Conserving and enhancing the resource base

[231] United Nations General Assembly (1987).
[232] World Commission on the Environment and Development (WCED) (1987).
[233] Ibid.
[234] Ibid.
[235] Ibid.

(v) Re-orienting technology and managing risk
(vi) Merging environment and economies in decision-making[236]

These critical objectives appeared in the discussions and latter legal texts that emerged from the United Nations Conference on Environment and Development in 1992 and subsequent other international meetings on environmental protection.

In December 1987, the UN General Assembly noted the Report and in 1988 called for the UN Conference on Environment and Development (UNCED) which was eventually held in Rio de Janeiro, Brazil, from 3–14 June 1992. The purpose of the Conference was to elaborate strategies and measures to halt and reverse the effects of environmental degradation in the context of strengthened national and international efforts to promote sustainable and environmentally sound development in all countries.

By the turn of the twenty-first century, global awareness of climate change, renewable energy, their effects and impacts have led to an understanding and awareness of the importance of sustainability. There is increasing global awareness of the threat posed by the human-induced enhanced greenhouse effect, produced largely by forest clearing and the burning of fossil fuels. This has led to climate change-induced impacts such as more heat waves, droughts and flooding, threatening food and water supplies.[237]

In March 2009, at a meeting of the Copenhagen Climate Council,[238] an international team of leading climate scientists, comprising 500 experts from 800 countries issued a keynote statement that there are now "no excuses" for failing to act on global warming and that without carbon reduction targets, "abrupt or irreversible" shifts in climate may occur that "will be very difficult for contemporary societies to cope with." To this end, the Council posits that:

> The climate system is already moving beyond the patterns of natural variability within which our society and economy have developed and thrived. These parameters include global mean surface temperature, sea-level rise, ocean and ice sheet dynamics, ocean acidification, and extreme climatic events. There is a significant risk that many of the trends will accelerate, leading to an increasing risk of abrupt or irreversible climatic shifts.[239]

The outcome of all these predictions and postulations is the emergence of an ecological economics perspective that has provided an inclusive and ethical economic model for society to combat environmental problems arising from human consumption habits. This has resulted in ecological economics. The main effort of ecological economics is that it sought to bridge the gap between ecology and traditional neoclassical economics. Emerging concepts include: car-free movement, Smart Growth, more sustainable urban environments, Life Cycle Assessment, the Cradle to Cradle (analysis of resource use and environmental impact over the life

---

[236] United Nations General Assembly (1987).

[237] Goudie (2013), p. 217.

[238] International Scientific Congress on Climate Change (2009).

[239] Ibid.

cycle of a product or process), Ecological Footprint Analysis, green building, dematerialisation (increased recycling of materials), and decarbonisation (removing dependence on fossil fuels). These concepts sought to provide us with basic platforms to protect the environment. They reminded us that rapidly advancing technologies mean it is now technically possible to achieve a transition of economies, energy generation, water and waste management, and food production towards sustainable practices using methods of systems ecology and industrial ecology and saving the human environment.[240]

3.7.4 *Sustainability Theory*

Sustainability is studied and managed over many scales (levels or frames of reference) of time and space and in many contexts of environmental, social and economic organisations. The focus ranges from the total carrying capacity[241] of planet Earth to the sustainability of economic sectors, countries, municipalities, neighbourhoods, home gardens, individual lives, individual goods and services, occupations, lifestyles, behaviour patterns and so on. Indeed, it can entail the full compass of biological and human activity or any part of it, especially the human consumption habit of biophysical resources. Human consumption can be divided into three key components: population numbers, levels of consumption (affluence), and impact per unit of resource use which depends on the technology used.[242] This has been expressed through an equation:

$$I = P \times A \times T:$$

where:

I = Environmental impact
P = Population
A = Affluence
T = Technology

According to the 2008 revision of the official United Nations population estimates and projections, the world population was projected to reach 7 billion early in 2012.[243] This estimate was up from 6.8 billion, and will surpass 9 billion people by 2050. Most of the additional 2.3 billion people will enlarge the population of developing countries, which is projected to rise from 5.6 billion in 2009 to 7.9

[240] International Scientific Congress on Climate Change (2009).

[241] Which if followed achieves sustainability.

[242] Ehrlich and Holden (1974), p. 282.

[243] Ironically, the world population hit the 7 billion mark on 31 October 2011, two clear months before 2012 and it has already reached 8.1 billion by August 2023.

billion in 2050, and will be distributed among the population aged 15–59 (1.2 billion) and 60 or over (1.1 billion) because the number of children under age 15 in developing countries will decrease. In contrast, the population of the more developed regions is expected to change minimally, passing from 1.23 billion to 1.28 billion, and would have declined to 1.15 billion were it not for the projected net migration from developing to developed countries, which is projected to average 2.4 million persons annually from 2009 to 2050.[244] Long-term estimates of the global population suggest a peak at around 2070 of nine to ten billion people, and then a slow decrease to 8.4 billion by 2100.[245] Population growth is therefore one of the driving factors in the prodigious use of Earth's resources. At a fundamental level, human impacts on the Earth are demonstrated through detrimental changes in the global biogeochemical cycles of chemicals that are critical to life, most notably those of water, oxygen, carbon, nitrogen and phosphorus.

The combination of population increase in the developing world and unsustainable consumption levels in the developed world presents a stark challenge to sustainability. The sustainability goal therefore is to raise the global standard of living without increasing the use of resources beyond globally sustainable levels; that is, to not exceed "one planet" consumption. The inclination of sustainability therefore is to control not only unbridled population growth but also our insatiable appetite for the consumption of biophysical resources. To this end, sustainable management is necessary at all phases of impact from the "direct" human impacts on land, water bodies and atmosphere to the "indirect" drivers of consumption, like natural capital[246] that initiate these direct impacts.

Thus, sustainability resists the usual tendency to meet resource demand by increasing supply. Instead, sustainability applies demand management of all goods and services by promoting reduced consumption, using renewable resources where possible, and encouraging practices that minimise resource intensity while maximising resource productivity. Resource management is therefore recommended for all phases in the life cycles of goods and services.

3.8 Market-Based Concepts in Environmental Legislation

3.8.1 Introduction

Largely, environmental pollution can be viewed as an economic problem. In addition, some economic policies and concepts can play important roles in environmental decision-making and the making of an environmental law. The use of these

[244] United Nations Department of Economic and Social Affairs, Population Division (2008).

[245] Ibid.

[246] Such as resources from the Earth's crust (i.e., minerals, oil), those produced by humans (synthetic substances) and those of the biosphere.

instruments is premised on a belief that the market can be used to provide incentives to guide adverse environmental human behaviours. This is on the premise that:

> If environmental resources are properly valued, the cost of using the environment will be fully taken into account in private economic decision making. This implies that environmental resources are used in "sustainable quantities," provided that their prices are based on their scarcity and place an appropriate value on non- renewable resources. Economic instruments are meant to correct current market prices by internalizing environmental costs which are treated by the market mechanism as external.[247]

It then follows that when air, water, scenery, wildlife, and the whole gamut of environmental resources we exploit, and depend on, are assigned an economic value, they are looked at from an entirely different point of view. The market-based approach can be found in the following policies.

3.8.2 Environmental Accounting Policy

Environmental accounting refers to the use of data about environmental costs and performance in business decisions and operations to enhance compliance with environmental regulations.[248] It has been claimed as a veritable management tool for internal business decisions,[249] and operated in recognising that cost of doing business should include environmental costs. Environmental cost has two major dimensions viz., the private costs and the societal costs.

The private costs are the costs a business incurs or for which a business can be held legally responsible, and therefore accountable.[250] Private costs arise from payments for damages and other forms of compensation in relation to non-compliance to environmental protection mechanisms and are borne either through an administrative settlement between the polluter and the victims or through court decisions.[251]

Societal costs on the other hand represent the costs of business impacts on the environment and the society for which business is not legally accountable. They are referred to as externalities or external costs.[252] Such societal costs include environmental degradation and adverse impacts on human beings, their property and their welfare. These impacts arise from damage caused to rivers because of pollution or pollution of the ecosystem from solid waste disposal.[253] These social costs a

---

[247] Report of the Working Group of experts from the E.C. member states on the use of Economic and Fiscal Instruments in EC Environmental Policy, cited in Phillipe Sands (2003), p. 130.

[248] United States Environmental Protection Agency (USEPA) (1999), p. 228.

[249] Ibid.

[250] United States Environmental Protection Agency (USEPA) (1999).

[251] Ibid.

[252] Ibid.

[253] Onyeabor (1995), p. 45.

business often does not pay. It is the social costs that are not internalised by business operations, that is, of interest to us and to which environmental accounting should seriously be applied.

The need for environmental accounting is to ensure that accounts reflect environmental costs so that stakeholders have information to enable them to make the best use of resources, taking account of the rights and obligations of shareholders, customers and local communities affected by environmental degradation.[254] To this end, environmental accounting allows corporations to internalise the full cost of production including environmental costs, contingent costs,[255] and potentially hidden costs,[256] and to calculate their "sustainable" income. It also enables a corporation to reflect the extent to which its environmental protection measures affect its financial position and performance including actual and potential environmental liabilities.

The essence of this policy is to make operators of activities that impact the environment more cautious in their operations. In addition, current accounting rules penalise, rather than encourage, the environmentally responsible corporation and the more a corporation spends on prevention and clean-up, the less per share it earns in the short run. It is based on this observation that environmental accounting is being advocated. This is because environmental accounting is used as a vehicle for recording "green assets" and monitoring their use and provides a corporation accounting incentives to improve environmental protection.

Thus, companies like the oil companies[257] operating in the Niger Delta of Nigeria that depend heavily on the extraction of natural resources as their main preoccupation should be made by the appropriate authorities to pursue the following environmentally related accounting policy:

i) recording liabilities and provisions
ii) setting up catastrophe reserves
iii) disclosing contingent liabilities (including liabilities provisions and reserves for the current period and amounts accumulated with an estimate of the amount involved)

3.8.3 Environmental or Pollution Tax Policy

Economic factors play a role in internationalising efforts to safeguard the environment. A state that enacts environmental measures must count the increased costs that are borne by its economy. In the long term, "green" investments are advantageous.

---

[254] Sands (2000), pp. 623–624.

[255] These costs include costs for natural resources damages, property damage, personal injury damage, legal expenses and remediation.

[256] Such as site studies, site preparation, permitting, installation, etc.

[257] Indeed, all companies in the extractive industry.

This is because it is more costly and, in some cases, impossible to repair environmental damage by, for example, cleaning up rivers or groundwater, rehabilitating the countryside, or reintroducing wildlife species than the green investment.

In economic theory, pollution is considered a negative externality because it has a negative effect on a party not directly involved in a transaction.[258] To confront parties with the issue, the economist Arthur Pigou[259] proposed taxing the goods, which are the source of the negative externality to accurately reflect the cost of the goods' production to society. In this way, the costs associated with the goods' production are internalised. A tax on a negative externality is termed a Pigouvian tax,[260] and should equal the marginal damage costs.[261] For example, a carbon tax, an environmental tax on emissions of carbon dioxide and other greenhouse gases is an example of a pollution tax. This type of tax is an indirect tax, that is, a tax on a transaction, as opposed to a direct tax, which taxes income. One advantage of this form of taxation is that it taxes at a fixed rate, independent of income.[262]

Accordingly, a carbon tax is effectively a tax on the use of fossil fuels.[263] As a result of its link with global warming, a carbon tax is sometimes assumed to require an internationally administered scheme.[264]

For instance, the European Union (EU) considered a carbon tax covering its Member States before starting its emissions trading scheme in 2005.[265] The United Kingdom (UK) has unilaterally introduced a range of carbon taxes and Climate Change levies to accompany the European Union Emission Trading Scheme (EU ETS) trading regime.[266]

The purpose of a carbon tax is to protect the natural environment by reducing emissions of carbon dioxide, thereby slowing climate change, at the global level, and the protection of the immediate environment from such adverse environmental impacts, arising thereto, such as acid rain.[267] A carbon tax can be implemented by taxing gas flaring[268] and the burning of fossil fuels, coal, and petroleum products such as gasoline, aviation fuel and natural gas, in proportion to their carbon content.

---

[258] Carbon Tax Centre (2018).

[259] Ibid.

[260] After Arthur Pigou who proposed taxing goods, such as petrol and gas.

[261] Carbon Tax Centre (2018).

[262] Dingell (2007), A21.

[263] Carbon atoms are present in every fossil fuel, coal, petroleum, and natural gas and are released as CO_2 when they are burnt.

[264] Dingell (2007).

[265] Debate is currently going on among airline operators on a proposed emissions tax from 2012 on all aircraft using the air space of EU member countries.

[266] Note that emissions trading systems do not constitute a Pigouvian tax because they entail the creation of a property right.

[267] Government of British Columbia (2018).

[268] Nigeria presently taxes gas flaring as a means of curbing gas flaring.

Is carbon tax feasible? The answer is yes. It is being implemented in the following countries: Finland, the Netherlands and Norway in 1990, and Sweden in January 1991. The United Kingdom Treasury imposed the Fuel Price Escalator, an incrementally increasing pollution tax, on retail petroleum products in 1993, Italy in 1998, the United States in 2006, New Zealand in 2007 and Canada in 2008. European Union (EU), as a regional group, in 2012 introduced carbon tax on airlines flying the EU air space.[269]

The benefit of carbon tax policy is succinctly captured in the opinion of Al Gore,[270] former Vice-President of the USA, in these words:

> We should start using the tax code to reduce taxes on employment and production, and make up the difference with pollution taxes, principally on CO_2. Now I fully understand that this is considered politically impossible. But part of our challenge is to expand the limits of what's possible. Right now we are discouraging work and encouraging the destruction of the planet's habitability.

Perceived advantages of a carbon tax are:

i) less complex, less expensive, and less time-consuming implementation. This advantage is especially great when applied to markets like petroleum products;
ii) reduced risk of certain types of cheating;
iii) reduced incentives for companies to delay efficiency improvements (when companies are given more carbon credits if they polluted less in the past;
iv) does not disadvantage new or growing companies relative to more established companies; and
v) it has greater transparency as tax is based on pollution output.[271]

Thus, revenue from environmental or pollution tax may be used to address adverse environmental impacts. Alternatively, such revenue may be used to fund environmental projects to redress environmental damage.

3.8.4 *Charges, Taxes, and Tax Relief Incentive Policy*

Charges and taxes form part of the economic instruments we recommend as part of our environmental protection policy. The rationale behind charges and taxes is that they create an incentive for polluters to limit activities that can be harmful to the environment such as emissions, generation of wastes and the excessive use of natural resources.

While taxes are commonly imposed on industries varying from production tax to income tax, charges on the other hand are not commonly imposed. Forms of charges advocated include: emission charges and user charges. Emission charges can be

[269] Carbon Finance (2012).
[270] Dingell (2007), A21.
[271] Government of British Columbia (2018).

levied on discharges of effluents and gases and can be calculated based on the quantity and/or quality of the pollution load. The user charges, on the other hand, are charges paid by dischargers for services rendered by environmental protection agencies in managing polluted environments and are only payable by firms or corporations who receive or are associated with the services.[272] Such services in issue include collection and removal of solid wastes, wastewater, and hazardous wastes; clean-up of spills and rehabilitation of contaminated soils.

It is suggested that the more a firm engages in activities that are inimical to a healthy environment, the more the charges are payable. In the same vein tax relief incentives and waiver of charges should be granted to firms that comply with environmental protection measures. The relief should also be granted to firms to cover the cost of new investment expenditure to improve the efficient use of natural resources and reduction in emissions and effluent discharges.

To this end, it is advocated that the current NESREA's Green Mark[273] instituted annually to the best environmentally performing facility and organisation be monetised or applied to such recipients as tax relief or waiver of charges instead of a mere certificate being issued to such organisation.

What is targeted is a shift towards using tax law to create incentives towards environmentally benign productions and activities, and disincentives against processes considered to be detrimental to the environment. Thus, gas-guzzler taxes, recycling tax credits, taxes on the use of virgin materials, taxes on hazardous waste generation and excise taxes on various products are approaches that can produce "green" products and development.

Overall, with a market-based incentive approach, the government sets firm environmental goals and defines them in specific responses and compliance strategies for each individual enterprise. In the words of Dudek et al.,[274] "the market-based incentive approach harnesses the economic self-interest of each business in service of environmental protection. . .and invites continuous environmental entrepreneurship in the private sector."

---

[272] Currently in Enugu State of Nigeria, the Enugu State Waste Management and Sanitation Authority Law 2004 has provisions for user charges paid by various waste generators to the Enugu State Waste Management and Sanitation Authority (ESWAMA) for refuse and waste collection. The same thing applies in Lagos State through the Lagos State Environmental Management Authority (LASEMA).

[273] Under the provisions of the National Environmental (Textile, Wearing Apparel, Leather and Footwear Industry) Regulations (2009), Regulation 55, the National Environmental (Chemical, Pharmaceutical, Soap and Detergent Manufacturing Industries) Regulations (2009), Regulation 53, and the National Environmental (Food, Beverages and Tobacco Sector) Regulations (2009), Regulation 53, among others.

[274] Dudek et al. (2007) cited in Anton et al. (2007), pp. 1254–1255.

3.9 Concepts of Strict Liability and Absolute Liability

3.9.1 *Introduction*

In the law of tort, it is trite that strict liability imposes liability on a party without a finding of fault (such as negligence or tortious intent). The claimant need only prove that the tort occurred and that the defendant was responsible. The law imputes strict liability to situations it considers to be inherently dangerous. It discourages reckless behaviour and needless loss by forcing potential defendants to take every possible precaution. It also has the effect of simplifying and thereby expediting court decisions in these cases. These postulations have found application in environmental matters under the concepts of strict liability and absolute liability.

3.9.2 *Concept of Strict Liability*

An offence is one of strict liability where it provides for people to be punished for doing something or failing to do something, whether they have a guilty intent. In other words, someone is held to be legally liable for their conduct irrespective of their moral responsibility.[275]

The rule of strict liability was laid down in 1868 in the case of *Rylands v. Fletc*her.[276] In that case, the defendants employed independent contractors to construct a reservoir on their land, the contractors found disused mines when digging but failed to seal them properly. They filled the reservoir with water and there was a blast. As a result, water flooded through the mineshafts into the plaintiff's mines on the adjoining property. The court held that if any person brings any hazardous substance onto his land, and if that substance is likely to cause some damage if it escapes then such person would be held liable, even if he had taken proper care and was not negligent in keeping the substance at his place.[277] Based on this judicial pronouncement, the concept of strict liability came into being.

3.9.2.1 Requirements for Proof of Liability Under Strict Liability Rules

According to Blackburn J who delivered the judgment of the Court of Exchequer Chamber, and the House of Lords in the case of *Ryland v. Fletcher*,[278] that for a claimant to succeed in the application of the strict liability, such claimant must show:

---

[275] Australian Senate Standing Committee for the Scrutiny of Bills (2018).

[276] (1868) L.R. 3 H.L. 330.

[277] Rylands v. Fletc*her* (1868), 330.

[278] In the case of Rylands v. Fletcher (1868) L.R. 3 H.L. 330.

(i) That the defendant brought something onto his land;
(ii) That the defendant made a "non-natural use" of his land (per Lord Cairns, LC);
(iii) The thing was something likely to do mischief if it escaped and did escape;
(iv) Damage must be foreseeable.[279]

3.9.2.1.1 The Defendant Brought Something onto His Land

In law, there is a difference between things that grow or occur naturally on the land, and those that are artificial and are accumulated therein by the defendant. For example, rocks and thistles naturally occur on land. However, the defendants in *Rylands v. Fletcher* brought a large amount of water stored onto his land. This was considered by the court as dangerous. Substances such as noxious fumes,[280] explosives,[281] and flag-pole,[282] had been considered as dangerous in other cases where the rule in *Rylands v. Fletcher* had been made applicable.

3.9.2.1.2 The Defendant Must Have Engaged in a Non-natural Use of Land

Another essential condition for the defendant to be held liable under the rule is that the defendant engaged in a non-natural use of his land. According to Blackburn J:

> We think the true rule of law is that the person who, for his own purposes, brings on his land and collects and keeps there anything likely to do mischief if it escapes, must keep it in at his peril, and if he does not do so, is prima facie answerable for all damages which is the non-natural use of land.[283]

Therefore, the rule in *Rylands v. Fletcher* would only apply where the defendant deliberately accumulated or brought onto his/her land a "dangerous thing" during some "non-natural" use of land. In *Giles v. Walker,*[284] it was held that there was no liability under the rule in respect of trees, shrubs and other plants that are naturally found on the defendant's land, even if part of these do escape to the claimant's land. Similarly, in the case of *Pontordawe RDC v. Moore-Gwyn,*[285] rocks that fell to the claimant's land because of weathering were held to be not deliberately accumulated and the defendant was held not liable.

[279] Rylands v. Fletcher (1868).
[280] West v. Bristol Tramways Co, (1908) 2 K.B. 14.
[281] TC Balakrishnan v. TR Subramanian, A.I.R. 1968 Kerela 151.
[282] Shiffman v. Graud Priory and Ors, (1936) 1 All ER 557.
[283] Rylands v. Fletcher (1868).
[284] (1890) 24 QBD 656.
[285] [1929] 1 Ch 656.

However, the decisions in the above cases[286] were overturned in the case of *Davey v. Harrow Corporation.*[287] In that case, the plaintiff's house was damaged by roots penetrating from trees on adjoining land. At the first instance, Sellers J found that the damage was caused by the trees, but they were not proven to be the property of the defendants. On appeal and after further evidence it was found that the trees had been growing for some time on the defendants' land. The court held that the defendants were liable in nuisance for damage caused by encroaching roots whether self-sown or planted. According to Lord Goddard CJ:

> Where a boundary hedge is delineated on an Ordnance Survey map by a line, the line indicates the centre of the existing hedge. This accords with the practice of the Ordinance Survey map and courts can take notice of that practice as prima facie evidence of what a line on a map indicates. 'After that Fisher -v- Winch and this, courts in future can take notice of this practice of the Ordnance Survey (that the boundary line on the map indicated the centre of the existing hedge) as at least prima facie evidence of what a line on the map indicates'. As to damage by roots: 'once it is established that encroachment by roots is a nuisance, it must follow that if damage is thereby caused, an action on the case will lie'.[288]

Although the bottom line is that the accumulation must be for a non-natural use of land for there to be a liability, there has been a clear intention by the courts to distinguish things that are naturally on land and something that is brought onto the land. In *Rickards v. Lothian,*[289] Lord Moulton explained that "It is not every use to which land is put that brings into play [the] principle. It must be some special use bringing with it increase danger to others, and must not merely be the ordinary use of land or such use as is proper for the general benefit of the community."[290] This was considered in the case of *Read v. J Lyon & Co Ltd.*[291]

In that case, the claimant was employed by the defendant in their factory which made explosives for the Ministry of Supply. During her employment, an explosion occurred which killed a man and injured others including the claimant. There was no evidence that negligence had caused the explosion. At trial, the judge held that the case was governed by the rule in *Rylands v. Fletcher* and liability was therefore strict. The Court of Appeals reversed this decision as the rule in *Rylands v. Fletcher* required an escape of the hazardous matter. The claimant appealed. The House of Lords dismissed the appeal and held that in the absence of any proof of negligence on behalf of the defendant or an escape of dangerous things, there was no cause of action on which the claimant could succeed.[292]

---

[286] Giles v. Walker (1890) and Pontordawe RDC v. Moore-Gwyn (1929).

[287] [1957] 2 WLR 941, [1957] 2 All ER 305, [1958] 1 QB 60.

[288] Ibid., 944.

[289] [1913] AC 263.

[290] Ibid.

[291] [1947] AC 156.

[292] Read v. J Lyon &Co Ltd (1947).

Again, in the case of *British Celanese Ltd v. A H Hunt Ltd*[293] Lawton J further commented that the use of land on an industrial estate for industrial purposes was an ordinary use of land. However, Lord Goff in the case of *Cambridge Water v. Eastern Counties Leather*[294] opined that "the storage of substantial quantities of chemicals on industrial premises should be regarded as an almost classic case of non-natural use."

In the case of *Transco plc v. Stockport MBC*,[295] Lord Bingham made it clear that the rule in *Rylands v. Fletcher* would only apply "where the defendant's use is shown to be extraordinary and unusual" and therefore the argument of "general benefit of the community" is not sufficient.[296] In that case, the claimant was the owner of a gas pipe that passed under the surface of an old railway between Stockport and Denton. The defendant was the local council which was responsible for a water pipe that supplied water to a block of flats in the nearby Brinnington Estate. In 1992, a leak developed in that water pipe, which was eventually fixed but which had not been immediately detected. At that time, the water had been leaking considerably (as the pipe was large) and had saturated the embankment where the Claimant's gas pipe was. The embankment eventually collapsed due to the saturation, which meant that the gas pipe was left unsupported. This caused a grave risk which necessitated immediate remedial work, which was costly. The claimant argued that the defendant council was liable without proof of negligence under *Rylands v. Fletcher.*[297]

The issue for determination before the court was whether the rule in *Rylands v. Fletcher* could be applied to this set of facts and specifically whether it could be held that the council's use of the land, to deliver water to the housing estate, was a non-natural use. The court held that the council was not liable for the damage as the council's use was a natural use of the land. The rule in *Rylands v. Fletcher* has limits and it is not possible to apply it to a burst pipe on council property. Supplying water was neither an unnatural nor specifically dangerous endeavour.[298]

What is therefore considered is that for the use to be non-natural such use must be for a special purpose and this brings with it increased danger to others. To this end, in the case of *Sochacki v. Sas*,[299] it was held that the fire in a house in a grate[300] is an ordinary natural use of the fireplace in a room. If this fire spreads to the adjoining premises, the liability under the strict liability rule will not arise as such use is a natural use of land.

---

[293] [1969] 2 All ER 1252, [1969] 1 WLR 959.

[294] 1994] 2 AC 264.

[295] [2004] 2 AC 1.

[296] Ibid.

[297] Transco plc v. Stockport MBC (2004).

[298] Transco plc v. Stockport MBC (2004).

[299] (1947) 1 All E.R. 344.

[300] The recess of a fireplace or furnace.

Again, in the case of *Ellison v. Ministry of Defence*,[301] the defendant constructed bulk fuel installations at Greenham Common airfield. This caused rainwater which had accumulated on the airfield to run off and flood neighbouring land. The court held that the construction work was an ordinary use of the land and necessary for the use of the land as an airfield and therefore there was no non-natural use. Also, the rainwater accumulated naturally and was not artificially kept there. The defendant was held not liable under *Rylands v. Fletcher*.[302]

3.9.2.1.3 The Thing Was Something Likely to Do Mischief If It Escaped

In this situation, the thing brought onto the land must be something likely to do mischief if it escapes. In such a situation the defendant keeps it in at his peril. For instance, where a defendant has some poisonous plant on his property and the leaves from the plant entered onto the property of the plaintiff. Where the plaintiff's cattle eat the leaves and die, the defendant will be liable for the loss. On the other hand, if the cattle belonging to the plaintiff entered the premises of the defendant, ate the poisonous leaves and died, the defendant would not be liable.[303]

In the judicial pronouncement in the case of *Reads v. Lyons & Co*[304] it was held that if there is no escape, the defendant cannot be held liable. In that case, the plaintiff was an employee at the defendant's ammunition factory. While she was experimenting at the defendant's premises a blast occurred from a shell which was manufactured in the factory. As a result, the plaintiff suffered an injury. It was held that the defendant was not held liable as the accident occurred within the premises of the defendant.

3.9.2.1.4 Damage and Foreseeability of the Defendant's Action

Foreseeability is the facility to perceive, know in advance or reasonably anticipate that damage or injury will probably ensue from acts or omissions.[305] For liability to arise on the part of the defendant under the rule in Rylands v. Fletcher, his acts or omissions should be reasonably foreseeable.

The foreseeability test was laid in *Re Polemis & Furness Withy & Company Ltd.*[306] In that case, some Stevedores carelessly dropped a plank of wood into the hold of a ship. The plank struck something as it was falling which caused a spark. The spark was ignited by petrol vapours destroying the ship. The arbitrator held that

---

[301] (1997) 81 BLR 101.

[302] E-Law Resources (2020).

[303] See the case of Ponting v. Noakes (1849) 2 Q.B. 281.

[304] Read v. J Lyons & Co (1947).

[305] Free Dictionary (2020).

[306] [1921] 3 KB 560.

the cause of the spark could not have been anticipated and therefore no liability arose. The claimant appealed. The court held that there was no requirement that the damage was foreseeable. The defendant was liable for all the direct consequences of their action.[307]

In the *Wagon Mound No. 1*[308] the defendant's vessel, The Wagon Mound, leaked furnace oil at a Wharf in Sydney Harbour. Some cotton debris became embroiled in the oil and sparks from some welding works ignited the oil. The fire spread rapidly destroying some boats and the wharf.

In its decision, the court laid the test for assessment of damages under the foreseeability rule. The test is whether the damage is of a foreseeable kind. If a foreseeable type of damage is present, the defendant is liable for the full extent of the damage, no matter whether the extent of damage was foreseeable.[309] Thus, a test of remoteness of damage was substituted for the direct consequence test and in this respect, the court held that *Re Polemis*[310] should no longer be regarded as good law.[311]

Again, in the case of *Cambridge Water v. Eastern Counties Leather plc*[312] foreseeability of the defendant's action was also tested. In that case, the defendant owned a leather tanning business. Spillages of small quantities of solvents occurred over a long period which seeped through the floor of the building into the soil below. These solvents made their way to the borehole owned by the Claimant water company. The borehole was used for supplying water to local residents. The water was contaminated at a level beyond that which was considered safe and Cambridge Water had to cease using the borehole. Cambridge Water brought actions based on negligence, nuisance and the rule in Rylands v. Fletcher.

The court held that Eastern Counties Leather were not liable as the damage was too remote. It was not reasonably foreseeable that the spillages would result in the closing of the borehole. The foreseeability of the type of damage is a pre-requisite of liability in actions of nuisance and claims based on the rule in *Rylands v. Fletcher* in the same way as it applies to claims based on negligence.

3.9.2.2 Defences under the Rule in Rylands v. Fletcher

A few defences have been developed to the rule in *Rylands v. Fletcher*. A defendant may escape liability if he can prove any of the following:

---

[307] The decision in the was overruled in Wagon Mound No. 1, [1961] AC 388.

[308] [1961] AC 388.

[309] Wagon Mound No. 1 (1961).

[310] *Re Polemis* (1921).

[311] Wagon Mound No. 1 (1961).

[312] [1994] 1 All E.R. 53 at 76.

3.9.2.2.1 Default of the Claimant

Damage caused by the escape due to the plaintiff's fault can be considered as a good defence. Thus, if the plaintiff suffers damage by his own intrusion into the defendant's property, then he has no right to complain about the damage so caused. In the case of *Ponting v. Noakes*[313] the horse of the plaintiff died because of nibbling the leaves of poisonous trees planted on the defendants' land. It was contended that the horse intruded onto the defendants' property where it ate leaves and died. The defendant was held not liable.

Again, if the damage suffered by the plaintiff was not because of escape but due to his incapacity to handle a situation in the ordinary course of things the defendant will not be held liable. As in the case of *Eastern and South African Telegraph Co. Ltd. v. Capetown Tramways Co*[314] where the defendant's submarine cable transmission was disturbed because of the escape current from the defendant's tramways. It was found that such would not have occurred in ordinary business, and that since it did occur, it was because of the sensitive nature of the plaintiff's apparatus. The defendant was held not liable.

3.9.2.2.2 Act of God

An act of God is an event which "no human foresight can provide against, and of which human prudence is not bound to recognise the possibility."[315] It has always been considered that where an incident occurs due to an unforeseeable event, which a human being does not have any control over, then in such circumstances the person cannot be held responsible for any liability arising thereto or any incident that occurs therefrom. In the case of *Nichols v. Marsland,*[316] the defendant made artificial lakes over his land by damming up a natural stream. Exceptionally heavy rain caused the artificial lakes, bridges and waterways to be flooded and damaged adjoining land. The defendant was held not liable since the event that happened was unforeseen.

However, in this case, *Nichols v. Marsland*[317] was doubted by the House of Lords in the case of *Greenock Corporation v. Caledonian Railway.*[318] In that case, the corporation constructed a concrete paddling pool for children in the bed of a stream and obstructed the natural flow of the stream. Owing to a rainfall of extraordinary violence the stream overflowed at the pond and damaged the property of the

[313](1849) 2 Q.B. 281.

[314](1902) A.C. 381.

[315]Lord Westbury in Tennent v. Earl of Glasgow (1864) 2 M (HL) 22 at 26–27.

[316](1876) 2 Ex. D 1.

[317]Nichols v. Marsland (1876).

[318][1917] AC 556.

plaintiffs. The court held that the extraordinary rainfall did not absolve the corporation from responsibility and that they were liable for damages.[319]

3.9.2.2.3 Consent of the Plaintiff

If the source of the danger was maintained for the benefit of both the claimant and the defendant, the defendant will not be liable for its escape. Thus, where the plaintiff had voluntarily consented to suffer the harm for the common benefit of the claimant and defendant, the defendant will not be liable for its escape. In the case of *Carstair v. Taylor*,[320] there was a two-storey building where the plaintiff acquired the ground floor of the building and the defendant acquired the first floor. There was a leakage of water from the upper floor of the building which both the plaintiff and defendant had agreed to store. The defendant was at no fault for the leakage. Due to the leakage, the plaintiff's goods were damaged. It was held that the defendant was not liable for the damage as it was a consented act by both parties.

3.9.2.2.4 The Act of the Third Party

If the damage is suffered by the defendant without the fault of the defendant but due to the third party, who was neither the defendant's servant nor was in any relation to the defendant then under those circumstances if any damage is suffered by the plaintiff defendant will not be held liable. In the case of *Box v. Jabb*[321] where there was an overflow of water from the defendant's reservoir causing damage to the plaintiff. It was revealed that the overflow so happened was due to the blocking of the drain done by a stranger, a third party. The defendant was held not liable under the strict liability rule. Also, in the case of *Rickards v. Lothian*,[322] the defendant was held not liable when an unknown person blocked a basin on his property and caused a flood, which damaged a flat below.

This issue of the negligent act of a third party was further highlighted in the case of *North-Western Utilities Ltd. v. London Guarantee and Accident Co. Ltd. & Others*.[323] The appellants in this case were a public utility company, supplying gas, under a statutory franchise, to consumers in the city of Edmonton. The Corona Hotel, owned and insured by the respondents respectively, was destroyed by fire caused by the ignition of the gas, which, escaping from the defendants' main, adjacent to the hotel, had percolated through the soil into the hotel basement. The court found that the gas escaped through a fractured joint in the main, and that the

[319] Greenock Corporation v. Caledonian Railway, ibid.

[320] (1871) LR 6 Ex. 217.

[321] (1879) 4 Ex. D 76.

[322] Rickards v. Lothian (1913).

[323] [1936] AC 108.

break was caused by the displacement of soil thereunder by workmen of the City of Edmonton in constructing a storm sewer.[324]

The action was brought (i) for permitting gas, a dangerous substance, to escape; (ii) for breach of a statutory duty; (iii) for negligence in that the appellants either knew, or ought to have known, what work the city was doing, and failed to take, as they could and should have done, all proper precautions to prevent the escape of the dangerous gas which they were carrying in their mains.[325] The appellant contended that it was not liable, because the real cause of the damage was the negligent construction of the storm sewer by the City of Edmonton, for which they were not responsible, and which it could not control and that they were guilty of no negligence in the matter.

Lord Wright delivered the judgment in the case, which was heard on appeal from the Supreme Court of Alberta. The court upheld the contention by the appellants that the act was perpetrated by a third party. "The defendant is excused," said Lord Wright, "where the casualty is due to the independent or conscious volition of a third party. . .and not to any negligence of the defendants."[326]

The main import of this case may be distilled from this statement of the court, "but this escape from liability under the rule in *Rylands v Fletcher* availed the appellant nothing." "He may still be held liable in negligence," said Lord Wright, "if he failed in foreseeing and guarding against the consequences to his works of that third party's act."[327]

Although the defendant may escape liability under the rule in *Rylands v. Fletcher*,[328] he may be held liable for negligence. The court added weight to this assertion when it acknowledged the damage to the plaintiff's property when it stated that the great damage to the respondent's property is an index of the risk attendant upon the escape of the gas from the mains. The duty of care owed to adjacent occupiers is high in proportion to that risk, and in this case, clearly involved a duty of inspection and the taking of precautions against possible interference with the mains by the city. The gas company had done nothing to fulfil this duty; it was, therefore, held liable for negligence, which is the breach of a duty of care.[329]

This preposition is prima facie within the rule laid down by Blackburn J in *Ryland v. Fletcher*. According to S T Frost,[330] "The gas constitutes an extraordinary danger, created by the appellants for their own purposes. . .they act at their peril, and must pay for damage caused by the gas if it escapes, even without any negligence on their part." Ownership of the land is not a necessary element of the liability. It is sufficient

---

[324] Ibid.

[325] Ibid.

[326] North-Western Utilities Ltd. v. London Guarantee and Accident Co. Ltd. & Others (1936), 119.

[327] Ibid., 125.

[328] Act of the third party.

[329] North-Western Utilities Ltd. v. London Guarantee and Accident Co. Ltd. & Others (1936).

[330] Frost (1938).

if the mains are laid in the exercise of a franchise to do so. The onus thus lay on the gas company to show that the case fell within one of the exceptions to the rule.

3.9.2.2.5 Statutory Authority

This is another defence in *Rylands v. Fletcher.* A statute may require a person or body to carry out a particular activity. Liability under *Rylands v. Fletcher* may be excluded upon the interpretation of the statute. Lord Wright speaking for the Privy Council in *Northwestern Utilities Ltd. v. London Guarantee and Accident Co. Ltd.*[331] allowed that *Rylands v. Fletcher* could apply to a statutory body although then in favour of such a body. He said, "The rule of strict liability has been modified by admitting as a defence that what was being done was properly done in pursuance of statutory powers, and the mischief that has happened has not been brought about by any negligence on the part of the undertakers."[332]

There was a divided opinion of the judges in the case of *Benning v. Wong*,[333] an Australian case. In that case, the plaintiff sued the defendant to recover damages for personal injuries sustained by her from gas whilst on land which at relevant times she occupied and which bounded a public street. According to the plaintiff, the gas escaped onto the land so occupied by her from pipes laid by the Australian Gas Light Co. in the public street under statutory powers and used by it for the conveyance of gas for domestic and industrial use.[334]

The defendant claims that because a statute authorised it to lay and to use the gas pipes in a public street, the rule that those who bring on to land dangerous things or substances likely to do harm if they escape from that land are bound to keep such things or substances on the land and are liable if the thing or substance escapes to other land and there does damage does not apply to it in relation to the escape of gas of which the plaintiff complains. The defendant says that the only relevant cause of action available to the plaintiff in the circumstances is for breach of a duty of care which would involve the plaintiff in affirmative proof on a balance of probabilities that the escape of gas of which the plaintiff complains was due to a want of care on the part of the defendant in or about the laying of the pipes or in their maintenance or otherwise in its operations as a supplier of gas using such pipes.[335]

In its decision, the minority[336] adopted the line of reasoning apparent in the *dicta* of the *Northwestern Utilities Ltd. v. London Guarantee and Accident Co. Ltd* case.[337] They held that the gas company was subject to *Rylands* v. *Fletcher* liability

[331] Northwestern Utilities Ltd. v. London Guarantee and Accident Co. Ltd (1936).

[332] Northwestern Utilities Ltd. v. London Guarantee and Accident Co. Ltd (1936) at 118.

[333] (1969) 122 CLR 249.

[334] Benning v. Wong (1969) at 254.

[335] Ibid., 255.

[336] Barwick C.J. and Windeyer J.

[337] Northwestern Utilities Ltd. v. London Guarantee and Accident Co. Ltd (1936).

unless it could show that its work was statutorily authorised. Since the statutory authority in this case only extended protection to works performed with technical skill and care, if the company were to prove statutory authorisation, it would have to prove that such skill and care had been exercised. For this reason, the onus of disproof of negligence properly fell on the company. Windeyer J. explained the railway spark cases on the ground that unlike the escape of gas the escape of sparks from a steam engine is inevitable and has always been held to be so. Hence a statutory authorisation to use a steam engine always displaces strict liability and the undertaker is only liable if the plaintiff proves negligence.[338]

Of the majority,[339] McTiernan J. confined his attention to the statutes. In His Honour's view, Section 61 of the 1837 Act[340] showed that the legislature plainly contemplated that escapes of gas would occur and hence could not have intended that the company should keep gas under pressure defined by statute in its pipes at its peril. Menzies J. found logical difficulty in having the *Rylands* v. *Fletcher* "strict liability" rule subject to a defence of disproof of negligence on the part of the company for as he saw it "the whole point of *Rylands* v. *Fletcher* liability is that the exercise of care is irrelevant."[341] Both Menzies and Owen JJ found assistance in the *dicta* from the Australian cases mentioned above and felt able to disregard Lord Wright's comments in reaching their conclusion that Mrs Wong was left to her remedy in negligence.[342]

In the words of Habersber,[343] the take from the case is that a statute only authorises those acts which it expressly nominates or which are necessarily incidental to the execution of such acts. Generally, even these acts are only authorised if they are performed with due care although it is always of course a matter of statutory construction to find if only carefully performed acts are within the statutory authority.

3.9.3 Concept of Absolute Liability

The rule of absolute liability, in simple words, can be defined as the rule of strict liability minus the exceptions.[344] According to the rule, "if any person is engaged in an inherently dangerous or hazardous activity and if any harm is caused to any

[338] Benning v. Wong (1969), 254.

[339] McTiernan, Menzies and Owen JJ.

[340] That section, that is s. 61, provides that: "When any gas shall be found to escape from any of the pipes which shall be laid down . . . the company . . . shall immediately . . . cause the most speedy and effectual measures to be taken to stop and prevent such gas from escaping."

[341] (1969) 43 A.L.J.R. 467, 477.

[342] Benning v. Wong (1969), 254.

[343] Habersber (1970), p. 576.

[344] Furtado (2020).

person due to any accident which occurred during carrying out such inherently dangerous and hazardous activity, then the person who is carrying out such activity will be held absolutely liable."[345] In such a situation the exceptions to the strict liability rule in *Rylands v. Fletcher* will not apply.

3.9.3.1 Genesis of Concept of Absolute Liability

The concept of absolute liability was laid down in the case of *MC Mehta v. Union of India.*[346] In that case, the claim arose from the leakage of oleum gas from the Shriram Food and Fertilizers Industries, in Delhi. The Shriram Foods and Fertiliser Plant, Delhi (Shriram) was situated amidst a population of 200,000 people. It manufactured items such as glycerine soap, and technical hard oil. The petitioner, M.C. Mehta, filed a writ petition in the Supreme Court to obtain an order for the closure of the plant and its relocation to an area where it would not be any real danger to the health and safety of the people.[347]

The Supreme Court permitted the plant to restart power and function, pending disposal of the petition. During the pendency of the petition, there occurred a leak in the Shriram industrial units on 4th and 6th December 1985. The oleum gas leak from the plant caused significant detrimental health effects, including loss of life and serious injuries to the local population, under which compensation claims were filed.[348]

An action in this application was filed by the Delhi Legal Aid & Advice Board and the Delhi Bar Association for the award of compensation to the persons who had suffered losses on account of this gas leak.[349] The leak in question was called the Bhopal gas tragedy.[350]

The Bhopal gas tragedy occurred in 1984 in the city of Bhopal, Madhya Pradesh. The disaster was a result of a leak of methyl isocyanate (MIC) which occurred in December in a pesticides manufacturing plant named Union Carbide India Ltd (UCIL). The MIC is considered the most hazardous chemical used for industrial purposes. On the night of 2–3 December 1984, there was a leak of the MIC gas in the plant. This leak had increased and contaminated the air and when people got exposed to it, they felt various symptoms like coughing, vomiting, severe eye irritation and suffocation. This led towards the death of thousands of people and a lot of people got permanently impaired in one way or another because of this disaster. The cases were filed against the majority holder UCC which was a United States (US) company. These criminal and civil cases were filed in the US courts. The government of India

[345] Ibid.

[346] AIR (1987) SC 1086.

[347] Ibid.

[348] Global Health Rights (2020).

[349] Dixit (2020).

[350] Ibid.

enacted the Bhopal Gas Tragedy Disaster Act to deal with the claims arising out of this tragedy. The sum of some USD 470 million was granted initially by the UCC as a part of the settlement with the government of India for compensation. This tragedy brought havoc and, after this, attention was brought to the need for various laws regulating environmental protection.[351]

One of the questions before the court was: What should be the applicable rule in determining liability and possible compensation to the victims? Should it be the rules established in the case of absolute liability or the rule in *Ryland v. Fletcher*? The court posed this question on the propriety or otherwise in following the rules set in the case of *Rylands v. Fletcher*:

> What is the measure of liability of an enterprise which is engaged in a hazardous or inherently dangerous industry, if by reason of an accident occurring in such industry, persons die or is injured? Does the rule in *Rylands v Fletcher* apply or is there any other principle on which the liability can be determined?[352]

To answer the above questions formulated by it, the court stated that:

> The rule in *Rylands v Fletcher* was evolved in the year 1866 and it provides that a person who for his own purposes being on to his land and collects and keeps there anything likely to do mischief if it escapes must keep it at his peril and, if he fails to do so, is prima facie liable for the damage which is the natural consequence of its escape. The liability under this rule is strict and it is no defence that the thing escaped without that person's wilful act, default or neglect or even that he had no knowledge of its existence. This rule laid down a principle of liability that if a person who brings on to his land and collects and keeps there anything likely to do harm and such thing escapes and does damage to another, he is liable to compensate for the damage caused. Of course, this rule applies only to non-natural user of the land and it does not apply to things naturally on the land or where the escape is due to an act of God and an act of a stranger or the default of the person injured or where the thing which escapes is present by the consent of the person injured or in certain cases where there is statutory authority.[353]

Thus, the court was reluctant to accept the concept of strict liability as embodied in the rules in *Rylands v. Fletcher*. The court held that:

> where an enterprise is engaged in a hazardous or inherently dangerous activity and harm results to anyone on account of an accident in the operation of such hazardous or inherently dangerous activity resulting, for example, in escape of toxic gas the enterprise is strictly and absolutely liable to compensate all those who are affected by the accident and such liability is not subject to any of the exceptions which operate vis-à-vis the tortious principle of strict liability under the rule in *Rylands v Fletcher*. We would also like to point out that the measure of compensation in the kind of cases referred to in the preceding paragraph must be co-related to the magnitude and capacity of the enterprise because such compensation must have a deterrent effect. The larger and more prosperous the enterprise, the greater must be the amount of compensation payable by it for the harm caused on account of an accident in the carrying on of the hazardous or inherently dangerous activity by the enterprise.[354]

---

[351] Dixit (2020).

[352] MC Mehta v. Union of India (1987).

[353] Ibid., 840.

[354] MC Mehta v. Union of India (1987).

The court believed that with the advancement and technological development, the involvement of hazardous and harmful material in the industry has increased manifold and this has posed a greater threat and to not make it easy enough for the industries to take the help of exceptions and get away easily, the court decided not to follow any foreign principle and came up with a new principle in this case. This principle is known as absolute liability.[355]

3.9.3.2 Main Kernel of the Concept of Absolute Liability

In enunciating the concept of absolute liability the court, in the case of *Mehta v. Union of India*,[356] stated that:

(i) Where an enterprise is engaged in a hazardous or inherently dangerous activity and harm results to anyone on account of an accident in the operation of such hazardous or inherently dangerous activity resulting, for example, in escape of toxic gas the enterprise is strictly and absolutely liable to compensate all those who are affected by the accident and such liability is not subject to any of the exceptions which operate vis-à-vis the tortious principle of strict liability under the rule in *Rylands v. Fletcher*.

(ii) The measure of compensation in the kind of cases referred to in the preceding paragraph must be co-related to the magnitude and capacity of the enterprise because such compensation must have a deterrent effect. The larger and more prosperous the enterprise, the greater must be the amount of compensation payable by it for the harm caused on account of an accident in the carrying on of the hazardous or inherently dangerous activity by the enterprise.

Regarding the liability of a corporation due to injurious consequences of hazardous activities conducted by it, the court held that a corporation owes an absolute and non-delegable duty to the community to ensure that no harm results to anyone on account of the hazardous or inherently dangerous nature of the activity which it has undertaken. Extending the principle of strict liability in *Rylands v. Fletcher*, the court, for the first time, enunciated the principle of absolute liability of corporations when they undertake hazardous and dangerous activity. Such activity, according to the court, should be allowed only on the condition that the enterprise indemnifies all those who suffer on account of the carrying on of such hazardous or inherently dangerous activity regardless of whether it is carried on carefully or not.[357]

In the final analysis, the court stated that the enterprise must be held to be under an obligation to provide that the hazardous or inherently dangerous activity in which it is engaged must be conducted with the highest standards of safety and if any harm results on account of such activity, the enterprise must be absolutely liable to

[355] Ibid.

[356] Ibid.

[357] MC Mehta v. Union of India (1987), 843.

compensate for such harm and it should be no answer to the enterprise to say that it had taken all reasonable care and that the harm occurred without any negligence on its part.[358]

Accordingly, under the rule of absolute liability, any person involved in inherently dangerous or hazardous activity, or any harm is caused to anyone because of any accident that occurred during carrying out those activities, the person who carried out those activities would be absolutely liable. Under the concept of absolute liability, it becomes the complete responsibility of the industry . . .to keep a check irrespective of the company's claim that it has taken all proper measures and there is no negligence on its part. The person harmed deserves justice and has Fundamental Rights which should be upheld in any condition.[359]

3.9.3.3 Nature of Absolute Liability

Absolute liability is a standard of tort liability. In other words, absolute liability is strict liability without any exception. According to the Supreme Court of Canada in the case of *R. v. Sault Ste. Marie*:[360]

> "Absolute liability" entails conviction on proof merely that the defendant committed the prohibited act constituting the *actus reus* of the offence. There is no relevant mental element. It is no defence that the accused was entirely without fault. He may be morally innocent in every sense, yet be branded as a malefactor and punished as such.

Various arguments have been advanced in the justification of absolute liability in public welfare offences. Two predominate. First, it is argued that the protection of social interests requires a high standard of care and attention on the part of those who follow certain pursuits and such persons are more likely to be stimulated to maintain those standards if they know that ignorance or mistake will not excuse them. The removal of any possible loophole acts, it is said, as an incentive to take precautionary measures beyond what would otherwise be taken, so that mistakes and mishaps be avoided.[361]

The second main argument is based on administrative efficiency. This was laid in the case of *R. v. Sault Ste. Marie*.[362] The court stated that:

> Having regard to both the difficulty of proving mental culpability and the number of petty cases which daily come before the Courts, proof of fault is just too great a burden in time and money to place upon the prosecution. To require proof of each person's individual intent would allow almost every violator to escape. This, together with the glut of work entailed in proving *mens rea* in every case would clutter the docket and impede adequate enforcement as virtually to nullify the regulatory statutes. In short, absolute liability, it is contended, is the

[358] Ibid.

[359] Global Health Rights (2020).

[360] [1978] 2 S.C.R. 1299 at 1310.

[361] Bronitt and McSherry (2001), p. 191.

[362] R. v. Sault Ste. Marie (1978) at 1311.

> most efficient and effective way of ensuring compliance with minor regulatory legislation and the social ends to be achieved are of such importance as to override the unfortunate by-product of punishing those who may be free of moral turpitude. In further justification, it is urged that slight penalties are usually imposed and that conviction for breach of a public welfare offence does not carry the stigma associated with conviction for a criminal offence.

The concept of absolute liability can therefore be said to be a strong legal tool against rogue corporations that were negligent towards health risks for the public. To this end, it can be said that the principle of absolute liability is much more powerful than the principle of strict liability developed in the case *Ryland v. Fletcher*. This is because the former is not subject to the exceptions applicable to the latter. What this portends is under absolute liability a defaulter could be held liable for even third-party errors when the public was at a realistic risk. This could ensure stricter compliance with standards that are meant to safeguard the public.

Typically, absolute liability is applied to offences of a regulatory nature and where it is particularly important to maximise compliance (e.g., public safety or protection of the environment). To this end, strict and absolute liability should be used in the following cases:

(i) regulatory offences, particularly those which relate to the environment or public health;
(ii) where it is difficult for the prosecution to prove a fault element because a matter is peculiarly within the knowledge of the defendant; and
(iii) to overcome the knowledge of law problem, where an element of the offence expressly incorporates a reference to a legislative provision.[363]

Arising from the above, situations in which absolute liability is considered justified should apply:

(i) where "greater efficacy in the supervision of regulatory schemes" is needed;
(ii) where overcoming "inability to prosecute effectively" in certain circumstances; and
(iii) to enable "matters to be dealt with expeditiously where this is necessary to ensure public confidence in the regulatory regime."[364]

Absolute liability offences therefore stem from the fact that such offences require a prosecuting authority to show only that the alleged act took place and not that the person concerned intended to do the act. They displace the common law presumption that the prosecutor must prove *mens rea* or a guilty mind. To this end, the application of strict and absolute liability rules in environmental matters is that society needs to maintain, through effective enforcement, high standards of public health and safety and that potential victims of those who carry on latently pernicious activities have a strong claim to consideration.

[363] Australian Senate Standing Committee (2018) at para 2.97.
[364] Ibid.

Therefore, enterprises that engage in a hazardous or inherently dangerous activity should be duty-bound to protect the environment from abuse and annihilation and should maintain an ecological balance by carrying on their productive processes and policies based on the concept of sustainable development. Otherwise, such enterprises should be absolutely liable not only for the costs and compensation to the victims but also to take all necessary precautions not to pollute the environment beyond the tolerable limits.[365]

As a result of the debilitating effects of environmental spoliation, it is recommended that the judiciary in Nigeria should in environmental pollution cases apply the concept of absolute liability. To this end, the advice of the Justices in India in the case of *M C Mehta v. Union of India*[366] should be heeded to. In that case, the Justices stated that:

> Although we are constrained to follow judicial pronouncements and laws in England, we cannot allow our judicial thinking to be constricted by reference to such laws. We no longer need the crotches of foreign legal order, and we cannot be constricted nor countenance an argument that merely because a new law does not recognize the rule of strict and absolute liability as laid down in the rules and laws inherited by us, we must venture to evolve new principles which are not in the law we inherited.

The view is that all operators of potentially dangerous substances that can cause death, mental or physical impairment to humans or cause irreversible damage to property and the environment, owe every person an absolute and non-delegable duty to ensure that no harm results to anyone on account of his operations with the highest standards of safety. If any harm results the operator must be absolutely liable to compensate for such harm. The fact that he has taken reasonable care or was not negligent or that it was an act of a third party must not be countenanced by the courts.

The operator must be held strictly liable for causing such harm.[367] The liability shall include compensation to victims of the pollution, rehabilitation of the damaged environment and clean-up cost, as the case may be. Therefore, the judiciary is expected to give priority to the doing of environmental justice.

---

[365] M.C. Mehta v. Union of India (1987).

[366] Ibid.

[367] See, for instance, the decisions in the cases of Alphacell Ltd v. Woodward (1972) AC, 824, CPC (UK) Ltd v. National Rivers Authority [1995] Env LR, 131, National Rivers Authority v. Wright Engineering Co. Ltd [1994] 4 All ER, 281, Empress Cars Arbertillery) Ltd v. National Rivers Authority [1998] Env LR, 369. These cases were discussed in sect. 7.5.2 of Chap. 7 of this book: "Cause or knowingly permitted a discharge."

3.9.4 Comparison Between Strict Liability and Absolute Liability

From the discussions on both rules, strict liability and absolute liability, a person is made liable only when he is at fault. But the principle governing these two rules is that a person can be made liable even without his fault. This is known as the principle of "no-fault liability."[368] Under these rules, the liable person may not have done the act, but he will still be responsible for the damage caused due to the acts. Although in the case of strict liability, there are some exceptions where the defendant may escape liable;[369] however, in the case of absolute liability, no exceptions are provided to the defendant. The defendant will be made liable under the absolute liability rule no matter what.

In addition, strict liability can be contrasted with absolute liability by the availability or otherwise of the defence of a mistake of fact. Under strict liability the defence allows an accused to raise "an honest and reasonable belief in a state of facts, which, if they existed, would render the act innocent."[370] This defence has several components to enable a defendant to escape liability. They are:

(i) there must be a mistake and not mere ignorance;
(ii) the mistake must be one of fact and not law;
(iii) the mistake must be honest and reasonable; and
(iv) the mistake must render the accused's act innocent.[371]

Thus, if these defences arise, either expressly or by implication, then the offence may not be an "absolute liability" offence.[372] In this respect absolute liability is used for certain regulatory offences in which it is necessary for individuals engaged in potentially hazardous or harmful activity to exercise extreme, and not merely reasonable, care.[373]

In the final analysis for the concept of strict and absolute liability to apply, the following should be borne in mind:

i) Strict and absolute liability offences should be applied only where the penalty does not include imprisonment.

---

[368] Furtado (2020).

[369] The exceptions applicable to the principle of strict liability are: the plaintiff's own mistake, plaintiff's consent, natural disasters, a third party's mistake (where such party is not an agent of the defendant), and part of a statutory duty. These defences have been discussed under strict liability in this chapter. See sect. 3.9.2.2 of this chapter.

[370] Bronitt and McSherry (2001).

[371] Ibid.

[372] Ibid.

[373] This is why absolute liability is advocated in the case of environmental pollution and in line with the concepts of environmental crime as discussed in sect. 3.4 of this chapter. Again, absolute liability is advocated because environmental abuses arise from carrying out potentially or harmful activities in which extreme care are needed.

ii) Strict and absolute liability offences should be regulatory (e.g., public safety or protection of the environment), not serious criminal offences.
iii) Generally, strict and absolute liability should be provided by primary legislation, with regulations used only for genuine administrative detail.
iv) Strict and absolute liability should depend as far as possible on the actions or lack of action of those who are actually liable for an offence, rather than be imposed on parties who must by necessity rely on information from third parties.
v) The intention to impose strict or absolute liability should be explicit.
vi) The size of the monetary penalty should reflect the fact that liability is imposed regardless of any mistake of fact.
vii) Absolute liability may be acceptable where an element is essentially a precondition of an offence and the state of mind of the offender is not relevant; such cases should be rare and carefully considered.
viii) Absolute liability offences may be acceptable where inadvertent errors, including those based on a mistake of fact, ought to be punished.

One thing is certain, the concept of strict liability and absolute liability has been given international recognition and states are urged to adopt the same. This is succinctly captured in the Report of World Environment and Development[374] in these words:

> States shall take all reasonable precautionary measures to limit the risk when carrying out or permitting certain dangerous but beneficial activities and shall ensure that compensation is provided should substantial transboundary harm occur even when the activities were not known to be harmful at the time they were undertaken.

3.10 Summary

The concept of environment includes the complex set of physical, social, cultural, and aesthetic factors affecting the individuals and the communities they belong to. However, the interactions and relationships between these complex sets have resulted in environmental pollution and the need to protect the environment. Environmental protection includes programmes and services that are aimed at reducing risks to the environment from contaminants from various sources. Various concepts and theories have been postulated to achieve an environmental end.

These concepts and theories illuminate an analysis of the various principles establishing standards in environmental legislation that have been accepted, and

[374] World Commission on Environment and Development (WCED) (1987) Report of the World Commission on Environment and Development: Our Common Future, Item 11 Annex 1, 287, https://sustainabledevelopment.un.org/content/documents/5987our-common-future.pdf (accessed on 11 May 2020).

adopted, as a benchmark amongst members of the international community and had over the years been infused in the enactment of environmental law.

For instance, under Free-market environmentalism, if industries internalised the costs of negative externalities, they would face an incentive to reduce them, perhaps even becoming enthusiastic about taking advantage of opportunities to improve profitability through lower costs. This would lead to the optimal balance between the marginal benefits of pursuing an activity and the marginal cost of its environmental consequences. This postulation may have given rise to the polluter-pays principle.

The Coase theorem has been used by jurists and legal scholars in the analysis and resolution of disputes involving both contract law and tort law. In contract law, Coase is often used as a method to evaluate the relative power of the parties during the negotiation and acceptance of a traditional or classical bargained-for contract. In modern tort law, the application of economic analysis has been used to assign liability for damages. In the case of the Kuznets Curve, although the theory was developed purely in economic scenarios, the Kuznets curve has applications in environmental protection.

In command and control as a theory, there is a perception of a problem and the solution for its control is developed and subsequently implemented. It encompasses a variety of methods that could elicit the required compliance with regulations on environmental pollution abatement. Emission trading is a prime example of a market externality and is a market-based approach to address pollution. The overall goal of an emission trading plan is to minimise the cost of meeting a set emissions target. This found expression in the reduction of carbon emissions.

The theory of sustainability, in general terms, is the ability to maintain a balance of a certain process or state in any system. It is now most frequently used in connection with biological and human systems. In an ecological context, sustainability can be defined as the ability of an ecosystem to maintain ecological processes, functions, biodiversity, and productivity in the future. This theory now guides the human quest in the use of natural resources.

Under the theory of market-based concepts in environmental legislation, it is believed that pollution control can be largely viewed as an economic problem and that some economic policies and concepts can play important roles in environmental decision-making and the enactment of environmental law. The use of these instruments is premised on a belief that the market can be used to provide incentives to guide adverse environmental human behaviours.

The concept of absolute liability can therefore be said to be a strong legal tool against rogue corporations that were negligent towards health risks for the public.

References

Adams TL (1999) Enforcement and liability. In: Sullivan TF (ed) Environmental law hand book, 15th edn. Government Institute, Rockville, Maryland

Anderson P (2014) Reforming law and economy for a sustainable earth: critical thought for turbulent times. Routledge, London
Australian House Committee (2019). http://www.aph.gov.au/house/committee/environ/charter/report/chapter2.pdf. Accessed on 30 June 2023
Australian Senate Standing Committee for the Scrutiny of Bills (2018) Report of the Work of the Committee during the 39th Parliament, at para 2.97. http://www.aph.gov.au/senate/committee/scrutiny/bills/2002/b06.pdf. Accessed on 28 May 2023
Ausubel K, Harpignies J (2004) Nature's operating instructions: the true biotechnologies. Sierra Club Books, San Francisco
Baldwin RCM, Lodge M (2011) Understanding regulation: theory, strategy and practice, 2nd edn. Oxford University, Oxford
Barbier EB (2014) Economics, natural-resource scarcity and development (Routledge revivals) conventional and alternative views. Routledge, London
Bell S, McGillivray D (2001) Environmental law, 5th edn. Blackstone, London
Berkeley Library (2019) Web: http://lib.berkeley.edu/ENVI/GreenAll.html U.C. Berkeley Library Web. Environmental Design Library Green Design / Sustainable Architecture: Resources. Accessed on 30 June 2023
Boswall J, Lee R (2002) Economics, ethics and the environment. Cavendish, London
Bronitt S, McSherry B (2001) Principles of criminal law. LBC Information Services, Sydney
Burdon PD (2014) Earth jurisprudence: private property and the environment. Routledge, London
Burton E, Sanjour W (1967) Applications of cost-effectiveness analysis to air pollution control, DHEW Contract No. CPA 22-69-17. Ernst and Ernst, Washington, D.C.
Burton E, Sanjour W (1969) An economic analysis of the control of sulphur oxides air pollution, DHEW Program Analysis Report No. 1967-69. Ernst and Ernst, Washington, D.C.
Burton E et al. (1969) Solving the air pollution control puzzle. Environ Sci Technol 7(5):412–415. Bibcode:1973EnST....7..412B. https://doi.org/10.1021/es60077a011. PMID 22283532
Carbon Finance (2006). http://carbonfinance.org/docs/StateoftheCarbonMarket2006.pdf. Accessed on 3 May 2023
Carbon Finance (2012). http://carbonfinance.org/docs/StateoftheCarbonMarket2012.pdf. Accessed on 3 February 2023
Carbon Finance (2019). http://carbonfinance.org/docs/StateoftheCarbonMarket2019.pdf. Accessed on 3 February 2023
Carbon Tax Centre (2018) Tax vs Cap-and-Trade. http://www.carbontax.org/issues/carbon-taxes-vs-cap-and-trade/. Accessed on 29 May 2023
Carbon Trade Watch (2019) http://www.carbontradewatch.orgltitle=Carbon Trade Watch. Accessed on 30 June 2023
Carey S (1991) Knowledge acquisition: enrichment or conceptual change? In: Carey S, Gelman R (eds) The epigenesis of mind: essays on biology and cognition. Lawrence Erlbaum Associates, Hillsdale, New Jersey, pp 257–291. https://bcs.mit.edu/research/cognitive-science. Accessed on 12 June 2023
Carlarne CP (2010) Climate change law and policy: EU and US approaches. Oxford University, Oxford
Center for American Progress (2019) Cap and Trade 101. http://www.americanprogress.org/issues/2008/01/capandtrade101.html January 16, 2008. Accessed on 30 June 2023
Clifford M (1998) Criminal law, and environmental crime. In: Clifford M (ed) Environmental crime: enforcement, policy, and social responsibility. McGraw Hills, New York
Coase RH (1960) The problem of social cost. J Law Econ 3(1):10. https://www.econlib.org/library/Enc/bios/Coase.html. Accessed on 25 June 2023
Commonwealth of Australia (2019) Defining sustainability. http://www.aph.gov.au/house/committee/environ/charter/report/chapter2.pdf 2007. Accessed on 30 June 2023
Daly HE, Farley J (2004) Ecological economics: principles and applications. Island, London
Dingell JD (2007) The power in the carbon tax. Washington Post, 2 August 2007, A21. http://www.washingtopost.com. Accessed on 30 May 2023

Dixit P (2020) MC Mehta v Union of India (1986) Case Analysis (Oleum gas leak case), 26 November 2020. https://lawcirca.com/mc-mehta-and-union-of-india-1986-case-analysis-oleum-gas-leak-case/. Accessed on 10 June 2023

Dudek DJ et al. (2007) Technology-based approaches versus market-based approaches, cited in Anton DK et al. (2007) International environmental law: cases materials and problems. Lexis Nexis, New York. ISBN 0-8205-4522-8, 1254-5

Earth Charter (2019). http://www.earthcharterinaction.org/2000/10/the_earth_charter.html. Accessed on 30 June 2023

Eboh M (2013) US proposes $16bn settlement with BP over Gulf spill. http://www.vanguardngr.com/2013/02/us-proposes-16bn-settlement-with-bp-over-gulf-spil/#sthash nZGVBs1L.dpuf. Accessed on 24 May 2023

Ehrlich PR, Holden JP (1974) Human population and the global environment. Am Sci 62(3):282

E-Law Resources (2020). http://www.e-lawresources.co.uk/cases/Ellison-v-Ministry-of-Defence.php. Accessed on 19 May 2023

Elinor O (2019). http://dlc.dlib.indiana.edu/archive/00000741/00/EOHO86AA.pdf. Accessed on 25 June 2023

Environmental Defense Fund (2019) How cap and trade works. http://www.edf.org/climate/how-cap-and-trade-works. Accessed on 30 June 2023

Freestone D, Streck C (2009) Legal aspects of carbon trading: Kyoto, Copenhagen and Beyond. Oxford University, Oxford

Frost ST (1938) The defence of act of stranger to the rule in Rylands v Fletcher: North-Western Utilities Ltd. v. London Guarantee and Accident Co. Ltd. & Others. http://classic.austlii.edu.au/au/journals/ResJud/1938/43.pdf. Accessed on 16 May 2023

Furtado R (2020) Concept of strict and absolute liability. https://blog.ipleaders.in/concept-strict-liability-absolute-liability/amp. Accessed on 13 May 2023

Giorgi F (2008) Climate change hot-spots. Geophys Res Lett 10:338

Global Health Rights (2020) M.C. Mehta v. Union of India and Ors (Oleum Gas Case 3). https://www.globalhealthrights.org/m-c-mehta-v-union-of-india-and-ors-oleum-gas-case-3. Accessed on 17 May 2023

Goudie A (2013) The human impact on the natural environment: past, present and future, 7th edn. Wiley-Blackwell, Oxford. ISBN 978-1-118-57657-1 (cloth) – ISBN 978-1-118-57658-8 (pbk.)

Government of British Columbia (2018) B.C.'s Revenue-neutral Carbon Tax. http://www.bcbudget.gov.bc.ca/2008/backgrounders/backgrounder_carbon_tax.htm. Accessed on 30 May 2023

Grimeaud D (2001) An overview of the policy and legal aspects of the international climate change regime. Environ Liabil 9(2):39

Habersber D (1970) Case Notes: Benning v Wong, Melbourne University Law Review 7:576

Hahnel R (2005) Economic justice and democracy: from competition to cooperation. Routledge, London

Halpin A (2007) Disproving the Coase Theorem. J Econ Philos 23(321):327

Hansmann H, Kraakman R (1991) Toward unlimited shareholder liability for Corporate Torts. Yale Law Rev 100:1879

Holling C, Meffe G (1996) Command and control and pathology of natural resource management. Conserv Biol 10(2):328

International Scientific Congress on Climate Change (2018) http://climatecongress.ku.dk/newsroom/congress_key_messages/ "Key Messages from the International Scientific Congress on Climate Change." University of Copenhagen, Denmark, 12th March 2009. Accessed on 15 June 2023

Jacoby DH, Ellerman AD (2004) The safety valve and climate policy. Energy Policy 32:481–449. http://www.sciencedirect.com. Accessed on 16 May 2023

Mandiberg SF, Faure MG (1995) A graduated punishment approach to environmental crimes: beyond vindication of administrative authority in the United States and Europe. Eur J Crime Crim Law Crim Justice 3(316):448

McManus P (2009) Environmental regulation. Australia Elsevier, Sydney

Meade J (2007) As cited by Andrew Halpin: "Disproving the Coase Theorem.". J Econ Philos 23(321):327

Mensah J (2019) Sustainable development: meaning, history, principles, pillars, and implications for human action: literature review. Cogent Soc Sci 5(1):75. https://doi.org/10.1080/23311886.2019.1653531. Accessed on 18 July 2023

Millennium Assessment (2019). http://www.millenniumassessment.org/documents/document.354.aspx.pdf. Accessed on 30 June 2023

Montgomery WD (1972) Markets in licenses and efficient pollution control programs. J Econ Theory 5:395–418

Newton AC, Cantarello E (eds) (2014) An introduction to the green economy: science, systems and sustainability. Routledge, London

O'Sullivan A, Sheffrin SM (2003) Economics: principles in action. Upper Saddle River, New Jersey. ISBN 0-13-063085-3

Onyeabor EU (1995) Rural development and environmental management: the case of Agip Nigerian Ltd Green River Project in ONELGA LGA of Rivers State. Dissertation, Department of Geography, University of Port- Harcourt, Nigeria

Onyeabor EU, Nnaji AC (2020) Making the punishment fit the crime in environmental pollution control and governance: a case for Nigeria. Int J Law 6(5):68–77. http://www.lawjournals.org/archives/2020/vol6/issue5 Academic Publications. ISSN: 2455-2194. https://www.academicpublications.net

Parliament of Australia (2019) Emissions trading schemes around the world, 2013. http://www.parlinfo.aph.gov.au. Accessed on 30 June 2023

Pope Benedict (2008) Pope Benedict Preaches Environmental Protection at World Youth Day. Environmental News Service, July 17, 2008. http://www.ens-newswire.com/ens/jul2008/2008-07-17-01.asp. Accessed on 30 May 2023

Porritt J (2006) Capitalism as if the world mattered. Earthscan, London

Ratner BD (2004) Sustainability as a dialogue of values: challenges to the sociology of development. Sociol Inq 74(1):50–52

Redmond WA (2009) Microsoft Encarta, 2009 (1993-2008 Microsoft Corporation). www.encarta.com. Accessed on 28 July 2023

Rothbard MN (1982) Law, property rights, and air pollution. Cato J 2(1). https://www.cato.org/sites/cato.org/files/serials/files/cato-journal/1982/5/cj2n1-2.pdf. Accessed on 10 May 2023

Russo MV (ed) (1999) Environmental management, readings and cases. Mifflin, Houghton

Sands P (2000) Principles of international environmental law, vol 1 frameworks, standards and implementation. Manchester University, Manchester

Sands P (2003) Principles of international environmental law. Manchester University, Manchester

The H C Coombs Policy Forum (2019) ANU College of Asia and the Pacific. http://coombs.anu.edu.au/~vern/caring/caring.html. Accessed on 30 January 2019

Tisdell C (2001) Globalisation and sustainability: environmental Kuznets Curve and WTO. Ecol Econ 30(2):190

United Nations Department of Economic and Social Affairs, Population Division (2008). http://www.un.org/esa/population/publications/wpp2008/wpp2008_highlights. Accessed on 6 May 2023

United Nations General Assembly (1987). http://www.un-documents.net/wced-ocf.htm, 1987. Accessed on 1 May 2023

United States Environmental Protection Agency (USEPA) (1999) An introduction to environmental accounting as a business management tool. In: Russo MV (ed) Environmental management readings and cases. Mifflin Coy, Houghton

United States Environmental Protection Agency (USEPA) (2019) The Economics of Clean Air, Annual Report of the Environmental Protection Agency to the Congress of the United States. U.-S. Government Printing Office, Washington, D.C. http://www.epa.org. Accessed on 31 May 2023

United States Environmental Protection Agency (USEPA) (2019) Cap and Trade 101. http://www.epa/captrade/captrade-101.html. Accessed on 30 June 2023

Westra L, Vilela M (eds) (2014) The Earth Charter, ecological integrity and social movements. Routledge, London

World Commission on Environment and Development (WCED) (1987) Report of the World Commission on Environment and Development: Our Common Future, Item 11 Annex 1, 287. https://sustainabledevelopment.un.org/content/documents/5987our-common-future.pdf. Accessed on 11 May 2023

World Commission on the Environment and Development (WCED) (1987) Our common future. Oxford University, Oxford

Chapter 4
International Law Principles Establishing Standards in Environmental Legislation

Abstract Over the years, principles of international law have established standards in environmental legislation that have been accepted and adopted, as a benchmark amongst members of the international community. What informs this position is that since the incident of environmental pollution spares no country the issue of its control should be sought from a global perspective. Discussions on these principles that have applied in establishing standards in environmental legislation enable us to have a more balanced focus on *raison d'etre* on the provisions of extant legal instruments. To this end, national, as well as regional and international legal instruments for environmental pollution abatement and control are at times guided by these established and universally accepted general principles and standards in order to achieve uniformity in environmental regulations, standards, guidelines and enforcement mechanisms. This chapter discusses some of these general principles and rules of international environmental law as reflected in treaties, binding acts of international organisations, state practices and soft law commitments. The principles in view and discussed in this chapter are: Principle of States' sovereignty over their natural resources and the responsibility not to cause transboundary environmental damage (The No Harm Rule), the Principle of Preventive Action, the Principle of Co-operation and Common but Differentiated Responsibilities, the Principle of Sustainable Development, the Precautionary Principle, and the Polluter-Pays Principle.

4.1 Basis for Environmental Legislation Standards: Setting Principles

References to principles and rules of general application have long been found in the preambular sections of treaties and other international acts, and in the jurisprudence of international courts and tribunals, and in recent times have been incorporated into the operative part of some treaties. For instance, the United Nations Framework

E. Onyeabor, *Environmental Law*, https://doi.org/10.1007/978-3-031-68956-7_4

Climate Change Convention (Climate Change Convention) 1992[1] lists "Principles" as intended to guide the parties "in their actions to achieve the objectives of the Convention and to implement its provisions." The Biodiversity Convention 1992[2] on its part introduces the text of Principle 21 of the Stockholm Declaration as the sole "Principle." The Umpire in the *Gentini* case[3] in 1903 provided some guidance about the legal effect of principles and their relationship to rule. "Principle expresses a general truth, which guides our action, serves as a theoretical basis for the various acts of our life, and the application of which to reality produces a given consequences."[4]

To this end, principles and rules

> point to particular decisions about legal obligations in particular circumstances, but they differ in the character of the direction they give. Rules are applicable in an all-or-nothing fashion... (A principle) states a reason that argues in one direction, but does not necessitate a particular decision ... All that is meant, when we say that a particular principle is a principle of our law, is that the principle is one which officials must take into account, it is relevant, as a consideration inclining in one way or another.[5]

It should be noted that some general principles reflect customary law, others may reflect emerging legal obligations and yet others might have a less developed legal status. In each case, however, the principle has broad support and is reflected in extensive state practice through repetitive use or reference in international legal content.[6]

The sources of these principles stem from resolutions, recommendations and declarations issued by international organisations such as the United Nations Environment Programme (UNEP), the World Health Organisation (WHO) or the Organisation for Economic Co-Operation and Development (OECD). The international organisations have made important contributions to the development of international environmental principles. The acts adopted at the United Nations Conference on Environment and Development (UNCED), particularly Agenda 21 and the Rio Declaration on Environment and Development, have helped to form these various principles and concepts into an increasingly comprehensive set of environmental principles for guiding the international community toward sustainable development.[7]

Environmental principles and concepts serve several purposes, most notably:

1) Legal and other implications are drawn from them by courts and tribunals in the interpretative process.

---

[1] United Nations Framework Convention on Climate Change (1992), Art. 3.

[2] United Nations Convention on Biological Diversity (1992), Art. 3.

[3] Gentini case (Italy v. Venezuela) MCC (1903).

[4] Dworkin (1985), p. 1201.

[5] Dworkin (1985), p. 1201.

[6] Sands (2003), p. 233.

[7] Organisation for Economic Co-Operation and Development (OECD) (1995), p. 4.

2) They provide a basis for negotiation and elaboration of future international environmental law.
3) In framing the debate for international environmental policy-making, these principles and concepts have also become increasingly important for discussions of trade and the environment.[8]

From the large body of international agreements and other acts, it is possible to discern general rules and principles that have broad, if not necessarily universal support and are frequently endorsed in practice and at times integrated into environmental legislation.

4.2 Principle of Sovereignty Over Natural Resources and the Responsibility Not to Cause Damage to the Environment of Other States or Areas Beyond National Jurisdiction

4.2.1 Introduction

This principle, also known as the "No Harm Rule," is succinctly captured in the Declaration of the United Nations Conference on the Human Environment in Stockholm 1972[9] (the Stockholm Declaration) and later by the United Nations Conference on Environment and Development (UNCED)[10] in the Rio Declaration on Environment and Development (Rio Declaration) 1992. The Stockholm Declaration 1972 in Principle 21 provides that:

> States have, in accordance with the character of the United Nations and the principles of international law, the sovereign right to exploit their own resources pursuant to **their own environmental policies**, and the responsibility to ensure that activities within their jurisdiction or control do not cause damage to the environment of other States or of areas beyond the limits of national jurisdiction.

However, at the UNCED, states negotiating the Rio Declaration 1992 were unable to improve significantly upon, develop, scale back or otherwise alter the language in adopting Principle 2 of the Rio Declaration 1992. Here, two words were added to recognise that states have the right to pursue their own environmental and developmental policies. The Rio Declaration 1992 under Principle 2 provides that:

> States have, in accordance with the Charter of the United Nations and the principles of international law, the sovereign right to exploit their own resources pursuant to **their own environmental and developmental policies**, and the responsibility to ensure that activities

[8] Ibid.

[9] Held in Stockholm, Sweden, between 5–16 June 1972.

[10] Held in Rio de Janeiro, Brazil, between 3–14 June 1992.

within their jurisdiction or control do not cause damage to the environment of other States or of areas beyond the limits of national jurisdiction.

Principle 21 of the Stockholm Declaration 1972 and Principle 2 of the Rio Declaration 1992 each comprise two elements that cannot be separated without fundamentally changing their sense and effect: the sovereign right of states to exploit their own natural resources; and the responsibility, or obligation, not to cause damage to the environment of other states or areas beyond the limits of national jurisdiction.

These two principles[11] establish the basic obligation underlying international environmental law and the source of its further elaboration in rules of greater specificity and are sufficiently well established that provide the basis for an international cause of action as they reflect international customary legal obligation whose violation could give rise to a free-standing legal remedy. For instance, in the *Trail Smelter Arbitration*,[12] a case between the United States of America (USA) v. Canada. In that case, the dispute arose from damage done to crops, pasture land, trees and agriculture in the USA from a smelting plant at the Consolidated Mining and Smelting Company of Canada at Trail, in British Columbia. It was damage caused by one state to the environment of another state that triggered the legal claim. The Tribunal held that:

> under the principles of International Law...no state has the right to use or permit the use of territory in such a manner as to cause injury by fumes in or to the territory of another, the properties or persons therein, when the case is of serious consequence and the injury is established by clear and convincing evidence.[13]

This principle has also been reaffirmed by the African Union.[14] In the Revised African Convention on the Conservation of Nature and Natural Resources 2003[15] it re-echoed the fact that:

> States have, in accordance with the Charter of the United Nations and the principles of international law, a sovereign right to exploit their own resources pursuant to their environmental and developmental policies, and the responsibility to ensure that activities within their jurisdiction or control do not cause damage to the environment of other States or of areas beyond the limits of national jurisdiction.

The two elements of the "No Harm Rule": the sovereign right of states to exploit their own natural resources; and the responsibility, or obligation, not to cause

---

[11] Stockholm Declaration (1972), Principle 21 and the Rio Declaration (1992), Principle 2.

[12] Trail Smelter Arbitration case (United States v. Canada) (1941) U.N. Rep. Int'l Arb. Awards 1905 (1949).

[13] Ibid.

[14] African Union (2003).

[15] African Nature Convention (2003), Preamble. This Convention was adopted by the 2nd Ordinary Session of the Assembly of the African Union in Maputo, Mozambique on 11 July 2003 and entered into force on 23 July 2016. The Convention replaces the earlier one adopted in 1968 in Algiers, Algeria.

damage to the environment of other states or areas beyond the limits of national jurisdiction were discussed below.

4.2.2 Sovereign Rights Over Natural Resources

The principle of state sovereignty allows states within limits established by international law to conduct or authorise such activities as they choose within their territories, including activities that may have adverse effects on their own environment. This fundamental principle underlies the first part of Principle 21 of the Stockholm Declaration 1972 and Principle 2 of the Rio Declaration 1992. The extension of the sovereignty principle into environmental affairs pre-dates the Stockholm Declaration and is rooted in the principle of permanent sovereignty over natural resources as formulated in various resolutions of the United Nations General Assembly (UNGA) regularly adopted after 1952. These resolutions were closely related to arrangements between states and foreign private companies for the exploitation of natural resources, particularly oil and minerals, in developing countries. They addressed the need to balance the rights of the sovereign state over its resources with the desire of foreign companies to ensure legal certainty in the stability of its investment.

A landmark resolution was adopted by the United Nations General Assembly (UNGA) in 1962 when it resolved that the "rights of peoples and nations to permanent sovereignty over their natural wealth and resources must be exercised in the interest of their national development of the well-being of the people of the State concerned."[16] The resolution reflects the right to permanent sovereignty over national resources as an international legal right, and has been accepted by some international tribunals as reflecting customary international law. This position is reflected in the case of *Texaco Overseas Petroleum Co. and California Asiatic Oil Co. v. Libya.*[17]

In that case, Libya promulgated a decree to nationalise all of Texaco's rights, interests and property in Libya. This action of the Libyan Government led Texaco to request arbitration, but Libya refused it. A sole arbitrator was however appointed by the International Court of Justice on Texaco's request, and Libya was found to have breached its obligations under the Deeds of Concessions and was also legally bound to perform in accordance with their terms. The issue was whenever reference is being made to general principles of law in the International arbitration context, can this be held to be a sufficient criterion for the internationalisation of a contract?[18] The question was answered in the affirmative. The Arbitral Tribunal states that:

---

[16] United Nations General Assembly (UNGA) (1962), Resolution 1803 (XVII).

[17] Texaco Overseas Petroleum Co. and California Asiatic Oil Co. v. Libya (1978) 53 ILR 389.

[18] Ibid.

> Whenever reference is been made to general principles of law in the international arbitration context, it is always held to be a sufficient criterion for the internationalization of a contract. The lack of adequate law in the state considered and the need to protect the private contracting party against unilateral and abrupt modifications of law in the contracting state is a justification to the recourse to general principles. Though international law involves subjects of a diversified nature, legal international capacity is not solely attributable to a state. A private contracting party, unlike a state, has only a limited capacity and is limited to invoke only those rights that he derives from his contract.[19]

By the 1970s, limits to the application of the principle of state sovereignty over natural resources were emerging as the international community recognised a need to co-operate to protect the environment. For instance, in 1971, UNGA declared that "each country has the right to formulate, in accordance with its own particular situation and in full enjoyment of its national sovereignty, its own national particular situation and in full enjoyment of its national sovereignty, its own national policies on the human environment."[20] The relationship between permanent sovereignty over natural resources and responsibilities for the environment was formally recognised by Principle 21 of the Stockholm Declaration 1972.

The importance placed by states on the principle of permanent sovereignty over natural resources is also reflected by its frequent invocation, in various forms, in international environmental agreements and during their negotiation. The Convention relative to the Preservation of Fauna and Flora in their Natural State (London Convention 1933) affirmed that all animal trophies were "the property of the Government of the territory concerned."[21]

Article 2(3) of the Convention on Wetlands of International Importance especially as Waterfowl Habitat (Ramsar Convention 1971) emphasises that the inclusion of national wetland sites in its List of Wetlands did "not prejudice the exclusive sovereignty rights of ... the party in whose territory the wetland is situated." The International Tropical Timber Agreement 1983 in its Article 1 recalled "the sovereignty of producing members over their natural resources."

Over time, more environmental treaties also refer to the sovereign rights of states over natural resources in their territory. For instance, the Basel Convention on the Control of Transboundary Movements of Hazardous Wastes and their Disposal (Basel Convention) 1989[22] recognised that "all States have the sovereign right to ban the entry or disposal of foreign hazardous wastes and other wastes in their territory."[23] The United Nations Framework Convention on Climate Change (Climate Change Convention 1992) also reaffirmed "the principle of sovereignty of States in international co-operation to address climate change."[24] The Convention on

---

[19] Texaco Overseas Petroleum Co. and California Asiatic Oil Co. v. Libya (1978) 53 ILR 389.

[20] UNGA (1971), Resolution 2849(XXVI).

[21] London Convention (1933), Art. 9(6).

[22] The Basel Convention (1989) was discussed in sect. 9.6.1 of Chap. 9 of this book under "International Law and Control of Hazardous Substances."

[23] Basel Convention (1989), Preamble.

[24] Climate Change Convention (1992), Preamble.

Biological Diversity 1992 more especially reaffirmed that states have "sovereign rights... over their natural resources," and that "the authority to determine access to genetic resources rests with the national governments and is subject to national legislation."[25]

The sovereign right to exploit natural resources includes the right to be free from external interference over their exploitation. This aspect is brought into question in disputes over the extra-territorial application of environmental laws of one state to activities taking place in areas beyond its national jurisdiction, either within the jurisdiction of another state or in activities beyond national jurisdiction. This issue was tested in the Bering Sea Arbitration of 1893[26] arose out of a fishery dispute between the United Kingdom of Great Britain and Ireland and the United States (US) in the 1880s.... This led to the US claiming exclusive jurisdiction over the sealing industry in the Bering Sea, which led to negotiations outside the courts. The Arbitral Tribunal rejected the claim by the US to be entitled to protect fur seals in areas beyond the three-mile limit of the territorial sea and the right to interfere in the internal affairs of other states to secure the enjoyment of their share in the "common property of mankind."

Again, in the case of *Mexico and Ors v. United States* (the Yellowfin Tuna-Dolphin case),[27] the US banned the importation of yellowfin tuna caught by Mexican vessels, in Mexico's exclusive economic zone and on the high seas, with purse-seine nets the compliance of which with US environmental protection standards could not be proved. In that case, key questions were: (a) Can one country tell another what its environmental regulations should be? (b) Do trade rules permit action to be taken against the method used to produce goods (rather than the quality of the goods themselves)?[28]

In eastern tropical areas of the Pacific Ocean, schools of yellowfin tuna often swim beneath schools of dolphins. Dolphins are trapped in the nets when tuna is harvested with purse seine nets. They often die unless they are released. The US Marine Mammal Protection Act 1972 was enacted on 21 October 1972. The Act established a national policy to prevent marine mammal species and population stocks from declining beyond the point where they ceased to be significant functioning elements of the ecosystems of which they are a part. It sets out dolphin protection standards for the domestic American fishing fleet and for countries whose fishing boats catch yellowfin tuna in that part of the Pacific Ocean.[29] If a country exporting tuna to the United States cannot prove to US authorities that it meets the

---

[25] Convention on Biological Diversity (1992), Art. 15(1).

[26] Bering Sea Arbitration: The Fur Seals Arbitration (UK and Ireland v. US) (1893) the Moore's International Arbitration, 755.

[27] Mexico and Ors v. United States (1991) World Trade Organisation (WTO).

[28] Ibid.

[29] United States National Oceanic and Atmospheric Administration (1972).

dolphin protection standards set out in US law, the US government must embargo all fish imports from that country.[30]

In this dispute, Mexico was the exporting country concerned and its tuna exports to the US were banned. The embargo also applies to "intermediary" countries[31] handling the tuna en route from Mexico to the United States. Often the tuna is processed and canned in one of these countries. Mexico complained under the General Agreement on Tariffs and Trade (GATT) dispute settlement procedure and asked for a panel in February 1991.[32] Several "intermediary" countries also expressed an interest.

The panel reported to General Agreement on Trade and Tariff (GATT) members in September 1991 which rejected the extra-jurisdictional application of US environmental standards and held that act of the US was contrary to GATT, holding that a country "can effectively control the production or consumption of an exhaustible natural resource only to the extent that the production or consumption is under its jurisdiction" and that to allow the "extra-jurisdictional" application of its environmental law would allow the US to "unilaterally determine the conservation policies" of Mexico. The Tribunal concluded:

i) that the US could not embargo imports of tuna products from Mexico simply because Mexican regulations on the way tuna was produced did not satisfy US regulations. (But the US could apply its regulations on the quality or content of the tuna imported.) This has become known as a "product" versus "process" issue.
ii) that GATT rules did not allow one country to take trade action for the purpose of attempting to enforce its own domestic laws in another country – even to protect animal health or exhaustible natural resources.[33]

Furthermore, in 1998 and 2001 in the *Shrimp/Turtle*[34] cases however, the WTO's Appellate Body has taken a broader approach and recognised the existence of a "sufficient nexus" between migratory and endangered populations of sea turtles located in Asian waters and the United States to allow the latter to claim an interest in their conservation. The traditional and absolute prohibition on extra-territorial (or extra-jurisdictional) application of national environmental laws recognised by the earlier decisions is consistent with the principle of absolute sovereignty over natural resources. Those decisions for not rest easily, however, with a more modern conception of an ecologically interdependent world in which limits are placed on

[30] Mexico and Ors v. United States (1991).

[31] In the dispute the "intermediary" countries facing the embargo were Costa Rica, Italy, Japan, and Spain, and earlier France, the Netherlands Antilles, and the United Kingdom. Others, including Canada, Colombia, the Republic of Korea, and members of the Association of Southeast Asian Nations.

[32] Mexico and Ors v. United States (1991).

[33] Ibid.

[34] Brack (2002), p. 491.

the exercise of sovereignty or sovereign rights, an approach with which the Appellate Body seemed sympathetic.

In the absence of generally accepted international standards of environmental protection and conservation, states with strict national environmental standards may seek to extend their application to activities carried out in areas beyond their territory, particularly where they believe that such activities cause significant environmental damage to share resources[35] or affect vital economic interests. For "shared natural resources"[36] it will often be difficult, if not impossible, to draw a clear line between natural resources over which a state does and does not have sovereignty or exercise sovereign rights. In such circumstances, it is unlikely that the principle of territorial sovereignty, or permanent sovereignty over natural resources, can provide much assistance in allocating rights and responsibilities of states over environmental policy.

The permissibility or the extra-territorial application of national laws remains an open question in international law. The right of states to exercise jurisdiction, either by legislation or adjudication, over activities in other states, or in areas beyond national jurisdiction that are harmful to the environment at the global, regional or local level, could be justified on several grounds.

First, corporations carrying on activities abroad might be subject to the environmental laws of their state of registration or incorporation, by application of the "nationality" principle of jurisdiction.[37] To this end, international law does not prevent a state from exercising jurisdiction within its own territory over its nationals, including corporations, who reside in a foreign state, although the power to enforce such laws depends upon the nationals being in the territorial jurisdiction or having assets therein against which judgment can be enforced. For instance, in the case of *Dow Chemical Co v. Alfaro*[38] a Texan court held that Costa Rican farm workers were entitled to bring a claim for injuries caused by a pesticide manufactured in the US and exported to Costa Rica.

However, the application of the "nationality" principle is likely to cause difficulty, where the foreigner abroad might be subject to the concurrent jurisdiction of the home state of registration or incorporation and the host state in which it carries out its activities, with the home state having more stringent rules of environmental protection. This will lead to jurisdictional disputes where some states use lower standards of environmental protection perhaps to gain economic advantage and attract foreign investment, and other states apply the nationality principle and require

---

[35] Such as migratory species, transboundary watercourses, or air quality and the climate system.

[36] Such as the high seas and atmosphere.

[37] The nationality principle is an international law tenet which recognised the right of countries to exercise sovereign jurisdiction over a national even if the national violates sovereign laws in another country. Thus, under this principle a sovereign can adopt criminal laws which govern the conduct of the sovereign's nationals while outside of the sovereign's borders.

[38] 768 SW 2d 674 at 681 (Texas 1990).

their companies to apply national environmental protection rules wherever they carry out their activities.[39]

In such circumstances, it has been suggested that the home state must not require compliance with its laws at the expense of its duty to respect the territorial sovereignty of the host state. When faced with such a conflict a court would be likely to balance the public policy of the home state, the interests of the host state, and the damage to international comity if it gave precedence to the laws of the home state, and only accord priority to those laws "where the balance of interest clearly lies in by reference to the environment which is being affected or damage was being caused to the environment of the home state or to areas beyond national jurisdiction, then the home state might have a stronger basis for asserting jurisdiction extra-territorially."[40]

This latter situation creates a second possible basis for allowing the extra-territorial application of national laws; where activities carried out in one state have, or are likely to have, "effects" in another state, recourse might be had to the "objective" application of the territorial principle, otherwise known as the "effects" doctrine. However, the application of the "effects" principle is said to have "doubtful consistency" with international law: the justification for assertions of jurisdiction on the basis of an alleged "effects" principle of jurisdiction has not been generally accepted, and the matter is still one of controversy.[41]

The extra-territorial application of national environmental laws has been particularly controversial in relation to trade issues. Principle 12 of the Rio Declaration 1992 declares those unilateral actions addressing environmental challenges "outside the jurisdiction of the importing country should be avoided" and that "environmental measures should, as far as possible, be based on an international consensus." The Rio Declaration and Agenda 21 do not, however, prohibit per se all unilateral environmental measures, an approach which now appears to have been endorsed by the WTO Appellate Body, subject to certain conditions being satisfied. The same approach has been taken in the World Summit on Sustainable Development (WSSD) Plan of Implementation 2002. The Plan commits states to "enhance corporate environmental and social responsibility and accountability" including actions at all levels to encourage industry:

> to improve social and environmental performance through voluntary initiatives, including environmental management systems, codes of conduct, certification and public reporting on environmental and social issues, taking into account such initiatives as the International Organisation for Standardization (ISO) standards and Global Reporting Initiative guidelines on sustainability reporting, bearing in mind Principle of the Rio Declaration.[42]

The challenge for the international community in coming years will be to determine the circumstances in which, in the absence of international consensus on agreed environmental standards, a state will be permitted, under the general rules

[39] Birne and Boyle (2002), p. 192.

[40] Ibid.

[41] Bell and McGillivray (2006), p. 201.

[42] United Nations Global Compact (2020).

of international law and specific WTO rules, to adopt unilateral environmental measures and apply them extra-territorially.

4.2.3 Responsibility Not to Cause Environmental Damage

This is the second arm of the "No Harm Rule" and the second element of Principle 21 of the Stockholm Declaration as well as Principle 2 of the Rio Declaration 1992 which reflects the view that states are subject to environmental limits in the exercise of their rights under the principle of permanent sovereignty over natural resources. This second element in the two Declarations: "the responsibility of State not to cause damage to the environment of other States or of areas beyond national jurisdiction" has been accepted as an obligation by all states as a rule of customary international law way back in time before 1972.

For instance, the responsibility of states not to cause environmental damage in areas outside their jurisdiction was relied upon, and elaborated on, by the arbitral tribunal in the *Trail Smelter Arbitration.*[43] Here, the Tribunal held that:

> under the principles of international law... no state has the right to use or permit the use of territory in such a manner as to cause injury by fumes in or to the territory of another of the properties or persons therein, when the case is of serious consequence and the injury is established by clear and convincing evidence.[44]

This formulation has been accepted as a rule of customary international law and was cited, with apparent approval, by Judge de Castro in his dissent in the *Nuclear Tests* case.[45] In that case, Australia had asked the ICJ to adjudge and declare that the carrying out of further atmospheric nuclear tests was inconsistent with applicable rules of international law and would be unlawful "in so far as it involves the modification of the physical conditions of and over Australian territory (and) pollution of the atmosphere and of the resources of the seas."

The general rule relied upon in the *Trail Smelter* case derives from an extension of the principle of good-neighbourliness. Although the UN Charter does not expressly address environmental issues, Article 74 of the Charter reflects the agreement of the UN members that "their policy in their metropolitan areas must be based on the general principle of good neighbourliness" and must take account of "the interests and well-being of the rest of the world, in social, economic and commercial matters." The principle of good-neighbourliness underlies the dicta of the ICJ in the *Corfu Channel* case.[46] The court stated in that case that the principle of sovereignty

---

[43] Trail Smelter Arbitration (United States v. Canada) (1941).

[44] Ibid.

[45] Nuclear Tests case (Australia v. France) (1974) ICJ Reports 253 at 389.

[46] Corfu Channel case (United Kingdom v. Albania) (1949) Merits, International Court of Justice (ICJ), 9 April 1949, ICJ Reports 4 at 22.

embodies "the obligation of every state not to allow its territory to be used for acts contrary to the rights of other state." Also in the *Lac Lanoux Arbitration,*[47] involving the proposed diversion of an international river by an upstream state, the arbitral tribunal affirmed that a state has an obligation not to exercise its rights to the extent of ignoring the rights of another:

> France [the upstream state] is entitled to exercise her rights; she cannot ignore the Spanish interests. Spain [the downstream state] is entitled to demand that her rights be respected and that her interests be taken into consideration.

The thread was further developed in 1961 when the UN General Assembly declared, specifically in relation to radioactive fallout, that:

> The fundamental principles of international law impose a responsibility on all states concerning actions which might have harmful biological consequences for the existing and future generations of peoples of other states, by increasing the levels of radioactive fallout.[48]

By 1972, shortly before the Stockholm Conference, the UN General Assembly was able to direct that the Conference must "respectfully the exercise of permanent sovereignty over natural resources, as well as the right of each country to exploit its own resources in accordance with its own priorities and needs and in such a manner as to avoid producing harmful effects on other countries."[49]

Ever since the wording of Principle 21 of the Stockholm Declaration in 1972, the responsibility of states not to cause environmental damage in areas outside their jurisdiction has found application in some international conventions. For instance, Principle 3 of the UNEP Draft Principles 1978 requires states to ensure that "activities within their jurisdiction or control do not cause damage to the natural systems located within other states or in areas beyond the limits of national jurisdiction."

The World Charter for Nature 1982 at Principle 22 declares the need to "safeguard and conserve nature in areas beyond national jurisdiction." Similar language to the second element of Principle 21 of the Stockholm Declaration 1972 also appears in the United Nations Convention on Law of the Sea (UNCLOS) 1982.[50] Article 193 of UNCLOS provides that "states have the sovereign right to exploit their natural resources pursuant to their environmental policies and in accordance with their duty to protect and preserve the marine environment." Under this provision, the emphasis shifted from a negative obligation to prevent harm to a positive commitment to preserve and protect the environment. To this end, however, Article 194 (2) provide that states:

[47] Lac Lanoux Arbitration (Spain v. France) (1957) 12 R.I.A.A. 281; 24 I.L.R. 101 Arbitral Tribunal, 285.

[48] United Nations General Assembly (UNGA) (1961), Resolution 1629 (XVI).

[49] UNGA (1972), Resolution 2849 (XXVI).

[50] United Nations Convention on Law of the Sea (UNCLOS) (1982).

> shall take all measures necessary to ensure that activities under their jurisdiction or control are so conducted as not to cause damage by pollution to other states and their environment, and that pollution arising from incidents or activities under their jurisdiction or control does not spread beyond the areas where they exercise sovereign rights in accordance with (the) Convention.

In subsequent years, especially after the UNCED and with the signing of Rio Declaration 1992, more compelling references to Principle 21 of the Stockholm Declaration 1972 and Principle 2 of the Rio Declaration 1992 were wholly incorporated in the preamble to several treaties. The Convention on Biological Diversity (Biodiversity Convention) 1992 in its preamble reaffirmed that "States have sovereign rights over their own biological resources." Again, these principles[51] were echoed in the Climate Change Convention 1992 as follows:

> that States have, in accordance with the Charter of the United Nations and the principles of international law, the sovereign right to exploit their own resources pursuant to their own environmental and developmental policies, and the responsibility to ensure that activities within their jurisdiction or control do not cause damage to the environment of other States or of areas beyond the limits of national jurisdiction.[52]

The provisions were also fully reproduced in the operational part of a treaty, for the first time. For instance, Article 3 of the Biodiversity Convention 1992 wholly incorporated the provisions, thus:

> States have, in accordance with the Charter of the United Nations and the principles of international law, the sovereign right to exploit their own resources pursuant to their own environmental policies, and the responsibility to ensure that activities within their jurisdiction or control do not cause damage to the environment of other States or of areas beyond the limits of national jurisdiction.

Against this background, the status of the obligation not to cause transboundary environmental harm could be said to have become a preposition of customary international law. This preposition can be found expression in the Order of the International Court of Justice (ICJ), oral arguments opened at the ICJ in the *Legality of the Threat or Use of Nuclear Weapons* Advisory Opinion proceedings.[53]

In that case, a request for an advisory opinion as to whether states are permitted to use nuclear weapons under international law was laid on the table of the International Court of Justice (ICJ) by the UN General Assembly (UNGA).[54] In that Resolution[55] UNGA asked the ICJ urgently to render its advisory opinion on the following

---

[51] Stockholm Declaration (1972), Principle 21 and the Rio Declaration (1992), Principle 2.

[52] Climate Change Convention (1992), Preamble.

[53] Legality of the Threat or Use of Nuclear Weapons, Advisory Opinion (1996) ICJ Reports, 226.

[54] UNGA (1994), Resolution A/RES/49/75K.

[55] Resolution was submitted to the ICJ on 19 December 1994, and was adopted by 78 states voting in favour, 43 against, 38 abstaining and 26 not voting.

question: "Is the threat or use of nuclear weapons in any circumstances permitted under international Law?"

Pleadings were submitted by a number of states. A review of the pleadings indicates that New Zealand's affirmation that Principle 21[56] and Principle 2[57] reflected a "well established proposition of customary international law" and this was not opposed by France. Citing Principle 21 of the Stockholm Declaration 1972 and Principle 2 of the Rio Declaration 1992 the ICJ expressed the common conviction of the states concerned that they have a duty "to ensure that activities within their jurisdiction or control do not cause damage to the environment of other States or of areas beyond the limits of national jurisdiction."[58]

These instruments and other provisions relating to the protection and safeguarding of the environment were said to apply at all times, in war as well as in peace, and it was contended that they would be violated by the use of nuclear weapons whose consequences would be widespread and would have transboundary effects.[59] The Judges of the ICJ in its Advisory Opinion on the question stated that: "the existence of the general obligation of States to ensure that activities within their jurisdiction and control respect the environment of other States or of areas beyond national control is now part of the corpus of international law relating to the environment."[60]

In the final analysis, the support given to the rule reflected in Principle 21 Stockholm Declaration 1972 and in Principle 2 of the Rio Declaration 1992 by states, by the ICJ and by other international actors over the past decades indicates the central role now played by the rule. The rule has been developed through the adoption of environmental agreements that establish specific and more detailed obligations giving effect to the basic objectives, as well as national environmental laws.

Although the principle reflects customary international law, its application in respect of claims may not be too helpful. This is because the scope and application in the context of activity that causes pollution and environmental degradation, to trigger liability and allow international claims to be brought, both principles have not addressed some of these questions:

1) What are the consequences of a violation and how are the measures of damages determined?
2) What constitutes environmental damage and when can the threshold for liability arise?
3) What environmental damage is prohibited, is it any damage, or just damage which is serious or significant and who should be liable for the damage?
4) To whom does the burden of proof lie and what is the type of liability?

---

56 Stockholm Declaration (1972).

57 Rio Declaration (1992).

58 Legality of the Threat or Use of Nuclear Weapons, Advisory Opinion (1996) 241, para 29.

59 Legality of the Threat or Use of Nuclear Weapons, Advisory Opinion (1996) 241, para 29.

60 Legality of the Threat or Use of Nuclear Weapons, Advisory Opinion (1996) 241, para 29.

5) What is expected from the person/s liable and what is the standard of care applicable to the obligation, is it strict, absolute or fault?
6) Where would the claim be instituted?
7) Are there time limitations for such a claim?[61]

These expected problems notwithstanding, Principle 21 of the Stockholm Declaration 1972 and Principle 2 of the Rio Declaration 1992 confirm that the rights of states over their natural resources in the exercise of permanent sovereignty are not unlimited, and are subject to significant constraints of an environmental character. Beyond that, the rule may provide a legal basis for bringing claims under customary international law asserting liability for environmental damage.

4.3 Principle of Preventive Action

Closely related to Principle 21 of the Stockholm Declaration 1972 obligation is the obligation requiring the prevention of damage to the environment, and otherwise to reduce, limit or control activities that might cause or risk such damage. This obligation, sometimes referred to as the "principle of preventive action" or the "preventive principle," is distinguishable from Principle 21 Stockholm Declaration 1972 and Principle 2 of the Rio Declaration 1992 in two ways.[62] First, the latter arises from the application of respect for the principle of sovereignty, whereas the preventive principle seeks to minimise environmental damage as an objective in itself. This difference of underlying rationale relates to the second distinction: under the preventive principle, a state may be under an obligation to prevent damage to the environment within its own jurisdiction, including using appropriate regulatory, administrative and other measures.[63]

The preventive principle requires action to be taken at an early stage and, if possible, before damage has actually occurred. For instance, in the *Gabcikovo-Nagymaros Project* case,[64] the ICJ noted that:

> it was mindful that, in the field of environmental protection, vigilance and prevention are required on account of the often irreversible character of damage to the environment and of the limitations inherent in the very mechanism of reparation of this type of damage.

The principle of preventive action is reflected in state practice concerning a broad range of environmental objectives. Broadly stated, it prohibits activity that causes or may cause damage to the environment in violation of the standards established under

[61] These issues were discussed under the "threshold of significance in claims for environmental damage" in sect. 10.5 of Chap. 10 of this book.

[62] Birne and Boyle (2002), p. 105.

[63] Ibid.

[64] Gabcikovo-Nagymaros Project (Hungary v. Slovakia) (1997) ICJ Reports 7 at 78, para 140.

the rules of international law. It has been described by Kramer[65] as being of "overriding importance in every effective environmental policy, since it allows action to be taken to protect the environment at an earlier stage. It is no longer primarily a question of repairing damage after it has occurred."

The preventive principle is supported by an extensive body of domestic environmental protection legislation which establishes authorisation procedures, as well as the adoption of international and national commitments on environmental standards,[66] access to environmental information,[67] and the need to carry out environmental impact assessments on the conduct of certain proposed activities.[68] The preventive principle may, therefore, take several forms, including the use of penalties and the application of liability rules.[69]

The preventive approach has been endorsed, directly or indirectly by some Multilateral Environmental Agreements. For instance, Principle 11 of the Rio Declaration 1992 requires states to enact "effective environmental legislation;" while Principle 14 calls on states "to prevent the relocation and transfer to other States of hazardous activities or substances" and Principle 15 specifically provides for precautionary approach by states in environmental matters. The Lome Convention 1989[70] in Article 35 provides for parties to agree to a "preventive approach aimed at avoiding harmful effects on the environment as a result of any programme or operation."

The preventive approach is endorsed by a large number of international environmental treaties, aiming to prevent inter alia: the spread of occupational disease, including radioactive contamination of workers;[71] pollution of the seas by oil,[72] hazardous waste and substances,[73] from land-based sources or from any source;[74] radioactive pollution of the atmosphere;[75] hostile environmental modification; adverse effects of activities that prevent the migration of species;[76] air pollution;[77]

---

[65] Kramer (1990), p. 61.

[66] As provided under the various National Environmental Regulations (discussed in sect. 16.2.5 of Chap. 16 as well as in Chap. 17 of this book).

[67] Discussed under sect. 5.1 of Chap. 5 of this book.

[68] As required by the provisions of the Environmental Impact Assessment Act Cap E12 LFN 2004 (discussed in sect. 16.2.3 of Chap. 16 of this book).

[69] See discussions on the various of liability for environmental damage in Chaps. 10, 11 and 15 of this book.

[70] Organisation of African, Caribbean and Pacific States (2020), Lome Convention 1989, ar. 35.

[71] Ionising Radiation Convention 1960, Art. 3(1).

[72] International Convention on Oil Pollution Prevention Convention 1969, Preamble.

[73] International Convention on Civil Liability for Oil Pollution MARPOL 73/78, Art. 1.

[74] UNCLOS (1982) Art. 194(1).

[75] Atmospheric Test Ban Treaty (1963), Art. 1(1).

[76] Convention on the Conservation of Migratory Species of Wild Animals (Bonn Convention 1979) Art. 111(4)(b)).

[77] Long Range Transboundary Air Pollution (LRTAP) (1979), Art. 2.

modification of the ozone layer;[78] degradation of the natural environment; significant adverse environmental impacts and transboundary impacts generally;[79] dangerous anthropogenic interference with the climate system;[80] and other biodiversity,[81] including as a result of the release of genetically modified organisms;[82] and damage to health and the environment from chemicals and persistent organic pollutants.[83]

The preventive principle is implicitly supported in relation to transboundary resources by the awards in the *Trial Smelter* case[84] and in the *Lac Lanoux Arbitration*.[85] It was supported in the pleadings of Australia in the *Nuclear tests* case[86] and in the claim by Nature that Australia had breached its legal obligation to administer the territory of Nauru in such a way as to not bring about changes in the territory that would cause irreparable damage to, or substantially prejudice, Nauru's legal interests in respect of that territory in the case *Concerning Certain Phosphate Lands*.[87] The principle of prevention may also be discerned in Hungary's Original Application to the ICJ in the case concerning the *Gabcikovo-Nagymaros Project*.[88]

Taken together, this extensive body of international commitments provides compelling evidence of: the wide support for the principle of preventive action; the different environmental media for which general preventive measures are required; the types of activities that should be regulated; and the basis upon which states should carry out their commitment to enact effective national environmental legislation under the general requirement of Principle 11 of the Rio Declaration 1992.

4.4 Principle of Co-operation and Common but Differentiated Responsibilities

There are two aspects to this principle: the principle of co-operation and that of common but differentiated responsibilities.

---

[78] Vienna Convention for the Protection of the Ozone Layer (1985), Art. 2(2)(b).

[79] Espoo Convention (1991), Preamble.

[80] Climate Change Convention (1992), Art. 2.

[81] Convention on Biological Diversity (1992), Preamble and Art. 1.

[82] Cartagena Protocol on Biosafety to the Convention on Biological Diversity (Biosafety Protocol) (2000), Art. 1.

[83] Persistent Organic Pollutant Convention (2001), Art. 1.

[84] Trail Smelter Arbitration (United States v. Canada) (1941)).

[85] Lac Lanoux Arbitration (Spain v. France) (1957).

[86] Legality of the Threat or Use of Nuclear Weapons, Advisory Opinion (1996).

[87] Nauru v. Australia (1992).

[88] Hungary v. Slovakia (1997).

4.4.1 *Principle of Co-operation*

The principle of cooperation relates to the principle of "good-neighbourliness" enunciated in Article 74 of the United Nations Charter 1945 in relation to social, economic and commercial matters and has been translated into the development and application of rules promoting international environmental co-operation.

The principle of "good-neighbourliness" is traditionally considered by reference to the application of the maxim *sic utere tuo et alienum non laedas*. This maxim was invoked, for example, as a fundamental rule by Hungary in its Original Application in the *Gabcikovo-Nagymaros Project* case[89] citing in support of the maxim the decision in the *Corfu Channel* case[90] and the *Trail Smelter Arbitration* case.[91] Also relied upon in the case were the provisions of the Stockholm Declaration 1972, the World Charter for Nature 1982 and the Rio Declaration 1992.

The principle of co-operation is reflected in many treaties and other international acts, and is supported also by state practice, particularly in relation to hazardous activities and emergencies. For instance, Principle 24 of the Stockholm Declaration 1972 reflects a general political commitment to international co-operation in matters concerning the protection of the environment, and Principle 27 of the Rio Declaration 1992 states rather more succinctly that "States and people shall co-operate in good faith and in a spirit of partnership in the fulfilment of the principles embodied in this Declaration and in the further development of international law in the field of sustainable development."

The importance attached to the principle of co-operation, and its practical significance, is reflected in many international instruments, such as the Convention on Biological Diversity 1992 which stressed the importance of, and the need to promote, international, regional and global cooperation among states and intergovernmental organisations and the non-governmental sector for the conservation of biological diversity and the sustainable use of its components.[92] This obligation to co-operate is affirmed in many international environmental agreements of bilateral and regional application, and global instruments – for instance, the provisions of Articles 123 and 197 of UNCLOS 1982, Article 2(2) of the Vienna Convention for the Protection of the Ozone Layer 1985 and Article 5 of the Convention on Biological Diversity 1992. The Convention on Biological Diversity 1992 specifically provides that each Contracting Party to the Convention shall,

> as far as possible and as appropriate, cooperate with other Contracting Parties, directly or where appropriate, through competent international organizations, in respect of areas beyond national jurisdiction and on other matters of mutual interest, for the conservation and sustainable use of biological diversity.[93]

---

[89] Hungary v. Slovakia (1997).

[90] United Kingdom v. Albania (1949), 4 at 22.

[91] Trail Smelter Arbitration (United States v. Canada) (1941).

[92] Convention on Biological Diversity (1992), Preamble.

[93] Convention on Biological Diversity (1992), Art. 5.

Furthermore, Article 4(1)(e) of the Climate Change Convention 1992 specifically provides for co-operation in preparation for adaptation to the impact of climate change.

The general obligation to co-operate has also been translated into more specific commitments through techniques designed to ensure information sharing and participation in decision-making. These include: rules on environmental impact assessment; rules ensuring that neighbouring states receive necessary information requiring information exchange, consultation and notification; the provision of emergency information; and transboundary enforcement of environmental standards. The extent to which these commitments are interrelated is reflected in Principle 7 of the UNEP Draft Principles 1978. It states that "Exchange of information, notification, consultation and other forms of co-operation regarding shared natural resources are carried out on the basis of the principle of good faith and in the spirit of good neighbourliness."

State practices supporting good-neighbourliness and international co-operation are also reflected in decisions and awards of international courts and tribunals.[94] The nature and extent of the obligation to co-operate is being invoked in international disputes. It was a central issue in the dispute between Hungary and Slovakia in the *Gabcikovo-Nagymaros Project* case,[95] at least as originally formulated by Hungary claiming that Czechoslovakia and then Slovakia had not co-operated in good faith in the implementation of principles affecting transboundary resources, including the obligation to negotiate in good faith and in a spirit of co-operation, to prevent disputes, to provide timely notification of plans to carry out or permit activities which may entail a transboundary interference or a significant risk thereof and to engage in good faith consultations to arrive at an equitable resolution of the situation.

The ICJ however did not address in any detail what the obligation to co-operate entailed, beyond recalling what it had said earlier in the *North Sea Continental Shelf* cases, as well as the principle of good faith which obliged the parties to apply their 1977 treaty "in a reasonable way and in such a manner that its purpose can be realized."[96]

The requirements of the obligation to co-operate are at the heart of the *MOX Plant* case.[97] In its application instituting arbitration proceedings under the UNCLOS 1982, Ireland claimed that the United Kingdom had failed to co-operate as required by Articles 123 and 197 of UNCLOS, for example by failing to reply to communications and request for information in a timely manner or at all, by withholding environmental information requested by Ireland, and by refusing to prepare a supplementary environmental statement. In its Provisional Measures Order, the International Tribunal for the Law of the Sea (ITLOS) affirmed that:

[94] Such as in the Lac Lanoux Arbitration (Spain v. France) (1957), 101.

[95] Hungary and Slovakia (1997).

[96] (1997) ICJ Reports 78–9, paras 141–142.

[97] Mox Plant case (Ireland v. United Kingdom) (2001) ITLOS Documents, 25 October 2001, para 33.

> the duty to co-operate is a fundamental principle in the prevention of pollution of the marine environment under Part XII of the Convention and general international law and that rights arise therefrom which the Tribunal may consider appropriate to preserve under Article 290 of the Convention.[98]

The Tribunal ordered the parties to co-operate and, for that purpose, to enter into consultations forthwith to:

(a) exchange further information with regard to possible consequences for the Irish Sea arising out of the commissioning of the MOX plan;
(b) monitor risks or the effects of the operation of the MOX plant for the Irish Sea; and
(c) devise, as appropriate, measures to prevent pollution of the marine environment which might result from the operation of the MOX plant.[99]

Above all, the duty to cooperate is well-established in international law, as exemplified in Articles 55 and 56 of Chapter IX of the Charter of the United Nations, to which all UN member states, subscribe, and applies on the global, regional and bilateral levels.

Key to the implementation of the principle of co-operation is hinged on the common but differentiated responsibilities aspect of the principle. Principle 7 of the Rio Declaration 1992 also speaks of common but differentiated responsibilities. This element is a way to take account of differing circumstances, particularly in each state's contribution to the creation of environmental problems and in its ability to prevent, reduce and control them. States whose societies have in the past imposed, or currently impose, a disproportionate pressure on the global environment and which command relatively high levels of technological and financial resources bear a proportionally higher degree of responsibility in the international pursuit of sustainable development.[100] This preposition in Principle 7 of the Rio Declaration is succinctly captured as follows:

> States shall cooperate in a spirit of global partnership to conserve, protect and restore the health and integrity of the Earth's ecosystem. In view of the different contributions to global environmental degradation, States have common but differentiated responsibilities. The developed countries acknowledge the responsibility that they bear in the international pursuit of sustainable development in view of the pressures their societies place on the global environment and of the technologies and financial resources they command.

Again, the Convention on Climate Change reiterated that the global nature of climate change calls for the widest possible cooperation by all countries and their participation in an effective and appropriate international response, in accordance with their common but differentiated responsibilities and respective capabilities and their social and economic conditions.[101]

---

[98] Ibid.

[99] Ibid.

[100] United Nations (2020).

[101] Convention on Climate Change (1992), Preamble.

Issues on co-operation in dealing with environmental problems are echoed in the Paris Agreement 2015 which provides that parties to the Agreement "Agree to uphold and promote regional and international cooperation in order to mobilize stronger and more ambitious climate action by all Parties and non-Party stakeholders, including civil society, the private sector, financial institutions, cities and other sub-national authorities, local communities and indigenous peoples."[102] The Agreement further requests "Parties to strengthen regional cooperation on adaptation where appropriate and, where necessary, establish regional centres and networks, in particular in developing countries. . . ."[103]

More specifically, the Paris Agreement 2015 provides that "Parties recognize the importance of support for and international cooperation on adaptation efforts and the importance of taking into account the needs of developing country Parties, especially those that are particularly vulnerable to the adverse effects of climate change."[104] In this regard, parties should strengthen their cooperation on enhancing action on adaptation, taking into account the Cancun Adaptation Framework, including with regard to:

a) Sharing information, good practices, experiences and lessons learned, including, as appropriate, as these relate to science, planning, policies and implementation in relation to adaptation actions.
b) Strengthening institutional arrangements, including those under the Convention that serve this Agreement, to support the synthesis of relevant information and knowledge, and the provision of technical support and guidance to parties.
c) Strengthening scientific knowledge on climate, including research, systematic observation of the climate system and early warning systems, in a manner that informs climate services and supports decision-making.
d) Assisting developing country parties in identifying effective adaptation practices, adaptation needs, priorities, support provided and received for adaptation actions and efforts, and challenges and gaps, in a manner consistent with encouraging good practices.
e) Improving the effectiveness and durability of adaptation actions.

In addition, Article 8.1 of the Paris Agreement 2015 notes that, "Parties recognize the importance of averting, minimizing, and addressing loss and damage associated with the adverse effects of climate change, including extreme weather events and slow onset events, and the role of sustainable development in reducing the risk of loss and damage." Article 8.3 notes that, "Accordingly, areas of co-operation and facilitation to enhance understanding, action and support may include:

---

[102] United Nations Framework Convention on Climate Change (UNFCCC) (2016), Preamble, para 15. The Paris Agreement 2015 was discussed under international legal instruments for the control of air pollution in sect. 6.4.2 of Chap. 6 of this book.

[103] United Nations Framework Convention on Climate Change (UNFCCC) (2016), item III, para 45.

[104] Paris Agreement (2015), Art. 7.6.

a) Early warning systems
b) Emergency preparedness
c) Slow onset events
d) Events that may involve irreversible and permanent loss and damage
e) Comprehensive risk assessment and management
f) Risk insurance facilities, climate risk pooling, and other insurance solutions
g) Non-economic losses
h) Resilience of communities, livelihoods, and ecosystems."[105]

4.4.2 *Principle of Common but Differentiated Responsibilities*

In practical terms, the principle of common but differentiated responsibilities is translated into the explicit recognition that different standards, delayed compliance timetables or less stringent commitments may be appropriate for different countries, to encourage universal participation and equity. This may result in differential legal norms, such as in the 1987 Montreal Protocol on Substances that deplete the Ozone Layer. In designing specific differentiated regimes, the special needs and interests of developing countries and countries with economies in transition, particularly in the least developed countries and those affected adversely by environmental, social and developmental considerations, should be recognised.[106]

According to the principle of common but differentiated responsibilities, developed countries bear a special responsibility in reducing and eliminating unsustainable production and consumption patterns and contributing to capacity-building in developing countries, inter alia by providing financial assistance and access to environmentally sound technology. In particular, developed countries should play a leading role and assume primary responsibility in matters of relevance to sustainable development.[107]

Several international agreements recognise a duty on the part of industrialised countries to contribute to the efforts of developing countries to pursue sustainable development and to assist developing countries in protecting the global environment. Such assistance may entail, apart from consultation and negotiation, financial aid, transfer of environmentally sound technology and cooperation through international organisations.

For example: Article 4 of the Climate Change Convention 1992 recognises the special circumstances and needs of developing countries and then structures the duties and obligations to be undertaken by states accordingly. The idea of common but differentiated responsibilities and respective capabilities is stated in Article 3 of the Climate Change Convention 1992 as the first principle to guide the parties in the

[105] Paris Agreement (2015), Art. 8.4.
[106] United Nations (2020).
[107] Ibid.

implementation of the Convention. Article 12 of the Convention allows for differences in reporting requirements. The provisions of the Convention on joint implementation under Article 4(2)(a) (b) and guidance provided on the issue by its Conference of the Parties (CoP) are also of relevance.

The Convention on Biological Diversity 1992 provides that the implementation of obligations undertaken by developing countries will depend on the commitments of developed countries to provide new and additional financial resources and to provide access to and transfer of technology on fair and most favourable terms.[108] The United Nations Convention to Combat Desertification (Convention on Desertification) 1994 contains specific obligations for affected country parties[109] and recognises additional responsibilities for developed country parties.[110]

From all indications, the goal of the Rio Declaration 1992 is, according to the fourth paragraph of its preamble, the establishment of a "...new and equitable global partnership..." The concept of global partnership can be seen as a more recent reformulation of the obligation to cooperate, and is becoming increasingly important. Principle 7 of the Rio Declaration refers to states, but the concept of global partnership may also be extended to non-state entities. International organisations, business entities (including in particular transnational business entities), NGOs and civil Society more generally should cooperate in and contribute to this global partnership. Polluters, regardless of their legal form, may also have responsibilities under the "Polluter-Pays Principle."[111]

The Paris Agreement 2015 reiterates the principle of common but differentiated responsibility in respect of adaptation to climate change and acknowledges that:

> adaptation action should follow a country-driven, gender-responsive, participatory and fully transparent approach, taking into consideration vulnerable groups, communities and ecosystems, and should be based on and guided by the best available science and, as appropriate, traditional knowledge, knowledge of indigenous peoples and local knowledge systems, with a view to integrating adaptation into relevant socioeconomic and environmental policies and actions, where appropriate.[112]

Notwithstanding the effort at providing for the application of the principle of common but differentiated responsibilities, the Paris Agreement 2015, however, "dismantles the firewall between developed and developing countries' obligations, at least partially."[113] This is anchored on the fact that the Paris Agreement for the first time unequivocally establishes that all parties "aim to reach global peaking of greenhouse gas emissions as soon as possible,"[114] asking each and all to undertake and communicate "ambitious efforts" to achieve the purpose of the Agreement.[115]

[108] Convention on Biological Diversity (1992), Art. 20 (4).

[109] Convention on Desertification (1994), Art. 5.

[110] Ibid., Art. 6.

[111] United Nations (2020).

[112] Paris Agreement (2015), Art. 7.5.

[113] Savaresi (2016), pp. 22–23.

[114] Paris Agreement (2015), Art. 4.1.

[115] Ibid., Art. 3.

Furthermore, while developed countries should still "continue taking the lead" in reducing their emissions, and are required to provide support to developing countries,[116] the agreement also "encourages" developing countries to move "towards economy-wide emission reduction of limitation targets, in light of different national circumstances."[117] The Paris Agreement therefore requests all parties to make efforts to reduce their emissions[118] and to submit information on the details. In this connection, the agreement introduces a nuanced approach to differentiation, providing less stringent requirements for least developing countries and small island developing states, while levelling the reporting obligations for the others.[119] This levelling is expected to engender a considerable secondary rules development process.[120]

4.5 Principle of Sustainable Development

There is a difference between sustainable development and sustainability. Sustainability[121] is often thought of as a long-term goal (i.e. a more sustainable world), while sustainable development refers to the many processes and pathways to achieve it (e.g. sustainable agriculture and forestry, sustainable production and consumption, good government, research and technology transfer, education and training, etc.).[122]

4.5.1 Introduction

The general principle that states should ensure that the development and use of their natural resources in a manner that is sustainable emerged in the run-up to UNCED. Sustainability is a paradigm for thinking about the future in which environmental, societal and economic considerations are balanced in the pursuit of an improved quality of life. For example, a prosperous society relies on a healthy environment to provide food and resources, safe drinking water and clean air for its citizens.[123]

Sustainable development ties together concern for the carrying capacity of natural systems with the social, political, and economic challenges faced by humanity. Sustainability Science is the study of the concepts of sustainable development and

---

[116] Ibid., Art. 4.4–4.5.

[117] Ibid., Art. 4.4.

[118] Ibid., Art. 3.

[119] Paris Agreement (2015), Art. 4.6.

[120] Savaresi (2016), p. 23.

[121] This was discussed in sect. 3.7 of Chap. 3 of this book.

[122] United Nations Scientific and Cultural Organisation (UNESCO) (2020).

[123] Ibid.

environmental science. There is an additional focus on the present generations' responsibility to regenerate, maintain and improve planetary resources for use by future generations.[124]

Following the publication of Rachel Carson's *Silent Spring* in 1962, the developing environmental movement drew attention to the relationship between economic growth and development and environmental degradation. Kenneth E. Boulding cited by Blewitt[125] identified the need for the economic system to fit itself into the ecological system with its limited pools of resources.

The term "sustainable development" in its present concept, is generally considered to have been coined by the 1987 Brundtland report,[126] which defined it as "development that meets the needs of the present without compromising the ability of future generations to meet their own needs." It contains within it two concepts:

(i) the concept of "needs," particularly the essential needs of the world's poor, to which overriding priority should be given; and
(ii) the idea of limitations imposed, by the state of technology and social organisation, on the environment's ability to meet present and future needs.[127]

An imperative of the Brundtland Report is a rational and controlled use of resources focused on renewable and long-term usage, protection and conservation of nature, raising ecological awareness, stricter national regulation and international co-operation, stopping population growth, using industry and technology in line with environmental requirements, developing technological innovations to reduce impact on environmental.[128] Thus, according to the Report, the underlying principles of the concept of sustainable development are assurance of human needs, while respecting certain environmental constraints. The Brundtland report marked the beginning of a new global socio-economic policy in which the concept of sustainable development has become a key element in environmental management and other areas of human activities.[129]

Since the Brundtland Report, the concept of sustainable development has developed beyond the initial intergenerational framework to focus more on the goal of "socially inclusive and environmentally sustainable economic growth."[130] For instance, at the United Nations Conference on Environment and Development (UNCED) the following documents were adopted: (i) Rio Declaration on Environment and Development, (ii) Agenda 21, (iii) Non-legally binding authoritative statement of principles for a global consensus on the management, conservation

---

[124] Finn (2009), p. 128.

[125] Blewitt (2014), p. 45.

[126] World Commission on Environment and Development (WCED) (1987).

[127] Ibid.

[128] Mensah (2019), p. 75.

[129] Ibid.

[130] Sachs (2015), p. 194.

and sustainable development of all types of forests, (iv) Climate Change Convention and (v) Convention on Biological Diversity.

Thus, at UNCED sustainable development formed the cornerstone underlying the conference and dominated Rio Declaration on Environment and Development (Rio Declaration) 1992. Perhaps most importantly, UNCED adopted Agenda 21, a five--hundred-page blueprint detailing the "new global partnership for sustainable development" in the twenty-first century. UNCED not only affirmed the goal of sustainable development but, through the Rio Declaration and Agenda 21, it added meaning and substance to this principle.[131]

The Rio Declaration 1992 emphasises that human beings are at the centre of concerns for sustainable development and they are entitled to a healthy and productive life in harmony with nature.[132] However, the right to development must be fulfilled to equitably meet the developmental and environmental needs of present and future generations.[133] Thus, to achieve sustainable development, environmental protection shall constitute an integral part of the development process and cannot be considered in isolation from it.[134]

Agenda 21 on the other hand, is a global programme with objectives of sustainable development and action plans and resources for their implementation set in 40 chapters. The document comprehensively provides guidelines for socio-economic development in line with environmental conservation.[135] The document highlights the need for international cooperation and consensus between development and environmental protection, whereby governments play an important role in the adoption and implementation of policies, plans and programmes, although the participation of all other stakeholders is also necessary. As a priority goal, the document emphasises the suppression of poverty, especially in poor countries where it is also necessary to preserve and protect natural resources. Agenda 21 further highlights the importance of educational programmes focused on raising awareness and promotion of sustainable development which are necessary for its implementation.[136]

In 2002, the World Summit on Sustainable Development (WSSD), known as Rio +10, was held in Johannesburg, South Africa, to review progress in implementing the outcomes from the Rio Earth Summit. WSSD developed a plan of implementation for the actions set out in Agenda 21, known as the Johannesburg Plan, and also launched a few multi-stakeholder partnerships for sustainable development.

In 2012, 20 years after the first Rio Earth Summit, the United Nations Conference on Sustainable Development (UNCSD) or Rio+20 was held. The conference focused on two themes in the context of sustainable development: a green economy and an

[131] OECD (1995), p. 5.

[132] Rio Declaration (1992), Principle 1.

[133] Ibid., Principle 3.

[134] Ibid., Principle 4.

[135] Agenda 21 (1992), Chapter 8.

[136] Ibid.

institutional framework.[137] Outcomes of Rio+20 included a process for developing new Sustainable Development Goals (SDGs), which took effect in 2015 and to encourage focused action on sustainable development in all sectors of the global development agenda.[138]

State practice, however, suggests that the idea of "sustainability" has been a feature in international legal relations since at least 1893, when the United States asserted a right to ensure the legitimate and proper use of seals and to protect them, for the benefit of mankind, from wanton destruction in the *Pacific Fur Seal Arbitration*.[139] The case involved an award between the United States (US) and the United Kingdom (UK) relating to the rights of the jurisdiction of the United States in the Bering Sea and the preservation of fur seals decided on 15 August 1893.[140] The arbitration was based on a Treaty between US and UK signed in Washington, on the 29th of February 1892.[141] Under Article 2 of the said treaty:

> The two Governments shall forbid their citizens and subjects respectively to kill, capture or pursue, in any manner whatever, during the season extending, each year, from the 1st of May to the 31th of July, both inclusive, the fur seals on the high sea, in the part of the Pacific Ocean, inclusive of the Behring sea, which is situated to the North of the 35th degree of North latitude, and eastward of the 180th degree of longitude from Greenwich till it strikes the water boundary described in Article 1 of the Treaty of 1867 between the United States and Russia, and following that line up to Behring straits.[142]

In the case, although the Tribunal rejected the US's claim on the right to protect seals outside her territory, the tribunal did adopt regulations for the conduct of sealing which incorporated some of the elements of what is now recognised as a "sustainable" approach to the use of natural resources.[143]

4.5.2 *Concept of Sustainable Development*

The term sustainable development, now appears with great regularity in international instruments of an environmental, economic and social character and has been invoked by various international courts and tribunals, and is now established as an international legal concept. It can therefore be said that the principle of sustainable development has entered the corpus of international customary law, requiring different streams of international law to be treated in an integrated manner.[144]

---

137 Allen et al. (2018), p. 438.

138 Ibid.

139 Macallister (2020), pp. 1192–1209.

140 Ibid.

141 Ibid.

142 Ibid.

143 Ibid.

144 Sands (2003), p. 338.

In the *Gabcikovo-Nagymaros Project*[145] case, the ICJ invoked the concept in relation to the future regime to be established by the parties. It said:

> Throughout the ages, mankind has, for economic and other reasons, constantly interfered with nature. In the past this was often done without consideration of the effects upon the environment. Owing to new scientific insights and to a growing awareness of the risks for mankind - for present and future generations-of pursuit of such interventions at an unconsidered and unabated pace, new norms and standards have been developed (and), set forth in a great number of instruments during the last two decades. Such new norms have to be taken into consideration, and such new standards given proper weight, not only when States contemplate new activities, but also when continuing with activities begun in the past. This need to reconcile economic development with protection of the environment is aptly expressed in the concept of sustainable development. For the purposes of the present case, this means that the Parties together should look afresh at the effects on the environment of the operation of the Gabcikovo power plant. In particular they must find a satisfactory solution for the volume of water to be released into the old bed of the Danube and into the side-arms on both sides of the river.[146]

By invoking the concept of sustainable development, the ICJ indicates that the term has a legal function and both a procedural/temporal aspect (obliging the parties to "look afresh" at the environmental consequences of the operation of the plant) and a substantive aspect (the obligation of result to ensure that a satisfactory volume of water is released from the by-pass canals into the main river and its original side arms).[147] Arising from this case therefore is that the correct formulation of the right to development is that that right does not exist in the absolute sense, but is relative always to its tolerance by the environment. To this end, this right to development as refined is clearly part of modern international law, which is compendiously referred to as sustainable development.[148]

The issue of sustainable development was found application in the *Shrimp/Turtle* case.[149] Here, the WTO Appellate Body noted that the Preamble to the WTO Agreement explicitly acknowledges "the objective of sustainable development," and characterises it as a concept which "has been generally accepted as integrating economic and social development and environmental protection." The concept appears to have informed the conclusion that sea turtles are an "exhaustible natural resource" within the meaning of Article XX (g) of the General Agreement on Trade and Tariff (GATT) and that they have a sufficient nexus with the United States to justify the later state's conservation measures, at least in principle.[150] The Appellate Body also invokes "sustainable development" in assessing whether those measures have been applied in a discriminatory fashion, as it concludes they have, and in this

[145] Hungary v. Slovakia [1997] ICJ Reports 7 at 78.

[146] Ibid., para 208.

[147] Sands (2003), p. 338.

[148] Ibid.

[149] United States – Import Prohibition of Certain Shrimp and Shrimp Products ['Shrimp-Turtle case'] WTO Appellate Body (1998) WT/DS58/AB/R and Art. 21.5 Report (2001) WT/DS58/AB/RW; Shrimp/Turtle case (1999) case 38 ILM 121, para 129.

[150] Shrimp/Turtle case (1999) case 38 ILM 121, para 129.

regard refers to "sustainable development" in the preamble to the WTO Agreement as adding:

> colour, texture and shading to our interpretation of the agreements annexed to the WTO Agreement, in this case the GATT 1994. We have already observed that Article XX(g) of the GATT 1994 is appropriately read with the perspective embodied in the above preamble.[151]

There are four dimensions to sustainable development – society, environment, culture and economy – which are intertwined, not separate.[152] Four recurring elements appear to comprise the legal elements of the concept of sustainable development as reflected in international agreements. They are:

(i) the need to preserve natural resources for the benefit of future generations (the principle of intergenerational equity);
(ii) the aim of exploiting natural resources in a manner which is "sustainable," or "prudent," or "rational," or "wise or 'appropriate" (the principle of sustainable use);
(iii) the "equitable" use of natural recourses, which implies that use by one state must take account of the needs of other states (the principle of equitable use, or intergenerational equity); and
(iv) the need to ensure that environmental considerations are integrated into economic and other development plans, programmes and projects, and that development needs are taken into account in applying environmental objectives (the principle of integration).[153]

These four elements are closely related and often used in combination (and frequently interchangeably), which suggests that they do not yet have a well-established, or agreed, legal definition or status. The Lomé Convention 1989 indicated how some of the elements of the concept of sustainable development can be brought together in a single legal text. Article 33 of the Convention provides that:

> in the framework of this Convention, the protection and the enhancement of the environment and natural resources, the halting of the deterioration of land and forests, the restoration ecological balances, the preservation of natural resources and their rational exploitation are basic objectives that the (states parties) concerned shall strive to achieve with Community support with a view to bringing an immediate improvement in the living conditions of their populations and to safeguarding those of future generations.

This position also found expression in the Cotonou Agreement 2002. Article 32 provides that:

> Co-operation on environmental protection and sustainable utilization and management of natural resources shall aim at mainstreaming environmental sustainability into all aspects of development co-operation and support programmes and projects implemented by the various actors.

---

[151] Ibid.

[152] UNESCO (2020).

[153] Ibid.

The different but related four elements of sustainable development were discussed hereunder.

4.5.3 Need to Preserve Natural Resources for Future Generation

The idea that we hold the earth in trust for future generations is expressly or implicitly referred to in many of the early environmental treaties. For example, the preamble to the International Whaling Convention 1946 recognises the "interest of the nations of the world in safeguarding for future generations the great nature resources represented by the whale stocks." The preamble to the African Conservation Convention 1968 on the other hand provides that natural resources should be conserved, utilised and developed "by establishing and maintaining their rational utilization for the present and future welfare of mankind." Article 4 of the World Heritage Convention 1972 provides that the parties agree to protect, conserve and transmit cultural and natural heritage to "future generations." Other, more recent treaties have sought to preserve particular natural resources and other environmental assets for the benefit of present and future generations. These include wild flora and fauna;[154] biological diversity;[155] and climate system.[156]

International declarations often refer to intergenerational equity as an important aspect of the concept of sustainable development. According to Principle 1 of the 1972 Stockholm Declaration, man bears "a solemn responsibility to protect and improve the environment for present and future generations," and UN General Assembly Resolution 35/8, adopted in 1980, affirmed that the responsibility to present and future generations is a historic one for the "preservation of nature." The Rio Declaration associates intergenerational equity with the right to development, providing in Principle 4 that the "right to development must be fulfilled so as to equitably met developmental and environmental needs of present and future generations."

In its Advisory Opinion on *The Legality of the Threat or Use of Nuclear Weapons*,[157] the ICJ recognised that "the environment is not an abstraction but represents the living space, the quality of life and the very health of human beings, including generations unborn." The purpose of the ICJ's reliance on the concept is not immediately apparent, and it is sometimes said that the undertakings in favour of future generations have limited practical legal consequences. They are considered by some to be closely associated with the civil and political aspects of the relationship between environmental protection and human rights protection. According to this

---

[154] Convention on International Trade on Endangered Species (CITES) (1973), Preamble.

[155] Convention on Biological Diversity (1992), Preamble.

[156] Climate Change Convention (1992), Preamble.

[157] The Legality of the Threat or Use of Nuclear Weapons (1996) ICJ Reports 241.

view, the rights of future generations to bring claims, in cases relying upon substantive rules of environmental treaties where doubt exists as to whether a particular treaty creates rights and obligations enforceable by individuals.[158]

4.5.4 Sustainable Use of Natural Resources

A second approach, reflected in treaties adopting a sustainable approach, is to focus on the adoption of standards governing the rate of use or exploitation of specific natural resources rather than on their preservation for future generations. "Sustainable use" means the use of components of biological diversity in a way and at a rate that does not lead to the long-term decline of biological diversity, thereby maintaining its potential to meet the needs and aspirations of present and future generations.[159]

In the case of marine living resources, a standard approach has emerged requiring exploitation to be conducted at levels that are "sustainable" or "optimal."[160] The failure of the International Whaling Convention 1946 to prevent the depletion of many whale species can be measured by reference to its stated objective of achieving: "the optimum level of whale stocks" and confining whaling operations "to those species best able to sustain exploitation in order to given an interval for recovery to certain species of whales now depleted in numbers."[161]

Sustainable use of natural resources also applies in the case of non-marine resources. For instance, the African Convention on the Conservation of Nature and Resources (African Nature Convention 2003) provides that in the utilisation of all natural resources, "States are responsible for protecting and conserving their environment and natural resources and for using them in a sustainable manner with the aim to satisfy human needs according to the carrying capacity of the environment."[162] The objectives of the Convention are to enhance environmental protection, foster the conservation and sustainable use of natural resources harmonise and coordinate policies in these fields and achieve ecologically rational, economically sound and socially acceptable development policies and programmes.[163] To achieve these objectives and implement its provisions, parties shall be guided by the right of all peoples to a satisfactory environment favourable to their development and that states, individually and collectively should ensure the enjoyment of the right to development and that developmental and environmental needs shall be met in a

[158] Sands (2003), p. 357.

[159] Convention on Biological Diversity (1992), Art. 2.

[160] Straddling Stocks Agreement (1995), Art. 2.

[161] Straddling Stocks Agreement (1995), Preamble.

[162] African Nature Convention (2003), Preamble.

[163] Ibid., Principle 2.

sustainable, fair and equitable manner.[164] In furtherance to the above, parties shall adopt and implement all measures necessary through preventive measures and the application of the precautionary principle, and with due regard to ethical and traditional values as well as scientific knowledge in the interest of present and future generations.[165]

Again, the International Tropical Timber Agreement 1983 encouraged "sustainable utilization and conservation of tropical forests and their genetic resources."[166] Further support for sustainable use or management as a legal term may be found in the preamble to the Zambezi Action Plan Agreement 1987,[167] Article 3(4) of the Climate Change Convention 1992, preamble to the Convention on Biological Diversity 1992 and Article 1 of its Biosafety Protocol 2000. The fact that so many species and natural resources are not sustainably managed illustrates the difficulty in translating the concept of sustainable development into a practical conservation tool.

Other acts of the international community have also relied upon the concept of "sustainable development," or the spirit that underlies it, without specifying precisely what it means. Although the Stockholm Declaration 1972 did not endorse "sustainable development," it did in Principles 3 and 5. Under these provisions, the Stockholm Declaration 1992 calls for the non-exhaustion of renewable natural resources and the maintenance and improvement of "the capacity of the earth to produce vital renewable resources."

The World Charter for Nature 1982[168] provides that the ecosystems and organisms, as well as the land, marine and atmospheric resources that are utilised by man, "shall be managed to achieve and maintain optimum sustainable productivity, but not in such a way as to endanger the integrity of those other ecosystems or species with which they coexist." The Charter also provides that living resources must not be utilised "in excess of their natural capacity for regeneration."[169]

The Rio Declaration 1992 in Principle 27 goes further than most instruments by expressly defining the content of the concept of sustainable development, and actively calls for the "further development of international law in the field of sustainable development," which suggests that international law in this field already existed. Apart from the environmental component of sustainable development, the Rio Declaration links environmental issues to matters which might previously be more properly considered as belonging to the realm of economics and development law. The issues increasingly considered for their environmental implications include: the eradication of poverty, the special responsibility of developed countries, the reduction and elimination of unsustainable patterns of production and

[164] Ibid., Principle 3.

[165] Ibid., Principle 4.

[166] International Tropical Timber Agreement (1983), Art. 1(h).

[167] Agreement on the action plan for the environmentally sound management of the Common Zambezi River system signed at Harare, Zimbabwe, 28 May 1987.

[168] World Charter for Nature (1982), Principle 4.

[169] Ibid., Principle 10(a).

consumption, the promotion of appropriate population policies, and a supportive and open international economic system.[170]

Treaties and other international acts have also supported the development of the concept of "sustainable use" through the use of closely related terms; international legal instruments have aimed for conservation measures and programmes which are "rational," or "wise," or "sound," or "appropriate," or a combination of the above. In some instruments, the preferred objective is the "conservation" of natural resources, which has been subsequently defined by reference to one or more of the terms identified above. Moreover, the term "conservation" itself includes elements similar to "sustainable development."[171] The Legal Experts Group of the World Commission on Environment and Development defined "conservation" in terms that recall the principle of sustainable development as:

> [the] management of human use of a natural resources or the environment in such a manner that it may yield the greatest sustainable benefit to present generations while maintaining its potential to meet the needs and aspirations of future generations. It embraces preservation, maintenance, sustainable utilization, restoration and enhancement of a natural resources or the environment.[172]

Sustainable use of resources therefore connotes "rational," "wise," "sound" and "appropriate" use. These are usually used without definition and often interchangeably, and accordingly the meaning of each term will depend upon its application in each instrument. Although attempts at definition have been made, no generally accepted definitions exist, and it is unlikely that distinguishable legal definitions could be agreed. The use of various terms in a single instrument is illustrated by the UNCLOS 1982: it requires conservation at "maximum sustainable yield" for the living resources found in the Exclusive Economic Zone (EEZ), and the "rational management" of the resources in the "Area" in accordance with "sound principles of conservation."[173]

To this end, "rational" utilisation and management of resources are the governing standard for migratory birds, fisheries, all natural resources, and hydro resources. They are the required standard called for by Principles 13 and 14 of the Stockholm Declaration 1972. While "proper" utilisation and management has been adopted as a governing standard for fisheries and forests, "wise use" has been generally been endorsed for flora and fauna, wetlands and natural resources. Other standards introduced by international agreements include: "judicious exploitation;" "sound environmental management;" "appropriate environmental management;" and "ecologically sound and rational" use of natural resources.[174]

The significance of these terms is that each recognises limits placed by international law on the rate of use or manner of exploitation of natural resources, including

---

[170] These are specifically provided in Principles 5, 7, 8 and 12 of the Rio Declaration (1992).

[171] Birne and Boyle (2002), p. 33.

[172] World Commission on Environment and Development Legal Principles (1986), para (i).

[173] UNCLOS (1982), arts 61(3), 62 (1), 119(1)(a) and 150(b).

[174] Sands (2003), p. 298.

those shared or are in areas beyond national jurisdiction. These standards cannot have an absolute meaning. Rather, their interpretation is, or should be, implemented by states acting co-operatively, or by decisions of international organisations, or, ultimately, by international judicial bodies if a dispute arises.

4.5.5 Equitable Use of Natural Resources (Concept of Intergenerational Equity)

Equity and equitable principles are terms that are frequently relied upon in international environmental texts. In the absence of detailed rules, equity can provide a conveniently flexible means of leaving the extent of rights and obligations to be decided at a subsequent date.

Intergenerational equity is often referred to in environmental contexts, as younger age cohorts will disproportionately experience the negative consequences of environmental damage. Two perspectives can be taken on what should be done to ameliorate environmental intergenerational equity: the "weak sustainability"[175] perspective and the "strong sustainability"[176] perspective. From the "weak" perspective, intergenerational equity would be achieved if gains in economic progress offset losses to the environment that future generations face. From the "strong" perspective, no amount of economic progress can justify leaving future generations with a degraded environment.

According to Beder,[177] the "weak" perspective is undermined by a lack of knowledge of the future, as we do not know which intrinsically valuable resources will not be able to be replaced by technology. We also do not know to what extent environmental damage is irreversible. Further, more harm cannot be avoided to many species of plants and animals.[178] Other scholars contest Beder's point of view. Professor Wilfred Beckerman for instance, insists that "strong sustainability" is "morally repugnant," particularly when it overrides other moral concerns about those alive today.[179] Beckerman insists that the optimal choice for society is to prioritise the welfare of current generations above future generations. He suggests placing a discount rate on outcomes for future generations when accounting for generational equity.[180]

However, Beckerman is extensively criticised by Barry.[181] Barry argues that only if inequalities of wealth and income are kept within a narrow range can equal

---

[175] Beder (2000), pp. 227–243.

[176] Beckerman (1994), pp. 191–209.

[177] Beder (2000), pp. 227–243.

[178] Ibid.

[179] Beckerman (1994), pp. 191–209.

[180] Ibid.

[181] Barry (1999), p. 117.

prospects for education, health and autonomy be realised. He proposes several policies to achieve a more equal society and argues that they are economically feasible. But are they politically possible? The apparent stability of the status quo is delusory, he responds: radical changes in our way of life are unavoidable. Whether these changes are for better or worse depends partly on the availability of a coherent set of principles and a programme flowing from them that can mobilise the growing discontent with business as usual.[182]

The concept of "intergenerational equity" recognises each generation's responsibility to be fair to the next generation by leaving a legacy of wealth no less than they themselves had inherited. Meeting this goal implies emphasising the sustainable use of natural resources for subsequent generations and avoiding any irreversible environmental damage.

Intergenerational equity is a value concept that focuses on the rights of future generations. It is a notion that is implicit in ecological sustainability. However, since skills to facilitate thinking about long-term consequences are not typically included in educational curricula, this value is presented as distinct from ecological sustainability to emphasise the need for thinking about how human actions that directly or indirectly degrade the environment in the present will affect future generations of humans and other life forms.

Intergenerational equity is a notion that views the human community as a partnership among all generations. Each generation has the right to inherit the same diversity in natural and cultural resources enjoyed by previous generations and to equitable access to the use and benefits of these resources. At the same time, the present generation is a custodian of the planet for future generations, obliged to conserve this legacy so that future generations may also enjoy these same rights. In this way, intergenerational equity extends the scope of social justice into the future.[183]

The concept of Intergenerational equity represents a widely recognised principle of international environmental law "providing for the preservation of natural resources and the environment for the benefit of future generations. It has roots in the Stockholm Declaration 1972 and forms a core tenet of sustainable development frameworks."[184]

The concept therefore has been important since the Stockholm Conference, where the first principle of the Stockholm Declaration provided that: "Man ... bears a solemn responsibility to protect and improve the environment for present and future generations."[185] Also, the Convention on Biological Diversity states that it is "determined to conserve and sustainably use biological diversity for the benefit of present and future generations."[186]

---

[182] Barry (1999), p. 117.

[183] Summer and Smith (2014), pp. 718–728.

[184] Venn (2018), p. 711.

[185] Stockholm Declaration (1972), Principle 1.

[186] Convention on Biological Diversity (1992), Preamble.

After being repeated in other environmental declarations and agreements including the United Nations Resolution on the Responsibility of States for the Protection of Nature for the Benefit of Present and Future Generations1980,[187] intergenerational equity was applied and reaffirmed during the negotiation and final wording of legal instruments that emerged at the United Nations Conference on Environment and Development (UNCED) in Rio de Janeiro, Brazil as a central component of the shift to sustainable development. Principle 3 of the Rio Declaration states that: "The right to development must be fulfilled so as to equitably meet developmental and environmental needs of present and future generations."

The principle of intergenerational equity has also found application in climate change discourse. Article 3 of the Convention on Climate Change (UNFCCC) frames the principle in terms of the need to "protect the climate system for the benefit of present and future generations of humankind," which is reinforced by the inclusion of sustainable development as a further core principle within the UNFCCC framework. According to Edith Brown Weiss,[188] "no longer can we ignore the fact that climate change is an intergenerational problem and that the well-being of future generations depends upon actions that we take today." She further reiterated that the basic concept is that "all generations are partners caring for and using the Earth." Thus, "every generation needs to pass the Earth and our natural and cultural resources on in at least as good condition as we received them."

The injunctions according to Weiss[189] leads to three principles of intergenerational equity: options, quality, and access. The first, comparable option, means conserving the diversity of the natural resource base so that future generations can use it to satisfy their own values. The second principle, comparable quality, means ensuring the quality of the environment on balance is comparable between generations. The third option, comparable access, means non-discriminatory access among generations to the Earth and its resources.[190] In the words of Venn,[191] all three of these climate obligations can be found within the international climate change regime, which has established a warming threshold commensurate with the prevention of dangerous interference with the climate system, and ascribes mitigation and adaptation assistance obligations to developed nations.

Although the continuing relevance of intergenerational equity as a guiding principle shaping climate action is reaffirmed by the preamble to the Paris Agreement,[192] its precise conceptualisation and implementation measures, beyond the implicit benefits of climate mitigation for future generations, generally, remain

---

[187] United Nations General Assembly (UNGA) (1989) Resolution A/RES/35/8.

[188] Weiss (2008), pp. 615–627 at 617.

[189] Ibid.

[190] Ibid.

[191] Venn (2018), p. 711.

[192] United Nations Framework Convention on Climate Change (UNFCCC) (2016), Paris Agreement, Preamble.

unclear.[193] It has been argued that intergenerational duties represent a core facet of global climate justice due to the temporal dimension of climate change, which means that the adverse impacts of current greenhouse gas emissions will be experienced by future generations of people. However, the way the principle should be defined and applied to climate change lacks agreement.[194]

At times, intergenerational equity is discussed within the realms of equity *simpliciter*. Equity involves understanding and giving people what they need to enjoy full, healthy lives. Equality, in contrast, aims to ensure that everyone gets the same things to enjoy full, healthy lives.[195]

Equity is an ethical term that represents fairness and has also been relied upon in relation to the participation of states in environmental organisations, financial and other contributions to activities, and the equitable distribution of the benefits of development.[196] In many respects, UNCED was about equity: how to allocate future responsibilities for environmental protection between states that are at different levels of economic development, which have contributed in different degrees to particular problems, and which have different environmental and developmental needs and priorities.[197] This is reflected in each UNCED instrument, which reflects efforts to apply equity to particular issues. Principle 3 of the Rio Declaration invokes the "right of development" as a means of "equitably" meeting the developmental and environmental needs of future generations.

Again, under the Climate Change Convention Articles 3(1) and 4(2)(a) provide that all the parties to the Convention undertake to be guided on "the basis of equity" in their actions to achieve the objective of the Convention, and Annex 1 Parties[198] agree to take into account the need for "equitable and appropriate contributions" by each of them to the global effort regarding the achievement of the objective of the Convention. The objectives of the Convention on Biological Diversity Convention 1992 include the "fair and equitable" sharing of the benefits arising out of the use of genetic resources.[199]

Furthermore, the Preamble to the Montreal Protocol 1987 reflects the aim of controlling "equitably total global emissions of substances that deplete the ozone layer," an aim usually translated into specific obligations through the process of intergovernmental negotiations.[200] The Climate Change Convention 1992 requires the equitable allocation of emission rights, and the Biodiversity Convention requires the determination of what constitutes an equitable sharing of the benefits arising out

193 Venn (2018), p. 711.

194 Ibid.

195 Summer and Smith (2014), pp. 718–728.

196 Sands (2003), p. 298.

197 Ibid.

198 Developed Economies of the World.

199 Convention on Biological Diversity (1992), arts 1 and 15(7).

200 These are reflected in the 1990 and 1992 Adjustments and Amendments to the Montreal Protocol 1987.

of the use of genetic resources. In each of these cases, the factors to be taken into account in establishing specific rights and obligations must be determined in the circumstances of each instrument, including its provisions, the context of its negotiation and adoption, and subsequent practice by the organs it establishes and by parties.

It is, however, in the allocation of shared natural resources that equity is likely to play an important role in coming years, as underscored by the ICJ's ruling in the *Gabcikovo-Nagymaros Project* case[201] that the then Czechoslovakia had violated international law by unilaterally assuming control of a shared resource and depriving Hungary of its right to an equitable and reasonable share of the natural resources of the Danube.

Despite the above position of the principle of intergenerational equity, Venn[202] opined that intergenerational equity, despite being widely referred to in the discourse and instruments of international institutions, is often provided for in the form of nonbinding "soft law" or remains undefined and open to interpretation, as in the UNFCCC. To this end, Bell, McGillivray et al.[203] observed that the status of the principle before the courts is contested and that the inherent difficulty in defining intergenerational equity means that it is very seldom invoked in judicial decisions.

4.5.6 *Integration of Environment and Development*

A fourth element of sustainable development is the commitment to integrate environmental considerations into economic and other development, and to take into account the needs of economic and other social development in crafting, applying and interpreting environmental obligations. This element is the main thrust of sustainable development and in many ways, it is the most important and the most legalistic element of the concept. Its formal application requires the collection and dissemination of environmental information, and the conduct of environmental impact assessment.

Environmental integration refers to the need for humans to increase their environmental awareness and to act upon it to minimise their environmental impact. The "need stems from the ecologically unspecialized nature of human beings and the fact that, unlike other species humans do not 'naturally' adapt to their environment but intervene in and change their environment to suit their own needs and wants."[204] To this end, environmental integration means that humans need to add an environmental

[201] Hungary v. Slovakia [1997].
[202] Venn (2018), p. 711.
[203] Bell and Mcgillivray (2001), pp. 588–589.
[204] Bührs (2009), p. 8.

"part" or dimension to their knowledge and awareness, actions and behaviour, and to the social institutions by which they are guided.[205]

Environmental integration depends on and requires the strengthening of environmental advocacy in the processes and institutions of collective decision-making with the ultimate aim that all policies and institutions are "greened" so that they no longer cause avoidable and unnecessary harm and can thus be considered environmentally rational.[206] This position will therefore require environmental policy integration.[207]

Environmental policy integration (EPI) is the process of placing environmental considerations at the heart of decision-making in other sectoral policies, such as energy and agriculture, rather than leaving them to be pursued separately through purely environmental policy instruments.[208] EPI also refers to the integration of environmental concerns into, and across, the array of policies pursued by governments. The reason being that many, if not most government policies have significant environmental implications, it is desirable or necessary that an environmental dimension is built into a broad range of policy areas.[209]

Integrating environment and development at the policy, planning and management levels includes the following areas to be addressed: (a) policy decisions for the highest good of all; (b) decision-making process for the highest good of all; and (c) creating cooperative and ethical partnerships.[210]

How do we improve decision-making processes to achieve environmental policy integration in development? Since the primary need is to integrate environmental and developmental decision-making processes, Governments should conduct a national review and, where appropriate, improve the processes of decision-making to achieve the progressive integration of economic, social and environmental issues in the pursuit of development that is economically efficient, socially equitable and responsible and environmentally sound.[211] Thus, national plans, policies and programmes for the following activities:

(i) Ensuring the integration of economic, social and environmental considerations in decision-making at all levels and in all ministries
(ii) Adopting a domestically formulated policy framework that reflects a long-term perspective and cross-sectoral approach as the basis for decisions, taking account of the linkages between and within the various political, economic, social and environmental issues involved in the development process

---

[205] Ibid.

[206] Ibid.

[207] Environmental policy integration is often treated as synonymous to environmental integration, and interpreted to include the integration of environmental concerns into institutions.

[208] Institute for European Environmental Policy in Bührs (2009), p. 8.

[209] This assertion can be buttressed by the provisions of Environmental Impact Assessment, Cap E12 Laws of the Federation of Nigeria (LFN) 2004, ss. 2 and 12.

[210] Peoples Agenda 21 (2020).

[211] An Architect's Guide to Designing Sustainability (2020).

(iii) Establishing domestically determined ways and means to ensure the coherence of sectoral, economic, social and environmental policies, plans and policy instruments, including fiscal measures and the budget; these mechanisms should apply at various levels and bring together those interested in the development process
(iv) Monitoring and evaluating the development process systematically, conducting regular reviews of the state of human resources development, economic and social conditions and trends, the state of the environment and natural resources; this could be complemented by annual environment and development reviews, with a view to assessing sustainable development achievements by the various sectors and departments of government
(v) Ensuring transparency of, and accountability for, the environmental implications of economic and sectoral policies
(vi) Ensuring access by the public to relevant information, facilitating the reception of public views and allowing for effective participation[212]

Achieving all these will involve: (a) researching environment and development interactions; (b) enhancing education and training; (c) promoting public awareness; (d) strengthening national institutional capacity and (e) providing an effective legal and regulatory framework.[213]

To this end, the major central economic and sectoral agencies of governments should now be made directly responsible and fully accountable for ensuring that their policies, programmes, and budgets support development that is ecologically as well as economically sustainable. What this means is that not only environmental issues and effects must be assessed and taken into account by sector authorities, but the objective and content of important policies, in reality, must be modified in substance to ensure long-term environmental protection and sustainable development.

Over the years, the integration of environmental concerns in developmental activities has been gaining some attention from the international community. In 1971, the General Assembly expressed its conviction that "development plans should be compatible with a sound ecology and that adequate environmental conditions can be ensured by the promotion of development, both at the national and international levels."[214] The Assembly further expressed its conviction that "rational planning procedures at both the national and the regional levels constitute an essential tool for an adequate equilibrium between the needs of development and the preservation and enhancement of the environment."[215] The Assembly then urged "the international community and the organizations of the United Nations system to

[212] Ibid.

[213] Ibid.

[214] United Nations General Assembly (1971), Resolution 2849(XXVI) (1971).

[215] Ibid.

strengthen international co-operation in the fields of environment, rational utilization of natural resources and preservation of adequate ecological balance."[216]

Again, the integration of environmental concerns echoed during the United Nations Conference on the Human Environment (Stockholm Conference). Principle 13 of the Stockholm Declaration calls on states to adopt "an integrated and co-ordinated approach to their development planning so as to ensure that their development is compatible with the need to protect and improve the human environment." The World Charter for Nature 1982, specifically in paras 7 and 8 provided that the conservation of nature was to be taken into account in the planning and implementation of economic and social development activities and that due account was to be taken of the long-term capacity of natural systems in formulating plans for economic development.

In 1987, the World Commission on Environment and Development (WCED)[217] in its report defines sustainable development and lists seven "strategic imperatives" to achieve it, including: "merging environment and economics in decision making."

The major push for integration of environment and development got a boost during the UNCED in 1992. For instance, the 27 principles of the Rio Declaration 1992 "define the rights and responsibilities of nations as they pursue human development and well-being."[218] Its many references to "sustainable development" suggest a form of development that integrates economic growth and environmental protection. Principle 4 of the Rio Declaration further provides that: "in order to achieve sustainable development, environmental protection shall constitute an integral part of the development process and cannot be considered in isolation from it."

Agenda 21 is a blueprint on how to make development socially, economically and environmentally sustainable. Under the document,

> The primary need is to integrate environmental and developmental decision-making processes. To do this, Governments should conduct a national review and, where appropriate, improve the processes of decision-making so as to achieve the progressive integration of economic, social and environmental issues in the pursuit of development that is economically efficient, socially equitable and responsible and environmentally sound.[219]

This is to ensure "the integration of economic, social and environmental considerations in decision-making at all levels and in all ministries."[220]

The Statement of Principles on Forests reiterates the integration of the environment in developments. The Principles on Forests is a report of the United Nations Conference on Environment and Development for a global consensus on the management, conservation and sustainable development of all types of forests. It is a nonbinding statement aimed at preserving the world's rapidly vanishing tropical rainforests and recommending that nations monitor and assess the impact of

---

[216] Ibid.

[217] WCED (1987).

[218] Rio Declaration (1992), Principle 3.

[219] Agenda 21 (1992), Chapter 1, para 8.4.

[220] Ibid., Chapter 1, para 8.4 (a).

development on their forest resources and take steps to limit the damage done to them. And avows the responsibility of countries to manage, conserve, and develop world forests in a sustainable manner.[221]

The United Nations Framework Convention on Climate Change (UNFCCC) 1992 on the other hand seeks "to stabilize greenhouse gases in the atmosphere at levels that would prevent dangerous anthropogenic interference with the climate system."[222] The Convention on Biological Diversity (CBC) implores nations to "adopt ways and means to conserve the variety of living species"[223] and that "each Contracting Party shall, in accordance with its particular conditions and capabilities: integrate, as far as possible and as appropriate, the conservation and sustainable use of biological diversity into relevant sectoral or cross-sectoral plans, programmes and policies."[224] In addition, "each Contracting Party shall, as far as possible and as appropriate: (a) Integrate consideration of the conservation and sustainable use of biological resources into national decision-making; (b) Adopt measures relating to the use of biological resources to avoid or minimize adverse impacts on biological diversity."[225]

At the national level, integrating environmental considerations in development has been captured by the Environmental Impact Assessment Act (EIA Act) 1992.[226] Under the Act, the objectives of any environmental impact assessment shall be: "to establish, before a decision is taken by any person, authority, corporate body or unincorporated body, including the Government of the Federation, State or local government intending to undertake or authorise the undertaking of any activity, those matters that may likely or to a significant extent affect the environment or have an environmental effect on those activities. . . ."[227]

Furthermore, Section 2 of the EIA Act 1992 restricts the commencement of "both public and private project without prior consideration of the environmental impact of such project." Thus, "all agencies, institutions (whether public or private) except if exempted pursuant to this Act, shall, before embarking on the proposed project, apply in writing to the Agency, so that subject activities can be quickly and surely identified and environmental assessment applied as the activities are being planned."[228]

From the foregoing sustainable development relates to the principle of meeting human development goals while at the same time sustaining the ability of natural systems to provide the natural resources and ecosystem services upon which the

[221] Statement of Principles on Forests (1992).

[222] Convention on Climate Change (1992), Art. 2.

[223] Convention on Biological Diversity (1992), Art. 10.

[224] Ibid., Art. 6(b).

[225] Convention on Biological Diversity (1992), Art. 10 (a) and (b).

[226] Environmental Impact Assessment Act (EIA) 1992, Cap E12 Laws of the Federal Republic of Nigeria (LFN) 2004.

[227] Ibid., s. 1(a).

[228] Ibid., s. 2(4).

economy and society depend. While the concept of sustainable development has been relevant since time immemorial, it can be argued that the relevance deepens with the dawn of every day because the population keeps increasing but the natural resources available to humankind do not. Conscious of this phenomenon, global concerns have always been expressed for judicious use of the available resources.

4.6 Precautionary Principle

4.6.1 Introduction

There is no clear and uniform understanding of the meaning of the precautionary principle among states and other members of the international community. The precautionary principle aims to guide the development and application of international environmental law where there is scientific uncertainty and some consider that it provides the basis for early international legal action to address highly threatening environmental issues such as ozone depletion and climate change.[229] For instance, the Alliance of Small Island States (AOSIS), a group of low-lying states, in support of the principle in relation to climate change negotiation, stated as follows:

> For us the precautionary principle is more than a semantic or theoretical exercise. It is an ecological and moral imperative. We trust the world understands our concerns for now. We do not have the luxury of waiting for conclusive proof, as some have suggested in the past. The proof, we fear, will kill us.[230]

According to Kiss and Shelton,[231] the precautionary principle can be considered as "the most developed form of prevention that remains the general basis for environmental law, because precaution is consideration and examination of the most likely or hypothetical threats, when there is no stringent proof that damage will occur."

The aim of the precautionary principle, as a general principle of international environmental law, is to minimise, and, if possible, eliminate, unnecessary human interference with a legitimate environmental interest.[232]

It means that where a law is set to prevent environmental harm,[233] a precautionary approach must be taken into consideration. It also means that a decision-making body must be aware of all the potential effects of what they are sanctioning and have all available information for the basis of its decision.[234] To have "all available" information and show due care and attention to the environmental consequences is

---

[229] Onyeabor (2011), p. 60.

[230] Ambassador Robert van Lierop (1991), p. 3.

[231] Kiss and Shelton (2007), p. 138.

[232] McIntyre and Mosedale (1997), p. 240.

[233] As is the intent of the environmental impact assessment practices.

[234] McIntyre and Mosedale (1997), p. 240.

to have: "appropriate procedures and mechanisms that incorporate a precautionary approach. It is contended that the precautionary principle has indeed crystallised into a norm of customary international law."[235]

4.6.2 *Core of the Precautionary Principle*

The core of the principle, which is still evolving, is reflected in Principle 15 of the Rio Declaration 1992, which provides that: "where there are threats of serious or irreversible damage, lack of full scientific certainty shall not be used as a reason for postponing cost-effective measures to prevent environmental degradation." Again, the Convention on Biological Diversity[236] noted that "where there is a threat of significant reduction or loss of biological diversity, lack of full scientific certainty should not be used as a reason for postponing measures to avoid or minimize such a threat."

At the most general level, the principle means that states agree to act carefully and with foresight when making decisions that concern activities that may have an adverse impact on the environment.[237] It therefore follows that activities and substances that may be harmful to the environment are to be regulated, and possibly prohibited, even if no conclusive or overwhelming evidence is available regarding the harm or likely harm they may cause to the environment. As the Bergen Ministerial Declaration put it, "lack of full scientific certainty should not be used as a reason for postponing measures to prevent environmental degradation."

Under the Rio Declaration 1992,[238] the requirement is stated to be mandatory: lack of full scientific certainty "shall not be used" to prevent action. What remains open is the level at which scientific evidence is sufficient to override arguments for postponing measures or at which measures might even be required as a matter of international law. What status does the principle have in international environmental law in terms of adaptation and application in environmental management and control?

The precautionary principle has been adopted in some international environmental treaties. However, its precise formulation is not identical in each instrument; nonetheless, the principle finds its roots in the more traditional environmental agreements which call on parties to such agreements, and the institutions they create, to act and to adopt decisions that are based upon "scientific findings" or methods,[239] or "in the light of knowledge available at the time."[240] Even in the International

[235] Ibid.

[236] Convention on Biological Diversity (1992), Preamble.

[237] Onyeabor (2011), p. 61.

[238] Rio Declaration (1992), Principle 15.

[239] As in the International Whaling Convention 1946.

[240] As provided in the Radiation Convention (1960), Art. 3(1).

Convention Relating to Intervention on the High Seas in Cases of Oil Pollution Casualties (Intervention Convention 1969), the position of the principle was not clearly stated, although it recognises the precautionary principle. Article 1(1) of the Convention states that the parties to the Convention:

> May take such measures on the high seas as may be necessary to prevent, mitigate or eliminate grave and imminent danger to their coastline or related interests from pollution or threat of pollution of the sea by oil, following upon a maritime casualty or acts related to such a casualty, which may reasonably be expected to result in major harmful consequences.

The standards set by these earlier treaties suggest that action shall only be taken where there is scientific evidence that significant environmental damage is occurring, and that in the absence of such evidence, no action would be required. This is exemplified by the Convention for the Prevention of Marine Pollution from Land-based Sources (Paris Convention 1974).[241] Under this Convention[242] contracting parties to the Convention may:

> …jointly or individually as appropriate, implement programmes or measures to forestall, reduce or eliminate pollution of the maritime area from land-based sources by a substance not then listed in Annex A to the Convention, **if scientific evidence has established that a serious hazard may be created in the maritime area by that substance and if urgent action is necessary**.[243]

This requires the party wishing to adopt measures to "prove" a case for action based on the existence of sufficient scientific evidence. For instance, under Annex A of the Convention, the allocation of substances takes account of the following criteria: (a) Persistence; (b) Toxicity or other noxious properties; (c) Tendency to bio-accumulation.[244] Thus, under Part 1 of the Annex the following substances: (i) Organohalogen compounds and substances which may form such compounds in the marine environment, excluding those that are biologically harmless, or which are rapidly converted in the sea into biologically harmless substances; (ii) Mercury and mercury compounds; (iii) Cadmium and cadmium compounds; (iv) Persistent synthetic materials which may float, remain in suspension or sink, and which may seriously interfere with any legitimate use of the sea; (v) Persistent oils and hydrocarbons of petroleum origin.

The reason for the inclusion of those substances is that (i) they are not readily degradable or rendered harmless by natural processes; and (ii) they may either give rise to dangerous accumulation of harmful material in the food chain, or endanger the welfare of living organisms causing undesirable changes in the marine eco-systems, or interfere seriously with the harvesting of seafood or with other legitimate uses of the sea; and finally it is considered that pollution by these substances necessitates urgent action.[245]

---

[241] Paris Convention (1974).

[242] Ibid., Art. 4(4).

[243] Emphasis mine.

[244] Paris Convention (1974), Annex, Part I.

[245] Paris Convention (1974).

Other substances such as: (i) organic compounds of phosphorous, silicon, and tin and substances that may form such compounds in the marine environment, excluding those that are biologically harmless, or which are rapidly converted in the sea into biologically harmless substances; (ii) elemental phosphorus; (iii) non-persistent oils and hydrocarbons of petroleum origin; and (iv) the following elements and their compounds, namely: arsenic; chromium; copper; lead; nickel and zinc.[246]

The import of this is that except so stated in the Annex of the Convention the precautionary principle can only apply in the case of other substances not mentioned "if scientific evidence has established that a serious hazard may be created in the maritime area by that substance and if urgent action is necessary" as stated in Article 4(4) of the Paris Convention 1974. As a result of difficulties that may be associated with obtaining such scientific proof, it became necessary over time to deviate from such a stringent approach.

A shift in the traditional approach to the application of the precautionary principle started gaining currency with time. For instance, developments in the mid-1980s to address ozone depletion reflected growing support for precautionary action. The Vienna Convention for the Protection of the Ozone Layer (Vienna Convention 1985)[247] was the first treaty which refers to the term when it reminded parties to be mindful of "the precautionary measures for the protection of the ozone layer which have already been taken at the national and international levels."[248]

By 1987, the parties to the Montreal Protocol on Substances that Deplete the Ozone Layer 1987 (Montreal Protocol to the Vienna Convention)[249] noted the "precautionary measures" to control emissions from certain CFCs which had already been taken at the national and regional levels and stated their determination to "protect the ozone layer by taking precautionary measures to control equitably total global emissions of substances that deplete it."[250]

At the United Nations Conference on Environment and Development in 1992 (UNCED) the application of the precautionary principle gave a boost in clear terms. For instance, the Rio Declaration 1992 states that: "where there are threats of serious or irreversible damage, lack of full scientific certainty shall not be used as a reason for postponing cost-effective measures to prevent environmental degradation."[251] The Convention on Climate Change 1992 added that the parties to the Convention should "take precautionary measures to anticipate, prevent or minimize the causes of

---

[246] Paris Convention (1974), Annex, Part II. It should be noted that the Paris Convention 1974 was replaced by the Convention for the Protection of the Marine Environment of the North-East Atlantic (OSPAR Convention) 1992 when the latter entered into force on 25 March 1998. This is pursuant to Article 31(1) of the OSPAR Convention.

[247] United Nations Environment Programme (UNEP) (2020a).

[248] Vienna Convention (1985), Preamble.

[249] United Nations Environment Programme (UNEP) (2020b).

[250] Montreal Protocol (1987), Preamble.

[251] Rio Declaration (1992), Principle 15.

climate change and mitigate its adverse effects."[252] The Convention further provides that:

> Where there are threats of serious or irreversible damage, lack of full scientific certainty should not be used as a reason for postponing such measures, taking into account that policies and measures to deal with climate change should be cost-effective so as to ensure global benefits at the lowest possible cost.[253]

To achieve this, such policies and measures should take into account different socio-economic contexts, be comprehensive, cover all relevant sources, sinks and reservoirs of greenhouse gases and adaptation, and comprise all economic sectors.[254]

The Convention on Biological Diversity 1992 also added support to the position of the applicability of the precautionary principle when it noted that "where there is a threat of significant reduction or loss of biological diversity, lack of full scientific certainty should not be used as a reason for postponing measures to avoid or minimize such a threat."[255]

These prepositions now attract broad support and some other environmental treaties, including some which are of global application on environmental matters of broad concern and applicable to almost all human activities, have adopted the precautionary principle or its underlying rationale. Among the earliest was the Convention on the Ban of Imports into Africa and the Control of Trans-boundary Movement and Management of Hazardous Wastes (Bamako Convention) 1991.[256] Article 4(3) (f) requires the parties to strive to adopt and implement:

> the preventive, precautionary approach to pollution which entails, inter alia, preventing the release into the environment of substances which may cause harm to humans or the environment without waiting for scientific proof the appropriate measures to implement the precautionary principle to pollution prevention through the application of clean production methods.

This formulation is one of the most far-reaching. It links the preventive and precautionary approaches, does not require damage to be serious or irreversible, and lowers the threshold at which scientific evidence might require action.

Furthermore, the Cartagena Protocol on Biosafety to the Convention on Biological Diversity (Biosafety Protocol) 2000 relies extensively on the precautionary approach. The objective of the Protocol is, however, stated to be "in accordance" with Principle 15 of the Rio Declaration, and, to that end, the Protocol affirms that "lack of scientific certainty due to insufficient relevant scientific information and knowledge regarding the extent of the potential adverse effects of a living modified

---

[252] Convention on Climate Change (1992), Art. 3(3).

[253] Ibid., Art. 3(3).

[254] Ibid.

[255] Convention on Biological Diversity (1992), Preamble.

[256] Access information on Multilateral Environmental Agreements (2020) Bamako Convention (1991).

organism on the conversation and sustainable use of biological diversity shall not prevent a party from prohibiting imports."[257]

Beyond the above Conventions, many others now commit their parties to apply the precautionary principle or approach. The Convention for the Protection of the Marine Environment of the North-East Atlantic (OSPAR Convention) 1992[258] links prevention and precaution: preventive measures are to be taken when there are "reasonable grounds for concern . . . even when there is no conclusive evidence of a causal relationship between the inputs and the effects."[259]

Another treaty that commits parties to apply the precautionary principle is the Straddling Stocks Agreement 1995. The Straddling Fish Stocks Agreement is a multilateral treaty created by the United Nations for the implementation of the provisions of the United Nations Convention on the Law of the Sea of 10 December 1982 relating to the conservation and management of straddling fish stocks and highly migratory fish stocks and enhancing the cooperative management of fisheries resources that span wide areas, and are of economic and environmental concern to a number of nations. It was signed on 4 December 1995 with 59 signatories and came into force on 11 December 2001.

The Agreement commits coastal states and states fishing on the high seas to apply the precautionary approach. To this end, "States shall apply the precautionary approach widely to conservation, management and exploitation of straddling fish stocks and highly migratory fish stocks in order to protect the living marine resources and preserve the marine environment."[260] In addition, the Agreement warns that "States shall be more cautious when information is uncertain, unreliable or inadequate. However, that the absence of adequate scientific information shall not be used as a reason for postponing or failing to take conservation and management measures."[261]

Guidelines for the implementation of the precautionary principle are provided under Article 6 of the Convention. Article 6(3) particularly posits that in implementing the precautionary approach, states shall:

a) improve decision-making for fishery resource conservation and management by obtaining and sharing the best scientific information available and implementing improved techniques for dealing with risk and uncertainty;
b) apply the guidelines set out in Annex II and determine, on the basis of the best scientific information available, stock-specific reference points and the action to be taken if they are exceeded;
c) take into account, inter alia, uncertainties relating to the size and productivity of the stocks, reference points, stock condition in relation to such reference points,

[257] Bamako Convention (1991), Art. 10.
[258] OSPAR Convention (1992).
[259] Ibid., Art. 2(2)(a).
[260] Straddling Stocks Agreement (1995), Art. 5(c).
[261] Ibid., Art. 6(2).

levels and distribution of fishing mortality and the impact of fishing activities on non-target and associated or dependent species, as well as existing and predicted oceanic, environmental and socio-economic conditions; and

d) develop data collection and research programmes to assess the impact of fishing on non-target and associated or dependent species and their environment, and adopt plans which are necessary to ensure the conservation of such species and to protect habitats of special concern.

The precautionary principle is receiving support from the international community in relation to a broad range of decisions and subject areas. The practice of international courts and tribunals, and states appearing before them, sheds some light on this respect. Before the International Court of Justice (ICJ) the principle appears to have first been raised in New Zealand's 1995 request concerning French nuclear testing.[262] New Zealand relied extensively on the principle, which it described as "a very widely accepted and operative principle of international law" and which shifted the burden onto France to prove that the proposed tests would not give rise to environmental damage.[263] Five "intervening" states (Australia, Micronesia, the Marshall Islands, Samoa and the Solomon Islands) also invoked the principle.

France responded that the status of the principle in international law was *tout a fait incertain*, but that in any event it had been complied with, and that evidentiary burdens were no different in the environmental field than any other area of international law.[264] The ICJ's order did not refer to these arguments, although Judge Weeramantry's dissent noted that the principle had "evolved to meet [the] evidentiary difficulty caused by the fact [that] information required to prove a proposition' may be 'in the hands of the party causing or threatening the damage'," and that it was "gaining increasing support as part of the international law of the environment."[265]

In the *Gabcikovo-Nagymaros Project*[266] case, Hungary and Slovakia also invoked the precautionary principle. Again, the ICJ did not feel the need to address the principle, limiting itself to a passing reference to Hungary's claim that the principle justified the termination of the 1977 treaty and its recognition of the parties' agreement on the need to take environmental concerns seriously and to take the required precautionary measures.[267] Of particular note was the failure of the ICJ to refer to or apply the principle in its consideration of the conditions under which Hungary could invoke the concept of ecological necessity to preclude the wrongfulness of its suspension of works on the two barrages in 1989.[268]

[262] The Legality of the Threat or Use of Nuclear Weapons (1996).

[263] Ibid., at 20–21.

[264] Ibid., at 71–72.

[265] The Legality of the Threat or Use of Nuclear Weapons (1996), 71–72.

[266] Hungary v. Slovakia [1997], 78.

[267] Ibid.

[268] Ibid.

Having acknowledged without difficulty "that the concerns expressed by Hungary for its natural environment in the region affected by the Gabcikovo-Nagymaros Project related to an 'essential interest' of the State," the ICJ nevertheless found that Hungary had not proved that "a real, 'grave' and 'imminent' 'peril' existed in 1989 and that the measures taken by Hungary were the only possible response to it." The ICJ found that there were serious uncertainties concerning future harm to freshwater supplies and biodiversity, but that these:

> could not, alone, establish the objective existence of a 'peril' in the sense of a component element of a state of necessity. The word 'peril' certainly evokes the idea of 'risk'; that is precisely what distinguishes 'peril' from material damage. But a state of necessity could not exist without a 'peril' duly established at the relevant point in time; the mere apprehension of a possible 'peril' could not suffice in that respect. It could moreover hardly be otherwise, when the 'peril' constituting the state of necessity has at the same time to be 'grace' and 'imminent'. 'Imminence' is synonymous with 'immediacy' or 'proximity' and goes far beyond the concept of 'possibility'... That does not exclude, in the view of the Court, that a 'peril' appearing in the long term might be held to be 'imminent' as soon as it is established, at the relevant point in time, that the realization of that peril, however far off it might be, is not thereby any less certain and inevitable.[269]

Although this wording is on the need to establish the certainty and inevitability of serious harm and may not precisely be regarded as precautionary language, however, it must be recognised that the ICJ was concerned here with the application of the law as it stood in 1989, when Hungary had wrongfully (in the view of the ICJ) suspended work on the project. At that time, the precautionary principle had not yet emerged and could not realistically be applied as general international law. It may be that the ICJ also had this in mind when it indicated later in the judgement that "what might have been a correct application of the law in 1989 or 1992, if the case had been before the Court then, could be a miscarriage of justice if prescribed in 1997."[270]

The International Tribunal on the Law of the Sea (ITLOS) has also been presented with arguments invoking precaution, and has shown itself to be notably more open to the application of the principle, albeit without express reliance. In 1999, in the *Southern Bluefin Tuna* cases,[271] Australia and New Zealand requested the Tribunal to order "that the parties act consistently with the precautionary principle in fishing for Southern Bluefin Tuna pending a final settlement of the dispute."[272] Japan, the respondent state, did not address the question of the status or effect of the principle.

In its Order, the Tribunal expressed the view that the parties should "act with prudence and caution to ensure that effective conservation measures are taken to prevent serious harm to the stock of southern bluefin tuna," that there was "scientific uncertainty regarding measures to be taken to conserve the stock of southern bluefin

[269] Hungary v. Slovakia [1997], 78.

[270] Hungary v. Slovakia [1997], 78 d.

[271] Southern Bluefin Tuna cases (New Zealand v. Japan and Australia v. Japan) (2000) 39 ILM 1359.

[272] Ibid.

tuna," and that, although it could not conclusively assess the scientific evidence presented by the parties, measures should be taken as a matter of urgency to preserve the rights of the parties and to avert further deterioration of the southern bluefin tuna stock.[273] In ordering the parties to refrain from conducting experimental fishing programmes, the Tribunal was plainly taking a precautionary approach, as Judge Treves recognised in his Separate Opinion where he said: "In the present case, it would seem to me that the requirement of urgency is satisfied only in the light of such precautionary approach. I regret that this is not explicitly in Order."[274]

In 2001, in the *MOX Plant* case,[275] Ireland claimed that the United Kingdom had failed to apply a precautionary approach to the protection of the Irish Sea in the exercise of its decision-making authority in relation to the direct and indirect consequences of the operation of the MOX plant and international movements of radioactive materials associated with the operation of the MOX plant.[276] The principle was invoked by Ireland at the provisional measures phase to support its claim that the United Kingdom had the burden of demonstrating that no harm would arise from discharges and other consequences of the operation of the MOX plant, and to inform the assessment by the Tribunal of the urgency of the measures it is required to take in respect of the operation of the MOX plant.[277]

For its part, Northern Ireland, and while accepting that in assessing the level of risk in any given case considerations of prudence and caution may be relevant.[278] The United Kingdom argued that in the absence of evidence showing a real risk of harm precaution could not warrant a restraint of the rights of the United Kingdom to operate a plant.[279] The Tribunal did not order the suspension of the operation of the plant, as Ireland had requested, but instead ordered the parties to co-operate and enter into consultations to exchange further information on possible consequences for the Irish Sea arising out of the commissioning of the marine environment which might result from the operation of the MOX plant.[280] That Order, which has a certain precautionary character, was premised on considerations of prudence and caution.

The precautionary principle has also been addressed by the World Trade Organisation (WTO) Appellate Body in a number of disputes under the WTO's Agreement on Sanitary and Phytosanitary Measures (the SPS Agreement).[281] In

---

[273] Southern Bluefin Tuna (New Zealand v. Japan and Australia v. Japan) (2000), para 77.

[274] Ibid., para 8.

[275] The MOX Plant case (Ireland v. United Kingdom) (2001), International Tribunal for The Law Of The Sea, Reports of Judgments, Advisory Opinions and Orders, Order of 3 December 2001.

[276] The MOX Plant case (Ireland v. United Kingdom) (2001), para 26.

[277] Ibid.

[278] Ibid., para 71.

[279] Ibid., para 75.

[280] The MOX Plant case (Ireland v. United Kingdom) (2001), paras 82 and 85.

[281] The SPS is an agreement on how governments can apply food safety and animal and plant health measures (sanitary and phytosanitary (SPS measures) sets out the basic rules in the WTO. The SPS Agreement tries to sort out genuine cases from those that are potentially excuses for protectionism. It does this by saying that measures either have to be based on scientific evidence of risk, or on

contention were the provisions of Articles 2.2, 3.3, 5.1, 5.2 and 5.7 of the SPS Agreement. Article 2.2 of the SPS Agreement[282] provides that: "Members shall ensure that any sanitary or phytosanitary measure is applied only to the extent necessary to protect human, animal or plant life or health, is based on scientific principles and is not maintained without sufficient scientific evidence, except as provided for in Article 5.7."

Under Article 3.3, the SPS Agreement requires that all possible less-restrictive solutions be exhausted before imposing protective measures, a requirement called the "necessary test." It further states that those actions produce more trade-restrictive effects than those generally expected from similar measures based on international standards.[283] must be corroborated by scientific justification. The issue of scientific justification implies that a risk assessment of the product under protection be performed. Thus, "Members shall ensure that their sanitary or phytosanitary measures are based on an assessment, as appropriate to the circumstances, of the risks to human, animal or plant life or health, taking into account risk assessment techniques developed by the relevant international organizations."[284]

However, the SPS Agreement provides an exception to this rule, which is included in Article 5.7 and considers a situation where scientific evidence is insufficient to conclude that there is a definite risk: "In cases where relevant scientific evidence is insufficient, 'a Member may provisionally adopt sanitary or phytosanitary measures on the basis of available pertinent information, including that from the relevant international organizations as well as from sanitary or phytosanitary measures applied by other Members'." It was on the basis of the above provisions of the SPS Agreement that the *European Communities – Measures Concerning Meat and Meat Products* (*Hormones case)*[285] and other disputes discussed below, were hinged upon.

In the *Hormones* case,[286] the European Community (EC) in 1998 invoked the precautionary principle to justify its claim that it was entitled to prohibit imports of beef produced in the United States and Canada with artificial hormones, where the

---

recognised international standards. If a country applies international standards, it is less likely to be challenged legally in the WTO than if it sets its own standards. But countries are free to set their own standards based on science. Sanitary or phytosanitary measures include all relevant laws, decrees, regulations, requirements and procedures including, inter alia, end product criteria; processes and production methods; testing, inspection, certification and approval procedures; quarantine treatments including relevant requirements associated with the transport of animals or plants, or with the materials necessary for their survival during transport; provisions on relevant statistical methods, sampling procedures and methods of risk assessment; and packaging and labelling requirements directly related to food safety. See Annex A (1)(d) SPS Agreements.

[282] United Nations (1995), vol 1, Annex 2 A, 1867 UN Treaty Ser 493.

[283] Sanitary and Phytosanitary Measures (SPS Agreement 1995), Art. 3.3.

[284] Ibid.

[285] World Trade Organization, Report of the Appellate Body (1998) 1 26, WTO Doc No WT/DS26/AB/R, WT/DS48/AB/R (16 January 1998) (EC Hormones), at 253.

[286] Ibid.

impacts on human health were uncertain.[287] The EC argued that the principle was already "a general customary rule of international law or at least a general principle of law," that it applied to both the assessment and management of a risk and that it informed the meaning and effect of Articles 5.1 and 5.2 of the SPS Agreement 1995.[288] The United States denied that the principle represented a principle of customary international law, and preferred to characterise it as an "approach" the content of which may vary from context to context. Canada referred to a precautionary approach as "an emerging principle of international law," which may in the future crystallize into one of the "general principles of law recognized by civilized nations," within the meaning of Article 38(1) (c) of the Statutes of the International Court of Justice (ICJ Statute) 1945.[289]

The WTO Appellate Body agreed with the United States and Canada that the precautionary principle did not override Articles 5.1 and 5.2 of the SPS Agreement, although it considered that it was reflected in the preamble to and Articles 3.3 and 5.7 of the SPS Agreement, which did not exhaust the relevance of the principle. Recognising that the status of the principle in international law was the subject of continued debate, and that it was regarded by some as having crystallised into a general principle of customary international environmental law, the Appellate Body said:

> Whether it has been widely accepted by Members as a principle of general customary International law appears less than clear. We consider, however, that it is unnecessary, and probably imprudent, for the Appellate Body in this appeal to take a position on this important, but abstract, question. We note that the Panel itself did not make any definitive finding with regard to the status of the precautionary principle in international law and that the precautionary principle, at least outside the field of international environmental law, still awaits authoritative formulation.[290]

The WTO Appellate Body concluded that, among other provisions, the EC had violated Article 5.1 of the Sanitary and Phytosanitary (SPS) Agreement, requiring that a member's SPS measures be based on a risk assessment.[291]

Another instance in which the precautionary principle was invoked in a trade dispute was in the European Community *(EC)-Measures Affecting the Approval and Marketing of Biotech Products* dispute *(EC-Biotech case).*[292] On 13 May 2003, the United States (US) requested consultations with the EC concerning certain measures taken by the EC and its member states affecting imports of agricultural and food imports from the United States. On 7 August 2003, the United States requested the establishment of a panel. At its meeting on 18 August 2003, the Dispute Settlement

---

[287] Ibid.

[288] Ibid.

[289] Ibid.

[290] World Trade Organization, Report of the Appellate Body (1998) at 253, para 123.

[291] Ibid.

[292] World Trade Organization, Report of the Panel (2003), 4.290-4.291, WTO Doc No WT/DS291 / R.

Body (DSB) deferred the establishment of a panel but at its meeting on 29 August 2003, the DSB established a single panel to examine this dispute.

In that dispute, a group composed of the US as Complainant and Argentina, Australia, Brazil, Canada, Chile, China, Chinese Taipei, Colombia, El Salvador, Honduras, Mexico, New Zealand, Norway, Paraguay, Peru, Thailand and Uruguay as third parties in the original proceeding accused the European Union (EU) of having imposed a de facto moratorium on the commercialisation of genetically modified organisms (GMOs)[293] since 1998 by "undue delay" in the approval procedure. Besides accusations of procedural failures, the complainants claimed that the European member states either never performed the risk assessments on GMOs or dismissed the positive results of risk assessments. Thus, according to the complainants, the European behaviour violated Article 5.1 of the SPS Agreement, which requires that SPS measures be based on scientific risk assessment. In the absence of such an assessment, the European delay amounted to a non-necessary and not science-based restrictive measure to trade.[294]

In their defence, the European Communities (EC) argued that to the extent that safeguard measures on the import of certain GMOs were adopted by six EC member states, the case of inconsistency was to be examined under Article 5.7 of the SPS Agreement instead of Article 5.1, the former contemplating the case of insufficient scientific evidence and better reflecting the precautionary principle.[295]

On 29 September 2006, the WTO Dispute Settlement Body issued its ruling on the complaints, on the one hand faulting the EC for "undue delay" in approving GMO products for a four-year period ending in 2003 and on the other accusing some EC member states of maintaining unjustified bans on genetically modified products already found safe by the European scientific committees. Indeed, the justification of the six European states that scientific results were not "convincing" and needed further evaluation before allowing the import of these products was not upheld by the Panel, which found no GMO case where scientific evidence was insufficient to perform an adequate risk assessment.[296] The Panel concluded that the EC member state safeguard measures violated Articles 5.1 and 2.2 of the SPS Agreement because they were not based on risk assessments and hence could be presumed to be maintained without sufficient scientific evidence.[297]

Again, in the *US-Continued Suspension* case,[298] the EC invoked the precautionary principle to justify a temporary ban on meat and meat products treated with five specific growth promotion hormones. Although it did not fault the EC for its

---

[293] GMOs are products that have been altered using recombinant DNA technologies.

[294] World Trade Organization, Report of the Panel (2003).

[295] World Trade Organization (WTO) (2003).

[296] Ibid.

[297] Ibid.

[298] WTO (2008), 85, WTO Doc No WT/DS320/AB/R.

conduct, the Appellate Body was unable to determine whether the risk assessments performed by the EC supported a case of insufficient scientific evidence.[299]

There are more recent trade disputes based on the SPS Agreement 1995. They include:

1) *Panama – Measures concerning the importation of certain products from Costa Rica*. The Complainant was Costa Rica, while Panama appeared as the Respondent. On 11 January 2021, Costa Rica requested consultations with Panama regarding measures on the importation of several products originating in Costa Rica, including: strawberries, dairy products, bovine, pork, poultry and turkey meat products, fish food, fresh pineapple, and plantains and bananas. Costa Rica claimed that the measures appear to be inconsistent with: Articles 2.1, 2.2, 2.3, 3.1, 3.3, 5.1, 5.4, 5.5, 5.6, 5.7, 5.8, 6.1, 7, 8 and Annexes B and C of the SPS Agreement. On 27 January 2021, Bolivia requested to join the consultations.[300]
2) *Russian Federation – Measures on the Importation of Live Pigs, Pork and Other Pig Products* from the European Union. The Complainant was the European Union, while the Russian Federation appeared as the Respondent. Australia, China, India, Japan, Korea, Republic of; Norway, Chinese Taipei, United States, Brazil and South Africa appeared as third parties in the original proceeding. On 8 April 2014, the European Union requested consultations with the Russian Federation concerning certain measures adopted by the Russian Federation affecting the importation of live pigs and their genetic material, pork, pork products and certain other commodities from the European Union, purportedly because of concerns related to cases of African swine fever. The European Union claims that the measures at issue are inconsistent with: Articles 2.2, 2.3, 3.1, 3.2, 3.3, 5.1, 5.2, 5.3, 5.4, 5.5, 5.6, 5.7, 6.1, 6.2, 6.3, 7, 8, Annex B, and Annex C of the SPS Agreement.[301]
3) *United States – Measures Affecting the Importation of Fresh Lemons*. The Complainant was Argentina while the Respondent was the US. On 3 September 2012, Argentina requested consultations with the United States concerning certain measures affecting the importation of fresh lemons from the Northwest region of Argentina. The specific measures challenged by Argentina:
    (i) a series of US measures allegedly maintained for the past 11 years, which Argentina argues constitute an import prohibition on citrus fruits affecting fresh lemons originating in the Northwest region of Argentina;
    (ii) the United States' failure to grant approval for the importation of fresh lemons from the Northwest region of Argentina; and
    (iii) alleged undue delays in the approval procedures for the importation of fresh lemons from the Northwest region of Argentina.[302]

---

299 Ibid., at 207–208.

300 WTO (2021).

301 WTO (2021).

302 Ibid.

Argentina claims that the challenged measures appear to be inconsistent with: Articles I:1, III:4, X:1, X:3 and XI:1 of the GATT 1994 and Articles 1.1, 2.2, 2.3, 3.1, 3.3, 5.1, 5.2, 5.4, 5.6 and 7, Annex B, 8, Annex C and Article 10.1 of the SPS Agreement 1995.[303]

The precautionary principle has also been raised before other courts, such as the European Court of Human Rights. In *Balmer-Schafroth v. Switzerland*,[304] the applicants claimed that the failure of Switzerland to provide for an administrative review of a decision extending the operation of a nuclear facility violated Article 6 of the European Convention on Human Rights. The claim was rejected by the majority because the connection between the government's decision and the applicants' rights was too remote and tenuous. The court ruled that the applicants had failed to:

> establish a direct link between the operating conditions of the power station ... and their right to protection of their physical integrity, as they failed to show that the operation of Muhleberg power station exposed them personally to a danger that was not only serious but also specific and, above all, imminent. In the absence of such a finding, the effect on the population of the measures which the Federal Council could have ordered to be taken in the instant case therefore remained hypothetical. Consequently, neither the dangers nor the remedies were established with a degree of probability that made the outcome of the proceedings directly decisive.[305]

A dissenting opinion by seven judges, however, criticised this finding, on the grounds that it "ignored the whole trend of international institutions and public international law towards protecting persons and heritage, as evident (inter alia) in ... the development of the precautionary principle."[306]

At the national level, there have also been several decisions addressing the status of the precautionary principle in international law. In the case of *Vellore Citizens' Welfare Forum v. Union of India and Others*,[307] for example, the Indian Supreme Court ruled that the precautionary principle was an essential feature of "sustainable development" and as such part of customary international law. By contrast, a United States Federal Court in the case of *Beanal v. Freeport-Mcmoran*,[308] appears more restrained in its approach, holding that the principle was not yet established in customary international law so as to give rise to a cause of action under the Allen Tort Claims Statute.

The legal status of the precautionary principle is evolving. There is certainly sufficient evidence of state practice to support the conclusion that the principle, as elaborated in Principle 15 of the Rio Declaration 1992 and various international conventions, has now received sufficiently broad support to allow a strong argument to be made that it reflects a principle of customary law, and that within the context of

---

[303] Ibid.

[304] (1998) 25 EHRR 598.

[305] Balmer-Schafroth v. Switzerland (1998), para 40.

[306] Ibid., para 45.

[307] AIR (1996) SC 2715 at 2722.

[308] 969 F Supp 362 at 384 (US District Court for Eastern District of Louisiana, 9 April 1997.

the European Union, it has now achieved customary status, without prejudice to the precise consequences of its application in any given case. Nevertheless, it must be recognised that international courts and tribunals have been reluctant to accept explicitly that the principle has a customary international law status, notwithstanding the preponderance of support in favour of that view, and diminishing opposition to it. The reluctance may be understandable, given its inherently commonsensical approach, even if the practical consequences of its application fail to be determined on a case-by-case basis.

From the above discussions, the application of the precautionary approach portents in litigating environmental damage is that an interpretation of the precautionary principle would tend to shift the burden of proof to the defendant. Accordingly, this will require the person who wishes to carry out an activity to prove that it will not cause harm to the environment. This interpretation would require polluters to establish that their activities and the discharge of certain substances would not adversely or significantly affect the environment before they are granted the right to release the potentially polluting substances or carry out the proposed activity.

There is growing evidence to suggest that this interpretation is beginning to be supported by state practices. Under the OSPAR Convention 1992, parties (France and the United Kingdom) that originally wanted to retain the option of dumping low – and intermediate-level radioactive wastes at sea were required to report to the OSPAR Commission on "the results of scientific studies which show that any potential dumping operations would not result in hazards to human health, harm to living resources or marine ecosystems, damage to amenities or interference with other legitimate uses of the sea."[309] However, "the precautionary approach shall be widely applied by States according to their capabilities."[310]

4.7 Polluter-Pays Principle

4.7.1 Introduction

The polluter-pays principle (PPP) is another principle that can be applied in environmental legislation to minimise, control, prevent, remediate and at times, punish behaviours or activities that may cause environmental damage. The meaning of the principle, and its application to particular cases and situations, remains open to interpretation, particularly on the nature and extent of the costs included and the circumstances, in which the principle will, perhaps exceptionally, not apply. According to Thornton and Beckwith,[311] the premise upon which the principle is based is its allocation of economic obligations on environmentally damaging

[309] OSPAR Convention (1992), Art. 3(3) (c).

[310] Rio Declaration (1992), Principle 15.

[311] Thornton and Beckwith (2004), p. 14.

activities, particularly on liability, the use of economic instruments, and the application of rules relating to competition and subsidy. The principle therefore imposes liability on a person who pollutes the environment to compensate for the damage caused and return the environment to its original state regardless of the intent.[312]

The polluter-pays principle has not received the same degree of support or attention accorded over the years to the principle of preventive action, or the attention more recently accorded to the precautionary principle. The strong objections of some countries to the further development of the polluter-pays principle, particularly for international relations, are evident from the compromise language adopted by Principle 16 of the Rio Declaration 1992, which provides that:

> National authorities should endeavour to promote the internalization of environmental costs and the use of economic instruments, taking into account the approach that the polluter should, in principle, bear the costs of pollution, with due regard to the public interests and, **without distorting international trade and investment**.

The polluter-pays principle in treaty law can be traced back to some of the first instruments establishing minimum rules on civil liability for damage resulting from hazardous activities. One such instrument is the Convention on Third Party Liability in the Field of Nuclear Energy (Paris Convention) 1960.[313] The Paris Convention 1960[314] is a 1960 Organisation for Economic Co-operation and Development (OECD) Convention on liability and compensation for damage caused by accidents occurring while producing nuclear energy.

Under Article 3 of the Paris Convention 1960, "the operator of a nuclear installation shall be liable for: (i) damage to or loss of life of any person; and (ii) damage to or loss of any property..."[315] and where the damage or loss is caused jointly by a nuclear incident and by an incident other than a nuclear incident, that part of the damage or loss which is caused by such other incident shall, to the extent that it is not reasonably separable from the damage or loss caused by the nuclear incident, be considered to be damage caused by the nuclear incident.[316]

In addition, the International Atomic Energy Agency (IAEA) Liability Convention 1963 was also influenced by the desire to channel compensation from those responsible for the activity causing damage to the victims.

Again, under Article V (2) International Convention on Civil Liability for Oil Pollution Damage 1969 (CLC 1969),[317] however, the ship owner is precluded from relying on the limitation of liability if the incident occurred as a result of his actual fault or privity. In the same vein, the preamble to the International Convention on the Establishment of an International Fund for Compensation for Oil Pollution Damage

---

[312] Rana and Co (2017).

[313] Ecolex (2020).

[314] The convention entered into force on 1 April 1968 and has been amended by protocols in 1964, 1982, and 2004.

[315] Paris Convention (1960), Art. 3(a).

[316] See also Paris Convention (1960), Art. 4.

[317] Discussed in sect. 15.1.2 of Chap. 15 of this book.

1971 (Fund Convention 1971)[318] reflects the consideration that the economic consequences of oil pollution damage should be borne by the shipping industry and oil cargo interests.

4.7.2 *Polluter-Pays Principle in International Environmental Law*

The first international instrument to refer expressly to the polluter-pays principle was the 1972 Organisation for Economic Co-operation and Development (OECD) Council Recommendation on "Guiding Principles Concerning the International Economic Aspects of Environmental Policies," which endorsed the polluter-pays principle to allocate costs of pollution prevention and control measures to encourage rational use of environmental resources and avoid distortions in international trade and investments and that the polluter should bear the expenses of carrying out the measures deemed necessary by public authorities to protect the environment. The 1972 Recommendation does not, on the face of it, apply to the costs of environmental damage.[319]

However, in 1974, the OECD Council adopted a further Recommendation on the "Implementation of the Polluter-Pays Principle," which reaffirmed that the principle constituted a "fundamental principle" for member countries, that aid given for new pollution control technologies and the development of new pollution abatement equipment was not necessarily incompatible with the principle, and that member countries should strive for uniform observance of the principle.[320]

The 1989 OECD Council "Recommendation on the Application of the Polluter-Pays Principle to Accidental Pollution,"[321] extends the principle to imply that the operator of a hazardous installation should bear the cost of reasonable measures to prevent and control accidental pollution from that installation which are introduced by public authorities in conformity with domestic law before the occurrence of an accident.

According to the 1989 OECD Council Recommendation, however, this does not necessarily require that "the costs of reasonable measures to control accidental pollution after an accident should be collected as expeditiously as possible from the legal or natural person who is at the origin of the accident." Examples of specific applications of the polluter-pays principle cited by the 1989 Recommendation include adjusting fees or taxes payable by hazardous installations to cover more fully the cost of certain exceptional measures taken by public authorities to prevent

---

[318] CLC 1969.

[319] Organisation for Economic Co-Operation and Development (OECD) (1975), p. 259.

[320] OECD (1995).

[321] OECD (2016).

and control accidental pollution, and charging to the polluter the cost of reasonable pollution control measures decided on by public authorities following an accident to avoid the spread of environmental damage and limit the release of hazardous substances (by ceasing emissions at the plant), the pollution as such (by cleaning or decontamination), or its ecological effects (by rehabilitating the polluted environment).[322]

The principle has been incorporated into some regional legal documents. For instance, the Niger Basin Charter 2012 enjoins member states "to set up tax incentives to help economic operators who implement procedures to use water resources in a manner which respects the environment" and that the polluter-pays principle should be taken into account and "applied to both legal persons and individuals, and under which the costs of prevention, control and pollution reduction are borne by the polluter."[323]

For Sadeleer,[324] the polluter-pays principle essentially reflects the "curative" and "preventive" model of thought. According to him, the curative model opposes the concept of nature as an ocean with unlimited resources. It canvasses the argument that natural resources are exhaustive and as such, humans should pay for the over-exploitation and unwise use of the environment. It espouses that everything is capable of being indemnified, restored, compensated and cured. In Sadeleer's opinion, as a wound inflicted on the environment cannot cure itself, help is required from the inflictor to help cure it (i.e., the polluter is required to finance the restoration of the environment he damaged).[325]

The preventive model of thought, on the other hand, posits that the polluter-pays principle should not be viewed as a principle that encourages arbitrary pollution once polluters can pay the cost of pollution. Rather, the principle should be seen as one that institutes a policy of pollution abatement such that polluters are encouraged to reduce their pollution and not remain content with paying pollution charges.[326]

4.7.3 *Integrating Polluter-Pays Principle in National Legislation*

The principle has also found application under regional and national laws. The need to legislate against environmental damage arose from the realisation that the environment is the most formidable source of national and international development and should be protected from damage, destruction and annihilation. In this respect,

---

[322] OECD (2016).

[323] Niger Basin Charter (2012), Art. 8.

[324] Sadeleer (2002), p. 15.

[325] Ibid.

[326] Sadeleer (2002), p. 36.

various environmental pollution abatement laws have been put in place to protect not only the environment but also to manage it for human survival.[327] These environmental pollution abatement laws generally deal with environmental damages caused by water pollution, oil and gas pollution, air quality and atmospheric protection, toxic and hazardous waste problems, noise control, and municipal waste disposal, among others.

The principle has also found application under regional and national laws. The Nigerian environmental laws[328] have provisions not only to protect the environment from damage and annihilation, but also provisions for punishing defiant behaviours that are responsible for such damage and compelling the polluter to pay for the resulting damages. Some of the Nigerian legislation that has provisions for the polluter-pays principle as an instrument for punishing perpetrators of activities that cause environmental damage include:

i) National Environmental (Sanitation and Wastes Control) Regulations 2009;
ii) National Environmental (Mining and Processing of Coal, Ores and Industrial Minerals) Regulations 2009;
iii) National Environmental (Food, Beverages and Tobacco Sector) Regulations 2009;
iv) National Environmental (Chemical, Pharmaceutical, Soap and Detergent Manufacturing Industries) Regulations 2009;
v) National Environmental (Electronic/Electrical Sector) Regulations 2011
vi) Harmful Waste (Special Criminal Provisions) (HWSCP) Act 1988
vii) Other Legislation

These laws and their provisions vis-à-vis polluter-pays principle are discussed below.

(i) National Environmental (Sanitation and Wastes Control) Regulations 2009[329]

Under the National Environmental (Sanitation and Wastes Control) Regulations, "all generators of wastes, owners or occupiers of premises where wastes are generated shall be legally and financially responsible for the safe and environmentally sound disposal of their wastes,"[330] all generators and managers of wastes shall apply sustainable practices to minimise pollution.[331]

---

[327] Onyeabor et al. (2017), p. 186.

[328] Some of these laws were discussed in sect. 16.2.5 of Chap. 16 of this book.

[329] Government Notice No. 281, S.I. No 28. Federal Republic of Nigeria Official Gazette No. 60 Vol. 96, 6 October 2009.

[330] National Environmental (Sanitation and Wastes Control) Regulations (2009), Regulation 14.

[331] Ibid., Regulation 15.

(ii) National Environmental (Mining and Process of Coal, Ores and Industrial Minerals) Regulations 2009[332]

Under the Regulations,[333] "all effluents are cleaned up and disposed of at an appropriate discharge point or waste treatment facility at the conclusion of each operation."[334] In line with the polluter-pays principle as one of the general principles and rules establishing standards in environmental protection as reflected in treaties, national laws, binding acts of international organisations, state practices and soft law commitments, Regulation 13 of the Regulations[335] provides that "collection, treatment, transportation and final disposal of wastes within the specified standards and guidelines, shall be the responsibility of the facility generating the waste."

Liability may arise if a facility fails to take reasonable measures to remove or treat and dispose of any effluent to minimise adverse effects,[336] to take measures required by the Agency after the unauthorised release of effluent,[337] to remediate the environment to the standard prescribed by the Agency[338] and to comply with guidelines with respect to the handling storing and transport of any effluent.[339]

Polluter-pays principle applies under Regulation 13(2) of the Regulations[340] states that in the event of pollution resulting in an impact on the environment whether socio-economically or health-wise, the facility that caused the pollution shall, as specified in Schedule 4 to these Regulations,[341] be responsible for: (a) the cost of clean-up; (b) remediation; (c) reclamation; (d) compensation to all affected parties; and (e) the cost of damage assessment and control.[342]

---

[332] Government Notice No. 284, S.I. No 28. Federal Republic of Nigeria Official Gazette No. 63 Vol. 96, 12 October 2009.

[333] National Environmental (Mining and Process of Coal, Ores and Industrial Minerals) Regulations (2009).

[334] Ibid., Regulation 10(5)(b).

[335] National Environmental (Mining and Process of Coal, Ores and Industrial Minerals) Regulations (2009).

[336] Ibid., Regulation 28(4)(a).

[337] Ibid., Regulation 28(4)(b).

[338] Ibid., Regulation 28(4)(c).

[339] Ibid., Regulation 28(4)(g).

[340] National Environmental (Mining and Process of Coal, Ores and Industrial Minerals) Regulations (2009).

[341] National Environmental (Mining and Process of Coal, Ores and Industrial Minerals) Regulations (2009).

[342] The provisions of the National Environmental (Mining and Process of Coal, Ores and Industrial Minerals) Regulations 2009 on polluter-pays principle under Regulation 13(4)(2) are similar in all respect as provided under the National Environmental (Food, Beverages and Tobacco Sector) Regulations 2009, Regulation 5 and the National Environmental (Chemical, Pharmaceutical, Soap and Detergent Manufacturing Industries) Regulations 2009, Regulation 5.

(iii) National Environmental (Electrical/Electronic Sector) Regulations 2011[343]

The principal thrust of the National Environmental (Electrical/Electronic Sector) Regulations 2011 as provided under Regulation 2 is to prevent and minimise pollution from all operations and ancillary activities of the electrical and electronic sector[344] to the Nigerian Environment.

To protect the Nigerian environment, the Regulations[345] place some responsibilities on those involved in the Electrical/Electronic Equipment (EEE) business. For instance, EEE imported into the country shall be functional, and must have the date of manufacture inscribed on them and warranty indicated,[346] must have the Personal Identification Number (PIN) and serial numbers inscribed on them.[347] In addition, such importer shall comply with the requirements specified in Schedule 11 to these Regulations which include the EEE being of comparative model of equipment; fit for purpose; functional and not scrap; such that the outward/external appearance of the item does not show any waste characteristics and properly packaged for protection during transport, loading and unloading.[348]

Again, under Regulation 34(1),[349] every importer and technician (involved in repair, dismantling and re-assembling) of used EEE shall ensure that e-waste is handled by a person and or corporate body registered to do so by the Agency.[350] The Regulations place a ban on the importation of End-of-life, unusable or unserviceable EEE,[351] as well as a ban on the importation of Cathode Ray Tubes (CRT).[352]

On the issue of storage, every person, corporate body or organisation in charge of a collection centre shall ensure that e-waste are: not stored longer than one year onsite, not disposed of in trash receptacles or at a dump site and or landfill, and that e-waste collected for recycling are transported to the designated recycling-centre.[353] The Regulations prohibit the open burning of EEE.[354]

---

[343] Government Notice No. 137, S.I. No 23. Federal Republic of Nigeria Official Gazette No. 50 Vol. 98, 25 May 2011.

[344] Electrical/electronic sector means organisation or corporate body involved in (a) manufacturing, assembling, processing or recycling any equipment contained in the categories of **EEE** listed in these Regulations and (b) operations in telecommunication, broadcasting, power (distribution, transmission and generation) facilities. This applies to both new (EEE) and used (UEEE). See National Environmental (Electrical/Electronic Sector) Regulations (2011), Regulation 69.

[345] National Environmental (Electrical/Electronic Sector) Regulations (2011).

[346] Ibid., Regulation 3(1).

[347] Ibid., Regulation 3(2).

[348] National Environmental (Electrical/Electronic Sector) Regulations (2011), Regulation 3(4).

[349] National Environmental (Electrical/Electronic Sector) Regulations (2011).

[350] The agency herein referred to is the National Environmental Standards and Regulations Enforcement Agency (NESREA).

[351] National Environmental (Electrical/Electronic Sector) Regulations (2011), Regulation 34(2).

[352] National Environmental (Electrical/Electronic Sector) Regulations (2011), Regulation 34(3).

[353] Ibid., Regulation 34(4) (a) (b) and (c).

[354] Ibid., Regulation 34(4)(d).

Elaborate handling and management of e-waste are provided under the Regulations. For instance, Regulation 8[355] provides for the application of best practices in handling EEE. The Regulations provide that implementation of cleaner production processes and pollution prevention measures shall be employed by handlers of EEE to yield economic, social and environmental benefits as specified in Schedule V to these Regulations.[356] Also, all EEE manufacturing, processing, assembling organisation or corporate bodies shall apply new technologies arising from the elimination of hazardous materials in many new-model EEE.[357]

Furthermore, for any EEE manufacturing, processing, assembling organisation or corporate body, pollution prevention measures shall focus on minimisation in the use of hazardous substances contained in Schedule XVI to these Regulations.[358] Thus, all damaged and disused equipment including wires, Cathode Ray Tubes (CRTs), metals, motors, transformers, plastics, etc., shall be amenable for recovery under the Extended Producer Responsibility Programme by NESREA's accredited Recyclers in an Environmentally Sound Manner (ESM).[359]

Also, operators of e-waste collection centres and transporters to recycling plants shall: maintain copies of all e-waste manifests and/or receipts and copies shall be made available for review during an inspection visit by officers of the Agency; forward a copy of the e-waste manifests to the Agency within 30 days of waste removal and sign copies of the e-waste manifest.[360]

The Regulations further provide that a person or corporate body or organisation shall not discard and or throw and or drop any e-waste anywhere except in a designated bin, collection centre and or point.[361] Therefore, every operator of a facility, technician, assembler or scavenger[362] of e-waste shall practice Environmentally Sound Management (ESM) of e-waste and shall not: burn e-waste in the Nigerian environment; dispose of e-waste alongside domestic and/or municipal waste; dispose of e-waste at clump sites, land-fill sites, water body, etc; break Cathode Ray Tubes (CRTs), in an unsound environmental manner; release Chlorofluorocarbons (CFCs) from fridges and other cooling systems and leach precious metals with acids and other hazardous waste from Printed Wire Boards (PWBs) or Printed Circuit Boards(PCBs).[363]

---

[355] National Environmental (Electrical/Electronic Sector) Regulations (2011).

[356] Ibid., Regulation 8(1).

[357] Ibid., Regulation 8(2).

[358] Ibid., Regulation 8(3).

[359] Ibid., Regulation 8(4).

[360] Ibid., Regulation 34(6).

[361] National Environmental (Electrical/Electronic Sector) Regulations (2011), Regulation 36 (1).

[362] "Scavenger," is defined as "a person who searches and picks waste that can be useful for recycling purposes by people that will convert them to other useful forms," National Environmental (Electrical/Electronic Sector) Regulations (2011), Regulation 69.

[363] National Environmental (Electrical/Electronic Sector) Regulations (2011), Regulation 36(2)(a)–(f).

In all, waste from electrical/electronic product assembly or manufacturing with hazardous properties shall be clearly labelled and stored separately from the general waste and contained in storage areas that are chemically resistant before disposal in an environmentally sound manner.[364] And that every corporate body or organisation that generates e-waste, shall separate such at source from other waste streams.[365]

In addition, waste from electrical/electronic product assembly or manufacturing with hazardous properties shall be clearly labelled and stored separately from the general waste and contained in storage areas that are chemically resistant before disposal in an environmentally sound manner.[366]

The essence of these directives placed on those involved in EEE business is geared towards the protection of both the physical and human environment from damage and destruction from hazards associated with EEE. To this end, offences are provided under Regulations 61–66 of the Regulations and penalties, ranging from fines to imprisonment are provided in Regulation 67.

Besides the penalties provided by the Regulations, the polluter-pays principle shall apply to everybody, corporate polluters, or organisations that pollute the environment with e-waste.[367] The collection, treatment, transportation and final disposal of wastes shall be the responsibility of the corporate body/organisation generating the wastes within the specified standards and guidelines.[368] In the event of an incident resulting in an adverse impact on the environment whether socio-economic or health-wise, the facility shall be responsible for: the cost of damage assessment, control and clean-up; remediation and reclamation and/or restoration.[369]

(iv) **Harmful Waste (Special Criminal Provisions) (HWSCP) Act 1988**

The HWSCP Act was promulgated as Degree No. 42 of 1988.[370] The Act prohibits the carrying, depositing and dumping of harmful waste on any land, territorial waters and matters related thereto and therefore prohibits all activities relating to the purchase, sale, importation, transit, transportation, deposit, and storage of harmful wastes.[371] An offence is committed under the Act if the person actually does the act or makes the omission which constitutes the crime; or does or omits to do any act for the purpose of enabling or aiding another person to commit the crime; or aids another person in committing the crime; or counsels or procures any person to commit the crime, in which case he may himself be charged with committing the crime or with counselling or procuring the commission of the

[364] Ibid., Regulation 8(5).

[365] Ibid., Regulation 34(7).

[366] Ibid., Regulation 8(5).

[367] National Environmental (Electrical/Electronic Sector) Regulations (2011), Regulation 7(1).

[368] Ibid., Regulation 7(2).

[369] National Environmental (Electrical/Electronic Sector) Regulations (2011), Regulation 7(3)(a)–(c).

[370] Currently retained as Cap H1 LFN 2004.

[371] HWSCP Act (1988), s. 1(1).

crime.[372] Sections 6 and 7 of the Act provide for penalties and punishment for individuals and corporate body.

In addition to the criminal liability, the Act also has provisions for civil liability against the person who carried out the unlawful act.[373] Thus, where any damage arises as a result of the depositing or dumping of wastes, any person who deposited, dumped or imported the harmful waste shall be liable for damages.[374] Damage in this respect includes the death of or injury to any person (including any diseases and any impairment of physical or mental condition).[375] In this respect, the polluter-pays principle is embedded in Section 12(1) of the Harmful Wastes (Special Criminal Provisions) Act 1988.

(v) **Other National Legislation on Polluter-Pays Principle**

In the oil industry, the Environmental Guidelines and Standards for the Petroleum Industry in Nigeria (EGASPIN)[376] embodies the polluter-pays principle in para 8.1 where it provides that "a spiller shall be liable for the damage from a spill for which he is responsible."

The National Oil Spill Detection and Response Agency (Establishment) Act, (NOSDRA) 2006, as amended,[377] states that "an oil spiller is to report an oil spill to the Agency[378] in writing, by fax or electronic mail not later than 24 hours after the occurrence of an oil spill."[379] The spiller shall be responsible for the cleanup and "failure to clean up the impacted site, to all practical extent including action plan for remediation within two weeks of the occurrence of the spill in accordance with the **polluter pays principle** shall constitute an offence."[380]

In addition, under Section 31(1) of the NOSDRA Act 2006, in the exercise of its functions, the Agency (NOSDRA) may demand by requisition from any person or organisation, any available equipment, facilities or personnel which may assist in a speedy and effective cleaning and rescue operation during an oil spill disaster. Under Section 31(2), any person or organisation that: (a) wilfully obstructs or impedes the Agency or any person acting under the authority of the Agency in the exercise of any

---

[372] Ibid., s. 2. See, also, the provisions of ss. 3–5 of the Act on crimes committed in prosecution of common purpose, mode of execution of the crime and accessories after the fact.

[373] HWSCP Act (1988), s. 12.

[374] Ibid., s. 12(1).

[375] HWSCP Act (1988), s. 12(2).

[376] Department of Petroleum Resources (2002).

[377] National Oil Spill Detection and Response Agency, established under National Oil Spill Detection and Response Agency (Establishment) Act 2006, as amended (NOSDRA Act 2006), s. 6(2).

[378] Ibid., s. 6(1).

[379] Failure to report shall attract penalty in the sum of =N=2,000,000 for each day of failure to report the occurrence.

[380] The spiller on conviction shall be liable to a fine not exceeding =N=5,000,000 or to imprisonment for a term not exceeding two years or to both such fine and imprisonment. NOSDRA Act (2006), s. 6(3).

powers or duties under this Act; or (b) without reasonable excuse fails to: (i) render assistance or release any available equipment, facility or personnel required for cleaning and rescue operation or other oil spill disaster curtailment activities, or (ii) comply with a directive of the Agency, is guilty of an offence.[381] When this situation arises, "the Agency shall ensure that the Polluter provides reasonable compensation for loss or damage arising from the use of any equipment, facility or personnel required under the Act."[382]

4.7.4 Applications of the Polluter-Pays Principles by the Courts

How has the case on the polluter-pays principle been handled by the Nigerian Judiciary? Unfortunately, despite all these provisions no known case that is on the polluter-pays principle had been handled by the Judiciary in Nigeria. To fill this lacunae recourse is had to decisions from other common law jurisdictions such as India.[383]

The Judiciary in India has incorporated the polluter-pays principle as a part of the country's environmental law regime. This is evident from the judgments passed by the Supreme Court of India in the cases discussed below.

The application of the polluter-pays principle and the precautionary principle in its decisions started on a gradual note. First, the Supreme Court inexplicitly, applied the principles, especially the polluter-pays principle in the case of *M C Mehta v. Union of India*[384] in the year 1986. In that case, five chemical industries were producing H-acid (l-napthol-8-amino, 6-disciphonic acid). An *azo* dye and untreated toxic sludge were discharged into the open compound which, in due course of time, flowed through a canal across the entire area and the rainwater washed the sludge deep into the bowels of the earth. It caused pollution of river water and underground water up to 70 feet below the ground within a radius of seven miles of the village of Bichhari. It further left the fields of this area infertile. As a result of which, residents of Bichhari and nearby villages had to migrate to other places. The case was taken up by the Supreme Court of India on a petition from the Indian Council for Enviro-legal Action of Udaipur as a public interest petition.

The court while making a landmark judgement kept in mind that any principle adopted by it must be simple, practical and suited to the conditions prevailing in the country. It was declared by the court that "we have to evolve new principles and lay

[381] Such person shall be liable on conviction to a fine not exceeding =N=500,000.00 or imprisonment for a term of two years or to both such fine and imprisonment.

[382] NOSDRA Act (2006), s. 31(3).

[383] The choice of India is predicated on the fact that Nigeria and India have similar legal system, common law jurisdiction.

[384] AIR (1986) SC 1086.

down new norms, which would adequately deal with the new problems which arise in a highly industrialised economy."[385] The significance of this judgement in the words of Satish C. Shastri[386] lies in the:

> Court's formulation of the principle of the measure of liability of industry engaged in 'hazardous or inherently dangerous activities.' Such measure must be correlated to the magnitude and capacity of the enterprise. Secondly, the court directed the industry either to shift from the present location or evolve a green belt around it as a condition precedent to restart the industry. Further, the industry was asked to deposit a sum of Rs. 3500000/- in a bank and a guarantee of rupees 1500000/- with the court for compensation to be paid to one who can prove before the court of law that he suffered because of the Oleum gas leakage from the Sri Ram Food and Fertiliser Corporation. Thus, an innovative remedy was evolved by the Supreme Court of India in this case which was indirect recognition and application of the 'polluter pays principle'.

Thus, in the *Oleum Gas Leak* case *(M.C. Mehta v. Union of India)*,[387] the court laid down that an enterprise engaged in a hazardous or inherently dangerous industry which poses a potential threat to the health and safety of persons working in the factory and to those residing in the surrounding areas, owes an absolute and non-delegable duty to the community to ensure that no harm results to anyone on account of hazardous or inherently dangerous nature of the activity which it has undertaken. The enterprise is absolutely liable to compensate for such harm irrespective of all reasonable care taken on its account. The larger and more prosperous the enterprise, the greater must be the amount of compensation payable for the harm caused on account of an accident in the carrying on of the hazardous or inherently dangerous activity by the enterprise.

The position of the court in the *Oleum Gas Leak* case *(M.C. Mehta v. Union of India)*[388] was applied in the case of *Indian Council for Enviro-Legal Action v. Union of India.*[389] Here, the court held that once the activity carried on is hazardous or inherently dangerous, the person carrying on such activity is liable to make good the loss caused to any other person by his activity irrespective of the fact whether he took reasonable care while carrying on his activity. The rule is premised upon the very nature of the activity carried on.

The position of the precautionary principle and the polluter-pays principle were again raised by the Supreme Court of India in the case of *Vellore Citizens Welfare Forum v. Union of India.*[390] In that case, more than 550 tannery units were discharging untreated effluent, thereby, causing water pollution and land pollution in 59 villages of three districts. Of the two districts, 467 wells which were used for drinking and irrigation purposes were polluted. This created an acute shortage of potable water. Looking at such a grave state of affairs the court ordered the closure of

---

[385] M C Mehta v. Union of India (1986) at 1099 per Bhagwati, C.J.

[386] Shastri (1987), p. 1.

[387] AIR (1987) SC 1086.

[388] M.C. Mehta v. Union of India (1987).

[389] AIR (1996) 3 SCC 212.

[390] Vellore Citizens Welfare Forum v. Union of India (1996).

industries involved in the tannery business. It was suggested by the court that the Central Government should constitute an "authority" under Section 3(3) of the Environment (Protection) Act 1986 and such authority, shall, with the help of the expert opinion assess the loss to the ecology/environment in the affected area. After making a proper assessment, such an authority shall further determine the compensation to be recovered from the polluters as the cost of reversing the damaged environment, after giving the polluter an opportunity to be heard.

The court reiterated and declared in unequivocal terms that the precautionary principle and the polluter-pays principle are part of the environmental jurisprudence of this country. These principles have been accepted as a part of the law of the land as Article 21 of the Constitution of India guarantees the protection of life and personal liberty. There is also a constitutional mandate to protect and improve the environment under Articles 48-A and 51-A(g). These are also supported by other statutory provisions. The court also observed that this principle has also been accepted as part of the customary international law, therefore, it automatically becomes a part of the basic jurisprudence of the land.[391]

To this end, the court interpreted the meaning of the polluter-pays principle as the absolute liability for harm to the environment extends not only to compensate the victims of the pollution but also the cost of restoring the environmental degradation. Remediation of the damaged environment is part of the process of "Sustainable Development" and as such the polluter is liable to pay the cost to the individual sufferers as well as the cost of reversing the damaged ecology.

Arising from this interpretation of the meaning of the polluter-pays principle as absolute liability for harm to the environment in the case of *Vellore Citizens' Welfare Forum v. Union of India*[392] the Supreme Court wasted no time in holding in the case of *M C Mehta v. Kamal Nath & Ors*[393] that pollution is a civil wrong and is a tort committed against the community as a whole. Thus, any person guilty of causing pollution has to pay damages (compensation) for the restoration of the environment and ecology. Further, under the polluter-pays principle, it is not the role of the government to meet the costs involved in either prevention of such damage, or in carrying out remedial action, because the effect of this would be to shift the financial burden of the pollution incident to the taxpayer.[394]

In addition, the Supreme Court of India had also in the case of *AP Pollution Control Board v. Prof M. V. Nayudu*,[395] declared that the precautionary principle and the polluter-pays principle have become a part of the environmental law of the country.

To this end, looking at the widespread ramifications of the hazardous or inherently dangerous activities, persons or institutions would be held "liable absolutely,"

---

[391] Vellore Citizens Welfare Forum v. Union of India (1996).

[392] Ibid.

[393] AIR (1997)1 SCC 388.

[394] Ibid.

[395] AIR (1999) SCW 434.

although they have taken all reasonable care while carrying out such activity. The liability to compensate is twofold; one, to compensate the victims of pollution for inconvenience and health loss; and the other, to restore the environmental degradation viz., of the soil, underground water and the vegetation cover of that area. Such remediation of damaged environment is part of the process of "sustainable development." It is also to be noted that all this does not absolve a person from criminal liability.[396]

4.7.5 Making Polluter-Pays Principle More Effective in Pollution Prevention

The increased attention being paid to the polluter-pays principle results, in part, from the greater consideration being given to the relationship between environmental protection and economic development, as well as recent efforts to develop the use of economic instruments in environmental protection law and policy. However, certain fundamental issues may arise in respect of the adaptation and application of the principle.

The first concerns the extent of the pollution control costs which should be paid by the polluter. Although it seems clear that the principle includes costs of measures required by public authorities to prevent and control pollution, it is less clear whether the costs of decontamination, clean-up and reinstatement would be included.

The second issue concerns exceptions to the principle, particularly in relation to rules governing the granting of subsidies. In this regard, consideration should be given to the practice of the EC and account taken of the potential role of the WTO in determining the impact of the polluter-pays principle on its subsidy rules. This is in view of the decision in the *Canada v. Dow Chemical Canada (US- Chemical Tax* case)[397] where it was held that GATT rules on tax adjustment allow contracting parties to apply the polluter-pays principle but do not require it.

The take here is that the polluter-pays principle can be applied as a veritable tool in the protection of the environment if entrenched in environmental legislation and seriously enforced. To this end, the polluter-pays principle should be applied in making environmental damage a strict and absolute liability affair and that a polluter must of necessity pay for his action or activity that damaged the environment.

To make the application of the polluter-pays principle to achieve its objectives certain inclusion should be made in our environmental legislation. For instance, that:

1) Any person, whether natural or juristic, who undertakes an activity that causes or is likely to cause damage to the environment shall take all reasonable and practicable measures to prevent or minimise any resulting adverse effects to the

[396] Shastri (1987), p. 1.

[397] Canada v. Dow Chemical Canada ULC, December 2020, Tax Court, Case No. 2020 TCC 139.

environment. Therefore, where such person discharges or causes or permits the entry into the environment, of any contaminant in any amount, concentration or level in excess of that prescribed by any regulations made under any environmental law in force or stipulated by any environmental authorisation made pursuant to any law, shall be strictly and absolutely liable for his conduct.

2) Any person responsible for the contaminant or for the process involving the contaminant or who causes or permits a discharge that caused the environmental damage, shall:

   (a) Immediately notify any appropriate authority responsible for environmental protection or management of:

      (i) the discharge;
      (ii) the concentration, nature and amount of contaminant;
      (iii) the circumstances of the discharge;
      (iv) what action the person had taken or intends to take to restore the natural environment.

   (b) Be responsible for:

      (i) cleaning or clean-up cost, cost of assessment and damage control;
      (ii) restoring the air, land and water to the condition they were before the discharge or the full cost of remediation, restoration, reclamation and rehabilitation of the damaged environment to the condition it were before the damage.

   (c) Be liable to:

      (i) pay compensation to those who suffered loss or damage as a consequence of his action;
      (ii) pay for the cost of an independent investigation into the discharge.

   (d) Do everything practicable to preserve, for investigation, evidence of the effects of the discharge.

3) Where the pollution in issue resulted in the course of the polluter carrying out any act permitted by any environmental laws for the time being in force, or any regulations made under any extant environmental laws, or that the harm to the environment cannot reasonably be avoided, such person shall take all reasonable measures to ensure that the pollution or degradation is minimised and rectified. Liability shall arise where the polluter fails to commence, continue or complete the measures to minimise and rectify the pollution or degradation of the environment or fails to comply with a directive from the Agency or Authority charged with environmental protection or management, the Agency or Authority shall take all reasonable measures to remedy the situation and recover all costs of assessment, assessment and damage control from such person.

4) In the event of any contravention of any of the provisions of any extant environmental laws it is further suggested that the Agency or Authority charged with

environmental protection or management, shall make an order directed to one or more of the following:

a) any person responsible for the contaminant; any person responsible for the process involving the contaminant;
b) any person whose assistance is necessary and can aid in the prevention, elimination, or ameliorating of the adverse effects or restore the natural environment.

Such order shall require the person so ordered to take such action as may be specified in the order in respect of the prevention, diminution or amelioration of the adverse effects and restoration of the natural environment within such period as may be specified in the order.

5) Again, where damage to the environment was caused by a permit holder under any law the court may enquire on whether the person was negligent or gained a monetary advantage in the process. And where the court finds that the permit holder was negligent or gained a monetary advantage, the court shall order that the holder shall pay to Agency or Authority charged with environmental protection or management a fine equal to the amount gained, and if the action was commenced by a person who suffered a loss or damage, the court shall order that such amount as would be necessary to restore him to the position he was before the act complained of occurred, be paid to him.[398]

4.8 Summary

Principles point to particular decisions about legal obligations in particular circumstances. Environmental principles and concepts serve several purposes, most notably: legal and other implications are drawn from them by courts and tribunals in the interpretative process; and they provide a basis for negotiation and elaboration of future international environmental law; and in framing the debate for international environmental policy-making, these principles and concepts have also become increasingly important for discussions of trade and environment.

The sources of these principles stem from resolutions, recommendations and declarations issued by international organisations such as the United Nations Environment Programme (UNEP), the World Health Organisation (WHO) or the Organisation for Economic Co-Operation and Development (OECD). The international organisations have made important contributions to the development of international environmental principles. For instance, the acts adopted at the UNCED conference,

[398] In this situation, legal proceedings may be commenced by the agency or authority charged with environmental protection or management or by any person who suffered any loss or damage as a result of the act of the permit holder.

particularly Agenda 21 and the Rio Declaration on Environment and Development, have helped to form these various principles and concepts into an increasingly comprehensive set of environmental principles for guiding the international community toward sustainable development.

From the large body of international agreements and other acts, it is possible to discern general rules and principles that have broad, if not necessarily universal support and are frequently endorsed in practice and at times integrated into environmental legislation and some have found application by judicial authorities.

References

Access information on Multilateral Environmental Agreements (2020) Bamako Convention (1991). https://www.informea.org/en/treaties/bamako/text. Accessed on 18 June 2023

African Union (2003) Revised African Convention on the Conservation of Nature and Natural Resources. https://au.int/en/treaties/african-convention-conservation-nature-and-natural-resources-revised-version. Accessed on 7 August 2023

Allen CM et al (2018) Prioritising SDG targets: assessing baselines, gaps and inter linkages. Sustain Sci 14(2):21–438. https://doi.org/10.1007/s11625-018-0596-81

An Architect's Guide to Designing Sustainability (2020). http://www.comarchitect.org/wp-content/architectsguide/integrating_environment_and_development_in_decision_making.htm. Accessed on 14 June 2023

Barry B (1999) Sustainability and intergenerational justice. In: Andrew Dobson A (ed) Fairness and futurity. Oxford University Press, Oxford

Beckerman W (1994) 'Sustainable development': is it a useful concept? Environ Values 3(3): 191–209. https://doi.org/10.3197/096327194776679700

Beder S (2000) Costing the earth: equity, sustainable development and environmental economics. New Zealand J Environ Law 4:227–243

Bell S, McGillivray D (2001) Environmental law, 5th edn. Blackstone, London

Bell S, McGillivray D (2006) Ball and Bell on environmental law: the law and policy relating to the protection of the environment, 6th edn. Blackstone, London

Birne PW, Boyle AE (2002) International law and the environment, 2nd edn. Oxford University, Oxford

Blewitt J (2014) Understanding sustainable development, 2nd edn. Routledge, London

Brack D (2002) The Appellate Body rulings in the Shrimp/Turtle Case: a new legal baseline for the trade and environmental debate. Columbia J Environ Law 27:491

Bührs T (2009) Environmental integration: our common challenge. Sunny, London

Department of Petroleum Resources (2002) Environmental Guidelines and Standards For The Petroleum Industry in Nigeria (EGASPIN) 1991, Revised Edition 2002. https://ngfcp.dpr.gov.ng/media/1066/dprs-egaspin-2002-revised-edition.pdf. Accessed on 16 June 2023

Dworkin R (1985) Taking rights seriously in Lord Lloyd et al.: introduction to jurisprudence, 5th edn. ELBS, London

Ecolex (2020) Convention on Third Party Liability in the Field of Nuclear Energy. https://www.ecolex.org/details/treaty/convention-on-third-party-liability-in-the-field-of-nuclear-energy-tre-000435/. Accessed on 19 June 2023

Finn D (2009) Our uncertain future: can good planning create sustainable communities? University of Illinois, Champaign-Urbana USA

Kiss A, Shelton D (2007) Guide to international environmental law. Martinus Nijhoff, Berlin

Kramer L (1990) EEC Treaty and Environmental Protection. Sweet and Maxwell, London

Macallister MIH (2020) Seals, empires and mass politics: the 1893 Fur Seal Arbitration. Int Hist Rev 42(6):1192–1209. https://doi.org/10.1080/07075332.2019.1689519

McIntyre O, Mosedale T (1997) The precautionary principle as norm of customary international law. J Environ Law 9(2):221–241

Mensah J (2019) Sustainable development: meaning, history, principles, pillars, and implications for human action: literature review. Cogent Soc Sci 5(1):75. https://doi.org/10.1080/23311886.2019.1653531. Accessed on 1 July 2023

Onyeabor EU (2011) Precautionary principles and environmental management and control: how far so far in international environmental law? Nigerian J Pet Nat Gas Environ Law (NJPNREL) 3(1):60. ISBN 2006 6791

Onyeabor EU et al (2017) Re-fortifying polluter-pays principle in addressing environmental damage in Nigeria. UNIPORT Law Rev 1:186

Organisation for Economic Co-Operation and Development (OECD) (1975) The polluter pays principle: definition, analysis and implementation. (OECD Publications, Paris, 20 OECD, C (72)128, reprinted in OECD (1975), 259

Organisation for Economic Co-Operation and Development (OECD) (1995) Environmental principles and concepts. OECD Publications, Paris

Organisation for Economic Co-Operation and Development (OECD) (2016) Recommendation of the Council on the Use of Economic Instruments in Environmental Policy (OECD Publications, Paris, [C (90)177/FINAL] https://legalinstruments.oecd.org/en/instruments/OECD-LEGAL-0434. Accessed on 1 July 2023

Organisation of African, Caribbean and Pacific States (2020) Lome Convention. http://www.acp.int/content/lome-convention. Accessed on 18 May 2023

Peoples Agenda 21 (2020) Integrating environment and development in decision making for the highest good of all. https://peoplesagenda21.com/integrating-environment-and-development-in-decision-making/. Accessed on 14 June 2023

Rana SS & Co (2017) "India: Polluter Pays Principle" 10 November 2017. https://www.lexology.com/library/detail.aspx?g=c832a88c-7f8c-4628-bb96-c3e7d9189b2d. Accessed on 28 June 2023

Robert van Lierop (1991) Permanent Representative of Vanuatu to the UN, Statement to the Plenary Session of the INC/FCCC, 5th February, 1991 at 3, http://www.un.org. Accessed 25 May 2023

Sachs JD (2015) The age of sustainable development. Columbia University, New York. ISBN 9780231173155

Sadeleer ND (2002) Environmental principles: from political slogans to legal principles. Oxford University, Oxford

Sands P (2003) Principles of international environmental law, 2nd edn. Cambridge University, Cambridge

Savaresi A (2016) The Paris agreement: a new beginning? J Energy Nat Res Law 34(1):16–26, https://doi.org/10.1080/02646811.2016.1133983

Shastri SC (1987) The Polluter Pays Principle and the Supreme Court of India. J Indian Law Inst 42:1

Summer JK, Smith LM (2014) The role of social and intergenerational equity in making changes in human well-being sustainable. Ambio 43(6):718–728. https://doi.org/10.1007/s13280-013-0483-6. Published online on 9 January 2014. https://www.ncbi.nlm.nih.gov/pmc/Articles/PMC4165836/. Accessed on 1 July 2023

Thornton J, Beckwith S (2004) Environmental law, 2nd edn. Sweet and Maxwell, London

UNGA (1962) Permanent Sovereignty Over Natural Resources. UNGA Resolution 1803 (XVII) (14 December 1962). http://www.worldlii.org/int/other/UNGA/1962/60.pdf. Accessed on 10 May 2023

UNGA (1971) Measures for protecting and enhancing the environment. UNGA Resolution 2849 (XXVI) (1971) 15 December 1972, A/RES/3000. https://www.refworld.org/docid/3b00f1cb38.html. Accessed on 9 May 2023

UNGA (1972) Co-operation between States in the field of Environment, UNGA Resolution 2849 (XXVI) (15 December 1972). http://www.worldlii.org/int/other/UNGA/1972/92.pdf. Accessed on 19 May 2023

UNGA (1989) Resolution on the Historical Responsibility of States for the Protection of Nature for the Benefit of Present and Future Generations (1980), G.A. Res. 8, 35 UN GAOR Supp. (No.48), UN Document A/RES/35/8; Declaration of the Hague, March 11, 1989; United Nations Framework Convention on Climate Change (1992), UN Document No. A/AC.237/18 (Part II)/Add.1

UNGA (1994) "Request for an advisory opinion from the International Court of Justice on the legality of the threat or use of nuclear weapons," Request for an advisory opinion from the International Court of Justice on the legality of the threat or use of nuclear weapons," Resolution A/RES/49/75K (15 December 1994). https://research.un.org/en/docs/ga/quick/regular/49. Accessed on 19 May 2023

United Nations (1995) Agreement on the Application of Sanitary and Phytosanitary Measures (SPS Agreement)1995, Final Act Embodying the Results of the Uruguay Round of Multilateral Trade Negotiations, Legal Instruments-Results of the Uruguay Round vol 1, Annex 2 A, 1867 UN Treaty Ser 493 (1995). http://www.un.org/documents. Accessed on 16 June 2023

United Nations (2020) Information Portal on Multilateral Environmental Agreements: Principles And Concepts Of International Environmental Law (Part II). https://globalpact.informea.org/. Accessed on 7 May 2023

United Nations Educational and Cultural Organisation (UNESCO) (2020) What is Sustainable Development? https://en.unesco.org/themes/education-sustainable-development/what-is-esd/sd#:~:text=Sustainable%20development. Accessed on 4 June 2023

United Nations Environment Programme (UNEP) (2020a) Vienna Convention. https://ozone.unep.org/treaties/vienna-convention/Articles/preamble. Accessed on 16 June 2023

United Nations Environment Programme (UNEP) (2020b) Montreal Protocol. https://ozone.unep.org/treaties/montreal-protocol. Accessed on 16 June 2023

United Nations Framework Convention on Climate Change (UNFCCC) (2016) Adoption of the Paris Agreement, Draft decision -/CP.21, FCCC/CP/2015/L.9/Rev.1, Conference of the Parties Twenty-first session Paris, 30 November to 11 December 2015. https://unfccc.int/process-and-meetings/the-paris-agreement/the-paris-agreement. Accessed on 3 May 2023

United Nations General Assembly (UNGA) (1961) Report of the United Nations Scientific Committee on the Effect of Atomic Radiation, Resolution 1629 (XVI) (27 October 1961). http://www.worldlii.org/int/other/UNGA/1961/. Accessed on 19 May 2023

United Nations Global Compact (2020). http://www.unglobalcompact.org/portal. Accessed on 25 June 2023

Venn A (2018) Social justice and climate change. In: Letcher TM (ed) Managing global warming: an interface of technology and human issues. Elsevier, London

Weiss EB (2008) Climate change, intergenerational equity and international law. Vermont J Environ Law 9:615–627, at 617. https://papers.ssrn.com/sol3/papers.cfm?abstract_id=2734420. Accessed on 10 May 2023

World Commission on Environment and Development (WECD) (1987) Report of the World Commission on Environment and Development: Our Common Future, 1987. https://sustainabledevelopment.un.org/content/documents/5987our-common-future.pdf. Accessed on 5 July 2023

World Trade Organization (WTO) (1998) Report of the Appellate Body, EC Measures Concerning Meat and Meat Products (Hormones) 1 26, WTO Doc No WT/DS26/AB/R, WT/DS48/AB/R (16 January 1998) (EC Hormones), at 253. https://www.wto.org/english/tratop_e/dispu_e/cases_e/ds26_e.htm. Accessed on 16 June 2023

WTO (2003) Report of the Pane, European Communities-Measures Affecting the Approval and Marketing of Biotech Products 4.290-4.291, WTO Doc No WT/DS291 /R. https://www.wto.org/english/tratop_e/dispu_e/cases_e/ds26_e.htm. Accessed on 16 June 2023

WTO (2008) Report of the Appellate Body, United States-Continued Suspension of Obligations in the EC-Hormones Dispute 85, WTO Doc No WT/DS320/AB/R (16 October 2008) (US-Continued Suspension). https://www.wto.org/english/tratop_e/dispu_e/cases_e/ds26_e.htm. Accessed on 16 June 2023
WTO (2021) Dispute Selection Index 2021. https://www.wto.org/english/tratop_e/dispu_e/dispu_agreements_index_e.htm?id=A19#selected_agreement. Accessed on 10 May 2023

Chapter 5
Tenets of Environmental Procedural Rights

Abstract The basis for environmental procedural rights is envisaged in a situation where the members of the public should not only have access to information about the environmental effects of a proposed project within their vicinity but also participate in shaping not only the environmental impact statement (EIS), but also contributing on possible remedial measures against possible impacts arising from a proposed project that may likely have significant environmental impact. In addition, members of the public as stakeholders are enabled to participate in the making of legislation on environment that may likely impact on their lives. Where these, access to information and public participation in decision making on environmental matters are denied, the members of the public should have access to justice. The focus of this chapter is on the major pillars of environmental procedural rights. These rights encapsulated as tenets of environmental procedural rights are discussed subsequently. They are: (i) access to information; (ii) public participation in decision making on environmental matters and (iii) access to justice.

5.1 Introduction

The main pillars of environmental procedural rights are: access to information, public participation and access to justice. These are guiding principles in achieving purposeful environmental protection. It should be noted that these three pillars depend on each other to enhance environmental procedural rights and environmental protection in general. The essence of these pillars was succinctly captured in Principle 10 of the Rio Declaration on Environment and Development (Rio Declaration) 1992.[1] It provides as follows:

> Environmental issues are best handled with the participation of all concerned citizens, at the relevant level. At the national level, each individual shall have appropriate access to information concerning the environment that is held by public authorities, including information on hazardous materials and activities in their communities, and the opportunity to participate in decision-making processes. States shall facilitate and encourage public

[1] United Nations (2020).

E. Onyeabor, *Environmental Law*, https://doi.org/10.1007/978-3-031-68956-7_5

awareness and participation by making information widely available. Effective access to judicial and administrative proceedings, including redress and remedy, shall be provided.

Principle 10, therefore, encapsulates these three environmental procedural rights pillars: access to information; public participation; and access to judicial and administrative proceedings in environmental matters. It is significant as the first clear global expression of these concepts together and provides an international benchmark against which the compatibility of national standards could be compared. It also foresaw the creation of new procedural rights that could be granted to individuals through international law and exercised at the national and possibly international level.[2]

5.2 Access to Environmental Information

5.2.1 Introduction

Environmental information means any information in written, visual, aural, electronic or any other material form.[3] The first pillar on environmental procedural rights, access to environmental information, sets rules and requirements for governments to disclose environmental and other relevant information to the public. The environmental information sought may be on:

a) The state of elements of the environment, such as air and atmosphere, water, soil, land, landscape and natural sites, biological diversity and its components, including genetically modified organisms, and the interaction among these elements.[4]
b) Factors, such as substances, energy, noise and radiation, and activities or measures, including administrative measures, environmental agreements, policies, legislation, plans and programmes, affecting or likely to affect the elements of the environment within the scope of subparagraph (a) above, and cost-benefit and other economic analyses and assumptions used in environmental decision-making.[5]
c) The state of human health and safety, conditions of human life, cultural sites and built structures, since they are or may be affected by the state of the elements of the environment or, through these elements, by the factors, activities or measures referred to in subparagraph (b) above.[6]

---

[2] Sands (2000), p. 99.

[3] European Union (1998), Aarhus Convention (1998) Art. 2, para 3.

[4] Aarhus Convention (1998), Art. 2, para 3(a).

[5] Ibid., Art. 2, para 3(b).

[6] Ibid., Art. 2, para 3(c).

Many environmental treaties have provisions for access to information among parties which includes obligations for parties to make government-held information accessible to members of the public. Many of these treaties have their basis in Principle 10 of the Rio Declaration on Environment and Development (Rio Declaration), which, inter alia, declares that "at the national level, each individual shall have appropriate access to information concerning the environment that is held by public authorities, including information on hazardous materials and activities in their communities."

Such treaties that have elements of access to information principles include global agreements, such as the Stockholm Convention on Persistent Organic Pollutants (Stockholm Convention),[7] the Rotterdam Convention on Prior Informed Consent, (Rotterdam Convention)1998 (as reversed in 2017),[8] Convention on Access to Information, Public Participation in Decision-Making and Access to Justice in Environmental Matters (Aarhus Convention) 1998[9] and the Cartagena Protocol on Biosafety to the Convention on Biological Diversity (Cartagena Protocol on Biosafety) 2000. The Cartagena Protocol on Biosafety 2000 requires parties to provide access to information on living modified organisms identified by the Protocol that may be imported.[10] Access to information forming part of the environmental procedural rights was discussed under:

1) International legal instruments
2) Domestic legislation

5.2.2 *Access to Information Under International Legal Instruments*

Discussions were based on the following international legal instruments:

a) Convention on Access to Information, Public Participation in Decision-Making and Access to Justice in Environmental Matters (Aarhus Convention) 1998
b) European Union Directive on Environmental Impact Assessment EIA Directive 2014/52/EU,[11] and
c) National Environmental Policy Act of the United States of America (NEPA) 1969

---

[7] Stockholm Convention (2001), para g.

[8] Rotterdam Convention (1998), Art. 15 para 2.

[9] Aarhus Convention (1998) Arts. 4 and 5.

[10] Cartagena Protocol on Biosafety (2000), Art. 23.

[11] European Union (2014) EIA Directive 2014/52/EU.

5.2.2.1 Access to Information Under Aarhus Convention

Of major relevance in this discourse are the provisions of the Convention on Access to Information, Public Participation in Decision-Making and Access to Justice in Environmental Matters (Aarhus Convention) 1998. The Aarhus Convention was adopted at the Fourth "Environment for Europe" Ministerial Conference in Aarhus, Denmark, on 25 June 1998. It entered into force on 30 October 2001.[12] Under the Aarhus Convention, access to information is of two folds: Access to environmental information[13] and collection and dissemination of environmental information.[14]

Article 4 of the Aarhus Convention 1998 sets out a framework through which members of the public can gain access to environmental information from public authorities, and in some cases, from private parties. Once a member of the public has requested for environmental information, Article 4 establishes criteria and procedures for providing or refusing to provide such information. Under the Convention, all persons have the right of access to such information.

The Aarhus Convention 1998 sets out a general rule of freedom of access to information. Parties are required to establish a system where a member of the public can request for environmental information from a public authority and receive that information within a reasonable amount of time. This general rule is protected by safeguards concerning the timing of responses, the conditions for refusals and the documentation of the process in writing. In addition, Article 9, para 1 of the Convention, provides for the review of information requests made under Article 4 of the Convention.

Most of the provisions in Article 4 are requirements that parties and public authorities must meet. However, paras 3 and 4[15] outline the circumstances when a party *may* allow public authorities to refuse a request for information. Indeed, paras 3 and 4 outline the only circumstances under which exceptions to the general rule apply. The Convention does not require parties to adopt these optional provisions and, even if the exceptions are adopted, parties may nevertheless allow the public authority to exercise discretion to provide the information requested. Moreover, if the information exempted from disclosure can be separated, parties are required to make available the remainder of the requested environmental information. To enable the public to request and receive environmental information from public authorities, Article 4 enjoins parties to:

i) Create an access to environmental information law or regulation
ii) Let the public know which public authority holds which type of information
iii) Have a system to help the public formulate properly directed requests
iv) Set clear standards for time limits

[12] The Convention has 47 parties from the United Nations Economic Commission for Europe (ECE) region, which includes 46 countries plus the European Union (EU).

[13] Aarhus Convention (1998), Art. 4.

[14] Ibid., Art. 5.

[15] Ibid., Art. 4.

v) Create a schedule for charges
vi) Clearly define any exemptions

To facilitate the implementation of this aspect of the Convention,[16] it sets out time limits for public authorities to respond and supply the requested information, which should be as soon as possible, but with a general time limit, at the latest one month, but if the document is voluminous and complex, possible extension, to two months, but the custodian must give reasons.[17] Under the Convention,[18] optional grounds for refusing disclosure are provided. For instance, where the requested information is not held by a public authority or request "manifestly unreasonable" or "too general" or requested material in the course of completion or concerns internal communications or may infringe intellectual property rights.[19] If disclosure would adversely affect listed public interests, the Convention sets out optional grounds for refusing disclosure.[20] However, such grounds are to be interpreted in a restrictive way, taking into account public interest in disclosure and whether the information relates to emissions into the environment.

Although the Convention does not provide specific guidance on how to balance the "public interest," in *Commission v. the Netherlands*,[21] the European Court of Justice (ECJ) held that Article 4 of Directive 2003/4/EC 2003 should be interpreted to require that the balancing exercise it prescribes between the public interest served by the disclosure of environmental information and the specific interest served by a refusal to disclose must be carried out in each individual case submitted to the competent authorities, even if the national legislature were by a general provision to determine criteria to facilitate that comparative assessment of the interests involved.

In the event of refusal to provide the information requested, such refusal shall be in writing, if the information request was in writing or if the applicant so requests, reasons for refusal to be stated and information on the review procedure to be provided. Such refusal must be as soon as possible and at the latest one month, unless the complexity of information justifies an extension to two months, in which case notice, including reasons, must be given.[22]

A public authority that cannot respond to a request for information because it does not hold the information requested is mandated to inform the applicant which public

---

[16] Access to environmental information.

[17] Aarhus Convention (1998), Art. 4, para 2.

[18] Ibid., Art. 4, para 3.

[19] Such as copyright, patent, trademark (including geographical indications) and trade secret. Sui generis forms include, inter alia, plant breeders' rights, database protection and industrial designs. Generally, patents protect novel ideas or inventions, copyrights protect original expressions (art, literature, music, etc.), trademarks and geographical indications protect symbols and names used in commerce and trade secrets protect proprietary business information of all kinds from improper acquisition and use.

[20] Aarhus Convention (1998), Art. 4, para 4.

[21] Case C-266/09, Judgement of the Court (Fourth Chamber) of 16 December 2010.

[22] Aarhus Convention (1998), Art. 4, para 7.

authority does hold the information, or to transfer the request to that authority and inform the applicant. In this respect, the public authority shall inform the applicant which public authority holds the information requested, or transfer the information request to that public authority and inform the applicant.[23]

Furthermore, a "request" can be any communication by a member of the public to a public authority asking for environmental information. The Convention[24] does not specify the form of the request, thus, implying that any request meeting the requirements of Article 4, whether oral or written, will be considered to be such under the Convention. In addition, under the Convention, public authorities must not impose any condition for supplying information that requires the applicant to state the reason he or she wants the information or how he or she intends to use it. Requests cannot be rejected because the applicant does not have an interest in the information.

Again, under Article 4, members of the public may request information in a specific form, such as paper, electronic media, videotape, recording, etc. In general, the public authority must honour the request for a specific form. What this means is that public authorities must provide copies of documents when requested, rather than simply providing the opportunity to examine documents. In addition, some applicants may prefer to examine the original documentation rather than receive copies. If they so request, public authorities must allow them to do so, subject to para 1(b)(i) and (ii). Under Article 4, para 1(b)(i), the public authority may decide on another form than the one requested if it is "reasonable." In any case, the public authority must state its reasons.[25]

A second exception is that the public authority is not required to give the information in the form requested if it is already publicly available in another form, such as in a government-published book that may be found in a public library. Instead, the public authority may refer to or give the already publicly available form. Clearly, the accessibility of the publicly available version of the information should be taken into account.[26]

However, the implementation standards set in Article 3, para 1 of the Convention make it clear that access to information should be effective in practice.[27] In addition, "another form" means that the available information is the functional equivalent of the form requested, not a summary; and that the information should be available in its entirety.[28]

In the end, each party may allow its public authorities to make a charge for supplying information, but such charge shall not exceed a reasonable amount. Public authorities intending to make such a charge for supplying information shall make

[23] Ibid., Art. 4, para 5.

[24] Ibid.

[25] Ebbesson et al. (2014), p. 80.

[26] Ibid.

[27] This means that the information is easily accessible to the members of the public requesting the information.

[28] Ebbesson et al. (2014), p. 81.

available to applicants a schedule of charges that may be levied, indicating the circumstances in which they may be levied or waived and when the supply of information is conditional on the advance payment of such a charge.[29]

Akin to access to information another aspect of access to environmental information under the Aarhus Convention is the Collection and dissemination of environmental information under Article 5. This article requires a system through which public authorities collect environmental information and actively disseminate it to the public without request. It requires record-keeping and reporting by public authorities and from operators to public authorities, making lists, registers and files publicly accessible free of charge, developing environmental information offices and identifying individual points of contact, using electronic databases and the Internet and creating incentives for operators to give information directly to the public.

Whereas Article 4 applies to "environmental information" generally, Article 5 contains obligations for specific categories of information. This includes, inter alia, information relevant to public authorities' functions, information about proposed and existing activities that may significantly affect the environment, information in times of emergencies, information on the state of the environment, product information, pollutant release and transfer information, information about laws, programmes, policies, agreements and other documents relating to the environment and information about how to get the information.

Article 5, para 1 (a), requires public authorities to possess and update environmental information[30] relevant to their functions, establish mandatory systems so that there is an adequate flow of information to public authorities about proposed and existing activities that may significantly affect the environment, and in the event of any imminent threat to human health or the environment, whether caused by human activities or due to natural causes, all information which could enable the public to take measures to prevent or mitigate harm arising from the threat and is held by a public authority is disseminated immediately and without delay to members of the public who may be affected.[31] Though the Convention does not give much guidance on how to implement this requirement it is suggested that parties can consider establishing systems that ensure a regular flow of information from operators, monitoring systems, researchers and others to the responsible public authorities.[32]

Specifically, Article 5, para 1(c), requires public authorities to inform the public in the event of environmental emergencies. Its requirement to disseminate information is triggered by any "imminent threat" to human health or the environment. This means that actual harm does not have to occur for the immediate dissemination of information to be required. The Convention does not distinguish between threats caused by human activities or by natural causes: both are treated with equal weight.

---

[29] Aarhus Convention (1998), Art. 4, para 8.

[30] As defined under the Aarhus Convention (1998), Art. 2, para 3.

[31] Aarhus Convention (1998), Art. 5, para 1(b) and (c).

[32] Ebbesson et al. (2014), p. 97.

The Convention also gives equal weight to whether the object of the threat is human health or the environment.[33]

Under the Convention, the information that public authorities must release includes all information that could enable the public to take measures to prevent or lessen harm arising from the threat. Information to enable the public to take preventive or mitigation measures can, inter alia, include safety recommendations, predictions about how the threat could develop, results of investigations and reporting on remedial and preventive actions taken. This aspect of the Convention is important especially when a new project is set to be commenced or through an environmental audit of an existing facility new threat of harm to the environment and human life may suffice. In this respect, the public authority must disseminate the information immediately.

Dissemination without delay can help save lives and prevent damage in situations involving an imminent threat to human health or the environment. This position was emphasised by the ECHR in 1998 in the case of *Guerra v. Italy*.[34] In that case, the Italian government had neglected to release essential information that would have enabled citizens to assess the risks they and their families might run into if they continued to live in their present location and were particularly exposed to danger from accidents at a local fertiliser production factory. The ECHR held that, by failing to provide timely information, the state did not fulfil its obligation to secure the applicant's right to respect for their private and family life.[35]

In another development, the Court of Appeal (UK) on 31 July 2006, held in the case of *David Edwards and Lilian Pallikaropoulos v. The Environment Agency, The First Secretary of State, Secretary of State for the Environment Food and Rural Affairs-and- Cemex UK Cement Limited (formerly Rugby Limited) (Interested Party) (David Edwards and Lilian Pallikaropoulos v. The Environment Agency and Ors)*[36] that the non-disclosure of reports held by a public authority containing information about the projected emissions from a cement factory that intended to change its processes to include the burning of waste tyres, left the public in a state of ignorance, until the agency's grant of the permit, regarding the full extent of the low-level emissions of dust and their possible impact on the environment. The court was of the view that such information was potentially material to the agency's decision and to the members of the public who were seeking to influence it. The court held that the failure of the agency to disclose it at the time was a breach of its common law duty of fairness to disclose it.[37]

To facilitate implementation of the dissemination of information requirement it will be pertinent to designate which public authority is responsible for the

[33] Ebbesson et al. (2014), p. 97.

[34] Application No. 14967/89, ECHR, Judgement of 19 February 1998.

[35] Guerra v. Italy (1998), para 60.

[36] 2006 EWCA Civ. 877.

[37] David Edwards and Lilian Pallikaropoulos v. The Environment Agency and Ors (2006) EWCA Civ. 877.

dissemination and which type of information and in what circumstances. To this end, the Aarhus Convention 1998 sets a minimum obligation to disseminate the information to members of the public who may be affected by the imminent threat, though, beyond this, public authorities may distribute the information as widely as they wish. In some cases, members of the public who may be affected may include the entire country, in others it may include members of the public in neighbouring countries, yet in others, it may be more localised to a specific region. The use of the word "may" indicates that there need only be a reasonable possibility that members of the public could be affected for the public authority to be obliged to inform them.[38]

Article 5, para 2(a) of the Convention, provides one example of the type of information covered under the article. Article 5, para 2, covers not only environmental information, but also information about how best to access environmental information. The reason for this is that the public will have much better access to environmental information if it knows what type of information is held, where it is held, the criteria for obtaining it, if any, and the procedures for obtaining it. Under the Convention, the information must be sufficient, or complete enough to ensure that it helps the public to effectively gain access to information. To achieve this, the public authority establishes and maintains practical arrangements such as publicly accessible lists, registers or files.

5.2.2.2 Access to Information Under European Union Directive on Environmental Impact Assessment

The European Union Directive on Environmental Impact Assessment (EU DIRECTIVES on EIA)[39] on the other hand provides that to strengthen public access to information and transparency, timely environmental information on the implementation of this Directive should also be accessible in electronic format. Member States should therefore establish at least a central portal or points of access, at the appropriate administrative level, that allow the public to access that information easily and effectively.[40]

---

[38] Ebbesson et al. (2014).

[39] European Union (2014).

[40] European Union (2014), Preamble, para 18.

5.2.2.3 Access to Information Under United States of America (USA) National Environmental Policy Act[41] (NEPA) 1969, as Amended

Under the United States of America's legislation, the National Environmental Policy Act (NEPA)1969,[42] federal agencies are directed to prepare publicly available detailed statement with every proposal for legislation or major Federal action significantly affecting the human environment. Statements must include:

i) Environmental impacts of proposed action
ii) Unavoidable adverse impacts of the proposal
iii) Alternatives to the proposed action
iv) Relationship between local short-term uses versus maintenance and enhancements of long-term productivity
v) Irreversible/irretrievable commitments of resources

5.2.3 Access to Information Under Domestic Legislation

Discussions under this sub-head were centred on:

i) Environmental Impact Assessment Act (EIA Act) of Nigeria 1992[43]
ii) Freedom of Information Act (FOI Act) of Nigeria 2011

5.2.3.1 Access to Information Under the Environmental Impact Assessment Act (EIA Act)

The EIA Act 1992 provides for the conduct of an environmental impact assessment of a proposed project, whether public or private.[44] The Act further requires that the proponent must, where the project falls under the mandatory list,[45] or is likely to have a significant environmental impact.[46] In addition, the proponent shall submit to

[41] NEPA (1969), as amended.
[42] Ibid., s. 102(2)(c).
[43] Cap E12 Laws of the Federation of Nigeria (LFN) 2004.
[44] EIA Act (1992), s. 2.
[45] Ibid., s. 12.
[46] Ibid., s. 18.

the Agency[47] an Environmental Impact Statement (EIS) on the project.[48] Under the EIA Act 1992, the Agency's decision on any proposed activity subject to environmental impact assessment shall: be in writing; state the reason therefore; and include the provisions, if any, to prevent, reduce or instigate damage to the environment.[49] Such report of the Agency shall be made available to any interested person or group,[50] and if no interested person or group requests for the report, it shall be the duty of the Agency to publish its decision in a manner by which members of the public or persons interested in the activity shall be notified.[51]

When information provided as part of an environmental impact assessment indicates that the environment within another state in the Federation or a local government area is likely to be significantly affected by a proposed activity, the state or the local government area in which the activity is being planned, shall, to the extent possible: notify the potentially affected state or local government of the proposed activity; transmit to the affected state or local government area any relevant information of the environmental impact assessment; and enter into timely consultations with the affected state or local government.[52]

Where the Agency receives a screening report and the Agency believes that the report could be used as a method in conducting screening of other projects within the same class, the Agency may declare the report to be a class screening report, any declaration made under subsection (1) of this Act shall be published in the Gazette and the screening report to which it relates shall be made available to the public at the registry maintained by the Agency.[53]

After receiving a mandatory study report in respect of a project, the Agency shall, in any manner it considers appropriate, publish in a notice setting out the following information: (a) the date on which the mandatory study report shall be available to the public; (b) the place at which copies of the report may be obtained and (c) the deadline and address for filing comments on the conclusions and recommendations

---

[47] Under the EIA Act (1992), s. 61, the Agency means the Federal Environmental Protection Agency established by the Federal Environmental Protection Agency (Establishment) Act 1988, now repealed by the National Environmental Standards Regulation and Enforcement Agency (Establishment) Act (NESREA Act), s. 37. A *lacuna* was left as a result. However, by the decision of the Court of Appeal (Kaduna Division) in the case of Helios Towers Nig. Ltd v. NESREA and Kaduna State Environmental Protection Agency. CA/K/123/2010 delivered on the 10th day of December 2014. The court while interpreting the purport of EIA Act, s. 61 and citing other laws held that NESREA should be regarded as the Agency meant in the EIA Act, s. 61. Thus, the Agency herein referred to means the National Environmental Standards Regulation and Enforcement Agency, established under the National Environmental Standards Regulation and Enforcement Agency (Establishment) Act (NESREA Act) 2007, s. 1.

[48] EIA Act (1992), s. 4.

[49] Ibid., s. 9(1).

[50] Ibid., s. 9(2).

[51] Ibid., s. 9(3).

[52] Ibid., s. 11.

[53] EIA Act (1992), s. 19(2).

of the report.[54] On receiving a report submitted by a mediator or a review panel, the Agency shall make the report available to the public in any manner the Council considers appropriate and shall advise the public that the report is available.[55]

Furthermore, to facilitate public access to records relating to environmental assessments, a public registry shall be established and operated under the provisions of this Act in respect of every project for which an environmental assessment is conducted.[56] The public registry in respect of a project shall be maintained by the Agency, from the commencement of the environmental assessment until any follow-up programme in respect of the project is completed; and where the project is referred to mediation or a review panel by the Agency, from the appointment of the mediator or the members of the review panel until the report of the mediator or review panel is submitted to the Agency or the Secretary to the Government of the Federation as the case may be.[57] The public registry shall contain all records and information produced, collected or submitted with respect to the environmental assessment of the project, including: (a) any report relating to the assessment; (b) any comments filed by the public in relation to the assessment; and (c) any record prepared by the Agency for Section 35 of the EIA Act 1992.[58]

However, the public registry in issue shall contain a record if the record falls within one of the following categories:

a) records that have otherwise been made available to the public carrying out the assessment under this Act and any additional records, that have otherwise been made publicly available;
b) a record or part of a record that the Agency, in the case of a record in its possession, or any other Ministry or government agency, determines would have been disclosed to the public if a request had been made in respect of that record at the time the record was filed with the registry, including any record that would be disclosed in the public interest;
c) any record or part of a record, except a record or part containing third party information, if the President in the case of a record in the Agency's possession, or the President believes on reasonable grounds that its disclosure would be in the public interest because it is required for the public to participate effectively in the assessment.[59]

It should be noted that under the duty to provide information, no civil or criminal proceedings shall lie against the Agency, or against any person acting on behalf of or under the direction of the Agency, and no proceedings shall lie against the state or any of its agencies, for the disclosure in good faith of any record or any part of a

---

[54] Ibid., s. 24(1).

[55] Ibid., s. 38.

[56] Ibid., s. 55(1).

[57] Ibid., s. 55(2).

[58] Ibid., s. 55(3), Section 35 of the Act refers to the appointment of review panel.

[59] EIA Act (1992), ibid., s. 55(4)(a)–(c).

record under the Act, for any consequences that flow from that disclosure and for failure to give any notice if reasonable care is taken to give the required notice.[60] This by implication includes disclosure of third-party information.

Under the EIA Act 1992[61] "third party information" means (a) trade secrets of a third party; (b) financial, commercial, scientific or technical information that is confidential information supplied to a government institution by a third party and is treated consistently in a confidential manner by the third party; (c) information, the disclosure of which could reasonably be expected to result in material financial loss or gain to, or could reasonably be expected to prejudice the competitive position of a third party; and (d) information, the disclosure of which could reasonably be expected to interfere with contractual or other negotiations of a third party.

5.2.3.2 Access to Information Under the Freedom of Information Act (FOI Act) of Nigeria 2011[62]

Besides the provisions of the EIA Act 1992, the Freedom of Information Act (FOI Act) 2011 has some general provisions on access to information. The purpose of the Act is aptly captured in its preamble as follows:

> An Act to make Public Records and Information more freely available; provide for public access to public records and information, protect public records and information to the extent consistent with the public interest and the protection of personal privacy, protect serving public officers from adverse consequences for disclosing certain kinds of official information without authorization and establish procedures for the achievement of those purposes and for related matters.

From the above the FOI Act 2011 empowers any person to access or request for information which is in the custody or possession of any public official, agency or institution, whether such information is contained in written form, notwithstanding anything contained in any other Act, law or regulation.[63] It should be noted that the applicant needs not demonstrate any specific interest in the information being applied for.[64]

Furthermore, illiterate or disabled applicants who because of their illiteracy or disability are unable to make an application for access to information or records may make that application through a third party.[65] To facilitate the unimpeded exercise of this right, all public institutions are required to keep records of all their activities, operations and businesses,[66] in such a manner as to enable the public to gain access

---

[60] Ibid., s. 55(5).

[61] Ibid., s. 55(6).

[62] Freedom of Information Act of Nigeria (FOI) (2011).

[63] Ibid., s. 1(1).

[64] Ibid., s. 1(2).

[65] Ibid., s. 3(3).

[66] Ibid., s. 2(1).

to it should the need arise. In addition, certain categories of information in the possession of the public institutions are to be widely disseminated and made readily available to members of the public through various means, including print, electronic online sources and physically at the offices of such institutions.[67]

Where a public institution receives an application for access to information, and the institution is of the view that another public institution has a greater interest in the information, the institution to which the application is made may within three days but not later than seven days after the application is received, transfer the application, and if necessary, the information, to the other public institution, in which case, the institution transferring the application shall give written notice of the transfer to the applicant, which notice shall contain a statement informing the applicant that such decision to transfer the application can be reviewed by the court.[68] Where an application is transferred such application shall be deemed to have been made to the public institution to which it was transferred on the day the public institution received it.[69]

However, the public institution may extend the time limit set out in respect of an application for a time not exceeding seven days if: (a) the application is for a large number of records and meeting the original time limit would unreasonably interfere with the operations of the public institution; or (b) consultations are necessary to comply with the application that cannot reasonably be completed within the original time limit, by giving notice of the extension stating whether the extension falls under the circumstances set out in the Act. Such notice shall contain a statement that the applicant has a right to have the decision to extend the limit reviewed by the court.[70]

Under the FOI Act 2011, a public institution may deny an application for any information and under those circumstances such denial may be legitimate. For instance, under Section 12 of the Act, a public institution may deny an application for any information which contains:

> Records compiled by any public institution for administrative enforcement proceedings and by any law enforcement or correctional agency for law enforcement purposes or for internal matters of a public institution, but only to the extent that disclosure would- interfere with pending or actual and reasonably contemplated law enforcement proceedings conducted by any law enforcement or correctional agency, interfere with pending administrative enforcement proceedings conducted by any public institution, deprive a person of a fair trial or an impartial hearing, unavoidably disclose the identity of a confidential source, constitute an invasion of personal privacy, except, where the interest of the public would be better served by having such record being made available, this exemption to disclosure shall not apply, and obstruct an ongoing criminal investigation.[71]

Other instances where information may be denied include where the disclosure of such information could reasonably be expected to be injurious to the security of

[67] Ibid., s. 2(3).

[68] FOI Act (2011), s. 5(1).

[69] Ibid., s. 5(2).

[70] Ibid., s. 6.

[71] Ibid., s. 12(1)(a) (i)–(vi).

penal institutions[72] and where such an application for information could reasonably be expected to facilitate the commission of an offence.[73] Again, denial of information requested may be legitimate under the provisions of Sections 14,[74] 15,[75] 16,[76] 17[77] and 19[78] of the FOI Act 2011.

Notwithstanding the aforesaid, the FOI Act 2011 provides that an application for information shall not be denied where the public interest in disclosing the information outweighs whatever injury that disclosure would cause.[79] Furthermore, where an application is made to a public institution for information which is exempted from disclosure, the institution shall disclose any part of the information that does not contain such exempted information.[80]

In the absence of any of the above exemptions, the government or public institution that refuses to give access to a record or information applied for under the FOI Act, the institution shall state in the notice given to the applicant the grounds for the refusal, the specific provision of the Act that it relates to.[81] Under this situation, a notification of denial of any application for information or records shall state the names, designation and signature, of each person responsible for the denial of such application.[82]

To this end, where the government or public institution fails to give access to information or records applied for within the time limit set out, the institution shall be deemed to have refused to give access.[83] Under such situation, the applicant has a right to challenge the decision refusing access and have it reviewed by a court.[84] And where a case of wrongful denial of access is established, the defaulting officer or institution commits an offence and is liable on conviction to a fine of ₦500,000.[85]

Access to information generally is now gaining increasing recognition as a human right, implicit in the right to freedom of expression as guaranteed by several global,[86]

---

[72] Ibid., s. 12(1)(b).

[73] FOI Act (2011), s. 12(3).

[74] Exemption of personal information.

[75] Exemption of third-party information.

[76] Exemption of personal or other privileges conferred by law.

[77] Exemption of course or research material.

[78] Denial by a public institution to disclose records.

[79] FOI Act (2011), s. 12(2).

[80] Ibid., s. 18.

[81] Ibid., s. 7(1).

[82] Ibid., s. 7(2).

[83] Ibid., s. 7(4).

[84] Ibid., s. 7(1).

[85] Ibid., s. 7(5).

[86] For instance, the Universal Declaration on Human Rights (UDHR) (1948), Art. 20(1), International Covenant on Civil and Political Rights, (ICCPR) (1966), Art. 19(2).

and regional treaties,[87] as well as national constitutions.[88] The move towards recognition of access to information as a human right had found expression in the case of *Claude-Reyes et al. v. Chile*,[89] where the Inter-American Court of Human Rights in 2006 held that Article 13 of the American Convention on Human Rights 1969[90] guarantees the right of all individuals to request, and be granted access to, government-held information, unless there is a specific justification for refusal. The case was brought by members of a Chilean environmental NGO who had been denied access to documents related to the environmental impact of a proposed logging project. Also in 2009, the European Court on Human Rights (ECHR) issued two rulings. In the case of *Társasága Szabadságjogokértv Hungary* and *Kenedi v. Hungary*,[91] the court recognised that a right of access to information held by public bodies is inherent in Article 10 of the European Convention on Human Rights.[92]

5.3 Public Participation in Environmental Decision-Making

5.3.1 Introduction

The second pillar, public participation in environmental matters, addresses issues related to how the public and public interest groups can participate in environmental decision-making. For the effectiveness of public participation in decision-making on environmental matters, reliance is placed on both access to information and access to justice. This is predicated on the fact that the public needs access to environmental information to ensure that their participation can be based on an informed fashion.

Public participation is premised that empowered public can help address various difficulties in confronting environmental issues.[93] In its ideal form, public participation involves the activity of members of the public in partnership with public authorities to reach an optimal result in decision-making and policy-making.[94] The importance of fully integrating environmental considerations into governmental

[87] For example, the African Charter on Human and Peoples' Rights, (ACHPR) (1981) Art. 10(1).

[88] For instance, Constitution of the Federal Republic of Nigeria (CFRN) 1999, Cap C23 Laws of the Federation of Nigeria (LFN) 2004, as amended, s. 39(1).

[89] Inter-American Court of Human Rights, judgement of 19 September 2006, Series C No. 151 (2006).

[90] That guarantees freedom of thought and expression.

[91] Application No. 37374/05, ECHR, judgement of 14 April 2009.

[92] That guarantees freedom of thought and expression.

[93] Toth (2010), p. 295.

[94] Hartmann (1994), p. 715.

decision-making requires public authorities to be in possession of accurate, comprehensive and up-to-date information.[95]

The public can be a major source of this information. Fortunately, the public often has the desire to take part in the process of gathering information and discussing options for decision-making, both out of self-interest and because of their wish to protect the environment. But this requires an open, regular and transparent process in which the public can have confidence. By providing such a framework in which the public can exercise its rights to information, association and participation, parties can achieve two goals simultaneously: improving the ability of authorities to carry out their responsibilities and providing the necessary conditions for the public to enjoy their rights and meet their own obligations.[96]

In addition, in the words of Tyler,[97] "public participation underscores the potential cost savings benefits. . . ." The reason being that while it may be tempting to cut corners to reach a result that might appear on the surface to be the best, there are countless cases where unexpected or hidden factors became apparent only through a public participation process, with the result that potentially costly mistakes were avoided.

Again, when governments enable the public to participate in decision-making, they help meet society's goal of sustainable and environmentally sound development. Public participation in environmental decision-making, particularly in EIA, may lead to some benefits in these processes. As a result of public participation, the process of decision-making, up to and including the final decision, becomes more transparent and legitimate. Public debate on proposed activities among all interested groups at an early stage of decision-making may prevent or mitigate conflicts and adverse environmental consequences of the decisions with transboundary impacts.[98] On a final note,

> The preamble also reminds us that public participation enhances the quality and implementation of decisions, contributes to public awareness of environmental issues, gives the public the opportunity to express its concerns and enables public authorities to take due account of such concerns. Public participation also furthers accountability of and transparency in decision-making and strengthens public support for decisions on the environment.[99]

Public participation as an aspect of environmental procedural rights were discussed hereunder based on the provisions of various legal instruments, both international[100] and domestic.[101]

---

[95] Ibid.

[96] Toth (2010), p. 295.

[97] Tyler (2003), p. 258.

[98] Economic Commission for Europe (ECE) (2006), p. 7.

[99] Ebbesson et al. (2014), p. 120.

[100] Under the Aarhus Convention, European Union Directive on EIA and National Environmental Policy Act of USA 1969, as amended.

[101] EIA Act (1992).

5.3.2 Public Participation Under Aarhus Convention

Under the Aarhus Convention, the public participation pillar is divided into three parts. The first part concerns the participation of the public that may be affected by or is otherwise interested in decision-making on a specific activity.[102] The second part concerns the participation of the public in the development of plans, programmes and policies relating to the environment.[103] The third part focuses on the participation of the public in the preparation of laws, rules and legally binding norms.[104] Article 6 of the Aarhus Convention sets out the general requirements and implementation guidelines for the conduct of public participation, these are:

a) Public participation is to be conducted early in decisions on activities with a possible significant environmental impact.
b) Public authorities[105] to give notice to the public concerned;[106] establish reasonable timeframes for phases of public participation; provide all relevant information to the public concerned; provide opportunities for the public to make comments; take due account of the outcome; and inform the public of the final decision with reasons.[107]

Implementation guidelines on the other hand enjoin public authorities to:

a) Develop criteria for evaluating the significance of non-listed activities
b) Identify which decisions "permit" activities and of these decisions, which should be subject to public participation requirements
c) Ensure that decision-makers have a legal basis to take environmental considerations into account;
d) Develop incentives for applicants to engage in early dialogue
e) Set guidelines and standards for the quality of relevant information
f) Establish clear procedures for submitting comments in writing or at hearings
g) Supervise how public authorities take comments into account
h) Clearly define any exemptions

---

[102] Aarhus Convention (1998), under Art. 6.

[103] Ibid., under Art. 7.

[104] Aarhus Convention (1998), under Art. 8.

[105] Aarhus Convention (1998), under Art. 2, para 2, "Public authority" means: (a) Government at national, regional and other levels; (b) Natural or legal persons performing public administrative functions under national law, including specific duties, activities or services in relation to the environment; (c) Any other natural or legal persons having public responsibilities or functions, or providing public services, in relation to the environment, under the control of a body or person falling within subparagraphs (a) or (b) above; and (d) The institutions of any regional economic integration organization referred to in Article 17 which is a party to the Convention.

[106] Aarhus Convention (1998), under Art. 2, para 5, "Public concerned" means the public affected or likely to be affected by, or having an interest in, the environmental decision-making; for the purposes of this definition, non-governmental organizations promoting environmental protection and meeting any requirements under national law shall be deemed to have an interest.

[107] Aarhus Convention (1998), Art. 6.

i) Be flexible in setting time frames
j) Facilitate public participation through early dialogue with the applicant
k) Apply information exemptions
l) Establish clear procedures for promptly informing the public of the final decision[108]

Article 7 of the Aarhus Convention 1998 provides for the participation of the public in the development of plans, programmes and policies relating to the environment and sets out the following general requirements that must be followed:

a) Establish a transparent and fair framework for public participation in plans and programmes relating to the environment
b) Identify participating public
c) Conduct public participation early in the development of plans and programmes relating to the environment
d) Give necessary information to the public
e) Establish reasonable timeframes for public participation
f) Take due account of the outcome[109]

In addition, the authorities should follow these implementation guidelines:

a) Develop a list or clear criteria for identifying plans, programmes and policies relating to the environment
b) Develop clear rules for participation
c) Develop mechanisms for notification
d) Set guidelines and standards for the quality of necessary information
e) Develop tools for the identification of the participating public
f) Supervise how public authorities take comments into account
g) Establish policies for public participation in policymaking
h) Flexibility in means (practical and/or other provisions)
i) Flexibility in setting timeframes
j) Broad latitude in how to provide public participation in the preparation of policies.[110]

The third part of the Aarhus Convention on the participation of the public[111] focuses on the preparation of laws, rules and legally binding norms. In respect of this, the public authority shall:

a) Strive to promote effective public participation in the preparation of laws and rules which may have a significant effect on the environment
b) Establish sufficient timeframes for effective participation
c) Publish or publicise drafts

---

[108] Aarhus Convention (1998).
[109] Ibid., Art. 7.
[110] Aarhus Convention (1998).
[111] Ibid., Art. 8.

d) Provide opportunities for the public to comment
e) Take account of the result as far as possible[112]

To make the above general guidelines feasible, the authority shall:

a) Develop clear rules for participation
b) Develop criteria for evaluating environmental significance
c) Establish are liable and regular vehicle for publishing drafts
d) Establish clear procedures for submitting comments in writing or at hearings
e) Supervise how public authorities take comments into account
f) Broad latitude in how to provide public participation in the preparation of laws and rules[113]

5.3.3 *Public Participation Under EU Directive on EIA*

In respect of public participation, the EU Directive on EIA provides as follows:

i) To stimulate more efficient decision-making and increase legal certainty, Member States should ensure that the various steps of the environmental impact assessment of projects are carried out within a reasonable period, depending on the nature, complexity, location and size of the project. Such time-frames should, under no circumstances, compromise the achievement of high standards for the protection of the environment, particularly those resulting from Union legislation on the environment other than this Directive, and effective public participation and access to justice.[114]
ii) To ensure the effective participation of the public concerned in the decision-making procedures, the public shall be informed electronically and by public notices or by other appropriate means, of the following matters early in the environmental decision-making procedures. . .and, at the latest, as soon as information can reasonably be provided.[115]
iii) Reasonable time-frames for the different phases shall be provided for, allowing sufficient time for informing the authorities and the public; and the authorities and the public concerned to prepare and participate effectively in the environmental decision-making, subject to the provisions of the article.[116]
iv) The time frames for consulting the public concerned on the environmental impact assessment report, shall not be shorter than 30 days.[117]

[112] Aarhus Convention (1998).
[113] Ibid., Art. 8.
[114] European Union (2014), Preamble, para 36.
[115] Ibid., Art. 6, para 2.
[116] Ibid., Art. 6, para 6.
[117] Ibid., Art. 6, para 7.

v) Furthermore, when a decision to grant or refuse development consent has been taken, the competent authority or authorities shall promptly inform the public and the authorities.[118]

Again, to ensure the effective participation of the public concerned in the decision-making procedures, the public shall be informed electronically and by public notices or by other appropriate means, of the following matters early in the environmental decision-making procedures referred to in Article 2(2) and, at the latest, as soon as information can reasonably be provided.[119]

Under Article 6(1),[120] Member States shall take the measures necessary to ensure that the authorities likely to be concerned by the project because of their specific environmental responsibilities or local and regional competences are given an opportunity to express their opinion on the information supplied by the developer and on the request for development consent, taking into account, where appropriate, the cases referred to in Article 8a(3).[121] To this end, Member States shall designate the authorities to be consulted, either in general terms or on a case-by-case basis. The information gathered under Article 5[122] shall be forwarded to those authorities. Detailed arrangements for consultation shall be laid down by the Member States.

Furthermore, Article 6(5)[123] provides the detailed arrangements for informing the public, for example by bill posting within a certain radius or publication in local newspapers, and for consulting the public concerned, for example by written submissions or by way of a public inquiry, shall be determined by the Member States. Member States shall take the necessary measures to ensure that the relevant information is electronically accessible to the public, through at least a central portal or easily accessible points of access, at the appropriate administrative level.

5.3.4 Public Participation Under the USA National Environmental Policy Act 1969, as Amended

Public participation under the Act requirements: transparency and public access to information; due diligence in engaging the public/stakeholders in all categories of environmental review, all project stages.[124]

[118] Ibid., Art. 9(1).

[119] European Union (2014), Art. 6, para (2)(b).

[120] European Union (2014).

[121] Ibid.

[122] Ibid.

[123] Ibid.

[124] United States Agency for International Development (USAID) (2012), p. 30.

Council for Environmental Quality (CEQ)[125] Regulations provide requirements for public participation. Federal Agencies are required to make diligent efforts to involve the public in preparing/implementing NEPA, provide public notice to agencies and the public meetings/hearings/availability/documents, hold or sponsor public hearings or meetings if substantial environmental controversy or request, solicit information and comments from the public, especially persons or organisations who might be interested or affected, explain where persons can get information or status reports, have a minimum 45 day comment period on draft EIS's and ensure public availability of public, agencies, Environmental Protection Agency (EPA) comments.[126]

Furthermore, CEQ Regulations[127] require public involvement before decisions are made. The Agency cannot issue a decision on a proposed action until 90 days after notice of filing of a Draft Environmental Impact Statement (EIS) and 30 days after notice of filing of a Final EIS, has elapsed since the publication of EPA's notice of availability in the Federal Register of filing an EIS with EPA. The filling involves accurate scientific analysis, expert agency comments, and public scrutiny documents.

Where the Agency filed a Finding of No Significant Impact (FONSI),[128] it must include the Environmental Assessment (EA) or a summary of it, and commit to mitigation measures needed to reduce impacts below significance thresholds. The Finding of No Significant Impacts must be circulated to the affected public or made available for review for 30 days before making a decision. The lead agency shall then prepare a Record of Decision (ROD)[129] where it shall state its decision which identifies alternatives considered, environmentally preferable mitigation measures all practicable were adopted or why the Agency should not commit to a monitoring and enforcement programme.[130]

5.3.5 Public Participation Under the Environmental Impact Assessment Act 1992 of Nigeria

The Environmental Impact Assessment Act (EIA Act 1992), on the other hand, has some provisions on public participation in decision-making on environmental

[125] Established under NEPA, s. 202 [42 USC § 4342].

[126] 40 Code of Federal Regulations (CFR) 1506.6.

[127] Ibid., 1506.6 (b).

[128] FONSI is a decision document supporting a determination that an action will not result in significant environmental impacts.

[129] ROD is a public document (i.e., be available for public review), but it need not be circulated for review.

[130] 40 CFR 1506.3.

matters. Under Section 7 of the EIA Act 1992, before the Agency[131] gives a decision on an activity to which an environmental assessment has been produced, the Agency shall give an opportunity to government agencies, members of the public, experts in any relevant discipline and interested groups to comment on the environmental impact assessment of the activity.

After receiving a mandatory study report in respect of a project, the Agency shall, in any manner it considers appropriate, publish in a notice setting out the following information: (a) the date on which the mandatory study report shall be available to the public; (b) the place at which copies of the report may be obtained; and (c) the deadline and address for filing comments on the conclusions and recommendations of the report.[132] However, before the deadline set out in the notice published by the Agency, any person may file comments with the Agency relating to the conclusions and recommendations of the mandatory study report.[133]

Again, where at any time the Agency, or the Council,[134] believes that (a) a project is likely to cause significant adverse environmental effects that may not be mitigable; or (b) public concerns respecting the environmental effects of the project warrant it, the Agency may refer the project to the Council for a referral to mediation or a review panel in accordance with Section 35 of this Act.[135] In addition, where a review panel is set up under Section 36 of the EIA Act 1992, a review panel shall not only ensure that the information required for an assessment by a review panel is obtained and made available to the public but also hold hearing in a manner that offers the public an opportunity to participate in the assessment.[136]

Under Section 38 of the EIA Act 1992, on receiving a report submitted by a mediator or a review panel, the Agency shall make the report available to the public in any manner the Council considers appropriate and shall advise the public that the report is available. Furthermore, the Council shall not approve a substitution under subsection 44 (1) of the EIA Act 1992 unless the Council is satisfied that. . .the public has been given an opportunity to participate in the assessment.[137]

Besides these specific national and regional laws, aspects of public participation can be found in a growing number of international legal instruments. As early as 1982, the World Charter for Nature, adopted by the United Nations General Assembly in its resolution 37/7 of 28 October 1982, provided persons with the opportunity to participate, individually or with others, in the formulation of decisions of direct concern to their environment.[138]

---

[131] See note 47 (pre) on the position of the Agency.

[132] 40 CFR 1506.3, s. 24(1)(a)–(c).

[133] Ibid., s. 24(2).

[134] Ibid., s. 29.

[135] Ibid., s. 26.

[136] EIA Act (1992), s. 36(b).

[137] Ibid., s. 45(b).

[138] United Nations General Assembly (UNGA) (1982), World Charter for Nature 1982, para 23.

The Rio Declaration 1992[139] states that environmental issues are best handled with the participation of all concerned citizens, and declares that each individual should have the opportunity to participate in decision-making processes, facilitated by the widespread availability of information. AGENDA 21 1992,[140] provides details on the methods and best practices for achieving sustainable development and gives a great deal of attention to public participation. For instance, Chapter 23 (2) of AGENDA 21 provides as follows:

> One of the fundamental prerequisites for the achievement of sustainable development is broad public participation in decision-making. Furthermore, in the more specific context of environment and development, the need for new forms of participation has emerged. This includes the need of individuals, groups and organizations to participate in environmental impact assessment procedures and to know about and participate in decisions, particularly those which potentially affect the communities in which they live and work. Individuals, groups and organizations should have access to information relevant to environment and development held by national authorities, including information on products and activities that have or are likely to have a significant impact on the environment, and information on environmental protection measures.

AGENDA 21[141] further provides that "countries should strengthen existing advisory bodies or establish new ones for public environment and development information, and should coordinate activities with, among others. . ., and they should encourage public participation in discussions of environmental policies and assessments. . . ."

More recently, international instruments have followed the direction taken by the Rio Declaration 1992. The United Nations Convention to Combat Desertification 1994 in its Articles 3(a) and 10(2)(e) and (f), repeats earlier formulations calling for public participation in relevant decision-making and the need for parties to facilitate action. It also specifically mentions public participation in several types of processes, including policy planning, decision-making, and implementation and review of national action programmes.

5.4 Access to Judicial and Administrative Proceedings in Environmental Matters

5.4.1 Introduction

The third pillar of environmental procedural rights, access to judicial and administrative proceedings in environmental matters, deals with the right of the public and public interest groups to seek judicial remedy for non-compliance by governments

---

[139] Rio Declaration (1992), Principle 10.

[140] United Nations Organisation (2020).

[141] AGENDA 21 (1992), Chapter 36.10(a).

and corporations within the legal obligations established by access to environmental information and public participation in environmental matters. Although the first two pillars create an enabling environment for public participation, the third, access to a judicial remedy, gives individuals and public interest organisations the capacity to enforce and actively seek the protection of their rights to information and input to decisions.[142]

Access to environmental justice is now one of the major issues on the international environmental law agenda. The relationship of access to environmental justice and good governance to sustainable development is becoming increasingly apparent. For instance, the preamble to the Rio Declaration 1992 refers to it as "the integrity of the global environmental and developmental system." The Rio Declaration 1992 further states that "in order to achieve sustainable development, environmental protection shall constitute an integral part of the development process and cannot be considered in isolation from it."[143] And under Principle 25, the Declaration further states that "peace, development and environmental protection are interdependent and indivisible." Whether courts, administrative appeals, or other possible access to justice mechanisms are considered, three aspects of access to justice need to be examined.

5.4.2 *Aspects of Access to Justice*

The first aspect of access to justice in environmental matters is a threshold issue. That is, under what circumstances does a person have standing to invoke substantive and procedural guarantees? The second is the question of which specific procedures and remedies should be available once the threshold is crossed. The third is the extent of judicial control through the procedures available, also referred to as the standard of review.[144]

Access to justice in environmental matters may be invoked under the following situations: (a) complaints and disputes arising out of the handling of information requests;[145] (b) the substance and procedure of environmental decision-making and other matters;[146] (c) attempts by members of the public to use various legal tools to enforce environmental law.[147] According to Article 9(1) of the Aarhus Convention 1998:

> Each Party shall, within the framework of its national legislation, ensure that any person who considers that his or her request for information under Article 4 has been ignored, wrongfully

---

[142] Ebbesson et al. (2014), p. 120.

[143] Rio Declaration (1992), Principle 4.

[144] Stec (2003), p. 18.

[145] Aarhus Convention (1998), Art. 9, para 1, FOI Act (2011), ss. 1(3) and 7(1).

[146] Aarhus Convention (1998), Art. 9, para 2.

[147] Ibid., Art. 9, para 3.

refused, whether in part or in full, inadequately answered, or otherwise not dealt with in accordance with the provisions of that Article, has access to a review procedure before a court of law or another independent and impartial body established by law.

In the same vein, the Freedom of Information Act of Nigeria 2011 provides that "any person entitled to the right to information under the Act, shall have the right to institute proceedings in the Court to compel any public institution to comply with the provisions of the Act."[148]

Accordingly, when public authorities hold information on the environment and do not provide it upon request, they disregard not only the information principle,[149] but also the participation principle.[150] Lack of access to information on environmental matters is a considerable obstacle to effective public participation.[151] In many cases, after initially denying access to the requested information, public authorities may decide to provide it "voluntarily" following the initiation of a court procedure, but before the court's ruling, perhaps to avoid a court judgement going against them.

The above position is illustrated by the Hungary Case 2 (the Metal Plant Case)[152] where a member of the public requested information from a public authority on emissions data for an enterprise. The Environmental Inspectorate of Northern Hungary first refused to provide the data on air pollution and noise emissions of this enterprise because the citizens had no right to participate in any government decisions relating to the enterprise. The individual in question filed a lawsuit at the local City Court of Miskolc to oblige the inspectorate to provide access to the requested information. During the process, the inspectorate "voluntarily" released a part of the requested data. While a final court judgement was avoided, in the view of one of the authors of the case study, the case proves that "the group of those who are entitled to have access to environmental data of a facility is not limited to the group of those who have standing in a particular case, which is the main idea behind public access to environmental information."

Another interesting case demonstrating a successful resolution where information was voluntarily released was the *Salisbury Bypass* case[153] in the United Kingdom (UK). The Department of Transport refused to deliver a copy of an "induced traffic assessment report" to Friends of the Earth,[154] arguing that the requested information was not related to the environment according to both the provisions of Directive 90/313/EEC8 and the UK's domestic legislation. Friends of the Earth brought a case for judicial review of the department's decision, and two weeks before the court hearing was due, the department provided Friends of the Earth with a copy of the report.

---

[148] FOI Act (2011), s. 1(3).

[149] Aarhus Convention (1998), Art. 4.

[150] Ibid., Arts. 6, 7 and 8.

[151] Savoia and Skrylnikov (2003), p. 23.

[152] Ibid.

[153] Savoia and Skrylnikov (2003), p. 23.

[154] An International Environmental Non-Governmental Organisation.

An incomplete response can be considered as a sub-category of "failure to respond." In fact, in such an event, the public authority releases only a part of the requested information. A synonym for "incomplete response" is "unsatisfactory response," as underlined in Ukraine Case 1 (the Ukrainian Right to Know Case).[155] In that case, a citizen expressed concern over the construction of a petrol filling station and asked the Oblast Chief Sanitary Doctor to provide information about its activities. Particularly, he demanded an assessment and forecast of health indices for Khmelnytsky residents and the results of laboratory research on air pollution. He received an unsatisfactory answer to his request. In fact, the doctor did not provide any information on the essence of the matter. The court declared the actions of the doctor illegal and obliged him to satisfy the inquiry. This case shows that although it is generally difficult for citizens and community organisations to obtain requested environmental information from officials, they can defend their entitlement to access to environmental information in court through a juridical procedure.

The challenge to claims of exemption is another basis for accessing the court. Exemption categories include the following: national defence; public security; international relations; commercial confidentiality; ongoing court proceedings or criminal and other investigations; personal privacy; and intellectual property rights, or that requested information was included in draft documents or data, or in internal communications.[156]

Depending on how these categories are applied and what other restrictions are in place, authorities have the potential to limit substantially the transparency that laws on access to information are supposed to ensure. In 1999, Friends of the Earth asked the European Commission (DG XI) for copies of two studies that had been conducted for the Commission into the UK's transposition of the habitats directive and various waste directives.[157] The Commission provided copies of the studies, but with page after page blacked out in thick ink. Friends of the Earth appealed to the Secretary-General of the Commission, as required by the Code of Conduct concerning public access to Commission and Council documents attached to Commission Decision 94/90/EC. The Secretary-General upheld the Commission's refusal to provide full copies. The Commission argued that the documents fell within the exception of "protection of the public interest (court proceedings, inspections and investigations)." In respect of the study on waste directives, DGXI also argued that the exception "for the protection of the Commission's interest in the confidentiality of its own proceedings" applied, but the Secretary-general dropped this argument.[158]

In 2000, Friends of the Earth appealed to the European Ombudsman against these refusals. It argued that the documents were studies, not investigations, and that the

---

[155] Savoia and Skrylnikov (2003), p. 24.

[156] Ibid.

[157] Roderick (2020).

[158] Ibid.

democratic accountability of the Commission meant that the public should be entitled to see an objective independent study on compliance with environmental law conducted for it. It also argued that the Commission was acting inconsistently with the Aarhus Convention.[159]

In March 2001, the Ombudsman ruled that the Commission was guilty of maladministration in refusing to provide full copies of the report and gave the Commission until 30 June 2001 to respond. The Ombudsman ruled that "it is reasonable to regard these reports as Commission documents, to which the rules of Decision 94/90/EC should apply," and went on to state as follows:

> An interpretation of the scope of 'inspections and investigations', as suggested by the Commission, could preclude public disclosure of any document held by the institution which might be relevant for its role of guardian of the treaty under Article 211 of the EC Treaty. Accordingly, whole categories of documents whose content relates to member states' compliance with Community law, and hence which may give factual or legal elements to the Commission in order to consider instituting infringements in the future, could be barred from public access . . .[160]

The Ombudsman therefore considers that the exception based on inspections and investigations should only be applied when the requested documents have been drawn up during an investigation connected to an infringement proceeding. The two reports in this case were commissioned before any investigation and with a view to solely considering the options available to the Commission. Therefore, the ombudsman ruled that the Commission was guilty of maladministration in refusing to provide full copies of the reports.[161]

At times, denial of access to information is based on an exemption for commercially confidential information. In certain cases, this exemption is used in a very broad way to suppress any information connected with business. For instance, under the FOI Act 2011,

> a public institution shall deny an application for information that contains trade secrets and commercial or financial information obtained from a person or business where such trade secrets or information are proprietary, privileged or confidential, or where disclosure of such trade secrets or information may cause harm to the interests of the third party. However, nothing contained in the Law shall be construed as preventing a person or business from consenting to disclosure.[162]

In the same vein, under the EIA Act 1992,[163] where a review panel is satisfied that the disclosure of evidence, documents or other things would cause specific, direct and substantial harm to a witness, the evidence, documents or things shall be privileged and shall not without the authorisation of the witness, knowingly be or

[159] Ibid.

[160] European Ombudsman Press Release (2020).

[161] Roderick (2020).

[162] FOI Act (2011), s. 15(1)(a).

[163] EIA Act (1992).

be permitted to be communicated, disclosed or made available by any person who has obtained the evidence, documents or other things under this Act.[164]

However, a public institution shall disclose any information that contains trade secrets and commercial or financial information, etc., if that disclosure would be in the public interest as it relates to public health, public safety or protection of the environment and, if the public interest in the disclosure clearly outweighs in importance any financial loss or gain to, or prejudice to the competitive position of or interference with contractual or other negotiation of a third party.[165]

In addition, the exemption is sometimes restricted when such information concerns impacts on the environment. In the *R v. Secretary of State for Environment Transport and The Regions and Another, exparte The Alliance Against The Birmingham Northern Relief Road & Others,*[166] the issue was whether a document, in this case an agreement for the construction of a toll-financed road scheme, fell under the exemption of commercial confidentiality. The Alliance Against the Birmingham Northern Relief Road opposed the proposal and sought to obtain a copy of the concession agreement from the Department of Environment. This was refused in writing on 23 September 1998 for reasons of commercial confidentiality. The Alliance sought to challenge this decision by way of judicial review.

The court decided that the agreement to construct the road was "information relating to the environment, and the fact that a document might contain confidential information that is truly commercial could not be used to prevent disclosure of the main body of the agreement. Moreover, the purpose of seeking the information was irrelevant."[167] This case illustrates that courts will examine the determinations made by public authorities with respect to confidentiality and will require public authorities to apply exemptions restrictively. In this case, the confidential information could not be used to justify the refusal to disclose other information that could be separated from the confidential information.

In all cases, where the information in issue falls into the category of information on ecological conditions (accidents and catastrophes endangering the safety and health of citizens, and their consequences) accordingly limiting access to information sought on any of those grounds should therefore not be considered. In the circumstances where a party provides for such a review by a court of law, it shall ensure that such a person also has access to an expeditious procedure established by law that is free of charge or inexpensive for reconsideration by a public authority or review by an independent and impartial body other than a court of law.

---

[164] Ibid., s. 37(4).

[165] FOI Act (2011), s. 15(4).

[166] (1998) High Court, Queen's Bench Division.

[167] R v. Secretary of State for the Environment, Transport and the Regions ex parte Holding and Barnes plc and others, in Slynn et al. (2001), pp. 275–276.

5.4.3 Substance and Procedure of Environmental Decision-Making and Other Matters

The second aspect of access to justice hinges on the substance and procedure of environmental decision-making and other matters. Under the Aarhus Convention 1998:

> Each Party shall, within the framework of its national legislation, ensure that members of the public concerned (a) having a sufficient interest or, alternatively, (b) Maintaining impairment of a right, where the administrative procedural law of a Party requires this as a precondition, have access to a review procedure before a court of law and/or another independent and impartial body established by law, to challenge the substantive and procedural legality of any decision, act or omission subject to the provisions of Article 6. . . .[168]

An examination of Article 6 of the Aarhus Convention 1998 shows several procedural requirements that could become the subject of a lawsuit or other appeal:

i) failure to provide access "to all information relevant to the decision-making" process, including data, a non- technical summary and alternatives;
ii) failure to provide early, timely and effective public notice;
iii) failure of the public notice to be clear about the activity, possible decisions and the public authority responsible;
iv) failure to provide notice of the procedure, including participation opportunities, where information can be obtained, and the nature of the information;
v) failure to provide an opportunity to submit comments, or failure of the authority to take due account of comments; and
vi) failure to inform the public (and to do so timely) of the final decision "along with the reasons and considerations on which the decision is based."[169]

These six requirements can be grouped into three categories of procedural errors:

i) failure to disclose all information to the public relevant to its participation;
ii) improper procedures for public participation, such as timely or adequate notice, opportunity to comment, timeframes, restrictions on "administrative standing," or other conditions; and
iii) inadequate response to comments received (failure to take due account), or failure to reveal the reasons or considerations for the decision.[170]

It is a basic principle of public participation that all documentation and information relevant to a proposed decision should be open for examination by the public concerned. Article 6 (2)(d) of the Aarhus Convention 1998 requires that a proponent/ applicant or public authority responsible for decision-making must notify the public concerned about public participation procedures, including "the public authority

[168] Aarhus Convention (1998), Art. 9, para 2.
[169] Ibid., Art. 6.
[170] Kravchenko et al. (2003), p. 27.

from which information can be obtained and where the relevant information has been deposited for examination by the public." What this connotes is that denying access to information not only harms the information principle, but also the participation principle.

Thus, information relating to proposed decisions must be available, according to Article 6(2) of the Aarhus Convention 1998, "early in an environmental decision-making procedure," when all possibilities and alternatives are open for consideration. Also, under Section 7 of the EIA Act 1992, before the Agency[171] gives a decision on an activity to which an environmental assessment has been produced, the Agency shall give an opportunity to government agencies, members of the public, experts in any relevant discipline and interested groups to comment on the environmental impact assessment of the activity.

The essence of these provisions is to give the public a chance to be prepared and to participate effectively. Furthermore, the information must be available "in an adequate, timely and effective manner." Lack of access to documentation can make public participation ineffective or even impossible.[172] Commenting on the possibilities of succeeding in an action on the above, Kravchenko et al.[173] posited as follows:

> It is likely to be easier to get judicial correction of some categories of violations than of others. Regarding disclosure, it appears to be difficult to persuade a judge that undisclosed information was relevant to the decision-making process. The second, improper participation procedures, asks courts to do the kind of work that is most familiar to them. If a member of the public can show that procedures were violated, courts can rule in their favour, without thinking that they are making policy decisions themselves about the environment. The third is the most difficult: to ask a court to determine that the government inadequately responded to a particular comment, or inadequately explained its reasons, requires the court to make a somewhat subjective judgement rather than a clear judgement about legal procedures. This is not to say that it is wrong for the court to do this. It is simply observed that judges may be reluctant to rule in such cases.

An occasion where the lack of opportunities for public participation in an Environmental Impact Assessment (EIA) that resulted in proceedings in court is illustrated in the case of Armenia Case 1 (the Victory Park Case).[174]

In the above case, the construction of a hotel complex started in a public park without an environmental impact assessment (EIA). When citizens saw trees being cut, the Environmental Public Advocacy Centre (EPAC) tried to obtain information about the project from the city. It asked whether an EIA existed, whether any hearings had been held, and whether the mayor of the city had given permission. However, access to the requested information was refused. Informally, EPAC discovered that the mayor of the city had permitted to start the construction, provided that an EIA first made a positive conclusion. EPAC also discovered that, despite this

[171] That is, the Agency charged with environmental protection under the EIA Act 1992 (see note 47).

[172] Kravchenko et al. (2003), p. 28.

[173] Ibid.

[174] Savoia and Skrylnikov (2003), p. 28.

condition, and the absence of an EIA, the general architect of the city made another order to start the construction two days later. The court dismissed EPAC's case, never addressing its demand for information. EPAC also sued the prime minister for failing to provide information, but the court proceedings were delayed, and again no injunction was issued to stop the ongoing construction.

A similar situation existed in the Nigerian case of *Oronto Douglas v. Shell Petroleum Development Company & 5 Ors*,[175] where the Federal High Court dismissed a suit instituted by the plaintiff against the five defendants[176] for breach of some provisions of the EIA Act. The five defendants were jointly engaged in a project for the production of liquefied natural gas (LNG) in Bonny. For the project to take off the defendants were required to do preliminary studies on the impact of the project[177] on the environment in compliance with the provisions of the EIA Act. The plaintiff was not satisfied that the defendants had satisfactorily adhered to the provisions of the Act hence the action in the Federal High Court. The plaintiff sought, among other things, the following reliefs:

(i) a declaration that the defendants cannot lawfully commission, carry out and operate their LNG projects without first complying strictly with the EIA Act
(ii) a declaration that the fifth defendant, FEPA, is bound to require the first to third defendants: SPDC; Nigeria LNG and NNPC to adequately publicise any proposed EIA report to all interested NGOs and the communities likely to be affected by the operation of the LNG project in accordance with the provisions of Section 7 of the EIA Act 1992[178]

However, during the action, the plaintiff discontinued the claim against FEPA, the fifth defendant. Subsequently, the plaintiff simultaneously filed originating summons for a declaration and an injunction restraining the first to fourth defendants from continuing and/or carrying on with the Liquefied Natural Gas project until a proper environmental impact assessment had been conducted strictly following the provisions of the EIA Act. The 1st, 2nd, 3rd and 4th defendants filed notices of preliminary objection contending that the plaintiff's actions were incompetent in that he lacked the requisite *locus standi* and that the mode of the commencement of the plaintiff's action was procedurally defective.

The court in its ruling by the trial judge, Belgore, CJ, delivered on 17 February 1997, struck out the plaintiff's claim on the ground that the procedure adopted was

---

[175] Suit No. FHC/25C/573/93 (unreported) delivered by FHC PH on 17 February 1997.

[176] (1st) Shell Petroleum Development Company Ltd (SPDC), (2nd) Nigerian National Petroleum Corporation (NNPC), (3rd) Nigerian Liquidified Natural Gas Ltd (LNG), (4th) Mobil Producing (Nig.) Unlimited and (5th) Federal Environmental Protection Agency (FEPA), represented by the office of the Attorney General of the Federation.

[177] Liquidified Natural Gas project is under EIA Act (1992), sch.1, item. 8(b) to which an environmental impact assessment is mandatory under the EIA Act (1992), s. 12.

[178] The section requires the Agency charged with environmental protection to adequately publicise any proposed EIA report to all interested persons before an approval is given for the project to take off.

"confused" and on the ground that the plaintiff had no legal standing to prosecute the action. The plaintiff appealed against this decision.

On appeal to the Court of Appeal, Lagos Division,[179] the Court held that since the *res* in the matter have not been validly determined it will be imprudent for it to discuss the issues raised in the appeal. So it set aside the learned trial Judge Belgore, C.J's decision of 17 February 1997.

In Germany Case 5 (the Baltic Sea Motorway Case)[180] which involved the question of whether documents were made available adequately to allow public participation to occur properly, the recognised conservation group, Bund fur Umwelt und Naturschutz (BUND) and the regional group Schleswig Holstein Association opposed the construction of a subsection of the A20 motorway, the so-called Baltic Sea motorway. During the procedure to approve the plan, a controversy arose about the extent of legal protection for the Wakenitz Valley. Since the conflict between the authority and BUND could not be resolved, BUND filed a case against the project.[181]

The association made procedural and substantive legal arguments in its suit. Procedurally, the association complained that important documents were not made completely accessible. The plan approval authority refused the inspection of the requested documents during the hearing procedure. The authority furthermore modified the documents several times, without allowing BUND to comment again.[182]

The court ruled that BUND could only challenge substantive violations of the nature protection law, and not violations of other laws, and apparently not procedural inadequacies such as the failure to provide information. Yet, adherence to proper procedures and the ability to challenge violations in the courts are fundamental to both the rule of law and the implementation of the principles of the Aarhus Convention.[183]

However, in Germany Case 2 (the Experts' Documents Case)[184] on the construction of a new and extended section of railway track between Erfurt and Leipzig/Halle, the courts were more attentive to citizen participation rights. A nature conservation association recognised under federal law, NABU Landesverband Sachsen-Anhalt (NABU), requested access to various documents in order to comment on the proposal. These particularly included an expert report by the planning office referring to a survey of the nature aspects of the surrounding countryside. The public authority rejected the NABU application to view the files. NABU sued. The court ruled that the defendant's public authority had infringed the plaintiff's participatory rights. The court rejected an argument by the defendant that, under the Administrative Procedure Act, the denial of access to documentation was an

[179] (1998) LPELR-CA/L/143/97.

[180] Savoia and Skrylnikov (2003), p. 24.

[181] Ibid.

[182] Ibid.

[183] Savoia and Skrylnikov (2003), p. 24.

[184] Ibid., 28.

insubstantial procedural error and therefore could not affect the legality of the development consent.

The court ruled that the Nature Conservation Act gave a right of consultation of independent weight and absolute character. This is an important statement, showing that access and participation rights under more recently promulgated environmental laws have to be treated seriously.[185]

Again, in the Poland Case 1 (the Highway and Housing Case)[186] the residents of the Muchobor Maly housing estate in Wroclaw claimed that a proposal to build a district highway near their housing estate would be illegal. They separately appealed the development consent and the building permit. Comments on the inadequacy of the EIA by residents living close to the new highway construction were rejected administratively. On appeal, the Supreme Administrative Court agreed with some of the residents' comments, however, apparently requiring new conditions for building the highway. This case illustrates the potential for judicial correction of a failure to take comments into account. In addition, there was an appeal to another independent body, the EIA Commission of the Ministry of Environment, which agreed that the EIA was not in compliance with the law, but the lack of citizen appeals at an earlier time resulted in allowing the EIA to stand.[187]

Another requirement for a proper public participation procedure is that the public must be able to understand the relevant environmental documents, as illustrated in United States Case 1 (the Telephone Case).[188] Without comprehensible documentation, public participation will be merely a formality, without any chance of benefiting either the public or public authorities. This case illustrates how such an improper procedure can be challenged. The highly technical language of the EIA in this case was difficult to understand by a layperson. Even a Harvard University professor, who helped to prepare the EIA, had difficulty explaining it. As a result, the court issued a nationwide injunction against a pesticide spraying programme, until proper procedures could be followed. This case upheld the right of the public to demand clear documents as part of their participation and comment in an EIA process, and showed that the court can be a bulwark in support of those rights.

These cases, whether failed or successful, suggest that citizens can challenge inadequate compliance with participation procedures in some countries, under certain circumstances. The fact that such cases are brought before the courts shows how important access to justice is to environmental law.

Generally, these three pillars or tenets for implementing environmental impact assessment emphasise the process rather than the outcome that provides an innovative model of policymaking and integrates environmental protection and governance norms. This integration is bound to benefit both the environment and democratic governance. It promotes citizens' involvement as a key to combating environmental

---

[185] Ibid.

[186] Ibid., 29.

[187] Ibid.

[188] Savoia and Skrylnikov (2003), p. 30.

mismanagement. Its principles of transparency and accountability are integral to the meaningful practice of democratic governance.

5.5 Summary

One of the fundamental prerequisites for the achievement of sustainable development as well as viable environmental protection revolves around these fundamental procedural rights such as access to information, broad public participation in decision-making and access to justice. These fundamental procedural rights include the need for individuals, groups and organisations should have access to information relevant to the environment and development held by national authorities, including information on products and activities that have or are likely to have a significant impact on the environment and information on environmental protection measures. Access to information generally is now gaining increasing recognition as a human right, implicit in the right to freedom of expression as guaranteed by several global, and regional treaties, as well as national constitutions.

Public participation requires individuals, groups and organisations to participate in procedures and to know about and participate in decisions, particularly those which potentially affect the communities in which they live and work. It also involves more specifically participation in several types of processes, including policy planning, decision-making, and implementation and review of national action programmes. The benefit of this is that when governments enable the public to participate in decision-making, they help meet society's goal of sustainable and environmentally sound development. Public participation in environmental decision-making, particularly in EIA, may lead to some benefits in these processes as environmental issues are best handled with the participation of all concerned citizens, at the relevant level.

Access to justice in environmental matters on the other hand, may be invoked under the following situations: (a) complaints and disputes arising out of the handling of information requests; (b) the substance and procedure of environmental decision-making and other matters; (c) attempts by members of the public to use various legal tools to enforce environmental law.

In sum, the main objective of procedural environment rights is that effective access to information, judicial and administrative proceedings, including redress and remedy, enhance the quality and implementation of decisions, contribute to public awareness of environmental issues, give the public the opportunity to express its concerns and enables public authorities to take due account of such concerns. These rights also further accountability and transparency in decision-making and strengthen public support for decisions on the environment.

References

Ebbesson J et al (2014) The Aarhus Convention: an implementation guide, 2nd edn. United Nations Publication

Economic Commission for Europe (ECE) (2006) Guidance on Public Participation in Environmental Impact Assessment in a Trans-boundary Context, ECE/MP.EIA/7, United Nations Publication

EU (2014) Directive on Environmental Impact Assessment EIA Directive 2014/52/EU. https://eur-lex.europa.eu/legal-content/en/text. Accessed on 10 May 2023

European Ombudsman Press Release (2020). https://www.euro-ombudsman.eu.int/recommen/en/000271.htm. Accessed on 16 June 2023

European Union (EU) (1998) Convention on Access to Information, Public Participation in Decision-Making and Access to Justice in Environmental Matters (Aarhus Convention) 1998, Art. 2, para 3. https://ec.europa.eu/environment/aarhus/. Accessed on 10 May 2023

Hartmann C (1994) NEPA: business as usual: the weaknesses of the National Environmental Policy Act. J Air Law Commerce 59:709, 715. https://scholar.smu.edu/jalc/vol59/iss3/6. Accessed on 10 May 2023

Kravchenko S et al (2003) Access to justice in cases involving public participation in decision-making. In: Stec S (ed) Handbook on Access to Justice under the Aarhus Convention. The Regional Environmental Center for Central and Eastern Europe, Szentendre, Hungary

Roderick P (2020) Friends of the Earth. https://www.foei.org. Accessed on 13 June 2020

Sands P (2000) Principles of International Environmental Law I: frameworks, standards and implementation. Manchester University, Manchester

Savoia R, Skrylnikov D (2003) Access to justice in cases involving access to environmental information. In: Stec S (ed) Handbook on Access to Justice under the Aarhus Convention. The Regional Environmental Center for Central and Eastern Europe, Szentendre, Hungary

Slynn LJ et al (2001) R v. Secretary of State for the Environment, Transport and the Regions ex parte Holding and Barnes plc and others. J Financ Regul Compliance 9(3):275–278. https://doi.org/10.1108/eb025081. ISSN: 1358-1988

Stec S (ed) (2003) Handbook on Access to Justice under the Aarhus Convention. The Regional Environmental Center for Central and Eastern Europe, Szentendre, Hungary

Toth B (2010) Public participation and democracy in practice—Aarhus Convention Principles as democratic institution building in the developing world. J Land Resour Environ Law 30(2):295. https://www.semanticscholar.org/paper/PUBLIC-PARTICIPATION-AND-DEMOCRACY-IN-CONVENTION-AS-Toth/13fd6ec45b271bd501360d57b3e4bbd2774c79bd. Accessed on 12 May 2023

Tyler N (2003) Practical experience of public participation: evidence from methodological experiments. INNOVATION 16(3):253, 258

United Nations (2020) Report of the United Nations Conference on Environment and Development. https://www.un.org/en/development/A/CONF.151/26 (Vol. I) Rio Declaration.pdf. Accessed on 14 May 2023

United Nations General Assembly (UNGA) (1982) World Charter for Nature 1982, para 23. https://digitallibrary.un.org/record/39295?ln=en. Accessed on 12 May 2023

United Nations Organisation (2020) AGENDA 21. http://www.un.org/esa/sustdev/agenda21.htm. Accessed on 10 June 2023

United States Agency for International Development (USAID) (2012) Public Participation: Environmental Impact Assessment in the United States. 5 September 2012, 30. https://www.usaid.gov. Accessed on 12 June 2023

Part II
Management and Control of Pollution of the Environmental Media

Chapter 6
Strategies for Atmospheric Pollution Abatement and Control

Abstract One of the main components of Earth's interdependent physical systems is the atmosphere which is made of layers of gases. The heat-trapping ability of the atmosphere helps to keep the Earth warm enough for life, and it also protects the Earth from harmful solar radiation and cosmic rays. Over the years, human activities such as the burning of fossil fuels, deforestation, industrialisation, urbanisation, and agricultural practices, among others, have had an impact on the atmosphere and are increasingly influencing the Earth's temperature and climate variability. Some of these activities add enormous amounts of greenhouse gases to those naturally occurring in the atmosphere, increasing the greenhouse effect and global warming. There are two variants of atmospheric pollution resulting from human activities: one associated with pollution of the air and the other on noise. This chapter discusses the strategies for atmospheric pollution abatement and control focusing on the nature of air pollution, its impact as well as strategies for abatement. Noise pollution, as a component of atmospheric pollution, is also discussed noting its concept, sources, effects, abatement strategies, and use of legislation in prosecuting offenders. Although air pollution is discussed generally using a mix of international and national legal instruments, the focus on noise pollution is mainly on Nigeria.

6.1 Introduction

The word "atmosphere" was coined by seventeenth-century scientists combining the Greek words for vapour, atmos, and sphere, sphaira.[1] The Earth's atmosphere is the air and gas surrounding our planet. Atmosphere also describes the feeling of a place. A coffee shop might have a cool, artsy atmosphere. Some plants grow best in a damp atmosphere. In physics, atmosphere is a unit of pressure equal to the air pressure at sea level.[2]

---

[1] Liddell and Scott (2015). See, also, Vocabulary.com (2020).

[2] Ibid.

E. Onyeabor, *Environmental Law*, https://doi.org/10.1007/978-3-031-68956-7_6

However, in this discourse, the word atmosphere refers to that part of the Earth that is a layer of gas or layers of gases that envelop it and hold it in place by the gravity of the planetary body. A planet retains an atmosphere when the gravity is great and the temperature of the atmosphere is low. The Earth's atmosphere is composed of about 78% nitrogen, 21% oxygen, and 1% other gases. These gases are found in layers (troposphere, stratosphere, mesosphere, thermosphere, and exosphere) defined by unique features such as temperature and pressure.[3]

The composition of Earth's atmosphere is determined by the by-products of the life that it sustains. Dry air (mixture of gases) from Earth's atmosphere contains 78.08% nitrogen, 20.95% oxygen, 0.93% argon, 0.04% carbon dioxide, and traces of hydrogen, helium, and other "noble" gases (by volume), but generally, a variable amount of water vapour is also present, on average about 1% at sea level.[4] The atmosphere of the Earth is made up of layers with different properties, such as specific gaseous composition, temperature, and pressure. The lowest layer of the atmosphere is the troposphere, which extends from the planetary surface to the bottom of the stratosphere. The troposphere contains 75% of the mass of the atmosphere, and is the atmospheric layer wherein the weather occurs; the height of the troposphere varies between 17 kilometres (km) at the equator and 7.0 km at the poles.[5]

The stratosphere extends from the top of the troposphere to the bottom of the mesosphere, and contains the ozone layer, at an altitude between 15 km and 35 km. It is the atmospheric layer that absorbs most of the ultraviolet radiation that Earth receives from the Sun. The mesosphere ranges from 50 km to 85 km, and is the layer wherein most meteors are incinerated before reaching the surface.[6]

The thermosphere extends from an altitude of 85 km to the base of the exosphere at 690 km and contains the ionosphere, where solar radiation ionises the atmosphere. The density of the ionosphere is greater at short distances from the planetary surface in the daytime and decreases as the ionosphere rises at night-time, thereby allowing a greater range of radio frequencies to travel greater distances. Moreover, located in the thermosphere is the Kármán line at 100 km, which is the boundary between outer space and Earth's atmosphere. The exosphere begins at 690 to 1000 km from the surface, and extends to roughly 10,000 km, where it interacts with the magnetosphere of Earth.[7]

The layered composition of the atmosphere minimises the harmful effects of sunlight, ultraviolet radiation, solar wind, and cosmic rays to protect organisms from genetic damage. The atmosphere protects life on Earth by shielding it from incoming ultraviolet (UV) radiation, keeping the planet warm through insulation, and preventing extremes between day and night temperatures. The sun heats layers of

---

[3] National Geographic Society (2020a), p. 25.

[4] Weaver and Villard (2020).

[5] Williams (2020).

[6] Ibid.

[7] Ibid.

the atmosphere causing it to convect driving air movement and weather patterns around the world.[8]

The current composition of the atmosphere of the Earth is the product of billions of years of biochemical modification of the paleoatmosphere by living organisms.[9] Man's unrelenting siege on the Earth over the years has led to some level of impairment of the Earth's atmosphere. Human actions on Earth's atmosphere have taken many forms and this has existed since humans first began to use fire for agriculture, heating, and cooking. The siege took a new dimension with the advent of the Industrial Revolution which relied, and still relies, on energy from various sources.

6.2 Air Pollution

6.2.1 Introduction

Air pollution became a major environmental problem since the beginning of the Industrial Revolution of the eighteenth and nineteenth centuries. Ever since, air pollution has increased in leaps and bounds. Although the National Environmental Standards and Regulations Enforcement Agency (Establishment) Act 2007 (NESREA Act 2007)[10] did not define air pollution, however, the National Environmental (Air Quality Control) Regulations 2014,[11] one of the regulations made under Section 34 of the NESREA Act 2007, defines air pollution as:

> the state of increased concentration of substances in the atmosphere which has or has the potential of adversely affecting the health of any living substance, ecosystem, natural or built environment, at a level that exceeds the carrying capacity of the atmospheric removal mechanisms to return the air to its natural background concentrations for such substance.[12]

Air pollution is also defined as the presence of contaminant or pollutant substances in the air that do not disperse and interfere with human health, or welfare, or produce other harmful environmental effects.[13] In the wordings of the National

[8] Ibid.

[9] Liddell and Scott (2015).

[10] National Environmental Standards and Regulations Enforcement Agency (Establishment) Act 2007 (NESREA Act 2007).

[11] National Environmental (Air Quality Control) Regulations (2014) Government Notice No. 225, S.I. 64.

Federal Republic of Nigeria Official Gazette No. 142, Vol. 101, 26 December 2014.

[12] Ibid., Regulation 41.

[13] Federal Environmental Protection Agency (FEPA) (1991), p. 199.

Environmental (Food, Beverages and Tobacco Sector) Regulations 2009,[14] it also means any change in the composition of the air caused by smoke, soot, dust (including fly-ash), cinders, solid particle of any kind, gases, fumes, aerosols and odorous substances.[15]

Air is said to be polluted when the atmospheric composition of nitrogen, oxygen, carbon dioxide and other gases exceeds the threshold level of 70% nitrogen, 20% oxygen and carbon dioxide exceeds 300 parts per million.[16]

6.2.2 Sources of Air Pollution

Anthropogenic (man-made) air pollution comes from many sources and can have numerous components including various sulphurous oxides (SOx), nitrous oxides (NOx), ozone (O_3), hydrocarbons, chloroflouro-carbons (CFCs), and heavy metals. Naturally occurring pollution, such as forest fires and volcanic eruptions, can also cause significant deterioration in air quality but cannot be controlled or mitigated by policy action.[17]

Human contamination of Earth's atmosphere can take many forms and has existed since humans first began to use fire for agriculture, heating, and cooking. During the Industrial Revolution of the eighteenth and nineteenth centuries, however, air pollution became a major problem. As early as 1661, John Evelyn[18] reported the dark London smog. Smog is an urban air pollution that is generally a smoky mixture of carbon monoxide and organic compounds from incomplete combustion (burning) of fossil fuels such as coal, and sulphur dioxide from impurities in the fuels.[19] As the smog ages and reacts with oxygen, organic and sulphuric acids condense as droplets, increasing the haze. Smog developed into a major health hazard by the twentieth century. In 1948, 19 people died and thousands were sickened by smog in the small US steel-mill town of Donora, Pennsylvania. In 1952, about 4000 Londoners died of its effects.[20]

A second type of smog, photochemical smog, is caused by combustion in car, truck and airplane engines, which produce nitrogen oxides and release hydrocarbons from unburned fuels. Sunlight causes the nitrogen oxides and hydrocarbons to combine and turn oxygen into ozone, a chemical agent that attacks rubber, injures

[14] National Environmental (Food, Beverages and Tobacco Sector) Regulations (2009) Government Notice No. 286, S.I. 33. Federal Republic of Nigeria Official Gazette No. 65 Vol. 96, 14 October 2009.

[15] Ibid., Regulation 54.

[16] Godish (2001), p. 26.

[17] Strahler and Strahler (1977), p. 45.

[18] British author and founding member of the British Royal Society.

[19] Strahler and Strahler (1977), p. 45.

[20] Ibid.

plants, and irritates the lungs. Hydrocarbons are oxidised into materials that condense and form a visible, pungent haze.[21]

Air pollution released from readily identifiable sources is referred to as primary pollution while pollutants that occur because of a chemical reaction with or in the atmosphere are secondary pollutants. The categories of primary pollution sources are mobile or stationary, combustion or non-combustion, area or point sources, direct or indirect. Mobile sources include automobiles, trains, and airplanes. A point source is a stationary source whose emissions have a significant impact on air quality while an area source is not a significant polluter by itself but contributes to air pollution as part of a group of relatively small polluters.[22]

Overall, primary air pollutants are carbon monoxide (CO), hydrocarbons (HC), particulates,[23] sulphur dioxide (SO_2) and nitrogen compounds, such as nitrogen oxide (NO) and nitrogen dioxide (NO_2). These materials may interact with one another in the presence of sunlight to form new secondary pollutants, such as ozone and other reactive materials. Secondary pollutants can also form from reactions with natural chemicals in the atmosphere.[24]

It should be noted that not all forms of air pollution can be accounted for by "traditional" gaseous and particulate matter. Non-traditional forms of air pollution include noise,[25] odour, heat, ionising radiation, and electromagnetic fields.[26] Again, large quantities of pollutants are by-products of fossil-fuel-burning industries, particularly coal-fired power plants and metal smelters.[27]

6.3 Impact of Air Pollution

6.3.1 Introduction

Air pollution is a major global environmental issue and one of the most serious environmental dangers to human health, causing an estimated seven million premature deaths per year.[28] Environmental and health issues are brought on by it. Additionally, it makes new health problems appear when none would have,

---

[21] Enger and Smith (2002), p. 320.

[22] Godish (2001), p. 27.

[23] These are minute pieces of solid materials dispersed into the atmosphere such as smoke particles from fires, bits of asbestos from brake linings and insulation, dust particles and ash from industrial plants.

[24] Strahler and Strahler (1977), p. 46.

[25] Noise pollution as a major aspect of atmospheric pollution was discussed in Sect. 6.5 of this chapter.

[26] These forms of pollution were mentioned for the sake of thoroughness but were not discussed in this book.

[27] Godish (2001), p. 27.

[28] United Nations Environment Programme (UNEP) (2021a).

aggravates existing health issues, and, in extreme situations, results in death. In addition to harming crops and trees, acid deposition (acid rain), and broad loss of acid-sensitive aquatic ecosystems and creatures, air pollution is also to blame for a wide range of other environmental issues.[29]

Air pollution is not a recent phenomenon. It has been linked to many negative impacts on human health and on the immediate environment of its impact. Contamination of the atmosphere has been a constant side effect of industrialisation. The severity of air pollution and the public's acute awareness of it, however, are relatively recent. As industrialisation has taken on a global dimension since the end of World War II, so has air pollution.[30]

Overall, air pollution has been identified as a causal factor in building deterioration, lowered visibility, fish kills, global warming, and widespread tree and plant damage, all of which have serious economic consequences.[31] To this end, the effects of air pollution are divided into two categories: impact within a territory and influence across borders.

6.3.2 *Territorial Impact of Air Pollution*

The most severe episodes of air pollution have impacted human health, and in some cases caused significant loss of life. For instance, some researchers believe that the combination of sulphur dioxide and water in the air allows people to breathe toxic metals and gasses deep into their lungs causing as many as 50,000 deaths in the United States every year—2% of annual mortality.[32] In 1986, when Lake Nyos in Cameroon erupted releasing dangerous gases such as sulphur dioxide (SO_2), carbon monoxide (CO) and methane (CH_4) into the atmosphere that killed about 1700 persons in both Cameroon and Nigeria.[33]

Recent studies revealed that air pollution from farms leads to death. According to one of the reports:[34]

> Animal agriculture is the worst emitter, researchers say, responsible for 80 percent of deaths from pollution related to food production. Gases associated with manure and animal feed produce small, lung-irritating particles capable of drifting hundreds of miles. These emissions now account for more annual deaths than pollution from coal power plants. Yet while pollution from power plants, factories and vehicles is restricted under the Clean Air Act, there is less regulation of air quality around farms.

[29] Enger and Smith (2002), p. 322.

[30] J and K ENVIS Centre (2021).

[31] J and K ENVIS Centre (2021).

[32] World Watch Institute (2004), p. 17.

[33] United States Geological Surveys (2019).

[34] Hill et al. (2021).

A first-of-its-kind study shows that air pollution from Duplin County farms, North Carolina in the United States of America (USA) is linked to roughly 98 premature deaths per year, 89 of which are linked to emissions directly caused by hogs. Those losses are among more than 17,000 annual deaths attributable to pollution from farms across the USA.[35]

The most insidious kinds of air pollutants are known as particulate matter, especially $PM_{2.5}$ and PM_{10}.[36] Exposure to $PM_{2.5}$ can lead to asthma and other breathing problems and over the long term increases the risk of dying of heart disease, cancer and stroke. These particles are directly produced when farmers till fields or burn crops before harvest. They can also come in the form of dust kicked up by livestock in large animal feeding operations.[37] This "primary" $PM_{2.5}$ is associated with about 4800 premature deaths per year, the study found. But "secondary" particulate matter, which is generated when emissions from farms interact with other gases in the atmosphere, is even more problematic. This is especially true for ammonia, a highly reactive molecule released by manure and fertiliser, which can combine with other pollutants such as nitrogen and sulphur compounds to create small, hazardous particles.[38]

The health effects of air pollution are dependent on atmospheric chemistry, local weather, and the size and health of communities living nearby. Only with advanced new air-quality models has it become possible to pinpoint the consequences of pollution produced hundreds of miles away.[39]

"Of all pollutants, ammonia is the one that has the greatest impact on mortality and that its emissions contribute to about 12,400 deaths per year," the report revealed.[40] "This is what makes pollution from animal agriculture so dangerous," the report further added. The source of ammonia in livestock farms comes from animal waste which is stored in massive "lagoons." Here, the microbes that break down faeces release huge amounts of ammonia. Again, many facilities spray nitrogen-rich liquid waste on nearby farm fields, making it another source of contamination. In addition, ammonia is also produced from the over-application of fertiliser on such crops.[41] "Now that we know this is an important source, what can we do about it?" Kaplan[42] queried. Accordingly,

---

[35] Kaplan (2021).

[36] $PM_{2.5}$ are tiny particles one-thirtieth the width of a human hair, which can become lodged in the lungs or absorbed into the bloodstream. PM_{10} on the other hand describes inhalable particles, with diameters that are generally 10 micrometers and smaller. Exposure to high concentrations of PM_{10} can result in some health impacts ranging from coughing and wheezing to asthma attacks and bronchitis to high blood pressure, heart attack, strokes and premature death.

[37] Hill et al. (2021).

[38] Ibid.

[39] Ibid.

[40] Ibid.

[41] Ibid.

[42] Kaplan (2021).

> Farmers could halve the number of air-pollution deaths from food production by changing their practices. Instead of leaving manure to decompose in lagoons, they could incorporate it into soil as fertilizer. Covering lagoons, separating urine from feces, and controlling the acidity and temperature of lagoons would also reduce ammonia emissions. Furthermore, targeted fertilizer applications would reduce the amount of ammonia released into the air on croplands, reducing tillage and burning of waste and cutting emissions from equipment could also lead to small health gains.

The high death rate recorded in certain places in the wake of the coronavirus pandemic (COVID-19) in 2020 and beyond has been attributed to high air pollution experienced in such cities. At the end of 2019, Wuhan (China) reported a new coronavirus disease (COVID-19) for the first time. The virus was found all over the world in a very short time. At the end of January 2020, the World Health Organisation (WHO) declared a state of public health emergency and COVID-19 widespread concern in the international community.[43] According to the United Nations Environment Programmes (UNEP),[44]

> One of the most terrifying things about the early weeks of the COVID-19 pandemic was the realisation that the air we breathe could also make us sick. And yet, for millions of people around the world, breathing potentially deadly air is a daily reality because of noxious pollution caused by everything from factories, to cars, to cooking fires.

In the words of Kissi-Debrah,[45] "air pollution is linked to diabetes, strokes, heart attacks, asthma attacks, and those with underlying health conditions are dying more from COVID-19." Several studies have been conducted on whether there were links between air pollutants, atmospheric variables and COVID-19 cases and fatalities.

In a study by Shahzad et al.,[46] the researchers explored the effects of environmental and weather variables on daily COVID-19 cases and COVID-19 fatalities in Istanbul, Turkey. Turkey has the eighth highest number of COVID-19 cases globally, with the highest number of infections and deaths in Istanbul. The authors conducted a comprehensive investigation for environmental quality (air quality pollutants, e.g. $PM_{2.5}$ and PM_{10}, ozone (O_3), nitrogen dioxide (NO_2), sulphur dioxide (SO_2), carbon monoxide (CO), etc.), weather parameters (temperature, humidity) and COVID-19 in Turkey using meteorological data from 11 March 2020 to 8 February 2021 and COVID-19 data from Istanbul and other regions. The results from empirical estimations, correlation analysis, and quantile-on-quantile techniques support that "air quality and temperature significantly influence COVID-19 deaths in Istanbul." According to the authors, "this research may help policymakers and health scientists to take specific measures to reduce the spread of corona virus across different global cities."[47]

---

[43] World Health Organization (WHO) (2020).

[44] United Nations Environment Programme (UNEP) (2021b).

[45] Kissi-Debrah (2020).

[46] Shahzad et al. (2021).

[47] Ibid.

In another study by Cai et al.,[48] air pollutant data were collected from national environmental monitoring stations across four metropolises in China (Shanghai, Wuhan, Guangzhou, and Tianjin) and were used to address to evaluate the interruption-recovery patterns of urban air pollution under COVID-19, and to further analyse the impacts of different lockdown policies on urban air quality at different response stages. Three air pollutants: Nitrogen dioxide (NO_2); particulate matter ($PM_{2.5}$) and ozone (O_3) were selected due to the typical and differing characteristics in the variation of concentrations of these three air pollutants. The findings[49] revealed, among other things, that:

1. The general trends for pollutant concentrations across the four cities were similar. To be specific, the NO_2 concentrations showed the most significant variation as the different lockdown policies shifted among response stages. The O_3 concentrations presented an opposite pattern compared with the other air pollutants. Both NO_2 and O_3 were strongly affected by traffic emissions. However, the sulphur dioxide (SO_2) concentrations were maintained at a relatively stable level during the pandemic, indicating that pollutant levels are determined less by traffic emissions and more by industrial sources.
2. Except for O_3, air pollutant concentrations during the lockdown period in 2020 first decreased significantly at the time cutoff of Level I and then gradually recovered at the time cutoff of Reopen, while O_3 showed the opposite pattern. The differences in NO_2 concentrations between during the lockdown period in 2020 and the same time in 2018–2019 were more pronounced than those for $PM_{2.5}$ and O_3.

The results therefore suggested that the effects of different lockdown policies under COVID-19 in 2020 on urban air quality were greater during peak hours than non-peak hours. A plausible reason is that lockdown policies restricted people's travel demands and the enterprises were not allowed to reopen until 10 March 2020. These results also suggest that anthropic activities can have large and negative impacts on urban air quality.[50]

In another study by Linares et al.,[51] the authors analysed the role of meteorological variables and the role played by air pollutants on the incidence and severity of COVID-19. The authors analysed data corresponding to the period from 1 February to 31 May 2020 for the City of Madrid, Spain. In that study, the independent variables consisted of meteorological data and air pollution data. Meteorological data were the values of daily maximum temperature (Tmax), minimum temperature (Tmin), and average temperature (Tmed) in Celsius and daily average relative humidity (RH) in percent. The values of average absolute daily humidity (AH) in g/m^3 were obtained based on average relative humidity and average daily humidity.

---

[48] Cai et al. (2021).

[49] Ibid.

[50] Ibid.

[51] Linares et al. (2021).

These values constitute the average value of the observations corresponding to the State Meteorological Agency (AEMET) stations located in the Community of Madrid and were provided by the AEMET.[52]

The air pollution data were the average daily values of the concentrations of PM_{10} and NO_2 in $\mu g/m^3$, obtained by using the average of the values measured in the stations located in the Community of Madrid.[53] These data were provided by the Ministry of Ecological Transition and Demographic Change (MITECO). Fourteen-day average values were calculated based on the average daily values for these independent variables.[54]

The dependent variables were daily incidence, daily hospital admissions per 100,000 inhabitants, daily Intensive Care Unit (ICU) admissions and daily death rates per million inhabitants. These data were provided by the ISCIII Spanish National Epidemiology Centre. The data were calculated based on the number of positive cases of COVID-19. Cases diagnosed as positive for COVID-19 were defined based on positive PCR test[55] results in 99.74% of the data. The remaining cases were diagnosed based on the presentation of symptoms compatible with the disease. Cases defined as such refer to the daily cases that occurred in the Community of Madrid during the period between 1 February 2020 and 31 May 2020. The state of alarm and subsequent confinement of the population was decreed by the Spanish State on 14 March 2020, with the application of measures for restricted movements and social interaction. This state of alarm remained in place until 21 June.[56]

Data corresponding to the number of cases diagnosed as positive for COVID-19 in different categories: number of cases, number of emergency hospital admissions, number of ICU admissions and the number of deaths due to COVID-19 were obtained. The data were provided by the National Center for Epidemiology at the Carlos III Institute. The data for this period related to the population of the Community of Madrid were supplied by the National Statistics Institute (INE). Based on these data, the authors calculated the following: COVID-19 incidence rate per 100,000 inhabitants; rate of emergency hospital admissions for COVID-19 per 100,000 inhabitants; rate of ICU hospital admissions for COVID-19 per 1,000,000 inhabitants and COVID-19 death rate per 1,000,000 inhabitants.[57]

---

[52] Linares et al. (2021).

[53] μg in the metric system, a microgram or microgramme is a unit of mass equal to one millionth (1×10^{-6}) of a gram.

[54] Linares et al. (2021).

[55] PCR test means polymerase chain reaction. It is a test to detect genetic material from a specific organism, such as a virus. The test detects the presence of a virus if you have the virus at the time of the test.

[56] Linares et al. (2021).

[57] Linares et al. (2021).

The authors used generalised linear models with a Poisson link between the dependent and independent variables, controlling for seasonality, trend and the autoregressive nature of the series.[58]

The results of the single-variable models showed a negative association between Tmax and all the dependent variables considered, except in the case of deaths, in which lower temperatures were associated with higher rates. Average absolute daily humidity (AH) also showed the same behaviour with the COVID-19 variables analysed, similar to those obtained with Tmax. In terms of atmospheric pollutants PM_{10} and NO_2, both showed a positive association with the dependent variables. Only PM_{10} was associated with the death rate. Associations were established between lags 12 and 21 for PM_{10} and between 0 and 28 for NO_2, indicating a short-term association of NO_2 with the disease. In the two-variable models, the role of NO_2 was predominant compared to PM_{10}.[59]

In conclusion, the study indicated that the environmental variables analysed are related to the incidence and severity of COVID-19 in the Community of Madrid. In general, low temperatures and low humidity in the atmosphere affect the spread of the virus. Air pollution, especially NO_2, is associated with a higher incidence and severity of the disease.[60]

Again, Marquès and Domingo,[61] in their study, concluded that there is a significant association between chronic exposure to various outdoor air pollutants such as $PM_{2.5}$, PM_{10}, O_3, NO_2, SO_2 and (carbon monoxide (CO), and the incidence/risk of COVID-19 cases, as well as the severity/mortality of the disease.

According to Carrington,[62] patients with severe COVID-19 are twice as likely to have had pre-existing respiratory diseases and three times as likely to have had cardiovascular problems. He opined that:

> Although the principal risk of catching Covid-19 is contact with an infected person, and the quality of healthcare is vital in determining the outcome, but air pollution may be important in three ways, studies show. Higher death rates due to lungs and hearts weakened by dirty air is the best understood. Pollutants also inflame lungs, potentially making catching the virus more likely and raising concern about rising pollution levels after lockdowns are lifted. Finally, particles of pollution might even help carry the virus further afield.[63]

Other aspects of the deleterious health effects of air pollution have been reported. For instance, Pothirat et al.[64] investigated the association between daily average seasonal air pollutants and daily mortality of hospitalised patients and community dwellers, as well as emergency and hospitalisation visits for serious respiratory, cardiovascular, and cerebrovascular diseases. It was found that air pollutants were associated with

[58] Ibid.

[59] Ibid.

[60] Ibid.

[61] Marquès and Domingo (2022).

[62] Carrington (2020).

[63] Carrington (2020).

[64] Chaicharn et al. (2019).

higher mortality of hospitalised patients and community dwellers, with varying effects on severe acute respiratory, cardiovascular, and cerebrovascular diseases. In relation to the age of the individuals who are affected by outdoor air pollution, with particular attention to the respiratory system, the elderly ages were especially found to be one of the most sensitive groups.[65]

Air pollution weakens the immune system in the short term. There is growing evidence that pollution can induce oxidative stress, resulting in the production of free radicals, which in turn, may damage the respiratory system, reducing the resistance to viral and bacterial infections.[66]

Air pollutants could influence the immune system and affect its ability to limit the spread of infectious agents like the Respiratory Syncytial Virus (RSV). According to Vandini et al.,[67] Respiratory Syncytial Virus (RSV) is the most important cause of severe respiratory infections in infants with seasonal epidemics. Environmental factors (temperature, humidity, air pollution) could influence RSV epidemics through their effects on virus activity and diffusion.

Exposures to levels of air pollution that do not cause immediate acute illness or death are more difficult to assess.[68] However, ambient air pollution has been implicated as a causal factor in:

1. chronic respiratory and cardiovascular disease,
2. alteration of body functions such as lung ventilation and oxygen transport,
3. reduced work and athletic performance,
4. sensory irritation of the eyes, nose, and throat,
5. aggravation of existing diseases such as asthma.[69]

Air pollution also impacts the natural environment. On impact on the natural environment, air pollution may result in the formation of acid "rain" with its destructive propensity on property and impact on human health. Acid "rain" makes dangerous metals such as aluminium, cadmium, lead, and mercury more soluble. These metals can be leached from soils and lake sediments into aquatic environments where they contaminate water supplies and edible fish. Acidic water can also dissolve toxic metals from municipal and home water systems thereby poisoning drinking water.[70]

The precursors of acid deposition, sulphur and nitrogen oxides are emitted from fossil-fuel-fired power plants, industrial boilers, gas flaring, metal smelters, and automobiles. In Nigeria, acid rain is caused when compounds such as sulphur, carbon monoxide and methane are released into the air by power plants, industrial smoke chains, exhaust from vehicles and gas flaring resulting in the formation of

---

[65] Ibid.

[66] Ciencewicki and Jasper (2007), pp. 1135–1146.

[67] Vandini et al. (2013).

[68] World Watch Institute (2004).

[69] Ibid.

[70] Ibid.

sulphur oxide and methane oxide. This is a phenomenon found in most urban cities and the Niger Delta region of Nigeria mainly due to gas flaring.[71] Acid deposition in the United States is primarily due to sulphuric (65%) and nitric (30%) acids, and approximately 60–70% of the sulphur oxide (SO_X) emissions are reported to be associated with large electric power plants which burn high-sulphur coal.[72]

Acidification is a worldwide problem that impacts negatively on the environment. In some regions such as American northeast and eastern Canada, much of Europe, Africa, Asia and South America biologists have extrapolated experimental findings to conclude that more than half the sensitive species such as molluscs, leeches, and crustaceans have been eliminated in acidified areas.[73]

Acidification may also reduce total phytoplankton biomass while increasing certain algae species. In severely acidified lakes, these algae species cover all surfaces with thick mats (algae blooms) which inhibit the life and feeding cycles of other aquatic organisms, contributing to the decrease in species diversity. Strong acidity leads to the binding of nutrient ions to minerals, preventing their absorption by phytoplankton—the primary component of the food chain.[74]

Clearly, acidification has drastic consequences on acidified watersheds. In addition to this severe disruption of the food chain and the ensuing ecological problems, acidification is more detrimental to smaller and younger fish due to their large body and gill surface per unit weight. Fish mortality is also caused by the toxic effects of aluminium ions and heavy metals such as mercury which can be mobilised from lake sediments through acidification.[75] Some researchers suggest that coastal waters are at risk as well as freshwater sources.[76]

Vegetation is also subject to damage destruction from acid deposition. Particularly severe damage is associated with the high concentration of SO_2 and heavy metal emissions from primary metal smelters.[77]

In addition to the direct damage from acid deposition, the mixture of acid deposition, ozone, and toxic metals makes vegetation more vulnerable to naturally occurring stresses such as drought, temperature extremes, and blight.[78]

Acidification through soot pollution can also stain the stone and erode it, slowly discolouring and damaging important national monuments and iconic buildings.[79] For instance, acid derivatives of SO_2 emission corrode monuments and historical artefacts. Skoulikidis,[80] a Greek expert on acid corrosion estimates that pollution has

---

[71] Ibid.

[72] Godish (2001), p. 133.

[73] Weidman and Marshall (2012).

[74] Godish (2001), p. 133.

[75] Ibid.

[76] Ibid.

[77] World Watch Institute (2004).

[78] Ibid.

[79] Weidman and Marshall (2012).

[80] United States Geological Surveys (2019).

caused more deterioration of Athenian monuments in the last 20–25 years than has occurred during the previous 2400 years.

Acidification also affects paper and leather, significantly reducing their usable life span. For instance, fabrics and textile dyes are adversely affected by acidification. Other problems associated with acidification include metal corrosion, odour pollution, and rubber deterioration. Building stones and masonry are susceptible to the corrosive action of sulphuric acid. Metals, fabrics, leather, rubber and paint works deteriorate under the impact of exposure to polluted air.[81]

In addition, through gaseous pollutants, a considerable amount of heat is emitted into the atmosphere causing thermal pollution and this could affect the heat balance of the affected areas. This is because heat discharges can drastically alter the ecology of a stream or lake. The deleterious effects of heat include a lessening of dissolved oxygen solubility and increased metabolic activity of aquatic animals.[82]

Again, soot experienced in Port Harcourt, Nigeria, since 2016 may be linked to the impact of air pollution. The presence of black soot in the air had been raging in Port Harcourt for some time. In its Editorial, the Nigerian Tribune[83] reported that since November 2016 residents of Port Harcourt suddenly discovered black soot covering everything from cars to houses, plants and clothes.

According to the report,[84] "breathing, wiping one's face with a handkerchief and even cooking is now risky endeavours. It has been difficult to breathe clean air in the city. White handkerchiefs turn black very quickly and homes are full of soot even when doors and windows are shut." The report further stated, "as a matter of fact, the report of the technical team it set up in 2019 indicated that about 22,077 persons had suffered from respiratory-related ailments in the last five years."[85]

The report[86] revealed that there were two major causes of the soot; the activities of illegal oil thieves who employ crude and primitive techniques and the inappropriate burning of these illegal refineries by security operatives during their trail and raid on the criminals. These are in addition to the burning of refuse and roast meat with tyres by residents. All these result in particulate pollution.

Particle pollution, commonly referred to as "soot," is one of the deadliest forms of air pollution. Soot is the common term for a type of particle pollution called $PM_{2.5}$,[87] particulate matter that is 2.5 μm in diameter or smaller. Such fine particles are even smaller than dust and mould particles, or approximately 1/30 of the size of a human hair. It is comprised of a variety of pollutants, including chemicals, acids, metals,

[81] Strahler and Strahler (1977), p. 63.
[82] Ibid.
[83] The Nigerian Tribune Editorial (2022).
[84] Ibid.
[85] Ibid.
[86] Ibid.
[87] See note 36.

soils, and dust, which are suspended in the air after emission. Soot can come in solid, liquid, or gaseous ("aerosols") states.[88]

Soot is a byproduct of burning fossil fuels, particularly coal. It is emitted by a variety of sources, including burning coal for electricity or industrial fuel, manufacturing, oil refining, and motor vehicles. Soot is released into the air as either extremely small particles or liquid droplets. Some solid particles are emitted directly into the air while others are formed when gases form particles as they are carried thousands of miles from pollution sources.[89]

Soot causes several environmental problems, such as haze and the acidification of lakes and rivers. Haze is an atmospheric phenomenon where dust, smoke, and dry particles in the air obscure the sky's clarity. It is formed when sunlight interacts with small particles in the atmosphere. When seen from afar, and depending upon the direction of view, haze can have a bluish or brownish tint. Although haze is mostly a dry air phenomenon, some of its particles tend to create condensation, subsequently giving form to mist droplets. This phenomenon is known as wet haze, or visibility-reducing aerosols of the wet type. The process of aerosol creation occurs due to the chemical reactions between the atmosphere and the sulphur dioxide gas emissions, which create small droplets of sulfuric acid. Sunlight, high humidity, and stagnant airflow may enhance this process.[90]

Human activities like forest burning, factory emissions, automobile traffic pollution, and the burning of coal and other fossil fuels are said to outweigh natural sources in the production of hazes. Soot is the primary cause of haze.[91]

Exposure to particulate matter can cause respiratory symptoms, aggravate existing heart or lung disease and may also cause irritation of the eyes, nose and throat in healthy individuals. Among healthy individuals, short-term exposure (i.e., continuous exposure to unhealthy daily average Pollutant Standards Index (PSI) levels for a few days) to high levels of haze particles may irritate the eyes, nose, and throat. Such irritation resolves on its own in most cases. Haze particles can sometimes affect the heart and lungs, especially in people who already have chronic heart or lung disease, e.g. asthma, chronic obstructive pulmonary disease (COPD), or heart failure.[92]

Particle pollution is also correlated to acid rain. The same compounds from soot react in the air to form a haze of sulphur dioxides and nitrogen oxides and these can mix with atmospheric moisture to acidify precipitation. Carried by the wind or in the water, this acidified pollution degrades water quality by making lakes and rivers more acidic, depleting the nutrients in the soil and damaging sensitive farm crops, and changing the nutrient balance in river basins, along coastlines, and in forests.

[88] Weidman and Marshall (2012).

[89] Ibid.

[90] Ralls (2010).

[91] Ibid.

[92] Ministry of Health, Singapore (2022).

More importantly, soot poses tremendous harm to public health, particularly because of its size. Particulate matter is so small that it can easily enter your lungs and bloodstream, potentially causing damage in a few ways. The United States Environmental Protection Agency (US EPA)[93] describes the process of soot harming the human body:

> Microscopic particles can penetrate deep into the lungs and have been linked to a wide range of serious health effects, including premature death, heart attacks, and strokes, as well as acute bronchitis and aggravated asthma among children.

The American Lung Association adds that breathing particle pollution can potentially cause "cancer and developmental and reproductive harm."[94]

The economic costs of widespread damage due to air pollution are equally large. All of air pollution's negative impacts have significant economic effects, both direct and indirect. Health costs are already staggering and placed in greater demand by pollution-related illnesses and exacerbations of existing medical problems. Damaged trees actually cost money in the form of lost revenue in addition to tourism decline in heavily impacted areas. Regions impacted by pollution odour experience declines in property value. Farmers experience reductions in crop yield driving up produce prices. Clothes and paper products deteriorate faster and require more frequent washing which also hastens their deterioration and contributes to higher demand for textiles.[95]

6.3.3 *Transboundary Impact of Air Pollution*

Air pollution can expand beyond a regional area. When this happens, it causes transboundary and at times global effects. Transboundary impacts of air pollution have resulted in a few environmental problems. For instance, air pollution has been indicted as being responsible for the damage to the upper atmospheric region known as the stratosphere causing depletion of the stratospheric ozone and being responsible for global warming and climate change.

6.3.3.1 Depletion of the Stratospheric Ozone Layer

Ozone is both a human-made greenhouse and a natural gas. Human-made ozone can be found in the lower atmosphere. In the lower atmosphere is a component of smog, a severe type of air pollution. Nitrogen oxides and volatile organic gases emitted by automobiles and industrial sources combine to form the ozone in smog. This type of

[93] United States Environmental Protection Agency (US EPA) (2017).

[94] Weidman and Marshall (2012).

[95] Ibid.

ozone is poisonous in that it damages vegetation, kills trees, irritates lung tissues, and attacks rubber. It is also a greenhouse gas that contributes about a fourth as much as carbon dioxide to global warming. Unlike the natural ozone, ozone in the lower atmosphere tends to be limited to industrialised regions.[96]

Ozone is also found in the upper atmosphere.[97] The stratosphere is the layer of the atmosphere between 16 km and 50 km above sea level. It is rich in ozone, the same molecule that acts as a pollutant when found at lower levels of the atmosphere in urban smog. Up at the stratospheric level, however, ozone forms a protective layer that serves a vital function: it absorbs the wavelength of solar radiation known as ultraviolet-B (UV-B). UV-B damages deoxyribonucleic acid (DNA), the genetic molecule found in every living cell, increasing the risk of such problems as cancer in humans.[98] Because of its protective function, the ozone layer is essential to life on Earth.

The ozone hole is formed each year in the Southern Hemisphere Spring (September–November) when there is a sharp decline (currently up to 60%) in the total ozone over most of Antarctica. During the cold dark Antarctic winter, stratospheric ice clouds (PSCs, polar stratospheric clouds) form when temperatures drop below −78 °C. These clouds are responsible for chemical changes that promote the production of chemically active chlorine and bromine. When sunlight returns to the Antarctic in the Southern Hemisphere Spring, this chlorine and bromine activation leads to rapid ozone loss, which then results in the Antarctic ozone hole. Although some ozone depletion also occurs in the Arctic during the Northern Hemisphere Spring (March–May), wintertime temperatures in the Arctic stratosphere are not persistently low for as many weeks which results in less ozone depletion.[99]

Between 1981 and 1983, meteorologists with the British Antarctic Survey noticed that ozone levels began dropping in the late 1970s. In 1984, it was found that the ozone layer over Antarctica's Halley Bay research station had lost one-third of its thickness compared to previous decades.[100] The researchers, Jonathan D Shanklin, Joe Farman and Brian Gardiner[101] published their findings in October 1985 suggesting a link to a human-made compound called chlorofluorocarbons (CFCs),[102] used in aerosols and cooling devices. Their discovery, the thinning of the ozone layer over Antarctica, came to be known as the ozone hole. Satellite

[96] World Watch Institute (2004).

[97] This is known as stratospheric ozone.

[98] National Oceanic and Atmospheric Administration (NOAA) (2008).

[99] Ibid.

[100] British Broadcasting Corporation (BBC) (2022).

[101] Farman et al. (1985), pp. 207–210.

[102] Compounds formerly used in refrigerators, air-conditioning systems, cleaning solvents, and aerosol sprays, and in the manufacture of polystyrene products are now banned under the Montreal Protocol on ODS 1987.

measurements then confirmed that the springtime ozone loss was a continent-wide feature.[103]

Research conducted by the National Oceanic and Atmospheric Administration[104] during the National Ozone Expeditions to the U.S. McMurdo Station in 1986 and 1987 and National Aeronautics and Space Authority (NASA) stratospheric aircraft flights into the Antarctic region from Chile in 1987 showed conclusively that the ozone loss was related to halogen (chlorine)-catalysed chemical destruction which takes place following spring sunrise in the Antarctic polar region.[105]

The chlorine is derived from manmade CFCs which have migrated to the stratosphere and have been broken down by solar ultraviolet light, freeing chlorine atoms.[106]

The CFCs, nitrous oxide from fertilisers, pesticides and methyl bromide, among others, are known to destroy ozone molecules in the upper atmosphere, causing them to break down, or deplete in thickness.[107] Particularly, the CFC molecules are the major destroyers of ozone since they are virtually indestructible until they reach the stratosphere. Here, intense ultraviolet radiation breaks the CFC molecules apart; releasing the chlorine atoms they contain which in turn break the ozone molecules. Because chlorine is not affected by its interaction with ozone, each chlorine molecule can destroy a large amount of ozone for an extended period. These chlorine atoms now break the ozone down into ordinary oxygen molecules that do not absorb UV-B. The chlorine acts as a catalyst—that is, it takes part in several chemical reactions—yet in the end emerges unchanged and able to react again. A single chlorine atom can destroy up to 100,000 ozone molecules in the stratosphere.[108]

In the stratosphere, the region of the Earth's atmosphere from 6 to 30 miles (10–50 km) above the surface, the chemical compound ozone plays a vital role in absorbing harmful ultraviolet radiation from the sun. During the past 20 years, concentrations of this important compound have been threatened by human-made gases released into the atmosphere, including those known as CFCs. These chemical compounds as well as meteorological conditions in the stratosphere affect the concentration of stratospheric ozone.[109]

Excessive production of this chlorine-containing compound (CFCs) has depleted the stratospheric ozone layer, creating a hole above Antarctica that lasts for several weeks each year. As a result, exposure to the Sun's harmful rays has damaged aquatic and terrestrial wildlife and threatened human health in high-latitude regions

---

[103] National Oceanic and Atmospheric Administration (NOAA) (2008).

[104] The National Oceanic and Atmospheric Administration is an American scientific and regulatory agency within the United States Department of Commerce that forecasts weather, monitors oceanic and atmospheric.

[105] National Oceanic and Atmospheric Administration (NOAA) (2008).

[106] NOAA (2022).

[107] NOAA (2008).

[108] Ibid.

[109] NOAA (2022).

of the northern and southern hemispheres. Depletion of the ozone layer actually causes a slight cooling, offsetting a small part of the warming from greenhouse gases. Scientists have found that under this assault the protective ozone layer in the stratosphere is thinning.[110]

The consequences of continued depletion of the ozone layer include increased ultraviolet radiation which may lead to a growing number of skin cancers and cataracts and reduce the ability of immune systems to respond to infection. Additionally, the growth of the world's oceanic plankton, the base of most marine food chains, would decline. Plankton contains photosynthetic organisms that break down carbon dioxide. If plankton populations decline, it may lead to increased carbon dioxide levels in the atmosphere and thus to global warming.[111]

Even in light of the ban on the use and manufacture of CFCs, the chlorine already released into the atmosphere will continue to destroy the ozone layer for many decades. Although CFC use has been greatly reduced in recent years as a result of the Montreal Protocol, CFC molecules already released into the lower atmosphere will be making their way to the stratosphere for decades, and further ozone loss is expected. As a result, experts anticipate an increase in skin cancers, more cataracts (clouding of the lens of the eye), and reduced yields of some food crops.[112]

As news of the discovery of the Antarctic ozone hole spread, alarm rippled around the world. Projections that the destruction of the ozone layer would adversely impact the health of humans and ecosystems sparked public fear mobilised scientific investigation and galvanised the world's governments to collaborate in an unprecedented way.[113]

Depletion of the ozone aside, one of the greatest global challenges caused by air pollution in a transboundary fashion is global warming and climate change.

6.3.3.2 Global Warming and Climate Change

Air pollution through the emission of Greenhouse Gases (GHGs) such as carbon dioxide, methane, nitrous oxide, hydrofluorocarbons, perfluorocarbons, sulphur hexafluoride and chlorofluorocarbon (indirect greenhouse gases),[114] has been

[110]NOAA (2022).

[111]NOAA (2008).

[112]Ibid.

[113]British Broadcasting Corporation (2022). Efforts at such collaboration yielded various international treaties such as the Vienna Convention on the Protection of the Ozone Layer and the Montreal Protocol on ODS 1987 put in place to control the use and manufacture of CFCs. At the Domestic level, in 2009 NESREA pursuant to its mandate under the NESREA Act (2007) set out the National Environmental (Ozone Layer Protection) Regulations, No. 642009, for the control of ozone-depleting substances. These legal instruments were discussed below (see Sects. 6.4.2.2 and 6.4.2.3, and 6.4.3.1 and 6.4.3.2, respectively).

[114]Climate Change Act of Nigeria (2021), s. 35.

indicted as being responsible for global warming and climate change, with their attendant impacts.

Global warming is the long-term heating of Earth's climate system observed since the pre-industrial period (between 1850 and 1900) due to human activities, primarily fossil fuel burning, which increases heat-trapping greenhouse gas levels in Earth's atmosphere. It is most commonly measured as the average increase in Earth's global surface temperature.[115] Global warming is therefore the phenomenon of increasing average air temperatures near the surface of the Earth over the past one to two centuries.[116]

Climate change on the other hand means a change of climate, which is attributed directly or indirectly to human activity or natural climate variability that alters the composition of the global atmosphere and which is in addition to natural climate variability observed over comparable periods.[117] Climate change therefore is a long-term shift in temperatures and change in the average weather patterns that have come to define Earth's local, regional and global climates. These shifts may be natural, such as through variations in the solar cycle. But since the 1800s, human activities have been the main driver of climate change, primarily due to burning fossil fuels like coal, oil and gas.[118] This act of burning fossil fuels in the cause of human activities is responsible for a wide variety of environmental problems. As the Intergovernmental Panel on Climate Change (IPCC) pointed out, "most of the observed increase in globally averaged temperatures since the mid-twentieth century is very likely due to the observed increase in anthropogenic (man-made) greenhouse gas concentrations via the greenhouse effect."[119]

Human-induced climate change may result in severe impacts, including more frequent and intense extreme events, and changes in the amount and pattern of precipitation that may result in rising sea levels, flooding and drought. Other effects may include changes in agricultural yields, the addition of new trade routes, reduced summer streamflows, species extinctions, and increases in the range of disease vectors.[120]

All these have caused widespread adverse impacts and related losses and damages to nature and people, beyond natural climate variability. Some development and adaptation efforts have reduced vulnerability. Across sectors and regions, the most vulnerable people and systems are observed to be disproportionately affected. The rise in weather and climate extremes has led to some irreversible impacts as natural and human systems are pushed beyond their ability to adapt.[121]

---

[115] National Aeronautics and Space Authority (NASA) (2021).

[116] Mann (2022).

[117] Climate Change Act of Nigeria (2021), s. 35.

[118] United Nations Climate Action (2022).

[119] Intergovernmental Panel on Climate Change (IPCC) (2022), pp. 8–9.

[120] Ibid.

[121] Intergovernmental Panel on Climate Change (IPCC) (2022), pp. 8–9.

Thus, the associated impacts of global warming and climate change entail significant economic costs to mitigate and adapt. The damage and attendant costs are becoming increasingly evident and increasingly large. As these costs become widely known, mitigating climate change becomes increasingly important and very necessary to adopt strategies to control and abate activities that contribute to air pollution generally.

6.4 Air Pollution Abatement Strategies

6.4.1 Introduction

Air pollution abatement has become increasingly important. Given the need to reduce air pollution, the question becomes one of finding the most effective pollution abatement techniques and the best way to implement them. This effort is compounded by the global nature of the problem and the transboundary impacts of particular pollution sources. There are several different air pollution abatement techniques available. These include the use of national legislation, the application of international legal instruments and the adoption of some policies. These were discussed below.

6.4.2 International Legal Instruments for the Control of Air Pollution

Air pollution freely crosses political boundaries making it an issue of multi-national importance. The transboundary nature of air pollution makes it a problem of global dimensions whether at international, regional or national levels. Of importance are:

1. West and Central Africa Regional Framework Agreement on Air Pollution 2009.
2. Vienna Convention on Ozone Depleting Substances (ODS) 1985.
3. Montreal Protocol on ODS 1987.
4. United Nations Framework Convention on Climate Change (UNFCCC) 1992.
5. Kyoto Protocol on UNFCCC 1997.
6. Paris Agreement to Climate Change 2015.

6.4.2.1 West and Central Africa Regional Framework Agreement on Air Pollution 2009 (Abidjan Agreement 2009)

The Abidjan Agreement of 2009 is a sub-regional agreement for West and Central Africa that seeks to address and reduce the release of toxic and air-polluting substances into the atmosphere, most especially from forest burning practices, truck and motor transportation and other pollution from extractive and industrial processes in the sub-region that elevate the release of air pollutants (especially particulate matter, sulphur dioxide, oxides of nitrogen, ammonia, volatile organic compounds, persistent organic pollutants, carbon monoxide and heavy metals).[122]

Although not legally binding, the agreement develops actionable targets to address air pollution issues in transport; industry and mining; household pollution; waste disposal; bushfires, uncontrolled burning and deforestation; urban planning and management; and national and regional environmental governance.[123]

The Abidjan Agreement 2009 brought together 21 African countries, namely: Angola, Benin, Burkina Faso, Cameroon, Cape Verde, Chad, Republic of Congo, Côte d'Ivoire, Democratic Republic of Congo, Equatorial Guinea, Gambia, Ghana, Guinea, Guinea Bissau, Liberia, Mali, Niger, Nigeria, Senegal, Sierra Leone and Togo and the Economic Community of West African States (ECOWAS).[124]

In setting out its targets, the agreement took cognizance of the increase in atmospheric pollutants from socio-economic development in the sub-region, the growing incidence of transboundary air pollution; the atmospheric transformations associated with emissions of volatile organic compounds and oxides of nitrogen that may have adverse impacts on human health and the environment; the linkage between air pollution and climate change amongst other things. To achieve the set targets, the state parties agree to cooperate in the preparation of flexible and differentiated agreements to control and reduce agreed air pollutants; consider the benefits of taking joint measures against the emission of air pollutants and greenhouse gases; harmonise national air quality management legislation, standards, where practicable; and promote the exchange of educational and research information on air quality management.[125]

Other governance tools include setting standards for motor vehicles, which include restricting the age of imported vehicles and ensuring that all imported gasoline vehicles are equipped with functioning converters by 2011, establishing harmonised emission standards, and adopting modern technologies that promote vehicle fuel efficiency and reduce emissions.[126]

On the activities in industries and the mining sectors, the parties agree to elaborate and adopt policy and legal frameworks to promote the adoption of the best available technology and standards, facilitate and promote the use of cleaner fuels and efficient utilisation of energy; conduct environmental and social impact assessment and environmental audit process on activities that impact on air quality; encourage air pollution and climate change mitigation projects; enact emission standards and regulations for industrial activities; build capacity for national monitoring of emissions from industrial and mining activity; and harmonise industrial and mining

[122] Abidjan Agreement (2009).

[123] Ibid.

[124] Ibid.

[125] Ibid., Art. 1.

[126] Abidjan Agreement (2009).

emission standards and regulations to address the effects of transboundary air pollution.[127]

The parties also agree, on a national and regional level, to promote the coordination of the development and implementation of air quality policies and emission management strategies.[128] In addition, the state parties will also enhance public awareness of air pollution issues; enhance stakeholder participation in air quality management; and promote access to and exchange of information on air pollution.[129] Other measures include capacity building and research development.[130]

6.4.2.2 Vienna Convention for the Protection of the Ozone Layer (Vienna Convention on ODS) 1985

The Conference of Plenipotentiaries on the Protection of the Ozone Layer was convened by the Executive Director of the United Nations Programme on Environment pursuant to decision 12/14, Section 1, para 4 adopted by the Governing Council of the United Nations Programme on Environment on 28 May 1984.[131] The Vienna Convention for the Protection of the Ozone Layer was adopted.

The Vienna Convention for the Protection of the Ozone Layer (Vienna Convention on ODS) 1985 is a framework convention that was adopted in Vienna in March 1985 and entered into force on 22 September 1988. The main focus of the Convention is that the parties to the Convention shall take appropriate measures in accordance with its provisions and of the protocols in force to which they are party to protect human health and the environment against adverse effects resulting or likely to result from human activities which modify or are likely to modify the ozone layer.[132] To this end, parties are requested to take appropriate measures under the provisions of the Convention and according to the means at their disposal and their capacities to:

(a) Co-operate by systematic observations, research and information exchange to better understand and assess the effects of human activities on the ozone layer and the effect on human health and the environment from modification of the ozone layer.
(b) Adopt appropriate legislative or administrative measures and co-operate in harmonising appropriate policies to control, limit, reduce or prevent human activities under their jurisdiction or control should it be found that these activities

[127] Ibid., Art. 4.
[128] Ibid., Art. 7.
[129] Ibid., Art. 8.
[130] Ibid., Art. 9.
[131] United Nations (1985).
[132] Vienna Convention on ODS (1985), Art. 2(1).

have or are likely to have adverse effects resulting from modification or likely modification of the ozone layer.

(c) Co-operate in the formulation of agreed measures procedures and standards for the implementation of this Convention with a view to the adoption of protocols and annexes.
(d) Co-operate with competent international bodies to implement effectively this Convention and protocol to which they are party.[133]

To this end, parties shall: (a) adopt appropriate legislative and administrative measures[134] and (b) cooperate:

1. on research and scientific assessment, scientific observations and information exchange;[135]
2. in the development and transfer of technology and knowledge;[136]
3. in the formulation of agreed measures, procedures and standard for the implementation of the Convention;
4. transmission of information on measures adopted in implementing the Convention.[137]

All these are geared towards identifying the physical and chemical processes that may affect the ozone layer, human health and other biological effects deriving from any modifications of the ozone layer, particularly those resulting from changes in ultra-violet solar radiation having biological effects (UV-B) as well as climatic effects deriving from any modifications of the ozone layer. Other aspects of the obligations point to identifying the effects deriving from any modifications of the ozone layer and any consequent change in UV-B radiation on natural and synthetic materials useful to mankind; as well as identifying substances, practices, procedures and activities that may affect the ozone layer, and their cumulative effects; and determine alternative substances and technologies and related socio-economic matters.[138]

To ensure the effective implementation of the Convention, two bodies are established. Namely:

(a) Conference of the Parties (CoP): The CoP has to keep under continuous review the implementation of the Convention. In addition, the CoP shall promote the harmonisation of policies and measures; establish necessary subsidiary bodies for the implementation of the Convention; review the various scientific information, among others.[139]

[133] Ibid., Art. 2(2).

[134] Ibid.

[135] Ibid., Arts. 3(1)(2)(3) and 4(1).

[136] Ibid., Art. 4(2).

[137] Ibid., Art. 5.

[138] Vienna Convention on ODS (1985), Art. 3(1).

[139] Ibid., Art. 6(4).

(b) A Secretariat: The Secretariat is established under Article 7 of the Convention and has the duty to arrange for and service meetings, prepare and transmit reports on countries' implementation of the Convention and its own activities, as well as ensuring coordination with other relevant international bodies.

A dispute resolution mechanism was also established by the Convention. A dispute as to the interpretation or application of the Convention shall be sought by negotiating, failing which the parties may jointly seek mediation by a third party.[140] However, on ratification, acceptance, approval or accession to the Convention, a party may declare in writing to the Depository (UN Secretary-General) that where mediation fails, it accepts compulsory settlement by arbitration or submission to the International Court of Justice (ICJ), otherwise the dispute shall be submitted to conciliation, and a Conciliation Commission shall on request of the parties be created.[141]

6.4.2.3 Montreal Protocol on Substances that Deplete the Ozone Layer 1987 and Its Amendments (Montreal Protocol)[142]

The Vienna Convention on ODS 1985 is a framework agreement. Although it provides a structure for action to protect the ozone layer, it neither specifies particular measures to be taken nor mentions any substance that might harm the ozone. As a result of this gap, it became necessary for more concrete action if the objectives of the Vienna Convention on ODS 1985 were to be achieved.

Consequently, the Conference of Plenipotentiaries on the Protocol on Chlorofluorocarbons to the Vienna Convention for the Protection of the Ozone Layer was convened by the Executive Director of the United Nations Environment Programme (UNEP) pursuant to decision 13/18 adopted by the Governing Council of UNEP on 23 May 1985.[143] The parties to the Conference of Plenipotentiaries in Montreal, Canada in 1987 and adopted the Montreal Protocol on substances that deplete the ozone layer. The adoption was on 15 September 1987.

According to the UNEP,[144] the Montreal Protocol on Substances that Deplete the Ozone Layer is the landmark multilateral environmental agreement that regulates the production and consumption of nearly 100 man-made chemicals referred to as ozone-depleting substances (ODS). When released into the atmosphere, those chemicals damage the stratospheric ozone layer, Earth's protective shield that protects humans and the environment from harmful levels of ultraviolet radiation from the sun. The Protocol is to date the only United Nations Treaty ever that has been

[140] Ibid., Art. 11(1)(2).

[141] Ibid., Art. 20.

[142] United Nations (1989) Montreal Protocol on ODS 1987.

[143] Ibid.

[144] United Nations Environment Programme (UNEP) (2021b).

ratified by every country on Earth as all the 198 UN Member States have adopted it.[145]

The objective of the Protocol is "to protect the ozone layer by taking precautionary measures to control global emissions of substances that deplete the ozone layer."[146] To this end, the Protocol adopted control measures that regulate the "production" of "controlled substances"[147] by the freezing of their consumption and production. To achieve its objectives, the Protocol provides for mechanisms through which certain ozone-depleting substances (ODS) can be regulated.[148] Such mechanisms include:

(a) setting up control measures among parties and non-parties;
(b) regulating the level of consumption of Chlorofluorocarbon (CFCs) and other fully halogenated CFCs, halons, carbon tetrachloride, 1,1,1-trichloroethane (methyl chloroform), hydro chlorofluorocarbons (HCFC), hydrobromofluorocarbons (HBFC) and methyl bromide;
(c) requesting parties to report data on their production, imports and exports of the controlled substances;
(d) promoting research, development, public awareness and exchange of information;
(e) establishing a financial mechanism, namely the Multilateral Fund, to meet all agreed incremental costs of parties operating under Articles 5(1) and 10;
(f) establishing an Implementation Committee, and,
(g) requiring all parties to take every practicable step to transfer the best available, environmentally safe substitutes and related technologies to parties operating under Article 5(1).

A few control measures are also adopted by the Protocol.[149] These include control of trade measures on ODS among parties and control of trade measures with non-parties to the Vienna Convention on ODS and its Protocol.

Under control of trade among parties, the Protocol recognises that all parties must take appropriate measures to protect human health and the environment against adverse effects resulting or likely to result from human activities which modify or are likely to modify the ozone layer. Thus, each party shall ensure that for 12 months commencing on the first day of the seventh month following the date of the entry into force of the Protocol, and every 12 months thereafter, its consumption of the controlled substances does not exceed its calculated level of consumption in 1986.

---

[145] Ibid.

[146] Montreal Protocol on ODS (1987), Preamble.

[147] The Protocol defines production as "the amount of controlled substances produced minus the amount destroyed by technologies approved by the parties," while controlled substances include substances existing as a mixture or alone and consumption as "production plus import minus exports of controlled substances." Montreal Protocol on ODS (1987), Art. 1.

[148] Montreal Protocol on ODS (1987), Arts. 2(a)–(h), 5, 7, 9 and 10.

[149] Ibid., Art. 4.

However, the Protocol differentiates the level of obligation between parties that are developing countries and whose annual calculated level of consumption of controlled substances in Annexes A and B is less than 0.3 kg per capita and 0.2 kg per capita respectively.

Under control of trade measures on ODS with non-parties, the Protocol enjoins each party to ban the import and export of any controlled substances after a specified period for each substance or group of substances. This ban also extends to the import of products containing controlled substances and products produced with, but not containing, controlled substances from non-parties.[150]

Furthermore, parties are obliged to facilitate safe alternative substances and technology for developing country parties and to facilitate the provisions of subsidies, aids, credits, etc., to them for the use of technology and substitute products. Parties shall equally cooperate in promoting research development and information exchange and promote awareness of the environmental effects of the substances.[151] To this end, the Protocol sets out for the establishment of a Multilateral Fund as a financial mechanism for the implementation of the provisions of the Protocol.[152] The Fund, which is financed by contributions from parties operates under the authority of the parties who decides its overall policies. The Fund aims at, among other things:

1. meeting, on a grant or concessional basis as appropriate, and according to criteria decided upon by the parties, the agreed incremental costs;
2. financing clearing-house functions to identify and facilitate possible technical cooperation to assist parties operating under Article 5(1).

The Protocol provides for the establishment of several bodies for the implementation of its provisions. The bodies are:

1. Meeting of the Parties (MoP) which shall inter alia; approve procedures and mechanisms for determining non-compliance and treatment of non-complying parties. It also has the mandate to review and assess the Protocol.[153] To carry out its functions there is established an Implementation Committee which receives, considers and reports to the MoP on reservations expressed by one or more parties regarding another party's implementation of its obligations under the Convention, as well as on information reviewed or observations made by the Secretariat regarding the information it receives under Articles 7 and 9. The Meeting of the Parties is the governance body for the treaty, with technical support provided by an Open-ended Working Group, both of which meet on an annual basis. The parties are assisted by the Ozone Secretariat, which is based at UN Environment Programme headquarters in Nairobi, Kenya.

[150] Montreal Protocol on ODS (1987).

[151] Ibid., Art. 5.

[152] Ibid., Art. 10(2).

[153] Ibid., Art. 12.

2. The Secretariat: The Vienna Convention and the Montreal Protocol share the same secretariat, called the Ozone Secretariat based at UNEP headquarters in Nairobi, Kenya.
3. Executive Committee of the Multilateral Fund: It consists of fourteen parties, seven parties operating under Article 5(1), and seven parties from a group of parties not so operating. The Committee which meets at least twice a year has the following functions: to develop the plan and budget of the Multilateral Fund and monitor expenditures incurred under the Fund; to develop the criteria for project eligibility; to review the performance reports on the implementation of activities supported by the Fund; to review any disagreement by a party operating under Article 5(1), on small projects; and to report to the meeting of the parties on its activities.

Some of the noticeable flaws in the Vienna Convention such as no fixed date for phasing out Ozone Depleting Substances, trading with non-parties, and setting up of multilateral funds to help developing country parties fulfil their obligations under the Protocol, among others, were cured by the Protocol.

First, it sets firm targets for reducing and eventually eliminating consumption and production of a range of ozone-depleting substances. For instance, developed countries phased out CFCs by 1996. The substances controlled by the Protocol are listed in Annexes A (CFCs, halons), B (other fully halogenated CFCs, carbon tetrachloride, methyl chloroform), C (HCFCs), E (methyl bromide) and F (HFCs).

Second, acknowledging the inequity of equal treatment for all and the very small contribution to ozone depletion made by developing country parties,[154] the Protocol through the establishment of the Multilateral Funds, makes special provisions for them.[155] Thus, developing country parties by 2005 were made to phase out CFCs reduce halons by 50%, the fumigant methyl bromide by 20% and the solvents carbon tetrachloride and methyl chloroform by 85% and 30% respectively.

Third, the Protocol dealt with the problem of non-parties by banning trade in controlled substances or products containing such substances. Akin to this, the parties must also discourage the exportation of CFC production technology. Fourthly, the power enjoyed by the Meeting of Parties to the Protocol is unique among environmental treaties. For instance, certain decisions taken by a two-thirds majority will bind all parties to the Protocol who voted against such decision, provided efforts to reach consensus had been exhausted. The Protocol has been amended in the light of experience and new information a few times:

The Protocol had evolved over time in light of new scientific, technical and economic developments, and it continues to be amended and adjusted. To this end, the Protocol had undergone several amendments. These include:

[154] Nigeria, for instance, consumes less than 0.3 kg of controlled substances per capita pursuant to Article 5 of the Protocol.

[155] Some industries in developing countries such as Nigeria's Adebowale, Eleganza, Vitafoam, etc., had at one time or the other benefited from this fund.

6.4.2.3.1 London Amendment

This amended the Montreal Protocol at the second meeting of the parties to the Protocol held in London in 1990 and came into force on 10 August 1992. The London Amendment introduced control measures for both the production and consumption of three new groups of substances: other halogenated CFCs, carbon tetrachloride and methyl chloroform by the year 2000 and gradual phasing out of controlled substances by 2005. Under the Amendment, a financial mechanism was established for providing financial and technological assistance to the developing country parties to enable their compliance with their obligations under the Protocol. The Fund has dispersed some $1.5 billion of the $1.6 billion approved in previous replenishments on projects and activities in developing countries since 1991. In November 2002, parties to the Protocol added the sum of $573 million to the Fund to help the developing country parties to the Protocol comply with their phase-out obligation under the Protocol.[156]

6.4.2.3.2 Copenhagen Amendment

This was adopted at the fourth meeting of the parties to the Protocol in 1992 in Copenhagen and entered into force on 14 June 1994. It introduced control measures for the consumption of HCFCs and control measures for both the production and consumption of two new groups of substances, namely HBFC and methyl bromide. Also, an Implementation Committee established under a declaration adopted in Helsinki in 1989 was enlarged and the Multilateral Fund already established was adopted on a permanent basis.[157]

6.4.2.3.3 Montreal Amendment

This was adopted in 1997 at the ninth meeting of parties to the Protocol held in Montreal and came into force on 10 November 1994. It introduced the requirement for licensing systems to allow control and monitoring of trade in substances controlled under the Protocol.[158]

6.4.2.3.4 Beijing Amendment

This was adopted in Beijing in 1999 at the 11th meeting of parties to the Protocol. The amendment introduced and imposed restrictions on trade with non-parties for

[156] United Nations Environment Programme (UNEP) (2002), p. 11.

[157] Ibid.

[158] Ibid.

the HCFCs. It also introduced control measures for both the production and consumption of one new group of substances: Bromo chloromethane (BCM).[159]

Owing to regulations on the production and use of certain ozone-destroying chlorinated compounds, which went into effect in January 1996, the atmospheric concentration of some of these man-made substances has begun to decline. Chlorine/bromine should reach maximum levels in the stratosphere in the first few years of the twenty-first century, and ozone concentrations should correspondingly be at their minimum levels during that period. It is anticipated that the recovery of the Antarctic ozone hole can then begin. But because of the slow rate of healing, it is expected that the beginning of this recovery will not be conclusively detected for a decade or more, and that complete recovery of the Antarctic ozone layer will not occur until the year 2050 or later. The exact date of recovery will depend on the effectiveness of present and future regulations on the emission of CFCs and their replacements. It will also depend on climate change in the intervening years, such as long-term cooling in the stratosphere, which could exacerbate ozone loss and prolong the recovery of the ozone layer.[160]

6.4.2.4 United Nations Framework Convention on Climate Change (Climate Change Convention) 1992[161]

Controlling GHG emissions was one of the efforts of the international community to protect the Earth's atmosphere. With the passage of time and more scientific discoveries and evidence, the international community came to realise GHG emissions have affected the Earth's atmosphere. That the world's weather has gone berserk is a fact as this act has led to many weather-related and induced catastrophes around the globe. It became necessary that efforts should be made to tackle this new phenomenon caused by air pollution that is resulting in climate change globally, with its attendant impacts. As Robert B. Zoellick[162] pointed out: "no country alone can take on the interconnected challenges posed by climate change…tackling the immense and multidimensional challenge of climate change demands extraordinary ingenuity and cooperation…such a transformation requires us to act now, act together, and act differently."[163]

One such effort of the international community to tackle air pollution relating to climate change was at the World Conference on Environment and Development (WCED) in 1992.[164] The WCED was seen as a watershed in the fight against climate

[159] United Nations Environment Programme (UNEP) (2002), p. 11.

[160] National Oceanic and Atmospheric Administration (2008).

[161] United Nations (1992).

[162] Former President of the World Bank.

[163] The World Bank (2010), p. xiii.

[164] This conference, also known as the Earth Summit, was held in Rio de Janeiro, Brazil, in June 1992.

change, and in the same vein air pollution. At the WCED the United Nations Framework Convention on Climate Change (Climate Change Convention 1992)[165] was adopted. As of 21 March 1994,[166] when it came into force, it had about 165 signatories, ratified by 50 countries.

The purpose of the Climate Change Convention 1992 is to establish an instrument to address the adverse effects of climate change and ensure that countries, particularly those most vulnerable can prepare adequately for adaptation to the adverse effect of climate change. This means changes in the physical environment or biota resulting from climate change which has significant deleterious effects on the composition of global atmosphere resilience or productivity of natural and managed ecosystems or the operation of socio-economic systems or on human health and welfare.[167]

The Climate Change Convention 1992 is made up of 26 articles and sets out a framework for the reduction of GHG emissions that will help to protect the atmosphere. The salient provisions of the Convention can broadly be separated into: the introductory provision setting forth the basic definitions,[168] objective of the Convention[169] and principles.[170] Other provisions are those relating to the commitments of parties to the Convention to the sources and sinks of greenhouse gases;[171] scientific cooperation, public information, and education; and financial resources and technology transfer among members,[172] and institutional and procedural mechanisms to implement the Convention.[173]

The ultimate objective of the Climate Change Convention 1992 is to "stabilize greenhouse gas concentration in the atmosphere at a level that would prevent dangerous anthropogenic interference with the climate system."[174] The climate system is defined as "the totality of the atmosphere, hydrosphere, biosphere and geosphere and their interactions."[175] While recognising that some climate change is inevitable, the objective of the Convention however, is to be achieved in such a way as to allow the ecosystem to adapt naturally to climate change to ensure that food production is not threatened and to enable economic development to proceed in a sustainable manner.[176] It therefore defines climate change as "a change of climate which is attributed directly or indirectly to human activity that alters the composition

[165] Hereinafter referred to as the Climate Change Convention 1992.

[166] United Nations Framework Convention on Climate Change Secretariat (2021).

[167] Climate Change Convention (1992), Art. 1(1).

[168] Ibid., Art. 1.

[169] Ibid., Art. 2.

[170] Ibid., Art. 3.

[171] Ibid., Art. 4.

[172] Ibid., Arts. 5 and 6.

[173] Ibid., Arts. 7 and 8.

[174] Ibid., Art. 2.

[175] Climate Change Convention (1992), Art. 1(3).

[176] Ibid., Art. 2.

of the global atmosphere and which is, in addition to natural climate variability observed over comparable period."[177]

To enable parties to achieve the objective of the Climate Change Convention 1992, the Convention sets out a few "principles" that will guide them in the implementation of its provisions. Thus, "Parties should protect the climate system for the benefit of present and future generations of humankind, on the basis of equity and in accordance with their common but differentiated responsibilities and respective capabilities. Accordingly, the developed country Parties should take the lead in combating climate change and the adverse effects thereof."[178]

Again, parties should take precautionary measures to anticipate, prevent or minimise the causes of climate change and mitigate its adverse effects.[179] Thus,

> where there are threats of serious or irreversible damage, lack of full scientific certainty should not be used as a reason for postponing such measures, taking into account that policies and measures to deal with climate change should be cost-effective so as to ensure global benefits at the lowest possible cost. To achieve this, such policies and measures should take into account different socio-economic contexts, be comprehensive, cover all relevant sources, sinks and reservoirs of greenhouse gases and adaptation, and comprise all economic sectors. Efforts to address climate change may be carried out cooperatively by interested Parties.[180]

Although the parties have a right to, and should, promote sustainable development, however, policies and measures to protect the climate system against human-induced change should be appropriate for the specific conditions of each party and should be integrated with national development programmes, taking into account that economic development is essential for adopting measures to address climate change.[181]

Overall, the parties should cooperate to promote a supportive and open international economic system that would lead to sustainable economic growth and development in all parties, particularly developing country parties, thus enabling them better to address the problems of climate change. Measures taken to combat climate change, including unilateral ones, should not constitute a means of arbitrary or unjustifiable discrimination or a disguised restriction on international trade.[182]

Besides the above principles, all parties taking into account their common but differentiated responsibilities and their specific national and regional development priorities, objectives and circumstances are committed to take certain measures in order to achieve the objective of the Convention. Such measures include: developing national inventories of anthropogenic emissions by sources and removals by

---

[177] Ibid., Art. 1(2).

[178] Ibid., Art. 3(1).

[179] Ibid., Art. 3(3).

[180] Ibid., Art. 3(3).

[181] Ibid., Art. 3(4).

[182] Climate Change Convention (1992), Art. 3(5).

sinks,[183] as well as formulating, implementing, publishing and regularly updating national and, where appropriate, regional programmes containing measures to mitigate climate change by addressing anthropogenic emissions by sources and removals by sinks of all greenhouse gases not controlled by the Montreal Protocol, and measures to facilitate adequate adaptation to climate change.[184]

In addition, parties are enjoined to "promote and cooperate in the development, application and diffusion, including transfer, of technologies, practices and processes that control, reduce or prevent anthropogenic emissions of greenhouse gases. . .in all relevant sectors, including the energy, transport, industry, agriculture, forestry and waste management sectors."[185] The parties are also required to promote sustainable management conservation and enhancement of sinks and reservoirs of these greenhouse gases,[186] cooperate in preparing for the adoption of the impacts of climate change,[187] and are further required to take climate change into account to the extent feasible, in their social, economic and environmental policies.[188]

To achieve all these, parties are to promote and cooperate in research, systematic observation and development of data archives to the further understanding of climate change, climate system and response strategies[189] as well as in education and public awareness.[190] This shall involve full, open and prompt exchange of relevant scientific, technological, technical, socio-economic and legal information related to the climate system and climate change, and to the economic and social consequences of various response strategies.[191]

All these commitments are to be periodically updated, published and made available to the Conference of the Parties, in accordance with Article 12 of the Climate Change Convention 1992.[192]

In addition to the above general commitments, the Convention sets out specific commitments. At the heart of these commitments are those relating to sources and sinks of greenhouse gases binding on all developed country parties.[193] To this end, each developed country party and each other party included in Annex I shall incorporate in its communication the following elements of information: (a) a detailed description of the policies and measures that it has adopted to implement its commitment and (b) a specific estimate of the effects such policies and measures

---

[183] Ibid., Art. 4(1)(a).
[184] Ibid., Art. 4(1)(b).
[185] Ibid., Art. 4(1)(c).
[186] Ibid., Art. 4(1)d).
[187] Ibid., Art. 4(1)(e).
[188] Ibid., Art. 4(1)(f).
[189] Ibid., Art. 4(1)(g).
[190] Ibid., Art. 4(1)(i).
[191] Climate Change Convention (1992), Art. 4(1)(h).
[192] Ibid., Art. 4(1)(j).
[193] Ibid., Art. 4(2).

will have on anthropogenic emissions by its sources and removals by its sinks of greenhouse gases during the period.[194]

The Climate Change Convention 1992 established institutions and arrangements for the implementation of its provisions. These institutions are the Conference of the Parties (CoP),[195] a Secretariat;[196] and two subsidiary bodies, namely: a subsidiary body for Scientific and Technological Advice,[197] and a subsidiary body for Implementation[198] and Financial Mechanism.[199]

The CoP is the supreme body of the Convention entrusted with keeping the implementation of the Convention under regular review and making decisions to promote its effective implementation. It has several functions set out under Article 7(2)(a–m) among which are:

1. To periodically examine the obligations of the parties.[200]
2. To facilitate the coordination of measures designed to promote the objectives of the Convention.[201]
3. To promote and guide compatible methodologies for preparing inventories of greenhouse gas emissions.[202]
4. To assess the implementation of the Convention by all parties and the overall effect of measures taken.[203]
5. To consider and adopt regular reports on the implementation of the Convention;[204]
6. Seek to mobilize financial resources in accordance with Article 4, paras 3, 4 and 5, and Article 11.[205]
7. Establish such subsidiary bodies as are deemed necessary for the implementation of the Convention[206]
8. Review reports submitted by its subsidiary bodies and provide guidance to them.[207]

[194] Ibid., Art. 12(2).

[195] Ibid., Art. 7(1). The CoP has been a prime mover in efforts to contain climate change. Through its instrumentality, the Kyoto Protocol on emission reduction was adopted in 1997 at the CoP3, and the Paris Agreement on Climate Change agreed upon by the parties in 2015 during the CoP21—two legal instruments for climate change mitigation and adaptation.

[196] Climate Change Convention (1992), Art. 8(1).

[197] Ibid., Art. 9.

[198] Ibid., Art. 10.

[199] Ibid., Art. 11(1)–(4).

[200] Ibid., Art. 12(2)(a).

[201] Ibid., Art. 12(2)(c).

[202] Climate Change Convention (1992), Art. 12(2)(d).

[203] Ibid., Art. 12(2)(e).

[204] Ibid., Art. 12(2)(f).

[205] Ibid., Art. 12(2)(h).

[206] Ibid., Art. 12(2)(i).

[207] Ibid., Art. 12(2)(j).

9. Agree upon and adopt, by consensus, rules of procedure and financial rules for itself and for any subsidiary bodies.[208]
10. Seek and utilize, where appropriate, the services and cooperation of, and information provided by, competent international organisations and intergovernmental and non-governmental bodies.[209]

The subsidiary body for Scientific and Technological Advice is multidiscipline and it is established to provide information on scientific and technological matters to the Conference of the Parties, as well as under the guidance of CoP, provide various functions to other international bodies.[210] The subsidiary body for implementation on the other hand will assist the CoP in the assessment and review of the implementation of the Convention.[211]

The Financial Mechanism entails the provision of financial resources to parties on a grant or concessional basis including technology. The mechanism functions under the guidance of, and is accountable to, the CoP.

Envisaging disputes arising during the implementation of the Convention, the Convention provides for the establishment of a multilateral consultative process for the resolution of implementation questions.[212] The Convention[213] also provides for possible compulsory recourse to arbitration or the International Court of Justice with the consent of the relevant parties to a dispute as well as the possibility for the compulsory establishment of a conciliation commission with the power to make a recommendatory award at the request of one of the parties to a dispute 12 months after notification of the dispute.

6.4.2.5 Kyoto Protocol to the United Framework Convention on Climate Change (Kyoto Protocol) 1997[214]

When the Climate Change Convention 1992 was adopted specific commitments to target emission levels of greenhouse gases were not included as the Convention did not set any legally binding limitations on emissions or provide any enforcement mechanisms. In 1995, the Conference of Parties (CoP) to the Climate Change

[208] Ibid., Art. 12(2)(k).

[209] Ibid., Art. 12(2)(l).

[210] Ibid., Art. 9(1)(2)(a)–(e).

[211] Ibid., Art. 10(2)(a)–(c).

[212] Climate Change Convention (1992), Art. 13.

[213] Ibid., Art. 14.

[214] With the signing of the Paris Climate Agreement in 2015, although the life span of the Kyoto Protocol 1997 was extended beyond 2012 to 2020 under the Doha Amendment, the regime of the Kyoto Protocol came to an end. The discussions on the Kyoto Protocol were merely done to highlight efforts of the international community, since the adoption of the Climate Change Convention in 1992 in mitigating global warming and climate change and in effect managing air pollution.

Convention 1992 launched a new round of talks, aimed at producing stronger and more detailed commitments from the parties, especially from the industrialised countries.

At the first session of the CoP held in Berlin in that year, 1995, negotiations were commenced and this led to the drafting of further legal instruments to give "teeth" to the implementation of the Climate Change Convention 1992. The result was the Kyoto Protocol to the Climate Change Convention 1992 adopted in Kyoto, Japan, on 11 December 1997 and entered into force on 16 February 2005. There were 192 parties to the Protocol in 2020 (Canada withdrew from the protocol, effective December 2012).[215]

The Kyoto Protocol 1997 implemented the objective of the Climate Change Convention 1992, that is, to reduce the onset of global warming by reducing greenhouse gas concentrations in the atmosphere to "a level that would prevent dangerous anthropogenic interference with the climate system."[216]

The main goal of the Kyoto Protocol 1997 therefore, was to control emissions of the main anthropogenic greenhouse gases (GHGs), namely: carbon dioxide (CO_2); methane (CH_4); nitrous oxide (N_2O); hydrofluorocarbons (HFCs); perfluorocarbons (PFCs) and sulphur hexafluoride (SF_6).[217]

At the Doha Round in 2012 (CoP18),[218] the seventh anthropogenic greenhouse gas, Nitrogen trifluoride, was added for the second compliance period for the Kyoto Protocol 1997 (2012 to 31 December 2020). However, this should be done in ways that reflect underlying national differences in GHG emissions, wealth, and capacity to make the reductions.[219] This position acknowledged the fact that individual countries have different capabilities in combating climate change, owing to economic development, and therefore placed the obligation to reduce current emissions on developed countries on the basis that they are historically responsible for the current levels of greenhouse gases in the atmosphere. The Protocol had two commitment periods. The first started in 2008 and ended in 2012 and the second started in 2012 and ended in 2020.[220]

To achieve its objectives, the Kyoto Protocol 1997 provided three compliance mechanisms that allowed flexibility in how countries chose to meet their targets on stabilisation of GHG emissions. The compliance mechanisms were: the joint implementation of specific projects, emission trading and clean development mechanisms.

[215] United Nations (1997).

[216] Climate Change Convention (1992), Art. 2.

[217] Listed in Annex A to the Kyoto Protocol (1997).

[218] United Nations (2012).

[219] Grubb (2004), p. 2.

[220] The life span of the Kyoto Protocol was extended under the Doha Amendment at Doha, United Arab Emirates in 2012 under the CoP18. It came into force on 31 December 2020 following its acceptance by the mandated minimum number of at least 144 state parties. Ironically, the Agreement ended on the same day, 31 December 2020, when it came into force. See United Nations (2012).

6.4.2.5.1 Joint Implementation

Joint Implementation (JI)[221] involves specific projects being undertaken by Annex 1 Party to the Climate Change Convention 1992 which will reduce another Annex 1 party's greenhouse gas emissions. This could include energy efficiency measures or the transfer of clean technology, or increased removals of greenhouse gases by creating a sink. The country setting up the project can then use the resulting reduction in emissions to reach its own target.

The formal crediting period for Joint Implementation (JI) was aligned with the first commitment period of the Kyoto Protocol, and did not start until January 2008.[222] In November 2008, only 22 JI projects had been officially approved and registered. The total projected emission savings from JI by 2012 were about one-tenth that of the CDM. Russia accounts for about two-thirds of these savings, with the remainder divided up roughly equally between Ukraine and the European Union's (EU) new Member States. Emission savings included cuts in methane, HFC, and N_2O emissions.[223]

6.4.2.5.2 Clean Development Mechanism

Article 12 of the Kyoto Protocol 1997 contains a flexibility tool called the Clean Development Mechanism (CDM). The idea for the CDM originated with the Brazilian government's proposal for a Clean Development Fund. In its initial conception, the provision would have required countries that exceeded their emissions targets during a period to pay a fine to the Fund, which would then be used to finance sustainable development in non-Annex I countries. During negotiations, however, the idea of the Fund was modified and the CDM emerged in its place.[224]

Under the CDM, an Annex I country can earn Certified Emissions Reductions (CERs) by investing in an emissions reduction project in a non-Annex I country. The CERs can either be applied to the developed country's emissions reduction goal or sold to other Annex I countries. The Protocol specifies that to qualify for CERs, each project must be voluntarily undertaken by both parties, the project's benefits must be measurable, and the project must create reductions that are additional to any that would occur in the absence of the CDM project.[225] Beyond laying out these three requirements, the Kyoto Protocol only skeletally describes how the CDM will work in practice. Further details of the mechanism's operation are spelled out in the Marrakesh Accords, adopted at the CoP7 in 2001.

---

[221] Provided under Kyoto Protocol (1997), Art. 6.

[222] Carbon Trust (2009), p. 20.

[223] Ibid.

[224] Prouty (2009), pp. 513–540.

[225] Kyoto Protocol (1997), Art. 12.

Although similar to the JI mechanism, the CDM, however, involves emission reduction projects in developing countries, financed by industrialised countries. Such projects could be in relation to sources of greenhouse gases like "cleaner" power stations or reductions in overall emission levels. This stems from the fact that developing countries are not subjected to any reduction targets, and there was concern that there was little incentive for them to adopt measures that would contribute to the overall achievement of the aims of the Climate Change Convention 1992. Thus, the Annex 1 party can gain credit for assisting the developing countries in the creation of projects that result in certified emission reductions. This in turn counts for such countries' efforts toward meeting their own targets.

Each Annex I country was required to submit an annual report of inventories of all anthropogenic greenhouse gas emissions from sources and removals from sinks under the Climate Change Convention 1992 and the Kyoto Protocol 1997. These countries nominate a person (called a "designated national authority") to create and manage their greenhouse gas inventory. Virtually all the non-Annex I countries have also established a designated national authority to manage their Kyoto obligations, specifically the "CDM process." This determines which GHG projects they wish to propose for accreditation by the CDM Executive Board. The CDM is therefore designed to encourage the production of emission reductions in non-Annex I parties, while JI encourages the production of emission reductions in Annex I parties.

The production of emission reductions generated by the CDM and JI can be used by Annex I parties in meeting their emission limitation commitments.[226] The emission reductions produced by the CDM and JI are both measured against a hypothetical baseline of emissions that would have occurred in the absence of a particular emission reduction project. The emission reductions produced by the CDM are called Certified Emission Reductions (CERs); reductions produced by JI are called Emission Reduction Units (ERUs). The reductions are called "credits" because they are emission reductions credited against a hypothetical baseline of emissions.[227]

At the time of the original Kyoto targets, studies suggested that the flexibility mechanisms could reduce the overall aggregate cost of meeting the targets.[228] Studies also showed that national losses in Annex I gross domestic product (GDP) could be reduced by the use of the flexibility mechanisms.[229]

The economic basis for providing the flexibility mechanism is that the marginal cost of reducing (or abating) emissions differs among countries.[230] "Marginal cost" is the cost of abating the last tonne of CO_2-eq for an Annex I/non-Annex I party.

It should be noted that only emission reduction projects that do not involve using nuclear energy are eligible for accreditation under the CDM, to prevent nuclear

[226] Bashmakov et al. (2001).

[227] Quesada (2013).

[228] Hourcade et al. (2012).

[229] Ibid.

[230] Toth et al. (2001).

technology exports from becoming the default route for obtaining credits under the CDM.

6.4.2.5.3 Emission Trading System[231]

Under this mechanism, Annex 1 party to the Convention can participate in emission trading to fulfil their commitment under the Protocol. This would enable countries with a significant "surplus" of emissions reduction as a result of exceeding targets, either to sell that surplus to countries that have a "deficit" or "stockpile" it to safeguard against meeting future reduction targets. The "surplus" can be acquired through carbon credits, joint implementation activities or clean development.

Besides these flexible mechanisms, parties to the Kyoto Protocol could use Land Use, Land Use Change, and Forestry (LULUCF) to meet their targets.[232] LULUCF activities are also called "sink" activities. Changes in sinks and land use can influence the climate,[233] and indeed the Intergovernmental Panel on Climate Change's Special Report on LULUCF estimates that since 1750 a third of global warming has been caused by land use change.[234] Particular criteria apply to the definition of forestry under the Kyoto Protocol. Forest management, cropland management, grazing land management, and re-vegetation are all eligible LULUCF activities under the Protocol.[235] Annex I parties use of forest management in meeting their targets is capped.[236]

6.4.2.5.4 Criticisms of the Kyoto Protocol

A criticism of the Kyoto Protocol, and other international conventions, is that of the right of indigenous peoples' right to participate. This position is buttressed by Bruce E Johansen's[237] quote from The Declaration of the First International Forum of Indigenous Peoples on Climate Change. It states that:

> Despite the recognition of our role in preventing global warming, when it comes time to sign international conventions like the United Nations Framework Convention on Climate Change, once again, our right to participate in national and international discussions that directly affect our Peoples and territories is denied.

Additionally, later in the declaration, it reads:

---

[231] Emission trading is provided under the Kyoto Protocol (1997), Art. 17, and was discussed in full in Sect. 3.5 of Chap. 3 of this book.

[232] Dessai (2001), p. 3.

[233] Baede (2010).

[234] Watson et al. (2000).

[235] Dessai (2001), p. 9.

[236] Ibid.

[237] Johansen (2003), pp. 115–116

> We denounce the fact that neither the United Nations nor the Kyoto Protocol recognises the existence or the contributions of Indigenous Peoples. Furthermore, the debates under these instruments have not considered the suggestions and proposals of the Indigenous Peoples nor have the appropriate mechanisms to guarantee our participation in all the debates that directly concern the Indigenous Peoples has been established.[238]

The above position clearly represents the dilemma of developing countries in the implementation of the various commitments and effective participation in the flexibility mechanisms. This assertion is buttressed by some environmentalists and scientists who have criticised the existing commitments under the Kyoto Protocol for being too weak.[239] This has particularly centred on the balance between the low emissions and high vulnerability of the developing world to climate change, compared to high emissions in the developed world.

Another area of criticism of the provisions of the Kyoto Protocol was the requirement that parties could reduce their emissions by increasing the amount of greenhouse gases removed from the atmosphere by the use of sinks. Under this arrangement for every tonne of carbon that is stored in a tree, an equivalent tonne of carbon from fossil fuels can be released into the atmosphere. Through this means such a country can acquire carbon credit which can be traded under the emissions trading system.

However, as pointed out by Ball and McGillivray,[240] this approach is replete with problems as regards the calculation of the actual extent of the reduction. According to them the amount of reduction in heavily forested countries could be significant in the overall total reduction. It is estimated that Russia could claim over 25% reduction of its overall target from the use of managed forests. Activities that may create such sinks include afforestation, re-forestation and preventing deforestation,[241] as well as forest management, crop-land management, grazing-land management and re-vegetation.[242]

Some critics therefore claimed that the Kyoto Protocol did not promote long-term solutions to reduce greenhouse gas emissions, but rather short-term solutions in having countries try to meet emission reduction standards, either by lowering emissions or finding ways to obtain trading credits.[243] In the same way, there had been criticism that the Kyoto Protocol did not address the concentration of atmospheric greenhouse gases, but rather greenhouse gas emissions, focusing on the short-term over the long-term[244]—again, the Kyoto Protocol focused too much on carbon emissions and did not address other pollutants, such as sulphur dioxide and

[238] Ibid.

[239] Grubb (2004), p. 5.

[240] Ball and McGillivray (2008), p. 640.

[241] Those sink mechanisms were introduced as eligible activities under the Kyoto Protocol.

[242] Those sink mechanisms were introduced as eligible activities under the Marrakesh Accords in 2001.

[243] ThoughtCo (1997).

[244] Ibid.

nitrogen oxides, which either do direct harm to human health and/or can be addressed using technology.[245]

World Bank[246] commented on how the Kyoto Protocol had only had a slight effect on curbing global emissions growth. The treaty was negotiated in 1997, but in 2006, energy-related carbon dioxide emissions had grown by 24%.[247] World Bank also stated that the treaty had provided only limited financial support to developing countries to assist them in reducing their emissions and adapting to climate change.[248]

The Kyoto Protocol was also criticised based on nationalistic considerations. For instance, Sobisevich[249] expressed the opinion that "since human civilisation is based on the consumption of hydrocarbons, the adoption of the Kyoto agreements could have a negative impact on Russian economy." He regarded the Kyoto agreement "as discriminatory and not universal, since the main sources of carbon dioxide emissions like the US, China, India, Brazil, Mexico and Korea, as well as a number of developing countries, did not impose any restrictions on themselves."

In the same vein, the United States queried the exemption of developing countries, such as China and India, from having to reduce their greenhouse gas emissions under the Kyoto Protocol.[250] In this respect, the Bush Administration criticised the Kyoto Protocol on the basis that 80% of the world is exempt from emissions reduction standards as well as the potential for economic harm to the United States.[251] Further argument was that developing countries at the time of the creation of the treaty and now have been large emitters of greenhouse gases.[252]

Greenhouse gases do not remain in the area in which they are emitted, but rather move throughout the atmosphere of Earth. Therefore, some say that even if the world's largest greenhouse gas emitter tackled the issue of climate change, there would be minimal impact on the atmosphere if other countries around the world did not work on reducing their emission levels as well.[253] It was therefore argued that the costs of the Kyoto Protocol outweighed the benefits, believing that the standards that Kyoto set were too optimistic and that the Kyoto Protocol was a highly inequitable and inefficient agreement that would do little to curb greenhouse gas emissions.[254]

[245] Maich (2013).

[246] World Bank (2010), p. 233.

[247] Ibid., 248.

[248] World Bank (2010), p. 233.

[249] Sobisevich (2020), pp. 74–75.

[250] Sanger (2001).

[251] Presidency (2022) "George W. Bush: Letter to Members of the Senate on the Kyoto Protocol on Climate Change," www.presidency.ucsb.edu (accessed on 29 April 2022).

[252] American Council for Capital Formation (ACCF) (1999a).

[253] Intergovernmental Panel on Climate Change (2013).

[254] American Council for Capital Formation (ACCF) (1999b).

To this end, the true impact of the Kyoto Protocol in the long run on the reduction of greenhouse gas emissions was insignificant. Coon[255] questioned how much-developed countries could offset their emissions while developing countries continue to emit these greenhouse gases was criticised. A criticism on this issue is that climate change is a unique environmental issue, but the Kyoto Protocol followed the format of the other international treaties (not necessarily useful for environmental issues) instead of promoting innovation in approaching the issue of global warming.[256]

However, Gupta et al.[257] described the Kyoto first-round commitments as "modest," stating that they acted as a constraint on the treaty's effectiveness. It was suggested that subsequent Kyoto commitments could be made more effective with measures aimed at achieving deeper cuts in emissions, as well as having policies applied to a larger share of global emissions. In 2008, countries with a Kyoto cap made up less than one-third of annual global carbon dioxide emissions from fuel combustion.[258]

Notwithstanding criticisms, the Kyoto Protocol can be considered an important first step towards a really worldwide emission reduction system that will stabilise GHG emissions. Some of the principal concepts of the Kyoto Protocol were:

1. Mandating binding commitments for the Annex I parties by establishing legally binding commitments to reduce emissions of greenhouse gases for Annex I parties.[259]
2. To meet the objectives of the Protocol, Annex I parties were required to prepare policies and measures for the reduction of greenhouse gases in their respective countries. In addition, they are required to increase the absorption of these gases and utilise all mechanisms available, such as joint implementation, the clean development mechanism and emissions trading, to be rewarded with credits that would allow more greenhouse gas emissions at home.[260]
3. While urging for concerted efforts in stabilising GHGs emission, the Protocol maintained that all parties, taking into account their common but differentiated responsibilities and their specific national and regional development priorities, objectives and circumstances, shall formulate, implement, publish and regularly update national and, where appropriate, regional programmes containing measures to mitigate climate change and measures to facilitate adequate adaptation to climate change.[261]

[255] Coon (2001).

[256] The Independent (2007).

[257] Gupta et al. (2007), p. 2.

[258] International Energy Agency (IEA) (2011), p. 12.

[259] Kyoto Protocol (1997), Arts. 3 and 5.

[260] Ibid., Art. 4.

[261] Ibid., Art. 10(b).

4. To minimise the effects of implementing the objectives of the Protocol on Developing Countries an adaptation fund for climate change was established.[262]
5. To ensure the integrity of the Protocol, provisions for accounting, reporting and review were provided.[263]
6. For purposes of compliance, a Compliance Committee to enforce compliance with the commitments under the Protocol was established.[264]

In addition, the Kyoto Protocol provided the architecture for the future international agreement on climate change. In 2015, at the sustainable development summit held in Paris, all UNFCCC participants adopted yet another pact, the Paris Agreement, which effectively replaced the Kyoto Protocol.

6.4.2.6 Paris Agreement to Climate Change Convention (Paris Agreement) 2015

At the Conference of Parties (CoP21) to the UNFCCC held in Paris, France, between 30 November 2015 and 12 December 2015, the parties to the Climate Change Convention 1992 were tasked to set the world on a path to address the issue of climate change by adopting a new climate agreement to replace the Kyoto Protocol 1997 that was billed to come to an end on 31 December 2020. After a series of debates, negotiations, disagreements and horse-trading, on 12 December 2015, the Paris Agreement as a treaty was formally adopted. The Agreement was based on the parties to the UNFCCC, pursuant to the Durban Platform for Enhanced Action, and was opened for signature on 22 April 2016.[265]

On 5 October 2016, the threshold for the entry into force of the Paris Agreement was achieved. The Paris Agreement entered into force on 4 November 2016, 30 days after the date on which at least 55 parties to the Convention accounting in total for at least an estimated 55% of the total global greenhouse gas emissions have deposited their instruments of ratification, acceptance, approval or accession with the Depositary. About 193 parties out of 197 parties to the Convention are parties to the Paris Agreement.[266]

The Paris Agreement 2015[267] consists of 29 articles and 16 preambular paragraphs. The treaty text is annexed to a 20-page CoP decision[268] that formally adopts the agreement and addresses some technical and substantive matters to give effect to it. The operative provisions of the Paris Agreement cover the substantive issues of

[262] Ibid., Art. 11(2)(a)(b).

[263] Ibid., Arts. 7 and 8.

[264] Kyoto Protocol (1997), Art. 9.

[265] United Nations Framework Convention on Climate Change (UNFCCC) (2015), Draft decision -/CP.21, FCCC/CP/2015/L.9/Rev.1.

[266] Ibid.

[267] United Nations Framework Convention on Climate Change (UNFCCC) (2022).

[268] Ibid.

mitigation, adaptation and means of implementation (capacity-building, finance, and technology transfer). The remainder of the Agreement includes a host of procedural and institutional arrangements.[269]

The Agreement covers most greenhouse gas emissions, but does not apply to international aviation and shipping, which fall under the responsibility of the International Civil Aviation Organisation and the International Maritime Organisation, respectively.[270] Discussions on the Paris Agreement were divided into:

1. Aim and Goal of the Agreement.
2. Substantive Issues in the Agreement.
3. Means of Implementation of the Agreement.
4. Procedural and Institutional Arrangements.

6.4.2.6.1 Aim and Goal of the Agreement

The aim of the Paris Agreement 2015, as provided in Article 2(1) is to have a stronger response to the danger of climate change; it seeks to enhance the implementation of the United Nations Framework Convention on Climate Change 1992 through:

(a) Holding the increase in the global average temperature to well below 2 °C above pre-industrial levels and pursuing efforts to limit the temperature increase to 1.5 °C above pre-industrial levels, recognising that this would significantly reduce the risks and impacts of climate change;
(b) Increasing the ability to adapt to the adverse impacts of climate change and foster climate resilience and low greenhouse gas emissions development, in a manner that does not threaten food production;
(c) Making finance flows consistent with a pathway towards low greenhouse gas emissions and climate-resilient development.

Therefore, the Paris Agreement's long-term temperature goal is to keep the rise in mean global temperature well below 2 °C (3.6 °F) above pre-industrial levels, and preferably limit the increase to 1.5 °C (2.7 °F), recognising that this would substantially reduce the effects of climate change. Emissions should be reduced as soon as possible and reach net zero by the middle of the twenty-first century.[271] Achieving the aim and goals of the Paris Agreement is predicated on several salient provisions.

---

[269] Savaresi (2016), pp. 16–263.

[270] Dessler and Parson (2020), pp. 190–191.

[271] Dessler and Parson (2020), p. 191.

6.4.2.6.2 Substantive Issues in the Agreement

6.4.2.6.2.1 Nationally Determined Contributions (NDC)

The Paris Agreement introduces a "bottom-top" approach to climate change governance as against the hitherto "top-down" governance under the Kyoto Protocol. This is because, under the Paris Agreement, no mechanism is provided that forces a country to set specific emission targets. Here, the distinction between developed and developing countries is blurred, so that the latter have to also submit plans for emission reductions under its Nationally Determined Contributions (NDC). This contrasts with the Kyoto Protocol 1997 where emission targets were set for the Annex 1 countries. By decision 1/CP.21,[272] the Conference of the Parties (CoP) invited parties to communicate their first nationally determined contribution (NDC) no later than when the party submits its respective instrument of ratification, acceptance, approval or accession. If a party has communicated an intended nationally determined contribution (INDC) before joining the Agreement, that party shall be considered to have satisfied this provision unless that party decides otherwise.

Under the Paris Agreement therefore, "each Party shall prepare, communicate and maintain successive nationally determined contributions (NDCs) that it intends to achieve and parties shall pursue domestic mitigation measures, with the aim of achieving the objectives of such contributions."[273] Article 3 therefore requires NDCs to make "ambitious efforts" towards "achieving the purpose of this Agreement" and to "represent a progression over time." To this end, "each Party's successive nationally determined contribution will represent a progression beyond the Party's then current nationally determined contribution and reflect its highest possible ambition, reflecting its common but differentiated responsibilities and respective capabilities, in the light of different national circumstances."[274]

However, the Paris Agreement does not prescribe the exact nature of the NDCs. At a minimum, they should contain mitigation provisions, but they may also contain pledges on adaptation,[275] financial support,[276] technology development and transfer,[277] capacity building[278] and transparency.[279] Some of the pledges in the NDCs are unconditional, but others are conditional on outside factors such as getting finance and technical support, the ambition of other parties, or the details of rules

[272] United Nations Framework Convention on Climate Change (UNFCCC) (2022), para 22.

[273] Paris Agreement (2015), Art. 4(2).

[274] Ibid., Art. 4(3).

[275] See the provisions of the Paris Agreement (2015), Art. 7.

[276] Paris Agreement (2015), Art. 9.

[277] Ibid., Art. 10.

[278] Ibid., Art. 11.

[279] Ibid., Art. 13.

of the Paris Agreement that are yet to be set. Most NDCs have a conditional component.[280]

6.4.2.6.2.2 Principle of Common but Differentiated Responsibilities

Another salient provision of the Paris Agreement is that in one of its preambles[281] it states that the Agreement is "in pursuit of the objective of the Convention,[282] and being guided by its principles, including the principle of equity and common but differentiated responsibilities and respective capabilities, in the light of different national circumstances."[283] However, it does not set out a specific division between developed and developing nations.[284] This division is blurred as all parties, whether Annex I richer countries with historical responsibility for climate change and non-Annex I countries as per the Kyoto Protocol are required to submit emissions reduction plans.[285]

In the words of Savaresi,[286] the Agreement dismantles the firewall between developed and developing countries' obligations, at least partially. While developed countries should still "continue taking the lead" in reducing their emissions, and are required to provide support to developing countries,[287] the agreement also "encourages" developing countries to move "towards economy-wide emission reduction of limitation targets, in light of different national circumstances."[288]

Thus, the Paris Agreement 2015 for the first time unequivocally establishes that all parties "aim to reach global peaking of greenhouse gas emissions as soon as possible,"[289] asking each and all to undertake and communicate "ambitious efforts" to achieve the purpose of the agreement.[290] It therefore requests all parties to make efforts to reduce their emissions[291] and to submit information on the details. In this connection, the Agreement introduces a nuanced approach to differentiation, providing less stringent requirements for least developing countries and small island developing states.[292] At the same time, levelling the reporting obligations for the

[280] Fatima-Zahra et al. (2020), p. 17.

[281] Paris Agreement (2015), Preamble, para 3.

[282] That is, the Climate Change Convention (1992), Art. 2.

[283] Paris Agreement (2015), Preamble, para 3.

[284] Sinhah (2015).

[285] Ibid.

[286] Savaresi (2016), p. 22.

[287] Paris Agreement (2015), Art. 4(4)(5).

[288] Ibid.

[289] Ibid., Art. 4(1).

[290] Ibid., Art. 3.

[291] Ibid.

[292] Savaresi (2016), p. 22.

others[293] is expected to engender a considerable secondary rules development process.[294]

6.4.2.6.2.3 *Pathways for Climate Change Mitigation*

Climate change mitigation refers to efforts to reduce or prevent the emission of greenhouse gases. Mitigation can mean using new technologies and renewable energies, making older equipment more energy efficient, or changing management practices or consumer behaviour.[295]

The issue of climate change mitigation is addressed in the Paris Agreement. It recognises that some parties may choose to pursue voluntary cooperation in the implementation of their NDCs to allow for higher ambition in their mitigation and adaptation actions and to promote sustainable development and environmental integrity.[296] To achieve this, Article 6 of the Paris Agreement establishes a framework for voluntary international cooperation for countries to reduce emissions and meet their NDCs, recognising the potential of international carbon markets to achieve emission reductions in a cost-efficient way and to spur private sector investment.

In this respect, an accounting framework for a cooperative approach to using credits from emissions reduction projects, known in the Agreement as international transferred mitigation outcomes (ITMOs) is established.[297] This framework includes linking the emissions-trading schemes of two or more countries. It also allows for the bilateral transfer of carbon credits between countries.

A central United Nations mechanism to certify tradable credits from emissions reductions generated through specific projects is established under the Agreement. The mechanism aims to promote the mitigation of greenhouse gas emissions while fostering sustainable development, incentivise and facilitate participation in the mitigation of greenhouse gas emissions by public and private entities authorised by a party, contribute to the reduction of emission levels in the host party, which will benefit from mitigation activities resulting in emission reductions that can also be used by another party to fulfil its nationally determined contribution and deliver an overall mitigation in global emissions is established under the Paris Agreement.[298]

However, the initial problem with the provisions of Article 6 was getting agreement between the parties to the framework and detailed rules needed for the provisions, especially Article 6(2) and (4), to work. This problem was somehow solved at the CoP26[299] where nations reached new agreements for market mechanisms,

[293] Paris Agreement (2015), Art. 4(6).

[294] Ibid., Art. 4(8)–(13).

[295] United Nations Environment Programme (UNEP) (2022).

[296] Paris Agreement (2015), Art. 6(1).

[297] Ibid., Art. 6(2).

[298] Ibid., Art. 6(4).

[299] Held in Glasgow, Scotland, between 31 October—13 November 2021.

essentially supporting the transfer of emission reductions between countries while also incentivising the private sector to invest in climate-friendly solutions. Simultaneously, parties decided on non-market approaches enabling stronger cooperation between countries on mitigation and adaptation.[300] The outcome of CoP26 therefore unified and internationally controlled standards including provisions to avoid situations where the same emissions reductions are claimed by multiple companies or countries. Overall, Article 6 broadly outlines the cooperative approach that parties can take in achieving their nationally determined carbon emissions reductions. In doing so, it helps establish the Paris Agreement as a framework for a global carbon market.[301]

6.4.2.6.2.4 Adaptation Procedures

Climate change adaptation received more focus in Paris negotiations than in previous climate treaties. Adapting to climate change means taking action to prepare for and adjust to both the current effects of climate change and the predicted impacts in the future.[302]

Collective, long-term adaptation goals are included in the Agreement, and countries must report on their adaptation actions, making it a parallel component with mitigation.[303] The adaptation goals focus on enhancing adaptive capacity, strengthening resilience and reducing vulnerability to climate change, to contribute to sustainable development and ensure an adequate adaptation response in the context of the temperature goal under the Agreement.[304]

However, adaptation action should follow a country-driven, gender-responsive, participatory and fully transparent approach, taking into consideration vulnerable groups, communities and ecosystems, and should be based on and guided by the best available science and, as appropriate, traditional knowledge, knowledge of indigenous peoples and local knowledge systems, to integrate adaptation into relevant socioeconomic and environmental policies and actions, where appropriate.[305]

Under the adaptation mechanism, parties are encouraged to strengthen their cooperation in enhancing action on adaptation with regard to sharing information and strengthening institutional arrangements and scientific knowledge on climate, including research, systematic observation of the climate system and early warning systems. Parties are also encouraged to assist developing country parties in identifying effective adaptation practices, adaptation needs, priorities, support provided and received for adaptation actions and efforts, and challenges and gaps, in a manner

[300] United Nations Framework Convention on Climate Change (UNFCCC) (2021).
[301] Stavins (2016).
[302] European Union (EU) (2022).
[303] Mogelgaard (2015).
[304] Paris Agreement (2015), Art. 7(1).
[305] Ibid., Art. 7(5).

consistent with encouraging good practices and improving the effectiveness and durability of adaptation actions.[306]

The global stocktake (GST)[307] shall recognise adaptation efforts of developing country parties; enhance the implementation of adaptation action by taking into account the adaptation communication, review the adequacy and effectiveness of adaptation and support provided for adaptation; and review the overall progress made in achieving the global goal on adaptation.[308]

6.4.2.6.2.5 Issue of Compensation for Loss and/or Damage

Another element introduced under the Paris Agreement in pursuit of climate change mitigation and adaptation is the issue of compensation for loss and/or damage resulting from impacts of human-induced climate change.

"Loss" applies to the "complete disappearance of something such as human lives, habitats, or even species."[309] These are gone forever and cannot be brought back. "Damage" on the other hand, refers to "something that can be repaired, such as a road or building or embankment."[310] Thus, loss and damage from climate change refers to the complete and irrecoverable loss of some things and the repairable damage of other things due to the impacts of human-induced climate change. It can stem from extreme weather or slow-onset events such as the loss of land to sea level rise for low-lying islands.[311]

Before the CoP21 in Paris France, compensation and liability/loss and damage from climate change-induced impact remained a bone of contention in climate change governance. The issue of compensation and liability or loss and damage from climate change impact had been muted during the CoP16 (held at Cancun, Mexico from 29 November 2011 to 10 December 2011)[312] and CoP17 (held in Durban, South Africa from 28 November 2011 to 11 December 2011).[313] During the CoP16, the Conference of the Parties decided to establish a work programme in order to consider approaches to address loss and damage associated with climate change impacts in developing countries that are particularly vulnerable to the adverse effects of climate change.[314]

---

[306] Paris Agreement (2015), Art. 7(7).

[307] GST was discussed below.

[308] Paris Agreement (2015), Art. 7(14).

[309] Huq and DeSouza (2016).

[310] Ibid.

[311] Taraska (2015).

[312] United Nations Framework Convention on Climate Change (UNFCCC) (2010), Decision 1/CP.16 FCCC/KP/CMP/2010/12/Add.1.

[313] United Nations Framework Convention on Climate Change (UNFCCC) (2011), Decision 7/CP.17, FCCC/CP/2011/9/Add.2.

[314] United Nations Framework Convention on Climate Change (UNFCCC) (2010), Decision 1/CP.16 FCCC/KP/CMP/2010/12/Add.1.

However, at the CoP17, the Conferences of Parties then recognised the need to strengthen international cooperation and expertise to understand and reduce loss and damage associated with the adverse effects of climate change, including impacts related to extreme weather events and slow onset events.[315] Parties were then encouraged to make use of the relevant information contained in the *Special Report on Managing the Risks of Extreme Events and Disasters to Advance Climate Change Adaptation* of the Intergovernmental Panel on Climate Change (IPCC) in considering approaches to address loss and damage, as appropriate.[316]

The Subsidiary Body for Implementation of the UNFCCC[317] was therefore requested by the parties to continue the implementation of the work programme on approaches to address loss and damage associated with climate change impacts in developing countries that are particularly vulnerable to the adverse effects of climate change and to make recommendations on loss and damage to the Conference of the Parties for its consideration at its eighteenth session.[318]

The eighteenth session of the Conference of Parties (CoP18) was held in Doha, Qatar.[319] For the first time, the issue that rich nations should move towards compensating poor nations for losses due to climate change was given some modicum of attention. This was contained in the proposed Loss and Damage mechanism tagged "Approaches to address loss and damage associated with climate change impacts in developing countries that are particularly vulnerable to the adverse effects of climate change to enhance adaptive capacity."[320]

However, the Conference acknowledged that further work to advance the understanding of and expertise on loss and damage should include enhancing the understanding of:

1. The risk of slow onset events, and approaches to address them.
2. Non-economic losses and damages.
3. How loss and damage associated with the adverse effects of climate change affect those segments of the population that are already vulnerable owing to geography, gender, age, indigenous or minority status, or disability, and how the implementation of approaches to address loss and damage can benefit those segments of the population.
4. How to identify and develop appropriate approaches to address loss and damage associated with the adverse effects of climate change, including to address slow onset events and extreme weather events, including through risk reduction, risk

315 United Nations Framework Convention on Climate Change (UNFCCC) (2011), Decision 7/CP.17, FCCC/CP/2011/9/Add.2.

316 United Nations Framework Convention on Climate Change (UNFCCC) (2011), para 4.

317 Established under Climate Change Convention (1992), Art. 10.

318 United Nations Framework Convention on Climate Change (UNFCCC) (2011), para 1.

319 Held from 26 November 2012–8 December 2012.

320 United Nations Framework Convention on Climate Change (UNFCCC) (2012), Decision 3/CP.18FCCC/CP/2012/8/Add1, 21.

sharing and risk transfer tools, and approaches to rehabilitate from loss and damage associated with the adverse effects of climate change.

5. How approaches to address loss and damage associated with the impacts of climate change may be integrated into climate-resilient development processes.
6. How impacts of climate change are affecting patterns of migration, displacement and human mobility.[321]

However, the proposal did not go without some politicking where national interests prevailed over collective global interests. For instance, the then United Kingdom (UK) Climate Secretary, Ed Davey, posited that "we haven't agreed to set up a new institution and there's no blank cheque, but there is clearly an issue if, say, an island state is lost underwater."[322] Reacting to this assertion by the then UK Climate Secretary, Ronald Jumeau from Seychelles, the spokesman of the Alliance of Small Island States (AOSIS), condemned wealthy countries for their lack of urgency and opined that there would be no need for talk about compensation if the rich had cut their emissions in previous meetings.[323] To him:

> The Doha caravan seems to be lost in the sand. As far as ambition is concerned, we are lost. We're past the mitigation (emissions cuts) and adaptation eras. We're now right into the era of loss and damage. What's next after that? Destruction? Disappearance of some of our islands? We're already into the era of re-location. But after loss and damage there will be mass re-locations if we continue with this loss of ambition.[324]

In the end, the Conference decided to establish, at its nineteenth session, institutional arrangements, such as an international mechanism, including functions and modalities, to address loss and damage associated with the impacts of climate change in developing countries that are particularly vulnerable to the adverse effects of climate change.[325]

At the CoP19 in Warsaw, Poland[326] the Warsaw International Mechanism (WIM) for loss and damage associated with climate change impacts was established.[327] The purpose of WIM is to address loss and damage associated with the impacts of climate change, including extreme events and slow onset events, in developing countries that are particularly vulnerable to the adverse effects of climate change in a comprehensive, integrated and coherent manner.[328]

---

[321] United Nations Framework Convention on Climate Change (UNFCCC) (2012), para 7.

[322] Harrabin (2012).

[323] Harrabin (2011).

[324] Ibid.

[325] United Nations Framework Convention on Climate Change (UNFCCC) (2012), Decision 3/CP.18, FCCC/CP/2012/8/Add1, 21.

[326] Held from 11–13 November 2013.

[327] United Nations Framework Convention on Climate Change (UNFCCC) (2013) 3/CP.18, Decision 2/CP.19FCCC/CP/2013/10/Add,1.

[328] Ibid., para 1.

The WIM promotes the implementation of approaches to address loss and damage associated with the adverse effects of climate change by undertaking the following functions:

1. Enhancing knowledge and understanding of comprehensive risk management approaches to address loss and damage associated with the adverse effects of climate change.
2. Fostering dialogue, coordination, coherence and synergies among all relevant stakeholders, institutions, bodies, processes and initiatives outside the Convention, to promote cooperation and collaboration across relevant work and activities at all levels.
3. Enhancing action and support, including finance, technology and capacity building, to address loss and damage associated with the adverse effects of climate change.[329]

To carry out its functions an executive committee of WIM was established, which shall function under the guidance of, and be accountable to the Conference of the Parties through the Subsidiary Body for Scientific and Technological Advice and the Subsidiary Body for Implementation established under Climate Change Convention 1992.[330] The Executive Committee shall make recommendations, as appropriate.[331]

When the parties met during CoP21,[332] the push to address loss and damage as a distinct issue in the Paris Agreement came from the Alliance of Small Island States (AOSIS) and the Least Developed Countries (LDC), whose economies and livelihoods are most vulnerable to the negative effects of climate change.[333]

At the CoP21, the parties decided on the continuation of the Warsaw International Mechanism for Loss and Damage associated with Climate Change Impacts, following the review in 2016.[334] The Executive Committee of the Warsaw International Mechanism was further requested to establish a clearinghouse for risk transfer that serves as a repository for information on insurance and risk transfer to facilitate the efforts of parties to develop and implement comprehensive risk management strategies.[335]

In addition, the Executive Committee was also requested to establish, according to its procedures and mandate, a task force to complement, draw upon the work of and involve, as appropriate, existing bodies and expert groups under the Convention including the Adaptation Committee and the Least Developed Countries Expert

[329] Ibid., para 5.

[330] Both bodies are established pursuant to the Climate Change Convention (1992), Arts. 9 and 10, respectively.

[331] United Nations Framework Convention on Climate Change (UNFCCC) (2013), para 3.

[332] Conference of Parties to UNFCCC, held in Paris, France, from 30 November 2015–11 December 2015.

[333] Taraska (2015).

[334] United Nations Framework Convention on Climate Change (UNFCCC) (2015), para 48.

[335] Ibid., para 49.

Group, as well as relevant organisations and expert bodies outside the Convention, to develop recommendations for integrated approaches to avert, minimise and address displacement related to the adverse impacts of climate change.[336]

Although the Warsaw International Mechanism, which was established during the CoP19, categorises loss and damage as a subset of adaptation, was unpopular with many countries, under the Paris Agreement, it is recognised as a separate pillar.[337] Article 8 of the Paris Agreement anchors loss and damage. Recognising that parties may be affected not only by climate change, but also by the impacts of the measures taken in response to it[338] and noting the importance of ensuring the integrity of all ecosystems, including oceans, and the protection of biodiversity, recognised by some cultures as Mother Earth, and noting the importance for some of the concept of "climate justice," when taking action to address climate change,[339] the parties in Article 8 agreed to the inclusion of loss and damage as a way of supporting the less developed country parties.

The areas of cooperation and facilitation to enhance understanding, action and support under the Agreement include:

(a) Early warning system.
(b) Emergency preparedness.
(c) Slow onset events.
(d) Events that may involve irreversible and permanent loss and damage.
(e) Comprehensive risk assessment and management.
(f) Risk insurance facilities, climate risk pooling and other insurance solutions.
(g) Non-economic losses.
(h) Resilience of communities, livelihoods and ecosystems.[340]

In the end, the Agreement coming out of the CoP21 adopted the Warsaw International Mechanism, an institution that will attempt to address questions about how to classify, address, and share responsibility for loss,[341] and calls for "averting, minimising, and addressing loss and damage."[342] The Paris Agreement therefore gave breakthrough recognition to the concept of "loss and damage," sorting through thorny discussions and politically charged negotiating positions. However, the thorny issue of liability and compensation, which developing countries called for but developed countries were unwilling to have it included, was not captured in the Paris Agreement.[343] The Agreement specifies that recognising loss

[336] United Nations Framework Convention on Climate Change (UNFCCC) (2013), para 50.
[337] Pidcock (2017).
[338] United Nations Framework Convention on Climate Change (UNFCCC) (2015), para 7.
[339] Ibid., para 13.
[340] Paris Agreement (2015), Art. 8(4).
[341] Mogelgaard and McGray (2015).
[342] Paris Agreement (2015), Art. 8(1).
[343] Huq and De Souza (2016).

and damage "does not involve or provide a basis for any liability or compensation."[344]

These notwithstanding, ultimately, the Paris Agreement 2015 included anticipatory compensation mechanisms through risk insurance; assured the continuation of a global mechanism on loss and damage, the Warsaw International Mechanism and gave recognition to the long-articulated position of many countries that have been arguing for support of short-term coping and longer-term adaptation when mitigation and adaptation efforts are insufficient to deal with the effects of climate change.

6.4.2.6.3 Means of Implementing the Agreement

Other salient elements provided under the Paris Agreement 2015 revolve around how countries can support one another to achieve both the aim and the goal of the Agreement. In this respect, the Agreement provides a framework for the following: financial support, technology development and transfer, and capacity-building support.

The Paris Agreement 2015 provides a framework for financial support to those countries that need it. It thus provides for and reaffirms that developed countries should take the lead in providing financial assistance to countries that are less endowed and more vulnerable. To this end, developed country parties shall provide financial resources to assist developing country parties with respect to both mitigation and adaptation in continuation of their existing obligations under the Climate Change Convention 1992.[345] The Paris Agreement for the first time also encourages voluntary contributions by other parties.[346] Climate finance is needed for mitigation because large-scale investments are required to significantly reduce emissions. Climate finance is equally important for adaptation, as significant financial resources are needed to adapt to the adverse effects and reduce the impacts of a changing climate.

Also provided in the Paris Agreement is a framework for technology development and transfer.[347] Realising the need for technology development and transfer as a means of improving both the resilience to climate change and reducing GHG emissions,[348] it establishes a technology framework to provide overarching guidance to the well-functioning Technology Mechanism.[349] The mechanism is to accelerate technology development and transfer through its policy and implementation arms.[350]

[344] United Nations Framework Convention on Climate Change (UNFCCC) (2013), para 52.
[345] Paris Agreement (2015), Art. 9(1).
[346] Ibid., Art. 9(2).
[347] Ibid., Art. 10.
[348] Ibid., Art. 10(1).
[349] Ibid., Art. 10(4).
[350] Ibid., Art. 10(2).

Realising that not all developing countries have sufficient capacities to deal with many of the challenges brought by climate change, the Agreement provides a framework for capacity-building support.[351] Capacity-building under the Agreement is meant to enhance the capacity and ability of developing country parties, in particular countries with the least capacity, such as the least developed countries, and those that are particularly vulnerable to the adverse effects of climate change, such as small island developing states, to take effective climate change action, including, inter alia, to implement adaptation and mitigation actions, and should facilitate technology development, dissemination and deployment, access to climate finance, relevant aspects of education, training and public awareness, and the transparent, timely and accurate communication of information.[352]

However, such capacity-building should be country-driven, based on and responsive to national needs, and foster country ownership of parties, particularly for developing country parties, including at the national, subnational and local levels. Capacity-building should be guided by lessons learned, including those from capacity-building activities under the Convention, and should be an effective, iterative process that is participatory, cross-cutting and gender-responsive.[353]

As a result, the Paris Agreement places great emphasis on climate-related capacity-building for developing countries and requests all developed countries to enhance support for capacity-building actions in developing countries[354] and through appropriate institutional arrangements.[355]

6.4.2.6.4 Procedural and Institutional Arrangements

The next salient provision of the Paris Agreement borders on its implementation. While the NDCs themselves are not binding, the procedures surrounding them such as the obligation to prepare, communicate and maintain successive NDCs and set a new one every five years, and provide information about the implementation are binding.[356] However, there is no mechanism to force a country to set an NDC target by a specific date,[357] nor to meet their targets,[358] all that is required is that countries must increase their ambition every 5 years and such contributions are to be registered by the UNFCCC Secretariat.[359] How then can this be assessed? In order words are there means of tracking progress made in the implementation of the NDCs?

---

[351] Ibid., Art. 11.

[352] Ibid., Art. 11(1).

[353] Paris Agreement (2015), Art. 11(2).

[354] Ibid., Art. 11(3).

[355] Ibid., Art. 11(5).

[356] Bodansky (2016), pp. 142–150.

[357] Reguly and McCarthy (2015).

[358] Mark (2015).

[359] Paris Agreement (2015), Art. 4(9).

To review the implementation of the Agreement and to assess the collective progress towards the collectively agreed goals, the Paris Agreement has institutionalised a transformative ambition as countries are urged to establish an enhanced transparency framework (ETF).[360] The ETF provides a clear understanding including clarity and tracking of progress by relevant individual parties in the context of climate change actions towards achieving parties' individual NDC and progress made in implementing and achieving the NDC[361] and parties' actions related to climate change impacts and adaptation,[362] aggregate financial,[363] technology transfer[364] and capacity-building support[365] received.

Under the ETF arrangement the developed country parties shall, and other parties that provide support should, provide information on financial, technology transfer and capacity-building support provided to developing country parties. The developing country parties, on the other hand, should provide information on financial, technology transfer and capacity-building support needed and received under Articles 9, 10 and 11, respectively.[366] The Agreement provides for international procedures for the review of the submitted reports.[367] The information gathered through the ETF will feed into the Global stocktake (GTS) under Article 14 of the Agreement.

The Global Stocktake (GST) assesses progress made by the Parties to the Agreement. The GST is a process that establishes a feedback mechanism connecting short-term, contemporary climate action with the overall long-term targets of the Agreement.[368] The purpose is to review the implementation of the Agreement and to "assess the collective progress towards the collectively agreed goals."[369] Its outcome is to be used as input for new nationally determined contributions of parties.[370]

To this end, the GST is the primary explicit institutional feature of the Paris Agreement that is supposed to catalyse dynamic increases in the level of ambition over time as it is supposed to transfer this momentum and galvanise national governments into more ambitious climate action represented in significantly more progressive subsequent NDCs.[371] This is in line with the provisions of Article 14(3) that provides that "the outcome of the global stocktake shall inform parties in updating and enhancing, in a nationally determined manner, their actions and

---

[360] Ibid., Art. 13.

[361] Ibid., Art. 4.

[362] Ibid., Art. 7.

[363] Paris Agreement (2015), Art. 9.

[364] Ibid., Art. 10.

[365] Ibid., Art. 11.

[366] Ibid., Art. 13(9) and (10).

[367] Ibid., Art. 13(11) and (12).

[368] Hermwille et al. (2019), pp. 988–1001.

[369] Paris Agreement (2015), Art. 14(1).

[370] Ibid., Art. 14(2).

[371] Hermwille et al. (2019).

support in accordance with the relevant provisions of this Agreement, as well as in enhancing international cooperation for climate action."

The importance of the GST is that limiting global warming to well below 2 °C or even 1.5 °C as aspired to in the Agreement's long-term temperature goal requires a fundamental transformation of global economies and societies. The question is, how can transformational change occur and, more specifically, how can the GST support the required transformational change? According to Hermwille et al.,[372] there are four different functions by which the GST can drive this required change. These are: (1) acting as a pacemaker to synchronise and stimulate national and subnational policy processes, (2) ensuring accountability, (3) driving NDC ambition, and (4) providing guidance and signal. In performing these functions under GST, it can be said that the Paris Agreement has institutionalised a transformative ambition.

The GST therefore works as part of the Paris Agreement's effort to create a "ratcheting up" of ambition in emissions cuts. While ratcheting up the ambition of NDCs is a major aim of the global stocktake, it assesses efforts beyond mitigation.[373] The 5-year reviews will also evaluate adaptation, climate finance provisions, and technology development and transfer. First, the evaluation of NDCs using the GST is slated for 2023.

These elements introduced under Article 13 of the Paris Agreement have been described as one of the most innovative features of the Agreement.[374] The author asserted that is an obligation concerning the reporting not only of action undertaken, but also of support provided and received. Again, the modalities and procedures for such reporting remain to be determined. However, the agreement establishes a technical review process, which will consider both the implementation and achievement of NDCs, as well as the support provided. This review is entrusted to identify areas of improvement, thus providing an element of novelty compared with extant arrangements, which it is eventually meant to supersede.[375]

6.4.2.6.5 Paris Agreement as a Human Rights Issue and Source of Climate Change Litigation

A court in New Zealand in 2002 in the case of *Environmental Defence Society v. Auckland Regional Council and Contact Energy Ltd*[376] acknowledged and accepted the fact that "the present scientific consensus is that the cumulative anthropogenic emission of carbon dioxide on a global basis contributes to climate change." The adverse effects of climate change threaten the enjoyment of a range of human rights, such as the right to life, adequate food, the highest attainable standard

[372] Hermwille et al. (2019), pp. 988–1001.

[373] Yeo (2016).

[374] Savaresi (2016), p. 23.

[375] Ibid.

[376] [2002] NZRMA 492.

of health, adequate housing, and to safe drinking water and sanitation. Thus, the need to protect these human rights. As Mr. Justice Edson Fachin of the Federal Supreme Court of Brazil pointed out in the case of *Partido Socialista Brasileiro (PSB), Partido Socialismo e Liberdade (PSOL), Partido dos Trabalhadores (PT) e Rede Sustentabilidade v. União Federal* (*PSB* et al. *v. Brazil*),[377] decided on 4 July 2022:

> If we recognize that environmental damage has, strictly speaking, multiple causes, such as those listed in Agenda 21 - natural disasters, heavy economic activities, atmospheric pollution, contamination by chemical products, intensive use of natural resources, among others - it is imperative to repeat that human action is now scientifically recognized as responsible for the increase in temperature of the planet and that this increase is due, in large part, to carbon emissions resulting from burning fossil fuels. Recognizing human activity as the cause of environmental damage has important legal consequences. By recognizing the right to a balanced environment as a fundamental right of the present and future generations, the constituent legislator called on the Public Powers and the collectivity to fulfill the duty to defend and preserve it. This duty of defence and protection logically also extends to the necessary protection in the face of human actions that degrade the planet[378]

According to the Office of the High Commissioner for Human Rights (OHCHR),[379] "the deepening impacts of climate change and environmental degradation are perhaps the greatest risk to human rights we face in the world today." Commenting further OHCHR[380] opined that

> An estimated one in six premature deaths are caused by pollution. Climate change directly contributes to harmful effects impacting human rights across the globe, such as droughts, floods, sea-level rises, heatwaves, and extreme weather events. In Europe, the "canicule" heat wave is killing people, particularly older people. Biodiversity loss threatens the collapse of entire ecosystems. The alarm bell rang a long time ago.

In the words of Boyd,[381] "the health and quality of life of everyone directly depend on clean air to breathe, safe water to drink, sustainably produced food to eat, non-toxic environments, a safe climate, and healthy biodiversity and ecosystems." He concluded that:

> The human right to a clean, healthy and sustainable environment, as recognised universally today, includes all of those substantial elements. Similarly, the recognition of the right to a healthy environment should lead to constitutional and legislative improvements at the regional, national, and sub-national levels, with positive implications for air quality, safe and sufficient water, healthy soil, sustainably produced food, green energy, climate change, biodiversity and the regulation of toxic substances.[382]

The Paris Agreement 2015[383] acknowledges that climate change is a common concern of humankind and that parties should:

---

[377] PCB et al. v. Brazil (2022).

[378] Ibid., 4.

[379] Office of the High Commissioner for Human Rights (OHCHR) (2022).

[380] Ibid.

[381] Boyd (2022).

[382] Ibid.

[383] United Nations Framework Convention on Climate Change (UNFCCC) (2015), para 11.

> when taking action to address climate change, respect, promote and consider their respective obligations on human rights, the right to health, the rights of indigenous peoples, local communities, migrants, children, persons with disabilities and people in vulnerable situations and the right to development, as well as gender equality, empowerment of women and intergenerational equity.

The Agreement thus became the first global environmental pact to explicitly mention human rights, but the sole mention is relegated to the preamble.[384] The Paris Agreement has therefore provided a marginal victory for those advocating for building bridges between the climate regime and human rights law.[385] This assertion is shared with Duyck[386] when he opined that "as the first global environmental agreement that includes an explicit reference to human rights, the Paris Agreement confirms the international community's recognition that human rights obligations apply in the context of climate change."

However, "when the Paris Agreement was negotiated, much disagreement ensued over the adoption of human rights obligations in the substantive part of the text."[387] Some scholars such as Knox[388] and Caney[389] have argued that the Paris Agreement is a human rights treaty. Knox, after examining the Paris Agreement on climate change in light of international human rights law, with particular attention to the human rights language included in the Paris Agreement, concluded that "the Paris Agreement is consistent with the human rights obligations relating to climate change in many respects, but that states must strengthen their commitments in order to fulfil those obligations completely."[390] Caney on the other hand explored the relationship between human rights, population and climate change and came to the same conclusion as Knox.[391]

History was made on 4 July 2022 when the Federal Supreme Court of Brazil recognised the Paris Agreement as a human right treaty. By this act of the Supreme Federal Court of Brazil, the country became the first to formally recognise the Paris Agreement as a human right treaty.

This landmark decision was made in the case of *PSB* et al. *v. Brazil*.[392] On 5 June 2020, four political parties[393] filed a Direct Action of Unconstitutionality for Omission, before the Federal Supreme Court to challenge the Federal Union's alleged

---

384 Tigre (2022).

385 Savaresi (2016), p. 24.

386 Duyck (2017), pp. 3–45.

387 Tigre (2022).

388 Knox (2020).

389 Caney (2020).

390 Knox (2020).

391 Caney (2020).

392 Partido Socialista Brasileiro (PSB), Partido Socialismo e Liberdade (PSOL), Partido dos Trabalhadores (PT) e Rede Sustentabilidade v. União Federal (PSB et al. v. Brazil) (2022), ADPF 708/2022.

393 Namely: Brazilian Socialist Party, the Socialism and Freedom Party, the Workers' Party and the Rede Sustentabilidade.

failure to adopt administrative measures concerning the Climate Fund. The National Climate Change Fund (Fundo Clima), created by Law 12.114/2009, is an instrument of the National Policy on Climate Change (PNMC, Law 12.187/2009) and aims to ensure that resources support projects or studies and finances activities aimed at mitigating and adapting to climate change and its effects.

The petitioners alleged that although there is a legal obligation for the Ministry of the Environment to prepare an annual plan for the Climate Fund, it has been inoperative since 2019. The petitioners rely on the obligation of the Union, the States, the Federal District and the Municipalities to "protect the environment and fight pollution in any of its forms" and "to preserve forests, fauna and flora" per the Federal Constitution, as well as the precautionary principle.[394]

The petitioners also alleged a violation of Article 225 of the Federal Constitution, regarding the state's duties to: preserve and restore ecological processes; promote the ecological management of ecosystems; define territorial spaces and their components to be specially protected; and protect fauna and flora.[395]

The petitioners then sought an injunction to require the Federal Union to: (1) undertake the necessary administrative measures to reactivate the operation of the Climate Fund, with the due availability of resources related to the Climate Fund (including the non-refundable and refundable modalities); (2) prepare and present the appropriate annual plans for the application of the Fund's resources; and (3) refrain from making new contingencies of resources from the Climate Fund.[396]

In response, the government first argued that (a) there was no constitutional question as the Constitution does not explicitly mandate the creation of a Climate Fund, (b) the facts in question relate to the management of funds, a federal government's prerogative and (c) the court's interference would violate the doctrine of separation of powers.[397]

Second, the federal government had also argued that the Climate Fund, deriving from Brazil's international commitments within the scope of multilateral treaties on climate change, does not bind the federal government to its mandatory compliance since it is not a Brazilian law.[398]

On 30 June 2022, the Supreme Court rejected the government's arguments and ruled that the executive branch cannot ignore the mandate of the legislative branch. Instead, the executive branch has a constitutional duty to execute and allocate the funds of the Climate Fund to mitigate climate change, based on both the separation of powers and the constitutional right to a healthy environment. The court further found that the judiciary, in turn, must act to avoid the regression of environmental protection.[399]

[394] PCB et al. v. Brazil (2022).

[395] Ibid.

[396] Ibid.

[397] Ibid.

[398] PCB et al. v. Brazil (2022).

[399] Ibid.

The court clarified that environmental law treaties constitute a particular type of human rights treaty, which enjoys "supranational" status. This "supralegality" of human rights treaties means that they are above "regular" laws in the legal hierarchy. Accordingly, any Brazilian law or decree that contradicts the Paris Agreement, including the nationally determined contribution, may be invalidated. Any action or omission contrary to this protection is a direct violation of the Constitution and human rights. The constitutional duty to allocate the funds effectively means that there is a duty to mitigate climate change considering the international commitments under the climate change framework.[400]

Another case that arose out of the Paris Agreement on the protection of human rights from impacts associated with climate change is the case of *Luisa Neubauer and Others*[401] *v. Germany.*[402] The case known as the German Klimaklage actually consists of four separate lawsuits that were brought to the German Federal Constitutional Court between 2018 and 2020 in suits Nos. 1 BvR 2656/18, 1 BvR 78/20, 1 BvR 96/20 and 1 BvR 288/20. When, in February 2020, a group of German youths filed a legal challenge to Germany's Federal Climate Protection Act ("Bundesklimaschutzgesetz" or "KSG"), arguing that the KSG's target of reducing GHGs by 55% by 2030 from 1990 levels was insufficient, the court decided to join the cases for a unitary trial and decision.[403]

The four lawsuits essentially challenge the emission reduction targets set by the Klimaschutzgesetz as too low. The Plaintiffs argue that the legislator is accepting the risk of dangerous climate change, thereby threatening their rights to life, physical integrity, personal development, property and occupation under the German Basic Law *(Grundgesetz—GG).*[404]

The complaints alleged that the KSG's 2030 target did not take into account Germany's and the EU's obligation under the Paris Agreement to limit global temperature rise to "well below 2 degrees Celsius." The complainants argued that in order to "do its part" to achieve the Paris Agreement targets, Germany would need to reduce GHGs by 70% from 1990 levels by 2030. Their claims principally arose out of the principle of human dignity allegedly enshrined in Article 1 of the Basic Law; Article 2 of the Basic Law, which protects the right to life and physical integrity; and Article 20a of the Basic Law, which protects the natural foundations of life in responsibility for future generations; and that young people will therefore be forced to drastically change their lifestyle and limit their free development in the

[400] Ibid.

[401] (1) Luisa Neubauer, (2) Sophie Backsen, (3) Paul Backsen, (4) Hannes Backsen, (5) Jakob Backsen, (6) Lucas Lütke Schwienhorst, (7) Franziska Blohm, (8) Johannes Blohm and (9) Lueke Recktenwald who are teenagers and young adults.

[402] Luisa Neubauer and Others v. Germany (2021) ECLI:NL:RBDHA:2021:5339 l, District Court The Hague, Judgment of 26 May 2021.

[403] Ibid.

[404] Luisa Neubauer and Others v. Germany (2021).

future. Essentially, current generations are living at the expense of young people and future generations.[405]

Complainants argued that by requiring insufficient short and medium-term GHG reductions and allowing for the transfer of emission allocations between Germany and other EU Member States despite the inadequacy of the overall EU emissions reduction target, the KSG allowed climate impacts that violate these human rights.[406]

The complaints asked the Federal Constitutional Court to declare that the legislature violated the Basic Law by requiring only a 55% reduction in GHGs by 2030; declare that the legislature is required to issue new reduction quotas to ensure that Germany's emissions are kept as low as possible, taking into account the principle of proportionality; and prohibit the transfer of emissions allocations in the new regulatory regime.[407]

On 29 April 2021, the Federal Constitutional Court struck down the parts of the KSG as incompatible with fundamental rights for failing to set sufficient provisions for emissions cuts beyond 2030. The court found that Article 20a of the Basic Law obliges the legislature to protect the climate and aim towards achieving climate neutrality. Further, the court stated that Article 20a "is a justiciable legal norm that is intended to bind the political process in favour of ecological concerns, also with a view to the future generations that are particularly affected."[408]

Accepting arguments that the legislature must follow a carbon budget approach to limit warming to well below 2 °C and, if possible, to 1.5 °C, the court found that the legislature had not proportionally distributed the budget between current and future generations. The court held that "the regulations at stake would be unconstitutional if they allowed so much of the remaining budget to be consumed that the future loss of freedom would inevitably assume unacceptable proportions from today's perspective, because there would be no time left for mitigating developments and transformations."[409]

The court ordered the legislature to set clear provisions for reduction targets from 2031 onward by the end of 2022. Accordingly, the German government announced on 30 April 2021 that it would move quickly to adjust its climate law in response to the decision.[410]

In the case of *Friends of the Earth Netherlands (Milieudefensie* et al.*) v. Royal Dutch Shell*,[411] environmentalists instituted action to compel multinational

[405] Ibid.

[406] Ibid.

[407] Ibid.

[408] Luisa Neubauer and Others v. Germany (2021).

[409] Ibid.

[410] Ibid.

[411] Friends of the Earth Netherlands (Milieudefensie et al.) v. Royal Dutch Shell (2021) BvR 2656/18/1, BvR 78/20/1, BvR 96/20/1, BvR 288/20/1, Judgement on 29 April 2021.

corporations to curtail carbon dioxide emissions within the tenets of the Paris Agreement and the protection of human rights.

As the Paris Agreement was being developed, Shell evaluated its businesses to determine what it could do to address emissions, but had stated in 2014 that it believed that the Paris targets were unattainable and did not plan to change its business model away from oil and gas. Following the signing of the Agreement in 2015, Shell stated that it would address its emissions, releasing a plan that called for reductions of its carbon dioxide emissions by 30% by 2035, compared to 2016 levels, and by 65% by 2050.[412]

Environmental activists saw this plan as far slower than the requirements set out by the Paris Agreement. Seven environmental foundations, Friends of the Earth (Milieudefensie)[413] and 17,379 individual claimants in the Netherlands filed a class-action lawsuit against Shell in April 2019, arguing that Shell could change its business model to invest more in renewable energy, and reach an emissions reduction target of 45% by 2030.[414] By failing to change to this alternative model, the suit argued, Shell had failed to uphold the unwritten standard of care laid down in Book 6 Section 162 of the *Burgerlijk Wetboek* (Dutch Civil Code) as well as Articles 2 and 8 of the European Convention on Human Rights.[415]

Shell stated in response to the lawsuit that it was doing its part to address climate change, and that "What will accelerate the energy transition is effective policy, investment in technology and changing customer behaviour. None of which will be achieved with this court action and that addressing a challenge this big requires a collaborative and global approach."[416]

Hearings at the district court at The Hague were held in December 2020. The plaintiffs were required under Dutch law to demonstrate that a viable alternative business model existed for Shell to achieve the suggested 45% reduction goal, and had used the recent transformation of Danish company Ørsted from fossil fuels to renewables as a viable example. During the trial, Shell issued a pledge in February 2021 to be net zero by 2050. Plaintiffs considered Shell's pledge to be inadequate as the company would fail to meet the Paris Agreement goals.[417]

The court issued its decision on 26 May 2021. In its ruling, the court found Shell's current sustainability policy to be insufficiently "concrete," and that its emissions were greater than that of most countries. The court then ordered that Shell must

[412] Friends of the Earth Netherlands (Milieudefensie) v. Royal Dutch Shell in Climate case chart (2021).

[413] Comprising Greenpeace, Fossielvrij, Waddenvereniging, Both ENDS, Jongeren Milieu Actief, and ActionAid.

[414] Friends of the Earth Netherlands (Milieudefensie) v. Royal Dutch Shell (2021).

[415] Friends of the Earth Netherlands (Milieudefensie) v. Royal Dutch Shell (2021).

[416] Ibid.

[417] Ibid.

reduce its global emissions by 45% by 2030 compared to 2019 levels; the reduction targets include emissions from its suppliers and buyers.[418]

In the court's view, global warming poses a significant risk to the present and future generations of the world, and of the Netherlands in particular. Regarding the latter, the court noted:

> The risks associated with climate change for Dutch residents [. . .] concern health risks and deaths due to climate change-induced hot spells as well as health problems and an increased mortality risk due to increasing infectious diseases, deterioration of air quality, increase of UV exposure, and an increase of water-related and foodborne diseases. They also concern water-related health risks, which the Netherlands [. . .] will face, including flooding along the coast and rivers, excess water, water shortage, deterioration of water quality, salinization, raised water levels and drought.[419]

The court declared the order provisionally enforceable, meaning that the order has immediate effect, even if one of the parties appeals the ruling.[420]

The Dutch District Court basically agreed with claimants that Shell was doing too little to reduce greenhouse gas emissions and prevent serious climate damage (global warming of over 1.5 °C). In the court's view, Shell was thereby acting unlawfully, and it was under an obligation to significantly reduce its greenhouse gas emissions and bring them in line with the global climate objective of the Paris Agreement.[421]

More specifically, the court ordered Shell, both directly and via its companies and legal entities with which it jointly forms the Shell group, to limit or cause to be limited the aggregate annual volume of all greenhouse gas emissions into the atmosphere, due to the business operations and sold energy-carrying products of the Shell group, to such an extent that this volume will have reduced by at least net 45% at the end of 2030, relative to 2019 levels.[422]

The case of *West Virginia et al v. Environmental Protection Agency et al.*[423] was yet another landmark case on climate change and its associated impacts on human rights. The US Supreme Court was asked to rule in that case on the US Environmental Protection Agency's (EPA) authority to control carbon dioxide emissions linked to climate change under the Clean Air Act of 1990.

The case centred on the Clean Power Plan (CPP) proposed by the EPA in 2015 by the Obama Administration. Among the provisions, the CPP had included regulation at existing power plants under Section 7411(d) of Title 42 of the United States Code to implement "within the fence line" emissions reduction technology and "outside the fence line" generation shifting to alternative clean energy sources such as solar and wind power. The generation-shifting aspects of the CPP were challenged by

[418] Ibid.

[419] Ibid.

[420] Friends of the Earth Netherlands (Milieudefensie) v. Royal Dutch Shell (2021).

[421] Spijkers (2021).

[422] Ibid.

[423] West Virginia et al. v Environmental Protection Agency et al. (2022) 597 U.S. (2022), No. 20-1530, decided on 30 June 2022 by the Supreme Court of USA.

several states and coal industry companies, and the CPP was stayed by the courts and never came into enforcement.[424]

The Trump administration's EPA put forth a less-aggressive Affordable Clean Power (ACP) rule in 2019 which was similarly challenged by other states and stayed by courts. The stay was challenged by multiple states and coal industry companies,[425] seeking to question the EPA's ability to regulate existing power plants under 7411(d) as proposed in the CPP.[426]

In a 6–3 ruling issued on 30 June 2022, the court ruled that the regulation of existing power plants in Section 7411(d) fell under the major question doctrine, and within that, Congress did not grant the EPA authority to regulate emissions from existing plants based on generation shifting mechanisms, which would have invalidated the Clean Power Plan. The EPA may continue to regulate emissions at existing plants through emissions reduction technologies.[427]

Earlier case decided on the basis of the impact of climate change on human rights is the case of *Urgenda Foundation c. s. v. The Kingdom of the Netherlands and Ministry of Infrastructure and the Environment*[428] In that case, Urgenda Foundation, an environmental group and 900 Dutch citizens sued the Dutch government to require it to do more to prevent global climate change and that the Dutch state is acting unlawfully by not contributing its proportional share to preventing global warming of more than 2 °C. The plaintiffs, among others, sought the following:

1. A declaration from the court that global warming of more than 2 °C will lead to a violation of fundamental human rights worldwide.
2. An order that the Dutch state drastically and no later than 2020, reduce carbon dioxide (CO_2) emissions coming from within the boundaries of the Netherlands, to the level that has been determined by scientists to be in line with less than 2 °C of global warming.

The second relief will involve a reduction of CO_2 emissions by 40% by 2020 below 1990 levels to prevent the risk of dangerous climate change, or at least reduce this risk.[429]

The district court in its judgement decided on 24 June 2015, ordered the Dutch government to limit annual greenhouse gas emissions from the country to 25% below 1990 levels by 2020. The government had pledged a 17% reduction, but the court found that insufficient. The court undertook a detailed examination of reports

[424] West Virginia et al. v. Environmental Protection Agency et al. (2022).

[425] In The North American Coal Corporation v. Environmental Protection Agency et al., No. 20–1531, Westmoreland Mining Holdings LLC v. Environmental Protection Agency et al., No. 20–1778, North Dakota v. Environmental Protection Agency et al., No. 20–1780, also on certiorari to the same court.

[426] West Virginia et al. v. Environmental Protection Agency et al. (2022).

[427] Ibid.

[428] Urgenda Foundation c. s. v. The Kingdom of the Netherlands and Ministry of Infrastructure and the Environment [2015] Case C/09/456689/HA ZA 13–1396.

[429] Urgenda Foundation v. The Kingdom of the Netherlands [2015].

of the Intergovernmental Panel on Climate Change, the United Nations Environment Programme, and various Dutch institutions, and concluded that the mandated 25% reduction was the level needed to meet the country's fair contribution toward the UN goal of keeping global temperature increases within 2 °C of pre-industrial conditions.[430]

The court held that due to the severity of the consequences of climate change and the great risk of hazardous climate change occurring, the state has a duty of care to take mitigation measures. The court reached its decision cited without directly applying, several legal documents, viz: Article 21 of the Dutch Constitution,[431] the emissions reduction targets of the European Union, principles under the European Convention on Human Rights, the "no harm" principle of international law, the doctrine of hazardous negligence, the principle of fairness, the precautionary principle generally, and the sustainability principle embedded in the UN Framework Convention on Climate Change, and the principle of a high protection level, the precautionary principle, and the prevention principle embedded in the European Climate Policy.

The Dutch government submitted 29 grounds of appeal contesting that Urgenda cannot directly invoke Articles 2 and 8 of the European Convention on Human Rights (EHCR) in the proceedings. On 8 October 2018, the Hague Court of Appeal upheld the ruling of the district court, concluding that by failing to reduce greenhouse gas emissions by at least 25% by the end of 2020 the Dutch government is acting unlawfully in contravention of its duty of care under Articles 2 and 8 of the European Convention on Human Rights (EHCR). The court further recognised Urgenda's claim under Article 2 EHCR which protects the right to life and Article 8 which protects the right to private life, family life, home and correspondence, and that the Dutch government has an obligation under ECHR to protect these rights from the real threat of climate change.

The Dutch government appealed to the Netherlands's Supreme Court. The court heard the case on 24 May 2019 and on 20 December 2019 upheld the decision of the lower court.[432] Opinion has it that the 2 °C temperature target of the Paris Agreement was thought to have provided part of the judgement's legal basis.[433]

In *Mataatua District Maori Council v. New Zealand*,[434] representatives of the Mataatua District Maori Council filed a claim alleging that New Zealand breached its obligations to the Maori by failing to implement policies to address climate change, which violates provisions of the Waitangi Treaty that make the government responsible for the "active protection" of natural resources such as forests and fisheries on behalf of the Maori. In 2019, New Zealand passed the Climate Change Response

[430] Urgenda Foundation v. The Kingdom of the Netherlands [2015].

[431] The article provides that: "It shall be the concern of the authorities to keep the country habitable and to protect and improve the environment."

[432] Appeal No. ECLI:ECLI:NL:HR:2019:2006.

[433] Backes and van der Veen (2020).

[434] Mataatua District Maori Council v. New Zealand [2019] WAI 2607.

(Zero Carbon) Amendment Act 2019, setting ambitious mid-century climate mitigation targets. Plaintiffs filed an amended pleading that argues that the act still fails to adequately guard against climate change because its targets are insufficient and unenforceable.[435]

There are several cases on the implementation of the provisions of the Paris Agreement and human rights violations now pending in various jurisdictions across the globe. Such cases pending before the European Court of Human Rights (ECtHR) include: *Duarte Agostinho and Others v. Portugal and 32 Other States,*[436] *KlimaSeniorinnen v. Switzerland (ECtHR),*[437] *Carême v. France,*[438] among others.

In *Duarte Agostinho and Others v. Portugal and 32 Others*, six Portuguese youths on 2 September 2020 filed a complaint with the European Court of Human Rights against 33[439] countries. The complainants allege that the respondents have fallen short of their human rights obligations by failing to agree to emissions reductions that will keep temperature rise to 1.5 °C, as envisioned by the Paris Agreement. By this failure the complaint alleges that the respondents have violated their human rights, particularly Articles 2, 8, and 14 of the European Convention on Human Rights, which protect the right to life, right to privacy, and right to not experience discrimination based on the respondents' failure to take sufficient action on climate change. The complainants claimed that their right to life is threatened by the effects of climate change in Portugal such as forest fires; that their right to privacy includes their physical and mental well-being, which is threatened by heat waves that force them to spend more time indoors; and that as young people, they stand to experience the worst effects of climate change. The complainants then sought an order requiring the respondents to take more ambitious action.[440]

On 30 June 2022, the Chamber of the European Court of Human Rights relinquished jurisdiction in favour of the Grand Chamber. The case is now going to be examined by the EctHR's Grand Chamber of 17 judges because the case raises a serious question affecting the interpretation of the Convention (Article 30 ECHR).[441]

The case of *KlimaSeniorinnen v. Switzerland (ECtHR)* hinges on the adequacy of the Swiss government's climate change mitigation targets and implementation measures and possible infringement on human rights. In 2016, a group of senior

[435] Mataatua District Maori Council v. New Zealand [2019], Second Amended Statement of Claims at 19(d).

[436] Application No. 39371/20.

[437] Application No. 53600/20.

[438] Application No. 7189/21.

[439] The case is brought against the Member States of the European Union (EU) (Austria, Belgium, Bulgaria, Cyprus, Czech Republic, Germany, Greece, Denmark, Estonia, Finland, France, Croatia, Hungary, Ireland, Italy, Lithuania, Luxembourg, Latvia, Malta, the Netherlands, Poland, Portugal, Romania, Slovak Republic, Slovenia, Spain and Sweden) as well as Norway, Russia, Switzerland, Turkey, Ukraine and the United Kingdom.

[440] Duarte Agostinho and Others v. Portugal and 32 Others (2020).

[441] Ibid.

women, filed a suit against the Federal Council, the Federal Department of the Environment Transport, Energy and Communications (DETEC), The Federal Office for the Environment, and the Federal Office for Energy, alleging that these bodies of the Swiss government had failed to uphold obligations under the Swiss Constitution[442] and the European Convention on Human Rights (ECHR)[443] by not steering Switzerland onto an emissions reduction trajectory consistent with the goal of keeping global temperatures well below 2 °C above pre-industrial levels.[444]

The petitioners alleged that their demographic group is especially vulnerable to the heat waves expected to result from climate change. They called upon the Swiss parliament and the relevant federal agencies to develop a regulatory approach to several sectors that would achieve greenhouse gas emissions reductions of at least 25% below 1990 levels by 2020, and at least 50% below 1990 levels by 2050. The petition criticised both the targets under discussion at the time in parliament (20% by 2020, and 30% by 2030) and the measures by which the government would pursue those targets.[445]

The petition was dismissed by DETEC on 25 April 2017. DETEC found that petitioners lacked standing because their rights were not affected as required by Article 25a (1) APA (Administrative Procedure Act, Verwaltungsverfahrensgesetz, VwVG). DETEC determined that petitioners sought regulation of global CO2 emissions through general regulations rather than seeking a remedy for an infringement of their specific legal rights. DETEC further found that petitioners did not have victim status under the ECHR because they sought an injunction to serve the wider public interest of adoption of legislative reform to reduce CO_2 emissions. Petitioners appealed the dismissal on 26 May 2017, and on 27 November 2018, the Swiss Federal Administrative Court rejected the appeal holding that Swiss women over 75 years of age are not exclusively affected by climate change impacts (thus echoing DETEC's determination that the injury and remedy were not specialised to claimants).[446]

In January 2019, the claimants appealed against the judgment with the Swiss Supreme Court. On 20 May 2020, the Supreme Court rejected the appeal. The court held that the plaintiffs' asserted rights had not been affected with sufficient intensity, and that the remedy they seek must be achieved through political rather than legal means.[447] However, on 26 November 2020, having exhausted all available legal remedies in Switzerland, the claimants filed an application to the European Court of Human Rights, where the suit is pending.

[442] Articles 10 (right to life), 73 (sustainability principle), and 74 (environmental protection), respectively.

[443] Articles 2 (right to life) and 8 (right to privacy), respectively.

[444] KlimaSeniorinnen v. Switzerland (ECtHR) (2020).

[445] Ibid.

[446] KlimaSeniorinnen v. Switzerland (ECtHR) (2020).

[447] Ibid.

In the case of *Carême v. France*, the municipality of Grande-Synthe, which is located in an area considered at very high risk of exposure to climate risks, and the applicant, acting in his capacity of Grande-Synthe Mayor and private resident, in 2019 asked the Council of State to cancel the government's refusal to take additional measures to meet the Paris Agreement objective of reducing GHG emissions by 40% by 2030. The cities of Paris and Grenoble, as well as several environmental protection associations, have intervened in the procedure.[448]

In its first decision, dated 19 November 2020, the Council of State declared the application admissible insofar as it was introduced by the municipality of Grande-Synthe and allowed the interventions of Paris, Grenoble and eNGOs. The court rejected, however, the application insofar as it was brought by the applicant, because he did not show any interest in the case since his claims were limited to the argument that, as an individual, his home was situated in an area likely to be subject to flooding by 2040.[449]

On 1 July 2021, the Council of State ruled on the merits, finding for the claimants. It observed that the drop in emissions in 2019 was too small and that it was not significant in 2020 because the economic activity had been reduced by the health crisis. It also held that adherence to the trajectory, which provides for a 12% drop in emissions for the period 2024–2028, did not appear to be achievable unless new measures were not quickly adopted. The Council of State therefore ordered the government to take additional measures by 31 March 2022 to achieve the goal of reducing GHG emissions by 40% by 2030.[450]

Further recognition of the relationship between climate change and human rights, besides judicial pronouncements, received a boost on 7 July 2022 when the United Nations Human Rights Council in a resolution on human rights and climate change,[451] adopted without a vote, "urged States that had not yet ratified the Paris Agreement to do so and called upon all States to adopt a comprehensive, integrated, gender-responsive, age-inclusive, and disability-inclusive approach to climate change adaptation and mitigation policies."[452] By this action, the Office of the United Nations High Commissioner for Human Rights officially recognised that "Climate change threatens the effective enjoyment of a range of human rights including those to life, water and sanitation, food, health, housing, self-determination, culture and development."[453]

The above-cited cases hinged mainly on the violation of the right to life as a result of non-adherence to the mandate of the Paris Agreement in mitigating climate change. Now that the Federal Supreme Court of Brazil has raised the bar on the Paris Agreement 2015 being recognised as a human rights treaty and the recognition

[448] Carême v. France (2021).

[449] Ibid.

[450] Carême v. France (2021).

[451] United Nations Human Rights Council (2022) A/HRC/RES/50/9.

[452] Ibid., paras 3 and 4, p. 5.

[453] Ibid.

by the Office of the United Nations High Commissioner for Human Rights that climate change threatens the effective enjoyment of a range of human rights, liability for harms attributable to human-induced allegedly caused by climate change impact may raise another crop of legal issues. Litigable areas on the impact of climate change on human rights may revolve around:

(a) Water shortages thought to be induced by climate change likely will lead to litigation over the nature of water rights.
(b) Sea level rise and extreme precipitation linked to climate change may raise questions as to: (1) the effect of sea level rise on the beachfront owner's property line; (2) whether public beach access easements migrate with the landward movement of beaches; (3) design and operation of levees; and (4) government failure to take preventive measures against climate change harms.
(c) Persons forced to relocate because of climate change impacts such as drought or sea level rise (environmental refuges) as these are not covered under Refuge Laws.
(d) Some adaptation responses to climate change are often property-rights related such as beach armouring (seawalls, bulkheads, etc.), beach re-nourishment, and "managed retreat" measures, retreat measures seek to move existing development away from areas likely to be affected by floods and sea level rise, and to discourage new development there, may also give rise to litigation where harm arises.
(e) Natural disasters to which climate change contributes may prompt questions as to whether response actions taken in an emergency are subject to relaxed requirements and, similarly, as to the rebuilding of structures destroyed by such disasters just as they were before.

6.4.3 Domestic Regulatory Frameworks in Combating Air Pollution

From the analysis of UNEP data,[454] a set of key policy actions were identified that, if adopted, would significantly improve air quality.

In Nigeria, a few efforts at regulating air pollution to control its attendant consequences on the human and nature environment, including global warming and climate change, have been put in place. Such measures can be found in the following legal instruments:

(a) The National Environmental Standards and Regulations Enforcement Agency (Establishment Act 2007) (NESREA 2007).
(b) National Regulations on Air pollution abatement made pursuant to the NESREA Act 2007.

[454] United Nations Environment Programme (UNEP) (2021a).

(c) Climate Change Act 2021.
(d) Petroleum Industry Act 2021.[455]

6.4.3.1 The National Environmental Standards and Regulations Enforcement Agency (Establishment Act 2007) (NESREA 2007)

The NESREA Act 2007[456] provides for the establishment of the National Environmental Standards and Regulations Enforcement Agency (NESREA).[457] The Agency is charged with several responsibilities some of which include: "powers to submit for the approval of the Minister in charge of Environmental matters proposals for the evolution and review of existing guidelines, regulations and standards on... air quality and atmospheric protection, and ozone depleting substances...."[458]

Specifically, Section 20 of the NESREA Act 2007 mandates the Agency[459] to make regulations setting specifications and standards to protect and enhance the quality of Nigeria's air resources, to promote the public health or welfare and the natural development and productive capacity of the nation's human, animal, marine or plant life. In this respect, the Agency shall: set minimum essential air quality standards for human, animal, marine or plant health; control the concentration of substances in the air which separately or in combination are likely to result in damage or deterioration of property or human, animal, marine or plant health; set out the most appropriate means to prevent and combat various atmospheric pollution; control atmospheric pollution originating from energy sources, including that produced by aircraft and other self-propelled vehicles, industries, factories and power generating situations or facilities; set standards applicable to emissions from any new mobile or stationary source which in the Agency's judgement causes or contributes to air pollution which may reasonably be anticipated to endanger public health or welfare and device the use of appropriate means to reduce emission to permissible levels.[460]

To achieve these goals, in addition to establishing specifications and regulations, the Agency is required to create monitoring stations or networks to discover sources of atmospheric pollution and assess their actual or prospective hazard.[461]

A person who violates the regulations made thereto commits an offence and shall on conviction, in the case of an individual, be liable to a fine not **less than** $= N =$ 200,000 or to imprisonment for a term not **less than six months** or to

[455] Petroleum Industry Act 2021, Act No.6 2021

[456] NESREA Act 2007.

[457] Established pursuant to NESREA Act 2007, s. 1.

[458] NESREA Act (2007), s. 8(k)(i)–(iii).

[459] The Agency referred to is the National Environmental Standards and Regulations Enforcement Agency (NESREA) established by the NESREA Act 2007, s. 1.

[460] NESREA Act (2007), s. 20(1)(a)–(f).

[461] Ibid., s. 20(2).

both such fine and imprisonment and an additional fine of = *N* = 20,000 for every day the offence subsists.[462] And where a body corporate contravenes the regulations made thereto, it commits an offence and is liable on conviction to a fine not **less than** = *N* = 2,000,000 and an additional fine of = *N* = 50,000 for every day the offence subsists.[463]

To protect the stratospheric ozone, the Agency shall in collaboration with other relevant agencies undertake to study data and recognise development in force in other countries regarding the cumulative effects of all substances, practices, processes and activities which may affect the stratosphere.[464] In addition to the above, the Agency shall **make regulations** for the control of any substance, practice, process or activity which may reasonably be anticipated to affect the stratosphere, especially ozone in the stratosphere, when such effects may reasonably be anticipated to endanger public health or welfare.[465] A body corporate that violets this provision, shall on conviction, be liable to a fine not **less than** = *N* = 2,000,000 and an additional fine of = *N* = 50,000 for every day the offence subsists.[466]

Note, all the words in bold such as **"less than"** and **"less the six months,"** etc. were inserted into the NESREA Act 2007 pursuant to the National Environmental Standards and Regulations Enforcement Agency (Establishment) Amendment) (Amendment Act) 2018 (NESREA Amendment Act 2018).[467]

6.4.3.2 National Regulations on Air Pollution Abatement

The NESREA Act 2007 mandates the Agency[468] to make regulations setting specifications and standards to protect and enhance the quality of Nigeria's air resources to promote public health or welfare,[469] protect the ozone layer[470] and control noise pollution.[471] In line with the above mandate, the Minister of

---

[462] Ibid., s. 20(3).

[463] Ibid., s. 20(4).

[464] NESREA Act (2007), s. 21(1).

[465] Ibid., s. 21(2).

[466] Ibid., s. 21(3).

[467] NESREA (Amendment Act) 2018, ss. 7 and 8, Government Notice No. 106, Act No. 26, 2018, Federal Republic of Nigeria Official Gazette No. 146, Vol. 105, 14 November 2018.

[468] NESREA Act (2007).

[469] Ibid., s. 20.

[470] Ibid., s. 21.

[471] Ibid., s. 22.

Environment between 2009 and 2014 made a few regulations.[472] Some of these regulations set out emission standards for various air-polluting facilities. Other efforts at air pollution abatement include regulations on ozone layer protection. These regulations were discussed below.

6.4.3.2.1 National Environmental (Textile, Wearing Apparel, Leather and Footwear Industry) Regulations 2009

For the textile, wearing apparel, leather and footwear industries, the National Environmental (Textile, Wearing Apparel, Leather and Footwear Industry) Regulations 2009[473] provide for national environmental standards on emissions limita-

---

[472] National Environmental (Chemical, Pharmaceutical, Soap and Detergent Manufacturing Industries Regulations (2009), Government Notice No. 289, S.I. No. 36. Federal Republic of Nigeria Official Gazette No. 68 Vol. 96, 10 October 2009.

National Environmental (Ozone Layer Protection) Regulations 2009, Government Notice No. 283, S.I. No. 32. Federal Republic of Nigeria Official Gazette No. 64, Vol. 96, 13 October 2009.

National Environmental (Food, Beverages, and Tobacco Sector) Regulations 2009, Government Notice No. 286, S.I. 33. Federal Republic of Nigeria Official Gazette No. 65 Vol. 96, 14 October 2009.

National Environmental (Textile, Wearing Apparel, Leather, and Footwear Industry) Regulations (2009), Government Notice No. 287, S.I. No. 34. Federal Republic of Nigeria Official Gazette No. 66 Vol. 96, 16 October 2009.

National Environmental (Base Metal, Iron and Steel Manufacturing/Recycling Industries Sector) Regulations 2011, Government Notice No. 127, S.I. No. 14. Federal Republic of Nigeria Official Gazette No. 41 Vol. 98, 4 May 2011.

National Environmental (Domestic and Industrial Plastic, Rubber and Foam Sector) Regulations 2011, Government Notice No. 131, S.I. No. 17. Federal Republic of Nigeria Official Gazette No. 44 Vol. 98, 5 May 2011.

National Environmental (Control of Bush, Forest Fire and Open Burning) Regulations 2011, Government Notice No. 219, S.I. No. 15. Federal Republic of Nigeria Official Gazette No. 92 Vol. 98, 6 May 2011.

National Environmental (Control of Vehicular Emissions from Petrol and Diesel Engines) Regulations 2011, Government Notice No. 134, S.I. 20. Federal Republic of Nigeria Official Gazette No. 47, Vol. 98, 17 May 2011.

National Environmental (Non-Metallic Minerals Manufacturing Industries Sector) Regulations 2011, Government Notice No. 134, S.I. No. 21. Federal Republic of Nigeria Official Gazette No. 48 Vol. 98, 23 May 2011.

National Environmental (Pulp and Paper, Wood and Wood Products Sector) Regulations 2013, Government Notice No. 214, S.I. No. 34. Federal Republic of Nigeria Official Gazette No. 98 Vol. 100, 1 November 2013.

National Environmental (Energy Sector) Regulations 2014, Government Notice No. 254, S.I. No. 63. Federal Republic of Nigeria Official Gazette No. 141, Vol. 102, 22 December 2014.

National Environmental (Air Quality Control) Regulations 2014, Government Notice No. 225, S.I. 64. Federal Republic of Nigeria Official Gazette No. 142, Vol. 101, 26 December 2014.

[473] Government Notice No. 287, S.I. No. 34. Federal Republic of Nigeria Official Gazette No. 66 Vol. 96, 16 October 2009.

tions,[474] measuring priority air pollutants,[475] treatment technologies for air emissions[476] and measurement of air quality standards using appropriate sampling techniques.[477] Standards are also set for noise, noise abatement and noise monitoring.[478] Under the regulations aforesaid, it shall be an offence where a facility fails to comply with abatement measures, including failure to remediate the environment to the standard prescribed by the Agency, particularly as provided under Schedule V[479] to the regulations,[480] or engage in the operation of listed activities in Schedule V.[481]

6.4.3.2.2 National Environmental (Chemical, Pharmaceutical, Soap and Detergent Manufacturing Industries) Regulations 2009

In respect of the chemical, pharmaceutical, soap and detergent manufacturing industries, the National Environmental (Chemical, Pharmaceutical, Soap and Detergent Manufacturing Industries) Regulations 2009[482] provide for national environmental standards in relation to emission standards,[483] measuring priority air pollutants,[484] treatment technologies for air emissions[485] and measurement of air quality standards using appropriate sampling techniques.[486]

Under Schedule III,[487] industry-specific pollutants that may be emitted from the point or fugitive sources during routine operations consist of numerous organic and inorganic compounds, including sulphur oxides (SO_X), ammonia (NH_3), ethylene, propylene, aromatics, alcohols, oxides, acids, chlorine, other volatile organic compounds (VOCs), semi-volatile organic compounds (SVOCs), etc. To this end,

---

[474] National Environmental (Textile, Wearing Apparel, Leather and Footwear Industry) Regulations (2009), Regulation 19.

[475] Ibid., Regulation 20.

[476] Ibid., Regulation 21.

[477] Ibid., Regulation 33.

[478] Ibid., Regulations 23, 24 and 26.

[479] Maximum values for various particulate matter are set under the Schedule. For instance, ammonia (NH_3) 150 mg/Nm3, for H_2S, 30 mg/Nm3, for CS_2–150 mg/Nm3, for chlorine, 5 mg/Nm3, for cyanide, 10 mg/Nm3, for phenol, 5 mg/Nm3, for formaldehyde, 5 mg/Nm3, etc.

[480] National Environmental (Textile, Wearing Apparel, Leather and Footwear Industry) Regulations (2009), Regulation 47.

[481] Ibid., Regulation 50.

[482] National Environmental (Chemical, Pharmaceutical, Soap and Detergent Manufacturing Industries) Regulations (2009) Government Notice No. 289, S.I. No. 36. Federal Republic of Nigeria Official Gazette No. 68 Vol. 96, 10 October 2009.

[483] Ibid., Regulation 20.

[484] Ibid., Regulation 21.

[485] Ibid., Regulation 22.

[486] Ibid., Regulation 34.

[487] National Environmental (Chemical, Pharmaceutical, Soap and Detergent Manufacturing Industries) Regulations (2009).

emission parameters are set for pharmaceutical manufacturing and for petroleum-based and chemical industries beyond which an offence is committed. Noise standards,[488] noise abatement[489] and noise monitoring are also regulated.[490] Thus, it shall be an offence where a facility fails to comply with abatement measures, including failure to remediate the environment to the standard prescribed by the Agency, particularly as provided under Schedule III to the regulations.[491]

6.4.3.2.3 National Environmental (Food, Beverages and Tobacco Sector) Regulations 2009

For the food, beverages and tobacco industries, the National Environmental (Food, Beverages and Tobacco Sector) Regulations 2009[492] also provide for national environmental standards for emission standards and control,[493] treatment technologies for air emissions[494] and measurement of air quality standards using appropriate sampling techniques.[495] Also provided are regulations for noise standards,[496] noise abatement[497] and noise monitoring.[498]

Under the regulations aforesaid, it shall be an offence where a facility fails to comply with abatement measures, including failure to remediate the environment to the standard prescribed by the Agency, particularly as provided under Schedule III[499] to the regulations,[500] or engage in the operation of listed activities in Schedule III.[501]

---

[488] National Environmental (Chemical, Pharmaceutical, Soap and Detergent Manufacturing Industries) Regulations (2009), Regulation 24.

[489] Ibid., Regulation 25.

[490] Ibid., Regulation 27.

[491] Ibid., Regulations 46–50, penalties are provided under Regulation 51.

[492] Government Notice No. 286, S.I. 33. Federal Republic of Nigeria Official Gazette No. 65 Vol. 96, 14 October 2009.

[493] National Environmental (Food, Beverages and Tobacco Sector) Regulations (2009), Regulations 19 and 20.

[494] Ibid., Regulation 21.

[495] National Environmental (Food, Beverages and Tobacco Sector) Regulations (2009), Regulation 32.

[496] Ibid., Regulation 22.

[497] Ibid., Regulation 23.

[498] Ibid., Regulations 25.

[499] Under the Schedule, National Environmental (Food, Beverages and Tobacco Sector) Regulations (2009), air emissions shall be in line with ambient air quality standards for Nigeria. For SO_X, the duration of effluents shall be 1 h and in a concentration of 425 μg/M3; for NO_2, the duration shall be 1 h and concentration shall be 313 U/M3; for CO, the duration shall be 1 h and concentration shall be 30,000, and for particulate matter, the duration shall be 1 h and concentration shall be 250 μg/M3.

[500] National Environmental (Food, Beverages and Tobacco Sector) Regulations (2009), Regulation 46.

[501] Ibid., Regulation 49.

Any person who violates the provisions of any of these regulations has committed an offence and shall on conviction be liable to a fine of = N = 200,000 or to imprisonment for a term not exceeding 1 year or to both such fine and imprisonment.[502] In addition, the person is fined = N = 20,000 for every day the offence subsists.[503] Where the offender is a body corporate the penalty shall be a fine of = N = 2,000,000 and an additional = N = 50,000 for each day the offence subsists.[504]

6.4.3.2.4 National Environmental (Base Metal, Iron and Steel Manufacturing/Recycling Industries Sector) Regulations 2011

Another set of regulations that have provisions for setting standards to protect and enhance the quality of Nigeria's air resources is the National Environmental (Base Metal, Iron and Steel Manufacturing/Recycling Industries Sector) Regulations 2011.[505] The main thrust of the regulations is to prevent and minimise pollution from all operations and ancillary activities of the sector.[506]

The regulations provide for national environmental standards on emissions standards,[507] as set out under Schedule III,[508] measuring priority air pollutants,[509] treatment technologies for air emissions[510] and measurement of air quality standards using appropriate sampling techniques.[511] Standards are also set for noise,[512] noise abatement[513] and noise measurement.[514]

[502] NESREA (Amendment) Act (2018) increased the threshold of the penalties prescribed in the NESREA Act 2007 and substituted maximum punishment with minimum punishment, by substituting for a term not "exceeding" with not "less than" in respect of penalties under ss. 20(3), 21(3), 22(3) and (4), 23(3) and 26(3) and (4) of the original Act.

[503] NESREA Act 2007, s. 20(3).

[504] Ibid., s. 20(4).

[505] Government Notice No. 127, S.I. No. 14. Federal Republic of Nigeria Official Gazette No. 41 Vol. 98, 4 May 2011.

[506] National Environmental (Base Metal, Iron and Steel Manufacturing/Recycling Industries Sector) Regulations (2011), Regulation 1.

[507] Ibid., Regulation 21.

[508] National Environmental (Base Metal, Iron and Steel Manufacturing/Recycling Industries Sector) Regulations (2011).

[509] Ibid., Regulation 22.

[510] Ibid., Regulation 24.

[511] Ibid., Regulation 37.

[512] Ibid., Regulation 26.

[513] Ibid., Regulation 27.

[514] Ibid., Regulation 38.

Under the regulations, it shall be an offence where a facility contravenes permit conditions,[515] makes false statements to the Agency,[516] fails to comply with abatement measures,[517] fails to submit an atmospheric pollution prevention plan or Air quality impact report arising from its operations,[518] including where the facility engages in the operation of listed activities as prescribed in Schedule XI of the regulations without a permit from the Agency.[519] Penalties are provided under Regulation 56.[520]

6.4.3.2.5 National Environmental (Domestic and Industrial Plastic, Rubber and Foam Sector) Regulations 2011

The National Environmental (Domestic and Industrial Plastic, Rubber and Foam Sector) Regulations 2011[521] is yet another set of regulations that have provisions for setting standards to protect and enhance the quality of Nigeria's air resources. The regulations provide for national environmental standards on emissions standards,[522] emission control,[523] dust/particulate matter emission control,[524] measurement of air quality standards using appropriate abatement technologies[525] and air sampling analysis.[526]

Again, all facilities in the industry should install pollution abatement equipment,[527] and implement cleaner production processes and pollution prevention measures.[528]

---

[515] National Environmental (Base Metal, Iron and Steel Manufacturing/Recycling Industries Sector) Regulations (2011), Regulation 50.

[516] Ibid., Regulation 51.

[517] Ibid., Regulation 52.

[518] National Environmental (Base Metal, Iron and Steel Manufacturing/Recycling Industries Sector) Regulations (2011), Regulation 53(d).

[519] Ibid., Regulation 55.

[520] The penalties are similar to those set out under NESREA Act (2007), s. 20(4).

[521] Government Notice No. 131, S.I. No. 17. Federal Republic of Nigeria Official Gazette No. 44 Vol. 98, 5 May 2011.

[522] National Environmental (Domestic and Industrial Plastic, Rubber and Foam Sector) Regulations (2011), Regulation 21.

[523] Ibid., Regulation 22.

[524] Ibid., Regulation 24.

[525] Ibid., Regulation 26.

[526] Ibid., Regulation 37.

[527] Ibid., Regulation 5(2).

[528] Ibid., Regulation 17(1).

The regulations also set standards for noise,[529] noise abatement,[530] noise monitoring,[531] and noise measurement.[532] In addition, while Schedule II[533] provides for air emission levels for plastic and rubber manufacturing industries, and Schedule V of the same regulations provides for emission limitation for petroleum-based polymer industries.[534]

In the same vein, Schedule VII[535] sets out recommended pollution prevention and control techniques for the emission of particulate matter.[536] Under the regulations,[537] it shall be an offence where a facility contravenes permit conditions,[538] makes false statements to the Agency,[539] fails to comply with abatement measures[540] fails to maintain records of all discharges and file quarterly and annual reports of all discharges[541] Penalties are provided under Regulation 55.[542]

6.4.3.2.6 National Environmental (Non-Metallic Minerals Manufacturing Industries Sector) Regulations 2011

The National Environmental (Non-Metallic Minerals Manufacturing Industries Sector) Regulations 2011[543] is yet another set of regulations that have provisions for setting standards to protect and enhance the quality of Nigeria's air resources. The main thrust of the National Environmental (Non-Metallic Minerals Manufacturing Industries Sector) Regulations 2011 is to prevent and minimise pollution from all operations and ancillary activities of the non-metallic minerals manufacturing

[529] Ibid., Regulation 27.

[530] Ibid., Regulation 28.

[531] Ibid., Regulation 30.

[532] Ibid., Regulation 38.

[533] National Environmental (Domestic and Industrial Plastic, Rubber and Foam Sector) Regulations (2011).

[534] These Schedules (II and V) are made with reference to the National Environmental (Domestic and Industrial Plastic, Rubber and Foam Sector) Regulations (2011), Regulations 21, 22 and 26.

[535] National Environmental (Domestic and Industrial Plastic, Rubber and Foam Sector) Regulations (2011).

[536] Particulate matter is defined as contaminants in solid and liquid phases in suspension in the atmosphere, National Environmental (Air Quality Control) Regulations (2014), Regulation 41.

[537] National Environmental (Domestic and Industrial Plastic, Rubber and Foam Sector) Regulations (2011).

[538] Ibid., Regulation 49.

[539] Ibid., Regulation 50.

[540] Ibid., Regulation 52.

[541] Ibid., Regulation 53.

[542] This is similar to the penalty under the NESREA Act (2007), s. 20(4).

[543] Government Notice No. 134, S.I. No. 21. Federal Republic of Nigeria Official Gazette No. 48 Vol. 98, 23 May 2011.

industries sector to the Nigerian environment.[544] The regulations[545] provide that every facility within the sector shall install pollution abatement equipment to enable such facility to engage in effective effluent and emission discharges to meet the prescribed effluent and emission discharge permissible limits.[546]

Again, all facilities shall have some built-in pollution control features for the dry process precalciner.[547] In addition, national environmental standards on emissions control,[548] priority air pollutants,[549] measurement of air quality standards using appropriate abatement technologies and air sampling analysis[550] and in compliance with National Ambient Air Quality Standards.[551]

The regulations also set standards for noise,[552] noise abatement,[553] noise monitoring,[554] and noise measurement.[555]

Other provisions in those regulations for the protection of Nigeria's air quality include: prevention and control techniques to reduce SO_2 emissions in the ceramics industries,[556] prevention and control techniques to reduce SO_2 emissions for glass industries,[557] reduction of nitrogenous gas emissions in the ceramics and tiles industries,[558] reduction of nitrogenous gas emissions in the glass industries,[559] prevention and control techniques to reduce fugitive particulate matter emissions in the ceramics and tiles industries[560] and management strategies for Green House Gases (GHGs) control in ceramic industries.[561]

The regulations also provide for air emissions levels for the various industries in the non-metallic minerals manufacturing industries sector, namely: cement

---

[544] National Environmental (Non-Metallic Minerals Manufacturing Industries Sector) Regulations (2011), Regulation 1.

[545] National Environmental (Non-Metallic Minerals Manufacturing Industries Sector) Regulations (2011).

[546] Ibid., Regulation 5.

[547] Ibid., Regulation 8.

[548] Ibid., Regulation 22.

[549] Ibid., Regulation 23.

[550] National Environmental (Non-Metallic Minerals Manufacturing Industries Sector) Regulations (2011), Regulation 44.

[551] Ibid., Sch. IX.

[552] Ibid, Regulation 33.

[553] Ibid., Regulation 34.

[554] Ibid., Regulation 36.

[555] Ibid., Regulation 45.

[556] Ibid., Regulation 25.

[557] Ibid., Regulation 26.

[558] Ibid., Regulation 27.

[559] Ibid., Regulation 28.

[560] Ibid., Regulation 29.

[561] Ibid., Regulation 30.

manufacturing,[562] lime manufacturing,[563] ceramics and tiles manufacturing,[564] and glass manufacturing.[565]

Under the regulations,[566] it shall be an offence where a facility contravenes permit conditions,[567] makes false statements to the Agency,[568] fails to comply with abatement measures[569] or fails to maintain records of all discharges and file quarterly and annual reports of all discharges[570] Penalties are provided under Regulation 62.[571]

6.4.3.2.7 National Environmental (Control of Vehicular Emissions from Petrol and Diesel Engines) Regulations 2011

The National Environmental (Control of Vehicular Emissions from Petrol and Diesel Engines) Regulations 2011[572] main thrust is to restore, preserve and improve air quality. . .provide protection of the air from pollutants as well as take into account (a) citizens' right of access to clean air, (b) reducing and preventing air pollution through the improvement of the quality of automobiles that operate in the roadway and (c) improve the health of Nigerians, especially in the urban areas with high incidence of air pollution due to increased number of vehicles that ply the roads.[573]

To achieve these objectives, the regulations set out control levels for gaseous emission from petrol engines[574] to be achieved through the conduct of emission tests for the petrol engine which is in use.[575]

---

[562] Ibid., Sch. IV.

[563] Ibid., Sch. V.

[564] Ibid., Sch. VII.

[565] Ibid., Sch. VIII.

[566] National Environmental (Non-Metallic Minerals Manufacturing Industries Sector) Regulations (2011).

[567] Ibid., Regulation 57.

[568] Ibid., Regulation 58.

[569] Ibid., Regulation 59.

[570] Ibid., Regulation 60.

[571] National Environmental (Non-Metallic Minerals Manufacturing Industries Sector) Regulations (2011).

[572] Government Notice No. 134, S.I. 20. Federal Republic of Nigeria Official Gazette No. 47, Vol. 98, 17 May 2011.

[573] National Environmental (Control of Vehicular Emissions from Petrol and Diesel Engines) Regulations (2011), Regulation 1 (a)–(c).

[574] Ibid., Regulation 8.

[575] Ibid., Regulation 9.

A similar test shall also apply to diesel engines.[576] Where a vehicle fails these tests, the Agency[577] or any authorised officer[578] may issue a prohibition order in respect of such vehicles whether of a petrol engine[579] or diesel engine.[580] The order shall cause the vehicle not to be in operation/use until the defects have been remedied to the satisfaction of the Agency or any authorised officer.[581]

Furthermore, the regulations set out emission standards for pollutants such as carbon monoxide (CO), hydrocarbons (HC), nitrogen oxide (NOx) and particulate matter (PM) in respect of:

(a) Petrol engine under Schedule I to the regulations.[582]
(b) New models of petrol engines manufactured on/after 1 January 2015 under Schedule II to the regulations.[583]
(c) Petrol engine in use under Schedule III to the regulations.[584]
(d) Diesel engine under Schedule VII to the regulations.[585]
(e) New models of diesel engine manufacture on/after 1 January 2015 under Schedule VIII to the regulations.[586]

Added to the above, maximum concentrations of smoke[587] and a maximum density of smoke[588] permitted are set out under the regulations.

---

[576] Ibid., Regulation 17.

[577] The Agency means the National Environmental Standards, Regulation and Enforcement Agency (NESREA) National Environmental (Control of Vehicular Emissions from Petrol and Diesel Engines) Regulations (2011), Regulation 31.

[578] Authorised officer means an officer duly authorised by the Agency to enforce the provisions of these Regulations and includes a Road Traffic Officer (RTO), Police officer, Federal Road Safety Corp (FRSC) or any other officer to whom the Agency has delegated this power. See National Environmental (Control of Vehicular Emissions from Petrol and Diesel Engines) Regulations (2011), Regulation 31.

[579] National Environmental (Control of Vehicular Emissions from Petrol and Diesel Engines) Regulations (2011), Regulation 10.

[580] Ibid., Regulation 24.

[581] National Environmental (Control of Vehicular Emissions from Petrol and Diesel Engines) Regulations (2011), Regulation 10, in respect of a petrol engine and Regulation 23(1) in respect of a diesel engine.

[582] The emission standard is set out pursuant to National Environmental (Control of Vehicular Emissions from Petrol and Diesel Engines) Regulations (2011), Regulations 3, 3(2), 5(1) and 8(1).

[583] The emission standard is set out pursuant to National Environmental (Control of Vehicular Emissions from Petrol and Diesel Engines) Regulations (2011), Regulation 3(6).

[584] The emission standard is set out pursuant to National Environmental (Control of Vehicular Emissions from Petrol and Diesel Engines) Regulations (2011), Regulations 8(1) and 10.

[585] The emission standard is set out pursuant to National Environmental (Control of Vehicular Emissions from Petrol and Diesel Engines) Regulations (2011), Regulations 17(1) and 19(1).

[586] The emission standard is set out pursuant to National Environmental (Control of Vehicular Emissions from Petrol and Diesel Engines) Regulations (2011), Regulation 17(2).

[587] National Environmental (Control of Vehicular Emissions from Petrol and Diesel Engines) Regulations (2011), Regulation 22(1).

[588] Ibid., Regulation 23(1).

To further control the emission of gaseous pollutants, the regulations prohibit the engine of a motor vehicle from idling for more than 5 min in an enclosed or partially enclosed parking area or terminus.[589] In addition, the regulations impose a ban on the manufacture, assembly or importation of any vehicle with a diesel engine without a certified emission reduction technology for the control of emissions from such vehicle. This ban took effect from the 28th day of April 2011.[590]

Any person who fails to comply with any of the provisions of these regulations has committed an offence. In the case of an individual, such a person shall be liable on conviction to a fine not exceeding $= N =$ 50,000 or imprisonment for a term not exceeding 1 year or both such fine and imprisonment. In addition, a fine of $= N =$ 1000 shall be imposed for every day the offence subsists.[591] In the case of a body corporate, the fine shall be $= N =$ 500,000 and an additional $= N =$ 20,000 for every day the offence subsists.[592]

6.4.3.2.8 National Environmental (Control of Bush, Forest Fire and Open Burning) Regulations 2011

The National Environmental (Control of Bush, Forest Fire and Open Burning) Regulations 2011[593] main thrust is to prevent and minimise the destruction of the ecosystem through fire out break and burning of any material that may affect the health of the ecosystem through the emission of hazardous air pollutants.[594] The regulations shall apply to any person or body corporate who engages in bush/forest/ opening burning for whatsoever purpose ranging from hunting and clearing farmland to destroying any of the items listed in Regulation 2 (c)(i)–(xi). To this end, the regulations place a ban, without a permit duly obtained from the Agency,[595] on bush/ forest fires,[596] burning of plant waste,[597] burning of forest for hunting[598] and open

[589] Ibid., Regulation 13.

[590] Ibid., Regulation 26.

[591] Ibid., Regulation 30(1).

[592] Ibid., Regulation 30(2).

[593] Government Notice No. 219, S.I. No. 15. Federal Republic of Nigeria Official Gazette No. 92 Vol. 98, 6 May 2011.

[594] National Environmental (Control of Bush, Forest Fire and Open Burning) Regulations (2011), Regulation 1.

[595] The Agency means the National Environmental Standards, Regulation and Enforcement Agency (NESREA), see National Environmental (Control of Bush, Forest Fire and Open Burning) Regulations (2011), Regulation 23.

[596] Ibid., Regulation 3.

[597] Ibid., Regulation 8(1).

[598] Ibid., Regulation 19.

burning activities.[599] The regulations also restrict the use of the following: engines;[600] bee smoker devices;[601] explosives;[602] and fireworks.[603]

However, there are some exceptions to this ban under Regulation 22 of these regulations.[604] These exceptions include: barbecue grills and outdoor cooking; small cooking and campfires; on-site burning of organic agricultural wastes for subsistence farming, but not pesticides, plastics or other non-organic materials; ceremonial or celebratory bonfires; individual open fire to control plant and animal diseases; and open fires as necessary to control invasive plant and insect species.[605]

As part of the efforts in achieving the main thrust of the regulations, any activity placed under a ban, except those activities under the exemption lists, shall only be embarked upon where such person had obtained a permit from the Agency.[606] The application for such permit shall be made to the Agency and in the forms specified under Schedule I in respect of bush/forest fire,[607] Schedule III in respect of the burning of plant wastes[608] and Schedules V and VI in respect of opening burning of plant wastes.[609] To keep track on incidental fire, the regulations further mandate the owner or occupier of the land to give notification of any such bush/forest fire as well as on losses caused by the fire incident.[610]

Violation of any of the provisions of the regulations amounts to an offence.[611] It is also an offence for a person to fail to comply with any condition on which a permit to burn is granted.[612] In the case of an individual, such a person shall be liable on conviction to a fine not exceeding $=N=$ 50,000 or imprisonment for a term not exceeding 3 months or both such fine and imprisonment.[613] Where the offence is committed by a body corporate, the fine shall be $=N=$ 1,000,000 and an additional $=N=$ 20,000 for every day the offence subsists.[614] In addition, the Agency is

---

[599] Ibid., Regulation 11(1).

[600] Ibid., Regulation 15(1).

[601] Ibid., Regulation 16.

[602] Ibid., Regulation 17.

[603] Ibid., Regulation 18.

[604] National Environmental (Control of Bush, Forest Fire and Open Burning) Regulations (2011).

[605] Ibid., Regulation 22(1)(a)–(f).

[606] See National Environmental (Control of Bush, Forest Fire and Open Burning) Regulations (2011), Regulation 3(1) in respect of bush/forest fire, Regulation 8(1) in respect of burning of plant waste and Regulation 11(1) in respect of open burning of plant waste.

[607] National Environmental (Control of Bush, Forest Fire and Open Burning) Regulations (2011), Regulation 3(2).

[608] Ibid., Regulation 8(2).

[609] Ibid., Regulation 11(2).

[610] National Environmental (Control of Bush, Forest Fire and Open Burning) Regulations (2011), Regulation 20.

[611] Ibid., Regulation 21(1).

[612] Ibid., Regulation 21(2).

[613] Ibid., Regulation 21(3).

[614] Ibid., Regulation 21(4).

empowered to enter and seal the premises/facilities contravening the provisions of the regulations.[615]

6.4.3.2.9 National Environmental (Pulp and Paper, Wood and Wood Products Sector) Regulations 2013

National Environmental (Pulp and Paper, Wood and Wood Products Sector) Regulations 2013[616] is yet another set of regulations that have provisions for setting standards to protect and enhance the quality of Nigeria's air resources. The main thrust of the regulations[617] is to prevent and minimise pollution from all operations and ancillary activities of the sector.[618]

The regulations have provisions for national environmental standards on emissions standards,[619] measuring priority air pollutants,[620] air quality permit,[621] measurement of air quality standards using appropriate sampling techniques,[622] and gaseous emissions from facilities.[623] Standards are also set for noise standards,[624] noise abatement,[625] noise monitoring,[626] and noise measurement.[627]

Under the regulations,[628] it shall be an offence where a facility contravenes permit conditions,[629] makes false statements to the Agency,[630] fails to comply with abatement measures[631] or fails to maintain records of all discharges and file quarterly and annual reports of all discharges.[632] Operating without a permit is also an offence under the regulations.[633] Penalties are provided under Regulation 61.[634]

[615] Ibid., Regulation 20(5).

[616] Government Notice No. 214, S.I. No. 34. Federal Republic of Nigeria Official Gazette No. 98 Vol. 100, 1 November 2013.

[617] National Environmental (Pulp and Paper, Wood and Wood Products Sector) Regulations (2013).

[618] Ibid., Regulation 1.

[619] Ibid., Regulation 27.

[620] Ibid., Regulation 28.

[621] Ibid., Regulation 31.

[622] Ibid., Regulation 42.

[623] National Environmental (Pulp and Paper, Wood and Wood Products Sector) Regulations (2013), Sch. III.

[624] Ibid., Regulation 32.

[625] Ibid., Regulation 33.

[626] Ibid., Regulation 35.

[627] Ibid., Regulation 43.

[628] National Environmental (Pulp and Paper, Wood and Wood Products Sector) Regulations (2013).

[629] Ibid., Regulation 55.

[630] Ibid., Regulation 56.

[631] Ibid., Regulation 57.

[632] Ibid., Regulations 58.

[633] Ibid., Regulation 60.

[634] National Environmental (Pulp and Paper, Wood and Wood Products Sector) Regulations (2013).

6.4.3.2.10 National Environmental (Air Quality Control) Regulations 2014

Another set of regulations that have provisions for setting standards to protect and enhance the quality of Nigeria's air resources is the National Environmental (Air Quality Control) Regulations 2014.[635] The main purpose of the regulations is to improve control of the nation's air quality to such an extent that would enhance the protection of flora, fauna, human health and other resources affected by air quality deterioration.[636]

The regulations provide against accidental discharge of air pollutants[637] and set out maximum air contaminants concentration[638] which shall not be higher than the concentrations set out in Schedules III, IV, V and VII of the regulations.[639] To this end, Regulation 9[640] requires a person[641] operating an industrial plant or facility to forward to the Agency information related to its point source emissions[642] for criteria pollutants annually within 3 months of the end of each year.[643] In addition, the regulations require that a person shall install air pollution control devices on new equipment, installations or retrofit an existing facility with technology or technologies that enable the facility to meet the national air quality emissions standard.[644]

As a result of the insidious effects of indoor air pollution, regulations are provided for the control of indoor air pollution in offices, public places and homes,[645] including banning smoking in public places, except designated areas.[646] Thus, the maximum concentration of air contaminants in offices and public places is set out under Schedule XI and Schedule XII of the regulations[647] sets out the maximum concentration for homes. Again, control of fugitive particulate matter[648] is set out

[635] Government Notice No. 225, S.I. 64. Federal Republic of Nigeria Official Gazette No. 142, Vol. 101, 26 December 2014.

[636] National Environmental (Air Quality Control) Regulations (2014), Regulation 1(a).

[637] Ibid., Regulation 5.

[638] Ibid., Regulation 6.

[639] National Environmental (Air Quality Control) Regulations (2014).

[640] Ibid.

[641] A person means any legal entity including an individual, association, corporate body, organisation, government and government agency, or institution that owns facility or facilities which emit pollutants into the atmosphere. National Environmental (Air Quality Control) Regulations (2014), Regulation 41.

[642] This means a single source emissions into the atmosphere contributing not less than 500 metric tonnes of CO_2 or 100 metric tonnes of NO, SO_2 and PM into the atmosphere during full operational annual circle.

[643] National Environmental (Air Quality Control) Regulations (2014), Regulation 41.

[644] Ibid., Regulation 10.

[645] Ibid., Regulations 18–24.

[646] Ibid., Regulation 24.

[647] National Environmental (Air Quality Control) Regulations (2014).

[648] This is defined under the National Environmental (Air Quality Control) Regulations (2014), Regulation 41 as "pollutants discharged into the atmosphere from sources other than combustion or

under Regulation 26[649] and subject to levels as prescribed in Schedule X of the regulations.[650] Furthermore, a person undertaking a business or activity releasing emissions into ambient air[651] should ensure that the ambient air quality within its premises or operational areas associated with emissions from its own facilities does not exceed 60% of the ambient air quality standard prescribed in Schedule XIII of the regulations.[652]

Any person who violates the provisions of any of these regulations[653] has committed an offence and shall on conviction be liable to a fine of $= N =$ 100,000 or to imprisonment for a term not exceeding 6 months or to both such fine and imprisonment. In addition, the person is fined $= N =$ 10,000 for every day the offence subsists. Where the offender is a body corporate the penalty shall be a fine of $= N =$ 1,000,000 and an additional $= N =$ 50,000 for each day the offence subsists.[654]

6.4.3.2.11 National Environmental (Energy Sector) Regulations 2014

National Environmental (Energy Sector) Regulations 2014[655] is yet another set of regulations that have provisions for setting standards to protect and enhance the quality of Nigeria's air resources. The main purpose of the regulations[656] is to prevent and minimise pollution and encourage energy efficiency in all operations and ancillary activities of the energy sector in achieving sustainable economic development in Nigeria.[657] The regulations have provisions for national environmental standards on emissions standards,[658] measuring priority air pollutants,[659] pollution abatement for air emissions,[660] emission control[661] and measurement of air

production processes but related to general processes such as evaporation, frictional processes leading to wears, system leakages in a stationary area or line source."

[649] National Environmental (Air Quality Control) Regulations (2014).

[650] Ibid.

[651] This is defined under the National Environmental (Air Quality Control) Regulations (2014), Regulation 41 as the "planetary boundary layer or the troposphere (outdoor air) in which humans and other organisms live and breathe."

[652] National Environmental (Air Quality Control) Regulations (2014), Regulation 33.

[653] National Environmental (Air Quality Control) Regulations (2014).

[654] Ibid., Regulation 40.

[655] Government Notice No. 254, S.I. No. 63. Federal Republic of Nigeria Official Gazette No. 141, Vol. 102, 22 December 2014.

[656] National Environmental (Energy Sector) Regulations (2014).

[657] Ibid., Regulation 1(1).

[658] National Environmental (Energy Sector) Regulations (2014), Regulation 17.

[659] Ibid., Regulation 18.

[660] Ibid., Regulation 19.

[661] Ibid., Regulation 24.

quality standards using appropriate sampling techniques.[662] Standards are also set for noise[663] and noise measurement.[664]

Under the regulations,[665] it shall be an offence where a facility contravenes the operator's conditions,[666] permit conditions,[667] makes false statements to the Agency,[668] fails to comply with guidelines and standards.[669] It is also an offence where a facility fails to comply with abatement measures[670] or fails to maintain records of all discharges and file quarterly and annual reports of all discharges.[671] Penalties are provided under Regulation 51.[672]

6.4.3.2.12 National Environmental (Ozone Layer Protection) Regulations 2009

To protect the stratospheric ozone,[673] the Agency is enjoined to collaborate with other relevant agencies to embark on programmes for the control of any substance, practice, process or activity which may reasonably be anticipated to affect the stratosphere, especially ozone in the stratosphere.[674]

Protection of the ozone layer is governed by the provisions of the National Environmental (Ozone Layer Protection) Regulations 2009.[675] Under the regulations[676] "no person shall import, manufacture in part or in whole, install, offer for sale, sell or buy new or refurbished facilities intended to be used for the production of any ozone depleting substance (ODS), unless for the recovery and recycling of substances already in use."[677]

---

662 Ibid., Regulation 28.

663 Ibid., Regulation 22.

664 Ibid., Regulation 29.

665 National Environmental (Energy Sector) Regulations (2014).

666 Ibid.

667 Ibid., Regulation 45.

668 Ibid., Regulation 46.

669 Ibid., Regulation 47.

670 Ibid., Regulation 48.

671 Ibid., Regulation 49.

672 National Environmental (Energy Sector) Regulations (2014).

673 Depletion of the ozone is said to be responsible for global warming and climate change and there are a series of international instruments targeted at combating these environmental problems, such as the Vienna Convention for Substances Depleting the Ozone Layer 1985, Montreal Protocol on Ozone Depleting Substances 1987, UN Framework Convention on Climate Change 1992 and the Kyoto Protocol on Climate Change 1997 and the Paris Agreement on Climate Change 2015. Some of these were discussed in Sect. 6.4.2 of this chapter.

674 NESREA Act (2007), s. 21(2).

675 Government Notice No. 283, S.I. No. 32. Federal Republic of Nigeria Official Gazette No. 64, Vol. 96, 13 October 2009.

676 National Environmental (Ozone Layer Protection) Regulations (2009).

677 Ibid., Regulation 1.

Again, the release of ODS from any source is prohibited, except from a purging device.[678] In addition, no person shall work with an ODS, whether by way of servicing, dismantling, installing or repairing, importing, manufacturing, offering for sale, selling,[679] and supply or lease a pressurised container which contains 10 kg or less of an ODS listed in Schedule 3 to the regulations, either alone or in a mixture.[680] There are however some exemptions to the application of the provisions of Regulation 5(1) of these regulations.[681] This is in respect of pressurised containers which are used to contain: a prescription drug; a topical anaesthetic; a bronchial dilator; a veterinary powder wound spray; a cytospray; or a spermicidal foam.[682]

As a further step to protect the ozone layer, the regulations[683] under discussion provide that the sale, use, storage, and possession of ODS will be strictly controlled after the phase-out dates as specified under Schedule 6 to the regulations.[684] Thus, from the phase-out date, 1 January 2010, it is now an offence to handle or deal in ODS refrigerant[685] or being in possession of a halon[686] without a special permit from the Agency.

Where any person engages in any practice, process or activity which violates the programmes for the control of ozone-depleting substance in such a way that the effects may reasonably be anticipated to endanger public health or welfare, an offence is committed under Section 21(2) of the NESREA Act 2007. Where the offence is committed by an individual, he shall on conviction be liable to a fine not less than $= N =$ 200,000 or to imprisonment for a term not less than 6 months or to both such fine and imprisonment and an additional fine of $= N =$ 20,000 for every day the offence subsists.[687] And where a body corporate contravenes the regulations made thereto, it commits an offence and is liable on conviction to a fine not **less than** $= N =$ 2,000,000 and an additional fine of $= N =$ 50,000 for every day the offence subsists.[688]

6.4.3.3 Climate Change Act 2021

Over the years, Nigeria has been affected by some of the climate change-induced impacts such as flooding, rising sea levels, drought, desertification, and desert

[678] Ibid., Regulation 2.
[679] Ibid., Regulation 3.
[680] Ibid., Regulation 5(1).
[681] National Environmental (Ozone Layer Protection) Regulations (2009).
[682] Ibid., Regulation 5(2).
[683] National Environmental (Ozone Layer Protection) Regulations (2009).
[684] Ibid., Regulations 6, 9 and 17.
[685] Ibid., Regulation 16.
[686] Ibid., Regulation 18.
[687] NESREA Act (2007), s. 20(3) as amended by the NESREA (Amendment) Act (2018), s. 8.
[688] Ibid., s. 8.

encroachment and has set out several policies and programmes on mitigating these climate change-induced impacts. In the same vein, Nigeria has ratified several international legal instruments on mitigating Climate change.[689] Under Vision 2020, a National Development Plan, the Nigerian government recognises climate change as threatening her economic prosperity and future development. On this note, efforts were geared towards mitigating the impacts of climate change through the Climate Change Law.

Climate change law has been defined as "Legislation, or regulations, policies and decrees with a comparable status, that refer specifically to climate change or that relate to reducing energy demand, promoting low carbon energy supply, tackling deforestation, promoting sustainable land use, sustainable transportation, or adaptation to climate impacts."[690] National efforts to address climatic change are guided by some principles including the following:

1. Strategic climate change response is consistent with national development priorities.
2. Climate change is addressed within the framework of sustainable development, which ensures that climate change response must be sensitive to issues of equity, gender, youth, children and other vulnerable groups.
3. The use of energy as a key driver for high economic growth is pursued within the broad context of sustainable development.
4. Mitigation and adaptation are integral components of the policy response and strategy to cope with climate change.
5. Climate change policy is integrated with other policies to promote economic and environmental efficiency.
6. Climate change is cross-cutting and demands integration across the work programmes of several government ministries/agencies/parastatals and stakeholders, and across sectors of industry, business and the community.
7. Climate change response provides viable entrepreneurship opportunities.[691]

The journey to legislating climate change in Nigeria started in 2011. In that year, Nigeria published the National Adaptation Strategy and Plan of Action on Climate Change for Nigeria (NASPACCN). The strategy outlined responses to climate change in key areas such as agriculture (crops and livestock), freshwater resources, coastal water resources and fisheries, forests, biodiversity, health and sanitation, human settlements and housing, energy, transportation and communications, industry and commerce, disaster, migration and security, livelihoods, vulnerable groups, and education.[692] However, the policy document did not find official support.

[689] Such as the United Nations Framework Convention on Climate Change 1992; Kyoto Protocol on Convention on Climate Change 1997; the Paris Agreement on Climate Change 2015; and other standards and guidelines relevant to climate change adaptation and mitigation.

[690] Nachmany et al. (2014), p. 18.

[691] Nachmany et al. (2014), p. 18.

[692] Ibid., 18.

In September 2012, approval was given for the adoption of a National Climate Change Policy and Response Strategy (NCCP-RS). The NCCP-RS aimed at providing Nigeria with a framework for responding to climate change-related challenges such as increased flooding and sea level rise. This was followed in October 2013 when the Federal Executive Council approved and adopted the National Policy on Climate Change. The objectives of the policy were to foster a low-carbon, high-growth economic development path and build a climate-resilient society through the attainment of set targets. This was with a view of advancing GHG mitigation and/or adaptation.[693]

From thence, policies and programmes for mitigating climate change-induced impacts went into a top gear. These programmes and action plans according to Climate Action Tracker started in 2015.[694]

In 2015, the programme/action plan was the National Integrated Master Plan (NIIMP). The NIIMP intended to serve as a blueprint for infrastructure development and investment for the period 2014–2043. In 2017 the Economic Recovery and Growth Plan (ERGP) (2017–2020) programme/action plan was launched. The ERGP was adopted following Nigeria's 2016 recession to promote sustainable economic development and includes multiple climate-related projects.[695] Also in 2017, the Sectoral Action Plans for Nigeria's Nationally Determined Contribution (NDC) to the United Nations Framework Convention on Climate Change (UNFCCC) was put in place. Under this programme, Nigeria adopted five sectoral action plans (agriculture, power generation, industrial energy efficiency, oil and gas, and transport) to support the implementation of its first NDC.[696]

In 2020, Nigeria launched the Economic Sustainability Plan (ESP). The ESP is Nigeria's stimulus plan in response to COVID-19. The ESP proposes key projects including the installation of solar home systems and the promotion of domestic gas utilisation.[697] In the same year, the National Action Plan on Gender and Climate Change for Nigeria was launched. The action plan aims to mainstream gender considerations in national climate change processes to guarantee inclusivity in climate change initiatives, programmes and policies.[698]

In 2021, Nigeria launched several ambitious programmes on climate change mitigation. These were:

1. The Medium Term National Development Plan (MTNDP) that will span from 2021 to 2025. This MTNDP is the successor to the ERGP and was approved in November 2021. The plan prioritises the implementation of the Climate Change Act, which will spur the development of decarbonisation pathways.[699]

---

[693] Ibid.

[694] Climate Action Tracker (CAT) (2022), p. 19.

[695] Climate Action Tracker (CAT) (2022), p. 19.

[696] Ibid.

[697] Ibid.

[698] Ibid.

[699] Ibid.

2. Revised National Climate Change Policy (NCCP) and the National Climate Change Programmes for Nigeria. The revised NCCP was approved in June 2021 along with a programmatic plan of action, replacing the 2012 climate policy. The NCCP outlines sectoral policy measures for mitigation and adaptation, as well as enabling conditions and means of implementation needed.[700]
3. The 2050 Long-Term Vision (LTV) for Nigeria (2021) Nigeria's Long-Term Vision (LTV). This action plan was submitted to the UNFCCC as Nigeria's Long-Term Strategy, aimed at reducing the current level of emissions by 50% by 2050 and moving towards net-zero emissions across all sectors. The LTV includes sectoral targets and measures.[701]
4. The Energy Transition Plan that laid out a roadmap to achieve Nigeria's net-zero target.[702]

To actualise her commitment to both her international and domestic obligations on climate change and in pursuit of her climate change mitigation programmes/action plans, Nigeria took a bold step in 2021 by enacting the Climate Change Act 2021. The Act was signed on 18 November 2021 by the then President Muhammadu Buhari.

The Act provides a framework for mainstreaming Climate Change actions, providing for a system of carbon budgeting and the establishment of the National Council on Climate Change.[703] This it is hoped will address the synergy between the various agencies of government in mainstreaming climate change into development planning.

The Climate Change Act provides a framework for achieving low greenhouse gas emissions (GHG) inclusive green growth and sustainable economic development. This is to be achieved by (a) ensuring that Nigeria formulates programmes for achieving its long-term goals on climate change mitigation and adaptation; (b) facilitating the coordination of climate change action needed to achieve long-term climate objectives; (c) mainstreaming climate change actions in line with national development priorities; (d) facilitating the mobilisation of finance, and other resources necessary to ensure effective action on climate change; (e) ensuring that climate change policies and actions are integrated with other related policies for promoting socio-economic development and environmental integrity; (f) setting a target for year 2050–2070 for the attainment of a net-zero GHG emission, in line with Nigeria's international climate change obligations; (g) identifying risks and vulnerabilities, building resilience and strengthening existing adaptive capacities to the impacts of climate change; (h) implementing mitigation measures that promote low carbon economy and sustainable livelihood;

---

[700] Ibid.

[701] Climate Action Tracker (CAT) (2022), p. 19.

[702] Ibid.

[703] Climate Change Act (2021), explanatory memorandum.

and (i) ensuring that private and public entities comply with stated climate change strategies, targets and National Climate Change Action Plan.[704]

One of the key provisions of the Act in driving to its objectives is the establishment of the National Council on Climate Change (NCCC) which shall be vested with powers to make policies and decisions on all matters concerning climate change in Nigeria.[705] The NCCC is a body corporate with perpetual succession and a common seal; and may sue and be sued in its corporate name.[706]

The NCCC has the President of Nigeria as the Chairman, with members from both the public and private sectors, including members of the civil society, women, youth, and persons with disabilities.[707] It empowers the Council with significant powers to coordinate national climate actions, administer the newly established Climate Change Fund, mobilise resources to support climate actions, and collaborate with the Nigerian Sovereign Green Bond in meeting Nigeria's NDC. The Climate Change Fund is envisioned as a financing mechanism for prioritised climate actions and interventions. The promotion and adoption of nature-based solutions to reduce GHG emissions and mitigate climate change is encouraged.[708]

For purposes of administration and control the Act provides for the establishment of a Secretariat for the NCCC. The Secretariat shall be the administrative (including secretarial and clerical) scientific and technical arm of the NCCC and perform the functions and discharge the duties assigned to it under this Act.[709] In addition, the Act empowers the NCCC to establish the Secretariat, offices, including zonal and state offices, committees, and such other administrative apparatus, as it may deem necessary to facilitate the proper implementation of the provisions and purpose of the Act.[710] Section 8 of the Act sets out the functions of the Secretariat,[711] while Section 9 sets out its powers, subject to the approval of the NCCC.[712]

Funding had always been the bane of public agencies in Nigeria in implementing their mandates under the various laws establishing them. This, it is hoped, shall not impede in the case of bodies established under the Climate Change Act 2021 and saddled with the implementation of the provisions of the Act. To facilitate the mobilisation of finance, and other resources necessary to ensure effective action on climate change,[713] the Act provides for the establishment of a Climate Change Fund.[714] Major sources of funding for the NCCC shall come from: (a) sums

---

[704] Ibid., s. 1(a)–(i).

[705] Climate Change Act (2021), s. 3(1).

[706] Ibid., s. 3(2)(a) and (b).

[707] Ibid., s. 5(1)(a)–(u).

[708] Ibid., s. 4.

[709] Ibid., s. 7(1).

[710] Ibid., s. 7(2).

[711] Ibid., s. 8(a)(k).

[712] Ibid., s. 9(a)–(e).

[713] As stated under the Climate Change Act (2021), s. 1(d).

[714] Climate Change Act (2021), s. 15(1).

appropriated by the National Assembly for the running of the Council; (b) subventions, grants and donations, fees and charges for services rendered or publications made by the Council; (c) funding from International Organisations and funds due to Nigeria for meeting her NDCs; (d) fines and charges from private and public entities for flouting their climate change mitigation and adaptation obligations; (e) carbon tax and emissions trading; and (f) such other funds, as the NCCC may prescribe from time to time.[715]

In addition to the above sources of funds, the NCCC may borrow money from financial organisations or other institutions to execute its mandate under this Act.[716] It may also accept gifts of land, money, or other property on such terms and conditions; as may be specified by the person or organisation making the gift, provided that these conditions are consistent with the functions of the NCCC under the Act.[717]

As part of Nigeria's efforts to mitigate climate change, the Act mandates the Federal Ministry of Environment, in consultation with the Federal Ministry of National Planning to do the following: (a) set a carbon budget for Nigeria, to keep average increases in global temperature within 2 °C and pursue efforts to limit the temperature increase to l.5 °C above pre-industrial levels; and (b) by an order set the carbon budget and budgetary period, and periodically revise the carbon budget, in line with Nigeria's NDCs and to comply with Nigeria's international obligations.[718] In addition, the Federal Ministry of Environment shall publish detailed national, regional and sectoral climate vulnerability and risk assessments that will serve as the basis for the adaptation components of the action plan;[719] and may by an order publish guidelines for measurement, reporting and verification of national emissions that will serve as the basis for the setting and annual review of the carbon budget.[720]

Furthermore, the Secretariat, in consultation with the Federal Ministries Environment, and Budget and National Planning, respectively, shall formulate an action plan in every 5-year cycle[721] and the pilot action plan shall be produced, not later than 12 months from the commencement of the Act.[722] The action plan shall:

(a) serve as a basis for: (1) identifying the activities aimed at ensuring that the national emissions profile is consistent with the carbon budget goals, and (2) establishing national goals, objectives and priorities on climate adaptation;
(b) prescribe measures and mechanisms: (1) for identifying and assessing risks, vulnerabilities and extremes of the impact of climate change on vulnerable

[715] Climate Change Act (2021), s. 15(a)–(f).
[716] Ibid., s. 17.
[717] Ibid., s. 18.
[718] Ibid., s. 19(1).
[719] Ibid., s. 19(5)(a).
[720] Ibid., s. 19(5)(b).
[721] Ibid., s. 20(1).
[722] Ibid., s. 20(2).

communities and populations, and eco-systems, (2) for setting out actions for mainstreaming climate change responses into sector functions, (3) for identifying actions for adaptation and mitigation against climate change, (4) geared towards mainstreaming climate change disaster risk reduction actions in development programmes, (5) for setting out a structure for public awareness and engagement in climate change actions, (6) for identifying strategic areas of national infrastructure requiring climate proofing, (7) to enhance energy conservation, efficiency and use of renewable energy in industrial, commercial, transport, domestic and other uses, (8) for reviewing levels and trends of greenhouse gas emissions, and (9) for achieving Nigeria's climate change goals;

(c) make provision for research, planning, and action on climate change mitigation and adaptation; and,

(d) contain a projection of fiscal and budgetary needs, for the execution of climate change projects and related activities.[723]

In addition, the components of the action plan include: (a) an articulated carbon budget for the 5-year cycle, consistent with the carbon budget; (b) an articulated annual carbon budget for each of the years that make up the 5-year cycle; (c) past, current and projected GHG emission profile of GHG emission sectors of the economy; (d) details of past, current and proposed climate mitigation and adaptation actions across the ·sectors of the economy including the rationale., costs, funding source and benefit of such action; (e) details on the level of compliance with international climate commitments; and (f) proposed incentives for private and public entities, which achieve GHG emission reduction.[724]

In furtherance of Nigeria's efforts to achieve short, medium, and long-term goals on climate mitigation and adaption the Act imposes certain obligations on (1) Ministries, Departments and Agencies (MDAs), (2) public entities and (3) private entities. This is in line with one of the objectives of the Act that private and public entities comply with stated climate change strategies, targets and the National Climate Change Action Plan.[725] Thus, ministries, departments and agencies (MDAs) are required under the Act to establish a climate change desk which should be under the supervision of a director. This Desk would carry out all compliance and planning activities relating to the climate change obligations. Furthermore, the Act states that sanctions and fines determined by the NCCC could be levied on the Principal of MDAs if a compliance failure is noted during evaluation.[726]

In the same vein, the Act provides that organisations providing services to the public on behalf of the Nigerian government are required to comply with the periodic regulations issued by the NCCC.[727] To cap it all, the Act provides that private

[723] Climate Change Act (2021), s. 20(4)(a)–(d).

[724] Ibid., s. 20(5)(a)(f).

[725] Ibid., s. 1(i).

[726] Climate Change Act (2021), s. 22.

[727] Ibid., s. 23.

entities that employ fifty (50) or more employees are required to develop a process to achieve the annual carbon emission reduction target as stated in the action plan. Furthermore, they are required to appoint a Climate change Officer or an Environmental Sustainability Officer with the responsibility to prepare and submit annual reports detailing the company's efforts at climate change obligations for the review period.[728] It should be noted that a private entity that fails to meet its target, as specified, shall be liable to a fine to be determined by the NCCC, relying on a system of Environmental Economic Accounting with attention on the health impacts, impact on climate variation, and total damage to ecosystem services.

Besides the above provisions, there are some other far-reaching provisions under the Act that if well enforced will establish the governance structures needed in climate change mitigation and adaptation in Nigeria. For instance, under Section 25(l) the Secretariat, with the approval of the Council, shall work in partnership with the Federal Ministry of Environment, Civil Society Organisations (CSOs), women, youths, and others, to monitor plans, programmes, projects, engage in climate advocacy and related activities. Again, under Section 26(1) the Secretariat shall, with the approval of the NCCC, advise the MDAs responsible for regulating educational curriculum in Nigeria on the integration of climate change into the various disciplines and subjects across all educational levels.

The Act also introduces an element of public participation in decision-making. Thus, the Secretariat shall, not later than 6 months to the end of every year, prepare and publish its public engagement strategy for the following year.[729] The public engagement strategy shall set out the modalities to be adopted towards achieving the objectives under the Act by (a) informing the public about the action plan; and (b) identifying actions and encouraging the public to contribute to the achievement of the objectives of the action plan and the Act.[730] When the need arises, the NCCC shall review the public engagement strategy; and within 1 month of the review, publish the reviewed public engagement strategy in the Federal Government Gazette.[731]

Furthermore, the Act provides for the promotion and adoption of nature-based solutions to reducing GHG emissions and mitigating climate change issues in Nigeria.[732] To this end, the Federal Ministry of Environment is mandated to set up a registry with sub-national nodes for capturing REDD+[733] activities in Nigeria including updates from the Forest Reference Emission Level (FREL).[734] In addition,

---

[728] Ibid., s. 24.

[729] Ibid., s. 30(1).

[730] Climate Change Act (2021), s. 30(2).

[731] Ibid., s. 30(3).

[732] Ibid., s. 27.

[733] "REDD+" means Reducing Emissions from Deforestation and Forest Degradation and the role of conservation, sustainable management of forests and the enhancement of forest carbon stocks. See Climate Change Act 2021, s. 28(2).

[734] Climate Change Act (2021), s. 28(1).

the NCCC shall collaborate with and equip the National Bureau of Statistics for developing Nigeria's Natural Capital Accounts.[735] The data from the Natural Capital Accounts shall be made available to MDAs, and used in policy formulation and development of an action plan, in line with the carbon budget and the Ministry of Finance, Budget, and National Planning shall ensure that the data generated is captured in the National Development Plan and expenditure framework, as a means of measuring the impact of climate change on sustainable development.

The Act empowers a Federal or State High Court, before which a suit regarding climate change or environmental matters is instituted, to make an order to: (a) prevent, stop or discontinue the performance of any act that is harmful to the environment; (b) compel any public official to act to prevent or stop the performance of any act that is harmful to the environment; (c) compensate victims directly affected by the acts that are harmful to the environment.[736]

The Act in Section 34(1) sets out offences thus, "a person, or private or public entity that acts in a manner that negatively affects efforts towards mitigation and adaptation measures made under this Act commits an offence and is liable to a penalty to be determined by the Council (that is the NCCC)." The Act therefore did not specify the nature of the penalty but left it at the discretion of NCCC. This is a negation of principles under environmental crime or even traditional criminal law where the legislature specifically sets out a penalty for contravening any of the provisions of the Act of Parliament. It should be noted that the NCCC being of the Executive branch should not determine any penalty for infringing any provisions of a Law made by the Legislature. The Climate Change Act is an Act of Parliament and the Legislature should have included in the Act appropriate penalty for infringing on the provisions of the Act. The Legislature is urged at the earliest opportunity to amend this Section 34(1) of the Act.

Be it as it may be, the Climate Change Act 2021, notwithstanding any noticeable limitations, falls within the following broad categorisation used in classifying legislation on climate change. They include: carbon pricing; energy demand; energy supply; REDD+ and Land Use, Land-Use Change, and Forestry (LULUCF); transportation; adaptation; research and development; and institutional or administrative arrangements.[737]

As pointed out by CAT,[738] "the Climate Change Act, passed in November 2021, marks a significant step forward in developing a Paris-compatible decarbonisation pathway for Nigeria. . .if fully implemented, will go a long way to establishing the governance structures needed to accelerate the transition to net zero emissions."[739] Where these are achieved, they may in the end help in mitigating some of the air pollution-related impacts such as global warming and climate change.

[735] Ibid., s. 29(1).

[736] Ibid., s. 34(2).

[737] Nachmany et al. (2014), p. 30.

[738] Climate Action Tracker (CAT) (2022), p. 19.

[739] Ibid., 20.

6.4.4 Policy Instruments in Controlling Air Pollution

Balancing the needs of polluters (who provide many products upon which industrial societies depend) with the public's need for clean air calls for thoughtful policy instruments that take the needs of all sides into account—not the least of which is the political sustainability of any particular policy instrument over time. Some of such policies are embedded in what is described as market-based policies. The policies include environmental accounting policy, environmental or pollution tax policy, charges, taxes, and tax relief incentive policy.[740] These policies are not necessarily mutually exclusive although there are positive and negative aspects of each that must be considered when formulating effective policy. Nonetheless, they may be applied as an air pollution abatement strategy.

In addition to the adoption of policy instruments, private litigation may be an added option in air pollution abatement strategies. By allowing private concerns (extra-national as well national) to sue violators of international pollution agreements, regulatory costs would be minimised since enforcement would be provided, perhaps sporadically, through litigation by interested/injured parties. The ability of wealthy polluters to stall legal proceedings, the uncertainty of compliance with an international court and the sovereignty issue such a body raises are obvious disadvantages to this system. It should be noted, however, that international law relating to oil spills at sea and European transboundary pollution treaties have established some legal precedents upon which to base a greater role for private litigation. While private litigation may be insufficient to lower toxic emissions and improve air quality, it may prove to be a valuable addition to the other strategies by providing an additional compliance incentive for polluters.

Much of the current literature barely touches or ignores several other alternatives that would complement all these measures. Greater education, particularly combined with the availability of information regarding polluter's emission levels, about pollution, would promote awareness and greater citizen oversight of pollution sources. As public awareness increases, its interest in environmentally sound products increases leading to a competitive advantage for firms able to advertise their goods as environmentally friendly.

6.5 Noise Pollution

This segment of the chapter discusses noise, noise emission and pollution, impact, and noise control and abatement measures.

[740] These were discussed in Sect. 3.8 of Chap. 3 of this book under "Market-Based Concepts in Environmental Legislation."

6.5.1 *Concept of Noise*

The word noise is derived from the Latin word "Nausea" implying "unwanted sound" or sound that is loud, unpleasant or unexpected and can be defined as a wrong sound, in the wrong place and at the wrong time.[741]

Noise means "any unwanted and annoying sound that is intrinsically objectionable to human beings or which can have or is likely to have an adverse effect on human health or the environment."[742] The South African Department of Minerals and Energy (2000) defined noise as "sound that is deemed undesirable, either because it annoys, distracts or interferes with those hearing it, or because it has the potential to damage the hearing mechanism and cause hearing loss for those exposed to it."[743]

Noise is usually machine-created sound that disrupts activity or balance of the human's way of life. It is a growing environmental problem that is increasingly becoming an omnipresent, yet unnoticed form of pollution not only in developed countries but also in developing countries.[744] To this end, "noise is physical form of pollution. It is not harmful to air, soil and water but affects the animals including humans. Noise is therefore unwanted sound, that is unpleasant, loud and disruptive."[745] Noise pollution is an invisible danger. It cannot be seen, but it is present nonetheless, both on land and under the sea. Noise pollution is considered to be any unwanted or disturbing sound that affects the health and well-being of humans and other organisms.[746]

6.5.2 *Sources of Noise Pollution*

Noise pollution is commonly generated inside many industrial facilities and some other workplaces, but it also comes from highway, railway, and airplane traffic and from outdoor construction activities.[747] There are many sounds in the environment, from rustling leaves (20–30 dB) to a thunderclap (120 dB) to the wail of a siren (120–140 dB). Sounds that reach 85 dB or higher can harm a person's ears. Sound sources that exceed this threshold include familiar things, such as power

---

[741] Firdaus and Ahmad (2010).

[742] National Environmental (Noise Standards and Control) Regulations 2009, Government Notice No. 67, S.I. No. 35. Federal Republic of Nigeria Official Gazette No. 288, Vol. 96, 19 October 2009, Regulation 19.

[743] Wirespace (2006).

[744] Jariwala (2018).

[745] Gandhinagar (2020).

[746] National Geographic Society (2020b).

[747] Berg and Nathanson (2020).

lawnmowers (90 dB), subway trains (90–115 dB), and loud rock concerts (110–120 dB).[748]

In his study, Ijaiya[749] identified the following as the main sources of noise pollution in Nigeria. They are electricity generating plants, vehicular traffic, noise engine and pressure horns, construction/industrial noise, machinery noise, noise from religious worship, institutions and household noise.

Generally, sources of noise include: industrialisation, poor urban planning, social events, transportation, construction activities, household chores,[750] fireworks, agricultural machines, defence equipment and launching of satellites[751] and miscellaneous sources such as automobile repair shops, marketplaces, schools, colleges, bus stands, and railway stations, etc.[752]

The oceans are also affected by noise pollution. Major sources of noise pollution in the oceans include ships, oil drills, sonar devices, and seismic tests. These have made the once tranquil marine environment loud and chaotic. Some of the loudest underwater noise comes from naval sonar devices. Sonar, like echolocation, works by sending pulses of sound down into the depths of the ocean to bounce off an object and return an echo to the ship, which indicates a location for object. Sonar sounds can be as loud as 235 dB and travel hundreds of miles underwater, interfering with whales' ability to use echolocation.[753]

Seismic surveys also produce loud blasts of sound within the ocean. Ships looking for deep-sea oil or gas deposits tow devices called air guns and shoot pulses of sound down to the ocean floor. The sound blasts can damage the ears of marine animals and cause serious injury. Scientists believe this noise may also be contributing to the altered behaviour of whales.[754]

6.5.3 Effects of Noise Pollution

Noise pollution is unwanted or excessive sound that can have deleterious effects on human health, wildlife, and environmental quality.[755] Thus, to understand the effects

[748] National Geographic Society (2020b).

[749] Ijaiya (2014), pp. 1–6.

[750] Such as gadgets like televisions, mobile phones, mixer grinders, pressure cookers, vacuum cleaners, washing machines and dryers, coolers, and air conditioners used extensively in our daily life are contributors to the amount of noise that is produced, but many times they affect the quality of life of our neighborhood.

[751] A lot of noise pollution is added to the atmosphere by artillery, tanks, launching of rockets, explosions, exercising of military airplanes and shooting practices. Screams of jet engines, the launching of satellites, and sonic booms have a deafening impact on the ears.

[752] Gandhinagar (2020).

[753] National Geographic Society (2020b).

[754] Ibid.

[755] Berg and Nathanson (2020).

of noise pollution, it will be pertinent to first discuss the means of measuring and perceiving loudness that results in excessive sound that affects the environment and human well-being.

6.5.3.1 Measuring and Perceiving Loudness of Noise

Sound waves are vibrations of air molecules carried from a noise source to the ear. Sound is typically described in terms of the loudness (amplitude) and the pitch (frequency) of the wave. Loudness (also called sound pressure level, or SPL) is measured in logarithmic units called decibels (dB).[756] The normal human ear can detect sounds that range between 0 dB (hearing threshold) and about 140 dB, with sounds between 120 dB and 140 dB causing pain (pain threshold). The ambient SPL in a library is about 35 dB, while that inside a moving bus or subway train is roughly 85 dB; building construction activities can generate SPLs as high as 105 dB at the source. SPLs decrease with distance from the source.[757]

The rate at which sound energy is transmitted, called sound intensity, is proportional to the square of the SPL. Because of the logarithmic nature of the decibel scale, an increase of 10 dB represents a tenfold increase in sound intensity, an increase of 20 dB represents a 100-fold increase in intensity, a 30-dB increase represents a 1000-fold increase in intensity, and so on. When sound intensity is doubled, on the other hand, the SPL increases by only 3 dB.[758]

It should be noted that precise measurement and scientific description of sound levels differ from most subjective human perceptions and opinions about sound. Subjective human responses to noise depend on both pitch and loudness. People with normal hearing generally perceive high-frequency sounds to be louder than low-frequency sounds of the same amplitude. For this reason, electronic sound-level meters used to measure noise levels take into account the variations of perceived loudness with pitch.[759]

Frequency filters in the meters serve to match meter readings with the sensitivity of the human ear and the relative loudness of various sounds. The so-called A-weighted filter, for example, is commonly used for measuring ambient community noise. SPL measurements made with this filter are expressed as A-weighted decibels, or dBA. Most people perceive and describe a 6- to 10-dBA increase in an SPL reading to be a doubling of "loudness." Another system, the C-weighted (dBC) scale, is sometimes used for impact noise levels, such as gunfire, and tends to be more accurate than dBA for the perceived loudness of sounds with low-frequency components.[760]

---

[756] Ibid.

[757] Ibid.

[758] Berg and Nathanson (2020).

[759] Ibid.

[760] Ibid.

Noise levels generally vary with time, so noise measurement data are reported as time-averaged values to express overall noise levels. There are several ways to do this. For example, the results of a set of repeated sound-level measurements may be reported as $L_{90} = 75$ dBA, meaning that the levels were equal to or higher than 75 dBA for 90% of the time. Another unit, called equivalent sound levels (L_{eq}), can be used to express an average SPL over any period of interest, such as an eight-hour workday. (L_{eq} is a logarithmic average rather than an arithmetic average, so loud events prevail in the overall result.) A unit called day-night sound level (DNL or L_{dn}) accounts for the fact that people are more sensitive to noise during the night, so a 10-dBA penalty is added to SPL values that are measured between 10:00 p.m. and 7:00 a.m. DNL measurements are very useful for describing overall community exposure to aircraft noise, for example.[761]

6.5.3.2 Impact of Noise Pollution

Noise is more than a mere nuisance. Noise pollution impacts millions of people on a daily basis. Excessive noise exposure can raise blood pressure and pulse rates, cause irritability, anxiety, and mental fatigue, and interfere with sleep, recreation, and personal communication.[762] These health problems can affect all age groups, especially children. Many children who live near noisy airports or streets have been found to suffer from stress and other problems, such as impairments in memory, attention level, and reading skills.[763]

The most common health problem caused by noise pollution is Noise Induced Hearing Loss (NIHL). At certain levels and durations of exposure, it can cause physical damage to the eardrum and the sensitive hair cells of the inner ear and result in temporary or permanent hearing loss, known as noise-induced hearing loss. Hearing loss does not usually occur at SPLs below 80 dBA (eight-hour exposure levels are best kept below 85 dBA), but most people repeatedly exposed to more than 105 dBA will have permanent hearing loss to some extent.[764]

World Health Organisation (WHO)[765] estimates that 1.1 billion young people worldwide could be at risk of hearing loss due to unsafe listening practices. Nearly half of all teenagers and young adults (12–35 years old) in middle- and high-income countries are exposed to unsafe levels of sound from the use of personal audio devices and some 40% of them are exposed to potentially damaging sound levels at clubs, discotheques and bars.

Noise pollution also impacts the health and well-being of wildlife. Studies have shown that loud noises cause caterpillars' hearts to beat faster and bluebirds to have

[761] Ibid.

[762] Berg and Nathanson (2020).

[763] National Geographic Society (2020b).

[764] Berg and Nathanson (2020).

[765] World Health Organisation (WHO) (2015).

fewer chicks. Animals use sound for a variety of reasons, including to navigate, find food, attract mates, and avoid predators. Noise pollution makes it difficult for them to accomplish these tasks, which affects their ability to survive.[766]

Noise pollution also impacts wildlife. A wide range of animals, including insects, frogs, birds and bats, rely on sound for a variety of reasons. Noise pollution can interfere with an animal's ability to attract a mate, communicate, navigate, find food, or avoid predators and thus can even be an existential threat to vulnerable organisms.[767]

Again, increasing noise is not only affecting animals on land, it is also a growing problem for those that live in the ocean. The problem of noise pollution is especially serious for marine animals, particularly those that rely on echolocation, such as certain whales and dolphins, and much of the world's oceans are polluted with chaotic sounds from ships, seismic tests, and oil drills. Some of the loudest and most detrimental sounds in the sea are from naval sonar devices, whose noise can travel hundreds of miles through the water and is associated with mass stranding of whales and dolphins.[768]

Whales and dolphins are particularly impacted by noise pollution. These marine mammals rely on echolocation to communicate, navigate, feed, and find mates, and excess noise interferes with their ability to effectively echolocate.[769]

Based on the above, noise pollution control is therefore important in the workplace and the community. What then are the legal instruments for regulating and mitigating noise pollution?

6.5.4 Noise Abatement and Control Strategies

As a result of the adverse effects of noise on human health, the National Environmental Standards Regulation Enforcement Agency (Agency) is mandated under the National Environmental Standards Regulation Enforcement Agency 2007 (NESREA Act) to identify major sources of noise, noise criteria and noise control technology and make regulations on noise, emission control and abatement as may be necessary to preserve and maintain public health and welfare.[770] These regulations are targeted at identifying major sources of noise, specifying permissible levels for such noise and setting out control and mitigating mechanisms.

To give effect to these provisions the Minister charged with the responsibility for the environment in 2009 made the National Environmental (Noise Standards and

[766] National Geographic Society (2020b).

[767] Berg and Nathanson (2020).

[768] Berg and Nathanson (2020).

[769] National Geographic (2020b).

[770] NESREA Act (2007), s. 22(1)(a) and (b).

Table 6.1 Permissible noise levels for general environment

	Column 1	Column 2	
		Maximum permissible noise limits dB (A) (Leg)	
	Facility	Day [a]	Night [b]
A	Any building used as a hospital, convalescence home, home for the aged, sanatorium and institutions of higher learning, conference rooms, public library, environmental or recreational sites	45	35
B	Residential buildings	50	35
C	Mixed residential (with some commercial and entertainment)	55	45
D	Residential + industry or small-scale production + commerce	60	50
E	Industrial (outside perimeter fence)	70	60

[a] Between the hours of 6:00 a.m. and 10:00 p.m., National Environmental (Noise Standards and Control) Regulations (2009) First Schedule
[b] Between the hours of 10:00 p.m. and 6:00 a.m., National Environmental (Noise Standards and Control) Regulations (2009)

Control) Regulations 2009,[771] for setting noise standards and noise control. The purpose of the regulations is to ensure the maintenance of a healthy environment for all the people of Nigeria, maintain the tranquility of their surroundings and their psychological well-being by regulating noise levels generally, and elevate the standard of living of the people. These objectives are to be achieved by prescribing the maximum permissible noise levels in a facility or activity to which a person may be exposed, providing for the control of noise and setting out mitigating measures for the reduction of noise.[772] Thus, the main thrust of noise control and abatement are:

(a) Setting the standards for permissible noise levels for various activities; and.
(b) Setting regulations to control noise pollution.

6.5.4.1 Setting the Standards for Permissible Noise Level for Various Activities

The maximum permissible noise level for various facilities and activities in Nigeria has been set out under Regulation 2 of the Noise Regulations.[773] These levels are expressed in the Tables 6.1, 6.2, 6.3, 6.4, 6.5, 6.6, 6.7, 6.8 and 6.9.[774]

Table 6.1 is pursuant to Regulation 2(1) of the Noise Regulations. Under the regulations, the maximum permissible noise level for the facilities specified in

[771] National Environmental (Noise Standards and Control) Regulations (2009).
[772] National Environmental (Noise Standards and Control) Regulations (2009), Regulation 1.
[773] National Environmental (Noise Standards and Control) Regulations (2009).
[774] Source for all the tables (6.1, 6.2, 6.3, 6.4, 6.5, 6.6, 6.7, 6.8 and 6.9): National Environmental (Noise Standards and Control) Regulations (2009).

Table 6.2 Maximum noise levels (continuous or intermittent noise) from factory or workshop

Column 1	Column 2	Column 3
dB (A) (Leg)	Duration (Daily)	Duration (Weekly)
85	8 h	40 h
88	4 h	20 h
91	2 h	10 h
94	1 h	5 h
97	30 min	2.5 h
100	15 min	1.25 h
106	7.5 min	37.5 min
109	1.875 min	9.375 min

Table 6.3 Maximum noise levels from impulsive noise

Column 1	Column 2
Sound level dB (A) (Lmax) [a]	Permitted number of impulses or impact per day
140	100
130	1000
120	10,000

[a] This means the maximum level of A-weighted individual noise events, see the National Environmental (Noise Standards and Control) Regulations (2009), Regulation 18

Table 6.4 Maximum permissible noise levels from construction site

Column 1	Column 2	
	Maximum noise level permitted in dB (A) (Leq)	
Facility	Day	Night
Hospitals, schools, institutions of higher learning, homes for the disabled, etc.	60	50
Buildings other than those prescribed above	75	65

Table 6.5 Maximum permissible noise levels for public announcement system or device

Column 1	Column 2	
Noise control zone	Sound level dB (A) (Leq) day	Sound level dB (A) (Leq) night
Residential	60	40
Commercial	75	50
Industrial	85	65

Table 6.6 Maximum permissible noise levels for places of entertainment

Column 1	Column 2	
Noise control zone	Sound level dB (A) (Leq) day	Sound level dB (A) (Leq) night
Residential	60	40
Commercial	75	50
Industrial	85	65

Table 6.7 Maximum permissible noise levels for places or areas of worship

Column 1	Column 2	
Noise control zone	Sound level dB (A) (Leq) day	Sound level dB (A) (Leq) night
Residential	60	40
Commercial	75	50
Industrial	85	65

Table 6.8 Maximum permissible noise levels for accelerating vehicle

Column 1	Column 2
Vehicle category	Maximum sound level in dB(A)
1. Vehicles intended for carriage of passengers and equipped with no more than nine seats, including the driver's seat	78
2. Vehicles intended for the carriage of passengers and equipped with not more than nine seats, including the driver's seat and having a maximum permissible mass of more than 3.5 tonnes:	
(a) With an engine power of more than 150 kW,	80
(b) With an engine power of less than 150 kW.	83
3. Vehicles intended for the carriage of passengers and equipped with more than nine seats, including the driver's seat and vehicles intended for carriage of goods:	
(a) With a maximum permissible mass not exceeding 2 tonnes,	79
(b) With a maximum permissible mass exceeding 2 tonnes but not exceeding 3.5 tonnes.	80
4. Vehicles intended for the carriage of goods and having a maximum permissible mass exceeding 3.5 tonnes:	
(a) With an engine power of less than 75 kW,	81
(b) With an engine power of not less than 75 kW but not less than 150 kW,	83
(c) With an engine power of not less than 150 kW.	84

Table 6.9 Maximum permissible noise levels from mines and quarries

Column 1	Column 2
Facility affected areas	Limit value in dB (C) [a]
1. For any building used as a hospital, school, convalescent home, old age home or residential	109 dB (C)
2. For any building in an area used for residential and one or more of the following purposes: Commerce, small-scale production, entertainment, or any residential apartment in an area that is used for purposes of industry, commerce or small-scale production, or any building used for industry, commerce or small-scale production	114 dB (C)

[a] This means C-weighted sound pressure reading especially for peak noise level, see the National Environmental (Noise Standards and Control) Regulations (2009), Regulation 18

column 1 shall not exceed the decibel (dB (A))[775] stated in column 2. Once the permissible level is exceeded, an offence is committed under the Noise Regulations, except where the person had applied for a permit for noise emission in excess of the permissible level.

Table 6.2 is pursuant to Regulation 2(2) of the Noise Regulations. Under Regulation 18, intermittent noise means a noise whose level suddenly drops to several times the level of the background noise. Arising from the table noise levels shall not exceed a Leg of 85 dB (A) for Factory/Workshops, 75 dB (A) for Factory/Workshop compound and 50 dB (A) for offices. Any noise in excess of these specifications for the facilities amounts to any offence except if the noise generator had applied for noise emission in excess of the permissible levels.[776]

Table 6.3 is pursuant to Regulation 2(3) of the Noise Regulations. Under the Noise Regulations,[777] impulsive noise means a noise consisting of one or more bursts of sound energy of a duration of less than one second. Where the sound level is up to 140 dB the permitted number of impulses or impact per day is 100, at 130 dB, it is 1000 impacts and at 120 dB, it is 10,000 impacts. What this means is that the higher the sound level the less the impact. An offence is committed once the impact exceeds the appropriate sound level.

Table 6.4 is pursuant to Regulation 2(4) of the regulations sets out permissible noise levels from construction sites as it affects facilities specified in column 1 of the table. Measurements are to be made at the receptor's sites.

Table 6.5 is pursuant to Regulation 2(5) of the Noise Regulations. This table specifically protects designated areas considered by the Agency as noise control zone (NCZ). A noise control zone means a geographical area so designated which under no conditions noise levels should exceed the permissible noise level designated for such area. It is the considered opinion of the Agency that such areas so designated require special consideration for noise control. Thus, in respect of the public announcement system or device, the sound level shall not be exceeded as specified for the various areas in column 1 of Table 6.5.

Table 6.6 is pursuant to Regulation 2(6) of the Noise Regulations. It sets to control noise levels from places of entertainment by setting out the permissible noise level, be it day or night, especially with reference to the noise control zone.

Table 6.7 is pursuant to Regulation 2(7) of the Noise Regulations. It sets to control noise levels from places or areas of worship by setting out the permissible noise level, be it day or night, especially with reference to the noise control zone.

Table 6.8, made pursuant to Regulation 2(8) of the Noise Regulations 2009, sets out permissible noise levels for various accelerating vehicles with reference to such vehicle's tonnes or horsepower (kW).

---

[775]This means average equivalent A-weighted continuous sound energy over a period, see the National Environmental Regulations (2009), Regulation 18.

[776]Application for noise emission over the permissible levels is controlled by the provisions of National Environmental (Noise Standards and Control) Regulations (2009), Regulations 7 and 8.

[777]National Environmental (Noise Standards and Control) Regulations (2009), Regulation 18.

Table 6.9, made pursuant to Regulation 2(9) of the Noise Regulations 2009, sets out permissible limits for mines and quarries.

In addition to the permissible noise levels set out by the Noise Regulations, some other national regulations made by NESREA 2007[778] set out noise standards and noise control measures for several activities and facilities. For instance, the National Environmental (Textile, Wearing Apparel, Leather and Footwear Industry) Regulations 2009[779] set standards for noise, noise abatement and noise monitoring[780] emanating from the textile, wearing apparel, leather and footwear industry. Under the National Environmental (Chemical, Pharmaceutical, Soap and Detergent Manufacturing Industries) Regulations 2009[781] noise standards,[782] noise abatement[783] and noise monitoring[784] are also regulated in the chemical, pharmaceutical, soap and detergent manufacturing industries.

The National Environmental (Food, Beverages and Tobacco Sector) Regulations 2009[785] also provide regulations for noise standards,[786] noise abatement[787] and noise monitoring[788] for facilities under the food, beverages and tobacco sector.

Again, under the National Environmental (Base Metal, Iron and Steel Manufacturing/Recycling Industries Sector) Regulations 2011,[789] standards are also set for noise,[790] noise abatement[791] and noise measurement[792] in respect of the base metal, iron and steel manufacturing/recycling industries sector. Similar standards are also set for noise,[793] noise abatement,[794] noise monitoring,[795] and noise measurement[796] in respect of domestic and industrial plastic, rubber and foam

---

[778] NESREA Act (2007).

[779] National Environmental (Noise Standards and Control) Regulations (2009).

[780] Ibid., Regulations 23, 24 and 26.

[781] National Environmental (Chemical, Pharmaceutical, Soap and Detergent Manufacturing Industries) Regulations (2009).

[782] Ibid., Regulation 24.

[783] Ibid., Regulation 25.

[784] Ibid., Regulation 27.

[785] National Environmental (Food, Beverages and Tobacco Sector) Regulations (2009).

[786] Ibid., Regulation 22.

[787] Ibid., Regulation 23.

[788] Ibid., Regulations 25.

[789] National Environmental (Base Metal, Iron and Steel Manufacturing/Recycling Industries Sector) Regulations (2011).

[790] Ibid., Regulation 26.

[791] National Environmental (Base Metal, Iron and Steel Manufacturing/Recycling Industries Sector) Regulations (2011), Regulation 27.

[792] Ibid., Regulation 38.

[793] National Environmental (Domestic and Industrial Plastic, Rubber and Foam Sector) Regulations (2011), Regulation 27.

[794] Ibid., Regulation 28.

[795] Ibid., Regulation 30.

[796] Ibid., Regulation 38.

sectors under the National Environmental (Domestic and Industrial Plastic, Rubber and Foam Sector) Regulations 2011.[797] In the same vein, the National Environmental (Non-Metallic Minerals Manufacturing Industries Sector) Regulations 2011[798] in respect of noise,[799] noise abatement,[800] noise monitoring,[801] and noise measurement.[802]

Other regulations such as the National Environmental (Pulp and Paper, Wood and Wood Products Sector) Regulations 2013[803] have provisions for noise standards,[804] noise abatement,[805] noise monitoring,[806] and noise measurement,[807] so also is the National Environmental (Energy Sector) Regulations 2014[808] in respect of noise[809] and noise measurement.[810]

6.5.4.2 Regulating Noise Pollution

In addition to the setting out of permissible noise levels and standards for various activities in respect of specified facilities and activities set out under Regulation 2(1)–(9),[811] and other national regulations, the Noise Regulations 2009 under Regulation 5 provides that:

> no person shall emit or cause to be emitted, or permit the emission of noise resulting from any action or activity, if that noise is a disturbance to the receptor or in the neighbourhood for more than two minutes or is within the prohibited time in a residential area or Noise Control Zone.

Actions or activities being referred to are:

(a) yelling, laughing, clapping, shouting. Hooting, pounding, whistling and singing;
(b) selling or advertising by shouting or outcry or amplified sound;

---

[797] National Environmental (Domestic and Industrial Plastic, Rubber and Foam Sector) Regulations (2011).

[798] National Environmental (Non-Metallic Minerals Manufacturing Industries Sector) Regulations (2011).

[799] Ibid., Regulation 33.

[800] Ibid., Regulation 34.

[801] Ibid., Regulation 36.

[802] Ibid., Regulation 45.

[803] National Environmental (Pulp and Paper, Wood and Wood Products Sector) Regulations (2013).

[804] Ibid., Regulation 32.

[805] Ibid., Regulation 33.

[806] Ibid., Regulation 35.

[807] Ibid., Regulation 43.

[808] National Environmental (Energy Sector) Regulations (2014).

[809] Ibid., Regulation 22.

[810] Ibid., Regulation 29.

[811] National Environmental (Noise Standards and Control) Regulations (2009).

(c) operating any equipment in connection with construction;
(d) detonating fireworks or explosive devices not used in construction;
(e) operating any auditory signaling device, including the ringing of bells or gongs and the blowing of horns or sirens or whistles or the production, reproduction or amplification of any similar sound by electronic means; and,
(f) operating or playing a radio or musical instrument or any electronic device or group of connected devices incorporating one or more loudspeakers, transducers or other electro-mechanism, which is intended for the production, reproduction or amplification of sound.[812]

However, the Agency[813] may permit the operation of an electronic device or loudspeakers or the emission of noise to create public awareness, demonstration, religious assembly, political debate, cinematography, and musical or other theatrical entertainment, beauty competition, handicraft show, fair, circus, private dance party, lecture or public hearing.[814] Again, no offence is committed where the:

(a) noise is caused by the operation of a loudspeaker or siren for fire brigade, ambulance or police purposes;
(b) noise is caused by emergency measures undertaken to safeguard the health, safety, or welfare of the people;
(c) noise is caused, or continuance of noise is caused by a person as a result of temporary or accidental cause which could not have been prevented by the exercise of due diligence and care on the part of that person;
(d) noise is caused by the horn of a vehicle to give sufficient warning of the approach or position of the vehicle;
(e) noise is caused at or by an educational class or recreation in or around a school, college, university or other educational institutions;
(f) noise is caused at or by athletics or sports;
(g) noise is caused at a cultural activity or cultural show, funeral service or rite, or marriage ceremony held between the hours of 10:00 a.m. and 8:00 p.m. of the same day in an area;
(h) noise is caused during a period, or by such a cause or for a purpose as the Agency may by notice specify.[815]

In the absence of the exceptions as specified under Regulation 5(3) and (4),[816] or the noise emission is expressly permitted under Regulations 7 and 8, of the said regulations, any violation of these regulations, especially emitting noise in excess of the permissible levels specified in Regulations 2(1)–(9) and contrary to the provisions of Regulation 5(1) and (2), an offence is committed. For the avoidance of

[812] National Environmental (Noise Standards and Control) Regulations (2009), Regulation 5(2).

[813] Agency means the National Environmental Standards Enforcement and Regulation Agency, established under the NESREA Act (2007), s. 1(1).

[814] National Environmental (Noise Standards and Control) Regulations (2009).

[815] National Environmental (Noise Standards and Control) Regulations (2009), Regulation 5(4).

[816] National Environmental (Noise Standards and Control) Regulations (2009).

doubts, Regulation 17 clearly captures the catalogue of offences under the regulations. These include: contravention of the provisions of Regulations 2, 3 and 5 including failure to immediately reduce excessive noise to a permissible level; failure to comply with a notice to abate noise issued under Regulation 6; contravention or failure to carry out any requirement of an improvement notice under Regulation 11; among others.

6.5.4.3 Mitigating Noise Pollution

Low levels of noise may be overcome using additional absorbing material, such as heavy drapery or sound-absorbent tiles in enclosed rooms. Where low levels of identifiable noise may be distracting or where privacy of conversations in adjacent offices and reception areas may be important, the undesirable sounds may be masked. A small white-noise source such as static or rushing air, placed in the room, can mask the sounds of conversation from adjacent rooms without being offensive or dangerous to the ears of people working nearby. This type of device is often used in offices of doctors and other professionals. Another technique for reducing personal noise levels is through the use of hearing protectors, which are held over the ears in the same manner as an earmuff. By using commercially available earmuff-type hearing protectors, a decrease in sound level can be attained ranging typically from about 10 dB at 100 Hz to more than 30 dB for frequencies above 1000 Hz.[817]

Outdoor noise limits are also important for human comfort. Standard house construction will provide some shielding from external sounds if the house meets minimum standards of construction and if the outside noise level falls within acceptable limits. These limits are generally specified for particular periods of the day—for example, during daylight hours, during evening hours, and at night during sleeping hours. Because of refraction in the atmosphere owing to the nighttime temperature inversion, relatively loud sounds can be introduced into an area from a rather distant highway, airport, or railroad.[818]

One interesting technique to control highway noise is the erection of noise barriers alongside the highway, separating the highway from adjacent residential areas. The effectiveness of such barriers is limited by the diffraction of sound, which is greater at the lower frequencies that often predominate in road noise, especially from large vehicles. To be effective, they must be as close as possible to either the source or the observer of the noise (preferably to the source), thus maximising the diffraction that would be necessary for the sound to reach the observer. Another requirement for this type of barrier is that it must also limit the amount of transmitted sound to bring about significant noise reduction.[819]

---

[817] Berg and Nathanson (2020).

[818] Berg and Nathanson (2020).

[819] Ibid.

6.5.5 *Prosecuting Noise Pollution Offences*

How then can noise pollution offences be prosecuted? To do this, the following questions were set out:

1. Who may complain that an offence has been committed?
2. Whom shall such complaint be laid before?
3. How is the complaint to be laid?

Under Regulation 10 of the Noise Regulations[820] any person may complain to the Agency in writing if such a person considers that the noise levels being emitted, or likely to be emitted, may be higher than the permissible noise levels under the regulations. It should be noted that such complainant need not show or prove personal loss, injury or discomfort caused by the emission of the alleged noise.[821]

This is a deviation from the Common Law Tort of nuisance where a complainant needs to show that he had suffered some harm for him to be heard by the courts. Thus, in line with the new trend in environmental protection which hinges on seeing the protection of the environment as everybody's problem, and that a complainant need not show that he had suffered any harm, is a welcomed provision. And by this singular act citizen suit is enthroned under the Noise Regulations.

Citizen suit is a key enforcement tool for environmental protection which allows any person, group or organisation to bring a civil suit against any alleged violator of environmental protection laws or environmental protection agencies for a failure to perform a non-discretionary duty. It also enables individuals to enforce statutory, regulatory and permit requirements through suits seeking compliance orders and/or penalties.[822] Where this is enthroned the role of the judiciary in environmental protection is enhanced, and as Rt Hon. Justice A.T.M. Afzal, the Chief Justice of Bangladesh, pointed out "citizens suits must be encouraged as the role of the judiciary can be undermined if vigilant civil society does not play the role of watchdog."[823]

Under the regulations aforesaid, outside the Noise Regulations, it shall be an offence where a facility or any activity fails to comply with noise abatement measures, including failure to remediate the environment to the standard prescribed by the Agency.

However, under the Noise Regulations,[824] an offence is committed where any person (a) contravenes the provisions of Regulations 3 and 5 of these regulations; (b) fails to comply with a notice issued under Regulation 6 of these regulations; (c) contravenes or fails to carry out any requirement of an improvement notice under

[820] National Environmental (Noise Standards and Control) Regulations (2009).

[821] Ibid., Regulation 10(2).

[822] In Natural Resources Defence Council v. Texaco refining and Marketing 2, F. 3d 493 (third Cir 7993) over US$1.5 million in penalties was paid resulting from a citizen suit.

[823] United Nations Environment Programme (UNEP) (2018), 3.

[824] National Environmental (Noise Standards and Control) Regulations (2009), Regulation 17.

Regulation 11 of these regulations; (d) fails, neglects or refuses to control excessive noise in accordance with these regulations; (e) fails to immediately reduce excessive noise to a permissible level when required to do so; (f) causes or contributes to the emission of noise in excess of the maximum permissible levels from or within the vicinity of the premises during a prohibited period; (g) fails, without lawful justification, to comply with any term or condition of a noise permit or order issued under these regulations; (h) makes a statement, or produces a document, that is false or misleading in a material particular or (i) obstructs the Agency or its authorised agents in the execution of their duties to ensure enforcement of these regulations; (j) carriers out works or activities, or permit works or activities to be carried out without due authority, permit or necessary permit; (k) or contravenes any requirements or condition of a permit.

Penalties for violation are provided under the various regulations pursuant to Section 22(3) and (4) of the NESREA Act 2007[825] as amended by the NESREA (Amendment) Act 2018.[826] Where a person violates the regulations such a person shall on conviction be liable to a fine not less than $=N=$ 50,000 or to imprisonment for a term not exceeding 1 year or to both such fine and imprisonment and an additional fine of $=N=$ 5000 for every day the offence subsists.[827] And where the offence is committed by a body corporate, it shall on conviction be liable to a fine not less than $=N=$ 500,000 and an additional fine of $=N=$ 10,000 for every day the offence subsists.[828]

6.6 Summary

The atmosphere of the Earth is made up of layers with different properties, such as specific gaseous composition, temperature, and pressure, and comprising of the troposphere, the stratosphere, the thermosphere, the exosphere and the ionosphere. The composition of Earth's atmosphere is determined by the by-products of the life that it sustains. These layered compositions of the atmosphere minimise the harmful effects of sunlight, ultraviolet radiation, the solar wind, and cosmic rays that protect organisms from genetic damage. The atmosphere thus protects life on Earth by shielding it from incoming ultraviolet (UV) radiation, keeping the planet warm through insulation, and preventing extremes between day and night temperatures.

---

[825] NESREA Act (2007).

[826] NESREA (Amendment) Act (2018) increased the threshold of the penalties prescribed in the NESREA Act (2007) and substituted maximum punishment with minimum punishment, by substituting for a term not "exceeding" with not "less than" in respect of penalties under ss. 20(3), 21(3), 22(3) and (4), 23(3) and 26(3) and (4) of the original Act.

[827] NESREA Act (2007), s. 22(3), see also National Environmental (Noise Standards and Control) Regulations (2009), Regulation 17(1).

[828] NESREA Act (2007), s. 22(4), see also National Environmental (Noise Standards and Control) Regulations (2009), Regulation 17(2).

However, because of human activities over the millennia, the atmosphere is now polluted through air pollution and noise pollution, each having a distinct impact on both the natural environment and the human environment. Air is said to be polluted when the atmospheric composition of nitrogen, oxygen, carbon dioxide and other gases exceeds the threshold level of 70% nitrogen, 20% oxygen and carbon dioxide exceeds 300 parts per million.

Air pollution is a major global environmental issue and one of the most serious threats to human health. It can make new health problems appear when none would have, aggravate existing health issues, and, in extreme situations, result in death. In addition to harming crops and trees, acid deposition (acid rain), and broad loss of acid-sensitive aquatic ecosystems and creatures, air pollution is also to blame for a wide range of other environmental issues. It has been identified as a causal factor in building deterioration, lowered visibility, fish kills, global warming, and widespread tree and plant damage, all of which have serious economic consequences.

The good news is that what humans had helped to create strenuous efforts are being made to amend. This has resulted in several Multi-lateral Environment Agreements (MEAs) as well as regional and national laws to address the anomaly.

References

Abidjan Agreement (2009) West and Central Africa Regional Framework Agreement on Air Pollution 2009 (Abidjan Agreement 2009). https://unterm.un.org/unterm/Display/record/UNHQ/West_and_Central_Africa_Regional_Framework_Agreement_on_Air_Pollution/C0AF9B6390F9EB8685257C9800705878. Accessed 24 May 2023

American Council for Capital Formation (ACCF) (1999a) The impact of the Kyoto Protocol on U.S. Economic Growth and Projected Budget Surpluses. https://www.accf.org/publications/testimonies/test-impactkyoto-March25-1999. Accessed 30 May 2023

American Council for Capital Formation (ACCF) (1999b) An economist's view of the Kyoto Climate Treaty. https://www.accf.org/templates/story/story.php?storyId=4504298. Accessed 30 May 2023

Backes CW, van der Veen GA (2020) Urgenda: the final judgment of the Dutch Supreme Court. J Eur Environ Plann Law 17(3)spiepr A3B2 twbch ":":spiepr A3B2 twbch307–321. ISSN 1876-0104. https://doi.org/10.1163/18760104-01703004. Accessed 27 May 2023

Baede APM (ed) (2010). "Annex II," Glossary: Land use and Land-use change, archived from the original on 1 May 2010, retrieved 28 May 2010. In: Core Writing Team, Pachauri RK, Reisinger A (eds) Climate Change 2007: Synthesis Report (SYR), Contribution of Working Groups I, II and III to the Fourth Assessment Report (AR4) of the Intergovernmental Panel on Climate Change (IPCC), IPCC, Geneva, ISBN 978-92-9169-122-7

Ball S, McGillivray D (2008) Environmental law, 6th edn. Oxford University, Oxford

Bashmakov I et al (2001). "6.Policies, Measures, and Instruments," 6.3.2 Project-based Mechanisms (Joint Implementation and the Clean Development Mechanism). In: Metz B et al (eds) Climate Change 2001: Mitigation, Contribution of Working Group III to the Third Assessment Report of the Intergovernmental Panel on Climate Change. Cambridge University, Cambridge. ISBN 978-0-521-80769-2, https://www.ipcc.ch/ipccreports/tar/wg3/english/index.htm. Accessed 29 May 2023

Berg RE, Nathanson JA (2020) Noise pollution. https://www.britannica.com/science/noise-pollution. Accessed 18 July 2023

Bodansky D (2016) The legal character of the Paris Agreement. Rev Eur Comp Int Environ Law 25(2)spiepr A3B2 twbch ":":spiepr A3B2 twbch142–150. https://doi.org/10.1111/reel.12154. ISSN 2050-0394. https://www.onlinelibrary.wiley.com/doi/abs/10.1111/reel12154. Accessed 8 May 2023

Boyd DR (2022) Historic day for human rights and a healthy planet: UN expert. Office of the High Commissioner for Human Rights (OHCHR), New York, 28 July 2022. https://www.ohchr.org/en/press-releases/2022/07/historic-day-human-rights-and-healthy-planet-un-expert. Accessed 28 June 2023

British Broadcasting Corporation (BBC) (2022) What happened to the world's ozone hole? BBC News, 21 March 2022. https://www.bbc.com/future/article/20220321-what-happened-to-the-worlds-ozone-hole. Accessed 24 May 2023

Cai W et al (2021) Characterizing the interruption-recovery patterns of urban air pollution under the COVID-19 lockdown in China. Build Environ. https://doi.org/10.1016/j.buildenv.2021.108231. https://www.ncbi.nlm.nih.gov/pmc/articles/PMC8354860/. Accessed 18 May 2023

Caney S (2020) Human rights, population, and climate change, Ch 16. In: Akande D et al (eds) Human rights and 21st century challenges. Oxford University, Oxford

Carbon Trust (2009) Global carbon mechanisms: emerging lessons and implications (CTC748). Carbon Trust, p 20. https://www.carbontrust.com/resources/report/advice/global-carbon-mechanism. Accessed 29 May 2023

Carrington D (2020) Is air pollution making the coronavirus pandemic even more deadly? Guardian, United Kingdom, 4 May 2020. https://enveurope.springeropen.com/articles/10.1186/s12302-021-00548-1. Accessed 18 May 2023

Chaicharn PC et al (2019) Acute effects of air pollutants on daily mortality and hospitalizations due to cardiovascular and respiratory diseases. J Thorac Dis 11(7). https://jtd.amegroups.com/article/view/30220/21811. Accessed 18 May 2023

Ciencewicki J, Jasper I (2007) Air pollution and respiratory viral infection. Inhalation Toxicology, International Forum for Respiratory Research 19(14)spiepr A3B2 twbch ":":spiepr A3B2 twbch1135–1146. Received on 22 June 2007. Accepted on 16 August 2007. Published online: 06 October 2008. https://doi.org/10.1080/08958370701665434. Accessed 19 May 2023

Climate Action Tracker (CAT) (2022) Climate Governance Assessment of the government's ability and readiness to transform Nigeria into a zero emissions society, CAT Climate Governance Series NIGERIA, February 2022, p 19. https://climateactiontracker.org/documents/1014/2022_02_CAT_Governance_Report_Nigeria.pdf. Accessed 10 May 2023

Climate Case Chart (2021) Friends of the Earth Netherlands (Milieudefensie) v. Royal Dutch Shell. https://climatecasechart.com/non-us-case/milieudefensie-et-al-v-royal-dutch-shell-plc. Accessed 11 May 2023

Climate Change Act of Nigeria (2021) Climate Change Act of Nigeria, Act No. NG0038 of November 2021

Coon C (2001) Why President Bush Is Right to Abandon the Kyoto Protocol. Heritage Foundation Backgrounder No. 1437, May 11, 2001. https://www.heritage.org/. Accessed 30 May 2023

Dessai S (2001) Tyndall Centre working paper 12: The climate regime from The Hague to Marrakech: saving or sinking the Kyoto Protocol? Tyndall Centre, Norwich, 2001, p 3. https://www.tyndall.ac.uk/content/climate-regime-hague-marrakesh-saving-or-sinking-kyoto-protocol. Accessed 30 May 2023

Dessler A, Parson EA (2020) The science and politics of global climate change: a guide to the debate. Cambridge University, Cambridge, pp. 190–191. ISBN 978-1-316-63132-4. https://doi.org/10.1093/oso/9780198824770.003.0016. https://academic.oup.com/book/36650/chapter-abstract/321665452?redirectedFrom=fulltext. Accessed 23 May 2023

Duyck S (2017) The Paris climate agreement and the protection of human rights in a changing climate (2015). Yearb Int Environ Law 26:3–45. https://doi.org/10.1093/yiel/yvx011. Accessed 24 May 2023

Enger ED, Smith BF (2002) Environmental science, a study of interrelationships, 8th edn. McGraw Hill, Boston

European Union (EU) (2022) EU adaptation strategy. https://ec.europa.eu/clima/eu-action/adaptation-climate-change_en#:~:text. Accessed 13 May 2023

Farman JC et al (1985) Large losses of total ozone in Antarctica reveal seasonal ClO_x/NO_x interaction. Nature spiepr A3B2 twbch ":"315:207spiepr A3B2 twbch–210. https://www.nature.com/articles/315207a0. Accessed 24 May 2023

Fatima-Zahra T et al (eds) (2020) Pocket guide to NDCs: 2020 edition. European Capacity Building Initiative 2020, 17. https://ecbi.org/sites/default/files/2020. Pocket Guide to NDCs.pdf. Accessed 8 May 2023

Federal Environmental Protection Agency (FEPA) (1991) Guidelines and standards for environmental pollution control in Nigeria. F E PA, Lagos

Firdaus G, Ahmad A (2010) Noise pollution and human health: a case study of municipal Corporation of Delhi, indoor and built environment. Sage, Delhi

Gandhinagar GCW (2020) Noise pollution. https://gcwgandhinagar.com/econtent/document/15876178200EVSAECC01_Noise%20pollution.pdf. Accessed 18 June 2023

Godish T (2001) Air quality. Lewis Publishers, Chelsea

Grubb M (2004) Kyoto and the future of international climate change responses: from here to where? Int Rev Environ Strateg 5(1)spiepr A3B2 twbch ":":spiepr A3B2 twbch2. https://www.econ.cam.ac.uk/rstaff/grubb/publications/J37/pdf. Accessed 29 May 2023

Gupta S et al (2007) Chapter 13: Policies, instruments, and co-operative arrangements. Executive Summary. In: Metz B et al (eds) Climate Change 2007: Mitigation of Climate Change, Contribution of Working Group III (WG3) to the Fourth Assessment Report (AR4) of the Intergovernmental Panel on Climate Change (IPCC). Cambridge University, Cambridge, ISBN 978-0-521-88011-4. https://www.ipcc.ch/publications_and_data/ar4/wg3/en/ch13s13-es.html. Accessed 29 May 2023

Harrabin R (2011) Climate compensation row at Doha. https://www.bbc.co.uk/news/correspondent/2012/08/11. Accessed 28 May 2023

Harrabin R (2012) UN climate talks extend Kyoto Protocol, promise compensation. https://www.bbc.co.uk/news/science-environment/2012/23/12. Accessed 28 April 2023

Hermwille L et al (2019) Catalyzing mitigation ambition under the Paris Agreement: elements for an effective Global Stocktake. Climate Policy 19(8)spiepr A3B2 twbch ":":spiepr A3B2 twbch988–1001. https://doi.org/10.1080/14693062.2019.1624494. ISSN 1469-3062. S2CID 197773078. https://www.tandfonline.com/doi/full/10.1080/14693062.2019.1624494. Accessed 8 May 2023

Hill JD et al (2021) Air quality–related health damages of food. Proc Natl Acad Sci. https://www.pnas.org/doi/full/10.1073/pnas.2013637118. Accessed 11 February 2022

Hourcade JC et al (2012) 8.Global, Regional, and National Costs and Ancillary Benefits of Mitigation. 8.3.1 International Emissions Quota Trading Regimes, archived from the original on 11 January 2012, in Intergovernmental Panel on Climate Change (IPCC) Third Assessment Report (TAR), Watson RT, Core Writing Team (eds.), Climate Change 2001: Synthesis Report (SYR), Contribution of Working Groups I, II, and III to the Third Assessment Report (TAR) of the Intergovernmental Panel on Climate Change (IPCC). Cambridge University, Cambridge, ISBN 978-0-521-80770-8. https://www.ipcc.ch/ipccreports/tar/wg3/english/index.htm. Accessed 29 May 2023

Huq S, De Souza R (2016) Not fully lost and damaged: how loss and damage fared in the Paris agreement. Wilson Centre, 12 January 2016. https://gbv.wilsoncenter.org/article/not-fully-lost-anddamaged-how-loss-and-damage-fared-the-paris-agreement. Accessed, 28 May 2023

Ijaiya H (2014) The Legal Regime of Noise Pollution in Nigeria. Beijing Law Rev spiepr A3B2 twbch ":"5:1spiepr A3B2 twbch–6. http://www.scirp.org/journal/blr. https://doi.org/10.4236/blr.2014.51001. Accessed 28 May 2023

Intergovernmental Panel on Climate Change (2013). https://www.ipcc.ch/publications_and_data/ar4/wg3/en/ch13s13-es.html. Accessed 29 May 2023

Intergovernmental Panel on Climate Change (IPCC) (2022) Climate Change 2022: impacts, adaptation and vulnerability (summary for policymakers), Working Group II (WGII)

Contribution to the Sixth Assessment Report (AR6), 27 February 2022, pp 8–9. https://www.ipcc.org. Accessed 17 May 2023

International Energy Agency (IEA) (2011) CO2 emissions from fuel combustion: highlights, 2011th edn. IEA, Paris, p 12. https://www.osti.gov/etdeweb/servlets/purl/21589332. Accessed 29 May 2023

J and K ENVIS Centre (2021) Air pollution. http://www.jkenvis.nic.in/air.html. Accessed 17 June 2023

Jariwala H et al (2018) Noise pollution and human health: a review. Conference Paper: Noise and Air Pollution: Challenges and Opportunities, March 2017. https://www.researchgate.net/publication/319329633_Noise_Pollution_Human_Health_A_Review#fullTextFileContent. Accessed 19 June 2023

Johansen BE (2003) Indigenous peoples and environmental issues: an encyclopedia. Greenwood Press, Santa Barbra, pp 115–116. ISBN 9780313323980 OCLC 51559162

Kaplan S (2021) Air pollution from farms leads to 17,900 U.S. deaths per year, study finds. The Washington Post, 10 May 2021. https://www.washingtonpost.com/climate-environment/2021/05/10/farm-pollution-deaths/. Accessed 11 May 2023

Kissi-Debrah R (2020) Omission on Air Pollution from Report on Covid 19 and Race Astonishing. Guardian, United Kingdom, 7 June 2020. https://www.theguardian.com/environment/2020/jun/07/omission-of-air-pollution-from-report-on-covid-19-and-race-astonishing. Accessed 18 July 2023

Knox J (2020) The Paris agreement as a human rights treaty, Ch 15. In: Akande D et al (eds) Human rights and 21st century challenges. Oxford University, Oxford

Liddell HG, Scott R (2015) ἀτμός. A Greek-English Lexicon, Perseus Digital Library. http://www.perseus.tufts.edu/hopper/text. Accessed 23 June 2023

Linares C et al (2021) Short-term associations of air pollution and meteorological variables on the incidence and severity of COVID-19 in Madrid (Spain): a time series study. Environ Sci Eur 33: Article number 107

Maich S (2013) Kyoto protocol's shortcomings. The Canadian Encyclopedia. https://www.thecanadianencyclopedia.ca/en. Accessed 28 May 2023

Mann ME (2022) Global warming. Earth Science. https://www.britannica.com/science/global-warming. Accessed 18 June 2023

Mark K (2015) COP21: what does the Paris climate agreement mean for me? BBC News. BBC, 14 December 2015. https://www.bbc.com/news/science-environment-35092127. Accessed 8 May 2023

Ministry of Health, Singapore (2022) FAQS on Haze health advisory. https://www.moh.gov.sg/resources-statistics/educational-resources/haze/faqs-on-haze-health-advisory#:~:text=Haze%20particles%20can%20sometimes%20affect,haze%20and%20health%20effects%2F%20symptoms. Accessed 12 May 2023

Mogelgaard K (2015) What does the Paris Agreement mean for climate resilience and adaptation. World Resources Institute, 23 December 2015. https://www.wri.org/blog/2015/12/what-does-the-paris-agreement-mean-for-climate-resilience-and-adaptation. Accessed 18 May 2023

Mogelgaard K, McGray H (2015) When adaptation is not enough: Paris Agreement recognizes 'Loss and Damage'. World Resources Institute, 24 December 2015. https://www.wri.org/insights/when-adaptation-not-enough-paris-agreement-recognizes-loss-and-damage. Accessed 20 May 2023

Montreal Protocol on ODS (1987). https://treaties.un.org/doc/Treaties/1989/01/19890101%2003-25%20AM/Ch_XXVII_02_ap.pdf. Accessed 30 July 2023

Marquès M, Domingo JL (2022) Positive association between outdoor air pollution and the incidence and severity of COVID-19. A review of the recent scientific evidences. Environ Res spiepr A3B2 twbch ":"203:111930spiepr A3B2 twbch. https://reader.elsevier.com/reader/sd/pii/S0013935121012251. Accessed 22 May 2023

Nachmany M et al (2014) The GLOBE Climate Legislation Study: a review of climate change legislation in 66 countries, 4th edn. GLOBE International and the Grantham Research Institute,

London School of Economics, London, p 37. https://www.globeinternational.org. Accessed 17 May 2023
National Aeronautics and Space Authority (NASA) (2021) Global climate change. https://climate.nasa.gov/resources/global-warming-vs-climate-change/. Accessed 18 June 2023
National Environmental (Air Quality Control) Regulations (2014) Government Notice No. 225, S.I. 64. Federal Republic of Nigeria Official Gazette No. 142, Vol. 101, 26 December 2014
National Environmental (Noise Standards and Control) Regulations (2009) Government Notice No. 67, S.I. No. 35. Federal Republic of Nigeria Official Gazette No. 288, Vol. 96, 19 October 2009
National Geographic Society (2020a) Atmosphere. https://www.nationalgeographic.org/topics/resource-library-atmosphere/?q=&page=1&per_page=25. Accessed 23 June 2023
National Geographic Society (2020b) Noise pollution. https://www.nationalgeographic.org/encyclopedia/noise-pollution/. Accessed 18 June 2023
National Oceanic and Atmospheric Administration (NOAA) (2008) Science: the Antarctic ozone hole. Last updated on 20 March 2008 by Karin.L.Gleason@noaa.gov. https://www.ozonelayer.noaa.gov/science/ozhole.htm. Accessed 24 May 2023
NESREA Act (2007) National Environmental Standards and Regulations Enforcement Agency (Establishment) Act (NESREA) Act No. 25, 2007, as amended by Act No. 26, 2018
Paris Agreement (2015) United Nations Framework Convention on Climate Change (UNFCCC): Adoption of the Paris Agreement, Draft decision -/CP.21, FCCC/CP/2015/L.9/Rev.1, Conference of the Parties Twenty-first session Paris, 30 November to 11 December 2015. https://unfccc.int/processand-meetings/the-paris-agreement/the-paris-agreement. Accessed 3 May 2023
Pidcock R (2017) Explainer: dealing with the 'loss and damage' caused by climate change. Carbon Brief, 9 May 2017. https://www.carbonbrief.org/explainer-dealing-with-the-loss-and-damage-caused-by-climate-change/. Accessed 20 May 2023
Prouty AE (2009) The Clean Development Mechanism and its Implications for Climate Justice. Columbia J Environ Law 34(2)spiepr A3B2 twbch ":":spiepr A3B2 twbch513–540. HeinOnline. https://scholar.google.com/scholar_lookup?title=The+Clean+Development+Mechanism+and+Its+Implications+for+Climate+Justice&author=Prouty+Ann+E.&publication+year=2009&journal=Columbia+Journal+of+Environmental+Law&volume=34. Accessed 30 May 2023
Quesada NF (2013) Kyoto Protocol, emissions trading and reduction technologies for climate change mitigation. GRIN Verlag, Munich, GmbH. ISBN 978-3-656-47173-8. OCLC 862 560217
Ralls E (2010) What is Haze? Earth.com staff writer. https://www.earth.com/earthpaedia-articles/haze/. Accessed 12 May 2023
Reguly E, McCarthy S (2015) Paris climate accord marks shift toward low-carbon economy. Globe and Mail Toronto, Canada, 14 December 2015. https://www.theglobeandmail.com/news/world/optimism-in-paris-as-final-draft-of-global-climate-deal-tabled/article27739122. Accessed 8 May 2023
Sanger DE (2001) Bush will continue to oppose Kyoto Pact on global warming. The New York Times, 12 June 2001. ISSN 0362-4331
Savaresi A (2016) The Paris agreement: a new beginning? J Energy Nat Resour Law 34(1)spiepr A3B2 twbch ":":spiepr A3B2 twbch16–26. https://doi.org/10.1080/02646811.2016.1133983
Shahzad KF et al (2021) Does environmental quality and weather induce COVID-19: case study of Istanbul, Turkey? Environ Forensic. https://doi.org/10.1080/15275922.2021.1940380. Accessed 18 May 2023
Sinhah A (2015) Paris climate talks: differentiation of developed and developing stays, India happy. Indian Express, 14 December 2015. https://www.indianexpress.com/article/india/india-news-india/paris-climate-talks-differentiation-of-developed-and-developing-stays-india-happy. Accessed 10 May 2023
Sobisevich A (2020) The activities of the Russian Academy of Science's Council Concerning the Kyoto Protocol and discussions around climate change. Abstracts of the Second Eurasian RISK-

2020 Conference and Symposium RISK-2020, 12–19 April 2020, Balrampur, pp 74–75. https://www.academia.edu/42881316. Accessed 30 May 2023
Spijkers O (2021) Friends of the Earth Netherlands (Milieudefensie) v. Royal Dutch Shell. Chin J Environ Law 5(2)spiepr A3B2 twbch ":":spiepr A3B2 twbch237–256. https://doi.org/10.1163/24686042-12340073. https://brill.com/cjel. Accessed 27 May 2023
Stavins R (2016) Market mechanisms in the Paris Climate Agreement: international linkage under Article 6.2. Harvard Project on Climate Agreements, 19 November 2016. https://www.belfercenter.ksg.harvard.edu/files/2016-10_paris-agreement-beyond_v4.pdf. Accessed 17 May 2023
Strahler AH, Strahler AN (1977) Geography and man's environment. Wiley, New York
Taraska G (2015) The Paris Climate Agreement. Center for American Progress, 15 December 2015. https://americanprogress.org/wp-content/uploads/2015/12/ParisClimateAgreement.pdf. Accessed 20 May 2023
The Independent (2007). Scientists say Kyoto protocol is 'outdated failure'. The Independent, 25 October 2007. https://www.independent.co.uk/environment/climate-change/scientists-say-Kyoto-protocol-is-outdated-failure-5328805.html. Accessed 30 May 2023
The Nigerian Tribune Editorial (2022) The Port Harcourt Soot Scourge. Tribune Online, 13 January 2022. https://tribuneonlineng.com/the-port-harcourt-soot-scourge/. Accessed 12 June 2023
ThoughtCo (1997) How does the Kyoto Protocol fight climate change? ThoughtCo, 11 December 1997. https://m.facebook.com/thoughtcodotcom/posts/718829205275079. Accessed 29 May 2023
Tigre MA (2022) Advancements in climate rights in courts around the world. Climate Law Blog, Sabin Center for Climate Change Law, Columbia Law School, 1 July 2022. https://blogs.law.columbia.edu/climatechange/2022/07/01/advancements-in-climate-rights-in-courts-around-the-world/. Accessed 26 June 2023
Toth FL et al (2001) "10.Decision-making Frameworks," 10.4.4. Where should the response take place? The relationship between domestic mitigation and the use of international mechanisms. In: Watson RT, Core Writing Team (eds) Climate Change 2001: Synthesis Report (SYR), Contribution of Working Groups I, II, and III to the Third Assessment Report (TAR) of the Intergovernmental Panel on Climate Change (IPCC), Cambridge University, Cambridge. ISBN 978-0-521-80770-8. https://www.ipcc.ch/ipccreports/tar/wg3/english/index.htm. Accessed 29 May 2023
United Nations (1985) Final Act of the Conference of Plenipotentiaries on the Protection of the Ozone Layer, United Nations 1985, 1. https://treaties.un.org/doc/Treaties/1988/09/19880922%2003-14%20AM/Ch_XXVII_02p.pdf. Accessed 30 May 2023
United Nations (1989) Montreal Protocol on ODS 1987. https://treaties.un.org/doc/Treaties/1989/01/19890101%2003-25%20AM/Ch_XXVII_02_ap.pdf. Accessed 30 June 2023
United Nations (1992) United Nations Framework Convention on Climate Change, United Nations, New York. https://unfccc.int/resource/docs/convkp/conveng.pdf. Accessed 30 June 2023
United Nations (1997) Kyoto Protocol. https://unfccc.int/resource/docs/convkp/kpeng.pdf. Preamble to the Kyoto Protocol, 1997. Accessed 30 May 2023
United Nations Climate Action (2022) What is climate change? https://www.un.org/en/climatechange/what-is-climate-change#. Accessed 18 June 2023
United Nations Environment Programme (UNEP) (2018) Biannual of environmental law, special issue no. 2, 3. UNEP Publications, London
UNEP (2001) About Montreal Protocol. https://www.unep.org/ozonaction/who-we-are/about-montreal-protocol. Accessed 30 June 2023
UNEP (2002) Environment for development. UNEP Publications, London
United Nations Environment Programme (UNEP) (2021a) Actions on air quality: a global summary of policies and programmes to reduce air pollution. UNEP Publications, London. https://www.unep.org/resources/report/actions-air-quality-global-summary-policies-and programmes-reduce-air-pollution. Accessed 17 May 2023

UNEP (2021b) Actions on air quality in Africa: executive summary. UNEP Air Pollution Series 7 September 2021, 2. https://www.unep.org/resources/report/actions-air-quality-global-summary-policies-and-programmes-reduce-air-pollution. Accessed 17 May 2023

UNEP (2022) Mitigation. UNEP Publications, Nairobi. https://www.unep.org/explore-topics/climate-action/what-we-do/mitigation#:~:text. Accessed 13 May 2023

United Nations Framework Convention on Climate Change (UNFCCC) (2010) Decision 1/CP.16: The Cancun Agreements: Outcome of the work of the AdHoc Working Group on Further Commitments for Annex I Parties under the Kyoto Protocol at its fifteenth session, Cancun Climate Change Conference—29 November 2010–12 December 2010, United Nations FCCC/KP/CMP/2010/12/Add.1. https://unfccc.int/resource/docs/2010/cmp6/eng/12a01.pdf. Accessed 19 May 2023

UNFCCC (2011) Decision 7/CP.17: work programme on loss and damage. Durban Climate Change Conference, 28 November 2011–11 December 2011, para 3, United Nations FCCC/CP/2011/9/Add.2. https://unfccc.int/resource/docs/2011/cop17/eng/09a02.pdf. Accessed 19 May 2023

UNFCCC (2012) Decision 3/CP.18: Report of the Conference of the Parties on its eighteenth session, held in Doha from 26 November to 8 December 2012, United Nations, FCCC/CP/2012/8/Add1, 21. https://unfccc.int/resource/docs/2012/cop18/eng/08a01.pdf#page=21. Accessed 19 May 2023

UNFCCC (2013) Decision 3/CP.18, Decision 2/CP.19: Report of the Conference of the Parties on its nineteenth session, held in Warsaw from 11 to 23 November 2013, United Nations, FCCC/CP/2013/10/Add1. https://unfccc.int/resource/docs/2013/cop19/eng/10a01.pdf#page=6. Accessed 19 May 2023

UNFCCC (2015) Adoption of the Paris Agreement, Draft decision -/CP.21, FCCC/CP/2015/L.9/Rev.1, Conference of the Parties Twenty-first session Paris, 30 November to 11 December 2015. https://unfccc.int/process-and-meetings/the-paris-agreement/the-paris-agreement. Accessed 3 May 2023

UNFCCC (2021) COP26 Outcomes: Market mechanisms and non-market approaches (Article 6). https://unfccc.int/process-and-meetings/the-paris-agreement/the-glasgow-climate-pact/cop26-outcomes-market-mechanisms-and-non-market-approaches-article-6. Accessed 15 May 2023

UNFCCC (2022) Paris Agreement 2015. https://unfccc.int/files/essential_background/convention/application/pdf/english_paris_agreement.pdf. Accessed 30 June 2023

United Nations Framework Convention on Climate Change Secretariat (2021) Bonn, Germany http://unfccc.int/resource/cd_roms/na1/contact_us.htm. Accessed 30 June 2023

United Nations Framework Convention on Climate Change. New York: United Nations 1992. https://unfccc.int/resource/docs/convkp/conveng.pdf. Accessed 30 July 2023

United Nations Human Rights Council (2022) Resolution A/HRC/50/L.10/Rev.1, 7 July 2022. https://www.ohchr.org/en/hr-bodies/hrc/regular-sessions/session50/res-dec-stat. Accessed 26 July 2023

United Nations Office of the High Commissioner for Human Rights (OHCHR) (2022) Climate Change as a New Frontier of Human Rights. Bangladesh Institute of International and Strategic Studies, 17 August 2022. https://www.ohchr.org/en/statements/2022/08/bangladesh-institute-international-and-strategic-studies-climate-change-new. Accessed 28 June 2023

United States Environmental Protection Agency (US EPA) (2017). https://yosemite.epa.gov/opa/admpress.nsf/d0cf6618525a9efb85257359003fb69d/f51c2fdeda736ea285257a1e0050c45f!opendocument. Accessed 12 June 2023

United States Geological Surveys (2019). www.encarta.com. Accessed 30 June 2023

Vandini S et al (2013) Respiratory syncytial virus infection in infants and correlation with meteorological factors and air pollutants. Italian J Pediatr. https://ijponline.biomedcentral.com/articles/10.1186/1824-7288-39-1. Accessed 17 June 2023

Vocabulary.com (2020) Atmosphere-definition, meaning and synonyms. https://www.vocabulary.com/dictionary/atmosphere. Accessed 23 June 2023

Watson RT, Noble IR et al (eds) (2000) Intergovernmental panel on climate change special report on land use, land-use change and forestry. Cambridge University, Cambridge

Weaver D, Villard R (2020) Hubble probes layer-cake structure of alien world's atmosphere. Hubble News Center. https://hubblesite.org/news/news-releases. Accessed 23 June 2023

Weidman J, Marshall S (2012) Soot Pollution 101. Centre for American Progress, 10 August 2012. https://www.americanprogress.org/article/soot-pollution-101/. Accessed 11 June 2023

Williams M (2020) What is the atmosphere like on other planets? Universe Today, https://www.universetoday.com. Accessed 23 June 2023

Wirespace (2006). https://wiredspace.wits.ac.za/bitstream/handle/10539/1546/06Bomela_Chapter1to6.pdf?sequence=6. Accessed 18 July 2023

World Bank (2010) World development report 2010: development and climate change. The World Bank, Washington, DC

World Health Organisation (WHO) (2015) Hearing loss due to recreational exposure to loud sounds: a review. WHO, Geneva, 2015, ISBN 978 92 4 150851 3 (NLM classification: WV 270). https://apps.who.int/iris/bitstream/handle/10665/154589/9789241508513_eng.pdf. Accessed 19 July 2023

World Health Organization (WHO) (2020) Coronavirus disease (COVID-19), January 2020. https://www.who.int/emergencies/diseases/novel-coronavirus-2019. Accessed 19 June 2023

World Watch Institute (2004) Cleaning the air: a global agenda. W W Norton, New York

Yeo S (2016). The Paris Agreement 'Ratchet Mechanism'. Carbon Brief, 19 January 2016. https://www.carbonbrief.org/timeline-the-paris-agreements-ratchet-mechanism/. Accessed 8 May 2023

Chapter 7
Water Pollution Abatement Strategies

Abstract Water is essential to life and one of human's fundamental needs. Although 70% of the Earth's surface is covered by water bodies, water is still in short supply, difficult to access, and unevenly distributed. Unfortunately, water is easily overused, resulting in pollution. This chapter discusses the nature of water, water pollution, water pollutants and their sources, the impact of water pollutants on human health and on the environment as well as strategies for water pollution control, particularly through the use of legal instruments. Although the chapter discusses water pollution generally, noting water pollutants and their sources, the impact of such water pollutants on human health and on the environment, the use of legal instruments as strategies for water pollution control focuses on Nigeria.

7.1 Introduction

Before delving into what amounts to water pollution, and attendant abatement strategies, first, let us understand the water issue. Water in its liquid form is the material that makes life possible on Earth. All living organisms are composed of cells that contain 60% water and their metabolic activities take place in a water solution.[1] According to Colbert,[2] "water is the main transport media of the body that delivers nutrients to all the cells," and to humans, "water is also essential to digestion in that it helps us to absorb, assimilate and eliminate," Thus, organisms can exist only where there is access to adequate supplies of water. As the saying goes, "ubiquity of water leads to ubiquity of settlement."[3] Water's ability to act as a solvent and its capacity to store heat, which is the direct consequence of its polar

---

[1] Colbert (2004), pp. 26–27.

[2] Ibid.

[3] This can be attested to by looking back to the early civilisations of Egypt, Mesopotamia, and the Mekong Valleys, among others, where the availability of water led to the springing up and the thriving of such civilisation.

E. Onyeabor, *Environmental Law*, https://doi.org/10.1007/978-3-031-68956-7_7

nature,[4] makes water extremely valuable for human, societal and industrial activities.

The importance of water cannot be overemphasised. Water dissolves and carries substances ranging from nutrients to industrial and domestic wastes. Because water heats and cools more slowly than other substances, it is used in large quantities for cooling in electric power generation plants and in other industrial processes. Water's ability to retain heat also modifies local climatic conditions in areas near large water bodies. Water pervades all aspects of human development. When people are denied access to clean water at home or when they lack access to water as a productive resource their choices and freedoms are constrained by ill health, poverty and vulnerability. Water gives life to everything, including human development and human freedom. In fact, water is vital for everything we do. The cradles of early civilisations were as a matter of fact found along water courses. As the saying goes, "ubiquity of water leads to ubiquity of settlement."

The importance of water dates to Biblical and historic times. In the beginning, God created water to make fields fruitful and to refresh and cleanse our bodies. Water was also made the instrument of God's mercy: through water, the prophets proclaimed the new covenant God was to enter with humans; Christ made water holy in the Jordan as our corrupted nature was regenerated.

For most human uses, as well as some commercial and industrial ones, the quantity of water is as important as its quality. Water must be substantially free of dissolved salts, plant and animal waste, and bacterial contamination to be suitable for human consumption. Unfortunately, only a small fraction of the Earth's freshwater is available for human and industrial use as a large percentage is found in the oceans which, although covering approximately 70% of the Earth's surface, contain over 97% of its water.[5] The ocean water is salty and therefore it cannot be used for domestic and most industrial purposes as well as other daily uses by humans. Again, less than 0.01% of water exists as surface water in lakes, marshes, and rivers, and only 2.5–2.75% of it is freshwater, including 1.75–2% that is frozen in glaciers, ice, and snow, 0.5–0.75% as fresh groundwater, and the remainder as soil moisture.[6] To this end, only about 0.006% of this freshwater is actually useable, which is water that is immediately accessible and safe for human consumption.[7]

The fact that some parts of the world have rich freshwater supplies while others have few adds to the difficulty. For example, two-thirds of the world's population lives in locations that receive only a quarter of the world's annual rainfall.[8] This is more acute in the developing world. Reports[9] show that one in five people living in the developing world lack access to clean water. This situation makes the quest for

[4] Water has two molecules; one part of the molecules is slightly positive and the other slightly negative.

[5] Gleick (1993), p. 3.

[6] Byju (2022).

[7] National Geographic Society (2022).

[8] Ibid.

[9] Watkins (2006), p. 15.

freshwater a serious issue and this usually results in abuse. The sum total is that because of the various needs to which water is put efforts are being made at using technology to augment its shortages.

Today, despite advances in drilling, irrigation, and purification, the location, quantity, quality, ownership and control of potable waters remain important human concerns. Unfortunately, there is still increased demand for water because of increases in human population and limitations on supply available. With a population of about 8.1 billion people[10] struggle for over half of all accessible freshwater contained in rivers, lakes, and underground aquifers, the future of water availability is gloomy.

Researches show that by the year 2025, humankind's share of water resources will be at least 70%. But this is due to population growth alone. However, if per capita consumption of water continues to rise at its current rate, humankind could be using over 90% of all available freshwater leaving just 10% for the rest of the world's species.[11] Thus, the supply of freshwater on Earth is finite, and only recently have we begun to understand that humans will probably exhaust the usable water supply. This reality is compounded by various human activities that have had a significant impact on most oceans, lakes, and rivers, resulting in water pollution.

Understanding how this impacts water quality and how to address the issues it raises is urgently needed. This fundamental reality was acknowledged by the United Nations Environment Assembly (UNEA) at its third session in December 2017 when it adopted Resolution 3/10,[12] and requested the Executive Director of the UN Environment Programme (UNEP) to develop a World Water Quality Assessment for UNEA's consideration. In November 2018, a workshop was held by UNEP with assistance from the World Meteorological Organisation (WMO) to kick off the creation of the Assessment. About 50 organisations (UN, research, civil society, and private sector) that had indicated an interest in participating in the assessment and working with UNEP to co-design objectives and actions on emerging problems of concern influencing water quality were gathered by UNEP during the workshop. The World Water Quality Alliance (WWQA), an open community of practise with numerous workstreams currently in operation, was established through this approach.[13]

[10] United Nations (2023).

[11] Postel et al. (1996), pp. 785–788.

[12] United Nations Environment Assembly (UNEA) (2017), Resolution 3/10 (UNEP/EA.3/Res.10).

[13] United Nations Environment Programme (UNEP) (2018).

7.2 Defining Water Pollution

Water is vital to human existence. The pollution of water poses serious environmental challenges, which need to be addressed to secure the continuing availability of a sufficient quantity of freshwater that is fit for human use. Unclean water and its effects on sanitation are directly implicated in the huge gulf in life chances at birth that separates children born in poor countries from children born in rich countries. Water pollution occurs when something enters water that changes the natural ecosystem and/or interferes with water use by segments of society.[14] According to the United Nations Convention on Law of the Sea (UNCLOS) 1982, water pollution is defined as:

> the introduction by man directly or indirectly, of substances or energy into the marine environment, including estuaries, which results or is likely to in such deleterious effects as harm to living resources and marine life, hazards to human health, hindrance to marine activities, including fishing and other legitimate use of the sea; impairment of quality for uses of seawater and reduction of amenities.[15]

National Environmental Standards and Regulations Enforcement Agency (Establishment) Act 2007 (NESREA Act),[16] also defines pollution. It means "man-made or man-aided alteration or chemical, physical, or biological quality of the environment beyond acceptable limits."

Water pollution is the contamination of water sources by substances that make the water unusable for drinking, cooking, cleaning, swimming, and other activities. Pollutants include chemicals, trash, bacteria, and parasites. All forms of pollution eventually make their way to water. Air pollution settles onto lakes and oceans. Land pollution can seep into an underground stream, then to a river, and finally to the ocean. Thus, waste dumped in a vacant lot can eventually pollute a water supply.[17] Water pollution therefore occurs when harmful substances, often chemicals or microorganisms, contaminate a stream, river, lake, ocean, aquifer, or other body of water, degrading water quality and rendering it toxic to humans or the environment.[18]

To this end, water pollution occurs when the water becomes overloaded with too much of one thing and the aquatic organisms cannot keep up with their cleaning responsibilities.[19] Under this condition when it is loaded with waste materials or heat its natural ability for self-purification can no longer cope with the situation.[20] The net effect is that the quality of water deteriorates as undesirable changes take place in its

---

[14] Enger and Smith (2002), p. 349.

[15] United Nations Convention on Law of the Sea (UNCLOS) 1982, Art. 1(4).

[16] NESREA Act (2007), s. 37.

[17] The Harvard T. H. Chan School of Public Health (2017).

[18] Denchak (2023).

[19] Dozier (2005).

[20] Nigerian Environmental Study/Action Team (NEST) (1991), p. 76.

physical, chemical and biological properties. These changes may be sufficient to render the water unsafe or inconvenient for domestic, industrial, recreational and other uses.

7.3 Water Pollutants and Their Sources

To understand human activities, which are chiefly responsible for water pollution and the substances that are discharged by those activities into the aquatic environment, four key questions must be asked:

i) Which activities are the main polluters?
ii) What substances do these activities discharge into the aquatic environment?
iii) What properties do these substances possess which are problematic?
iv) What factors will affect the impact of such pollutants upon the waters into which they are discharged?

Sources of pollutants are classified as either point sources or non-point sources. When a source of pollution can be readily identified because it has a definite source and place where it enters the water, it is said to come from a point source. Point source therefore means any discernible, confined and discrete conveyance, including but not limited to any pipe, ditch, channel, tunnel, conduit, well, discrete fissures, container rolling stock, concentrated animal feeding operation or vessel or other floating craft from which pollutants are or may be discharged.[21] Thus, point source includes all dry weather pollutants that enter watercourses through pipes or chemicals and mainly come from industrial facilities and municipal wastewater treatment plants.[22]

Non-point sources on the other hand are difficult to identify because of the mechanisms involved. This is because non-point source pollution comes from indiscernible sources, especially over land flow associated with rain events. As rain falls and strikes the ground, a complex runoff process begins and non-point source water pollution unavoidably results.[23] To this end, as raindrops pick up soil particles, muddy streams form and major watercourses become clogged with sediments.

In addition to the above natural process, accidental spillages of chemical substances such as oils and fuels from industrial activities, pollution from agriculture, especially in regards to fertiliser and pesticide usage which "run off" the land and are carried into the river systems, run offs from mining waste tips which are rich in metals, etc, are other non-point sources.

[21] NESREA Act (2007), s. 37.

[22] Singh and Gupta (2016), p. 2; Denchak (2023).

[23] Enger and Smith (2002), p. 350; Singh and Gupta (2016), pp. 2–5; Denchak (2023).

Non-point source pollutants may also leach out from the base of waste sites, especially old landfills and cause contamination of ground waters. Again, abandoned mines cause pollution when old mine workings fill up with water, become contaminated, and then discharge into surface water.[24]

Substances that, when discharged into the aquatic environment, can cause pollution come in the following forms:

i) Oxygen-demanding wastes
ii) Heat
iii) Agricultural wastes
iv) Industrial effluent
v) Sediment from land erosion
vi) Urbanisation
vii) Pollution from petroleum compounds
viii) Global warming[25]

Oxygen-demanding wastes, such as what might be discharged from breweries, paper mills and other organic wastes as well as municipal wastewater treatment plants, make up one of the most important types of pollutants. These materials decompose in the watercourses and can deplete the water's oxygen and create anaerobic conditions. The anaerobic bacteria begin to break down wastes. This produces chemicals that have a foul odour and unpleasant taste and that generally interfere with the well-being of humans.[26]

Heat, which comes as industrial wastes, that is discharged into water, may drastically alter the ecosystem of a stream or lake. Power plants are the greatest culprits. Power plants heat water to convert it into steam that drives the turbines that generate electricity. For steam turbines to function efficiently, the steam must be condensed into water after it leaves the turbine. This condensation is usually accomplished by taking water from lakes, streams, or oceans to absorb the heat. The heated water is then discharged into the aquatic environment. Heat lowers the solubility of oxygen in water. This is because gas solubility in water is inversely proportional to temperature, thereby reducing the amount of dissolved oxygen available to gill-breathing species. As the level of dissolved oxygen decreases, the metabolic activity of aerobic aquatic species increases, thus increasing oxygen demand.[27]

Agricultural wastes as a source of water pollutants come mainly from plant nutrients. Such plant nutrients include: nitrates; phosphates and other plant nutrients that come from fertilised farmlands. When they are washed into water bodies, they encourage the growth of algae and phytoplankton. These aquatic plants may become

---

[24] Denchak (2023).

[25] Carson (2002), p. 389; Singh and Gupta (2016), pp. 2–5; Denchak (2023).

[26] Singh and Gupta (2016), pp. 2–5.

[27] Carson (2002); Singh and Gupta (2016), pp. 2–5; Denchak (2023).

so abundant that their decomposition drastically cuts down the amount of dissolved oxygen.[28]

Industrial effluents arise from discharges from the industries into the aquatic environment. Almost all our industries discharge their effluent, without prior or proper treatment, into the river system. Run-offs from mining waste tips, which are rich in metals, also cause pollution. Pollutants may leach out from the base of waste sites, especially old landfills, and cause contamination of ground waters. Again, abandoned mines also cause pollution when old mine workings fill up with water, become contaminated and then discharged into surface waters. Many of these effluents are toxic as they include DDT, dyes, mercury, lead,[29] cadmium and other heavy metals.[30]

Sediments from land erosion may also be classified as a pollutant. Sediment consists of mostly inorganic materials washed into a stream as a result of land cultivation, construction, demolition, and mining operations. Sediment interferes with fish spawning because it can cover gravel beds and block light penetration, making food harder to find. Some of the solid wastes decay only slowly while others are virtually indestructible. These constitute physical pollution commonly clogging up water bodies, converting them into unsightly junkyards, unsuitable for almost any use and promoting destructive flooding.[31]

Urbanisation has a strong impact on water quality. Ions are introduced into the surface water from rainwater. Such ions include sulphate and nitrate ions representing the washout of air pollutants produced by fuel combustion. In addition, although some sewage collected by sewer systems in urban areas are treated before being released into the river system, such treatments do not remove the ions. These ions eventually find their way into the river systems.[32]

In addition, individuals are also partly responsible for the discharge of treated and untreated sewage into rivers and streams. These wastes are typically dumped in available open spaces, on streets, and in gutters, streams, and rivers. The biodegradable components decompose to yield soluble material, including stains, poisonous and corroding substances. When these substances find their way into sources of water supply, they make water unsafe to use for any purpose.[33]

Pollution from petroleum compounds also forms a major source of water pollutants. Petroleum exploration, exploitation, and refining as well as transportation, storage, marketing and use of petroleum products create water pollution. For instance, during exploration and exploitation, drill cuttings, drilling mud, and accidental discharges of crude petroleum constitute serious water pollutants. During

[28] Singh and Gupta (2016), pp. 2–5.

[29] Impact, and the insidious effect of lead, especially on growing children, has been in the news in Zamfara State of Nigeria in the last decades.

[30] Clarke and King (2004), p. 22.

[31] Ibid.

[32] Enger and Smith (2002), p. 380; Singh and Gupta (2016), p. 4; Denchak (2023).

[33] Enger and Smith (2002), p. 380.

refining refinery effluents in the form of oil, grease, phenol, cyanide, sulphide, suspended solids, chromium and biological oxygen-demanding organic matter may pollute the river system. During transportation, storage, marketing and use of petroleum products, accidental spills of petrol, lubricating oil as well as sludge and bitumen slops from tank cleaning operations are commonly discharged onto the landscape. These wastes, which have a high BOD[34] and COD,[35] often find their way through runoff and erosion of contaminated soil into water bodies, thus polluting them.[36]

Global warming has also an impact on water resources. It affects water resources through increased evaporation, and geographical changes in precipitation intensity, length, and frequency, all of which affect average runoff, soil moisture, and the frequency and severity of droughts and floods.[37]

7.4 Impact of Water Pollutants on the Human and Natural Environment

The effect of any potential pollutant on the environment will vary according to: the rate of flow of the river of receiving water; the volume of the receiving water system, the geology and topography of the relevant area in which the river is situated, and the upstream and downstream uses of a river.

7.4.1 Impact of Water Pollution on Human Health

Specifically, water pollution causes deleterious health problems. Globally, 2.3 billion people suffer from diseases linked to water.[38] Again, in 2015, the World Health Organisation/United Nations International Children's Emergency Fund (WHO/UNICEF) Joint Monitoring Programme (JMP) estimated that 660 million people still do not have access to improved drinking-water sources, and over 2.4 billion people do not have access to improved sanitation.[39]

---

[34] Biological Oxygen Demand.

[35] Chemical Oxygen Demand.

[36] NEST (1991), p. 87; Singh and Gupta (2016), pp. 2–5; Denchak (2023).

[37] Singh and Gupta (2016), pp. 2–5.

[38] Population Information Centre (2000), p. 7.

[39] World Health Organization (WHO) (2017).

Water-borne diseases[40] result from using water contaminated by human, animal or chemical wastes. These diseases cause an estimated 12 million deaths a year, 5 million of them from diarrheal diseases.[41]

Heavy metals[42] such as lead, mercury, cadmium, arsenic, copper, zinc and chromium which are found naturally in the soil in trace amounts, can pose problems when concentrated in a particular area. Arsenic and cadmium for instance can cause cancer.

Most unfortunately, those that are mostly affected by water pollution are children. It has been estimated, through expert opinion, that 26% of childhood deaths and 25% of the total disease burden in children under five could be prevented through the reduction of environmental risks, including by reducing unsafe water, sanitation and inadequate hygiene. Specifically, diarrheal diseases are among the main contributors to global child mortality, causing about 10% of all deaths in children under five years.[43]

Mercury can cause mutations and genetic damage. For instance, in Minamata Bay, Japan, mercury waste from Chisso Corporation, a plastic manufacturing company in 1966 afflicted 397 persons with mercury poison, resulting in 60 deaths, $3.8 million was paid as compensation to 45 survivors and the company Executives charged with "professional negligence resulting in death."[44] Copper, lead and mercury can cause brain-bone damage. A study in Thailand in 1990 found that some 70,000 children in Bangkok risked losing four or more points on the Intelligence Quotient (I.Q.) test because they were heavily exposed to lead emissions from motor vehicles.[45]

Again, on health impacts, the visible impacts were exposure to unknown or uncertain complex risks (such as radiation), while the potential impacts spanned through malnutrition, mental problems including stress, depression and suicide, infectious diseases, and other environmental-related diseases. The socio-economic impacts included displacement, lack of work security, labour absenteeism, firings, unemployment, loss of livelihood, loss of traditional knowledge/practices/cultures, land dispossession, loss of landscape/sense of place and violations of human rights.[46]

Aside from these direct effects of water pollution on human health, water pollutants resulting from oil production activities may also indirectly affect human health. For instance, due to the acidification of water bodies arising from acidic precipitation from the polluted atmosphere with subsequent mobilisation of heavy

[40] Also known as "dirty water" disease.

[41] Population Information Centre (2000), p. 7.

[42] Heavy metals also come from uncontrolled emissions by metal smelters and other industrial activities, unsafe disposal of industrial wastes and lead in water pipes, paints and gasoline.

[43] World Health Organisation (WHO) (2017).

[44] Enger and Smith (2002), p. 289.

[45] Ibid.

[46] BBC News (2012).

metals, there may be an increase in the risk of exposure to these potently toxic substances through drinking water and the food chain. This is because heavy metals like cadmium, lead, mercury and arsenic that are always present in the region may enter the food chain and biomagnify to the detriment of man.[47]

Added to the above, the heavy metals may corrode the plumbing systems of water supplies and subsequently release toxic heavy metals, particularly lead, into the water supplies. This according to an observation may likely be the source of the frequent reports of food poisoning.[48]

7.4.2 *Impact of Water Pollution on the Environment*

One major water pollutant is from petroleum products. Petroleum products in the form of oil pollution have impacted the environment in no small ways, especially during transportation. Oil pollution from this source first came to public attention with the *Torrey Canyon* disaster in 1967. The oil tanker, loaded with crude oil, ploughed into a reef in the English Channel spilling about 100,000 metric tons of oil with lethal effects upon ecosystems of the shore zone of France and England. Despite efforts at cleaning using straw to soak up the oil and detergents to disperse it the oil leaked out and fouled the beaches. Worse still, the detergents used in the cleanup were found to be more harmful to the coastal ecology.[49]

A more serious oil spillage occurred on 24 March 1989, when an oil tanker, *Exxon Valdez*, loaded with crude oil, veered off course and hit a submerged reef, spilling 42 million litres of oil (about 11 million gallons of oil) into Prince William Sound in Alaska. The spill devastated the fragile ecosystem. About 40,000 birds died, including about 150 bald eagles. The effect on the local economy was more than $100 million and the clean-up by Exxon cost about $2 billion.[50] There was also the "Prestige" disaster in 2002 off the coast of Spain in which large quantities of crude oil were spilt along the Spanish and French Coasts causing extensive damage to the coastline ecology and the environment.[51]

Again, in the Funima 5 blowout at Bonny, Nigeria on 17 January 1980, over 400,000 barrels of crude oil was spilt causing the pollution of 23,390.9 km^2 of estuaries, lagoons, lakes, rivers, rivulets, creeks and other watercourses. It rendered 55 sources of drinking water unsafe for human consumption. The spills also affected 230,000 people of which there were 180 deaths and caused damages estimated at =N=554,494,658 out of which a total sum of =N=12.5 million was paid as

[47] Singh and Gupta (2016), pp. 2–5; Denchak (2023).

[48] Kaladumo (1996), p. 24.

[49] Bell and Cacciottolo (2017).

[50] History Channel (2018), see also Peirce et al. (1998), p. 33.

[51] Safety 4 Sea (2018).

compensation. These were in addition to the dislocation of social and economic activities in the Sangana area.[52]

On 20 April 2010 in the Deepwater Horizon oil rig explosion operated by British Petroleum (BP) off New Orleans in the United States of America (US), 11 people were killed and hundreds of millions of gallons of crude oil were spilt into the Gulf of Mexico in the four months it took to cap the well. The explosion caused extensive damage to the ecosystem and property, resulting in economic loss to the affected region.[53] Between April and November 2012, BP paid various sums in US dollars in the form of compensation and for damages.[54]

There was also the Bonga oil spill in Nigeria in December 2011. The Shell Bonga oil spill of 2011 involved the spilling of over 40,000 barrels on 20 December 2011. The spill affected over 20 riverine communities across Akwa Ibom, Bayelsa and Delta States in Nigeria. The spill was considered that at least 168,000 people have been affected by the Bonga spill, one of the worst of the decade in the Niger Delta.[55]

The Bonga oil spill impacted the communities in various ways, namely environmental, health and socio-economic impacts. The environmental impacts of the spill are of two dimensions, namely: visible and potential impacts. The visible impacts included: biodiversity loss (wildlife, agro-diversity); food insecurity (crop damage); loss of landscape/aesthetic degradation; oil spills, surface water pollution/decreasing water (physico-chemical, biological) quality; groundwater pollution or depletion. The potential impacts on the other hand were: air pollution; fires, floods (river, coastal, mudflow); genetic contamination; soil contamination; soil erosion; waste overflow; large-scale disturbance of hydro and geological systems and reduced ecological/hydrological connectivity.[56]

Oil spills on water have been found to cause the death of mangrove seedlings and trees, reduce the productivity of phytoplankton and other aquatic flora, and disrupt detritus-based food webs of fish, all of which result in reduced fish yields. This is connected with the fact that oil films on water surfaces could prevent natural aeration and can lead to the death of marine organisms trapped below. In some cases, fish may ingest the spilled oil, or other food materials impregnated with oil. Such fish often are very unpalatable. Where the death of marine life is not the case, oil

[52] Shell Petroleum Development Company (1995), p. 6.

[53] Michael Eboh (2013).

[54] BP paid out $10 billion to businesses, individuals and local governments impacted by the spill and spent more than $14 billion on the response and cleanup. In April 2012, BP reached a $7.8 billion settlement to cover the bulk of the outstanding private claims for economic loss, property damage and medical problems. The company in November 2012 pleaded guilty to criminal charges, including felony manslaughter and agreed to pay a record $4.5 billion in criminal fines. At present, the US is proposing a $16 billion settlement to cover fines BP owes under the Clean Water Act, a federal water pollution law, as well as payments under the Natural Resources Damage Assessment, an environmental evaluation. The oil firm also remains on the hook for billions in additional damages, including the cost of environmental rehabilitation.

[55] BBC News (2012).

[56] Ibid.

pollution leads to reduced growth rate and reproductive rate of estuarine fishes, as well as causing the fishes to suffer from increased incidence of fin rot disease.[57]

In addition, research have shown that water bodies with sulphate and nitrate deposition are likely to be acidic.[58] A water body is said to be acidic when its buffering capacity is zero. The effect of this is acidification of the regional water bodies and contamination of groundwater by iron sulphate and other metallic radicals making the water polluted. Polluted water imparts taste and odour to drinking water. This constitutes danger to health as the water body is now loaded with waste materials and heat thus reducing its natural ability for self-purification, as undesirable changes take place in its physical and biological properties. The result is the eutrophication of water bodies and the consequent loss of drinking and industrial water which procurement or derivation will be at extra cost.[59]

Enger and Smith[60] identified various sources and impacts of some pollutants on both the human and natural environment. For instance, acids sourced from atmospheric decomposition, mining, drainage, and decomposing organic matter reduce the availability of fish and shellfish, increase heavy metal in fish and result in the death of sensitive aquatic organisms; increase the release of trace metals from soils, rock, and metal surfaces such as water pipes.[61]

Chlorides which are sourced from runoff from roads, irrigation runoff, and brine produced in oil extraction, and mining reduce the availability of drinking water supplies; reduce the availability of shellfish and cause high levels of toxicity to freshwater organisms.[62]

Dumping of raw and partially treated sewage; runoff of animal wastes from feed lots toxic chemicals may introduce disease-causing organisms resulting in increased costs of water treatment; reduced availability of and contamination of fish, shellfish, and associated species and disease. Death of the organisms may result due to reduced survival and reproduction of the aquatic organisms due to disease.[63]

Heat trapped by cities that is transferred to water; unshaded streams; solar heating of reservoirs; warm-water discharges from power plants and industrial facilities may result in elevated temperatures of the water body causing reduced availability of fish because of elimination of availability of fish due to inappropriate spawning behaviour.[64]

Heavy metals form another source of water pollutants. These come from atmospheric deposition; road runoff; discharges from sewage treatment plants and

[57] BBC News (2012). Further discussions on the impact of pollution on the marine environment can be found in sect. 13.5 of Chap. 13 of this book.

[58] Kaladumo (1996), p. 21.

[59] Ibid.

[60] World Resources in Enger and Smith (2002), p. 349.

[61] Ibid.

[62] Ibid.

[63] Ibid.

[64] World Resources in Enger and Smith (2002), p. 349.

industrial sources; the creation of reservoirs; and acidic mining effluents. They result in increased costs of water treatment; disease and death; reduced availability and health fullness of fish and shellfish; biomagnifications, lower fish population due to failed reproduction and death of invertebrates leading to reduced prey for fish.[65]

Runoff from agricultural fields; pastures, and livestock feedlots; landscaped urban areas; dumping of raw and treated sewage and industrial discharges, phosphate detergents, agricultural fields and pastures; landscaped urban areas; logged areas; discharges from chemical manufacturing and other industrial processes, combined sewers, are all sources of pollutants into the water body. These introduce Nutrient enrichment, Organic molecules and Sediments into the water body. Algal blooms occur, causing the death of algae because of low oxygen levels. This in turn results in the reduction of the diversity and growth of large plants, animals and other aquatic life. Death may result therefrom.[66]

Taken together, water pervades all aspects of human development. When people are denied access to clean water at home or when they lack access to water as a productive resource their choices and freedoms are constrained by ill health, poverty and vulnerability. According to the United Nations Development Programme (UNDP),[67] "water gives life to everything, including human development and human freedom." Thus, the need to overcome the crisis in water and sanitation calls for some measures of control through the instrumentality of the law.

7.5 Use of Statutes in the Control of Water Pollution

Overcoming the crisis in water and sanitation is one of the greatest human development challenges of the twenty-first century.

Thus, in 2000 the international community came up with the Millennium Development Goals (MDGs).[68] With the passage of time and by the end of 2015, a lot of the indices on water and sanitation were not met. In that year, that is, 2015 the international community again set out new development goals targeting 2030.[69]

---

[65] Ibid.

[66] Ibid.

[67] United Nations Development Programme (UNEP) (2006).

[68] The Millennium Development Goals (MDGs) 2000, Goal number 7 ensures environmental sustainability as one of the targets in this respect, Target number 10 sets to halve, by 2015, the proportion of people without sustainable access to safe drinking water and basic sanitation. Indicators for achieving this target are: an increased proportion of the population with sustainable access to an improved water source, urban and rural and an increased proportion of the population with access to improved sanitation, urban and rural. Sustainable Development Goals (SDGs) in 2015 replaced the MDGs.

[69] United Nations Department of Economic and Social Affairs (2020).

Goal 6 of the Sustainable Development Goals (SGDs)[70] states that by 2030 availability and sustainable management of water and sanitation for all, achieve universal and equitable access to safe and affordable drinking water for all, achieve access to adequate and equitable sanitation and hygiene for all and end open defecation, paying special attention to the needs of women and girls and those in vulnerable situations, improve water quality by reducing pollution, eliminating dumping and minimising release of hazardous chemicals and materials, halving the proportion of untreated wastewater and substantially increasing recycling and safe reuse globally, substantially increase water use efficiency across all sectors and ensure sustainable withdrawals and supply of freshwater to address water scarcity and substantially reduce the number of people suffering from water scarcity, implement integrated water resources management at all levels, including through transboundary cooperation as appropriate, protect and restore water related ecosystems, including mountains, forests, wetlands, rivers, aquifers and lakes, expand international cooperation and capacity building support to developing countries in water and sanitation related activities and programmes, including water harvesting, desalination, water efficiency, wastewater treatment, recycling and reuse technologies, support and strengthen the participation of local communities in improving water and sanitation management.[71]

Based on the above it becomes necessary to control water pollution. This is so because without pollution control water would become grossly polluted and unusable for a wide range of human and non-human needs with its attendant consequences on human health and development. Once water has been used it is returned to the aquatic environment as an effluent. These effluents discharged into surface waters and sewers must be regulated to maintain a sufficiently high quality of the receiving waters to meet our needs. It is in light of the above that various control measures were put in place to regulate water pollution. For our purpose, emphasis was based on the use of legislation to control water pollution.[72]

Legislating against water pollution has been one of the means through which water pollution is combated. This involves statutes,[73] regulations, standards and guidelines.[74] These laws create water pollution offences whose breach attracts sanctions.

---

[70] Ibid.

[71] Ibid.

[72] Common law tort can also be applied in controlling water pollution by punishing offenders. See discussions in sect. 2.2.2 of Chap. 2 of this book.

[73] The following laws have been put in place to control water pollution: National Environmental Standards and Regulations Enforcement Agency Act, (NESREA Act) 2007, Act No. 25 2007, ss. 23 and 24, Harmful Wastes (Special Criminal Provisions) Act 1988, Cap H1 Laws of the Federation of Nigeria (L F N) 2004, s. 1, Oil in Navigable Waters Act 1968, Cap O6 L F N 2004, ss. 1 (1), 3(1), 7(3) (b), and Criminal Code, Cap C.38 L F N 2004, s. 245.

[74] National Environmental Standards and Regulations Enforcement Agency Act 2007, s. 8 (k) (vi) empowers NESREA to set up water quality standards. While Sections 23 and 24 enjoin

Water pollution offences are therefore means of imposing criminal liability on those who may discharge polluting materials into the water bodies without authority[75] or discharge polluting materials, although with a lawful permit, but not in accordance with laid down regulations, or below the standards specified or contrary to existing guidelines on the discharge of such pollutants. By imposing criminal liability on water polluters, water pollution offences ensure the maintenance of a safe water system through a system of prohibitions, sanctions and procedures that deal fairly with culpable conduct that causes or threatens serious harm to both human and natural environments.

To successfully establish criminal liability for underwater pollution offences the following considerations are usually taken into account:

1) Was the discharge with the consent of the appropriate authority (consent discharge)?
2) Did the culprit cause or knowingly permit the discharge?[76]

7.5.1 *Provisions of Consent Discharges Under the Law*

The laws creating some water pollution offences usually provide for consent discharge.[77] Where this is so provided any person who discharges particulate matters into a water body with the consent of the appropriate authority and in accordance with set out regulations, guidelines and practices set out by the relevant Authority will escape liability. On the converse where the discharge, although with the consent of the Authority, was done not in accordance with laid down regulations, or below the standards specified or contrary to existing guidelines on the discharge of such pollutants, the polluter will be culpable.

The yardstick for water pollution offences under consent discharges is based on those offences created under Section 245 of the Criminal Code, Sections 1(1), 3(1) and 7(3)(b) of the Oil in Navigable Waters Act, Section 1 of the Harmful Wastes (Special Criminal Provisions) Act, and Sections 23 and 24 of the National Environmental Standards and Regulations Enforcement Agency (Establishment) Act (NESREA Act) 2007.

Offences under consent discharges can also be committed where the polluter discharges polluting materials into the aquatic environment contrary to the

the Agency to make regulations to protect public health and enhance quality of water, and effluent limitations, respectively.

[75] For instance, where substances are illicitly dumped into a river or there is a pollution spill after an accident.

[76] Bell and McGilliviray (2008), p. 607.

[77] Consent discharge entails being permitted by or with the authority of appropriate Environmental Protection Agency, to discharge particulate materials into a water body.

provisions of some of the 33 regulations made by the National Environmental Standards and Regulations Enforcement Agency (NESREA) between 2009 and 2014.[78]

Under the NESREA Act 2007,[79] the Agency, NESREA, is mandated to make regulations and standards for water quality,[80] review effluent limitations for existing point sources and set up schedules for compliance,[81] make regulations to protect public health and promotion of environmental sanitation,[82] and make regulations, guidelines and standards for the protection and enhancement of the quality of land resources, natural watersheds, coastal zone dams and reservoirs, including prevention of flood and erosion.[83]

To achieve the purpose of protecting the water bodies and enhancing water quality, discussions were based on the provisions of those regulations made by NESREA, using aggregates of human activities and specific industries, to which the regulations relate. To this end, legal control and culpability of polluters of the water bodies under consent discharges is established under the following economic activities:

7.5.1.1 Activities Involving Mining and Process of Coal, Ores and Industrial Minerals

For the mining and process of coal, ores and industrial minerals, regulation on effluent discharges is controlled by the National Environmental (Mining and Process of Coal, Ores and Industrial Minerals) Regulations 2009.[84] Effluent is defined under Regulation 47 of these regulations as "any liquid waste, discharge from mining facilities including mine water, tailings, acid leaching, acid mine drainage, fuels and lubricants." Part 111 of the regulations[85] set out effluent limitation procedures for this industrial sector. Under the regulations,[86] no facility shall cause to be discharged, any effluent into the natural water system and land without a permit from the Agency.

---

[78] Some of these regulations were discussed in sect. 16.2.5 of Chap. 16 of this book.

[79] NESREA Act (2007), s. 34.

[80] Ibid., s. 23(1) and (2).

[81] Ibid., s. 24(1) and (2).

[82] Ibid., s. 25(1).

[83] Ibid., s. 26(1) and (2).

[84] Government Notice No. 284, S.I. No. 28. Federal Republic of Nigeria Official Gazette No. 63 Vol. 96, 12 October 2009.

[85] National Environmental (Mining and Process of Coal, Ores and Industrial Minerals) Regulations (2009).

[86] Ibid., Regulation 12.

Flowing from this, every facility which discharges effluent shall treat it to an acceptable limit.[87] Thus, no waste material beyond permissible limits is released from the premises at which the operation is being carried out.

Furthermore, all effluents are cleaned up and disposed of at an appropriate discharge point or waste treatment facility after each operation.[88] In line with the polluter-pays principle as one of the general principles and rules establishing standards in environmental protection as reflected in treaties, national laws, binding acts of international organisations, state practices and soft law commitments, Regulation 13 of the regulations[89] provides that collection, treatment, transportation and final disposal of wastes within the specified standards and guidelines, shall be the responsibility of the facility generating the waste. In addition, in the event of pollution resulting in an impact on the environment whether socio-economically or health-wise, the facility shall as specified in Schedule 4 to these regulations, be responsible for: (a) the cost of clean-up; (b) remediation; (c) reclamation; (d) compensation to all affected parties; and (e) cost of damage assessment and control.[90]

The above liabilities notwithstanding, it shall be an offence, in addition to other offences, if a facility fails to comply to take reasonable measures to remove or treat and dispose of any effluent, remediate the environment, comply with guidelines on handling, storing and transport of any effluent, releases effluent and sludge into the environment above permissible level, take reasonable measures to prevent, reduce or remedy the adverse effect of effluent and sludge on the environment.[91] Any person who violates any of the provisions of Regulation 28 of these regulations, commits an offence and shall on conviction be liable to a fine of =N=100,000 or imprisonment for two years or both such fine and imprisonment. In addition, the offender shall be liable to an additional fine of =N=5000 for each day the offence subsists. Where the offender is a body corporate, the fine shall be =N=1,000,000 and an additional fine of =N=50,000 each day the offence subsists.[92]

The fine provided under Regulation 29(1) of these regulations for individual offenders in the sum of =N=100,000 is below the sum provided in the parent statute. Under Section 24 (4) of the NESREA Act, the fine provided in respect of an individual offender is the sum of =N=200,000. One wonders why this disparity as the regulations is subsidiary to the Act which is the parent statute. This is not

[87] What constitutes an acceptable limit in the treatment of effluent is specified in the National Environmental (Mining and Process of Coal, Ores and Industrial Minerals) Regulations (2009), Sch. 1.

[88] National Environmental (Mining and Process of Coal, Ores and Industrial Minerals) Regulations (2009) Regulation 10 (1) and (5).

[89] National Environmental (Mining and Process of Coal, Ores and Industrial Minerals) Regulations (2009).

[90] Ibid., Regulation 13(2).

[91] Ibid., Regulation 28.

[92] National Environmental (Mining and Process of Coal, Ores and Industrial Minerals) Regulations (2009), Regulation 29.

supposed to be so because a subsidiary law shall not contradict the provisions of the parent law from which the former takes its authority. This in essence shall be deemed *ultra vires* the powers of the Minister of Environment to make regulations under the provisions of Section 34 of the NESREA Act 2007. This anomaly as contained in Regulation 29(1) of these regulations[93] should be amended to fall in line with the provisions of Section 24 (4) of the Act.

7.5.1.2 Activities Under Textile, Wearing Apparel, Leather and Footwear Industry

For the textile, wearing apparel, leather and footwear industry the National Environmental (Textile, Wearing Apparel, Leather and Footwear Industry) Regulations 2009,[94] set out the effluent limitation. For this industry, effluent is defined in Regulation 56 of these regulations as "waste water treated or untreated; that flows out of a treatment plant, sewer, or industrial outfall resulting from the commercial or industrial use of water, generally to as waste discharged into surface waters."

Schedule 1 to the regulations sets out effluent limitation standards for the industry in respect of various parameters such as the appearance of wastewater, temperature, Total Suspended Solids (TSS), Chemical Oxygen Demand (COD), Biological Oxygen Demand (BOD), metals Chlorine, phenol, Dissolved Oxygen, etc. Under the regulations, an effluent shall be deemed to be a pollutant if the concentration of any of these parameters exceeds the permissible limits as specified in column 2 of Schedule 1 to the regulations.[95] To this end, such a facility shall not discharge the wastewater onto the land, into watercourses or a water body unless the facility ensures that the parameters of the effluent do not exceed the permissible limits set out in Schedule 1 to the regulations.

It shall therefore be an offence if a facility fails, inter alia, to take reasonable measures to remove or otherwise treat and dispose of any effluent to minimise adverse environmental impact, release effluent and sludge into the environment above permissible level, take reasonable measures to prevent, reduce or remedy adverse effect of effluent, sludge and emissions released into the environment to the standard prescribed by the Agency.[96] Any person who violates any of the provisions of Regulation 47 of these regulations, commits an offence and shall on conviction be liable to a fine of =N=200,000 or imprisonment for two years or both such fine and imprisonment. In addition, the offender shall be liable to an additional fine of

[93]National Environmental (Mining and Process of Coal, Ores and Industrial Minerals) Regulations (2009).

[94]Government Notice No. 287, S.I. No. 34. Federal Republic of Nigeria Official Gazette No. 66 Vol. 96, 16 October 2009.

[95]National Environmental (Textile, Wearing Apparel, Leather and Footwear Industry) Regulations (2009), Regulation 15(2).

[96]National Environmental (Textile, Wearing Apparel, Leather and Footwear Industry) Regulations (2009), Regulation 47.

=N=5000 for each day the offence subsists. Where the offender is a body corporate, the fine shall be =N=1,000,000 and an additional fine of =N=50,000 each day the offence subsists.[97]

In line with the polluter-pays principle, Regulation 5 of the regulations provides that collection, treatment, transportation and final disposal of wastes within the specified standards and guidelines, shall be the responsibility of the facility generating the waste. In addition, in the event of pollution resulting in an impact on the environment whether socio-economically or health-wise, the facility shall as specified in these regulations, be responsible for: (a) the cost of clean-up; (b) remediation; (c) reclamation; (d) compensation to all affected parties; and (e) cost of damage assessment and control.

7.5.1.3 Activities Under Chemical, Pharmaceutical, Soap and Detergent Manufacturing Industries

For chemical, pharmaceutical, soap and detergent manufacturing industries, effluent discharges are controlled by National Environmental (Chemical, Pharmaceutical, Soap and Detergent Manufacturing Industries) Regulations 2009.[98] Effluent is defined under Regulation 54 of these regulations as "waste water treated or untreated; that flows out of a treatment plant, sewer, or industrial outfall resulting from the commercial or industrial use of water, generally to as waste discharged into surface waters." National environmental standards on effluent limitations for this industry are set out in Schedule 1 to these regulations. Thus, any effluent arising from this industry shall be deemed to be non-compliant and polluted if:

(a) the concentration of any of its parameters exceeds the permissible limits as specified in the first column of Schedule 1 aforesaid;
(b) it does not comply with corresponding limit specified in the second or third column of Schedule 1 to these regulations;
(c) it is discharged from a facility without treatment.[99]

Arising from the above, no facility shall discharge effluent onto land, into a watercourse or a water body unless the facility ensures that the parameters of the effluent do not exceed the permissible limits specified in Schedule 1 to these regulations.[100] To this end, facilities that discharge effluent into the environment shall treat the effluent to the permissible level to ensure assimilation by the receiving medium. It is therefore an offence for any person to release effluent and sludge, or

[97] Ibid., Regulation 51.

[98] Government Notice No. 289, S.I. No. 36. Federal Republic of Nigeria Official Gazette No. 68 Vol. 96, 10 October 2009.

[99] National Environmental (Chemical, Pharmaceutical, Soap and Detergent Manufacturing Industries) Regulations (2009), Regulation 16.

[100] Ibid., Regulation 17.

fail to report the release of effluent and sludge, into the environment above the permissible level in these regulations. An offence is also committed when any person fails to take reasonable measures to prevent, reduce or remedy the adverse effect of effluent, sludge and emissions into the environment.[101]

Any person who violates any of the provisions of Regulation 50 of these regulations,[102] commits an offence and shall on conviction be liable to a fine of =N=200,000 or imprisonment for two years or both such fine and imprisonment. In addition, the offender shall be liable to an additional fine of =N=5000 for each day the offence subsists. Where the offender is a body corporate, the fine shall be =N=1,000,000 and an additional fine of =N=50,000 each day the offence subsists.[103]

In addition to the above liabilities, and in line with the polluter-pays principle, Regulation 5 of the regulations provides that collection, treatment, transportation and final disposal of wastes within the specified standards and guidelines, shall be the responsibility of the facility generating the waste. In addition, in the event of pollution resulting in an impact on the environment whether socio-economically or health-wise, the facility shall as specified in these regulations,[104] be responsible for: (a) the cost of clean-up; (b) remediation; (c) reclamation; (d) compensation to all affected parties; and (e) cost of damage assessment and control.

7.5.1.4 Activities Under the Food, Beverages and Tobacco Industrial Sector

For the food, beverages and tobacco sector, the National Environmental (Food, Beverages and Tobacco Sector) Regulations 2009[105] set out the effluent limitation. For this industry, effluent is defined in Regulation 54 of these regulations as "waste water treated or untreated; that flows out of a treatment plant, sewer, or industrial outfall resulting from the commercial or industrial use of water, generally to as waste discharged into surface waters." National environmental standards on effluent limitations for this industry are set out in Schedule 1 to these regulations. Thus, any effluent arising from this industry shall be deemed to be non-compliant and polluted if:

(a) the concentration of any of its parameters exceeds the permissible limits as specified in the first column of Schedule 1 aforesaid;

[101] Ibid., Regulation 50.

[102] National Environmental (Chemical, Pharmaceutical, Soap and Detergent Manufacturing Industries) Regulations (2009).

[103] Ibid., Regulation 51.

[104] National Environmental (Chemical, Pharmaceutical, Soap and Detergent Manufacturing Industries) Regulations (2009).

[105] Government Notice No. 286, S.I. No. 33. Federal Republic of Nigeria Official Gazette No. 65 Vol. 96, 14 October 2009.

(b) it does not comply with corresponding limit specified in the second or third column of Schedule 1 to these regulations;
(c) it is discharged from a facility without treatment.[106]

Based on the above no facility shall discharge effluent onto land, into a watercourse or a water body unless the facility ensures that the parameters of the effluent do not exceed the permissible limits specified in Schedule 1 to these regulations.[107] To this end, facilities that discharge effluent into the environment shall treat the effluent to the permissible level to ensure assimilation by the receiving medium. It is therefore an offence for any person to release effluent and sludge, or fail to report the release of effluent and sludge, into the environment above the permissible level in these regulations. An offence is also committed when any person fails to take reasonable measures to prevent, reduce or remedy the adverse effect of effluent, sludge and emissions into the environment.[108]

Thus, any person who violates any of the provisions of Regulation 48 of these regulations, commits an offence and shall on conviction be liable to a fine of =N=200,000 or imprisonment for two years or both such fine and imprisonment. In addition, the offender shall be liable to an additional fine of =N=5000 for each day the offence subsists. When the offender is a body corporate, the fine shall be =N=1,000,000 and an additional fine of =N=50,000 each day the offence subsists.[109]

There are also provisions for the polluter-pays principle. Regulation 5 of these regulations[110] provides that collection, treatment, transportation and final disposal of wastes within the specified standards and guidelines, shall be the responsibility of the facility generating the waste. In addition, in the event of pollution resulting in an impact on the environment whether socio-economically or health-wise, the facility shall as specified in these regulations, be responsible for: (a) the cost of clean-up; (b) remediation; (c) reclamation; (d) compensation to all affected parties; and (e) cost of damage assessment and control.

[106] National Environmental (Food, Beverages and Tobacco Sector) Regulations (2009), Regulation 15.

[107] Ibid., Regulation 16.

[108] Ibid., Regulation 48.

[109] National Environmental (Food, Beverages and Tobacco Sector) Regulations (2009), Regulation 49.

[110] National Environmental (Food, Beverages and Tobacco Sector) Regulations (2009).

7.5.1.5 Activities Under Base Metal, Iron and Steel Manufacturing/Recycling Industries Sector

The National Environmental (Base Metal, Iron and Steel Manufacturing/Recycling Industries Sector) Regulations 2011[111] control effluent limitations in the sector. The main thrust of these regulations is to prevent and minimise pollution from all operations and ancillary activities of the sector. The regulations require all facilities to provide pollution abatement equipment.[112] To minimise waste generation, the regulations require operators of facilities to engage best practices in waste minimisation by ensuring that pollution prevention programmes are directed towards the use of the 5 Rs[113] as well as the efficient use of reduction and recycling of water.[114]

The regulations[115] also provide for effluent limitation,[116] restrictions on the release of toxic effluent[117] and encourage engagement in effluent treatment[118] and treatment of sludge before disposal.[119] In addition, the regulations[120] provide for effluent levels for the metal manufacturing industries[121] as well as effluent pollution abatement measures.[122]

Under the regulations,[123] it shall be an offence where a facility contravenes permit conditions[124] makes false statements to the Agency,[125] fails to comply with

[111] Government Notice No. 127, S.I. No. 14. Federal Republic of Nigeria Official Gazette No. 41 Vol. 98, 4 May 2011.

[112] National Environmental (Base Metal, Iron and Steel Manufacturing/Recycling Industries Sector) Regulations (2011), Regulation 5.

[113] Ibid., Regulation 7(1). 5Rs as stated under this regulation means Reduce, Repair, Reuse, Recycle and Recover.

[114] Ibid., Regulation 7(2)(b).

[115] National Environmental (Base Metal, Iron and Steel Manufacturing/Recycling Industries Sector) Regulations (2011).

[116] Ibid., Regulation 17.

[117] Ibid., Regulation 18.

[118] Ibid., Regulation 19.

[119] Ibid., Regulation 20(1).

[120] National Environmental (Base Metal, Iron and Steel Manufacturing/Recycling Industries Sector) Regulations (2011).

[121] National Environmental (Base Metal, Iron and Steel Manufacturing/Recycling Industries Sector) Regulations (2011), Sch. I.

[122] Ibid., Sch. VIII.

[123] National Environmental (Base Metal, Iron and Steel Manufacturing/Recycling Industries Sector) Regulations (2011).

[124] Ibid., Regulation 50.

[125] Ibid., Regulation 51.

abatement measures,[126] and discharge effluent beyond the permissible level.[127] Penalties are provided under Regulation 56.[128]

The National Environmental (Base Metal, Iron and Steel Manufacturing/ Recycling Industries Sector) Regulations 2011 also have provisions for the application of the polluter-pays principle.[129]

7.5.1.6 Activities Under the Domestic and Industrial Plastic Rubber and Foam Industries Sector

Water pollution abatement in this industrial sector is controlled by the National Environmental (Domestic and Industrial Plastic Rubber and Foam Sector) Regulations 2011.[130] The main thrust of the regulations is to prevent and minimise pollution from all operations and ancillary activities of the domestic and industrial plastic rubber and foam sector to the Nigerian environment.[131] The regulations require all facilities to provide pollution abatement equipment.[132] To minimise waste generation, the regulations require operators of facilities to engage best practices in waste minimisation and ensure that pollution prevention programmes focus on the reduction of the use of water and more efficient use of process chemicals.[133]

The regulations[134] also provide for effluent limitation,[135] restrictions on the release of toxic effluent[136] and encourage engagement in effluent treatment[137] and

[126] Ibid., Regulation 52.

[127] Ibid., Regulation 54.

[128] The penalties are similar to those set out under NESREA Act 2007, s. 24(4)(5).

[129] National Environmental (Base Metal, Iron and Steel Manufacturing/Recycling Industries Sector) Regulations (2011), Regulation 6. Similar provisions can be found in the National Environmental (Mining and Process of Coal, Ores and Industrial Minerals) Regulations (2009), Regulation 5, National Environmental (Textile, Wearing Apparel, Leather and Footwear Industry) Regulations (2009), Regulation 5, National Environmental (Chemical, Pharmaceutical, Soap and Detergent Manufacturing Industries) Regulations (2009), Regulation 5 and the National Environmental (Food, Beverages and Tobacco Sector) Regulations (2009), Regulation 5.

[130] Government Notice No. 131, S.I. No. 17. Federal Republic of Nigeria Official Gazette No. 44 Vol. 98, 5 May 2011.

[131] National Environmental (Domestic and Industrial Plastic Rubber and Foam Sector) Regulations (2011), Regulation 2.

[132] Ibid., Regulation 5.

[133] Ibid., Regulation 7(2)(b).

[134] National Environmental (Domestic and Industrial Plastic Rubber and Foam Sector) Regulations (2011).

[135] Ibid., Regulation 17.

[136] Ibid., Regulation 18.

[137] Ibid., Regulation 19.

treatment of sludge before disposal.[138] In addition, the regulations[139] provide for effluent limitation standards for plastic and rubber manufacturing industries,[140] effluent limitation standards for petroleum-based polymer industries,[141] pollution prevention and control techniques,[142] as well as sludge disposal permissible limits.[143]

Under the regulations,[144] it shall be an offence where a facility contravenes permit conditions,[145] makes false statements to the Agency,[146] uses banned chemicals,[147] fails to comply with abatement measures,[148] fails to maintain records of all discharges and file quarterly and annual reports of all discharges.[149] Other offences arise where there are discharges of effluent beyond the permissible level.[150] Penalties are provided under Regulation 55.[151] The regulations also have provisions for the application of the polluter-pays principle.[152]

7.5.1.7 Activities Involving Non-metallic Minerals Manufacturing Industries Sector

The National Environmental (Non-Metallic Minerals Manufacturing Industries Sector) Regulations 2011[153] is yet another set of regulations that have provisions for

---

[138] Ibid., Regulation 20(1).

[139] National Environmental (Domestic and Industrial Plastic Rubber and Foam Sector) Regulations (2011).

[140] Ibid., Sch. 1.

[141] Ibid., Sch. IV.

[142] Ibid., Sch. VII.

[143] Ibid., Sch. XIV.

[144] National Environmental (Domestic and Industrial Plastic Rubber and Foam Sector) Regulations (2011).

[145] Ibid., Regulation 49.

[146] Ibid., Regulation 50.

[147] Ibid., Regulation 51.

[148] Ibid., Regulation 52.

[149] Ibid., Regulation 53.

[150] Ibid., Regulation 54.

[151] This is similar to the penalty under the NESREA Act (2007), s. 24(4)(5).

[152] National Environmental (Domestic and Industrial Plastic Rubber and Foam Sector) Regulations (2011), Regulation 6. This is similar to the provisions of Similar the provisions can be found in the National Environmental (Mining and Process of Coal, Ores and Industrial Minerals) Regulations (2009), Regulation 5, National Environmental (Textile, Wearing Apparel, Leather and Footwear Industry) Regulations (2009), Regulation 5, National Environmental (Chemical, Pharmaceutical, Soap and Detergent Manufacturing Industries) Regulations (2009), Regulation 5 and the National Environmental (Food, Beverages and Tobacco Sector) Regulations (2009), Regulation 5.

[153] Government Notice No. 134, S.I. No. 21. Federal Republic of Nigeria Official Gazette No. 48 Vol. 98, 23 May 2011.

setting standards to protect and enhance water quality in Nigeria. The main thrust of the National Environmental (Non-Metallic Minerals Manufacturing Industries Sector) Regulations 2011 is to prevent and minimise pollution from all operations and ancillary activities of the non-metallic minerals manufacturing industries sector to the Nigerian environment.[154]

The regulations[155] provide that every facility within the sector shall install pollution abatement equipment to enable such facility to engage in effective effluent and emission discharges to meet the prescribed effluent and emission discharge permissible limits.[156] Again, all facilities shall have a few built-in pollution control features for the dry process precalciner.[157]

To minimise waste generation, the regulations[158] require operators of facilities to engage best practices in waste minimisation and ensure that pollution prevention programmes, including the application of 5Rs.[159] Operators of such facilities are therefore enjoined to employ cleaner production processes and pollution prevention measures that would yield both economic and environmental benefits.[160]

The regulations[161] also provide for effluent limitation,[162] restrictions on the release of toxic effluent[163] and encourage engagement in effluent treatment[164] and treatment of sludge before disposal.[165] Other provisions for enhancing water quality standards in Nigeria include: provisions for maximum permissible effluent level for ceramics and tiles manufacturing,[166] cement and limes manufacturing,[167] glass manufacturing[168] and sludge disposal permissible limits.[169]

---

[154] National Environmental (Non-Metallic Minerals Manufacturing Industries Sector) Regulations (2011), Regulation 1.

[155] National Environmental (Non-Metallic Minerals Manufacturing Industries Sector) Regulations (2011).

[156] Ibid., Regulation 5.

[157] Ibid., Regulation 8.

[158] National Environmental (Non-Metallic Minerals Manufacturing Industries Sector) Regulations (2011).

[159] Ibid., Regulation 7(2).

[160] Ibid., Regulation 7(3).

[161] National Environmental (Non-Metallic Minerals Manufacturing Industries Sector) Regulations (2011).

[162] Ibid., Regulation 18.

[163] Ibid., Regulation 19.

[164] Ibid., Regulation 20.

[165] Ibid., Regulation 21.

[166] Ibid., Sch. I.

[167] Ibid., Sch. II.

[168] Ibid., Sch. III.

[169] Ibid., Sch. X.

Under the regulations,[170] it shall be an offence where a facility contravenes permit conditions,[171] makes false statements to the Agency,[172] fails to comply with abatement measures[173] fails to maintain records of all discharges and file quarterly and annual reports of all discharges[174] and discharges effluent beyond the permissible level.[175] Penalties are provided under Regulation 62.[176]

7.5.1.8 Activities Under the Pulp and Paper, Wood and Wood Products Sector

Polluting incidents in this sector are controlled by the National Environmental (Pulp and Paper, Wood and Wood Products Sector) Regulations 2013.[177] The regulation is yet another set of regulations that have provisions for setting water quality standards and for the protection of Nigeria's water resources. The main thrust of the regulations[178] is to prevent and minimise pollution from all operations and ancillary activities of the pulp and paper, wood and wood products sector.[179]

The regulations[180] require all facilities to provide pollution abatement equipment.[181] To minimise waste generation, the regulations require operators of facilities to engage best practices in waste minimisation by ensuring that pollution prevention programmes are directed towards the use of the 5 Rs[182] as well as engage in pollution prevention programmes that shall focus on the reduction of the use of water and more efficient use of process chemicals.[183] The regulations[184] also provide for

[170] National Environmental (Non-Metallic Minerals Manufacturing Industries Sector) Regulations (2011).

[171] Ibid., Regulation 57.

[172] Ibid., Regulation 58.

[173] Ibid., Regulation 59.

[174] National Environmental (Non-Metallic Minerals Manufacturing Industries Sector) Regulations (2011), Regulation 60.

[175] Ibid., Regulation 61.

[176] This is similar to the penalty under the NESREA Act (2007), s. 24(4)(5).

[177] Government Notice No. 214, S.I. No. 34. Federal Republic of Nigeria Official Gazette No. 98 Vol. 100, 1 November 2013.

[178] National Environmental (Pulp and Paper, Wood and Wood Products Sector) Regulations (2013).

[179] Ibid., Regulation 1.

[180] National Environmental (Pulp and Paper, Wood and Wood Products Sector) Regulations (2013).

[181] Ibid., Regulation 6.

[182] Ibid., Regulation 8(1). 5Rs as stated under this regulation means Reduce, Repair, Reuse, Recycle and Recover.

[183] National Environmental (Pulp and Paper, Wood and Wood Products Sector) Regulations (2013), Regulation 8(3).

[184] National Environmental (Pulp and Paper, Wood and Wood Products Sector) Regulations (2013).

effluent limitation,[185] restrictions on the release of toxic effluent,[186] encourages engagement in effluent treatment[187] and treatment of sludge before disposal.[188] In addition, the regulations[189] provide for effluent limitation standards[190] and sludge disposal.[191]

Under the regulations,[192] it shall be an offence where a facility contravenes permit conditions[193] makes false statements to the Agency,[194] fails to comply with abatement measures,[195] discharge effluent beyond permissible level.[196] Operating without a permit is also an offence under the regulations.[197] Penalties are provided under Regulation 61.[198]

7.5.1.9 Activities Involving the Energy Sector

Polluting incidents in the energy sector are controlled by the National Environmental (Energy Sector) Regulations 2014.[199] The main purpose of the regulations is to prevent and minimise pollution and encourage energy efficiency in all operations and ancillary activities of the energy sector in achieving sustainable economic development in Nigeria.[200]

The regulations[201] require all facilities to install anti-pollution abatement equipment,[202] prohibit discharge of hazardous waste on water or land without prior treatment,[203] and provide for effluent limitation,[204] treatment of sludge before

[185] Ibid., Regulation 23.
[186] Ibid., Regulation 24.
[187] Ibid., Regulation 25.
[188] Ibid., Regulation 26.
[189] National Environmental (Pulp and Paper, Wood and Wood Products Sector) Regulations (2013).
[190] Ibid., Sch. I.
[191] Ibid., Sch. II.
[192] National Environmental (Pulp and Paper, Wood and Wood Products Sector) Regulations (2013).
[193] National Environmental (Pulp and Paper, Wood and Wood Products Sector) Regulations (2013), Regulation 55.
[194] Ibid., Regulation 56.
[195] Ibid., Regulation 57.
[196] Ibid., Regulation 59.
[197] Ibid., Regulation 60.
[198] National Environmental (Pulp and Paper, Wood and Wood Products Sector) Regulations (2013).
[199] Government Notice No. 254, S.I. No. 63. Federal Republic of Nigeria Official Gazette No. 65 Vol. 102, 22 December 2014.
[200] National Environmental (Energy Sector) Regulations (2014), Regulation 1(1).
[201] National Environmental (Energy Sector) Regulations (2014).
[202] Ibid., Regulation 8.
[203] Ibid., Regulation 15.
[204] Ibid., Regulation 13.

disposal[205] and place restrictions on the release of toxic effluent.[206] Under the regulations,[207] it shall be an offence where a facility contravenes the operator's conditions,[208] contravenes permit conditions,[209] makes a false statement to the Agency,[210] fails to comply with guidelines and standards,[211] abatement measures[212] or fails to maintain records of all discharges and file quarterly and annual reports of all discharges[213] and discharges effluent beyond the permissible level.[214] Penalties are provided under Regulation 51.[215]

In addition to discussions on specific provisions of the regulations, as they affect various industrial sectors, every facility shall carry out effective treatment of effluent and sludge throughout the operation of the plant or unit, ensure environmentally sound management of sludge containing heavy metals or other toxins, and dispose of same in a landfill or designated disposal site approved by the Agency. Thus, wastes containing harmful organics must be thermally treated to effectively destroy or remove 99.99% of the toxic organics, and the residuals must be disposed of in accordance with the regulations.[216]

In so far as these regulations are in line with the current trend in effluent limitation efforts at the global level, it is hoped that the Agency will not only have the will to enforce these provisions decisively but avoid being hemmed in by its own bureaucracy, thus stultifying all efforts at the protection of water bodies and assuring good water quality standard.

7.5.2 *Cause or Knowingly Permitted a Discharge*

This is another legal approach adopted to successfully establish the criminal liability of a culprit in underwater pollution offences. The question to be asked in this case is: Did the defendant or the accused person or culprit "cause or knowingly permit" the

205 Ibid., Regulation 16.

206 Ibid., Regulation 14.

207 National Environmental (Energy Sector) Regulations (2014).

208 Ibid., Regulation 44.

209 Ibid., Regulation 45.

210 Ibid., Regulation 46.

211 Ibid., Regulation 47.

212 Ibid., Regulation 48.

213 Ibid., Regulation 49.

214 Ibid., Regulation 50.

215 National Environmental (Energy Sector) Regulations (2014).

216 National Environmental Regulations 2009 National Environmental (Textile, Wearing Apparel, Leather and Footwear Industry) Regulations (2009), Regulation 17, National Environmental (Chemical, Pharmaceutical, Soap and Detergent Manufacturing Industries) Regulations (2009), Regulation 17 and the National Environmental (Food, Beverages and Tobacco Sector) Regulations (2009), Regulation 18.

discharge of effluent into the water body? This question was discussed in two parts: "cause" polluting incident and "knowingly permitted" the polluting incident.

7.5.2.1 Cause Polluting Incident

In water pollution cases, an offence is deemed to have been committed where a person causes or knowingly permits the discharge of any poisonous, noxious or any other form of effluent or polluting matter, or any solid matter into the aquatic environment. When can one be said to have "caused or knowingly permitted" the discharge of effluent, what act amounts to discharge and when are substances regarded as poisonous, noxious or polluting, needed to be addressed before a conviction is made for underwater pollution offences.[217]

The word "cause" lays down an offence of strict liability. This is because the word is not conditioned by any requirement of knowledge.[218] In applying this in prosecuting water pollution offences what needed to be proved is that the accused carried out an activity that gave rise to a pollution incident being complained of. Once it can be shown that the discharge was intentional all that is necessary to prove liability is to establish a link between the defendant's activities and the pollution of the water body. The test therefore is that "causing" must involve some active operation or chain of operations involving the defendant resulting in the pollution of the aquatic environment.

This test was laid in the case of *Alphacell Ltd v. Woodward*.[219] In that case, the defendant, a paper manufacturing company, was charged with causing polluting matter to enter a river. Settling tanks in the paper factory overflowed, when vegetation clogged up the pumps which maintained the level of effluent in the tanks. The tanks filled up and overflowed causing polluting matter to enter the river. An overflow channel led directly from the tanks to the river. The defendant claimed it did not cause polluting matter to enter the river rather presence of vegetation in the settling tank was the real cause of the incident. The court held that the act of constructing and operating the effluent tank was a positive and deliberate act which led to the overflow which caused the pollution. According to Lord Wilberforce,[220]

> ...the appellants abstract water, pass it through their works where it becomes polluted, conduct it to a settling tank communicating directly with the stream, into which the polluted will inevitably flow if the level rises over the flowing point.

Where the defendant is found to have caused the polluting incident what then is the scope of his liability? There must be active involvement of the defendant in the

---

[217] Bell and McGillivray (2008), p. 607.

[218] Ibid.

[219] (1972) AC 824, see also the case of FJH Wrothwell v. Yorkshire Water Authority [1984] Crim LR, 43.

[220] Alphacell Ltd v. Woodward (1972), 835.

operations or chain of events. Thus, in the case of *CPC (UK) Ltd v. National Rivers Authority*,[221] a factory operator was held to have caused polluting matter to enter a stream when a pipe carrying cleaning fluid fractured, allowing the fluid to flow into a river via a storm drain – although the cause of the fracture was a defective work carried out by subcontractors for the previous owner, which was not exposed by environmental audit. The court still held the current owners liable because they were actively operating the storm drain at the time of the polluting incident.

There are however limits to the applicability of the concept of causing pollution. Where it can be shown that the defendant had no active involvement in the chain of events that led to the polluting incident, he will not be liable. That is, he had been passive. Thus, in the case of *Price v. Cromack*,[222] a farmer had a contract permitting an animal firm to discharge waste into lagoons on his land. One lagoon wall failed and the resulting escape severely polluted a river. The farmer was charged with polluting the river. He was acquitted because he only permitted the accumulation and had not caused the pollution.

Again, in the case of *Wychavon District Council v. National Rivers Authority*,[223] raw sewage escaped from a sewer under the control of the appellant Council acting as an agent of the water company in maintaining and repairing the sewerage system. The immediate cause of the escape was a blockage in the sewer. The court held that the Council was not guilty of causing the pollution since it had mainly remained inactive.

Furthermore, where a third party or intervening act was thought to have interrupted the chain of causation, and the defendant had taken appropriate steps, yet the polluting incident occurred, the defendant shall not be liable. In the case of *National Rivers Authority v. Wright Engineering Co. Ltd*,[224] vandals had interfered with an oil tank, which then leaked into a water body. The company was held not to have caused the entry of the polluting matters and therefore not liable.

Also, in the case of *Shell Petroleum Development Co. Ltd v. Graham Otoko and Ors*,[225] plaintiffs/respondents sued for injurious affection to and deprivation of the use of the Andoni River and Creek because of the spillage of crude oil caused by the negligence of the appellant/defendant and claimed damages for their polluted drinking water and destruction of fish and other living creatures in the river. The lower court found in favour of the plaintiffs and awarded =N=491,700 as damages. On appeal, the Court of Appeal, while upholding the appeal, held inter-alia, that to sustain the action, it must be shown that the negligence found by the court is the proximate cause of the damage and where the proximate cause is the malicious act of a third person, against which precautions would have been in operative, the

[221] [1995] Env LR 131.

[222] [1975] 1WLR 988.

[223] [1993] 1WLR 125, see also the case of National Rivers Authority v. Welsh Development Agency [1993] Env LR 407.

[224] [1994] 4 All ER 281.

[225] (1990) 6NWLR (pt. 159) 693.

defendant is not liable in the absence of a finding either that he instigated it or that he ought to have foreseen and provided against it.

However, in situations where the defendant fails to take appropriate steps to guard against actions of trespassers and other third parties, equipment failure or natural events, the defence of break in the chain or the defendant being passive in the operation that caused the polluting incident, shall not avail him. In the case of *Empress Cars (Arbertillery) Ltd v. National Rivers Authority,*[226] the defendants maintained an oil storage tank on their site. A bund wall protected the tank. Standing outside the bund was a much smaller oil drum which was connected to the oil tank by a rubber hose. The open/close valve on the tank was not lockable and site security was poor. A trespasser entered the site and opened the valve on the oil tank. Oil flowed from the tank to the drum which rapidly filled up and overflowed. The escaped oil found its way into the surface water drains and from there entered the river. The defendants argued that it had not caused the oil pollution but had merely created circumstances whereby a trespasser could enter the site, turn on the oil storage tank and cause the pollution. The defendant further submitted that the act of the trespasser broke the chain of causation linking the defendant to the pollution and absolved its liability. The court rejected this defence and found the defendant liable.

Furthermore, where the nature of an intervening act of a third party is clearly foreseeable, it will not enable the defendant to escape liability. In *National Rivers Authority v. Yorkshire Water Service Ltd,*[227] the defendants were responsible for a sewer into which an unidentified industrial customer of theirs had discharged solvents. The court held that there was sufficient evidence on which the court could conclude that the defendants were prima facie guilty of causing the pollution.

In recent times, however, the courts, especially in England, have taken the stand that lack of culpability on the part of the defendant shall not be taken into account in sentencing. In *Hart v. Anglian Water Services Ltd,*[228] the company pleaded guilty to causing sewage effluent to enter the River Crouch. In a hearing of appropriate sentence, the company sought to make the point that, since the offence did not require *mens rea*, it should be distinguished from most other acts of a criminal nature, and that lack of culpability should be an important factor in determining the level of the fine. In rejecting this contention, the court noted that sewage treatment works carried a high risk of damage to adjoining waters, and that Parliament had imposed on water companies, with responsibility for sewage treatment, a heavy burden to do everything possible to ensure that they do not cause pollution.

[226] [1998] Env LR 369.

[227] [1984] Crim LR, 43.

[228] [2003] EWCA Crim 2243.

7.5.2.2 Knowingly Permitted the Polluting Incident

While "cause" imports an element of strict liability, "knowingly permit" on the other hand involves knowledge requirement. It has two arms: "knowingly" and "permitting." The essence of the "knowingly permit" is designed to catch the offender who knows that pollution is occurring, has the power to do something about it, and yet does nothing. In the case of "knowingly," the defendant must be aware of the discharge or the polluting incident. This is because a party must know about a problem before it can be guilty of failing to take reasonable steps to correct it.

The case of *Price v. Cromack*[229] provides a useful illustration of the difference between the "causing" offence and the offence of "knowingly." A farmer was charged with "causing" pollution when a lagoon on his land failed and waste animal products were released into a river. The farmer had a contract with an animal product firm which allowed the firm to discharge animal waste products into the lagoons on the farmer's land. The farmer was acquitted of the "causing" charge on the basis that he had not caused the pollution. Whilst he had permitted the building of the waste on his land, he could not be said to have caused the pollution. Had he been charged with knowingly permitting pollution, then the verdict would probably have been different. The basis for this is that he had knowingly permitted the accumulation of the waste on his land. Again, a defendant could be affixed with constructive knowledge of facts of which he ought to have been aware in circumstances where he had deliberately turned a blind eye to the obvious, or had refrained from inquiry because he did not wish his suspicions to be confirmed.[230]

Where the defendant is a company, the question arises: who must know about the pollution in order for the company to knowingly permit its presence? Does the pollution need to be known about by a director or a senior manager of such a standing who can be said to constitute the mind of the company? In environmental cases, as in the present, knowledge need not be by the director or a senior manager, provided the person who acquires the knowledge has some power to make relevant decisions. In the case of *Shanks and McEwan (Teeside) Ltd v. Environment Agency,*[231] a prosecution for an illegal deposit of waste, the court held a company in the business of accepting waste had corporate knowledge in respect of a specific illegal deposit when it was accepted by a site supervisor in the absence of the site manager.

In the case of "permitting," its meaning depends upon the context under which it is being considered. It could be confined to "allows," or "authorises" or it could carry the wider meaning of failure to take reasonable steps to prevent the occurrence of that which should not be permitted.[232] In *Berton v. Alliance Economic Investment*

---

[229] Price v. Cromack [1975], 988.

[230] [1993] Env L.R.D. 1.

[231] [1997] Env LR 629.

[232] Thornton and Beckwith (2004), p. 234.

Co. Ltd,[233] "permitting" was held to mean either giving leave for an act which, without that leave, could not legally be done, or to abstain from taking reasonable steps to prevent an act, where it is within a person's power to do so. However, the bottom line is that for a defendant to be liable for permitting a polluting incident such a defendant must be in control.

What act then amounts to discharge one may ask? Having shown that a defendant caused or knowingly permitted the discharge of poisonous, noxious or polluting matter into an aquatic environment, what act constitutes discharge? Although no Nigerian law on environmental protection defines the word discharge, according to the Water Resources Act of the United Kingdom (UK) 1991,[234] the term discharge refers to discharges from pipes, channels, or similar features into controlled waters, while entry refers to a situation in which polluting matter is deliberately introduced into the aquatic environment.[235] Such acts may include: a deliberate pouring of the content of a drum of pesticides into a stream, accidental spillages of polluting matter into surface drains, leaky pipes and tanks which cause polluting matter to escape into groundwater, and "run-off" from farmers' fields entering a river over a wide area.[236]

From the foregoing, for there to be a conviction the polluter must have caused or knowingly caused the discharge of a poisonous, noxious or polluting matter into the water. The term "poisonous" has a wide meaning. This is because what is poisonous is a matter of degree. It is a popularly held belief that all substances are poisons and that there is none which is not a poison, the right dose differentiates a poison and a remedy.[237] The word poisonous will therefore be considered in relation to the organisms on which a substance may have an impact. "Noxious" on the other hand is arguably somewhat broader than "poisonous," in that noxious may cover physically unpleasant effects without necessarily being dangerous in any respect. The term polluting requires the substance which has entered the aquatic environment to have the likelihood or capability of causing harm to humans, animals and plants.[238]

The gist therefore is that the substance introduced into the aquatic environment is hazardous, whether poisonous, noxious or toxic, what is important is that the substance in issue is hazardous. What amounts to a hazardous substance is defined in the Harmful Wastes (Special Criminal Provisions) (HWSCP) Act 1988[239] as: "Any injurious, poisonous, toxic or noxious substance...which can subject any person to the risk of death, fatal injury or incurable impairment of physical and mental health..."

---

[233] [1992] 1 K.B.724 at 759.

[234] Water Resources Act of the United Kingdom (UK) (1991), s. 85(3).

[235] Ibid., s. 85(1).

[236] Wolf et al. (2002), p. 81.

[237] Paracelsus in Thornton and Beckwith (2004), p. 226.

[238] National Rivers Authority v. Egger (UK) Ltd (1992) Env LR 130.

[239] HWSCP Act (1988), s. 15.

Flowing from the above definition of a hazardous substance, it then follows that introducing any hazardous waste into the aquatic environment will suffice for the defendant to be liable for the offence of water pollution. For the avoidance of doubt, hazardous waste according to Regulation 106 of the National Environmental (Sanitation and Wastes Control) Regulations 2009,[240] means, "any waste or combination of wastes that exhibits ignitability, corrosive, reactive, or toxic characteristics and poses a substantial danger, now or in future, to human, plant or animal life, and which therefore cannot be handled or disposed of without special precautions."

Other approaches may be used in addition to using legislative laws to control polluting incidents. In this circumstance, those who have been harmed by the offender's actions or polluting activities may file a civil lawsuit against him or her to seek any of the following remedies: Compensation and damage (under the Riparian Right Doctrine or violation of the right to water under the Human Rights Doctrine); Abatement; Injunction; Restitution; Rehabilitation/Restoration,[241] or invoke the application of the polluter-pays principle.[242]

7.6 Summary

Water in its liquid form is the material that makes life possible on Earth. Water's ability to act as a solvent and its capacity to store heat, which is the direct consequence of its polar nature, makes water extremely valuable for human, societal and industrial activities. Water gives life to everything, including human development and human freedom. In fact, water is vital for everything we do. The cradles of early civilisations were as a matter of fact found along water courses.

Unfortunately, potable water is scarce and unevenly distributed as only about 0.006% of fresh water is actually usable. Thus, the supply of freshwater on Earth is finite and only recently have we begun to understand that humans will probably exhaust the usable water supply.

It should be noted that for most human uses, as well as some commercial and industrial ones, the quantity of water is as important as its quality. This reality is compounded by various human activities that have had a significant impact on most oceans, lakes, and rivers, resulting in water pollution. To understand human activities, which are chiefly responsible for water pollution and the substances that are discharged by those activities into the aquatic environment, four key questions must be asked: Which activities are the main polluters? What substances do these activities discharge into the aquatic environment? What properties do these substances

[240]Government Notice No. 281, S.I. 28. Federal Republic of Nigeria Official Gazette No. 68 Vol. 98, 10 October 2009.

[241]These remedies were discussed in sects. 12.3–12.8 of Chap. 12 of this book.

[242]Polluter-pays principle was discussed in sect. 4.7 of Chap. 4 and sect. 12.9 of Chap. 12 of this book.

possess which are problematic? What factors will affect the impact of such pollutants upon the waters into which they are discharged?

These questions became necessary because water must be substantially free of dissolved salts, plant and animal waste, and bacterial contamination to be suitable for human consumption. Again, unwholesome water has been found to have had effects on human health. Understanding how this impacts water quality and how to address the issues it raises is urgently needed. It is as a result that water pollution abatement strategies become imperative.

Overcoming the crisis in water and sanitation became one of the greatest human development challenges of the twenty-first century. Various strategies have been put in place by the international community in overcoming water stress from the Millennium Development Goals (MDGs) of 2000 to 2015 to the current Sustainable Development Goals (SDGs) (2015–2030), especially Goal 6. In addition, nations have also, through the instrumentalities of the law set up strategies to combat water pollution. These laws provide regulations, standards and guidelines for effluent limitation, and criminalising discharges of polluting materials into the water body, among others.

References

BBC News (2012) Shell urged to pay Nigeria $5bn over Bonga oil spill, 17 July 2012. https://www.bbc.com/news/world-africa-Nigeria. Accessed on 17 May 2023

Bell B, Cacciottolo M (2017) Torrey Canyon oil spill: the day the sea turned black. BBC News Published 17 March 2017. https://www.bbc.com/news/uk-england-39223308. Accessed on 18 May 2023

Bell S, McGilliviray D (2008) Environmental law, 7th edn. Oxford University, Oxford

Byju (2022) What percentage of the total water available on earth is actually used by humans. https://byjus.com/question-answer/what-percentage-of-the-total-water-available-on-earth-is-actually-used-by-humans-0-1/. Accessed on 29 July 2023

Carson R (2002) In: Eldon DE, Bradley FS (eds) Environmental science, a study of interrelationships, 8th edn. McGraw Hill, Boston

Clarke R, King J (2004) The Atlas of water: mapping the world's most critical resource. Earthscan, London

Colbert D (2004) What you don't know may be killing you. A Strang Company, Lake Mary, Florida

Denchak M (2023) Water pollution: everything you need to know Natural Resources Defense Council (NRDC) 11 January 2023. https://www.nrdc.org/stories/water-pollution-everything-you-need-know#whatis. 28 July 2023

Dozier MC (2005) What is water pollution? The Texas A & M University System, Produced by Soil and Crop Sciences Communications, February 2005. http://waterandme.tamu.edu/WaterPollution/waterpollution.pdf. Accessed on 29 July 2023

Eboh M (2013) US proposes $16bn settlement with BP over Gulf spill. http://www.vanguardngr.com/2013/02. Accessed on 24 May 2023

Enger ED, Smith BF (2002) Environmental science, a study of interrelationships, 8th edn. McGraw Hill, Boston

Gleick P (1993) An introduction to global fresh water issues. In: Gleick P (ed) Water in crisis. Oxford University, New York

History Channel (2018) Exxon Valdez Oil Spill, 9 March 2018. https://www.history.com/topics/1980s/exxon-valdez-oil-spill. Accessed on 17 June 2023

Kaladumo COK (1996) The implication of gas flaring on the Niger Delta Environment. A Paper presented at the 8th Biennial International Seminar on Petroleum Industry and the Nigerian Environment, Hotel Presidential, Port Harcourt, November 18–21, 1996

National Geographic Society (2022) Earth's Freshwater, Educator Guide, 22 September 2022. https://education.nationalgeographic.org/resource/earths-fresh-water/. Accessed on 29 July 2023

Nigerian Environmental Study/Action Team (NEST) (1991) Nigeria's threatened environment, a national profile. NEST, Ibadan

Peirce JJ et al (1998) Environmental pollution and control, 4th edn. Butterworth- Heinemann, Boston

Population Information Centre (2000) Population and the environment; The Global Challenge. Population Reports, vol XXXV111, no 3, Fall 2000, 7

Postel S et al (1996) Human appropriation of renewable freshwater. Science 271(5256):785–788

Safety 4 Sea (2018) Learn from the past: Prestige sinking, one of the worst oil spills in Europe, 13 November 2018. https://safety4sea.com/cm-learn-from-the-past-prestige-sinking-one-of-the-worst-oil-spills-in-europe/. Accessed on 17 June 2023

Shell Petroleum Development Company (1995) Nigeria brief: the environment. S P D C, Lagos

Singh MR, Gupta A (2016) Water pollution-sources, effects and control, ResearchGate. https://www.researchgate.net/publication/321289637_WATER_POLLUTION-SOURCESEFFECTS_AND_CONTROL. Accessed on 29 July 2023

The Harvard T. H. Chan School of Public Health (2017) Water Pollution. https://www.hsph.harvard.edu/ehep/82-2/#:~:text=Water%20pollution%20is%20the%20contamination,make%20their%20way%20to%20water. Accessed on 28 July 2023

Thornton J, Beckwith B (2004) Environmental law, 2nd edn. Sweet and Maxwell, London

United Nations (2023) Data based on United Nations Population Division estimates. https://www.worldometers.info/world-population/population-by-country/. Accessed on 29 July 2023

United Nations Department of Economic and Social Affairs (2020) Sustainable Development Goals (SGDs). https://sustainabledevelopment.un.org/content/documents/21252030%20Agenda%20for%20Sustainable%20Development%20web.pdf. Accessed on 25 May 2023

United Nations Development Programme (UNEP) (2006) Beyond scarcity: power, poverty and the global water crisis. Human Development Report, UNEP Publications Geneva

United Nations Environment Assembly (UNEA) (2017) Resolution 3/10 (UNEP/EA.3/Res.10), Addressing water pollution to protect and restore water-related ecosystems. 3rd session of UNEA, Nairobi, 20 December 2017. https://wedocs.unep.org/bitstream/handle/20.500.11822/22773/K1800216%20-%20UNEP-EA-3-RES-10%20-%20Advance.pdf?sequence=21&isAllowed=y. Accessed on 20 July 2023

United Nations Environment Programme (UNEP) (2018) The World Water Quality Alliance (WWQA) – uniting society to protect the future. https://www.unep.org/explore-topics/water/what-we-do/improving-and-assessing-world-water-quality-partnership-effort? Accessed on 20 July 2023

Watkins K (2006) Beyond scarcity: power, poverty and the global water crisis. In United Nations Development Programme, Human Development Report

Wolf S et al (2002) Principles of environmental law, 3rd edn. Cavendish, London

World Health Organization (WHO) (2017) UN-Water global analysis and assessment of sanitation and drinking-water (GLAAS) 2017 report: financing universal water, sanitation and hygiene under the sustainable development goals. World Health Organization, Geneva. ISBN 978-92-4-151219-0

Chapter 8
Land Use Planning and Development Control

Abstract Land is scarce, limited in supply and relatively fixed in quantity, and in the face of unbridled population growth, rapid urbanisation and industrialisation, land is readily depleted. To permit anyone to do what he absolutely likes with his property. . .will be to make property generally valueless, thus, the need for land use control. This chapter discusses the concept of development, zoning and land use policies as well as various aspects of land use regulations and the mechanisms for development control. Jurisdiction covered in the discussions include the United Kingdom and Nigeria.

8.1 Introduction

"Land use" is the term used to describe the human use of land. It represents the economic and cultural activities (e.g., agricultural, residential, industrial, mining, and recreational uses) that are practiced at a given place. Public and private lands frequently represent very different uses. For example, urban development seldom occurs on publicly owned lands (e.g., parks, wilderness areas), while privately owned lands are infrequently protected for wilderness uses.[1] Land use planning, on the other hand, refers to the process by which land is allocated between competing and sometimes conflicting uses to secure the rational and orderly development of land in an environmentally sound manner to ensure the creation of sustainable human settlements.[2]

But why control land use? This is not farfetched. All development is earthbound and land upon which such developmental activities take place is scarce, limited in supply and relatively fixed in quantity, and in the face of unbridled population growth, rapid urbanisation and industrialisation, the land is readily depleted. Two other factors also compound these problems of land. First, humans being gregarious in nature may want to utilise land unrestrained, unchallenged and undisturbed.

[1] United States Environmental Protection Agency (EPA) (2023).

[2] Organisation of American States (2023).

E. Onyeabor, *Environmental Law*, https://doi.org/10.1007/978-3-031-68956-7_8

Second, it is a notorious fact that land which makes up only 30% of the Earth's entire surface is not only fixed but is also currently under serious threats from the vagaries of weather and climate, which unfortunately is attributed to human activities through exploitation and usage of natural resources found on land.

Where this unpleasant situation is allowed to continue, especially allowing humans to develop land unrestrained, will affect the value of land in the long run, thus the need for land use control. The reason for this is that rational planning is a crucial instrument for resolving any conflict between development needs and the need to protect and improve the environment.[3]

Planning law is enacted for land use control to create a benign, friendly and aesthetically pleasing environment. The law requires that all developmental activities that may have significant environmental impact shall not be commenced except where such a developer has obtained a planning permit from the appropriate planning authority. What this portends is that once an activity is considered to be development, it shall not be commenced until a development permit is first had and obtained from the appropriate town planning authority. In discussing land use and land use control, the concept of development will be addressed first.

8.2 Concept of Development

Under the Town and Country Planning Act of the United Kingdom (UK) (Act of UK) (1990), as amended, "development" means, "the carrying out of building, engineering, mining or other operations in, on, over or under land, or the making of any material change in the use of any buildings or other land."[4] This definition is further expanded by the Nigerian Urban and Regional Planning Act (NURPA) (1992).[5] Under the NURPA (1992),[6] development is defined as:

> the carrying out of any building, engineering, mining or other operations in, on, over or under any land, **or the making of any environmentally significant change in the use of any land or demolition of buildings including the felling of trees and the placing of free-standing erections used for the display of advertisement on the land.**

From these definitions, the following activities are considered as development:

(a) Building, engineering, mining or other operations
(b) Environmentally significant change in the use of any land
(c) Demolition of buildings

[3] United Nations (1972) Stockholm Declaration (1972), Principle 14.

[4] The Act of UK (1990), s. 55.

[5] Nigerian Urban and Regional Planning Act (NURPA) 1992, Cap N138 Laws of the Federation of Nigeria (LFN) 2004.

[6] Ibid., s. 91.

(d) Felling of trees
(e) Placing of free-standing erections used for advertisement

Any act that falls under any of the above "five legs" of the definition amounts to development. The proponent shall therefore be required by law to obtain planning permission from the appropriate planning authority before embarking on such act. Of greatest significance in land use control are activities under: (a) operations and (b) the making of environmentally significant changes in the use of land. Each of these two activities separately determines: (i) when each of the activities can amount to development and (ii) how the carrying out of such activities can affect the environment, as discussed below.

8.2.1 Operations

For development control and within the ambit of the definition of the word development, Lord Parker, C.J. defines operations as, "some acts which change the physical characteristic of the land, or of what is under it, or of the air above it."[7] According to Lord Denning in *Parkes v. Secretary of State for the Environment*,[8] the word "operations" "comprises activities which result in some physical alteration of the land which has some degree of permanence in relation to the land itself." Such acts on the land must result in some physical alteration of the land, which has some degree of permanence in relation to the land itself. At times, "development" can occur even where the land in question is not physically altered. In addition, the following four matters are specifically mentioned as constituting development in this respect:

(a) the use of a single dwelling-house for two or more separate dwellings;
(b) the deposit of refuse or waste materials on an existing on an existing dump if either:
    (i) the superficial area of the dump is extended, or
    (ii) the height of the dump is extended and exceeds the level of the land adjoining the dump;
(c) the placing or assembly of a tank in any inland waters for fish farming;
(d) the display of an advertisement on an external part of a building not normally used for such display.[9]

---

[7]Cheshire County Council v. Woodward (1962) All ER, 517.
[8](1978) I WLR 1308 at 1311.
[9]Onyeabor (2016), pp. 43–44.

Some activities which can alter the physical characteristics of the land that have some degree of permanence in relation to the land itself have been recognised. Such activities are:

(a) Building operations
(b) Engineering operations
(c) Mining operations
(d) Other operations

8.2.1.1 Building Operations

To determine what amounts to building operations we must first delimit what a building is. The NURPA (1992) offers some help. According to the Act, a building means any structure (whether of a temporary nature or not), erected or made on, in, over or under any land.[10] The Act of UK (1990)[11] defines a building to include "any structure or erection and any part of a building so defined, but does not include plant, or machinery comprised in a building." The Nigerian Building Code 2006 on the other hand defines a building as "any structure or enclosure of space with a roof and walls for protection of life and property,"[12] and a structure as "that which is built or constructed of parts joined together in some definite manner."[13]

Elucidating further as to what amounts to a building, Lord Parker CJ[14] stated that a building includes any structure including walls, fences hoarding, masts[15] or any erection. In *Buckingham County Council v. Callingham*,[16] it was held that a model village of buildings constructed to scale was a structure or erection and therefore subject to planning control. In *Cooper v. Bailey*,[17] an advertisement was displayed in a garage. The garage consisted of a central building and petrol pump with two walls on either side running from the building in a curve towards the road. In front of the walls was a kerb marking the limits of the pull-in. The advertisement signs were fixed to the kerb or displayed on the concrete between the kerb and the walls. The question was whether the advertisement signs constituted a structure that would require a planning permit. It was held that these advertisements were displayed on part of the building or structure of the garage and therefore did not constitute a different operation, meaning that no planning permission was needed to display the advertisements.

---

[10] NURPA (1992), s. 91.
[11] The Act of UK (1990), s. 336(1).
[12] Nigerian Building Code 2006, s. 2.19.
[13] Ibid., s. 2.104.
[14] Cheshire County Council v. Woodward (1962), 517.
[15] Masts here may include GSM Operators' base stations.
[16] (1952) I ALL ER, 1166.
[17] (1956) 6 P & CR 261.

The importance of the above decisions is that it does not mean that anything placed on land is to be treated as a building or structure for purposes of planning control. Although there is apparently no simple test for determining whether some object or installation is a building, Lord Parker CJ concluded that "any structure or erection which may be said to form part of the reality and to change the physical character of the land could be regarded as a building or structure."[18]

However, these positions have imported some levels of controversies as to what is a building. Some judicial decisions have tried to offer some help in resolving the controversies. First, a building or structure will be something of a size that has either been in fact or would normally be built or constructed on the site as opposed to being brought on it ready-made. In *Cheshire County Council v. Woodward,*[19] large hoppers and a conveyor for coal in a coal yard were held by the court not to constitute a "building" within the meaning of the word development since the equipment was brought to the site intact.

Second, such a building or structure will have some degree of permanence, once installed it will normally remain *in situ* and can only be removed by pulling down or taking to pieces. This position was applied in the case of *R v. Swansea City Council, ex parte Elitestone Ltd*[20] where it was noted that the degree of permanence is a highly material factor. In that case, the question arose as to whether some 27 self-built wooden chalets were "building" for the purpose of planning law. The chalets were of varying degrees of substance and some were little more than sheds and nearly all were suspended on pillars. It was held that the chalets were structures or erections, since it could be assumed that they had been erected with a prospect of permanence and that they had survived over many years and their erection had affected the physical quality of the land.

Third, the question of whether the thing is, or is not physically attached to the site to constitute a building or structure is relevant but not conclusive. In *Barvis Ltd v. Secretary of State for the Environment,*[21] the appellants who are specialists in the erection of pre-cast concrete structures had erected at their depot a mobile tower crane some 89 feet high which ran on rails fixed in concrete. It had previously been used on contract work and they intended to use it again for contract work when required. The dismantling and re-erection of the crane was carried out by specialists, the whole operation took several days and cost about £2,000. The respondents concluded that the erection of the crane with all that it entails did alter the physical characteristics of the land and amounted to development. This decision was upheld on appeal.

It should be noted that a limited degree of motion does not prevent a thing from being regarded as a building or structure. This criterion was applied in the case of

[18] Cheshire County Council v. Woodward (1962), 517.

[19] Cheshire County Council v. Woodward (1962), 517.

[20] [1993] JPL 1019.

[21] (1971) 22 P & CR 710.

Bendles Motors Ltd v. Bristol Corporation.[22] In that case, the court held that the minister was entitled to find that the installation of a free-standing egg-vending machine in the forecourt of a garage and petrol filling station constituted development.

Since the above criteria have provided guides in determining what constitutes a building, it should be noted that building operations may also include rebuilding operations, structural alterations of or additions to buildings, demolition of buildings and other operations.

However, building operation does not arise where an activity or act is done to the exterior of a building that does not alter its external appearance. In *Kensington and Chelsea Royal London Borough Council v. C. G. Hotels,*[23] the owners of a hotel installed floodlights in the basement areas and on the first-floor balconies. The council served an enforcement notice requiring the removal of the floodlights. On appeal, the inspector quashed the enforcement notice in that:

(i) the "works" did not amount to building or other operations; and
(ii) the floodlights were virtually invisible during the daylight.

This decision was upheld on appeal to the Division Court – the floodlights did not materially affect the external appearance of the building.

In *Burroughs Day v. Bristol City Council,*[24] the question arose as to whether some proposed roof alterations would materially affect the external appearance of a building. The works in question would have super-imposed two areas of flat roofs instead of slopes running down to a valley gutter. The court in arriving at its decision maintained that what must be affected is the external appearance, not the exterior, thus held that the works could not have been visible from any of the surrounding streets and therefore not development.

At times a problem may arise as to whether a work on a building is work of maintenance or work of improvement. Where the act is the former, that is, work of maintenance, it does not constitute building operations, but if the latter, work of improvement, it amounts to reconstruction, and therefore a building operation. The question before the court in the case of *Street v. Essex County Council*[25] was whether the demolition of an existing building down to a damp course and rebuilding it from there amounted to works of maintenance. The local authority opined that the act amounted to development and since Streets did not obtain a planning permit it served an enforcement notice requiring Streets to remove the "new building." The enforcement notice was upheld on appeal to the Minister. On further appeal to the High Court, it was contended on behalf of Streets that the work done did not constitute development provided that design and some part, however small, of the original structure remained, thus the act of Streets should be work of maintenance. This

[22] (1963) I ALL ER 578.
[23] (1980) 41 P & CR 40.
[24] (1997) JPL 107.
[25] (1965) 193 Estates Gazette 537.

argument was not upheld by the court. It held that the minister was entitled to hold as a matter of fact that what took place was reconstruction and as such involved development. The reasoning of the court in this respect is that in reality there was no longer a building to be maintained or improved.

8.2.1.2 Engineering Operations

The Act of UK (1990)[26] defines engineering operations to include "the formation or laying out of means of access to highway." This definition does not give much guidance to planners in the present context. To overcome this inadequacy the court in the case of *Fayrewood Fish Farms v. Secretary of State for the Environment,*[27] laid out the test to be followed to determine when an act constitutes engineering operations. One of such tests for engineering operations is an activity of the kind usually undertaken by, or calling for the skills of, an engineer.

In its ordinary meaning, however, engineering operations may include the building and maintenance of roads, the laying of sewers, water mains and other public utility apparatus.[28] Thus, in the case of *Coleshill and District Investment Co Ltd v. Minister of Housing and Local Government,*[29] the removal of earth embankments was held to constitute an engineering operation.

It should be noted that not every aspect of public utility maintenance shall constitute engineering operations. Therefore, where the maintenance or improvement of a road by the appropriate authority, for instance, the Ministry of Works, within the existing boundaries of the road, is doubtful whether such shall constitute development within the meaning of engineering operations. Again, the inspection, repair and removal of sewers, mains, cables, etc, by any statutory or corporate undertaker may also not come within the meaning of engineering operations.

8.2.1.3 Mining Operations

Both the NURPA (1992) and the Act of UK (1990) did not provide any definition of mining operations. As a result of these shortcomings of the Acts in use, this question may arise: when can an activity amount to mining operations to constitute development? Perhaps the removal of materials of any description from mineral deposits and waste tips, including quarrying and other extractive operations, whether of surface or underground operations may be regarded as constituting mining operations.[30]

[26] The Act of England 1990, s. 55(2) (9).

[27] (1984) JPL 267.

[28] Such as the laying of GSM optic fibres, water pipelines, oil/gas pipelines, etc.

[29] (1967) 2 ALL ER 525.

[30] Onyeabor (2016), p. 48.

This assertion is predicated on the fact that the removal of all minerals and substances that are on, in or under the land by surface or underground working will have an environmentally significant impact on the land bearing the minerals. It is, perhaps, against this background that mining of minerals (in any form) is included in the mandatory list of the Environmental Impact Assessment Act (EIA Act) 1992,[31] as one of the development projects where an environmental impact assessment is a must before the commencement of the project.[32]

8.2.1.4 Other Operations

There is uncertainty as to the meaning of the phrase, "other operations." Bell and McGillivray[33] regard it as "catch-all category apparently designed to ensure that matters such as waste disposal and drill are covered." Because of the uncertainty of what "other operations" stands for, Duxbury[34] suggested that the phrase can be interpreted in different ways:

(a) It might be taken as meaning any operation affecting the physical characteristics of the land (perhaps outside building, engineering and mining operations).
(b) In applying the *ejusdem generis* rule,[35] the phrase may be limited to operations of the classes of a genus as building, engineering and mining.
(c) Applying the rule of interpretation known as *noscitur a sociis*, other operations would be restricted to operations similar to building, engineering or mining, but in a less strict manner than would be required by the *ejusdem generis* rule.

Applying the rule of interpretation known as *noscitur a sociis*[36] is however preferable in that other operations invariably would be within the classes of a genus of building, engineering and mining operations, but less strict in manner.[37] In applying the rule of *noscitur a sociis*, the English Court of Appeal in *Cambridge*

[31] Cap E12 L F N 2004.

[32] EIA Act (1992), s. 12. See Schedule 1 to the EIA Act (1992).

[33] Bell and McGillivray (2006), p. 310.

[34] Duxbury (1999), pp. 91 and 92.

[35] The meaning of "Ejusdem Generis" is "of the same kind." It is generally used in courts for deciding or classification of entities or bodies that come under a specific definition. It is generally used when ambiguity or confusion on the statutes arises.

[36] *Noscitur a sociis* is a rule of construction and it is used by the court to interpret legislation. It means that the meaning of an unclear word or phrase must be determined by the words that surround it. In other terms, the meaning of a word must be judged by the company that it keeps. The questionable meaning of a doubtful word will be derived from its association with other words. It is used when two or more words susceptible of analogous meaning are coupled together, they are understood to be used in their cognate sense. The words take their color from and are quantified by each other, the meaning of the general words being restricted to a sense analogous to that of the less general.

[37] Onyeabor (2016), p. 49.

City Council v. Secretary of State for the Environment[38] held that the demolition of two dwelling houses constituted development as an operation normally undertaken by a person carrying on business as a builder.

Again, the Nigerian Building Code 2006[39] defines demolition works as "work carried out in the process of pulling down of the super-structure of a building and/or the removal of, or material alteration to the sub-structure, as may be required." In the same vein, the removal of topsoil as in the case of excavating of gravels and laterites, in such a circumstance may be deemed to constitute "other operations" within the meaning of the word development. The reason is that demolition works and the act of removing topsoil may have a significant impact on the environment and therefore may be of interest to the planning authority.

8.2.2 Change in Use of Land

The second important arm of the definition of development under Section 91 of NURPA 1992 is… "the making of any material or environmentally significant change in the use of any building or land." Under the Nigerian Building Code 2006,[40] change in use means "an alteration in the use of an existing building to a new use which imposes other special provisions of law governing design building construction, equipment or means of egress." Use in this sense refers to the purpose to which the building or land is devoted to. This preposition is supported by the Nigerian Building Code 2006. In Section 2.116 of the Code, use means "the purpose for which the building or structure is designed, used or intended to be used."

The "use" here comprises activities that are done in, alongside or on the land, but do not interfere with the actual physical characteristics of the land.[41] It should be noted that the use, and therefore the change arising therefrom, must be material in planning sense and falls within the authority of a Development Control Department.[42] Material change of use therefore shall mean the alteration of the use of land or after occupancy of a building or structure for a purpose other than for which it was originally designed or approved.[43] For a change in use to be considered material therefore according to Bell and McGillivray,[44] the change in issue must have:

[38] (1992) JPL 644.

[39] Nigerian Building Code 2006, s. 2.37.

[40] Ibid., s. 2.28.

[41] Parkes v. Secretary of State for the Environment (1978), 1311.

[42] The establishment of the Development Control Department is provided under the various planning laws, e.g. under the NURPA (1992), s. 27.

[43] Nigerian Building Code (2006), s. 2.75.

[44] Bell and McGillivray (2006) p. 465.

(a) a physical impact on the land;
(b) such impact must be a substantial impact; and
(c) the impact must be relevant to the Development Control Department.

In considering whether there has been a change in the use of land, the planning unit of the land in question is usually considered. The planning unit is normally the unit of occupation before the change of use. In some cases, building or land in the same occupation may be divided into two or more planning units. For instance, where the occupier carries on more than one activity within the same planning unit, the "use" of the building or land comprised in it will depend on the nature of the activities. Thus, it is quite common for one activity to be ancillary to a primary activity and this use may be regarded as included in the primary use, for example, a factory and office block, storage facility in respect of a supermarket, parking space and office complex, etc. In all these cases separate planning permission is not required for the commencement of the ancillary activity.[45] Note that the right to use the building or land for an ancillary activity will be lost on the cessation of the primary activity.[46]

At times the planning unit may accommodate two or more activities neither of which is ancillary to the other. In such a case the planning unit may be said to have mixed or composite use. Therefore, the deposit of refuse or other waste materials, including the extension of an existing tip, if the superficial area is extended or the height is extended above the level of the adjoining ground, may constitute a material change in the use of the land.[47] Again, the display of advertisements on any external part of a building not previously used for that purpose in the wordings of Section 91 of NURPA (1992), amounts to a material change in the use of the building or land. It should be noted that under Section 73 of the Act of UK (1990), the planning authority shall regulate the dimensions, appearances, display, sitting and manner in which an advertisement billboard shall be affixed to the land.

In all these cases, for there to be a change in use the new use must be material. Issues declared to be material must be assessed by reference to their effect on the appropriate area of land or building in question. To this end, the new use must be substantially different from the old use. For any use to be regarded as substantial, the new use must be considerable, solid or big. Determining whether a new use is substantial and therefore material employs a high level of subjectivity. Help is however offered by the courts. Certain questions are asked in respect of the use in issue and the answers provided thereto may help in ascertaining whether the new use is substantial and therefore material to warrant the attention of the Development Control Department. These questions include:

First, will the new use completely alter the character of the land or building? In answering this question, what is relevant is not the particular purpose to which the

[45] (1984) JPL, 183.
[46] (1980) JPL 594.
[47] Duxbury (1999), p. 94.

occupier puts the land or building but whether the use is of such a character that it matters having regard to the objects of planning control.[48] In *Guildford RDC v. Penny*[49] where a field of caravans was increased from 8 to 29 caravans, it was held that that did not amount to material change. In *Marshall v. Nottingham City Council,*[50] Flynn-Jones, J, while elucidating further on the issue stated that:

> If the business of a retail dealer is being carried on in any building, it may be that there is a change of use, if, for example, the business of a baker is substituted for a different business, for example, that of a grocer.... I am unable to see why or how such a change can be material from a point of view which could legitimately be taken by a planning authority.

In that case, land used for the manufacturing and sale of modern portable buildings was converted to the selling of caravans and portable buildings were held not to amount to material change of use.

Again, in *East Barnett v. British Transport Commission,*[51] a land used for storage of coal was changed for storage of caravans was held not to constitute material change of use. The reason being that the purpose of the land at all times had been as storage and transit depot. In all these cases the decision of the courts was predicated on the fact that the new use did not alter the character of the land in question, nor did they fall within the requirements for a planning permit.

However, in the case of *M K O Abiola v. Felix O Ijeoma*[52] the plaintiff who lived with his family at No. 7 Shofidiya Close, Surulere, Lagos, brought this action against the defendant who owned and occupied the adjoining property at No. 8 Shofidiya Close, Surulere, Lagos. The two houses were situated in an area zoned for residential purposes only. The defendant kept a poultry farm at the back of his house as a hobby but in 1969 he increased the number of day-old chickens to 400. These were kept in pens erected on the boundary wall that separated his own building from that of the plaintiff. The plaintiff brought an action for an injunction to restrain the defendant's act of nuisance and damages. While granting the injunction, Dosunmu, J. stated as follows:

> every person is entitled as against his neighbour to the comfortable and healthy enjoyment of the premises occupied by him... but it is necessary to take into account the circumstances and character of the locality in which the complainant is living....The making or causing of such a noise materially interfering with the comfort of a neighbour, ...constitutes an actionable nuisance ....[53]

The bottom line in the above case is that the defendant's action in keeping poultry in an area zoned for residential purposes constituted a change in use and when viewed from the fact that by the plaintiff's claim, the defendant's action has changed

---

[48] Burdle v. Secretary of State for the Environment (1972), 240.

[49] (1959) 2 ALL ER 111.

[50] (1960) I ALL ER 659 at 665.

[51] (1960) 3 ALL ER 878.

[52] (1970) ALL NLR 569.

[53] M K O Abiola v. Felix O Ijeoma (1970), 570.

the character of the building and the adjoining land and therefore amounted to a material change in the use of the building. To this end, the defendant's action ordinarily in planning parlance required a planning permit as his act constituted objects of interest to the Development Control Department.[54]

The second question arises where a new use does not completely alter the character of a building or land. The question that follows is whether the new use is material for any other reasons. The test here revolves around answers to the following questions:

(i) Is the change likely to involve a great increase in the number of persons calling at the building?
(ii) What is the effect of the new use on the neighbourhood; will there be a great deal of noise from callers?
(iii) For what purpose is the change in use, that is, whether the new use is for profit?

Where the answers to the above questions are in the affirmative then the new use is regarded as material and therefore a change in the use of land within the meaning of development under both the Act of UK (1990) and the NURPA (1992). It is immaterial that the change in use did not altogether or completely alter the character of the building or land.[55]

The third question centres on where the existing use has been intensified, in other words, no new use was introduced. The question is: has there been a complete change in the character of the building or land because of the intensification of the old use? The test here is whether the intensification of use of building or land is such as to amount to a material change of use so as to draw the attention of the Development Control Department. In the case of *Brooks and Burton Ltd v. Secretary of State for the Environment*,[56] an increase in the production of cement blocks from 300,000 to 1,200,000 was held to amount to an intensification of use.

Also, in *Peake v. Secretary of State for Wales,*[57] the plaintiff's changed the use of his garage from part-time to full-time usage was held to amount to intensification of use. The reason for this decision stemmed from the fact that initially, the act of using the garage for car maintenance was merely a hobby but changing to full-time usage amounted to a trade or business. In this regard, the new use (of full-time mechanic) is material and therefore a change in the use of the building.

Furthermore, in the case of *Birmingham Corporation v. Minister of Housing and Local Government and Habbib Ullah*,[58] the conversion of a single dwelling house into two or more separate dwellings and whereby several families were installed into hitherto single-family occupation was held to amount to intensification of use.

---

[54] It was in the light of this that the Lagos City Council ordered the demolition of the pens.

[55] Onyeabor (2016), p. 52.

[56] (1976) 35 P and CR. 27.

[57] Peake v. Secretary of State for Wales (1971), 501.

[58] (1963) 3 ALL ER 368.

The fourth question is on the nature of the planning zone under consideration. Whether a change of use is material under this head must be assessed by reference to the planning unit where the building or land is situated. Three ways of dealing with the situation were enunciated in the case of *Burdle v. Secretary of State for the Environment.*[59]

First, where an occupier has a single main purpose with or without ancillary uses, the whole of the unit of occupation constitutes a planning unit. Therefore, any additional use outside the main use to which the area has been zoned amounts to a material change in use. This principle was applied in the case of *M K O Abiola v. Felix O Ijeoma.*[60]

Second, if there is a variety of uses or composite uses where activities may vary or fluctuate, the whole unit is a planning unit. But where the use of the composite use conflicts irreconcilably with the other uses an actionable wrong may arise. In the case of *Tebite v. Nigerian Marine Trading Co Ltd,*[61] the plaintiff, a legal practitioner, had his office and residence in an area in Warri designated as a mixed-use zone where the defendant company engaged in the manufacturing of steel products and servicing of boats. The plaintiff complained that the defendant worked round the clock thereby disturbing him from the use of his chambers at night, also denying him a good night's sleep and causing sooth to be deposited on his window blinds and room. He therefore brought the present action for an injunction restraining the defendants and for damages. The court found for the plaintiff holding that although the area is a mixed-use zone, the defendant's use of his land unreasonably interfered with that of the plaintiff. The injunction was therefore granted.

Third, where within a holding physically separate and distinct areas are occupied for different and unrelated purposes; each separate area is regarded as a separate planning unit. The test here is whether the material change of use is physically and functionally separate, then the new use is regarded as separate use and as such a separate planning unit, thus amounting to development.

For instance, in *Wood v. Secretary of State for the Environment,*[62] the use of a conservatory attached to a dwelling house was used for the sale of produce from small-holding was held not to amount to a separate planning unit as one cannot dissect a dwelling house and regard each room in it as a separate planning unit. However, the court expressed that what the defendant would have considered was whether the sale of produce amounted to a material change in the use of the whole of the premises. This opinion of the court may apply in cases concerning the use of part of a dwelling house for a professional practice or business. For example, a lawyer who is using part of his dwelling house for legal practice, or a medical doctor who is using part of his dwelling house as a clinic, or the case of an occupier using one room

[59] Burdle v. Secretary of State for the Environment (1972).

[60] M K O Abiola v. Felix O Ijeoma (1970), 571.

[61] (1971) UILR 432.

[62] (1973) 2 ALL ER 404.

of his flat for the sale of drinks and other provisions or man using part of his apartment for religious services.

Again, where a block of flats in single ownership is let to separate and different tenants, the planning unit would normally be the individual flats in question. However, where there is a complex of buildings such as in a housing estate or commercial development, although a single planning permission covers the complex of buildings, each building or use therein is treated as a planning unit. In the case of *Hertsmere Borough Council v. Secretary of State for the Environment,*[63] an office that formed part of a larger complex of offices in multiple occupations, had been turned into a wholesale warehouse without planning permission. On appeal against the enforcement notice, the inspector took the planning unit to be the whole complex on the fact that the whole complex was covered by a single planning permission. The court held that this conclusion was unreasonable and perverse since the grant of planning permission does not necessarily dictate the planning unit.

The fifth question in deciding whether there was a material change in the use of land is, having established use rights, have such rights been lost or abandoned? Under this step, the following must be considered:

(a) Whether the use right has been extinguished; and
(b) Whether the use right has been abandoned.

In deciding whether a use right has been extinguished in assuming a change of use because of new development, there have been some controversies. In one instant, where there is extinguishment of use rights because of new development the continuation of previous uses would be wholly inconsistent with the new development and often indeed impracticable giving rise to the fact that the use right has been extinguished. For instance, in the case of *Petticoat Lane Rental v. Secretary of State for the Environment*[64] a cleared bomb site had been used throughout the week as a market. The entire site was redeveloped by the erection of a building, the ground floor was open, the building was supported by pillars, and was to be used as a car park and loading area. Planning permission was given for the use of the ground floor as a market on Sundays, but it continued to be used as a market throughout the week. The court held that the previously existing land had merged into the new building, and a new planning unit had been created which had no previous planning permission (except on Sundays) and that there was therefore a breach of planning control. In other words, the new development has extinguished the old use right, and the new use amounts to a change of use thus requiring fresh planning permission.

In the case of *Aston v. Secretary of State for the Environment,*[65] a building was erected as part of the original planning unit. In 1952, the plaintiff bought some land which he began to use for the keeping of pigs and as a base for vehicles for his transport business. In 1956, he built a large barn which he used for both purposes.

[63](1991) JPL 552.
[64](1971) 2 ALL ER 793.
[65](1973) 43 P & CR 331.

However, because of a storm, the barn was blown down in 1961 and there was no use of this part of the site until 1969. In that year, he built a larger barn on the former site without planning permission and claimed that he had the right to use the barn for the maintenance of his vehicles (as he had done previously). The court held that where a new building is erected on part of the land, that part of the land becomes a new planning unit.

Thus, where there are no permitted uses apart from the previous planning permission, the prior existing use rights have been extinguished with the new development. Lord Lane summarised this situation in the case of *Newbury District Council v. Secretary of State for the Environment,*[66] where he pointed out that "the holder of planning permission will not be allowed to rely on any existing use rights if the effect of the permission when acted on has been to bring one phase of the planning history of a site to end and to start a new one . . . ."

These prepositions border on the theory of "new planning unit" and it appears to be inflexible in its application. Application of the theory at times leads to hardship on the part of the developer. The reason being that although at times the previous use rights may not be impracticable and not necessarily inconsistent with the new development the courts had held otherwise. To ameliorate this hardship, a school led by Lord Denning MR had come up with a new way of dealing with the situation. The test, according to him, in determining whether a use right had been extinguished by new development was enunciated in the case of *Jennings Motors Ltd v. Secretary of State for the Environment.*[67] According to Lord Denning, "the test now is whether there is a radical change in the nature of the buildings on the site or the uses to which they are put so radical that it can be looked on as a fresh start altogether in the character of the site."[68]

In that case, the site had an established use as a taxi, car and coach hire business and for vehicle repairs and car sales. Most of the site was used for access and parking, there was a garage workshop in one corner occupying one-twelfth of the site, and there was a showroom and office in another corner occupying one-thirteenth of the site. There had also been a second garage workshop but the appellants pulled it down and put up a new building notwithstanding a refusal of planning permission to do so. The new building occupied about one-seventeenth of the site and the appellants began to use it for the repair and servicing of vehicles. The local planning authority took enforcement proceedings to prevent the building from being used for repair and maintenance work. This was upheld by the Secretary of State for the Environment, noting that when the new building was erected, a new planning history had commenced in respect of it and the building on completion had a "nil" use. This decision was appealed against at the High Court. The court held that:

---

[66] (1981) AC 578.

[67] (1982) I ALL ER 471.

[68] Ibid.

(i) The erection of the new building did not necessarily create a "new planning unit" nor give rise to a "new planning unit" nor give rise to a "new chapter" in the planning history.
(ii) The question of whether a new planning history was about to begin was one of fact and degree in each case.
(iii) In the present case, there had been no change in the planning history and the appellants were entitled to the existing use rights attaching to the site inside the new building.

In the case of *Gray v. Minister of Housing and Local Government*,[69] the plaintiff owned a seaside café which was gradually converted to predominantly amusement use. The café was destroyed by fire and he applied for and obtained planning permission for the re-erection of the café. The plaintiff subsequently used the new building for amusement. An enforcement notice was issued to him to convert the building into a café. The plaintiff failed to comply, thus the present action. It was held that as a result of the fire, any use rights attaching to the original café building were extinguished when the building was destroyed by fire. This means that the plaintiff ought to have applied for a permit to use the site as an amusement park.

Where a use right has not been extinguished, the issue of change in use under the fifth head may considered on the basis as to whether the use right had been abandoned. The question of whether existing use rights have been lost through abandonment arises where a use has ceased for a time and the land has not been used for any other purpose in the meantime. If the circumstances justify a finding that the use has been abandoned, the land will be termed to have a nil use and a resumption of the previous use will require planning permission. However, as was held in the case of *Young v. Secretary of State for the Environment*[70] where the previous use is immediately followed by another positive use, the previous use rights are deemed not to have been abandoned. But where the new use right amounts to a material change of use in any other material particular it is unlikely that the previous use could thereafter be resumed without planning permission as the previous use is deemed to have been abandoned.

There are several ways of considering whether existing use rights have in fact been abandoned.[71] First, if the sole use to which the land is put is suspended and thereafter resumed without there being any intervening different user, prima facie the resumption does not constitute development. This assertion is based on the fact that, as Lord Parker CJ pointed out in the case of *McKellan v. Minister of Housing and Local Government*,[72] at all times there is no material change in the use of the land or building. Therefore, where a change moved from A to X and then from X to A does not involve development either way if X is completely nil, no use at all.

[69] (1969) 68 L GR 50.
[70] (1983) JPL 465.
[71] After Ashworth J in Hartley v. Minister of Housing and Local Government (1969) I ALL ER 309.
[72] (1966) 198 Estates Gazette, 683.

Second, where the land remained unused for a considerable time in such circumstances that a reasonable man might conclude that the previous use has been abandoned, the court may hold the same. In the case of *Ratcliffe v. Secretary of State for the Environment*,[73] a quarry site had been used by a local authority for tipping refuse from 1920–1961, and thereafter some sporadic tipping was done but not by the local authority but by a purchaser who proposed to use the reclaimed land for chicken farming. In 1970, the appellant applied for a determination as to whether filling the quarry for reclamation purposes would amount to development. The Secretary of State for the Environment decided that the tipping use had been abandoned in 1961. This decision was upheld on appeal. At times a reasonable man's test is applied in determining whether an old use has been abandoned. In applying the reasonable man's test, the intention of the occupier and other surrounding circumstances must be taken into consideration. In the case of *Hale v. Lichfield District Council*,[74] Mrs. H. had spent the last 13 years of her life in hospital leaving her house empty and it seems no repairs were done. On her death, her personal representatives sought to repair the house and applied for a declaration that the house was not abandoned. The court found in favour of the applicants and declared that the residential use of the house had not been abandoned.

Third, where the land might have been put to a composite use the cessation of one of the composite uses does not of itself constitute development, nor can it be said that the change from dual use to single use is of itself a material change of use. After the cessation of one of the uses, the continuing use absorbs some or all the remaining land, which has been held in the case of *Hartley v. Minister of Housing and Local Government*[75] as amounting to a material change in the use of the whole site.

Fourth, one of the component uses may be discontinued without any subsequent intensification of the other component use or uses, if the discontinued use is later resumed without planning permission it will be necessary to consider whether that use has in fact been abandoned. According to Duxbury[76] relevant considerations will include:

(a) The nature of the uses.
(b) What portion of the site was devoted to the discontinued use?
(c) What use, if any, was made of that portion during the period of discontinuance?
(d) How long does the discontinuance last?
(e) When the resumption occurred, was there a material change in the use of land?

From the above analyses, the issue of development as defined by the NURPA (1992) is a matter taken very seriously as the essence is not only to control land use but also to protect the environment. It should however be noted that not all activities that involve the use of land amount to development. Therefore, to protect the

---

[73] (1975) JPL 728.
[74] (1979) JPL 425.
[75] Hartley v. Minister of Housing and Local Government (1969), 309 at 315.
[76] Duxbury (1999), p. 123.

environment from abuse and degradation and at the same time allow for development only activities that fall within the ambit of the definition of development under planning law are controlled. It follows therefore that there are activities that may affect and touch the land but are not considered development. Such activities can be allowed to commence without any insistence by the planning authority for a planning or development permit.

8.2.3 Activities Not Considered Development

In the preceding discussions, efforts were made to highlight instances where an activity may be regarded as development either under "operations" or "change in use of land." There are certain situations in which the use of land for all intents and purposes would not constitute development. Some of such situations are discussed below.

Where an occupier uses a dwelling house for any purpose incidental to the enjoyment of such a dwelling house, for instance, the use of an existing garden shed as a garage for the owner's car or as additional sleeping accommodation. However, it should be noted that this does not authorise the erection of a building or shed for these purposes, as this action would amount to building operations, thus development. However, where such enjoyment amounts to a hobby that may be of a kind and requires such a space that the enjoyment of the dwelling house becomes incidental to the indulgence of the hobby, such incidental enjoyment has been held in the case of *Wallington v. Secretary of State for Wales*[77] to constitute development. In that case, a householder kept 44 dogs at her home, which made considerable noise. The dogs were not kept commercially but as a hobby. The argument that because it was a hobby it was incidental to enjoyment of the dwelling house was rejected.

Also, in the case of *M KO Abiola v. Felix O Ijeoma*[78] the defendant argued strenuously that the poultry was kept as a hobby. This argument was however rejected by the court. In arriving at these decisions, the courts took into consideration what would be a normal use of a dwelling house. In another vein, the courts have held that where the performance of the following activities such as the maintenance, improvement or alterations to a building affecting only its interior or not materially affecting the external appearance do not amount to development.[79]

Certain works carried out by highway authorities to maintain and improve roads, including works by local authorities, Ministry of Works or statutory undertakers for the repair or removal of sewers, public water involving breaking open of streets (such as by Water Corporation), etc, do not amount to development. Furthermore, the use of any land for agriculture or forestry (including afforestation and

[77] (1990) JPL 112.

[78] M K O Abiola v. Felix O Ijeoma (1970), 571.

[79] Kensington and Chelsea Royal London Borough Council v. C G Hotels (1980).

re-forestation) and the use for any of these purposes of any building occupied with land so used. Also, other uses connected with or pertaining to or arising from agricultural practices are included not to constitute development.[80]

Although the demolition of a building comes within the purview of the definition of development under NURPA (1992),[81] however, the demolition of any description of the building specified in a direction given by the appropriate Development Control Department especially the application of the provisions of Section 62 of the NURPA (1992) does not amount to development. Under Section 61 of the NURPA (1992), the Development Control Department shall have the power to serve on a developer a demolition notice if a structure erected by the developer is found to be defective as to pose danger or constitute a nuisance to the occupier and the public.

To this end, after the expiration of the notices served on the developer under the provisions of Section 61, the Development Control Department shall take such necessary action to effect the demolition of the defective structure.[82] Once this is carried out, although demolition is regarded as development under Section 91 of the NURPA (1992), this will not in itself be regarded as such because of the provisions of Section 62 of the same Act.

However, it should be noted that planning does not fully control development. It aims to steer and guide development. The extent to which development follows a more sustainable trajectory depends on a range of factors (politics, market forces, social norms and standards, etc.) that can influence development in both positive and negative ways.[83]

8.3 Land Use and Zoning Policy

Besides the provisions of the NURPA (1992) in regulating the use of land, various planning policies are employed by planning authorities that operate to govern land development and control in a given society along its urban and rural regions. Such regulations impose operationally, a system of restrictions upon the general rights of every landowner to use or develop his land not based on the way he likes but on the pre-conceived socio-economic pattern to achieve a purposeful utilisation of land in the interest of the general welfare of the community to which the land situates or relates.[84] One of the most veritable policies used by planning authorities to control land use and development is zoning.

[80] The Act of UK (1990), s. 55(2) (a)-(g).

[81] NURPA (1992), s.91.

[82] NURPA (1992), s 62.

[83] Van der Berg (2019), p. 18.

[84] Royal Town Planning Institute (RTPI) (2004).

8.3.1 Concept of Zoning

Zoning has a relatively short history as a tool for land-use planning. It determines the location, size, and use of buildings and decides the density of city blocks. Zoning is a planning control tool for regulating the built environment and creating functional real estate markets. It does so by dividing land that comprises the statutory area of a local authority into sections, permitting particular land uses on specific sites to shape the layout of towns and cities and enable various types of development.[85]

Zoning can also be regarded as the restrictions on land use imposed on landowners by a governmental agency are codified in a zoning plan.[86] A zoning plan is a detailed map that designates restrictions placed on the use of each piece of property under a government's jurisdiction. Zoning restrictions can limit the type and amount of development that may take place on a land parcel. For example, zoning may prohibit the construction of a warehouse or industrial plant on a parcel of land in a residential neighbourhood. Zoning may also specify the maximum size of the house that may be constructed with limits on height and volume. The zoning regulations may also specify the "setbacks," the distance of any structures from the boundaries of the property.[87]

According to a judge in Vermont, United States of America (USA) in the case of *Kalakowski v. John A. Russell Corporation,*[88]

> Zoning is a process by which the Planning Authority determines what people propose to do with their land, and decide whether or not it will be permitted. More importantly, zoning promotes the health, safety, morals and general welfare of the town. It is specific and regulatory and must deal with the present realities of the community. Zoning bylaws are the most practical means to implement the town plan. Though the plan may recommend many desirable approaches to development, only those provisions incorporated in the bylaws are legally enforceable

Zoning according to the Nigerian Building Code[89] means "the reservation of certain specific areas within a community or city for specific types of buildings and structures, or use of land for certain purposes with limitations such as height, plot coverage, and other stipulated requirements." Zoning therefore is a regulatory device aimed at classifying land within an entity into areas, layouts and districts or zones and prescribing and applying in each area, layout, district or zone regulations concerning building and structure design, building and structure placement, and use to which land, building and structures within such designated areas, layouts, districts or zones may be used for. It is a system of land use regulation that designates the permitted uses of land based on location.[90] Zoning therefore helps to protect

[85] The World Bank (2015).

[86] Glickman (2014).

[87] Glickman (2014).

[88] [1979] 137 Vt. 219, 401 A.2d 906, 4401.

[89] Nigerian Building Code 2006, s. 2.127.

[90] Royal Institute of Town Planners (2004).

public and private interests, preserve critical areas, promote orderly growth, and encourage development to occur at a rate and manner that the community desires.[91]

Typically, the zoning regulation will include the following categories of uses which will be acceptable on particular areas or layouts, such as: residential, commercial, industrial, office, open space, recreational, public/institutional, and agricultural. There may be several subcategories as well such as detached or attached residential zones of various sizes or densities or heavy or light industrial uses.

Each zone is regulated by a few conditions in addition to use. These may include the densities at which those activities can be performed, such as: low-density housing such as single-family homes to high density such as apartment buildings, the building heights, the amount of space structures that may be occupied by limiting how close a building may be from the edge of the plot, the proportions of the types of space on a plot, for example, setbacks and set-offs, and how much landscaped space and how much paved space, and how much parking space must be provided. In addition, as indicated above, there may be zones that are based on environmental conditions such as open space, flood plains, and steep slopes.[92] Under zoning policy, each land use zone is subject to a series of regulations depicting what can be built regarding criteria such as nature, function, and density, giving municipal governments tools to influence urban development.[93]

Zoning therefore is a classification of land uses that limits what activities can or cannot take place on a parcel by establishing a range of development options and can be a valuable tool for directing and controlling growth within a city. When utilised as a tool for achieving planning goals, rather than serving as the plan itself, zoning has proven to have a positive impact on the environment.[94] On the whole, zoning as a land use policy informs a land owner what to do with his or her land to have a decent and convenient environment. In *Penn Control Transportation Company v. New York City*,[95] the court opined that zoning laws are the classic example of laws by which health, safety morals or general welfare would be promoted.

In this respect, zoning can be regarded as a form of "police power," which is delegated to the planning authority through enabling legislation to ensure the welfare of the community where the land is situated by regulating the most appropriate use of the land. Although there may be a variable number of zones designated as part of the zoning regulation, depending upon the size and complexity of a given city or jurisdiction, the traditional concept behind zoning is to separate potential conflicts among incompatible land uses. The zoning regulation is therefore the mechanism by

---

[91] Rostron (2001), p. 41.

[92] Rostron (2001), p. 41.

[93] Rodrigue (2020), p. 292.

[94] Rostron (2001), p. 41.

[95] (1978) 438 US 104, 125, see also Newtown v. Cambridge (1928) 277 US 183 to 188.

which new development is controlled as growth occurs.[96] On a general note, a zoning regulation has the force and effect of a legislative enactment.[97]

8.3.2 *Utility and Purposes of Zoning*

The purpose of zoning is to allow local and national authorities to regulate and control land and property markets to ensure complementary uses. Zoning can also provide the opportunity to stimulate or slow down development in specific areas.[98]

From all indications, zoning can be a valuable and useful tool for directing and controlling development and growth within a city. When utilised as a tool for achieving planning goals, zoning may have a positive impact on the protection of the environment from prodigious use and abuse. If applied appropriately, zoning may achieve purposeful utilisation of land in the interest or general welfare of the people and the locality to which the land situates and relates. These can be buttressed by the following cases.

In *Ademola v. Rutili and Ors*,[99] the defendants attempted to build a school on a piece of land zoned as an open space in the approved Victoria Island (Lagos) Scheme. The court restrained the defendants from continuing with the project on the ground that the purported development contravened what was approved on the planning scheme.

In another instance, in the case of *M K O Abiola v. Felix O Ijeoma*[100] both plaintiff and defendant were neighbours living at adjoining properties in the Surulere Area of Lagos State zoned for residential purposes. The defendant operated a poultry in the compound of his house which made excessive noise and smell to the annoyance of the plaintiff. The court granted the injunction sought by the plaintiff restraining the defendant from the use of his compound to keep poultry. The decision of the court was based on the fact that the area is zoned for residential purposes only.

Also, in the case of *Defactor Bakeries and Catering Services Ltd. v. Ajilore & Anor*[101] the plaintiff overdeveloped their plot and wrongly inserted a few doors and windows as well as other outlets along the boundary adjoining the 1st defendant's property, contrary to the Ilupeju Planning Scheme in Lagos State. However, when the 1st defendant developed his land in accordance with the planning schemes the plaintiffs brought the present action that they were entitled to a right of easement of

---

[96] Onyeabor (2016).

[97] Murphy Motor Sales, Inc. v. First National Bank of St. Johnsbury (1960) 122 Vt. 121, 124, 165 A.2d 341, 343.

[98] The World Bank (2015).

[99] Suit No. LD/784/84 (Unreported) delivered on 21 September 1985. See also JPPL Vol. 4, 1985, 43.

[100] M K O Abiola v. Ijeoma (1970) 572.

[101] (1974) ALL NLR, 385.

light as the defendant's building obstructed the enjoyment of this right. The court dismissed this claim. This was affirmed on appeal to the Court of Appeal. On appeal to the Supreme Court, the appeal was again dismissed on the ground that the appellants were in contravention of the planning scheme of the area and therefore should not be heard to complain.

At times an area may be zoned not as a single-use but as a mixed-use zone. This notwithstanding the law enjoins land owners to use their land in such a way that one use should not conflict irreconcilably with other landowners' use of his land nor should it interfere with his enjoyment of the land or degrade the said property or the environment where the land situates. Where such a situation arises, the law is usually invoked against the defaulting land owner for the protection of the other landowner's use. This state of affairs is aptly illustrated by the following cases.

In *Tebite v. Nigerian Marine & Trading Co. Ltd.*[102] the plaintiff, a legal practitioner, had his office and residence in an area in Warri designated as a mixed-use zone where the defendant company engaged in the manufacturing of steel products and servicing of boats. The plaintiff complained that the defendant worked round the clock thereby disturbing him from the use of his chambers at night, also denying him a good night's sleep and causing sooth to be deposited on his window blinds and room. He brought an action for injunction against the defendant. The court in granting the injunction held that the defendants' use of their land unreasonably interfered with that of the plaintiff.

Also, in the case of *Karagulamus v. Kolawole Oyesile*,[103] plaintiff brought this action against the defendant on the ground that fumes from the defendant's machines caused damages to his bedroom and that such fumes were offensive. The court granted the injunction sought.

To preserve and protect the environment, in extreme situations the contravention of the zoning policy may attract an order for the demolition or dismantling of the offending building or structure. In *Ipadiola and Ibadan Metropolitan Planning Authority v. Abiodu*,[104] the first appellant obtained a planning permit from the second appellant. This planning approval was however in contravention of the Federal Highway Building Lines Regulation. The respondent had earlier obtained approval from the 2nd appellant and had developed his land in accordance with the building lines, plans and setback of 46 metres. Now with the construction work of the 1st Appellant, the respondent's view of the highway was blocked. Consequently, the respondent sought a declaration that the first appellant built in contravention of the building line regulation through the active connivance of the second appellant. Both the lower courts and the Supreme Court decided in favour of the respondent. The planning authority, the second appellant, was ordered to enforce the approved planning scheme of the area. The 1st appellant's building was subsequently demolished.

---

[102] Tebite v. Nigerian Marine & Trading Co. Ltd (1971) 432.

[103] (1973) 3 UILR.

[104] (1987) 3 NWLR (Pt. 59) 18.

Again, in the case of *Chika Ibeneme v. Governor of Anambra State*,[105] the plaintiff who was a Commissioner in Anambra State (1992–1993), in abuse of her office connived with the planning authority who had her official residential quarters carved out into plots, allotted it to her and gave a planning approval for the development of the plot. When the military struck in 1993, a review panel was set up to review all land allocations by the ousted civilian administration. The panel found that the allocation of the plot to the plaintiff and approval of the planning permit application were in contravention of the zoning policy of the area as it offends the maximum building space applicable to the Government Residential Area (GRA). The Governor ordered the demolition of the building. The plaintiff then brought the present action for damages and trespass. The action was dismissed.

8.3.3 Benefits of Zoning Policy Vis-a-Vis Environmental Protection

What then are the benefits of zoning policy vis-à-vis environmental protection? Without zoning no property owner can complain about encroachment on his property. For instance, in the case of *Oladehin v. Continental Textiles Mills*,[106] while construction work was going on in the plaintiff's land poisonous fumes and effluents escaped from the defendant's property and caused damages to the building materials in the plaintiff's land. The lower court found the defendant liable. This was upheld on appeal to the Supreme Court.

In *Ojo Eholor v. Idemudia Idahosa*,[107] the defendant in contravention of the planning regulation which required specific setbacks and offsets developed his property wall to wall. The roof from the building jolted into the plaintiff's compound and when it rained the plaintiff's compound was flooded causing damages therein. In the present action, the court held that the defendant's use of his land encroached on the plaintiff's and granted the relief sought.

Furthermore, without zoning policy, the concept of a material change in the use of land would never be applicable. To this end, landowners would not have been constrained by the courts to guide against altering the character of an area by changing its use or intensifying an approved use. Thus, in *M K O Abiola v. Felix Ijeoma*,[108] because the use to which the defendant subjected his land changed the character of the building and adjoining land, his act amounted to a material change in use. Based on this the planning authority (Lagos City Council) demolished the pens.

Moreover, without zoning no specific use might have been designated for a property. In this respect, where a developer in the course of developing a project

[105] Unreported, decided by the Anambra State High Court siting at Onitsha, in 1993.

[106] (1978) 2 SC, 23.

[107] (1992) 2 NWLR (pt 223), 327, see also Ige v. Taylor Woodrow (Nig) Ltd. ((1963) LLR 140.

[108] M K O Abiola (1970), see also the case of Tebite (1971).

used the land for the purpose in which it was not designated the offending project is usually ordered to be pulled down. In the case of *Anthony Savage and Anor v. Akinrinade*,[109] the defendant erected a store building along a public highway in Sureulere, Lagos, in contravention of the planning scheme of the area. The building blocked the only access road to the school in the neighbourhood. In an action by the residents of the area, the court ordered for demolition of the offending building.

Again, without planning law and the use of zoning policy exercise of individual rights as to the injury likely to be suffered as a result of encroachment would simply be subject to the general common law liabilities and all that it entails, usually to the detriment of other land users. For instance, in *Adediran & Ors v. Interland Transport Ltd.*[110] an action to restrain the defendants failed as the court disregarded the purpose of zoning policy under planning law and relied on the common law liability principle of public nuisance. The case failed because according to the court, the plaintiffs could not show that they suffered any wrongs over and above other residents of the area. The court disregarded the fact that the area was zoned as purely residential and that the activities of the defendants: parking of trucks, along the entrance to the estate, rattling of trucks day and night and the noise from the workers loading and off-loading cargo, among others, impinged on the plaintiffs use and enjoyment of their land.

The decision that a case may fail because the plaintiff could not show that he suffered any wrongs over and above other residents of the area,[111] although reared up again in the case of *Justice Peter Obiorah v. Helios Towers Nigeria Ltd,*[112] is no longer tenable. This is by virtue of the decision of the Nigerian Court of Appeal, Asaba Division in the above case. In that case, the respondent/defendant erected a big Collocation Base Transceiver Station (Mast) of above 35 meters height on Plot 1 Extract of Phase 1, Core Area Layout, GRA, Asaba, a high-brow low-density residential area. The appellant/plaintiff instituted an action against the respondent/defendant at a High Court in Asaba seeking reliefs and arguing that:

(i) The mast was unlawfully erected without necessary and appropriate approval from the Town Planning Authority of Delta State and contrary to Nigeria Communications Commission (NCC) Guidelines on Technical Specifications.
(ii) The noises and thick smoke from the power generating sets and other equipment installed by the respondent constitute a nuisance and interfere with the quiet enjoyment of his land and pose a health challenge and great danger to the lives of his family members who live in perpetual fear, anxiety and apprehension of death in the event of collapse of the illegal mast on them.

[109] (1964) ALL NLR, 238, see also Ademola v. Rutili (1985).

[110] (1991) 9 NWLR (pt 244), 155.

[111] That is undue reliance by courts on common law liabilities over and above statutory provisions in land use control.

[112] (Unreported) Suit No. CA/AS/573/2018, delivered by the Court of Appeal, Asaba Division on 25 March 2022 by Justices M O Bolaji-Yusuff, Justice Ekanem, and Obaseki-Adejumo, JJCA.

The trial High Court presided over by Justice T O Diai in its judgment delivered on 2 May 2018 agreed that the base station was erected without compliance with the NCC Guidelines or Town Planning Law of Delta State **but held that the case fell within the realm of public nuisance and that the claimant did not establish that he sustained any particular damage.**

Dissatisfied with the judgment, the appellant approached the Court of Appeal urging the appellate court to reverse the judgment of the High Court at Asaba. The Court of Appeal in its judgment delivered on 25 March 2022 by Justice M. O. Bolaji-Yusuff, JCA, in which Justice Ekanem and Obaseki-Adejumo, JJCA concurred, allowed the appeal and set aside the judgment of the High Court at Asaba delivered on 2 May 2018. The court declared that the location and erection of the respondent's Collocation Base Transceiver Station (Mast) on Plot 1 Extract of Phase 1, Core Area Layout, Asaba which is a residential area and adjacent to the compound of the appellant is unlawful and illegal and constitutes a nuisance to the appellant. **The court then directed the respondent (Helios Towers Nigeria Ltd) to dismantle, shut down, remove and stop the use and operation of the Collocation Base Transceiver Station (Mast) immediately**.

The purport of this case is that for a claimant to succeed in an action against contravention of zoning policy, contrary to the decision of Justice T. O. Diai, he need not establish that he suffered any particular damage by the action/activity of the defendant being complained of. Such a claimant may succeed in his action once he can show that the action or activity of a defendant being complained of was not only contrary to laid down guidelines and/or specifications set out by an appropriate authority but also constituted a nuisance. Overall, zoning sets to:

(i) Achieve purposeful utilisation of land in the interest or general welfare of the community to which the land situates and relates.[113]
(ii) Improve and protect man's environment from prodigious abuse.[114]
(iii) Attempt at a rational apportionment scheme among the various uses which often conflict with each other.[115]
(iv) Ensuring harmonious inter-relationship between those, often, competing land uses.[116]
(v) Controlling nuisance and protecting against damages to property of other land users due to wrong use.[117]
(vi) Relieves the environment from overcrowding, congestion, pollution and disease conditions which is always common in an unrestrained exercise over the right of property.

[113] See the following cases of Anthony Savage and anor (1964), Ojo Eholor (1992) and Ige v. Taylor Woodrow Nig. Ltd (1963) LLR 140.

[114] Ipadiola and anor (1987), M K O Abiola (1970), Justice Peter Obiorah v. Helios Towers Nigeria Ltd (2022).

[115] Abiola v. Ijeoma (1970) and Defactor Bakeries & Catering Services Ltd (1974).

[116] See Tebite v. Nigerian Marine & Trading Co (1971).

[117] Oladehin v. Continental Textiles Ltd (1978), 23.

(vii) Informs a land owner what to do with his or her land to have a decent and convenient environment to promote the health, safety morals or general welfare of the land users/owners.

Generally, zoning serves to prevent new development from harming existing residents or businesses or an activity of land use having an overbearing preponderance on another. In this way, planning ensures that the environment is protected from prodigious abuse. This may lead to the conclusion that planning decisions and environmental protection are intricately linked. As Thorton and Beckwith[118] put it:

> It is sometimes unclear where the dividing line is to be drawn between 'planning' and 'environmental' controls. What is clear, however, is that very often the purposes of the two regimes converge, so that 'environmental' issues must form part of planning policy and procedure.

Alluding further to the nexus between planning and environmental protection, the case of *California Coastal Commission v. Granite Rock Company*[119] is instructive. In that case, the court stated as follows:

> The line between environmental regulation and land-use planning will not always be bright, for example, one may hypothesize state environmental regulation so severe that a particular land use may become commercially impracticable. However; the core activity described by each phrase is undoubtedly difference. Land-use planning in essence chooses uses for the land; environmental regulation at its core, does not mandate particularly uses for the land, but requires only that, however, the land is used, damage to the environment is kept within prescribed limits.

Despite the above position, it is unclear why the Supreme Court of Nigeria per Umaru Atu Kalgo JSC in *Attorney General of Lagos State v. Attorney General of the Federation and 35 Ors*[120] asserted that the Nigerian Urban and Regional Planning Law was deliberately dealing with planning policy and development control and is not aimed at protecting or improving the environment as envisaged by Section 20 of the Constitution of the Federal Republic of Nigeria 1999 (CFRN 1999),[121] as amended. Section 20 of CFRN 1999 provides as follows: "the State shall protect and improve the environment and safeguard water, air and land, forests and wildlife of Nigeria."

It should be noted that environmental law encompasses all the laws within our legal system that are directed towards achieving an environmental end. To this end, since planning law, and the whole gamut of the planning system, are directed towards achieving an environmental end, it follows that planning law and regulations are integral parts of environmental law.[122] It has been pointed out that environmental protection and land use development are inextricably linked, an

---

[118] Thornton and Beckwith (2004), p. 355.

[119] (1987) 40 US 572.

[120] [2003] 35 WRN 1 at 179.

[121] Cap C23 LFN 2004.

[122] Onyeabor (2016), p. 82.

understanding of how the planning system works is vital to an appreciation of the specific environmental controls which it supplements.[123]

From all indications, there is a correlation between planning law and environmental protection. This is based on the fact that the basis of planning law is to control development whose essence is to improve and protect the environment. This position was recognised in the Declaration of the United Nations Conference on the Human Environment in Stockholm 1972.[124] For instance, Principle 13 of the Stockholm Declaration provides that, "in order to achieve a more rational management of resources and thus to improve the environment States should adopt an integrated and coordinated approach to their development planning."[125] Once an activity falls under any of the categories of development such activity shall not be commenced until a development or planning permit is first had and obtained from the appropriate Development Control Department (DCD).[126] In breach of this options against the developer include:

(i) an order for stop work and enforcement notices;[127] and
(ii) in extreme cases, an order for the demolition of the offending structure or building.[128]

The implication of the above options is that the developer shall be criminally liable where he fails to comply with the terms of an enforcement notice or disregards a stop-work order issued and served under the law. Such person shall be liable on conviction to a fine of not exceeding =N = 10,000, in the case of an individual and in the case of a corporate body to a fine not exceeding =N = 50,000.[129] Again, where notice for demolition is served and the developer fails to comply with such notice, he shall be liable for the cost of demolition if carried out by the planning authority.[130]

Furthermore, where a developer contravenes the provisions of the NURPA (1992) or any regulations made pursuant to it, the DCD shall have the power to require the developer to: prepare and submit his building plans for approval; or to carry out such alterations to a building as may be necessary to ensure compliance; or to pull down the building; or to re-instate a piece of land to the state in which it was before the commencement of building as required under Section 60 of the Act,[131] an

[123] Thornton and Beckwith (2004), p. 355.

[124] Held in Stockholm, Sweden between 5–16 June 1972, United Nations (1972).

[125] Stockholm Declaration (1972).

[126] NURPA (1992), ss. 28, 29, 30 and 33.

[127] NURPA (1992), ss. 47–60. See also THE Act of UK (1990), Part VII on enforcement.

[128] NURPA (1992), ss. 61–63, 70 and 71, see also the cases of Ikpadiola and anor (1987) 18, Chika Ibeneme (1993).

[129] Ibid., s. 59.

[130] Ibid., s. 63.

[131] NURPA (1992).

offence is committed.[132] To this end, a person guilty of an offence under Section 60 shall:

(a) on summary conviction be liable to imprisonment for a term not exceeding three months or to a fine not exceeding =N = 1000 or both such imprisonment and fine;
(b) on conviction on indictment be liable to imprisonment for a term not exceeding twelve months or to a fine not exceeding =N = 2000 or both such imprisonment and fine;
(c) in the case of a body corporate to a fine of =N = 5000;
(d) be liable to a fine not exceeding =N = 200 for every day the offence continues or to imprisonment for a term not exceeding one month.[133]

Finally, under Section 70 of the NURPA (1992) a person shall be guilty of an offence if he:

(a) executes or causes to be executed any work aimed at the demolition, alteration; or
(b) extension in any manner which changes the character of a listed building;[134] or
(c) fails to comply with any condition attached to a written consent of the DCD.

8.4 Land Use Regulations

Certain land use regulations form part of the instruments for land use control. Land use policies are part of planning schemes used to control the use of land. The idea of land use policies is intended to reduce overcrowding and congestion and have a more decent and convenient environment. The following are some of the land use policies that are applied by a planning authority.

8.4.1 Prescription of Minimum Land Area

The prescription of minimum plot size and the room dimensions for every type of building, whether in residential, commercial, industrial, mixed-use, educational, medical institutional or places of worship, is an important device for checking over-crowded in an urban neighbourhood. In the case of Lagos State, for instance, the maximum coverage area in respect of dwelling houses is 40%. However, in

[132] Ibid., s. 60.

[133] Ibid., s. 71.

[134] NURPA (1992), s. 64 empowers the Development Control Department to compile a list of buildings of special architectural or historical interest; these buildings shall under Section 67 of the Act be deposited with appropriate state or local government.

respect of commercial or industrial buildings, the maximum coverage is 70% while a petrol filing station of 45 × 45 metres is 35%.[135]

Disregarding the minimum land area may lead to the demolition of the offending structure. The case of *Chika Ibeneme v. Governor of Anambra State*[136] is instructive. In that case, the plaintiff was allocated a building in GRA, Onitsha where she lived as a commissioner during the civilian regime in 1993. During her tenure in office, she got the planning office to carve out and approve more than half of the compound in her name, which was in direct contravention of the minimum building space as well as the zoning policy of the area. When the military struck in November 1993, a panel was set up which found that the allocation was made in contravention of the planning scheme as well as the minimum building space. The Governor ordered a demolition, which was carried out. Her action for damages and trespass at the High Court, Onitsha was dismissed.

8.4.2 Developable Space

This is necessary for there to be adequate circulation of air in erecting any building. For instance, developable space ensures that residential plots are large enough to allow for the erection of residential buildings with good cross ventilation, light and privacy and for front and rear gardens. The space required for all these is a minimum of 25 meters for frontage and 50 metres depth. Areas marked as high-density development areas are 30 metres for frontage and 50 metres depth.

Therefore, no developer is allowed to encroach on the right of others such as building on a place proposed as open space to the detriment and annoyance of the land owners within the vicinity. In *Ademola v. Rutili & Ors*,[137] the defendant attempted to build a school on a piece of land zoned as an open space in the approved Victoria Island Scheme. The defendant was restrained on the ground that the purported development contravened what was approved in the scheme. The planning law empowers the planning authority to "remove," "pull down" or "alter" so as to bring into conformity with the provisions of the scheme.[138]

---

[135] Lagos State Town and Country Planning (Building Plan) Regulations 1986, s. 15(a)(b).
[136] Chika Ibeneme v. Governor of Anambra State (1993).
[137] Ademola v. Rutili (1985).
[138] NURPA (1992), s. 61.

8.4.3 *Building Line and General Setbacks*[139]

This generally refers to the distance from either side of a lot (front, back or side of a lot beyond which a construction or improvements may not extend without permission from the planning authorities. This means that a building should not be close to the road or public pathway.

A planning scheme or master plan indicates what a building line or setback is in relation to any building. The general limit between buildings in residential areas is at least six (6) metres. For commercial and industrial buildings, the setback is 9 metres. The right of way within a building for major roads should be a minimum of 60 to 80 meters and for minor roads 20 to 50 metres.[140] Building lines and general setbacks serve many purposes.

First, one of the essences of building lines is to avoid buildings encroaching upon roads and streets within a planning area, as the relevant planning scheme or master plan prescribes a building line in relation to buildings abutting streets or highways. Contravention of this provision may attract either sanction from the planning authority or a suit from other owners or occupiers of other buildings within the planning area. The case of *Ipadeola and Ibadan Metropolitan Planning Authority v. Abiodun*[141] alludes to this assertion. In that case, the appellant built a house in contravention of the building setback and blocked the respondent's view of the highway. The respondents sought a declaration in the High Court that the appellant's building was in contravention of the setback through the active connivance and support of the authority. Both the trial court, the Court of Appeal and the Supreme Court found the appellant guilty and ordered the demolition of the building.

Second, another purpose of building lines and setbacks is for the right to access light or air. This right is imposed by the planning scheme or master plan. For instance, in Lagos State, the general air space permissible in relation to residential buildings has been fixed at a distance of not less than six (6) metres at the front line and in the case of commercial or industrial buildings at a distance of not less than nine or ten meters on the sides and rear.[142] This right restricts the owner of a building not to unreasonably block off light or air to the detriment of an adjoining tenement or building as a result of over-development or ignoring this planning policy, that is, building line and setback.

Contravention may either attract sanctions by the planning authority or legal action from owners or occupiers of other tenements within the planning scheme. For

---

[139] For appropriate setbacks from the road in Nigeria, see Opera news online https://www.operanewsapp.com/ng/en/share/detail?news_id=6fd5cef56fe9bb1227305beec373c8a5&news_entry_id=s688e12b5211226en_ng&open_type=transcoded&from=news&request_id=share_reques (accessed on 17 August 2023).

[140] Lagos State Town and Country Planning (Building Plan) Regulations 1986, s. 15(a)(b).

[141] Ipadeola and Ibadan Metropolitan Planning Authority v. Abiodun (1987) 18.

[142] Lagos State Town and Country Planning (Building Plan) Regulations 1986, s. 15(a)(b).

instance, in the case of *Bryant v. Leefever,*[143] the court believed that a right of way by having access to air over the general unlimited surface of a neighbour's land cannot be acquired as mere enjoyment. In the case of *Defacto Bakeries and Catering Services Limited v. Ajilore,*[144] the plaintiffs/appellants had overdeveloped their plot. As a result of this contravention of the approved scheme, there was no airspace left between the defendant's property and that of the plaintiffs'. The Supreme Court held that the appellant's house was in contravention of the planning regulation and must be demolished. In the case of *Ipadiola and Anor v. Oshowole and Anor,*[145] the issue was on the right of way. In that case, the defendant built a house in front of the plaintiff's house which blocked the plaintiff's access to the highway and obstructed the easement of light. The court ordered the defendant to conform with the provisions of the planning scheme.

It should be noted that the planning policy of building lines and general setbacks may appear to be similar to the common law principle of easement, the former is a bit different from the latter. While building lines and general setbacks are a creation of law and imposed on a developer, easement, on the other hand, is a right attached to land which allows the land owner (referred to as the dominant owner) either to use the land of another person (known as the servient owner) in a particular way or to restrict its user by that other person to a particular extent but does not allow him to take any part of its natural produce or its soil.[146]

Easement is also a right annexed to one piece of land exercisable over the land of another and capable of being the subject matter of a grant.[147] These rights may be right of way as in the case of *Wheeldon v. Burrow*[148] or right to access to light as in the case of *Colls v. Home & Colonial Stores Ltd.*[149] The right of easement may be either positive or negative easements. Positive easement involves the right to use the land of another person in a rightful and lawful manner. In the case of *Okunzua v. Amisu* and *Anor,*[150] the court reiterated that easement generally confers rights inclusive and not exclusive to its owner and not proprietary rights of the owner of the land.[151] In that case, the appellant argues that under an oral agreement between him and the 2nd respondent, the 1st respondent had been excluded from the use of a driveway thereby creating an easement that only favours the appellant. The Supreme

[143] (1879) 4 CPD, 170.

[144] Defacto Bakeries and Catering Services Limited v. Ajilore (1974), 385, see also Savage v. Akinrinade (1964) 238.

[145] (1987) 5SC 376 at 389.

[146] Manning v. Wasdale ER vol. iii, 1353.

[147] As against the land use policy of building lines and setbacks that restrict the owner of a building not to unreasonably block off light or air to the detriment of an adjoining tenement or building because of over-development or ignoring this planning policy. This is a right imposed by law rather than being granted by the other landowner.

[148] (1878) 12 CH, 31.

[149] (1904) AC 179.

[150] (1992) 6NWLR (pt. 48) 417 at 436–437.

[151] Ibid.

Court in dismissing the appeal held, inter alia, that where a person claims the right to the exclusive and restrictive use of a piece of land, it is not an easement.

The following conditions as laid down by the court in *Re Ellenborough Park*[152] must be fulfilled for there to be an easement:

(i) A tenement must be in existence over which the easement is exercisable. This means that there must be a servient tenement and another tenement before any easement is said to exist. Also, a person seeking to enforce a right in easement must have land to be benefited from as the law does not recognise an easement in gross; it must have a link or attached to a land.[153]

(ii) An easement must benefit the dominant tenement. There should be a direct link between the enjoyment of the right and the user of the dominant tenement such as where a residential house being the dominant tenement has annexed to it by express grant a right to use an adjoining garden for purposes of relaxation and pleasure. But if the easement is not beneficial to the land owner but rather the land is acquired for the exploitation of the right, there is no easement but a mere license.[154]

(iii) The dominant and servient tenements must be owned by different persons. Therefore, where a person owns two adjoining but separate proprieties, any rights exercised over one or other of them are not easements because they derive from his ownership not of the quasi-dominant land but of the quasi-servient land itself.[155]

(iv) The right claimed as an easement must be capable of being the subject of a grant. The nature and extent of a claim must show the exact description and its sphere of operation must be precise and certain.

(v) If any rights exhibit these four characteristics the right is treated as an easement that will run with the dominant land owner against the servient land owner even though its aim may be enforceable between the parties who created it but cannot be enforceable by or against any third party or parties.

8.4.4 Provision of Drainage and Waste Disposal System

Every scheme or master plan provides that a building should have toilets, and bathrooms with appropriate soak-away pits and drainage systems. This was first initiated by the various Public Health Acts as a means of preventing waste and effluent from being discharged into open spaces and streets.[156] The operation of the device eliminates the lodgement of waste matters in our urban communities.

---

[152] (1956) CH 131.

[153] Rangelly v. Midland Railway Corporation, 3CH. App, 306 at 311.

[154] Hill v. Tupper E.R vol. 159, 5.

[155] Bolton v. Bolton (1879) 11Ch 968.

[156] Public Health Act 1917, s. 19(1).

8.4.5 Issue of Ventilation

Under the Building Code 2006[157] ventilation means "the natural or mechanical process of supplying conditioned or unconditioned air to, or removing stale or foul air from any space." Ventilation is the act of allowing fresh air to enter a building. It is the policy of the government that every dwelling house should be properly ventilated. Accordingly, every dwelling house must have ventilation for natural lighting through window openings directing to the external air and doors.[158]

8.5 Mechanisms for Development Control

There are various means provided under the NURPA (1992), in which development control strategies may be employed. These mechanisms are strategies for controlling development to ensure stability in planning and land use. The discussions on mechanisms for development control sought to answer the following questions:

(a) What is development control?
(b) Who controls development?
(c) How is development control achieved?

8.5.1 What Is Development Control?

This is the control of the use of land, character, appearance and arrangement of buildings and facilities to ensure economy, convenience and aesthetics. Development control involves the regulation of the detailed aspect of physical development about which precise guidance cannot be given in the master plan, layout or local plan. To this extent, development control is the formal voice of the planning authority regarding such matters as permitted density, height limitation, users' restriction, assets, preservation, conservation, etc. It can therefore be said that development control in planning and land use control is an instrument of overall environmental quality control since development control sets the standards and regulations guiding the bulk and use of the structures as well as the air space around buildings.[159]

[157] Nigerian Building Code 2006, s. 2.120.
[158] Lagos State Town and Country Planning (Building Plan) Regulation 1986, ss. 2(1)(k), 27(11)(9).
[159] Onyeabor (2016), p. 77.

8.5.2 Who Controls Development?

Section 27 of the NURPA (1992) provides for the establishment and jurisdiction of the Development Control Department (DCD) to be established at the various Planning Control levels. Such Control Department shall be a multi-disciplinary department charged with the responsibility for matters relating to development control and implementation of physical development plans.[160] To this end, the Development Control Department at the federal level shall have power over the development control of federal lands and estates,[161] the Development Control Department at the state level shall have power over the development control on state lands[162] and the Development Control Department at the local government level shall have power over the control of development on all land within the jurisdiction of the local government.[163]

8.5.3 How Is Development Control Achieved?

To appreciate how the DCD controls development, recourse is had to the various powers and functions of the DCD as provided under Sections 28–85 of the NURP Act 1992. Generally, the functions and powers of the DCD can broadly be segregated into three (3) broad heads:

(a) Issuance of development permits and other issues thereto for land use.
(b) Monitoring of conditions contained thereto in the permit granted.
(c) Enforcement of breaches of conditions.

8.5.3.1 Issuance of Development Permit

Section 30 of the NURP Act 1992 provides that no development shall commence without a permit granted for that purpose. To this end, there must be approval by the DCD for any land development.[164] This also extends to any development to be undertaken by the government or its agencies.[165] According to Section 30 (1), a developer (whether private or government) shall apply for a development permit in such manner using such forms and providing such information including:

---

[160] NURPA (1992), s. 27(2).
[161] Ibid., s. 27(3).
[162] Ibid., s. 27(4).
[163] Ibid., s. 27(5).
[164] NURPA (1992), s. 28(1).
[165] Ibid., s. 29.

(i) Plans
(ii) Designs
(iii) Drawings
(iv) Any other information as may be prescribed by regulation made under this section

Under this provision, any plan required to be made shall be prepared by a registered architect, town planner or engineer.[166] At the time of submitting the application for development in the case of:

(i) Residential land in excess of 2 hectares; or
(ii) Permission to build or expand a factory or for the construction of an office building in excess of four floors or 5000 m^2 of a lettable space; or
(iii) Permission for a major recreational development.

A developer, according to Section 33 of the Act, shall submit to an appropriate DCD a detailed environmental impact statement.

A plan, once submitted, may be rejected or approved by the DCD.[167] The Act sets out grounds for rejection of an application[168] and the circumstances under which the DCD may delay the approval of an application for a development permit.[169] A DCD may, subject to such directives as may be given by the federal, state or local government, delay the approval of an application for a development permit for a period not exceeding three months.[170] The reason for the delay in the decision for the application shall be communicated to the applicant in writing.[171] The refusal or rejection of an application for a development permit shall not confer on a developer any legal or other rights until it has been communicated to the applicant in writing.[172] Where the DCD decides not to approve an application, it shall give reasons for its decision[173] and that decision shall be conclusive evidence of information stated therein.[174]

8.5.3.2 Monitoring of Conditions Attached to a Permit

This is the second aspect in the control of development. Once a permit is granted and is subsisting, the DCD shall enforce all the conditions attached to the permit against

[166] Ibid., s. 30(3).
[167] Ibid., s. 34(1).
[168] Ibid., s. 31.
[169] NURPA (1992), s. 34(2).
[170] Ibid., s. 34(4).
[171] Ibid., s. 34(5).
[172] Ibid., s. 34(8).
[173] Ibid., s. 34(5).
[174] Ibid., s. 34(7).

the developer.[175] Section 35 (2) (a) of the Act provides that a development permit granted to a developer shall remain valid for two years from the date of communication of the approval of such permit to a developer. Where a developer fails to commence development within two years the permit shall be subject to re-validation by the DCD which issued the original permit.[176]

It should be noted that the conditions attached to the grant of a development permit by a DCD must not conflict with the conditions attached to a grant of a certificate of occupancy or a customary right of occupancy.[177] However, such conditions attached to the grant of a development permit may be altered, amended, varied or revoked by the DCD but it shall serve a notice of its intention on the holder for the time being of a development.[178] This notice, according to Section 37 (2) of the Act, shall state the reasons for the proposed action of the DCD. The DCD must consider any representation made to it by the developer or holder of the development permit.[179] Its decision must be communicated in writing to them.[180] A dissatisfied developer or holder of the development permit, according to Section 38 of the NURP Act 1992, may appeal to a tribunal set up to hear appeals within 28 days of service of a notice by the DCD.

The DCD may revoke a permit already granted and communicated to a developer or holder of a development permit where it can be observed that the grantee or a holder of the permit is developing contrary to the conditions attached to the permit or contrary to the land use policy of the area. To this effect, it shall serve a notice of its intention to revoke the development permit, state reasons for the revocation of the development permit on the notice and consider any representation made by a developer to it.[181] In revoking a development permit, the DCD shall have regard to all matters and conditions specified by the provisions of the NURPA (1992) before granting a development permit and shall take into account matters of overriding public interest as provided for in Section 28 (2), (3) of the Land Use Act 1978.[182] An appeal against this decision of the DCD shall lie in the first instance to the Minister or Commissioner charged with responsibilities for matters relating to planning.[183] An appeal against the decision of the Minister or Commissioner shall be to a tribunal set up to hear appeals within 28 days of service of a notice by a DCD.[184]

Upon revocation of a development permit, compensation shall be payable to a developer or the holder of the permit for the time being if:

---

[175] Ibid., s. 35(1).

[176] Ibid., s. 35(2)(b).

[177] Ibid., s. 36.

[178] Ibid., s. 37(1).

[179] Ibid., s. 37(3).

[180] Ibid., s. 37(4).

[181] NURPA (1992), s. 39.

[182] Ibid., s. 41.

[183] Ibid., s. 40(1).

[184] Ibid., s. 40(2).

(a) Development has commenced; or
(b) The developer or holder is liable under an existing contract to a third party for damages for a breach of contract; or
(c) The developer has incurred any expense or has suffered a loss during the process of obtaining the development permit.[185]

This compensation payable shall be to reimburse the developer or holder of the development permit for the losses incurred because of the revocation. It is not in the form of payment of damages or in excess of the sum incurred by the developer.[186] However, there are grounds upon which compensation is not payable. These grounds are where:

(a) A development is not in accordance with the terms and conditions under which the development permit was granted; or
(b) The right of occupancy of the land on which development was to take place has been cancelled or revoked on the ground that the applicant did not comply with the requirements of the Land Use Act 1978;[187] or
(c) A compensation claim is made 28 days after a notice of revocation is served on the developer or the holder for the time being of a development permit.[188]

Where compensation is to be paid, it shall not be paid later than 90 days after the compensation claim has been made.[189] In the event of a dispute arising as to the amount of compensation payable to a developer, the dispute may be referred to a Planning Tribunal.[190] An appeal against the decision of the Planning Tribunal in respect of an amount payable to a developer shall lie as of right to the High Court in the State or the Federal Capital Territory, Abuja, as the case may be.[191]

8.5.3.3 Enforcement of Breaches and Conditions

Besides revocation of a development permit granted to a development, the DCD may while monitoring how development is taking place finds out that a developer has derailed from the conditions attached to a permit or is in breach of such conditions, he may be called to order by the DCD through any of the following ways:

[185] Ibid., s. 42.
[186] Ibid., s. 43(1).
[187] Cap L 4 LFN 2004.
[188] NURPA (1992), s. 43(2).
[189] Ibid., s. 44.
[190] Ibid., s. 45. Planning Tribunal is established pursuant to NURPA (1992), s. 85.
[191] Ibid., s. 46.

8.5.3.3.1 Service of Enforcement Notice

The service of an enforcement notice as provided under Section 47 of the Act may be made on a developer where he has commenced development without approval. An enforcement notice may require a developer to alter, remove or discontinue a development to ensure that the development becomes a lawful development or becomes compatible with the use for which an adjoining land has been put.[192] The DCD may impose additional conditions as it may deem fit in each circumstance.[193]

However, under Section 48 (3) of the Act,[194] before the enforcement notice is issued or served, the DCD shall have regard to the existing conditions for granting a development permit; the likely environmental degradation or impact of a development carried out or being carried out, and; consider the over-riding public interest without prejudice to the likely environmental degradation or impact of a development carried out or being carried out. Such enforcement notice should be in writing and communicated to the developer and it shall state the reasons for the proposed action of the DCD as well as consider any representation made by a developer or on behalf of a developer.[195]

The DCD or its authorised agent shall enforce an order of the Planning Tribunal or High Court against a developer or holder of a devilment permit who fails to comply with such an order.[196] In enforcing this, the developer or holder of the development permit is liable for all expenses reasonably incurred by the DCD or any of its officers or agents, as the case may be.[197]

8.5.3.3.2 Issuance of Stop-Work Order

Where it appears to the DCD that an unauthorised development is being carried out or where the development does not comply with a development permit issued by the DCD, the DCD issues a stop-work order pending the service of an enforcement notice on the owner, occupier or holder as specified in Section 50 of the NURP Act 1992 provided that where the development is a minor development or use, the DCD shall have the power to order the developer to alter, remove or discontinue the development or use without reference of the matter to a court of law.[198] This stop-work order, under Section 55 of the Act[199] shall also inform the developer or

[192] Ibid., s. 50(2).
[193] Ibid., s. 48(2).
[194] NURPA (1992).
[195] NURPA (1992), s. 50(1).
[196] Ibid., s. 51.
[197] Ibid., s. 52.
[198] Ibid., s. 53.
[199] NURPA (1992).

occupier of the development that is required to be stopped and the work to be done on the site to conform to the development permit issued thereto.

A stop-work order shall take immediate effect upon service on a developer or the occupier of the development for the time being. The DCD shall give a reasonable time not exceeding 21 days within which the developer shall be required to comply with the stop-work order.[200]

However, a stop-work order shall cease to have effect if within 21 days of its issue, the enforcement notice is not served on a developer.[201] Under Section 58 of the Act,[202] where an enforcement notice is served in respect of a development in which a stop-work order is served, a Planning Tribunal may on the application of the DCD extend the period during which a stop-work order shall remain in force.

A person who fails to comply with the terms of an enforcement notice or disregards a stop-work order issued and served is guilty of an offence and liable on conviction to a fine not exceeding ₦10,000 in the case of an individual and in the case of a corporate body, to a fine not exceeding ₦50,000.[203]

8.5.3.3.3 Issuance of Contravention Notice

Where a developer contravenes the provisions of a planning law or any regulation made pursuant to a law, Section 60 of the Act[204] provides that the DCD shall have the power to require the developer to:

(a) prepare and submit his building plan for approval; or
(b) carry out such alterations to a building as may be necessary to ensure compliance; or
(c) pull down the building; or
(d) reinstate a piece of land to the state in which it was before the commencement of building.

8.5.3.3.4 Revocation of Certificate of Occupancy

Another means through which enforcement of breaches against a developer may be effected is by revocation of the certificate of occupancy to which the land relates. Upon recommendation of the appropriate authority, any right of occupancy subsisting on a land shall be revoked where it appears to the National Urban and Regional Planning Commission (the Commission), the State Urban and Regional

---

[200] Ibid., s. 54.
[201] Ibid., s. 57.
[202] NURPA (1992).
[203] NURPA (1992), s. 59.
[204] NURPA (1992).

Planning Board (the Board) or the Local Planning Authority (the Authority) that it is necessary to obtain any land in connection with planned urban or rural development following the policies and proposals of any approved plan.[205] However, Section 75 (2) of the NURPA (1992) provides that any right of occupancy held in pursuance of subsection (1) above shall be revoked following the relevant provisions of the Land Use Act 1978.

However, Section 75 of the NURPA (1992) is a limitation on the right of the DCD or the Commission, Board or Authority to revoke a right of occupancy. Section 75 (2) of the NURP Act 1992 provides that revocation should be under the relevant provisions of the Land Use Act. This suffices that the revocation is not automatic but that the provisions of Section 28 and Section 6 (3) of the Land Use Act which relates to revocation of a right of occupancy are to be followed.

8.5.3.3.5 Demolition of the Offending Structure

This is another means through which the DCD carries out development control. Accordingly, if a structure erected by a developer is found to be defective as to pose danger or constitute a nuisance to the occupier and the public, the DCD shall have the power to serve on the developer a demolition notice. This notice shall contain a date not later than 21 days on which the DCD shall take steps to commence demolition action on the defective structure.[206]

After the expiration of the time specified in the demolition notice served, the DCD shall take such necessary action to effect the demolition of the defective structure.[207] A developer shall reimburse the DCD for the expenses incurred reasonably in the exercise of its powers of demolishing the structure.[208]

8.6 Land Use Control and Rights of a Developer[209]

It should be noted that the NURP Act 1992 did not create a leviathan against a developer in establishing the Development Control Department. Thus, while exercising its powers in the issuance of a development permit, a developer is protected by the following provisions of the NURPA (1992).

[205] Ibid., s. 75(1).

[206] NURPA (1992), s. 61.

[207] Ibid., s. 62.

[208] Ibid., s. 63.

[209] See generally the Act of UK (1990), Part VI.

(a) Section 32 of NURPA (1992) provides that the DCD may consider representations made to it by a person, body or organisation to be affected by an intended development.
(b) Section 34 of the Act sets out a time limit of three months as the maximum period for which the DCD may delay approval of an application for a development permit.
(c) Where the DCD is to communicate its decision after the delay, it should be in writing according to Section 34 (5) of the NURPA (1992), and where it does not approve an application, it shall give reasons for its decision under Section 34 (6) of the NURP Act.
(d) Where the DCD decides to alter, vary or amend conditions attached to a development permit, Section 38 of the NURPA (1992) provides for a right of appeal.
(e) Section 40 of the NURPA (1992) provides for an appeal against the decision of the DCD to revoke a development permit
(f) Where the development permit is finally revoked, Section 42 of the NURPA (1992) sets out the grounds on which compensation is payable and Section 43 (2) of the NURP Act 1992 sets out the grounds upon which compensation is not payable. Thus, anything outside this box will amount to contravention of the Act.[210]
(g) Where there is an agreement for compensation, Section 44 of the NURPA (1992) provides for a time limit of 90 days.
(h) In the event of any dispute as to the amount of compensation payable to a developer, Section 45 of the NURPA (1992) provides that the dispute may be referred to a Planning Tribunal and further appeal shall lie as of right to the High Court of a State or the Federal Capital Territory (FCT) according to Section 46 of the NURPA (1992).
(i) According to Section 50 (1) of the NURPA (1992), the enforcement notice should be in writing and communicated to the developer, it shall state the reasons for the proposed action of the DCD and consider any representation made by a developer or on behalf of a developer.

Under Section 54 of the NURPA (1992), a stop-work order shall take immediate effect upon service on a developer or the occupier of the development for the time being. However, the DCD shall give a reasonable time not exceeding 21 days within which the developer shall be required to comply with the stop-work order.

[210] NURP Act 1992.

8.7 Summary

All development is earthbound and land upon which such developmental activities take place is scarce, limited in supply and relatively fixed in quantity, and in the face of unbridled population growth, rapid urbanisation and industrialisation, the land is readily been depleted. Two other factors also compound these problems of land. First, a man by his gregarious nature may want to utilise his land in any way he may deem fit, unrestrained, unchallenged and undisturbed. Second, it is a notorious fact that land which makes up only 30% of the Earth's entire surface is not only fixed but is also currently under serious threats from the vagaries of weather and climate, which unfortunately is attributed to human activities through exploitation and usage of natural resources found on land. Where this unpleasant situation is allowed to continue, especially allowing humans to develop land unrestrained, will affect the value of land in the long run, thus the need for land use control. The reason for this is that rational planning is a crucial instrument for resolving any conflict between development needs and the need to protect and improve the environment

Planning law was therefore enacted for land use control to create a benign, friendly and aesthetically pleasing environment. The law requires that all developmental activities that may have significant environmental impact shall not be commenced except where such a developer has obtained a planning permit from the appropriate planning authority. What this portends is that once an activity is considered to be development, it shall not be commenced until a development permit is first had and obtained from the appropriate town planning authority. Thus, in engaging in land use and land use control, the concept of development must be first addressed. Once this is done, under the various planning laws no spatial development shall be commenced without approval of the appropriate planning authority.

A planning authority employs various mechanisms to control spatial development and therefore land use. These mechanisms include: the issuance of development/planning permits; enforcement of various land use regulations prescription of a minimum land area such as: developable space; building line and general setbacks; provision of drainage and waste disposal system; and issue of ventilation, issuance of development permits and other issues thereto for land use, monitoring of conditions contained thereto in the permit granted, enforcement of breaches of conditions and service of enforcement notice such as: issuance of stop-work order; issuance of contravention notice; revocation of certificate of occupancy and in extreme cases demolition of the offending structure.

Taken together, the whole gamut of the planning land use control is directed towards achieving an environmental end. Again, the devices discussed under planning and land use policy impose minimum standards for the erection of buildings that are considered to be consistent with public safety as well as to ameliorate the environmental impairment otherwise inherent in the uncontrolled right of a land owner to build in the way he likes thereby helping in environmental protection. It has been pointed out that environmental protection and land use development are inextricably linked. To this end, an understanding of how the planning system works is vital to an appreciation of the specific environmental controls to which it supplements.

References

Bell S, McGillivray D (2006) Ball and bell on environmental law: the law and policy relating to the protection of the environment, 6th edn. Blackstone, London

Duxbury RMC (1999) Telling and Duxbury's Planning Law and Procedure, 11th edn. Butterworths, London, http://www.landuse2/cdweb/glossary/htm/#Environment. Accessed 30 Apr 2019

Glickman EA (2014) An Introduction to Real Estate Finance. https://www.sciencedirect.com/topics/social-sciences/zoning-plan. Accessed 7 Aug 2023

Onyeabor EU (2016) Fundamentals of planning law in Nigeria, Lambert Academic, Saarbrucken, Germany, ISBN 978-3-659-95317-0, September 2016

Organisation of American States (2023) The importance of Development Plans/Land Use Policy for Development. https://www.oas.org/pgdm/document/BITC/papers/dthomas.htm#:~:text=Land%20use%20planning%20refers%20to,creation%20of%20sustainable%20human%20settlements. Accessed 7 Aug 2023

Rodrigue JP (2020) The geography of transportation system, 5th edn. Routledge, New York. ISBN 978-0-367-36463-2. https://doi.org/10.4324/9780429346323

Rostron J (2001) Environmental law for built environment, 1st edn. Cavendish, London

Royal Town Planning Institute (RTPI) (2004) Mediation of space-making of place. RPTI, London

The World Bank (2015) Zoning and land use planning. https://urban-regeneration.worldbank.org/. Accessed 7 Aug 2023

Thornton J, Beckwith S (2004) Environmental law, 2nd edn. Sweet and Maxwell, London

United Nations (1972) Declaration of the United Nations Conference on the Human Environment in Stockholm 1972 https://sustainabledevelopment.un.org/milestones/humanenvironment. Accessed 12 May 2023

United States Environmental Protection Agency (EPA) (2023) What are the trends in land use and their effects on human health and the environment? https://www.epa.gov/report-environment/land-use#. Accessed 7 Aug 2023

Van der Berg A (2019) Can South African planning law and policy promote Urban sustainability in the anthropocene? In: Lim M (ed) Charting environmental law futures in the anthropocene. Springer, Singapore. https://doi.org/10.1007/978-981-13-9065-4_18

Chapter 9
Waste Management Strategies

Abstract Waste is a significant environmental issue on a global scale, and it is closely related to human growth on all fronts, socially, economically, and technologically. The composition of various wastes has changed over time and location, with waste products being directly related to industrial development and innovation. This chapter discusses the concept of waste, waste sources, solid waste, its nature and environmental impact, electrical/electronic waste (e-waste), including the concept of why e-waste is an environmental and health problem, trending options in e-waste management, and how hazardous waste can be controlled through the use of legal instruments. The focus is on the use of both international and national legal instruments in the management of waste, especially the hazardous types.

9.1 Concept of Waste

Waste is often referred to as rubbish, trash, garbage or junk, depending upon the type of material and the regional terminology. But in living organisms, waste relates to unwanted substances or toxins that are expelled from them.[1] In other words, waste may be regarded as an unwanted or undesired material, substance or object. According to the European Union Waste Framework Directive (WFD) 2008[2] waste is defined as "an object the holder discards, intends to discard or is required to discard."[3]

To understand the nature of waste, recourse is had to the definition of waste provided under the WFD. Under that definition, the key component in answering the question of when a substance or object becomes waste lies in the word "discard." The key term "discard" in that definition is used in three alternatives: any substance or object, which, (a) the holder discards, (b) intends or (c) is required to discard. This definition is in *pari materia* with Article 2(1) of the Basel Convention on the Control

[1] Colbert (2004), pp. 26–27.

[2] European Union (2018) (WFD 2008).

[3] This is the working definition of "waste" adopted in this book.

E. Onyeabor, *Environmental Law*, https://doi.org/10.1007/978-3-031-68956-7_9

of Transboundary Movements of Hazardous Wastes and their Disposal (Basel Convention) 1989 which provides that "Wastes are substances or objects which are disposed of or are intended to be disposed of or are required to be disposed of by the provisions of national law." thus, this definition shall be the working definition of waste in this book.

The fulcrum upon which the definition hinges is the issue of "discard." Discard here has a special meaning which is not necessarily the same as its dictionary meaning. It includes not only the disposal of a substance or object but also its recovery or recycling.[4] The decision on whether something is discarded or not must take into account all the circumstances at the material time the discarding was done. This means that every case must be assessed on its merits to determine when a substance or object has become waste and when wastes should be considered to have ceased to be waste.

9.1.1 When Can It Be Said That a Substance or Object Has Been Discarded

A general test for determining when a substance or object is to be regarded as waste or not revolves around this issue: whether the substance or object in question has been discarded by its holder. Discard describes an action or activity[5] of the holder of the substance or the object, which can involve a positive, neutral, or negative commercial value. A holder may discard a substance or object for a variety of reasons: it may be intentional or accidental, it may be voluntary or required and it may even occur without the holder's realising it.[6]

The dictionary definition of discard is to get rid of something as useless or unwanted.[7] That definition covers disposal operations but not recovery operations where waste is put to some use. In the case of *ARCO Chemie Nederland Ltd v. Minister van Volkshuisvesting, Ruimtelijke Ordening en Milieubeheer et al. (ARCO Chemie),*[8] the European Court of Justice (ECJ) considered that waste in the form of wood which was impregnated with toxic substances did not lose its classification as waste when it was transformed into chips or those chips were reduced to wood powder since it did not purge the wood of the toxic substances. The court held, inter alia, that to determine whether the use of a substance such as LUWA bottoms as a fuel is to be regarded as constituting discarding, it is irrelevant

[4]Department for Environment, Food and Rural Affairs (Defra) (2012), p. 15.

[5]For example, (a) an item is thrown into a waste bin, (b) a company transfers material to a waste collector.

[6]The Director-General European Union Directorate-General Environment (2008), p. 11.

[7]Merriam-Webster Dictionary (2019).

[8]ARCO Chemie case (2000) Joined Cases C- 418/97 and C-419/97 delivered by the European Court of Justice on 15 June 2000, para 96.

that that substance may be recovered in an environmentally responsible manner for use as fuel without substantial treatment. Thus,

> The fact that a substance used as fuel is the residue of the manufacturing process of another substance, that no use for that substance other than disposal can be envisaged, that the composition of the substance is not suitable for the use made of it or that special environmental precautions must be taken when it is used may be regarded as evidence that the holder has discarded that substance or intends or is required to discard it.[9]

Therefore, a person may be regarded as discarding a substance or object if he is carrying out a recycling or other recovery operation in the course of his business even though the substance or object has a commercial value to them.[10] And it makes no difference whether a disposal or recovery operation is carried out by the person who produced the waste or someone else. In both cases, the substance or object will be "discarded" and will be waste.[11]

The next question is when a substance or object is to be classified as waste if the holder intends to discard that substance or object. Here, the state of mind of the holder is not the key as the holder's intention is to be inferred from his actions. For instance, (a) in its decommissioning plan in the event of future closure, an operating site indicates that it will send off-site for appropriate disposal or recovery any of its stock of raw materials that cannot be returned, (b) the holder of leftover quarried stone which has been stored for an indefinite length of time to await possible use discards or intends to discard that leftover stone. The third alternative, required to discard imposes a legal obligation to perform the act. Thus, the requirement to discard arises where there is an imposition of the law to do so.[12]

9.1.2 *When Then Does a Substance or Object Become a Waste?*

The following criteria had been set out by the Department for Environment, Food and Rural Affairs (Defra), UK[13] to help with this assessment:

On the first issue: Has the substance or object become waste criteria? The following questions are posed:

Q.1: Is the substance or object produced with the intention that it will be used or marketed or is it being reused for the same purpose for which it was originally conceived? If the answer to either of these questions is "yes" then it is likely that the substance or object is not waste.

---

[9] ARCO Chemie case (2000), para 47.

[10] ARCO Chemie case (2000), para 96.

[11] Ibid.

[12] Defra (2012), p. 15.

[13] Ibid., 16–23.

Q.2: Is the substance or object a by-product of a production process? If a substance or object is a by-product it is not waste. If the answer "yes" can be given to all of the following four questions, this will help indicate that a residue is a by-product and not waste:

i) Is further use of the substance or object not just a possibility but a certainty?
ii) Can it be used directly, without any further processing before its use?
iii) Has it been produced as an integral part of a production process?
iv) Is its further use lawful in the sense that:

- it fulfils all relevant product, environmental and health requirements for the specific use to be made of it; and
- it will not have an adverse impact on the environment or human health.

The answers to the following questions are likely to help decide whether the four basic conditions for classification as a by-product have been met:

- Is the substance or object fully suitable for the proposed use?
- Can it be used without any special precautions being taken to ensure the protection of the environment or human health?
- Is there a genuine market for it?
- Is it free of any contaminants that could have an adverse effect on its use?
- Can it be used without any additional risk to the environment or human health, when compared with an equivalent raw material?

Q.3: Does the substance or object need to be disposed of?

A substance or object might have to be disposed of because of a legal requirement (e.g. mercury or some animal by-products). It might also have to be disposed of because of its condition or its continued use might be dangerous (e.g. some out-of-date medicines). If so, it is waste.

Q.4: Has the substance or object been transferred to a disposal or recovery operation? If a substance or object is sent on for disposal or recovery that will indicate that it is waste. It is sometimes difficult to tell what a "recovery operation" is and what just the normal use of a product is. For example, "use as a fuel" could be either, depending on the circumstances. However, if a particular operation is generally accepted as being a common way of recovering waste, that may indicate that it is a recovery operation.

Q.5: Does the substance or object have a low economic value? If the substance or object has a low or negative economic value, this points to its being waste since it is a burden on the producer or holder who then may have an incentive to get rid of it; although it does not follow that a substance or object with a good economic value to the producer is not a waste.

Q.6: Is the substance or object hazardous or polluting? Wastes can be quite harmless in themselves, and they may be processed without harmful impacts on the environment. On the other hand, some non-waste products are polluting or hazardous (e.g. poisonous chemicals). So this question of harm is not always relevant to the issue of whether something is waste. The question does become relevant where the substance or object has become or is contaminated, is leftover, unwanted, or a burden on its holder. It is also relevant when a substance or object has become contaminated with something that presents a risk. In these circumstances, the hazardous or polluting nature of the substance or object can indicate that it is waste.

Q.7: Is the substance or object still suitable for its use? Substances or objects that can no longer be used for their original purpose (e.g. because they are out-of-date) or have become damaged or unsuitable for use are likely to be waste.

Q.8: Is the substance or object being passed on as second-hand goods? A substance or object may be unwanted by one owner, but it is passed on to be used for its original purpose without needing any processing or treatment. If so, it is generally not waste.

On the second issue: when the substance or object ceases to be waste criteria, the following questions are relevant:

Q.9: Has the waste only been pre-treated, rather than fully recovered or recycled? If waste has gone through one treatment but needs further treatment before being ready for reuse, this will indicate that it has not ceased to be waste. Sorting and size reduction often fall into this category.

Q.10: Have all unwanted substances been removed from the waste? Often, waste is contaminated because of its origins or previous use. It will not cease to be waste until the contamination is removed – either so that it can be used again for its original purpose or made into a new product.

Q.11: Is recovered/recycled material fully suitable as a replacement for a non-waste material? To cease to be waste, the material that results from the recovery or recycling of waste must be fully suitable as a replacement for the non-waste material for which it is substituting.

Q.12: If the waste has been fully recovered/recycled, is it certain to be used? Only if there is a genuine market for the recovered or recycled material and its future use is certain, it is likely to cease to be waste. Otherwise, it will remain a waste.

Q.13: Can the recovered/recycled material be used? The recovered or recycled material will not cease to be waste if it poses a greater risk to the environment or human health than the non-waste material it replaces, as this would undermine the aims of the Directive.

Q.14: Has the waste been converted or transformed into a distinct product? On the other hand, if the waste has been converted or transformed to the extent that it has become a new product in its own right, it may no longer be waste. The new product needs to be distinct from the original waste and minor changes to its composition are unlikely to be sufficient.

In addition to the above postulations, how can the court arrive at a decision that a discarded substance or object has become waste? This is predicated on the fact that "one man's waste may be another man's raw material." Thus, it may be difficult at a pinpoint accuracy for the court to draw a line between when a substance or object is waste (thereby needing disposal in an environmentally sound manner) and when such a substance or object may be regarded as a raw material,[14] and therefore not waste. This process requires some levels of scientific and economic certainty which the court may not be fully disposed to.

Some of the questions[15] the court may be required to address to conclude that a particular substance or object is waste or not are:

i. Where a manager of a laundry stored sludge from dry-cleaning machines in his laundry, on a temporary basis, is the temporary storage of the sludge a waste management activity?
ii. Is acid, discarded by one person, having been used to strip metal surfaces, but very useful to another person, who transports it from one locality to another, a waste to which a waste management permit is necessary?
iii. Is left-over rock from the extraction of ore, which is stored near the ore mine, a waste when some of the rock will remain there permanently, a small amount will be used as raw material for aggregates, some will be landscaped, and some will be used to fill in underground parts of the mine?
iv. Are powered wood residues from the construction and demolition industry which are treated and then used as a fuel to generate electricity or other form of energy (for example, for cooking purposes), to be regarded as waste?
v. Does the fact that the disposal or recovery of a substance forms part of an industrial process (being carried out by the undertaking which produced the substance, at the place of production, as opposed to elsewhere by a specialist disposal or recovery company) remove it from the scope of waste?
vi. Does the concept of waste exclude objects that possess an economic value, or are dealt with as part of a continuous commercial cycle (especially in this era of "scavengers")?

9.1.3 Why Regulate Waste?

Waste is by definition something that is not wanted by its producer or owner and by its nature has the potential to pollute the environment and harm human health. Waste can constitute a burden to its holder which may lead to its being dealt with in socially or environmentally unacceptable ways or in its being abandoned or dumped. The composition of waste is often uncertain and it is sometimes hazardous. Waste also often attracts a stigma that is not traditionally associated with products that are manufactured, and can be sold only if consumers are willing to pay for them. In other words, it is often the case that the producers and holders of waste do not have the same self-interest to ensure the provision of appropriate safeguards as those who extract raw materials or manufacture and place products on the market.

[14] For purposes of recovery, reuse or recycling.

[15] Adopted from Thornton and Beckwith (2004), pp. 185–186.

Waste is therefore regulated because it may present a risk to the environment and human health. This risk derives from waste's collective qualities, its nature and composition, the variety of sources from which it originates, and its potential to cause harm to the environment and human health. To this end, all necessary measures are to be taken to ensure that waste management is carried out without endangering human health, without harming the environment, particularly:

i) without risk to water, air, soil, plants or animals;
ii) without causing a nuisance through noise or odours; and
iii) without adversely affecting the countryside or places of special interest.[16]

However, waste is also a resource, albeit one which may present risks to the environment and human health. However, the environment is to be protected not only through the application of waste management controls but also by promoting the efficient use of resources. But to achieve a high level of environmental protection, action should not only be taken to ensure the safe recovery and disposal of waste but also to give priority to the prevention of waste, which may include the reuse of products and the recycling of substances and objects that have been discarded and are waste.

9.1.4 Environmentally Friendly Option to Reducing the Amount of Waste

Achieving a high level of environmental protection from substances or objects discarded as waste therefore would require the most sustainable and environmentally friendly option to reduce the amount of waste which is produced in the first place. What is then required is to seek and encourage the efficient use of waste as a resource through (i) recovery, (ii) reuse and (iii) recycling. These processes, i.e., recovery, reuse and recycling are encouraged as part of the 5Rs (Reduce, Repair, Reuse, Recycle and Recover) recommended for certain sectors of the economy under the various provisions of the National Environmental Regulations of Nigeria made pursuant to the NESREA Act 2007.[17] Besides the use of 5Rs, adopting efficient disposal of waste generated is another means of waste management. To these, we now turn.

[16]European Union (2018) (WFD 2008), Art. 13.

[17]For example, the National Environmental (Non-Metallic Minerals Manufacturing Industries Sector) Regulations 2011, Regulation 8, the National Environmental (Base Metal, Iron and Steel Manufacturing/Recycling Industries Sector) Regulations 2011, Regulation 7(1), the National Environmental (Pulp and Paper, Wood and Wood Products Sector) Regulations 2013, Regulation 8(1) (discussed in sect. 16.2.5 of Chap. 16 of this book).

9.1.4.1 Recovery

Recovery has been defined under Regulation 106 of the National Environmental (Sanitation and Wastes Control) Regulations 2009[18] as "the processing of waste material into a new product of similar chemical composition." The WFD[19] on the other hand defines recovery as:

> . . .any operation the principal result of which is waste serving a useful purpose by replacing other materials which would otherwise have been used to fulfill a particular function, or waste being prepared to fulfill that function, in the plant or in the wider economy.

The principal objective of a recovery operation is to ensure that the waste serves a useful purpose by replacing other substances that would have had to be used for that purpose and thereby conserving natural resources.

It should be noted that the fact that a substance or object undergoes a process which is a common method of recovering or disposing of waste may be taken as evidence that it is being discarded and hence is waste. For example, a lot of waste burns well and it is a common way of getting rid of it. So if you have something that is unwanted or cannot be used for its original purpose, and you decide to burn it, that is a strong indication that the item is waste.

However, in the case of *Mario Antonio Saetti and Andrea Frediani* (Petroleum Coke)[20] the ECJ held that, petroleum coke (petcoke) produced in an oil refinery and used to produce electricity which met the needs of the refinery was the result of technical choice and intended for use as a fuel, that is, that the petcoke was a product and not a production residue. In such cases, the fact that use as a fuel for energy production is a standard waste recovery method is not evidence of discarding, since the intention is to produce a type of fuel that can be burned. Therefore, the petroleum coke that is produced intentionally or in the course of producing other petroleum fuels in an oil refinery and is certain to be used as fuel to meet the energy needs of the refinery and those of other industries does not constitute waste. Thus, if the fuel had not been regarded as a product, the conclusion may have been different.[21]

Another point to be noted is that recovery may take place over several stages. This means that submission to a recovery operation may not result in the substance or object being declassified as waste. If further recovery is necessary then it remains waste until it is the subject of a complete recovery operation and is fully recovered. Only in those examples of recovery operations that result in a final use of the substance (e.g. where waste is used as fuel to generate energy or as a fertiliser to benefit agriculture) will the waste always cease to be waste. In other cases, it will be necessary to assess whether the resulting substance needs to be controlled.

---

[18] Government Notice No. 281, S.I. 28. Federal Republic of Nigeria Official Gazette No. 68 Vol. 98, 10 October 2009.

[19] European Union (2018) (WFD 2008), Art. 3(15).

[20] Case C- 235/02, Judgment delivered by ECJ on 14 January 2004.

[21] Case of Mario Antonio Saetti and Andrea Frediani (2004).

9.1.4.2 Reuse

Reuse simply means "waste used again with or without cleaning or repairing."[22] The WFD[23] on the other hand defines reuse as "any operation by which products or components that are not waste are used again for the same purpose for which they were conceived." To this end, a substance or object is not waste when it is being used for the purpose for which it was conceived, unless the circumstances are exceptional (e.g. the use is unlawful).

A distinction should be made between reuse as a waste prevention operation and reuse following a recovery operation. In the former, the substance or object in question never becomes waste because it is designed or used in such a way as to enable reuse. For example, an empty bottle of soft drink or beer. When the liquid content is drunk by a purchaser and the bottle is kept in the room, this makes the bottle a waste having been discarded by the purchaser. However, when the bottle is returned to the seller who would then collect the same and send to the manufacturers of the soft drink or beer, the bottle at this time ceases to be a waste as it is then recovered in some way so that it can once again be used for the purpose for which it was conceived. This is a classic example of "preparing for re-use" which does not involve waste.

"Preparing for re-use" is an activity by which products or components of products that have become waste are prepared so that they can be reused without any other pre-processing. It involves checking, cleaning or repairing recovery operations.[24] Another example of "preparing for re-use" is the case of electrical equipment which is discarded by its holder at a dump site. At that stage, it is a waste. But if the waste is sorted[25] to identify the equipment that is still fully functional and ready for use, then that equipment may cease to be waste once it is certain to be reused.[26]

One thing that must be noted in the issue of reuse is that a substance or object having become waste, such substance or object remains waste unless something happens to alter its status. This view is consistent with the approach taken by a court (in the UK) in the case of *R. v. W, C and C.*[27] This case arose out of the deposit at a farm of a large quantity of soil and subsoil, extracted from neighbouring farmland in the course of construction on that land of new hotel premises. In assessing whether the material was "waste" the court found that the question of immediate reuse could not determine the status of the material regardless of other considerations. The term "discard" had to be interpreted in the light of the aims of the WFD and material

---

[22] National Environmental (Sanitation and Wastes Control) Regulations (2009), Regulation 106.

[23] European Union (2018) WFD, Art. 3(13).

[24] Defra (2012), p. 42.

[25] For instance, "scavenger" is defined as "a person who searches and picks waste that can be useful for recycling purposes by people that will convert them to other useful forms." See National Environmental (Electrical/Electronic Sector) Regulations (2011), Regulation 70.

[26] Defra (2012), p. 42.

[27] [2010] EWCA Crim 927.

which was originally waste needed to continue to be so treated until acceptable recovery or disposal has been achieved.

9.1.4.3 Recycling

Recycling is a form of recovery and as such pursues the same objective of saving natural resources. The National Environmental (Sanitation and Wastes Control) Regulations 2009[28] defines recycling as "the processing of waste material into a new product of similar chemical composition." The WFD[29] on the other hand defines recycling as follows:

> . . .any recovery operation by which waste materials are reprocessed into products, materials or substances whether for the original or other purposes. It includes the reprocessing of organic material but does not include energy recovery and the reprocessing into materials that are to be used as fuels or for backfilling operations.

The implication of the above definitions is that recycling can only ever be carried out on substances or objects that are classified as waste. To this end, the definition of recycling requires the waste to be re-processed to obtain a product, material or substance whether for the original or other purposes. This differs from recovery operations which result merely in a change in the nature or composition of the waste so that the waste can serve a useful purpose. In the case of recovery a new product, material or substance has been recovered and so all the material has re-entered the productive cycle. No further processing is required. But in a recycling operation, it will always result in the substance in question ceasing to be waste when it is transformed. The substance will cease to be waste before its final use.[30]

9.1.4.4 Disposal

Disposal operations on the other hand are primarily aimed at getting rid of waste. It is defined as the "final destination of wastes including put away, sales, transformation burial, etc. excluding open burning of refuse."[31] According to WFD,[32] disposal is "any operation which is not recovery even where the operation has as a secondary consequence the reclamation of substances or energy. Annex I sets out a non-exhaustive list of disposal operations."

Thus, any benefit that results as a secondary consequence will not affect the nature of the operation. There will usually be very little debate as to whether an operation that looks like disposal involves waste or not. If the ultimate aim of the

---

[28] National Environmental (Sanitation and Wastes Control) Regulations (2009), Regulation 106.

[29] European Union (2018) WFD, Art. 3(17).

[30] Defra (2012), p. 41.

[31] National Environmental (Sanitation and Wastes Control) Regulations (2009), Regulation 106.

[32] European Union (2018) WFD, Art. 3(19).

operation is to get rid of the waste, there is a clear intent to discard it; although sometimes it will not necessarily be obvious. For instance, the use of animal droppings as a fertiliser does not amount to the disposal or recovery of waste. The reason for this is that animal faeces amount to a by-product of keeping animals and comprise a traditional fertiliser for which proprietary fertilisers may be regarded as a substitute.

9.1.5 Characteristics of a Substance or Object Vis-à-Vis Being Classified as a Waste

The environmental impact of a substance or object does not in itself determine the waste status of that substance or object. This is consistent with the notion that any substance or object can be waste if its holder decides to discard it. The discard test relates to the conduct of the holder and not to the intrinsic characteristics of the substance or object. The consequence of this is that the characteristics of the substance or object cannot by themselves determine whether a substance or object is waste or not.

For instance, neither the potential to pollute nor the harmlessness of the substance or object in question is a decisive criterion for determining what its holder intends to do with it and hence whether it is waste. In the *Palin Granit* case,[33] leftover stone resulting from stone quarrying had very little potential to pollute as it was inert. However, it was stored for an indefinite length of time to await possible use and so was waste. The European Court of Justice[34] found that the long-term stockpiling which was necessary was a burden to the holder and also presented the type of nuisance which the law seeks to address.

Again, there are also substances with hazardous properties that are not waste even if they cause pollution. An ordinary fuel may be burned without becoming waste even if it causes pollution. But waste that is recovered by burning as a fuel will be classified as waste and hence subject to regulation even if it presents a lower pollution risk when burned. This position was recognised by the European Court of Justice (ECJ) in the *Arco Chemie* case[35] when it explained that the polluting characteristics are only relevant to the level of control to be applied when it held that, "the fact that substances may be recovered as fuel in an environmentally responsible manner and without substantial treatment is, indeed, material to the question whether the use of that substance as fuel should be authorised or encouraged or to the decision as to the degree of control to be exercised."

Although the characteristics of the substance or object cannot by themselves determine whether a substance or object is waste or not, this does not mean that the

[33] Palin Granit case (2000) Case C-9/00, European Court of Justice.

[34] Ibid.

[35] Arco Chemie case (1997) Joined Cases C-418/97 and C-419/97.

characteristics of the substance or object are not relevant at all. For instance, the concept of waste does not exclude substances or objects even if they have a commercial value. This applies to the use of waste in recovery operations and in such circumstances, the waste often has an economic value. To this end, substances and objects which have been discarded remain waste even though they have value to their current holder who collected them on a commercial basis for recycling.

For instance, scrap metal is not recycled until it meets end-of-waste criteria[36] or is re-processed[37] into a new product. So someone who purchases scrap metal with the intention of its being re-processed into steel is taken to have the intention to discard that material even though they may regard it as a valuable secondary raw material.[38] In the joined Cases C-206/88 and C-207/88, *Vessoso and Zanetti*[39] and C-359/88 *Zanetti and Others,* delivered by the ECJ.[40] The court held that:

> The concept of waste, within the meaning . . .is not to be understood as excluding substances and objects which are capable of economic re- utilization. The concept does not presume that the holder disposing of a substance or object intends to exclude all economic re-utilization of the substance or object by others. And that National legislation which defines waste as excluding substances and objects which are capable of economic re-utilization is not compatible with European Council Directives 75/442 and 78/319.[41]

9.1.6 If a Substance or Object Is Waste When Does It Cease to Be Waste?

Once a substance or object has been discarded and is waste, something usually needs to be done to it for it to cease to be waste. This can range from something relatively minor to quite extensive processing, comprising one or more recovery operations. To this end, it may be necessary for waste to undergo a series of recovery operations before it ceases to be waste.

Thus, in *Antonio Niselli,*[42] the issue before the court was to determine the point at which waste streams are considered to be recycled. The ECJ reiterated that it is only

[36] This means a post-consumer waste of products appliances, equipment, and machinery that may have physical integrity but have lost their utility value (e.g., tyre, vehicle, television, cooker, refrigerator, mobile phones, etc.) which the owner has discarded, intends to discard or is required to discard. See National Environmental (Sanitation and Wastes Control) Regulations 2009, Regulation 106.

[37] This involves the processing of waste into a new product of different chemical composition. See National Environmental (Sanitation and Wastes Control) Regulations 2009, Regulation 106.

[38] Case of Zanetti and others (1988), European Court of Justice Case C-359/88, para 9.

[39] [1990] 2 LMELR 133.

[40] 28 March 1990.

[41] Case of Zanetti and others (1988), European Court of Justice, Case C-359/88, para 9.

[42] Antonio Niselli (2004) European Court of Justice, Case C- 457/02, delivered on 11 November 2004.

in exceptional circumstances that recycled substances, like products, will be waste and it is not possible to distinguish products derived from recycled material from those made from primary raw materials. The court held that:

> subject to the case where the products obtained are in their turn abandoned, the point at which the materials in question cease to be classified as 'waste' cannot be fixed at an industrial or commercial stage subsequent to their reprocessing into steel products, because, from that point, they can hardly be distinguished from other steel products made from primary raw materials.[43]

It further held that "secondary raw materials derived from scrap metal and used in steel making continued to be classified as waste until they had actually been recycled into steel products, and that in the earlier phases, they cannot yet be regarded as recycled, since the reprocessing has not yet been concluded."[44]

In another situation, the issue was can waste-derived fuel ceased to be waste prior to use as a fuel? The Court of Appeal of the UK set out a three-part test in *R (on the application of OSS Group Ltd) v. Environment Agency and others* (OSS case).[45] In that case, the court was asked whether it was possible for waste lubricating oil which is to be used as fuel to cease to be waste before it is burnt. The court concluded that "waste lubricating oil was no different from any other waste and that it might cease to be waste if it had been completely recovered." Accordingly, the court discussed at what point complete recovery will have occurred and proposed the following three-part test: "It should be enough that the holder has converted the waste material into a distinct, marketable product, which can be used in exactly the same way as an ordinary fuel and with no worse environmental effects."[46]

At times, a substance or object that becomes waste may not need very much to be done to it to rid it of its waste status.[47] In this case, recovery operations that make the waste suitable for reuse are often very minor operations. Thus, if it is certain that the substance or object can be used in the same way it was used before it became waste, it will have been recovered and should not be regarded as waste. In the case of *Environment Agency v. Thorn International UK Ltd,*[48] a UK Divisional Court considered the case of electrical equipment collected by distributors of electrical equipment under new-for-old schemes, where the collected old equipment was then bought and refurbished for resale by a repair company. The court held that the items bought by the repair company were not waste even though they needed repair before resale.

As a result of this judgement where discarded electrical and electronic equipment is obtained for refurbishment, there is a very high degree of probability that all the

---

[43] Antonio Niselli (2004) European Court of Justice, Case C- 457/02.

[44] Ibid.

[45] [2007] EWCA Civ 611.

[46] OSS case (2007).

[47] For example, a sorting operation may identify those substances and objects that can still be used for their original purpose.

[48] [2008] WLR (D) 219.

items selected will be repaired and reused. In this regard, waste electrical and electronic equipment (WEEE) remains waste until it has been completely recovered. Recovery will commonly involve recycling of materials or dismantling items to obtain parts, but can also occur, in limited circumstances, where WEEE is subject to a competent assessment and segregated for immediate reuse or for reuse following repair. If WEEE is segregated for reuse, the reusable WEEE will only cease to be waste at the time of segregation if the holders have an auditable system that ensures that almost all of the items will in fact be reused (following repair if needed).[49]

In the final analysis, waste includes any substance that constitutes a scrap material, effluent or other unwanted surplus arising from the application of any process or any substance or article that requires to be disposed of which has been broken, worn out, contaminated or otherwise spoiled; this is supplemented with anything which is discarded otherwise dealt with as if it were waste shall be presumed to be waste unless the contrary is proved.[50]

9.2 Sources of Waste

Substances or objects that are discarded or intended to be discarded or required to be discarded come from various sources. These sources are:

9.2.1 Oxygen-Demanding Wastes

Oxygen-demanding wastes, such as might be discarded from breweries, or paper mills and other sources such as municipal wastewater treatment plants, make up one of the most important sources of waste. Pollutants from these sources when discarded or discharged into water bodies decompose and can deplete the water's oxygen and create anaerobic conditions. The anaerobic bacteria begin to break down wastes. This produces chemicals that have a foul odour and unpleasant taste and that generally interfere with the well-being of humans.[51]

9.2.2 Heat

Heat, which are discarded as industrial effluents may drastically alter the ecosystem of a stream or lake. Power plants are the greatest culprits. Power plants heat water to

[49] Defra (2012), p. 53.

[50] Thornton and Beckwith (2004), p. 187.

[51] Goudie (2013), p. 54.

convert it into steam that drives the turbines that generate electricity. For steam turbines to function efficiently, the steam must be condensed into water after it leaves the turbine. This condensation is usually accomplished by taking water from lakes, streams, or oceans to absorb the heat. The heated water is then discharged into the aquatic environment. Heat lowers the solubility of oxygen in water. This is because gas solubility in water is inversely proportional to temperature, thereby reducing the amount of dissolved oxygen available to gill-breathing species. As the level of dissolved oxygen decreases, the metabolic activity of aerobic aquatic species increases, thus increasing oxygen demand.[52]

9.2.3 Agricultural Activities

Agricultural activities also form a source of pollutants. This comes mainly from plant nutrients such as nitrates; phosphates and other plant nutrients that come from fertilised farmlands. When they are washed into water bodies, they encourage the growth of algae and phytoplankton. These aquatic plants may become so abundant that their decomposition drastically cuts down the amount of dissolved oxygen.[53]

9.2.4 Industrial Effluents

Industrial effluents arise from discharges from the industries into the environment. Almost all our industries discharge their effluent, without prior or proper treatment, into the river system. Run-offs from mining waste tips, which are rich in metals, also serve as a source of waste. Pollutants may leach out from the base of waste sites, especially old landfills, and cause contamination of ground waters. Again, abandoned mines also cause pollution when old mine workings fill up with water, become contaminated, and then discharged into surface waters. Many of these effluents are toxic as they include dichloro-diphenyl-trichloroethane (DDT), dyes, mercury, lead,[54] cadmium and other heavy metals.[55]

[52] Ibid.

[53] Adinna (2001), p. 67.

[54] Impact and the insidious effect of lead, especially on growing children, have been in the news in Zamfara state of Nigeria since 2010.

[55] Adinna (2001), p. 77.

9.2.5 *Sediments from Land Erosion*

Sediment from land erosion may also be classified as a pollutant. Sediment consists of mostly inorganic materials washed into a stream as a result of land cultivation, construction, demolition, and mining operations. Sediment interferes with fish spawning because it can cover gravel beds and block light penetration, making food harder to find. Some of the solid wastes decay only slowly while others are virtually indestructible. These constitute physical pollution commonly clogging up water bodies, converting them into unsightly junkyards, unsuitable for almost any use, and promoting destructive flooding.[56]

9.2.6 *Burgeoning Population and Economic Growth*

The flow of such refuse has increased enormously as a result of burgeoning economic growth and social mobility (both acquired and accrued). Junked automobiles, refrigerators, cans, stoves, packaging materials, metal scraps, eggshells, vegetable peelings, empty cartons, plastics, furniture, animal wastes, etc, are discarded and they end up littering the sides of roads, floating in lakes and streams, and sitting in unsightly dumps causing aesthetic perturbation. These refuse are what people throw away each year.[57]

Life magazine in 1995,[58] pictured a happy family in an article entitled "Throw – away – living." In that article, a disposable lifestyle was marked as the way of the future and as a way to cut down on household chores. This attitude of "use it once and throw it away" became a very popular advertising slogan. Because of this new lifestyle, the lack of space for dumping waste has become a problem for many large metropolitan areas throughout the world, including Nigeria. Communities are now concerned about the increasing costs of waste disposal, possible hazards to groundwater and maintaining air quality.

The waste problem has increased dramatically over the past several decades because of the alarming increase in population.[59] The implication of this is "more people, more garbage." In addition, industries and government facilities add millions of tons of other types of waste, such as blood, diseased body parts, syringes and bandages from hospitals. Builders throw away construction debris. Factories discard thousands of poisonous chemicals. Nuclear power plants produce radioactive waste. Corporate bodies using the latest inventions of science and technology have also

---

[56] Enger and Smith (2002), p. 389.

[57] Enger and Smith (2002), p. 389.

[58] The Watch Tower (2002), p. 3.

[59] Unbridled population growth is getting worse as the world hit 7 billion persons on 31 October 2011, and it is recently estimated to be about 8.1 billion as of 11 August 2023 according to World Data Lab (2023).

been added to the list. We now see discarded and junk electronic gadgets[60] littering the dump sites. The list goes on and on.

9.3 Managing Solid Waste Pollution

9.3.1 Nature of Solid Waste

The National Environmental (Sanitation and Wastes Control) Regulations 2009[61] define solid waste to mean, "all putrescible and non-putrescible solid and semi-solid waste including garbage, rubbish, ashes, industrial waste, swill, demolition or construction waste, abandoned vehicles or parts thereof and discarded commodities."

Solid wastes are unwanted solid materials such as garbage (decomposable wastes from food), rubbish: non-decomposable wastes, either combustible (such as paper, wood, and cloth) or non-combustible (such as metal, glass, and ceramics); ashes: residues of the combustion of solid fuels; large wastes: demolition and construction debris and trees; dead animals; sewage-treatment solids: material retained on sewage-treatment screens, settled solids, and biomass sludge; industrial wastes: such materials as chemicals, paints, and sand; mining wastes: slag heaps and coal refuse piles; and agricultural wastes: farm animal manure and crop residues. These are collectively referred to as municipal waste.[62]

9.3.2 Environmental Impact of Solid Waste

Solid wastes have negative impacts on the wider natural environment. Typical materials that are found in household waste, and which have specific environmental impacts, include biodegradable wastes, batteries, aerosols, oils, acids, cellophane and garbage. Biodegradable waste is of specific concern because it breaks down in landfills to form methane, a potent greenhouse gas. If this gas is not prevented from entering the atmosphere, by implication, it contributes to climate change.[63]

Littering can be considered the most visible form of solid waste pollution. Litter means "any material including scrap paper, newspaper, sweet rapper, water sachet, fruit skins etc, left or abandoned in a place other than a receptacle or place intended

[60] These are commonly referred to as electrical/electronic waste or e-waste. This was discussed later in this chapter.

[61] National Environmental (Sanitation and Wastes Control) Regulations (2009), Regulation 106.

[62] National Environmental (Sanitation and Wastes Control) Regulations (2009), Regulation 106.

[63] Green Ontario (2019).

or approved for receiving such material. . ."[64] The act of littering for the most part constitutes disposing of waste inappropriately, typically in public places. Littering itself may or may not be an intentional action, but is still an environmental crime in most government jurisdictions, with punitive consequences if cited by authorities.

For instance, under Regulation 3 of the National Environmental (Sanitation and Wastes Control) Regulations 2009, "no person is to discard, throw or drop any litter or any similar refuse anywhere except in designated litter bins." It shall therefore be an offence for an owner or occupant in care of premises or control or management of a business to release or cause litter to be released into the environment.[65] Penalty for violation is a fine of =N=20,000 or imprisonment for six months or both.[66]

Marine debris, also known as marine litter, is human-created waste that has been deliberately dumped, or accidentally become afloat, in a lake, sea, ocean or waterway. Although it was originally assumed that most oceanic marine waste stemmed directly from ocean dumping, it is now thought that around four-fifths of the oceanic debris is from rubbish blown seaward from landfills, and washed seaward by storm drains.[67]

Other forms of pollution associated with solid waste materials include illegal dumping or "fly-tipping" and leaching. "Fly-tipping" means "the illegal dumping of all kinds of waste such as household, animal carcass, disused vehicle parts and tyres, and those from building and demolition work."[68] Illegal dumping or fly-tipping often involves unregulated disposal of materials on private or public land. Remote sites with road access, coupled with limited surveillance, often provide the perfect opportunity for this form of dumping, which often goes unpunished and leaves others, such as the community or developer, to properly dispose of the waste. Leaching is the process by which contaminants from solid waste enter the soil and often groundwater systems, contaminating them.

9.3.3 Approaches to Solid Waste Management

Waste management encompasses a whole gamut of activities. It means planning, handling, treatment, processing and disposal, including the supervision of these operations, as well as the measures for the protection of the environment and human life and health during the operation of the facilities and installations for waste disposal. . . .[69] Waste management therefore involves the collection, transport,

---

[64] National Environmental (Sanitation and Wastes Control) Regulations (2009), Regulation 106.

[65] Ibid., Regulation 71(a).

[66] Ibid., Regulation 94.

[67] British Broadcasting Corporation (BBC) (2008).

[68] National Environmental (Sanitation and Wastes Control) Regulations (2009), Regulation 106.

[69] British Broadcasting Corporation (2008).

processing, recycling or disposal, and monitoring of waste materials.[70] It involves the management of solid, liquid, gaseous or radioactive substances, with different methods and fields of expertise for each. The purpose of waste management is to reduce the effect of waste on health, the environment or aesthetics. At times solid waste management is carried out to recover resources from it.

Waste management practices differ for developed and developing nations, for urban and rural areas, and for residential and industrial producers. Management of non-hazardous residential and institutional waste in metropolitan areas is usually the responsibility of local government authorities,[71] while management of non-hazardous commercial and industrial waste is usually the responsibility of the generator. In Nigeria, Schedule 4 item 1(h) to the Constitution of the Federal Republic of Nigeria 1999 (CFRN 1999),[72] as amended, empowers the local government to maintain public conveniences and engage in sewage and refuse disposal. However, this function is being performed by various State Waste Management Agencies or Environmental Protection Authorities. It should be noted that effective waste management involves the collection, transport, processing, recycling or disposal, and monitoring of waste materials. This is clearly out of the capabilities of most, if not all, local government authorities in Nigeria, as presently constituted.

Various waste management methods can be employed to reduce the impact of waste pollution. These methods are discussed below.

9.3.3.1 Landfill

Disposing of waste in a landfill involves burying the waste, and this remains a common practice in most countries. Landfills were often established in abandoned or unused quarries, mining voids or borrow pits. In a modern landfill, refuse is spread in thin layers, each of which is compacted by a bulldozer before the next is spread. When about 3 m (about 10 ft) of refuse has been laid down, it is covered by a thin layer of clean Earth, which also is compacted. Pollution of surface and groundwater is minimised by lining and contouring the fill, compacting and planting the cover, selecting proper soil, diverting upland drainage, and placing wastes in sites not subject to flooding or high groundwater levels.[73]

A properly designed and well-managed landfill can be a hygienic and relatively inexpensive method of disposing of waste materials. Older, poorly designed or poorly managed landfills can create many adverse environmental impacts such as wind-blown litter, attraction of vermin (such as mice or rats), and generation of liquid leachate. Leachate may contaminate surface water. Another common

[70] Wanless Waste Management (2021).

[71] As in Nigeria, see Schedule 4 item 1(h) to the Constitution of the Federal Republic of Nigeria 1999, as amended.

[72] Cap C23 Laws of the Federation of Nigeria (LFN) 2004.

[73] Enger and Smith (2002), p. 401.

by-product of landfills is gas (mostly composed of methane and carbon dioxide), which is produced as organic waste breaks down anaerobically. This gas can create odour problems, kill surface vegetation, and is a greenhouse gas and at times, if a significant amount of methane is present, it may be explosive. However, proper venting eliminates this latter problem.[74]

Design characteristics of a modern landfill include methods to contain leachate such as clay or plastic lining material. Deposited waste is normally compacted to increase its density and stability, and covered to prevent attracting vermin. Many landfills also have landfill gas extraction systems installed to extract the landfill gas. Gas is pumped out of the landfill using perforated pipes and flared off or burnt in a gas engine to generate electricity.[75]

9.3.3.2 Incineration

Incineration is a disposal method that involves combustion of waste material. Incineration and other high-temperature waste treatment systems are sometimes described as "thermal treatment." Incinerators convert waste materials into heat, gas, steam, and ash. Incineration is carried out both on a small scale by individuals and on a large scale by industry. It is used to dispose of solid, liquid and gaseous waste. It is recognised as a practical method of disposing of certain hazardous waste materials (such as biological medical waste). Incineration is common where land is scarce, as these facilities generally do not require as much area as landfills. Incineration may involve waste-to-energy (WtE) or energy-from-waste (EfW), a process through which waste is burnt in a furnace or boiler to generate heat, steam and/or electricity.[76]

However, incineration is a controversial method of waste disposal, due to issues such as the emission of gaseous pollutants. Combustion in an incinerator is not always perfect and there have been concerns about micro-pollutants in gaseous emissions from incinerator stacks. Although incineration of waste reduces the volume of solid waste it however produces dense ashen wastes that often contain dangerous concentrations of hazardous materials such as heavy metals and toxic compounds. Particular concern has focused on some very persistent organics such as dioxins[77] which may be created within the incinerator and which may have serious environmental consequences in the area immediately around the incinerator.[78]

Moreover, incineration contributes to air pollution by generating dust, acidic and greenhouse gases. It also produces dense ashen wastes (some of which become

[74] Ibid.

[75] Ibid.

[76] Reddy et al. (1981), p. 25.

[77] Toxic chemical: a heterocyclic hydrocarbon that is a carcinogen and toxic environmental pollutant.

[78] Ausubel and Harpignies (2004), p. 59.

airborne) that often contain dangerous concentrations of hazardous materials and toxic compounds such as vaporised metals, metal salts, and furans.[79] These notwithstanding, incineration of waste may produce heat that can be used as a source of energy.

9.3.3.3 Recycling Methods

Recycling, extracting and reusing certain waste materials, has become an important part of municipal solid waste strategies in both developed countries and developing countries. To this end, recycling plays a significant but informal role in solid waste management. In Nigeria for instance, organised waste-pickers comb streets and waste dumpsites for items such as plastics, iron and metal scraps which they reuse or resell. Plastics, polythenes, and other resin-based products are easy to recycle. The reason is that these items are usually composed of a single type of material, making them relatively easy to recycle into new products. The recycling of complex products, such as computers and electronic equipment, is more difficult, due to the additional dismantling and separation required.[80]

9.3.3.4 Biological Reprocessing

This process involves composting and anaerobic digestion of bio-degradable waste matters. Biological processing in waste management intends to control and accelerate the natural process of decomposition of organic matter. Waste materials that are organic in nature, such as plant material, food scraps, and paper products, can be recycled using biological composting and digestion processes to decompose the organic matter. There is a large variety of composting and digestion methods and technologies varying in complexity from simple home compost heaps, to industrial-scale enclosed-vessel digestion of mixed domestic waste. Methods of biological decomposition are differentiated as aerobic or anaerobic methods, although hybrids of the two methods also exist.[81]

Composting, using natural biological processes to speed the decomposition of organic wastes, is an effective strategy for dealing with organic garbage and produces a material that can be used as a natural fertiliser. In addition, the resulting organic material is then recycled as mulch or compost for agricultural or landscaping purposes. Furthermore, waste gas from the process, such as methane, can be captured and used for generating electricity.[82]

---

[79] A colourless flammable liquid.

[80] Enger and Smith (2002), p. 402.

[81] Ibid.

[82] Reddy et al. (1981), p. 25.

What should be done to make this effective is for the waste management authorities or agencies to dedicate containers where household organic waste, such as kitchen scraps and plant cuttings, are collected in a dedicated container and then composted. A compositing site is then established where the refuse are dumped and appropriate methods of decomposition are applied. The solid aspect is then bagged as natural fertiliser while the escaping gas is captured in appropriate containers for use in generating electricity.[83]

9.3.3.5 Energy Recovery (Waste to Energy, WtE)

The energy content of waste products can be harnessed directly by using them as a direct combustion fuel, or indirectly by processing them into another type of fuel. Recycling can also be done through thermal treatment. This ranges from using waste as a fuel source for cooking or heating and for boilers to generate steam and electricity in a turbine. Pyrolysis[84] and gasification are two related forms of thermal treatment where waste materials are heated to high temperatures with limited oxygen availability. The process typically occurs in a sealed vessel under high pressure. Pyrolysis of solid waste converts the material into solid, liquid and gas products. The liquid and gas can be burnt to produce energy or refined into other products.[85] The solid residue, char, can be further refined into products such as activated carbon. Gasification and advanced Plasma arc gasification are used to convert organic materials directly into a synthetic gas, syngas, composed of carbon monoxide and hydrogen. The gas is then burnt to produce electricity and steam.[86]

9.3.3.6 Avoidance and Reduction Methods

This process involves waste minimisation. An important method of waste management is the prevention of waste material being created. This method is also known as waste reduction. Methods of avoidance include the reuse of second-hand products, repairing broken items instead of buying new ones, and designing products to be refillable or reusable, such as the use of cotton or paper materials to produce shopping bags, instead of plastic or cellophane. Other aspects of this method include: encouraging consumers to avoid using disposable products, such as disposable cutlery; removing any food/liquid remains from cans, packaging, and designing

[83] Ibid.

[84] The use of heat to break down complex chemical substances into simpler substances.

[85] A form of biofuel.

[86] Reddy et al. (1981), p. 25.

products that use less material to achieve the same purpose, for example, lightweighting of beverage cans.[87]

Achieving the above processes requires education of the populace and creation of awareness in this environmentally sound management of waste. Education and awareness in the area of waste and waste management is increasingly important from a global perspective of resource management. People should be discouraged from engaging in throw-way culture but made to embrace the culture of reuse. Globally, there is a sustainability concern about the unprecedented scale and speed of environmental pollution and degradation, and the depletion of natural resources. Local, regional, and global air pollution; accumulation and distribution of toxic wastes; destruction and depletion of forests, soil, and water; depletion of the ozone layer and emission of "greenhouse" gases threaten the survival of humans and thousands of other living species, the integrity of the Earth and its biodiversity, the security of nations, and the heritage of future generations.

9.4 Electrical/Electronic Waste (E-Waste)

9.4.1 Introduction

Every product has a life cycle. From plastic bags to ships, electrical/electronic equipment and gadgets, among others, sooner or later they reach the end of their useful life. Then, unless they are recycled into other products, they are discarded and become waste. Initially, waste regulation was concerned with controlling the management of waste within the domestic context. But as the world becomes more developed and societies become more consumer-oriented in nature, giving rise to a wide range of industrial, commercial, agricultural and even domestic activities, the inevitable consequence is a parallel increase in waste, amounting to thousands of tonnes every year, making its management an arduous task. This situation is further compounded by the fact that some of the wastes are hazardous as they are potentially dangerous to the environment and human health. These hazardous wastes are toxic, noxious, poisonous, explosive, corrosive, exotoxic, flammable or infectious in nature.

Simply defined, hazardous waste is a waste with properties that make it dangerous or capable of having a harmful effect on human health or the environment. Hazardous waste is generated from many sources, ranging from industrial manufacturing process wastes to batteries and may come in many forms, including liquids, solids gases, and sludges.[88] A hazardous substance includes liquid, semi-solid or solid substances as well as "any injurious, poisonous toxic or noxious substance... which

[87] This is already in use by some beverage companies such as Nigerian Breweries, Coca-Cola, Pepsi, and other makers of soft drinks, alcoholic beverages, and canned food.

[88] United States Environmental Protection Agency (USEPA) (2009).

can subject any person to the risk of death, fatal injury or incurable impairment of physical and mental health. . . ."[89]

As a result of the insidious effects of hazardous substances, it has become imperative that any form of dealing with them, be it buying, selling, transporting, dumping and depositing be controlled. One of the most common sources of hazardous waste is that coming from discarded electrical/electronic equipment and gadgets popularly referred to as electrical/electronic waste or e-waste.

9.4.2 *Concept of Electrical/Electronic Waste (E-Waste)*

Electronic waste is one of the emerging environmental problems that is of interest to environmental law. With growth in the use of electrical and electronic equipment and gadgets in virtually every home and human endeavour in recent years, coupled with the speed to which they become obsolete and discarded, electrical and electronic equipment and gadgets, have become a new wave of hazardous waste which is now of serious environmental concern to the international community, especially in the developing countries. This new wave of hazardous waste coming from obsolete and discarded electrical and electronic equipment and gadgets is generally referred to as "e-waste."[90]

The term e-waste can be used when it comes to electrical/electronic equipment, gadgets and devices that are away from order or electronically dead and form a loose category of surplus, obsolete, broken, or discarded electrical or electronic devices.[91] E-waste may be defined as all secondary computers, entertainment devices, electronics, mobile phones, and other items such as television sets and refrigerators, which might be in working condition or at the conclusion of their electronic life,[92] whether sold, donated, or discarded by their original owners.[93] This definition includes used electronics which are destined for reuse, resale, salvage, recycling, or disposal. It is also seen as the fastest growing component of municipal waste worldwide with 20–50 million tonnes generated annually.[94]

According to Günzel,[95] e-waste is electronic equipment and its components that no longer sparkle and are therefore disposed of. E-waste in the words of Tomlinson[96] is the metal components of any electronic device: the chips, the wiring, the solder,

[89] Harmful Waste (Special Criminal Provisions) Act (HWSCP Act) 1988, Cap H1 LFN 2004, s. 15.

[90] E-waste is also known variously as "electronic waste," "e-scrap," or "Waste Electrical and Electronic Equipment" ("WEEE").

[91] Green Peace International (2001).

[92] Spelch (2016).

[93] Ibid.

[94] Ibid.

[95] Günzel (2019).

[96] Tomlinson (2019).

circuit boards, transistors, capacitors, batteries, etc. These components contain a wide range of heavy metals that are highly toxic, and will poison soil, groundwater, and waterways.

Many components of these electronic equipment and its components can be recycled or reused. However, there is a dearth of recycling facilities in many countries or even a slow procedure of recycling. This makes the rate of reuse much less than the rate of disposal. As a result, many of these electronic equipment and their components are mostly discarded.[97]

Morgan[98] however opined that the reusable (working and repairable electronics) and secondary scrap (copper, steel, plastic, etc.) should be regarded as "commodities," and reserved the term "waste" for residue or material which was represented as working or repairable but which is dumped or disposed or discarded by the buyer rather than recycled. Other aspects to be regarded as "waste" include residue from reuse and recycling operations. Because loads of surplus electronics are frequently commingled (good, recyclable, and non-recyclable), several public policy advocates apply the term "e-waste" broadly to all surplus electronics.[99]

Debates have continued over the distinction between "commodity" and "waste" electronics definitions. It should be noted that both types of e-waste have raised considerable concern because many components of electrical/electronic equipment are considered toxic and non-biodegradable. Some exporters may deliberately leave difficult-to-spot obsolete or non-working equipment mixed in with loads of working equipment (through ignorance, or to avoid more costly treatment processes). All the same, obsolete household electronic and electrical gadgets, such as computers, are termed "hazardous household waste" by the United States Environmental Protection Agency (EPA).[100]

It is estimated that weight for weight, the average computer chip does more harm to the environment than a car. To make a 2-gram memory chip, over 1400 grams of materials and fossil fuels are needed.[101] Computers, which have a high rate of obsolescence, also contain cadmium, lead and mercury and when they are no longer required are dumped, recycled or disassembled to recover precious metals such as gold and copper, the rest are discarded as wastes.[102] Since this class of waste was not envisaged by the Basel Convention in 1989, the sixth Conference of Parties to the Convention met in Geneva, in December 2002 to address a wide number of topics, including the growing issue of "e-waste," among others. During the conference technical guidelines were adopted on the disposal and recycling of "e-waste," lead-acid batteries, plastic wastes and obsolete ships.[103]

---

[97] Spelch (2016).

[98] Morgan (2006).

[99] Morgan (2006).

[100] Ibid.

[101] United Nations Environment Programme (UNEP) (1997), p. 46.

[102] Ibid.

[103] Ibid.

E-waste as a form of toxic waste was first exposed by Basel Action Network (BAN) in their 2002 report and film entitled "Exporting Harm: The High-Tech Trashing of Asia."[104] The film placed a spotlight on the global dumping of e-waste, primarily from North America, particularly the United States, in a township area of China known as Guiyu, since the United States has not ratified the Basel Convention[105] or the Ban Amendment to the Convention,[106] and has no domestic laws forbidding the export of toxic waste.

The e-waste is one of the most rapidly growing waste problems in the world today. There is increased regulation of electronic waste and concern over the environmental harm that can result from toxic electronic waste in developed economies and this has raised disposal costs. The regulation creates an economic disincentive to remove residues before export. In extreme cases, brokers and others calling themselves recyclers export unscreened electronic waste to developing countries, avoiding the expense of removing items like bad cathode ray tubes (CRT), the processing of which is expensive and difficult. As a result, electronic waste is often exported to developing countries that are ill-prepared to tackle technologies that they do not possess relevant capacities to manage. In June 2008, a container of electronic waste, destined from the Port of Oakland in the USA to Sanshui District in mainland China, was intercepted in Hong Kong by Greenpeace.[107]

In July 2009, containers from the United Kingdom (UK) loaded with all sorts of waste, including e-waste, found their way into Brazil. Concerns over exports of electronic waste were raised in press reports in India, Ghana, Ivory Coast and Nigeria.[108] In addition, countries such as Ghana, Nigeria, Pakistan, India and China have in recent past become hot spots for e-waste dumping; although recycling occurs, this happens illegally.[109]

Defenders of the trade in used electronics argue that extraction of metals from virgin mining such as hard-rock mining of copper, silver, gold and other materials extracted from electronics is considered far more environmentally damaging than the recycling of electronic materials.[110] They further argued that repair and reuse of computers and televisions has become a "lost art" in wealthier nations, and that refurbishing has traditionally been a path to development in developing countries.[111] To this end, countries such as South Korea, Taiwan, and southern China have excelled in finding "retained value" in used goods, and in some cases have set up

---

[104] National Geographic Society (2008).

[105] As of date, only the United States of America (USA) and Haiti have not ratified the Basel Convention.

[106] This came into force on 5 December 2019.

[107] Greenpeace International (2016).

[108] Carney (2006).

[109] Junior Scholastic Magazine (2009).

[110] Greenpeace International (2016).

[111] Carney (2006).

billion-dollar industries in refurbishing used ink cartridges, single-use cameras, and working CRTs.[112]

Refurbishing has traditionally been a threat to established manufacturing, and simple protectionism explains some criticism of the trade. To this end, proponents of the trade argue that thousands of men, women, and children are employed in reuse, refurbishing, repair, and remanufacturing, sustainable industries in decline in developed countries. It is held that denying developing nations access to used electronics denies them not only affordable products and internet access but also means of employment and income.[113]

Opponents of surplus electronics exports however argue that lower environmental and labour standards, cheap labour, and the relatively high value of recovered raw materials lead to a transfer of pollution-generating activities, such as the burning of copper wire. In China, Malaysia, India, Kenya, Nigeria, and various African countries, electronic waste is being sent to these countries for processing, sometimes illegally. Many surplus laptops are routed to developing nations as "dumping grounds for e-waste," especially from the USA.[114]

The top 5 e-waste producing countries include the USA, China, Japan, Germany and India. According to a study conducted by ASSOCHAM-KPMG, 70% of e-waste is constituted by computers, 12% is telecommunication equipment, 8% electrical equipment and 7% medical equipment.[115]

The Institute for Scrap Recycling Industries, and the World Reuse, Repair and Recycling Association argue that whatever the figure, the truth of the matter is that large consignments of obsolete electronic equipment are shipped to developing countries under various guises by the United States and other Western countries.[116] In fact, "e-waste" has become the most rapidly growing waste problem in the world today. It is estimated that weight for weight, the average computer chip does more harm to the environment than a car. For instance, to make a 2-gram memory chip, over 1400 grams of materials and fossil fuels are needed.[117]

9.4.3 Why the Increase in E-Waste Generation

Several reasons, although appearing separate but are interlinked with each other, contribute to the increasing wave of e-waste in our society. Some of the identified major causes of increasing e-waste are:

[112]Guiyu in the Shantou region of China, and Delhi and Bangalore in India, have electronic waste processing areas.

[113]Morgan (2006).

[114]UNEP (1997).

[115]Chauhan (2019).

[116]Greenpeace International (2016).

[117]Ibid.

Green[118] opines that the main causes of e-waste are: people's lack of care for cheap electronic items, low cost of electronic items, and replace rather than respect attitude; for example, people will insure their phone, and get it replaced if damaged, rather than buy a protective case and actually looking after it. "Cloud" type backup for contacts and photos makes it all too easy to do this. Another reason adduced by him is the inability to repair or recycle electronic items. According to him,[119] electronics are harder to recycle than a lot of waste because they contain many different substances smooched together. Metals, semi-metals, and plastics all spun together as microscopically small composites. Also, many electronic items are not built to be repairable. Because it is so difficult to economically recycle e-waste, it is often exported to countries where there is little environmental protection or worker safety.

Another cause is the issue of development. It is estimated that there are over a billion personal computers in the world.[120] In developed countries, these have an average life span of only two years. In the United States alone, there are over 300 million obsolete computers. Not only developed countries, the developing countries too have faced a steep rise in sales or moreover wastage in this industry. It is believed that sales of computers and internet usage have gone up by 400% in developing countries as well.[121] The electronic industry especially is globalising at a fast and alarming rate narrowing the digital divide. The result is large numbers of "end of life" computers and other IT equipment that are not easily disposed of.

Again, Chauhan[122] added as to the causes of e-waste. According to him, electronics are made using various metals, precious metals, chemicals, plastics, glass, etc. The processing of recovering the commodities from these electronics devices is known as e-waste recycling. While plastics, aluminium, steel, iron, copper, gold, silver, gold, palladium, etc. are recovered as good commodities; mercury, cadmium, arsenic, cartridge inks, and leads fall under the hazardous category. So, if the recycling is not done in a proper way these hazardous materials get into the waste stream and can pollute air, water and soil which can adversely affect the environment.

Another reason adduced on the cause of e-waste because of its frequency in discarding of electronic devices. The high obsolesce of electrical equipment and electronic devices has created the mentality of "upgrading" and using the "latest" equipment or devices. This has culminated in "disposable" lifestyle and has generated an attitude of "use it once and upgrade." The result is that nowadays, people change their personal old computers, mobiles and other electronic devices very frequently, which results in the rapid increase of e-waste.[123] But some of these

---

[118] Green (2019).

[119] Green (2019).

[120] Biju (2017).

[121] Ibid.

[122] Chauhan (2020).

[123] Kohli (2017).

electrical equipment and electronic devices might be in working condition and not at the conclusion of their electronic life. Thus, many components of these devices can be reused or recycled but only a few countries are taking decent measures in this regard. Due to the dearth of recycling facilities in many countries or even the slow procedure of recycling many of the devices are mostly discarded. As a result of this, the rate of reuse is much less than the rate of disposal. This is regarded as "Planned Obsolescence"[124] and it compounds the existing problem.

Planned obsolescence (or built-in obsolescence) is a policy of planning or designing a product with an artificially limited useful life, so it will become obsolete (that is, unfashionable or no longer functional) after a certain period.[125] It is therefore a strategy used in product marketing that intentionally helps reduce the lifetime of a product.[126]

> This means that your electronics are being built to last shorter and shorter periods of time. We have seen this being used in various industries from fashion to phones, a calculated behaviour change introduced and sustained by big business. Simply, so that they can sell more.[127]

On why companies do it, Shahan[128] opined that technology companies are notorious for forcing you to upgrade, but other companies also do their best to make things obsolete so you will upgrade and buy more from them. That is just how companies make money. To be fair, because technology is constantly improving, and technology companies want to continue to offer the latest and greatest, sometimes the "older" equipment just does not work as well anymore. But that is normal and no one has a problem with things getting old. The problem occurs when a company intentionally slows down older devices or takes other measures to actively "strongly encourage" you to upgrade.[129] That is why planned obsolescence is here to stay. In fact, one could argue that planned obsolescence is good for investors, but not for consumers, Shahan intoned.[130]

From the foregoing, the cause of accumulating e-waste in the words of Mathur[131] is that:

> We aren't cleaning up the waste we are generating at the same rate that we are buying new products. This essentially means a huge surplus of electronic waste. In 2017, 44 million tonnes of e-waste was generated. This is 4500 times that of the volume of Eiffel tower and a distance from New York to Bangkok and back long.

---

[124] Mathur (2018).

[125] Sarhan (2017).

[126] Ibid.

[127] Mathur (2018).

[128] Mathur (2018).

[129] For instance, Apple just got smacked with a class action lawsuit after the tech giant admitted it slowed down older iPhones. This act is also known as planned obsolescence.

[130] And one may be forced to add, not good for the environment especially applying that policy to electrical/electronic devices.

[131] Mathur (2018).

9.4.4 Why Is E-Waste an Environmental and Health Problem

Electronic waste by its very nature causes serious health and pollution problems. This is because electronic equipment contains some very serious contaminants such as lead, cadmium, beryllium and brominated flame-retardants. If treated properly, electronic waste is a valuable source of secondary raw materials.[132] For instance, "White box computers"[133] which are often assembled by small-scale manufacturers utilising refurbished components of electronic materials. However, if not treated properly, electronic waste is a major source of toxins and carcinogens. Rapid technology change, low initial cost and planned obsolescence have resulted in a fast-growing surplus of electronic waste around the globe.[134]

Electronic waste is of concern largely due to the toxicity and carcinogenicity of some of its substances, if processed improperly.[135] Toxic substances in electronic waste may include lead element, mercury element, and cadmium. Carcinogenic substances in electronic waste may include polychlorinated biphenyls (PCBs). Capacitors, transformers, and wires insulated with or components coated with polyvinyl chloride (PVC), manufactured before 1977, often contain dangerous amounts of PCBs.[136] Up to 38 separate chemical elements are incorporated into electronic waste items.[137]

Substances found in large quantities include epoxy and electronics resins, fiberglass, PCBs, PVC, thermosetting plastics, lead, tin, copper, silicon, beryllium, carbon, iron and aluminium.[138] While elements found in small amounts include cadmium, mercury and thallium. Elements found in trace amounts include americium, antimony, arsenic, barium, bismuth, boron, cobalt, europium, gallium, germanium, gold, indium, lithium, manganese, nickel, niobium, palladium, platinum, rhodium, ruthenium, selenium, silver, tantalum, terbium, thorium, titanium, vanadium, and yttrium. Almost all electronics contain lead and tin (as solder) and copper (as wire and printed circuit board tracks), although the use of lead-free solder is now spreading rapidly.[139]

Again, many of the plastics used in electronic equipment contain flame retardants. These are generally halogens added to the plastic resin, making the plastics difficult to recycle. Due to the flame retardants being additives, they easily leach off the material in hot weather, which is a problem because when disposed of, electronic

[132] Greenpeace International (2016).

[133] Off-brand or no-name computers.

[134] Greenpeace International (2016).

[135] Kaley et al. (2018).

[136] Ibid.

[137] Ibid.

[138] Chemical Fact Sheet (2020).

[139] Ibid.

waste is generally left outside. The flame retardants leach into the soil and recorded levels were 93 times higher than soil with no contact with electronic waste.[140]

Hazards also associated with electronic waste include health problems such as occupational safety and health effects among those directly involved due to the methods of processing the waste.[141] Thousands of men, women, and children are employed in highly polluting, primitive recycling technologies, extracting metals, toners, and plastics from computers and other electronic waste.[142] Even in developed countries disposal of e-waste involves significant risk to workers and communities and great care is taken to avoid unsafe exposure in recycling operations and leaching of materials such as heavy metals from landfills and incinerator ashes. It is as a result of these and other hazards associated with hazardous substances that there is a need to protect the environment from the adverse effects of e-waste.[143]

In addition, developing countries utilise methods that are more harmful and more wasteful. In most developing countries, including Nigeria, electronic waste processing usually first involves dismantling the equipment into various parts – metal frames, power supplies, circuit boards and plastics, which are separated often by hand. Alternatively, materials are shredded and sophisticated expensive equipment separates the various metal and plastic fractions, which then are sold to various smelters and plastic recyclers. However, an expedient and prevalent method is simply to toss equipment onto an open fire, to melt plastics and burn away invaluable metals. This releases carcinogens and neurotoxins into the air, contributing to acrid, lingering smog. These noxious fumes include dioxins and furans. Bonfire refuse can be disposed of quickly into drainage ditches or waterways feeding the ocean or local water supplies. This has a deleterious effect on the water bodies.[144]

After the end of useful life electronic products result in e-waste. Computers, desktops, washing machines, mobile phones, printers, etc. contribute to e-waste generation. Major compositions of e-waste include consumer electronics, IT communication technology, and large household appliances, among others.

The effect of the various components of e-waste on human health has been identified. For instance, components such as the motherboard contain beryllium that affects the skin and lungs. Switches and flatscreen monitors contain mercury that affects the skin and the brain. Cable coating contains PVC which affects the human immune system. Also, the computer batteries, containing cadmium affect the kidney and liver.[145]

While plastics, aluminium, steel, iron, copper, gold, silver, gold, palladium etc. are recovered as good commodities, mercury, cadmium, arsenic, cartridge inks, and

---

[140] Ibid.

[141] Kaley et al. (2018).

[142] Ibid.

[143] Kaley et al. (2018).

[144] Ibid.

[145] Chauhan (2019).

leads fall under the hazardous category and are very toxic.[146] These toxic materials pose a threat to human health. The presence of materials in the environment causes breathing problems, nervous disorders, different types of allergies and cancers, blood anaemia, physical and mental weakness and many other dangerous diseases.[147]

At times, the toxic materials from the electronic devices are released into bodies of water, groundwater, soil and air, affecting both land and sea animals. When you throw out your e-waste they wind up in landfills, causing toxic materials to seep into groundwater. This is because toxins from disposed of electronics like lead, mercury, arsenic, cadmium, chlorine and bromine, leak into the groundwater and bio-accumulate in the food chain causing detrimental damage to the soil, water supply, vegetation, animals and humans. For instance, exposure to lead can cause damage to the reproductive, blood and nervous systems; so also is mercury used in cellphones.[148] Overall, the results of e-waste are grave and injurious to human health.

Besides the impact of e-waste on the environment and human health, improper recycling and disposal of electronic equipment, especially laptops, cellphones, tablets, etc., also have a big impact on data and information security as well. When e-waste is disposed of improperly and without the use of a company that specialises in proper data destruction, there is a severe risk of identity theft, data breaches and massive liability for the companies involved. This poses a potential security threat to both individuals and businesses. Thus, if a hard drive is not properly erased before it is thrown away, it can be opened, potentially putting sensitive information in the hands of the wrong people. Credit card numbers, financial data and bank account information can all be obtained by those trained to do so.[149]

Again, working on e-waste may lead to human exploitation. According to the Borgen Report,[150] an estimated 29.8 million people are living in slavery across the globe. There are even more people who submit themselves to dangerous and gruelling work for a demeaning wage, as it may be the only work available. Since 90% of e-waste is illegally traded, there are many criminals worldwide benefiting from the stripping and processing of e-waste by poorer labourers. These workers are without rights, as they are exposed to hazardous materials on a daily basis. Some may also be intimidated into working long hours, putting them at even more risk.[151]

E-waste is not a problem that is going away any time soon. In fact, it is only going to get worse. By 2017, the volume of our thrown-away e-products throughout the world rose by 33% from 2012, and we can expect the weight of this garbage to equal

[146] Ibid.

[147] Spelch (2016).

[148] Mathur (2018).

[149] Stokes (2017).

[150] Borgen Magazine (2018).

[151] Ibid.

eight of the Great Pyramids of Egypt. The amount of e-waste that we produce, including computers, DVD players, cellphones and global positioning products, could rise by a whopping 500% over the next decade in many countries.[152]

It is crucial now that some of the effects of e-waste on both the natural and human environment have been known, the next discussion centred on how to determine what can be done to control the e-waste menace.

9.5 Trending Options in E-Waste Management

Waste electrical and electronic equipment (WEEE or E-waste) is defined as, "the electrical or electronic equipment which is waste within the meaning of Article 3(1) of Directive 2008/98/EC,[153] including all components, sub-assemblies and consumables which are part of the product at the time of discarding.[154] WEEE or e-waste is becoming major threat to the whole world. Its toxic emissions mixed with virgin soil and air and causing harmful effects to the entire bioscope either directly or indirectly. Direct impacts include release of acids, toxic compounds including heavy metals, carcinogenic chemicals and indirect effects such as bio magnification of heavy metals,[155] thus, the need for e-waste management. E-waste management can be defined as the practical and holistic approach and the founding pillar of cutting down waste from our mother Earth. It is reusing and recycling of e-waste which is no longer in use and can be salvaged for some of its components.[156]

In the developed and some of the developing economies trending options in managing e-waste is through legislation.[157] Technical solutions are available, but in most cases, a legal framework, a collection system, logistics, and other services need to be implemented before a technical solution can be applied.[158] In the United States, an estimated 70% of heavy metals in landfills come from discarded electronics, while electronic waste represents only 2% of America's trash in landfills.[159] Discarded electronics represented 5 to 6 times as much weight as recycled electronics.[160] The Consumer Electronics Association said that U.S. households spend an average of US$ 1400 annually on an average of 24 electronic items, leading to

[152] Borgen Magazine (2018).

[153] European Union (2018) (WFD 2008), Art. 3(1).

[154] European Union (2012) (WEEE 2012), Art. 3(1)(e).

[155] Sahu (2019).

[156] Ibid.

[157] However, there are other options which include: recycling, donation, take back, exchange and consumer awareness. For this work, the legislative option is advocated and relevant international and domestic instruments are reviewed in the subsequent segment of this chapter.

[158] Silicon Valley Toxic Corporation (2019).

[159] Ibid.

[160] United States Environmental Protection Agency (EPA) (2008).

speculations of millions of tons of valuable metals sitting in desk drawers.[161] U.S. National Safety Council estimates that 75% of all personal computers ever sold are now gathering dust as surplus electronics. While some recycle, 7% of cellphone owners still throw away their old cellphones.[162]

In the United States of America (USA), the main federal law governing waste is the Resource Conservation and Recovery Act of 1976.[163] It covers only CRTs, although some states' regulations may differ. For instance, in 2001, the State of Arkansas enacted the Arkansas Computer and Electronic Solid Waste Management Act, which requires that state agencies manage and sell surplus computer equipment, establish a computer and electronics recycling fund, and authorise the Department of Environmental Quality to regulate and/or ban the disposal of computer and electronic equipment in Arkansas landfills.[164]

California state implemented a broader waste ban, with advance recovery fee funding, two years later. Electronic waste in California may neither be disposed of in a landfill nor be exported overseas. The 2003 Electronic Waste Recycling Act in California introduced an Electronic Waste Recycling Fee on all new monitors and televisions sold to cover the cost of recycling. The fee ranges from six to ten dollars. California went from only a handful of recyclers to over 60 within the state and over 600 collection sites. The amount of the fee depends on the size of the monitor; it was adjusted on 1 July 2005 to match the real cost of recycling. Cellphones are "considered hazardous waste" in California; many chemicals in cellphones leach from landfills into the groundwater system.[165]

State of Colorado legislation requires education programmes that address its electronic waste problem. In 2004, Maine passed Maine Public Law 661, an Act to Protect Public Health and the Environment by providing for a System of Shared Responsibility for the Safe Collection and Recycling of Electronic Waste. It necessitated that after 2006; computer manufacturers take responsibility for handling and recycling computer monitors, and pay the handling costs as well. Massachusetts was the first in the United States to make it illegal to dispose of CRTs in landfills in April 2000, most similar to the European disposal bans of the 1990s.[166]

Minnesota state enacted a law-making vendors responsible for the disposal of their branded electronics. Minnesota legislation also outlaws the dumping of cathode ray tubes in landfills. A law in the State of Washington took effect on 1 January

[161] Martin (2019).

[162] Ibid.

[163] Although efforts were made to enact laws on e-waste, for example, the National Computer Recycling Bill (H.R. 425) 2002, Electronic Device Recycling Research and Development Act H.R. 1580) and the Green Energy Education Act (H.R. 957) 2009, the bills were passed but were not signed into law.

[164] House of Representatives (1999).

[165] Nate (2006).

[166] Maine Legislature (2012).

2009, requiring manufacturers of electronic goods to pay for recycling, and establishing a state-wide network of collection points.[167]

In Canada, some Canadian provinces have implemented a broader waste ban with advance recovery fee funding on all new monitors and televisions sold to cover the cost of recycling. The fee ranges from six to ten Canadian dollars. The fee was added to the cost of purchasing new televisions, computers, and computer components in Alberta in February 2004, the first of its kind in Canada. Saskatchewan also implemented an electronics recycling fee in February 2007, followed by British Columbia in August 2007, Nova Scotia in February 2008, and Ontario in April 2009.[168]

In the 1990s, some European countries banned the disposal of electronic waste in landfills. This created an electronic waste processing industry in Europe. In Switzerland, the first electronic waste recycling system was implemented in 1991, beginning with the collection of old refrigerators. Over the years, all other electric and electronic devices were gradually added to the system.[169] Legislation followed in 1998, and since January 2005 it has been possible to return all electronic waste to the sales points and other collection points free of charge. There are two established producer responsibility organisations: SWICO,[170] mainly handling information, communication, and organisation technology, and SENS, mainly responsible for electrical appliances. The total amount of recycled electronic waste exceeds 10 kg per capita per year.[171]

The European Union implemented a similar system in February 2003, under the Waste Electrical and Electronic Equipment Directive (WEEE Directive, 2002/96/EC).[172] The WEEE Directive has now been transposed into national laws in all member countries of the European Union. It was designed to make equipment manufacturers financially or physically responsible for their equipment at the end of its life, under a policy known as extended producer responsibility (EPR). Under this policy users of electrical and electronic equipment from private households should have the possibility of returning WEEE at least free of charge. To this end, manufacturers must dispose of electrical and electronic equipment in an environmentally friendly manner, by ecological disposal, reuse, or refurbishment. The EPR policy was therefore seen as a useful policy as it internalised the end-of-life costs and provided a competitive incentive for companies to design equipment with fewer costs and liabilities when it reached its end of life.

---

[167] Californians Against Waste (2009).

[168] Katalin (2010).

[169] Ibid.

[170] Swico Recycling is a voluntary, cooperative system for taking back waste equipment. It is operated successfully by Swiss manufacturers and importers in the IT, office equipment, consumer electronics and photo/film sectors.

[171] European Union (2015).

[172] European Union (2003).

Since 13 August 2005, electronics manufacturers became financially responsible for compliance with the WEEE Directive. Under the directive, from the end of 2006, every country must recycle at least 4 kg of electronic waste per capita per year. The intention was that the Directive should decrease e-waste and e-waste exports within and outside the European Union. In December 2008, a draft revision to the Directive proposed a market-based goal of 65%, which is 22 kg per capita in the case of the United Kingdom. A decision on the proposed revisions resulted in a new WEEE Directive in 2012.[173]

The purpose of the WEEE Directive 2012 is to contribute to sustainable production and consumption by, as a first priority, the prevention of WEEE and, in addition, by the reuse, recycling and other forms of recovery of such wastes to reduce the disposal of waste and to contribute to the efficient use of resources and the retrieval of valuable secondary raw materials. It also seeks to improve the environmental performance of all operators involved in the life cycle of EEE, e.g. producers, distributors and consumers and, in particular, those operators directly involved in the collection and treatment of WEEE.[174]

The WEEE Directive of 2012 has far-reaching provisions for the management of e-waste. For instance, the provisions of the Directive apply to products and producers irrespective of selling technique, including distance and electronic selling. In this connection, the obligations of producers and distributors using distance and electronic selling channels should, as far as is practicable, take the same form, and should be enforced in the same way, as for other distribution channels, to avoid those other distribution channels having to bear the costs resulting from the Directive arising from WEEE for which the equipment was sold by distance or electronic selling.[175]

In addition, under the Directive,[176] the collection, storage, transport, treatment and recycling of WEEE as well as its preparation for reuse shall be conducted with an approach geared to protecting the environment and human health and preserving raw materials and shall aim at recycling valuable resources contained in EEE.[177]

Again, appropriate priority should be given to preparing for reuse of WEEE and its components, sub-assemblies and consumables. Where this is not preferable, all WEEE collected separately should be sent for recovery, in the course of which a high

[173] European Union (2012).

[174] European Union (2012) (WFD 2012), Preamble, para 6.

[175] Ibid., Preamble, para 7.

[176] Ibid., Preamble, para 19.

[177] "Electrical and electronic equipment" or "EEE" means equipment that is dependent on electric currents or electromagnetic fields to work properly and equipment for the generation, transfer, and measurement of such currents and fields and designed for use with a voltage rating not exceeding 1000 volts for alternating current and 1500 volts for direct current. See European Union (2012) (WFD 2012), Art. 3(1)(a). See also the Nigerian National Environmental (Electrical/Electronic Sector) Regulations 2011, Regulation 70.

level of recycling and recovery should be achieved. In addition, producers should be encouraged to integrate recycled material into new equipment.[178]

Furthermore, users of EEE from private households should have the possibility of returning WEEE at least free of charge. WEEE from private households means:

> WEEE which comes from private households and WEEE which comes from commercial, industrial, institutional and other sources which, because of its nature and quantity, is similar to that from private households. Waste from EEE likely to be used by both private households and users other than private households shall in any event be considered to be WEEE from private households.[179]

Producers are therefore urged to finance at least the collection from collection facilities, and the treatment, recovery and disposal of private household WEEE.

In line with the polluter-pays principle, producers are encouraged to take full responsibility for the WEEE collection, particularly by financing the collection of WEEE throughout the entire waste chain, including from private households, to avoid separately collected WEEE becoming the object of sub-optimal treatment and illegal exports, to create a level playing field by harmonising producer financing and to shift payment for the collection of this waste from general taxpayers to the consumers of EEE.

To give maximum effect to the concept of producer responsibility, each producer should be responsible for financing the management of the waste from his own products. The producer should be able to choose to fulfil this obligation either individually or by joining a collective scheme. Each producer should, when placing a product on the market, provide a financial guarantee to prevent costs for the management of WEEE from orphan products from falling on society or the remaining producers.

The responsibility for the financing of the management of historical waste should be shared by all existing producers through collective financing schemes to which all producers that exist on the market when the costs occur contribute proportionately. Collective financing schemes should not have the effect of excluding niche and low-volume producers, importers and new entrants. Collective schemes could provide for differentiated fees based on how easily products and the valuable secondary raw materials that they contain could be recycled. In the case of products which have a long life cycle and which are now covered by the Directive, such as photovoltaic panels, the best possible use should be made of existing collection and recovery systems, provided that they meet the requirements laid down in the Directive.[180]

Information to users about the requirement not to dispose of WEEE as unsorted municipal waste and to collect WEEE separately and about the collection systems and their role in the management of WEEE is indispensable for the success of WEEE collection. Such information necessitates the proper marking of EEE which could

[178] European Union (2012) (WFD 2012), Preamble, para 20.

[179] Ibid., Art. 3(1)(h).

[180] European Union (2012) (WFD 2012), Preamble, para 23.

end up in rubbish bins or similar means of municipal waste collection.[181] Thus, producers could be allowed to show purchasers, on a voluntary basis at the time of sale of new products, the costs of collecting, treating and disposing of WEEE in an environmentally sound way.[182]

However, the application of the WEEE Directive has been criticised for implementing the EPR concept in a collective manner, thereby losing the competitive incentive of individual manufacturers to be rewarded for their green design.[183]

Other efforts of the EU in curbing problems of e-waste include: The Directive on the Restriction of the Use of Certain Hazardous Substances in Electrical and Electronic Equipment (2002/95/EC), Restriction of the Use of Certain Hazardous Substances in Electrical and Electronic Equipment, commonly referred to as the Restriction of Hazardous Substances Directive (RoHS Directive), was also adopted in February 2003 by the European Union. The RoHS Directive took effect on 1 July 2006. This directive restricts the use of six hazardous materials in the manufacture of various types of electronic and electrical equipment.[184]

Several countries in the Asian continent have made some strides in the control of e-waste. South Korea, Japan, India and Taiwan require that sellers and manufacturers of electronics be responsible for recycling 75% of them.[185]

Besides all these efforts by the government and its agencies, many private firms are involved in the battle against the e-waste scourge especially in the areas of collecting, dismantling, separating and exporting e-waste for recyclers. One such agency is the Basel Action Network (BAN).

Basel Action Network (BAN) is a toxic trade watchdog organisation founded in 1997. It is a USA-based charity organisation involved in public awareness programmes on e-waste, championing global environmental health and justice by eliminating toxic trade, catalysing a toxics-free future, and campaigning for everyone's right to a flourishing environment. BAN's vision focuses on a bright future where "we live harmoniously with ourselves, our technology, and our planet."[186] It engages in Basel Convention advocacy. As the only non-profit that regularly attends Basel Convention meetings, BAN's speeches are often instrumental in defending existing policies and advocating for just decisions.[187] Throughout 2014, BAN investigated negligence and illegal activity after fires at multiple Stone Castle Recycling sites in Utah. The investigation included site visits to assess the damage.[188]

[181] Ibid., Preamble, para 25.

[182] European Union (2012) (WFD 2012), Preamble, para 24.

[183] Greenpeace International (2006).

[184] Deepali et al. (2006).

[185] Ibid.

[186] Basel Action Network (BAN) (2013).

[187] For instance, BAN played a prominent role in the Basel Ban Amendment in 1995.

[188] Basel Action Network (BAN) (2013).

It may be just a coincidence that BAN is USA-based. First, the USA and Haiti are the only countries that have failed to ratify the Basel Convention that had been in force since 5 May 1992. Again, the USA, among other countries, has also refused to ratify the Ban Amendment to the Basel Convention that came into force on 5 December 2019. Since the USA has not ratified the Basel Convention or its Ban Amendment, and has no domestic laws forbidding the export of toxic waste, the Basel Action Network estimates that about 80% of the electronic waste directed to recycling in the USA does not get recycled there at all, but is put on container ships and sent to countries such as China.[189]

The USA is taking in and throwing out an astonishing number of devices every year: millions of tonnes of televisions, phones, computers, and appliances, and they rarely see the aftermath. To handle its waste, the USA has turned to other nations, funnelling discarded electronics to South Asia and Africa, where labourers scrap products for salvageable metals. The workers might burn the material in the open air, or treat it in an acid bath, sifting through the remains for small amounts of potentially valuable metals, like gold.[190]

The USA is an extreme producer of e-waste, but has done next to nothing about regulating it. Despite signing on to the Basel Convention, the country has failed to ratify it, and nearly all e-waste can be lawfully shipped overseas, many years after the first countries agreed to abide by the Basel Convention. America has "this distinction all the time of being the jerk in the room," Scott Cassel said.[191] Europe, by contrast, has much stricter rules about how manufacturers dispose of the electronics they produce. States have taken on some of the burden, and about half have passed some form of law regulating electronics dumping in the country.[192]

Again, according to *Down To Earth*,[193] not only does the USA produce the most waste per capita, but it has also failed to ratify the Basel Convention and has actively opposed the BAN Amendment. This non-adherence of the USA to international waste trade rules has allowed unscrupulous "recyclers" to export many hundreds of containers of hazardous electronic waste each week to developing countries for so-called recycling, according to BAN.[194] BAN estimates that about 80% of the e-waste directed to recycling in the United States does not get recycled there at all but is put in containers and sent to developing countries and that nearly 40% of e-waste delivered to USA recyclers is exported to Asian and African countries.[195]

To this end, BAN has revealed that large quantities of obsolete computers, televisions, mobile phones, and other used electronic equipment exported from the USA and Europe to Lagos, Nigeria for "reuse and repair" are ending up gathering

[189] Ibid.

[190] Lecher (2019).

[191] Cassel (2001).

[192] Ibid.

[193] Down To Earth Magazine (2018).

[194] Basel Action Network (BAN) (2013).

[195] Basel Action Network (BAN) (2013).

dust in warehouses or being dumped and burned near residences in empty lots, roadsides and in swamps creating serious health and environmental contamination from the toxic leachate and smoke.[196] According to Puckett et al.:[197]

> …Because of widespread usage of toxic chemicals in today's high-tech equipment most electronic wastes are hazardous wastes… Much of the growth in the information technology (IT) sector in developing countries has been fueled by the importation of hand-me-down, used equipment from rich, developed countries… BAN's latest investigation in Lagos, Nigeria, a new hotbed of high-tech growth…reveals…a growing environmental and health disaster… While supposedly closing the "digital divide," we are opening a "digital dump."… The following is a partial list of brand names of imported computers, copy machines, and high-tech peripherals found in the markets, warehouses and dumps of Lagos: AEG, Agfa, Apple, Compaq [part of HP], Dell, Epson [part of Seiko], Gateway, Hewlett-Packard [HP], IBM, Panasonic [part of Matsushita], Pitney-Bowes, Ricoh, Sharp, Sony, Toshiba [also refers to Intel].

To help everyone tackle their toxic footprint, BAN introduced e-Stewards Programme.[198] Under this programme, BAN certifies socially and environmentally responsible electronics recyclers. With recyclers, enterprises, and auditors, "we're creating a successful and growing market solution which provides a viable alternative to e-waste export."[199] After years of consultation with leading recycling experts, certification bodies, and occupational health experts, BAN published the updated e-Stewards Certification Standard Version 2.0 in November 2013.

Recognising that auditors are central to the certification's success, BAN partnered with SAI Global[200] to train auditors to the new standard. Together, they also created top-notch implementation training to help e-stewards recyclers comply with the enhanced new version.[201] BAN also created the e-Stewards Marketplace, a secure business-to-business online trading platform that connects any company or group with e-waste to an e-Stewards recycler. Now anyone can easily dispose of used electronics with the world's most responsible recyclers.[202]

Did the e-Stewards Programme make any impact on recyclers, one may be tempted to ask. The answer is in the affirmative. For instance, Arrow Electronics achieved certification in all of its recycling plants worldwide. LG Electronics updated its consumer take-back programme to ensure all electronics are recycled responsibly. On Earth Day 2013, Staples began offering free drop-off for e-Stewards recycling in all of its stores in the USA. To elicit more support and participation in

[196] Basel Action Network (2005).

[197] Puckett et al. (2005).

[198] E-Stewards certified recyclers adhere to the industry's gold standard for occupational health and safety.

[199] Basel Action Network (2005).

[200] SAI Global is a multinational business services company based in Chicago, Illinois, United States. It offers risk management services, quality assurance audit and certification, auditor training, standards information services, and property services.

[201] Basel Action Network (2005).

[202] Ibid.

the e-Steward Programme, BAN designed the new, easy-to-use e-Stewards E-waste Calculator App (Apple IOS and Android). This App helps companies quantify the value of their e-Stewards commitment. "Enter in how much e-waste you have recycled responsibly, and you will see the greenhouse gas emissions saved and the amount of toxic chemicals diverted."[203]

9.6 Controlling Hazardous Substances Through the Law

"Hazardous wastes" are a subset of wastes that include a wide range of wastes capable of causing harm to human health, the environment, or both. Hazardous wastes include by-products that are explosive, flammable, radioactive, liable to spontaneous combustion, emit flammable gases upon contact with water, poisonous, infectious, corrosive, toxic, and those that are capable of yielding another harmful substance after disposal. They also include wastes containing harmful compounds, such as arsenic, cadmium, mercury, lead, acidic solutions, organic phosphorus, halogenated organic solvents and phenols. Such wastes originate from a variety of sources including a wide range of production processes, medical care in hospitals and domestic garbage.[204]

As already stated hazardous wastes may subject a person to harm; including death or bodily injury. These generated wastes require proper handling and disposal if their adverse impacts on human health and the environment are to be avoided. One way through which hazardous wastes may be controlled is legal approaches. Legal approaches to the control of hazardous substances are twofold: the application of international conventions on hazardous substances and the use of national legislation.

9.6.1 International Law and Control of Hazardous Substances

9.6.1.1 Introduction

Hazardous substances may come from solid waste, e-waste and other types of waste that are poisonous, toxic, and noxious that may subject a person to harm, including death or bodily injury.

As the problem of waste generation and management becomes more pronounced both nationally and internationally, the management of hazardous waste has acquired a prominent position in environmental protection. Again, as waste

[203] Basel Action Network (2005).

[204] UNEP (2006), p. 125.

regulations became tighter in some countries, the costs of disposal rose and it became common practice to export these hazardous wastes, especially to developing countries where they could be disposed of at a lower cost. As a result, there was increasing pressure for the introduction of controls over the transboundary movement of waste, especially those that are potentially harmful or hazardous,[205] between countries. These pressures gave rise to a legal approach to the control of hazardous substances through the application of international conventions on hazardous substances.

9.6.1.2 The Basel Convention on the Control of Trans-boundary Movements of Hazardous Wastes and Their Disposal (Basel Convention) 1989

The Basel Convention is an international treaty that was designed to reduce the movements of hazardous waste between nations, and specifically to prevent the transfer of hazardous waste from more developed countries (MDCs) to less developed countries (LDCs). It does not, however, address the movement of radioactive waste or e-waste. The Convention is also intended to minimise the amount and toxicity of wastes generated, to ensure their environmentally sound management as closely as possible to the source of generation, and to assist LDCs in the environmentally sound management of the hazardous and other wastes they generate.[206] The Convention was opened for signature on 22 March 1989, and entered into force on 5 May 1992. Of the 185 parties to the Convention, Haiti and the United States, although have signed the Convention, are yet to ratify it.[207]

With the tightening of environmental laws in developed nations in the 1970s, disposal costs for hazardous waste rose dramatically. At the same time, the globalisation of shipping made the transboundary movement of waste more accessible, and many LDCs were desperate for foreign currency. Consequently, the trade in hazardous waste, particularly to LDCs, grew rapidly. One of the incidents that led to the creation of the Basel Convention was the *Khian Sea* waste disposal incident, in which a ship carrying incinerator ash from the city of Philadelphia in the United States after having dumped half of its load on a beach in Haiti, was forced away where it sailed for many months, changing its name several times. Unable to unload the cargo in any port, the crew was believed to have dumped much of it at sea.[208]

The objective of the Convention is to regulate the transboundary movements of hazardous and other wastes and it imposes obligations on the parties to the Convention to ensure that environmentally sound management, in particular, the disposal of hazardous wastes is pursued. "Transboundary movement" means any movement of

[205] Such as e-waste.

[206] Birne and Boyle (2002), p. 383.

[207] Basel Convention (1994).

[208] Birne and Boyle (2002), p. 383.

hazardous wastes or other wastes from an area under the national jurisdiction of one state to or through an area under the national jurisdiction of another state or to or through an area not under the national jurisdiction of any state, provided at least two states are involved in the movement.[209]

The Convention stipulates three main interdependent and mutually supportive goals that have to be fulfilled. They are:

(i) transboundary movements of wastes should be reduced to a minimum consistency with their environmentally sound management;
(ii) hazardous wastes should be treated and disposed of as close as possible to their source of generation and
(iii) hazardous waste generation should be reduced and minimised at its source.[210]

9.6.1.2.1 Obligations of Parties Under the Basel Convention

The Basel Convention contains general obligations requiring parties, inter alia, to ensure that the transboundary movements of hazardous wastes are reduced to the minimum consistent with environmentally sound and efficient management. This, according to Birnie and Boyle,[211] places three important and far-reaching restrictions on international trade in hazardous wastes.

First, the Convention confirms the sovereign right to ban imports; either on an individual, bilateral or regional basis, provided the exercise of this right to prohibit trade in waste is notified to other parties through the secretariat.[212]

Second, the Convention has adopted the principle of minimising the generation of hazardous waste and promoting disposal at the source. Indeed, the primary obligation is to manage the transboundary movement of waste in an environmentally sound manner. Thus, transboundary movement is permitted between parties to the Basel Convention but only in circumstances where the state of export does not have the capacity or facilities to dispose of the wastes in an environmentally sound manner itself, or unless the wastes are intended for recycling.[213]

The Convention while recognising the importing states' responsibility under international law for the protection of their environments places on importing states' parties an obligation of environmentally sound management.[214] However, the exporting state may not under any circumstances discharge its obligation to manage

[209] Basel Convention (1989), Art. 2 (3).
[210] Ibid., Preamble.
[211] Birne and Boyle (2002), p. 383.
[212] Basel Convention (1989), Preamble and Art. 4(1)(a).
[213] Ibid., Art. 4(9)(a) and (b).
[214] Basel Convention (1989), Arts. 4(8) and 9(3).

the wastes in an environmentally sound manner and must permit re-import if necessary.[215]

To enhance the application of this concept (environmentally sound management of hazardous wastes) the Convention requires the establishment of technical guidelines.[216] The development and implementation of these guidelines create less hazardous waste and/or improve existing technologies to eliminate the generation of hazardous waste.

To achieve this aim, a technical working group was established directly after the adoption of the Convention. What amounts to environmentally sound management was defined in general terms in Article 2(8). It means, "taking all practicable steps to ensure that hazardous wastes or other wastes are managed in a manner which will protect human health and the environment against the adverse effects which may result from such wastes."

Before the coming into effect of the Basel Convention in 1992, the Cairo Guidelines and Principles of Environmentally Sound Management of Hazardous Wastes of 1985, adopted by the United Nations Environment Programme (UNEP) in 1987, provided a more detailed functional definition of the term. It means, "the use of best practicable means, approval of sites and facilities, disposal plans, monitoring, public access to information and contingency planning."[217]

Third, the Convention under Articles 4 and 6 requires prior, informed and written consent of both transit and import states, in the conduct of international trade in hazardous wastes. The basis for this provision, according to Sunkin et al.,[218] is that a state's sovereignty over its territory places a duty upon other states using its territory not to cause damage or interfere with other uses of the territory. To this end, Birnie and Boyle[219] regard this prior consent provision as the crowning achievement of the Convention as really does international law require prior consent of other states before environmentally harmful activities may be undertaken.

Although the Basel Convention places a general prohibition on the exportation or importation of wastes between parties and non-parties, the exception to this rule is where the waste is subject to another treaty that does not take away from the Basel Convention. This makes a nonsense of this provision and allowes non-party members to trade with a party member of the Basel Convention. For instance, the United States of America (USA) is a notable non-party to the Convention and has a number of such agreements for allowing the shipping of hazardous wastes to Basel party countries. The Organisation of Economic Co-operation and Development (OECD) Council also has its own control system that governs the transboundary movement of hazardous materials between OECD member countries. This allows, among other

[215] Ibid., Art. 4(10).

[216] Ibid., Art. 4(8).

[217] UNEP (2012).

[218] Sunkin et al. (1998), p. 296.

[219] Birne and Boyle (2002), p. 385.

things, the OECD countries to continue trading in wastes with countries like the United States that have not ratified the Basel Convention.[220]

Article 4 of the Basel Convention 1989 calls for an overall reduction of waste generation, by encouraging countries to keep wastes within their boundaries and as close as possible to its source of generation, the internal pressures should provide incentives for waste reduction and pollution prevention. Parties are generally prohibited from exporting covered wastes to, or importing covered waste from, non-parties to the convention. The Convention states that illegal hazardous waste traffic is criminal but contains no enforcement provisions.

In addition, under Article 4 (6), parties to the Basel Convention 1989 agree not to allow the export of hazardous wastes or other wastes for disposal within the area south of Latitude 60 degrees whether or not such wastes are subject to transboundary movement. Other far-reaching general obligations imposed by the Convention are provided under Article 4(7).[221] Under this article, each party shall:

(i) prohibit all persons under its national jurisdiction from transporting or disposing of hazardous wastes or other wastes unless such persons are authorised or allowed to perform such types of operations;
(ii) require that hazardous wastes and other wastes that are to be the subject matter of a transboundary movement be packaged, labelled, and transported in conformity with generally accepted and recognised international rules and standards in the field of packaging labelling and transport, and that due account is taken of relevant internationally recognised practices;
(iii) require that hazardous wastes or other wastes be accompanied by a movement document from the point at which a transboundary movement commences to the point of disposal.[222]

Thus, any transboundary movement of hazardous wastes or other wastes without notification to all states concerned; or without consent of a state concerned; or consent obtained from states concerned through falsification, misrepresentation or fraud; or that does not conform in a material way with the documents; or that results in deliberate disposal of hazardous wastes or other wastes will be in contravention of the Convention and principles of international law and be deemed to be illegal traffic.[223] To this end, parties shall consider illegal traffic in hazardous wastes or other wastes criminal.[224] However, a Protocol adopted in 1999[225] provides for a

[220]Birne and Boyle (2002), p. 385.

[221]General overview of other obligations is provided in the Basel Convention (1989), Art. 4(8–13).

[222]Basel Convention (1989), Art. 7.

[223]Ibid., Art. 9.

[224]Ibid., Art. 4(3).

[225]Basel Protocol on Liability and Compensation for Damage resulting from Transboundary Movements of Hazardous Wastes and their Disposal (Basel Protocol on Liability and Compensation) 1999.

liability scheme compensation for damage resulting from transboundary movements of hazardous wastes.

9.6.1.2.2 Implementation Mechanisms of the Basel Convention

For effective implementation of the Convention, state parties to the Convention should aim towards activities for the reduction and minimisation of all risks of harm caused by hazardous wastes to health and the environment. Such activities should include, among other things:

a) steps to reduce or avoid the generation of hazardous wastes;
b) steps to ensure proper recovery of wastes;
c) steps to reduce to a minimum or eliminate the export/import of hazardous wastes.

This entails the planning of environmentally sound disposal facilities, located as close as practicable to the source of generation, and identification of the generators.[226]

The Convention, like other Conventions before it, has provisions for institutional arrangements for purposes of implementation. They are:

a) Conference of Parties (CoP), which shall keep under continuous review and effective implementation of the Convention, among others.[227]
b) A Secretariat, which shall, inter alia, compile information on national sites and facilities of parties; receive and convey information to parties on sources of technical assistance, etc.[228]
c) Settlement of disputes mechanism which shall involve submission of disputes to the International Court of Justice or to arbitration in accordance with the procedures set out in Annex V1. Such disputes include matters on interpretation, application or compliance with the provisions of the Convention.[229]

The Basel Convention can be said to be the most comprehensive international environmental instrument on hazardous and other wastes and is almost universal, with 187 parties. With an overarching objective of protecting human health and the environment against the adverse effects of hazardous wastes, its scope covers a wide range of wastes defined as hazardous based on their origin and/or composition and characteristics. It had also by its various provisions laid down global standards for the control of transboundary movements of hazardous wastes and other wastes.

---

[226] Sunkin et al. (1998), p. 297.
[227] Basel Convention (1989), Art. 5(5)(a–e).
[228] Basel Convention (1989), Art. 16.
[229] Ibid., Art. 20.

All these notwithstanding, in the words of Sunkin et al.,[230] the Basel Convention nevertheless leaves open the possibility of national, bilateral or regional treaties incorporating stricter obligations, even amounting to total prohibitions against the imports of hazardous wastes. This assertion may be unconnected with the strong protestations made by developing country parties to the Convention as it did not provide for the banning of transboundary movements of hazardous wastes and other wastes. Perhaps, this was the impetus needed by African countries that gave birth to the Bamako Convention on the Ban of Imports into Africa and the Control of Trans-boundary Movement and Management of Hazardous Wastes, Bamako Convention.[231] To this we now turn.

9.6.1.3 Bamako Convention on the Ban of Imports into Africa and the Control of Trans-boundary Movement and Management of Hazardous Wastes (Bamako Convention) 1991

Although African countries are parties to the Basel Convention, they remained conscious of their particularly vulnerable situation since the continent had become a dumpsite for developed countries where most of the hazardous wastes are produced. They were therefore conscious of the need for control measures, stricter than the Basel Convention, to protect the lives of Africans and their environment taking advantage of Article 11 of the Basel Convention, which provides that:

> Nothing in this Convention shall prevent a Party from imposing additional requirements that are consistent with the provisions of this Convention, and are in accordance with the rules of international, in order better to protect human health and the environment.

The Bamako Convention is a treaty of African nations prohibiting the import of any hazardous (including radioactive) waste. The Convention was negotiated by twelve nations of the Organisation of African Unity[232] at Bamako, Mali in January 1991, and came into force on 30 January 1998. It uses a format and language similar to that of the Basel Convention, but is much stronger in prohibiting all imports of hazardous waste. Additionally, it does not make exceptions on certain hazardous wastes (like those for radioactive materials) made by the Basel Convention.

Impetus for the Bamako Convention arose from the failure of the Basel Convention to prohibit trade on hazardous waste to less developed countries. This was from the realisation that many developed nations were exporting toxic wastes to Africa. This impression was strengthened by several prominent cases. One important case,

---

[230] Sunkin et al. (1998), p. 297.

[231] Perhaps with hindsight the need for the Bamako Convention on the Ban of Imports into Africa and the Control of Trans-boundary Movement and Management of Hazardous Wastes, would not have arisen if the Basel Ban Amendment that came into force on 5 December 2019 had been accepted by the parties to the Basel Convention before 1991.

[232] As it was then called, now known as the African Union.

which occurred in 1988, concerned the importation into Nigeria of 18,000 barrels of hazardous waste from the Italian companies Ecomar and Jelly Wax, which had agreed to pay local farmer Sunday Nana $100 per month for storage. The barrels, found in storage in the port of Lagos, contained toxic waste including polychlorinated biphenyls (PCB) and their eventual shipment back to Italy led to protests closing three Italian ports.

The objective of the Bamako Convention is to protect the human health of the African population and the environment against the adverse effects which may result from the generation of hazardous wastes to and within Africa.[233] Under the Convention the scope of hazardous wastes are as contained in Article 2. These include:

i) wastes that belong to any category contained in Annex 1 of the Convention;
ii) wastes not covered by the Annex but are defined as or considered to be hazardous waste by domestic legislation of the party of import, export or transit;
iii) wastes that possess any of the characteristics contained in Annex 11 of the Convention; and
iv) hazardous substances which have been banned, cancelled or refused registration by government regulatory action for health or environmental reasons or voluntarily withdrawn from registration in the country of manufacture for the same reason.[234]

It should be noted that radioactive wastes that are subject to any international control system are covered by the Convention.[235] However, if wastes are derived from normal operation of a ship such wastes are not covered by the Convention.[236] Article 4 spells out general obligations to the parties under the Convention. Parties shall:

i) take appropriate legal, administrative and other measures within the area under their jurisdiction to prohibit the import of all hazardous wastes for any reason into Africa from non-contracting parties. Such import shall be deemed illegal and a criminal act.
ii) prohibit dumping or incineration of the wastes at seabed and sub-seabed and not even contracting parties shall engage in such, whether in internal waters, waterways, territorial seas, exclusive economic zone or high seas and where these happen, they shall be deemed illegal.
iii) ensure that generators of wastes submit to the secretariat reports in respect of the generation and impose strict, unlimited, joint and several liability on the generators and as well ensure that the generation is reduced to a minimum taking into account social, economic and technological aspects.

---

233 Bamako Convention (1991), Preamble.

234 Bamako Convention (1991), Art. 2.

235 This was an improvement to the Basel Convention.

236 Bamako Convention (1991), Arts. 2(1)(2) and (3).

iv) ensure the availability of adequate treatment and disposal facilities for the Environmentally Sound Management of the wastes and that within their jurisdiction persons involved in the management of the wastes take necessary steps to prevent pollution arising from the wastes and where pollution occurs to ensure the minimisation of the consequences thereof.

In addition to the above each party shall strive to adopt and implement the preventive precautionary approach to pollution problems and to this end shall promote Clean Production Method. This involves production or industrial systems that avoid or eliminate the generation of wastes.[237]

9.6.1.4 Basel Ban Amendment 2019

Electrical/electronic waste (E-waste) has been identified as a form of toxic waste and was first exposed by Basel Action Network in their 2002 report and film entitled "Exporting Harm: The High-Tech Trashing of Asia."[238] Trade in electronic waste is controlled by the Basel Convention.

However, the Basel Convention specifically exempts repair and refurbishment of used electronics in Annex IX. However, the parties to the Convention have considered the question of whether exports of hazardous used electronic equipment for repair or refurbishment are considered as Basel Convention hazardous waste, subject to import and export controls under that Convention. In the guidance document produced on that subject, that question was left up to the parties, however in the working group all the parties present believed that when material is untested, or contains hazardous parts that would need to be replaced as part of the repair process, then the Convention did apply.[239]

It should be noted that since e-waste contain toxins and carcinogens it is considered hazardous thus the texts of the Basel Convention should apply. This is so because computers as noted earlier have a high rate of obsolescence, contain cadmium, lead and mercury and when they are no longer required are dumped, recycled or disassembled to recover precious metals such as gold and copper, the rest are discarded as waste.[240] Increased trade in recyclable materials has led to an increase in a market for used products such as computers. This market is valued in billions of dollars. At issue is the distinction when used computers stop being a "commodity" and become a "waste." The Basel Convention did not envisage this class of waste in 1989.[241] This gave impetus to glamour for the amendment of the Basel Convention to reflect this environmental hazard.

[237] Ibid., Arts. 4(1), (2), (3)(a–h).

[238] BAN (2005), see also National Geographic Society (2008).

[239] BAN (2005).

[240] UNEP (2012).

[241] Ibid.

After the initial adoption of the Basel Convention 1989, some least developed countries and environmental organisations argued that it did not go far enough. Many nations and non-governmental organisations (NGOs), such as Green Peace International, argued for a total ban on shipment of all hazardous wastes to LDCs. More impetus for the amendment was provided by Basel Action Network (BAN), an NGO. In particular, the original Basel Convention 1989 did not prohibit waste exports to any location except Antarctica but merely required a notification and consent system known as "prior informed consent" or PIC. Further, many waste traders sought to exploit the good name of recycling and begin to justify all exports as moving to recycling destinations. Many believed a full ban was needed including exports for recycling. These concerns led to several regional waste trade bans.[242]

The "Ban Amendment" provides for the prohibition by each party included in the proposed new Annex VII (parties and other states which are members of the OECD, European Community (EC), Liechtenstein) of all transboundary movements to states not included in Annex VII of hazardous wastes covered by the Basel Convention 1989 that are intended for final disposal, and of all transboundary movements to states not included in Annex VII of hazardous wastes covered by para 1 (a) of Article 1 of the Basel Convention 1989 that are destined for reuse, recycling or recovery operations.[243]

The Ban Amendment to the Basel Convention 1989 was originally adopted as a decision of the second meeting of the Conference of the Parties (CoP2) in March 1994. At that time, some members felt that the Ban Amendment was a way to address challenges faced by developing countries and countries with economies in transition in controlling imports of hazardous and other wastes they were unable to manage in an environmentally sound manner but continued to receive.[244]

Parties agreed that parties listed in Annex VII (members of OECD, EU, Liechtenstein) prohibit immediately all transboundary movements of hazardous wastes which are destined for final disposal operations from OECD to non-OECD states.[245] In the same decision, it was agreed that such "Annex VII Parties" phase out by 31 December 1997, and prohibit as of that date, all transboundary movements of hazardous wastes destined for recovery or recycling operations from OECD to non-OECD states.[246]

At the next meeting (CoP3) in 1995, parties adopted a further decision as an amendment to the Convention (the "Ban Amendment").[247] The decision was as a result of the lobbying at that conference by LDCs, Greenpeace and several European countries such as Denmark. This led to the adoption of an amendment, termed the

[242] This also led to the signing of the Bamako Convention in 1991 by the African countries under the auspices of the then Organisation of African Unity (now the African Union).

[243] Basel Convention (1989).

[244] Ibid.

[245] Conference of Parties to Basel Convention (1997).

[246] Ibid.

[247] Conference of Parties to Basel Convention (1995).

Basel Ban Amendment to the Basel Convention, at that meeting in 1995. Thus, during the meeting of the sixth Conference of Parties to the Convention (CoP6) in Geneva, it addressed a wide number of topics, including the growing issue of "e-wastes," among others. During the conference technical guidelines were adopted on disposal and recycling of "e-wastes," lead-acid batteries, plastic wastes and obsolete ships. This gave birth to the Ban Amendment to the Basel Convention.[248]

For some years after, there were differing views among parties about the interpretation of the provision on the Ban amendments to the Convention, with many considering it to be ambiguous. After several meetings without agreement in this regard, the President of the ninth meeting of the Conference of the Parties (CoP9) in 2000 issued a Statement on the possible way forward on the Ban Amendment. In this statement, the President called on parties to create enabling conditions, through among other measures, country-led initiatives conducive to the attainment of the objectives of the Amendment. Based on the statement of the President of CoP9, Indonesia and Switzerland announced their readiness to organise a "Country-led Initiative" (CLI).[249]

At its tenth meeting (CoP10), the Conference of the Parties adopted proposal on the Indonesian-Swiss country-led initiative to improve the effectiveness of the Basel Convention.[250] Section A of this decision addresses the entry into force of the Ban Amendment and agreed an interpretation of Article 17(5) of the Basel Convention on amendments to the Convention.[251] This was an important step in the development of the Convention that then led to follow up to the Country-led initiative being adopted at the eleventh meeting (CoP11) of the Conference of the Parties in 2002.[252]

With passage of time the Ban Amendment was accepted by 86 countries and the European Union, but did not enter into force based on the requirement that it must be ratified by 3/4 of the member states to the Convention. There was however a twist of luck. On 6 September 2019, Croatia became the 97th country to ratify the Amendment thus bringing up the required 3/4 of number of states that ratified it. The Ban Amendment entered into force on 5 December 5, 2019, 90 days, after ratification by Croatia.[253] Jim Puckett,[254] commenting on this development said that the BAN Amendment coming into force is, "the most important idea ever conceived to promote environmental justice at the global level." He added further, "we applaud Croatia and all of the 97 countries that have ratified the agreement to date and hope

[248] Conference of Parties to Basel Convention (2002).

[249] Basel (2011).

[250] Conference of Parties to Basel Convention (2011).

[251] For the Ban Amendment to the Basel Convention to enter into force, it requires ratification by 3/4 of the member states to the Convention and will become law 90 days after such ratification. See Basel Convention (1989), Art. 17(5).

[252] Basel (2011).

[253] Basel Convention (2020).

[254] Executive director at Basel Action Network (BAN) in Seattle, USA.

that all others will now do so at the earliest opportunity."[255] However, countries like the USA, Canada, Japan, Australia, New Zealand, South Korea, Russia, India, Brazil, and Mexico are yet to ratify the Ban Amendment.

With this amendment, BAN became a new article in the Basel Convention. The objective of the amendment is to protect human health and the environment against the adverse effects of hazardous wastes.[256] The Amendment prohibits the export of hazardous waste from a list of MDCs, mostly OECD countries to LDCs.

The Basel Ban Amendment applies to export for any reason, including recycling. The recycling involves the burning, melting and chemically stripping electronic waste by desperate, unprotected workers in highly polluting operations. Further, wastes from the shipping companies, old ships, hazardous asbestos and flammable gases and oils, end up on beaches in South Asia where they create pollution, occupational disease and death due to fires and explosions.[257]

"There can be no excuse for using the developing world as the dumping ground for the toxic effluent of the affluent," said Puckett, and that, "with the Ban Amendment now a legal certainty, we hope the countries that have to date refused to ratify will do so and close the sad chapter of toxic colonialism done in the name of recycling.," he concluded.[258]

Also, reflecting on these latest developments, the Executive Secretary of the Basel Convention, Payet,[259] had this to say,

> Today that public awareness of the scale and impact of our waste problem has risen enormously in recent years and Parties are stepping up their efforts to collectively tackle this, both at home through innovative measures and also globally through international, multilateral action. The Basel Convention has continually evolved to reflect these new challenges and the entry into force of the Ban Amendment is another milestone towards minimising risks from the adverse effects of transboundary movements of hazardous waste. Quite simply, the world will be a safer, healthier place from now on.

The Ban Amendment was strenuously opposed by a number of industry groups as well as nations including Australia and Canada. However, the European Union (EU) fully implemented the Basel Ban in its Waste Shipment Regulation (EWSR), making it legally binding in all EU Member States. Norway and Switzerland have similarly fully implemented the Basel Ban in their legislation.

The Basel Convention Secretariat provides assistance to parties that are facing difficulties in ratifying the Ban Amendment, on request and within available resources. This includes provision of information and documentation to relevant stakeholders and decision makers; the provision of legal and practical advice;

[255] Puckett et al. (2005).

[256] Basel Convention (1989), Preamble.

[257] Puckett et al. (2005).

[258] Ibid.

[259] Basel (1994).

organisation of electronic and face to face activities (workshops and webinars); and facilitation of exchange of information and experiences between parties.[260]

9.6.2 Domestic Legislation in the Control of Hazardous Substances

Neither the National Environmental Standards and Regulation Enforcement Agency (Establishment) Act (NESREA Act) 2007, nor the National Environmental (Sanitation and Wastes Control) Regulations 2009, made pursuant to the NESREA Act, provides any legal definition of waste generally.

Prior to 1988 in Nigeria no efforts were made at having laws that addressed the protection of the Nigerian environment in its entirety. There were therefore no adequate legal responses to the emerging grave problems of environmental abuse not only from the growing oil and gas sector but also from all segments of the Nigerian economy, include those associated with electrical/electronic equipment. Therefore, the environmental problems associated with economic and developmental activities were never given adequate national recognition until 1988.[261] The then military government in quick succession two laws were promulgated two laws.[262] Among the legislation for the control of hazardous substances in Nigeria are:

9.6.2.1 Harmful Waste (Special Criminal Provisions, etc) Act 1988

The Act was promulgated as Degree No. 42 of 1988[263] in the wake of Koko incident in June 1988. It defines harmful waste under Section 15 to include semi-solid, liquid or solid substance as well as "any injurious, poisonous toxic or noxious substance… which can subject any person to the risk of death, fatal injury or incurable impairment of physical and mental health. . . ."

The Act prohibits the carrying, depositing and dumping of harmful waste on any land, territorial waters and matters related thereto and therefore prohibits all activities

[260] Basel (1994).

[261] Nigerians woke up in the morning of June 1988 and found that an Italian, with some Nigerian collaborators, had dumped tonnes of toxic waste in the "sleeping" port of Koko in the then Bendel State (now in Delta State). Efforts to prosecute the "dead merchants" were abortive as there were no laws banning the importation, dumping, or depositing of harmful wastes on the Nigerian environment. It was only through diplomatic means that the deadly cargo was eventually evacuated from Nigerian soil, but not after it had taken its first victim, Nana Sunday, the landlord where the cargo was dumped.

[262] Harmful Wastes (Special Criminal Provisions, etc.) Act (1988) and the Federal Environmental Protection Agency (Establishment) Act (FEPA Act) 1988 (The FEPA Act (1988) had been repealed by NESREA Act (2007), s. 37).

[263] Currently retained as Cap H1 LFN 2004.

relating to the purchase, sale, importation, transit, transportation, deposit, storage of harmful wastes.[264] It is therefore an offence for any person who, without lawful authority carries, deposits, dumps or causes to be carried, deposited or dumped, or is in possession for the purpose of carrying, depositing or dumping, any harmful waste on any land or in any territorial waters or contiguous zone or Exclusive Economic Zone of Nigeria or its inland water ways.[265] It is also an offence "to transport, or cause to be transported or is in possession of transporting; imports, or causes to be imported or negotiates for the purposes of importing; or sell, offer for sale, buy or otherwise deal in any harmful waste."[266]

Under the Act a person shall be deemed to deposit or dump harmful waste if he deposits or dumps the harmful waste ... in such circumstances, or for such period that he may be deemed to have abandoned it where it is deposited or dumped; or to have brought it to the place where it is so deposited or dumped for the purpose of its being disposed of or abandoned whether by him or any other person.[267] An offence is committed under the Act if the person actually does the act or makes the omission which constitutes the crime; or does or omits to do any act for the purpose of enabling or aiding another person to commit the crime; or aids another person in committing the crime; or counsels or procures any person to commit the crime, in which case he may himself be charged with committing the crime or with counselling or procuring the commission of the crime.[268]

Penalty on conviction include life imprisonment, forfeiture of vessel and of land on which harmful wastes was dumped.[269] Where the crime is committed by a body corporate and it is proved that it was committed with the consent or connivance of or is attributable to any neglect on the part of a director, manager, secretary or similar officer of the body corporate, or any other person purporting to act in the capacity of a director, manager, secretary or similar officer, he as well as the body corporate, shall be guilty of the crime and shall be liable to be proceeded against and punished accordingly.[270]

In addition to criminal liability, the Act provides for civil liability.[271] Thus, where any damage arises as a result of the depositing or dumping of wastes, any person who deposited, dumped or imported the harmful waste shall be liable for damages.[272] Damage in this respect includes death of or injury to any person (including

[264] HWSCP Act (1988), s. 1(1).

[265] Ibid., s. 1(2)(a).

[266] Ibid., s. 1(2)(b)–(d).

[267] Ibid., s. 1(3).

[268] Ibid., s. 2, see also the provisions of ss. 3–5 of the Act on crimes committed in prosecution of common purpose, mode of execution of the crime and accessories after the fact.

[269] HWSCP Act (1988), s. 6.

[270] HWSCP Act (1988), s. 7.

[271] Ibid., s. 12.

[272] Ibid., s. 12(1).

any diseases and any impairment of physical or mental condition).[273] It should be noted that it is immaterial whether the offences were committed by individuals or body corporate.[274] Furthermore, immunity from prosecution conferred on certain persons by or under the Diplomatic Immunities and Privileges Act[275] shall not extend to any crime committed under the Act by any of those persons.[276]

9.6.2.2 National Environmental Standards, Regulations and Enforcement Agency Act (NESREA Act) 2007[277]

Discharging harmful quantities of any hazardous substance into the air or upon land and the waters of Nigeria or the adjoining shorelines is an offence under Section 27 of the NESREA Act.

Punishments are provided under Section 27 (2)–(3).[278] For an individual the punishment is a fine of =N=1,000,000 or imprisonment for 5 years. Where the offender is a body corporate every person who at the time the offence was committed was in charge of the body corporate shall be deemed to be guilty of such offence and shall be liable to be proceeded against and punished accordingly as if he committed the offence in his personal capacity. However, where such a person can show that the offence was committed without his knowledge or that he exercised all due diligence to prevent the commission of the offence, such person shall not be liable.[279]

9.6.2.3 National Environmental (Sanitation and Wastes Control) Regulations 2009

The regulations were made pursuant to Section 34 of NESREA Act. Types of hazardous waste are classified in Schedule XIII to the regulations as:

(a) Waste that exhibits any of the following hazardous properties: explosive; flammable liquids and solids; poisonous; toxic; ecotoxic; and infectious.
(b) Wastes that belong to any of the following categories: clinical wastes; waste oils/water, hydrocarbon/water mixtures, emulsions; wastes from the production, formulation and use of resins, latex, plasticisers, glues or adhesives; wastes resulting from surface treatment of metals and plastics; waste from industrial

[273] Ibid., s. 12(2).

[274] HWSCP Act (1988), s. 7.

[275] Cap D 9 Laws of the Federation of Nigeria (LFN) 2004.

[276] HWSCP Act (1988), s. 9.

[277] Government Notice No. 61, Act No. 25 2007, Federal Republic of Nigeria Official Gazette No. 92, Vol. 97, 31 July 2007.

[278] NESREA Act (2007).

[279] Ibid., s. 27(3).

processes, waste disposal operations and wastes which contain compounds such as copper, zinc, cadmium, mercury, lead and asbestos.

(c) End-of-life waste of household electrical and electronic appliances or residues arising from the incineration of the same.

(d) Waste that contains dangerous substances above standard limits based on scientific factors or as a result of international commitments.

(e) Special wastes which are highly dangerous substances or objects that are under the concurrent control of both federal and state governments such as: radioactive waste; decommissioned explosives, waste resulting from prospecting, extraction, treatment, and storage of mineral resources; waste deposited or discharged into waterways under federal jurisdiction; and any other waste so defined.

The regulations[280] prohibit activities relating to hazardous substances. It is an offence for any person who generates toxic or hazardous waste as classified under Schedule XIII to the regulations not to treat or cause to be treated such hazardous waste using methods acceptable to the conditions approved by the Agency.[281]

Again, an offence is committed where any person exporting or transiting hazardous wastes to do so without a valid permit issued by the Agency in consonance with international conventions, or to transit toxic or hazardous waste destined for another country through the territory of Nigeria without a valid Prior Informed Consent for such movement issued by the Agency.[282] Any person who violates the provisions of Regulations 80–83 of the regulations shall be guilty of an offence and shall on conviction be liable to a fine of =N=5,000,000 or imprisonment for five years or to both fine and imprisonment.[283]

9.6.2.4 National Environmental (Electrical/Electronic Sector) Regulations 2011[284]

The regulations were also made pursuant to Section 34 of NESREA Act. The principal thrust of these regulations[285] under Regulation 2 is to "prevent and minimize pollution from all operations and ancillary activities of the Electrical and Electronic sector[286] to the Nigeria Environment." Under the regulations, all new

[280] National Environmental (Sanitation and Wastes Control) Regulations (2009).

[281] Ibid., Regulation 80.

[282] Ibid., Regulations 81 and 82.

[283] National Environmental (Sanitation and Wastes Control) Regulations (2009), Regulation 103.

[284] Government Notice No. 137, S.I. 23. Federal Republic of Nigeria Official Gazette No. 50 Vol. 98, 25 May 2011.

[285] National Environmental (Electrical/Electronic Sector) Regulations (2011), Regulation 2.

[286] Electrical/electronic sector means organisation or body corporate involved in (a) manufacturing, assembling, processing or recycling any equipment contained in the categories of **EEE** listed in these Regulations and (b) operations in Telecommunication, broadcasting, power (distribution,

electrical/electronic equipment (EEE)[287] imported into the country shall be functional and importation have the date of manufacture inscribed on them and warranty indicated.[288]

Again, all EEE imported into the country or assembled in the country shall have the Pin and Serial numbers inscribed on them.[289] In addition, all used EEE (UEEE) imported into the country shall comply with the provisions as specified in Schedule 11 to these regulations and shall be: of comparative model of equipment; fit for purpose; functional and not scrap; such that the outward/external appearance of the item does not show any waste characteristics and Properly packaged for protection during transport, loading and unloading.[290]

In addition, under Regulation 34(1), every importer and technician (involved in repair, dismantling and re-assembling) of used EEE shall ensure that e-waste is handled by a person and or body corporate registered to do so by the Agency.[291] The regulations place a ban on End-of-life, unusable or unserviceable EEE as these are prohibited from being imported into Nigeria.[292] The regulations[293] also ban the importation of Cathode Ray Tubes (CRT) into the country.[294]

On the issue of storage, every person, body-corporate or organisation in charge of a collection centre shall ensure that e-waste are: not stored longer than one year onsite, not disposed in trash receptacles or at a dump-site and or landfill and that e-waste collected for recycling are transported to the designated recycling-centre.[295] The regulations prohibit open burning of EEE.[296]

Elaborate handling and management of e-waste are provided under the regulations. For instance, Regulation 8 provides for application of best practices in handling EEE. The regulations provide that implementation of cleaner production

---

transmission and generation) facilities. This applies to both new (EEE) and used (UEEE). See National Environmental (Electrical/Electronic Sector) Regulations (2011), Regulation 70.

[287] Electrical/electronic equipment (EEE) means:

(a) Equipment that is dependent on electric currents/voltage or electromagnetic fields to function properly and equipment for the generation, transfer and measurement of such currents and fields falling under the categories set out in Schedule 2 to these Regulations and designed for use with a voltage rating; not exceeding I, 000 volts for alternating current and 1,500 volts for direct current and (b) Equipment for the generation, transfer, distribution and measurement of these currents and fields, including the components necessary for the cooling, heating, protection, etc., of the electrical or electronic components. See National Environmental (Electrical/Electronic Sector) Regulations (2011), Regulation 70.

[288] National Environmental (Electrical/Electronic Sector) Regulations (2011), Regulation 3(1).

[289] Ibid., Regulation 3(2).

[290] Ibid., Regulation 3(4).

[291] The Agency herein referred to is the National Environmental Standards and Regulations Enforcement Agency (NESREA).

[292] National Environmental (Electrical/Electronic Sector) Regulations (2011), Regulation 34(2).

[293] National Environmental (Electrical/Electronic Sector) Regulations (2011).

[294] Ibid., Regulation 34(3).

[295] Ibid., Regulation 34(4)(a)(b) and (c).

[296] Ibid., Regulation 34(4)(d).

processes and pollution prevention measures shall be employed by handlers of EEE to yield economic, social and environmental benefits as specified in Schedule V to these regulations.[297] Also, all EEE manufacturing, processing, assembling organisation or corporate body shall apply new technologies arising from the elimination of hazardous materials in many new-models EEE.[298]

Furthermore, for any EEE manufacturing, processing, assembling organisation or body corporate, pollution prevention measures shall focus on minimisation in the use of hazardous substances contained in Schedule XVI to these regulations.[299] Thus, all damaged and disused equipment including wires, Cathode Ray Tubes (CRTs), metals, motors, transformers, plastics etc, shall be amenable for recovery under Extended Producer Responsibility Programme by NESREA's accredited Recyclers in an Environmentally Sound Manner (ESM).[300]

To this end, operator of e-waste collection centres and transporter to recycling plants shall: maintain copies of all e-waste manifests and/or receipts and copies shall be made available for review during an inspection visit by officers of the Agency; forward a copy of the e-waste manifests to the Agency within 30 days of waste removal and sign copies of the e-waste manifest.[301]

The regulations[302] further provide that a person or body corporate or organisation shall not discard and or throw and or drop any e-waste anywhere except in designated bin, collection centre and or point.[303] Therefore, every operator of a facility, technician, assemblers or scavengers[304] of e-waste shall practice Environmentally Sound Management (ESM) of e-waste and shall not: burn e-waste in the Nigerian environment; dispose of e-waste alongside domestic and/or municipal waste; dispose e-waste at clump site, land-fill site, water body, etc; break Cathode Ray Tubes (CRTs), in an unsound environmental manner; release Chlorofluorocarbons (CFCs) from fridges and other cooling systems and leach precious metals with acids and other hazardous waste from Printed Wire Boards (PWBs) or Printed Circuit Boards (PCBs).[305]

In all, waste from electrical/electronic product assembly or manufacturing with hazardous properties shall be clearly labelled and stored separately from the general waste and contained in storage areas that are chemically resistant before disposal in

[297] Ibid., Regulation 8(1).

[298] Ibid.

[299] Ibid., Regulation 8(3).

[300] Ibid., Regulation 8(4).

[301] Ibid., Regulation 34(6).

[302] National Environmental (Electrical/Electronic Sector) Regulations (2011).

[303] Ibid., Regulation 36(1).

[304] Ibid., Regulation 70.

[305] Ibid., Regulation 36(2)(a)–(f).

an environmentally sound manner.[306] And that everybody corporate or organisation, which generates e-waste, shall separate such at source from other wastes streams.[307]

Under the regulations, it shall be an offence for a person to import end-of-life, unusable or unserviceable electrical/electronic equipment or import electrical/electronic equipment or manufacture any electrical/electronic equipment without registration with the Agency or import Cathode Ray Tube into the country.[308] It shall also be an offence for a person to manufacture, import, assemble, or distribute electrical/electronic equipment or operate electrical/electronic equipment facility without providing e-waste collection centre for take-back of the e-waste in Nigeria.[309]

In addition, it shall be an offence if a person, body corporate or organisation: discards, throws, drops e-waste anywhere except in designated authorised collection centre or point; burns e-waste in the Nigerian environment; disposes e-waste alongside domestic and or municipal waste; disposes e-waste at dump site, land-fill site, water body, or any other place except at the designated recycling plant; breaks Cathode Ray Tubes (CRTs), improperly; releases Chlorofluorocarbons (CFCs) from fridges and other cooling system in an environmentally unsound manner; leaches precious metals with acids and other hazardous waste from Printed Wire Boards (PWBs); transports e-waste to non-designated recycling plant; stores e-waste longer than one year onsite; fails to supply information as required for approval to operate e-waste facility; fails to maintain e-waste facility in a sanitary manner; fails to comply with the decommissioning conditions of e-waste facility as may be prescribed by the Agency; fails to submit to the Agency within a specified period, information/data about materials received at its facility and fails to submit an Environmental Audit Report as required by these regulations.[310]

Other offences provided under the regulations are contravention of permit condition,[311] making false and misleading statement or have in possession a document that is likely to mislead or deceive the Agency,[312] failure to comply with abatement measures,[313] failure to report[314] and discharge of effluent beyond permissible limit.[315]

Penalties are provided under Regulation 67. Thus, any person who violates the provisions of Regulation 61(1)(a) of these regulations commits an offence and of conviction be liable to a fine not exceeding Five hundred Thousand Naira

[306] Ibid., Regulation 8(5).

[307] Ibid., Regulation 34(7).

[308] Ibid., Regulation 61(1)(a)–(c).

[309] Ibid., Regulation 61(2).

[310] National Environmental (Electrical/Electronic Sector) Regulations (2011), Regulation 61(3) (a)–(n).

[311] Ibid., Regulation 62.

[312] Ibid., Regulation 63.

[313] Ibid., Regulation 64.

[314] Ibid., Regulation 65.

[315] Ibid., Regulation 66.

(=N=500,000), or to imprisonment for a term not exceeding two years or to both such term and imprisonment.[316] Further, any person who violates the provisions of Regulation 61(1) (b) to Regulation 66 of these regulations commits an offence and shall on conviction, be liable to a fine not exceeding =N=200,000 or to imprisonment for a term not exceeding six months or to both such fine and imprisonment and an additional fine of =N=5000 for every day the offence subsists.[317] Where an offence is committed by a body corporate, it shall on conviction, be liable to a fine not exceeding =N=1,000,000 and an additional fine of =N=50,000 for every day the offence subsists.

In addition to the above penalties, the Polluter-Pays-Principle shall apply to everybody, corporate Polluter, or organisation that pollutes.[318] The collection, treatment, transportation and final disposal of wastes shall be the responsibility of the body corporate/organisation generating the wastes within the specified standards and guidelines.[319]

In the event of an incident resulting in an adverse impact on the environment whether socio-economic or health wise, the facility shall be responsible for: the cost of damage assessment, control and clean-up; remediation and reclamation and/or restoration.[320]

In all, waste from electrical/electronic product assembly or manufacturing with hazardous properties shall be clearly labelled and stored separately from the general waste and contained in storage areas that are chemically resistant before disposal in an environmentally sound manner.[321]

9.6.2.5 National Environmental (Hazardous Chemicals and Pesticides) Regulations 2014

The National Environmental (Hazardous Chemicals and Pesticides) Regulations 2014[322] is another of the regulations on hazardous waste. The objectives of the regulations[323] are to protect human health and the environment from harmful effects of hazardous chemicals and pesticides and other agro-chemicals,[324] implement the

---

[316] Ibid., Regulation 67(1).

[317] Ibid., Regulation 67(2).

[318] Ibid., Regulation 7(1).

[319] Ibid., Regulation 7(2).

[320] National Environmental (Electrical/Electronic Sector) Regulations (2011), Regulation 7(3)(a)–(c).

[321] Ibid., Regulation 8(5).

[322] Government Notice No. 256, S.I. 65. Federal Republic of Nigeria Official Gazette No. 143 Vol. 101, 30 December 2014.

[323] National Environmental (Hazardous Chemicals and Pesticides) Regulations (2014).

[324] Ibid., Regulation 1(a).

Rotterdam Convention,[325] enforce the ban on Persistent Organic Pollutants (POPs),[326] control the transboundary movement of hazardous chemical wastes and their disposal,[327] enforce the provisions of the HWSCP Act 1988,[328] among others.

In the regulations[329] a substance is regarded as hazardous if contains the characteristics listed under Schedule X to the regulations. That is being explosive, corrosive, flammable or inflammable, poisonous, toxic, ecotoxic, infectious or reactive. Once a substance shows any of the above characteristics its importation or exportation is either banned or restricted under Regulation 5. A list of restricted chemical and pesticides are provided under Schedule II.[330]

Where a substance is placed under the restricted or banned chemical and pesticides no one shall import, export or being in possession of such substance unless a permit is issued or obtained,[331] and the permittee shall comply with a few guidelines. Some of these guidelines include engaging the services of a Chartered Chemist,[332] labelling the containers,[333] affixing appropriate signs,[334] and following the guidelines for labelling and packaging of such substance.[335] Besides the provisions for the importation or exportation of restricted or banned chemicals and pesticides, there are provisions to guide the storage or handling of the substance.[336]

Under the regulations,[337] it shall be an offence where a facility contravenes permit conditions,[338] makes false statements to the Agency,[339] fails to comply

---

[325] Ibid., Regulation 1(c). The Rotterdam Convention is a multilateral treaty to promote shared responsibilities on the importation of hazardous chemicals, signed on 10 September 1998 and came into force on 24 February 2004.

[326] National Environmental (Hazardous Chemicals and Pesticides) Regulations (2014), Regulation 1(d). Persistent Organic Pollutants (POPs) are controlled by the Stockholm Convention on Persistent Organic Pollutants. The Convention was signed on 22 May 2001 and came into force on 17 May 2004. Currently, 22 chemicals or groups of chemicals are regulated as POPs.

[327] National Environmental (Hazardous Chemicals and Pesticides) Regulations (2014), Regulation 1(e).

[328] Ibid., Regulation 1(f).

[329] National Environmental (Hazardous Chemicals and Pesticides) Regulations (2014).

[330] Ibid.

[331] National Environmental (Hazardous Chemicals and Pesticides) Regulations (2014), Regulation 5 (2).

[332] Ibid., Regulation 6(a).

[333] Ibid., Regulation 7.

[334] Ibid., Regulation 8.

[335] Ibid., Sch. XII.

[336] While National Environmental (Hazardous Chemicals and Pesticides) Regulations (2014), Sch. VIII sets out guidelines for storage, Sch. IX provides guidelines for handling.

[337] National Environmental (Hazardous Chemicals and Pesticides) Regulations (2014).

[338] Ibid., Regulation 27.

[339] Ibid., Regulation 28.

with abatement measures,[340] fails to report accidental release and emergencies,[341] operates without permit[342] and violates registration requirements.[343] Under the regulations[344] where the offence is committed by an individual, he shall on conviction be liable to a fine of =N=1,000,000 or 5 years imprisonment and where the offender is a body corporate the penalty shall be a fine of =N=1,000,000 and an additional =N=50,000 for each day the offence subsists.[345]

There appears to be some confusion in respect of offences and penalties as provided within the extant laws[346] and these regulations[347] and between those laws and the regulations, for the control of hazardous substances in Nigeria.

For instance, under the NESREA Act 2007,[348] the discharge in such harmful quantities of any hazardous substance into the air or upon the land and the waters of Nigeria or at the adjoining shorelines is prohibited, except where such discharge is permitted or authorised under any law in force in Nigeria, amounts to an offence. Such a person is liable on conviction, to a fine, not exceeding =N=1,000,000 or to imprisonment for a term not exceeding 5 years.[349] Where the offence is committed by a body corporate, it shall on conviction, be liable to a fine not exceeding =N=1,000,000 and an additional fine of =N=50,000 for every day the offence subsists.[350]

In the case of a body corporate, every person who at the time the offence was committed was in charge of the body corporate shall be deemed to be guilty of such offence and shall be liable to be proceeded against and punished accordingly provided that nothing contained in this subsection shall render any person liable to any punishment if he proves that the offence was committed without his knowledge or that he exercised all due diligence to prevent the commission of such offence.[351]

The HWSCP Act 1988, on the other hand, prohibits the carrying, depositing and dumping of harmful waste on any land, territorial waters and matters related thereto and therefore prohibits all activities relating to the purchase, sale, importation, transit, transportation, deposit, storage of harmful wastes.[352] It is therefore an offence for any person who, without lawful authority carries, deposits, dumps or

---

340 Ibid., Regulation 29.

341 Ibid., Regulation 30.

342 Ibid., Regulation 31.

343 Ibid., Regulation 32.

344 National Environmental (Hazardous Chemicals and Pesticides) Regulations (2014).

345 Ibid., Regulation 33.

346 HWSCP Act (1988) and NESREA Act (2007).

347 National Environmental (Sanitation and Wastes Control) Regulations (2009) and National Environmental (Hazardous Chemicals and Pesticides) Regulations (2014).

348 NESREA Act (2007), s. 27(1).

349 NESREA Act (2007), s. 27(2).

350 Ibid., s. 27(3).

351 Ibid., s. 27(4).

352 HWSCP Act (1988), s. 1(1).

causes to be carried, deposited or dumped, or is in possession for the purpose of carrying, depositing or dumping, any harmful waste on any land or in any territorial waters or contiguous zone or Exclusive Economic Zone of Nigeria or its inland waterways.[353] In addition, it is also an offence "to transport, or cause to be transported or is in possession of transporting; imports, or causes to be imported or negotiates for the purposes of importing; or sell, offer for sale, buy or otherwise deal in any harmful waste."[354]

Penalties on conviction include life imprisonment, forfeiture of the vessel and of land on which harmful wastes were dumped.[355] Where the crime is committed by a body corporate and it is proved that it was committed with the consent or connivance of or is attributable to any neglect on the part of a director, manager, secretary or similar officer of the body corporate, or any other person purporting to act in the capacity of a director, manager, secretary or similar officer, he as well as the body corporate, shall be guilty of the crime and shall be liable to be proceeded against and punished accordingly.[356]

Under the NESREA Act discharging of such harmful quantities of any hazardous substance into the air or upon the land and the waters of Nigeria or at the adjoining shorelines is an offence, except where such discharge is permitted or authorised under any law in force in Nigeria.[357] Penalty includes a fine, not exceeding =N=1,000,000 or imprisonment for a term not exceeding 5 years in the case of an individual[358] and a fine not exceeding =N=1,000,000 and an additional fine of =N=50,000 for every day the offence subsists in the case of a body corporate.[359]

But in the case of the HWSCP Act on the same offence[360] penalty on conviction includes life imprisonment, forfeiture of vessel and of land on which harmful wastes was dumped.[361]

The same punishment awaits the alter ego of a body corporate if proven that the offence was committed with his consent or connivance.[362] That is the confusion and it is irrespective of the provisions of Section 27(5).[363] It provides that, "Notwithstanding the provisions of this section or any other sections of this Act, **the provisions of the Harmful Waste (Special Criminal Provisions, etc.) Act shall apply in respect of any hazardous substance constituting harmful waste as defined in**

[353] Ibid., s. 1(2)(a).

[354] Ibid., s. 1(2)(b)–(d).

[355] Ibid., s. 6.

[356] HWSCP Act (1988), s. 7.

[357] NESREA Act (2007), s. 27(1).

[358] Ibid., s. 27(2).

[359] NESREA Act (2007), s. 27(3).

[360] . . .depositing, dumping . . . any harmful waste without lawful authority.

[361] HWSCP Act (1988), s. 6.

[362] Ibid., s. 7.

[363] NESREA Act (2007).

section 37 of this Act."[364] There is a need for the legislature to harmonise the penalties provided in Sections 27(2)(3) and (4)[365] and Sections 6 and 7.[366] The penalties in the NESREA Act should be subordinated to those of the HWSCP Act under the said provisions of Section 27(5) of the NESREA Act.

Again, the same problem of different penalties for the same offence appears in respect of the National Environmental (Sanitation and Wastes Control) Regulations 2009 and the National Environmental (Hazardous Chemicals and Pesticides) Regulations 2014. In respect of the National Environmental (Sanitation and Wastes Control) Regulations 2009, it is an offence for any person who generates toxic or hazardous waste[367] not to treat or cause to be treated such hazardous waste using methods acceptable to the conditions approved by the Agency.[368] Again, an offence is committed **where any person exporting or transiting hazardous wastes does so without a valid permit issued by the Agency**[369] in consonance with international conventions,[370] or transits toxic or hazardous waste destined for another country through the territory of Nigeria without a valid Prior Informed Consent (PIC) for such movement issued by the Agency.[371] Any person who violates the provisions of Regulations 80–83 of the regulations shall be guilty of an offence and shall on conviction be liable to a fine of =N=5,000,000 or imprisonment for five years or to both fine and imprisonment.[372]

Under the National Environmental (Hazardous Chemicals and Pesticides) Regulations 2014, it shall be an offence where a facility contravenes permit conditions,[373] makes false statements to the Agency,[374] fails to comply with abatement measures,[375] fails to report accidental release and emergencies,[376] **operates without permit**[377] and violates registration requirements.[378] And where the offence is committed by an individual, he shall on conviction be liable to a fine of

[364] That is, the NESREA Act (2007).

[365] NESREA Act (2007).

[366] HWSCP Act (1988).

[367] As classified under the National Environmental (Sanitation and Wastes Control) Regulations (2009), Sch. XIII.

[368] National Environmental (Sanitation and Wastes Control) Regulations (2009), Regulation 80.

[369] National Environmental (Hazardous Chemicals and Pesticides) Regulations (2014), Regulation 31.

[370] National Environmental (Sanitation and Wastes Control) Regulations (2009), Regulation 81.

[371] Ibid., Regulation 82.

[372] National Environmental (Sanitation and Wastes Control) Regulations (2009), Regulation 103.

[373] National Environmental (Hazardous Chemicals and Pesticides) Regulations (2014), Regulation 27.

[374] Ibid., Regulation 28.

[375] Ibid., Regulation 29.

[376] National Environmental (Hazardous Chemicals and Pesticides) Regulations (2014), Regulation 30.

[377] Ibid., Regulation 31.

[378] Ibid., Regulation 32.

=N=1,000,000 or 5 years imprisonment and where the offender is a body corporate the penalty shall be a fine of =N=1,000,000 and an additional =N=50,000 for each day the offence subsists.[379]

Under the National Environmental (Sanitation and Wastes Control) Regulations 2009, an offence is committed where any person exporting or transiting hazardous wastes does so without a valid permit issued by the Agency.[380] In the same vein, under the National Environmental (Hazardous Chemicals and Pesticides) Regulations 2014, "it shall be an offence where a facility operates without permit."[381]

Curiously, these two regulations have different penalties for committing the same offence.[382] Under the National Environmental (Sanitation and Wastes Control) Regulations 2009, "any person who violates the provisions of regulations 80 – 83 (of which regulation 81 is inclusive) shall be guilty of an offence and shall on conviction be liable to a fine of =N=5,000,000 or imprisonment for five years or to both fine and imprisonment."[383]

But under the National Environmental (Hazardous Chemicals and Pesticides) Regulations 2014, "where the offence is committed by an individual, he shall on conviction be liable to a fine of =N=1,000,000 or 5 years imprisonment and where the offender is a body corporate the penalty shall be a fine of =N=1,000,000 and an additional =N=50,000 for each day the offence subsists."[384]

The question is which of these two penalties should be imposed by the Agency. The Minister charged with the responsibility of environmental matters should look into this to create harmony in the implementation of the regulations by the Agency. Besides, the penalties under these regulations[385] should not be at variance with the parent legislation.[386] The regulations are subsidiary to the parent legislation and made under it. Therefore, the regulations being executive made law should have penalties that refer to the parent legislation, otherwise, such penalties should be null and void, being inconsistent with the penalties provided under the parent legislation.

---

[379] Ibid., Regulation 33.

[380] National Environmental (Sanitation and Wastes Control) Regulations (2009), Regulation 81.

[381] National Environmental (Hazardous Chemicals and Pesticides) Regulations (2014), Regulation 31.

[382] That is, where a facility operates without a permit from the Agency under both regulations under discussion.

[383] National Environmental (Sanitation and Wastes Control) Regulations (2009), Regulation 103.

[384] National Environmental (Hazardous Chemicals and Pesticides) Regulations (2014), Regulation 33.

[385] National Environmental (Sanitation and Wastes Control) Regulations (2009), and National Environmental (Hazardous Chemicals and Pesticides) Regulations (2014).

[386] NESREA Act 2007 (n221). The regulations, that is National Environmental (Sanitation and Wastes Control) Regulations (2009) and National Environmental (Hazardous Chemicals and Pesticides) Regulations (2014) were made pursuant to s. 34.

9.7 Summary

Waste is often referred to as rubbish, trash, garbage or junk, depending upon the type of material and the regional terminology. But in living organisms, waste relates to unwanted substances or toxins that are expelled from them. In other words, waste may be regarded as an unwanted or undesired material, substance or object, particularly when the holder of such substance or object discards, intends to discard or is required to discard it. In determining when a substance or object becomes a waste, the Department for Environment, Food and Rural Affairs (Defra) of the UK set out some criteria to help with such assessment. All said and done waste could therefore be regarded as something that is not wanted by its producer or owner and by its nature has the potential to pollute the environment and harm human health. It therefore constitutes a burden to its holder which may lead to its being dealt with in socially or environmentally unacceptable ways or in its being abandoned or dumped.

The composition of waste is often uncertain and it is sometimes hazardous. It is on this premise that waste is regulated as it may present a risk to the environment and human health. This risk derives from waste's collective qualities, its nature and composition, the variety of sources from which it originates and its potential to cause harm to the environment and human health. To this end, all necessary measures must be taken to ensure that waste management is carried out without endangering human health or harming the environment.

To do this the environment is to be protected not only through the application of waste management controls but also by promoting the efficient use of resources through the application of the 5Rs (Reduce, Repair, Reuse, Recycle and Recover). To achieve a high level of environmental protection, action should not only be taken to ensure the safe recovery and disposal of waste but also to give priority to the prevention of waste, which may include the reuse of products and the recycling of substances and objects that have been discarded and are waste.

Although there is no scientific certainty about all wastes, especially hazardous wastes, studies and research confirmed fears about the dangers of many kinds of wastes by revealing their toxicity, carcinogenicity, mutagenicity, corrosivity and other characteristics harmful to human health and the environment. The revelations, which later provided a basis for international legal actions, led to a tightening of environmental regulations in industrialised countries, beginning in the early 1970s. This, in turn, led to a dramatic rise in the cost of hazardous waste disposal. Inevitably, the situation led to a search for alternative, cheaper ways to dispose of waste within countries of origin and abroad.[387]

There are twofold legal strategies to control waste generation and disposal: the application of international conventions on hazardous substances and the use of national legislation. No doubt, there are ample legal instruments to combat the

[387] UNEP (2006), p. 125.

menace of waste, especially those that are hazardous, but the will to enforce those laws becomes the major obstacle.

References

Adinna EN (2001) Environmental hazard and management. Snaap, Enugu

Ausubel K, Harpignies J (2004) Nature's operating instructions: the true biotechnologies. Sierra Club Books, San Francisco

Basel Action Network (2005) High-Tech Toxic Trash Exported to Africa- USA and Europe Creating a "Digital Dump" from "Re-Use and Repair" Trade. https://www.business-humanrights.org, 24 October 2005. Accessed on 31 May 2023

Basel Action Network (2013) Turn Back the Toxic Tide. Basel Action Network 2013 – 2014 Annual Report, www.ban.org. Accessed on 31 May 2023

Basel Convention (1994) Implementation, Legal Matters, Ban Amendment Overview. http://www.basel.int/Implementation/LegalMatters/BanAmendment/Overview/tabid/1484/Default.aspx. Accessed on 31 May 2023

Basel Convention (2011) Implementation legal matters. https://www.basel.int/implementaion/legalmatters. Accessed on 31 March 2020

Basel Convention (2020) Ratification of the Basel Convention Ban Amendment. https://www.basel.int. Accessed on 31 May 2023

Biju H (2017) Causes of e-waste. https://www.quora.com/profile/hii-biju, 13 July 2017. Accessed on 20 May 2023

Birne PW, Boyle AE (2002) International law and the environment, 2nd edn. Oxford University, Oxford

Borgen Magazine (2018) Borgen Project. https://www.borgenproject.org. Accessed on 28 May 2023

British Broadcasting Corporation (BBC) (2008) Marine Debris. BBC News. http://www.bbc.co.uk/news/science. Accessed on 6 June 2023

Californians Against Waste (2009) E-waste laws in other states. http://www.cawrecycles.org. Accessed on 28 May 2023

Carney L (2006) Nigeria fears e-waste toxic legacy, BBC World Service's Dirty Business 19 December 2006, British Broadcasting Corporation (BBC). http://news.bbc.co.uk/2/hi/africa/6193625.stm. Accessed on 14 June 2023

Cassel S (2001) EU Waste, Guardian Newspaper. https://www.theguardian.com/environment/201/aud/14/eu-waste. Accessed on 31 May 2023

Chauhan N (2019) E-waste marketing. https://www.quora.com/profile/nisha-chauhan-282, 10 July 2019. Accessed on 21 May 2023

Chauhan A (2020) What causes E-waste. https://www.quora.com/profile/anand-chauhan. Accessed on 20 May 2023

Chemical Fact Sheet (2020) Thallium (Spectrum Laboratories). http://www.speclab.com/elements/thallium.htm. Accessed on 21 May 2023

Colbert D (2004) What you don't know may be killing you. A Strang Company, Lake Mary, Florida

Conference of Parties to Basel Convention (1995) Decision III/I, COP-3. https://www.basel.int. Accessed on 31 May 2023

Conference of Parties to Basel Convention (1997) Decision II/12, COP-2. https://www.basel.int. Accessed on 31 May 2023

Conference of Parties to Basel Convention (2002) COP-6. https://www.basel.int. Accessed on 31 May 2023

Conference of Parties to Basel Convention (2011) Decision BC-10/3, COP-10. https://www.basel.int. Accessed on 31 May 2023

Deepali SK et al (2006) Legislating e-waste management: progress from various countries, ResearchGate. ELNI Rev 1(2):27–36. https://doi.org/10.46850/elni.2006.006. https://www.researchgate.net/publication/294690378_Legislating_e-waste_management_Progress_from_various_countries. Accessed on 28 May 2023

Department for Environment, Food and Rural Affairs (Defra) (2012) Guidance on the Legal Definition of Waste and Its Application, August 2012. http://www.defra.gov.uk, 15. Accessed on 5 June 2023

Down To Earth Magazine (2018). https://www.downtoearth.org.int. Accessed on 25 May 2023

Enger ED, Smith BF (2002) Environmental science, a study of interrelationships, 8th edn. McGraw Hill, Boston

EU (2012) Waste Electrical Electronics Equipment (WEEE) Directive 2012/19/EU. https://eur-lex.europa.eu/legal-content/EN/TXT/PDF/. Accessed on 12 June 2023

EU (2015) WEEE. http://eur-lex.europa.eu/LexUriServ/LexUriServ. Accessed on 29 June 2023

EU (2018) Waste Framework Directive 2008 (WFD) (Directive 2008/98/EC), as amended by Directive (Eu) 2018/851 of The European Parliament and of the Council of 30 May 2018, Amending Directive 2008/98/EC on Waste. https://eur-lex.europa.eu/legal-content/EN/TXT/PDF/, Art. 3(1). Accessed on 5 June 2023

European Union (EU) (2003) DIRECTIVE 2002/96/EC of the European Parliament and of the Council. https://eur-lex.europa.eu/resource.html? Accessed on 20 June 2023

Goudie A (2013) The human impact on the natural environment, 6th edn. Blackwell, Oxford

Green K (2019) Anything electronic. https://www.quora.com/profile/kermit-greem, 29 January 2019. Accessed on 20 May 2023

Green Ontario (2019) Strategy for solid waste. http://www.greenontario.org/strategy/solid_waste.html. Accessed on 6 June 2023

Green Peace International (2001) E. Waste Toxic- Not in Our Backyard. https://www.greenpeace.org. Accessed on 17 June 2023

Greenpeace International (2006) Lost in transposition? Greenpeace Report, dated 27 September 2006. http://www.greenpeace.org/international/press/reports/lost-in-transposition. Accessed on 28 May 2023

Greenpeace International (2016) Illegal e-waste exposed. http://www.greenpeace.org/international/news/illegal-e-waste-exposed. Accessed on 14 June 2023

Günzel K (2019) What are E-waste, causes and effects? https://www.quora.com/profile/kay-g%c3%bcnzel, 28 September 2019. Accessed on 20 May 2023

House of Representatives (1999) H.R. 1580: Electronic Waste Research and Development Act Legislative Digest. www.govtrack.us. Accessed on 28 May 2023

Junior Scholastic Magazine (2009) 13 April 2009, vol. 111, No. 16

Kaley KB et al. (2018) Health concerns and environmental issues with PVC-containing building materials in green buildings. http://www.ciwmb.ca.gov/publications/GreenBuilding/43106016.pdf. Accessed on 3 August 2023

Katalin F (2010) Canada moves to WEEE compliance. http://www.greensupplyline.com, 28 May 2023

Kohli A (2017) E-Waste Causes. https://www.quora.com/profile/akanksha-kohli-19, 7 November 2017. Accessed on 21 May 2023

Lecher C (2019) American Trash: How an E-Waste Sting Uncovered a Shocking Betrayal. https://www.theverge.com/author/colin-lecher/2019/12/4. Accessed on 31 May 2023

Maine Legislature (2012) Maine Public Law 661. http://www.mainelegislature.org/legis/bills/bills_123rd/chapters/PUBLIC661.asp. Accessed on 28 May 2023

Martin L (2019) Got a gadget gathering dust? http://news.cnet.com. Accessed on 29 June 2019

Mathur A (2018) Health, Sustainability & Ethics. https://www.quora.com/profile/avantika-mathur-12, 29 May 2018. Accessed on 20 May 2023

Merriam Webster Dictionary (2019). https://www.merriam.webster.com. Accessed on 5 June 2023

Morgan R (2006) Tips and tricks for recycling old computers. http://www.smartbiz.com/article/articleprint/1525/-1/58/21/08/2006. Accessed on 17 June 2023

Nate A (2006) California to electronics industry: no toxins for you! http://arstechnica.com/news.ars/post/20060224-6254.html. Accessed on 28 May 2023
National Geographic Society (2008) "High-Tech-Trash" National Geographic Magazine, January 2008
Puckett J et al. (2005) Basel Action Network, "The Digital Dump: Exporting Re-use and Abuse to Africa," https://www.business-humanrights.org/enpdf-full-report-the-digital-dump-exporting-re-use-and-abuse-to-africa, 24 October 2005. Accessed on 31 May 2023
Reddy AKN et al (1981) Southern perspectives on the rural energy crisis. Nautilus of America Inc, Bolinas, California
Sahu M (2019) What is e-waste management. https://www.quora.com/profile/manoj-sahu-505, 16 March 2019. Accessed on 20 May 2023
Sarhan A (2017) Planned Obsolescence: Apple Is Not the Only Culprit. www.forbes.com/sites/adamsarhan, 22 December, 2017. Accessed on 20 May 2023
Silicon Valley Toxic Corporation (2019) Poison PCs/Toxic TVs Executive Summary. http://www.svtc.org/cleancc/pubs/pctvexecsum.htm. Accessed on 29 June 2023
Spelch C (2016) What are E-waste, causes and effects? https://www.quora.com/profile/craig-spelch, June 16, 2016. Accessed on 20 May 2023
Stokes N (2017) Electronic-Waste. www.eridirect.com/norman-stokes/ 16 February 2017. Accessed on 21 May 2023
Sunkin M et al (1998) Source book on environmental law. Cavendish, London
The Director-General European Union Directorate-General Environment (2008) Guidelines on the interpretation of key provisions of Directive 2008/98/EC on waste. http://eur-lex.europa.eu. Accessed on 5 June 2023
The Watch Tower (2002) Awake Magazine, 22 August 2002
Thornton J, Beckwith S (2004) Environmental law, 2nd edn. Sweet and Maxwell, London
Tomlinson V (2019) What is E-waste? https://www.quora.com/profile/valerie-tomalinson, 29 September 2019. Accessed on 20 May 2023
UNEP (2006) UNEP Training Manual on International Environmental Law. https://wedocs.unep.org/20.500.11822/20599. Accessed on 28 July 2023
UNEP (2012) Basel Basics. http://www.basel.int/Pub/basic. Accessed on 25 July 2023
United Nations Environment Programme (UNEP) (1997) Environmental Law Training Manual. UNEP, Nairobi
United States Environmental Protection Agency (USEPA) (2008) Donate. http://www.epa.gov/epaoswer/hazwaste/recycle/ecycling/donate.htm. Accessed on 29 June 2023
USEPA (2009) Learn the basics of hazardous waste. https://www.epa.gov/hw/learn-basics-hazardous-waste. Accessed on 19 June 2023
Wanless Waste Management (2021) What is waste management. http://www.wanless.com.au/what_is_waste_management.html. Accessed on 6 June 2023
World Data Lab (2023) Population 1.0, https://population.io/? Accessed on 11 August 2023

Part III
Liabilities and Remedies for Environmental Damage

Chapter 10
Liabilities and Compensation for Environmental Damage Under International Law

Abstract Environmental pollution by its very nature causes extensive damage to the environment, human lives and property. The aim of environmental law is to prevent damage, protect and preserve the environment and impose liability on actors for their illegal acts, or for the adverse consequences of their lawful activities. Liability is an obligation of a person to provide compensation or take redress measures for damage resulting from an action or a situation for which that person is deemed to be responsible under the applicable law. This chapter discusses the issue of liability for damage to the environment under international law laying emphasis on defining environmental damage under multi-lateral environmental agreements, state liability for environmental damage, guidelines for state responsibility for internationally wrongful act, especially under the United Nations Compensation Commission, noting the threshold of significance in claims for environmental damage as well as reparations for environmental damage. The chapter also discusses criminal liability for environmental damage under international environmental law, especially in areas of crime against the environment, including wildlife and forest crimes.

10.1 Defining Environmental Damage Under Multi-Lateral Environmental Agreements

Liability rules generally serve a variety of purposes. They may be preventive as a form of economic instrument that provides an incentive to encourage compliance with environmental obligations. They may be punitive when used to impose sanctions against wrongful conduct. They may also be corrective measures when applied to restore a given environmental asset to its pre-damage condition. Finally, they may provide a technique for internalising environmental and other social costs into production processes and other activities.[1] What then constitutes environmental damage to which liability may apply?

[1] Secretariat of the Convention on Biological Diversity (2011).

E. Onyeabor, *Environmental Law*, https://doi.org/10.1007/978-3-031-68956-7_10

One major problem in addressing environmental damage is how to define it. Defining environmental damage, in order to impose liability, remains a complex issue. In defining environmental damage, treaties and state practice reflect various approaches. A narrow definition of environmental damage is limited to damage to natural resources alone (air, water, soil, fauna and flora, and their interaction); a more extensive approach includes damage to natural resources and property which forms part of the cultural heritage; the most extensive definition includes landscape and environmental amenity.[2] The early efforts at defining "environmental damage" were based on reference to the words "damage," "pollution damage" and "adverse effects."

Under the Convention on International Liability for Damage caused by Space Objects (Space Liability Convention) 1972,[3] "damage" means "loss of life, personal injury or other impairment to health; or loss of or damage to property of states or of persons, natural or juridical, or property of international intergovernmental organizations."[4]

Another approach in defining environmental damage with reference to the word "damage" can be found in the Convention on the Regulation of Antarctic Mineral Resource Activities (CRAMRA) 1988. It establishes the basic rules governing responsibility and liability for damage to the Antarctic environment resulting from mineral resource activities. Under CRAMRA[5] damage to the Antarctic environment or dependent or associated ecosystems means "any impact on the living or non-living components of that environment or those ecosystems, including harm to atmospheric, marine or terrestrial life, beyond that which is negligible or which has been assessed and judged to be acceptable pursuant to this Convention."

The above definition under CRAMRA according to Khalatbari and Poorhashemi[6] not only involves the definition of damage, but also that of environmental damage. To this end, it is possible to generalise this definition to argue that the concept of environmental damage is the damage that is caused to the environment. In the words of Larsson,[7] "environmental damage is considered as a change in a specific section

---

[2] Mackenzie and Khalastchi (1996), p. 283.

[3] United Nations Office for Outer Space Affairs (1972) Space Liability Convention (1972). The Convention on International Liability for Damage Caused by Space Objects, also known as the Space Liability Convention, is a 1972 treaty that expanded on the liability rules created in the Outer Space Treaty of 1967. The Space Liability Convention was concluded and opened for signature on 29 March 1972 and it entered into force on 1 September 1972. As of 1 January 2019, 96 states have ratified the Liability Convention, 19 have signed but not ratified and four international intergovernmental organisations (the European Space Agency, the European Organisation for the Exploitation of Meteorological Satellites, the Intersputnik International Organisation of Space Communications, and the European Telecommunications Satellite Organization) have declared their acceptance of the rights and obligations provided for in the Agreement.

[4] Space Liability Convention (1972), Art. 1(a).

[5] CRAMRA (1988), Art. 1(15).

[6] Khalatbari and Poorhashemi (2019), 21–28 at 21.

[7] Larsson (2009), p. 159.

or the entire environment, that has a significant detrimental impact on the quality of the environment, or a change in its ability to maintain an acceptable quality of life or a lasting and stable balance of ecosystems."

To Wolfrum,[8] the term "damage" in the definition under CRAMRA means "any impact on the living or non-living components of the Antarctic environment or it's dependent or associated ecosystems beyond those which are either negligible or which have been assessed and judged acceptable to CRAMRA." An impact on the Antarctic environment will only be deemed not to constitute damage if it is either negligible or if it was foreseen in *concreto* and judged to be acceptable in the respective authorisation procedure.

Accordingly, an operator undertaking any mineral resource activity (which includes prospecting) is responsible for taking the necessary and timely response action if the activity results or threatens to result in damage to the Antarctic environment or its dependent or associated ecosystems. The responsibility of the operator is unconditional. The operator cannot invoke any defences or limitations and the failure to comply with such responsibility entails liability of the operator on the basis of strict liability. It follows therefore that such operator shall be strictly liable for:

(i) damage to the Antarctic environment or dependent or associated ecosystems arising from its Antarctic mineral resource activities, including payment in the event that there has been no restoration to the status quo ante;
(ii) loss of or impairment to an established use, or loss of or impairment to an established use of dependent or associated ecosystems, arising directly out of damage. . .;
(iii) loss of or damage to property of a third party or loss of life or personal injury of a third party arising directly out of damage. . . and
(iv) reimbursement of reasonable costs by whomsoever incurred relating to necessary response action, including prevention, containment, clean up and removal measures, and action taken to restore the *status quo ante* where Antarctic mineral resource activities undertaken by that Operator result in or threaten to resulting damage to the Antarctic environment or dependent or associated ecosystems.[9]

Under the International Convention on Liability and Compensation for Damage in Connection with the Carriage of Hazardous and Noxious Substances by Sea (HNS Convention) 2010, "damage" includes loss of life or personal injury on board or outside the ship carrying HNS, loss of or damage to property outside the ship, loss or damage caused by contamination of the environment, loss of income in fishing and tourism, and the costs of preventive measures and further loss or damage caused by

[8] Wolfrum (1990), pp. 27–31.
[9] CRAMRA (1988), Art. 8(1).

such measures.[10] The HNS Convention 2010 goes further to define preventive measures as "any reasonable measures taken by any person after an incident has occurred to prevent or minimize damage. These include measures such as clean-up or removal of HNS from a wreck if the HNS present a hazard or pollution risk."[11]

A legal definition of "damage" is also mentioned in the Basel Protocol on Liability and Compensation for Damage resulting from Transboundary Movements of Hazardous Wastes and their Disposal (Basel Protocol on Liability and Compensation) 1999. The objective of the Protocol is to provide for a comprehensive regime for liability and for adequate and prompt compensation for damage resulting from the transboundary movement of hazardous wastes and other wastes and their disposal including illegal traffic in those wastes.[12] Under the Protocol, "damage" means:

(i) Loss of life or personal injury;
(ii) Loss of or damage to property other than property held by the person liable under the present Protocol;
(iii) Loss of income directly deriving from an economic interest in any use of the environment, incurred as a result of impairment of the environment, taking into account savings and costs;
(iv) The costs of measures of reinstatement of the impaired environment, limited to the costs of measures actually taken or to be undertaken; and
(v) The costs of preventive measures, including any loss or damage caused by such measures, to the extent that the damage arises out of or results from hazardous properties of the wastes involved in the transboundary movement and disposal of hazardous wastes and other wastes subject to the Convention.[13]

The provisions of the Protocol shall apply to damage due to an incident occurring during a transboundary movement of hazardous wastes and other wastes and their disposal, including illegal traffic, from the point where the wastes are loaded on the means of transport in an area under the national jurisdiction of a state of export. Any contracting party may by way of notification to the Depositary exclude the application of the Protocol, in respect of all transboundary movements for which it is the state of export, for such incidents which occur in an area under its national jurisdiction, as regards damage in its area of national jurisdiction.. . .[14]

The Convention on Civil Liability for Damage Resulting from Activities Dangerous to the Environment (Lugano Convention) 2007[15] offers some help on the

[10] HNS Convention (2010), Art. 1(6). HNS Convention was discussed in Sect. 15.2.3 of Chap. 15 of this book.

[11] HNS Convention (2010), Art. 1(7).

[12] Basel Protocol on Liability and Compensation (1999), Art. 1.

[13] Ibid., Art. 2(c).

[14] Ibid., Art. 3(1).

[15] The Lugano Convention was signed by member states of the Council of Europe on 21 June 1993. The Convention provides for the possibility of accession by non-member states. In fact, a dangerous

subject matter. Under Article 2(7) of the Convention, "damage" may be characterised as follows:

(a) loss of life or personal injury;
(b) loss of or damage to property other than to the installation itself or property held under the control of the operator, at the site of dangerous activity;
(c) loss or damage by impairment of the environment in so far as this is not considered to be damage within the meaning of subparagraphs a or b above provided that compensation for impairment of the environment, other than for loss of profit from such impairment, shall be limited to the costs of measures of reinstatement actually undertaken or to be undertaken; and
(d) the costs of preventive measures and any loss or damage caused by preventive measures.

There has been an increasing interest in international environmental agreements rather than using the word "damage" with reference to the subject matter: "environmental damage," used the word "pollution damage" to define the environmental damage. For instance, the Convention On Civil Liability For Oil Pollution Damage Resulting From The Exploration For And Exploitation Of Seabed Mineral Resources (London Convention 1977) defines "pollution damage," as "loss or damage outside the installation caused by contamination resulting from the escape or discharge of oil from the installation and includes the cost of preventive measures and further loss or damage outside the installation caused by preventive measures."[16]

To the Institute of International Law, also known as the Institut de Droit International (IDI)[17] "pollution," "means any physical, chemical or biological alteration in the composition or quality of waters which results directly or indirectly from human action and affects the legitimate uses of such waters, thereby causing injury."[18] The injury in question may result in environmental damage which could be interpreted to include injury to both the natural environment and the human environment.

Under the Convention on Long-range Transboundary Air Pollution (LRTAP Convention) 1979, "air pollution" is defined by reference to deleterious effects on living resources and ecosystems, human health and material property, as well as interference with amenities and other legitimate uses of the environment.[19]

---

activity carried out in one country may threaten to cause or indeed cause damage in another country. Therefore, the problems are not necessarily confined to the territory of the Council of Europe member states. See European Treaty Series (ETS) (1993).

[16] Civil Liability Convention (1977), Art. 1.

[17] The Institute of International Law (IIL), also known as the Institut de Droit International (IDI), is an organisation devoted to the study and development of international law, whose membership comprises the world's leading public international lawyers. The organisation is generally considered the most authoritative world academy of international law founded in September 1873 in Ghent, Belgium, with Headquarters in Geneva, Switzerland.

[18] Institute of International Law (IIL) (2017a), Art. I.

[19] LRTAP (1979), Art. 1(a).

The distinction between environmental damage (and compensable environmental damage) and pollution is illustrated by the Lugano Convention 1993[20] which provides that an operator of a dangerous activity will not be liable for damage (impairment of the environment) caused by pollution at "tolerable" levels under local relevant circumstances.

Under the Convention on Civil Liability for Bunker Oil Pollution Damage (BUNKER 2001), "pollution damage" means:

(a) loss or damage caused outside the ship by contamination resulting from the escape or discharge of bunker oil from the ship, wherever such escape or discharge may occur, provided that compensation for impairment of the environment other than loss of profit from such impairment shall be limited to costs of reasonable measures of reinstatement actually undertaken or to be undertaken; and
(b) the costs of preventive measures and further loss or damage caused by preventive measures.[21]

Other treaties require "adverse effects," rather than "pollution," to define the consequences of activities that are to be avoided that may cause some environmental damage or harm. Like pollution, the term "adverse effects" provides some assistance in establishing a basis for, but cannot be used interchangeably with, a general definition of environmental damage.

The Vienna Convention on Substances that Deplete the Ozone Layer (Vienna Convention on ODS) 1985 defines "adverse effects" in relation to the depletion of the ozone layer, inter alia, "changes in the physical environment or biota, including changes in climate, which have significant deleterious effects on human health or on the composition, resilience and productivity of natural and managed ecosystems, or on materials useful to mankind."[22]

The United Nations Convention on Climate Change (Climate Change Convention) 1992 introduces a similar definition. However, it reverses the order by placing deleterious effects on the environment before effects on human health, and extends the definition to include effects on socio-economic systems and human welfare.[23]

Although "pollution" and "adverse effects" help in determining the threshold beyond which environmental damage might trigger liability, they do not actually define it. As pointed out by the United Nations Environment Programmes (UNEP) Working Group of Experts on Liability and Compensation for Environmental Damage in 1998,[24] that terms such as "pollution" or "adverse effects" simply describe the threshold beyond which environmental damage may entail liability, and are not synonymous with environmental damage.

---

[20] Lugano Convention (1993), Art. 2(7) (a) (b) (d).

[21] Bunker Oil (2001), Art. 1(9).

[22] Vienna Convention on ODS (1985), Art. 1(2).

[23] Climate Change Convention (1992), Art. 1(1).

[24] United Nations Environment Programmes (UNEP) (2002).

A broader approach in defining environmental damage was provided by the United Nations Environment Programmes (UNEP). According to the UNEP Working Group 1996,[25] "environmental damage" relates to injury caused to components of the environment to which typically no commercial value attaches. It further suggested that environmental damage could relate to "impairment of the environment," which may be defined as: "a change which has a measurable adverse impact on the quality of a particular environment or any of its components including its use and non-use values and its ability to support and sustain an acceptable quality of life and a viable ecological balance."[26] The Group on the issue of "depletion of natural resources," as an aspect of environmental damage, that it could be desirable to it as referring to the destruction of natural resource assets which occur in their natural state . . . and which have a primarily commercial use or commercial value rather than a non-commercial use or value.[27]

According to this UNEP Working Group,[28] environmental damage is:

> A change that has a measurable adverse impact on the quality of a particular environment or any of its components, including its use and non-use values, and its ability to support and sustain an acceptable quality of life and a viable ecological balance. In this sense, environmental damage does not include damage to persons or property, although such damage could be consequential to the damage caused to the environment.

In addition, international environmental regulations and some national environmental legislation[29] tried to define the standards and procedures with a view to protect the environment and avert any damage. In this logic, if polluters are to repair the damage caused to the environment by paying the corresponding costs, they will reduce pollution as long as the cost of de-pollution remains below the amount of compensation for the damage. The principle of environmental liability thus prevents environmental damage. The principle of liability may also encourage different actors to apply precautionary principles by avoiding risks and damages to the environment and improve the environmental knowledge and best available technology in environmental protection.[30]

10.2 State Liability for Environmental Damage

The law of state responsibility outlines the principles governing when and how a state is responsible for the breach of its international obligation. State responsibility refers to the situation where "one state commits an internationally unlawful act

[25] UNEP (1996).

[26] UNEP (2002).

[27] Ibid.

[28] Ibid.

[29] Some national regulations on the Nigerian environment were discussed in Chap. 16 of this book.

[30] Khalatbari and Poorhashemi (2019), p. 25.

against another state, international responsibility is established between the two. A breach of international obligation gives rise to a requirement for reparation."[31] Under the international legal system, states are responsible for breaches of their obligations and shall compensate affected states for any damage caused by their violation of international law. This rule forms the basis of the law of state responsibility.[32]

Accordingly, the law of state responsibility is focused on the secondary aspects of procedure, liability and other legal consequences resulting from a breach of a substantive rule of international law.[33] This position was succinctly captured by the Permanent Court of International Justice (PCIJ)[34] in 1927 in the *Factory at Chorzow* case.[35]

The issue in this case involved a dispute between Germany and Poland on paying reparation by Poland to Germany for having breached an agreement entered between them. After World War I, a bipartite agreement was entered wherein the control of the Upper Silesia area was transferred by Germany to Poland on the condition that Poland would not forfeit any property of Germany. However, Poland in breach of the agreement sold two German factories located in that area. In that case, PCIJ stated as follows: "It is a principle of international law that the breach of an engagement involves an obligation to make reparation in an adequate form. Reparation therefore is an indispensable complement of a failure to apply a convention."[36]

Although it has been recognised that "a State is under an obligation to make full reparation for the injury caused by the international wrongful act,"[37] certain gaps and inadequacies exist in respect of state liability for environmental damage under some multi-lateral environmental agreements (MEAs). The United Nations Conference on the Human Environment in Stockholm (Stockholm Declaration) 1972[38] recognised some of these gaps. Principle 22 calls on states to: "Co-operate to develop further the international law regarding liability and compensation for victims of pollution and other environmental damage caused by activities within the jurisdiction or control of such states to areas beyond their jurisdiction."

---

[31] Shaw (2014), p. 566.

[32] Dendle (2018).

[33] Shaw (2014), p. 566.

[34] The Permanent Court of International Justice (PCIJ), often called the World Court, existed from 1922 to 1946. It was an international court attached to the League of Nations. Created in 1920, the court was initially well-received from states and academics alike, with many cases submitted to it for its first decade of operation. Between 1922 and 1940, the court heard a total of 29 cases and delivered 27 separate advisory opinions. By a resolution from the League of Nations on 18 April 1946, both the court and the league ceased to exist and were replaced by the International Court of Justice and the United Nations.

[35] Factory at Chorzów, Case Concerning Factory at Chorzow (Germany v. Poland), (1927) PCIJ, Series A, Collection of Judgments (1923 – 1930) No. 17, 1929.

[36] Factory at Chorzów (1927), p. 21.

[37] Draft Articles on the Responsibility of States for Internationally Wrongful Acts, Art. 31(1). See International Law Commission (ILC) (2001a).

[38] Held in Stockholm, Sweden between 5–16 June 1972.

The World Charter for Nature 1982,[39] although did not directly address liability, called for degraded areas to be rehabilitated and for individuals to have access to means of redress when "their environment has suffered damage or degradation."[40] The Basel Convention on the Control of Trans-boundary Movements of Hazardous Wastes and their Disposal (Basel Convention) 1989, on the other hand, enjoined parties to the Convention to co-operate with a view to adopting, as soon as practicable, a protocol setting out appropriate rules and procedures in the field of liability and compensation for damage resulting from the trans-boundary movement and disposal of hazardous waste and other wastes.[41]

The Rio Declaration on Environment and Development (Rio Declaration) 1992 emphasises the development of national rules in addition to the further development of international rules for all adverse effects of environmental damage including, implicitly, liability for damage to the environment itself. The Rio Declaration provides that:

> States shall develop national law regarding liability and compensation for the victims of pollution and other environmental damage. States shall also co-operate in an expeditious and more determined manner to develop further international law regarding liability and compensation for adverse effects of environmental damage caused by activities within their jurisdiction or control to areas beyond their jurisdiction.[42]

A number of non-binding instruments have sought to restate the general principles on state liability for environmental damage. For instance, the United Nations Environment Programme in 1978 adopted the Draft Principles of Conduct in the Field of the Environment for the Guidance of States in the Conservation and Harmonious Utilisation of Natural Resources Shared by Two or More States (UNEP Draft Principles 1978).[43] The UNEP Draft Principles 1978 affirms that states are responsible for the fulfilment of their international environmental obligations relating to the utilisation of shared natural resources, and that they "are subject to liability in accordance with applicable international law for environmental damage resulting from violations of these obligations caused to areas beyond their jurisdiction."[44]

The World Commission on Environment and Development Experts on Environmental Law (WCED Legal Principles Group) 1996[45] states that:

> if one or more activities create a significant risk of substantial harm as a result of a transboundary environmental interference, and if the overall technical and socio-economic cost or loss of benefits involved in preventing or reducing such risks far exceeds in the long

[39] World Charter for Nature (1982).

[40] Ibid., paras 11(c) and 23.

[41] Ibid., Art. 12.

[42] Rio Declaration (1992), Principle 13.

[43] UNEP Draft Principles (1978), see United Nations Environment Programme (UNEP) (1978).

[44] Draft Principles (1978), Principle 12.

[45] World Commission on Environment and Development Experts on Environmental Law (WCED 1996).

> run the advantage which such prevention or reduction would entail... the state which carried out or permitted the activities shall ensure that compensation is provided should substantial harm occur in an area under national jurisdiction of another state or in an area beyond the limits of national jurisdiction.[46]

Article 11(2), WCED Legal Principles Group, particularly provides that states "shall ensure that compensation is provided for substantial harm caused by transboundary environmental interferences resulting from activities carried out or permitted by that state notwithstanding that the activities were not initially known to cause such interferences."

Some international institutes on environmental law have lent support for state responsibility and liability on the issue of environmental damage and have made some contributions on the subject matter. One such institute is the Institute of International Law (IIL).[47]

The IIL is deeply concerned by the effects of transboundary air pollution on the environment and human health, on soil, agriculture and production, forests, life in lakes, rivers and the sea, and the ozone layer and equally concerned by irreparable damage to buildings, monuments and sites, many of which are part of the cultural and natural heritage of mankind passed a resolution on state responsibility on transboundary air pollution.[48]

In this respect, IIL resolved that, "States shall take, and adapt to the circumstances, all appropriate and effective measures, in particular: (a) to prevent any new form of transboundary air pollution or any increase in the existing degree of pollution; and (b) progressively to eliminate existing transboundary air pollution within the shortest possible time."[49] Such measures can be especially rigorous in the case of activities that (a) involve particularly dangerous materials; or (b) threaten areas or environments requiring special protection.[50]

To this end, IIL recognised that "States incur responsibility under international law for any breach of their international obligations with respect to transboundary air pollution."[51] It therefore calls on states to conclude international treaties and enact laws and regulations "with a view to ensuring an effective system of prevention and of compensation for victims of transboundary air pollution, and that States should conclude international treaties and enact laws and regulations concerning, in particular: (a) systems of strict liability and compensation funds; (b) environmental norms, whether regional or universal, in particular quality and safety norms; and (c) the jurisdiction of courts, the applicable law and the enforcement of judgments."[52]

---

[46] WCED Legal Principles Group, Art. 11, see WCED (1996).

[47] Institute of International Law (IIL) (see note 18).

[48] IIL Resolutions (1987), Preamble. See Institute of International Law (IIL) (2017b).

[49] IIL Resolutions (1987), Art. 3(1).

[50] Ibid., Art. 3(2).

[51] Ibid., Art. 6.

[52] Ibid., Art. 7.

Again, in 1997, the IIL unanimously adopted a resolution on responsibility and liability under international law for environmental damage.[53] This resolution seeks to "identify, harmonize and to the necessary extent develop the principles of international law applicable to responsibility and liability in the context of environmental damage."[54] The resolution affirms that "the breach of an obligation of environmental protection established under international law engages responsibility of the State... entailing as a consequence the obligation to re-establish the original position or to pay compensation."[55] "The latter obligation may also arise from a rule of international law providing for strict responsibility on the basis of harm or injury alone, particularly in case of ultra-hazardous activities (responsibility for harm alone)."[56] In addition, civil liability of operators can be engaged under domestic law or the governing rules of international law regardless of the lawfulness of the activity concerned if it results in environmental damage.[57]

In recent years, the issue of state responsibility and liability as a principle of international law has been recognised and codified by the International Law Commission (ILC) in the International Law Commission Articles on the Responsibility of States for Internationally Wrongful Acts 2001 (ILC Draft Articles on Responsibility of States 2001).[58]

Under Article 1 "every internationally wrongful act of a state entails the international responsibility of that state."[59] The same principle applies to other international persons, including international organisations. A state responsible for an internationally wrongful act is under an obligation to cease that act, if it is continuing, and to offer appropriate assurances and guarantees of non-repetition if the circumstances so require, and to make full reparation for the injury caused by the internationally wrongful act.[60]

State liability for environmental damage is therefore premised upon a breach of an international legal obligation established by treaty, or by the rule of customary international law, or possibly under general principles of international law. This is so because both responsibility and liability have in addition to the traditional role of ensuring restoration and compensation that of enhancing the prevention of environmental damage.[61] For instance, the ILC Articles on State Responsibility[62] states that "there is an internationally wrongful act of a State when conduct consisting of an act

[53] IIL Resolutions (1997), see Institute for International Law (IIL) (2001c).

[54] Ibid., Preamble, para (f).

[55] Ibid., Art. 1.

[56] Ibid.

[57] IIL Resolutions (1997).

[58] Draft Articles on the Responsibility of States for Internationally Wrongful Acts, see International Law Commission (ILC) (2001a).

[59] Ibid.

[60] Draft Articles on the Responsibility of States for Internationally Wrongful Acts, Arts. 30 and 31.

[61] IIL Resolutions (1997), Preamble, para (e), see Institute for International Law (IIL) (2001c).

[62] Draft Articles on the Responsibility of States for Internationally Wrongful Acts.

or omission: (a) is attributable to the State under international law; and (b) constitutes a breach of an international obligation of the State."[63]

The ILC Articles on State Responsibility elaborate on the circumstances in which an act or omission will be attributable to a state, and indicate the circumstances in which a breach of an obligation will have occurred and that the state must be bound by the obligation in question at the time that act occurs. They elaborated on the conditions which must be satisfied for one state to incur responsibility in connection with the acts of another state, for example where one state aids or assists another in the commission of an internationally wrongful act. Therefore, under the ILC Articles, it is an international wrong "for the international responsibility where aid or assistance is provided with knowledge of the circumstances of an internationally wrongful act."[64]

To this end, the most pertinent international obligation requires a state to prevent particular environmental harm, or to refrain from carrying out or permitting activities that could lead to environmental damage. To a large extent discussions of state liability are likely to be concerned with the consequences of a breach of this obligation, which encompasses the obligation not to cause significant harm.

Also, responsibility and liability may arise on other substantive obligations, as well as procedural requirements pertaining, for example, to access to information and the duty to carry out an environmental impact assessment.[65]

Additionally, some regimes, for example, the World Trade Organisation (WTO) Appellate Body in a number of disputes under the WTO's Agreement on Sanitary and Phytosanitary Measures (the SPS Agreement) establish their own rules and remedies governing the consequences of a failure to comply with the obligations that are established.[66]

10.3 Guidelines for State Responsibility for Internationally Wrongful Act

Over the years, some guides for state responsibility for internationally wrongful acts have been provided. For state responsibility to be invoked, there needs to be an international obligation in force between the two states. According to Voigt,[67] the "responsibility in environmental cases will normally arise because of the breach of a treaty or a customary obligation." Kysar[68] adds that "a primary obligation refers to

[63] Ibid., Art. 2.

[64] Ibid., Art. 16.

[65] See the discussions on these in Sect. 5.1 of Chap. 5 of this book.

[66] See the discussions on the "No Harm Rule" and polluter-pays principle in Sects. 4.1 and 4.7 generally in Chap. 4 of this book.

[67] Voigt (2008), p. 3.

[68] Kyar (2013), p. 16.

the positive law that is being breached, or the substantive obligations of States in the subject areas of international law."

For instance, a failure to comply with the provisions of an environmental agreement by a signatory state or a breach of the transboundary harm principle may give an injured state the right to invoke state responsibility. This notwithstanding, an injured state must prove that the responsible state was under a primary obligation not to commit or allow the internationally wrongful act. The Convention on International Liability for Damage Caused by Space Objects (Space Liability Convention) 1972 provides some guides in this respect. Subject to the exceptions set out in Articles VI and VII, a state that launches a space object is "absolutely liable to pay compensation for damage caused by its space object on the surface of the earth or to aircraft in flight."[69] Under Article XII of the Convention, "compensation is to be determined in accordance with international law and the principles of justice and equity, in order to provide such reparation in respect of the damage as will restore the person, natural or judicial, state or international organization on whose behalf the claim is presented to the condition which would have existed if the damage had not occurred."

A party will be liable for damage other than on the surface of the earth to another space object or persons or property on board only if the damage is due to fault.[70] In some situations, states may be jointly and severally liable, notably where damage is caused on the surface of a third state as a result of damage by one space object to another.[71]

The only claim under the Convention was presented by Canada in 1979 to the former Union of Soviet Socialist Republics (USSR) for damage caused by the crash of Cosmos 954, a nuclear-powered satellite that disintegrated over Canada. Canadian authorities took steps to locate, recover, remove and test the radioactive debris and to clean up the affected areas of the Northwest Territories and the Provinces of Alberta and Saskatchewan, claiming some C$6 million from the USSR.[72]

The Canadian claim was based on relevant international agreements[73] and general principles of international law. Canada claimed that the deposit and presence of hazardous radioactive debris over large areas of Canadian territory rendering part of it unfit for use constituted damage to property within the meaning of the Space Liability Convention 1972.[74] Canada also claimed the USSR had failed to minimise the effects by providing timely and complete answers to its questions, and under general principles of international law the USSR was bound to prevent and reduce harmful consequences and mitigate damage. The claim covered the costs of restoring Canadian territory, to the extent possible, to the condition that would have existed if

[69] Space Liability Convention (1972), Art. II.

[70] Space Liability Convention (1972), Art. III.

[71] Ibid., Arts. IV and V.

[72] The Cosmos 954 case, ILM 899-908 (1979).

[73] Space Liability Convention (1972), Art. VIII and Outer Space Treaty (1967), Art. VII.

[74] The Cosmos 954 case (1979).

the intrusion had not occurred.[75] In calculating the costs, Canada applied "the relevant criteria established by general principles of international law and has limited the costs included in the claim to those costs that are reasonable, proximately caused by the intrusion of the satellite and deposit of debris and capable of being calculated with a reasonable degree of certainty."[76]

Canada also claimed under Article VII of the Outer Space Treaty 1967, the USSR must compensate under international law for the consequences of the intrusion of the satellite into Canadian air space and the deposit on Canadian territory of hazardous radioactive debris.[77]

Finally, Canada claimed under general principles of international law that the violation of its sovereignty was established by "the mere fact of the trespass of the satellite, the harmful consequence of hazardous radioactive debris and the interference with the sovereign right of Canada to determine the acts that will be performed on its territory."[78] This violation gave rise to an obligation to pay compensation and was based on a standard of absolute liability for space activities, which applied to activities in common having a high degree of risk and had been accepted as a general principle of international law.

The measure of compensation under this head was the same as that applied under the 1972 Convention. Canada additionally reserved its rights to present additional claims for compensation for damage not yet identified, for the costs incurred in establishing a Compensation Commission under the 1972 Convention, and for interest.[79]

The matter was settled in 1981 when the USSR agreed to pay C$3 million in full and final compensation, and Canada agreed to accept such payment in full and final settlement of its claim. Although the settlement agreement was silent as to the basis of the settlement, the reference in Article II of the agreement to Canada's claim allows a conclusion that the settlement was agreed on the basis of all the legal arguments proposed by Canada.[80]

United Nations Convention on Law of the Sea (UNCLOS) 1982 contains two rules on state responsibility for internationally wrongful acts. Under Article 139, which applies to the "Area,"[81] states parties and international organisations have the responsibility to ensure that activities in the area carried out by them, by their nationals or by those effectively controlled by them or their nationals, comply with the UNCLOS rules on the area. Moreover:

> Without prejudice to the rules of international law and Annex III, Article 22, damage caused by the failure of a State Party on international organization to carry out its responsibilities

[75] Ibid.

[76] Ibid.

[77] The Cosmos 954 case (1979).

[78] Ibid.

[79] Cambridge University (1979), pp. 899–930.

[80] Ibid.

[81] The seabed, ocean floor and subsoil beyond the limits of national jurisdiction.

> under this Part shall entail liability; State Parties or international organizations acting together shall bear joint and several liability.[82]

A state party may argue, as a defence, that it has taken all necessary and appropriate measures to secure effective compliance under the relevant provisions of UNCLOS. State parties are also required to take appropriate measures to ensure that international organisations of which they are members implement their responsibilities under Article 139.

The second provision is under Article 235 of UNCLOS. Accordingly, states are themselves "responsible for the fulfillment of their international obligations concerning the protection and preservation of the marine environment. They shall be liable in accordance with international law." Article 235 incorporates existing rules of state liability into the Convention and does not create a new rule of liability for damage to the marine environment. UNCLOS does not define "damage" to the marine environment and, except for the provisions for the measure of damage on the liability of contractors or the enterprise, does not establish a measure of compensation. The definition of marine "pollution" in Article 1(4) provides some guidance as to the standard of damage that might be applied: "deleterious effects" envisaged include the harm to living resources and marine life, hazards to human health, hindrance to marine activities, impairment of water quality, and reduction of amenities.

Under CRAMRA 1988, a sponsoring state mineral resource activities in the Antarctic environment will be liable, under international law, if damage under Article 8(2) of the Convention would not have occurred or continued if it had "carried out its obligations under the Convention" with respect to the operator. Although liability may be limited to that not satisfied by the operator or otherwise, this provision establishes potentially unlimited state liability for environmental damage.

Although the Climate Change Convention 1992 does not contain a rule on the consequences of activities by states which harm the environment, Article 3 emphasises on prevention of adverse climatic impacts. It encourages states "to take precautionary measures to anticipate, prevent or minimize the causes of climate change and mitigate its adverse effects." While Article 4(2)(a) commits developed countries to limit their anthropogenic emissions of greenhouse gases, Article 4 (4) requires developed country parties listed in Annex II and the European Community (EC) to "assist the developing countries parties that are particularly vulnerable to the adverse effects of climate change in meeting costs of adaptation to those adverse effects."

However, there are differing opinions as to whether the various commitments within the Climate Change Convention are legally binding or merely aspirational objectives. Von Stein[83] is of the view that "the Climate Change Convention seeks to establish a set of principles, norms, and goals . . . for cooperation on the issue . . .

[82] United Nations Convention on Law of the Sea (UNCLOS) 1982, Art. 139(2).

[83] Stein (2008), pp. 243, 247.

rather than to impose major binding obligations." Verheyen,[84] on the other hand, opined that judging from the provisions of Article 2, the Convention should not be merely viewed as "a non-binding policy statement and is instead the source of a binding, long-term commitment for all Parties to prevent climate change." In addition, Kysar[85] states that "the Climate Change Convention's status as a framework agreement with seemingly aspirational 'objectives' and 'principles' and its almost universal acceptance and ratification among states is an indication to some that the treaty contains few actual legal obligations."

Whether an individual obligation under this Climate Change Convention is legally binding is a crucial issue for invoking state responsibility. While the provisions of the Convention are novel, it is not a formal expression of liability under the principles of state responsibility. It however reflects an admission of responsibility with financial consequences. Thus, for an injured state to invoke state responsibility it must prove that the responsible state was under a primary obligation not to commit or allow the international wrongful act.

Another guideline on state responsibility for internationally wrongful acts is provided in the Works of the International Law Commission (ILC).[86] By its various works, the International Law Commission (ILC) has codified the law of state responsibility.[87] Apart from its now completed work on state responsibility, the ILC began working in the late 1970s on the issue of the liability of states for acts not prohibited by international law, and in 1990 prepared a first set of Draft Articles.[88] In 1992, the ILC divided the topic of international liability into prevention and remedial measures and decided to focus initially on developing Draft Articles on prevention.[89] Two of such Draft Articles[90] are discussed below.

The first Draft Article was on the Prevention of Trans-boundary Harm from Hazardous Activities.[91] The Draft Articles were intended to establish basic principles applicable to the activities carried out in the territory of a state, or in other places under its jurisdiction, or under its control, "not prohibited by international law which involve a risk of causing significant transboundary harm through their physical

[84] Verheyen (2005), pp. 56–58.

[85] Kyar (2013), p. 20.

[86] International Law Commission (ILC) (2001a).

[87] Various aspects of customary international law applicable in the event of environmental damage were touched by the articles.

[88] Barboza (1990), p. 39.

[89] Rao (1998).

[90] United Nations General Assembly (UNGA) (2001).

[91] International Law Commission Draft Articles on Prevention of Transboundary Harm from Hazardous Activities 2001(I LC Draft Articles on Harm from Hazardous Activities 2001), see ILC (2001c).

consequences,"[92] the physical consequences of which cause, or create a risk of causing, transboundary harm throughout the process.

The activities envisaged include those which involve the handling, storage, production, carriage, unloading or other similar operation of one or more dangerous substances; or which use technologies that produce hazardous radiation, or which introduce into the environment genetically altered organisms and dangerous micro-organisms.[93]

The provisions of the ILC Draft Articles 2001 echoed the elements of Principle 21 of the Stockholm Declaration[94] in recognising the sovereign freedom of states to carry out or permit human activities that may likely cause transboundary harm. However, "the State of origin shall take all appropriate measures to prevent significant transboundary harm or at any event to minimize the risk thereof."[95] Furthermore, the "States concerned shall cooperate in good faith and, as necessary, seek the assistance of one or more competent international organisations in preventing significant transboundary harm or at any event in minimizing the risk thereof."[96]

In the event of any harm arising thereto, the state of origin of the harm shall be required to make reparation for appreciable harm caused by activities following negotiation between states and guided by the criteria set out in the ILC Articles.[97] Such reparation should restore the balance of interests affected by the harm. A principle of non-discrimination would require state parties to "treat the effects of an activity that arise in the territory or under the jurisdiction or control of another state in the same way as effects arising in their own territory."[98]

The ILC Draft Articles further proposes procedural rules for the prevention of transboundary harm, including provisions on assessment,[99] notification and information (including provision for industrial and other confidentiality),[100] consultations[101] and dispute resolution.[102] Although not binding, they reflect one considered approach to the identification and application of principles of equity in environmental matters, and provide a point of reference for courts or tribunals faced with a balancing exercise.

The second Draft Articles considered was the ILC Draft Articles on Responsibility of States for Internationally Wrongful Acts 2001. Under the Draft Articles

[92] ILC Draft Articles on Harm from Hazardous Activities 2001, Art. 1.

[93] International Law Commission Draft Articles on Prevention of Transboundary Harm from Hazardous Activities, with Commentaries 2001, see ILC (2001d).

[94] Stockholm Declaration (n46).

[95] ILC Draft Articles on Harm from Hazardous Activities 2001, Art. 3, see ILC (2001c).

[96] Ibid., Art. 4.

[97] ILC Comments on Draft Articles on Harm from Hazardous Activities 2001, see ILC (2001d).

[98] ILC Draft Articles on Harm from Hazardous Activities 2001, Art. 15.

[99] ILC Draft Articles on Harm from Hazardous Activities 2001, Art. 7.

[100] Ibid., Art. 8.

[101] Ibid., Art. 9.

[102] Ibid., Art. 19.

"every internationally wrongful act of a State entails the international responsibility of that State."[103] The term "internationally wrongful act" includes an omission and extends to conduct consisting of several actions or omissions which together amount to an internationally wrongful act.[104] This is premised on the fact that every state, by its membership in the international community, has a legal interest in the protection of certain basic rights and the fulfilment of certain essential obligations.

Therefore the term "international responsibility" in Article 1 covers the relations that arise under international law from the internationally wrongful act of a state, whether such relations are limited to the wrongdoing state and one injured state or whether they extend also to other states or indeed to other subjects of international law, and whether they are centred on obligations of restitution or compensation or also give the injured state the possibility of responding by way of countermeasures.[105]

The principle set out in Article 1 of ILC Draft Articles on Responsibility of States 2001 has a long history. The Permanent Court of International Justice (PCIJ) applied the principle set out in Article 1 in several cases. For example, in the *Phosphates in Morocco* case,[106] PCIJ affirmed that when a state commits an internationally wrongful act against another state international responsibility is established "immediately as between the two States."[107]

The International Court of Justice (ICJ) has also applied the principle on several occasions, for example in the *Corfu Channel* case,[108] in the *Military and Paramilitary Activities in and against Nicaragua* case,[109] and in the *Gabčíkovo-Nagymaros Project* case.[110] The court also referred to the principle in its advisory opinions on *Reparation for Injuries*,[111] and on the *Interpretation of Peace Treaties (Second Phase)*,[112] in which it stated that "refusal to fulfil a treaty obligation involves international responsibility."[113]

It should be noted that the consequences of an internationally wrongful act cannot be limited either to reparation or to a "sanction." In international law, as in any

---

[103] Draft Articles on Responsibility of States, Art. 1, see ILC (2001a).

[104] ILC Comments on Draft Articles on Responsibility of States for Internationally Wrongful Acts (2001b).

[105] ILC Comments on Draft Articles on Responsibility of States 2001, 33, para 5. See ILC (2001b).

[106] Phosphates in Morocco (Italy v. France) Judgment, 1938, PCIJ, Series A/B, No. 74, 10 at 28.

[107] Ibid.

[108] Corfu Channel case, United Kingdom v. Albania; Merits, International Court of Justice (ICJ), 9 April 1949, (1949) ICJ Reports, 4 at 23.

[109] Military and Paramilitary Activities in and against Nicaragua (Nicaragua v. United States of America), Merits, Judgment, ICJ Reports 1986, 14 at 142, para 283, and 149 para 292.

[110] Gabčíkovo-Nagymaros Project case, Hungary v. Slovakia (1997) ICJ Reports 7 at 38, para 47.

[111] Reparation for Injuries Suffered in the Service of the United Nations, Advisory Opinion, (1949) ICJ Reports, 174 at 184.

[112] Interpretation of Peace Treaties with Bulgaria, Hungary and Romania, Second Phase, Advisory Opinion (1950) ICJ Reports, 221.

[113] Ibid., 228.

system of law, the wrongful act may give rise to various types of legal relations, depending on the circumstances. Increasingly it has been recognised that some wrongful acts engage the responsibility of the state concerned towards several or many states or even towards the international community as a whole.[114] A significant step in this direction was taken by ICJ in the *Barcelona Traction* case[115] when it noted that:

> an essential distinction should be drawn between the obligations of a State towards the international community as a whole, and those arising vis-à-vis another State in the field of diplomatic protection. By their very nature the former are the concern of all States. In view of the importance of the rights involved, all States can be held to have a legal interest in their protection; they are obligations *erga omnes*.[116]

It should be noted that the fact that under Article 1 every internationally wrongful act of a state entails the international responsibility of that state does not mean that other states may not also be held responsible for the conduct in question, or for injury caused as a result. The same conduct may be attributable to several states at the same time. For instance, one state may be responsible for the internationally wrongful act of another, if the act was carried out under its direction and control. Nonetheless, the basic principle of international law is that each state is responsible for its own conduct in respect of its own international obligations.[117]

Article 2[118] specifies the conditions required to establish the existence of an internationally wrongful act of the state, i.e. the constituent elements of such an act. Two elements are identified. First, the conduct in question must be attributable to the state under international law. Second, for responsibility to attach to the act of the state, the conduct must constitute a breach of an international legal obligation in force for that state at that time.

For particular conduct to be characterised as an internationally wrongful act, it must first be attributable to the state. The state is a real organised entity, a legal person with full authority to act under international law. But to recognise this is not to deny the elementary fact that the state cannot act of itself. An "act of the State" must involve some action or omission by a human being or group: "States can act only by and through their agents and representatives." The question is which persons should be considered as acting on behalf of the state, i.e. what constitutes an "act of the State" for the purposes of state responsibility.[119]

Conduct attributable to the state can consist of actions or omissions. Cases in which the international responsibility of a state has been invoked based on an omission are at least as numerous as those based on positive acts, and no difference

[114] ILC Comments on Draft Articles on Responsibility of States 2001, 33, para 3. See ILC (2001b).

[115] Barcelona Traction, Light and Power Company Limited (New Application, 1962), (Belgium v. Spain), Judgment, Merits, Second Phase, ICJ Rep 3, (1970) 5th February 1970.

[116] Ibid., 32, para 33.

[117] ILC Comments on Draft Articles on Responsibility of States 2001, 33, para 3. See ILC (2001b).

[118] Draft Articles on Responsibility of States, see ILC (2001a).

[119] ILC Comments on Draft Articles on Responsibility of States 2001, 35, para 5. See ILC (2001b).

in principle exists between the two. Moreover, it may be difficult to isolate an "omission" from the surrounding circumstances that are relevant to the determination of responsibility. For example, in the *Corfu Channel* case, ICJ held that it was a sufficient basis for Albanian responsibility that it knew, or must have known, of the presence of the mines in its territorial waters and did nothing to warn third states of their presence.[120]

In the *United States Diplomatic and Consular Staff in Tehran* case,[121] the court concluded that the responsibility of the Islamic Republic of Iran was entailed by the "inaction" of its authorities which "failed to take appropriate steps," in circumstances where such steps were evidently called for. In other cases, it may be the combination of an action and an omission which is the basis for responsibility.[122]

The second condition for the existence of an internationally wrongful act of the state is that the conduct attributable to the state should constitute a breach of an international obligation of that state. The terminology of breach of an international obligation of the state is long established and is used to cover both treaty and non-treaty obligations.[123]

The arbitral tribunal in the "*Rainbow Warrior*"[124] affair referred to "any violation by a State of any obligation." In practice, terms such as "non-execution of international obligations," "acts incompatible with international obligations," "violation of an international obligation" or "breach of an engagement" are also used. All these formulations have essentially the same meaning. The phrase preferred in the articles is "breach of an international obligation" corresponding as it does to the language of Article 36, para 2(c), of the ICJ Statute.[125]

These two elements were specified, for example, by PCIJ in the *Phosphates in Morocco* case.[126] The court explicitly linked the creation of international responsibility with the existence of an "act being attributable to the State and described as contrary to the treaty right[s] of another State," ICJ has also referred to the two elements on several occasions.

In the *United States Diplomatic and Consular Staff in Tehran* case,[127] it pointed out that, to establish the responsibility of the Islamic Republic of Iran:

> first, it must determine how far, legally, the acts in question may be regarded as imputable to the Iranian State. Secondly, it must consider their compatibility or incompatibility with the

---

[120] Ibid., 35, para 4.

[121] United States of America v. Iran, ICJ Reports 1980, 3 at 29, para 56.

[122] Ibid., 3 at 29, para 56.

[123] ILC Comments on Draft Articles on Responsibility of States 2001, 35, para 7. See ILC (2001b).

[124] New Zealand v. France, (1990) UNRIAA, Vol. XX (Sales No E/F.93.V.3) (1990), 215 at 251, para 75.

[125] ILC Comments on Draft Articles on Responsibility of States 2001, 35, para 7. See ILC (2001b).

[126] Phosphates in Morocco (1938).

[127] United States Diplomatic and Consular Staff in Tehran (1980), p. 90.

> obligations of Iran under treaties in force or under any other rules of international law that may be applicable.[128]

Similarly in the *Dickson Car Wheel Company* case,[129] the Mexico-United States General Claims Commission noted that the condition required for a state to incur international responsibility is "that an unlawful international act be imputed to it, that is, that there exist a violation of a duty imposed by an international juridical standard."

Under Article 3,[130] the characterisation of a given act as internationally wrongful is independent of its characterisation as lawful under the internal law of the state concerned. There are two elements to this. First, an act of a state cannot be characterised as internationally wrongful unless it constitutes a breach of an international obligation, even if it violates a provision of the state's own law. Second and most importantly, a state cannot, by pleading that its conduct conforms to the provisions of its internal law, escape the characterisation of that conduct as wrongful by international law. An act of a state must be characterised as internationally wrongful if it constitutes a breach of an international obligation, even if the act does not contravene the state's internal law, even if, under that law, the state was actually bound to act in that way.[131]

In theory, the conduct of all human beings, corporations or collectivities linked to the state by nationality, habitual residence or incorporation might be attributed to the state, whether or not they have any connection to the government. In international law, such an approach is avoided, both with a view to limiting responsibility to conduct which engages the state as an organisation, and also to recognise the autonomy of persons acting on their own account and not at the instigation of a public authority. Thus, the general rule is that the only conduct attributed to the state at the international level is that of its organs of government, or of others who have acted under the direction, instigation or control of those organs, i.e. as agents of the state.[132]

Article 4[133] states the basic rule attributing to the state the conduct of its organs. Thus, the conduct of any state organ shall be considered an act of that state under international law, whether the organ exercises legislative, executive, judicial or any other functions, whatever position it holds in the organisation of the state, and whatever its character as an organ of the central government or of a territorial unit of the state.[134] Here, an organ includes any person or entity that has that status under

[128] Ibid., 3 at 29, para 56.

[129] Dickson Car Wheel Company (USA) v. United Mexican States, (1931) UNRIAA, vol. IV (Sales No. 1951.V.1), 669 at 678.

[130] Draft Articles on Responsibility of States 2001, see ILC (2001a).

[131] ILC Comments on Draft Articles on Responsibility of States 2001, 38, para 1. See ILC (2001b).

[132] Ibid., 38, para 2.

[133] Draft Articles on Responsibility of States, see ILC (2001a).

[134] Ibid., Art. 4(1).

the internal law of the state.[135] To this end, the principle of the unity of the state entails that the acts or omissions of all its organs should be regarded as acts or omissions of the state for the purposes of international responsibility.

Thus, there is no category of organs specially designated for the commission of internationally wrongful acts, and virtually any state organ may be the author of such an act. The diversity of international obligations does not permit any general distinction between organs that can commit internationally wrongful acts and those that cannot.[136]

This clearly reflects the rule of international law in the matter as no distinction is made for this purpose between legislative, executive or judicial organs. Thus, in the *Salvador Commercial Company* case,[137] the tribunal said that: "a State is responsible for the acts of its rulers, whether they belong to the legislative, executive, or judicial department of the Government, so far as the acts are done in their official capacity."[138]

Article 5 of ILC Draft Articles[139] deals with the conduct of entities empowered to exercise the governmental authority of a state. Under this article, the conduct of a person or entity which is not an organ of the state under Article 4 but which is empowered by the law of that state to exercise elements of the governmental authority shall be considered an act of the state under international law, provided the person or entity is acting in that capacity in the particular instance.

According to ILC,[140] the generic term "entity" reflects the wide variety of bodies which, though not organs, may be empowered by the law of a state to exercise elements of governmental authority. They may include public corporations, semi-public entities, public agencies of various kinds and even, in special cases, private companies, provided that in each case the entity is empowered by the law of the state to exercise functions of a public character normally exercised by state organs, and the conduct of the entity relates to the exercise of the governmental authority concerned.[141]

Furthermore, the conduct of an organ placed at the disposal of a state by another state shall be considered an act of the former state under international law if the organ is acting in the exercise of elements of the governmental authority of the state at whose disposal it is placed.[142]

The ILC stated that two criteria must be met for Article 6 to apply. First, the organ in question must possess the status of an organ of the sending state. What this means

[135] Ibid., Art. 4(2).

[136] ILC Comments on Draft Articles on Responsibility of States 2001, para 5. See ILC (2001b).

[137] Claim of the Salvador Commercial Company ("El Triunfo Company") UNRIAA, vol. XV (Sales No. 66.V.3), (1902) 467–479.

[138] Salvador Commercial Company case (1902), at 477.

[139] Draft Articles on Responsibility of States 2001, see ILC (2001a).

[140] ILC Comments on Draft Articles on Responsibility of States 2001, see ILC (2001b).

[141] Ibid., 43, para 2.

[142] Draft Articles on Responsibility of States 2001, Art. 6, see ILC (2001a).

is that these conditions excluded from the ambit of Article 6 the conduct of private entities or individuals that have never had the status of an organ of the sending state. For example, experts or advisers placed at the disposal of a state under technical assistance programmes do not usually have the status of organs of the sending state.[143]

The second is that the conduct must involve the exercise of elements of the governmental authority of the receiving state. Under this criteria, the condition is that the organ placed at the disposal of a state by another state must be "acting in the exercise of elements of the governmental authority" of the receiving state. There will only be an act attributable to the receiving state where the conduct of the loaned organ involves the exercise of the governmental authority of that state. By comparison with the number of cases of cooperative action by states in fields such as mutual defence, aid and development, Article 6 covers only a specific and limited notion of "transferred responsibility." Yet, in state practice the situation is not unknown.[144]

Internationally wrongful acts of a state may arise where the conduct of organs or entities empowered to exercise governmental authority is attributable to the state even if it was carried out outside the authority of the organ or person concerned or contrary to instructions.[145] Thus, the conduct of an organ of a state or of a person or entity empowered to exercise elements of the governmental authority shall be considered an act of the state under international law if the organ, person or entity acts in that capacity, even if it exceeds its authority or contravenes instructions. Therefore:

> The State cannot take refuge behind the notion that, according to the provisions of its internal law or to instructions which may have been given to its organs or agents, their actions or omissions ought not to have occurred or ought to have taken a different form. This is so even where the organ or entity in question has overtly committed unlawful acts under the cover of its official status or has manifestly exceeded its competence. It is so even if other organs of the State have disowned the conduct in question. Any other rule would contradict the basic principle stated in article 3, since otherwise a State could rely on its internal law in order to argue that conduct, in fact carried out by its organs, was not attributable to it.[146]

The Inter-American Court of Human Rights applied this rule in *Velásquez Rodríguez v. Honduras*.[147] Here, the Inter-American Court of Human Rights states that:

> This conclusion [of a breach of the Convention] is independent of whether the organ or official has contravened provisions of internal law or overstepped the limits of his authority: under international law a State is responsible for the acts of its agents undertaken in their official capacity and for their omissions, even when those agents act outside the sphere of their authority or violate internal law.[148]

---

[143] ILC Comments on Draft Articles on Responsibility of States 2001, 44, para 5. See ILC (2001b).

[144] ILC Comments on Draft Articles on Responsibility of States 2001, 44, para 5. See ILC (2001b).

[145] Draft Articles on Responsibility of States 2001, Art. 7, see ILC (2001a).

[146] ILC Comments on Draft Articles on Responsibility of States 2001, 45, para 2. See ILC (2001b).

[147] Inter-American Court of Human Rights, Series C No. 4, 29 July 1989, ILR, vol. 95, 232.

[148] Velasquez Rodriguez v. Honduras (1989) 232, at 296, para 170.

Again, under Article 8, ILC Draft Articles on Responsibility of States 2001, the conduct of a person or group of persons shall be considered an act of a state under international law if the person or group of persons is in fact acting on the instructions of, or under the direction or control of that state in carrying out the conduct. It should be noted that Article 8 uses the words "person or group of persons," reflecting the fact that conduct covered by the article may be that of a group lacking separate legal personality but acting on a de facto basis. Thus, while a state may authorise conduct by a legal entity such as a corporation, it may also deal with aggregates of individuals or groups that do not have legal personality but are nonetheless acting as a collective.

At what point shall the conduct of private persons bind the state? As a general principle, the conduct of private persons or entities is not attributable to the state under international law. According to ILC,[149] circumstances may arise, however, where such conduct is nevertheless attributable to the state because there exists a specific factual relationship between the person or entity engaging in the conduct and the state. The first circumstance involves private persons acting on the instructions of the state in carrying out wrongful conduct. The second deals with a more general situation where private persons act under the state's direction or control.

At times the question may arise as to a state's responsibility for actions going beyond the scope of the authorisation. For example, where an agent while carrying out lawful instructions or directions, engages in some activity, which contravenes both the instructions or directions given and the international obligations of the instructing state. Under this situation, the issue may be resolved by asking whether the unlawful or unauthorised conduct was really incidental to the mission or clearly went beyond it. The answer to this scenario is provided by ILC[150] where it asserted that:

> In general a State, in giving lawful instructions to persons who are not its organs, does not assume the risk that the instructions will be carried out in an internationally unlawful way. On the other hand, where persons or groups have committed acts under the effective control of a State, the condition for attribution will still be met even if particular instructions may have been ignored. The conduct will have been committed under the control of the State and it will be attributable to the State in accordance with article 8.

Another aspect of state responsibility for internationally wrongful act is provided under Article 9.[151] It provides that the conduct of a person or group of persons shall be considered an act of a state under international law if the person or group of persons is in fact exercising elements of the governmental authority in the absence or default of the official authorities and in circumstances such as to call for the exercise of those elements of authority. The article established three conditions that must be met for conduct to be attributable to the state: first, the conduct must effectively relate to the exercise of elements of the governmental authority, second, the conduct must have been carried out in the absence or default of the official authorities, and

[149] ILC Comments on Draft Articles on Responsibility of States 2001, 47, para 1. See ILC (2001b).

[150] Ibid., 49, para 9.

[151] Draft Articles on Responsibility of States 2001, see ILC (2001a).

third, the circumstances must have been such as to call for the exercise of those elements of authority.[152]

State responsibility may arise where conduct acknowledged and adopted by a state as its own conduct is not attributable to it under the preceding articles.[153] Under this condition, the conduct shall nevertheless be considered an act of that state under international law if and to the extent that the state acknowledges and adopts the conduct in question as its own.[154] However, conduct will not be attributable to a state under Article 11 where a state merely acknowledges the factual existence of conduct or expresses its verbal approval of it.[155]

The responsibility of a state may also arise where there is a breach consisting of a composite act. This may happen where:

(1) The breach of an international obligation by a state through a series of actions or omissions defined in aggregate as wrongful occurs when the action or omission occurs which, taken with the other actions or omissions, is sufficient to constitute the wrongful act.
(2) In such a case, the breach extends over the entire period starting with the first of the actions or omissions of the series and lasts for as long as these actions or omissions are repeated and remain not in conformity with the international obligation.[156]

Again, a state which aids or assists another state in the commission of an internationally wrongful act by the latter is internationally responsible for doing so.[157] Such situations arise where a state voluntarily assists or aids another state in carrying out conduct which violates the international obligations of the latter, for example, by knowingly providing an essential facility or financing the activity in question. Other examples include providing means for the closing of an international waterway, facilitating the abduction of persons on foreign soil, or assisting in the destruction of property belonging to nationals of a third country.[158] The state primarily responsible in each case is the acting state, and the assisting state has only a supporting role.[159]

A state which directs and controls another state in the commission of an internationally wrongful act by the latter is internationally responsible for that act if: (a) that

[152] ILC Comments on Draft Articles on Responsibility of States 2001, 49, para 3. See ILC (2001b).

[153] ILC Draft Articles on Responsibility of States 2001, Art. 11, see ILC (2001a).

[154] Ibid., Art. 11.

[155] ILC Comments on Draft Articles on Responsibility of States 2001, 53, para 6. See ILC (2001b).

[156] Draft Articles on Responsibility of States 2001, Art. 15, see ILC (2001a).

[157] Ibid., Art. 16.

[158] This gives rise to the issue of co-perpetrators or co-participants in an internationally wrongful act.

[159] ILC Comments on Draft Articles on Responsibility of States 2001,66, para 1. See ILC (2001b).

state does so with knowledge of the circumstances of the internationally wrongful act; and (b) the act would be internationally wrongful if committed by that state.[160]

In the same vein, a state which coerces another state to commit an act is internationally responsible for that act if: (a) the act would, but for the coercion, be an internationally wrongful act of the coerced state; and (b) the coercing state does so with knowledge of the circumstances of the act.[161]

Arising from the above, a state shall be liable where there is a breach of an international obligation by a state when an act of that state is not in conformity with what is required of it by that obligation, regardless of its origin or character.[162] This is so because any breach of an international engagement entails international responsibility.[163]

It should be noted however that an act of a state does not constitute a breach of an international obligation unless the state is bound by the obligation in question at the time the act occurs.[164] To this end, there are situations where the state in question may escape responsibility for the internationally wrongful act. The wrongfulness of an act of a state is precluded under the following circumstances:

1. Where there was valid consent by a state to the commission of a given act by another state precludes the wrongfulness of that act in relation to the former state to the extent that the act remains within the limits of that consent.[165]
2. If the act constitutes a lawful measure of self-defence taken in conformity with the Charter of the United Nations. Article 51 of the Charter of the United Nations preserves a state's "inherent right" of self-defence in the face of an armed attack and forms part of the definition of the obligation to refrain from the threat or use of force laid down in Article 2, para 4. Thus, a state exercising its inherent right of self-defence as referred to in Article 51 of the Charter is not, even potentially, in breach of Article 2, para 4.[166]

However, as to obligations under international humanitarian law and on non-derogable human rights provisions, self-defence does not preclude the wrongfulness of conduct. The ICJ, in its advisory opinion on the *Legality of the Threat or Use of Nuclear Weapons*,[167] provided some guidance on this question. One issue before the court was whether the use of nuclear weapons would necessarily be a

[160] Draft Articles on Responsibility of States 2001, Art. 17, see ILC (2001a).
[161] Ibid., Art. 18.
[162] Ibid., Art. 12.
[163] Factory at Chorzow case (1927).
[164] Draft Articles on Responsibility of States 2001, Art. 13, see ILC (2001a).
[165] Ibid., Art. 20.
[166] ILC Comments on Draft Articles on Responsibility of States 2001, 74, para 1. See ILC (2001b).
[167] Legality of the Threat or Use of Nuclear Weapons (1996) Advisory Opinion, ICJ Report, 1996, 241-242.

breach of environmental obligations because of the massive and long-term damage such weapons can cause.[168] The court said:

> The issue is not whether the treaties relating to the protection of the environment are or are not applicable during an armed conflict, but rather whether the obligations stemming from these treaties were intended to be obligations of total restraint during military conflict. The Court does not consider that the treaties in question could have intended to deprive a State of the exercise of its right of self-defence under international law because of its obligations to protect the environment. Nonetheless, States must take environmental considerations into account when assessing what is necessary and proportionate in the pursuit of legitimate military objectives. Respect for the environment.[169]

3. The wrongfulness of an act of a state not in conformity with an international obligation towards another state is precluded if and to the extent that the act constitutes a countermeasure taken against the latter state.[170]
4. Force majeure may also be a defence for an internationally wrongful act of a state where (1) the wrongfulness of an act of a state not in conformity with an international obligation of that state is precluded if the act is due to force majeure, that is, the occurrence of an irresistible force or of an unforeseen event, beyond the control of the state, making it materially impossible in the circumstances to perform the obligation. However, para 1 does not apply if: (a) the situation of force majeure is due, either alone or in combination with other factors, to the conduct of the state invoking it; or (b) the state has assumed the risk of that situation occurring.[171]

A situation of force majeure precluding wrongfulness only arises where three elements are met: (a) the act in question must be brought about by an irresistible force or an unforeseen event; (b) which is beyond the control of the state concerned; and (c) which makes it materially impossible in the circumstances to perform the obligation.[172]

The adjective "irresistible" qualifying the word "force" emphasises that there must be a constraint that the state was unable to avoid or oppose by its own means. To have been "unforeseen" the event must have been neither foreseen nor of an easily foreseeable kind. Further the "irresistible force" or "unforeseen event" must be causally linked to the situation of material impossibility, as indicated by the words "due to force majeure . . . making it materially impossible." Subject to para 2, where these elements are met, the wrongfulness of the state's conduct is precluded for so long as the situation of force majeure subsists.[173]

---

[168] ILC Comments on Draft Articles on Responsibility of States 2001, 74, para 4. See ILC (2001b).

[169] Legality of the Threat or Use of Nuclear Weapons (1996).

[170] Draft Articles on Responsibility of States 2001, Art. 22, see ILC (2001a).

[171] Ibid., Art. 23.

[172] ILC Comments on Draft Articles on Responsibility of States 2001, 77, para 2. See ILC (2001b).

[173] Ibid.

Material impossibility of performance giving rise to force majeure may be due to a natural or physical event (e.g. stress of weather which may divert state aircraft into the territory of another state, earthquakes, floods or drought) or to human intervention (e.g. loss of control over a portion of the state's territory as a result of an insurrection or devastation of an area by military operations carried out by a third state), or some combination of the two.[174]

Certain situations of duress or coercion involving force imposed on the state may also amount to force majeure if they meet the various requirements of Article 23 of ILC Draft Articles 2001. In particular, the situation must be irresistible, so that the state concerned has no real possibility of escaping its effects.[175]

Force majeure does not include circumstances in which the performance of an obligation has become more difficult, for example due to some political or economic crisis. Nor does it cover situations brought about by the neglect or default of the state concerned, even if the resulting injury itself was accidental and unintended.[176]

5. Distress may also offer some defence. The defence of distress may arise where the wrongfulness of an act of a state was not in conformity with an international obligation of that state and if the author of the act in question has no other reasonable way, in a situation of distress, of saving the author's life or the lives of other persons entrusted to the author's care. However, this defence may not arise if: (a) the situation of distress is due, either alone or in combination with other factors, to the conduct of the state invoking it; or (b) the act in question is likely to create a comparable or greater peril.[177]
6. Necessity in performing the wrongful act may be a defence.[178] However, necessity may not be invoked by a state as a ground for precluding the wrongfulness of an act not in conformity with an international obligation of that state unless the act: (a) is the only way for the state to safeguard an essential interest against a grave and imminent peril; and (b) does not seriously impair an essential interest of the state or states towards which the obligation exists, or of the international community as a whole.

For instance, in March 1967, the Liberian oil tanker *Torrey Canyon* went aground on submerged rocks off the coast of Cornwall outside British territorial waters, spilling large amounts of oil which threatened the English coastline. After various remedial attempts had failed, the British government decided to bomb the ship to burn the remaining oil. This operation was carried out successfully. The British government did not advance any legal justification for its conduct, but stressed the

---

[174] Ibid., para 3.

[175] Ibid.

[176] Ibid.

[177] Draft Articles on Responsibility of States 2001, Art. 24, see ILC (2001a).

[178] Ibid., Art. 25.

existence of a situation of extreme danger and claimed that the decision to bomb the ship had been taken only after all other means had failed.[179]

In any case, necessity may not be invoked by a state as a ground for precluding wrongfulness if: (a) the international obligation in question excludes the possibility of invoking necessity; or (b) the state has contributed to the situation of necessity.[180]

10.4 State Liability and the United Nations Compensation Commission

Clear support for the provision of compensation for environmental damage under rules of state liability was provided by the resolutions of the United Nations Security Council (UNSC) in 1991[181] when it reaffirmed that Iraq…"is liable under international law for any direct loss, damage, including environmental damage and the depletion of natural resources or injury to foreign Governments, nationals and corporations' occurring as a result of its unlawful invasion and occupation of Kuwait."[182]

Although the UN Security Council Resolution 687 unequivocally determines that a state can be liable for the environmental damage and depletion of natural resources which resulted from unlawful use of force, it did not, however, define environmental damage or depletion of natural resources, or provide guidance on assessment, or the measure of reparation or compensation for the environmental damage. This task was however left in the hands of the United Nations Compensation Commission (the Commission).

The Commission was established in 1991[183] to deal with compensation claims resulting from the consequences of Iraq's unlawful invasion and occupation of Kuwait in 1990. The Resolution 692(1991)[184] also provided for the establishment of a Governing Council for the Commission. The Commission pursuant to the decision of the Governing Council in para 35 of Decision 7[185] established criteria

[179] ILC Comments on Draft Articles on Responsibility of States 2001, 82, para 9. See ILC (2001b).

[180] Ibid.

[181] United Nations Security Council Resolution (UNSC) (1991).

[182] Ibid., para 16. On 2 August 1990, the Iraqi Army invaded and occupied Kuwait, which was met with international condemnation. Iraqi's refusal to vacate Kuwait led to the Gulf War that began with an extensive aerial bombing campaign by allied forces on 16 January 1991 and ended with an Iraqi defeat and retreat from Kuwait on 28 February 1991. The retreating Iraqi soldiers ignited hundreds of oil well fires and the release of million barrels of crude oil into the Persian Gulf resulted in one of the largest deliberate man-made disasters on record.

[183] The Commission was officially established in 1991 pursuant to United Nations Security Council (UNSC) Resolution 692 of 20 May 1991 and adopted at the 2987th meeting on 20 May 1991. See UNSC (1992).

[184] United Nations Security Council (UNSC) (1992).

[185] United Nations Compensation Commission Governing Council (UNCCGC) (1992).

for claims in respect of environmental damage and the depletion of natural resources.[186] It provided that "direct environmental damage and the depletion of natural resources" includes losses or expenses resulting from:

(a) Abatement and prevention of environmental damage, including expenses directly relating to fighting oil well fires and stemming the flow of oil in coastal and international waters;
(b) Reasonable measures already taken to clean and restore the environment or future measures which can be documented as reasonably necessary to clean and restore the environment;
(c) Reasonable monitoring and assessment of the environmental damage to evaluate and abate the harm and restore the environment;
(d) Reasonable monitoring of public health and performing medical screenings for investigation and combating increased health risks as a result of the environmental damage; and
(e) Depletion of or damage to natural resources.[187]

The Commission accepted for filing claims of individuals, corporations and governments, submitted by governments and international organisations and received approximately 2.69 million claims seeking a total of approximately US$352.5 billion in compensation, of which 1.5 million were awarded a total of US$52.4 billion. Nearly one hundred governments submitted claims for their nationals, corporations and/or themselves. Thirteen offices of three international organisations, the United Nations Development Programme (UNDP), the United Nations High Commissioner for Refugees (UNHCR) and the United Nations Relief and Works Agency for Palestine Refugees in the Near East (UNRWA), also submitted claims for individuals who were not in a position to have their claims filed by governments.[188]

The Rules[189] provided for the appointment of Commissioners[190] who shall be appointed for specific tasks and terms by the Governing Council upon nomination by the Secretary-General on the basis of recommendations of the Executive Secretary of the Commission. In considering the claims, Article 31 of the Rules[191] provides that:

> Commissioners will apply Security Council resolution 687 (1991) and other relevant Security Council resolutions, the criteria established by the Governing Council for particular

---

[186] The language was drawn from a Working Paper submitted by the United States, which drew upon its domestic legislation, including provisions of the Oil Pollution Act of 1990 adopted following the *Exxon Valdez* oil spill in 1989.

[187] UNCCGC (1992), para 35, Decision 7.

[188] UNCC (1991).

[189] United Nations Compensation Commission Provisional Rules for Claims Procedures (1992), Art. 18.

[190] Commissioner means experts appointed by the Governing Council for the verification and evaluation of claims. See United Nations Compensation Commission Provisional Rules for Claims Procedures (1992), Art. 1(5).

[191] UNCCGC (1992).

categories of claims (such as that provided under Paragraph 35 of Decision 7 of the Governing Council to the Commission), and any pertinent decisions of the Governing Council. In addition, where necessary, Commissioners shall apply other relevant rules of international law.

At the first meeting in August 1991, the Governing Council identified six categories of claims: Category A: claims from individuals forced to flee Kuwait between the invasion and the cease-fire; Category B: claims from individuals who (or whose family) suffered injuries or death as a result of the invasion; Category C: claims from individuals for business losses, pain and anguish, property damage, etc. less than US$100,000; Category D: claims from individuals for business losses, pain and anguish, property damage etc. more than $100,000; Category E: claims from corporations and other entities for business (including oil sector) losses; and Category F: claims filed by governments and international organisations, including those for damages to the environment.[192]

Deadlines were established for the filing of the various categories of claims. The deadline of 1 January 1995 was set for the filing of category "A", "B", "C" and "D" claims and 1 January 1996 for the filing of category "E" and "F" claims, except for environmental claims in category "F" which had to be filed before 1 February 1997. After the expiration of these deadlines, the Governing Council, based on certain criteria it established, accepted some claims for late filing from individuals who had not been able to file their claims during the regular filing period.[193]

In 2004, the Governing Council adopted Decision 219 (S/AC.26/Dec. 219 (2004)[194] in which it decided that the Council would not consider or accept any further requests for the late filing of a claim in any claims category.

Category "F" claims were claims filed by governments and international organisations for losses incurred in evacuating citizens; providing relief to citizens; damage to diplomatic premises and loss of, and damage to, other government property; and **damage to the environment**. The Commission received approximately 400 category "F" claims, submitted by forty-three governments and six international organisations, seeking a total of approximately US$236 billion in compensation.[195]

The Commission organised the category "F" claims into four main sub-categories: "F1,"[196] "F2,"[197] "F3"[198] and "F4." "F4" claims were claims for

---

[192] UNCC (1991).

[193] UNCC (1991).

[194] United Nations Security Council (UNSC) (2004).

[195] Ibid.

[196] Claims here were for losses incurred in connection with the departure and evacuation of individuals and for damage to property belonging to governments and to international organisations. The Commission received approximately 100 "F1" claims seeking a total of approximately US$30 billion in compensation.

[197] Claims here were claims filed by the governments of Jordan and Saudi Arabia. The Commission received 63 "F2" claims seeking US$18.4 billion in compensation.

[198] Claims in this category were claims filed by the government of Kuwait, excluding environmental claims. The Commission received 62 "F3" claims submitted on behalf of Kuwaiti ministries and

damage to the environment. The Commission also established a corresponding Secretariat team and Panel of Commissioners (the Panel) for each category of claims.[199]

The "F4" claims are relevant to the discussions on state liability for environmental damage. The Commission received approximately 170 claims seeking a total of approximately US$85 billion in compensation. The "F4" claims consisted of five instalments.

10.4.1 The First Instalment of "F4" Claims

The first instalment of "F4" claims consisted of monitoring and assessment claims submitted under para 35 of the Governing Council of the Commission Decision 7.[200] The total compensation claimed was US$ 1,007,412,574 from 107 claims.[201]

The claimants[202] under this instalment sought compensation for expenses resulting from monitoring and assessment activities undertaken or to be undertaken to identify and evaluate damage or loss suffered by them as a result of Iraq's invasion and occupation of Kuwait. These activities related to, inter alia, damage from air pollution; depletion of water resources; damage to groundwater; damage to cultural heritage resources; oil pollution in the Persian Gulf; damage to coastlines; damage to fisheries; damage to wetlands and rangelands; damage to forestry, agriculture and livestock; and damage or risk of damage to public health.[203]

The claimants alleged that environmental damage, depletion of natural resources and increased health risks resulted from, inter alia:

(a) The release and transport, into the claimants' territories, of airborne pollutants caused by oil fires resulting from the ignition of hundreds of oil wells in Kuwait by Iraqi forces during Iraq's invasion and occupation of Kuwait;
(b) Numerous oil rivers and lakes formed by oil from the destroyed oil wells that did not ignite;
(c) The release, by Iraqi forces, of millions of barrels of oil into the sea from oil pipelines, off-shore terminals and oil tankers;

other government entities seeking a total of approximately US$114 billion in compensation. Most of the "F3" claims included multiple types of loss, such as damage to government buildings, loss of equipment, loss of the value of work carried out by contractors prior to the invasion and relief provided to the Kuwaiti population.

199 UNCC (1991).

200 UNCCGC (1992).

201 UNCCGC (2001), para 12.

202 The Islamic Republic of Iran, Hashemite Kingdom of Jordan, the State of Kuwait, the Kingdom of Saudi Arabia, the Syrian Arab Republic and the Republic of Turkey.

203 UNCCGC (2001), para 13.

(d) Disruption of fragile desert and coastal terrain caused by the movement of military vehicles and personnel, coupled with the construction of thousands of kilometres of military trenches and the emplacement of mines, weapons caches and other fortifications; and
(e) Adverse impacts on the environment resulting from the transit and settlement of the thousands of persons who departed from Iraq and Kuwait as a result of Iraq's invasion and occupation of Kuwait.[204]

The first "F4" instalment assessment of claims bordered on monitoring and assessment of expenses incurred by the claimants as a result of Iraq's unlawful invasion and occupation of Kuwait was based on the provisions of para 35 of Decision 7 of the Governing Council to the Commission.[205] Reference is made specifically to para 35(b) that recognises a liability in respect of "reasonable measures . . . to clean and restore the environment," and para 35(e) that recognises an additional liability in respect of loss relating to "depletion of or damage to natural resources." Thus, to qualify for compensation the monitoring and assessment of expenses should be based on those resulting from: (a) monitoring and assessment of environmental damage that is reasonable for any of the purposes specified in subparagraph (c) of para 35 of Governing Council Decision 7; and (b) monitoring of public health and performing medical screenings that is reasonable for any of the purposes set out in subparagraph (d) of para 35 of the same decision.[206]

As a result, the Panel held the view that compensation should not be awarded for monitoring and assessment activities that were purely theoretical or speculative, or which have only a tenuous link with damage resulting from Iraq's invasion and occupation of Kuwait.[207] Furthermore, for claims to succeed, there should be a sufficient nexus between the activity and environmental damage or risk of damage that may be attributed directly to Iraq's invasion and occupation of Kuwait.

However, the Panel did not consider that conclusive proof of environmental damage was a prerequisite for a monitoring and assessment activity to be compensable, rather, "the purpose of monitoring and assessment is to enable a claimant to develop evidence to establish whether environmental damage has occurred and to quantify the extent of the resulting loss."[208]

In assessing the strength of the nexus, and hence the reasonableness of the monitoring and assessment activity, the Panel took into account, inter alia, the following considerations:

(a) Whether there is a possibility that environmental damage or depletion of natural resources could have been caused as a result of Iraq's invasion and occupation of Kuwait. This entails an inquiry regarding the plausibility that pollutants released

[204] Ibid., para 14.
[205] UNCCGC (1992).
[206] UNCCGC (2001), para 11.
[207] Ibid.
[208] Ibid., para 30.

as a result of Iraq's invasion and occupation of Kuwait, or other effects of the invasion, could have impacted the territories of the claimants;

(b) Whether the particular areas or resources in respect of which the monitoring and assessment activity is undertaken could have been affected by pollutants released as a result of Iraq's invasion and occupation of Kuwait, or other effects of the invasion. This entails, in appropriate cases, an examination of the possible pathways and media by which pollutants resulting from Iraq's invasion and occupation of Kuwait could have reached the areas or resources concerned;

(c) Whether there is evidence of environmental damage or risk of such damage as a result of Iraq's invasion and occupation of Kuwait; and

(d) Whether, having regard to the stated purpose of the monitoring and assessment activity and the methodologies to be used, there is a reasonable prospect that the activity will produce results that can assist the Panel in reviewing any related substantive claims.[209]

Although the Panel recognised the difficulty of ascertaining whether and to what extent damage as identified was attributable to Iraq's invasion, and the inadequacy of documented baseline information on the state of the environment or of conditions and trends regarding natural resources before the invasion, it however confirmed that loss or damage occurring outside Kuwait and Iraq was compensable. The Panel also noted that some of the monitoring and assessment activities may need to be conducted for several years. Under such circumstances, the Panel recommended awards of compensation for monitoring and assessment activities even though the results of the activities may not become available in time for use in the review of any substantive claims or may not be needed for such review.[210]

The Panel also determined that "environmental damage" was not limited to losses or expenses resulting from the activities and events, but could also cover other direct losses or expenses, such as measures undertaken to prevent or abate harmful impacts of airborne contaminants, provided that they were a direct result of the invasion. The Panel therefore decided that Iraq cannot be exonerated from liability because other factors may have contributed to the loss or damage, and that expenses resulting from activities undertaken by military personnel will be compensable if there is evidence to show that the predominant purpose of the activity engaged in was to respond to environmental damage or threats of damage to the environmental or health.[211]

On the basis of above, out of US$1007 million claimed under the first instalment "F4" claims Iran, Jordan, Kuwait, Saudi Arabia, and Syria were awarded a combined amount of more than US$243 million for activities that included shoreline surveys of oil-spill damage (Kuwait and Saudi Arabia); a study of bioaccumulation of oil spill-related pollutants in fisheries stocks (Iran); evaluation of damage to cultural heritage sites caused by oil fire pollutants (cities in Iran and Syria); and studies of pollution in

[209] UNCCGC (2001), para 31.

[210] Ibid., para 40.

[211] UNCCGC (2001).

groundwater and springs caused by the presence of refugees (Jordan). For Iran, US$17 million was recommended out of US$42.9 million claimed; Jordan, US$7 million out of US$12.5 million claimed, Kuwait, US$109.5 million out of US$460.4 million claimed; Saudi Arabia, US$109.5 million out of US$482 million claimed; and Syria, US$0.67 million out of US$5.6 million claimed.[212]

10.4.2 The Second Instalment of "F4" Claims

The second "F4" instalment consisted of 31 claims for expenses incurred for measures to abate and prevent environmental damage, to clean and restore the environment, to monitor and assess environmental damage, and to monitor public health risks alleged to have resulted from Iraq's invasion and occupation of Kuwait.[213] There were two groups of claimants.

The first group of claimants was those countries directly affected by the impact of the invasion and occupation of Kuwait: the Islamic Republic of Iran, the State of Kuwait, the Kingdom of Saudi Arabia and the Republic of Turkey (Regional claims). The second group consisted of non-regional claims but governments that offered assistance to abate and prevent environmental damage. They were the governments of Australia, Canada, the Federal Republic of Germany, the United Kingdom of Great Britain and Northern Ireland and the United States of America.[214]

Iran, Kuwait and Saudi Arabia sought compensation in the amount of US$ 829,458,298 for measures to respond to environmental damage and human health risks from:

(a) Mines, unexploded ordnance and other remnants of war;
(b) Oil lakes formed by oil released from damaged wells in Kuwait;
(c) Oil spills in the Persian Gulf caused by oil released from pipelines, offshore terminals and tankers; and
(d) Pollutants released from oil well fires in Kuwait.[215]

Australia, Canada, Germany, the Netherlands, the United Kingdom and the United States, on the other hand, sought compensation for expenses incurred for assistance to abate and prevent environmental damage resulting from Iraq's invasion and occupation of Kuwait. The expenses are for measures to respond to the oil spills, oil fires and other environmental damage or threats of environmental damage resulting from the invasion and occupation, including monitoring and assessment of the impacts of the oil spills and oil fires.[216] The total amount of compensation

---

212 UNCCGC (2001).

213 UNCCGC (2002), para 5.

214 Ibid., para 2.

215 Ibid., para 6.

216 Ibid., para 211.

sought in the non-regional claims was US$ 43,302,236.[217] The procedural orders focused on the following questions:

(a) May compensation be awarded for environmental damage or depletion of natural resources even if such damage or depletion may not have been caused solely as a result of Iraq's invasion and occupation of Kuwait?
(b) Where environmental damage or depletion of natural resources may not have resulted solely from Iraq's invasion and occupation of Kuwait, what factors should the Panel take into account in determining that: (i) a portion of the damage or depletion is compensable, or (ii) no portion of the damage or depletion is compensable?
(c) Does "environmental damage and the depletion of natural resources" under Security Council Resolution 687 (1991) and Governing Council Decision 7 include loss or damage to elements such as cultural property, human health, aesthetic values of landscapes, etc.?
(d) To what extent, if any, should the procedure and criteria used for selecting contractors to undertake the removal of mines and ordnance affect the compensability of expenses arising from these activities?[218]

In respect of the second instalment "F4" claims, the Panel also relied on Article 31 of the Rules[219] in addition to para 16 of Security Council Resolution 687 (1991).[220]

On compensable losses or expenses, the Panel relied on the provisions of the Governing Council Decision 7[221] for guidance. The Panel regarded losses or expenses that may be considered as "direct loss, damage, or injury" resulting from Iraq's invasion and occupation of Kuwait, under para 16 of Security Council Resolution 687 (1991). However, on the issue of "direct environmental damage and depletion of natural resources," the Panel relied on the provisions of para 35 of Governing Council Decision 7.[222]

The Panel further recommended that compensation should be payable to cover expenses resulting from assistance rendered to countries in the region to respond to damage or threats, provided it did not duplicate compensation paid to any country in the region. In reviewing the second instalment of claims, the Panel was assisted by a multidisciplinary team of independence experts retained by the Commission, having regard to the complexity of the issues and the need to consider scientific, legal, social, commercial and accounting issues. The Panel therefore recommended compensation under the second "F4" instalments payments of US$711 million, out of US$872 million claimed as follows:

---

[217] Ibid., para 212.

[218] UNCCGC (2002), para 13.

[219] United Nations Compensation Commission Provisional Rules for Claims Procedures (1992).

[220] UNSC (1991).

[221] UNCCGC (1992).

[222] Ibid.

For Iran, US$67,000 million was recommended out of US$64.3 million claimed;[223] Kuwait, US$694 million out of US$715 million claimed for the removal and disposal of ordnance left in its[224] and US$1.255 million as total compensable expenses for the restoration and remediation of the Garden;[225] Saudi Arabia, US$8.2 million out of US$49.7 million claimed;[226] Australia, US$7,700 out of US$20,000 claimed;[227] Canada, US$529,000 was recommended out of US$1.25 million claimed;[228] Germany, US$2 million out of US$28.7 million claimed;[229] UK, US$1.8 million out of US$2.2 million claimed;[230] and US, US$3.8 million out of US$9.1 million claimed.[231]

10.4.3 The Third Instalment of "F4" Claims

The third "F4" instalment consisted of three claims by the government of the State of Kuwait and two claims by the government of the Kingdom of Saudi Arabia.[232] The claims were for expenses resulting from measures already taken or to be undertaken in the future to clean and restore the environment alleged to have been damaged as a direct result of Iraq's invasion and occupation of Kuwait.[233] The claimants sought compensation for expenses resulting from cleaning and restoration measures undertaken or to be undertaken by them to remediate damage from:

(a) Oil released from damaged oil wells in Kuwait;
(b) Pollutants released from oil well fires and firefighting activities in Kuwait;
(c) Oil spills into the Persian Gulf from pipelines, offshore terminals and tankers;
(d) Laying and clearance of mines;
(e) Movements of military vehicles and personnel; and
(f) Construction of military fortifications.[234]

In its claim, Kuwait alleged that the detonation of oil wells by Iraqi forces during the final days of their occupation of Kuwait resulted in the release of over 1 billion barrels of crude oil into the environment, much of which was ignited and burned for

223 UNCCGC (2002), para 72.
224 Ibid., para 106.
225 Ibid., para 150.
226 Ibid., para 154.
227 Ibid., para 218.
228 Ibid., para 231.
229 Ibid., para 248.
230 Ibid., para 282.
231 Ibid., para 341.
232 UNCCGC (2003).
233 Ibid., para 5.
234 UNCCGC (2003), para 6.

many months. According to Kuwait, the fallout from the burning oil, in the form of soot and oil droplets, contaminated the soil as well as buildings and other structures in Kuwait. In addition, seawater used to fight the oil well fires, together with oil and dissolved hydrocarbons, seeped into the soil and infiltrated the aquifers in Umm-Al Aish and Raudhatain in the northeast of the country.[235]

According to Kuwait, the desert soil and vegetation were severely disrupted by the construction of military fortifications, including ditches, berms, bunkers, trenches, and pits; the laying and clearance of mines; and the extensive movement of military vehicles and personnel. These activities are alleged to have resulted in, inter alia, accelerated soil erosion, increased sand movement and increased incidence of dust and sand storms. Kuwait asserts that the construction of military fortifications and the movement of military vehicles and personnel also caused significant damage to natural vegetation and wildlife.[236] Kuwait also claimed for expenses incurred for the cleaning and restoration of the exterior of the Central Bank of Kuwait's building.[237]

In the case of Saudi Arabia, it sought compensation in the amount of US$ 4,748,292,230 for expenses of future measures to remediate damage to its coastal environment resulting from Iraq's invasion and occupation of Kuwait. This amount represents a decrease of the original amount claimed; reflecting amendments made by Saudi Arabia on the basis of new information obtained from its monitoring and assessment projects.[238]

Saudi Arabia stated that its coastal environment was damaged by (a) more than 10 million barrels of oil deliberately released into the Persian Gulf by Iraqi forces; (b) contaminants released from oil wells in Kuwait that were set on fire by Iraqi forces; and (c) other releases of oil into the Persian Gulf as a result of Iraq's invasion and occupation of Kuwait.[239]

Again, Saudi Arabia asserted that the oil released as a result of Iraq's invasion and occupation of Kuwait dwarfed all previous inputs of oil into the Persian Gulf from spills, refinery operations, natural seeps, exploration and production activities, operational discharges from vessels, urban run-offs and similar sources.[240]

On 24 January 2003, the Panel issued Procedural Order No. 4 and listed the issues to be considered at the oral proceedings as follows:

(a) On what basis should the Panel determine whether and to what extent environmental damage resulted from causes other than the effects of Iraq's invasion and occupation of Kuwait?
(b) What should be the appropriate objectives of remediation measures?

[235] UNCCGC (2003), para 61.
[236] Ibid., para 62.
[237] Ibid., para 60.
[238] Ibid., para 169.
[239] Ibid., para 170.
[240] UNCCGC (2003), para 171.

(c) What standards should be applied in determining remediation goals in particular circumstances?
(d) To what extent will remediation goals and standards be affected where there is evidence that the environment was not in "pristine condition" before Iraq's invasion and occupation of Kuwait?[241]

For the claims in the third "F4" instalment, the Panel also relied on Article 31 of the Rules[242] in addition to para 16 of Security Council Resolution 687 (1991),[243] holding that the Security Council Resolution 687 (1991) and the relevant decisions of the Governing Council provided sufficient legal guidance. The key issues for decision in connection with the claims in the third "F4" instalment were:

(a) whether the environmental damage for which compensation is sought resulted directly from Iraq's invasion and occupation of Kuwait;
(b) whether measures already taken by a claimant to remediate environmental damage were "reasonable;" and
(c) whether measures proposed to be undertaken by a claimant qualify as "future measures which can be documented as reasonably necessary to clean and restore the environment."[244]

As a general rule, in considering the reasonableness of remediation measures, it is appropriate to have regard to the extent of the damage involved. However, in the view of the Panel, "this is not the only factor to be considered. Other factors, such as the location and nature of the damage and its actual or potential effects on the environment may also be relevant."[245] The Panel further stated that "where damage that might otherwise be characterised as 'insignificant' is caused to an area of special ecological sensitivity, or where the damage, in conjunction with other factors, poses a risk of further or more serious environmental harm, it may not be unreasonable to take remediation measures in order to prevent or minimize potential additional damage."[246]

For the claims in the third "F4" instalment, the Panel considered that the appropriate objective of remediation was to restore the damaged environment or resource to the condition in which it would have been if Iraq's invasion and occupation of Kuwait had not occurred. In applying this objective to a particular claim, regard must be had to a number of considerations. These include, inter alia, the location of the damaged environment or resource and its actual or potential uses; the nature and extent of the damage; the possibility of future harm; the feasibility of the proposed

[241] Ibid., para 15.
[242] United Nations Compensation Commission Provisional Rules for Claims Procedures (1992).
[243] UNSC (1992).
[244] UNCCGC (2003), para 15.
[245] Ibid., para 16.
[246] UNCCGC (2003).

remediation measures; and the need to avoid collateral damage during and after the implementation of the proposed measures.[247]

In the view of the Panel, such an approach was appropriate even where there is evidence that the environment was not in pristine condition before Iraq's invasion and occupation of Kuwait. The contribution of any pre-existing or subsequent causes of damage (where such causes can be identified) should be considered, not in determining the restoration objective to be achieved by remediation, but in determining the proportion of the costs of remediation that can reasonably be attributed to Iraq's invasion and occupation of Kuwait.[248]

The Panel considered that, in assessing what measures were "reasonably necessary to clean or restore" damaged environment, primary emphasis must be placed on restoring the environment to pre-invasion conditions, in terms of its overall ecological functioning rather than on the removal of specific contaminants or restoration of the environment to a particular physical condition.[249] The Panel asserted that "even if sufficient baseline information were available to determine the exact historical state of the environment prior to Iraq's invasion and occupation of Kuwait, it might not be feasible or reasonable to fully recreate pre-existing physical conditions."[250]

Accordingly, the Panel recommended for the award in the third instalment "F4" claims a sum of USD$ 685,381,727(US$ 41,531,463 for damage to groundwater resources, US$ 643,814,034 for damage to terrestrial resources and US$ 36,230 for damage to the Central Bank of Kuwait building, in respect of claims by Kuwait[251] and the sum of US$ 463,319,284 for damage to coastal resources in respect of claims by Saudi Arabia.[252]

10.4.4 The Fourth Instalment of "F4" Claims

The fourth instalment of "F4" total claims was US$16,305,459,098, consisted of nine claims: government of the State of Kuwait (3 claims: US$33,901,560 and US$695,119,160); the government of the Kingdom of Saudi Arabia (2 claims: US$ 9,470,667,058 and US$1,844,497,435); the government of the Islamic Republic of Iran (1 claim: US$2,484,623,669); the government of the Hashemite Kingdom of Jordan (1 claim: US$136,761,897); the government of the Syrian Arab Republic (1 claim: US$1,634,619,154); and the government of the Republic of Turkey (1 claim: US$5,269,165).[253]

[247] Ibid., para 46.
[248] Ibid.
[249] Ibid., para 47.
[250] Ibid.
[251] Ibid., para 168.
[252] UNCCGC (2003), para 197.
[253] UNCCGC (2004a).

The claims in the fourth "F4" instalment were for expenses resulting from measures already taken or to be undertaken to clean and restore the environment alleged to have been damaged as a direct result of Iraq's invasion and occupation of Kuwait. The claimants sought compensation for expenses resulting from measures already taken or to be undertaken by them to remediate damage caused, inter alia, by:

(a) Oil released from damaged oil wells in Kuwait;
(b) Pollutants released from the oil well fires and fire-fighting activities in Kuwait;
(c) Oil released from pipelines onto the land;
(d) Oil-filled trenches;
(e) Oil spills into the Persian Gulf from pipelines, offshore terminals and tankers;
(f) Movement and presence of refugees who departed from Iraq and Kuwait;
(g) Mines and other remnants of war;
(h) Movement of military vehicles and personnel; and
(i) Construction of military fortifications, encampments and roads.[254]

As in other claims, the Panel relied on Governing Council Decision 7[255] guidance regarding the losses or expenses that may be considered as "direct loss, damage, or injury" resulting from Iraq's invasion and occupation of Kuwait under para 16 of Security Council Resolution 687 (1991).[256] Legal reliance was also placed on para 35 of Governing Council Decision 7 which provides that "direct environmental damage and the depletion of natural resources" includes losses or expenses.. . ..[257]

The fourth "F4" instalment only concerns claims for compensation for expenses of measures to remediate alleged environmental damage,[258] and in the following areas: (i) expenses for measures to remediate environmental damage that it alleges resulted from Iraq's invasion and occupation of Kuwait; (ii) future measures to remediate damage to sand beaches caused by oil pollution in the Persian Gulf; and (iii) future measures to remediate damage to terrestrial resources from stockpiled ordnance and unexploded ordnance, and from open burning/open detonation pits.[259]

Although some claims in the fourth "F4" instalment related to environmental damage was alleged to have occurred outside Kuwait or Iraq, the Panel noted that neither Security Council Resolution 687 (1991) nor any decision of the Governing Council restricted eligibility for compensation to damage that occurred only in Kuwait or Iraq.

Iraq contended that some of the damage for which the claimants seek compensation in the fourth "F4" instalment had been caused or contributed to by the claimants themselves, either because they failed to take steps to mitigate damage resulting from the invasion and occupation of Kuwait or because the damage had

[254] Ibid., para 9.
[255] UNCCGC (1992).
[256] UNSC (1991).
[257] UNCCGC (2004a), para 28.
[258] Ibid., para 51.
[259] Ibid., para 156.

been aggravated by the acts or omissions of the claimants after the invasion and occupation.[260] Iraq also reiterated its view that failure by a claimant to take reasonable and timely measures to mitigate damage from the invasion and occupation of Kuwait amounts to contributory negligence and justifies the rejection of the claim for compensation or a corresponding reduction in the compensation to be awarded to the claimant.[261]

However, the Panel found that losses or expenses that meet the criteria set forth in para 35 of Governing Council Decision 7 were compensable in principle, even if they occurred outside Kuwait or Iraq.[262] This is because Iraq was not exonerated from liability for loss or damage that resulted directly from the invasion and occupation simply because other factors might have contributed to the loss or damage.[263] Thus, "whether or not any environmental damage or loss for which compensation was claimed was a direct result of Iraq's invasion and occupation of Kuwait depended on the evidence presented in relation to each particular loss or damage."[264]

On the whole, the Panel reiterated its view that, in determining what remediation measures were necessary, "primary emphasis must be placed on restoring the environment to pre-invasion conditions, in terms of its overall ecological functioning rather than on the removal of specific contaminants or restoration of the environment to a particular physical condition."[265] In the end, the Panel recommended an award for compensation in respect of part one of the fourth instalment "F4" claims as follows:

(i) Award to Kuwait was US$ 4,152,411 (US$ 3,990,152 for damage to marine resources and US$ 162,259 for damage to terrestrial resources).[266]
(ii) Saudi Arabia total award was US$ 625,146,707 (US$ 618,974,433 damage to terrestrial resources and US$ 6,172,274 for damage to marine resources).[267]
(iii) To Iran, compensation was US$ 188,760 for damage to terrestrial resources only.[268]
(iv) Although Jordan laid claims for damage to water resources, agricultural resources, wetland resources and marine resources, no compensation was awarded.[269]

---

[260] Ibid., para 41.
[261] Ibid., para 42.
[262] Ibid., para 37.
[263] Ibid., para 39.
[264] UNCCGC (2004a).
[265] Ibid., para 50.
[266] Ibid., para 241.
[267] Ibid., para 321.
[268] Ibid., para 101.
[269] Ibid., para 155.

(v) Also no award for compensation was recommended by the Panel in respect of claims by Syria and Turkey.[270]

In addition to the compensation to Kuwait stated above,[271] Kuwait also sought another claim for compensation in Claim No. 5000454.[272] Claim No. 5000454 comprised two claim units:

The first claim unit was for expenses of proposed measures to remediate environmental damage in Kuwait alleged to have been damaged by oil contamination in the form of oil lakes, oil-contaminated piles, oil trenches and oil spills from pipelines as a result of Iraq's invasion and occupation of Kuwait.[273]

In respect of this claim unit Kuwait sought compensation in the amount of US$ 5,863,998,176 for expenses of future measures to remediate areas alleged to have been damaged by oil contamination (oil lakes, oil-contaminated piles, oil trenches and oil spills).[274] In this claim, Kuwait alleged that over 114 square kilometres of its desert had been damaged by oil that was released when retreating Iraqi troops detonated 798 oil wells in Kuwait. The oil flowing from the damaged oil wells formed oil lakes, which contaminated over 40 million cubic metres of soil. Kuwait alleges that contamination of the desert altered soil properties, caused extensive plant and animal mortality and continues to impair ecosystem functioning.[275]

Kuwait also stated that oil discharged from the damaged oil wells accumulated in depressions in the desert areas and that subsequent evaporation of lighter oil fractions resulted in the formation of a thick sludge with an underlying layer of contaminated soil. Kuwait describes the oil lakes as areas of "wet oil contamination" or areas of "dry oil contamination."[276]

According to Kuwait, oil contamination destroyed the vegetative cover of the affected areas and posed a risk to groundwater. Kuwait also alleged that the chemical and physical effects of the oil lakes have had adverse impacts on wildlife. For example, Kuwait stated that animals continue to be trapped in oil-contaminated areas.[277]

To escape liability, Iraq however contended that Kuwait did not take adequate measures to mitigate the environmental damage caused by the oil lakes; and argued that there was undue delay in extinguishing the oil well fires and that earlier action could have reduced the amount of released oil.[278]

[270] Ibid., para 360.
[271] See note 266.
[272] UNCCGC (2004b), para 5.
[273] Ibid., para 54.
[274] UNCCGC (2004b), para 58.
[275] Ibid., para 59.
[276] Ibid., para 60.
[277] Ibid., para 68.
[278] Ibid., para 71.

Rejecting this contention, the Panel noted that from available literature, Kuwait made efforts to control the oil well fires suggesting that the oil well fires were extinguished much sooner than originally predicted. This was added to the fact that "removal of the oil was initially prevented by mine clearance and further delayed by oil field reconstruction operations." Thus, the evidence available showed that "the measures taken by Kuwait to mitigate environmental damage from the oil spills and oil well fires were reasonable and adequate," the Panel concluded.[279]

The Panel further noted that extensive contamination of Kuwait's environment by the oil lakes was directly caused by the actions of Iraqi forces and that the oil lakes posed acute threats to wildlife and possibly to Kuwait Oil Company (KOC) employees working in and around these areas. Site visits to the affected areas confirm that the existing damage from oil contamination is severe since hardly any live vegetation is currently present in either areas of wet or dry oil contamination or in piles of oil-contaminated material. The barren oil-contaminated areas stand in sharp contrast to the surrounding desert areas, which have experienced ecological recovery. In addition to the visible damage to vegetation and soil, the oil lakes continue to impair water transport and nutrient cycling because water is unable to penetrate the pools of oil and crusts of weathered sludge that cover the oil lakes. In the view of the Panel, near-term recovery of vegetation or ecological processes will not occur in the oil-contaminated areas without some form of active remediation.[280]

The Panel, therefore, found that damage to Kuwait's desert areas from oil lakes, oil-contaminated piles, oil trenches and oil spills constitutes environmental damage directly resulting from Iraq's invasion and occupation of Kuwait, and a programme to remediate the damage would constitute reasonable measures to clean and restore the environment.[281] Accordingly, the Panel recommended compensation for part two fourth instalment "F4" claims in the amount of US$ 1,975,985,580 for remediation of areas damaged by oil contamination resulting from Iraq's invasion and occupation of Kuwait.[282]

The second claim unit was for expenses of proposed measures to re-vegetate desert areas alleged to have been damaged by oil contamination and areas alleged to have been physically disturbed by the construction and subsequent backfilling of oil trenches by Iraqi forces and by the construction of pipelines by Iraqi forces to transfer oil to fill those trenches.[283] In that claim Kuwait proposed to re-vegetate the areas affected by oil lakes; oil-contaminated piles; oil trenches; oil spills; and the areas physically disturbed by the construction and backfilling of oil trenches and pipelines. Kuwait stated that a re-vegetation programme was critical to the sustainability of the desert ecosystem, and would contribute to stabilisation of the desert

[279] Ibid., para 72.

[280] UNCCGC (2004b), para 73.

[281] Ibid., para 79.

[282] Ibid., para 102.

[283] Ibid., para 55.

surface and minimise erosion.[284] Kuwait therefore sought compensation in the amount of US$ 904,312,445.[285]

Against this unit of claim Iraq not only argued that the re-vegetation plan proposed by Kuwait "is necessary only because of the destructive remediation method chosen by the Claimant," but also that the proposed programme "goes far beyond the restoration of vegetation to the pre-Conflict levels and seeks substantial improvements with respect to density and quality of the vegetation."[286] The Panel noted that the areas of the oil lakes and oil-contaminated piles were devoid of vegetation, and re-vegetation measures were essential for the restoration of ecological functioning in those areas.[287] The Panel however noted that while re-vegetation of the areas damaged by oil lakes and oil-contaminated piles was appropriate, planting density should be reduced, and the application of chemical fertilisers and soil inocula would not be necessary.[288]

Accordingly, the Panel recommended compensation in the amount of US$ 283,300,389 for re-vegetation of the areas affected by oil lakes and oil-contaminated piles; by oil trenches and oil spills; by the construction and subsequent backfilling of oil trenches; and by the construction of oil pipelines by Iraqi forces.[289]

The third claim unit was for expenses incurred by Kuwait Oil Company ("KOC"). Kuwait sought compensation in the amount of US$ 31,180,905 for expenses incurred or to be incurred by KOC to recover or remove large quantities of oil released from the many oil wells in Kuwait that were damaged or destroyed by Iraqi troops during Iraq's invasion and occupation of Kuwait. The compensation was claimed for expenses of the oil recovery programme after 31 December 1992. These expenses include labour costs, the costs of oil tank refurbishment and costs of materials and contracts.[290]

The Panel found that the activities undertaken by KOC to recover and remove oil from its operational areas before 31 December 1992 constituted abatement and prevention of environmental damage and measures reasonably necessary to clean and restore the environment, and that expenses resulting from these activities qualified for compensation under para 35(a) and (b) of Governing Council Decision 7,[291] and that expenses of the programme that were incurred after 31 December 1992 also qualify for compensation.[292] Accordingly, the Panel recommended compensation for this claim under the part two fourth instalment "F4" claims the sum of US$

[284] Ibid., para 105.
[285] Ibid., para 104.
[286] UNCCGC (2004b), para 115.
[287] Ibid., para 116.
[288] Ibid., para 117.
[289] Ibid., para 122.
[290] Ibid., para 124.
[291] UNCCGC (1997).
[292] UNCCGC (2004b), para 126.

17,920,420 for the oil recovery programme undertaken by KOC to remediate damage resulting from Iraq's invasion and occupation of Kuwait.[293]

10.4.5 The Fifth Instalment of "F4" Claims

The claims in the fifth "F4" instalment were for compensation for damage to or depletion of natural resources, including cultural heritage resources; measures to clean and restore damaged environment; and damage to public health.[294] There were 19 claims submitted by six governments: Islamic Republic of Iran (5 claims); Hashemite Kingdom of Jordan (2 claims); State of Kuwait (4 claims); Kingdom of Saudi Arabia (4 claims); Syrian Arab Republic (3 claims); and Republic of Turkey (1 claim).[295] The claims related to damage resulting from, inter alia:

(a) Pollutants from the oil well fires and damaged oil wells in Kuwait;
(b) Oil spills into the Persian Gulf from pipelines, offshore terminals and tankers;
(c) Influx of refugees into the territories of some of the claimants;
(d) Operations of military personnel and equipment;
(e) Mines and other remnants of war; and
(f) Exposure of the populations of the claimants to pollutants from the oil well fires and oil spills in Kuwait and to hostilities and various acts of violence.[296]

The compensation sought therefrom amounting to US$ 49,936,562,997,[297] included compensation for loss of use of the resources during the period between the occurrence of the damage and the full restoration of the resources, either through natural recovery or as a result of remediation or restoration measures undertaken by a claimant.[298]

As was the case in other "F4" instalment claims, the Panel relied on Article 31 of the Rules,[299] para 16 of Security Council Resolution 687 (1991)[300] and para 35 of Decision 7[301] to consider the claims. During the hearing, Iraq made several contentions to avoid liability: first was on contributory negligence and second, on compensating natural resources that have no commercial value.

[293] Ibid., para 130.
[294] UNCCGC (2005), para 2.
[295] Ibid., para 1.
[296] Ibid., para 4.
[297] Ibid., para 6.
[298] Ibid., para 44.
[299] United Nations Compensation Commission Provisional Rules for Claims Procedures (1992).
[300] UNSC (1991).
[301] UNCCGC (1992).

10.4.5.1 Contributory Negligence

On the issue of contributory negligence Iraq contended that some of the damage for which claimants seek compensation in the fifth "F4" instalment had been caused or contributed to by the claimants themselves, either because they failed to take steps to mitigate damage resulting from the invasion and occupation of Kuwait or because the damage was aggravated by the acts or omissions of the claimants after the invasion and occupation.[302]

Iraq further reiterated its view that failure by a claimant to take reasonable and timely measures to mitigate damage from the invasion and occupation amounts to contributory negligence and justifies rejection of the compensation claim, or a corresponding reduction in the compensation to be awarded.[303]

In response to the evidence laid by the claimants, the Panel stressed that claimants had a duty to mitigate damage to the extent possible and reasonable in the circumstances. Indeed, the Panel asserted that "in the case of environmental claims, the duty to prevent and mitigate damage was a necessary consequence of the common concern for the protection and conservation of the environment, and entails obligations toward the international community and future generations."[304] This duty according to the Panel "encompasses both a positive obligation to take appropriate measures to respond to a situation that poses a clear threat of environmental damage, as well as the duty to ensure that any measures taken do not aggravate the damage already caused or increase the risk of future damage."[305]

However, the Panel had clarified that "whether an act or omission of a claimant constitutes failure to mitigate damage depended on the circumstances of each claim and the evidence available."[306] The test therefore was "whether the claimant acted reasonably, having regard to all the circumstances with which it was confronted, including the information available to it at the time regarding the nature and extent of damage and the measures appropriate to respond to the damage in each case."[307]

To this end, the Panel has considered whether appropriate measures of mitigation would have reduced the damage in any particular claim. To the Panel, "where the evidence demonstrates that the claimant has failed to take timely action to mitigate damage, account has been taken of the failure in determining the compensation recommended, where appropriate, adjustments are made to account for the loss that is attributable to the failure to mitigate."[308]

[302] UNCCGC (2005), para 39.
[303] UNCCGC (2005).
[304] Ibid., para 40.
[305] Ibid.
[306] UNCCGC (2005).
[307] Ibid.
[308] Ibid., para 41.

10.4.5.2 Natural Resources That Have No Commercial Value

On this issue, Iraq contended that there was no legal justification for compensating claimants for "interim loss" of natural resources that have no commercial value; i.e., resources that "are not traded in the market."[309] It argued that compensation for damage to non-commercial resources was limited to the costs of reasonable measures of remediation or restoration. Specifically, Iraq argued that there was no evidence that the Security Council[310] intended that Iraq be held liable for temporary damage to a natural resource that has been or will be restored at its expense.[311]

Iraq thus maintained that interpretation and application of Security Council Resolution 687 (1991)[312] must be carried out by applying the relevant rules of international law. It therefore asserted that claims for interim loss of natural resources without commercial value have no precedent in general international law and that compensation in international law can only be paid for damage that is "financially assessable." To this end, Iraq concluded that that, "under current international law, interim loss of non- commercial environmental resources is not financially assessable."[313] Iraq, therefore, argued that all claims for compensation for interim loss of non-commercial environmental resources should be rejected. In the view of Iraq, awarding compensation for any such claim, even if only for a small amount, would constitute a revolutionary change in international law.[314]

For their part, the claimants contended that temporary loss of the use of natural resources, such as the loss of biomass in the marine environment or the presence of long periods of oil contamination on beaches, clearly represents "environmental damage" within the language and meaning of Security Council Resolution 687 (1991) and Governing Council Decision 7. According to the claimants, the absence of a specific reference to interim loss in Security Council Resolution 687 (1991) or Governing Council Decision 7 did not in any way suggest a limitation.[315]

They pointed out that the criteria enumerated in Governing Council Decision 7 were not intended to resolve every issue that might arise with respect to claims presented under Security Council Resolution 687 (1991), and they referred to the conclusion of the Panel, in the third "F4" report, that the term "environmental damage" in para 16 of Security Council Resolution 687 (1991) was not limited to losses or expenses resulting from the activities and events listed in para 35 of Governing Council Decision 7.[316]

---

[309] UNCCGC (2005), para 45.

[310] UNSC (1991) or under the UNCCGC (1992).

[311] UNCCGC (2005), para 45.

[312] UNSC (1991).

[313] UNCCGC (2005), para 46.

[314] Ibid., para 47.

[315] Ibid., para 48.

[316] UNCCGC (2005) para 48.

The claimants further argued that, under general international law, it would be an absurd and unreasonable result to deny compensation for temporary loss of resources resulting from a deliberate internationally wrongful act of aggression. They asserted that entitlement to compensation for such damage under international law is mandated by the fundamental principle articulated by the Permanent Court of International Justice in the *Factory at Chorzów* case[317] that "reparation must, as far as possible, wipe out all the consequences of the illegal act and re-establish the situation which would, in all probability, have existed if that act had not been committed."[318] They pointed out that this principle, which predates 1991 and Security Council Resolution 687 (1991), had been accepted by the International Law Commission of the United Nations[319] and many other international authorities.[320]

According to the claimants, "all losses that were a direct result of Iraq's illegal acts must be compensated in order to wipe out all the consequences of those illegal acts. In their view, compensation for temporary losses pending remediation or restoration is an appropriate form of compensation because it 'mirrors' the restitution in kind that is favoured as a matter of principle by international law authorities such as the judgement in the *Factory at Chorzów* case."[321]

In the final analysis, the claimants, therefore, maintained that they were entitled to recover compensation for "ongoing losses" of natural resources resulting from Iraq's invasion and occupation of Kuwait, and that such compensation should be measured from the time that the resources were damaged up to the time when recovery to pre-invasion conditions had been or would be completed.[322]

According to the Panel "the fundamental issue to be resolved was whether, pursuant to Security Council resolution 687 (1991), claimants who suffered damage to natural resources that have no commercial value are entitled to compensation beyond reimbursement of expenses incurred or to be incurred to remediate or restore the damaged resources."[323] In other words, the question is whether the term "environmental damage," as used in Security Council Resolution 687 (1991), includes what is referred to as "pure environmental damage"; i.e. damage to environmental resources that have no commercial value.[324]

In this regard, the Panel noted that Iraq did not deny that claimants were entitled to claim compensation for the temporary loss of resources which have an economic value ("which are traded in the market"), such as fisheries and crops. The Panel,

---

[317] Factory at Chorzów case (1927).

[318] UNCCGC (2005).

[319] Under ILC Draft Articles on the Responsibility of States for Internationally Wrongful Acts, Art. 31(1) provides that the "State is under an obligation to make full reparation for the injury caused by the international wrongful act," see ILC (2001a).

[320] UNCCGC (2005), para 49.

[321] Ibid., para 50.

[322] Ibid., para 51.

[323] UNCCGC (2005), para 52.

[324] UNCCGC (2005).

therefore, concluded that Iraq's objection to the claims for the temporary losses in the fifth "F4" instalment was based on the fact that the resources involved are "non-commercial" in nature, rather than on the fact that the losses were of a temporary duration.[325]

The Panel, therefore, found that "a loss due to depletion of or damage to natural resources, including resources that may not have a commercial value is, in principle, compensable in accordance with Security Council resolution 687 (1991) and Governing Council decision 7 if such loss was a direct result of Iraq's invasion and occupation of Kuwait. It follows, therefore, that temporary loss of the use of such resources is compensable if it is proved that the loss resulted directly from Iraq's invasion and occupation of Kuwait."[326]

In the end, the Panel recommended award for compensation in respect of the fifth instalment "F4" claims as follows:

(i) The award to Kuwait was US$ 7,943,030 for the loss of natural resources.[327]
(ii) Saudi Arabia's total award was US$ 46,113,706 for damage to other natural resources.[328]
(iii) To Iran, compensation awarded was US$ 24,034,892 for damage to agricultural resources and US$ 46,596 for damage to other resources[329]
(iv) Jordan was awarded compensation in the sum of US$161,926,734 for the loss of natural resources.[330]
(v) No award for compensation was recommended by the Panel in respect of claims by Syria[331] and Turkey.[332]

The outcome of the recommendations of the United Nations Compensation Commission (UNCC) is that the practice of the Claims Commission in defining environmental damage could provide assistance to other international bodies, including courts and tribunals, which may be required to deal with this issue in the future. Several legal principles could be gleaned from the decisions. For instance, under para 16 of Security Council Resolution 687 (1991)[333] the UNCC Panel reaffirms that Iraq is "liable under international law for any direct loss, damage, including environmental damage and the depletion of natural resources, or injury to foreign governments, nationals and corporations, as a result of Iraq's unlawful invasion and occupation of Kuwait."[334] Thus, liability for environmental damage may extend

[325] Ibid.
[326] Ibid., para 57.
[327] Ibid., para 544.
[328] Ibid., para 718.
[329] Ibid., para 311.
[330] Ibid., para 410.
[331] Ibid., para 764.
[332] Ibid., para 771.
[333] UNSC (1991).
[334] UNCCGC (2004a), para 25.

to all damage and losses related to the environment and any consequences of such damage or losses that can reasonably be attributable to the activities or acts of the defendant.

Again, the UNCC environmental decisions focused on the protection and restoration of environmental integrity and were based on the principles of precaution, common concern, obligations to future generations, and the value of the ecosystems, in addition to long-standing principles of international law. In making awards for environmental monitoring and assessment costs, the UNCC acknowledged the precautionary need to identify potential risks in order to plan future action, especially for the protection of human health, and to obtain information that could inform the substantive claim review.[335] In the words of the environmental panel, the mitigation of environmental damage is the duty of injured states; it is "a necessary consequence of the common concern for the protection and conservation of the environment, and entails obligations towards the international community and future generations."[336]

10.5 Threshold of Significance in Claims for Environmental Damage

What is the threshold at which environmental damage may entail liability? Whilst all pollution or human activity having adverse effects might give rise to environmental damage, it is unlikely that all environmental damage results in liability. In determining the threshold of significance in claims for environmental damage, some questions needed to be addressed. These questions are:

(1) When can the threshold for liability arise?
(2) Who should be liable for the damage?
(3) To whom does the Burden of Proof lie and what is the type of liability?
(4) What is expected from the person/s liable?
(5) Where would the claims be instituted?
(6) Are there time limitations for claims?

10.5.1 When Can the Threshold for Liability Arise?

No agreed international standards establish a threshold for environmental damage that triggers liability and allows claims to be brought. For instance, in the Gulf War claims against Iraq,[337] Iraq had argued that "damage resulting from the invasion and

[335] Schneider (2016), p. 736.

[336] Ibid.

[337] See note 194.

occupation of Kuwait is not compensable unless it reaches the 'threshold' that is generally accepted in international law for compensation in cases of state responsibility for transboundary environmental damage," which, according to Iraq, was damage that is at least "significant."[338] The above position might have been based on decisions of international tribunals, the provisions of some international legal instruments and state practice suggest that environmental damage must be "significant" or "substantial" for liability to be triggered.

For example, in the exchange between the then President of the ICJ, Sir Humphrey Waldock, and the government of Australia in the *Nuclear Tests* case,[339] reflecting a view that not every transmission of chemical or other matter into another state's territory, or into the global commons, will create a legal cause of action in international law.

The tribunal in the *Trail Smelter* case[340] held that the injury must have a "serious consequence" to justify a claim. In its claim against Australia, Nauru[341] argued for general principle based upon an obligation not to bring about changes in the condition of territory which will cause "irreparable damage to, or substantially prejudice" the legal interest of another state.

A similar approach underlies Hungary's Original Application in the Case Concerning the *Gabčíkovo-Nagymaros* Project.[342] The Canadian claim following the crash of *Cosmos 954*[343] was brought in the context of damage to the land which made it "unfit for use," a level of damage which supports the view that the impact on the environment must be more than nominal to establish a claim.

Again, several international legal instruments point out that for the threshold to environmental damage to give rise to liability, the damage must have adverse effects which are: "significant;"[344] or "serious;"[345] or above "tolerable levels;"[346] or "substantial injury."[347] This approach provides for a *de minimis* rule which allows for the discarding of tolerated, minor or transitory damage, and only includes the damage above the defined threshold or significance. The justification for excluding minor

[338] UNCCGC (2003), para 33.

[339] Legality of the Threat or Use of Nuclear Weapons (1996).

[340] Trail Smelter Arbitration case (United States v. Canada) 1941, U.N. Rep. Int'l Arb. Awards 1905 (1949).

[341] Legality of the Threat or Use of Nuclear Weapons (1996).

[342] Gabčíkovo-Nagymaros Project case (1997).

[343] The Cosmos 954 case (1979).

[344] United Nations Economic Commission on Europe (UNECE) Watercourses Convention (1992), Art. 1(2).

[345] UNECE Industrial Accidents Convention (1992), Art. 1(d).

[346] Lugano Convention (1993), Art. 8(d).

[347] International Law Association Rules Montreal Rules on Water Pollution in an International Drain age Basin (ILA Montreal Rules) (1982), Art. 3 (1).

impacts from the definition of damage and hence from liability is based on the fact that the cost of evaluating small impacts might exceed its benefits.[348]

A different approach altogether is to allow for an exemption from liability for damage that is "insignificant"[349] or "negligible."[350] This approach may entail an important shift in the burden of proof since the evidence to justify the exemption will have to be provided by the operator and not by the claimant.[351] Instruments that deal with environmental damage by allowing clean-up and restoration costs,[352] on the other hand, have been able to avoid the threshold issue altogether by evaluating each response project on its technical merits. This approach facilitates the implementation of technically reasonable measures without the need for first proving some level of ecological "significance."[353] The implication of these cases and Conventions above demonstrate that there is no general consensus or consistency at an international level as to the level of damage required to incur liability.

However, the key issue in determining the threshold for liability should not be whether the damage reached a particular threshold, but whether the damage was a direct result of the defendant's illegal acts, the actual or potential effects of such acts on the environment and whether the proposed methods and costs of remediation were reasonable. Consideration of the reasonableness of the cost of remediation should be based on the location, nature, and extent of the damage caused by the defendant's acts. For instance, where the damage that might otherwise be characterised as "insignificant" is caused to an area of special ecological sensitivity, or where the damage, in conjunction with other factors, poses a risk of further or more serious environmental harm, it may not be unreasonable to take remediation measures to prevent or minimise potential additional damage.[354] Thus, the possibility of areas of special ecological sensitivity is an important interpretation of the standard for the threshold admissibility of environmental claims.

10.5.2 Who Should Be Liable for the Damage?

Another aspect of the threshold requirements is the determination of the person/s that should be liable or to whom the liability may be channelled to. The question as to which actor should be made responsible for damage is the cornerstone of an effective

[348] United Nations Environment Programme (UNEP) (2003), p. 54.

[349] Vienna Convention on Civil Liability for Nuclear Damage (Vienna Convention 1963), Art. 1(2).

[350] CRAMRA (1988), Art. (1)(15).

[351] UNEP (2003), p. 54.

[352] Such as the Civil Liabilities Convention 1969 as amended by the Protocol (International Convention on Civil Liability for Oil Pollution Damage 1992, discussed in Sect. 15.1.2 of Chap. 15 of this book.

[353] UNEP (2003), p. 55.

[354] Payne (2016), p. 736.

liability regime. In most Conventions, the "operator" or "owner" of the activity that caused the damage may be held liable for the environmental damage. Operators and owners have been defined to include: persons "exercising control" over a dangerous activity;[355] persons "in charge" of the activity;[356] states in which a dangerous activity takes place.[357]

Again, under the Convention on Civil Liability for Oil Pollution Damage resulting from Exploration for and Exploitation of Seabed Mineral Resources (Seabed Mineral Resources Convention 1977), "operator" means the person, whether licensee or not, designated as operator for the purposes of this Convention by the controlling state, or, in the absence of such designation, the person who is in overall control of the activities carried on at the installation.[358] Under the same Convention, "person" means any individual or partnership or any public or private body, whether corporate or not, including a state or any of its constituent subdivisions.[359]

In some of the Conventions dealing with oil pollution and the marine environment,[360] liability is expressly focused on the shipowner.[361] Under the United Nations Economic Commission for Europe (UNECE) Convention on Civil Liability for Damage Caused During Carriage of Dangerous Goods by Road, Rail and Inland Navigation Vessels (CRTD 1989) the owner of the vehicle transporting the goods is liable, since such person is presumed to be in control of the use of the vehicle.[362] However, liability is imposed on the carrier if the owner is clearly not in control of the vehicle.[363]

Under the Basel Protocol on Liability and Compensation for Damage Resulting from Transboundary Movements of Hazardous Wastes and their Disposal (Basel Protocol 1999)[364] the liability is strict and the notifier or exporter is liable for damage until the disposer has taken possession of the wastes. However, fault-based liability can be imposed for intentional, reckless or negligent acts or omissions. The notifier is exonerated from liability if he/she proves that damage was the result of an armed conflict or war, a natural phenomenon of exceptional character, compliance with state law, or the intentional conduct of a third party. In any case, all transboundary

---

[355] Lugano Convention (1993), Art. 2(5).

[356] UNECE Industrial Accidents Convention (1992), Art. 1(e).

[357] Vienna Convention (1963), Art. 1(a) (c).

[358] Seabed Mineral Resources Convention 1977, ibid., Art. 1(3).

[359] Ibid., Art. 1(5).

[360] Such as Civil Liabilities Convention 1969 as amended by the Protocol (International Convention on Civil Liability for Oil Pollution Damage 1992 (CLC 1969) and International Convention on Liability and Compensation for Damage in Connection with the Carriage of Hazardous and Noxious Substances by Sea (HNS 2010) (discussed in Sect. 15.2.3 of Chap. 15 of this book).

[361] CLC (1969), Art. 3(1), HNS (2010), Art. 7(1).

[362] CRTD 1989, Art. 5(1) (2).

[363] Ibid., Art. 6(1).

[364] Basel Protocol (1999).

hazardous waste movements must be covered by insurance.[365] Sometimes legal instruments provide for a third-party liability, for example, insurance companies.[366]

In addition, the polluter-pays principle (PPP)[367] may also be used in identifying such an operator or owner. The reason is that the PPP recognises the key position of the operator or owner to take preventive steps to eliminate or reduce the risk of damage, and thus internalise the environmental costs derived from those activities.[368]

In some cases, operators, owners and other parties will be jointly or severally liable.[369] This means that the plaintiff can bring an action against either all or only one of the perpetrators of the damage. This not only provides the person bringing forth the claim with the option to seek out the perpetrator with the deepest pockets, but also means that the accused party bears the financial risk if the other perpetrators do not have enough money to pay their share of the compensation. In any case, joint and several liability weakens the link between diligence in operation and payment of liability, thus weakening the incentive mechanism of the polluter-pays principle.[370]

10.5.3 To Whom Does the Burden of Proof Lie and What Is the Type of Liability?

Another salient issue in the threshold of environmental damage is the determination of both the burden of proof and the type of liability. Under international law, a direct legal interest is required for the affected party to be entitled to make an environmental claim and demand the termination of an activity causing damage.[371] With regard to civil liability,[372] three types of liability, namely: fault liability;[373] strict liability;[374] and absolute liability,[375] may be imposed, depending on what the extant law provides. It has been suggested that strict and absolute liability be invoked in the case of liability for environmental damage, for example liability is absolute under the

[365] Ibid., Art. 4(14).

[366] Civil Liabilities Convention 1969 as amended by the Protocol (International Convention on Civil Liability for Oil Pollution Damage (1992), Art. 2(7).

[367] Discussed in Sect. 4.7 of Chap. 4 of this book.

[368] UNEP (2003).

[369] For instance, CRTD (1988), Art. 5(3), Lugano Convention (1993), Art. 6(2) and HNS (2010), Art. 8(1).

[370] UNEP (2003), p. 56.

[371] UNEP (2003), p. 56.

[372] Involving the traditional concept of personal injury and damage to property state liability.

[373] Based upon intention or negligence.

[374] Prima facie responsibility with defences available.

[375] Responsibility with no mode of exculpation (absolute liability was discussed in Sect. 3.9.3 of Chap. 3 of this book).

Vienna Convention on Civil Liability for Nuclear Damage (Vienna Convention 1963). Article IV provides that "the liability of the operator for nuclear damage under this Convention shall be absolute."[376]

The distinction between imposing absolute or strict liability is usually based on a distinction between ultra-hazardous activities. It is however suggested that due to the debilitating effect of environmental damage on both the natural and human environment, strict liability should be imposed.[377] This is so because from a law and economics perspective imposing strict liability for environmental damages has several advantages. These include:

(i) Preventing damage in the first place: Because compensation can be expensive operators will try to avoid environmentally unsound economic actions that can add to the costs in the running of their business.
(ii) Quick response time to minimise environmental damage: Because strictly liable operators know from the start that they must pay compensation, they will always have the incentive to respond quickly to an incident and keep damage to a minimum.
(iii) Speeding payment of compensation: Victims and responders will receive compensation more promptly under a system of strict liability because there is much less need for litigation as it will be much less likely that the potential plaintiff will need to establish a nexus between the activity and the damage caused.[378]

An important aspect for the proper operation of an environmental regime is to provide access by states, international organisations and individuals to formal and informal mechanisms of dispute resolution. Under international law, a direct legal interest is required for the affected party to be entitled to make an environmental claim and demand the termination of an activity causing damage.[379] Access to justice denotes the expeditious and equal access to domestic courts and remedies on a non-discriminatory basis. The Aarhus Convention 1998[380] requested parties to ensure that members of the public having "a sufficient interest" have access to justice.

Claims for personal injury, damage to private property, or commercial losses, may be handled in the standard civil system of the affected state. However, this poses a problem when the resulting damage is pure environmental damage, entailing damage to an animal or plant species or to the air or water.

To this end, it is suggested that where the litigation to recover for natural resource damages, public trustees system should be adopted as they are designated to act on

[376] Vienna Convention on Civil Liability for Nuclear Damage (Vienna Convention 1963).

[377] UNEP (2003), p. 56.

[378] Ibid.

[379] UNEP (2003), p. 56.

[380] Convention on Access to Information, Public Participation in Decision-Making and Access to Justice in Environmental Matters (Aarhus Convention) (1998), Art. 9.

behalf of the public interest. The advantages of the public trustee system with integrated public review and comment are that: (i) it allows the government to undertake one of its standard roles, that of protecting the public interest and (ii) it allows for the creation of agencies with the high level of technical expertise necessary to undertake meaningful restoration planning and implementation.[381] Claims for compensation for damage using the public trustees system on behalf of the public interest were adopted by the Governing Council of the United Nations Compensation Commission (UNCC).[382] This approach permitted the submission of consolidated claims and receiving payments on behalf of individuals affected, including claims on behalf of third parties[383]

Even where it is not possible to designate a trustee to represent the collective interest, other solutions may be explored. For instance, there is a push for the right to class actions which would allow environmental organisations and other non-owners to bring forward an action.

The need for class actions is stressed since access to justice is often hampered by unaffordable costs and the fact that there is often no one to represent the rights of the environment. Enhancing access to justice may mean granting *locus standi* to environmental organisations or other persons with sufficient interests in the damage so that they may bring forth the claim on behalf of the environment.[384]

10.5.4 What Is Expected from the Person/s Liable?

To be able to cover the risk of liability, most civil liability regimes require the operator to establish financial security and this is most commonly done by purchasing insurance. For instance, The Paris Convention on Third Party Liability in the Field of Nuclear Energy (Paris Convention 1960) provides that the maximum liability of the operator in respect of damage caused by a nuclear incident shall be 15,000,000 Special Drawing Rights ("Special Drawing Rights") as defined by the International Monetary Fund and used by it for its own operations and transactions.[385] To cover the liability under the Convention, the operator shall be required to have and maintain insurance or other financial security of 15,000,000 Special Drawing Rights and of such type and terms as the competent public authority shall specify.[386] Under the Vienna Convention 1963, the liability of the operator may be

---

[381] UNEP (2003), p. 56.

[382] See UNCCGC (2001), UNCCGC (2002), UNCCGC (2003), UNCCGC (2004a), UNCCGC (2004b) and UNCCGC (2005) at notes 201, 213, 232, 253, 272 and 294, respectively.

[383] UNCCGC (1992).

[384] UNEP (2003), p. 56.

[385] Paris Convention (1960), Art. 7(a).

[386] Ibid., Art. 10(a).

limited by the installation state to not less than US$5 million for any one nuclear incident.[387]

Again, under the Seabed Mineral Resources Convention 1977,[388] to cover his liability the operator shall be required to have and maintain insurance or other financial security to such amount, of such type and on such terms as the controlling state shall specify, provided that the amount shall not be less than 22 million Special Drawing Rights until five years have elapsed from the date on which the Convention is opened for signature and not less than 35 million Special Drawing Rights thereafter. However, the controlling state may exempt the operator wholly or in part from the requirement to have and maintain such insurance or other financial security to cover his liability for pollution damage wholly caused by an act of sabotage or terrorism.[389]

However, the operator shall be entitled to limit his liability under the Seabed Mineral Resources Convention 1977 for each installation and each incident to the amount of 30 million Special Drawing Rights until five years have elapsed from the date on which the Convention is opened for signature and to the amount of 40 million Special Drawing Rights thereafter.[390] But the operator shall not be entitled to limit his liability if it is proved that the pollution damage occurred as a result of an act or omission by the operator himself, done deliberately with actual knowledge that pollution damage would result.[391]

The chief advantage of a compulsory insurance regime is the certainty that is provided that victims will receive compensation, even if the operator is undercapitalised or becomes bankrupt. An objection to having a regime based on compulsory insurance is that this could reduce the incentive for potential perpetrators to avoid causing damage, a situation known as "moral hazard."[392]

A potential problem may be that insurers will shy away from general, compulsory insurance for every potential type of environmental damage to counteract this effect, insurance companies may demand upper-limit premiums and or significant damage thresholds to restrict their own financial risk.[393]

---

[387] Vienna Convention (1963), Art. V.

[388] Seabed Mineral Resources Convention (1977).

[389] Ibid., Art. 8(1). Similar provisions can be found in CLC (1969), Art. VII (1), CTRD (1989), Art. 13(1), Lugano Convention (1993), Art. 12, HNS (1996), Art. 12(1), Basel Protocol (1999), Art. 14(1).

[390] Seabed Mineral Resources Convention (1977), Art. 6(1).

[391] Ibid., Art. 6(4).

[392] UNEP (2003), p. 6.

[393] Ibid.

10.5.5 Where Would the Claims Be Instituted?

This refers to where compensation claims may be brought, bordering on the issue of court with jurisdiction to entertain such claims. International regimes generally provide the criteria for establishing jurisdiction in multinational cases. For instance, the jurisdiction for the nuclear conventions is vested in the domestic (national) courts of the state where the incident has occurred.[394] In the case of pollution of the sea by oil, authority is vested in the domestic courts of the affected state.[395] However, some conventions offer a choice between the courts of the state where the pollution occurred or those of the affected state.[396]

This notwithstanding, UNEP[397] opined that certain issues in the area of jurisdiction needed further clarification. Such issues include: the international jurisdiction of courts, the reciprocal recognition and enforcement of judgments of courts or tribunals, and an expeditious procedure for securing the enforcement of judgements and court settlements. Questions of concurrent jurisdiction and forum shopping should also be taken into account in this context to prevent abuse.

10.5.6 Are There Time Limitations for Claims?

Although an operator is liable for environmental damages resulting from his activities, his liability could be negated by a lapse of time; consequently, persons affected by any damages are required by law to proceed against such an operator within a specified time. Most Conventions therefore have limitation periods in place to relieve the burden on operators or owners from having stale claims hanging over them years after the damage was caused. The overall length of time within which an action must be brought varies from Convention to Convention most with regard to the form of damage or the activity leading to it.

For instance, time limitation ranges from one year under the Space Objects Convention 1972[398] in which to bring forth a claim must be brought within one year following the date of the occurrence to 30 years under the Lugano Convention 1993.[399] However, under the Lugano Convention 1993, where the incident consists of a continuous occurrence the 30 years' period shall run from the end of that occurrence. And where the incident consists of a series of occurrences having the same origin the 30 years' period shall run from the date of the last of such

[394] Paris Convention (1960), Art. 13(a), Vienna Convention (1963), Art. XI(1) and the Seabed Mineral Resources Convention (1977), Art. 11(1).

[395] CLC (1969) as amended by the 1992 Protocol, Art. IX(1) and HNS (1996), Art. 38(1).

[396] CRTD (1989), Art. 19(1), Lugano (1993), Art. 19, Basel Protocol (1999), Art. 8.

[397] UNEP (2003), p. 179.

[398] Space Objects Convention (1972), Art. X(I).

[399] Lugano Convention (1993), Art. 17(2).

occurrences. In respect of a site for the permanent deposit of waste, the 30 years' period shall at the latest run from the date on which the site was closed under the provisions of internal law.[400] The Seabed Mineral Resources Convention 1977 provides that liability extends for five years after abandonment of the installation.[401]

The Nuclear Conventions[402] have a time limit of ten years. For instance, under the Vienna Convention 1963 rights of compensation shall be extinguished if an action is not brought within ten years from the date of the nuclear incident. If, however, under the law of the installation state the liability of the operator is covered by insurance or other financial security or by state funds for a period longer than ten years, the law of the competent court may provide that rights of compensation against the operator shall only be extinguished after a period which may be longer than ten years, but shall not be longer than the period for which his liability is so covered under the law of the installation state.[403]

However, the Protocol to Vienna Convention 1997 extends the period during which claims may be brought for loss of life and personal injury to 30 years.[404] Furthermore, with the Nuclear Conventions, states have the option to shorten the limitation periods to periods of not less than three years under the Vienna Convention 1963[405] and not less than two years under the Paris Convention 1960[406] from the date the claimant knew or ought to have known of the damage and that the operator was liable.

Although there is no uniform time limit, it appears from existing and proposed international agreements that liability does not extend beyond 30 years after the harmful event. It should be stressed that this period is distinct from the period during which a victim should be permitted to bring a claim after the discovery of the harm and the identification of the source of the harm. For this time limit, most Conventions provide a period of three years.[407] There are some exceptions. For example, under the Seabed Mineral Resources Convention 1977, the time limit is only 12 months,[408] two years in respect of the Paris Convention 1960[409] and five years under the Basel Protocol 1999.[410]

Establishing the appropriate threshold on liability for environmental damage depends on the facts of each case, and may vary according to local or regional circumstances. It is posited that under international law there should be a call for full

---

[400] Ibid.

[401] Seabed Mineral Resources Convention (1977), Art. 3(4).

[402] Such as the Paris Convention (1960) and the Vienna Convention (1963).

[403] Vienna Convention (1963), Art. VI.

[404] Protocol to Vienna Convention (1997), Art. VI(I)(a).

[405] Vienna Convention (1963), Art. VI(1).

[406] Paris Convention (1960), Art. 8(c).

[407] CLC (1969), CRTD (1989), Lugano Convention (1993), HNS (1996).

[408] Seabed Mineral Resources Convention (1977), Art. 10.

[409] Paris Convention (1960), Art. 8.

[410] Basel Protocol (1999), Art. 13(2).

reparation of all consequences of an operator's or owner's or other parties' or state's illegal acts as stated by the tribunal in the *Factory at Chorzów* case.[411] In that case, the tribunal stated that "reparation must, as far as possible, wipe out all the consequences of the illegal act and re-establish the situation which would, in all probability, have existed if that act had not been committed."[412]

10.6 Reparation for Environmental Damage

In the event of environmental damage, the victim is likely to seek financial reparation to cover a variety of costs arising from the material damage to environmental resources. These may include lost income or costs related to emergency response, clean-up, impact studies, restoration, or monitoring.[413]

Various approaches have been adopted to compensate victims of environmental damage. These approaches span through reparation, restitution, compensation and rehabilitation of damaged environment. Most notable of these approaches however is that of reparation which, invariably may be combined with restitution and compensation in the final analysis to remediate the damaged environment and/or losses suffered.

The International Law Commission (ILC) in the ILC Articles on State Responsibility[414] envisages that reparation for the injury caused by an internationally wrongful act shall take the form of restitution, compensation and satisfaction, either singly or in combination.[415] Continuing, restitution accordingly is aimed at "re-establishing the situation which existed before the wrongful act was committed, provided and to the extent that it is not materially impossible and does not involve a burden out of all proportion to the benefit deriving from restitution instead of compensation."[416]

Compensation on the other hand is to be provided for damage which is not made good by restitution, and should cover "any financially assessable damage including loss of profits in so far as it is established."[417] Satisfaction is to be provided if the injury cannot be made good by restitution or compensation, for example by an acknowledgment of the breach, an expression of regret or a formal apology.[418] This approach was adopted in the *Rainbow Warrior* case.[419] In that case, France was

[411] Factory at Chorzów case (1927).

[412] Ibid., para 29.

[413] UNEP (2003), p. 59.

[414] Draft Articles on State Responsibility 2001, see ILC (2001a).

[415] Draft Articles on State Responsibility 2001, Art. 34.

[416] Ibid., Art. 35.

[417] Ibid., Art. 36.

[418] Ibid., Art. 37.

[419] New Zealand v. France (1990).

required to give a formal and unqualified apology to New Zealand for the sinking of Greenpeace's vessel in Auckland Harbour, and ordered to pay US$7 million in compensation.[420]

The principle of reparation is well established that the perpetrator of an internationally wrongful act is under an obligation to make reparation for the consequences of such violation. This position was succinctly put by the Permanent Court of International Justice (PCIJ) in its judgement in the *Factory at Chorzow* case.[421] The court stated that:

> The essential principle contained in the actual notion of an illegal act – a principle which seems to be established by international practice and in particular by the decisions of arbitral tribunals – is that reparation must, as far as possible, wipe out all the consequences of the illegal act and re-establish the situation which would, in all probability, have existed if that act had not been committed restitution in kind, or, if this is not possible, payment of a sum corresponding to the value which a restitution in kind would bear; the award, if need be, of damages for loss sustained which would not be covered by restitution in kind or payment in place of it – such are the principles which should serve to determine the amount of compensation due for an act contrary to international law.[422]

In most environmental cases, the victim will be seeking an end to the harmful act, or restitution, or financial compensation to cover the costs associated with material damage to environmental resources (pure environmental damage) and consequential damage to people and property (consequential environmental damage), including restoration or reinstatement.

For example, in its Original Application in the *Gabčíkovo-Nagymaros Project* case[423] Hungary claimed that Czechoslovakia was under an obligation to cease the internationally wrongful act, re-establish the situation which would have existed if the act had not taken place and provide compensation for the harm which resulted from the wrongful act. On restitution, it will be necessary to identify the baseline conditions prior to which the damage occurred, which may be difficult.

The International Court of Justice (ICJ) in that case confirmed that Hungary was entitled to "compensation for the damage sustained as a result of the diversion of the Danube," but did not specifically indicate that Hungary was entitled to reparation for purely environmental damages. As regards the measure of compensation, the court merely observed that "the issue of compensation could satisfactorily be resolved in the framework of an overall settlement if each of the parties were to renounce or cancel all financial claims and counter-claims."[424]

In April 2002, in the *Marshall Island Nuclear Claims*,[425] the Tribunal made an award of US$324,949,311 to the People of Enewatak, as "just and adequate"

[420] Ibid., 215 at 250.

[421] Factory at Chorzow case (1927).

[422] Ibid., at 47.

[423] Gabčíkovo-Nagymaros Project case (1997).

[424] Ibid.

[425] 39 ILM (2000) 1214.

settlement for claims of Marshall Islanders in respect of damages to land arising out of the nuclear testing programme carried out by the United States between 1946 and 1958. The award included payments in respect of past and future loss of use (US$199,154,811), restoration to a "safe and productive state" (US$91,710,000), and hardship as a result of relocation (US$34,084,500). The tribunal applied standards agreed by the parties, in particular standards applicable under US law. On restoration, the Tribunal accepted the position adopted by the IAEA to the effect that "policies and criteria for radiation protection of populations outside national borders from releases of radioactive substances should be at least as stringent as those for the population within the country of release,"[426] and accordingly applied the current standards applied by the US Environmental Protection Agency.

It should be noted that the rules of international law relating to reparation for environmental damage remain undeveloped, as evidenced by the lack of legal precedents. In addition, the few judgements provided no practical guidance on how to calculate the measure of such environmental damage. This reluctance is consistent with the limited international practice concerning reparation for environmental damage at the inter-state level. Part of this problem hinges on:

(a) Valuing the environment to assess claims includes the price that the environmental resource commands in the market.
(b) The economic value attached to the use of environmental resources (such as methods of costing travel relying on expenditures made by an individual to visit and enjoy a resource, or a hedonic pricing method which takes the extra market value enjoyed by private property with certain environmental amenities and assumes that public resources with comparable amenities have similar economic values).
(c) Contingent valuation methods to measure the willingness of individuals to pay for environmental goods such as clean air or water or the preservation of endangered species.[427]

Besides the above, problems may arise with the concept of pure environmental damage as it does not fit easily with the traditional approaches of civil liability and it may be incapable of calculation in economic terms. However, an accepted solution to this problem is to link liability for harm to the environment to the payment of the reasonable costs of restoration measures, reinstatement measures or preventative measures.[428] In recent years, the work of the UN Compensation Commission

[426] Ibid.

[427] Sands (2003), p. 884.

[428] CRTD (1989), Art. 10(c)(d), Lugano (1993), Art. 2(7)(c)(d), HNS (1996), Art. 1(6)(c)(d), Protocol to the Vienna Convention (1997), Art. I(k)(iv)(v)(vi)(m)(n)(o) and Basel Protocol (1999), Art. 2(2)(c) (iii)(iv)(v).

(UNCC) in applying Security Council Resolution 687 (1991)[429] provides some guidance on resolving the above issues.

In presenting their claims for temporary loss of natural resources, some claimants[430] in the UNCC claims utilised the methodology known as "Habitat Equivalency Analysis" ("HEA") to determine the nature and extent of compensatory restoration that is necessary to compensate for the loss of ecological services that were provided by the resources before they were damaged. Based on the results of the HEA, these claimants proposed to undertake compensatory restoration projects that were intended to offset the ecological services that had been lost between the time of initial damage to the resources and the time of their full recovery. The compensatory restoration projects were aimed at providing equivalent ecological service gains either in the same area or at other locations.[431]

However, Iraq objected to the use of HEA by the claimants. It contended that in international law, compensation can only be paid for financially assessable damage; and it claims that both the proof of damage and the assessment of damage must be made under established principles of international law.[432]

The Panel[433] in rejecting the Iraqi's contention stated that international law does not prescribe any specific and exclusive methods of measurement for awards of damages for internationally wrongful acts by states. The general rule is to restore what has been damaged to integrity or, if this is not possible, to provide an equivalent for it. The overall criterion is always that of effective reparation for the wrongful act. Hence, even in the absence of precise rules or prescriptions on the methods for evaluating damage, courts and tribunals are entitled and required to evaluate the damage and determine appropriate compensation, relying on general principles for guidance, particularly the principle that reparation must, as far as possible, wipe out all the consequences of the illegal act.[434]

The take however is that as the Tribunal in the *Trail Smelter Arbitration*[435] stated in its interim award:

> Where the wrongful act itself is of such a nature as to preclude the ascertainment of the amount of damages with certainty, it would be a perversion of fundamental principles of justice to deny all relief to the injured person, and thereby relieve the wrongdoer from making any amend for his acts. In such case, while the damages may not be determined by mere speculation or guess, it will be enough if the evidence show the extent of the damages as a matter of just and reasonable inference, although the result be only approximate.[436]

---

[429] UNSC (1991), see the discussions on claims against Iraq in the aftermath of the Gulf war in Sect. 10.4 of this chapter.

[430] Such as Iran, Kuwait, Saudi Arabia (Sect. 10.4 of this chapter).

[431] UNCCGC (2005), p. 23, para 73.

[432] UNCCGC (2005), p. 23, para 74.

[433] Panel of Commissioners set up by the UNCC under the "F4" claims against Iraq (see the discussions in Sect. 10.4 of this chapter).

[434] UNCCGC (2005), p. 24, para 80.

[435] Trail Smelter Arbitration (USA v. Canada) (1941).

[436] Ibid.

Again, the PCIJ in the *Factory at Chorzów* case[437] provides the touchstone definition as well as the fundamentals of reparation. To the court, "reparation must, as far as possible, wipe out all the consequences of the illegal act and re-establish the situation which would, in all probability, have existed if that act had not been committed."[438] Remediation measures for damaged resources should therefore focus on primary restoration, in terms of the restoration of ecological functioning. Consequently, compensatory restoration measures should be considered only where there is sufficient evidence that primary restoration will not fully compensate for any identified losses.[439]

Furthermore, in determining what remediation measures are necessary, "primary emphasis must be placed on restoring the environment to pre-invasion conditions, in terms of its overall ecological functioning rather than on the removal of specific contaminants or restoration of the environment to a particular physical condition."[440] Thus, in the event of any harm arising thereto the state of origin of the harm shall be required to make reparation for appreciable harm caused by activities following negotiation between states and guided by the criteria set out in the ILC Articles. Such reparation should restore the balance of interests affected by the harm.

A principle of non-discrimination would require state parties to "treat the effects of an activity that arise in the territory or under the jurisdiction or control of another state in the same way as effects arising in their own territory."[441] Thus, "the fact that environmental damage is irreparable or unquantifiable shall not result in exemption from compensation."[442]

In the end, "compensation is to be determined in accordance with international law and the principles of justice and equity, in order to provide such reparation in respect of the damage as will restore the person, natural or judicial, state or international organisation on whose behalf the claim is presented to the condition which would have existed if the damage had not occurred."[443]

---

[437] Factory at Chorzów case (1927).

[438] Ibid., at 47.

[439] UNCCGC (2005), p. 25, para 82.

[440] UNCCGC (2003), p. 16, para 43.

[441] ILC (2001c) Draft Articles on Harm from Hazardous Activities 2001, Art. 15.

[442] IIL (2017c), Art. 29.

[443] Space Liability Convention (1988), Art. XII.

10.7 Criminal Liability for Environmental Damage Under International Environmental Law

10.7.1 Introduction

Modern times demonstrate that the environment, representing the "... living space, the quality of life and the very health of human beings, including generations unborn,"[444] is threatened daily. Such threats occur both in the context of armed conflicts,[445] and in peacetime constellations. Peacetime threats to the environment can, inter alia, be large amounts of carbon dioxide emissions, deforestation, contamination of natural resources by pollution or the unsustainable extraction of natural resources.[446] These may become an imminent threat not only to flora and fauna, and natural resources but also to whole ecosystems, and consequently to the peace and security of humankind.[447] To this end, environmental damage may not only result in civil liability but may also trigger liability of a criminal nature.

The need for criminalising environmental damage was succinctly captured by the Convention on the Protection of the Environment through Criminal Law 1998[448] where it was emphasised that whilst the prevention of the impairment of the environment must be achieved primarily through other measures, criminal law has an important part to play in protecting the environment, environmental violations having serious consequences must be established as criminal offences subject to appropriate sanctions and as such effective measures be taken to ensure that the perpetrators of such acts do not escape prosecution and punishment and desirous of fostering international co-operation to this end. Thus, imposing criminal or administrative sanctions on legal persons can play an effective role in the prevention of environmental violations and noting the growing international trend in this regard.

To this end, criminalising environmental infractions and seeking appropriate sanctions for serious norm violations of a nation's laws that seek to protect public health and ·natural resources is a vital role for government to play in a democratic polity.[449]

There are different perspectives among states in tackling environmental damage. Many states, such as the USA and Canada, adopt more Civil Liability for Environmental Damage (CLED) as a method, while countries, such as France, Russia and Brazil, adopt Criminal Liability for Environmental Damage (RLED). Nigeria, on the

[444] Legality of the Threat or Use of Nuclear Weapons (1996), p. 226, para 29.

[445] International Committee of the Red Cross (IRCC) (2019).

[446] Higgins et al. (2013), p. 251 at 252–254.

[447] INTERPOL-UNEP (2016).

[448] Convention on the Protection of the Environment through Criminal Law (1998), Preamble.

[449] Blomquist (2011), p. 83.

other hand, adopts the two variants, CLED and RLED, in its environmental legislation to address issues of environmental violations.[450]

The purpose of Criminal Liability for Environmental Damage (RLED) is not only restorative and remedial actions that are available; but also disciplinary action. Governments play a major role in minimising environmental harm through RLED, while preventing the defendant from gaining any potential economic profit.[451] Criminalising environmental damage may be because "certain environmental damage may be so serious in the eyes of the international community that it should be categorised as criminal, or delictual."[452]

10.7.2 International Law and Crime Against the Environment

First proposals to include a crime against the environment into international criminal law were made in the 1970s in response to the massive environmental damages inflicted by the US Army during the Vietnam War.[453] Further, in the development of the Rome Statute of the International Criminal Court 1998 (Rome Statute),[454] the International Law Commission (ILC) considered the "wilful and severe damage to the environment" as a major crime against the peace and security of mankind, regardless of its connection to an armed conflict.[455]

Article 26 of the ILC Draft Code of Crimes against the Peace and Security of Mankind (ILC Draft Code of Crimes) stipulates that wilfully causing or ordering to cause "... widespread, long-term and severe damage to the natural environment..." by an individual is an international crime. This assertion was based on the consideration that "environmental damage would not only encompass serious consequences for the present generations, but also for future generations, and thus needed to be addressed separately from other crimes pursuing the protection of human beings."[456]

---

[450] In Nigeria, liability for environmental damage could be a crime and can lead to a civil wrong, for instance, the provisions of the Harmful Wastes (Special Criminal Provisions) Act, Cap H1, LFN 2004, particularly at ss. 6, 7 and 12. Environmental crimes can be found in the provisions of the National Environmental Standards and Regulations Enforcement Agency (Establishment) (Amendment) Act (NESREA) Act 2018, particularly ss. 20–27 (these Acts, among others, were discussed in Chap. 16 of this book).

[451] Bodansky (2010), pp. 22–23.

[452] ILC (1995).

[453] Bustami and Hecken (2021), p. 154.

[454] Rome Statute of the International Criminal Court (1998).

[455] ILC Draft Code of Crimes against the peace and security of mankind (ILC Draft Code of Crimes) (1996), Art. 26, paras 119–121, see United Nations (1996).

[456] ILC Draft Code of Crimes (1996), para 120. Despite long and intensive discussions to include the serious violation of environmental obligations into the realm of the international criminal law

The Rome Statute 1998 provides for the protection of the environment in times of war. It criminalises intentionally launching an attack with the knowledge that such an attack will cause widespread, long-term and severe damage to the natural environment. Such an attack is regarded as a war crime. Under the Statute, a war crime is defined as an international attack with the knowledge that it will cause "widespread, long term and severe damage to the natural environment which would be clearly excessive in relation to the concrete and direct overall military advantage anticipated."[457] The prohibition of environmental degradation in international humanitarian law, as found in Articles 35(3) and 55(1) of the Additional Protocol I (AP I) forms the basis for this crime. People like Sharp[458] have therefore suggested that the Rome Statute 1998 by virtue of Article 8(2)(b)(iv) be interpreted to include environmental crimes in relation to acts of genocide or crimes against humanity.

The Convention on the Protection of the Environment through Criminal Law (CPECL)[459] adopted at Strasbourg on 4 November 1998 is the first International Convention to criminalise acts causing or likely to cause environmental damage. Articles 2 and 3 of CPECL require parties to criminalise under their domestic law intentional or grossly negligent acts falling within certain categories which cause substantial environmental damage. Under Article 2(1)(a)–(e) of CPECL, intentional unlawful acts include:

(a) the discharge, emission or introduction of a quantity of substances or ionising radiation into air, soil or water which causes death or serious injury to any person, or creates a significant risk of causing death or serious injury to any person;[460]
(b) the discharge, emission or introduction of a quantity of substances or ionising radiation into air, soil or water which causes or is likely to cause their lasting deterioration or death or serious injury to any person, or substantial damage to protected monuments, other protected objects, property, animals or plants;[461]
(c) unlawful disposal, treatment, storage, transport, export or import of hazardous waste;[462]
(d) unlawful operation of a plant in which dangerous activity is carried out;[463] and
(e) manufacture, treatment, storage, use, transport, export or import of nuclear materials or other hazardous radioactive substances.[464]

---

draft, Article 26 was not adopted and the protection of the environment, as a separate provision and was not incorporated in the final draft of the Rome Statute.

457 Rome Statute (1998), art, 8(2) (b) (iv).

458 Sharp (1999), p. 217.

459 Convention on the Protection of the Environment Through Criminal Law (CPECL) (1998).

460 Ibid., Art. 2(1)(a).

461 Ibid., Art. 2(1)(b).

462 Ibid., Art. 2(1)(c).

463 Ibid., Art. 2(1)(d).

464 Ibid., Art. 2(1)(e).

Other acts in respect of which sanctions or other measures may be appropriate include: unlawful introduction of substances or iodising radiation; causing of noise; disposal, treatment, storage, transport, export or import of waste; operation of a plant; manufacture, treatment, use, transport export or import of nuclear materials, other radioactive substances or hazardous chemicals; causing of changes detrimental to natural components of a national park, nature reserve, water conservation area or other protected areas; and possession, taking, damaging, killing or trading of or in protected wild flora and fauna species.[465] Article 1 (a) of the CPECL defines "unlawful" as: "infringing a law, an administrative regulation or decision taken by a competent authority, aiming at the protection of the environment." The CPECL, under Articles 6 and 9, identifies sanctions, imprisonment, fines and reinstatement of the environment, and allows parties to establish criminal liability for corporations.

In addition to the provisions above, an environmental crime may be committed where a person is deemed to have exploited a natural resource above the allowable quantity as stated in a permit granted to the person.

A case in point is the *Tomimaru* case.[466] In the *Tomimaru* case,[467] the vessel, the *Tomimaru,* a Japanese flag ship, was licensed to fish for walleye Pollock and herring between 1 October and 31 December 2006. The vessel was only permitted to fish in the Western Bering Sea, which is located in the exclusive economic zone (EEZ) of the Russian Federation. The vessel was allowed a maximum load of 1,163 tonnes of walleye Pollock, as well as 18 tonnes of herring.[468]

On 31 October 2006, the *Tomimaru,* while fishing in the area of Russia's exclusive economic zone (EEZ) designated above, was boarded by officers from the patrol boat *Vorovskii* and inspected by officials from the Northeast Border Coast Guard Directorate of the Federal Security Service of the Russian Federation. An examination of the holds of the vessel revealed that there was an unaccounted amount of 5.5 tonnes of walleye pollack. The vessel was then re-routed and escorted to Avachinskiy Bay for further investigation.[469]

As a result of the inspection of the ship on 8 November 2006, not less than 20 tonnes of gutted walleye pollack that were not listed in the logbook were found on

---

[465] CPECL (1998), Art. 4.

[466] Earlier and similar cases on this subject matter were (i)The "Volga" Case: Russian Federation versus Australia, 2002, Prompt Release Judgment, International Tribunal for the Law of the Sea (ITLOS) Case No. 11 (ii) The "Grand Prince" Case: Belize versus France, 2001, Prompt Release Judgment, International Tribunal for the Law of the Sea (ITLOS) Case No. 8.

(iii) The "Monte Confurco" Case: Seychelles versus France, Prompt Release Judgment, International Tribunal for the Law of the Sea (ITLOS) Case No. 6, 2000.

(iv) The "Camouco" Case: Panama versus France, 2000, Prompt Release Judgment, International Tribunal for the Law of the Sea (ITLOS) Case No. 5.

[467] Tomimaru (Japan v. Russian Federation), Prompt Release Judgment, International Tribunal for the Law of the Sea (ITLOS) Case No. 15, Judgement of 6 August 2007, ITLOS Reports (2005–2007), 74.

[468] Tomimaru case, (2007), para 23.

[469] Tomimaru case, (2007), para 24.

board the vessel, and "some kinds of fish products which are forbidden to catch."[470] Later, by a letter dated 22 December 2006, the Inter-district Prosecutor's Office for Nature Protection in Kamchatka informed the Consulate-General of Japan in Vladivostok that the accurate quantity of fish illegally caught was "established at 62,186.9 kg and the damage to the living marine resources in the Russian Federation amounted to 8,800,000 Russian Rubles" (approximately US$ 345,000).[471]

A criminal case was therefore instituted against the Master of the *Tomimaru* on 8 November 2006 for "exploitation without permission of the natural resources in the exclusive economic zone of the Russian Federation, causing enormous environmental damages to the living [marine] resources equivalent to not less than 8,500,000 rubles" a crime stipulated in Article 253, para 2, of the Criminal Code of the Russian Federation.[472]

The prosecutor in the criminal case fixed the bond on 12 December 2006.[473] Two days later, the owner sent a letter noting this fact and requesting that bond be also fixed for the administrative offenses with which the owner was charged.[474] On 19 December 2006, the court hearing the administrative charges rejected the petition for bond.[475] On 28 December 2006, the court imposed a fine and confiscated the vessel and its equipment. This decision was affirmed on appeal by the Kamchatka District Court.[476]

10.7.3 International Law, Wildlife and Forest Crime

Akin to criminalising the exploitation of natural resources in excess of the allowable quantity, environmental crime may be committed when a person commits "acts contrary to national and international laws and regulations for the protection of natural resources and to manage their sustainable use."[477] Such acts may be against "wildlife and forest." Wildlife and forest refer to "all fauna and flora, including animals, birds and fish, as well as timber and non-timber forest products."[478]

---

[470] That is not less than 19.5 tonnes of various sorts of frozen halibut, 3.2 tonnes of ray, 4.9 tonnes of cod as well as not less than three tonnes of other kinds of bottom fish.

[471] Tomimaru case (2007), para 25.

[472] Tomimaru case (2007), para 26.

[473] Ibid., para 36.

[474] Ibid., para 37.

[475] Ibid., para 39.

[476] Ibid., para 42.

[477] United Nations Office on Drugs and Crime (UNODC) (2016a).

[478] UNODC (2019).

10.7.3.1 Introduction

"Wildlife and forest crime" refers to the taking, trading (supplying, selling or trafficking), importing, exporting, processing, possessing, obtaining and consumption of wild fauna and flora, including timber and other forest products, in contravention of national or international law. Broadly speaking, wildlife and forest crime is the illegal exploitation of the world's wild flora and fauna.[479]

The crime may also involve poaching including sport hunting of a fully protected species, unauthorised netting or trapping of protected bird species for consumption or for illegal trade, trade in fully protected species, poisoning, illegal trade and hunting either outside the legal season or within protected areas, illegal shooting, poisoning, netting, liming and snaring of bird species, killing protected dolphins to use as bait for fishing, or increasingly, consuming dolphins as a response to falling fish catches and killing of marine turtles and collection of their eggs for consumption and use of their shells for ornamental products. Any act bordering on the enumerated situations above may amount to wildlife crime.[480]

Wildlife and forest crimes threaten biodiversity and endangered species, the livelihood of people, and severely impact national security, social and economic development. The transnational and organised nature of wildlife and forest crime necessitates a common and coordinated global response. To this end, some international frameworks[481] for combating wildlife trafficking had been put in place to combat wildlife trafficking. There is no universally accepted definition of the term wildlife trafficking and different jurisdictions and organisations employ different terminology. However, wildlife trafficking involves the illegal trade, smuggling, poaching, capture, or collection of endangered species, protected wildlife (including animals or plants that are subject to harvest quotas and regulated by permits), derivatives, or products thereof.[482]

10.7.3.2 International Conventions on Wildlife and Forest Crime

Wildlife crime also involves violations of intergovernmental treaties such as the Convention on International Trade in Endangered Species of Wild Fauna and Flora (CITES) 1973 as well as the Convention on the Conservation of Migratory Species of Wild Animals (Bonn Convention) 1979. These treaties regulate exports and imports of wildlife, a violation of their provisions in this respect may amount to an environmental crime with the attendant liability on the offender. Provisions of those treaties as they relate to when criminal liability may arise as a result of their violation are discussed below.

---

[479] Ibid.

[480] UNODC (2016a).

[481] These include International Conventions and International organisations discussed in this part.

[482] Biegus and Bueger (2017), p. 29.

10.7.3.2.1 Convention on International Trade in Endangered Species of Wild Flora and Fauna (CITES 1973)

The Convention on International Trade in Endangered Species of Wild Flora and Fauna (CITES) regulates and moderates international trade in plants and animals to ensure that such trade does not threaten their survival. As of June 2019, CITES regulates the trade of some 30,000 plants and 5,800 animal species. As of 1 March 2019, 183 states have signed this treaty.[483] The Convention is legally binding on ratifying parties, which must adopt domestic laws to ensure CITES compliance at the national level.

CITES's scope is limited to international trade and species affected by that international trade.[484] However, state parties are free to regulate domestic trade involving CITES-listed species as they see fit.[485] CITES seeks to achieve this by placing various restrictions and requirements on legal trade in certain flora and fauna. Its system of permits and certificates, which relate to three lists of protected species in the Convention's Appendices, enables state parties to reciprocally protect one another's species according to a common set of rules.[486] In addition, CITES provides a framework to combat trade that occurs outside these limits. CITES is the only international instrument mandating penalisation of illegal trade in protected species.[487]

CITES appendices contain a list of species for which the international community has agreed on common rules and standards to regulate their trade and transboundary movement. CITES does not address all aspects of wildlife crime, but it is the single most coherent approach to a topic of considerable international complexity.

CITES is so important because wildlife protection laws are usually situated in broader national environmental legislation. As a result, these laws focus on native species, and they do so in a wide variety of ways. Since wildlife populations are dynamic, most wildlife-related legislation leaves it to the executive branch of the government to issue regulations determining when and how wildlife can be harvested. Species can be added and removed from protected species lists, licenses issued allowing the legal taking of wildlife, and quotas established to ensure sustainability. As a result, the domestic legality of any given wildlife product is a matter of considerable complexity.[488]

As mentioned earlier, CITES requires parties to "penalise" violations of the agreement. CITES violations are punished in different ways and degrees depending on the seriousness of the infraction and the different national legal systems. Some

---

483 UNODC (2016a).

484 Convention on International Trade in Endangered Species of Wild Flora and Fauna (CITES 1973), Art. 1(c), (e).

485 UNODC (2016b).

486 UNODC (2020), p. 23.

487 UNODC (2012).

488 UNODC (2020), p. 30.

countries are more inclined to sanction with a fine, while in others, offenders can be sentenced to more than four years in prison.[489]

10.7.3.2.2 Convention on the Conservation of Migratory Species of Wild Animals (Bonn Convention) 1979

The Bonn Convention works for the conservation of a wide array of endangered migratory animals worldwide through the negotiation and implementation of agreements and species action plans. It has 120 member states. It engages all relevant stakeholders in addressing wildlife crime in concert with all other aspects of wildlife conservation and management and provides a global platform for the conservation of migratory species of wild animals and their habitats. The Bonn Convention brings together countries through which migratory animals pass and lays the legal foundation for conservation measures.[490]

Unfortunately, both CITES, Bonn Convention, and indeed any other international treaty at present, have no specific provisions for the prevention and suppression of wildlife trafficking. Nonetheless, treaties such as the *United Nations Convention Against Transnational Organised Crime (UNTOC)* and the *United Nations Convention Against Corruption* (UNCAC) serve as platforms to seek assistance in matters involving organised crime or corruption linked to wildlife trafficking.

10.7.3.2.3 United Nations Convention against Transnational Organised Crime (UNTOC) 2000

The UNTOC 2000[491] was opened for signature in December 2000 and entered force on 29 September 2003. The purpose of the Convention is to promote cooperation to prevent and combat transnational organised crime more effectively.[492] Due to the impact of Wildlife trafficking on both flora and fauna the UNTOC 2000, although not explicitly made to combat wildlife trafficking, can be a veritable instrument applied to combat wildlife trafficking. This assertion is premised on the fact that wildlife trafficking is not only a transnational organised crime but also a serious crime against the environment.

---

[489] Ibid.

[490] UNODC (2016a).

[491] Since its entry into force, *UNTOC* has enjoyed a high level of adherence; 190 states are party to the Convention as of June 2019.

[492] UNTOC (2000), Art. 1.

Although the Convention does not explicitly define organised crime, it sets out four offences: corruption,[493] money-laundering,[494] obstruction of justice[495] and participation in an organised criminal group.[496] Furthermore, the Convention defines the actors involved in the commission of organised criminal activities and, in doing so, it introduces a concept that is central for the delimitation of its scope of application: the concept of "serious crime."[497] The concept of "serious crimes" is defined as "conduct constituting an offence punishable by a maximum deprivation of liberty of at least four years or a more serious penalty."[498]

Again, two additional elements are crucial in the assertion that UNTOC 2000 can be applied in combating wildlife trafficking. Article 3 specifies the element of transnationality and the involvement of an organised criminal group so defined in Article 2(a) as "a structured group of three or more persons, existing for a period of time and acting in concert with the aim of committing one or more serious crimes or offences established in accordance with this Convention, in order to obtain, directly or indirectly, a financial or other material benefit." This is apt as wildlife trafficking can be regarded as a transnational crime, which is planned, executed, or has effects across national borders, thus providing a broad definition of transnationality, and involving a group with the characteristics defined in Article 2(a) of UNTOC 2000.

Transfering this reflection to the application of UNTOC to wildlife trafficking however, depends on whether the relevant offences are criminalised under national legislation and whether the penalty attached to them is punishable by a maximum deprivation of liberty of at least four years (i.e. whether the offences constitute a "serious crime"). Thus, state parties to UNTOC 2000 have been urged by the United Nations Economic and Social Council (ECOSOC) and the CITES Conference of the Parties (CoP) to make wildlife trafficking a serious crime, as defined under the Convention.[499] In addition, available tools provided by *UNTOC* 2000 that are relevant to combating wildlife trafficking, and can be used when such crimes reach the necessary threshold include provisions regarding cooperation between states parties,[500] extradition,[501] transfer of sentenced persons,[502] mutual legal

[493] Ibid., Art. 8.

[494] Ibid., Art. 6.

[495] Ibid., Art. 23.

[496] Ibid., Art. 5.

[497] UNODC (2016b).

[498] UNTOC (2000), Art. 2(b).

[499] UNGA (2013).

[500] UNTOC (2000), Art. 27.

[501] Ibid., Art. 16.

[502] Ibid., Art. 17.

assistance,[503] joint investigations,[504] transfer of criminal proceedings,[505] and confiscation and seizure,[506] among others.

10.7.3.2.4 United Nations Convention Against Corruption (UNCAC) 2003

Corruption is a major enabler of wildlife trafficking. The UNCAC 2003 was adopted on 31 October 2003 and entered into force on 14 December 2005. As of June 2018, the Convention had 186 state parties. It contains provisions on criminalisation, prevention, cooperation, asset recovery, and technical assistance and information exchange.[507] As a result, this is where UNCAC 2003 comes into play in combating wildlife trafficking. This is because the Convention criminalises corruption and sets out various measures to combat it, and therefore is complementary to broader efforts to combat wildlife trafficking under the other international instruments discussed in this sub-chapter. The purposes of the Convention are to:

(a) promote and strengthen measures to prevent and combat corruption more efficiently and effectively;
(b) promote, facilitate and support international cooperation and technical assistance in the prevention of and fight against corruption, including in asset recovery; and
(c) promote integrity, accountability and proper management of public affairs and public property.[508]

The UNCAC 2003 contains several criminalisation provisions that may be relevant in combating wildlife trafficking. It requires criminalisation of bribery of national public officials,[509] bribery of foreign public officials and officials of public international organisations,[510] embezzlement,[511] money-laundering,[512] and obstruction of justice.[513] The Convention further encourages criminalisation of trading in influence,[514] abuse of functions[515] and bribery in the private sector.[516]

---

[503] Ibid., Art. 18.
[504] Ibid., Art. 19.
[505] Ibid., Arts. 12 and 13.
[506] Ibid., Art. 12.
[507] UNCAC (2003).
[508] Ibid., Art. 1.
[509] UNCAC (2003), Art. 15.
[510] Ibid., Art. 16.
[511] Ibid., Art. 17.
[512] Ibid., Art. 23.
[513] Ibid., Art. 25.
[514] Ibid., Art. 18.
[515] Ibid., Art. 19.
[516] Ibid., Art. 21.

The role of the UNCAC 2003 in preventing and combating wildlife trafficking is emphasised in numerous international materials. In 2013, the United Nations General Assembly (UNGA) stated that "coordinated action is critical to eliminate corruption and disrupt the illicit organized criminal groups that drive and enable trafficking in wildlife."[517] In July 2015, the UNGA called on states to "prohibit, prevent and counter any form of corruption that facilitates illicit trafficking in wildlife and wildlife products."[518]

The need to combat wildlife crime is predicated on the fact that "wildlife crime ranks alongside drug smuggling, human trafficking and illegal arms trade as one of the most lucrative activities funding organized crime and terrorism. It undermines legitimate activities such as eco-tourism or sustainable hunting, which provide long-term livelihoods and generate foreign exchange income."[519] There had been many efforts at enforcing relevant international conventions and domestic laws that had yielded convictions. Some of such cases are discussed below.

10.7.3.3 Some Cases on Wildlife and Forest Crime

Several convictions had been made across jurisdictions to curb the menace of illegal wildlife trade. Convictions were based on various acts that came within the purview of wildlife crime, such as:

(i) Illegal trafficking of protected species
(ii) Illegal export of protected species
(iii) Illegal sale of protected species
(iv) Illegal purchase and sale of protected species
(v) Aiding and abetting the illegal transport of protected species
(vi) Smuggling and conspiracy to smuggle protected species
(vii) Poaching of protected species

The following are some of the cases in issue.

A large number of convictions in the cases discussed below fall under the illegal trafficking of protected species. For instance, in the case of *United States v. Arongkron Malasukum*,[520] Arongkron "Paul" Malasukum on 1 August 2018 was sentenced to nine months in prison to be followed by one year of supervised release for illegally trafficking parts from endangered African lions and tigers. Malasukum admitted that between 9 April 2015 and 29 June 2016, he purchased and exported from the United States to Thailand approximately 68 packages containing skulls, claws, and parts from endangered and protected species, with a total fair market value in excess of US$150,000. He admitted to purchasing a tiger

517 UNGA (2014).
518 Ibid.
519 UNODC (2016a).
520 Department of Justice U.S. Attorney's Office Eastern District of Texas (2018).

skull from undercover agents and purchasing lion skulls from an auction house in Texas through the undercover agents. After the purchases, Malasukum shipped the tiger and lion skulls from Texas to his home in Woodside, New York. From New York, Malasukum shipped the skulls to Thailand for sale to a wholesale buyer.

In the case of *United States v. William Sheldon et al.,*[521] three men, William Sheldon, Timothy Lewis, and Thomas Reno, were on 3 May 2018, sentenced to six months' incarceration, followed by three years' supervised release, for illegally trafficking juvenile eels. Sheldon will pay a US$10,000 fine and Lewis will pay US$2500. Reno will complete a one-year term of probation, and Sheldon will further forfeit US$33,200 in lieu of a truck he used during the criminal acts. Both Sheldon and Lewis were prohibited from possessing a license to purchase or export elvers. The defendants bought, sold, and transported elvers, knowing that they had been taken, possessed, transported, and sold in violation of the laws and regulations of numerous states including New Jersey, Massachusetts, Rhode Island, and Connecticut.

Again, in the case of *United States v. Yarann Im et al.*[522] prior to 2016, the defendants knowingly illegally harvested American eels and illegally transported and sold them in interstate commerce in contravention of the Lacey Act. The eels in question were juvenile and amounted to a value of US$ 1.9 million. The defendants conducted their illegal business with eels sourced in a variety of U.S. East Coast states, knowing that these states had prohibited harvesting glass eels. To cover up the origin of the fish, the defendants used harvesting licenses from Florida and Maine, which are among the last states to allow eel harvesting, to claim that the eels were in fact fished legally. This illegal documentation was included in export declarations to facilitate the shipment of the eels to East Asia. In October 2016, the seven defendants pleaded guilty to trafficking more than $1.9 million worth of juvenile American eels, a felony under 16 U.S.C. §§ 3372, 3373. They were sentenced in December 2017.

In the case of *United States v. Travis Leger and Jason Leckelt,*[523] Travis Leger, his half-brother Jason Leckelt, and Rickey Simon were on 15 December sentenced to 21 months and 16 months in prison, respectively, followed by three years of supervised release for conspiring to violate the Lacey Act by illegally trafficking alligator snapping turtles. The third defendant in the case, Rickey Simon of Sulphur, Louisiana, was sentenced to three years of probation. As part of his guilty plea, Leger admitted to selling a live, illegally taken 171-pound turtle for US$1000, and another live, illegally taken 168-pound turtle, for US$500 in May and June of 2016. The turtles were later seized by U.S. Fish and Wildlife Agents from the buyer. Simon admitted that he sold an illegally-trafficked, 120-pound turtle to an undercover Special Agent of the U.S. Fish and Wildlife Service on 19 May 2016.

Leger admitted that the market value of all the turtles that he caught illegally in Texas and then sold in Louisiana during the course of the conspiracy was between

---

[521] Environment and Natural Resources Division, U.S. Department of Justice (2018b).

[522] UNODC (2017).

[523] Department of Justice U.S. Attorney's Office Eastern District of Texas (2017).

US$40,000 and US$95,000. The market value of the turtles that were illegally trafficked by Leckelt was between US$15,000 and US$40,000. In July 2016, Federal agents seized about 30 large turtles from ponds located at Leger's property in Sulphur, Louisiana, pursuant to a federal search warrant. As part of his guilty plea, Leger agreed to forfeit all of the seized turtles and will permit the U.S. Fish and Wildlife Service to return to his property, drain the ponds, and seize any turtles remaining in the ponds. All of the turtles seized by the government, in this case, will be cared for at the U.S. Fish and Wildlife Service Natchitoches Fish Hatchery in Louisiana and used as part of a breeding program to restock the species in its native waterways in the southwestern United States.

In the *United States v. Tommy Water Zhou,*[524] Tommy Water Zhou was on 3 November 2017 sentenced to 18 months' imprisonment for trafficking juvenile American eels in violation of the Lacey Act. In April 2017, Zhou pleaded guilty to violating the Lacey Act by trafficking more than US$150,361 worth of elvers in interstate commerce that had been harvested illegally in Virginia. Court documents indicate that Zhou trafficked at least 105 pounds of elvers, which is approximately 210,000 individual eels. Zhou subsequently sold these elvers to international buyers and exported them from the United States.

On 18 September 2017, in the case of *United States v. Fengyi Zhou,*[525] Fengyi Zhou was sentenced to 24 months' incarceration, followed by three years' supervised release, and ordered to pay a US$5,000 fine and US$112,133 in restitution, for illegally trafficking black rhinoceros horns. Zhou owned a business that specialised in Asian art. Between November 2010 and January 2011, he purchased approximately five uncarved rhinoceros horns from another Asian art dealer in New York. Along with the horns, Zhou was given an "Endangered Species Bill of Sale," which informed him that four of the horns were purchased in Texas and unlawfully transported to New York. Zhou sold the horns to a Chinese associate in China for more than US$130,000.

In the *United States v. Tim Davis,*[526] Tim Davis was on 13 July 2017 sentenced to complete a three-year term of probation, including one month of home confinement. He was also ordered to pay a US$20,000 fine. Davis previously pleaded guilty to a Lacey Act violation for trafficking in ivory products made from sperm whales, elephants, and walruses. Davis advertised on internet sites such as Etsy, EBay, and Craigslist, offering to purchase and sell various ivory products. He sold ivory to buyers outside the U.S., particularly in Asia. To conceal his international transactions, Davis fraudulently labelled the ivory packages, stating that they contained "ox bone" products. He participated in approximately 74 transactions involving the purchase and sale of whale, elephant, and walrus ivory between May 2006 and June 2015. In May 2015, he sold an undercover agent a collection of sperm whale teeth for US$2000 and purchased four walrus tusks from the agent in June 2015.

---

[524] Department of Justice, US Office of Public Affairs (2017c), see also Department of Justice, US Office of Public Affairs (2017a).

[525] Case Number: 1:16-cr-00363-WFK-RER, 19 September 2017.

[526] Criminal Case No. 3:20-CR-00113 (REP) (E.D. Va. 30 December 2020).

In the case of illegal sale of protected species, the case of *United States v. Guan Zong Chen*[527] comes handy. Guan Zong Chen, a Chinese national, was on 14 February 2018 sentenced to 19 months' incarceration, which was time served, for leading a conspiracy to illegally export US$700,000 worth of endangered and protected wildlife items made from rhinoceros horn, elephant ivory, and coral from the United States to China.

The court ordered him to forfeit the seized ivory and pay US$700,000 in substituted assets. Chen, who owned an antique business in China, was previously arrested in Chengdu, China, and convicted in China in 2009 for trafficking ivory carvings that had been purchased in the United States. Unable to travel outside of China due to his conviction, Chen continued to traffic wildlife by procuring the help of others to smuggle wildlife merchandise to China that he purchased at U.S. auction houses located in California, Florida, Ohio, Pennsylvania, New York, and Texas. Jin Jie Yang, a Chinese national, and Carla Marsh, who owned a shipping business in Concord, Massachusetts, both aided Chen in his illegal activities. In December 2014, Yang pleaded guilty to his role in the conspiracy and was sentenced in May 2015 to time-served. Marsh pleaded guilty in May 2015 and was sentenced to one year of probation in April 2016.

On the other hand, in the case of *United States v. Edward Levine and Anor,*[528] Edward N. Levine was on 23 March 2018 sentenced to 27 months in prison followed by three years of supervised release for illegally selling two black rhinoceros horns in Las Vegas. Levine will be prohibited from wildlife and antique sales. Levine was convicted under the Lacey and Endangered Species Acts for conspiring to and knowingly selling the horns to an undercover agent from the United States Fish and Wildlife Service. Levine and co-defendant Lumsden Quan had negotiated the sale of two black rhinoceros horns by e-mail and telephone, ultimately communicating with an undercover agent. Levine offered to sell two horns for US$55,000 and agreed to meet the buyer in Las Vegas. Quan and Levine flew from California to complete the sale in a Las Vegas hotel room. Quan had been sentenced previously.

At times the conviction may be based on both illegal purchase and sale of protected species. In the case of *United States v. Andrew A. Praskovsky,*[529] the defendant, Andrew A. Praskovsky was on 26 January 2017 sentenced to pay a US$5000 fine, complete a two-year term of probation, and perform 250 hours of community service for a multi-defendant scheme involving the illegal purchase and sale of paddlefish eggs. Praskovsky and his co-defendants Arkadiy Lvovskiy, Dmitri Elitchev, Felix Baravik, Bogdan Nahapetyan, Fedor Pakhnyuk and Artour Magdessian in 2011 and 2012, travelled to Missouri, and engaged in numerous transactions with agents posing as fishermen for the purchase and sale of female paddlefish. They then processed the paddlefish eggs into caviar which was then

[527] Criminal No. 15-cr-10348-RWZ, Document 33 filed on 24 October 2017.

[528] See Environment and Natural Resources Division, U.S. Department of Justice (2018a).

[529] Department of Justice (2016).

transported to Colorado. The retail value of the caviar was estimated to be betweenUS$30,000 and US$50,000.

In some cases, the conviction may not be based on the illegal wildlife trade but on some offences ancillary to it like aiding and abetting the commission of an offence under the illegal wildlife trade. The case of *United States v. Timothy Lewis et al.*[530] comes to mind. While Timothy Lewis and William Sheldon were on 3 May 2018 sentenced to serve six months incarceration, and to pay a US$2500 fine having previously pled guilty to Lacey Act trafficking violations, Charles Good pleaded guilty to aiding and abetting the illegal transport of juvenile American eels, or "elvers." Between 2011 and 2014, Sheldon purchased elvers (also called "glass eels") from individuals who he knew had harvested them illegally. He then transported those elvers to an exporter, who shipped them to Hong Kong and Korea to be raised to adulthood and sold for food. From 2012 to 2014, Lewis fished for elvers illegally, purchased glass eels that he knew had been harvested illegally, and arranged for their transport and export. Good, whose home served as a base of operations, conspired with Lewis to illegally harvest, transport, and sell elvers. Among those dealers is Thomas Choi, who pleaded guilty to related crimes in the District of Maine in 2016, and who was subsequently sentenced to six months' imprisonment for those offences.

Smuggling is another offence under which a conviction had been secured as in the case of *Salvius Francis Matembo, Manase Julius Philemon and Yang Feng Glan v. Republic.*[531] In that case, the Appellants were charged in a Tanzanian court, to wit: (i) Leading organised crime contrary to para 4(1) of the first schedule to Section 57 (1) & 60(2) of the Economic and Organized Crime Control Act Cap. 200 RE 2002 and (ii) Unlawful Dealing in Trophies contrary to Section 80(1) and Part 1 of the schedule of Wildlife and Conservation Act No. 5 of 2009 read together with para 14 (b) of the 1st Schedule to Section 57 (1) and 60 (2) of the Economic and Organized Crime Control Act Cap 200 R.E 2002.

On 19 February 2019, the court delivered a landmark ruling and sentenced the Appellants to 15 years imprisonment for smuggling hundreds of elephant tusks. In addition, the "shamba and buildings in Muheza Maili Saba" were confiscated by the government of Tanzania. Yang Feng Glan[532] the 3rd Defendant/Appellant was accused of running one of Africa's biggest ivory trafficking rings. Having moved to Tanzania in the 1970s, she was secretary-general of the Tanzania China-Africa Business Council and owned a popular Chinese restaurant in Dar es Salaam. She used her knowledge of Tanzanian culture, her Swahili language skills, and her ties to the Chinese and Tanzanian establishment to run a sophisticated organised criminal group.

[530] Case No.3:19-cr-29 (TBR) (W.D. Ky. 27 January 2022). See also Department of Justice, Office of Public Affairs (2018a).

[531] Criminal Appeal 95 of 2019, [2019] TZHC 11 (16 October 2019).

[532] A Chinese business woman nicknamed the "Ivory Queen."

The three convicts then filed an appeal at Dar Es Salaam District Registry at Dar es Salaam challenging the conviction. The appeal was struck out as being incompetent in its entirety with costs.

Poaching is another instance in South Africa, in the case of *The State v. Ndlovu*[533] three individuals were found guilty of more than 50 counts of rhino poaching between 2013 and 2016 by the Grahamstown High Court in South Africa. The members of the group, also known as the Ndlovu Trio, will each serve a minimum of 25 years in prison. After an investigation, the trio was convicted in early 2019. During the arrests, several items were recovered, including a freshly harvested rhino horn, a darting rifle, saws and knives and two rental vehicles.

It should be noted that there is a thin line demarcating these offences when it comes to prosecuting offenders under illegal wildlife trade or trafficking. The reason is that in several cases, as in some cases discussed below, the offender/s was/were charged under more than one of the offences above specified. The following cases may buttress this assertion.

In the case of *United States v. David Sommers,*[534] a federal grand jury in July 2018 indicted David Sommers for trafficking in protected diamondback terrapins. The indictment charges Sommers with smuggling turtles and submitting false records for a package shipped to Canada and four violations of the Lacey Act for trafficking over 3500 turtles in interstate commerce. The indictment alleges that throughout 2017 Sommers poached diamondback terrapins and their eggs from coastal marshes in New Jersey, and then sold them, in violation of the Lacey Act. The indictment also charges that in 2014, Sommers smuggled turtles to Canada and falsely labelled the package by claiming it contained a book. The United States seized over 3,400 diamondback terrapin hatchlings from Sommers' house in October and they were able to return the hatchlings to their New Jersey native habitat. If convicted, Sommers faces a maximum sentence of ten years' incarceration on the smuggling charge and five years for the Lacey Act violations.

On 18 January 2018 in the case of *United States v. Joseph Kelley et al.,*[535] Joseph Kelley and James Lewis were charged in a seven-count indictment with conspiracy, smuggling, and Lacey Act charges for their involvement in the illegal trafficking of juvenile eels. Between January 2013 and May 2014, Kelley, Lewis, and others bought, sold, and transported young eels, knowing that they had been taken, possessed, transported, and sold in violation of the laws and regulations of the states of New Jersey, Massachusetts, Rhode Island, Connecticut, and other states.

In the case of *United States v. Michael Hegarty and Anor,*[536] Michael Hegarty, an Irish national was on 14 November 2017, sentenced to 18 months' incarceration, followed by three years' supervised release, for facilitating the transportation and

---

[533] 59/2020) [2021] ZAKZPHC 46 (30 July 2021).

[534] Department of Justice U.S. Attorney's Office Eastern District of Pennsylvania (2019).

[535] Case No. 18-CR-00022 (D.N.J.), see Department of Justice (2018).

[536] Department of Justice, US Office of Public Affairs (2017b).

concealment of a libation cup carved from an endangered rhinoceros horn that was illegally smuggled from the United States to Great Britain.

In mid-April 2012, Hegarty and a co-conspirator joined a Miami resident to attend an auction in North Carolina where a second co-conspirator worked as the bidder, making a winning bid for a rhinoceros horn libation cup. After Hegarty and his first co-conspirator received the cup in Florida, the co-conspirator smuggled it out of the United States in his luggage. The co-conspirator, along with two other Irish nationals, was arrested in London while attempting to sell the cup to a Hong Kong native. Hegarty was arrested via an INTERPOL Red Notice and extradited to the United States from Belgium. His co-conspirator was convicted of unrelated charges in England, is currently incarcerated there, and will face wildlife trafficking charges in Florida.

Again, in the case of *United States v. Aristides Sanchez,*[537] the defendant, Aristides Sanchez on 23 August 2017, pleaded guilty to two felony violations of the Lacey Act for collecting, purchasing, falsely labelling, and shipping protected marine invertebrate species as part of an effort to subvert Puerto Rican law designed to protect corals and other reef species. Sanchez was the owner of the Arecibo-based saltwater aquarium business, Wonders of the Reef Aquarium. A large part of the business was devoted to the sale of native Puerto Rican marine species that are popular in the saltwater aquarium trade.

In another development, Yunhua Lin, a Chinese national, regarded as the head of the "Lin-Zhang gang," which has been operating out of Malawi for at least a decade, was arrested in August 2019 alongside Malawian national James Mkwezelemba following a three-month manhunt by the authorities. They were arraigned before a court in Malawi and on 28 September 2021 Yunhua Lin was sentenced to 14 years for dealing in rhino horn, 14 years for possession of rhino horn and six years for money laundering; the sentences will run concurrently so he will serve a total of 14 years. He will be deported back to China on completion of the jail term.[538]

10.8 Summary

Environmental pollution by its very nature causes extensive damage to the environment, human lives and property. Where environmental damage occurs liability may ensure. Liability rules may be preventive as a form of economic instrument which provides an incentive to encourage compliance with environmental obligations. They may be punitive when used to impose sanctions against wrongful conduct. They may also be corrective measures when applied to restore a given environmental asset to its pre-damage condition. Finally, they may provide a technique for

[537] Environment and Natural Resources Division, U.S. Department of Justice (2017).

[538] Environmental Investigation Agency (UK) (2021).

internalising environmental and other social costs into production processes and other activities.

However, one problem in the application of the liability rules is the determination of what constitutes environmental damage to which liability may apply. Many attempts were made at defining what amounts to environmental damage to which liability will apply. The attempts were based on the provisions of some international legal instruments. The take from these provisions is that the concept of environmental damage is the damage that is caused to the environment and as a change in a specific section or the entire environment that has a significant detrimental impact on the quality of the environment, or a change in its ability to maintain an acceptable quality of life or a lasting and stable balance of ecosystems. Liability for environmental damage could be civil or criminal.

At the international level, civil liability is focused on the responsibility of the state for internationally wrongful acts that result in environmental damage. It is an established principle that a breach of international obligation by a state gives rise to a requirement for reparation as states are responsible for breaches of their obligations and shall compensate affected states for any damage caused by their violation of international law. This rule forms the basis of the law of state responsibility.

Guidelines for ascertaining the level of state liability for wrongful acts that caused environmental damage focused on the United Nations Compensation Commission framework for compensation that was set up by the UN after the 1991 invasion of Kuwait by Iraq. To establish state liability major hurdle is where to draw the threshold of significance in such claims for environmental damage. The posers here are: when can the threshold for liability arise; who should be liable for the damage; to whom does the burden of proof lie and what is the type of liability, what is expected from the person/s liable; where would the claims be instituted; and whether there are time limitations for claims?

Criminal liability for environmental damage under international environmental law addressed the issue of wildlife and forest crime (as part of environmental crime).

The liability logic is therefore premised on the fact that if polluters are to repair the damage caused to the environment by paying the corresponding costs, they will reduce pollution as long as the cost of de-pollution remains below the amount of compensation for the damage. The principle of environmental liability thus prevents environmental damage. The principle of liability may also encourage different actors to apply precautionary principles by avoiding risks and damages to the environment and improve the environmental knowledge and best available technology in environmental protection.

In all, the use of international law in creating liability for environmental damage and the pursuit of compensation for victims has gone through a long process over the years. It is heartwarming to note that with the plethora of multi-lateral environmental agreements (MEAs), customary international law, judicial decisions and case laws from diverse jurisdictions, there is hope that polluters may think twice before unleashing their pollution-causing activities on the environment and on its natural resources.

References

Barboza J (1990) Sixth Report, UN Documents A/CN.4/428, 39 (1990), http://www.un.org. Accessed 1 May 2023

Biegus O, Bueger C (2017) Poachers and pirates, improving coordination of the global response to wildlife crime. South Africa Crime Q 60:29

Blomquist RF (2011) The logic and limits of environmental criminal law in the global setting: Brazil and the United States--comparisons, contrasts, and questions in search of a Robust theory. Tulane Environ Law J 25:83, https://scholar.valpo.edu/cgi/viewcontent.cgi?article=1119&context=law_fac_pubs. Accessed 11 June 2023

Bodansky D (2010) The art and craft of international environmental law. Harvard University, Cambridge

Bustami A, Hecken MC (2021) Perspectives for a New international crime against the environment: international criminal responsibility for environmental degradation under the Rome Statute. Gottingen J Int Law 11(1):154, https://www.gojil.eu/issues/111/BustamiHecken_Final.pdf. Accessed 18 June 2023

Cambridge University (1979) Canada: Claim Against The Union Of Soviet Socialist Republics For Damage Caused By Soviet Cosmos 954. Int Legal Mater 18(4):899–930, Cambridge University Press, https://www.jstor.org/stable/20692062, Accessed 10 May 2023

Dendle B (2018) State responsibility for climate change—a legal assessment. https://www.academia.edu/14883718/STATE_RESPONSIBILITY_FOR_CLIMATE_CHANGE_A_LEGAL_ASSESSMENT. Accessed 15 May 2023

Department of Justice (2016) United States v. Andrew A. Praskovsky, No. 13-CR-04015 (W.D. Mo.), Environmental Crimes Section Monthly Bulletin, September 2016, 6. https://www.eksservices.com/wp-content/uploads/2013/01/doj-env-crimes.pdf. Accessed 19 July 2023

Department of Justice (2018) United States v. Joseph Kelley et al., No. 18-CR-00022 (D.N.J.),: Environmental Crimes Section Monthly Bulletin, September 2018, 10. https://www.justice.gov/enrd/page/file/1105646/download. Accessed 19 July 2023

Department of Justice U.S. Attorney's Office Eastern District of Pennsylvania (2019) Levittown Man Sentenced for Trafficking Protected Turtles. Justice News, 29 August 2019, https://www.justice.gov/usao-edpa/pr/levittown-man-sentenced-trafficking-protected-turtles. Accessed 19 July 2023

Department of Justice U.S. Attorney's Office Eastern District of Texas (2017) Two brothers sentenced to 21 months and 16 months in prison for illegally trafficking threatened alligator snapping turtles. Justice News, 15 December 2017, https://www.justice.gov/usao-edtx/pr/two-brothers-sentenced-21-months-and-16-months-prison-illegally-trafficking-threatened. Accessed 19 July 2023

Department of Justice U.S. Attorney's Office Eastern District of Texas (2018) New York man sentenced to prison for trafficking in endangered lion and tiger parts. Justice News, Wednesday, 1 August 2018. https://www.justice.gov/usao-edtx/pr/new-york-man-sentenced-prison-trafficking-endangered-lion-and-tiger-parts. Accessed 19 July 2023

Department of Justice, US Office of Public Affairs (2017a) Two Men Indicted in Maine for Illegally Trafficking American Eels. Justice News, 3 March 2017, https://www.justice.gov/opa/pr/maine-fisherman-sentenced-illegally-trafficking-american-eels-0. Accessed 19 July 2023

Department of Justice, US Office of Public Affairs (2017b) Foreign National Pleads Guilty to Smuggling Rhinoceros Horn. Justice News, 29 September 2017, https://www.justice.gov/opa/pr/foreign-national-pleads-guilty-smuggling-rhinoceros-horn. Accessed 19 July 2023

Department of Justice, US Office of Public Affairs (2017c) Maine Fisherman Sentenced for Illegally Trafficking American Eels. Justice News, 3 November 2017, https://www.justice.gov/opa/pr/maine-fisherman-sentenced-illegally-trafficking-american-eels-0. Accessed 19 July 2023

Environment and Natural Resources Division, U.S. Department of Justice (2017) Summary of Recent Wildlife Trafficking Enforcement Cases, October 2018 ... United States v. Aristides Sanchez, 23 August 2017, https://www.justice.gov/opa/pr/owner-arecibo-aquarium-business-pleads-guilty-two-federallacey-act-felonies-illicit. Accessed 19 July 2023

Environment and Natural Resources Division, U.S. Department of Justice (2018a) Summary of Recent Wildlife Trafficking Enforcement Cases, October 2018 ... United States v. Edward Levine and Anor, 23 March 2018, https://www.justice.gov/opa/pr/california-man-sentenced-27-months-prison-sale-blackrhinoceros-horns. Accessed 19 July 2023

Environment and Natural Resources Division, U.S. Department of Justice (2018b) Summary of Recent Wildlife trafficking Enforcement Cases, October 2018 ... United States v. William Sheldon et al. (D. Maine) 3 May 2018, https://www.justice.gov/opa/pr/maine-men-sentenced-illegally-trafficking-american-eels. Accessed 19 July 2023

Environmental Investigation Agency (UK) (2021) Yunhua Lin, a notorious kingpin of wildlife crime syndicate is jailed 14 years in Malawi. 28 September 2021, https://eia-international.org/news/yunhua-lin-notorious-kingpin-of-wildlife-crime-syndicate-is-jailed-for-14-years-in-malawi/. Accessed 19 May 2023

European Treaty Series (ETS) (1993) 150-Environment, 21.VI.1993, https://rm.coe.int/168007c079. Accessed 22 May 2023

Higgins P et al. (2013) Protecting the planet: a proposal for a law of ecocide. Crime Law Soc Change 59(3):251 at 252–254

ILC (2001a) Draft Articles on the Responsibility of States for Internationally Wrongful Acts, Report of the ILC on the Work of its Fifty-third Session, UNGA resolution 56/83 (12 December 2001), Supp No 10, 43, UN Doc A/56/10 (2001), https://legal.un.org/ilc/texts/instruments/english/commentaries/9_6_2001.pdf. Accessed 9 May 2023

ILC (2001b) Draft Articles on Responsibility of States for Internationally Wrongful Acts, with Commentaries 2001 (ILC Comments on Draft Articles on Responsibility of States 2001), Text adopted by the at its fifty-third session, in 2001, and submitted to the General Assembly as a part of the Commission's report covering the work of that session (A/56/10). https://legal.un.org/ilc/texts/instruments/english/commentaries/9_6_2001.pdf. Accessed 9 May 2023

ILC (2001c) Draft Articles on Prevention of Transboundary Harm from Hazardous Activities 2001 (I LC Draft Articles on Harm from Hazardous Activities 2001). https://legal.un.org/ilc/texts/instruments/english/draft_articles/9_7_2001.pdf. Accessed 9 May 2023

ILC (2001d) ILC Comments on Draft Articles on Harm from Hazardous Activities 2001), Text adopted by the at its fifty-third session, in 2001, and submitted to the General Assembly as a part of the Commission's report covering the work of that session (A/56/10). https://legal.un.org/ilc/texts/instruments/english/commentaries/9_7_2001.pdf. Accessed 9 May 2023

Institute of International Law (IIL) (2017a) The Pollution of Rivers and Lakes and International Law. IDI Resolutions, Session of Athens, 12 September 1979, https://www.idi-iil.org/app/uploads/2017/06/1979_ath_02_en.pdf, Accessed 18 May 2023

Institute of International Law (IIL) (2017b) Transboundary Air Pollution. IDI Resolutions, Session of Cairo, Egypt, 20 September 1987, preamble. https://www.idi-iil.org/app/uploads/2017/06/1987_caire_03_en.pdf. Accessed 18 May 2023

Institute of International Law (IIL) (2017c) Responsibility and Liability under International Law for Environmental Damage. IDI Resolutions, Session of Strasbourg, 4 September 1997. https://www.idi-iil.org/app/uploads/2017/06/1997_str_03_en.pdf. Accessed 18 May 2023

International Committee of the Red Cross (IRCC) (2019) Natural environment: Neglected victim of armed conflict. https://www.icrc.org/en/document/natural-environment-neglected-victim-armed-conflict. Accessed 25 June 2023

International Law Commission (ILC) (1995) Report of the ILC on the work of its 47*th* session, UN Doc A/50/10, 21 July 1995. https://legal.un.org/ilc/texts/7_4.shtml. Accessed 18 June 2023

INTERPOL-UN Environment (2016) Strategic Report: Environment, Peace and Security – A Convergence of Threats, Perspectives for a New International Crime Against the Environment, http://www.interpol.int and www.unep.org. Accessed 20 July 2023

Khalatbari Y, Poorhashemi A (2019) Environmental damage: challenges and opportunities in international environmental law. CIFILE J Int Law (CJIL), 1(1):21–28 at 21. https://www.cifilejournal.com. Accessed 25 May 2023

Kyar DA (2013) Climate change and the International Court of Justice: seeking an advisory opinion on transboundary harm from the court (14 August 2013). Yale Law School, Public Law Research Paper No. 31, 16, http://www.un.org/press/en/2012/120203_ICJ.doc.htm. Accessed 19 May 2023

Larsson ML (2009) Legal definition of the Environment and Environmental Damage. Stockholm Institute Law, 159, http://www.scandinavianlaw.se/pdf/38-7.pdf. Accessed 25 May 2023

Mackenzie R, Khalastchi R (1996) Liability and compensation for environmental damage in the context of the work of the United Nations Compensation Commission. RECIEL 5(4):283, https://onlinelibrary.wiley.com/doi/epdf/10.1111/j.1467-9388.1996.tb00291.x. Accessed 15 May 2023

Payne CR (2016) Legal liability for environmental damage: the United Nations Compensation Commission and the 1990-1991 Gulf War. In: Muffett BC, Nichols SS (eds) Governance, natural resources, and post- conflict peace building. Earthscan, London

Rao R (1998) First report on prevention of trans-boundary damage from hazardous activity. UN Documents A/CN.4/487, 3–4, http://www.un.org. Accessed 1 June 2023

Rome Statute of the International Criminal Court (1998), A/CONF.183/9 of 17 July 1998, https://www.icc-cpi.int/nr/rdonlyres/add16852-aee9-4757-abe7-9cdc7cf02886/283503/romestatuteng1.pdf. Accessed 18 June 2021

Sands P (2003) Principles of international environmental law, 2nd edn. Cambridge University, New York

Schneider M (2016) In Cymie R, Payne CR "Legal Liability for Environmental Damage: The United Nations Compensation Commission and the 1990-1991 Gulf War.". In: Muffett BC, Nichols SS (eds) Governance, natural resources, and post- conflict peace building. Earthscan, London

Secretariat of the Convention on Biological Diversity (2011) Liability and Redress: Some Basic Concepts and Facts. Workshop Material No. 1 2011, http://bch.cbd.int/protocol/. Accessed 30 July 2023

Sharp P (1999) Prospects for environmental liability in the international criminal court. Virginia Environ Law J 18:217

Shaw MN (2014) International law, 7th edn. Cambridge University, London

Stein J (2008) The international law and politics of climate change: ratification of the United Nations framework convention and the Kyoto Protocol. J Confl Resol 52(243):247

UNCCGC (2001) Report and Recommendations Made by the Panel of Commissioners Concerning the First Instalment of "F4" Claims, Security Council S/AC.26/2001/16, 22 June 2001, https://uncc.ch/sites/default/files/attachments/documents/r2001-16.pdf. Accessed 8 June 2023

UNCCGC (2002) Report and Recommendations Made by the Panel of Commissioners Concerning the Second Instalment of "F4" Claims, Security Council S/AC.26/2002/26, 3 October 2002, https://uncc.ch/sites/default/files/attachments/documents/r2002-26.pdf. Accessed 8 June 2023

UNCCGC (2003) Report and Recommendations Made by the Panel of Commissioners Concerning the Third Instalment of "F4" Claims, Security Council S/AC.26/2003/31, 18 December 2003. https://uncc.ch/sites/default/files/attachments/documents/r2003-31.pdf. Accessed 8 June 2023

UNCCGC (2004a) Report and Recommendations Made by the Panel of Commissioners Concerning the Part One of the Fourth Instalment of "F4" Claims, Security Council S/AC.26/2004/16, 9 December 2004. https://uncc.ch/sites/default/files/attachments/documents/r2004-16.pdf. Accessed 8 June 2023

UNCCGC (2004b) Report and Recommendations Made by the Panel of Commissioners Concerning Part Two of the Fourth Instalment of "F4" Claims, Claim No. 5000454, Security Council S/AC.26/2004/17, 9 December 2004. https://uncc.ch/sites/default/files/attachments/documents/r2004-17.pdf. Accessed 8 June 2023

UNCCGC (2005) Report and Recommendations Made by the Panel of Commissioners Concerning the Fifth Instalment of "F4" Claims, Security Council S/AC.26/2005/10, 30 June 2005. https://uncc.ch/sub-category-f4-claims-environmental-damage. Accessed 8 June 2023
UNEP (1996) Report of Working Group of Experts on Liability and Compensation for Environmental Damage Arising from Military Activities. https://www.ecolex.org/details/literature/report-on-liability-and-compensation-for-environmental-damage-arising-from-military-activities-mon-070472/. Accessed 20 May 2023
UNEP (2002) Report of Working Group of Experts on Liability and Compensation for Environmental Damage, Report of the Meeting, 8 August 2002, UNEP/DEPI/L&C Expert Meeting 1/1. https://wedocs.unep.org/. Accessed 20 May 2023
UNEP (2003) Liability and Compensation Regimes Relating To Environmental Damage: A Review, UNEP-Division of Environmental Policy Implementation, December 2003, 54, ISBN Number 92-807-2395-4. https://wedocs.unep.org/. Accessed 20 May 2023
UNGA (2013), Crime prevention and criminal justice responses to illicit trafficking in protected species of wild fauna and flora, Resolution E/RES/2013/40, 17 October 2013 https://documents-dds-ny.un.org/doc/UNDOC/GEN/N13/435/70/PDF/N1343570.pdf?OpenElement. Accessed 19 July 2023
UNGA (2014) Resolutions adopted by the General Assembly at its 69th session, A/69/49 Vol III, 14 February 2014, https://research.un.org/en/docs/ga/quick/regular/69. Accessed 11 July 2023
United Nations (1996) ILC Draft Code of Crimes against the peace and security of mankind (1996) https://legal.un.org/ilc/texts/instruments/english/draft_articles/7_4_1996.pdf. Accessed 25 July 2023
United Nations Compensation Commission (1991) The Claims, https://uncc.ch/claims. Accessed 30 May 2023
United Nations Compensation Commission Governing Council (UNCCGC) (1992) Security Council S/AC.26/1991/7/Rev.1, 17 March 1992. https://uncc.ch/sites/default/files/attachments/S-AC.26-DEC%207%20-.pdf. Accessed 8 June 2023
United Nations Compensation Commission Provisional Rules for Claims Procedures (1992) UN Security Council Documents S/AC 26/1992/10, 26th June 1992. http://unscr.com/en/resolutions/692, Accessed 2 June 2023
United Nations Environment Programme (UNEP) (1978) UNEP Draft Principles 1978, https://wedocs.unep.org/bitstream/handle/20.500.11822/17274/78_05_GC6_report_k7803325.pdf. Accessed 22 May 2023
United Nations General Assembly (UNGA) (2001) Draft Articles on the Prevention of Transboundary Harm from Hazardous Activities 2001 and the Draft Articles on Responsibility of States for Internationally Wrongful Acts 2001, UNGA fifty-third session in 2001, and submitted to the General Assembly as a part of the Commission's report covering the work of that session (A/56/10). https://legal.un.org/ilc/texts/instruments/english/commentaries/9_6_2001.pdf. Accessed 9 June 2023
United Nations Office for Outer Space Affairs (1972) Space Liability Convention 1972, Convention on International Liability for Damage Caused by Space Objects. https://treaties.un.org/doc/Publication/UNTS/Volume%20961/volume-961-I-13810-English.pdf. Accessed 22 May 2023
United Nations Office on Drugs and Crime (UNODC) (2012) Wildlife and Forest Crime Analytic Toolkit. UNODC, Vienna
United Nations Security Council (UNSC) (1991) Resolution 687 1991, adopted at its 2981st Meeting of 3 April 1991, UN Security Council Documents S/AC.26/1991/WP.20, 20 November 1991. http://unscr.com/en/resolutions/691,pdf. Accessed 2 June 2023
UNODC (2016a) CITES and the international trade in endangered species https://www.unodc.org/e4j/en/wildlife-crime/module-2/key-issues/cites-and-the-international-trade-in-endangered-species.html. Accessed 12 July 2023
UNODC (2016b) Organized crime and corruption. https://www.unodc.org/e4j/en/wildlife-crime/module-2/key-issues/organized-crime-and-corruption.html. Accessed 18 July 2023

UNODC (2017) Sharing Electronic Resources and Laws on Crime (SHERLOC) Case Law and Database, https://sherloc.unodc.org/cld/case-law-doc/wildlifecrimetype/usa/2017/united_states_v._yarann_im_et_al..html. Accessed 19 July 2023

UNODC (2019) Wildlife and Forest Crime: Overview 2019 https://www.unodc.org/unodc/en/wildlife-and-forest-crime/overview.html. Accessed 10 July 2023

UNODC (2020) World wildlife crime report: trafficking in protected species. UNODC, Vienna

UNSC (1992) Resolution 692 of 20 May 1991, adopted at the 2987th meeting on 20 May 1991. UN Security Council Documents S/AC 26/1992/10, 26 June 1992, http://unscr.com/en/resolutions/692. Accessed 2 June 2023

UNSC (2004) Decision concerning requests for the late filing of claims taken by the Governing Council of the United Nations Compensation Commission at its 135th meeting, on 11 March 2004, https://uncc.ch/sites/default/files/attachments/S-AC.26-DEC%20219%20%5B2004%5D.pdf. Accessed 19 July 2023

Verheyen R (2005) Climate change damage and international law: prevention, duties and state responsibility. 56–58

Voigt C (2008) State responsibility for climate change damages. NORDIC J Int Law 77:1, 3

Wolfrum R (1990) The unfinished task: CRAMRA and the question of liability. International Challenges, Norway, 10(1):27–31

World Commission on Environment and Development Experts on Environmental Law (1996) "Summary of proposed legal principles for environmental protection and sustainable development" Principles of Environmental Conservation and Sustainable Development: Summary and Survey. http://www.onlyoneplanet.com/Env_principles_WCED1996.htm. Accessed 21 May 2023

Chapter 11
Liabilities and Compensation for Environmental Damage Under the Domestic Legal System

Abstract Man's effort at exploiting nature for his numerous needs has left some indelible scars on the environment. Over the years, environmental legislation has provided provisions to minimise, prevent, punish and remedy the consequences of actions that damage or threaten the environment, public health and public safety. This chapter discusses liabilities for environmental damage under domestic legal system, such as Nigeria, focusing on the nature of environmental damage, for which liabilities may be imposed; the types of environmental liabilities, from both civil and criminal perspectives, under domestic legislation; as well as obstacles to environmental litigation in situations where such liabilities are to be challenged in a court of law.

11.1 Nature of Environmental Damage

Man, in his quest for development, had laid, and has continued to lay, an unrestrained siege to the environment. The degree of assault differs from region to region and from one developmental activity to another. The tempo of this assault increases with every passing day, so much so that it is being speculated that if the present trend continues and is unchecked, man may destroy himself and join the dinosaurs. The result of the above scenario is a high level of environmental damage with its attendant pollution, leading to dire consequences for the survival of both the physical environment and the human environment.

As a result of the debilitating effects of environmental damage, environmental law imposes liabilities on actors for their illegal acts or for the adverse consequences of their lawful activities. Liability rules at the domestic or international level serve a variety of purposes. They may be used to impose sanctions for wrongful conduct or to require corrective measures to restore a given environmental asset to its pre-damage condition. They may also be a form of economic instrument that provides an incentive to encourage compliance with environmental obligations.[1]

[1] Sands (2003), p. 338.

E. Onyeabor, *Environmental Law*, https://doi.org/10.1007/978-3-031-68956-7_11

Finally, they may provide a technique for internalising environmental and other social costs into production processes and other activities in the implementation of the polluter-pays principle.[2] Environmental damage in this case refers to damage to the environment that can lead to possible destruction and includes one of four possible elements within the environment, namely:

(i) fauna, flora, soil, water and climatic factors
(ii) material assets (including archaeological and cultural heritage)
(iii) the landscape and environmental amenity, and
(iv) the interrelationship between the above factors[3]

Although environmental damage as defined above does not include people and their property, it should be noted that it is difficult for environmental damage to occur without, in the final analysis, affecting people and their property, as exemplified by various environmental laws on environmental liability. This is so because environmental damage occasioned by human activities infringes on the rights of others, incurring liability on the part of the offender. These in turn become a veritable source of claims by victims of such environmental damage.

However, for there to be a valid cause of action that may result in an enforceable claim for damages, there must be rights guaranteed and protected by law, a breach of which amounts to environmental liability. Environmental liability may arise where there is non-compliance with the provisions of environmental laws by the defendant/s or where a person suffers environmental damage caused by acts of the defendant/s. Damage resulting therefrom could be:

(a) loss of life or personal injury;
(b) loss of or damage to property;
(c) loss or damage by impairment of the environment;
(d) the costs of preventive measures and any loss or damage caused by preventive measures. . . .[4]

---

[2] Ibid.

[3] Sands (2003), p. 338.

[4] Convention on Civil Liability for Damage Resulting from Activities Dangerous to the Environment (Luguano Convention) (1993), art 2(7) (a)–(d). The Convention was signed by the member states of the Council of Europe on 21 June 1993. The Convention provides for the possibility of accession by non-member states. In fact, a dangerous activity carried out in one country may threaten to cause or indeed cause damage in another country. The problems are, therefore, not necessarily confined to the territory of the Council of Europe member states. See European Treaty Series (1993).

11.2 Civil Liability for Environmental Damage

There are two ways through which civil liabilities may arise. The first is through the application of common law tort. The second is through a violation of the provisions of relevant environmental statutes.

11.2.1 Civil Liability Under Common Law Tort

Common law torts were the precursors of codified civil liabilities and had created a number of tortuous liabilities.[5] Tortuous liability, according to Winfield, 'arises from the breach of a duty primarily fixed by law; this duty is towards persons generally and its breach is repressible by an action for unliquidated damage'.[6] It is on the basis of the above premise that the various tortuous liabilities were discussed as platforms for civil liabilities for environmental damage. The common law torts that relate to the discussion on civil liability are:

(a) Tort of nuisance
(b) The rule in *Ryland v Fletcher* and
(c) Tort of negligence

11.2.1.1 Tort of Nuisance

A tort of nuisance is an unreasonable use by man of his land to the detriment of his neighbour.[7] "It is also an act or omission that is an interference with, disturbance of or annoyance to a person in the exercise or enjoyment of a right . . ."[8] where the right of a person interfered with is a right belonging to him as a member of the public, it is a public nuisance, and where what is disturbed is the ownership or occupation of land or of some easement, profit, or other right used or enjoyed in connection with land, then it is private nuisance.[9]

A public nuisance is an unlawful act or omission in the discharge of a legal duty, which act or omission endangers the lives, safety, health, property or comfort of the public. According to Karibi-Whyte, J.S.C. (as he then was), in the case of *Adediran and Ors v Interland Transport Ltd*,[10] a public nuisance is one that inflicts damage, injury or inconvenience to the generality of the population or upon all of a class who

---

[5] Such as nuisance, the rule in Ryland v Fletcher, trespass and negligence.

[6] Rogers (2006), p. 50.

[7] Court of Appeal in the case of *Ojo Eholor v Idemudia Idahosa* (1992) 2 NWLR (pt 223) 327.

[8] Supreme Court of Nigeria in the case of *Ipadeola v Oshowole* (1987) 3 NWLR (pt 59) 18.

[9] *Ipadeola v Oshowole* (1987), p. 18.

[10] (1991) 9 NWLR (pt 214) 164.

come within its ambit. In an action under public nuisance, a private individual must establish that he had sustained particular damage other than and beyond the general inconvenience and injury suffered by the public and that the particular damage is direct and substantial. A failure to show this will lead to the action being dismissed by the court.

Thus, in the case of *A S Amos and 4 Others v Shell B. P Nig. Ltd.*,[11] the plaintiff claimed general and special damages from the defendant for the 'unlawful damage caused by the defendants by deliberately and negligently blocking, for about three months, the Kolo Creek new water way'. The Supreme Court dismissed the action on the ground that, *inter alia*, the plaintiffs failed to prove that they suffered damage over and above that suffered by the general public.[12]

However, in the case of *Ejowhomu v Edok-Eter Mandilas Ltd*,[13] the plaintiff who sued the defendant for blocking a public road, which consequently barred access to his poultry farm and caused him some loss, recovered compensation. The court found that the plaintiff's injury was 'beyond the general inconvenience and injury suffered by the public'. Also in the case of *Savage v Akinrinnade*,[14] the defendant caused a public nuisance by blocking a public highway. The plaintiff's action was based on the fact that the blockage interfered particularly with the access of the staff, parents and pupils to his school. The court held that this amounted to particular damage to the plaintiff over and above that suffered by other users of the highway.

At times, an action for public nuisance may be commenced in a representative capacity. The Supreme Court, in the case of *Oganioba v Oghene and Ors*,[15] laid the following grounds for such action:

(i) there must be a common interest;
(ii) there must be a common grievance; and
(iii) the relief claimed must be beneficial to all.

In the case of *Shell Petroleum Development Company Limited v Graham Otoko and Ors*,[16] the plaintiffs/respondents sued for injurious affection to and deprivation of the use of the Andoni River and creeks as a result of the spillage of crude oil caused by the negligence of the appellant/defendant. They also claimed, in the alternative, for nuisance and mandatory injunction to restrain the defendant/appellant and its agents from further committing unlawful acts. They further claimed damages for the desecration of their juju shrines, for polluted drinking water and for the destruction of fish and other living creatures in the river. The lower court found in favour of the plaintiffs and awarded the sum of ₦491,700 as damages. The Court of

[11] (1977) 6 SC 109.

[12] The same reason was applied by the Supreme Court to dismiss the claims in *Adediran & Ors v Interland Transport Ltd* (1991).

[13] (1986) 5 NWLR (pt 39), 1, or (1986) 9 S.C. 41 at 107–118.

[14] (1964) All NLR, 238.

[15] (1961) 1 SC. NLR 115.

[16] (1990) 6 NWLR (pt 159), p. 693.

Appeal, in upholding the appeal, held inter alia that the six villages that were represented were not one community and that the spillage that was injuriously affecting the fishermen, farmers, persons bathing and washing in the Andoni River and adjoining creeks and persons using the river and adjoining creeks for cassava processing showed a diversity of interests, that there was no joint tort and that the damage caused to each of them could only be personal to each.[17]

A nuisance is private if it does not cause damage or inconvenience to the public at large but interferes with a person's use or enjoyment of land or of some right connected to the land in his possession.[18] To this end, a private nuisance may be caused by a person who, although doing a lawful act on his land, produces, by reason of such lawful act, consequences that are not confined to his own land but extends to the land of his neighbour by encroaching upon his neighbour's land, or building, or by unduly interfering with his neighbour in the comfort and convenient enjoyment of his land.[19]

In the case of *Ojo Eholor v Idahosa*,[20] the respondent/plaintiff built his house in line with the building regulations. When, however, the appellant/defendant built his, the building was high, and having overdeveloped his land by building the house wall to wall, it caused rainwater from his roof to drip on the roof and onto the premises of the respondent's house, causing deterioration and a considerable reduction in the value of the house. The lower court awarded ₦56,429 and ₦43,671 as special and general damages, respectively, on the ground that the appellant's/defendant's action constituted a nuisance. On appeal, the Court of Appeal dismissed the appeal and upheld the judgment of the trial court.

At times in the case of private nuisance, the plaintiff need not prove physical damage to his property. All he needs to prove is that there was substantial interference with the use or enjoyment of his land. In *M K O Abiola v Felix Ijeoma*,[21] the parties occupied adjoining premises in Surulere Lagos. The plaintiff complained that excessive noise made by the defendant's chickens in the early hours of the morning disturbed his sleep that and the nauseating smell emanating from the pens interfered with his comfort. The court found that the plaintiff had suffered more than a trifling inconvenience than an ordinary person living in that part of Surulere. The injunction sought was granted, although the plaintiff suffered no physical damage.

---

[17] The case of *Adeniran and Ors v Interland Transport Ltd* (1991) was also dismissed by the Supreme Court on the same ground. However, by virtue of this case, it is no longer necessary to join the Attorney General (AG) in relator actions under section 6(6)(b) of the Constitution of the Federal Republic of Nigeria, 1979, in *pari materia* with section 6(6)(b) of the Constitution of the Federal Republic of Nigeria, 1999, as amended, and Cap C3 Laws of the Federation of Nigeria (LFN) 2004.

[18] Tort Law of Enugu State (2004), s. 235.

[19] Akpata J.C.A. in *Abdullah v Governor of Lagos State* (1989) NWLR (pt 97), 358, and applied in the case of *Ojo Eholor v Idahosa* (1992) and in the case of *Ige v Taylor Woodrow Nig. Ltd.* (1963) LLR, 140.

[20] *Ojo Eholor v Idahosa* (1992), p. 327.

[21] (1970) ALL NLR 569.

However, in arriving at this conclusion, when no physical damage is shown, the court must consider the locality in question in order to establish the standard for the particular locality. The defendant will be liable only if his conduct or the nuisance created by him falls short of the standard of that locality. This is because the court considers a nuisance not merely based on elegant and dainty attitudes and habits of living but according to plain and sober and simple notions obtaining among the members of the community. Therefore, the inconvenience suffered must be substantial, and substantial interference is given an objective construction.

In *Tebite v Nigeria Marine and Trading Co. Ltd.*,[22] the plaintiff, a legal practitioner with an office at 11 Robert Road Warri (a mixed-use zone), succeeded in an action in nuisance against the defendants, who run a workshop for boat building and repair at 9 Robert Road, Warri. The defendants, by operating their machines continuously for several hours a day, persistently caused to emit from their workshop loud and excessive noise and noxious fumes, which diffused to the plaintiff's premises and caused him much discomfort and inconvenience. The court held that the noise was completely out of character with that ordinarily produced by ordinary people in any neighbourhood in the country.

The basis for the above decision, and other decisions, is that a just balance must be struck between the rights of the defendant and those of the plaintiff to the undisturbed enjoyment of their property; it is a compromise that borders on social coexistence. It is immaterial whether the plaintiff brought himself to the nuisance, that is, that the act complained of was already in existence even before the plaintiff commenced his occupation of the land. What is important is that the plaintiff had suffered some physical damage to his property. This was buttressed in the case of *St. Helen's Smelting Company v Tipping*,[23] where the defendant's plea that the locality in question was devoted to industries was rejected, and the plaintiff recovered damages.

Again, the fact that the act of the defendant is usually in the locality or is beneficial or useful to the community will not in itself act as a bar or deny the plaintiff the claims sought. In the case of *Rushmer v Polsue and Alfieri Ltd*,[24] the court granted the plaintiff's claim for injunction to restrain the use by the defendants of their printing presses at night, even though the premises were in the printing area of London. Again, in the case of *Bellew v Cement Co. Ltd*,[25] the court was unmoved by the defendants' argument that their cement production was vital to the public interest at a time when building was an urgent public necessity. While granting the injunction sought,[26] the court held that the argument that the plaintiff should put up with the harm caused because it is beneficial to the community as a whole was

[22] (1971) UILR, 432. Also in the case of *Moore v Nnado* (1967) FNLR 156.

[23] (1865) 11 ER 1483.

[24] (1906) 1 Ch 234 (1907) AC 121.

[25] (1948) R 61.

[26] Closure of the factory for 3 months.

unacceptable. According to the court, that would amount to requiring him to carry alone the burden of an activity for which many others benefit.

11.2.1.2 The Rule in *Ryland v Fletcher*

Another means through which environmental damage is awarded under common law tort is by the application of the rule in *Ryland v Fletcher.*[27] Under this rule, a defendant who, in the course of the non-natural use of his land, accumulates thereon, for his own purpose, anything that is likely to do mischief, if it escapes, is liable for all the direct damage to or interference with the use of the land of another which results from the escape of the thing from his land.[28] Things likely to do mischief on escape include not only inherently dangerous materials, such as explosives, gas, petrol, fire or petroleum chemicals, but also reasonably safe things that become dangerous when accumulated in large quantities, such as water, crude oil, sewage and slag heaps.

For the rule to apply, the question is whether the thing was dangerous under the circumstances of the particular case and not whether the thing was dangerous *per se*. In the case of *Oladehin v Continental Textile Mills Ltd*,[29] industrial waste accumulated by the defendant escaped from its factory premises into the uncompleted house of the plaintiff, flooding it. It was found that the factory was in the habit of storing large quantities of water on the premises in order to facilitate its job. This was deemed to be a special use of the premises. The defendants were held liable under the rule in *Ryland v Fletcher.*

Also, in the case of *Machine Umudje v Shell BP Petroleum Development Company*,[30] oil escaped from the defendants' premises, destroying the plaintiff's fish and fishpond. The oil was crude oil waste previously accumulated in a pit burrowed by, and in the control of, the defendants. The rule was applied to hold the defendants liable.

Besides the accumulation of dangerous substances, for the rule to apply, the plaintiff must also show that the defendant engaged in a non-natural use of the land. A 'non-natural user' was classically defined in the case of *Rickards v Lothian*[31] as follows: 'a non-natural user must be some special use bringing with it increased danger to others and must not merely be ordinary use of the land or such a use as is proper for the general benefit of the community'.[32]

---

[27] (1868) LR H.L. 330.

[28] Ibid.

[29] (1977) 2 SC, 23.

[30] (1975) 9–11 SC. 155.

[31] (1913) A.C. 263 at 280.

[32] *Rickards v Lothian* (1913) 263 at 280.

To this end, in the case of *San Ikpede v Shell BP Development Company Ltd*,[33] where the plaintiffs suffered damage as a result of the escape of crude oil from the pipelines of the defendant, the court held that laying pipelines carrying crude oil through swamp land is a non-natural use of land.

There is no objective universal test for determining 'non-natural' use as it varies from place to place and from time to time. Therefore, the court, in so determining, has to look not only at the thing or activity in isolation but also at the place and manner in which it is maintained and its relation to its surroundings. This proposition was applied in the case of *Rainham Chemical Works Ltd v Belvedere Fish Guano Co.*,[34] wherein the court took the view that the defendants manufacturing explosives, in peacetime, constituted a non-natural use of land. However, in the case of *Read v Lyons & Co Ltd*,[35] the court expressed the view that manufacturing explosives in time of war for the purpose of defeating the King's enemies was not a non-natural use of the land. It has to be borne in mind that a defendant may escape liability by proving that:

(i) It has statutory authority, provided that the public authority kept or accumulated the substance in their efforts to provide public service, but it can be found to be negligent if the substance is not properly kept.[36]
(ii) The escape was caused by a deliberate act of a third party or stranger which could not reasonably have been anticipated by the defendant.[37]
(iii) The escape was caused by an act of God in circumstances in which no human foresight can provide against and of which human prudence is not bound to recognize the possibility.

However, in claiming that the escape was caused by a deliberate act of a third party or stranger which could not reasonably have been anticipated by the defendant, this defence may fail in situations where he failed to take appropriate steps to guard against actions of trespassers and other third parties; equipment failure or natural events, the defence of deliberate act of a third party or stranger, or a break in the chain of events shall not avail him.

In the case of *Empress Cars (Arbertillery) Ltd v National Rivers Authority*,[38] the defendants maintained an oil storage tank on their site. A bund wall protected the tank. Standing outside the bund was a much smaller oil drum, which was connected to the oil tank by a rubber hose. The open/close valve on the tank was not lockable, and the site security was poor. A trespasser entered the site and opened the valve on the oil tank. Oil flowed from the tank to the drum, which rapidly filled up and

[33] (1973) MWSJ 61.

[34] (1921) 12 AC 465.

[35] (1947) AC 156 at 168.

[36] As in *Green v Chelsea Waterwork Co* (1894) 70 LF, 547.

[37] As in *Shell Petroleum Development Company Limited v Otoko and Ors* (1990) 693, where the defendant/appellant successfully raised the defence that the act of a third party caused the spillage.

[38] [1998] Env LR, 369.

overflowed. The escaped oil found its way into the surface water drains and, from there, entered the river. The defendants argued that it had not caused the oil pollution but had merely created circumstances whereby a trespasser could enter the site and turned on the oil storage tank, which caused the pollution. The defendant further submitted that the act of the trespasser broke the chain of causation linking the defendant to the pollution and absolved it of liability. The court rejected this defence and found the defendant liable.

Again, where the nature of an intervening act of a third party is clearly foreseeable, the defendant will not escape liability by relying on the act of a third party. In the case of *National Rivers Authority v Yorkshire Water Service Ltd*,[39] the defendants were responsible for a sewer into which an unidentified industrial customer of theirs had discharged solvents. It was held that there was sufficient evidence on which the court could conclude that the defendants were *prima facie* guilty of causing the pollution.

11.2.1.3 Tort of Negligence

Negligence is another common law tort that is usually applied in order to obtain compensation for environmental damage. Here, the plaintiff maintains that the defendant owed him a duty of care and that the duty had been breached through either the negligent performance of the duty or omission to perform such duty. To sustain an action in negligence, it must be shown that the negligence found by the court is the proximate cause of the damage, and where the proximate cause is the malicious act of a third person, against which precautions would have been inoperative, the defendant is not liable in the absence of a finding that either he instigated it or he ought to have foreseen and provided against it.[40]

In the case of *Chief G.B.A. Tiebo VII and Ors v Shell Petroleum Development Company Limited*,[41] the plaintiffs succeeded in proving negligence against the defendant when the defendant's act caused a spill of crude oil into the Peremabiri creek in Yenogoa, causing damages. The court awarded the sum of ₦6 million as damages.

Where it is impossible to prove negligence, the plaintiff can rely on the doctrine of *res ipsa loquitur*. This doctrine is applicable to actions for injury by negligence where no proof of such negligence is required beyond the accident itself.[42] This act amounts to shifting the burden of proof.

---

[39] [1995] 1 All E.R. 225.

[40] As in the case of *Shell Petroleum Development Company Limited v Otoko and Ors* (1990) at 725.

[41] (1996) 4 NWLR, (pt 445), 657.

[42] Per Obaseki (J.S.C., as he then was) in *Management Enterprises v Otusanya* (1987) 2 NWLR (pt 55), 181.

Put in its simplest terms, the doctrine simply means 'the fact speaks for itself'. The pendulum upon which this doctrine revolves was stated by Erle, C.J., in the case of *Scott v London and St Katherine Docks Co*,[43] where he stated as follows:

> Where the thing is shown to be under the management of the defendant or his servants, and the accident is such as in the ordinary course of things does not happen if those who have the management use proper care, it affords reasonable evidence in the absence of explanation by the defendants, that the accident arose from want of care.

In all civil matters, it is trite law that the evidential burden lies within the doorsteps of the plaintiff. Where this burden is not discharged, the claim sought may be lost. Environmental cases, by their very nature, require the application of scientific knowledge for successful litigation. Here, the plaintiff is required to prove that there is a correlation between the harm or damage suffered and the act of the defendant/s. This is usually replete with problems as plaintiffs most of the time fail to discharge this evidential burden.[44] By this act, the pollution victim is left without a remedy, not minding that he had suffered a wrong, a negation of one of the time-honoured maxims of equity: equity will not suffer a wrong to be without a remedy.

To this end, in recognition of the difficulty that pollution victims experience in gathering such evidence and in order to achieve an environmental end and punish the polluter for his polluting actions, the judiciary is urged to whittle down the evidential burden of proof of causation. This should be reversed, and plaintiffs should no longer have to prove a causal connection between the polluting act and the damage suffered. This is where the doctrine of *res ipsa loquitur* can come into play.

It should, however, be noted that it is possible for a plaintiff to institute an action under one head of common law tort and another head in the alternative. This is because a single act may give rise to liability under the rule in *Ryland v Fletcher*[45] and under negligence. In this situation, if things within the defendant's control are dangerous things and likely to escape and do damage, any resulting damage constitutes liability for negligence on the part of the owner.[46] Also, an action may be commenced based on nuisance and, as an alternative, on negligence.[47]

11.2.2 Civil Liability Under Statutes

A number of domestic environmental statutes have provisions for environmental liability. They are:

---

[43] (1865) 3 H&C, 590.

[44] This is one of the obstacles facing a litigant in Nigeria in claims for environmental damage (these obstacles are discussed below).

[45] *Ryland v Fletcher* (1868).

[46] *Shell Petroleum Development Company Limited v Otoko and Ors* (1990) at 724.

[47] *Shell Petroleum Development Company Limited v Otoko and Ors* (1990) at 724 and also in *G B A Tiebo VII v Shell Petroleum Development Company Limited* (n 41) at 657.

(a) Oil Pipelines Act 1956
(b) Harmful Wastes (Special Criminal Provisions) Act 1988
(c) Nigerian Urban and Regional Planning Act 1992
(d) Nigerian Minerals and Mining Act 2007
(e) Petroleum Industry Act 2021

These laws provide various liability and compensation for damages to the environment.

11.2.2.1 Oil Pipelines Act 1956

The Oil Pipelines Act (OPA) was enacted in 1956 as Act No. 31 and was amended by Act No. 24 of 1965. Its commencement period was 4 October 1956.[48] The Act,[49] in section 11(1), (2) (3) and (4), provides for the rights and obligations of a holder of a licence. Such holder is enjoined to 'take all reasonable steps to avoid unnecessary damage to any land entered upon and any buildings, crops or profitable trees thereon, shall make compensation to the owners or occupiers for any damage done under such authority and not made good'.[50]

Section 11(5) (a) (b) and (c) of the Act provides for persons to be entitled to the payment of compensation in the event of damage by a holder of an oil pipeline licence. It provides as follows: a holder of a licence shall pay compensation to:

(a) any person whose land or interest in land (whether or not it is land respect of which the licence has been granted) is injuriously affected by the exercise of the rights conferred by the licence, for any such injurious affection not otherwise made good;[51] and
(b) any person suffering damage by reason of any neglect on the part of the holder or his agents, servants or workmen to protect, maintain or repair any work structure or thing executed under the licence, for any such damage not otherwise made good;[52] and
(c) any person suffering damage (other than on account of his own default or on account of the malicious act of a third person) as a consequence of any breakage of or leakage from the pipeline or an ancillary installation, for any such damage not otherwise made good.[53]

Besides the person/s mentioned in section 11(5) of the Act, where the interests injuriously affected are those of a local community, the court may order the

[48] Currently retained as Cap 07 LFN 2004.

[49] The Act is saved under the Petroleum Industry Act 2021, s. 311(9)(c), Act No. 6 2021, Federal Republic of Nigeria Official Gazette Lagos, No. 42, Vol. 108, 27 August 2021.

[50] Oil Pipelines Act 1956 (n 48), s. 6.

[51] Ibid., s. 11(5)(a).

[52] Oil Pipelines Act (1956), s. 11(5)(b).

[53] Ibid., s. 11(5)(c).

compensation to be paid to any chief, headman or member of that community on behalf of such community or to be paid in accordance with a scheme of distribution approved by the court or to be paid into a fund to be administered by a person approved by the court on trust for application to the general, social or educational benefit and advancement of that community or any section thereof.[54]

In furtherance of the provisions of section 11 on compensation, section 20-(2) provides that the court shall award such compensation as it considers appropriate, having regard to:

(a) any damage done to any buildings, crops or profitable trees by the holder of the licence in the exercise of the rights conferred by the licence;[55] and
(b) any disturbance caused by the holder in the exercise of such rights;[56] and
(c) any damage suffered by any person by reason of any neglect on the part of the holder or his agents, servants or workmen to protect, maintain or repair any work, structure or thing executed under the licence;[57] and
(d) any damage suffered by any person (other than as stated in such subsection (5) of this section) as a consequence of any breakage of or leakage from the pipeline or an ancillary installation;[58] and
(e) loss (if any) in value of the land or interests in land by reason of the exercise of the rights as aforesaid, and also having regard to any compensation already awarded in accordance with subsection (1) of this section.[59]

In determining the loss in value of the land or interest inland of a claimant arising from any damage, the court shall assess the value of the land or the interests injuriously affected at the date immediately before the grant of the licence and shall assess the residual value to the claimant of the same land or interests consequent upon and at the date of the grant of the licence and shall determine the loss suffered by the claimant as the difference between the values so found, if such residual value is a lesser sum.[60] 'It should be noted that no compensation shall be awarded in respect of unoccupied land as defined in the Land Use Act...'.[61]

In recent years, the courts have lent a voice with regard to the quest for environmental protection in Nigeria. In the case of *Centre for Oil Pollution Watch v Nigerian National Petroleum Corporation*,[62] the Supreme Court of Nigeria, in its judgment, considered the provisions of Article 24 of the African Charter on Peoples

[54] Ibid., s. 21.
[55] Ibid., s. 20(2)(a).
[56] Ibid., s. 20(2)(b).
[57] Ibid., s. 20(2)(c).
[58] Ibid., s. 20(2)(d).
[59] Ibid., s. 20(2)(e).
[60] Oil Pipelines Act (1956), s. 20(3).
[61] Ibid., s. 20(4).
[62] [2019] 5 NWLR [pt 1666] 518.

and Human Rights (ACPHR) (Ratification and Enforcement) Act,[63] sections 20 and 33(1) of the Constitution of the Federal Republic of Nigeria (CFRN) 1999 (as amended),[64] section 17(4) of the Oil Pipelines (OPA) Act[65] and regulation 9(a)(ii) and (b)(ii) and (iii) of the Oil and Gas Pipeline Regulations of 1995[66] to arrive at its decision.

While Article 24 of the ACPHR (Ratification and Enforcement) Act provides that 'all peoples shall have the right to a general satisfactory environment favourable to their development', section 20 of CFRN 1999 provides that 'the State shall protect and improve the environment and safeguard the water, air and land, forest and wild life of the country'. Section 17(4) of OPA, on the other hand, provides as follows:

> Every licence shall be subject to the provisions contained in this Act as in force at the date of its grant and to such regulations concerning public safety, the avoidance of interference with works of public utility in, over and under the land included in the licence and the prevention of pollution of such land or any waters as may from time to time be force.

The court noted that regulation 9(a)(ii) and (b)(ii) and (iii) of the Oil and Gas Pipeline Regulations of 1995 was made pursuant to the provisions of section 17(4) of OPA and that a combined reading of all the above provisions, that is, section 24 of the ACPHR (Ratification and Enforcement) Act, section 20 of CFRN 1999 and section 17(4) of OPA, with regulation 9(a)(ii) and (b)(ii) and (iii), would reveal that they require the oil pipeline licence holder to institute mechanisms for the prevention of accidents like crude oil spill and for remedial action for the protection of the environment and the control of accidental discharge from the pipeline.

11.2.2.2 Harmful Wastes (Special Criminal Provisions) Act (HWSCP Act) 1988

The Harmful Wastes (Special Criminal Provisions) (HWSCP) Act 1988[67] has provisions for civil liability under section 12. This section provides that where any damage has been caused by any harmful waste that has been deposited or dumped on any land, etc., any person who deposited, dumped or imported the harmful waste or caused the harmful waste to be so deposited, dumped or imported shall be liable for the damage suffered by the victim. Damage in this case includes death or injury to a person, including any diseases and any impairment of one's physical or mental condition.[68] However, claims for damages shall not avail any person where the damage:

---

[63] Cap A9 Laws of the Federal Republic of Nigeria (LFN) 2004.

[64] Cap C23 LFN 2004.

[65] Oil Pipelines Act (1956).

[66] S.I. No. 14 of 1995.

[67] Cap H 1 LFN 2004.

[68] HWSCP Act (1988), s. 12(2).

(a) was due wholly to the fault of the person who suffered it, or
(b) was suffered by a person who voluntarily accepted the risk thereof.[69]

11.2.2.3 Nigerian Urban and Regional Planning Act (NURP Act) 1992

Under the Nigerian Urban and Regional Planning Act (NURPA) 1992,[70] a liability may arise for failure to:

(i) obtain a planning or development permit before the commencement of development of land.
(ii) observe necessary planning regulations, especially issue of zoning, as may be set out by appropriate planning authority.

NURPA 1992 sets out procedures for the establishment of various authorities charged with land use control.[71] It also sets out various methods for land use control, the non-compliance of which may result in liability on the part of the landowner or developer.[72] Methods employed by the planning authorities include the following measures:

(i) determining what is development and what activities amount to building, engineering or mining operations;
(ii) enforcing zoning policy and
(iii) ensuring compliance with other planning regulations by the developers.

The importance of determining whether a developmental activity amounts to a building, engineering or mining operation is that once an activity falls under any of the mentioned, such activity shall be considered development and shall not be commenced until a development or planning permit is first obtained from the appropriate Development Control Department.[73] Again, liability may also arise where a landowner or occupier engages in an environmentally significant change in the use of land or building.

The bottom line is that under NURPA 1992, a developer that does not obtain a development or planning permit before commencing development or a landowner or occupier of any land[74] or building that engages in an environmentally significant change in the use of land or building incurs liability.[75]

---

[69] Ibid., s. 12(1)(a), (b).

[70] Cap N138 LFN 2004.

[71] Such as the Urban and Regional Commission, Board and Authority provided under NURPA (1992), s. 5(a), (b) and (c) and the Development Control Department under NURPA (1992), s. 27.

[72] As set out under NURPA (1992), ss. 28–76.

[73] NURPA (1992), ss. 28, 29, 30 and 33.

[74] Ibid., s. 28.

[75] Ibid., s. 91.

In addition, where a land developer has obtained a development or planning permit, it shall comply with the terms and conditions contained in such permit.[76] To this end, a developer must observe the planning regulations applicable to the area where the land is situated. Where a developer fails to comply with these regulations,[77] a cause of action may arise against him. This is so because any aggrieved person or group of persons may bring an action against him.

For instance, in the case of *Ipadiola and Anor v Oshowole and Anor*,[78] the defendants built a house in front of the plaintiffs' house, which not only blocked the plaintiff's access to the highway but also obstructed the easement of light, contrary to building regulations. Again, in *Abiola v Ijeoma*,[79] the defendant built a poultry farm in a single-use residential area against the planning regulation of the area. In all the former cases, the court granted the injunction sought, while in the *Abiola* case, the planning authority ordered the demolition of the pens.

Developing land contrary to the zoning policy of the area in which the land is situated may give rise to liability on the part of the developer. Through this policy, the rights of citizens are protected from abuse and any infringement is protected by law. The purpose of zoning is to achieve purposeful utilisation of land in the interest or for the general welfare of the locality in which the land is situated. Once a developer encroaches on the rights of others, an actionable wrong may arise, such as in the following scenarios:

(i) building on a place designated as open space to the annoyance of other land owners within the vicinity;[80]
(ii) denial of access to public utilities such as a high way;[81]
(iii) using a building or land against the use designated for such area[82] and
(iv) cause damages to property of other land owners;[83]

These contraventions form a veritable avenue for environmental claims. Other areas where infringements on planning regulations may give rise to a cause of action include non-adherence to setbacks and set-offs,[84] easements[85] and overdevelopment.[86]

---

[76] Ibid., s. 35.

[77] Such as setbacks, set-offs, building heights, developable space, easements, covenants, etc. (see Appendix I for details).

[78] *Ipadiola and Anor v Oshowole and Anor* (1987) 376 at 389; see also the case of *Ojo Eholor v Idemudia Idahosa* (1992) 327.

[79] *Abiola v Ijeoma* (1970), 569.

[80] *Ademola v Rutili and Ors* (unreported) Suit No. LD/784/84, delivered on 21 September 1985.

[81] *Anthony Savage and Anor v Akinrinade* (1964) 238.

[82] *Karagulamus v Kolawole Oyesile* (1973) 3UILR, I. Also, as in *Abiola v Ijeoma* (1970).

[83] *Oladehin v Continental Textiles Ltd* (1977), 23.

[84] *Defactor Bakeries & Catering Services Ltd v Ajilore and Anor* (1974) All NLR 385.

[85] *Metro Gas Ltd v Eferakaye* (2000) 14 NWLR (pt 686) 1.

[86] *Anthony Savage v Akinrinade* (1964), 238.

11.2.2.4 Nigerian Mineral and Mining Act 2007

The Nigerian Mineral and Mining Act 2007,[87] on the other hand, deals with the protection of the environment against abuses resulting from mining operations, the violation of which may lead to a cause of action. For instance, section 123[88] prohibits the pollution of water courses in the area within the mining lease or beyond that area and requires the licensee to make sure that the water used does not contain injurious substances in quantities likely to prove detrimental to animal or vegetation life when the water leaves the mining area in which it has been used.[89]

Again, 'no person shall make or permit any other person to make, without the permission of the Mines Inspectorate Department, any alterations in the water supply of any land so as to prejudicially affect the water supply enjoyed by any other person or land'.[90] Also, the Act[91] further enjoins holders of a mining title to exercise their rights under the licence or lease, having regard to the effect of mining operations on the environment, and to take such steps as may be necessary to prevent pollution of the environment as a result of the mining operation.

Under the Act,[92] an offence is deemed to have been committed where a person conducts exploration or mines minerals or carries out quarrying operations otherwise than in accordance with the provisions of the Act.[93] Such a person shall, on conviction, have his licence revoked and, on conviction at first instance, pay a fine of not less than ₦20,000,000 and be subject to imprisonment of not less 5 years if the offence is a continuing one, whether or not it is a first offence; in addition, the person convicted shall be liable to a fine of ₦20,000 for each day during which the offence continues.[94] In the end, a licensee or lessee shall pay compensation to the owner or occupier who suffers damage as a result of the pollution of any source of water used for domestic or other purposes, or as a consequence of the exploration of or the operations carried out in connection with the property, for any damage not otherwise made good.[95]

[87] Act No. 20 2007, Federal Republic of Nigeria Official Gazette Lagos.

[88] Nigerian Minerals and Mining Act (2007).

[89] Ibid., s. 124.

[90] Ibid., s. 127.

[91] Nigerian Minerals and Mining Act (2007), s. 111.

[92] Nigerian Minerals and Mining Act (2007).

[93] Ibid., s. 131(1)(a).

[94] Ibid., s. 133.

[95] Ibid., s. 125 (b).

11.2.2.5 Petroleum Industry Act 2021

The Petroleum Industry Act 2021 (PIA 2021)[96] has some provisions for liability and compensation. Under section 101(2), a person shall not in the course of petroleum operations:

(a) injure or destroy a tree or object which is of commercial value or the object of veneration to the people resident within the license or lease area;
(b) damage or destroy any building or property; or
(c) disturb or damage the surface of the land or any other rights to any person who owns or is in lawful occupation of the surface area covered by the license or lease.

Where a licensee or lessee causes any damage, in contravention of the provisions under section 101(2) of the Act,[97] liability will arise against such person, and he shall be liable to pay fair and adequate compensation to the persons or communities directly affected by the damage or injury.[98] The amount payable shall be determined by the Commission.[99] The payment of compensation shall be effected within 30 days; in the case of failure to do so, the Commission[100] may be compelled to apply sanctions against the licensee or lessee.[101]

The Act mandates a licensee or lessee that engages in upstream and midstream petroleum operations to, within (a) 1 year from the date of effectivity or (b) 6 months after the grant of the applicable licence or lease, 'submit for approval an environmental management plan in respect of the projects which requires Environmental Impact Assessment to the Commission or Authority,[102] as the case may be'.[103] The environmental management plan shall be in accordance with extant Acts.[104] As a way of eliciting compliance and as a means of protecting and managing the environment, it is provided under the Act that as a condition for the grant of a licence or lease and prior to the approval of the environmental management plan by the Commission or Authority, a licensee or lessee shall pay a prescribed financial contribution to an environmental remediation fund established by the Commission

[96] Act No. 6, 2021, Federal Republic of Nigeria Official Gazette Lagos, No. 42, Vol. 108, 27 August 2021.

[97] Nigerian Minerals and Mining Act (2007).

[98] Petroleum Industry Act (2021), s. 101(3).

[99] Ibid., s. 101(4).

[100] 'Commission' means the Nigerian Upstream Petroleum Regulatory Commission established under the Petroleum Industry Act (2021), s. 4. See Petroleum Industry Act (2021), s. 318.

[101] Petroleum Industry Act (2021), s. 101(5).

[102] 'Authority' means the Nigerian Midstream and Downstream Petroleum Regulatory Authority established under the Petroleum Industry Act (2021), s. 29. See Petroleum Industry Act (2021), s. 318.

[103] Petroleum Industry Act (2021), s. 102(1).

[104] Ibid., s. 102(2).

or Authority, as the case may be, for the rehabilitation or management of negative environmental impacts with respect to the licensee or lessee.[105]

Where the licensee or lessee fails to rehabilitate or manage or is unable to undertake the rehabilitation or management of any negative impact on the environment, the Commission or Authority, as the case may be, may, upon written notice to the holder of the licence or lease, apply the fund to rehabilitate or manage the negative environmental impacts.[106]

In addition to these express provisions for liability and compensation, the Act also empowers the Commission or the Authority, as the case may be, to impose administrative penalties against any person for prescribed contraventions of the Act, regulations or an order made pursuant to the Act.[107] The conditions for the imposition and operation of such penalties are provided under section 231(2)–(50) of the Act.

In the event of environmental damage arising from the flaring of gas, the Petroleum Industry Act contains some provisions. Under section 104(1), penalties are imposed in the case of gas flaring, except as permitted by the Commission or Authority under section 104(1)(a)–(c). The penalties shall be in the form of a fine, and money recovered by the Commission from such penalties shall be for the purposes of environmental remediation and the relief of the host communities of the settlor[108] in which the penalties are levied.[109]

In addition to these laws, a number of national environmental regulations[110] have introduced the polluter-pays principle as another means through which environmental pollution victims may be compensated and the rehabilitation of the environment *per se* may be achieved. For instance, regulation 13 of the National Environmental (Mining and Process of Coal, Ores and Industrial Minerals) Regulations, 2009, provides that the collection, treatment, transportation and final disposal of wastes within the specified standards and guidelines shall be the responsibility of the facility generating the waste. In addition, in the event of pollution resulting in an impact on the environment, whether socio-economically or health wise, the facility shall, as specified in Schedule 4 to these Regulations, be responsible for:

(a) the cost of clean-up;
(b) remediation;
(c) reclamation;

---

[105] Ibid., s. 103(1).

[106] Ibid., s. 103(4).

[107] Ibid., s. 231(1).

[108] A settler is a holder of an interest in a petroleum prospecting licence or petroleum mining lease whose area of operation is located in or appurtenant to any community or communities. See Petroleum Industry Act (2021), s. 318.

[109] Petroleum Industry Act (2021), s. 104(4).

[110] These Regulations (33 in number) were made by the Minister in charge of environmental matters pursuant to the National Environmental Standards and Regulations Enforcement Agency (Establishment) (NESREA) Act No. 25, 2007, s. 34.

(d) compensation to all affected parties; and
(e) cost of damage assessment and control.[111]

11.3 Obstacles to Litigating Claims for Environmental Damage

One thing is to have an enforceable right; another is to know how to best pursue it in order to achieve the desired objective. Various obstacles lie in wait for not only claimants seeking compensation for environmental damage but also pollution victims seeking environmental compliance from environmental polluters. The following, though not exhaustive, are considered essential factors to be considered before one can pursue a successful claim for environmental damage under the domestic legal system

11.3.1 Issue of Court with Jurisdiction

It is trite law that for the machinery of the court to be activated, such court must have jurisdiction to entertain such matters. Where a court lacks jurisdiction in respect of a subject matter and assumes jurisdiction on that subject matter, the decision of the court is a nullity.[112] As J.O. Ogebe (JCA) observed in the case of *Shell Petroleum Development Company Limited v Helleluja Bukuma Fishermen Multi-Purpose Co-operative Society Ltd,*[113]

> A plaintiff may have a good cause of action supported by existing law and if he takes his case to a court which has no jurisdiction over the subject matter or the cause of action, he cannot ventilate his claims before the court . . . once the jurisdiction of a court to determine a matter had been ousted any further hearing in the matter is indeed null and void because any decision it makes amounts to nothing.

[111] National Environmental (Mining and Process of Coal, Ores and Industrial Minerals) Regulations 2009, regulation 13(2); National Environmental (Food, Beverages and Tobacco Sector) Regulations, 2009, regulation 5; and National Environmental (Textile, Wearing Apparel, Leather and Footwear Industry) Regulations, 2009, regulation 5, among others. These Regulations and others were discussed in Sect. 6.4.3.2 of Chap. 6, Sect. 9.6.2.3 of Chap. 9, Sect. 14.6.2.1 of Chap. 14 and Sect. 16.2.2.5.2.1 to 16.2.2.5.3 of Chap. 16 of this book.

[112] See the following cases: *Madukolu v Nkemdilem* (1992) I ALL NLR, 587, and *Anisminic v Foreign Compensation Corp.* (1962) 2 AC 147.

[113] (Unreported) Suit No. CA/PH/84/96, delivered on 12 July 2001 by the Court of Appeal Port Harcourt Division.

Most legislation on environmental matters[114] and section 251(1)(n)[115] give exclusive jurisdiction to the Federal High Court, especially in respect of matters arising from or connected to mines and minerals (including oil fields, oil mining and geological surveys and natural gas). Where a litigant institutes an action on any matters as provided by various environmental protection laws or matters provided under section 251(1) of the Nigerian Constitution in a State High Court, the decision of the court is a nullity and shall be upturned on appeal.[116] In the case of *Abel Isaiah and Two Ors v Shell Petroleum Development Company Ltd.*,[117] the Supreme Court of Nigeria finally laid to rest any doubt as to whether the State High Court has jurisdiction to entertain matters arising from activities in the oil industry. According to Uthman Mohammed (J.S.C.), issues forming the interpretation of now section 251(1) (n) of the Constitution of the Federal Republic of Nigeria 1999, as amended,[118] cover every facet of activities within the oil industry:

> I think it cannot be dispute if I say that installation of pipelines, producing treatment and transmitting crude oil to the storage tanks is part of petroleum mining operations, therefore, if any incident happens during the transmission of petroleum to the storage tanks it can be explained as having arisen from or connected with or pertaining to mines and minerals including oil fields and oil mining.[119]

The effect of these judicial pronouncements, especially those of the Supreme Court of Nigeria, is that where any right is violated arising from environmental pollution problems, especially from the oil industry, which is a major source of environmental pollution in Nigeria, the victim can only seek redress from the Federal High Court. This is not withstanding the fact that this court is sparsely located across the country, which adds to the cost of litigation. The result is that access to justice is inadvertently denied to the victims in ventilating their claims or seeking compliance with the environmental protection provisions of environmental laws against the violators.

11.3.2 Locus Standi

Another major problem that may be faced by a claimant in pursuit of claims for environmental damage is the issue of undue attachment to technicalities by the courts. Technicalities that the courts had been warned against on several occasions

---

[114] Such as Harmful Wastes (Special Criminal Provisions, etc.) Act 1988, National Environmental Standards and Regulations Enforcement Agency Act 2007, etc.

[115] CFRN 1999, as amended.

[116] *Impidi Barry and Ors v Obi A Eric and Ors* (1998) 8 NWLR (pt 562) 404 at 416.

[117] (2001) 6 NSCQR, 542.

[118] CFRN 1999, as amended.

[119] *Abel Isaiah and Two Ors v Shell Petroleum Development Company Ltd* (2001) 6 NSCQR, 542 at 550.

should not be unduly relied upon by courts to short-circuit the course of justice, for, as Kayode Eso (J.S.C., as he then was) pointed out in the case of *State v Salihu Mohammed Gwonto*,[120] 'the court has for some time now laid down as a guiding principle in that it is more interested in substance than in mere form. Justice can only be done if the substance of the matter is examined. Reliance on technicalities leads to injustice'.

In spite of the above injunctions, potential litigants, on a number of occasions, had their pursuit of justice defeated because of the reliance on technicalities by the courts. Most notable of these legal technicalities used by the courts to frustrate environmental claims is the vexed issue of *locus standi.*[121]

Reduced to its bare bones, *locus standi* means standing to sue. The fundamental aspect of *locus standi* is that it focuses on the party seeking to get his complaint before the court and not on the issues he wished to have adjudicated.[122] The concept of *locus standi* therefore concerns the capacity of a person to institute legal proceedings in a court of law or other competent tribunals. It follows that such a person must have an interest that is sufficiently affected by the action and that it is not enough that such a person merely claims that he falls within the class of persons for whose general interest that statute was passed. He must go forward to show that he has some personal interest that has been, or is most likely or certain to be, affected by the action complained of.[123]

Undue reliance on *locus standi* by the courts has had a toll on a number of environmental cases. The general rule for public nuisance is that the Attorney General is the proper plaintiff where a public right is involved. A private individual does not have the locus standi to sue in public nuisance cases unless the interference with the public right is such that some private right of his is at the same time interfered with, and where no private right is interfered with, he, in respect of his public right, suffers special damages peculiar to himself from the interference with the public right.[124] The onus is on the victim to prove that he has suffered damages beyond those of the members of the public.

In *A. S Amos and 4 Others v Shell B. P Nig. Ltd.*,[125] the plaintiff claimed damages from the defendant (among others) for public nuisance. They alleged that the defendant made a large earth dam across their creek during oil mining operations and that this resulted in the flooding of the upstream, while the downstream was dry. Consequently, the plaintiffs were put at a disadvantage with respect to the use of waterways for navigating barges, rivers crafts and canoes; the disruption of commercial activities; and the use of water for drinking and other commercial purposes. The trial court and the Supreme Court found that the conduct of the defendant

[120] (1983) 1 AII NLR, 109.

[121] Onyeabor (2010), pp. 67–85 at 77.

[122] Obaseki (J.SC) in *Thomas v Olufosoye* (1986) 2 S.C. 325 at 350.

[123] Owoade (1999), p. 111.

[124] *Dumez (Nig.) Ltd. v Ogboli* (1972) ALL NLR, 241.

[125] *A S Amos and 4 Others v Shell B. P Nig. Ltd.* (1977), 109.

amounted to public nuisance. However, there was no evidence from the plaintiffs showing that they suffered damages over and above those suffered by the general public. The action was therefore dismissed. This is in spite of the fact that environmental problems linger and know no personal boundaries or individual enclaves. To this end, *locus standi* remains the plaintiff's most difficult task in environmental litigation involving public nuisance.[126]

Another area where *locus standi* has compounded environmental litigation is in the use of tort of trespass to pursue environmental claims. Trespass to land arises from an unjustifiable interference with a plaintiff's possession of land.[127] The slightest direct physical interference with land in possession of another person is actionable, for example walking on another man's land. It is not necessary to prove actual physical damage because trespass to land is actionable per se.[128]

In *Onasanya v Emmanuel*,[129] Omolulu-Thomas J. held that trespass is committed when, without lawful justification, a defendant directly places or projects any material object upon such land. It is also considered trespassing to place anything upon the plaintiff's land or cause a physical object or noxious substance to come into physical contact with his land. For an action in trespass to arise from the placing of an object on the plaintiff's land, such placing must be direct; otherwise, the action will lie only in nuisance, in which case damage must be established to ground liability. This requirement, however, excludes all cases of industrial or human waste discharges not directly introduced into the plaintiff's premises by the defendant.[130] In spite of this, however, for the plaintiff to be entitled to sue, he must be in possession.[131] But the possession that entitles the plaintiff to sue must be actual and effective in order to maintain an action against anyone except the true owner or one who can trace his title to the true owner.[132]

The issue of *locus standi* also influenced the decision of the Federal High Court, Port Harcourt Division, in the case of *Oronto Douglas v Shell Petroleum Development Company and 5 Ors*.[133] In that case, the plaintiff brought an action asserting that the provisions of the Environmental Impact Assessment Act 1992[134] requires all environmental impact assessments submitted by a proponent to be made available to members of the public for comments before the Agency charged with environmental protection allows the take-off of such project as it affects mandatory environmental impact assessment in case the Nigerian Liquefied Natural Gas Project had not been carried out by the proponents. The defendants filed a preliminary objection,

---

[126] Onyeabor (2010), p. 77.

[127] *Anyabunsi v Ugwunze* (1995) 6 NWLR (pt 401) 26.

[128] *Ashby v White (1703)* 87 ER 810, *Dabira v Adelaja* (1973) II CCHCJ, 100.

[129] (1973) 4 CCHCJ 1477 at 1481.

[130] *Onasanya v Emmanuel* (1973), p. 1481.

[131] *Oya v Ikaile* (1995) 7 NWLR (pt 406), 155; *Lamidi v Oyedele* (1994) 6 NWLR (pt 348) 25.

[132] *Nwosu v Otumola* (1974) I ALL NLR (pt 1), 153.

[133] Suit No. FHC/25C/573/93 (unreported) delivered by FHC PH on 17 February 1997.

[134] Cap E12 Laws of the Federation of Nigeria (LFN) 2004, s. 7.

contending that the plaintiff lacks *locus standi* in the matter and therefore cannot institute the action. After reviewing various authorities, Belgore C.J. (as he then was), while agreeing with the defendants, held, *inter alia*, that the plaintiff had no *locus standi* to institute the action since he had shown no *prima facie* evidence that his right was affected or any direct injury was caused to him or that he suffered any injury more than the generality of the people. Hence, the action was dismissed.

With this decision, an opportunity to make a concrete pronouncement in respect of the pursuit of environmental justice was lost. Adherence to undue legal technicalities has held sway, and justice lies prostrate. It should, however, be borne in mind that environmental wrongs, unlike other legal wrongs, carry with them special species of implications. This is because environmental wrongs know no national boundaries or individual enclaves. They affect any person within or in remote areas of their occurrence.[135]

Therefore, where a statute clearly provides for public or private participation by any person interested in any environmental issue, it stands to reason that the draftsmen intended that such group or individual fall within the class of persons for whose general interest the statute was passed. Such persons therefore have some special or personal interest that has been or is most likely or certain to be affected where the provisions of that statute are not complied with. This confers on the person the right to sue, and he need not show any other *prima facie* evidence that his right was affected or that he suffered any injury more than the generality of the people before his complaint is heard on the merits.[136]

All he needed to show is that non-compliance with the requirements of the statute would impinge on his rights to a clean, benign, disease-free, aesthetically pleasing and friendly environment and that he is entitled to an environment not flagrantly abused as to violate his rights.[137] To this end, issues of technicalities, especially *locus standi*, should be downplayed in environmental litigation, and courts should adhere to the views expressed by Chukwudifu Oputa (J.S.C., as he then was) when he said:

> The picture of law and its technical rules triumphant and justice prostrate may no doubt have its admirers. But the spirit of justice does not reside in forms and formalities, nor in technicalities, nor in the triumph of the successfully picking one's way between pitfalls or technicalities.[138]

---

[135] Onyeabor (2010), p. 81.

[136] Onyeabor (2010), p. 81.

[137] There appears to be a shift to this suggestion under the National Environmental (Noise Standards and Control) Regulations, 2009, regulation 10(2), which provides that any person may complain to the Agency in writing if such a person considers that the noise levels being emitted, or likely to be emitted, may be higher than the permissible noise levels under the Regulations; such complainant need not show or prove personal loss or injury or discomfort caused by the emission of the alleged noise.

[138] As cited by Kayode Eso in 'Thoughts on Human Rights Norms Vis-à-Vis the Courts and Justice: An African Court or Domestic Court' (Lagos, NIALS, 1995) 26.

In the end, the courts, as Obaseki (J.S.C, as he then was) pointed out, will listen to any person whose circumstances are of an oppressive or hostile nature and whose rights guaranteed under the law and Constitution are curtailed or invaded or breached by non-compliance with the Constitution.[139]

It is gratifying to note that the Supreme Court of Nigeria, in its decision in the case of *Centre for Oil Pollution Watch v Nigerian National Petroleum Corporation*,[140] has extended the scope of application of the doctrine of *locus standi* to environmental matters and the right to institute an action for the protection of the environment. The court also noted in that decision that operators, owners and oil pipeline license holders have a duty to maintain and repair their oil pipelines so as to safeguard the water, air, land, forest and wildlife from environmental degradation.[141]

In that case, the appellant, a non-governmental organisation (NGO) as the plaintiff, instituted the action at the Federal High Court, Lagos, against the Nigerian National Petroleum Corporation (NNPC) regarding an alleged oil spillage in the Acha autonomous community of Isuikwuato Local Government Area of Abia State of Nigeria. At the High Court, the appellant claimed, among other reliefs, the reinstatement, restoration and remediation of the impaired and contaminated environment in the Acha autonomous community and the provision of portable water supply as a substitute for the soiled and contaminated Ineh/Aku streams, which were greatly affected by the spillage and which serves as the major source of water supply to the community.[142]

In response, the NNPC, as the defendant before the High Court, filed a motion seeking to challenge the suit *in limine* on the ground that the appellant lacked the requisite *locus standi* to institute the action. The trial court, in its ruling, agreed with the respondent/defendant's motion and struck out the suit for want of *locus standi* on the part of the appellant/plaintiff. The appellant filed an appeal to the Court of Appeal, Lagos Division. The court dismissed the appeal, reaffirming the ruling of the trial court.

Dissatisfied with the judgment of the Court of Appeal, the appellant turned to the Supreme Court. The issue for determination revolved solely on whether the learned justices of the Court of Appeal were right in dismissing the appellant's claim for want of *locus standi* to maintain the suit. The court allowed the appeal and held that in environmental matters such as this, NGOs such as the appellant have the requisite *locus standi* to sue.[143]

The court noted that the suit being of public interest, litigation is instituted in the interest of the general public and is an action brought for the benefit of a group or class of persons who have suffered a general wrong or are about to suffer such a wrong as a result of the activities of other persons, usually corporate institutions or

---

[139] Owoade (1999), p. 113.

[140] *Centre for Oil Pollution Watch v Nigerian National Petroleum Corporation* (2019), p. 518.

[141] *Centre for Oil Pollution Watch v Nigerian National Petroleum Corporation* (2019), p. 518.

[142] Ibid.

[143] Ibid.

governments, for political, religious or economic gains. The court further held that the responsibility of the state to protect the environment is now a well-accepted notion in all countries. The court was of the view that the provisions of section 20 of the Constitution of the Federal Republic of Nigeria (CFRN) 1999, as amended,[144] and sections 16 and 24 of the African Charter on Peoples and Human Rights (ACPHR) (Ratification and Enforcement) Act[145] recognise the fundamental rights of the citizenry to a clean and healthy environment to sustain life.

The gist of this judgment is that the outdated technical rules of *locus standi* should not be used to prevent an individual or group from bringing a matter of unlawful environmental conduct to the attention of the court. More so, every person, including NGOs, that seek in good faith the due performance of statutory functions or the enforcement of statutory provisions or public laws, especially laws designed to protect human lives, public health and the environment, should be regarded as having the *locus standi* to request adjudication on issues of public nuisance that are injurious to human lives, public health and the environment.

11.3.3 Procuring Credible and Compelling Expert Witness

Environmental problems, by their very nature, import a high-level scientific approach in their analysis, and the court, in most cases, is not versed in scientific analysis. In order to discharge the evidential burden, the victim of environmental pollution must place such violation in concrete scientific proof within the doorsteps of the defendant if he is to succeed. In this respect, the plaintiff is required to procure the services of professionals versed in such scientific analysis. This is not easy to come by as these professionals charge highly, and in the end, the court is now left with the expert evidence procured by the violators, whose enormous resources make hiring the services of these experts easy.

An expert for the purposes of giving credible and compelling evidence in matters before a court "is a person who is specially skillful in the field in which he is giving evidence, and he is required where he can furnish the court with scientific or other information of a technical nature that is likely to be outside the experience of the judge of facts."[146] Failure to secure the services of an expert may be fatal to a plaintiff's claim. This state of affairs is exemplified in the following cases.

For instance, in the case of *Seismograph Services Ltd v Benedict Onokposa*,[147] the respondent/plaintiff alleged that the damage caused to his building was a result of the negligent act of the appellant/defendant while carrying out shooting operations during a seismic party. To succeed, the respondent/plaintiff had to prove that the

---

[144] CFRN (1999) as amended.

[145] ACPHR (Ratification and Enforcement) Act (2004).

[146] *Shell Petroleum Development Company v Otoko and Ors* (1990) at 712–713.

[147] (1992) 4SC, 123.

defendant's negligent act caused the damage. He was unable to prove his claim to the satisfaction of the court as the witnesses called by him were no match to the experts (properly) called by the defendant. The matter was thrown out.[148]

In the case of *Seismograph Services Ltd. v Akpruoyo*,[149] with similar facts, the lower court found in favour of the plaintiff/respondent, but this decision was reversed on appeal. The Supreme Court held that the trial judge ought to have accepted and acted on the unchallenged expert evidence of the appellant. This decision also guided the Supreme Court in a sister case.[150]

But where the plaintiffs were able to secure the services of experts, the decision of the court is usually different. For instance, in the case of *Shell Petroleum Development Company Ltd. v Councilor Farah and 7 Ors*,[151] the respondent/plaintiff alleged that the defendant, by its negligent act, caused oil spillage, which damaged the land and economic trees and crops of the plaintiffs. The defendant provided evidence that the land had been rehabilitated. The plaintiffs procured the services of experts, who found that the land in question had not been rehabilitated. When the court appointed its expert to look into the matter, it concurred with the expert opinion of the plaintiffs. The court awarded the damages claimed and ordered the rehabilitation of the land by the defendants. The plaintiffs succeeded in this matter because they were able to match the expert evidence of the defendants.

11.3.4 Limitation of Action and Pre-action Notice

Limitation of action[152] and pre-action notice are other obstacles that lie on the part of a litigant in pursuit of claims for environmental damage. Where a statute provides that certain acts be done by the person initiating an action before invoking the jurisdiction of the court, it is only after compliance with such law that the court's jurisdiction to adjudicate on it can be activated. The requirement of pre-action notice, where the law prescribes it, for instance section 32(1) of the National Environmental Standards Regulation and Enforcement Agency (Establishment) (NESREA) Act 2007[153] and also section 308 of the Petroleum Industry Act 2021,[154] is known to have one rationale. It is to appraise the defendant beforehand of the nature of the action contemplated and to give him enough time to consider or reconsider his position in the matter as to whether to comprise or contest it.[155]

---

[148] Also in the case of *Shell Development Company v Otoko and Ors* (1990), 711.

[149] (1974) 6 SC 119.

[150] *Seismograph Services Ltd. v Kwarbi Ogbeni* (1976) 4 SC 85.

[151] (1995) 3 NWLR (pt 382) 148.

[152] This serves as a statute of limitation, as was held by the Supreme Court in the case of *Mobil Producing (Nig) Unlimited v LASEPA, FEPA and Ors*. See the NESREA Act (2007), s. 32(1).

[153] Act No. 25, 2007.

[154] Petroleum Industry Act (2021).

[155] *Eze v Okechukwu* (1985) 5 NWLR (pt 548) 43.

Although statutory provisions prescribing pre-action notice are mandatory, non-compliance with such mandatory provisions can be waived.[156] To this end, the Supreme Court, in the case of *Mobil Producing (Nig) Unlimited v LASEPA, FEPA and Ors*,[157] held that:

> service of a pre-action notice on the party intended to be sued pursuant to a statute is, best, a procedural requirement and not an issue of substantive law on which the rights of the plaintiff depend. It is not an integral part of the process of initiating proceedings...

The decision of the Supreme Court in the case of *Nigercare Development Company Ltd v Adamawa State Government and Ors*,[158] which stated that an issue of pre-action notice, being a jurisdictional issue, can be raised at any stage of the proceeding, even for the first time on appeal, adds to the problem of the litigant.

Ogbuabor[159] posited that the requirement of pre-action notice is a procedural requirement in the nature of a privilege and that the privilege could be waived and indeed would be deemed to have been waived if it was not timorously and properly raised. His reasoning is that pre-action notice, being a privilege and not a right *stricto sensu*, could, like any other privilege, be waived. Arising from this position, Ogbuabor,[160] in another instance, argued that the decision of the Supreme Court in the case of *Nigercare Development Co. Ltd v Adamawa State Government and Ors*, judging from its earlier decisions,[161] 'is manifestly erroneous' when he said:

> It is arguable whether the decision is *per incuriam* since *Katsina Local Authority v Makudawa* was cited but it definitely presents a case of conflicting decisions from the apex court on the same point without any attempt at resolving the conflict. However, when it is remembered that in-between *Katsina Local Authority v Makudawa* and *Mobil Producing (Nig) Un Ltd v LASEPA, FEPA and Ors,* there were conflicting opinions of the Court of Appeal until the Supreme Court seized the opportunity offered by *Mobil Producing (Nig) Un Ltd v LASEPA, FEPA and Ors* to explain *Makudawa*'s case, then there is an almost irresistible urge to conclude that the decision in *Nigercare Development Co. Ltd v. Adamawa State Government and Ors* in forgetfulness of *Mobil Producing (Nig) Unlimited v LASEPA, FEPA and Ors* is *per incuriam* especially when the latter decision conflicts with that in *Mobil Producing (Nig) Unlimited v LASEPA, FEPA and Ors.*

In the opinion of Fagbohun,[162] 'interesting as this development would appear to be', making reference to the decision of the Supreme Court of Nigeria in the case of *Mobil Producing (Nig) UnLimited v LASEPA, FEPA and Ors*,[163] he expressed as follows:

---

[156] *Katsina Local Authority v Makudawa* (1971) 7 NSCC 119.

[157] (2002) 1 S C (pt1) 26, (2002) 18 NWLR (pt 798) 1.

[158] (2008) 9 NWLR (pt 1093) 498.

[159] Ogbuabor (2008), p. 149.

[160] Ogbuabor (2010), pp. 224 and 225.

[161] As in the cases of *Katsina Local Authority v Makudawa* (1971) NSCC 119 and *Mobil Producing (Nig) Unlimited v LASEPA, FEPA and Ors* (2002) (2002) 1 S C (pt1) 26.

[162] Fagbohun (2012), p. 65.

[163] *Mobil Producing (Nig) Unlimited v LASEPA, FEPA and Ors* (2002), p. 26.

> it has little promise in that non-compliance with pre-action notice still renders an action incompetent, except where it is not raised by a defendant in which case it would be taken as a mere irregularity. It is my respectful submission that it is time for the Supreme Court to lift the stakes in purposive construction, and at the minimum allow for stay of proceedings while the notice is being served. This will enable courts to be in position to grant orders of injunction in deserving situations.

The bottom line, however, is that whether the court considers the non-service of pre-action as a condition precedent or a mere procedural requirement, for smooth and effective litigation, it is advisable that where a claim lies against a body required by law to be served pre-action notice, it will be necessary to do so timorously to avoid any unnecessary delay of the substantive issue that has been canvassed by the litigant.

11.3.5 Undue Delays by the Courts and Defendants

As the cliché goes, 'justice delayed is justice denied'. Delays plagued the course of litigation against environmental claims, especially in the oil industry. For instance, a case of an oil spill at Peremabiri, Bayelsa State, which caused extensive damage to the environment and property in January 1987, came to the High Court in 1992 and to the Court of Appeal in 1996.[164]

In the case of *John Eboigbe v Nigerian National Petroleum Company*,[165] damage caused in 1979 and followed by correspondence leading to a writ of summons in 1984 was first heard in 1987. It was appealed in 1989 and was heard by the Supreme Court in 1994.

Again, the case of *Shell Petroleum Development Company Limited v George Uzoaru and 3 Ors*,[166] which was heard in the High Court in 1985 in relation to damages suffered on a continuous basis since 1972, was heard in the Court of Appeal in 1994. An issue of undue delay also reared in the case of *Elf Nigeria Ltd. v Opere Silo and Daniel Etsemi*.[167] In that case, damage had been suffered since 1967; the case was heard in the High Court in 1987 at the Court of Appeal in 1990 and in the Supreme Court in 1994.

In *Shell Petroleum Development of Nigeria Ltd. v Councillor Farah*,[168] the delay was caused by the defendant, now appellant. An action was filed by Ejama-Ebubu communities in Tai Eleme Local Government Area of Rivers State, seeking damages against Shell Petroleum Development Company of Nigeria Limited (SPDC) for an oil spillage incident. In that suit, environmental NGOs, including the Movement for

---

[164] *Shell Petroleum Development Company Ltd v HRH Chief G.B.A. Tiebo VII and 4 Ors* (1996), 657.

[165] (1994) 5 NWLR (pt 347) 649.

[166] (1994) 9 NWLR (pt 366) 51.

[167] (1994) 6 NWLR (pt 350) 258.

[168] (1995) 3 NWLR (pt. 382) 148 at 192.

the Survival of the Ogoni People (MOSOP), accused SPDC of more than 20 years of environmental degradation and negligence in Ogoni communities, a region of the Niger Delta with mangroves devastated by oil pollution.[169]

The community obtained judgment at the Federal High Court in Port Harcourt, which awarded damages in their favour on 14 June 2010, but the case went on appeal up to the Supreme Court. On 11 January 2019, the Supreme Court affirmed the judgment in favour of the community. 'But since then, the multinational had been resisting the Supreme Court verdict.'[170] On 27 November 2020, SPDC filed an application for a review of the verdict, but the Supreme Court dismissed the request.[171]

Unrelented, SPDC subsequently brought the case back to the Federal High Court in Abuja in continuation of its pushback against the verdict. However, on 11 August 2021, SPDC finally agreed to pay the court-ordered ₦45.9 billion compensation to the community.[172] Shell's Nigerian subsidiary, the Shell Petroleum Development Company of Nigeria Limited (SPDC), said in a statement: 'The order to pay 45.9 billion Naira (£94.9 million) to the plaintiffs is intended to fully and finally satisfy the judgment.'[173]

On the whole, these undue delays in the administration of justice portent a veritable source of frustration in pursuing legal redress by pollution victims for the violation of rights or in eliciting environmental compliance.

11.3.6 Problem of Enforcement of Judgment

At times, environmental pollution victims may be able to prove their cases and compensation for damages is awarded by the courts but the enforcement of such judgment becomes a problem. This state of affairs had resulted in threats and protests to enforce such judgment after the violators vehemently refused to pay. A case in point is *Chief Joel Anare and Others v Shell Petroleum Development Company Ltd.*[174] In that case, the Delta State High Court, Holden at Ughelli, awarded four communities in Burutu Local Government Council—Sokebelou, Obotogo, Ofoghene and Ekeremorzion—the sum of ₦30 million as compensation in connection with a claim relating to a spill in 1982.

Shell claimed non-liability, asserting that the spill was an act of sabotage, and refused to pay on the pretence that it was appealing against the judgment. Shortly

[169] Odour (2021).

[170] Premium Times (2021).

[171] Ibid.

[172] Michael Odour (2021).

[173] Ibid.

[174] (Unreported) Suit No. HCB/35/89 Delta High Court, Ughelli Division, delivered on 27 May 1997.

after the decision, Chief Matthew Saturday Eregbene, head of the Oil Producing Communities Development Organisation and spokesperson for the communities, announced that Shell had a deadline of 8 July 1997 to pay the judgment sum or to cease production; otherwise, production would be forcibly closed. Before the deadline, on 7 July 1997, Eregbene was arrested and taken to Asaba, where he was detained by men of the State Security Service. A meeting with Eregbene and other representatives of the communities was later convened by the then Military Administration of Delta State in respect of the case. While this was going on, Shell called a meeting in which it warned those present that the consequences for the communities would be serious if the threat to shut down Shell's production were carried out.[175] The amount awarded to the plaintiffs in the sum of =N=30 million by the High Court in 1997 was not paid by the defendant. The defendant rather appealed against the judgement up to the Supreme Court, where judgement was given in 2015. There is no evidence that the judgement sum had been paid therefore making nonsense to the extra mile the judge went in realising the devastating effect of environmental violations and awarded exemplary damage.

Taken together, the quest for legal redress in respect of environmental damage had not been a smooth ride for the victims of environmental damage. The victims had not been fully compensated, nor are there real concerted efforts to ameliorate the harsh situations created by such environmental spoliation. Since it appears to some of them that the rule of law had failed them in seeking redress, they at times, as an alternative, resort to protests to rub in their demands. This is usually met with repression and suppression, especially where such action may impinge on revenue-yielding avenues for the government.

11.4 Criminal Liability for Environmental Damage

Under existing environmental legislation in Nigeria, criminal liabilities have been put in place to ensure environmental sustainability. The extant environmental laws tend to punish environmental damage caused by the following acts:

1. Illegal dumping or depositing of or dealing in hazardous wastes/substances
2. Non-compliance with legislative provisions on environmental impact assessment prior to the commencement of projects that may impact or have a likelihood of causing a significant environmental impact
3. Failure to comply with legislation protecting various environmental media
4. Illegal wildlife trade and trafficking of endangered species

These pieces of legislation criminalising environmental degradation are discussed below.

[175] Human Rights Watch (1999), p. 158.

11.4.1 Illegal Dumping or Depositing of or Dealing in Hazardous Wastes/Substances

Harmful waste is defined under the Harmful Wastes (Special Criminal Provisions etc.) (HWSCP) 1988 Act[176] as 'Any injurious, poisonous, toxic or noxious substance . . . which can subject any person to the risk of death, fatal injury or incurable impairment of physical and mental health. . .'.[177] Under the HWSCP Act, it is an offence for any person, without lawful authority, to carry, deposit, dump or cause to be carried, deposited or dumped; transport or cause to be transported; import or cause to import; negotiate for the purpose of importing; sell; offer for sale; buy; or otherwise deal in any harmful waste.[178]

A person shall be deemed to have committed the offence if he actually does the act or enables, aids, counsels or procures any person to commit the crime.[179] It is immaterial, in the case of counselling, that the act committed is the same as the one counselled or a different one or is committed in the way counselled or in a different way, provided that in either case, the facts constituted a probable consequence of carrying out the counsel.[180] Such a person shall, on conviction, be liable to the same punishment prescribed in the Act.[181] The punishment prescribed under the Act is imprisonment for life, and in addition:

(a) any carrier, including aircraft, vehicle container and any other thing whatsoever used in the transportation or importation of the harmful waste, and
(b) any land on which harmful waste was deposited or dumped, shall be forfeited and vest in the Federal Government without any further assurance.[182]

Where the offence is committed by a body corporate and it is proved that it was committed with the consent or connivance of or it is attributable to a neglect on the part of any director, manager, secretary or other similar officer or any person purporting to act in the same capacity, he, as well as the body corporate, shall be guilty of the crime and shall be liable to be proceeded against and punished accordingly.[183]

[176] HWSCP Act (1988).

[177] Ibid., s. 15.

[178] Ibid., s. 1(2).

[179] Ibid., s. 2(1).

[180] Ibid., s. 4.

[181] Ibid., s. 2(2)(3).

[182] Ibid., s. 6.

[183] Ibid., s. 7.

11.4.2 Non-compliance with Legislative Provisions on Environmental Impact Assessment

Non-compliance with legislative provisions on environmental impact assessment may result in criminal sanction against the offender, especially under the provisions of the Environmental Impact Assessment Act 1992.[184]

The rationale underlying its importance is that 'rational planning constitutes an essential tool for reconciling development and environmental needs and that planning must be applied to human settlements and urbanisation with a view to avoiding adverse effects on the environment and obtaining maximum social, economic and environmental benefits for all'.[185] Thus, the United Nations Environment Programme (UNEP)[186] asserts that the major functions of EIA include 'to identify, predict and to describe in appropriate terms the pros and cons (penalties and benefits) of a proposed development...'. Environmental impact assessment can therefore be seen as a procedure that seeks to ensure the acquisition of adequate and early information on the likely environmental consequences of development projects, on possible alternatives and on measures to mitigate harm. It is generally a prerequisite decision to be undertaken before a designated authority or agency can authorise a designated construction, process or activity.

The Environmental Impact Assessment (EIA) Act 1992,[187] in section 1, sets out the goals and objectives of environmental impact assessment. Section 2 of the EIA Act restricts public or private projects from being commenced without prior consideration of the environmental impact of such projects. It is immaterial whether the project is being undertaken by the federal, state or local government or any of its agencies or institutions.[188] Once such a project falls within the mandatory study list[189] and does not fall under the excluded projects,[190] failure to conduct an environmental impact assessment amounts to non-compliance with the provisions of the Act.[191] A proponent is found liable for non-compliance with the provisions of the Act once there is a failure to conduct an environmental impact assessment as required by the Act. [192] Here, the penalty prescribed under section 60 of the EIA Act 1992 shall be paid to the appropriate Agency of the government.

However, under certain circumstances, an environmental claim may arise not from actual damage to the environment nor from non-compliance by proponents

[184] EIA Act (1992).

[185] United Nations (1972) (Stockholm Declaration 1972), principles 14 and 15.

[186] United Nations Environment Programme (1982), p. 13.

[187] EIA Act 1992 (n 134).

[188] Ibid., s. 2(4).

[189] Ibid., s. 12.

[190] Ibid., s. 14.

[191] Ibid., s. 60.

[192] With respect to a project proponent, it means the person or body or authority that proposes a project.

with the provisions of the EIA Act 1992 but from failure by the relevant Agency or Authority to act in accordance with the provisions of the Act. The EIA Act 1992 requires the implementing Authority to give opportunity to government agencies, members of the public, experts in any relevant discipline and interested groups to make comments on the environmental impact assessment of an activity.[193] Failure to do this is a source of a cause of action. Again, under section 24 of the EIA Act 1992, after receiving a mandatory study report of a project,[194] the Authority shall, in any manner considered appropriate, publish a notice setting out the following information:

(i) the date on which the mandatory study report shall be available to the public.
(ii) the place at which copies of the report may be obtained; and
(iii) the deadline and address for filing comments on the conclusions and recommendations of the report.

Furthermore, on receiving a report submitted by a mediator[195] or a review panel,[196] the Authority shall make the report available to the public in any manner considered appropriate and shall advise the public that the report is available.[197] It would appear that failure on the part of the Authority to notify the public under either section 7, 24 or 38 of the Act might attract a cause of action against the Authority. A case in point is *Oronto Douglas v Shell Petroleum Development Company Limited and 5 Ors.*[198] In that case, the plaintiff brought an action in which he sought, among other things, the following reliefs:

(i) A declaration that the defendants cannot lawfully commission, carry out and operate their LNG projects without first complying strictly with the EIA Act
(ii) A declaration that the fifth defendant, FEPA, is bound to require the first to third defendants—SPDC, Nigeria LNG and NNPC—to adequately publicise any proposed EIA report to all interested NGOs and the communities likely to be affected by the operation of the LNG project in accordance with the provisions of section 7 of the Act.

At times, a cause of action may arise where the Authority in charge of the implementation of the Act fails to take the required steps to carry out the purpose of the Act. For instance, where the Authority is of the opinion that a project is not described in the mandatory study list[199] or any exclusion list,[200] the Authority is enjoined by section 18 to ensure that a screening[201] of the project is conducted and a

[193] EIA Act (1992) s. 7.
[194] Mandatory study made pursuant to the EIA Act (1992), s. 22.
[195] Set up pursuant to the EIA Act (1992), s. 31, and conducted under s. 33.
[196] Set up pursuant to s. 35 and conducted under the EIA Act (1992), ss. 36 and 37.
[197] EIA Act (1992), s. 38.
[198] Suit No. FHC/25C/573/93 (unreported), delivered by FHC PH on 17 February 1997.
[199] As contained in the Schedule to the EIA Act (1992).
[200] EIA Act (1992), s. 14.
[201] An inquiry as to whether a project is likely to have significant effects on the environment.

screening report prepared. After the completion of the screening report, the Authority shall take a course of action or decision on whether the project may have significant environmental effects or not and how such effects, if any, may be mitigated.[202]

The EIA Act 1992 also enjoins the Authority to ensure that where a project is described in the mandatory study list, a mandatory study is conducted and a mandatory study report prepared and submitted to it by the proponent.[203] Furthermore, if based on the screening report and the mandatory study report the Authority is of the opinion that a project is likely to cause significant adverse environmental effects that may not be mitigated or that public concerns respecting the environmental effects of the projects warrant it, the Authority is mandated by section 26 of the EIA Act 1992 to bring the matter to the Council for referral for mediation or panel review. In this respect, the Council shall appoint mediators.[204] But where in the opinion of the Council or Authority mediation is not likely to produce a result that is satisfactory to all parties, the Authority is empowered to terminate the mediation and refer the project to a review panel.[205]

The bottom line in all of the above situations, and other situations,[206] is that the failure of the implementing Authority to act or take appropriate steps is a veritable source of environmental claims, which may be for a declaration, injunction, mandamus or *certiorari*, as the case may be. Through this process, environmental abuses may be minimised.

11.4.3 Failure to Comply with Legislation Protecting Various Environmental Media

Some legislation, such as the National Environmental Standards Regulation and Enforcement Agency (Establishment) (NESREA) Act 2007,[207] the Criminal Code[208] and the Oil in Navigable Waters Act 1968,[209] have provisions for the

---

[202] EIA Act (1992), s. 21.

[203] Ibid., s. 22.

[204] Ibid., s. 31.

[205] Ibid., ss. 34 and 35, for the appointment of a review panel.

[206] Such as the establishment of a Public Registry under the EIA Act 1992 (n 134), s. 55; prohibiting a proponent under the EIA Act (1992), s. 51; and failure to take steps required under the EIA Act (1992), s. 39.

[207] Government Notice No. 61, Act No. 25, 2007, Federal Republic of Nigeria Official Gazette No. 92, Vol. 94, 31 July 2007 and amended in 2018 vide Government Notice No. 106, Act No. 26 2018, Federal Republic of Nigeria Official Gazette No. 146, Vol. 105, 14 November 2018.

[208] Cap C38 LFN 2004.

[209] This Act was discussed in Sect. 16.2.3.1 of Chap. 16 of this book.

protection of various environmental media. Under such legislation, non-compliance with their provisions may lead to criminal sanctions.

11.4.3.1 National Environmental Standards Regulation and Enforcement Agency (Establishment) (Amendment) (NESREA) Act 2007[210]

This is one of the legislation through which criminal liability may arise for failure to comply with its legislative provisions for the protection of the various environmental media. The NESREA Act 2007 repealed the Federal Environmental Agency Act[211] and established the National Environmental Standards and Regulations Enforcement Agency (NESREA).[212] Of interest to us is the provisions of sections 20–27. It is from these eight sections[213] that it can be said that the NESREA Act 2007 is used as a mechanism to impose environmental liability for environmental damage.

Under section 20(1) of the NESREA Act 2007, the Agency[214] is mandated to make regulations setting standards to protect and enhance the quality of Nigeria's air resources so as to promote public health or welfare. Any person who violates the regulations commits an offence and shall, on conviction, be liable to a fine of ₦200,000 or to imprisonment for a term of not exceeding 1 year or to both such fine and imprisonment. In addition, the person is fined ₦20,000 for every day the offence subsists.[215] Where the offender is a body corporate, the penalty shall be a fine of ₦2,000,000 and an additional ₦50,000 for each day the offence subsists.[216]

In order to protect the stratospheric ozone,[217] the Agency is enjoined to collaborate with other relevant agencies to embark on programmes for the control of any substance, practice, process or activity that may reasonably be anticipated to affect the stratosphere, especially the ozone in the stratosphere.[218] Where a person engages in any practice, process or activity that violates programmes for the control of

---

[210] NESREA Act (2007).

[211] Ibid., s. 36.

[212] Ibid., s. 1.

[213] In addition, various Regulations (33 in number) made by NESREA have provisions for criminal sanctions for environmental damage.

[214] National Environmental Standards and Regulations Enforcement Agency (NESREA).

[215] NESREA Act (2007), s. 20 (3).

[216] Ibid., s. 20 (4).

[217] The depletion of the ozone is said to be responsible for global warming and climate change, and there are a series of international instruments targeted at combating these environmental problems, such as the Vienna Convention for Substances Depleting the Ozone Layer, 1985; Montreal Protocol on Ozone Depleting Substances, 1987; United Nations Framework Convention on Climate Change, 1992; Kyoto Protocol to the United Nations Framework Convention on Climate Change (Kyoto Protocol), 1997; and Paris Agreement 2015 under the United Nations Framework Convention on Climate Change.

[218] NESREA Act (2007), s. 21(2).

ozone-depleting substances in such a way that the effects may be reasonably anticipated to endanger public health or welfare, such a person commits an offence under section 21(2). Where the offence is committed by an individual, he shall, on conviction, be liable to a fine of ₦200,000 or to 1-year imprisonment or to both fine and imprisonment and to an additional fine of ₦20,000 for each day the offence subsists.[219] Where the offender is a body corporate, the penalty shall be a fine of ₦2,000,000 and an additional ₦50,000 for each day the offence subsists.[220]

As a result of the adverse effect of noise, the Agency is mandated to identify major sources of noise, noise criteria and noise control technology and to make regulations on noise, emission control and abatement, as may be necessary to preserve and maintain public health and welfare.[221] Any violation of the regulations constitutes an offence. With respect to an individual, the penalty is a fine of ₦50,000 and an additional fine of ₦5000 for each day the offence subsists. Where the offender is a body corporate, the penalty shall be a fine of ₦500,000 and an additional ₦10,000 for each day the offence subsists.[222]

The Agency[223] is also mandated to make regulations and standards for water quality,[224] review effluent limitations for existing point sources and set up schedules for compliance;[225] make regulations for the purpose of protecting public health and promoting environmental sanitation;[226] and make regulations, guidelines and standards for the protection and enhancement of the quality of land resources, natural watershed, coastal zone dams and reservoirs, including the prevention of flood and erosion.[227] A violation of the regulations amounts to an offence. Penalties for individual offenders are set out in sections 23(3), 24(4) and 26(3), and fines range from ₦50,000 to ₦200,000. Body corporate penalties are set out in sections 23(4), 24(5) and 26(4), and fines range from ₦5000,000 to ₦1,000,000.

Discharging harmful quantities of any hazardous substance into the air or upon land and the waters of Nigeria or the adjoining shorelines is an offence under section 27. Punishments are provided under section 27(2)–(4). For an individual, the punishment is a fine of ₦1,000,000 or imprisonment for 5 years. Where the offender is a body corporate, the penalty shall be a fine of ₦1,000,000 and an additional ₦15,000 for each day the offence subsists.[228]

---

[219] NESREA Act (2007), s. 21(3).

[220] Ibid., s. 21(4).

[221] Ibid., s. 22(1)(a) and (b).

[222] Ibid., s. 22(3) and (4), respectively.

[223] National Environmental Standards, Regulations and Enforcement Agency (NESREA).

[224] NESREA Act (2007), s. 23(1) and (2).

[225] Ibid., s. 24 (1) and (2).

[226] Ibid., s. 25(1).

[227] Ibid., s. 26(1) and (2).

[228] Ibid., s. 27(3).

11.4.3.2 Criminal Code

The Criminal Code[229] also provides for criminal sanctions under sections 245 and 247. Under section 245, 'any person who corrupts or fouls water of any spring, stream, well, reservoir so as to render it less fit for the purpose for which it is ordinary used, is guilty of a misdemeanour and is liable to imprisonment for six months'. Section 247, on the other hand, proscribes noxious acts. Thus, any person who:

(a) vitiates the atmosphere in any place so as to make it noxious to the health of persons in general dwelling or carrying on business in the neighbourhood or passing along a public way; or
(b) does any act which is, and which he knows or has reason to believe to be likely to spread the infection of any disease dangerous to life whether human or animal is guilty of a misdemeanor, and is liable to imprisonment for six months.

11.4.4 Illegal Wildlife Trade and Trafficking in Endangered Species

11.4.4.1 Introduction

Wildlife trafficking and illegal wildlife trade are not new societal challenges; however, there is a broadening recognition of the problem as being an environmental crime with implications for socio-environmental security.[230] While species extinction and animal abuse are major problems, wildlife trafficking is also associated with corruption, national insecurity, the spread of zoonotic disease, undercutting of sustainable development investments and erosion of cultural resources, among others.[231]

Wildlife trafficking and illegal wildlife trade are transnational environmental crimes that pose diverse harms to Indigenous peoples and local communities, biodiversity conservation and sustainable development, and they are associated with violence against people and animals, which can be associated with other forms of criminality, such as drug trafficking.[232]

An increasing amount of research on wildlife trafficking has been documented, which includes what species are being trafficked, where species are being transported and who is driving demand for trafficked wildlife.[233] To this end, wildlife trafficking has been documented in over 120 countries around the world.[234]

---

[229] Criminal Code (1916), as amended.
[230] Gore and Agu (2022), p. 2.
[231] Agu and Gore (2022).
[232] Gore et al. (2019), pp. 784–786.
[233] Andrew and Agu (2022), p. 11.
[234] Gore and Agu (2022), p. 2.

11.4.4.2 Offences Bordering on Illegal Wildlife Trade and Trafficking in Endangered Species

Although there is no universal treaty defining wildlife crime and, therefore, there is no universally accepted definition of the term, the term 'wildlife crime' can be referred to as 'harvesting and trade contrary to national law, particularly, but not exclusively, the national laws implemented in fulfillment of Convention on International Trade in Endangered Species of Wild Fauna and Flora 1973 (CITES) obligations'.[235]

Reports show that Nigeria, in recent years, has evolved into a primary transit hub for trafficking in illicit wildlife and forest products, in particular for global illegal pangolin trade, sourced primarily from Central Africa. In the World Wildlife Crime Report (WWCR) 2020,[236] launched by the United Nations Office on Drugs and Crime (UNODC), Nigeria was significantly indicted as a compromise country in the increasing dimensions of illegal trade in wildlife and forestry products, corroborating earlier reports.

In 2013, in a report by the Environmental Investigation Agency and Africa Nature Investors,[237] Nigeria was one of the 11 countries identified as being of a 'secondary concern' by the CITES Standing Committee on the basis of evidence identifying it as a transit point for the illegal trafficking of elephant ivory and other wildlife products. In 2019, Nigeria's status was escalated to the category of highest concern, owing to its increasing role in transnational ivory trafficking. In addition, as of May 2021, Nigeria is subject to compliance proceedings upon application of Article XIII of the CITES Convention.

The findings in those reports referred to above can be corroborated by recent seizures of illegal wildlife products in Nigeria. For instance, Nigeria made its largest seizure of pangolin scales in January 2020 when officials recovered 9.5 metric tons of scales estimated to be worth ₦10.6 billion ($25.9 million). In 2021, the Nigeria Customs Service intercepted 18.7 metric tons of elephant tusks, rhino horns, pangolin scales and claws at various exit points across the country. In February 2022, it seized 145 kilograms (kg) (about 320 pounds (lbs)) of elephant tusks and 840 kg (about 1852 lbs) of pangolin scales at a notorious market in the affluent Lekki district of Lagos.[238]

The reason for this intensification is not far-fetched. Activities bordering on illegal wildlife trade and trafficking in endangered species are becoming increasingly criminalised. Though CITES does not define wildlife crime as such, it strongly influences national legislation on wildlife crime and provides a means for international cooperation against trafficking. In this respect, CITES provides a framework for the protection of certain species against over-exploitation through international

---

[235] United Nations Office on Drugs and Crime (UNODC) (2020), p. 30.

[236] Ibid.

[237] Environmental Investigation Agency and Africa Nature Investors (2021).

[238] Ekott (2022), p. 30.

trade. Parties to CITES are required to 'penalise' illegal trade, which may include the criminalisation of serious offences.[239] This includes offences that might not attract criminal sanctions in some parts of the world.[240] It is in respect of this injunction that Nigeria had enacted some pieces of legislation that criminalise illegal wildlife trade and trafficking in endangered species. Some of the offences on illegal wildlife trade and trafficking in endangered species that can be found in those legislation include:

(i) Trade/sale or export/import of wildlife products and related offences
(ii) Offences bordering on the hunting of wildlife
(iii) Offence of possession of wildlife and forest products
(iv) Offences of money laundering
(v) Offences of corruption practices in relation to illegal wildlife trade and trafficking in endangered species

These offences and applicable legislation are discussed below.

11.4.4.2.1 Trade/Sale or Export/Import of Wildlife Products and Related Offences

Trade/sale- or export/import-related offences are provided under the following legislation:

(i) Endangered Species (Control of International Trade and Traffic) Act 1985, as amended in 2016
(ii) National Environmental (Protection of Endangered Species in International Trade) Regulation 2011, and
(iii) Custom and Excise Management Act 1959, as amended in 2003

11.4.4.2.1.1 Endangered Species (Control of International Trade and Traffic) Act 1985

One of the pieces of legislation that criminalises illegal trade/sale or dealing in wildlife is the Endangered Species (Control of International Trade and Traffic) Act 1985 (or the 'Endangered Species Act').[241] The Act provides for the conservation and management of Nigeria's wildlife[242] and the protection of some of its

---

[239] Ekott (2022), p. 30.

[240] Ibid.

[241] The Act was promulgated in 1985, retained as Cap E9 LFN 2014 and amended in December 2016.

[242] Under the Endangered Species Act (1985) at s. 8, 'wild life' includes (a) wild animals and plants, whether or not they are indigenous to Nigeria; (b) wild animals and plants that are indigenous to the continental shelf of Nigeria or the super-adjacent waters; (c) migratory wild animals and birds that temporarily make their habitation in, pass through or overfly, Nigeria and (d) any animal or plant other than domesticated animals or usually cultivated plants.

endangered species in danger of extinction as a result of over-exploitation, as required under certain international treaties to which Nigeria is a signatory.[243] The Act prohibits the hunting of/trading in wild animals.

Under section 1(1) of the Act, the hunting or capture of, or trade in, the animal species specified in the First Schedule to the Act (being animal species threatened with extinction) is absolutely prohibited. Again, under section 2(1) of the Act, no person shall trade in any animal specified in the Second Schedule to this Act except where he complies with the following provisions, that is, to say:

(a) he has obtained an export permit granted by the Minister;[244]
(b) the Minister is satisfied that such export will not be detrimental to the survival of that specimen;
(c) the Minister is satisfied that the specie is to be exported alive, it will be so prepared and transported as to minimise the risk of injury, damage to health, cruel treatment or death of the animal;
(d) the Minister is satisfied that an import permit has been or will be granted for the specimen by the country of importation.

In the same vein, no person shall import any species specified in the Second Schedule to the Act, except where he has first obtained an import permit or a re-export certificate for that purpose.[245] No import permit shall, however, be issued unless the Minister is satisfied that:

(a) the import shall be for a purpose which is not detrimental to the survival of the specimen;
(b) the specimen is not to be used for a primarily commercial purpose; and
(c) the proposed recipient of a living specimen is suitably equipped to house and care for it.[246]

Notwithstanding the provisions of section 2(3) of the Act,[247] no re-export certificate shall be granted in respect of any specimen specified in the Second Schedule to this Act unless the minister is satisfied that:

(a) the specimen was imported in accordance with the provisions of this Act;
(b) any living specimen shall be so prepared and shipped as to minimise the risk of injury, damage to health, cruel treatment or death thereto; and
(c) an import permit has been obtained for any such living specimen.[248]

---

[243] Endangered Species Act (1985), preamble.

[244] The Minister referred to is the Minister of the Government of the Federation charged with responsibility for matters relating to wildlife. Endangered Species Act (1985), s. 8.

[245] Endangered Species Act 1985 (n 241), s. 2(2).

[246] Ibid., s. 2(3).

[247] Endangered Species Act (1985).

[248] Ibid., s. 2 (4).

To this end, no certificate for the removal from any waters of any specimen under the Second Schedule to this Act shall be issued unless the Minister is satisfied that:

(a) the removal shall not be detrimental to the survival of the specimen concerned;
(b) the recipient of a living specimen is fully and suitably equipped to receive and care for it; and
(c) the specimen shall not be used for a primarily commercial purpose.[249]

From the foregoing, any person who, in contravention of the above provisions of the Act, trades in, or is in possession of, or otherwise deals with a specimen specified in the First and Second Schedules to the Act shall be guilty of an offence and liable, on conviction, to:

(a) in respect of any specimen under the First Schedule to this Act, a fine of ₦5,000,000 for a first offence and for a second and subsequent offence to imprisonment for 1 year without the option of a fine;[250] and
(b) in respect of any specimen under the Second Schedule to this Act, to a fine of ₦1,000,000 for a first offence and for a second or subsequent offence, to imprisonment for six months without the option of a fine.[251]

In addition, where a person is convicted of an offence under section 5(1) above, the court may:

(a) order the forfeiture of any specimen which is the subject of such prosecution and
(b) make such orders (including the upkeep of live specimens at the expense of the person so convicted) as the court may deem fit.

11.4.4.2.1.2 National Environmental (Protection of Endangered Species in International Trade) Regulation 2011

Another legislation that criminalises illegal wildlife trade and trafficking in endangered species is the National Environmental (Protection of Endangered Species in International Trade) Regulation 2011.[252] The prohibition of trafficking in endangered species under the National Environmental (Protection of Endangered Species in International Trade) Regulation 2011 apply to specimen of wildlife species listed in Appendices I, II and III to the Convention on International Trade in Endangered

[249] Endangered Species Act (1985), s. 2(5).

[250] Endangered Species (Control of International Trade and Traffic) (Amendment) Act (2016), s. 3. This Act amended the penalty of ₦1000 specified under the Endangered Species Act (1985), s. 5(1)(a).

[251] Endangered Species (Control of International Trade and Traffic) (Amendment) Act (2016), s. 4. This Act amended the penalty of ₦500 specified under the Endangered Species Act (1985), s. 5(1)(b).

[252] Government Notice No. 130, S.I. No. 16. Federal Republic of Nigeria Official Gazette No. 43 Vol. 98, 9 May 2011.

Species of Wild Fauna and Flora (CITES) 1973 (or 'the Convention') domesticated by the Endangered Species (Control of International Trade and Traffic) Act 1985 (Endangered Species Act)[253] include wildlife species included under the Convention and also those listed in the Schedules I and II to the Act.[254]

The requirements for the import, introduction from sea, export and re-export of the specimens of wildlife species listed in Appendices I, II and III to the Convention and of wildlife species listed in Schedules I and II to the Endangered Species Act are provided under regulation 4 of the Regulations.[255]

In order to import into the Federal Republic of Nigeria any specimen of wildlife species listed in Appendix I of the Convention from any foreign country, an import permit issued pursuant to section 3 of the Act and a valid foreign re-export permit issued by the country of origin or a valid foreign re-export certificate issued by the country of re-export must be obtained and presented prior to such importation. To import any specimen of wildlife species listed in Appendix I of the Convention taken in a marine environment not under the jurisdiction of any country, a certificate of introduction from the sea issued in accordance with section 3 of the Act must be obtained prior to such introduction.

Where any person wishes to import any specimen of wildlife species listed in Appendix II of the Convention or Schedule II to the Act, taken from any foreign country, a valid foreign export permit issued by the country of origin or a valid foreign re-export certificate issued by the country of export must be obtained and presented prior to such importation. Appendix II of the Convention or Schedule II of the Act also states that in order to import any specimen of wildlife species listed therein and taken in a marine environment that is not under the jurisdiction of any country, an introduction from the sea certificate issued in accordance with the provisions of the Act and these Regulations must be obtained prior to such introduction.

Before importing any specimen of species included in Appendix III of the Convention from a foreign nation that has listed such specimen of wildlife, a valid foreign export permit or re-export certificate issued by such country must be obtained. And where such foreign land has not listed such specimen of a wildlife species, a valid foreign certificate of origin or foreign re-export certificate must be obtained prior to such importation.[256]

Before exporting or re-exporting any specimen of a wildlife species listed in Appendix I or II of the Convention from the Federal Republic of Nigeria, an export permit or re-export certificate granted under section 3 of the Act must be obtained. Where the specimen of wildlife species is listed in Appendix III of the Convention or

---

[253] See note 251.

[254] National Environmental (Protection of Endangered Species in International Trade) Regulation 2011, regulation 1.

[255] National Environmental (Protection of Endangered Species in International Trade) Regulation 2011.

[256] Ibid., regulation 4(1).

Schedule II to the Act, an export permit issued pursuant to section 3 of the Act must be obtained prior to such exportation or re-exportation. In the case that such specimen of wildlife species has not been listed by the Federal Republic of Nigeria, a certificate of origin, issued pursuant to section 3 of the Act, must be obtained prior to such exportation.[257]

Furthermore, in order to re-export from the Federal Republic of Nigeria any specimen of wildlife listed in Appendix III of the Convention, a certificate issued pursuant to the provisions of the Act and these Regulations that the specimen was processed in the Federal Republic of Nigeria or is being re-exported must be obtained prior to such re-exportation.[258] From the foregoing, it is therefore unlawful:

(a) To import into the Federal Republic of Nigeria any specimen of a wildlife species listed in Appendices I, II and III of the Convention or Schedule I and II to the Act from any foreign country
(b) To introduce directly into the Federal Republic of Nigeria any specimen of a wildlife species listed in Appendix I or II of the Convention or Schedules I and II of the Act taken in a marine environment not under the jurisdiction of any country
(c) To export from the Federal Republic of Nigeria any specimen of a wildlife species listed in Appendices I, II and III of the Convention or Schedules I and II of the Act
(d) To re-export from the Federal Republic of Nigeria any specimen of a wildlife species listed in Appendix I, II or III of the Convention or Schedules I and II to the Act, and
(e) For any person to possess any specimen of a wildlife species listed in Appendix I, II or III of the Convention or Schedules I and II to the Act imported into the Federal Republic of Nigeria or exported or re-exported from the Federal Republic of Nigeria contrary to the provisions of the Convention and the Act.[259]

Based on the above provisions under regulation 3 of these Regulations,[260] it shall be an offence to import, export, re-export or introduce from the sea or attempt to import, export, re-export or introduce from the sea any specimen listed in Appendices I, II and III to the Convention and to Schedules I and II to the Endangered Species Act.[261] Any person found guilty of contravening this provisions shall, on conviction, be liable to a fine not exceeding 5 million naira (₦5 m) or to

[257] National Environmental (Protection of Endangered Species in International Trade) Regulation 2011, regulation 4(2).

[258] Ibid., regulation 4(3).

[259] Ibid., regulation 3(2).

[260] National Environmental (Protection of Endangered Species in International Trade) Regulation 2011.

[261] National Environmental (Protection of Endangered Species in International Trade) Regulation 2011, regulation 7(1).

imprisonment for a term not exceeding 3 years or to both such fine and imprisonment.[262]

It shall also be an offence under these Regulations for any person to have in his possession or under his control or to offer or expose for sale or display to the public any specimen of the species listed in Appendices I, II, and III of the Convention or the Schedules to the Act and these Regulations which was acquired in contravention of the provisions of the Convention, the Act and/or these Regulations.[263] Any person found guilty of contravening the provisions shall be guilty of an offence and shall, on conviction, be liable to a fine not exceeding 5 million naira (₦5 m) or to imprisonment for a term not exceeding 3 years or to both such fine and imprisonment.[264]

Under the Regulations,[265] it shall also be an offence to make or attempt to make either oral or written false or misleading statements in connection with an application for a permit or certificate or registration. Any person found guilty of contravening these provisions shall, on conviction, be liable to a fine not exceeding 3 million naira (₦3 m) or to imprisonment for a term not exceeding 3 years or to both such fine and imprisonment.[266]

Again, it shall be an offence to obstruct or otherwise hinder an officer in the performance of his duties.[267] A person found guilty of contravening these provisions shall, on conviction, be liable to a fine not exceeding 1 million naira (₦l m) or to imprisonment for a term not exceeding 1 year or to both such fine and imprisonment.[268]

Where any unauthorised person alters, defaces or erases a mark used by the Authority to individually and permanently identify specimens, such person is deemed to have committed an offence under these Regulations.[269] The penalty for such contravention is a fine not exceeding 2 million naira (₦2 m) or imprisonment for a term not exceeding 2 years or both such fine and imprisonment.[270]

Where a body corporate is found guilty of contravening any of the provisions of these Regulations, such body corporate or any person purporting to act in any such capacity shall, on conviction, be liable to a fine not exceeding 20 million naira (₦20 m), and its principal officers shall be liable to a term of imprisonment not exceeding 7 years or to both such fine and imprisonment.[271]

---

262 Ibid., regulation 7(2).

263 Ibid., regulation 7(3).

264 Ibid., regulation 7(4).

265 Ibid., regulation 7(5).

266 Ibid., regulation 7(6).

267 Ibid., regulation 7(7).

268 Ibid., regulation 7(8).

269 Ibid., regulation 7(9).

270 Ibid., regulation 7(10).

271 National Environmental (Protection of Endangered Species in International Trade) Regulation 2011, regulation 7(11).

In addition to the above penalties, when a person is convicted of an offence against these Regulations, any cage, container, boat, aeroplane, vehicle or other articles and equipment in respect of or by means of which the offence was committed shall be forfeited to the Federal Republic of Nigeria.[272]

Again, expenses incurred as a result of the seizure, including custody costs and costs for the transporting and disposing of specimens or for maintaining live animals and plants during the time of seizure shall be recoverable from the offender.[273]

11.4.4.2.1.3 Customs and Excise Management Act 1959, as Amended in 2003

The Customs and Excise Management Act was enacted as Act No. 55 of 1958 and commenced on 1 April 1959. The Act was amended by the Customs and Excise Management (Amendment) Act No. 20 of 10 July 2003.[274] It is an Act to regulate the management and collection of duties of customs and excise and for purposes ancillary thereto.[275] Although the Act was not specifically enacted for the purposes of regulating illegal trade and trafficking in wildlife, some of its provisions can be applied in controlling the import and export of wildlife and endangered species. This is so because under the Nigeria Customs Service Export Prohibition List wildlife animals are classified as endangered species and their products (e.g. crocodile, elephant, lizard, eagle, monkey, zebra, lion, etc.) under item 7 as well as timber (rough and sown) under item 2.

In the case of importation, for instance under section 47(1)(a)(ii), it is an offence if any person lands or unloads in Nigeria or removes from their place of importation or from any approved wharf, examination station, customs station or customs area any goods imported contrary to any prohibition;[276] assists or is otherwise concerned in such landing, unloading or removal;[277] or imports or is concerned in importing any goods contrary to any prohibition, whether or not the goods are landed or unloaded.[278] Any person that does any of the above prohibited acts and with intent to evade any such duty or any prohibition shall be liable and sentenced to imprisonment for 5 years without the option of a fine.

An offence is also committed if any person (a) imports or causes to be imported any goods concealed in a container holding goods of a different description or (b) directly or indirectly imports or causes to be imported or entered any goods found, whether before or after delivery, not to correspond with the entry delivered

---

[272] Ibid., regulation 8(4).

[273] Ibid., regulation 7(12).

[274] The Act is currently retained as Cap C 45 Laws of the Federation of Nigeria (LFN) 2004.

[275] Customs and Excise Management Act (1959), preamble.

[276] 'Prohibition', in relation to goods, means any prohibition or restriction on the importation, exportation or carriage coastwise of goods imposed by or under this or any other enactment, and 'prohibited' shall be construed accordingly; see Customs and Excise Management Act (1959), s. 2.

[277] Customs and Excise Management Act (1959), s. 47(1)(b).

[278] Ibid., s. 47(1)(c).

thereof. Such a person shall be sentenced to imprisonment for 5 years without the option of a fine.[279]

In addition to the penalties specified in section 47(1) and (2), the offender is liable to the forfeiture of goods improperly imported where the goods are imported, landed or unloaded contrary to any prohibition[280] or the goods imported are concealed in a container holding goods of a different description[281] or the imported goods are concealed or packed in a manner that appears to intend to deceive an officer[282] or the imported goods are found, whether before or after delivery, to not correspond with the entry made therefor.[283]

Similarly, the improper exportation of goods is penalised. A penalty is imposed under section 64(1) of the Act[284] if any person, except as provided by or under the Act, exports or is concerned in exporting any goods contrary to any prohibition[285] or loads for exportation or as stores or brings to any place in Nigeria for the purpose of exporting or loading as stores any goods the exportation of which is **contrary to any prohibition** or assists or is otherwise concerned in such loading or bringing.[286]

The phrase '**contrary to any prohibition**', as provided under section 64(1)(b) of the Act,[287] can be loosely interpreted to apply to goods that fall under the specimen of wildlife species listed in Appendices I, II and III to the Convention on International Trade in Endangered Species of Wild Fauna and Flora (CITES) 1973 and also those listed in Schedules I and II to the Endangered Species (Control of International Trade and Traffic) Act 1985.

In such a situation, as provided above, any person who does any of those acts and with intent to evade any such duty or any prohibition as provided under the Act, is deemed to have committed an offence and shall be liable, on conviction, to imprisonment for 5 years without the option of a fine. In addition, an offence is committed if any person, except as provided by or under the Act,

(a) loads or causes to be loaded any goods into a ship or aircraft for exportation or as stores, or removes or causes to be removed any goods from a customs station for exportation before entry outwards thereof has been signed by the proper officer;[288]

[279] Ibid., s. 47(2).

[280] Ibid., s. 46(b).

[281] Ibid., s. 46(d).

[282] Ibid., s. 46(e).

[283] Ibid., s. 46(f).

[284] Customs and Excise Management Act (1959).

[285] Ibid., s. 64(a)(ii).

[286] Ibid., s. 64(1)(b).

[287] Customs and Excise Management Act (1959).

[288] Customs and Excise Management Act (1959), s. 64(2)(a).

(b) exports or causes to be exported, or brings or causes to be brought to any place in Nigeria for exportation, any goods concealed in a container holding goods of a different description;[289] or
(c) directly or indirectly exports or enters outwards or causes to be exported or entered outwards any goods found not to correspond with the entry made thereof.[290]

The penalty for contravention is imprisonment for a term of 5 years without the option of a fine.

Furthermore, forfeiture as a penalty under the Act shall apply to any goods, being goods chargeable with any duty on exportation or goods the exportation of which is prohibited, are found after having been loaded for exportation to have been concealed in any manner on board any ship or aircraft or in any vehicle;[291] or any goods are exported or brought to any place in Nigeria for exportation concealed in a container holding goods of a different description;[292] or any goods are exported or brought to any place in Nigeria for exportation concealed or packed in any manner appearing to be intended to deceive an officer;[293] or any goods entered outwards are found, whether before or after loading, not to correspond with the entry made thereof.[294]

It should be noted that the offences specified in sections 47 and 64 and the acts done under sections 46 and 63 if committed by an agent shall be affixed to the agent's principal. Under section 155 of the Act,[295]

> any person who authorises an agent to act for him in relation to any goods for any of the purposes of the customs and excise laws shall be liable for the acts and declarations of his agent, and may accordingly be prosecuted for any offence against the customs and excise laws committed by the agent in respect of any such goods in the same manner as if he had himself committed the offence.

However, it shall be a good defence if the principal can prove that he had used due diligence to secure compliance with the provisions of the customs and excise laws, as the case may be, and that the offence was committed without his consent, connivance or wilful default.[296] Where this is established, the agent shall be liable to be prosecuted for any of the offences in issue.[297]

---

289 Ibid., s. 64(2)(b).

290 Ibid., s. 64(2(c).

291 Ibid., s. 63(d).

292 Ibid., s. 63(e).

293 Ibid., s. 63(f).

294 Ibid., s. 63(g).

295 Customs and Excise Management Act (1959).

296 Customs and Excise Management Act (1959), s. 155(i).

297 Ibid., s. 155(ii).

11.4.4.2.2 Offences Bordering on Hunting of Wildlife

The main legislation prohibiting the hunting of wildlife is the National Park Service Act 1999, as amended in 2006.[298] This is an Act to establish the National Park Service, to be responsible for the preservation, enhancement and protection of wild animals and plants and other vegetation in national parks and for matters connected therewith. The Act was enacted in 1999 as Act No. 46 and came into effect on 26 May 1999 and was amended in 2006 by the National Park Service (Amendment) Act, 2006. To safeguard wildlife and endangered species, the Act has provisions criminalising acts bordering on hunting, wounding, killing or capturing wildlife as well as prohibiting certain methods of hunting in national parks.

It is an offence under section 30(1) of the Act[299] for a person who, unless authorised to do so under the Act or the regulations made pursuant to the Act, hunts or captures an animal[300] or destroys or collects an animal[301] or removes from or damages the nest of a bird or reptile[302] or fishes or attempts to kill any fish.[303] A person who engages in any of these offences bordering on the hunting, wounding, killing or capturing of the mother of a young animal, large mammal or any endangered, protected or prohibited species shall be liable, on conviction, to imprisonment for a term of not less than 3 months but not exceeding 5 years without the option of a fine.[304]

Again, a person who, unless authorised to do so under the Act or the regulations made pursuant to the Act, does an act likely to harm or disturb the fauna or flora[305] is guilty of an offence and shall, on conviction, be liable to imprisonment for a term of not less than 6 months but not exceeding 10 years without the option of a fine.[306]

Likewise, a person who uses any bait, decoy, hide, blind or any calling device whatsoever to bring animals closer for the purpose of hunting them[307] or uses or is in possession of a motor vehicle's dazzling or artificial light or radio communication[308] is guilty of an offence. An offence is also committed when a person flies any kind of aircraft at an altitude lower than 200 metres over a national park.[309] Such a person shall, on conviction, be liable to a fine of not less than ₦10,000 but not exceeding

[298] Cap N 65 LFN 2004.

[299] National Park Services Act (1999).

[300] Ibid., s. 30(1)(a).

[301] Ibid., s. 30(1)(b).

[302] Ibid., s. 30(1)(h).

[303] Ibid., s. 30(1)(i).

[304] Ibid., s. 37(2)(a).

[305] Ibid., s. 30(1)(o).

[306] National Park Services Act (1999), s. 37(2)(b).

[307] Ibid., s. 30(1)(q).

[308] Ibid., s. 30(1)(r).

[309] Ibid., s. 30(2).

₦50,000 or to imprisonment for a term of not less than 1 year but not exceeding 5 years or to both such fine and imprisonment.[310]

Where any of these offences specified under section 30(1) bordering on the hunting, wounding, killing or capturing of a mother of a young animal, large mammal or any endangered, protected or prohibited species is committed by a body corporate, it shall, on conviction, be liable to a fine of not less than ₦100,000 but not exceeding ₦1,000,000.[311]

Furthermore, section 31 of the Act restricts the use of weapons in national parks, save as exempted under section 31(2)–(5) of the Act. Thus, a person in a national park who, (a) without a permit issued under this section or (b) in breach of any express condition of a permit issued under this Act or (c) in breach of a regulation made pursuant to this Act, conveys into the national park or, while within the confines of the national park, is in possession of, carries or uses for any purpose any firearm, spear, bow, arrow or other weapons, explosives, snares, net traps or poison or sets out any snare, net trap or other instruments for the purpose of capturing or killing an animal is guilty of an offence under this Act.[312] A person who does any of these prohibited acts is guilty of an offence and is liable, on conviction, to a fine of not less than ₦5,000 but not exceeding ₦25,000 or to imprisonment for a term of not less than 6 months but not exceeding 5 years or to both such fine and imprisonment.[313]

Subject to the provisions of section 29(1) (a)–(f) of the Act,[314] entry into national parks is restricted. Thus, under section 29(1), a person who enters into or resides, erects a building or camps in a national park is guilty of an offence. A person found guilty of this offence shall be liable, on conviction, to a fine not exceeding ₦20,000 or to imprisonment for a term not exceeding 2 years or to both such fine and imprisonment.[315]

Under the Act,[316] a person who aids, abets, procures or conspires with another person or attempts to commit any of the offences specified in the Act or regulations made pursuant to the Act is guilty of an offence as if he himself had committed the offence and shall be punished accordingly. Note that a person who aids, abets, procures or conspires with another person or attempts to commit any of the offences under the Act or regulations made pursuant to the Act is liable, on conviction, to the penalty to which the person who committed the offence is subject under the Act or regulations.[317]

---

[310] Ibid., s. 37(2)(c).

[311] Ibid., s. 37(2)(d).

[312] Ibid., s. 31(1).

[313] Ibid., s. 37(3).

[314] National Park Services Act (1999).

[315] National Park Services Act (1999), s. 37(1).

[316] Ibid., s. 36.

[317] Ibid., s. 37(8).

Where any of the offences specified under the Act is committed by a body corporate and it is proved to have been committed with the consent or connivance of or to be attributable to any neglect on the part of any director, manager, secretary or other similar officer of the body corporate or any person purporting to act in any of those capacities, he, as well as the body corporate, shall be deemed to be guilty of that offence and shall be liable to be proceeded against and punished accordingly.[318]

Besides the penalties provided under section 37(2)(c),[319] in a judicial proceeding under the Act, it shall be lawful for the court before which the proceeding is brought to order that any equipment, instrument and other things of a like nature used by the offender in committing the offence be forfeited to the national park.[320] And where under the Act a fine or imprisonment is imposed on a person, the court may order that compensation for the conservation value of a wild plant, wild animal or the ecosystem, where applicable, as stipulated in the regulations made under section 51 of the Act, be paid by the person to the national park.[321]

11.4.4.2.3 Offence of Possession of Wildlife and Forest Products

Although section 1 of the Endangered Species Act 1985[322] prohibits hunting, capturing, trading in or otherwise dealing with an animal species specified in the Second Schedule to the Act, the Endangered Species Act 1985 also punishes any person who is **in possession** of a specimen specified in Schedules I and II to the Act.[323] Thus, under section 5(1) of the Act,[324] 'any person who, in contravention of the provisions of the Act . . . is **in possession** of or otherwise deals with a specimen specified in the First and Second Schedules to this Act, shall be guilty of an offence. . .'. Such a person shall be liable, on conviction, to:

(a) In respect of any specimen under the First Schedule to this Act, a fine of ₦5,000,000 for the first offence and for the second and subsequent offence, to imprisonment for 1 year without the option of a fine,[325] and

[318] Ibid., s. 38.

[319] National Park Services Act (1999).

[320] Ibid., s. 39(1).

[321] Ibid., s. 39(2).

[322] Endangered Species Act (1985).

[323] Endangered Species Act (1985).

[324] Ibid.

[325] Endangered Species (Control of International Trade and Traffic) (Amendment) Act, 2016, s. 3. This Act amended the penalty of ₦1000 specified under the Endangered Species Act (1985), s. 5(1) (a).

(b) In respect of any specimen under the Second Schedule to this Act, a fine of ₦1,000,000 for the first offence and for the second or subsequent offence, to imprisonment for 6 months without the option of a fine[326]

In addition, where a person is convicted of an offence under 5(1) of the Act,[327] the court may (a) order the forfeiture of any specimen that is the subject of such prosecution and (b) make such orders (including the upkeep of live specimens at the expense of the person so convicted) as the court may deem fit.[328]

Under regulation 3(2) of the Regulations,[329] it is unlawful for any person to **possess** any specimen of a wildlife species listed in Appendix I, II or III of the Convention[330] or in Schedules I and II to the Act;[331] imported into the Federal Republic of Nigeria; or exported or re-exported from the Federal Republic of Nigeria contrary to the provisions of the Convention and the Act.

Furthermore, under regulation 7(3), it shall be an offence under these Regulations for any person to have in his **possession or under his control** or to offer or expose for sale or display to the public any specimen of the species listed in Appendices I, II and III of the Convention[332] or in the Schedules to the Act[333] and these Regulations which was acquired in contravention of the provisions of the Convention, the Act and/or these Regulations. Any person found guilty of contravening this provision shall be guilty of an offence and, on conviction, be liable to a fine not exceeding 5 million naira (₦5 m) or to imprisonment for a term not exceeding 3 years or to both such fine and imprisonment.[334]

Under section 30(1) of the National Park Services Act,[335] it is an offence to be **in possession** of a wild animal, bird or reptile, dead or alive,[336] or to be **in possession** of, use or set a snare, net trap or any other instrument for the purpose of capturing or killing an animal[337] or to use or be in possession of a motor vehicle's dazzling or

[326]Endangered Species (Control of International Trade and Traffic) (Amendment) Act, 2016, s. 4. This Act amended the penalty of ₦500 specified under the Endangered Species Act (1985), s. 5(1)(b).

[327]Endangered Species Act (1985).

[328]Ibid., s. 5(2).

[329]National Environmental (Protection of Endangered Species in International Trade) Regulation 2011.

[330]Convention on International Trade in Endangered Species of Wild Fauna and Flora 1973 (CITES).

[331]Endangered Species Act 1985.

[332]CITES.

[333]Endangered Species Act 1985.

[334]National Environmental (Protection of Endangered Species in International Trade) Regulation 2011, regulations 7(4).

[335]National Park Services Act (1999).

[336]Ibid., s. 30(1)(j).

[337]Ibid., s. 30(1)(k).

artificial light or radio communication.[338] Such a person shall, on conviction, be liable to a fine of not less than ₦10,000 but not exceeding ₦50,000 or to imprisonment for a term of not less than 1 year but not exceeding 5 years or to both such fine and imprisonment.[339]

Besides the penalties provided under section 37(2)(c) of the Act,[340] in any judicial proceeding under the Act, it shall be lawful for the court before which the proceeding is brought to make an order that any equipment, instrument and other things of a like nature used by the offender in committing the offence be forfeited to the national park.[341] Where a fine or imprisonment is imposed on a person under the Act the court may order that compensation for the conservation value of a wild plant, wild animal or the ecosystem, where applicable, as stipulated in regulations made under section 51 of the Act, be paid by the person to the National Park.[342]

11.4.4.2.4 Offence of Money Laundering

It would appear strange, and rightly too, to discuss the offence of money laundering as part of criminal liability for environmental damage, especially as part of the offences on illegal wildlife trade and trafficking in endangered species, the reason being that crimes bordering on illegal wildlife trade and trafficking in endangered species do not necessarily function in isolation of other crimes or other criminal activity, such as money laundering, human trafficking, and arms and drug smuggling.[343] In fact, these crimes can enable one another and exacerbate further crime; syndicates can exploit the same transportation routes and corrupt supply chains to fulfil orders.[344] Again, wildlife crimes also converge; for example, both timber exports and charcoal exports have been shown to facilitate the illegal transport of ivory and pangolin scales.[345]

International illegal wildlife trade and trafficking of large shipments require well-organised logistics, and illegal operations have unique requirements in terms of routing and transportation, which make them distinct from legal trade. Wildlife trafficking and illegal wildlife trade comprise all activities also found in the legal sphere, such as the procurement, production, transportation, sale and distribution of commodities, and all these activities are associated with expenditures for the organisers.[346]

---

[338] Ibid., s. 30(1)(r).

[339] Ibid., s. 37(2)(c).

[340] National Park Services Act (1999).

[341] Ibid., s. 39(1).

[342] Ibid., s. 39(2).

[343] Environmental Investigation Agency (UK) (2021).

[344] Ibid.

[345] Environmental Investigation Agency (UK) (2021).

[346] United Nations Office on Drugs and Crime (UNODC) (2020), p. 119.

Since an illegal wildlife trade requires more complex operations, the services of persons specialised in facilitating the movement of large amounts of money across borders may be required. Although illegal wildlife trade at the local level may be mostly financed by cash transactions, transferring larger amounts of money from destination to source countries requires formal or informal money service providers.[347] This is where money laundering offences and other financial crimes may come in.

Criminals resort to money laundering to make it appear that illicit funds have a legitimate origin. There are three major steps in money laundering (placement, layering and integration), and various controls should be put in place to monitor any suspicious activity that could be involved in money laundering.[348] In this respect, the Federal Government of Nigeria enacted the Anti Money Laundering (AML) Laws and Regulations[349] and established AML enforcement institutions.[350]

11.4.4.2.4.1 Money Laundering Legislation in Nigeria

The money laundering legislation in Nigeria has a chequered history. The key Nigerian AML law and regulations are as follows: the Money Laundering Act; the Terrorism Prevention Act, as amended; the Banks and Other Financial Institutions Act (BOFIA), as amended; the National Drug Law Enforcement Act; the Central Bank of Nigeria (CBN) Act 2017; the Regulations on Terrorism Prevention (Freezing of International Terrorist Funds and Other Matters) 2013; the CBN AML/Combating the Financing of Terrorism (CFT) Regulations; the CBN Risk-Based Supervision Framework for AML/CFT, 2011; CBN Circulars; and other regulatory messages.[351] Of interest in this discourse are the Money Laundering Act and the Cybercrime Act.

11.4.4.2.4.1.1 Money Laundering Act

The legal battle against money laundering in Nigeria started with the promulgation of the Money Laundering (Exchange Control (Anti Sabotage)) Decree No. 7 of 1984. This Decree was repealed in 1995 by the Money Laundering Decree. The 1995 Law was fine-tuned in 2002 as the Money Laundering Act No. 9 of 2002, repealing the 1995 Decree. The 2002 Act was repealed in 2003 by the Money Laundering (Prohibition) Act No. 7 of 2003. In 2004, the Act of 2003 was repealed by the Money Laundering (Prohibition) Act 2004. In 2011 and 2012, the Money

[347] Ibid., 122.

[348] Sanction Scanner (2021).

[349] For instance, the Money Laundering (Prevention and Prohibition) Act 2022 and the Cybercrimes (Prohibition, Prevention, etc.) Act, 2015 (discussed below), among others.

[350] Such as the Economic and Financial Crimes Commission (EFCC) and the Nigerian Financial Intelligence Unit (NFIU). These are discussed below.

[351] Sanction Scanner (2021).

Laundering (Prohibition) Act 2004 was repealed by the Money Laundering (Prohibition) Act No. 11 of 2011, which was amended by the Money Laundering (Prohibition) Act No. 1 of 2012, which consolidated the two laws. However, in May 2022, the Money Laundering (Prohibition) Act No. 11 of 2011, as amended, was repealed by the Money Laundering (Prevention and Prohibition) Act No. 14 of 2022.[352]

The current legislation on money laundering in Nigeria, therefore, is the Money Laundering (Prevention and Prohibition) Act, 2022.[353] The objectives of the Act[354] are to:

(a) provide for an effective and comprehensive legal and institutional framework for the prevention, prohibition, detection, prosecution and punishment of money laundering and other related offences in Nigeria;
(b) strengthen the existing system for combating money laundering and related offences ;
(c) make adequate provisions to prohibit money laundering ;
(d) expand the scope of money laundering offences and provide appropriate penalties; and
(e) establish the Special Control Unit Against Money Laundering under the Economic and Financial Crimes Commission for effective implementation of the money laundering provisions of the Act in relation to the designated non-financial businesses and professions.

The Act[355] makes a limitation to make or accept cash payments. To this end, no person or body corporate shall, except in a transaction through a financial institution, make or accept cash payments of a sum exceeding (a) ₦5,000,000 or its equivalent, in the case of an individual, or (b) ₦10,000,000 or its equivalent, in the case of a body corporate.[356] The Act[357] also imposes the duty to report the international transfer or transportation of funds, securities and cash. Such report shall indicate the nature and amount of the transfer and the names and addresses of the sender and receiver of the funds or securities.[358]

In addition, the transportation of cash or negotiable instruments in excess of US $10,000 or its equivalent by individuals in or out of Nigeria shall be declared to the Nigerian Customs Service.[359] To this end, any person who falsely declares or fails to make a declaration to the Nigerian Customs Service, as aforesaid, commits an

---

[352] See Money Laundering (Prevention and Prohibition) Act No. 14 of 2022, s. 29.

[353] Government Notice No. 67, Act No. 14, 2022, Federal Republic of Nigeria Official Gazette No. 90, Vol. 109, 13 May 2022.

[354] Money Laundering (Prevention and Prohibition) Act (2022), s. 1(1)(a)–(e).

[355] Money Laundering (Prevention and Prohibition) Act (2022).

[356] Money Laundering (Prevention and Prohibition) Act (2022), s. 2(1).

[357] Ibid., s. 3(1).

[358] Ibid., s. 3(2).

[359] Ibid., s. 3(3).

offence and is liable, on conviction, to the forfeiture of the undeclared funds or negotiable instrument or imprisonment for a term of at least 2 years or both.[360]

Under the Act, it is incumbent on any financial[361] and 'non-financial institution'[362] to report any suspicious transaction. Thus, where a transaction (a) involves a frequency that is unjustifiable or unreasonable, (b) is surrounded by conditions of unusual or unjustified complexity, (c) appears to have no economic justification or lawful objective, (d) is inconsistent with the known transaction pattern of the account or business relationship or, (e) in the opinion of the financial institution or non-financial business and profession, involves the proceeds of a criminal activity, unlawful act, money laundering or terrorist financing, that transaction shall be deemed to be suspicious, and the financial institution and designated non-financial business and profession involved in the transaction shall report to the Unit,[363] as the case may be, immediately.[364]

In this respect, the financial institution or designated non-financial business and profession shall, within 24 hours after the transaction above referred to, (a) draw up a written report containing all relevant information on the matters mentioned in section 7(1) of the Act, together with the reasons and identity of the principal and, where applicable, of the beneficiary or beneficiaries; (b) take appropriate action to prevent the laundering of the proceeds of a crime or an illegal act; and (c) report the suspicious transaction and actions taken to the Unit.[365] Failure to comply with the above provisions by the financial institution or designated non-financial business and profession amounts to an offence and subjects the offender, on conviction, to a fine of ₦1,000,000 for each day during which the offence continues.[366]

---

[360] Ibid., s. 3(5).

[361] Financial institutions include banks; body corporates; associations or groups of persons, whether corporate or incorporate, that carry on the business of investment and securities; virtual asset service providers; discount houses; insurance institutions; debt factorisation and conversion firms; bureau de change; finance companies; and money brokerage firms whose principal business includes factoring, project financing, equipment leasing, debt administration, fund management, private ledger service, investment management, local purchase order financing, export finance, project consultancy, financial consultancy, pension fund management and such other businesses as the Central Bank or other appropriate regulatory authorities may designate. See Money Laundering (Prevention and Prohibition) Act (2022), s. 30. See Economic and Financial Crimes Commission (Establishment) Act (2004), s. 46.

[362] Non-financial institutions mean dealers in 'jewellery, cars and luxury goods, chartered accountants, audit firms, tax consultants, clearing and settlement companies, legal practitioners, hotels, casinos, supermarkets or such other business as the Federal Ministry of Commerce or appropriate regulatory authorities may from time to time designate'. See Economic and Financial Crimes Commission (Establishment) Act (2004), s. 46.

[363] 'Unit' here refers to the Nigerian Financial Intelligent Unit responsible for the receiving, requesting, analysing and disseminating to competent authorities the disclosures of financial information concerning suspected proceeds of a crime and potential financing of terrorism. See Money Laundering (Prevention and Prohibition) Act (2022), s. 30.

[364] Money Laundering (Prevention and Prohibition) Act (2022), s. 7(1).

[365] Money Laundering (Prevention and Prohibition) Act (2022), s. 7(2).

[366] Ibid., s. 7(10).

Generally speaking, money laundering is prohibited in Nigeria.[367] Therefore, any person or body corporate, in or outside Nigeria, who directly or indirectly: (a) conceals or disguises the origin of (b) converts or transfers, (c) removes from the jurisdiction, or (d) acquires, uses, retains or takes possession or control of any fund or property, intentionally, knowingly or reasonably ought to have known that such fund or property is, or forms part of the proceeds of an unlawful act,[368] commits an offence of money laundering under this Act.[369]

A person found to have contravened any of these provisions is liable, on conviction, to imprisonment for a term of not less than 4 years but not more than 14 years or a fine of not less than five times the value of the proceeds of the crime or both.[370] Where the offence is committed by a body corporate, it shall be liable, on conviction, to a fine of not less than five times the value of the funds or the properties acquired as a result of the offence committed.[371] Where such body persists in the commission of the unlawful act[372] for which it was convicted in the first instance, the regulators may withdraw or revoke the certificate or licence of the body corporate.[373] Note that it is immaterial whether the various acts constituting the offence of money laundering were committed in different countries or places; the punishment prescribed therefor shall apply.[374]

The Act[375] also prohibits the retention of the proceeds of an unlawful act.[376] In this respect, an offence is deemed to have been committed where any person who: (a) conceals, removes from jurisdiction, transfers to nominees or otherwise retains the proceeds of an unlawful act on behalf of another person, where he knows or reasonably ought to have known or suspected that other person to be engaged in an unlawful act or has benefited from an unlawful act, or (b) knows or reasonably ought to have known or suspected that any property either in whole or in part directly or indirectly represents another person's proceeds of an unlawful act, acquires or uses that property or takes possession of it. Such a person is liable, on conviction, to a fine of at least five times the value of the proceeds of the unlawful act or to imprisonment for a term of at least 4 years but not more than 14 years or to both.

---

[367] Ibid., s. 18(1).

[368] Unlawful acts, among others, include participation in an organised criminal group, corruption, bribery, smuggling any other criminal act specified in the Act or any other law in Nigeria, including any act wherever committed in so far as such act would be an unlawful act if committed in Nigeria. See Money Laundering (Prevention and Prohibition) Act (2022), s. 18(6).

[369] Money Laundering (Prevention and Prohibition) Act (2022), s. 18(2).

[370] Ibid., s. 18(3).

[371] Ibid., s. 18(4).

[372] Ibid.

[373] Ibid., s. 18(5).

[374] Money Laundering (Prevention and Prohibition) Act (2022), s. 18(7).

[375] Money Laundering (Prevention and Prohibition) Act (2022).

[376] Ibid., s. 20.

Again, it is an offence when a person (a) conspires with, aids, abets or counsels any other person to commit an offence; (b) attempts to commit or is an accessory to an act or offence; or (c) incites, procures or induces any other person by any means whatsoever to commit an offence under the Act. The offender shall be liable, on conviction, to the same punishment as prescribed for that offence under the Act.[377]

Furthermore, where an offence under the Act which has been committed by a body corporate is proved to have been committed upon the instigation or with the connivance of or to be attributable to a neglect on the part of any director, manager, secretary or other similar officer of the body corporate or any person purporting to act in any such capacity, he, as well as the body corporate, where applicable, commits an offence and is liable to be proceeded against and punished accordingly.[378] In addition, where a body corporate is convicted of an offence under the Act, the court may order that the body corporate be wound up and all its assets and properties be forfeited to the Federal Government.[379]

11.4.4.2.4.1.2 Cyber Crime

Like many markets, illegal wildlife trade and trafficking in endangered species and wildlife products are moving online. Organised criminal groups are increasingly using a range of online platforms and technologies to facilitate the transnational trafficking of wildlife products. The monitoring of online trade, and using available technology to track key hubs, patterns and players involved in the illegal trade, is critical to disrupting the organisations exploiting online platforms.[380]

The Federal Republic of Nigeria, through the enactment of the Cybercrimes (Prohibition, Prevention, Etc) Act 2015,[381] has developed the capacity of law enforcement agencies to investigate the online sales of illegal wildlife; infiltrate existing online markets; collect relevant evidence, including using digital forensics; and develop enforcement countermeasures.

The Cybercrimes (Prohibition, Prevention, etc.) Act 2015 commenced on 15 May 2015. It is an Act to provide for the prohibition, prevention, detection, response, investigation and prosecution of cybercrimes and other related matters.[382] This intent is succinctly captured by the objectives of the Act. The main objectives of the Act[383] are to (a) provide an effective and unified legal, regulatory and institutional framework for the prohibition, prevention, detection, prosecution and punishment of cybercrimes in Nigeria; (b) ensure the protection of critical national information infrastructures; and (c) promote cybersecurity and the protection of

377 Ibid., s. 21.

378 Ibid., s. 22(1).

379 Ibid., s. 22(2).

380 United Nations Office on Drugs and Crime (UNODC) (2020).

381 Cybercrimes (Prohibition, Prevention, etc.) Act (2015).

382 Ibid., preamble.

383 Ibid., s. 1.

computer systems and networks, electronic communications, data and computer programmes, intellectual property and privacy rights.

Organised criminal groups spend money to commit crimes (for example, by paying for harvesting equipment (chainsaws, firearms, ammunition)), for transportation (for example, plane tickets for couriers), to establish front companies, etc., and these flows of money should also be used as indicators to detect potential illicit transactions and opportunities for disruption. To this end, basic information gleaned during law enforcement processes, such as details of the business structures of criminal groups and the financial transactions they enter into, must be collected.[384] Thus, the need to follow the flow of money may, at times, force the criminal gangs to hack into computers to evade detection or cover their tracks.

Under the Act,[385] any person who, with intent to commit an offence, uses any device to avoid detection or otherwise prevent identification or attribution to the act or omission commits an offence and shall be liable, on conviction, to imprisonment for a term of not more than 7 years or to a fine of not more than ₦7,000,000.00 or to both such fine and imprisonment.[386]

Furthermore, any person or organisation that knowingly and intentionally traffics in any password or similar information through which a computer may be accessed without lawful authority, if such trafficking affects public, private and/or individual interests within or outside the Federation of Nigeria, commits an offence and shall be liable, on conviction, to a fine of not more than ₦7,000,000.00 or imprisonment for a term of not more than 3 years or both such fine and imprisonment.[387]

To cover up its illicit transactions, a criminal organisation involved in illegal wildlife trade online may want to cover up its tracks. This may involve computer-related forgery or fraud. Computer-related forgery or fraud is punished under the Act.[388] In this respect, a person who knowingly accesses any computer or network and inputs, alters, deletes or suppresses any data resulting in inauthentic data, with the intention that such inauthentic data will be considered or acted upon as if it were authentic or genuine, regardless of whether or not such data is directly readable or intelligible, commits an offence and is liable, on conviction, to imprisonment for a term of not less than 3 years or a fine of not less than ₦7,000,000.00 or both.[389]

In the same vein, any employee of a financial institution found to have connived with another person or group of persons to perpetrate fraud using computer system (s) or network(s) commits an offence and shall be liable, on conviction, to imprisonment for a term of not more than 7 years and shall, in addition, refund the stolen

[384] United Nations Office on Drugs and Crime (UNODC) (2020).

[385] Cybercrimes (Prohibition, Prevention, etc.) Act (2015).

[386] Ibid., s. 6(3).

[387] Cybercrimes (Prohibition, Prevention, etc.) Act (2015), s. 6(4).

[388] Ibid., under ss. 13 and 14.

[389] Ibid., s. 13.

money or forfeit any property to which it has been converted into to either the bank, the financial institution or the customer from where the fraud was perpetrated.[390]

Notwithstanding that the act in issue was not carried out to fruition, the Act penalises any person who (a) attempts to commit any offence under the Act or (b) aids, abets, conspires with, counsels or procures another person(s) to commit any offence under the Act. Such a person shall be liable, on conviction, to the punishment provided for the principal offence under the Act.[391]

11.4.4.2.4.2 Institutional Framework on Money Laundry and Cybercrime

There are a number of institutions in Nigeria that are involved in the fight against money laundering and cybercrime, such as the Nigeria Police, the Office of the Attorney General of the Federation, the Nigerian Financial Intelligence Unit (NFIU) and the Economic and Financial Crimes Commission (EFCC). However, discussions were focused on the Economic and Financial Crimes Commission (EFCC) and the Nigerian Financial Intelligence Unit (NFIU) as the main institutions in the fight against money laundering and cybercrime in Nigeria. The selection of the two institutions is predicated on the fact that the EFCC is Nigeria's primary agency investigating and prosecuting money laundering crimes as it can investigate, arrest and prosecute individuals and entities suspected of engaging in money laundering activities. On the other hand, NFIU advises law enforcement and regulatory and supervisory agencies on the prevention and combating of money laundering, terrorist financing and predicate offences as well as conducts research into emerging threats of money laundering, terrorist financing and other predicate offences.

11.4.4.2.4.3 Economic and Financial Crimes Commission (EFCC)

The Economic and Financial Crimes Commission (or ‘the Commission’) is an anti-money laundering (AML) institution in Nigeria established under the Economic and Financial Crimes Commission (Establishment) Act 2002.[392] The Commission was established in 2003,[393] partially in response to pressure from the Financial Action Task Force on Money Laundering (FATF), which named Nigeria as one of the 23 countries that are not cooperative in the international community's efforts to fight money laundering.[394]

The Economic and Financial Crimes Commission (Establishment) (EFCC) Act 2004, mandates the Commission to combat financial and economic crimes. The

[390] Ibid., s. 14(5).

[391] Ibid., s. 27(1).

[392] Act No. 5 2002. The Act was repealed by the Economic and Financial Crimes Commission (Establishment) (EFCC) Act 2004, s. 44, and its section 1 establishes the Commission.

[393] When Former President Olusegun Obasanjo appointed Nuhu Ribadu as the first Chairman of the Commission in 2003.

[394] EFCC, the Establishment Act.

Commission is empowered to prevent, investigate, prosecute and penalise economic and financial crimes and is charged with the responsibility of enforcing the provisions of other laws and regulations relating to economic and financial crimes, including the Money Laundering Act.[395] The Commission in this respect coordinates anti-money laundering (AML) prosecutions and the sharing of information, gives the Central Bank of Nigeria (CBN) a wider power to deny bank licences and enables the CBN to freeze suspicious accounts.[396] The following provisions of the Act help the Commission to carry out its mandate in combating money laundering and, *a fortiori*, help in combating illegal trafficking and wildlife trade.

Under the Act,[397] a person who, being an officer of a bank or other financial institution or a designated non-financial institution, (a) fails or neglects to secure compliance with the provisions of this Act or (b) fails or neglects to secure the authenticity of any statement submitted pursuant to the provisions of this act commits an offence and is liable, on conviction, to imprisonment for a term not exceeding 5 years or to a fine of ₦500,000 or to both such imprisonment and fine.

Also, under the EFCC Act 2004, any person who, in the discharge of his duty under the Act, gives information that is false in any form, commits an offence under the Act, and the onus shall lie on him to prove that such information was supplied to him by another person and that he exercised due diligence to prevent the commission of the offence, having regard to the nature of his functions in that capacity and in all circumstances.[398] The penalty for these offences shall be imprisonment for a term of not less than 2 years but not exceeding 3 years, provided that where the offender is a public officer, the penalty shall be imprisonment for a term of not less than 3 years but not more than 5 years.[399]

Retention of the proceeds of criminal conduct also amounts to an offence under the EFCC Act 2004. Thus, a person who, (a) whether by concealment, removal from jurisdiction, transfer to nominees or otherwise, retains the control of the proceeds of a criminal conduct or an illegal act on behalf of another person knowing that the proceeds are a result of criminal conduct by the principal or, (b) knowing that any property in whole or in part directly or indirectly represents another person's proceeds of a criminal conduct, acquires or uses that property or has possession of it commits an offence and is liable, on conviction, to imprisonment for a term of not less than 5 years or to a fine equivalent to five times the value of the proceeds of the criminal conduct or to both such imprisonment and fine.[400]

Furthermore, a person commits an offence where, without lawful authority, (a) he engages in the acquisition, possession or use of property knowing that, at the time of its acquisition, possession or use, such property was derived from any offence under

[395] EFCC Act (2004), s. 6.

[396] Ibid., s. 7(2).

[397] EFCC Act (2004), s. 14(1).

[398] Ibid., s. 16(1).

[399] Ibid., s. 16(2).

[400] Ibid., s. 17.

the EFCC Act 2004 or (b) engages in the management, organisation or financing of any of the offences under the Act or (c) engages in the conversion or transfer of property knowing that such property is derived from any offence under the Act or (d) engages in the concealment or disguise of the true nature, source, location, disposition and movement of and rights with respect to the ownership of property knowing such property is derived from any offence referred to under the Act.[401] Such a person shall be liable, on conviction, to imprisonment for a term not less than 2 years but not exceeding 3 years.[402]

It should be noted that where a person is arrested for committing an offence under the Act,[403] such a person shall make full disclosure of all his assets and properties by completing the declaration of Assets Form, as specified in form A of the Schedule to the Act: (3) Any person who (a) knowingly fails to make full disclosure of his assets and liabilities or (b) knowingly makes a declaration that is false or (c) fails, neglects or refuses to make a declaration or furnishes any information required in the Declaration of Assets Form commits an offence and is liable, on conviction, to imprisonment for a term of 5 years.[404]

In addition, the Commission may approach the court for an interim forfeiture order under section 29 of the Act[405] and a final forfeiture order under section 30, as the case may be.

11.4.4.2.4.4 Nigerian Financial Intelligence Unit (NFIU)

The Nigerian Financial Intelligence Unit (NFIU) is the federal agency charged with the responsibility for requesting, receiving, analysing and disseminating financial and other related information to all law enforcement and security agencies and other relevant authorities.[406] This is with a view to producing financial intelligence to other agencies combating money laundering, terrorism financing and other financial crimes. The NFIU was established by virtue of the Nigerian Financial Intelligence Unit Act 2018.[407]

Prior to the NFIU Act 2018, the NFIU was established in 2004 as an autonomous unit within the central coordinating body for the country's Anti-Money Laundering, Counter-Terrorist Financing, and Counter-Proliferation Financing (AML/CFT/CPF) framework of the Central Bank of Nigeria and operated as part of the Economic and Financial Crimes Commission (EFCC). In 2007, the NFIU joined the Egmont Group of Financial Intelligence Units, an international organisation that facilitates

[401] EFCC Act (2004), s. 18(1).
[402] Ibid., s. 18(2).
[403] Ibid., s. 27(1).
[404] Ibid., s. 27(3).
[405] EFCC Act 2004.
[406] Nigerian Financial Intelligence Unit (NFIU) Act (2018), s. 2(1).
[407] Ibid.

cooperation and intelligence sharing between national financial intelligence units to investigate and prevent money laundering and terrorist financing.

Under the NFIU Act 2018, the NFIU is independent and operationally autonomous in discharging its duties and the performance of its functions under the NFIU Act.[408] However, for purposes of institutional location, the NFIU is domiciled in the Central Bank of Nigeria.[409] The functions of the NFIU are as spelt out under section 3(1)(a)–(s) of the NFIU Act 2018. The NFIU, among others, has the power to receive, collect and analyse reports concerning transactions under the Money Laundering (Prohibition) Act, the Terrorism Prevention Act and other relevant laws.[410]

In respect of money laundering, there are certain triggers or red flags that point to the occurrence of certain activities; these triggers, referred to as indicators,[411] caused the NFIU to set out some money laundering indicators classified under the appropriate predicate offence type, which when observed must be reported to the NFIU. Such indicators of fraud include, among others, different instrument deposits, huge cash withdrawals, dual/multiple identities, multiple deposits from different geographical locations, cash purchase of shares, transactions on nominee accounts, third-party payments, invisible payments/transactions (on non-performance), multiple individuals sending funds to one beneficiary, multiple cheques cashed into the one bank account and multiple transactions of a similar nature on the same day in different locations.

In respect of corruption and bribery, the following indicators were provided: unusual transactions from government accounts to personal accounts, cash withdrawals from government accounts, huge transactions involving minor accounts, transactions involving non-profit organisations, frequent early repayment of loans, huge lodgements, sudden inflow into a dormant account, transactions inconsistent with customer transaction profiles/patterns, frequent termination of investments, cash used to purchase large amounts of gold, insurance policy cashed outside the jurisdiction of purchase, company account doing large multiple cash transactions, elaborate movement of funds through different accounts, transfers to accounts on which there are no other transactions, transfers followed by cash withdrawals, more concern about speed than costs, high volume of transactions within a short period, sale of large amounts of gold from an individual, huge cash payments to Bureau De Change (BDCs), investments of ministry, department and agency (MDA) accounts and large and/or structured payments into individual accounts from MDAs, among others.[412]

[408] NFIU Act (2018), s. 2(2).

[409] Ibid., s. 2(3).

[410] Ibid., s. 4(e).

[411] Indicators are observable events that point to the possibility of specific activities occurring.

[412] Nigerian Financial Intelligence Unit (NFIU) (2021).

11.4.4.2.5 Offence of Corrupt Practices in Relation to Illegal Wildlife Trade and Trafficking in Endangered Species

Corruption remains the bedrock of the negative effects of wildlife trade in sub-Saharan Africa; the inability of laws to work effectively lies in corrupt practices in the system occasioned by officials who sneak through the laws to condone illegality.[413] The United Nations Office on Drugs and Crime (UNODC), in its report,[414] emphasised that addressing corruption is foundational to preventing wildlife crime. In that report, UNODC indicates that corruption exists across all stages of the wildlife supply chain and can facilitate the illegal trade of wildlife. Accordingly,

> Corruption manifests itself in various ways, ranging from officials receiving bribes and colluding with criminals, to abuse of office and embezzlement of resources allocated to wildlife management and protection. Bribes paid to officials can make up a significant part of the overall costs of wildlife trafficking; for example, customs officers may receive 4–10 per cent of the final wholesale value of ivory.[415]

Criminals engage in corruption to create the veneer of legitimacy; as a result, illegal enterprises can be presented as legitimate sources of wildlife. Corruption inhibits the ability of honest public officials to fulfil their mandates, whether those managing and protecting wildlife resources, protecting borders or managing and regulating markets for wildlife products.[416]

Corruption also interrupts the path towards criminal justice as the absence of controls may result in evidence being lost or concealed, as well as leaving witnesses, prosecutors and other judicial officers vulnerable to corruption. Delays in expedient trial processes may increase opportunities for wrongdoings.

Corruption has been found to be a critical enabler of the illicit wildlife trade, taking place at sourcing, transit and export stages and involving public and private sector abuse of power and trust. It can be ad hoc involving a small amount of money and low-level officials, or it can be systemic, involving larger amounts of money and higher-level officers and generally pre-planned.[417] Corruption can thus occur at any level of the supply chain, and this involves different actors.

A common theme generally in the illicit wildlife trade is corruption in the form of bribes. Thus, when corruption is mentioned, bribery comes to mind.[418] According to the Environmental Investigation Agency in the case of the Shuidong connection, 4–10 per cent of the ultimate cost of ivory in Asia is expended on bribing law enforcement officials.[419] The case in issue recorded US$90,000–210,000 expended on bribes alone. It was recorded that in 2012, the amount of money given to border

[413] Onyeabor et al. (2021).

[414] United Nations Office on Drugs and Crime (UNODC) (2020), p. 21.

[415] Ibid., 21.

[416] UNODC (2020), p. 20.

[417] Organisation for Economic Co-operation and Development (OECD) (2018), p. 11.

[418] Organisation for Economic Co-operation and Development (OECD) (2018), p. 11.

[419] Environmental Investigation Agency (UK) (2017).

officials in a single day along the Viet Nam-China border was between US$18,000 and US$30,000.[420] Here in Africa, the Financial Intelligence Unit (FIU) of Namibia[421] also recorded a case where a traveller from Namibia en route China was accosted in South Africa with a baggage containing 18 rhino horns weighing a total of 43 kilograms. Obviously, he was cleared by some officials who closed their eyes to the baggage. In several other places, fake permits are obtained with the aid of corrupt officials.[422]

In Nigeria, corruption has been viewed as a major problem in combating illegal trafficking in wildlife and illegal wildlife trade. Banned animal parts are easily transported, and traders and officials said illicit payments remain a crucial factor in greasing the supply chain.[423] Officials charged with the prevention of illegal trade alluded to 'big money' interests in the business, which can make it difficult for law enforcement officials to follow due process. According to one official in an interview conducted by Premium Times and Mongabay.com,[424] 'these types of cases require those involved to be able to resist a lot of temptation. Because we know a lot of money is involved'.

For more than a decade, poachers and traffickers were often not arrested or traced. Most of those who were detained were not prosecuted, and in the few cases that made it to court, defendants were asked to pay a nominal out-of-court settlement fee and continued to operate after release. On 21 January 2021, officials announced that they had recovered a haul of pangolin parts at the port of Apapa in Lagos. It was the second-largest ever seized by Nigerian authorities. On paper, the 20-foot container due to be exported to Haiphong, Vietnam, contained furniture, but inside, officials found that the woodwork was being used to conceal 162 sacks of pangolin scales and claws weighing 8.8 metric tons. They also found 57 bags of elephant ivory and lion bones. Court records show that customs officials notified the High Court in Lagos that they had completed their investigation on 28 June 2021. However, no suspects have been arraigned.[425]

It was also found that authorities, in most cases, do not investigate the owners of seized shipments, even when there are clues pointing to their identity. Also, 3 years after the government promised to investigate how 34 shipments of wildlife parts intercepted overseas left Nigeria's shores, no evidence that any such investigations had begun.[426]

An analysis of government records and interviews with officials showed that despite huge seizures over the past decade, no traffickers have served a jail term as a result. Records of 63 major interceptions at the country's ports between 2010 and

[420] Bennett (2014), pp. 54–60.

[421] Republic of Namibia Financial Intelligence Centre (2017).

[422] United Nations Office on Drugs and Crime (UNODC) (2017).

[423] Ekott (2022).

[424] Ibid.

[425] Ekott (2022).

[426] Ibid.

2021 that we reviewed show that only 11 cases went to court and many remain unresolved. No arrests were made in most cases. The three convictions that the authorities secured, all between 2012 and 2013, involved Chinese nationals caught with processed ivory. They were each fined ₦100,000 ($240) as an alternative to serving a three-year jail term. Under the country's Endangered Species Act, the fines could have been as high as ₦5 million ($12,000).[427]

The investigation further showed that many agencies, in particular Nigeria Customs Service (Customs), National Park Service (NPS) and the National Environmental Standards and Regulations Enforcement Agency (NESREA), hold the power to 'compound' rather than prosecute an offence.[428] The power to compound is a potential incentive for corrupt practices.[429] In spite of the above lapses, Nigeria has taken some steps in the fight against corruption generally under the Corrupt Practices and Other Related Offences Act 2000.[430]

The Act[431] seeks to prohibit and prescribe punishment for corrupt practices and other related offences.[432] It establishes the Independent Corrupt Practices and Other Related Offences Commission,[433] vesting it with the responsibility for the investigation and prosecution of the offenders thereof. Provision has also been made for the protection of anybody who gives information to the Commission in respect of an offence committed or likely to be committed by any other person.

The Act provides penalties against gratification[434] by officials,[435] corrupt offers to public officers,[436] corrupt demands by persons,[437] counselling offences relating to corruption,[438] deliberate frustration of investigation by the Commission,[439] making

---

[427] Ibid.

[428] On the admission of the accused and payment of a fine, these agencies discontinued any further action.

[429] Environmental Investigation Agency and Africa Nature Investors (2021), p. 5.

[430] Act No. 5 2000.

[431] Corrupt Practices and Other Related Offences Act (2000).

[432] 'Corruption' under the Act includes bribery, fraud and other related offences. See Corrupt Practices and Other Related Offences Act (2000), s. 2.

[433] Ibid., s. 3.

[434] Under the Corrupt Practices and Other Related Offences Act (2000), 'gratification', among others, include money, donation, gift, loan, fee, reward, valuable security, property of any description, whether movable or immovable, or any other similar advantage given or promised to any person with the intent to influence such a person in the performance or non-performance of his duties; any payment, release, discharge or liquidation of any loan, obligation or other liability, whether in whole or in part; any valuable consideration of any kind, such as any discount, commission, rebate, bonus deduction or percentage; etc. See Corrupt Practices and Other Related Offences Act (2000), s. 2.

[435] Corrupt Practices and Other Related Offences Act (2000), s. 8(1)(a)(b).

[436] Ibid., s. 9.

[437] Ibid., s. 10.

[438] Ibid., s. 11.

[439] Ibid., s. 15.

false statements or returns,[440] gratification by and through agents,[441] and bribery of public officers,[442] among others.

Note that where in any proceedings against any person for an offence under these sections[443] it is proved that any gratification has been accepted or agreed to be accepted, obtained or attempted to be obtained, solicited, given or agreed to be solicited or given, promised or offered, by or to the accused, the gratification shall be presumed to have been corruptly accepted, obtained, solicited, given, promised or offered as an inducement or reward for or on account of the matters set out in the particulars of the offence, until the contrary is proved.[444]

Again, where in any proceedings against any person for an offence under the Custom and Excise Management Act it is proved that any officer of customs or other person duly employed for the prevention of smuggling has accepted, agreed to accept or attempted to obtain any bribe, gratuity, recompense or reward, such officer or person shall be presumed to have done so in the neglect or non-performance of his duty, as set out in the particulars of the offence, until the contrary is proved.[445]

Thus, any person who corruptly does any of the prohibited acts under section 8(1)(a)(b) of the Act[446] is guilty of an offence of official corruption and is liable to imprisonment for seven (7) years.[447] In respect of offences under sections 8–19, without prejudice to any sentence of imprisonment imposed under the Act, a public officer or other persons found guilty of soliciting, offering or receiving gratification shall forfeit the gratification and pay a fine of not less than five times the sum of the value of the gratification that is the subject matter of the offence where such gratification is capable of being valued or is of a pecuniary nature or amounts to ₦10,000 (ten thousand naira), whichever is higher.[448]

It should be noted that in any proceedings under the Corrupt Practices and Other Related Offences Act 2000, evidence shall not be admissible to show that any such gratification mentioned in the Act is customary in any profession, trade, vocation or calling or on a social occasion.[449]

Other offences are related to the duty to report bribery transactions.[450] Under section 23 of the Act,[451] any public officer to whom any gratification is given,

---

[440] Ibid., s. 16.

[441] Ibid., s. 17.

[442] Ibid., s. 18.

[443] Those are sections 8, 9, 10, 11, 15, 16, 17 and 18 of the Corrupt Practices and Other Related Offences Act (2000).

[444] Corrupt Practices and Other Related Offences Act (2000), s. 53(1).

[445] Ibid., s. 53(4).

[446] Corrupt Practices and Other Related Offences Act 2000 (n 426).

[447] Ibid., s. 8(1)(b)(ii).

[448] Corrupt Practices and Other Related Offences Act (2000), s. 20.

[449] Ibid., s. 60.

[450] Ibid., s. 23.

[451] Corrupt Practices and Other Related Offences Act (2000).

promised or offered, in contravention of any provision of the Act, shall report such gift, promise or offer, together with the name, if known, of the person who gave, promised or offered such gratification to him, to the nearest officer of the Commission or police officer.[452]

Again, any person from whom gratification has been solicited or obtained or from whom an attempt has been made to obtain such gratification, in contravention of any provision of the Act,[453] shall, at the earliest opportunity thereafter, report such soliciting or obtaining or attempt to obtain the gratification, together with the name, if known, or a true and full description of the person who solicited or obtained or attempted to obtain the gratification from him to the nearest officer of the Commission or police officer.[454] Failure to comply with the above provisions amount to an offence and shall, on conviction, subject the offender to a fine not exceeding ₦100,000 or to imprisonment for a term not exceeding 2 years or to both fine and imprisonment.[455]

Notwithstanding the stifling of wildlife trade through the laws, the populations of wildlife have continued to deplete. This is because restrictive laws drive people to continue their activities in secret and make private money at the expense of collective economic advancement.[456] The reasons for this are not far-fetched.

Many governments do not see wildlife crimes as serious crimes worth the government's attention, and as such, there is little or no investment to curtail them. Rangers are not well equipped, and even when poachers are apprehended, they are either allowed to go free or handed weak sentences by the court, which is incapable of deterring future offenders.[457]

A weak legal and enforcement mechanism is a major factor in the illegal wildlife trade. Africa and, indeed, many developing countries have a track record of weak laws, governance and corruption.[458]

Institutional lapses coupled with other economic drivers[459] have made it a Herculean task to regulate the wildlife trade in Nigeria and Africa in general. The wildlife trade should have been a great resource in Africa, but because most African communities are bereft of the value of these resources, they keep wasting these resources under the guise of benefitting from them.[460]

The international community has recognised the significance of corruption in the prevention and combating of illegal wildlife trafficking and illegal trade of wildlife. For instance, at the 17th meeting of the Conference of the Parties to CITES in 2016, a

[452] Ibid., s. 23(1).

[453] Corrupt Practices and Other Related Offences Act (2000).

[454] Ibid., s. 23(2).

[455] Ibid., s. 23(3).

[456] Onyeabor et al. (2021).

[457] Williamson (2004), p. 11.

[458] Harrison et al. (2015).

[459] Such as poverty, the impact of wealth and ostentation, and food security, among others.

[460] Onyeabor et al. (2021).

resolution[461] was passed calling on the parties to take a broad range of measures to prevent and combat corruption linked to illegal wildlife trade. Again, in 2019, at the Eighth Conference of the States Parties to the United Nations Convention Against Corruption, they adopted a resolution[462] on preventing and addressing corruption linked to crimes that have an impact on the environment.

The resolutions recognise that corruption underpins the illegal trade in natural resources and constitutes a growing source of profits for various criminal actors and that addressing this connection is vital to target action to reduce illegal harvesting and trade and raise awareness of the detrimental effects of corruption.[463] In addition, these resolutions help create the policy environment in which to deepen and strengthen the much-needed practical work to combat and prevent corruption linked to wildlife management.[464]

On the whole, investigating and prosecuting corruption and other economic crimes will help target more senior members of criminal groups and actual beneficiaries of wildlife crimes and disrupt organised criminal groups, and in the end, it is hoped that this will help combat and prevent corruption linked to wildlife management.

11.5 Summary

Environmental law imposes liabilities on actors for their illegal acts or for the adverse consequences of their lawful activities. Environmental damage in this case may refer to damage to the environment that can lead to a possible destruction of the four elements within the environment, namely fauna, flora, soil, water and climatic factors; material assets (including archaeological and cultural heritage); the landscape and environmental amenities; and the interrelationship between the above factors. Damage also involves acts that may infringe on the rights of others, incurring liability on the part of the offender. These, when committed, become a veritable source of claim by victims of such environmental damage.

Environmental liability may therefore arise where there is non-compliance with the provisions of environmental laws by the defendant/s or where a person suffers environmental damage caused by the acts of the defendant/s. Damage resulting therefrom could include loss of life or personal injury, loss of or damage to property, loss or damage by impairment of the environment, the costs of preventive measures and any loss or damage caused by preventive measures.

Liability may be civil or criminal. In the case of civil liability, there are two ways through which it may arise. The first is through the commission of common law tort,

[461] Secretariat of the Convention on Biological Diversity (2016).

[462] Conference of the States Parties to the United Nations Convention Against Corruption (2019).

[463] United Nations Office on Drugs and Crime (UNODC) (2020).

[464] Ibid.

and the second is through a violation of the provisions of relevant environmental statutes. There are several obstacles to the litigation of claims for environmental damage, including the jurisdiction of courts; legal standing to sue (locus standi); the ability of the litigant to procure the services of a credible and compelling expert witness; adherence to the limitation of action and service of pre-action notice; and the problem of enforcement of judgment if the action is successful.

Criminal liability for environmental damage may arise where an offender may have been involved in various aspects of environmental crimes, such as illegal dumping, depositing or dealing in hazardous wastes/substances in the environment that resulted in environmental damage, non-compliance with legislative provisions on impact assessment, failure to comply with legislation protecting various environmental media and illegal wildlife trade and trafficking in endangered species. Various statutes prohibit those acts, and an offender may be liable to some terms of imprisonment or payment of specified fines if convicted.

In the end, it is hoped that liability rules may be used to achieve effective and efficient environmental protection as the rules tend not only to impose sanctions for wrongful conduct or to require corrective measures to restore a given environmental asset to its pre-damage condition. The rules may also be a form of economic instrument that provides an incentive to encourage compliance with environmental obligations or may provide a technique for internalising environmental and other social costs into production processes and other activities in implementing the polluter-pays principle.

References

Agu HU, Gore ML (eds) (2022) Women and wildlife trafficking: participants, perpetrators and victims, 1st edn. Routledge, New York. ISBN 978-0-367-64026-2. https://doi.org/10.4324/9781003121831

Andrew C, Agu HU (2022) Using a feminist political ecology lens to explore the gendered dimensions of wildlife trafficking literature. In: Agu HU, Gore ML (eds) Women and wildlife trafficking: participants, perpetrators and victims, 1st edn. Routledge, New York, ISBN 978-0-367-64026-2, https://doi.org/10.4324/9781003121831

Bennett E (2014) Legal ivory trade in a corrupt world and its impact in African elephant populations. Conserv Biol 29(1)spiepr A3B2 twbch ":":spiepr A3B2 twbch54–60

Conference of the States Parties to the United Nations Convention Against Corruption (2019) Draft resolution to be recommended by the Conference of the States Parties to the United Nations Convention against Corruption for adoption by the General Assembly, https://www.unodc.org/documents/treaties/UNCAC/COSP/session8/Advance_unedited_resolutions_final.pdf), Accessed 30 July 2023

Ekott I (2022) In Nigeria, a decade of payoffs boosted global wildlife trafficking hub. Mongabay Series: Illegal Trade, 4 March 2022 https://news.mongabay.com/2022/03/in-nigeria-a-decade-of-payoffs-boosted-global-wildlife-trafficking-hub/. Accessed 30 July 2023

Environmental Investigation Agency (UK) (2017) The Shuidong Connection: Exposing the Global Hub of the Illegal Ivory Trade [2017]. https://eia-international.org/wp-content/uploads/EIA-The-Shuidong-Connection-FINAL.pdf. Accessed 27 July 2023

Environmental Investigation Agency (UK) (2021) Double Impact – The Nexus Where Wildlife and Forestry Crime Overlap. https://eia-international.org/report/double-impact-the-nexus-where-wildlife-and-forest-crime-overlap/. Accessed 18 May 2023

Environmental Investigation Agency and Africa Nature Investors (2021) Combating Wildlife Crime in Nigeria: An Analysis of Criminal Justice Legislative Framework, August 2021. https://eia-international.org/wp-content/uploads/Combating-Wildlife-Crime-in-Nigeria-2021-FINAL.pdf. Accessed 28 May 2023

European Treaty Series (ETS) (1993) 150 – Environment, 21.VI.1993, https://rm.coe.int/168007c079. Accessed 22 May 2023

Fagbohun O (2012) Mournful Remedies, Endless Conflicts and Inconsistencies in Nigeria's Quest for Environmental Governance: Rethinking the Legal Possibilities for Sustainability. Inaugural Paper, Nigerian Institute of Advanced Legal Studies Abuja: NIALS Press 2012, 65 ISBN: 978-978-8407-57-7

Gore ML, Agu HU (2022) The roles of women in wildlife trafficking are mostly unknown, but not unknowable. In: Agu HU, Gore ML (eds) Women and wildlife trafficking: participants, perpetrators and victims, 1st edn. Routledge, New York., ISBN 978-0-367-64026-2,. https://doi.org/10.4324/9781003121831

Gore ML et al (2019) Transnational environmental crime threatens sustainable development. Nat Sustain 2(9)spiepr A3B2 twbch ":":spiepr A3B2 twbch784–786

Harrison M et al (2015) Wildlife crime: a review of the evidence on drivers and impacts in Uganda. [2015] IIED Research Report http://pubs.iied.org/pdfs/17576IIED.pdf. Accessed 20 July 2023

Human Rights Watch (1999) The price of oil: corporate responsibilities and human rights violations in Nigeria's oil producing communities, Human Rights Watch, New York

Nigerian Financial Intelligence Unit (NFIU) (2021) Money laundering indicators https://www.nfiu.gov.ng/images/Downloads/downloads/mlindicators.pdf. Accessed 28 July 2023

Odour M (2021) Justice at last: Shell agrees to pay US$110million over oil spills in Nigeria. https://www.africanews.com/2021/08/12/justice-at-last-shell-agrees-to-pay-110m-over-oil-spills-in-nigeria//. Accessed 30 July 2023

Ogbuabor CA (2008) Towards a consistent application of the law on pre-action notice in Nigeria. Nigerian J Public Law (NJPL) spiepr A3B2 twbch ":"2:149spiepr A3B2 twbch

Ogbuabor CA (2010) Can Jurisdiction be Waived? Waiver and Jurisdiction in Cases involving Pre-action Notice: Nigercare Development Company Ltd v. Adamawa State Government & Ors Revisited. Dec2009/Jan 2010 The Appellate Review, Vol. 1, No. 2, 224 and 225

Onyeabor EU (2010) Expanding the scope of Locus Standi in environmental litigation. Nnamdi Azikiwe Univ Law J 7(1)spiepr A3B2 twbch ":":spiepr A3B2 twbch67–85. at 77

Onyeabor EU et al (2021) Economic implications of trade in wildlife: from legality to illegality. Nigerian Juridical Rev spiepr A3B2 twbch ":"16:272spiepr A3B2 twbch, Faculty of Law University of Nigeria, Enugu Campus

Organisation for Economic Co-operation and Development (OECD) (2018) Strengthening governance and reducing corruption risks to tackle illegal wildlife trade: lessons from East and Southern Africa. OECD, Paris, 11, ISSN: 26175835 (online), https://doi.org/10.1787/26175835., https://www.oecd-ilibrary.org/trade/strengthening-governance-and-reducing-corruption-risks-to-tackle-illegal-wildlife-trade_9789264306509-en. Accessed 27 July 2023

Owoade MA (1999) Locus Standi, criminal law and the rights of the private prosecutor in Nigeria: Fawehinmi v Akilu and Togun revisited. Nigerian Juridical Rev Vol. 4, 111

Premium Times (2021) Oil Spillage Shell agrees to pay Ogoni community N45.9billion ordered by Supreme Court. Premium Times 11 August 2021, https://www.premiumtimesng.com/news/top-news/478762-oil-spillage-shell-agrees-to-pay-ogoni-community-n45-9billion-ordered-by-supreme-court.html. Accessed 30 July 2023

Republic of Namibia Financial Intelligence Centre (2017) Trends and typology report No 1 of 2017: Rhino and elephant poaching, illegal trade in related wildlife products and associated money laundering in Namibia, 2017

Rogers WH (2006) Winfield and Jolowicz on Tort, 17th edn. Sweet and Maxwell, London

Sanction Scanner (2021) Anti Money Laundering Guide in Nigeria. 15 June 2021 https://sanctionscanner.com/Aml-Guide/anti-money-laundering-aml-in-nigeria-434. Accessed 19 June 2023

Sands P (2003) Principles of international environmental law, 2nd edn. Cambridge University, Cambridge

Secretariat of the Convention on Biological Diversity (2016) Resolution Conf. 117.6 Prohibiting, preventing, detecting and countering corruption, which facilitates activities conducted in violation of the Convention, https://cites.org/sites/default/files/document/E-Res-17-06_0.pdf. Accessed 30 July 2023

United Nations (1972) Declaration of the United Nations Conference on Human Environment (Stockholm Declaration)1972, principles 14 and 15, UN Document A/CONF.48/14/Rev.1 https://www.un.org/en/conferences/environment/stockholm1972. Accessed 14 May 2023

United Nations Environment Programme (1982) Guidelines for Assessing Industrial Environmental Impact and Environmental Criteria for the Sitting of Industry - Supplementary Volume, https://wedocs.unep.org/20.500.11822/29827. Accessed 28 June 2023

United Nations Office on Drugs and Crime (UNODC) (2017) Sharing Electronic Resources and Laws on Crime (SHERLOC). Case Law Database, available at: https://sherloc.unodc.org. Case number ZAFx008, Accessed 27 July 2023

UNODC (2020). World Wildlife Crime Report, United Nations, New York, May 2020, ISBN: 978-92-1-148349-9, e ISBN: 978-92-1-005225-2, https://www.unodc.org/unodc/en/dat-analysis/wildlife.html. Accessed 17 May 2023

Williamson DF (2004) Tackling the ivories: the status of the US trade in elephant and Hippo Ivory [2004], 11 https://www.traffic.org/site/assets/files/4054/tackling_the_ivories.pdf. Accessed19 July 2023

Chapter 12
Remedies in Addressing

Abstract Where environmental damage has occurred, the law requires some remedial measures to heal the ill feelings of the victims and compensate for the damage they had suffered as a result. In seeking redress for environmental damage, various remedies are available to the victims. Such remedies include compensation, restraining order of a court, abatement, injunctions, damages, reparation, restitution, rehabilitation/restoration and application of the polluter-pays principle. These remedies are discussed in this chapter and are focused mainly on cases from the United Kingdom and Nigeria.

12.1 Compensation

12.1.1 Introduction

Compensation in environmental matters is founded on the legal maxim of *restitutio integrum*, which means to restore the injured party to the position he was in prior to the injury. The sum of money paid as compensation is meant to restore the victim of environmental damage to the same position as he would have been had he not sustained that wrong for which he is now being compensated.[1]

Compensation raises the problem of assessing the measure of environmental damage. For instance, should it be by reference to the costs of measures of reinstatement or on the basis of an abstract quantification calculated in accordance with a theoretical model or on some other basis?[2] The problem arises because environmental damage does not fit easily with the traditional approaches of civil and state liability, which are designed to compensate an injured person by requiring the responsible person to pay the economic costs of the resulting damage, which is frequently calculated by reference to depreciation of the economic value of the damaged item or the cost of repairing the damage. Pure damage to the environment

[1] *Shell Petroleum Development Company Limited v Tiebo VII* (1996) 4 NWLR (pt 445), 659.

[2] Sands (2003), p. 389.

E. Onyeabor, *Environmental Law*, https://doi.org/10.1007/978-3-031-68956-7_12

per se may be incapable of calculation in economic terms, although it may have a non-economic value requiring restoration to the state prior to the damage occurring.[3]

However, compensation could mean measures of reinstatement. This, according to the Convention on Civil Liability for Damage Resulting from Activities Dangerous to the Environment (Lugano Convention) 1993,[4] means 'any reasonable measures aiming to reinstate or restore damaged or destroyed components of the environment, or to introduce, where reasonable, the equivalent of these components into the environment. Internal law may indicate who will be entitled to take such measures.'[5]

This measure emphasises the relationship between damage and the restoration of damage in environmental issues. In this context, the Protocol to the International Convention for the Prevention of Pollution from Ships MARPOL Convention of 1973/78, 1992, used the reasonable costs of measures in the concept of damage.[6]

Claims for compensation for environmental damage may be brought under the riparian right doctrine or based on a violation of the human rights of pollution victims.

12.1.2 The Riparian Right Doctrine

The riparian right doctrine is a common law doctrine that is predicated on property rights arising from the ownership of property adjoining a river. It applies mainly to claims for damages arising from water pollution incidents. A riparian owner is a person whose land abuts a watercourse. He is entitled to water from the watercourse in its natural flow, without sensible diminution or increase and without sensible alteration to its character or quality.[7] These positions had been given a judicial nod in the case of *Miner v Gilmore*,[8] where Lord Kingsdown stated:

> By the general law applicable to running streams, every riparian proprietor has a right to what may be called the ordinary use of water flowing past his land; for instance to the reasonable use of the water for his domestic purposes and for his cattle, and this without regard to the effect which such use may have, in case of a deficiency on a proprietor lower down the stream.[9]

---

[3] Ibid.

[4] Convention on Civil Liability for Damage Resulting from Activities Dangerous to the Environment (Luguano Convention) (1993), art. 2(7)(a)–(d).

[5] Luguano Convention (1993), art. 2(8).

[6] Annex 111: Prevention of pollution by harmful substances carried by sea in packaged form. MARPOL came into force on 1 July 1992 (this legal instrument was discussed in Sect. 14.1.2 of Chap. 14 of this book).

[7] Rostron (2001), p. 28.

[8] (1859) 12 Moo PCC 131.

[9] Ibid.

However, the above position is qualified, in that ordinary uses of water can be enjoyed notwithstanding their effects on a lower owner. An owner can also use the water for some extraordinary purpose but must do so in a way that does not cause any sensible damage to another riparian interest. An extraordinary use that damages another riparian owner will be actionable. The discharge of pollution would be considered to be an extraordinary use of the land and would only be acceptable if it did not cause any danger.[10]

Therefore, if one riparian owner wishes to use water for what would be described as an extraordinary use, they could only do so if it would not harm the rights of others. This position is supported by the court in the case of *Rugby Joint Water Board v Walters*,[11] where the court stated that the water removed must either have no effect on the river or be returned to the river in substantially undiminished quantity or quality.

To this end, for a right of action to accrue to a landowner downstream and in order to pursue a pollution claim, he must show that his right to abstract water, which flows through or under his land, or his right to use water adjacent to his land has been affected by the polluting act of the defendant. This is because over the years, as far as common law is concerned, the definition of water pollution has traditionally depended on how the rights of others to use water are affected. For example, if the temperature of water in a stream is altered by the defendant's act so that a downstream user is unable to use the water as before, the common law will look upon the water as 'polluted' even though it may be free from harmful substances.[12] The bundle of rights that will enable a landowner to pursue a claim under common law is known as riparian rights.

To be a riparian owner, one must own or have an interest in land.[13] Such land in question must adjoin a river or a stream. He normally owns the bed of the river or owns it to a point equidistant from his neighbour on the opposite side, but he does not own the water itself.[14] Even under customary environmental law, as pointed out by Elias,[15] 'the generally accepted principle is that persons in the community have a right to use the water passing through it'.

The principle underlying the riparian right doctrine is that since the riparian owner owns the land adjoining or underlying the river or stream, he is, as such, entitled to use the water as long as the quantity is not depleted nor the quality degraded. He therefore has, as an incident of his ownership of the land, a right to receive waters in their natural state, free from impurities and in the same quantity and of the same natural character as he has come to expect. Riparian ownership therefore imposes a form of property right, and he is expected to a reasonable enjoyment of his

[10] Rostron (2001), p. 28.

[11] [1967] Ch. 234.

[12] Wolf (2002), p. 101.

[13] Lord Macnaghten, in the case of *John Young & Co v Bakier Distillery Co* [1893] AC 691.

[14] *Amachree v Kalio* (1914) 2 NLR and *Braide and Ors v Adoki and Ors* (1931) 10 WLR.15.

[15] Elias (1971), p. 46.

land, and any infringement is treated as being analogous to the commission of a nuisance, which can result in an environmental liability. In other words, once this right is affected, an actionable wrong has arisen. This state of affairs was aptly captured by Lord Macnaghten in *John Young & Co. v Bankier Distillery Co.*,[16] where he stated as follows:

> A riparian proprietor is entitled to have water of the stream, on bank of which his property lies, flow down as it has been accustomed to flow down to his property, subject to the ordinary use of the flowing water by upper proprietors, and to such further use, if any, on their part in connection with their property as may be reasonable in the circumstances. Every riparian owner is thus entitled to the water of his stream, in its natural flow, without sensible diminution or increase, and without sensible alteration in its character or quality.

In that case, discharges from a mine upstream of the plaintiff's land altered the chemistry of the water from soft to hard. This, in turn, caused changes to the quality of the plaintiff distiller's whisky. They were able to obtain an injunction to stop the defendants' activities, even though the defendants had not made the water impure.

Again, where the unreasonable interference complained of involves interference with the fishing rights of the riparian owner, he can also bring an action for damages. In the case of *Cook v South West Water plc*,[17] the plaintiff, Cook, owned three-quarters of a mile of riparian salmon and trout fishing rights. In 1990, the defendants, who operated three sewage works upstream from the plaintiff's stretch of the river, discharged detergent and phosphates into the river, which damaged the river's ecosystem and also seriously interfered with fishing. The plaintiff brought an action in nuisance against the defendants, claiming both damages and injunction. The court found in favour of the plaintiff.

In cases of oil spills, which is a common occurrence in the Niger Delta region of Nigeria, large quantities of crude oil are spilt almost from every facet of oil production. Spills can kill large numbers of fish in small areas, especially in creeks and freshwater swamps. This usually interferes with the fishing rights of the particular community in affected areas. At times, the spill affects individual fish ponds, causing an enormous loss of income and becoming a veritable source of litigation.[18]

Thus, the riparian owner is entitled to a reasonable use of the water, and it is only when the use is unreasonable such that the use interferes with the natural quantity or quality of the water that an actionable wrong would arise; otherwise, the riparian owner suffers no wrong that is actionable. In the case of *New York City v The States of Pennsylvania and New Jersey*,[19] New York City, in 1920, began to pipe drinking water from the upper reaches of the Delaware River, and as the city grew, the

---

[16] [1893] AC 691 at 698.

[17] [1992] Water Law 3(4) 103.

[18] *Shell Petroleum Development Company Limited v Chief Graham Otoko and 5 Ors* (1990) 6 NWLR (pt 159), 693, and *Ogiale and Ors v Shell Petroleum Development Company Limited* (1997) NWLR (pt 380), 148, are cases in point where the cause of action arose from an oil spill caused by the operations of Shell Petroleum Development Company.

[19] 187 N.Y Super, 210 (1921).

demand for water increased until the people downstream from these impoundments found that their rivers had disappeared. Many resort owners simply went out of business. After prolonged court battles, it was finally determined that since the city did own the land around the impounded streams and the use of the water was reasonable, the city could continue to use the water. Although there was some monetary compensation for the downstream riparian owners, in the long run, it did show that once your use of the water was reasonable, no actionable wrong has accrued.

Liability for damage may also arise under the riparian doctrine for polluting percolating groundwater, as long as causation can be shown. This was first established in the case of *Ballard v Tomlinson*,[20] where a brewery successfully sued for the contamination of its well caused by a neighbour who used his own well for the disposal of sewage, which polluted water percolating through the plaintiff's land.

However, with the passage of time, the test of foreseeability of harm, not just causation alone, was added as a necessary ingredient for the plaintiff to succeed. This was considered and applied in the case of *Cambridge Water Company Ltd v Eastern Counties Leather plc.*[21]

In that case, the plaintiff, a water company, abstracted water from a borehole, which had become contaminated when solvents had seeped into the watercourse beneath the defendant's tannery and had percolated towards the borehole. The plaintiff water company brought an action in nuisance and negligence and under the rule in *Ryland v Fletcher.*[22] The Court of Appeal of England, following the decision in *Ballard v Tomlinson*, held that the right to abstract unpolluted groundwater was a proprietary one and that, accordingly, once the water company had shown causation, liability will follow. This decision was, however, reversed by the House of Lords, holding that the action was proper to be categorised as an action in nuisance, of which the rule in *Ryland v Fletcher* was an offshoot, and that, following the dicta of Lord Reid in *The Wagon Mound (No. 2)*,[23] foreseeability of the type of harm was a necessary ingredient in the tort of nuisance. The court's decision was based on the fact that at the time the tannery had permitted the solvents to be spilt, their harmful effects were unknown.

Although the courts most commonly adopt a nuisance-based approach, liability for the infringement of riparian rights has sometimes been held to arise in trespass. Trespass involves an unjustifiable physical interference with land, arising from an intentional or negligent entry onto the land.[24] The key issues that must be present in order for an action in trespass to be brought are that the trespass was direct, that the act was intentional or negligent and that there is a causal link between the directness

---

[20](1885) 29 Ch. D 115.

[21][1994] 2 AC. 264.

[22]*Ryland v Fletcher* (1868) LR H.L. 330.

[23][1967] 1 AC 617.

[24]*Anyabunsi v Ugwunze* (1995) 6 NWLR (pt 401) 261.

of the act and the inevitability of the consequences.[25] Thus, in the case of *Jones v Llanrwst UDC*,[26] it was held that sewage which had been released into a river which had passed downstream and settled on the plaintiff's land was a direct interference and amounted to trespass. This again reflects the recognition of the riparian right as a proprietary right.

In addition to claims for nuisance and trespass, it may be possible for a riparian owner to make a claim for negligence. In the case of *Scott-Whitehead v National Coal Board*,[27] the defendant, a regional water authority, was found to be negligent for failing to advise a farmer that the water he was abstracting from a stream to irrigate his crops contained a strong chlorinated solution. The farmer's potato crop was damaged as a consequence of using the chlorinated water. The court held that the water authority was liable for negligence.

At times, the riparian owner may bring an action under the rules in *Ryland v Fletcher* to pursue his claims. Thus, in the case of *Machine Umudje v Shell B.P. Petroleum Development Company*,[28] oil escaped from the defendants' premises, destroying the plaintiff's fish and fish pond. The oil was crude oil waste previously accumulated in a pit burrowed by, and in control of, the defendants. The rule in *Ryland v Fletcher* was applied to find the defendants liable.

Taken together, it can be shown that although the riparian doctrine as a basis for compensating pollution victims is rooted in common law tort, its applicability in pollution damage goes a long way in assuaging the ill feelings suffered by a victim of environmental damage and his quest for environmental justice.

12.1.3 Violation of the Fundamental Rights of the Pollution Victim

Environmental problems, by their very nature, carry with them a wide range of infringements that adversely impact both the natural environment and the human environment, at times also leading to violations of human rights. Realising that human lives and well-being are affected, it became necessary to protect those adversely affected through legislation. Victims of such environmental damage may be compensated in the event of such violation. To this end, the nature, types and extent of human rights violations and how human rights violation principles are applied in determining the basis for compensation of the victims of such violations form the basis of the next discussions.

---

[25] Enemo (2007), p. 207.

[26] [1911] 1 Ch. 39.

[27] [1987] 2 EGLR 227.

[28] *Machine Umudje v Shell B.P. Petroleum Development Company* (1975) 9–11 SC. 155.

12.1.3.1 Nature of Human Rights Violated

First, what do human rights entail? Human rights are ‘those liberties, immunities and benefits which by accepted contemporary values, all human being should be able to claim as of right of the society in which they live’.[29] They therefore represent demands or claims that individuals or groups make on society, some of which are protected by law and have become part of *lex lata*, while others remain aspirations to be attained in future.[30] Human rights are therefore those rights held by all individuals merely by reason of their being humans without regard to status and position. Those rights are neither privileges granted by the state nor are contingent upon any duties owed to it but are entitlements against the state.[31] To this extent, human rights had been described by Kayode Eso (J.S.C., as he then was) in the case of *Ransome Kuti v Attorney General of the Federation*[32] as:

> A right which stands above the ordinary laws of the land and which in fact is antecedent to the political society itself. It is primary condition to a civilized existence and what has been done by our Constitution since independence is to have these rights enshrined in the constitution so that the rights could be immutable to the extent of the non-immutability of the constitution itself.

As Umozuruike[33] pointed out, human rights represent ‘an ambitious . . . attempts to bring rationality into political institutions and the societies of all states’. Rights demanded by peoples from states span from civil and political rights to economic, social and cultural rights, as well as solidarity rights. These rights are universal in nature, and they apply regardless of race, colour, sex or other distinctions. They may not be drawn or denied by governments, groups, organisations or individuals as the universal nature of these rights and freedom is beyond question.[34]

12.1.3.2 Types of Rights Violated That May Attract Litigation for Compensation

The next issues for discussion border on the types of rights that may be violated as a result of environmental damage, how these rights are protected by both international and domestic human rights instruments and how the violation of these rights may form a basis for compensation from environmental polluters. Those rights whose violation may attract compensation include the following:

---

[29] Hekin (1985), p. 268.

[30] Eze (1984), p. 5.

[31] International Committee of Red Cross (ICRC) (1978), p. 40.

[32] [1985] 2 NWLR (pt 6) 211.

[33] Umozuruike (1997), p. 3.

[34] Declaration and Programme of Action, World Conference on Human Rights, Vienna (1993), para. 1.

1. Civil and political rights
2. Economic and social rights and
3. Group rights

12.1.3.2.1 Civil and Political Rights

The first sets of rights protected by the various human rights instruments are referred to as civil and political rights, naturally called the first-generation rights. These rights, among others, include the following:

1. Right to life
2. Right to personal liberty
3. Freedom from torture or inhuman or degrading punishment
4. Right to peaceful assembly and association and
5. Right to freedom of expression

12.1.3.2.1.1 Right to Life

The right to life is guaranteed by various domestic and international human rights instruments. For instance, the Constitution of the Federal Republic of Nigeria 1999 (CFRN 1999),[35] as amended, guaranteed this right in these terms: 'Every person has a right to life, and no one shall be deprived intentionally of his life, save in execution of the sentence of a court in respect of a criminal offence of which he has been found guilty in Nigeria.'[36] Section 33(2)[37] goes further to indicate circumstances in which the deprivation of right to life may be warranted. It provides as follows:

> A person shall not be regarded as having been deprived of his life in contravention of this section, if he dies as a result of the use, to such extent and in such circumstances as are permitted by law, of such force as is reasonably necessary—
>
> (a) for the defence of any person from unlawful violence or for the defence of property:
> (b) in order to effect a lawful arrest or to prevent the escape of a person lawfully detained; or
> (c) for the purpose of suppressing a riot, insurrection or mutiny.

In addition to the Constitution of the Federal Republic of Nigeria (CFRN) 1999, as amended, a number of international human rights instruments have provisions for the protection of this right: the right to life. The Universal Declaration of Human Rights (UDHR) 1948 provides as follows: 'everyone has the right to life, liberty and security of person'.[38]

[35] Cap C23 Laws of the Federation of Nigeria (LFN) 2004.

[36] Ibid., s. 33(1).

[37] CFRN (1999).

[38] Universal Declaration of Human Rights (UDHR) (1948), art. 3.

The International Covenant on Civil and Political Rights (ICCPR) 1966, on the other hand, provides that 'every human being has the inherent right to life. This right shall be protected by law. No one shall be arbitrarily deprived of his life.'[39]

Under the African Charter on Human and Peoples' Rights (ACHPR) 1981, 'every human being shall be entitled to respect for his life and the integrity of this person. No one may be arbitrarily deprived of this right.'[40]

What all these instruments provide indicates that the right to life is an inviolable right and cannot arbitrarily, or without legal justification, be deprived. However, this had not been the case with regard to environmental damage resulting from environmental pollution. Environmental pollution carries with it life-threatening situations and, at times, causes death. This is more prevalent in oil-producing communities and in other areas with mineral-bearing rocks, for instance in the case of *Shell Petroleum Development Company Limited v Chief Caiphas Enoch and 2 Ors*,[41] in which five children are alleged to have died as a result of drinking oil-contaminated water.

At times, in order to protect both local interest and the interest of the multinational operators of the extractive industry, the right to life of some people in mineral-bearing communities had, on several occasions, been arbitrarily, and without legal justification, deprived. Examples of the occurrence of this act in the past years shall suffice to illustrate this. In October 1990, a protest that took place at Shell's facility at Umuechem in Etche L.G.A. of Rivers State resulted in the police killing some 80 unarmed demonstrators and destroying or badly damaging 495 houses. This led to the setting up of a judicial commission of inquiry by the government, which found no evidence of a threat by the villagers.[42]

On 24 August 1995, a conflict between a Shell contractor, Western Geophysical, and a local community (Iko in Akwa Ibom State) over employment led to the killing of one Emmanuel Nelson, a teacher, who had been interpreting during the meeting. He was beaten to death by the police.[43]

In July 1997, a youth named Gidikumo Sule was killed by the mobile police in Opuama, Delta State, in the course of a dispute with a Chevron contractor—Halliburton. Again, in May 1998, two youths were killed on Chevron's Parabe platform off Ondo State by members of the security forces transported to the platform by Chevron to remove 200 protesters who had closed down production. The protesters demanded to be compensated for environmental damage caused by the canals cut for Chevron, which opened local waterways to the sea.

At the Clough Creek flow station near Egbemo-Angalabiri in Rivers State, owned by Agip, a youth was beaten to death by security guards during a protest march. On 30 December 1998, soldiers shot dead about seven youths protesting in Yenogoa,

---

[39] International Covenant on Civil and Political Rights (ICCPR) (1966), art. 6(1).

[40] African Charter on Human and Peoples' Rights (ACHPR) (1981), art. 4.

[41] (1992) 8 NWLR (pt. 259) 335.

[42] Human Rights Watch (1999), p. 123.

[43] Ibid.

Bayelsa State. It was during a gathering of youths that the 'Kaiama Declaration' was adopted, asking the oil companies to pay up or shut out.[44]

Perhaps it would be most uncharitable to conclude violations of rights to life unleashed on the people of oil-producing communities without mentioning the Ogoni crisis. Since 1993, Ogoni had fought an unrelenting 'battle' with Shell to pay compensation for oil exploitation for the past 30 years or vacate Ogoni land. This saga led to the extrajudicial killing of several hundreds of Ogoni people by the mobile police and a military unit,[45] set up to crackdown Ogoni 'trouble shooters' and members of the Movement for the Survival of Ogoni People (MOSOP).

In one way or another, several prominent Ogonis had met their untimely and unwarranted death in the hands of this military unit. In some cases, a 'tribunal' was set up to try the MOSOP members. A case in mind is the 'Tribunal' that tried Ken Saro-Wiwa and eight others. They were charged with murder in connection with the May 1994 killing, in which four prominent Ogonis were slain. The trial, which has been variously described as being a travesty of law and justice,[46] found the accused persons guilty of murder and were sentenced to death by hanging. The execution was carried out on 10 December 1995 amidst international condemnations.[47]

In addition to these killings in the hands of security operatives protecting installations and interest in the oil industry, some activities in the industry had also created environmental hazards that had led to the unwarranted death of some people in such areas. In 1991, a causeway to carry a road to the well heads was built on behalf of Shell by Willbros West Africa Inc. The causeway initially had no passages for water to pass underneath, blocking the drainage channel. After a series of protests, culverts were eventually constructed. But being poorly constructed, the drainage was still disturbed, causing widespread environmental problems, among which was the turbulence generated by the flow of water to the lake. A young girl had her life terminated by drowning when her canoe was capsized by the turbulence.

Again, in 1997, at Esit Eket Akwa Ibom State, five children drowned in an unfenced flooded pit where Shell used to have a 'Christmas Tree' well head.[48]

All these cases of violation of the right to life were avenues for instituting legal actions for compensation, more especially where the loss of life is unwarranted under any law. In a twist of faith, the survivors of the late Ken Saro-Wiwa instituted a legal action against Shell Petroleum Development Company Limited (SPDC) in

[44] Ibid.

[45] This unit, known as the Internal Security Task Force, was set up by the Rivers State Government of Nigeria.

[46] Birnbaum (1995).

[47] As a result of this execution, Nigeria was suspended from the Commonwealth of Nations in 1995. This situation has not de-escalated as the Joint Task Force (JTF) continued in its operation of 'flushing out' militants and sacked many villages, killing and maiming innocent civilians. Many villages in the Niger Delta had been affected since the Odi debacle in 2000, and this trend has continued.

[48] Human Rights Watch (1999), p. 71.

the United States of America (USA) for compensation for the death of their father. The matter did not go into a full trial; SPDC, however, agreed to pay some amount in this respect.[49]

12.1.3.2.1.2 Right to Personal Liberty and Freedom from Torture or Inhuman or Degrading Punishment

These are another set of human rights that have been greatly violated in protesting against environmental damage, especially in the oil industry. CFRN 1999,[50] in guaranteeing the right to personal liberty, provides that 'every person shall be entitled to his personal liberty and no one shall be deprived of such liberty save in the following cases and in accordance with a procedure permitted by law'. The subsection in paragraphs (a)–(f) sets out conditions under which this right may be derogated, but it is set forth in subsections 2–5 and in subsection 6 that 'any person who is unlawfully arrested or detained shall be entitled to compensation and public apology from the appropriate authority or person . . . specified by law'.[51]

UDHR 1948,[52] in respect of this right, provides that 'everyone has the right to life, liberty and security of person and that no one shall be subjected to arbitrary arrest, detention or exile'. ICCPR 1966, on the other hand, states that 'everyone has the right to liberty and security of person. No one shall be subjected to arbitrary arrest or detention. No one shall be deprived of his liberty except on such grounds and in accordance with such procedure as are established by law.'[53] ACHPR 1981 also guarantees this right as Article 6 provides: 'every individual shall have the right to liberty and to the security of his person. No one may be deprived of his freedom except for reasons and conditions previously laid down by law. In particular, no one may be arbitrary arrested or detained.'

Akin to the right to personal liberty is the right to the dignity of the human person, especially freedom from torture and cruel, inhuman and degrading treatment. Section 34(1) of CFRN 1999 guarantees that 'every individual is entitled to respect for the dignity of his person'. Accordingly, paragraph (a) of the said section provides that 'no person shall be subjected to torture, or to inhuman or degrading treatment'.

UDHR 1948, on the other hand, states that 'no one shall be subjected to torture or to cruel, inhuman or degrading treatment or punishment'.[54] ICCPR 1966, in Article 10(1), provides that all persons deprived of their liberty shall be treated with

[49] SPDC, however, maintained that the act was not that of accepting liability but for 'good neighbourliness'.

[50] CFRN (1999), s. 35(1).

[51] CFRN (1999).

[52] UDHR (1948), arts. 3 and 9.

[53] ICCPR (1966), art. 9(1).

[54] UDHR (1948), art. 5.

humanity and with respect for the inherent dignity of the human person. Meanwhile, ACHPR 1981[55] declares as follows:

> Every individual shall have the right to respect of the dignity inherent in a human being and to the recognition of his legal status. All forms of exploitation and degradation of man particularly slavery, slave trade, torture, cruel, inhuman or degrading punishment and treatment shall be prohibited.

The idea of treating these rights together is that, more often than not, events have shown that where personal liberty is violated, this may invariably result in the violation of the right to the dignity of the human person. There is a plethora of violations against these rights, especially in the oil industry. For instance, in June and July 1995, at Egbema, Imo State, as a result of a disagreement between the community and ELF (an oil-producing company), a major disturbance ensued. The mobile police sent to safeguard installations carried out indiscriminate beatings and arrests. More than 30 people were hoarded in detention for several weeks without trial. They were eventually released on bail after being subjected to various inhuman treatments at the police cell.[56]

The rights in issue, such as the right to personal liberty and the right to dignity of human person, especially freedom from torture, cruel, inhuman and degrading treatment, were violated in respect of community leaders and environmental whistleblowers at different periods between 1996 and 1997. For example, Godwin Uyi Ojo, project officer at Environmental Right Action (ERA), was detained between 25 January and 10 February 1996 on the excuse that he had in his possession documents on the situation in Ogoniland. Between 5 June and 19 July 1996, Nnimmo Bassey, director of ERA, was detained in Lagos from 7 to 17 November 1996 by the State Security Service (SSS), while Patrick Naagbanton of the Rivers Coalition and Rivers State chapter of the Civil Liberties Organisation (CLO) and Uche Okwukwu of the Niger Delta Human and Environmental Rescue Organisation (ND-HERO) were detained in Uyo for distributing leaflets calling on students to commemorate the anniversary of the execution of the Ogoni Nine. Again, on 26 June 1996, Chief C O B Aliba of the Egbema community was arrested and detained for 2 weeks, in the company of 19 other community leaders, by members of the River State Internal Security Task Force. Their crime was that they demanded for the provision of electricity to the community from Agip Oil Company.[57]

Violations of the rights to personal liberty and dignity of the human person were not limited to community leaders and environmental whistleblowers. For instance, in March 1996, seven youths from Yenezue-Gene village near Shell's Gbaran oilfield in Rivers State went to Mife Construction, a contractor of Shell, to ask for employment. The youths were lured into the company's main site by the soldiers posted in the camp, who ordered the youths to strip, forced them to crawl on the road and beat

---

[55] ACHPR (1981), art 5.

[56] Human Rights Watch (1999), p. 16.

[57] Ibid., 131–132.

them with electric cable.[58] Similarly, on 4 January 1997, Prince Ugo, secretary of the Umugo Youth Association in Ogba-Egbema-Ndoni LGA in Rivers State, went looking for employment at the Obite gas project construction site, where C and C Construction was the main contractor. He was ordered out of the site. When he protested, he was beaten up for several hours by the mobile police stationed at the site and was later locked up for several hours in one of the trailers there.[59]

In January 1997, over 100 youths held a demonstration at Shell's Ahia flow station in Omudioga, Rivers State, demanding that Shell carry out development projects in their village, including the tarring of roads, completion of a water project and provision of electricity, as part of compensation for the environmental degradation the village suffered due to Shell's oil production activities. The youths went to the flow station and occupied the site. Later, about 15 members of the Internal Security Task Force came to the site and arrested 12 of the youths. They were taken to Bori camp near Port Harcourt, where they were detained for 1 month without trial. They were beaten up every morning, and they alleged that teargas canisters were filled into their cell on a number of occasions.[60]

On 22 March 1998, members of the Rivers State Internal Security Task Force and Operation Flush, an anti-crime unit in Rivers State, arrested many members of MOSOP. They were subsequently detained without trial until May 1998.[61] In 2000, the town of Odi was completely devastated by members of the security operatives. A large number of the inhabitants were assaulted, beaten, detained and even killed.

The list is endless and the atrocities bone chilling. Viewed from any angle, human rights instruments have made it abundantly clear that the deprivation of personal liberty must be made in accordance with the procedures laid down by law, and section 35(2)–(5)[62] laid out such procedures.

In spite of all the provisions, these rights have been flagrantly abused, especially by operators in the oil industry. Moreover, it is not on record that the provisions of section 35 (6)[63] of CFRN 1999, which indicates that 'any person who is unlawfully arrested or detained shall be entitled to compensation and public apology from the appropriate authority or person . . . specified by law', has been complied with. Thus, this provision offers a legitimate ground for suing for compensation where one's personal liberty has been abused in the course of protesting against environmental abuse and the damages arising therefrom.

---

[58] Ibid., 142.

[59] Human Rights Watch (1999), p. 143.

[60] Ibid., 144.

[61] Ibid., 128.

[62] CFRN (1999).

[63] Ibid.

12.1.3.2.1.3 Rights to Peaceful Assembly and Association and Right to Freedom of Expression

At times, as a result of adverse environmental damage caused by environmental pollution, victims may decide to go on a peaceful demonstration to bring to the fore the environmental damage they had suffered. These victims at times face brutal force. Their rights[64] are being severally abused and violated without any justification or without accordance to the circumstances provided by law, especially in the oil industry. For instance, the Ogoni people, in the exercise of their rights to a peaceful assembly and association and of their right to freedom of expression, formed MOSOP, through which they engaged in rallies and other forms of dissemination of information to express their ill feelings regarding the environmental degradation being suffered by them, which was met with brutal force by the security operatives employed by the oil companies and the Federal Government of Nigeria.[65]

Similar associations, like the Movement for the Survival of Izon Ethnic Nationality in Delta (MOSIEND), the Movement for Reparation to Ogba (Oloibiri) (MORETO) and the Chikoko Movement, among others, having similar aims and objectives, that is, to protest and express their opinion on how oil wealth should be shared and on the restitution of the devastated environment, met a similar faith as MOSOP. In all these associations, rallies held were broken up by the police and other security outfits, including soldiers, and prominent members were arrested, detained, brutalised and, in some cases, killed.[66]

After the MOSIEND rally on 30 December 1998, in support of the Kaiama Declaration adopted on 11 December 1998, a state of emergency was declared in Bayelsa State and a dusk-to-dawn curfew imposed; though it was lifted on 3 January 1999, a ban on meeting, processions and other gatherings remained in place. Acknowledging this development, then Military Head of State General Abdulsalami Abubakar,[67] while accepting that the government was committed to freedom of expression, the right to dissent and all other basic freedoms and rights that are the hallmark of a decent, civilised and open society, fired this salvo: 'The recent activities in the Niger Delta region are a flagrant abuse of our commitment to such rights and freedoms. This administration will not allow lawlessness and anarchy to camouflage as right or freedom. . . .'[68]

Notwithstanding this 'riot act', the people in the Niger Delta still believe in the use of protests, through rallies, to derive home their grievances. This assertion may be correct, as studies[69] have shown that there is a clear correlation between such

[64] Rights to peaceful assembly and association and the right to freedom of expression.

[65] Human Rights Watch (1999), p. 144.

[66] Ibid.

[67] June 1998 to May 1999.

[68] Nigerian Television Authority (NTA) (1999).

[69] Environmental Resources Manager Ltd (1997), p. 230.

protests and the subsequent provision of development projects, and many community members feel that protests are therefore the only way to be heard.

These acts of violation of the aforementioned rights form a basis for applying for compensation. This is so because those rights violated are protected by various human rights instruments and provide situations or circumstances under which they may be derogated. For instance, CFRN 1999[70] guarantees the right to a peaceful assembly and association in the following terms: 'Every person shall be entitled to assembly freely and associated with other persons, and in particular he may form or belong to any political party, trade union or any other association for the protection of his interests.'

UDHR 1948, as regards the same right, provides in Article 20(1) that everyone has the right to a peaceful assembly and association. ICCPR 1966,[71] on the other hand, declares that 'everyone shall have the right to freedom of association with others'. ACHPR 1981[72] also guarantees this right as follows: 'Every individual shall have the right to free association provided he abides by the law and the every individual shall have the right to assembly freely with other but subject to only to necessary restrictions provided by law. . . .'

With respect to right to freedom of expression, CFRN 1999, as amended, guarantees this: 'every person shall be entitled to freedom of expression, including freedom to hold opinions and to receive and impart ideas and information without interference'.[73] Under ICCPR 1966, the right is guaranteed thus: 'every one shall have the right to freedom of expression. . .'.[74]

ACHPR 1981 also guarantees this right, stipulating that 'every individual shall have the right to express and disseminated his opinions within the law'.[75] Circumstances under which these rights can be derogated are provided under section 45(1), CFRN 1999, as amended, which provides: 'Nothing in sections 37, 38, 39, 40 and 41 of this Constitution shall invalidate any law that is reasonably justifiable in a democratic society:

(a) in the interest of defence, public safety, public order, public morality or public health; or
(b) for the purpose of protecting the rights and freedom or other persons.'[76]

[70] CFRN (1999), s. 40.
[71] ICCPR (1966), art. 22.
[72] ACHPR (1981), arts. 10 and 11.
[73] CFRN (1999), s. 39(1).
[74] ICCPR (1966), art. 19(2).
[75] ACHPR (1981), art. 9(2).
[76] A similar provision can be found in ICCPR (1966), art. 22(2).

12.1.3.2.2 Economic and Social Rights

These are a bundle of rights referred to as second-generation rights. Within environmental management circles, they are those rights translating general economic and social rights into specific environmental standards that promise to allow human rights bodies to consider whether substantive environmental standards and conditions are being maintained at satisfactory levels or whether environmental dislocations have impinged on the enjoyment of those rights. In the context of environmental issues and for the purposes of this section of the work, the relevant rights include:

1. Proprietary rights
2. The right to family life
3. The right to a standard of living adequate to health and well-being
4. The right to the highest attainable standard of physical and mental health

The rights are, however, discussed under two headings, namely:

1. Proprietary Rights and
2. Other Aspects of Economic and Social Rights, in respect of sections 2–4 above.

12.1.3.2.2.1 Proprietary Rights

CFRN 1999, as amended, guarantees in section 43 the acquisition and ownership of immovable property anywhere in Nigeria. CFRN 1999 further guarantees that 'no moveable property or any interest in an immovable property shall be taken possession of compulsorily and no right over or interest in any such property shall be acquired in any part of Nigeria, except in the manner and for the purposes prescribed by a law'.[77]

CFRN 1999, as amended, further provides for the payment of compensation under section 44(1) (a) and (b) and when no compensation shall be paid.[78] UDHR 1948[79] also warrants this right, stating that 'everyone has the right to own property alone as well as in association with others; no one shall be arbitrarily deprived of his property'. ACHPR 1981,[80] in respect of this right, provides as follows: 'the right to property shall be guaranteed. It may only be encroached upon in the interest of public need or in the general interest of the community and in accordance with the provisions of appropriate laws.'

Exercising these proprietary rights in the mineral-ore-bearing areas of Nigeria, especially the oil-producing communities, is replete with problems.[81] One of the

[77] CFRN (1999), s. 44(1).

[78] Ibid., s. 44(2).

[79] UDHR (1948), art. 17.

[80] ACHPR (1981), art. 14.

[81] See, for instance, CFRN (1999), s. 44(3); Petroleum Act, Cap P10 LFN 2004, s. 1; Land Use Act, Cap L5 LFN. 2004, s. 28; and Petroleum Industry Act 2021, Act No 26, 2021, s. 1.

problems is that land, upon which the minerals are found, is heavily protected by various laws in Nigeria in favour of mineral extractions and, by so doing, expropriates the people's right to such lands where minerals are discovered. Thus, land is acquired for mineral ore extraction with no effective due process and without protection of the people whose livelihoods may be destroyed by such activities. Although some of these laws[82] provide for the payment of compensation to the persons affected, the quantum of compensation is at times left in the hands of the operators of the mineral-extracting industries or, in most cases, to the discretion of the court.

For instance, in the case of *Godpower Nweke v Nigerian Agip Oil Company Ltd*,[83] the issue before the court was compensation for economic trees, fish, ponds, lakes, juju shrines, damaged fishing creeks and lands belonging to the plaintiff. The damages were caused by the defendant's oil operations. After going through administrative procedures for compensation, the plaintiff brought this action on the ground that the compensation advanced by the defendant was inadequate. The Supreme Court of Nigeria disagreed with the approach adopted by the lower court for not dismissing the case since the defendant had offered an amount to the plaintiff and should have entered judgement for the plaintiff in the amount earlier agreed upon by the parties.

Again, an infringement on proprietary rights does not stop with the expropriation of land. Activities in mineral ore extraction, especially in the oil industry, by its various operations also impinge on the means of livelihood of the people. For instance, the most noticeable yet generally unremarked effect of gas flaring is light pollution. Across the oil-producing areas, the night sky is lit up by flares; villagers close to the flares complain that nocturnal animals are disturbed by this light and leave the area, making hunting more difficult and contributing to a loss of income. In cases of oil spills, which are a common occurrence in the area, spills can kill large numbers of fish in a small area, especially in creeks and freshwater swamps.

This usually affects the access of a particular community to fishing in the area. At times, the spill affects individual fish ponds, causing an enormous loss of income and becoming a veritable source of litigation.[84]

Furthermore, the forests of the Niger Delta, all types, provide important sources of food and income to the local communities. Besides, the mangrove forests are a source of, aside from timber, medicines, dyes, thatching and food species. In freshwater swamp forests, products like raffia palm, mango, *ogbono*, land snails, etc. are destroyed during oil operations, in addition to the destruction of cultivated land. A serious blow is dealt with on the people's search for income.

---

[82] CFRN (1999), s. 43.

[83] (1976) 9 & 10 S C, 107.

[84] See the cases of *Shell Petroleum Development Company Limited v Chief Graham Otoko and 5 Ors* (1990), 693, and *Ogiale and Ors v Shell Petroleum Development Company Limited* (1997), which are some cases in point.

Recourse to litigation is then had for compensation. Although compensation is paid in most cases, either through a court order or through administrative procedures, communities claim that the compensation they receive when a claim is finally agreed is nothing compared to the loss they suffered. This is contrary to the dictum of the Court of Appeal in the case of *Shell Petroleum Development Company Limited v Councilor F.B. Farah and 7 Ors*,[85] where the court stated that compensation should 'restore the person suffering the loss as far as money can do that to the position he was before the loss or would have been but for the loss'. Thus, where the compensation paid is less than the loss suffered, not only people's income is affected, but also the right to acquire property is destroyed.

Although some of the villagers may not be aware of the full environmental consequences of environmental pollution and other environmental hazards from mineral ore extractions, they are all aware of the economic effects of the resultant damages to the income they usually derive from farming, fishing and hunting as well as the attendant effects on their right to acquire property, which should form a basis for a claim for compensation against the polluters.

12.1.3.2.2.2 Other Aspects of Economic and Social Rights

Other aspects of economic and social rights that may be violated that may form the basis for compensation include:

1. The right to a standard of living adequate to health and well-being
2. The right to the highest attainable standard of physical and mental health, and
3. The right to family life

The first two rights, the right to a standard of living adequate to health and well-being and the right to the highest attainable standard of physical and mental health, are somewhat connected and are thus treated together. In respect of the right to a standard of living adequate to health and well-being, CFRN 1999, as amended,[86] provides as follows:

> The State shall, within the context of the ideals and objectives for which provisions are made in this Constitution, control the national economy in such a manner as to secure the maximum welfare, freedom and happiness of every citizen on the basis of social justice equality of status and opportunity.

On the same right, the UDHR guarantees that 'everyone has the right to a standard living adequate for the health and well-being of himself and of his family, including food, clothing, housing and medical care, and necessary social services'.[87] The International Covenant on Economic, Social and Cultural Rights (ICESCR) 1966, in similar words, recognises this right. It states that 'the state parties to the present

[85] (1995) 3 NWLR (pt. 382) 148 at 192.

[86] CFRN (1999), s. 16(1)(b).

[87] UDHR (1948), art. 25.

covenant recognize the right of everyone to an adequate standard of living for himself and his family'.[88]

In respect of the right to the highest attainable standard of physical and mental health, the ICESCR,[89] while enjoining states parties to the Covenant to recognise the right of everyone to the enjoyment of the highest attainable standard of physical and mental health, sets out the steps to be taken for such attainment. This shall include the improvement of all aspects of environmental and industrial hygiene. The ACHPR[90] also recognises this right in a similar language to that of the provisions of the ICESCR above.

One is not in doubt as to the debilitating effects that environmental pollution has on the environment and on human life. Environmental pollution affects the acquisition of proprietary interests on land and the means of subsistence and sustenance of the people, and it impinges on the health of those affected by it. The inability to acquire income, coupled with the devastation caused by pollution and the paucity or absence of compensation, as the case may be, and the repressions and suppressions especially coming from the extractive industries, may lead to the non-attainment of these two rights: the right to a standard of living adequate to health and well-being and the right to the highest attainable standard of physical and mental health. These violations may give room for victims of pollution to apply for compensation.

The right to private and family life, the third segment of other social rights being discussed, is guaranteed and protected under CFRN 1999, as amended.[91] UDHR 1948 also recognises this right. Under UDHR 1948,[92] 'no one shall be subjected to arbitrary interference with his privacy, family, home or correspondence nor to attacks upon his honour and reputation'.

ICCPR 1966,[93] while recognising family life as a right to be protected, states that the family is 'the natural and fundamental group unit of society and is entitled to protection by society and the state'. Again, ICESCR 1966[94] provides that the widest possible protection and assistance should be accorded to the family, which is the natural and fundamental group unit of society. In a similar language, ACHPR 1981[95] provides that 'the family shall be the natural unit and basis of society that it shall be protected by the state which will take care of its physical and moral health'.

This right, that is, the right to private and family life, may be infringed upon due to environmental pollution. The extractive industry[96] (especially the oil and gas

---

[88] International Covenant on Economic, Social, and Cultural Rights (ICESCR) (1966), art. 11(1).

[89] ICESCR (1966), art. 12(1) and (2)(b).

[90] ACHPR (1981), art. 16(1).

[91] CFRN (1999), s. 37.

[92] UDHR (1948), art. 12.

[93] ICCPR (1966), art. 23(1).

[94] ICESCR (1966), art. 10(1).

[95] ACHPR (1981), art. 18(1).

[96] The industry is one of the greatest sources of environmental pollution in Nigeria. The latest report by the United Nations Environment Programme (UNEP), entitled *Environmental Assessment of*

sector), through its various activities, leaves in its trail a high level of environmental dislocation and has caused environmental pollution through oil spills; the deposition of wastewater, chemicals and effluent; the emission of fumes, especially through gas flaring; the deposit of tailing; and the creation of borrow pits. These, in one way or the other, may impinge on the right to privacy and family life.

These environmental problems have created health problems and, at times, the evacuation and relocation of families.[97] In this respect the European Court on Human Rights (ECHR) in a number of cases based on Article 8 of the European Human Rights Act,[98] had decided in the case of *Lopes Ostra v Spain*[99] that environmental pollution from a treatment plant which was releasing fumes and smells that were causing health problems and nuisance, and where many locals were evacuated and re-housed violated right to family life.

Also, where the quality of life is affected due to environmental spoliation, as in the case of *Powell and Raynor v United Kingdom,*[100] and where the polluter fails to provide information on the risks from pollution, as in the case of *Guaerra and Others v Italy,*[101] the ECHR held that these acts amounted to a violation of the provisions of the right to private and family life and correspondence.

Commenting on the above decisions, Thornton and Tromans[102] concluded that although the Human Rights Act did not set out to establish environmental rights in its Article 8, the court and Commission have, however, accepted that the enjoyment of a certain quality of the environment is part of the enjoyment of the right to family life and to the peaceful enjoyment of possession. It can therefore be held that a violation of the right to private and family life in such manner as aforementioned constitutes a veritable source for environmental claims for compensation.

On the whole, the aforementioned economic and social rights may be violated in various ways. This can arise from the lack of access to drinking water that is free from toxic or other contaminants, the pollution of the atmosphere through gas flaring, the dumping of hazardous and toxic wastes in the vicinity of people's homes, the destruction of natural vegetation and source of food and income, the expropriation of land with the attendant paucity of compensation as well as repressions and suppressions, which can all be viewed and treated as violations of

---

Ogoniland, in August 2011, submitted to the President of Nigeria, said that it would take 30 years, costing US$30 billion annually, for Ogoniland to be rehabilitated as a result of the devastation caused by many years of pollution arising from oil exploitation in the area. See the United Nations Environment Programme (UNEP) (2011).

[97] The case of Funima in Bonny, where the Nigerian Liquefied Natural Gas firm is located, is a case in point; the case of the Bonga oil spill in December 2011 is another case in point. These are in addition to other cases of oil spills that are perennial in the oil-producing communities.

[98] This article guarantees the right to respect for private and family life and correspondence.

[99] (1994) 20 ECHR, 277.

[100] (1990) 172 ECHR 41.

[101] (116/1996/735/932) 4 BHRC 63.

[102] Thorton and Tromans (1999), p. 35.

fundamental economic and social rights. These violations had provided an impetus for a demand for compensation.

12.1.3.2.3 Group Rights

Group rights are referred to as solidarity rights and the third generation of rights in the sets of rights to be recognised. According to Karel Vasak,[103] these rights:

> Seek to infuse human dimension into areas where it has all too often been missing having been left to the states . . . They are new in that they may be both invoked against the state and demanded of it, but above all . . . they can be realized only through the concerted effort of all the actors on social scene: the individual, state, public, and private bodies and the international community.

Group rights include the following:

1. The right to be different
2. The right to share in the common heritage of mankind
3. The right to international peace and security
4. The right to communicate
5. The right to receive humanitarian assistance
6. The right to development and
7. The right to health and a healthy environment[104]

Relevant to the discussions on the violations of rights by environmental polluters that could provide the bases for compensation are:

1. The right to development and
2. The right to health and a healthy environment

12.1.3.2.3.1 Right to Development

Development in this case concerns the capacity and creative capability of a people to effectively transform the natural resources of their environment into goods and services through the imaginative and practical application of their creative talents and productive labour force. Development in this respect is human centred. This is because 'all human beings have a responsibility for development, individually and collectively, taking into account the need for full respect for their human rights and fundamental freedoms as well as their duties to the community, which alone can ensure the free and complete fulfilment of the human being, and they should therefore promote and protect an appropriate political, social and economic order for development'.[105]

---

[103] Quoted in Umozuruike (1997), p. 51.

[104] United Nations Declaration on the Right to Development (DRD) (1986).

[105] Ibid., art. 2(2).

To this end, development involves the development of man since it has to be woven around man and not man around it. This position is imaginatively expressed in the Third National Development Plan (1975–1980)[106] in these words:

> True development must mean the development of man—the unfolding and realization of his creative potential, enabling him to improve his material conditions of living through the use of resources available to him. It is a process by which man's personality is enhanced, and it is that enhanced personality—creative, organized and disciplined, which is the moving force behind the socio-economic transformation of any society.

It is therefore no gainsaying that for the right to development to be enjoyed, it involves the right of man to develop in economic, social and cultural matters. Thus, states are obliged to create a favourable atmosphere for development so as to imbue in man an enhanced personality not only for the enjoyment of other rights—civil, political, economic, social and cultural—but also for the transformation of his society. This assertion is captured by the late Leopold Senghor,[107] former President of Senegal, when he declared thus:

> Our overall concept of Human Rights is marked by the Right to Development since it integrates all economic, social and cultural rights, and also civil and political rights. Development is first and foremost a change of quality of life and not only an economic growth required at all costs, particularly in the blind repression of individuals and peoples. It is the full development of every man in his community.

Arising from the above, the Rio Declaration on Environment and Development (or 'Rio Declaration') 1992 provides that the right to development must be fulfilled so as to equitably meet the developmental and environmental needs of present and future generations.[108] In line with the above assertions, various international instruments and soft laws have guaranteed the enjoyment of this right. For instance, the Declaration on the Right to Development (DRD) 1986[109] provides thus:

> The right to development is an inalienable human right by virtue of which every human person and all peoples are entitled to participate in, contribute to, and enjoy economic, social, cultural and political development, in which all human rights and fundamental freedoms can only be fully realized.

ACHPR 1981, in Article 22(2), declares that 'states shall have the duty individually or collectively, to ensure the exercise of the right to development'.

The crux of the matter is that in the Nigerian environment, especially in communities where the extraction of mineral ores takes place, the people are marginalised in the scheme of things; their quest for development usually competes with the quest to exploit the natural resources in their environment. These two competing variables, the people's quest for self-determination in their search for development and

[106] Federal Ministry of National Planning (1976).

[107] Address to Meeting of Experts Preparing the Draft on African Charter on 28 November 1979, OAU DOC CAB? LEG?67/5, 5.

[108] Rio Declaration on Environment and Development (1992), principle 3.

[109] DRD (1986), art. 1(1).

exploration and exploitation of mineral ores, often clash. The latter, being stately protected,[110] overrides the former. The net effect is that the people's creative and organised energies are channelled not towards the transformation of their society but to never-ending protests to be heard and the attendant repressions and suppressions and the violation of other rights guaranteed by various human rights protection instruments.

Again, the right to development carries with it the right to participate in deciding the nature and direction of development projects within one's society. But apart from a few dispirited development projects embarked upon by oil companies, as they fancy or deem fit, much of what the people need and require for their development passes them by. The picture therefore is a society devoid of basic infrastructures, desolate, impoverished, marginalised and brutalised and an environment that is devastated. No wonder an Izombe chief[111] aptly described their situation as that of a snail picked by a hunter who takes away the meat and throws the shell carelessly away. Lamenting what had befallen the farming in Ogoniland, Rekiya Sha'aba[112] pointed out:

> Today farming in Ogoni land has become an exercise in futility. The land has been raped of its virginity, deprived of its fertility through the continuous exploitation . . . What remains of the once luxuriant rain forest are only shrub lands. Lakes, rivers and creeks have been and are still being polluted through spillage and leakage.

The sum of these assaults and deprivations is that they amount to a crime against both humanity and the environment. In this respect, a crime against the environment can be viewed as a crime against the right to development, for as Baxi[113] pointed out, 'crimes against the right to development are international acts or omissions or patterns of behaviour designed to defeat, distort, deflect, detract from laws directed to fulfil components of the right to development'.

The right to development therefore should be seen as the foremost and most far-reaching task in mineral-ore-bearing communities, especially the Niger Delta region. To this end, development must be seen in its many dimensions: peace, social justice, democracy, the economy and environmental protection.[114] But for peace, social justice and democracy to reign and for the economy to thrive, there must be adequate environmental protection.

Environmental protection in the Niger Delta, or at least adequate compensation for environmental damage, shall bring with it an avenue for development. Without development, however, there is no prospect for peace, and where there is no peace, restiveness holds sway, the state is not securely at peace and there will be no lasting development; insecurity will persist, and this itself is not good for the environment.

[110] Petroleum Industry Act (2021), s. 1; CFRN (1999), s. 45(3).

[111] Nigerian Environmental Study/Action Team (NEST) (1991), p. 87.

[112] Sha'aba (1998), p. 73.

[113] Unpendra (1984), pp. 63 and 64.

[114] United Nations General Assembly (UNGA) (1994).

The panacea for avoiding the above scenario is that there should be an avenue for compensating victims of environmental damage.

12.1.3.2.3.2 Right to Health and a Healthy Environment

This right connotes the right to enjoy a pollution-free, benign, friendly and aesthetically pleasing environment. The right to a decent environment has been recognised as one of man's fundamental rights.[115] Living in a healthy environment implies an environment protected from abuse and devastation, an environment free from pollution, whether solid, liquid or gas. A violation of this right is a veritable source for compensation. It will be pertinent to ask, with respect to the right to health and a healthy environment, the following questions:

1. Has this right ever been violated?
2. What had been the level of environmental damage resulting from this devastation?
3. Is this right protected under extant human rights legal instruments?
4. Had the victims of this environmental damage ever sought legal redress?
5. What had been the nature of compensation awarded to the victims?

The answers to these questions can be found in the United Nations Environment Programme (UNEP) Report[116] and in the following cases:

1. *Social and Economic Rights Action Centre and the Centre for Economic and Social Rights (SERAC) v Nigeria*
2. *Socio-Economic Rights and Accountability Project (SERAP) v Federal Republic of Nigeria*
3. The *Comunidad Yanomami* case

12.1.3.2.3.2.1 United Nations Environment Programme (UNEP) Report[117]

In 2011, at the request of the Federal Government of Nigeria, the United Nations Environment Programme (UNEP) conducted an independent environmental impact assessment on Ogoniland. A team of international experts, local experts and academics surveyed 122 km of pipelines and visited all oil spill sights, oil wells and other oil facilities in Ogoniland, including decommissioned and abandoned facilities.[118] The assessment covered the extent of contamination on the land and in the groundwater, surface water, sediments, vegetation, and air.[119] It also covered

[115] United Nations (1972).

[116] United Nations Environment Programme (UNEP) (2011).

[117] UNEP (2011), p. 8.

[118] Ibid.

[119] Ibid.

industry practices, institutional issues and the effects of contamination on public health.[120]

The findings of the report show that oil pollution in Ogoniland[121] is widespread and severely affects many parts of the environment. With respect to soil and groundwater, the report concluded that the pollution from petroleum hydrocarbons in Ogoniland is extensive in many land areas, sediments and swamps.[122] The report also found that the groundwater in Ogoniland is exposed to hydrocarbons spilt on the surface, noting that 'in 49 cases, [the] UNEP observed hydrocarbons in soil at depths of at least 5 m'.[123] As a result, the hydrocarbon pollution in the groundwater in many places exceeded Nigerian national standards as set out by the Environmental Guidelines and Standards for the Petroleum Industries in Nigeria (EGASPIN).[124]

Oil spills have also devastated the vegetation in Ogoniland as 'Oil pollution in many intertidal creeks has left mangroves denuded of leaves and stems, leaving roots coated in a bitumen-like substance sometimes 1 cm or more thick'.[125] As a result, oil pollution in many creeks has destroyed mangrove forests, which provide spawning areas and serve as nurseries for juvenile fish. Extensive pollution and the destruction of mangroves have a negative impact on the fish cycle. In addition, oil pollution has also damaged crops, leading to lower yields and making the remediation of vegetation difficult. The reason is that 'channels that have been widened and the resulting dredged material are clearly evident in satellite images, decades after the dredging operation and without proper rehabilitation, former mangrove areas which have been converted to bare ground were being colonised by invasive species such as nipa palm. . .'.[126]

The UNEP investigation concluded that surface water in the region's creeks contained varying levels of hydrocarbons, with some creeks having layers of thick black oil. This pollution has negatively affected the fishing sector due to the destruction of fish habitats in the mangroves and creeks. Because fish tend to leave polluted areas for cleaner waters, pollution has forced fishermen to relocate to stay in business.[127]

Finally, with respect to public health, the report found that oil spills have exposed the Ogoni people to high concentrations of hydrocarbons in the air and in drinking water.[128] According to UNEP, one community was drinking from a well contaminated with benzene, a known carcinogen, 'at levels over 900 times above the World

[120] Ibid.

[121] Which may be applicable to other oil-bearing communities in the Niger Delta region of Nigeria.

[122] UNEP (2011), p. 9.

[123] Ibid., 11.

[124] Ibid., 10.

[125] Ibid.

[126] UNEP (2011), 10.

[127] Ibid.

[128] Ibid.

Health Organization (WHO) guideline'.[129] Experts also found hydrocarbon contamination in 28 other wells in ten different communities.[130] In several samples, the hydrocarbon levels were 'at least 1,000 times higher than the Nigerian drinking water standard of 3 mg/l'.[131] In air samples, the UNEP team detected benzene in concentrations of 900 times higher than recommended levels.[132] Given the timeline of oil operations in the area and Nigeria's average life expectancy, the report concluded, 'it is a fair assumption that most members of the current Ogoniland community have lived with chronic oil pollution throughout their lives'.[133]

Under the various international legal instruments on human rights, there are provisions for the respect and protection of the right to health and the right to a healthy environment. For instance, Article 12 of ICESCR[134] guarantees that every man and woman has an inherent right to the 'highest attainable standard of physical and mental health'.

Although ICESCR recognises the right to health, it does not explicitly recognise the right to a healthy environment; instead, the existence of the right to a healthy environment is implicit in certain articles of the Convention, such as the right to self-determination and the right to control natural wealth and resources;[135] the right to safe and healthy working conditions and the right to a decent living;[136] the right to an adequate standard of living and the right to the continuous improvement of living conditions;[137] the right to health, including all aspects of environmental and industrial hygiene;[138] and the right to the benefits of scientific progress.[139]

In addition, the Committee on Economic, Social, and Cultural Rights (CESCR)[140] addressed the right to a healthy environment when it used its General Comments to recognise that the right to health is 'an inclusive right extending not only to timely and appropriate health care but also to the underlying determinants of health, such as … healthy occupational and environmental conditions …'.[141] In doing so, the CESCR has recognised that a healthy environment is a necessary condition for the enjoyment of the right to health.

---

[129] Ibid.

[130] Ibid.

[131] Ibid.

[132] Ibid.

[133] Ibid.

[134] ICESCR (1966).

[135] Ibid., art. 1.

[136] ICESCR (1966), art. 7.

[137] Ibid., art. 11.

[138] Ibid., art, 12(b).

[139] Ibid., art 15.

[140] The implementation body of the ICESCR.

[141] United Nations Economic and Social Council, Committee on Economic Social and Cultural Rights (2000), p. 11.

ACHPR 1981,[142] on the other hand, explicitly recognises the right to a healthy environment. It provides that 'all peoples shall have the right to a general satisfactory environment favorable to their development'.[143] The CESCR and the African Commission[144] both interpret the ICESCR and the African Charter as imposing certain core or minimum obligations on states, including the obligations to protect, respect and fulfil.

Interestingly, Nigeria is a party to both the ICESCR and the ACHPR. Both legal instruments require the Nigerian government to fulfil, respect and protect the right to health and the right to a healthy environment. The ICESCR requires states parties to use the maximum of their available resources to work progressively towards fully realising the rights under the Covenant.[145] Accordingly, a state's failure to respect, protect or fulfil constitutes a breach unless the state can show that it has used all available resources to meet its obligations.[146]

State compliance with the three core obligations is necessary to ensure that individuals can fully realise the right to health. First, the obligation **to respect** requires states to 'refrain from interfering directly or indirectly with the enjoyment of the right...".[147] A state fails to meet its obligation where it repeals or suspends legislation necessary for the full realisation of the right to health.[148]

Second, the obligation **to protect** imposes an affirmative duty on states to prevent third parties, including corporations, from interfering with the right to a healthy environment and, hence, the right to health.[149] States must adopt and enforce measures that require non-state actors to conduct their operations in a manner that respects the right to health.[150] States breach their obligation to protect when they fail to prevent or regulate the operations of individuals, groups, corporations or other third parties whose conduct violates the right to health.[151]

Finally, the obligation **to fulfil** requires that states 'take positive measures that enable and assist individuals and communities to enjoy the right to health'.[152] This obligation is more difficult to implement since it requires states to take affirmative steps to assist communities.[153] For example, concerning the right to water, states must take positive steps to assist communities to enjoy the right to water by assisting

---

[142] ACHPR (1981).

[143] Ibid., art. 24.

[144] The body responsible for implementing the African Charter (AFCPHR).

[145] ICESCR (1966), art. 2(1).

[146] Konne (2014), p. 187.

[147] Ibid.

[148] Konne (2014), p. 187.

[149] Ibid.

[150] Ibid.

[151] Ibid.

[152] Ibid.

[153] UNEP Report (2011), 188.

in the clean-up of polluted streams or wells.[154] To ensure that third parties respect the right to health, states must adopt proper domestic legislation that guarantees those rights.[155] Specifically, Article 2 of the ICESCR requires that states use 'all appropriate means' to adopt legislative measures and other programmes necessary to fulfil the right to health.

Unfortunately, as the UNEP Report[156] revealed, the Nigeria State had not only failed to prevent third parties, in this case multinational oil companies, from interfering with the right to a healthy environment and, hence, the right to health, but it had also failed to adopt and enforce measures that require non-state actors to conduct their operations in a manner that respects the right to health.

Again, the Nigeria State had also failed to take positive steps to assist communities to enjoy the right to water by assisting in the clean-up of polluted streams or wells. This is in spite of the adoption of some legislative measures and other programmes necessary to fulfil this right to health. Thus, the Nigerian State had failed in its obligation to fulfil the requirements that states should 'take positive measures that enable and assist individuals and communities to enjoy the right to health'.[157]

As a result of the failure of the operators of the activities that caused the damage and the failure of its partner[158] to enforce extant environmental protection laws, the victims, at times, were left with no other option than to seek legal redress. A number of such suits had been recorded.

12.1.3.2.3.2.2 Social and Economic Rights Action Centre and the Centre for Economic and Social Rights (SERAC) v Nigeria

One of the cases respecting the issue of violations of the right to health and a healthy environment is *Social and Economic Rights Action Centre and the Centre for Economic and Social Rights v Nigeria (SERAC v Nigeria).*[159] This matter was filed before the African Commission on Human and Peoples' Rights (or 'Commission') in 2001. The Commission was established by the African Union to adjudicate matters between member states and matters against member states where there is a violation of rights as contained in the African Charter on Human and Peoples' Rights (ACHPR) 1981 and any other international legal instruments on human rights. In that case, the plaintiff, a non-governmental organisation (NGO) representing the interests of the Ogoni people of Rivers State, Nigeria,

[154] Ibid.

[155] Ibid.

[156] Ibid.

[157] UNEP Report (2011), 188.

[158] Federal Government of Nigeria.

[159] Case No. ACHPR/COMM/A044/1, African Commission on Human and Peoples' Rights 44 (May 27, 2002).

filed Communications at the African Commission on Human and Peoples' Rights (or 'Commission') in compliance with its rules on procedure.

The Complaints

In the Communication forwarded to the Commission, the complainants alleged that the military government of Nigeria had been directly involved in oil production through the state oil company, the Nigerian National Petroleum Company (NNPC), a majority shareholder in a consortium with Shell Petroleum Development Corporation (SPDC); that these operations had caused environmental degradation and health problems among the Ogoni people as a result of the contamination of the environment;[160] and that the oil consortium had exploited oil reserves in Ogoniland with no regard to the environment and health of the local communities, disposing toxic wastes into the environment and local waterways in violation of applicable international environmental standards. It also neglected and/or failed to maintain its facilities, causing numerous avoidable spills in the proximity of the villages. The resulting contamination of water, soil and air had serious short- and long-term health impacts, including skin infections, gastrointestinal and respiratory ailments, increased risk of cancers and neurological and reproductive problems.[161]

In the Communication to the Commission, the complainants again alleged that the Nigerian government had condoned and facilitated these violations by placing the legal and military powers of the state at the disposal of the oil companies[162] and that the government neither monitored the operations of the oil companies nor required safety measures that are standard procedure within the industry. This was in addition to withholding from the Ogoni communities information on the dangers created by oil activities.[163] This position was further compounded as the Nigerian government did not require oil companies to consult communities before beginning operations, even if the operations posed direct threats to community or individual lands.[164]

Further complaints revolve around the fact that the government had not required oil companies or its own agencies to produce basic health and environmental impact studies regarding hazardous operations and materials relating to oil production, despite the obvious health and environmental crisis in Ogoniland. This state of affairs was further aggravated by the government's refusal to permit scientists and environmental organisations from entering Ogoniland to undertake such studies.[165]

Besides the health and environmental issues, the complainants further alleged that the Nigerian security forces have attacked, burned and destroyed several Ogoni villages and homes, destroyed crops and killed farm animals. The security forces

160 *SERAC v Nigeria* (2002), para. 1.

161 *SERAC v Nigeria* (2002), para. 2.

162 Ibid., para. 3.

163 Ibid., para. 4.

164 Ibid., para. 6.

165 Ibid., para. 5.

created a state of terror and insecurity, which made it impossible for many Ogoni villagers to return to their fields and animals. The destruction of farmlands, rivers, crops and animals has created malnutrition and starvation among certain Ogoni communities.[166] All these destructions were under the pretext of dislodging the officials and supporters of the Movement of the Survival of Ogoni People (MOSOP), and the complete failure of the Government of Nigeria to investigate these attacks, let alone punish the perpetrators, further implicates the Nigerian authorities.[167]

In summary, the complaints alleged violations of Articles 2, 4, 14, 16, 18(1), 21 and 24 of ACHPR 1981.[168]

The Communication was received by the Commission on 14 March 1996. The documents were sent with a video. On 13 August 1996, letters acknowledging the receipt of the Communication were sent to both complainants. On 13 August 1996, a copy of the Communication was sent to the Government of Nigeria. At the 20th Ordinary Session held in Grand Bay, Mauritius, in October 1996, the Commission declared the Communication admissible and decided that it would be taken up with the relevant Nigerian authorities during the planned mission to Nigeria. On 10 December 1996, the Secretariat sent a *Note Verbale* and letters to this effect to the Government of Nigeria and the complainants, respectively.[169]

Applicable Law on Admissibility

Article 56 of ACHPR 1981 governs admissibility generally. Article 56(5) of ACHPR 1981, in particular, requires that local remedies, if any, be exhausted, unless these are unduly prolonged. One purpose of the exhaustion of the local remedy requirement is to give domestic courts an opportunity to decide upon cases before they are brought to an international forum, thus avoiding contradictory judgements of law at the national and international levels. Where a right is not well provided for in domestic law such that no case is likely to be heard, a potential conflict does not arise. Similarly, if the right is not well provided for, there cannot be effective remedies or any remedies at all.[170]

Another rationale for the exhaustion requirement is that a government should have notice of a human rights violation in order to have the opportunity to remedy such a violation before being called to account by an international tribunal. The exhaustion of the domestic remedy requirement should be properly understood as ensuring that the state concerned has an ample opportunity to remedy the situation the applicants complain of. It is not necessary here to recount the international attention that Ogoniland has received to argue that the Nigerian government has

---

[166] Ibid., para. 9.

[167] Ibid., para. 7.

[168] *SERAC v Nigeria* (2002), para. 10.

[169] Ibid., paras. 11–15.

[170] Ibid., paras. 35–37.

had ample notice and, over the past several decades, more than sufficient opportunity to give domestic remedies.[171]

The Commission therefore took cognisance of the fact that Nigeria had incorporated the African Charter on Human and Peoples' Rights into its domestic law, with the result that all the rights contained therein can be invoked in Nigerian courts, including those violations alleged by the complainants. However, the Commission noted that at the time of submitting the Communication, the then military government of Nigeria had enacted various decrees ousting the jurisdiction of the courts and thus depriving the people in Nigeria of the right to seek redress in the courts for acts of the government that violate their fundamental human rights. In such instances, and as in the instant Communication, the Commission is of the view that no adequate domestic remedies are in existent.[172]

It should also be noted that the government of Olusegun Obasanjo,[173] in their *Note Verbale* reference 127/2000 submitted at the 28th session of the Commission held in Cotonou, Benin, admitted to the violations committed then by stating, 'there is no denying the fact that a lot of atrocities were and are still being committed by the oil companies in Ogoni Land and indeed in the Niger Delta area'.[174]

Arising from the above, the Commission therefore declared that all the conditions of Article 56 of ACPHR 1981 were met by the Communication as it alleged a concerted violation of a wide range of rights guaranteed under ACHPR 1981.[175] The Commission then went ahead to establish what is generally expected of governments under ACHPR 1981, and more specifically *vis-à-vis* the rights themselves, and noted as follows:

1. That it is internationally accepted ideas of the various obligations engendered by human rights indicate that all rights—both civil and political rights and social and economic—generate at least four levels of duties for a State that undertakes to adhere to a rights regime, namely the duty to respect, protect, promote, and fulfil these rights. These obligations universally apply to all rights and entail a combination of negative and positive duties. As a human rights instrument, the African Charter is not alien to these concepts and the order in which they are dealt with here is chosen as a matter of convenience and in no way should it imply the priority accorded to them. Each layer of obligation is equally relevant to the rights in question.[176]
2. That at a primary level, the obligation **to respect** entails that the State should refrain from interfering in the enjoyment of all fundamental rights; it should

[171] Ibid., para. 38.

[172] *SERAC v Nigeria* (2002), para. 41.

[173] Elected President of the Federal Republic of Nigeria in May 1999–May 2007.

[174] *SERAC v Nigeria* (2002), para. 42.

[175] As it alleged a concerted violation of articles 2, 4, 14, 16, 18(1), 21 and 24 ACHPR (1981); see *SERAC v Nigeria* (2002), para. 10.

[176] *SERAC v Nigeria* (2002), para. 44.

respect right-holders, their freedoms, autonomy, resources, and liberty of their action.[177]

3. With respect to socio economic rights, this means that the State is obliged to respect the free use of resources owned or at the disposal of the individual alone or in any form of association with others, including the household or the family, for the purpose of rights-related needs. And with regard to a collective group, the resources belonging to it should be respected, as it has to use the same resources to satisfy its needs.[178]
4. Again, that at a secondary level, the State is obliged **to protect** right-holders against other subjects by legislation and provision of effective remedies. This obligation requires the State to take measures to protect beneficiaries of the protected rights against political, economic and social interferences. Protection generally entails the creation and maintenance of an atmosphere or framework by an effective interplay of laws and regulations so that individuals will be able to freely realize their rights and freedoms. This is very much intertwined with the tertiary obligation of the State **to promote** the enjoyment of all human rights. The State should make sure that individuals are able to exercise their rights and freedoms, for example, by promoting tolerance, raising awareness, and even building infrastructures.[179]
5. Furthermore, that the last layer of obligation requires the State **to fulfil** the rights and freedoms it freely undertook under the various human rights regimes. It is more of a positive expectation on the art of the State to move its machinery towards the actual realisation of the rights. This is also very much intertwined with the duty to promote mentioned in the preceding paragraph. It could consist in the direct provision of basic needs such as food or resources that can be used for food (direct food aid or social security).[180]

To this end, the Commission further stated that states are generally burdened with the above set of duties when they commit themselves to human rights instruments. Emphasising the all-embracing nature of their obligations, ICESCR 1966,[181] for instance under Article 2(1), stipulates exemplarily that states should 'undertake to take steps ... by all appropriate means, including particularly the adoption of legislative measures'. Depending on the type of rights under consideration, the level of emphasis in the application of these duties varies. But sometimes, the need to meaningfully enjoy some of the rights demands concerted action from the state in terms of more than one of the said duties.[182]

[177] Drzewicki (1999), p. 31.

[178] *SERAC v Nigeria* (2002), para. 45.

[179] Ibid., para. 46.

[180] Ibid., para. 47.

[181] ICESCR (1966).

[182] *SERAC v Nigeria* (2002), para. 48.

Examination of the Complaints by the Commission

The complainants alleged that the Nigerian government violated the right to health and the right to a clean environment as recognised under Articles 16 and 24 of ACHPR 1981 by failing to fulfil the minimum duties required by these rights. This, the complainants alleged, the government had done by:

1. Directly participating in the contamination of air, water and soil and thereby harming the health of the Ogoni population
2. Failing to protect the Ogoni population from the harm caused by the NNPC Shell Consortium but instead using its security forces to facilitate the damage
3. Failing to provide or permit studies of potential or actual environmental and health risks caused by the oil operations[183]

The Commission then went ahead to examine the allegations contained in the Communication it received in accordance with Articles 60 and 61 of ACHPR 1981 and other relevant international and regional human rights instruments and principles.

On the issue of violation of Articles 16 and 24 of ACPHR 1981, the Commission reiterated that under Article 16, 'Every individual shall have the right to enjoy the best attainable state of physical and mental health'[184] and that 'State Parties to the present Charter shall take the necessary measures to protect the health of their people and to ensure that they receive medical attention when they are sick'.[185] Meanwhile, Article 24 reads: 'All peoples shall have the right to a general satisfactory environment favourable to their development.' Read together, the Commission stated that 'these rights[186] recognise the importance of a clean and safe environment that is closely linked to economic and social rights in so far as the environment affects the quality of life and safety of the individual'.[187]

The Commission then concluded that the right to a generally satisfactory environment, as guaranteed under Article 24 of ACHPR 1981, or the right to a healthy environment, as is widely known, therefore imposes clear obligations upon a government. It required the state to take reasonable and other measures to prevent pollution and ecological degradation, to promote conservation and to secure ecologically sustainable development and use of natural resources. It noted that Article 12 of ICESCR 1966, to which Nigeria is a party, requires governments to take the necessary steps for the improvement of all aspects of environmental and industrial hygiene.[188]

The right to enjoy the best attainable state of physical and mental health enunciated in Article 16(1) of ACHPR 1981 and the right to a general satisfactory

[183] Ibid., para. 50.

[184] ACPHR (1981), art. 16(1).

[185] Ibid., art. 16(2).

[186] That is, those rights provided under ACPHR (1981), arts. 16 and 24.

[187] *SERAC v Nigeria* (2002), para. 51.

[188] *SERAC v Nigeria* (2002), para. 52.

environment favourable to development[189] already obligate governments to desist from directly threatening the health and environment of their citizens. The state is under obligation to respect the just-noted rights, and this entails largely non-interventionist conduct from the state for example, not carrying out, sponsoring or tolerating any practice, policy or legal measures violating the integrity of the individual.[190]

The Commission further inferred that government compliance with the spirit of Articles 16 and 24 of ACHPR 1981 must also include ordering or at least permitting independent scientific monitoring of threatened environments, requiring and publicising environmental and social impact studies prior to any major industrial development, undertaking appropriate monitoring and providing information to those communities exposed to hazardous materials and activities and providing meaningful opportunities for individuals to be heard and to participate in the development of decisions affecting their communities.

Reasoning and Decisions

The Commission then examined the conduct of the Government of Nigeria in relation to Articles 16 and 24 of ACHPR 1981. It observed that undoubtedly and admittedly, the Government of Nigeria, through NNPC, has the right to produce oil, the income from which will be used to fulfil the economic and social rights of Nigerians. But the care that should have been taken, as outlined in the preceding paragraph, and that would have protected the rights of the victims of the violations complained of was not taken. To exacerbate the situation, the security forces of the government engaged in conduct in violation of the rights of the Ogonis by attacking, burning and destroying several Ogoni villages and homes.[191]

The complainants also alleged a violation of Article 21 of ACHPR 1981[192] by the Government of Nigeria. The complainants alleged that the military Government of Nigeria was involved in oil production and thus did not monitor or regulate the operations of the oil companies and, in so doing, paved the way for the oil consortiums to exploit oil reserves in Ogoniland.

Furthermore, in all their dealings with the oil consortiums, the government did not involve the Ogoni communities in the decisions that affected the development of Ogoniland. The destructive and selfish role played by oil development in Ogoniland, closely tied with repressive tactics of the Nigerian government and the lack of material benefits accruing to the local population,[193] may well be said to constitute a violation of Article 21 of the ACHPR 1981. The Commission then opined that governments have a duty to protect their citizens, not only through appropriate legislation and effective enforcement but also by protecting them from damaging

---

[189] ACPHR (1981), art. 16(3).

[190] *SERAC v Nigeria* (2002), para. 53.

[191] Ibid., para. 54.

[192] Ibid., para. 55.

[193] Singh et al. (1995), paragraph B (1.6–1.7), pp. 2–3.

acts that may be perpetrated by private parties. This duty calls for positive action on the part of governments in fulfilling their obligation under human rights instruments.[194]

It should be noted that the practice before other tribunals also enhances this requirement, as evidenced in the case of *Velàsquez Rodríguez v Honduras.*[195] In this landmark judgment, the Inter-American Court of Human Rights held that when a state allows private persons or groups to act freely and with impunity to the detriment of the rights recognised, it would be in clear violation of its obligation to protect the human rights of its citizens. Similarly, this obligation of the state is further emphasised in the practice of the European Court of Human Rights in *X and Y v Netherlands.*[196] In that case, the court pronounced that there was an obligation on the part of the authorities to take steps to make sure that the enjoyment of the rights is not interfered with by any other private person.

Arising from the above, the Commission noted that in the present case, despite its obligation to protect persons against interferences in the enjoyment of their rights, the Government of Nigeria facilitated the destruction of Ogoniland. Contrary to its Charter obligations and despite such internationally established principles, the Nigerian government has given the green light to private actors, and the oil companies in particular, to devastatingly affect the well-being of the Ogonis. And by any measure of standards, its practice falls short of the minimum conduct expected of governments and, therefore, is in violation of Article 21 of ACHPR 1981.[197]

The complainants had asserted that the military government of Nigeria massively and systematically violated the right to adequate housing of the members of the Ogoni community provided under Article 14 and implicitly recognised by Articles 16 and 18(1) of ACHPR 1981. Article 14 of ACPHR 1981 provides that 'the right to property shall be guaranteed. It may only be encroached upon in the interest of public need or in the general interest of the community and in accordance with the provisions of appropriate laws'. Article 18(1), on the other hand, stipulates: 'The family shall be the natural unit and basis of society. It shall be protected by the State. . . .' The Commission observed that although the right to housing or shelter is not explicitly provided for under the African Charter, as a corollary the combination of the provisions protecting the right to enjoy the best attainable state of mental and physical health, cited under Article 16, the right to property, and the protection accorded to the family forbids the wanton destruction of shelter because when housing is destroyed, property, health and family life are adversely affected.[198]

The Commission therefore noted that the combined effect of Articles 14, 16 and 18(1) of ACHPR 1981 reads into the Charter the right to shelter or housing, which

---

[194] *SERAC v Nigeria* (2002), para. 57.

[195] Inter-American Committee on Human Rights, *Velàsquez Rodrígeuz* case, Judgment of July 19, 1988, Series C, No. 4.

[196] 91 ECHR (1985) (Ser A) at 32.

[197] *SERAC v Nigeria* (2002), para. 58.

[198] *SERAC v Nigeria* (2002), para. 59.

the Nigerian government has apparently violated. It further observed that at the very minimum, the right to shelter obliges the Nigerian government not to destroy the housing of its citizens and not to obstruct efforts by individuals or communities to rebuild lost homes.[199]

The state's obligation to respect housing rights requires it, and thereby all of its organs and agents, to abstain from carrying out, sponsoring or tolerating any practice, policy or legal measure that violates the integrity of the individual or infringes upon his freedom to use those material or other resources available to him in a way that he finds most appropriate in order to satisfy individual, family, household or community housing needs.[200] The state's duty to protect obliges it to prevent the violation of any individual's right to housing by any other individual or non-state actors, like landlords, property developers and landowners, and where an infringement occurs, it should act to preclude further deprivations as well as guarantee access to legal remedies.[201] The right to shelter even goes further than a roof over one's head. It extends to embody the individual's right to be let alone and to live in peace—whether under a roof or not.[202]

Again, the Commission observed that the protection of the rights guaranteed in Articles 14, 16 and 18 (1) of ACHPR 1981 leads to the same conclusion. As regards the earlier right and in the case of the Ogoni people, the Government of Nigeria had failed to fulfil these two minimum obligations. The government had destroyed Ogoni houses and villages and then, through its security forces, obstructed, harassed, beaten and, in some cases, shot and killed innocent citizens who had attempted to return to rebuild their ruined homes. These actions, the Commission noted, constituted massive violations of the right to shelter, in contravention of Articles 14, 16, and 18(1) of ACHPR 1981.[203]

As a corollary, the Commission noted the violation by the Nigerian government of the right to adequate housing, as implicitly protected in the Charter, also encompasses the right to protection against forced evictions.[204] The Commission then drew inspiration from the definition of the term 'forced evictions' by the Committee on Economic Social and Cultural Rights, which defines this term as 'the permanent removal against their will of individuals, families and/or communities from the homes and/or which they occupy, without the provision of, and access to, appropriate forms of legal or other protection'.[205]

The Commission noted that wherever and whenever they occur, forced evictions are extremely traumatic. They cause physical, psychological and emotional distress;

---

[199] Ibid., para. 60.

[200] Leckie (1995), pp. 107–123 at p. 113.

[201] Ibid.

[202] *SERAC v Nigeria* (2002), para. 61.

[203] *SERAC v Nigeria* (2002), para. 62.

[204] Ibid., para. 63.

[205] See General Comment No. 7 (1997) on the right to adequate housing (Article 11.1): Forced Evictions.

they entail losses of the means of economic sustenance, and they increase impoverishment. As noted by Leckie,[206] 'eviction can also cause physical injury and in some cases sporadic deaths ... Evictions break up families and increase existing levels of homelessness." In this regard, 'all persons should possess a degree of security of tenure which guarantees legal protection against forced eviction, harassment and other threats'.[207] Thus, the conduct of the Nigerian government clearly demonstrated a violation of this right enjoyed by the Ogonis as a collective right.

As regards the complaint on the right to food, it was argued that the right to food is implicit in the African Charter—in such provisions as the right to life,[208] the right to health[209] and the right to economic, social and cultural development.[210] By violating these rights, the Nigerian government trampled upon not only the explicitly protected rights but also the implicitly guaranteed right to food.[211]

According to the Commission, the right to food is inseparably linked to the dignity of human beings and is therefore essential for the enjoyment and fulfilment of such other rights as the right to health, education and work and the right of political participation. Furthermore, the African Charter and international law require and bind Nigeria to protect and improve existing food sources and to ensure access to adequate food for all citizens. And without touching on the duty to improve food production and to guarantee access, the minimum core of the right to food requires the Nigerian government to not destroy or contaminate food sources.[212]

The Commission therefore reasoned that the Nigerian government should not allow private parties to destroy or contaminate food sources and prevent people's efforts to feed themselves. It noted that the government's treatment of the Ogonis violated all three minimum duties of the right to food. The government destroyed food sources through its security forces and state oil company, allowed private oil companies to destroy food sources and, through terror, created significant obstacles to Ogoni communities trying to feed themselves. The Nigerian government again fell short of what is expected of it under the provisions of the African Charter and international human rights standards and, hence, is in violation of the right to food of the Ogonis.[213]

On the allegation that the Nigerian government had also violated Article 4 of ACHPR 1981, which guarantees the inviolability of human beings and everyone's right to life and the respect for the integrity of the human person, given the widespread violations perpetrated by the Government of Nigeria and by private

---

[206] Leckie (1995), p. 113.

[207] General Comment No. 4 (1991) of the Committee on Economic, Social and Cultural Rights on the right to adequate housing states (E/1992/23, annex III, para. 8(a)).

[208] ACHPR (1981), art. 4.

[209] Ibid., art. 16.

[210] Ibid., art. 22.

[211] *SERAC v Nigeria* (2002), para. 64.

[212] Ibid., para. 65.

[213] Ibid., para. 66.

actors, the most fundamental of all human rights—the right to life—had been violated. The security forces were given the green light to decisively deal with the Ogonis, which was illustrated by the widespread terrorisation and killings. Pollution and environmental degradation, to a level humanly unacceptable, had made living in Ogoniland a nightmare. The survival of the Ogonis depended on their land and farms, which were destroyed by the direct involvement of the government. These and similar brutalities persecuted not only individuals in Ogoniland but also the whole of the Ogoni community. They affected the life of the Ogoni society as a whole.[214]

Although the Commission stated that it did not wish to fault governments that were labouring under difficult circumstances to improve the lives of their people, it, however, noted that the situation of the people of Ogoniland required, in its view, a reconsideration of the government's attitude to the allegations contained in the instant communication. The intervention of multinational corporations may be a potentially positive force for development if the state and the people concerned are ever mindful of the common good and the sacred rights of individuals and communities.[215]

In summary, the Commission concluded that the Nigerian government did not live up to the minimum expectations of the African Charter and stated as follows:

1. That the Federal Republic of Nigeria was in violation of articles 2, 4, 14, 16, 18(1), 21 and 24 of the African Charter on Human and Peoples' Rights 1981;
2. The Commission appealed to the government of the Federal Republic of Nigeria to ensure protection of the environment, health and livelihood of the people of Ogoniland by:

   (a) Stopping all attacks on Ogoni communities and leaders by the Rivers State Internal Securities Task Force and permitting citizens and independent investigators free access to the territory;
   (b) Conducting an investigation into the human rights violations described above and prosecuting officials of the security forces, NNPC and relevant agencies involved in human rights violations;
   (c) Ensuring adequate compensation to victims of the human rights violations, including relief and resettlement assistance to victims of government sponsored raids, and undertaking a comprehensive cleanup of lands and rivers damaged by oil operations;
   (d) Ensuring that appropriate environmental and social impact assessments are prepared for any future oil development and that the safe operation of any

[214]The Commission conducted a mission to Nigeria from 7 to 14 March 1997 and witnessed first-hand the deplorable situation in Ogoniland, including the environmental degradation therein. In 2011, a study conducted by UNEP on such environmental degradation revealed a devastated environment, in which the clean-up cost was put at US$30 billion per annum. See UNEP Report (2011).

[215]*SERAC v Nigeria* (2002), para. 69.

further oil development is guaranteed through effective and independent oversight bodies for the petroleum industry; and

(e) Providing information on health and environmental risks and meaningful access to regulatory and decision-making bodies to communities likely to be affected by oil operations.

3. The Commission then urged the government of the Federal Republic of Nigeria to keep the African Commission informed of the outcome of the work of:

(a) The Federal Ministry of Environment which was established to address environmental and environment related issues prevalent in Nigeria, and as a matter of priority, in the Niger Delta area including the Ogoni land;
(b) The Niger Delta Development Commission (NDDC) enacted into law to address the environmental and other social related problems in the Niger Delta area and other oil producing areas of Nigeria; and
(c) The Judicial Commission of Inquiry inaugurated to investigate the issues of human rights violations.[216]

The take in this case is that the Commission highlighted the Nigerian government's breaches of the obligations to respect, protect and fulfil the right to health and the right to a healthy environment under ACHPR 1981. First, in regard to the obligation to respect, the Commission reasoned that governments must not threaten the health and environment of their citizens and must refrain from interfering with the enjoyment of 'the best attainable state of physical and mental health'.[217] According to the Commission, this obligation requires states to desist from tolerating or carrying out practices or policies that violate the integrity of the individual.[218]

In other words, parties to the African Charter may not engage in conduct that undermines the right to health and the right to a healthy environment. Here, the Nigerian government breached that duty by sending security forces to attack villages and to destroy the environment and livelihood of the Ogoni people.[219]

Second, the Commission recognised that the obligation to fulfil the right to a generally satisfactory environment, as guaranteed under Article 24 of ACHPR 1981, or the right to a healthy environment, as is widely known, therefore imposes clear obligations upon a government. 'It requires the state to take reasonable and other measures to prevent pollution and ecological degradation, to promote conservation, and to secure an ecologically sustainable development and use of natural resources.'[220] Compliance with this obligation, according to the Commission, requires states to conduct environmental impact assessments in order to provide

[216] *SERAC v Nigeria* (2002), 9.
[217] Ibid., paras. 44–45.
[218] Ibid., para. 52.
[219] Konne (2014), p. 190.
[220] *SERAC v Nigeria* (2002), para. 52.

communities with information regarding their exposure to hazardous substances.[221] Here, the Nigerian government breached this obligation by failing to provide environmental impact assessments of Ogoniland and by preventing independent experts from conducting such assessments. This is so because according to the Commission, 'in all their dealings with the oil consortiums, the government did not involve the Ogoni communities in the decisions that affected the development of Ogoniland ... which may well be said to constitute a violation of Article 21 of ACHPR 1981'.[222]

Furthermore, failing to regulate the conduct of third parties, including corporations that interfere with the right to health[223] and the right to a healthy environment,[224] is a violation of the obligation to protect. In this respect, the Commission opined that:

> Government compliance with the spirit of Article 16 and Article 24 of the African Charter must also include ordering or at least permitting independent scientific monitoring of threatened environments, requiring and publicising environmental and social impact studies prior to any major industrial development, undertaking appropriate monitoring and providing information to those communities exposed to hazardous materials and activities and providing meaningful opportunities for individuals to be heard and to participate in the development decisions affecting their communities.[225]

The Commission then noted that the Government of Nigeria breached its responsibility by failing to (1) monitor the oil production activities of Shell and other multinational corporations operating in Ogoniland; (2) enforce domestic and international environmental standards, which require safety measures and prompt oil spill response to prevent further environmental pollution and ecological devastation; and (3) consult with Indigenous communities before commencing oil operations; therefore, the Nigerian government breached its obligations under Articles 16 and 24 of ACHPR 1981.

The Commission held that despite the Nigerian government's obligation to protect the rights of the Ogonis, it facilitated the destruction of Ogoniland.[226] The Commission concluded thus:

> Clearly, collective rights, environmental rights, and economic and social rights are essential elements of human rights in Africa. The African Commission will apply any of the diverse

---

[221] Ibid.

[222] *SERAC v Nigeria* (2002), para. 55.

[223] Under the ACHPR (1981), art. 16.

[224] ACPHR (1981), art. 24.

[225] *SERAC v Nigeria* (2002), para. 53.

[226] It should be noted that since the Commission's decision in 2001, Nigeria has taken some steps to address the issues discussed in the *SERAC* case. For example, the Nigerian government requested an independent assessment, which led to the UNEP's report. The government also established the National Oil Spill Detection and Response Agency (NOSDRA). Lastly, the country has enacted and revised several environmental laws and regulations intended to monitor and control the operations in the oil industry, for example the Petroleum Industry Act 2021, Act No. 26 2021 (discussed in Sect. 16.2.4.5 of Chap. 16 of this book).

rights contained in the African Charter. It welcomes this opportunity to make clear that there is no right in the African Charter that cannot be made effective.[227]

12.1.3.2.3.2.3 Socio-Economic Rights and Accountability Project (SERAP) v Federal Republic of Nigeria

Another case respecting the issue of violation of the right to health and a healthy environment is *Socio-Economic Rights and Accountability Project (SERAP) v Federal Republic of Nigeria.*[228] This case was filed before the Court of Justice of the Economic Community of West African States (ECOWAS) in 2012. The court is located in Abuja, Nigeria, and entertains matters from members of the ECOWAS or matters instituted against any of the member states.

The Complaints

The case originated from a complaint brought on 23 July 2009 by the Registered Trustees of the Socio-Economic Rights and Accountability Project (SERAP) pursuant to Article 10 of the Supplementary Protocol A/SP.1/01/05 against the President of the Federal Republic of Nigeria, the Attorney General of the Federation, the Nigerian National Petroleum Company, Shell Petroleum Development Company, ELF Petroleum Nigeria ltd, AGIP Nigeria PLC, Chevron Oil Nigeria PLC, Total Nigeria PLC and Exxon Mobil.[229]

In that case, SERAP averred that the Niger Delta had suffered for decades from oil spills, which destroy crops and damage the quality and productivity of soil, which communities use for farming, and contaminates water, which people use for fishing, drinking and other domestic and economic purposes, and that these spills, which result from poor maintenance of infrastructure, human error, deliberate vandalism or theft of oil have pushed many people deeper into poverty and deprivation, fuelled conflict and led to a pervasive sense of powerlessness and frustration.[230]

SERAP further contended that the devastating activities of the oil industries in the Niger Delta continued to damage the health and livelihoods of the people of the area, who are denied the basic necessities of life, such as adequate access to clean water, education, healthcare, food and a clean and healthy environment.[231]

Orders Sought

SERAP sought a declaration that the failure and/or complicity and negligence of the defendants to effectively and adequately clean up and remediate contaminated land and water and to address the impact of oil-related pollution and environmental damage on agriculture and fisheries is unlawful and a breach of international human rights obligations and commitments as it violates the Nigerian government's

---

[227] *SERAC v Nigeria* (2002), para. 68.

[228] Judgment No. ECW/CCJ/JUD/18/12, ECOWAS (Dec. 14, 2012).

[229] *SERAP v Federal Republic of Nigeria* (2012), at 2, para. 3.

[230] Ibid., at 3, para. 13.

[231] *SERAP v Federal Republic of Nigeria* (2012), at 4, para. 14.

international human rights obligations under the International Covenant on Economic, Social and Cultural Rights (ICESCR) 1966; the International Covenant on Civil and Political Rights (ICCPR) 1966; and the African Charter on Human and Peoples' Rights (ACHPR) 1981.[232] The complainant then sought, among others, the following Orders from the court:

1. An Order directing the defendants to ensure the full enjoyment by the people of Niger Delta of an adequate standard of living, including adequate access to food, to healthcare, to clean water, to a clean and healthy environment and to socio-economic development, and the right to life and human security and dignity[233]
2. An Order directing the defendants to hold the oil companies operating in the Niger Delta responsible for their complicity in the continuing serious human rights violations in the Niger Delta[234]
3. An Order compelling the defendants to solicit the views of the people of the area throughout the process of planning and policymaking on the Niger Delta[235]
4. An Order directing the Government of Nigeria to establish adequate regulations for the operation of multinationals in the Niger Delta and to effectively clean up and prevent pollution and avoid damage to human rights[236]
5. An Order directing the Government of Nigeria to carry out a transparent and effective investigation into the activities of oil companies in the Niger Delta and to bring to justice those suspected to be involved and/or complicit in the violation of the human rights highlighted above[237]
6. An Order directing the defendants individually and/or collectively to pay adequate monetary compensation of US$1 billion dollars to the victims of human rights violations in the Niger Delta and to execute other forms of reparation that the Honourable Court may deem fit to grant[238]

Preliminary Rulings by the Court

The government filed a preliminary objection contending that SERAP did not have the legal standing to sue (*locus standi*) and that the court did not have the jurisdiction to rule on alleged violations of the ICESCR or the ICCPR and that human rights violations were non-justiciable. Ruling on this, the court held that SERAP was a legal person and had the standing to institute the action. The court, however, ruled that it had no jurisdiction over the private oil corporations initially listed in the suit, and they were subsequently struck out from the suit.[239]

[232] Ibid., at 6, para. 19(b).

[233] Ibid., at 7, para. 1 9(e).

[234] Ibid., para. 19(f).

[235] Ibid., para. 19(g).

[236] Ibid., para. 19(h).

[237] Ibid., para. 19(i).

[238] *SERAP v Federal Republic of Nigeria* (2012), para. 19(j).

[239] Ibid., at 3, paras. 7 and 8.

On the issue of the non-justiciability or non-enforceability of economic, social and cultural rights, as canvassed by the Federal Republic of Nigeria,[240] the court was of the view that instead of a generalistic approach recognising or denying their enforceability, the appropriate way to deal with that issue is to analyse each right in concrete terms and to try to determine which specific obligation it imposes on the states and public authorities and whether that obligation can be enforced by the courts.[241] The court further held that once the concerned right for which the protection is sought before the court is enshrined in an international instrument that is binding on a member state, the domestic legislation of that state cannot prevail over the international treaty or covenant, even if it is its own Constitution.[242] Thus,

> the sources of Law that the Court takes into consideration in performing its mandate of protecting Human Rights are not the Constitutions of Member States, but rather the international instruments to which these States voluntarily bound themselves at the international level, including the Universal Declaration of Human Rights, the International Covenant on Civil and Political Rights, the International Covenant on Economic, Social and Cultural Rights and the African Charter on Human and Peoples' Rights.[243]

The court then asserted that the above position was consistent with paragraph 2, Article 5, of the International Covenant on Economic, Social and Cultural Rights (ICESCR) 1966, to which Nigeria has been a party by adhesion since 29 July 1993. Article 5 of the International Covenant on Economic, Social and Cultural Rights (ICESCR) 1966 provides:

> No restriction upon or derogation from any of the fundamental human rights recognised or existing in any country in virtue of law, conventions, regulations or custom shall be admitted on the pretext that the present Covenant does not recognise such rights or that it recognises them to a lesser extent.

The court therefore concluded that 'in these circumstances, invoking lack of justiciability of the concerned right, to justify non accountability before this Court is completely baseless'[244] and that the Federal Republic of Nigeria cannot invoke the non-justiciability or non-enforceability of ICESCR as a means to shirk its responsibility of ensuring protection and guarantee for its citizens within the framework of the commitments it has made vis-à-vis the Economic Community of West African States and the Charter.[245]

---

[240] By virtue of the Constitution of the Federal Republic of Nigeria 1999 (as amended), s. 6(6)(c), which makes the issue of socio-economic rights under Chapter 2 of the said Constitution non-justiciable.

[241] *SERAP v Federal Republic of Nigeria* (2012), at 10, para. 31.

[242] Ibid., para. 36.

[243] Ibid., at 11, para. 35.

[244] *SERAP v Federal Republic of Nigeria* (2012) at 12, para. 38.

[245] Ibid., at 12, para. 39.

Decision and Reasoning

The court reaffirmed the African Commission's essential holding in the *SERAC* case[246] and held that the Federal Republic of Nigeria had violated Articles 1 and 24 of ACHPR 1981 by their failure to protect the Niger Delta environment from degradation. Article 1 states that 'member States are required to recognize the rights enshrined in the Charter and to adopt legislative or other measures to give effect to these rights'. Article 24 of ACHPR, on the other hand, provides: 'All peoples shall have the right to a general satisfactory environment favourable to their development.'

Article 24 of the Charter thus requires every state to take every measure to maintain the quality of the environment understood as an integrated whole, such that the state of the environment may satisfy the human beings who live there and enhance their sustainable development. It is by examining the state of the environment and entirely objective factors that one judges, by the result, whether the state has fulfilled this obligation. If the state is taking all the appropriate legislative, administrative and other measures, it must ensure that vigilance and diligence are being applied and observed towards attaining concrete results.[247]

The Federal Republic of Nigeria, in its defence, had listed a series of measures it had taken to respond to the environmental situation in the Niger Delta and to ensure a balanced development of the region, including legislation.[248] The court noted that those numerous laws passed to regulate the extractive oil and gas industry and safeguard their effects on the environment, the creation of agencies to ensure the implementation of the legislation and the allocation to the region of 13% of the resources produced there to be used for its development were not sufficient to prevent the continued environmental degradation of the region.[249]

According to the court,

> the adoption of the legislation, no matter how advanced it may be, or the creation of agencies inspired by the world's best models, as well as the allocation of financial resources in equitable amounts, may still fall short of compliance with international obligations in matters of environmental protection if these measures just remain on paper and are not accompanied by additional and concrete measures aimed at preventing the occurrence of damage or ensuring accountability, with the effective reparation of the environmental damage suffered.[250]

The court therefore noted that all of these measures put in place by the Federal Republic of Nigeria 'did not prevent the continued environmental degradation of the region, as evidenced by the facts abundantly proven in this case and admitted by the very same Federal Republic of Nigeria'.[251] Thus,

---

[246] *SERAC v Nigeria* (2002).

[247] *SERAP v Federal Republic of Nigeria* (2012), at 25, para. 101.

[248] Ibid., at 21, para. 81.

[249] *SERAP v Federal Republic of Nigeria* (2012), at 25, para. 103.

[250] Ibid., at 26, para. 105.

[251] Ibid., at 26, para. 104.

> From what emerges from the evidence produced before this Court, the core of the problem in tackling the environmental degradation in the Region of Niger Delta resides in lack of enforcement of the legislation and regulation in force, by the Regulatory Authorities of the Federal Republic of Nigeria in charge of supervision of the oil industry.[252]

The court then maintained that Nigeria failed to monitor and enforce environmental laws and thus violated the rights to health and a healthy environment under Articles 1 and 24 of ACHPR 1981. This is because Articles 1 and 24 of ACHPR 1981 impose a positive obligation on member states to take every measure necessary to maintain the quality of the environment such that it can satisfy the human inhabitants and enhance their sustainable development. In addition, a breach of the right to health and the right to a healthy environment had led to the subsequent breach of other rights, including the rights to an adequate standard of living and economic and social development.

On the whole, the court ruled that the Federal Republic of Nigeria's failure to prevent environmental degradation and to hold the offenders of the damage accountable violated Articles 1 and 24 of ACHPR 1981. The court then ordered the Federal Republic of Nigeria to take all effective measures to ensure the restoration of the environment of the Niger Delta, prevent further damage to the environment and hold the perpetrators of the environmental damage accountable.[253]

Accordingly, the court ordered the Federal Republic of Nigeria to (1) take all effective measures, as quickly as possible, to restore the environment of the Niger Delta; (2) take all measures necessary to prevent the occurrence of further environmental pollution; and (3) take all measures to hold the perpetrators of the environmental damage, including Shell, accountable.[254]

On the relief for reparation, the court dismissed the plaintiff's request for reparations of US$1 billion. It reasoned that through the whole proceedings, the plaintiff failed to identify a single victim to whom the requested pecuniary compensation could be awarded.[255]

The take from this case is that what was in dispute was not a failure of the defendants to allocate resources to improve the quality of life of the people of Niger Delta but rather a failure to use state authority, in compliance with international obligations, to prevent the oil extraction industry from doing harm to the environment and the livelihood and quality of life of the people of that region.[256] This is predicated on the fact that the environment, as emphasised by the International Court of Justice,[257] 'is not an abstraction but represents the living space, the quality of life and the very health of human beings, including generations unborn'. Again, the environment must be considered an indivisible whole, comprising the biotic and

---

[252] Ibid., para. 108.

[253] *SERAP v Federal Republic of Nigeria* (2012), para. 108.

[254] Ibid., at 29, para. 121.

[255] Ibid., at 27, para. 113.

[256] Ibid., at 10, para. 33.

[257] Legality of the threat or use of nuclear arms, ICJ Advisory Opinion of 8 July 2006, para. 28.

abiotic natural resources, notably air, water, land, fauna and flora and the interaction between these same factors.[258]

The court further noted that the environment is essential to every human being and that the quality of human life depends on the quality of the environment.[259] And notwithstanding the fact that the environmental situation in the Niger Delta region has still been of continuous degradation despite measures the defendant alleges having been put in place, it concluded that there has been a failure on the part of the Federal Republic of Nigeria to adopt any of the measures required by the said Article 1 of the African Charter to ensure the enjoyment of the right laid down in Article 24 of the same instrument.[260]

The court acknowledged that the continuous environmental degradation in the Niger Delta region produced a devastating impact on the livelihood of the population; it may have forced some people to leave their area of residence in search of better living conditions and may even have caused health problems to many.[261]

12.1.3.2.3.2.4 Comunidad Yanomami *Case*

The *Comunidad Yanomami* case[262] is another case in point respecting the issue of the violation of the right to health and a healthy environment. On 15 December 1980, a petition against the Government of Brazil was presented to the Inter-American Commission on Human Rights (IACHR) in favour of the Yanomami Indigenous community.

The Indian Law Resource Center, the American Anthropological Association and the Survival International and Anthropology Resource Center filed a petition on behalf of the Yanomami Indigenous community alleging violations of the human rights of the Yanomami Indians, citing in particular the following guarantees of the American Declaration of the Rights and Duties of Man 1948 (or 'American Declaration 1948'): right to life, liberty and personal security;[263] right to equality before the law;[264] right to religious freedom and worship;[265] right to the preservation of health and to well-being;[266] right to education;[267] right to the recognition of juridical personality and civil rights;[268] and right to property.[269]

[258] International Law Commission (2001), art. 1.
[259] *SERAP v Federal Republic of Nigeria* (2012), at 25, para. 100.
[260] Ibid., at 26, para. 107.
[261] *SERAP v Federal Republic of Nigeria* (2012), at 27, para. 114.
[262] Resolution No. 12/85, Case No. 7615 Brazil, March 5, 1985.
[263] American Declaration (1948), art. I.
[264] Ibid., art. II.
[265] Ibid., art. III.
[266] Ibid., art. XI.
[267] Ibid., art. XII.
[268] Ibid., art. XVII.
[269] Ibid., art. XXIII.

Summary of the Petition
In the presentation made by the petitioners and in subsequent testimony and reports given to the Commission by them, the following allegations were made:

(a) The massive penetration of outsiders into the area has had devastating physical and psychological consequences for the Indians; it has caused the break-up of their age-old social organization; it has introduced prostitution among the women, something that was unknown; and it has resulted in many deaths, caused by epidemics of influenza, tuberculosis, measles, venereal diseases, and others.
(b) Despite repeated interventions in behalf of the Indians by many humanitarian, religious, and pro-Indian organizations, the authorities responsible for the Indians' health and for ensuring the implementation of the provisions of the Constitution and the law have done little.
(c) The agricultural development projects carried out by the Instituto Nacional de Colonizaçäo e Reforma Agraria (INCRANational Institute for Settlement and Agrarian Reform), established for the benefit of the Indians displaced from their lands, have not produced the desired effects. The result, on the contrary, has been the loss of their lands and their compulsory transfer to agricultural communities that do not correspond to their customs and traditions.
(d) The process of integration of the Indians, as it is established in the legislation and as it is applied by the responsible authorities, tends toward the disintegration and destruction of the Indian communities, instead of contributing to their economic and social well-being.
(e) The occupation and development of the area of Amazonas and the Territory of Roraima has resulted in the destruction of encampments and the disappearance and death of hundreds of Yanomami Indians and threatens to make them extinct.
(f) The proposal for the establishment of the 'Yanomami Indian Park,' while it has received the support of the Federal Government, on the other hand has been objected to by sectors primarily interested in the economic development of the State and the Territory of Roraima, which have expressed their opposition to the project, and so far this has resulted in noncompliance with Law 6001, which provided for the reservation of the Indians lands.[270]

All the Communications from the petitioners were duly transmitted to the Government of Brazil, and it responded via its Notes N° 127 of May 13, 1981; N° 316 of November 3, 1981; N° 101 of April 14, 1982; and N° 38 of February 13, 1985.[271] The issues considered, among others, were:

1. That the petitioners reported to the Commission the violation of the human rights of the Yanomami Indians by the Government of Brazil and by the National Foundation for Indians (FUNAI) the government agency of guardianship of the

[270] *Comunidad Yanomami* case (1985), para. 3(a)–(f).
[271] Ibid., para 4.

Indians established to administer the Government's Indian policy and to implement Law 6001 of December 19, 1973, called the 'Statute of the Indians.'[272]
2. That the reported violations have their origin in the construction of the trans-Amazonian highway BR-210 that goes through the territory where the Indians live; in the failure to establish the Yanomami Park for the protection of the cultural heritage of this Indian group; in the authorization to exploit the resources of the subsoil of the Indian territories; in permitting the massive penetration into the Indians' territory of outsiders carrying various contagious diseases that have caused many victims within the Indian community and in not providing the essential medical care to the persons affected; and finally, in proceeding to displace the Indians from their ancestral lands, with all the negative consequences for their culture, traditions, and costumes.[273]
3. That international law in its present state, and as it is found clearly expressed in Article 27 of the International Covenant on Civil and Political Rights, recognizes the right of ethnic groups to special protection on their use of their own language, for the practice of their own religion, and, in general, for all those characteristics necessary for the preservation of their cultural identity.[274]

Main Findings

The Inter-American Commission found that Brazil failed to take timely and effective measures to protect the Yanomami community's human rights and that such failure detrimentally impacted the community's traditional way of life. The Commission held that, resultantly, there were violations of the following rights in the American Declaration of the Rights and Duties of Man: the right to life, liberty, and personal security (Article I); the right to residence and movement (Article VIII); and the right to the preservation of health and to well-being (Article XI).[275]

The Commission made reference to international law, including in particular Article 27 of the International Covenant on Civil and Political Rights, and that the rights of Indigenous peoples to the protection of their culture and traditional way of life, comprising access to and control over their traditional land. As a remedy, the Commission required the demarcation of their traditional land and the creation of positive measures to protect and ensure their traditional way of life as well as ensure education, health protection and social integration programmes, all carried out in consultation with the community.[276]

Considering current international law, the IACHR acknowledged the right of Indigenous groups to special protection for the use of their language, their religion and, in general, all elements essential to the preservation of their cultural identity. The IACHR recommended that the state, in line with domestic legislation, to

[272] *Comunidad Yanomami* case (1985).
[273] Ibid.
[274] Ibid.
[275] United Nations Office of the High Commissioner on Human Rights (UN/OHCHR) (2015), p. 39.
[276] UN/OHCHR (2015).

proceed to demarcate the Yanomami Park, to continue adopting preventive and remedial sanitary measures aimed at protecting the life and health of the Yanomami, and to ensure education, health protection and social integration programmes aimed at the Yanomami were carried out in consultation with the Indigenous community, as well as expert scientific, medical and anthropological advisors.[277]

Enforcement of the Decision and Outcomes

In 1992, the land of the Yanomamis was finally demarcated as 'Yanomami Park'. In a 1995 visit to Brazil, the IACHR was able to prove onsite the presence of federal agency surveillance and healthcare stations in the Yanomami area. However, the Yanomamis' personal and collective integrity, as well as their environment, continues to be subject to aggression by intruding miners. State protection is weak and inconsistent.[278]

Significance of the Case

This is one of the first reports in which the IACHR outlined the doctrine on the right of Indigenous peoples to receive special protection aimed at enabling the preservation of their cultural identity. The IACHR also acknowledged their lack of title over their ancestral land as a key factor behind their situation of vulnerability.[279]

In all, the bottom line is that, virtually, all facets of human rights are affected by environmental degradation as there are disruptions of the waterways, causing water and air pollution, soil degradation, disruptions of the means of livelihood of the communities, etc. These formed some of the basis for legal redress for environmental damage.

As can be observed, major perpetrators of human rights violations causing environmental damage are multinational oil companies.[280] However, as noted by the United Nations General Assembly Human Rights Council,[281]

> International and local advocacies as well as national regulatory agencies have not been able to compel Shell to change and to respect human rights in the Niger Delta in any of these cases. None has been resolved in favor of the communities nor has any remedy been implemented. Shell refuses to respect the regulatory agencies, national governments and the laws of the land, making it look as if the regulated have become the regulator. This level of impunity demonstrates the dire need for an international mechanism to hold companies to account uniformly rather than allowing for voluntary company mechanisms that are not legally binding.

It[282] therefore concluded that 'the binding mechanism should be made uniformly applicable on a global scale. The treaty should involve preventive measures covering environmental and human rights violations rather than the current ineffective

[277] Ibid.

[278] Ibid.

[279] Ibid.

[280] Notably Shell Petroleum Development Company Ltd.

[281] United Nations General Assembly Human Rights Council (UNGAHRC) (2014).

[282] United Nations General Assembly Human Rights Council (2015).

manipulative compensation regime. Prior and informed consent must be a condition to negotiate with the communities.'

These and other lines of cases present judicial precedents for the pursuit of compensation in the event of violations of certain human rights.

12.2 Restraining Order of Court

At times, the relief sought by victims of environmental damage may not give rise to an award for damages, costs or compensations whatsoever against those whose activities caused the environmental damage. The victims may be more interested in a court order restraining the polluter from continuing with the activities that had caused the environmental damage. A case in point is *Jonah Gbemre v Shell Petroleum Development Company Nigeria Ltd, Nigerian National Petroleum Corporation and Attorney-General of the Federation.*[283] In that case, the applicant (for himself and representing Iwherekan community in Delta State, Nigeria) sued the defendants at the Federal High Court of Nigeria in the Benin Judicial Division in Suit No. FHC/B/CS/53/05.

The applicants claimed that the constitutionally guaranteed fundamental rights to life and dignity of the human person provided in sections 33(1) and 34(1)[284] and reinforced by Articles 4, 16 and 24[285] inevitably include the right to a clean, poison-free, pollution-free and healthy environment and that the actions of the first and second respondents in continuing to flare gas in the course of their exploration and production activities in the applicant's community is a violation of their fundamental rights to life (including a healthy environment) and dignity of the human person guaranteed by the said laws.

The applicants further averred that the failure of the first and second respondents to carry out an environmental impact assessment in the applicant's community concerning the effects of their gas flaring activities is a violation of section 2(2) of the Environment Impact Assessment Act[286] and contributed to the violation of the applicant's said fundamental rights to life and dignity of the human person.

The applicants further alleged that the provisions of section 3(2)(a), (b) of the Associated Gas Re-injection Act[287] and section 1 of the Associated Gas Re-Injection (continued flaring of gas) Regulations of 1984, under which the continued flaring of gas in Nigeria may be allowed, are inconsistent with the applicant's right to life and/or dignity of human person enshrined in sections 33(1) and 34(1)[288] and Articles

[283] (2005) AHRLR 151 (NgHC 2005).

[284] CFRN (1999).

[285] African Charter on Human and Peoples' Rights (Ratification and Enforcement) Act, Cap A9 Laws of the Federation of Nigeria (LFN) 2004.

[286] Environmental Impact Assessment Act 1992, Cap E12 LFN 2004.

[287] Cap A25 LFN 2004, now repealed by the Petroleum Industry Act 2021, s. 310.

[288] CFRN (1999).

4, 16 and 24[289] and are therefore unconstitutional, null and void by virtue of section 1(3) of the Constitution.[290]

Finally, the applicants argued that the activities of the first and second respondents, in continuing to flare gas in their community, seriously pollute the air, cause respiratory diseases and generally endanger and impair their health. The effect of this was that the gas flaring:

1. Poisons and pollutes the environment as it leads to the emission of carbon dioxide, the main greenhouse gas; the flares contain a cocktail of toxins that affect their health, lives and livelihood.
2. Exposes them to an increased risk of premature death, respiratory illness, asthma and cancer.
3. Contributes to adverse climate change as it emits carbon dioxide and methane, which causes warming of the environment and pollutes their food and water.
4. Causes painful breathing, chronic bronchitis, decreased lung function and death.
5. Reduces crop production and adversely impacts their food security.
6. Causes acid rain; their corrugated house roofs are corroded by the composition of the rain that falls as a result of gas flaring, saying that the primary causes of acid rain are emissions of sulphur dioxide and nitrogen oxides, which combine with atmospheric moisture to form sulphuric moisture to form sulphuric acid and nitric acid, respectively. The acidic rain consequently acidifies their lakes and streams and caused damages to the vegetation.[291]

The applicants therefore sought the solitude of the court and asserted that unless the court promptly intervenes, their said fundamental rights being breached by the first and second respondents will continue to be unabated and with impunity, while its members will continue to suffer various sicknesses, deterioration of health and premature death.

The court, upon evaluation of all the processes, submissions and judicial and statutory authorities, held that the actions of the first and second respondents in continuing to flare gas in the course of their oil exploration and production activities in the applicants' community are a gross violation of their fundamental right to life (including healthy environment) and dignity of the human person enshrined in the Constitution.[292] Nwokorie J held as follows: 'I hereby order that the 1st and 2nd respondents are accordingly restrained whether by themselves, their servants or workers or otherwise from further flaring of gas in applicants' community and are to take immediate steps to stop the further flaring of gas in the applicant's community.'[293]

---

289 ACHPR (1981).

290 CFRN (1999).

291 *Jonah Gbemre v Shell Petroleum Development Company Nigeria Ltd* (2005).

292 Ibid.

293 Ibid.

The court further ordered the Honourable Attorney General of the Federation and Ministry of Justice, third respondent, 'to immediately set into motion, after due consultation with the Federal Executive Council, necessary processes for the Enactment of a Bill for an Act of the National Assembly for the speedy amendment of the relevant sections of the Associated Gas Re-Injection Act and the Regulations made there under to quickly bring them in line with the provisions of chapter 4 of the Constitution, especially in view of the fact that the Associated Gas Re-Injection Act even by itself also makes the said continuous gas flaring a crime having prescribed penalties in respect thereof'.[294]

12.3 Abatement

Another means through which environmental damage may be redressed is through abatement. This is applied where the act creating the environmental problem amounts to a nuisance. A nuisance may be abated or removed. According to Winfield & Jolowicz,[295] 'This is a remedy which the law does not favour because, as St. Mathew Hale said, thus, many times occasions tumults and disorders, and its exercise may destroy any right of action in respect of the nuisance'.

In the case of nuisance, the law provides for abatement. However, one should not attempt abatement unless notice is given to the defendant to remedy the nuisance. But if the nuisance is one of omission, and the security of lives and property does not allow time for notice, or the nuisance can be removed by the person without entry into the defendant's land, then he need not give the notice. The abator of nuisance may cherish this remedy because he finds it a cheap way of eliminating a cause of interference without going to court; also, in cases of emergency, it may be the most efficient remedy, and it may be available where no actionable nuisance exists.

The abator must not do unnecessary damages, and the less mischievous way of abatement should always be followed, unless it would inflict injury on an innocent third party or on the public. The courts do not favour this method because it, more often than not, causes disorders and confusion, and its exercise destroys any right of action in respect of the nuisances.[296] Without committing other torts, a person affected by a nuisance has a right to abate it. Abatement is a limited form of self-help. In *Obasa v Saruwa Ors*,[297] it was held that the act of placing a gate across the highway constitutes a nuisance, and as such, any person affected by it has a right to abate it.

Thus, the branches of my neighbour's tree or his tree roots may be encroaching on my land, and they may cause no damage, but I may, nevertheless, sever them.

[294] *Jonah Gbemre v Shell Petroleum Development Company Nigeria Ltd* (2005).

[295] Bell and Mcgillivray (2008), p. 349.

[296] Enemo (2007), p. 165.

[297] (1931) 10 NLR 102.

However, I should not keep the served branches.[298] Traditionally, where a claimant is affected by a nuisance, he is entitled by law to take steps himself to abate the nuisance without recourse to legal proceedings. Thus, in *Lemon v Webb*,[299] the plaintiff was held to have acted legally when he trimmed the branch of a tree that overhung his land. The remedy of abatement, however, must be exercised until narrow confines. In particular, notice must be given to the defendant by the plaintiff prior to his taking action; unless he can abate the nuisance without going to the defendant's land, the abator must not do unnecessary damage to the defendant's land in abating the nuisance, and where there is more than one method of abating the nuisance, the abator must select the course of action that causes the least harm to the defendant financially, except where this would have a detrimental effect on innocent third parties or on the public.[300]

12.4 Injunctions

The granting of an injunction is a discretionary remedy that can either prohibit or restrict a defendant from carrying on an environmentally damaging activity. Normally, either the activity complained of has to be continuing at the date of claim, or there has to be a threat that the activity will continue.[301] An injunction has the effect of preventing the defendant from carrying out the activity that is being complained of or of restricting the scope of that activity. Exceptionally, an injunction may be mandatory in its terms, requiring the defendant to perform some positive act rather than to restrain him from doing the act complained of. Unlike an award of damage, an injunction is an equitable remedy, so that the claimant is not entitled to it as of right but must have the discretion of the court exercised in his favour. In exercising this discretion, the courts take the view that an injunction relief is generally preferable to an award of damages but that in certain circumstances, damages, in lieu of an injunction, are appropriate.[302]

In deciding whether or not to grant the claimant damages instead of an injunction, the traditional approach of the courts has been to grant an injunction without having regard to the social and economic effects of doing so on third parties. In *Shelfer v City of London Electric Co*,[303] the court refused to award the plaintiff damages instead of an injunction despite the defendant's argument that the public at large derived a benefit from their supplying electricity. Traditionally, then, the courts will

---

[298] *Lemon v Webb* (1894) 3 Ch. 1.

[299] *Lemon v Webb* (1894) 3 Ch. 1.

[300] Thornton and Beckwith (2004), p. 342.

[301] Bell and Mcgillivray (2008), p. 342.

[302] Ibid.

[303] (1895) 1 Ch. 287.

not grant damages instead of an injunction where this would amount to allowing the defendants to 'buy' the right to continue the nuisance.

The issue of an injunction cannot be demanded as of right. It is an equitable remedy, and its grant is governed by equitable principles, and therefore, it is discretionary. Whether the wrong suffered by the plaintiff, for which an injunction is sought, is trivial or of a very temporary nature, injunction would generally be refused.[304] Injunction therefore can sometimes perform the same function as specific performance. For this reason, injunction will not be granted where specific performance will not be granted. Injunctions are either restrictive (preventive) or mandatory (compulsive).

If the injunction is mandatory, then it is restorative in its effect and not merely preventive. It directs the defendant to undo what he has already done in breach. For example, he may be compelled to demolish a building that he has created in contravention of the contract. In practice, this type of injunction is very rarely granted.

There are situations in which it is possible to obtain an injunction before the occurrence of the event causing injury or damage. Such anticipatory injunctions do not require proof of environmental damage at all, but there must be sufficient proof of imminent damage, and it must be demonstrated that if the activity were to continue, the damage accruing would be significant enough to make it difficult to rectify.[305]

12.5 Damages

Unlike an injunction, a claimant can demand that the court award damages. The aim of such damages is to place the claimant as far as possible in the position in which he would have been had the wrongful act not occurred.

Damages might, however, be awarded for the loss of amenity, that is, interference with the enjoyment of the use of land on top of capital losses, although the courts try to restrict such awards to relatively modest sums. In the case of *Farley v Skiner*,[306] which arose from the interference of amenity due to noise from aircraft, for example, an award was made by the court because of the exceptional level of interference. But if there is actual damage, this will have to be compensated. An example of this is the case of *Marquis of Granby v Bakewell Ltd District Council.*[307] In that case, the defendant operated a gas work that discharged poisonous effluent into a river over which the claimant had fishing rights, killing numerous fish. The claimant received compensation equalling the cost of restocking the river, in addition to the loss of a

[304] *Armstrong v Sheppard and Short Ltd* (1959) 1 Q B 384.

[305] Bell and Mcgillivray (2008), p. 350.

[306] (2001) UKHL 49; see also ACHPR v Kenya (2022) (see note 301, post).

[307] (1923) 87 JP 105.

large amount of the food supply for other stocks. The court also took into account the effects of the pollution on higher-quality areas of the river and considered that the damages would be higher where environmental pollution was greater.

The purpose of the award of damages is to compensate the plaintiff for the injury he has suffered as a result of the defendant's act. An award of damages aims to evaluate the loss to the claimant resulting from the defendant's activities and to put the claimant in the position he would have been in if the nuisance had not occurred. The traditional method of quantifying damages is to access the diminutives in the market value of the claimant's properly. While this method has the advantage of relative simplicity, it may be criticised as often underestimating the subjective value of the property to the resident owner. The diminution in the value test assumes that the property is worth no more to the claimant than its market value and fails to take account of the emotional and psychological damage that can flow from a disturbance in the home.[308]

12.6 Reparation

Reparation refers to the process and result of remedying the damage or harm caused by an unlawful act. The purpose of reparation is generally understood to re-establish the situation that existed before the harm occurred. It can also serve as a measure to end ongoing breaches and to deter future ones, as a vehicle for reconciliation or to restore relations between the violator and injured parties as well as a basis to repair or rehabilitate physical and psychological integrity and dignity.[309]

Under the principles of international law, a state that is responsible for an international wrong is required to make full reparation for the damage caused. The Permanent Court of International Justice (PCIJ), in *The Factory at Chorzow*,[310] ably restated the position in the following words: 'It is a principle of international law that the breach of an engagement involves an obligation to make reparation in an adequate form. Reparation therefore is the indispensable complement of a failure to apply a convention, and there is no necessity for this to be stated in the convention itself.'

Reparation, therefore, is 'one of the fundamental principles of contemporary international law on State responsibility, which constitutes a customary norm of international law, is that, any violation of an international obligation that has caused harm entails the obligation to provide adequate reparation'.[311]

---

[308] Bell and Mcgillivray (2008), p. 342.

[309] Ferstman (2017).

[310] Factory at Chorzów, Case Concerning Factory at Chorzow (*Germany v Poland*), (1927) PCIJ, Series. A, Collection of Judgments (1923–1930) No. 17, 1929.

[311] *African Court on Peoples' Rights in Reverend Christopher Mtikila v United Republic of Tanzania* (14 June 2013) 1 AfCLR 72, 27–29.

In terms of quantifying the reparations, the applicable principle is that of full reparation, commensurate with the prejudice suffered. As stated by the PCIJ in *The Factory at Chorzow*, the state responsible for the violation needs to make an effort to 'wipe out all the consequences of the illegal act and re-establish the situation which would, in all probability, have existed if that act had not been committed'.[312]

Who is a victim to whom reparation claims may be awarded? The United Nations General Assembly[313] defined victims as '. . .persons who individually or collectively suffered harm, including physical or mental injury, emotional suffering, economic loss or substantial impairment of their fundamental rights, through acts or omissions that constitute gross violations of international human rights law, or serious violations of international humanitarian law'.

Where appropriate, and in accordance with domestic law, the term 'victim' also includes the immediate family or dependents of the direct victim and persons who have suffered harm in intervening to assist victims in distress or to prevent victimisation.[314] It is against this background that the Inter-American Court of Human Rights, in the case of *The Saramaka People v Suriname*,[315] which involves an Indigenous community, ordered the respondent to pay, into a development fund for the benefit of the applicants, the sum of US$75,000 (seventy-five thousand United States dollars) as compensation for the material prejudice suffered by the applicants. In this particular case, the material damage suffered by the applicants consisted primarily of the illegal exploitation of their lands and natural resources.

According to the United Nations General Assembly (UNGA),[316] the recognised forms of reparation are variably understood as restitution, compensation, rehabilitation, satisfaction and guarantees of non-repetition. These forms are afforded singly or in combination.

Again, the International Law Commission's (ILC's) Draft Articles on the Responsibility of States for Internationally Wrongful Acts 2001[317] lists restitution, compensation and satisfaction as forms of reparation. Accordingly, cessation and non-repetition are dealt with separately, as independent obligations stemming from the wrongful act. Restitution relates to the re-establishment of the situation that existed before the wrongful act was committed. Compensation is for any pecuniary and non-pecuniary losses, including the loss of profits and employment.

Rehabilitation refers to long-term medical and psychological care and surgeries, as well as legal care, whereas satisfaction refers to measures such as formal acknowledgement of the unlawful character of the breach, apologies and prosecutions. Guarantees of non-repetition are forward-looking remedies focusing on prevention, which can refer to either measures of deterrence aimed at protecting a victim

---

[312] PCIJ: The Factory at Chorzow (1929) 47.

[313] United Nations General Assembly (UNGA) (2005).

[314] Ibid.

[315] Judgment of November 28, 2007 (Preliminary Objections, Merits, Reparations and Costs).

[316] UNGA (2005).

[317] International Law Commission (2001), art. 34.

from further harm or broader measures, such as legal and institutional reform and vetting of public officials aimed at avoiding the wider conditions that allowed for the breach.[318]

It has been recognised that reparation must 'fully' make amends for any injury, including any material or moral damage caused by the wrongful act. It must, so far as possible, wipe out all the consequences of the illegal act and re-establish the situation that would, in all probability, have existed if that act had not been committed.[319]

It should be noted that reparation also applies to Indigenous people whose rights might have been trampled upon by the state. This is succinctly captured in Article 28 of the United Nations Declaration on the Rights of Indigenous Peoples (UNDRIP)[320] in the following words:

> Indigenous peoples have the right to redress, by means that can include restitution or, when this is not possible, just, fair and equitable compensation, for the lands, territories and resources which they have traditionally owned or otherwise occupied or used, and which have been confiscated, taken, occupied, used or damaged without their free, prior and informed consent. Unless otherwise freely agreed upon by the peoples concerned, compensation shall take the form of lands, territories and resources equal in quality, size and legal status or of monetary compensation or other appropriate redress.[321]

These assertions were buttressed in the *Matter of African Commission on Human and Peoples' Rights v Republic of Kenya.*[322] In its application filed on 12 July 2012, the African Commission on Human and Peoples' Rights (hereinafter referred to as 'the applicant' or the 'Commission') alleged that in October 2009, the Ogiek, an Indigenous minority ethnic group in the Republic of Kenya (hereinafter referred to as 'the respondent state'), received a thirty (30)-day eviction notice, issued by the Kenya Forestry Service, to leave the Mau Forest.[323]

The Commission filed this application after receiving, on 14 November 2009, an application from the Centre for Minority Rights Development and Minority Rights Group International, both acting on behalf of the Ogiek of Mau Forest. In the application, the Commission argued that the eviction notice failed to consider the importance of the Mau Forest for the survival of the Ogiek, leading to violations of Articles 1, 2, 4, 8, 14, 17(2) and (3), 21 and 22 of the African Charter on Human and Peoples' Rights (ACHPR) 1981.[324]

The court delivered its judgment on the merits on 26 May 2017. In the operative part of its judgment, the court pronounced itself as follows:

---

[318] Ibid.

[319] Ferstman (2017).

[320] UNGA (2007), Resolution 61/295.

[321] UNDRIP (2007), art. 28.

[322] *The Matter of African Commission on Human and Peoples' Rights (ACHPR) v Republic of Kenya*, Application No. 006/2012, Judgment (Reparations) 23 June 2022 (*ACPHR v Republic of Kenya* (2022)).

[323] *ACPHR v Republic of Kenya* (2022), at 2, para. 1.

[324] *ACPHR v Republic of Kenya* (2022), at 2, para. 1.

On the merits:

1. Declares that the Respondent has violated Articles 1, 2, 8, 14, 17(2) and (3), 21 and 22 of the Charter;
2. Declares that the Respondent has not violated Article 4 of the Charter;
3. Orders the Respondent to take all appropriate measures within a reasonable time frame to remedy all the violations established and to inform the Court of the measures taken within six (6) months from the date of this judgment.[325]

The Commission reserved its ruling on reparations and requested the applicant to file submissions on reparations within 60 days from the date of the judgment, and thereafter, the respondent shall file its response. The ruling on reparations was made by the Commission on 23 June 2022. The claim for reparation centred on:

1. Pecuniary reparations
   (a) Material prejudice
   (b) Moral prejudice
2. Non-pecuniary reparations
   (a) Restitution of Ogiek ancestral lands
   (b) Recognition of the Ogiek as an Indigenous people
   (c) Public apology
   (d) Erection of public monument
   (e) The right to effective consultation and dialogue
   (f) Guarantees of non-repetition
3. Development fund for the Ogiek[326]

On pecuniary reparation on material prejudice, the claim for compensation by the applicant related to the violation of Articles 14 and 21 of the Charter and specifically in relation to the following: the loss of non-moveable possessions from Ogiek land, both houses ($59,736,172) and farm buildings ($18,029,915); the loss of livestock that relies on the land from which the Ogiek were evicted ($97,923,370); the loss of household income generated from activities on Ogiek land ($14,137,888); and the loss of revenue generated from activities using the Mau Forest due to the eviction of the Ogiek ($14,777,233). The total claim was US$204,604,578 (two hundred four million, six hundred four thousand and five hundred seventy-eight United States dollars); the claim for compensation relates to the right to property (Article 14 of the Charter) and also the right to freely dispose of wealth and natural resources (Article 21 of the same instrument).[327]

The Commission, taking all factors into consideration, decided, in the exercise of its equitable jurisdiction, that the respondent state must compensate the Ogiek the

[325] Ibid., at 2, para. 2.

[326] *ACPHR v Republic of Kenya* (2022), at 2, para. 2.

[327] Ibid., at 23, para. 64.

sum of KES 57,850,000 (fifty-seven million, eight hundred and fifty thousand Kenyan shillings) for the material prejudice suffered.[328]

On the issue of pecuniary reparation on moral prejudice, the applicant prayed for the payment of compensation as a result of violations under the principle of non-discrimination (Article 2), the right to religion (Article 8), the right to culture (Article 17) and the right to development (Article 22) under the Charter. According to the applicant, the Ogiek have suffered routine discrimination at the hands of the respondent state, including the non-recognition of their tribal or ethnic identity and their corresponding rights. The Ogiek have not been able to practice their religion, including prayers and ceremonies intimately connected to the Mau Forest; to bury their dead in accordance with traditional spiritual rituals; and to access sacred sites for initiation and other ceremonies. They have also been denied access to an integrated system of beliefs, values, norms, traditions and artefacts closely linked to the Mau Forest and have had their right to development violated due to the respondent state's failure to consult with or seek their consent about their shared cultural, economic and social life within the Mau Forest.[329]

The Commission noted that, in its judgment on the merits,[330] it established that the respondent state violated the Ogiek's rights under Article 2 of the Charter by failing to recognise the Ogiek as a distinct tribe, like other groups; Article 8 of the Charter by making it impossible for the Ogiek to continue practising their religious practices; Article 17(2) and (3) of the Charter by evicting the Ogiek from the Mau Forest area, thereby restricting them from exercising their cultural activities and practice; and Article 22 of the Charter, due to the manner in which the Ogiek have been evicted from the Mau Forest.[331]

In the end, the Commission, in the circumstances of the application, noted that it was not contested that members of the Ogiek community had suffered from the lack of recognition as an Indigenous group; from the evictions from their ancestral land; from the denial of enjoyment of the benefits emanating from their ancestral land; and from the failure to practice their religion and culture, as well as the right to fully and meaningfully participate in their economic, social and cultural development.[332] The Commission therefore awarded, taking into account the exercise of its reasonable discretion in equity, and ordered the respondent to compensate the Ogiek the sum of KES 100,000,000 (one hundred million Kenyan shillings) for the moral prejudice suffered.[333]

---

[328] Ibid., at 27, para. 77. The respondent state opposed the award to be in United States dollars as submitted by the applicant and insisted that any award, if made, should be made in its currency. On this, the Commission agreed with the respondent, so the award was made in Kenyan shillings (KES).

[329] *ACPHR v Republic of Kenya* (2022), at 27, paras. 78–79.

[330] Delivered on 26 May 2017.

[331] *ACPHR v Republic of Kenya* (2022), at 29, para. 85.

[332] Ibid., at 30, para. 90.

[333] Ibid., at 31, para. 93.

The Commission, on non-pecuniary reparations, ordered the respondent state to take all necessary measures, legislative, administrative or otherwise, to identify the ancestral land of the Ogiek people, in consultation with the Ogiek and/or their representatives, and delimit, demarcate and title Ogiek ancestral land and to grant collective title to such land in order to ensure, with legal certainty, the Ogiek's use and enjoyment of the same.[334] And where concessions and/or leases had been granted over Ogiek ancestral land, it ordered the respondent state to commence dialogue and consultations between the Ogiek and their representatives and other concerned parties for purposes of reaching an agreement on whether or not they could be allowed to continue their operations by way of lease and/or royalty and benefit sharing with the Ogiek in line with all applicable laws. Where it proved impossible to reach a compromise, the respondent state was ordered to compensate the concerned third parties and return such land to the Ogiek.[335]

The respondent state must also take all appropriate measures, within one (1) year, to guarantee the full recognition of the Ogiek as an Indigenous people of Kenya in an effective manner, including but not limited to the full recognition of the Ogiek language and Ogiek cultural and religious practices.[336]

The Commission also ordered the respondent state to take all necessary legislative, administrative or other measures to recognise, respect and protect the right of the Ogiek to be effectively consulted, in accordance with their traditions/customs, with respect to all development, conservation or investment projects on Ogiek ancestral land, and the respondent state shall also ensure the full consultation and participation of the Ogiek, in accordance with their traditions/customs, in the reparation process as ordered in the judgment.[337]

The respondent state was again ordered to adopt legislative, administrative and/or any other measures to give full effect to the terms of the judgment as a means of guaranteeing the non-repetition of the violations identified.[338]

Finally, on the claim for the establishment of a development fund for the Ogiek, the Commission agreed with the application and ordered the respondent state to establish a community development fund for the Ogiek, which should be a repository of all the funds ordered as reparations in this case. The community development fund shall be used to support projects for the benefit of the Ogiek in the areas of health, education, food security, natural resource management and any other causes beneficial to the well-being of the Ogiek as determined from time to time by the committee managing the fund in consultation with the Ogiek. The respondent state must, therefore, take the necessary administrative, legislative and any other measures

[334] Ibid., at 39, para. 116.
[335] *ACPHR v Republic of Kenya* (2022), at 39, para. 117.
[336] Ibid., at 41, para. 126.
[337] *ACPHR v Republic of Kenya* (2022), at 47, para. 144.
[338] Ibid., at 48, para. 150.

to establish this fund within twelve (12) months of the notification of the judgment.[339]

12.7 Restitution

Restitution is said to be synonymous with reparation or indemnity. Restitution is a constructive act. While punishment may be painful or uncomfortable, restitution is constructive to the extent that the offender provides something of himself and also compensates the victim. It involves not only the payment of money but also the provision of services. The first major concern of restitution therefore is the damage done as a result of the crime committed to the victim, an attempt to make the situation better than before the crime was committed. It therefore goes beyond what any law or court requires, beyond what friends and family expect, beyond what a victim asks and beyond what conscience or superego demands.[340]

As a general rule, where the court orders restitution, it will order mutual restitution, that is, a giving back on both sides. The right of restitution is lost if something happens in which the party misled has participated that renders it impossible to restore the parties to their former position. However, the court may, in special circumstances, grant recession if substantial restitution can be made even though it is not precise. Restitution is synonymous with reparation or indemnity. It is said to contain the best features of punishment, deterrence and justice. The major concern of restitution is to repair the damage done to both the victim and society as a result of the crime(s) committed.

This position can be buttressed in the case of *The Matter of African Commission on Human and Peoples' Rights v Republic of Kenya*,[341] where Indigenous owners of land had been displaced by the state, and the people sought redress by way of restitution. In that case, the applicant submitted to the African Court on that the Government of Kenya should return to Ogiek Indigenous people of Kenya all twenty-two (22) forest blocks within the Mau Forest Complex by means of twenty-four (24) communally held titles. The applicant maintained that each community will hold title according to the procedure set out in the Community Land Act 2016 of Kenya and will manage the forested areas as community forests under the Forest and Conservation Management Act 2016, also of Kenya.[342]

In addition, the applicant also prayed for the rescission of such titles and concessions found to have been illegally granted with respect to the Ogiek ancestral land

---

[339] Ibid., at 49, para. 155.

[340] Dambazau (1999), p. 311.

[341] *The Matter of African Commission on Human and Peoples' Rights (ACHPR) v Republic of Kenya*, Application No. 006/2012, Judgment (Reparations) 23 June 2022 (*ACPHR v Republic of Kenya* (2022)).

[342] *ACPHR v Republic of Kenya* (2022), at 33, para. 99.

and for such land to be returned to the Ogiek with a common title within each location. Accordingly, the applicant submitted that the respondent state should enter into a dialogue with the Ogiek, via the 'original complaints', regarding the land to be returned from non-Ogiek to the Ogiek.[343]

To this end, the applicant filed a Road Map, which it submitted to serve as a guide in the quest for restitution. According to the applicant's Road Map, the court should order a process of restitution that revolves around four elements: firstly, the appointment of an independent gender-balanced panel of experts to oversee the settlement of all claims; secondly, the reclassification of the Mau Forest into three categories depending on the difficulty of resettlement; thirdly, the court to remain seized of the case until both the merits and reparations are fully implemented; and, lastly, the court to play an active role in overseeing the process of implementation of its judgments.[344]

Although the respondents adduced various reasons to scuttle these claims,[345] the court observed that, in the context of the Indigenous peoples' claims to land, demarcation is the formal process of identifying the actual locations and boundaries of Indigenous lands or territories and physically marking those boundaries on the ground. It noted that the demarcation was important and necessary because a mere abstract or legal recognition of Indigenous lands, territories or resources can be practically meaningless unless the physical identity of the land is determined and marked. The purpose was to remove any uncertainty on the part of the concerned Indigenous people in respect of the land to which they are entitled to exercise their rights.[346]

The court therefore took special notice of the fact that the protection of rights to land and natural resources remains fundamental for the survival of Indigenous peoples. It confirmed that the right to property includes not only the right to have access to one's property and not to have one's property invaded or encroached upon but also the right to the undisturbed possession, use and control of such property however the owner(s) deem(s) fit.[347]

The court then emphasised, though, that given the unique situation and way of life of Indigenous people, it was important to conceptualise and understand the distinctive dimensions in which their rights to property, like land, can be manifested when it said:

> Ownership of land for indigenous people, therefore, is not necessarily the same as other forms of State ownership such as the possession of a fee simple title. At the same time, however, ownership, even for indigenous people, entails the right to control access to

[343] *ACPHR v Republic of Kenya* (2022), at 34, para. 100.

[344] Ibid., para. 101.

[345] See *ACPHR v Republic of Kenya* (2022), at 34–35, paras. 102–105.

[346] *ACPHR v Republic of Kenya* (2022), at 35, para. 107.

[347] Ibid., at 35, para. 109.

> indigenous lands. It thus behooves duty bearers, like the Respondent State, to attune their legal systems to accommodate indigenous peoples' rights to property such as land.[348]

The court thus acknowledged that:

> Among indigenous peoples there is a communitarian tradition regarding a communal form of collective property of the land, in the sense that ownership of the land is not centred on an individual but rather on the group and its community.' Indigenous people, therefore, have, by the fact of their existence, the right to live freely in their own territory. The close ties that indigenous peoples have with the land must be recognised and understood as the fundamental basis of their cultures, spiritual life, integrity and economic survival.[349]

The court then reiterated its position and held that the Ogiek had a right to the land that they have occupied and used over the years in the Mau Forest Complex. However, in order to make the protection of the Ogiek's right to land meaningful, there must be more than an abstract or juridical recognition of the right to property. It was for this reason that physical delineation, demarcation and titling was important. This delineation, demarcation and titling must be premised on, among others, the respondent state's Community Land Act, 2016, and the Forest Conservation and Management Act, 2016, without undermining any of the protections accorded to Indigenous people by the applicable international law.[350]

To this end, the court held that the respondent state should undertake an exercise of delimitation, demarcation and titling in order to protect the Ogiek's right to property, which in this case revolved around their occupation, use and enjoyment of the Mau Forest Complex and its various resources. The court refused to agree with the respondent state's submission that delimitation, demarcation and titling were inimical to the ways of life of Indigenous people. While the court recognised that the Ogiek way of life, like that of many Indigenous peoples, had not remained stagnant, the evidence before it demonstrated that they had maintained a way of life in and around the Mau Forest, which distinguished them as Indigenous people. Securing their right to property, especially land, should create a conducive context for guaranteeing their continued existence.[351]

The court, therefore, ordered the respondent state to take all necessary measures be they legislative or administrative to identify, in consultation with the Ogiek and/or their representatives, to delimit, demarcate and title Ogiek ancestral land and to grant *de jure* collective title to such land in order to ensure the permanent use, occupation and enjoyment, by the Ogiek, with legal certainty. Where the respondent state is unable to restitute such land for objective and reasonable grounds, it must enter into negotiations with the Ogiek through their representatives, for purposes of either offering adequate compensation or identifying alternative lands of equal extension and quality to be given for Ogiek use and/or occupation. This process must be

---

[348] *ACPHR v Republic of Kenya* (2022), at 37, para. 111.

[349] Ibid., para. 112.

[350] Ibid., at 38, para. 114.

[351] Ibid., para. 115.

undertaken and concluded within two (2) years from the date of notification of the judgment.[352]

The court further ordered that, where concessions and/or leases have been granted over Ogiek ancestral land to non-Ogiek and other private individuals or corporations, the respondent state must commence dialogue and consultations between the Ogiek and/or their representatives and other concerned parties for purposes of reaching an agreement on whether or not they can be allowed to continue their operations by way of lease and/or royalty and benefit sharing with the Ogiek in line with the Community Land Act. In cases where land was allocated to non-Ogiek and where it proves impossible to reach a compromise, the respondent state must either compensate the concerned third parties and return the land to the Ogiek or agree on appropriate compensation for the Ogiek.[353]

12.8 Rehabilitation/Restoration

Under the Nigerian Mineral and Mining Act 2007, 'no lessee shall deposit a greater quantity of tailing[354] in any natural water course than that prescribed by regulations'.[355] In furtherance of the measures to protect the environment, the Act[356] provides that 'every holder of mineral title shall as far as it is reasonably practicable: (a) minimise, manage and mitigate any environmental impact resulting from his activity and (b) rehabilitate and reclaim, where applicable, the land disturbed, excavated, explored, mined or covered with tailings arising from mining operations to its natural or predetermined state.[357] What this entails is that where land which is the subject of a Mining Lease has been exploited, the mined out areas shall be restored by the applicant under the condition of its grant. . . .'[358]

Again, under the Act,[359] every holder of an Exploration Licence, Small-Scale Mining Lease, Mining Lease, Quarry Lease and Water Use Permit shall, (a) prior to the commencement of mining operations or (b) upon application for an extension of the term or (c) upon an application for the conversion of a mineral title, submit to the Mines Environmental Compliance Department an (1) environmental impact assessment statement approved by the Federal Ministry of the Environment in respect of the exploration or mining operations to be conducted within the Mineral Title Area and (2) an Environmental Protection and Rehabilitation Programme. Such

[352] *ACPHR v Republic of Kenya* (2022), at 39, para. 116.

[353] Ibid., para. 117.

[354] The waste left behind after ore had been extracted from a rock.

[355] Nigerian Minerals and Mining Act 2007, Act No. 20 2007, s. 126(1).

[356] Nigerian Minerals and Mining Act (2007).

[357] Ibid., s. 118.

[358] Ibid., s. 115.

[359] Ibid., s. 119.

Environmental Protection and Rehabilitation Programme shall (a) provide for specific rehabilitation and reclamation actions, inspections and annual reports; (b) a reasonable estimate of the total cost of rehabilitation; (c) cost estimates for each specific rehabilitation and reclamation action; and (d) a timetable for the orderly and efficient rehabilitation and reclamation of the Mineral Title Area to a safe and environmentally sound condition suitable for future economic development or recreational use.[360]

To this end, every holder of an Exploration Licence shall:

1. Maintain and restore the land that is the subject of the licence to a safe state from any disturbance resulting from exploration activities, including but not limited to filling up any shafts, wells, holes or trenches made by the titleholder and in compliance with applicable environmental laws and regulations[361]
2. Not abstract, divert or discharge water or effluent from any watercourse except in compliance with a Water Use Permit and Regulations[362]
3. Not explore any forest reserve except with the approval of the Minister and in consultation with other relevant authorities and subject to such conditions as may be specified in the Regulations.[363]

Furthermore, no person shall, in the course of exploration or mining, carry out operations, in or under any area held to be sacred, or permit injury or destruction of any tree or other thing that is the object of veneration.[364]

In the case of abandonment or permanent cessation of production within the title area, the mineral title holder shall (a) securely seal, fence or cover every mine shaft and adit; (b) make safe all tailings and water retention areas; and (c) demolish, fence or lock all potentially hazardous buildings, structures, plant and equipment.[365]

Restoration, on the other hand, involves a variety of strategies that aim to bring the offender and victim together, sometimes in 'conferencing' schemes, with a view to encouraging the offender to recognise the harm done by the offence and to make some direct reparation.[366] Restoration is envisioned by many as an alternative way to handle crime. The approach emphasises victim-offender mediation, where care victims have an opportunity to meet with the offenders.

Restoration may either be 'primary restoration' (which returns the damaged site itself to its baseline condition) or 'complimentary restoration' (which entails action in a different location designed to provide a similar level of natural resources and amenities elsewhere). Complimentary restoration will be appropriate where a damaged site cannot be restored to its baseline condition or where doing so will involve a

[360] Nigerian Minerals and Mining Act (2007), s. 120.

[361] Ibid., s. 61(1)(d).

[362] Ibid., s. 61(1)(e).

[363] Ibid., s. 61(1)(f).

[364] Ibid., s. 98(1).

[365] Nigerian Minerals and Mining Act (2007), s. 159(6).

[366] Bell and Mcgillivray (2008), p. 20.

disproportionate cost. The requirement of complementary remediation aims to avoid a situation where a person who has damaged a site beyond economic recovery pays less in restoration costs than someone who has only partially damaged it.[367]

At times, a polluter may be ordered to pay compensation by way of cost for the restitution of the environment and ecology of the area. This liability for harm is to compensate not only the victims of the environmental damage but also the cost of restoring the environmental degradation and of reversing the damaged ecology.[368] The reason is that pollution is a civil wrong, and by its very nature, it is a tort committed against the community as a whole.

12.9 Polluter-Pays Principle[369]

The essence of this principle requires that the polluter, rather than the society at large, must pay for the cost of environmental clean-up required as a result of his polluting activities. The difficulty surrounding the principle is twofold. First, in order to make the polluter pay, it must first be ascertained who is appropriate to be regarded as a polluter. Second, if the principle is to be applied fairly, it must be ascertained to what extent the polluter has degraded the environment, and the event of that degradation must then be given a precise monetary value.[370] This involves the 'valuing' of environmental amenities, which, as discussed below, is extremely difficult to accomplish with accuracy.

This principle embodies the idea that the polluter should bear the expense of carrying out measures decided upon by public authorities as necessary to ensure that the environment is in an acceptable state. One way of giving effect to this principle is to ensure that the costs of environmental protection measures are reflected in the prices of goods and services that were lost as a result of the polluting incident, through the use of economic instruments.[371] This principle is encouraged by the international community, as reflected in the Rio Declaration, which states:

> National authorities should endeavor to provide the internalization of environmental costs and the use of economic instruments, taking into account the approach that the polluter should, in principle, bear the cost of pollution, with due regard to the public interest and without distorting international trade and investment.[372]

The polluter-pays principle is mentioned in a number of National Environmental Standards and Regulations Enforcement Agency (NESREA) Regulations. Under the National Environmental (Sanitation and Wastes Control) Regulations 2009, for

---

[367] Thornton and Beckwith (2004), p. 94.

[368] Raju, J, in *M C Mehta v Kamal Nath and Others*, 2000(6) SCC 213.

[369] This principle was discussed in Sect. 4.7 of Chap. 4 of this book.

[370] Thornton and Beckwith (2004), p. 22.

[371] Ibid., 44.

[372] Rio Declaration on Environment and Development (1992), principle 16.

instance, 'all generators of wastes, owners or occupiers of premises where wastes are generated shall be legally and financially responsible for the safe and environmentally sound disposal of their wastes'.[373] To this end, 'all generators and managers of wastes shall apply sustainable practices to minimize pollution'.[374] Similar provisions for polluter pays can be found in the National Environmental (Mining and Process of Coal, Ores and Industrial Minerals) Regulations 2009, where 'all effluents are cleaned up and disposed of at an appropriate discharge point or waste treatment facility at the conclusion of each operation'.[375] Thus, regulation 13 of the Regulations[376] provides 'that collection, treatment, transportation and final disposal of wastes within the specified standards and guidelines, shall be the responsibility of the facility generating the waste'.

The above liabilities notwithstanding, it shall be an offence, in addition to other offences, if a facility fails to comply and take reasonable measures to remove or treat and dispose of any effluent; remediate the environment; comply with guidelines with respect to the handling, storing and transport of any effluent; release effluent and sludge into the environment in excess of the permissible level; and take reasonable measures to prevent, reduce or remedy the adverse effect of effluent and sludge on the environment.[377]

In addition, under the National Oil Spill Detection and Response Agency (Establishment) Act (NOSDRA) 2006, as amended,[378] 'an oil spiller is to report an oil spill to the Agency[379] in writing, by fax or electronic mail not later than 24 h after the occurrence of an oil spill'.[380]

The spiller shall be responsible for the clean-up, and 'failure to clean up the impacted site, to all practical extent including action plan for remediation within two weeks of the occurrence of the spill in accordance with the **polluter pays principle** shall constitute an offence'.[381]

---

[373] National Environmental (Sanitation and Wastes Control) Regulations (2009), regulation 14.

[374] Ibid., regulation 15.

[375] National Environmental (Mining and Process of Coal, Ores and Industrial Minerals) Regulations (2009), regulation 10 (1) and (5).

[376] National Environmental (Mining and Process of Coal, Ores and Industrial Minerals) Regulations (2009). Similar provisions can be found under regulation 5 of the National Environmental (Food, Beverages and Tobacco Sector) Regulations (2009) and regulation 5 of the National Environmental (Chemical, Pharmaceutical, Soap and Detergent Manufacturing Industries) Regulations (2009), among others.

[377] National Environmental (Mining and Process of Coal, Ores and Industrial Minerals) Regulations (2009), regulation 28.

[378] NOSDRA (2006), s. 6 (2).

[379] The National Oil Spill Detection and Response Agency, established under the National Oil Spill Detection and Response Agency (Establishment) Act (2006), as amended, s. 6(1).

[380] Failure to report shall attract a penalty in the sum of ₦2,000,000 for each day of failure to report the occurrence.

[381] The spiller, on conviction, shall be liable to a fine not exceeding ₦5,000,000 or to imprisonment for a term not exceeding 2 years or to both such fine and imprisonment. NOSDRA (2006), s. 6(3).

These provisions notwithstanding, Ezike[382] described these measures as 'so few in number, so shallow in effect'. This is further compounded by the fact that, at times, it is difficult to draw a dividing line as to whom the principle should apply. For instance, where a car causes pollution, is the 'polluter' the manufacturer of the car, the producer of the fuel or the driver of the car? This, of course, is one of the fundamental problems in applying the polluter-pays principle.

In all the approaches discussed above, one thing is clear: they target to compensate the victim of environmental damage and also to punish the polluter so as to make amends for his adverse activities that are damaging to the environment. It is trite that the purpose of compensation, just like damages in the law of contract, is to put the injured party, so far as money can do it, in the same position as he was before the pollution occurred. Environmental damages are far-reaching and devastating. Therefore, large sums of money must be awarded to the victim to regain his former position, as if nothing happened. Put in another way, where monetary compensation is paid for damaged properties in pollution-related cases, what the law gives to the victims is the right to be put, so far as money can do it, in the same position as if his land or property had not been destroyed. Truly, we know that this is difficult, that is, to put the victim in exactly the same position as he was before the devastation happened. It is not always possible. But an attempt must be made to get as near that position as possible. Sometimes, the courts appreciate this; at other times, they do not.

In the case of *Shell Petroleum Development Company Ltd v Councillor F.B. Farah*[383] the court of appeal affirmed the High Court's award of ₦4,621,307 against the appellant being special and general damages of an oil blowout which occurred in 1970 as lost income, general inconveniences and rehabilitation of land. Again, in the case of *Shell Petroleum Development Company Limited Ltd v Tiebo VII and Others*,[384] the respondents were awarded a total sum of ₦6,000,000 as special and general damages for an extensive oil spill caused by the appellant. But in the case of *R. Mon and Anor v Shell BP*,[385] the court awarded a paltry sum of ₦200.

12.10 Summary

To assuage the ill feelings of the victims of environmental damage requires some form of compensation. Compensation in environmental matters is founded on the legal maxim of *restitutio integrum*, which means to restore the injured party to the position he was in prior to the injury. The sum of money paid as compensation is meant to restore the victim of environmental damage to the same position as he

[382] Ezike (2011), p. 74.

[383] *Shell Petroleum Development Company Ltd v Councillor F.B. Farah* (1995) at 208.

[384] *Shell Petroleum Development Company Limited Ltd v Tiebo VII and Others* (1996), 657.

[385] (1970–72) I RSLR 7.

would have been had he not sustained that wrong for which he is now being compensated

Compensation raises a number of problems. First is the problem of assessing the measure of environmental damage. For instance, should it be by reference to the costs of measures of reinstatement or on the basis of an abstract quantification calculated in accordance with a theoretical model or on some other basis? The problem arises because environmental damage does not fit easily with the traditional approaches to civil and state liabilities, which are designed to compensate an injured person by requiring the responsible person to pay the economic costs of the resulting damage, This is frequently calculated by reference to a depreciation of the economic value of the damaged item or the cost of repairing the damage. Pure damage to the environment *per se* may be incapable of calculation in economic terms, although it may have a non-economic value requiring restoration to its state prior to the occurrence of the damage.

However, compensation could mean 'any reasonable measures aiming to reinstate or restore damaged or destroyed components of the environment, or to introduce, where reasonable, the equivalent of these components into the environment'. Internal law may indicate who will be entitled to take such measures.

Having assessed the measure for compensation for environmental damage, the second problem is the determination of the nature of the right violated or the damage suffered as well as determining what right the victim has in order to pursue the claims.

The next problem is determining the type of compensation that will adequately address the nature of the wrong suffered. Various types of measures for addressing the wrong suffered by the victim are available to choose from. They include a restraining order from the court, abatement, injunctions, damages, reparation, restitution, rehabilitation/restoration or the application of the polluter-pays principle.

The right to receive just compensation for the expropriation of private rights is a constitutionally guaranteed right under the Nigerian Constitution,[386] but like other legal regimes for compensation in pollution cases, the Constitution fails to provide a mode for assessing compensation.[387] The greatest problem faced by pollution victims is the determination of the quantum of compensation. This is a specialised area and needs experts to meaningfully tackle it and do justice to the matter.

It is regrettable that only a very few statutes on the environment expressly provide for compensation to the victims of environmental damage. For instance, section 11 (5)(c) of the Oil Pipelines Act[388] provides that the holder of a licence shall pay compensation to a person suffering damage as a consequence of any breakage of or leakage from a pipeline or an ancillary installation. The Petroleum Act, in paragraph 36 of Schedule 1, also provides that a holder of a licence, with respect to oil

[386] CFRN (1999), s. 44(1)(a), gives to any person whose property is compulsorily acquired the right to the prompt payment of compensation.

[387] Ezike (2011), p. 22.

[388] Cap 07 LFN 2004.

production activities, shall, in addition to any liability for compensation, be liable to pay fair and adequate compensation for the disturbance of the surface or other rights of any person who owns or is in lawful occupation of the licensed or leased land.

The Petroleum (Drilling and Productions) Regulations, in regulation 23, provide only for compensation for interference with fishing rights. The Mineral and Mining Act 2007, on the other hand, deals with the protection of the environment against abuse from mining operations and provides for the payment of compensation to any person whose rights have been violated by a mining operator. In addition, the Harmful Wastes (Special Criminal Provisions) Act provides for civil liability under section 12. The section provides that where any damage has been caused by any harmful waste that has been deposited or dumped on any land, territorial waters, including Exclusive Economic Zone (EEZ), etc., any person who deposited, dumped or imported such harmful waste shall be liable for the damage suffered by the victim. Compensating pollution victims should be better pursued and achieved if the absolute liability principle is adopted. Once the damage occurs, the polluter shall have no defence.[389]

References

Bell S, Mcgillivray D (2008) Environmental law, 7th edn. Oxford University Press, Oxford

Birnbaum M (1995) A travesty of law and justice: an analysis of the judgement in the case of Ken Sara-Wiwa and others. Article 19, London

Dambazau AB (1999) Criminology and criminal justice, 1st edn. Nigerian Defence Academy, Kaduna

Drzewicki K (1999) Internationalization of human rights and their juridization. In: Hanski R, Suksi M (eds) An introduction to the international protection of human rights: a textbook. 2nd revised edition. Åbo Akademi University. Institute for Human Rights, Åbo

Eide A (1995) Economic, social and cultural rights as human rights. In: Asbjørn Eide A et al (eds) Economic, social, and cultural right: a textbook. Martinus Nijhoff, London

Elias TO (1971) Nigerian land law. Sweet and Maxwell, London

Enemo IP (2007) The law of tort. Chenglo, Enugu

Environmental Resources Manager Ltd (1997) Niger delta environmental survey final report phase I, vol I. https://www.researchgate.net/publication/315800412_Niger_Delta_Environmental_Survey_1997_Vol_1_-_Environmental_and_Socio-Economic_Characteristics. Accessed 19 July 2023

Eze O (1984) Human rights in Africa. Macmillan, Lagos

Ezike EO (2011) Remediating environmental pollution damages in Nigeria: need to adopt the principle of absolute liability. Pet Nat Resour Environ Law J 3(1):74

Federal Ministry of National Planning (1976) The Third National Development Plans (1975 – 1980). Government Printers, Lagos

Ferstman C (2017) Reparations. Oxford Bibliographies, 13 June 2017. https://doi.org/10.1093/OBO/9780199796953-0003. https://www.oxfordbibliographies.com/view/document/obo-9780199796953/obo-9780199796953-0003.xml#:~:text=Reparation. Accessed 4 Aug 2023

Hekin L (1985) Human rights. In: Bbernhardt R (ed) Encyclopedia of international law, vol 8

[389] See discussions on absolute liability in Sect. 3.9.3 of Chap. 3 of this book.

Human Rights Watch (1999) The price of oil: corporate responsibilities and human rights violations in Nigeria's oil producing communities. Human Rights Watch, New York

International Committee of Red Cross (ICRC) (1978) Fundamental rules of international humanitarian law applicable in armed conflicts. ICRC, Geneva

International Law Commission (2001) Draft articles on the responsibility of states for internationally wrongful acts, Report of the ILC on the Work of its Fifty-third Session, UNGA resolution 56/83 (12 December 2001), Supp No 10, 43, UN Doc A/56/10 (2001), https://legal.un.org/ilc/texts/instruments/english/commentaries/9_6_2001.pdf. Accessed 9 May 2023

Kiss A (1993) Concept and possible implications of the right to environment. In: Mahoney KE, Mahoney P (eds) Human rights in the twenty first century: a global challenge. Martinus Nijhoff, London. ISBN: 9780792318101

Konne BR (2014) Inadequate monitoring and enforcement in the Nigerian oil industry: the case of Shell and Ogoniland. Cornell Int Law J 47:187. https://ww3.lawschool.cornell.edu/research/ILJ/upload/Konne-final.pdf. Accessed 11 June 2023

Leckie S (1995) The right to housing. In: Eide A et al (eds) Economic, social and cultural rights. Martinus Nijhoff, London

Nigerian Environmental Study/Action Team (NEST) (1991) Nigeria's threatened environment, a national profile. NEST, Ibadan

Nigerian Television Authority (NTA) (1999) Federal Government of Nigeria Budget Speech, NTA Network Programme, 1 January 1999

Rostron J (2001) Environmental law for built environment. Cavendish, London

Sands P (2003) Principles of international environmental law, 2nd edn. Cambridge University Press, Cambridge

Sha'aba RA (1998) MOSOP and the Ogoni struggle. EDHR, Ken-Saro Wiwa and the Crises of Nigerian State, EDHR Special, Ikeja

Singh J et al (1995) Defining an environmental development strategy for the Niger Delta, vol 1, paragraph B (1.6–1.7), pp 2–3. World Bank Industry and Energy Operations Division, West Central Africa Department, World Bank Group, Washington, D.C. https://books.google.com.ng/books/about/Defining_an_Environmental_Development_St.html?id=xofTzAEACAAJ&redir_esc=y. Accessed 28 June 2023

Thornton J, Beckwith S (2004) Environmental law, 2nd edn. Sweet and Maxwell, London

Thorton J, Tromans S (1999) Human rights and environmental wrongs – incorporating the European Convention on Human Rights: some thoughts on the consequences for U.-K. environmental law. J Environ Law 11(1):35

Umozuruike OU (1997) The African Charter on Human and Peoples' Rights. Kluwer Law International, The Hague

United Nations (1972) Stockholm Declaration, Declaration of the United Nations Conference on the Human Environment (Stockholm Declaration 1972) (1973), UN Document A/CONF.48/14/Rev.1. https://www.un.org/en/conferences/environment/stockholm1972. Accessed 14 May 2023

United Nations Economic and Social Council (2000) Committee on Economic Social and Cultural Rights, General Comment No. 14: The Right to the Highest Attainable Standard of Health, 33, U.N. Doc. E/C.12/2000/4 (Aug. 11, 2000). http://www.unhchr.ch/tbs/doc.nsf/. Accessed 10 June 2023

United Nations Environment Programme (UNEP) (2011) Environmental assessment of Ogoniland. UNEP, Nairobi. ISBN: 978-92-807-3130-9. http://postconflict.unep.ch/publications/OEA/UNEP_OEA.pdf. Accessed 10 June 2023

United Nations General Assembly (UNGA) (1994) Agenda for development: report to the UN Secretary General A/49/665, 11th November 1994. www.un.org. Accessed 26 June 2023

UNGA (2005) Basic principles and guidelines on the right to a remedy and reparation for victims of gross violations of international human rights law and serious violations of international humanitarian law, adopted and proclaimed by United Nations General Assembly (UNGA), Resolution 60/147 of 16 December 2005. https://www.ohchr.org/en/instruments-mechanisms/

instruments/basic-principles-and-guidelines-right-remedy-and-reparation. Accessed 4 Aug 2023
UNGA (2007) United Nations Declaration on the Rights of Indigenous Peoples, Resolution 61/295 adopted by the General Assembly on 13 September 2007. https://www.un.org/development/desa/indigenouspeoples/wp-content/uploads/sites/19/2018/11/UNDRIP_E_web.pdf. Accessed 29 May 2023
United Nations General Assembly Human Rights Council (UNGAHRC) (2014) Twenty-sixth session agenda item 3: promotion and protection of all human rights, civil, political, economic, social and cultural rights, including the right to development, A/HRC/26/NGO/100 26 May 2014. Being comments on joint written statement by Europe-Third World Centre (CETIM) and Environmental Rights Action/Friends of the Earth Nigeria (ERA/FoEN), "Cases of Environmental Human Rights Violations by Shell in Nigeria's Niger Delta," circulated in accordance with Economic and Social Council resolution 1996/31. https://www.ecoi.net/en/file/local/1245905/1930_1403101174_g1404473.pdf. Accessed 10 July 2023
United Nations Office of the High Commissioner on Human Rights (UN/OHCHR) (2015) Land and human rights: annotated compilation of case laws, (UN/OHCHR), Geneva. https://www.ohchr.org/Documents/Publications/Land_HR-CaseLaw.pdf. Accessed 14 June 2023
Unpendra B (1984) Crimes against right to development, human rights activism in Asia, some perspectives, problems and approaches. ACHRO, New York
Wolf S et al (2002) Principles of environmental law, 3rd edn. Cavendish, London

Part IV
Pollution Damage and the Marine Environment

Chapter 13
The Marine Environment

Abstract The marine environment is an essential component of the global life-support system. From deep oceans to coastal reefs, from mudflats to seagrass beds, oceans and marine systems provide us with essential services: carbon capture for climate mitigation and renewable energy and protection from storm surges, to name but a few. This chapter discusses the nature and extent of pollution in the marine environment, touching on the history of marine pollution, the types of pollutants, the pathways of marine pollution as well as the nature, impact and effects of pollution on the marine environment. The focus is on the marine environment generally.

13.1 Introduction

The most significant aspect of the marine environment is the coastal area. The coastal area means land and sea areas bordering the shoreline.[1] It is a low area lying with heights of not more than 3.0 m above sea level and is generally covered by freshwater swamps, mangrove swamps, lagoon marshes, tidal channels, beach ridges and sandbars.[2] The major distinguishing parameter that separates the brackish water from the freshwater environment is their different salinity ranges. The salinity of any water body is simply a measure of the sodium chloride content of that water body, and it is measured in parts per thousand (ppt). The salinity ranges of the fresh water, brackish water (estuarine mainly) and sea water are: fresh water: less than 0.5 parts per thousand (ppt); brackish water: 0.5–30 ppt; and seawater: 30–40 ppt, on average.[3]

Coastal areas are commonly defined as the interface or transition areas between land and sea, including large inland lakes.[4] The coast, also known as the coastline or

[1] Mangor et al. (2017).

[2] Dublin-Green and Hughes (2015), p. 226.

[3] Ralph (2015), p. 226.

[4] Walsh Medical Media (2023).

E. Onyeabor, *Environmental Law*, https://doi.org/10.1007/978-3-031-68956-7_13

seashore, is defined as the area where land meets the ocean or as a line that forms the boundary between the land and the ocean or a lake. The earth has around 620,000 km of coastline.[5]

Coastal areas are diverse in functions, forms and dynamics and do not lend themselves well to definition by strict spatial boundaries. Unlike watersheds, there are no exact natural boundaries that unambiguously delineate coastal areas. Geologically, continental margins are of two types: active margins, where the edge of a continent happens to be at the edge of an oceanic plate, and inactive margins, where the transition from continental lithosphere to oceanic lithosphere is within a plate rather than at a plate edge.[6]

13.2 Nature and Extent of the Marine Environment

The coastal environment generally refers to any piece of land next to, bordering or adjourning the seashore.[7] The extent of the coastal environment also varies immensely, depending on the object of the context within which it is being defined.[8] Sometimes, it simply means the narrow linear corridor of shoreline separating the continental shelf from the oceanic land mass. At other times, it may be considered to extend both largely inwards, towards the continental shelf, and outwards, farther away from the shoreline towards the terrestrial land mass.[9]

Consequently, the coastal environment can be said to transcend the shoreline up to the exclusive economic zone seawards and across the estuarine and intertidal zones to the lower reaches of the freshwater tributaries, sandy beaches and sometimes even arid continental land masses, landwards where such bound the world's seas and oceans.[10]

Nigeria covers a total of 923,768 km^2, with a land area of 910 km^2. It has a coastline of 853 km and inland waterways totalling 8575 km, consisting largely of Rivers Niger and Benue, as well as other smaller rivers and creeks.[11]

The Nigerian coastline lies on the West Coast of Africa between latitude 4°10′ to 6°20′N and longitude 2°45′ to 8°32′E, covering approximately 853 km, from the Seme border in Badagri to Ikang in Cross River State (from West to East) and gently descending into the Atlantic Ocean.[12] Some of the key maritime claims of Nigeria include a continental shelf of 200 m to the depth of exploitation, territorial water of

[5] Ibid.

[6] Ibid.

[7] Ralph (2015), p. 26.

[8] Ibid.

[9] Ibid.

[10] Ibid.

[11] Adewale (2015).

[12] Zabbey et al. (2019), pp. 835–854.

20 nautical miles from the shoreline and an exclusive economic zone (EEZ) of 200 nautical miles from its territorial water. This, alongside Nigeria's stretch of coastline, indicates clearly the vast maritime environment that subtends the Nigerian hinterland. The Nigerian maritime territory is 853 km of coastline, 12 nautical miles of territorial waters, 24 nautical miles of contiguous zone and 200 nautical miles of EEZ, with maximum water depths between 2600 m and 3000 m.[13]

The nature of coastal environments, which are often a complex mix of the different ecologies of both fresh- and saltwater habitats, makes it naturally one of the richest environments in terms of biodiversity resources and mineral deposits. The mangrove swamp of the Niger Delta (a coastal environment), for instance, is a highly productive area of the region in terms of fishery resources.[14] For example, a lot of brackish fin fish and shellfishes abound in this area; these include crabs, oysters, clams, periwinkles, etc. These fishery resources support a wide array of fishers and thus serve as a very important means of livelihood for the community. 'Nationally, almost 35% of all "threatened" and "endangered" species are either located in or dependent on wetland habitats and 90% of the species of commercially important fish and shellfish either pass their entire lives in estuarine habitats or require estuaries as nursery grounds.'[15]

However, oil production activities in the Niger Delta are a major source of land- and marine-based pollution of the coastal zone. Other threats include untreated effluent discharges, reclamation, deforestation, harmful fishing methods, invasive species and unregulated sand mining. These activities weaken climate resilience, delimit socio-economic opportunities and increase coastal erosion vulnerability. The region's tourism destination potential is also devalued.[16]

13.3 Nature of Marine Pollution

13.3.1 Introduction

The term pollution generally refers to the alteration of the natural physico-chemical characteristics of an entity, medium or matter as a result of the presence of substances or compounds that are not supposed to be present in it or that are present in quantities and qualities that would alter the natural balance of the particular entity, medium or matter.[17]

Pollution is the addition of any substance (solid, liquid or gas) or any form of energy (such as heat, sound or radioactivity) to the environment at a rate faster than it

---

[13] Adewale (2015).

[14] Akankali and Jamabo (2015), p. 226.

[15] Sulton and Shun (2015), p. 226.

[16] Zabbey et al. (2019).

[17] Akankali and Oronsaye (2015), p. 226.

can be dispersed, diluted, decomposed, recycled or stored in some harmless form. The major kinds of pollution, usually classified based on the environment, are air pollution, water pollution and land pollution. Modern society is also concerned about specific types of pollutants, such as noise pollution, light pollution and plastic pollution. Pollution of all kinds can have negative effects on the environment and wildlife and often impacts human health and well-being.[18]

Consequently, pollution can be classified in terms of where it occurs or its medium of occurrence, such as water or aquatic pollution (marine, brackish or freshwater pollution), atmospheric pollution and soil/land pollution.[19] Furthermore, pollution can be classified in terms of the type of the causative matter or compound, such as chemical pollution, noise pollution, air pollution, agrochemical pollution and industrial and domestic effluent pollution, to mention but a few.[20]

An acceptable definition of the term marine pollution is as drawn up by the working group of the Joint Group of Experts on the Scientific Aspects of Marine Pollution IMO/FAO/UNESCO/WMO/WHO/IAEA/UN/UNEP and World Health Organization.[21] To the Group, marine pollution is defined as:

> the introduction by man directly or indirectly of substances or energy into the marine (estuarine) environment resulting in such deleterious effects as harm to living resources, hazard to human health, hindrance to marine activities including fishing, impairment of quality for the use of sea water and reduction of amenities.[22]

Although these delineations exist, their precise boundary in reality overlaps over a wide area, especially from the fresh water through the brackish water to the saline or brine water. For the purpose of this review, the term marine pollution is meant to encapsulate the brackish water, saline or brine aquatic environment.

Marine pollution occurs when harmful, or potentially harmful, effects result from the entry into the ocean of chemicals; particles; industrial; agricultural; and residential waste; noise; or the spread of invasive organisms. Eighty per cent of marine pollution comes from land. Air pollution is also a contributing factor by carrying off pesticides or dirt into the ocean. Land and air pollution have proven to be harmful to marine life and its habitats.[23]

Pollution often comes from non-point source, such as agricultural run-off, windblown debris and dust. Nutrient pollution, a form of water pollution, refers to contamination by excessive inputs of nutrients. It is a primary cause of eutrophication of surface waters, in which excess nutrients, usually nitrogrn or phosphorus, stimulate algae growth.[24]

---

[18] Nathanson (2023).

[19] Nathanson (2023).

[20] Ibid.

[21] Joint Group of Experts on the Scientific Aspects of Marine Pollution (1989).

[22] Ibid.

[23] National Oceanic and Atmospheric Administration (NOAA) (2023).

[24] Ibid.

Many potentially toxic chemicals adhere to tiny particles, which are then taken up by plankton and benthos animals, most of which are either deposit or filter feeders. In this way, the toxins are concentrated upward within ocean food chain. Many particles combine chemically in a manner highly depletive of oxygen, causing estuaries to become anoxic.[25]

When pesticides are incorporated into the marine ecosystem, they quickly become absorbed into marine food webs. Once in the food webs, these pesticides can cause mutations, as well as diseases, which can be harmful to humans as well as the entire food web.[26]

Toxic metals can also be introduced into marine food webs. These can cause a change in tissue matter, biochemistry, behaviour and reproduction and suppress growth in marine life. Also, many animal feeds have a high fissh meal or fish hydrolysate content. In this way, marine toxins can be transferred to land animals and appear later in meat and dairy products.[27]

13.3.2 History of Marine Pollution

Although marine pollution has a long history, significant international laws to counter it were only enacted in the twentieth century. Marine pollution was a concern during several United Nations Conferences on the Law of the Sea beginning in the 1950s. Most scientists believed that the oceans were so vast that they had unlimited ability to dilute and thus render pollution harmless.[28]

In the late 1950s and early 1960s, there were several controversies about dumping radioactive waste off the coasts of the United States by companies licensed by the Atomic Energy Commission into the Irish Sea from the British reprocessing facility at Windscale and into the Mediterranean Sea by the French Commissariat à l' Energie Atomique. After the Mediterranean Sea controversy, for example, Jacques Cousteau became a worldwide figure in the campaign to stop marine pollution. Marine pollution made further international headlines after the 1967 crash of the oil tanker Torry Canyon and after the 1969 Santa Barbara oil spill off the coast of California.[29]

Marine pollution was a major area of discussion during the 1972 United Nations Conference on the Human Environment, held in Stockholm.[30] That year also saw the signing of the Convention on the Prevention of Marine Pollution by Dumping of Waste and Other Matters, sometimes called the London Convention. The London

[25] National Oceanic and Atmospheric Administration (NOAA) (2023).

[26] Ibid.

[27] Ibid.

[28] Joint Group of Experts on the Scientific Aspects of Marine Pollution (1989).

[29] Ibid.

[30] Hamblin (2008).

Convention did not ban marine pollution, but it established black and grey lists for substances to be banned (black) or regulated by national authorities (grey). Cyanide and high-level radioactive waste, for example, were put on the blacklist. The London Convention applied only to waste dumped from ships and, thus, did nothing to regulate waste discharged as liquids from pipelines.[31]

13.3.3 Types of Marine Pollutants

Pollutant types based on the nature of the polluting substance are often categorised fundamentally into physical, chemical, biological and radioactive pollutants. However, there is a further classification, based on the environment of occurrence, the source of the pollutant or even the mode of impact. This latter form of classification could be highly subjective, depending on what the classifier's perceptions and objectives may be. However, it is entirely well defined, and the importance of the classification is easily understood from the context of such classification. The following are the various marine pollutants.

13.3.3.1 Energy Pollutants

There are various forms of energy sources available to man, either naturally or enhanced and exploited by man as forms of artificial energy. Some of these forms of energy include noise, heat, nuclear, vibration and solar (both ultraviolet and other forms of radiation) energy.[32] These energy forms are utilizable by man and applied in various forms to drive the various forms of human socio-economic activities, with the exception of noise. Incidentally, a significant portion of these energy sources end up in the aquatic environment as what could be termed as thermal energy residues, which eventually constitute thermal pollutants. Thermal pollution occurs mainly through the creation of a phenomenon known as thermal plume. This creates thermal shock for the aquatic organisms, which can lead to either death or other physiologic problems.[33]

Perhaps one of the most insidious of all energy pollutants is radioactive waste. Radioactive waste is also dumped in the oceans and usually comes from the nuclear power process, medical use of radioisotopes, research use of radioisotopes and industrial uses. The difference between industrial waste and nuclear waste is that nuclear waste usually remains radioactive for decades.[34] The protocol for the disposal of nuclear waste involves special treatment, which requires keeping it in

[31] Hamblin (2008).

[32] Peirce et al. (1998), p. 122.

[33] Ibid.

[34] Ibid.

concrete drums so that it does not spread when it hits the ocean floor.[35] The dumping of radioactive material has reached a total of about 84,000 terabecquerels (TBq), a unit of radioactivity equal to 10^{12} atomic disintegrations per second or 27.027 curies. Curie (Ci) is a unit of radioactivity. One curie was originally defined as the radioactivity of 1 gram of pure radium. In 1953, scientists agreed that curie would represent exactly 3.7×10^{10} atomic disintegrations per second, or 37 gigabecquerels (GBq), this being the best estimate of the activity of a gram of radium.[36] The unit is named after Pierre and Marie Curie, who discovered radium. The high point of nuclear waste dumping was in 1954 and 1962, but this nuclear waste only accounts for 1% of the total TBq that has been dumped in the ocean. The concentration of radioactive waste in concrete drums varies, as does the danger to marine life and humans.[37]

13.3.3.2 Organic or Biological Pollutants

The life processes of organisms lead to the generation of a class of pollutants, which inevitably impact the aquatic environment. Some of these include urine, faeces and various other products of the decay process of organics from living or dead organisms.[38] Incidentally, geometric increases in human population and the need to keep up with the provision of food for the astronomically rising global population has led to corresponding increases in crop and animal productions. This increases the amount of biological pollutants that eventually get into our aquatic environment. Especially in urban areas and in highly industrialised cities that have water bodies, biological pollutants have rendered most municipal water bodies highly toxic.[39]

In Lagos, Nigeria, for example, most of the lagoons have become so badly polluted from the indiscriminate dumping of untreated human waste and open defecation and urination into the waters, among other pollutants. The water body is perpetually black in colour, with a stench-like strong ammonia (NH3) odour.[40] This is an indication of heavily polluted waters, mostly from biological pollutants. Aquatic life in such water is reduced to the barest minimum, as the primary producers are completely wiped out. Human wastes, in particular, generally cause serious problems to the marine environment. The disposal of untreated human waste is one of the largest contributors to the pollution of the marine environment. There are numerous health problems associated with it. Even in places where there are septic tanks and soak-away pits, they tend to overflow, including in many of the

[35] Ibid.

[36] Peirce et al. (1998), p. 122.

[37] Ibid.

[38] Goudie (2005).

[39] Ibid.

[40] Nigerian Environmental Study/Action Team (NEST) (1991), p. 79.

coastal villages in rural settings due to a lack of proper toilet facilities, especially in developing nations like Nigeria.[41] Human waste gets discharged into the sea or coastal waters either directly or through streams, rivers and storm drainages.

Furthermore, as the human population grows, more and more categories of pollutants impact both fresh- and brackish waters. One of the most common pollution in this category is the organic pollutant caused by oxygen-demanding wastes, such as domestic sewage, wood fibre from pulp and paper mills, effluent from food-processing plants and run-off from agricultural areas (especially hay, dairy and cattle farms). Dissolved oxygen is consumed either through the chemical oxidation of these substances or through the respiratory processes of biological decomposition.[42]

The decomposition of materials is a normal process in all aquatic ecosystems and is a function of decomposers such as bacteria and fungi. These organisms metabolise the organic matter as an energy and nutrient source and utilise dissolved oxygen in the process. However, serious consequences can result if these natural mechanisms are overloaded by large influxes of organic matter. Severe oxygen depletion can result in the loss of desirable aquatic life and may produce an odorous anaerobic system.[43]

13.3.3.3 Domestic Pollutants

For decades, communities, settlements and municipalities have utilised water courses for domestic chores and transportation and as a sink for waste. However, sewage depletes the much-needed dissolved oxygen and contains high concentrations of bacterial and viral life forms, some of which could be pathogenic.[44]

In addition, effluent from municipal domestic waste treatment plants, with unknown and unusual chemical contents found in the industrial process because of trade secrets, find their way into water courses. These substances affect both pelagic and benthic organisms and impair water quality for fish spawning and breeding, ultimately in coastal aquatic environments.[45]

13.3.3.4 Synthetic Pollutants

Synthetic pollution involves pollutants from substances that are manufactured or synthesised by man from factories and laboratories. In other words, they are artificially formulated compounds, which man utilises as raw materials, drugs, herbicides

---

[41] Nigerian Environmental Study/Action Team (NEST) (1991), p. 79.

[42] Enger and Smith (2002), p. 399.

[43] Ibid.

[44] Ibid.

[45] Ibid.

and pesticides.[46] Depending on the nature of the active ingredients of the synthetic pollutants, irrespective of where they are used, the residues may persist in the aquatic environment and have long-lasting impacts as they may not easily be biodegradable.[47] Pesticides constitute very good examples of synthetic pollutants.

There are two major categories of synthetic products: the organo-chlorine and organo-phosphorous groups. Organo-chlorine-based compounds include pesticides, pharmaceutical and cosmetic products and plastics.[48] For example, some pesticides, like dichloro-diphenyl-trichloroethane (DDT), are not only biologically active but also stable and persist for a long time in the aquatic environment. Some organo-phosphorous-based compounds are less stable and therefore of lesser persistence and impact the aquatic environment. Although most pesticides are often used on land in agricultural estates, the aquatic environment becomes the ultimate recipient of the residues.[49]

The heavy metals in them may be in very trace quantities, but aquatic organisms such as molluscs and crustaceans are able to raise the level of concentrations through their filter-feeding habits. When these substances bio-accumulate in such aquatic organisms and are consumed by man, they bio-magnify the adverse health hazards of the pollutants. It has been reported that over 90% of detergents that are the commonest in use today are biodegradable; many new pesticides, such as the organo-phosphorous group, break down readily in water, although not necessarily to simple inorganic salts. Even where a substance is biodegradable, it does not mean that it poses no problems as the products of its breakdown may be toxic or bio-accumulated to levels at which it becomes hazardous.[50]

13.3.3.5 Crude Oil Pollutants

Crude oil pollution, a type of chemical pollutant, deserves specific discussion as a type of pollutant. This is because it has become one of the most critical pollutants in the marine environment. Several factors make crude oil a top-polluting substance in the aquatic environment. Top among these factors is the global economic importance of crude oil as a product that drives most economies all over the world. Hence, its global demand and production have steadily been on the rise, thereby leading to the development of numerous oilfields all over the world.[51] Some of the major oil-producing facilities around the globe are located either onshore, near shore or

[46] Enger and Smith (2002), p. 399.

[47] Ibid.

[48] Ibid.

[49] Ibid.

[50] Ibid.

[51] This is notwithstanding the drop in the demand for oil and the push for alternative energy sources away from fossil fuels (of which oil is one of them).

offshore.[52] Furthermore, most oil refining and transportation facilities are sited close to and are carried on water, respectively.

13.3.3.6 Industrial Pollutants

The discussion on industrial pollution as a pollutant type centres mainly on industrial wastewater, even though thermal heat (such as from gas flaring), radiation and other forms of industrial pollutants impact negatively the aquatic environment. Industrial wastewater is given priority as a fundamental type of water pollutant due to its serious impact on the aquatic environment.[53] In virtually all industrial processes, water is required as an important catalyst ingredient and as a coolant, etc. The excess of such water is often released into the environment, especially into the aquatic environment, with all the dissolved constituents.

Most of the constituents include organics and inorganics. Undesirable industrial wastewater may be characterised based on the nature of the industry and the projected uses of the waters of the receiving stream.[54] These undesirable wastewater characteristics (pollutants) include soluble organics, suspended solids, heavy metals, cyanide and toxic organics, colour and turbidity, nitrogen and phosphorous, refractory substances, volatile material oil and floating material, and aquatic toxins.[55]

13.3.3.7 Precipitation Pollutants

Liquid precipitation such as rainfall constitutes a fundamental source of marine pollutants. This is because the processes that lead to the formation of precipitation are based on the crystallisation of moisture around suspended particulate matter. The particulate sources include salt particles from the field, ash emitted from volcanic eruption and dust particles such as chromium, asbestos, particulates from smokestacks, crystals of salt, pollens in the air or combustion by-products of coal or fossil fuel.[56] The increasing concentration of greenhouse gases (GHGs) containing carbon dioxide (CO_2) and oxides of nitrogen and sulphur beyond threshold levels is responsible for acid rain, which adversely affects fisheries and aquaculture, forestry and agricultural soil fertility in coastal environments.[57]

52 Ike (1991), p. 46.

53 Gerlach (2005), p. 99.

54 Ibid.

55 Ibid.

56 Ibid.

57 Ibid.

13.3.3.8 Extraneous Pollutants

There are pollutant types in the aquatic marine environment that are not easily recognisable and may not be easily classified. Consequently, they are termed as extraneous pollutants. When large tracts of land are ploughed, the exposed soil can erode during rainstorms. Much of this run-off flows to the sea, carrying with it loose earth material that may be contaminated. In the process of sedimentation, a considerable portion of such earth material may constitute silt pollutants. Extraneous pollutants occur mainly through the non-point source of pollution, which occurs as a result of run-off.[58]

Other extraneous pollutants include minor leakages from many small sources, like septic tanks, cars, trucks and boats, plus larger sources, such as farms, ranches and forest areas. Millions of motor vehicle engines drop small amounts of oil each day onto roads and parking lots. Much of these oil droplets make their way to water bodies or seas. Some water pollution actually starts as air pollution, which settles into waterways and oceans. Dirt and dust from road construction during dry weather also constitute extraneous pollutants, which impact the aquatic marine environment. Silt from fields or construction sites can run off into waterways, harming fish and wildlife habitats.[59]

13.4 Pathways of Marine Pollution

Pathways of pollution are often classed as either point source or non-point source pollution. Point source pollution occurs when there is a single, identifiable and localised source of pollution.[60] An example is directly discharging sewage and industrial waste into the ocean. Pollution such as this occurs particularly in our environment. Non-point source pollution occurs when the pollution comes from ill-defined and diffuse sources. These can be difficult to regulate. Agricultural run-off and wind-blown debris are prime examples.[61] There are many different ways to categorise and examine the inputs of pollution into our marine ecosystems. The following are the major pathways through which pollutants enter the marine environment.

---

[58] Gerlach (2005).

[59] Ibid.

[60] Enger and Smith (2002), p. 399.

[61] Ibid.

13.4.1 Direct Discharge

One common path of entry by contaminants to the sea is through rivers. The evaporation of water from oceans exceeds precipitation. The balance is restored by rain over the continents entering rivers and then being returned to the sea. The Hudson river in New York State and the Raritan river in New Jersey, which empty at the northern and southern ends of Staten Island, are a source of mercury contamination of zooplankton (copepods) in the open ocean. The highest concentration in the filter-feeding copepods is not at the mouths of these rivers but 70 miles south, nearer Atlantic city, because water flows close to the coast. It takes a few days before toxins are taken up by the plankton.[62]

Pollutants enter rivers and the sea directly from urban sewage and industrial waste discharges, sometimes in the form of hazardous and toxic wastes. Inland mining for copper, gold, etc., is another source of marine pollution. Most of the pollution is simply soil, which ends up in rivers flowing to the sea. However, some minerals discharged in the course of mining can cause problems, such as copper, a common industrial pollutant, which can interfere with the life history and development of coral polyps.[63] Mining has a poor environmental track record. For example, according to the United State Environmental Protection Agency, mining has contaminated portions of headwaters of over 40% of watersheds in the western continental United States.[64] Much of this pollution finishes up in the sea.

13.4.2 Pollution from Land Run-Off

Surface run-offs from farming, as well as urban run-off and run-off from the construction of roads, buildings, ports, channels and harbours, can carry soil and particles laden with carbon, nitrogen, phosphorus and minerals. This nutrient-rich water can cause fleshy algae and phytoplankton to thrive in coastal areas, known as algal blooms, which have the potential to create hypoxic conditions by using all available oxygen.[65]

Polluted run-off from roads and highways can be a significant source of water pollution in coastal areas. About 75% of the toxic chemicals that flow into Puget Sound are carried by storm water that runs off paved roads and driveways, rooftops, yards and other developed land.[66]

---

[62] Enger and Smith (2002), p. 120.

[63] Young (2003).

[64] Ibid.

[65] Washington State Department of Ecology (2008).

[66] Ibid.

13.4.3 Pollution from Ships

Ships can pollute waterways and oceans in many ways. Oil spills can have devastating effects. While being toxic to marine life, polycyclic aromatic hydrocarbon (PAHs), found in crude oil, are very difficult to clean up and last for years in the sediments and marine environment.[67]

Oil spills are probably the most emotive of marine pollution events. However, while a tanker wreck may result in extensive newspaper headlines, much of the oil in the world's seas comes from other smaller sources, such as tankers discharging ballast water from oil tanks used on return ships, leaking pipelines or engine oil disposed off from down sewers.[68]

The discharge of cargo residues from bulk carriers can pollute ports, waterways and oceans. In many instances, vessels intentionally discharge illegal wastes despite foreign and domestic regulations prohibiting such actions. It has been estimated that container ships lose over 10,000 containers at sea each year (usually during storms).[69] Ships also create noise pollution, which disturbs natural wildlife, and water from ballast tanks can spread harmful algae and other invasive species.[70]

Ballast water taken up at sea and released in ports is a major source of unwanted exotic marine life. The invasive freshwater zebra mussels, native to the Black, Caspian and Azov seas, were probably transported to the Great Lakes via ballast water from a transoceanic vessel.[71] Meinesz[72] believes that one of the worst cases of a single invasive species causing harm to an ecosystem can be attributed to a seemingly harmless jelly fish. Mnemiopsis leidyi is a species of comb jellyfish that spread, so it now inhabits estuaries in many parts of the world. It was first introduced in 1982 and was thought to have been transported to the Black Sea in a ship's ballast water. The population of the jellyfish shot up exponentially, and by 1988, it was wreaking havoc upon the local fishing industry. 'The anchovy catch fell from 204,000 tons in 1984 to 200 tons in 1993; sprat from 24,600 tons in 1984 to 12,000 tons in 1993; horse mackerel from 4000 tons in 1984 to zero in 1993.'[73] Now that the jellyfish have exhausted the zooplankton, including fish larvae, their numbers have fallen dramatically, yet they continue to maintain a stranglehold on the ecosystem.[74]

Invasive species can take over once occupied areas facilitate the spread of new diseases, introduce new genetic material, alter underwater seascapes and jeopardise the ability of native species to obtain food. Invasive species are responsible for about

---

[67] Panetta (2008), p. 22.

[68] Farmer (1998).

[69] Podsadam (2001).

[70] Meinesz (2003), p. 12.

[71] Ibid.

[72] Ibid.

[73] Ibid.

[74] Ibid.

$138 billion in lost revenue and management costs annually in the United States alone.[75]

13.4.4 Pollution from the Atmosphere

Another pathway of pollution occurs through the atmosphere. Wind-blown dust and debris, including plastic bags, are blown seawards from landfills and other areas. Dust from the Sahara moving around the southern periphery of the subtropical ridge moves into the Caribbean and Florida during the warm season as the ridge builds and moves northwards through the subtropical Atlantic.[76] Dust can also be attributed to a global transport from the Gobi and Taklamakan deserts across Korea, Japan and the Northern Pacific to the Hawaiian Islands. Since 1970, dust outbreaks have worsened due to periods of drought in Africa. There is a large variability in dust transport to the Caribbean and Florida from year to year; however, the flux is greater during positive phases of the North Atlantic Oscillation.[77] The United States Geological Survey (USGS) links dust events to a decline in the health of coral reefs across the Caribbean and Florida, primarily since the 1970s.[78]

Climate change is raising ocean temperatures and raising levels of carbon dioxide in the atmosphere. These rising levels of carbon dioxide are acidifying the oceans. This, in turn, is altering acquatic ecosystems and modifying fish distributions, with impacts on the sustainability of fisheries and the livelihoods of the communities that depend on them. Healthy ocean ecosystems are also important for the mitigation of climate change.[79]

13.4.5 Pollution from Deep-Sea Mining

Deep-sea mining is a relatively new mineral retrieval process that takes place on the ocean floor. Ocean mining sites are usually around large areas of polymetallic nodules or active and extinct hydrothemal vents at about 1400–3700 m below the ocean's surface.[80] The vents create sulphide deposits, which contain precious metals such as silver, gold, copper, manganese, cobalt and zinc. The deposits are mined using either hydraulic pumps or bucket systems that take ore to the surface to be

[75] Pimentel et al. (2005), pp. 273–288.

[76] United States Geological Survey (2010).

[77] Ibid.

[78] Intergovernmental Panel on Climate Change (IPCC) (2007).

[79] Ibid.

[80] Ahnert and Borowski (2000), pp. 299–315.

processed. As with all mining operations, deep-sea mining raises questions about environmental damages to the surrounding areas.[81]

Since deep-sea mining is a relatively new field, the complete consequences of full-scale mining operations are unknown. However, experts are certain that the removal of parts of the sea floor will result in disturbances to the benthic layer, increased toxicity of the water column and sediment plumes from tailings.[82] Removing parts of the sea floor disturbs the habitat of benthic organisms, possibly, depending on the type of mining and location, causing permanent disturbances.[83] Aside from the direct impact of mining the area, leakage, spills and corrosion would alter the mining area's chemical makeup.

Among the impacts of deep-sea mining, sediment plumes could have the greatest impact. Plumes are caused when the tailings from mining (usually fine particles) are dumped back into the ocean, creating a cloud of particles floating in the water.[84] Two types of plumes occur: near-bottom plumes and surface plumes.[85] Near-bottom plumes occur when the tailings are pumped back down to the mining site. The floating particles increase the turbidity, or cloudiness, of the water, clogging filter-feeding apparatuses used by benthic organisms. Surface plumes cause a more serious problem. Depending on the size of the particles and water currents, the plumes could spread over vast areas. The plumes could impact zooplankton and light penetration, in turn affecting the food web of the area.[86]

13.5 Nature of Pollution Impacts on the Marine Environment and Their Effects

The marine environment is impacted variously. Among the major impacts arise from the following: (1) shipping activities, (2) ocean acidification, (3) eutrophication, (4) plastic debris, (5) toxins, (6) mercury pollutants, (7) underwater noise and (8) impact from oil spillage. The nature of such impacts and their effects on the marine environment are discussed below.

[81] Halfar and Fujita (2007), p. 987.

[82] Ahnert and Borowski (2000), pp. 299–315.

[83] Halfar and Fujita (2007), p. 987.

[84] Ibid.

[85] Ibid.

[86] Ahnert and Borowski (2000), pp. 299–315.

13.5.1 Impact Resulting from Shipping Activities

What then are the environmental impacts of shipping activities? The environmental impact of shipping includes greenhouse gas emissions, acoustic pollution and oil pollution. A number of impacts on the marine environment result from shipping activities. They include the following.

13.5.1.1 Deposit from Ballast Water

Ballast water is fresh- or saltwater held in the ballast tanks and cargo holds of ships. It is used to provide stability and manoeuvrability during voyages when ships are not carrying cargo or heavy enough cargo or when more stability is required due to rough seas.[87] Cruise ships, large tankers and bulk cargo carriers use huge amounts of ballast water, which is often taken on in coastal waters in one region after ships discharge wastewater or unload cargo and is discharged at the next port of call, wherever more cargo is loaded. Ballast water discharge typically contains a variety of biological materials, including plants, animals, viruses and bacteria. These materials often include non-native, nuisance, invasive and exotic species, which can cause extensive ecological and economic damage to aquatic ecosystems, as well as serious human health problems.[88]

13.5.1.2 Sound Pollution

Noise pollution can cause health problems for people and wildlife, both on land and in the sea. From traffic noise to rock concerts, loud or inescapable sounds can cause hearing loss, stress and high blood pressure. Noise from ships and human activities in the ocean is harmful to whales and dolphins, which depend on echolocation to survive.[89]

Noise pollution caused by shipping and other human enterprises has increased in recent history. The noise produced by ships can travel long distances, and marine species that may rely on sound for their orientation, communication and feeding can be harmed by this sound pollution. The Convention on the Conservation of Migratory Species has identified ocean noise as a potential threat to marine life.[90]

---

[87] United States Department of Agriculture (USDA) (2020).

[88] Ibid.

[89] National Geographic Society (2023).

[90] Prideaux (2017).

13.5.1.3 Wildlife Collisions

Marine mammals such as whales and manatees, risk being struck by ships, causing injury and death. For example, if a ship is travelling at a speed of only 15 knots, there is a 79% chance of a collision being lethal to a whale.[91] One notable example of the impact of ship collisions is the endangered North Atlantic right whale, of which 400 or less remain. The greatest danger to the North Atlantic right whale is injury sustained from ship strikes.[92] Between 1970 and 1999, 35.5% of recorded deaths were attributed to collisions. During 1999–2003, incidents of mortality and serious injury attributed to ship strikes averaged one per year. In 2004–2006, that number increased to 2.6. Deaths from collisions have become an extinction threat.[93]

13.5.1.4 Pollution of the Atmosphere

The International Maritime Organisation (IMO) estimates that carbon monoxide emissions from shipping were equal to 2.2% of the global human-made emissions in 2012 and expects them to rise by as much as two to three times by 2050 if no action is taken.[94]

Exhaust gases from ships are considered to be a significant source of air pollution, both for conventional pollutants and for greenhouse gases. There is a perception that cargo transport by ship is low in air pollutants because, for equal weight and distance, it is the most efficient transport method, according to shipping researcher Amy Bows-Larkin.[95] This is particularly true in comparison to air freight; however, because sea shipment accounts for far more annual tonnage and the distances are often large, shipping's emissions are globally substantial. A difficulty is that the year-on-year increasing amount of shipping overwhelms gains in efficiency, such as from slow steaming or the use of kites. The growth in tonne-kilometres of sea shipment has averaged 4% yearly since the 1990s.[96] And it has grown by a factor of 5 since the 1970s. There are now over 100,000 transport ships at sea, of which about 6000 are large container ships.[97]

---

[91] Vanderlaan and Taggart (2007).

[92] Ibid.

[93] Ward-Geiger et al. (2005), pp. 263–278.

[94] International Maritime Organisation (IMO) (2009).

[95] Reilly et al. (2009).

[96] Ibid.

[97] Ibid.

13.5.1.5 Emission of Greenhouse Gas Pollutants

The First Inter-sessional Meeting of the IMO Working Group on Greenhouse Gas Emissions from Ships took place in Oslo, Norway, on 23–27 June 2008. It was tasked with developing the technical basis for the reduction mechanisms that may form part of a future IMO regime to control greenhouse gas emissions from international shipping and a draft of the actual reduction mechanisms themselves, for further consideration by IMO's Marine Environment Protection Committee (MEPC).[98]

About 3.5–4% of all climate change emissions are caused by shipping, primarily carbon dioxide. As a way to reduce the impact of greenhouse gas emissions from shipping, vetting agency RightShip developed an online 'Greenhouse Gas (GHG) Emissions Rating' as a systematic way for the industry to compare a ship's CO_2 emissions with peer vessels of a similar size and type. Based on the International Maritime Organization's (IMO's) Energy Efficiency Design Index (EEDI), which applies to ships built from 2013, RightShip's GHG rating can also be applied to vessels built prior to 2013, allowing for effective vessel comparison across the world's fleet.[99]

The GHG rating utilises an A to G scale, where A represents the most efficient ships. It measures the theoretical amount of carbon dioxide emitted per tonne nautical mile travelled based on the design characteristics of the ship at the time of build, such as cargo-carrying capacity, engine power and fuel consumption. Higher-rated ships can deliver significantly lower CO_2 emissions across the voyage length, which means they also use less fuel and are cheaper to run.[100]

In addition, large marine diesel engines are believed to contribute 7% of mobile source nitrogen oxide emissions in Baton Rouge/New Orleans. Ships can also have a significant impact in areas without large commercial ports: they contribute about 37% of total area nitrogen oxide emissions in the Santa Barbara area, and that percentage increased to 61% by 2015.[101] Again, there is little cruise-industry-specific data on this issue. They comprise only a small fraction of the world shipping fleet, but cruise ship emissions may exert significant impacts on a local scale in specific coastal areas that are visited repeatedly. Shipboard incinerators also burn large volumes of garbage, plastics and other waste, producing ash that must be disposed of. Incinerators may release toxic emissions as well.[102]

In 2005, the International Convention for the Prevention of Pollution from Ships 1973 (MARPOL), Annex VI,[103] came into force to combat this problem. As such, cruise ships now employ closed circuit television (CCTV) monitoring on the

---

[98] International Maritime Organisation (IMO) (2008a).

[99] Reilly et al. (2009).

[100] Ibid.

[101] Ibid.

[102] Ibid.

[103] MARPOL was discussed in Sect. 14.1.2 of Chap. 14 of this book.

smokestacks as well as recorded measuring via opacity metre, while some are also using clean burning gas turbines for electrical loads and propulsion in sensitive areas.

13.5.1.6 Conventional Pollutants

Air pollution from cruise ships is generated by diesel engines that burn high-sulphur content fuel oil, also known as bunker oil, producing sulphur dioxide, nitrogen oxide and particulate, in addition to carbon monoxide, carbon dioxide and hydrocarbons. Diesel exhaust has been classified by US Environmental Protection Agency (EPA) as a likely human carcinogen.[104] EPA recognises that these emissions from marine diesel engines contribute to ozone and carbon monoxide non-attainment (i.e. failure to meet air quality standards), as well as adverse health effects associated with ambient concentrations of particulate matter and visibility, haze, acid deposit and the euthrophication and nitrification of water.[105]

The US Environmental Protection Agency (EPA)[106] estimates that large marine diesel engines accounted for about 1.6% of mobile source nitrogen oxide emissions and 2.8% of mobile source particulate emissions in the United States in 2000. Contributions of marine diesel engines can be higher on a port-specific basis. Ultra low sulphur diesel (ULSD) is a standard for defining diesel fuel with substantially lowered sulphur content. As of 2006, almost all of the petroleum-based diesel fuel available in Europe and North America is of a ULSD type.[107]

Of the total global air emissions, shipping accounts for 18–30% of nitrogen oxide and 9% of sulphur oxides. Sulphur in the air creates acid rain, which damages crops and buildings.[108] When inhaled, sulphur is known to cause respiratory problems and even increases the risk of a heart attack. According to Irene Blooming,[109] a spokeswoman for the European environmental coalition Seas at Risk, the fuel used in oil tankers and container ships is high in sulphur and cheaper to buy compared to the fuel used for domestic land use. ‘A ship lets out around 50 times more sulphur than a lorry per metric tonne of cargo carried.’ Cities in the United States, like Long Beach, Los Angeles, Houston, Galveston and Pittsburgh, see some of the heaviest shipping traffic in the nation and have left local officials desperately trying to clean up the air. Increasing trade between the United States and China is helping increase the number of vessels navigating the Pacific and exacerbating many of the environmental problems.[110]

---

[104] Reilly et al. (2009).

[105] Ibid.

[106] Ibid.

[107] Ibid.

[108] Watson (2004).

[109] Ibid.

[110] Ibid.

13.5.1.7 Oil Spills from Ships

The most common impact on the marine environment associated with ship activities comes from oil spills from ships. While less frequent than the pollution that occurs from daily operations, oil spills have devastating effects. While being toxic to marine life, polycyclic aromatic hydrocarbons (PAHs), the components in crude oil, are very difficult to clean up and last for years in the sediment and marine environment. Marine species constantly exposed to PAHs can exhibit developmental problems, susceptibility to disease and abnormal reproductive cycles.[111]

13.5.1.8 Deposit of Sewage

The cruise line industry dumps 255,000 US gallons (970 m^3) of greywater and 30,000 US gallons (110 m^3) of blackwater into the sea every day. Blackwater is sewage and wastewater from toilets and medical facilities, which can contain harmful bacteria, pathogens, viruses, intestinal parasites and harmful nutrients.[112] Discharges of untreated or inadequately treated sewage can cause bacterial and viral contamination of fisheries and shellfish beds, producing risks to public health. Nutrients in sewage, such as nitrogen and phosphorus, promote excessive algal blooms, which consume oxygen in the water and can lead to fish kills and the destruction of other aquatic life. A large cruise ship (3000 passengers and crew) generates an estimated 55,000 L to 110,000 L of blackwater waste per day.[113]

Due to the environmental impact of shipping, and sewage in particular, MARPOL Annex IV was brought into force in September 2003, strictly limiting untreated waste discharge. Modern cruise ships are most commonly installed with a membrane bio-reactor type treatment plant for all blackwater[114] and greywater, such as Zenon or Rochem , which produces near-drinkable, quality effluent to be reused in machinery spaces as technical water.[115]

13.5.1.9 Deposits from Cleaning Waste

Waste from the cleaning of ships comes in the form of greywater. Greywater is wastewater from sinks, showers, galleys, laundry and cleaning activities aboard a ship. It can contain a variety of pollutant substances, including faecal coliforms, detergents, oil and grease, metals, organic compounds, petroleum, hydrocarbon,

[111] Prideaux (2017).

[112] Ibid.

[113] Ibid.

[114] Black wastewater from the vessel is all the water that comes from toilets and medical treatments.

[115] G&O Maritime Group (2021).

nutrients, food waste and medical and dental waste.[116] Sampling done by the US Environmental Protection Agency (EPA) and the state of Alaska found that untreated greywater from cruise ships can contain pollutants at variable strengths and can contain levels of faecal coliform bacteria several times greater than is typically found in untreated domestic wastewater.[117]

Greywater has the potential to cause adverse environmental effects because of concentrations of nutrients and other oxygen-demanding materials in particular. Greywater is typically the largest source of liquid waste generated by cruise ships (90–95% of the total). Estimates of greywater range from 110 L to 320 L per day per person or 330,000 L to 960,000 L per day for a 3000-person cruise ship.[118]

13.5.1.10 Deposit of Solid Waste

Solid waste generated on a ship includes glass, paper, cardboard, aluminium and steel cans and plastics. It can be either non-hazardous or hazardous in nature. Solid waste that enters the ocean may become marine debris and can then pose a threat to marine organisms, humans, coastal communities and industries that utilise marine waters. Cruise ships typically manage solid waste by a combination of source reduction, waste minimisation and recycling.[119]

However, as much as 75% of solid waste is incinerated on board, and the ashes are typically discharged at sea, although some are landed ashore for disposal or recycling. Marine mammals, fish, sea turtles and birds can be injured or killed from entanglement with plastics and other solid waste that may be released or disposed of from cruise ships. On average, each cruise ship passenger generates at least 2 pounds of non-hazardous solid waste per day.[120]

With large cruise ships carrying several thousand passengers, the amount of waste generated in a day can be massive. For a large cruise ship, about 8 tons of solid waste are generated during a 1-week cruise. It has been estimated that 24% of the solid waste generated by vessels worldwide (by weight) comes from cruise ships.[121] Most cruise ship garbage is treated on board (incinerated, pulped or ground up) for discharge overboard. When garbage must be offloaded (for example because glass and aluminium cannot be incinerated), cruise ships can put a strain on port reception facilities, which are rarely adequate to the task of serving a large passenger vessel.[122]

---

[116] Ibid.

[117] G&O Maritime Group (2021).

[118] Ibid.

[119] The Ocean Conservancy (2002), p. 13.

[120] Ibid.

[121] Ibid.

[122] Ibid.

13.5.1.11 Deposit of Bilge Water

On a ship, oil often leaks from the engine and machinery spaces or from engine maintenance activities and mixes with water in the blige, the lowest part of the hull of the ship, but there is a filter to clean bilge water before being discharged. Oil, gasoline and by-products from the biological breakdown of petroleum products can harm fish and wildlife and pose threats to human health if ingested. Oil in even minute concentrations can kill fish or have various sub-lethal chronic effects. Bilge water also may consist of solid wastes and pollutants containing high levels of oxygen- demanding material, oil and other chemicals. A typically large cruise ship will generate an average of 8 metric tons of oily bilge water for each 24 h of operation.[123]

To maintain ship stability and eliminate potentially hazardous conditions from oil vapours in these areas, the bilge spaces need to be flushed and periodically pumped dry. However, before a bilge can be cleared out and the water discharged, the oil that has been accumulated needs to be extracted from the bilge water, after which the extracted oil can be reused, incinerated and/or offloaded in port. If a separator, which is normally used to extract the oil, is faulty or is deliberately bypassed, untreated oily bilge water could be discharged directly into the ocean, where it can damage marine life. A number of cruise lines have been charged with environmental violations related to this issue in recent years.[124]

13.5.2 Impacts from Shipping Accidents

In the course of shipping activities, a number of accidents, referred to as incidents, have had enormous impacts on the marine environment. These incidents range from ships running aground to sinking, damage to the hull, breaking up, collision of ships, mishandling of oil discharge, mishandling of cargo, overflow from supply pipe, storm damage, ruptured discharge pipe and fire on board a ship. A few of such incidents may suffice.

The International Oil Pollution Compensation (IOPC) Funds[125] documented a number of ship incidents arising from shipping activities that had an impact on the marine environment. According to IOPC Funds, among the major ship incidents that had impacted the marine environment were the grounding of ships, the sinking of ships, collision and fire and explosion incidents during ship stranding, the overflow of oil during loading operations, the mishandling of oil supply and transfer, discharges from ships, a ruptured discharge pipe and de-ballasting. Some examples of

[123] National Research Council (1995), pp. 38–39.

[124] Ibid., 126.

[125] International Oil Pollution Compensation Funds (2022).

such ship incidents, such as the grounding of ships and fire and explosion incidents on ships are discussed below.

13.5.2.1 Grounding of Ship Incident

On 27 February 1979, *Antonio Gramsci*, a Union of Soviet Socialist Republic (USSR)-flagged ship, ran aground in Ventspils, USSR, spilling 5500 tonnes of oil. *Jose Marti*, a USSR-flagged ship, ran aground on 7 January 1981 at Dalarö, Sweden, spilling 1000 tonnes of oil. There was the grounding of *Globe Asimi*, a Gibraltar-flagged ship, on 22 November 1981, at Klaipeda, USSR, spilling 16,000 tonnes of oil. On 2 August 1985, *Jan*, a flagged ship of Germany, ran aground at Aalborg, Denmark, spilling 300 tonnes of oil. On 21 December 1986, *Thuntank 5*, a flagged ship of Sweden, ran aground at Gävle, Sweden, spilling about 150–200 tonnes of oil. *Antonio Gramsci*, a USSR-flagged ship, ran aground on 6 February 1987 at Borgå, Finland, spilling about 600–700 tonnes of oil. On 21 July 1987, El Hani, a flagged ship of Libya, ran aground at Indonesia, spilling 3000 tonnes of oil.[126]

Again, on 16 October 1990, there was the grounding of a flagged ship of the Cayman Islands, *Rio Orinoco*, at Anticosti Island, Canada, spilling 185 tonnes of oil. The *Hokunan Maru N°12*, a flagged ship of Japan, ran aground at Okushiri Island, Japan, on 5 April 1991. *Aegean Sea*, a flagged ship of Greece, ran aground on 3 December 1992 at La Coruña, Spain, and spilt 73,500 tonnes of oil. The *Braer*, a flagged ship of Liberia, ran aground at Shetland, United Kingdom, on 5 January 1993, spilling 84,000 tonnes of oil. *Kihnu*, a flagged ship of Estonia, ran aground on 16 January 1993 at Tallinn, Estonia, and spilt 140 tonnes of oil. *Iliad*, a flagged ship of Greece, ran aground at Pylos, Greece, on 9 October 1993 and spilt 200 tonnes of oil. The *Sea Prince*, a flagged ship of Cyprus, ran aground on 23 July 1995 at Yosu, Republic of Korea, and spilt 315 tonnes of oil. On 15 February 1996, *Sea Empress*, a Liberian-flagged ship, ran aground at Milford Haven, Wales, United Kingdom, spilling 72,360 tonnes of oil. *Nissos Amorgos*, a flagged ship of Greece, ran aground on 28 February 1997 at Maracaibo, Venezuela, spilling 3600 tonnes of oil. There was also the grounding of *Diamond Grace*, a flagged ship of Panama, on 2 July 1997 at Tokyo Bay, Japan, where 1500 tonnes of oil were spilt.[127] On 1 January 1998, *Santa Anna*, a flagged ship of Panama, ran aground at Devon, United Kingdom, spilling 280 tonnes of oil. On 31 July 2011, *MT Pavit*, a flagged ship of Panama, ran aground at Mumbai, Republic of India.[128]

In another incident, on 8 September 2019, a South Korean automobile carrier ship named *MV Golden Ray* capsized shortly after leaving Port of Brunswick. Though demolition works have been carried out since November, about half of the ship still remains partially submerged underwater. There has been periodical oil leakage from

[126] International Oil Pollution Compensation Funds (2022).

[127] Ibid.

[128] International Oil Pollution Compensation Funds (2022).

the ship of late that has become a huge concern for environmentalists. A large amount of oil gushed into the water along Georgia Beach in the United States from the overturned ship that was being dismantled. The oil leak can be a result of the cutting away of the sixth giant section of the ship. The oil gushed into the water as soon as the towering crane began lifting the segment of the ship, which was around 4 tons. According to the salvage team, the ship's ballast tanks had collected oil. It oozed out through the holes that were drilled to drain water from the partly submerged sections of the ship.[129]

13.5.2.2 Impact from Ship Fire Incident

In June 2021, a Singapore-registered ship, *X-Press Pearl*, which was on its way from Hazira Port, India, to Singapore, caught fire. The ship was carrying 1486 containers of harmful chemicals when it caught fire.[130] The ship's cargo comprised 25 tonnes of hazardous sodium methylate, nitric acid, caustic soda, plastic, lubricant oil, lead ingots and quick lime. It was also transporting inflammable chemicals like low-density polyethylene, vinyl acetate, sodium methoxide, high-density polyethylene, urea, methanol, bright yellow sulphur and cosmetics. This entire consignment comprised 46 types of chemicals categorised as dangerous goods per the International Maritime Dangerous Goods (IMDG). The ship also had 300 tonnes of bunker oil on board.[131]

The ship eventually sank off Sri Lanka's coast on 17 June 2021, emptying its deadly cargo into the sea. More than 60 dead turtles and other marine creatures, including dolphins and a blue whale, have been killed due to the disaster. The carcasses have been washed ashore the famed beaches of Sri Lanka.[132]

Beside the impact of the incident on the natural environment, about 6000 fishermen and their families residing along the stretch from Uswetakeiyawa to Negombo coastal and about 2000 boats go fishing in the ocean daily were affected by the incident.

Again, almost 7753 fishermen, those employed in fishing-related activities, and their families have lost their jobs due to the shipwreck. Meanwhile, more than 2000 families who had been employed in fisheries and related activities, like drying fish or fish netting, have no source of income at present. Furthermore, fishermen who are engaged in fisheries and related activities have been severely affected by the contamination of sea areas and the loss of fishing grounds.[133]

[129] MI News Network (2021).

[130] Marine Insight Network (2021a, b).

[131] Ibid.

[132] Ibid.

[133] Marine Insight Network (2021a).

As a result of this incident, tagged as the country's worst environmental disaster, a petition was filed on 23 June 2021 at the Sri Lankan Supreme Court by affected fishermen, asking for compensation for damages.

The petition filed by Rev. Fr. Sarath Iddamalgoda and two fishermen was a fundamental rights petition seeking the court to direct the authorities to compensate for Rs. 500,000 each fisherman affected by the burning and sinking of the container ship *X-Press Pearl*.

The petitioners cited the Minister of Fisheries Douglas Devananda, the Minister of Environment Mahinda Amaraweera, the Chairman of the Sri Lanka Ports Authority, the Marine Environment Protection Authority, the Minister of Ports and Shipping Rohitha Abeygunawardena, and X-Press Feeders—the shipowners represented by the Sea Consortium Lanka (Pvt) Ltd (local agent)—and others as respondents.[134]

The petitioners stated that their livelihood has been threatened due to the ecological restriction directed by the government as they upkeep lives from their daily wage as fishermen. As a result, they have been unable to conduct daily fishing activities for a fortnight.

The petitioners also feared that they may be suffering for years. They have sought a declaration stating that the respondents have violated the fundamental rights guaranteed under Articles 12(1) and 14(1)(g) of the Sri Lankan Constitution.[135]

While petitions were being filed at the Sri Lankan Supreme Court on 23 June 2021, another environmental disaster in Sri Lanka occurred on 25 June 2021 as another container ship that had been sailing towards Singapore caught fire. The ship, *MSC Messina*, a Liberian-flagged one, departed from the port of Colombo, Sri Lanka, on 22 June 2021, headed to Singapore.[136]

An explosion incident happened on 2 November 2020 on *MT Harcourt*, a registered ship from the Marshall Islands, in which an approximately 31 barrels of oil were spilt into the Benin River, Delta State, Nigeria.[137]

On 17 August 2019, *Stolt Groenland*, a Cayman Islands registered chemical/products tanker operated by Stolt Tankers B.V., sailed from Houston, USA, for passage to Kobe, Japan, via the Panama Canal. The tanker was carrying 20 different chemical cargoes in 37 of its 39 cargo tanks. After discharging four cargo tanks off Kobe on 23 September and six cargo tanks at the Odfjell Terminal in Ulsan, Republic of Korea, between 26 and 27 September, *Stolt Groenland* moored alongside Yeompo Quay in Ulsan. Two further cargo tanks were then discharged via a ship-to-ship transfer with *Stolt Voyager*. On completion, *Stolt Voyager* moored ahead of *Stolt Groenland*.[138]

At about 0600 hr on 28 September 2019, the Singapore-registered chemical/products tanker *Bow Dalian* secured alongside *Stolt Groenland*'s port side. The

---

[134] Ibid.

[135] Ibid.

[136] Marine Insight Network (2021b).

[137] International Oil Pollution Compensation Funds (IOPC Funds) (2022).

[138] Marine Accident Investigation Branch (MAIB) (2019).

purging of *Bow Dalian*'s cargo tanks with nitrogen supplied from shore-side vehicles was then commenced in preparation for a ship-to-ship cargo transfer with *Stolt Groenland*. At 1043 h, vapour started to release from the pressure vacuum valve of *Stolt Groenland*'s number 9 starboard (9S) cargo tank, which contained styrene monomer. About 2 min later, a high-level alarm indicated that the level in 9S cargo tank had reached 95%, soon followed by a high-high-level alarm indicating that the level had increased to 98%. By now, *Stolt Groenland*'s on-watch deck officer and chief officer had made their way to the cargo control room, and they saw from the cargo monitoring system that the pressure inside the 9S cargo tank was rapidly rising. Suddenly, at 1050 h, two explosions were seen and heard in rapid succession in the way of the tanker's cargo manifold. The resulting fireball passed very closely to a road bridge above the quay.[139]

On 28 September 2019, the Maritime Authority of the Cayman Islands requested the Marine Accident Investigation Branch (MAIB)[140] to investigate this accident in accordance with the International Maritime Organization Casualty Investigation Code.[141] The objective of this Code is to provide a common approach for states to adopt in the conduct of marine safety investigations into marine casualties and marine incidents. Marine safety investigations do not seek to apportion blame or determine liability. Instead, a marine safety investigation, as defined in this Code, is an investigation conducted with the objective of preventing marine casualties and marine incidents in the future.[142] However, the investigating authority should not refrain from fully reporting the causes because fault or liability may be inferred from the findings.[143]

Investigations by MAIB revealed that the explosions on board *Stolt Groenland* were probably caused by the rupture of the deck above the 9S cargo tank, followed immediately by the ignition of the styrene monomer vapour that was then released. The rupture was due to over-pressurisation, and the likely sources of the ignition were static electricity, spark or elevated steel deck plate temperatures resulting from the tank rupture. A large hole was found in the tank's common bulkhead with number 9 centre (9C) cargo tank, and its hatch cover had been blown off. No cargo operations or deck maintenance were in progress at the time. Voyage data recorder (VDR) data showed that the temperature of the styrene monomer had reached 100 °C at the time of the explosion. Such an elevated temperature indicates that the cargo was polymerising.[144]

---

[139] Ibid.

[140] Ibid.

[141] International Maritime Organisation (IMO) (2008b).

[142] IMO Resolution MSC.255 (84) adopted on 16 May 2008, chapter 1.1.

[143] Merchant Marine General Directorate Department of Maritime Casualty Investigations (2014).

[144] Styrene monomer is used to make plastics, paints and synthetic rubber. It is a colourless to yellowish oily liquid with an aromatic odour and is highly flammable. It has a flash point of 32 °C (90 °F). It is also toxic and reactive and is generally stable at ambient temperatures. The polymerisation of monomers is a chemical reaction in which two or more molecules combine to form larger molecules that contain repeating structural units. However, if a large amount of monomers are

Stolt Groenland loaded 5250 tonnes of styrene monomer at the LBC terminal in Houston, USA, between 7 and 8 August. The cargo was distributed between three stainless steel cargo tanks: numbers 9S, 6P and 6C. Prior to loading, the tanks had been washed and inspected and wall wash tests had been conducted; no problems were recorded. The tanks were not purged with nitrogen before loading, and none were adjacent to heated cargoes in accordance with cargo loading instructions.[145]

The concentration of the tert-butylcatechol (TBC) inhibitor in the styrene monomer in the shore tank was 11.3 ppm, but this was increased by the addition of 3 US gallons of liquid TBC to each of the destination tanks before loading was commenced. The target concentration of the TBC was 17 ppm. The loading was overseen by an American Cargo Assurers cargo surveyor acting on behalf of the supplier of the styrene monomer, Ineos Styrolutions, and the purchaser, Samsung C&T Corporation.[146]

The certificate of inhibitor, issued by the cargo surveyor at the time of loading, stated that the TBC should remain effective for between 60 and 90 days. It also stated that the inhibitor was oxygen dependent and that the ideal temperature for the styrene monomer was between 60 °F and 85 °F (15.5 °C–29.4 °C). *Stolt Groenland* did not carry additional inhibitors.[147]

As a result of the incident, besides extensive damage to *Stolt Groenland*'s cargo manifold and accommodation block, one crew member of *Stolt Groenland*, another crew member from *Bow Dalian* and 15 shore workers/officials were also reported to have been injured. Toxic fumes from the incident were released into the environment.[148]

13.5.3 Ocean Acidification

Ocean acidification is another source through which the marine environment is impacted. The oceans are normally a natural carbon sink, absorbing carbon dioxide

involved and if the reaction is strongly exothermic, the monomers may combine too quickly. Consequently, heat and pressure increase, initiated by heat or contact with peroxides. The polymerisation process is exothermic, and the monomer's temperature may rise to the point where the reaction becomes very rapid and self-sustaining (runaway polymerisation). Normally, temperatures above 65 °C (149 °F) are needed to initiate runaway polymerisations. To reduce the possibility of polymerisation during storage and transportation, a tert-butylcatechol (TBC) inhibitor is added to the styrene monomer, typically at a concentration of between 10 and 15 ppm, but higher levels might be needed depending on storage conditions and expected voyage duration. The depletion of TBC over time and its effectiveness as an inhibitor are affected by temperature, oxygen levels and water.

[145] Marine Accident Investigation Branch (MAIB) (2019).

[146] Marine Accident Investigation Branch (MAIB) (2019).

[147] Ibid.

[148] Ibid.

from the atmosphere. Because the levels of atmospheric carbon dioxide are increasing, the oceans are becoming more acidic. The potential consequences of ocean acidification are not fully understood, but there are concerns that structures made of calcium carbonate may become vulnerable to dissolution, affecting corals and the ability of shellfish to form shells.[149]

Oceans and coastal ecosystems play an important role in the global carbon cycle and have removed about 25% of the carbon dioxide emitted by human activities between 2000 and 2007 and about half of the anthropogenic CO_2 released since the start of the industrial revolution. Rising ocean temperatures and ocean acidification mean that the capacity of the ocean carbon sink will gradually get weaker, giving rise to global concerns expressed in the Monaco and Manado Declarations.[150]

A related issue is the methane clathrate reservoirs found under sediments on the ocean floors. These trap large amounts of greenhouse gas methane, which ocean warming has the potential to release. In 2004, the global inventory of ocean methane clathrates was estimated to occupy between 1 and 5 million cubic kilometres. If all these clathrates were to be spread uniformly across the ocean floor, this would translate to a thickness between 3 and 14 metres. This estimate corresponds to 500—2500 gigatonnes of carbon (Gt C) and can be compared with the 5000 Gt C estimated for all other fossil fuel reserves.[151]

13.5.4 Eutrophication

Euthrophication is an increase in chemical nutrients, typically compounds containing nitrogen or phosphorus, in an ecosystem. It can result in an increase in the ecosystem's primary productivity (excessive plant growth and decay) and further effects, including the lack of oxygen and severe reductions in water quality, fish and other animal populations.[152]

The biggest culprits are rivers that empty into the ocean and, with it, the many chemicals used as fertilisers in agriculture, as well as waste from livestock and humans. An excess of oxygen-depleting chemicals in the water can lead to hypoxia and the creation of a dead zone. [153]

Eustuaries tend to be naturally eutrophic because land-derived nutrients are concentrated where run-off enters the marine environment in a confined channel. The World Resources Institute has identified 375 hypoxic coastal zones around the world, concentrated in coastal areas in Western Europe, the Eastern and Southern

[149] Raven et al. (2005).

[150] Monaco Declaration and Ocean Acidification (2008).

[151] Milkov (2004), pp. 183–197.

[152] Ibid.

[153] Gerlach (2005), p. 34.

coasts of the United States and East Asia, particularly in Japan. In the ocean, there are frequent red tide algae blooms that kill fish and marine mammals and cause respiratory problems in humans and some domestic animals when the blooms reach close to shore.[154]

In addition to land run-off, atmospheric anthropogenic fixed nitrogen can enter the open ocean. A study in 2008 found that this could account for around one-third of the ocean's external (non-recycled) nitrogen supply and up to 3% of the annual new marine biological production. It has been suggested that accumulating reactive nitrogen in the environment may have consequences as serious as putting carbon dioxide in the atmosphere.[155]

One proposed solution to eutrophication in estuaries is to restore shellfish populations, such as oysters. Oyester reefs remove nitrogen from the water column and filter out suspended solids, subsequently reducing the likelihood or extent of harmful algal blooms or anoxic conditions. Filter-feeding activity is considered beneficial to water quality by controlling phytoplankton density and sequestering nutrients, which can be removed from the system through shellfish harvest, buried in the sediments or lost through denitrification.[156] Foundational work towards the idea of improving marine water quality through shellfish cultivation was conducted by Lindahl et al.[157] using mussels in Sweden.

13.5.5 Plastic Debris

Marine plastic debris is mainly discarded human rubbish that floats on, or is suspended in, the ocean. There is an incomprehensible amount of plastic in the ocean; estimates put the known total at 5 trillion individual pieces or around 150 million tonnes. An additional 8 million tonnes find their way into the ocean every year. That is only increased thanks to Covid-19 and the resulting surge in single-use items like masks and gloves.[158]

It is estimated that around 4% of the world's annual petroleum production is converted to plastics (synthetic organic polymers), while a similar amount of petroleum is used to provide energy for plastic manufacturing. The annual global production of plastics is about 280 million tons per year. Europe is using about 50 million tons of plastic, with almost 75% of the demand coming from four major sectors: packaging, construction, automotive and electrical/electronics. Packaging represents more than a third of European plastic consumption and consists of

[154] Eureka Alert (2008).
[155] Burkholder et al. (2001), p. 98.
[156] Burkholder et al. (2001).
[157] Lindahl et al. (2005), pp. 131–138.
[158] Bryce (2021).

products that have a very short life span. Less than 10% of the plastic is recycled; the rest is burned or sent to landfills.[159]

Discarded plastic bags, six-pack rings and other forms of plastic waste that finish up in the ocean present dangers to wildlife and fisheries; aquatic life can be threatened through entanglement, suffocation and ingestion. Fishing nets, usually made of plastic, can be left or lost in the ocean by fishermen. Fishing nets known as ghost nets entangle fish, dolphins, sea turtles, sharks, dugongs, crocodiles, sea birds, crabs and other creatures, restricting movement; causing starvation, laceration and infection; and, in those that need to return to the surface to breathe, suffocation.[160]

Most plastic enters the ocean via rivers, which carry vast amounts of waste from inland sources. Once in the ocean, plastic is broken down by the sun's rays and by wind and waves, eventually transforming into smaller fragments called microplastics. But the hardy nature of the material means that this process can take hundreds of years. In the meantime, plastic—both macro and micro—wreaks havoc on marine life. It brings the risk of entanglement and starvation (as species mistake plastics for food). As it enters the food chain, it also potentially leaches toxins into animals' bodies, with as-yet largely unknown effects on these creatures and the humans who consume them.[161]

Many animals that live on or in the sea consume flotsam by mistake as it often looks similar to their natural prey. Plastic debris, when bulky or tangled, is difficult to pass and may become permanently lodged in the digestive tracts of these animals, especially when evolutionary adaption makes it impossible for the likes of turtles to reject plastic bags, which resemble jellyfish when immersed in water, as they have a system in their throat to stop slippery foods from otherwise escaping, thereby blocking the passage of food and causing death through starvation or infection.[162]

Plastics accumulate because they do not biodegrade in the way many other substances do. They will photograde upon exposure to the sun, but they do so properly only under dry conditions, and water inhibits this process.[163] In marine environments, photodegraded plastic disintegrates into ever smaller pieces while remaining polymers, even down to the molecular level. When floating plastic particles photodegrade down to zooplankton sizes, jellyfish attempt to consume them, and in this way, the plastic enters the ocean food chain. Many of these long-lasting pieces end up in the stomachs of marine birds and animals, including sea turtles and black footed albatross.[164]

Plastic debris tends to accumulate at the centre of ocean gyres. In particular, the Great Pacific Garbage Patch has a very high level of plastic particulate suspended in the upper water column. In samples taken in 1999, the mass of plastic exceeded that

---

[159] Thevenon et al. (2014).

[160] Weiss (2006).

[161] Bryce (2021).

[162] Ibid.

[163] Moore (2002).

[164] Ibid.

of zooplankton (the dominant animal life in the area) by a factor of 6. Midway Atoll, in common with all the Hawaiian Island, receives substantial amounts of debris from the garbage patch.[165] Ninety per cent plastic, this debris accumulates on the beaches of Midway, where it becomes a hazard to the bird population of the island. Midway Atoll is home to two-thirds (1.5 million) of the global population of Laysan albatross. Nearly all of these albatross have plastic in their digestive system, and one-third of their chicks die.[166]

Toxic additives used in the manufacture of plastic materials can leach out into their surroundings when exposed to water. Waterborne hydrophobic pollutants collect and magnify on the surface of plastic debris, thus making plastic far more deadly in the ocean than it would be on land. Hydrophobic contaminants are also known to bio-accumulate in fatty tissues, bio-magnifying up the food chain and putting pressure on apex predators. Some plastic additives are known to disrupt the endocrine system when consumed; others can suppress the immune system or decrease reproductive rates.[167]

Floating debris can also absorb persistent organic pollutants from seawater. These persistent organic pollutants are varied. They include:

1. Polychlorinated biphenyls (PCBs)[168]
2. Dichlorodiphenyltrichloroethane (DDT)[169]
3. Tributyltin (TBT)[170] and

[165] Ibid.

[166] Hawaii Newspaper (2005).

[167] Hawaii Newspaper (2005).

[168] PCB is an organic chlorine compound and was once widely deployed as dielectric and coolant fluids in electrical apparatus, carbonless copy paper and heat transfer fluids. PCB remnants cycle between the air, water and soil and finally settle into water and sediment, where they are taken up by small organisms and increasingly accumulate in fats and organs, such as the liver in fish and animals (including humans) that eat fish.

[169] DDT is a colourless, tasteless and almost odourless crystalline chemical compound, an organochloride. Originally developed as an insecticide, it became infamous for its environmental impacts. DDT was first synthesised in 1874 by the Austrian chemist Othmar Zeidler. DDT's devastating effect on the aquatic environment has been thoroughly studied. Due to its low solubility, it has a greater rate of bio-accumulation in water and, thus, poses a great long-term threat to aquatic wildlife. It is highly toxic to both aquatic invertebrate species, like stoneflies and crayfish, and fish. Being able to affect all kinds of wildlife, and given its low decay rate, it proliferates through the entire web of life until it reaches the species inhabiting the throne of the great chain of life.

[170] TBT is an umbrella term for a class of organotin compounds that contain the $(C_4H_9)_3Sn$ group, with a prominent example being tributyltin oxide. For 40 years, TBT was used as a biocide in anti-fouling paint, commonly known as bottom paint, applied to the hulls of ocean-going vessels. Bottom paint improves ship performance and durability as it reduces the rate of bio-fouling (the growth of organisms on the ship's hull). TBT slowly leaches out into the marine environment, where it is highly toxic towards non-target organisms. TBT is also an obesogen. After it led to the collapse of local populations of organisms, TBT was banned.

4. Polycyclic aromatic hydrocarbons (PAHs).[171]

Aside from toxic effects, when ingested, some of these are mistaken by the animal brain for oestradiol,[172] causing hormone disruption in the affected wildlife.[173]

13.5.6 Impact from Toxins

Apart from plastics, there are particular problems with other toxins that do not disintegrate rapidly in the marine environment. Examples of persistent toxins are PCBs, DDT, TBT, persticides, furans, dioxins, phenols and radio active waste.[174] Heavy metals are metallic chemical elements that have a relatively high density and are toxic or poisonous at low concentrations. Examples are mercury, lead, nickel, arsenic and cadmium. Such toxins can accumulate in the tissues of many species of aquatic life in a process called bio-accumulation. They are also known to accumulate in benthic environments, such as estuaries and bay-muds: a geological record of human activities of the last century.[175] Specific examples include:

1. Chinese and Russian industrial pollutants, such as phenols and heavy metals in the Amur River, have devastated fish stocks and damaged its estuary soil.[176]
2. Wabamun Lake in Alberta, Canada, once the best whitefish lake in the area, now has unacceptable levels of heavy metals in its sediment and fish.
3. Acute and chronic pollution events have been shown to impact southern California kelp forests, though the intensity of the impact seems to depend on both the nature of the contaminants and the duration of exposure.[177]
4. Due to their high position in the food chain and the subsequent accumulation of heavy metals from their diet, mercury levels can be high in larger species such as bluefin and albacor. As a result, in March 2004, the United States Food and Drug Administration (FDA) issued guidelines recommending that pregnant women, nursing mothers and children limit their intake of tuna and other types of predatory fish.[178]

[171] PAHs are a class of chemicals that occur naturally in coal, crude oil and gasoline. They also are produced when coal, oil, gas, wood, garbage and tobacco are burned. PAHs generated from these sources can bind to or form small particles in the air. ... Cigarette smoke contains many PAHs.

[172] Oestradiol, also spelt estradiol, is an oestrogen steroid hormone and the major female sex hormone. It is involved in the regulation of the oestrous and menstrual female reproductive cycles.

[173] Weiss (2006).

[174] Rios et al. (2007), pp. 1230–1237.

[175] Rios (2007).

[176] Arctic Network for the Support of the Indigenous Peoples of the Russian Arctic (2006).

[177] Grigg and Kiwala (1970), pp. 145–155.

[178] Ibid.

5. Some shellfish and crabs can survive polluted environments, accumulating heavy metals or toxins in their tissues. For example, mitten crabs have a remarkable ability to survive in highly modified aquatic habitats, including polluted waters. The farming and harvesting of such species need careful management if they are to be used as a food.[179]
6. Surface run-off of pesticides can alter the gender of fish species genetically, transforming male into female fish.[180]
7. Heavy metals enter the environment through oil spills —such as the Prestige oil spill on the Galician coast—or from other natural or anthropogenic sources.[181]
8. In 2005, the Ndrangheta, an Italian mafia syndicate, was accused of sinking at least 30 ships loaded with toxic waste, much of it radioactive. This has led to widespread investigations into radioactive waste disposal rackets.[182]
9. Since the end of World War II, various nations, including Russia, the United Kingdom, the United States and Germany, have disposed of chemical weapons in the Baltic Sea, raising concerns about environmental contamination.[183]

It will be pertinent at this point to take a closer look at one of the most insidious heavy metals that impact the marine environment. That heavy metal is mercury. The issue of mercury in the ocean is the next focus of the discussion.

13.5.7 Mercury Pollutants and Their Impacts

Mercury is a toxic heavy metal that cycles through the atmosphere, water, and soil in various forms to different parts of the world. Due to this natural cycle, irrespective of which part of the world releases mercury, it could affect an entirely different part of the world, making mercury pollution a global concern. Mercury pollution is now identified as a global problem, and awareness has been raised on an international action plan to minimise anthropogenic mercury emissions and clean up mercury pollution. 'The Global Mercury Assessment 2002 concluded that International actions to address the global mercury problem should not be delayed'.[184] Among many environments that are under the impact of mercury pollution, the ocean is one that cannot be neglected as it has the ability to act as a 'storage closet' for mercury.[185]

---

[179] Ibid.

[180] Ibid.

[181] Ibid.

[182] Ibid.

[183] Grigg and Kiwala (1970).

[184] United Nations Environment Programme (UNEP) (2002).

[185] Oskin (2014).

According to a recent model study, the total anthropogenic mercury released into the ocean is estimated to be around 80,000 to 45,000 metric tons, and two-thirds of this enormous amount is estimated to be found in waters shallower than 1000 m level, where many consumable fish live.[186] Mercury can get bio-accumulated in marine food chains in the form of highly toxic methylmercury, which can cause health risks to human seafood consumers.[187] According to statistics, about 66% of global fish consumption comes from the ocean.[188] Therefore, it is important to monitor and regulate oceanic mercury levels to prevent more and more mercury reaching human population through seafood consumption.

13.5.7.1 Sources of Mercury

Mercury release occurs by both natural and anthropogenic processes. Natural processes are mainly geogenic, such as volcanic activities and land emissions through the soil. Volcanoes release mercury from underground reservoirs upon eruption. Land emissions are usually observed in regions closer to plate tectonic boundaries, where soils are enriched with minerals such as cinnabar containing mercury sulphide (HgS). This mercury is released by either natural weathering of the rocks or by geothermal reactions.[189] While natural phenomena account for a certain percentage of present-day emissions, anthropogenic emissions alone have increased mercury concentration in the environment by threefold.[190]

The Global Mercury Assessment 2013 states that the main anthropogenic sources of mercury emission are artisanal and small-scale gold mining, fossil fuel burning and the primary production of non-ferrous metals. Other sources, such as cement production, consumer product waste, contaminated sites and the chlor-alkali industry, also contribute in relatively small percentages.[191]

13.5.7.2 Mercury Species in the Ocean

Mercury enters the ocean in different ways. Atmospheric deposition is the largest source of mercury in the oceans. Atmospheric deposition introduces three types of mercury to the ocean. Gaseous elemental mercury (Hg0) enters the ocean through air-water exchange. Inorganic mercury (Hg2+/HgII) and particle-bound mercury (Hg(P)) enters through wet and dry deposition. In addition, mercury enters the

[186] Lamborg et al. (2014), pp. 65–68.
[187] Weiner et al. (2006); see also Clarkson and Magos (2006), p. 609.
[188] Food and Agricultural Organisation (FAO) (2015).
[189] Selin (2009), pp. 43–63.
[190] United Nations Environment Programme (UNEP) (2013).
[191] United Nations Environment Programme (UNEP) (2002).

ocean via rivers, estuaries, sediments, hydrothermal vents, etc.[192] These sources also release organic mercury compounds such as methylmercury. Once they are in the ocean, they can undergo many reactions primarily grouped as redox reactions (the gain or loss of electrons), adsorption processes (binding to solid particles), methylation and demethylation (the addition or removal of a methyl group).[193]

13.5.7.3 Chemical Reactions of Mercury in the Ocean

The reduction and oxidation of mercury mostly occur closer to the ocean water's surface. These are driven either by sunlight or by microbial activity. Under ultraviolet (UV) radiation, elemental mercury oxidises and dissolves directly in ocean water or binds to other particles. The reverse reaction reduces some mercury Hg2+ to elemental mercury Hg(0) and returns to the atmosphere. Fine aerosols in the atmosphere, such as ocean water droplets, can act as small reaction chambers in this process, providing the special reaction conditions required. The oxidation and reduction of mercury in the ocean are not very simple reversible reactions.[194]

Photo oxidation is suspected of being driven by hydroxyl (OH) radicals, and reduction is driven by wind and surface layer disturbances. In the dark, mercury redox reactions continue due to microbial activity. The biological transformations are different and have a smaller rate compared to sunlight-driven processes.[195] Inorganic mercury Hg2+ and methylmercury have the ability to get adsorbed into particles. A positive correlation of binding is observed for the amount of organic matter vs. the concentration of these mercury species, showing that most of them bind to organic matter.[196] These phenomena can determine the bioavailability and toxicity of mercury in the ocean. Some methylmercury is released to the ocean through river run-off. However, most of the methylmercury found in the ocean is produced in situ (inside the ocean itself).[197] The methylation of inorganic mercury can occur via biotic and abiotic pathways. However, biotic pathways are more predominant. The reactions illustrated in a simplified scheme below are actually parts of complex-enzyme-driven metabolic pathways taking place inside microbial cells.

In abiotic reactions, humic substances act as methylating agents, and therefore this process occurs at shallow sea levels, where decomposing organic matter is available to combine with inorganic mercury Hg2+9. Interestingly, mercury methylation studies in polar regions have also shown a positive correlation between

[192] Mason et al. (2012), pp. 101–117.

[193] Batrakova et al. (2014), pp. 1047–1063.

[194] Qureshi et al. (2010), pp. 644–649.

[195] Batrakova et al. (2014).

[196] Boszke et al. (2002), pp. 285–298.

[197] Mason et al. (2012).

methylation and chlorophyll content in water, showing there could also be biogenic pathways for methylmercury production.[198]

Produced methylmercury gets accumulated in microbes. Due to the high permeability and absence of degradation for methylmercury in other species that depend on those microbes, this very toxic compound gets bio-magnified through marine food chains to the top predators. The human population consumes many types of marine fish that are top predators in the food chains, which puts their health in great danger. Therefore, finding possible solutions to minimise further mercury emissions and cleaning up the already-existing mercury pollution are extremely important.[199]

13.5.7.4 Prevention and Cleaning of Mercury Pollution in the Ocean

Cleaning up the existing mercury pollution could be a tedious process. Nevertheless, there is some promising ongoing research bringing hope to the challenging task. One such research is based on nanotechnology.[200] It uses synthesised aluminium oxide nanoparticles (Al2O3) mimicking the coral structures. These structures absorb heavy metal toxins effectively due to the high surface/volume ratio and the quality of the surface. In nature, it has been long observed that corals can absorb heavy metal ions due to their surface structure, and this new technique has used nanotechnology to create 'synthetic corals', which may help clean mercury in the ocean.[201]

Another novel material, 'Patent application PCT/US15/55205',[202] is still under investigation, which looks at the possibility of cleaning mercury pollution using orange peels as raw material. This technology produces sulphur limonene polysulphide (proposed material) with the use of sulphur and limonene. Using industrial by-products to manufacture this polymer makes it a highly sustainable approach. Scientists say that 50% of the mercury content could be reduced with a single treatment using this polymer.[203]

In addition to the cleaning processes, minimising the usage of coal power and shifting to cleaner energy sources, reducing small-scale artisanal gold mining, proper treatment of industrial mercury waste and implementation of policies are sound approaches to reduce mercury emissions in the long-term/large-scale plan. Public awareness is critical in achieving this goal. The proper disposal of mercury-containing items, such as medicinal packaging and thermometers; using mercury-free bulbs and batteries; and buying consumer products with zero or minimum

[198] Kirk et al. (2012), pp. 64–87. Note that dimethylmercury degradation also produces some of the methylmercury present in the ocean.

[199] Kirk et al. (2012).

[200] Wang et al. (2015), pp. 244–251.

[201] Ibid.

[202] The Patent Cooperation Treaty (*PCT*) assists applicants in seeking patent protection . . . By filing one international *patent application* under the *PCT*.

[203] The Conversation (2015).

mercury emission to the environment can make a significant difference in recovering the world's ecosystems from mercury pollution, leaving a minimum legacy of mercury pollution in the ocean for our future generations.[204]

13.5.8 Marine Impacts from Underwater Noise

Marine life can be susceptible to noise or sound pollution from sources such as passing ships, oil exploration seismic surveys and naval low-frequency active sonar. Sound travels more rapidly and over larger distances in the sea than in the atmosphere. Marine animals, such as cetaceans, often have weak eyesight and live in a world largely defined by acoustic information. This applies also to many deeper-sea fishes, which live in a world of darkness.[205] Between 1950 and 1975, ambient noise at one location in the Pacific Ocean increased by about 10 decibels (that is, a tenfold increase in intensity).[206]

Noise also makes species communicate louder, which is called the Lombard vocal response. Whale songs are longer when submarine detectors are on.[207] If creatures do not 'speak' loud enough, their voice can be masked by anthropogenic sounds. These unheard voices might be warnings, finding of prey or preparations of net bubbling. When one species begins speaking louder, it will mask other species' voices, causing the whole ecosystem to eventually speak louder.[208] According to oceanographer Earle,[209]

> Undersea noise pollution is like the death of a thousand cuts. Each sound in itself may not be a matter of critical concern, but taken all together, the noise from shipping, seismic surveys, and military activity is creating a totally different environment than existed even 50 years ago. That high level of noise is bound to have a hard, sweeping impact on life in the sea.

13.5.9 Impact from Oil Spillage

Oil spill disasters have been one of the major concerns of the marine world for a long time now. They are environmental catastrophes. As a result of an accident involving ships or oil rigs or pipelines transporting oil, the ocean water became contaminated by liquid petroleum hydrocarbon, causing damage to the environment for decades to come. In addition to killing fish, marine mammals and birds, oil spills damage

[204] Ibid.

[205] National Geographic Society (2023).

[206] Institute of Acoustics (2014), p. 18.

[207] Ibid.

[208] Ibid.

[209] Earle (2005).

beaches and wildlife habitats, among others. When an oil slick reaches the beach, it also affects human settlement on the beaches and mangrove forests, etc.[210]

Oil pollution arising from oil spills has impacted the oil-producing environment in no small ways, especially during transportation.[211] Oil spills on water have been found to cause the death of mangrove seedlings and trees, reduce the productivity of phytoplankton and other aquatic flora and disrupt detritus-based food webs of fish, all of which result in reduced fish yields. This is not unconnected with the fact that oil films on the water surface could prevent natural aeration and can lead to the death of marine organisms trapped below. In some cases, fish may ingest the spilt oil or other food materials impregnated with oil. Such fish often are very unpalatable. Where the death of marine life is not the case, oil pollution leads to a reduced growth rate and the reproductive rate of estuarine fishes, as well as causes fishes to suffer from an increased incidence of fin rot disease.[212]

The world has been racked by major oil spill disasters many times. While only major accidents that result in spills receive most of the attention, a number of smaller and chronic incidents take place on a regular basis. Below are some of the largest and worst oil spills in world history and in Nigeria.

13.5.9.1 Global Incident of Oil Spills

The following are some of the incidents of oil spills that impacted the marine environment, including the oceans.

13.5.9.1.1 Amoco Cadiz

On 16 March 1978, an oil tanker named Amoco Cadiz ran aground and started a major oil spill off the coast of Brittany, France. The very large crude carrier (VLCC) was run aground after the failure of its steering due to a storm.

The vessel later broke in half and sunk, letting its cargo of 246,000 tons of light crude oil spill into the waters of the English Channel. The oil spill cleaning was a massive and rather futile effort. The slick spread quickly, covering an area of 18 miles with 80 miles in length. As 76 beaches suffered oil spill effects, it killed more marine life than any other oil spills recorded till then.[213]

---

[210] Ike (1991).

[211] Nigerian Environmental Study/Action Team (NEST) (1991), p. 89.

[212] Nigerian Environmental Study/Action Team (NEST) (1991), p. 89.

[213] Mohit in Marine Environment (2021).

13.5.9.1.2 Atlantic Empress

In July 1979, two oil tankers collided in the Caribbean Sea, off the coast of Tobago, during a tropical storm. When the accident occurred, the Atlantic Empress was en route to Beaumont from Saudi Arabia, while the Aegean Captain was sailing from Aruba to Singapore. Immediately after the accident, the cargo of the supertankers—the Atlantic Empress and Aegean Captain—started to leak and caught fire. According to reports, around 88.3 million gallons of crude oil was discharged into the sea, making the accident the largest ship-sourced oil spill in the world. In addition, the accident also claimed the lives of 26 crew members as the Atlantic Empress exploded later.[214]

13.5.9.1.3 Ixtoc 1 Oil Well

In June 1979, the Bay of Campeche of the Gulf of Mexico saw the collapse of an oil well operated by the Mexican petroleum company Pemex. Around 140 million gallons of oil—almost 10,000 to 30,000 barrels of oil was gushing out per day—were discharged into the sea during a 10-month period of time. The oil slick resulted from the accident, measured around 1100 square miles, and it was surrounded by Rancho Nuevo, a prominent nesting site for Kemp's ridley sea turtles on Mexican coasts. Moreover, as a measure to reduce the impact on marine life, thousands of baby sea turtles were moved to the cleaner part of the ocean.[215]

13.5.9.1.4 Nowruz Field Platform

During the Iran-Iraq war in 1983, an oil tanker hit the Nowruz Field platform situated in the Persian Gulf, leading to a major oil spill. The damage the accident made to the well resulted in the leaking of oil. It is estimated that about 80 million gallons of oil—around 1500 barrels a day—flowed into the Persian Gulf during a 7-month period after the accident. The capping could be done only in September as the continuous war meant that the oil spill pollution could not be controlled soon enough. At the cost of 11 lives, a huge amount of oil that went to waste and many unfavourable effects on marine life, the oil spill was finally controlled.[216]

---

[214] Ibid.

[215] Mohit in Marine Environment (2021).

[216] Ibid.

13.5.9.1.5 Castillo de Bellver

The Spanish tanker Castillo de Bellver was en route to Spain from the Persian Gulf when the tanker caught fire around 70 miles northwest of South Africa's Capetown. The tanker was carrying 250,000 tonnes (around 79 million gallons) of light crude oil at the time of the accident in August 1983. The burning vessel was abandoned later, only to break in half eventually. Following this, the stern of the vessel sank with 110,000 tons of oil inside its tanks. According to environmentalists, though the impact of this oil spill on the fish stock was less, the incident affected thousands of gannets gathered on a nearby island for their breeding season.[217]

13.5.9.1.6 Odyssey Oil Spill

Odyssey, a Liberian tanker loaded with around 43 million gallons of North Sea crude oil in its cargo, broke in half and sunk off the coast of Canada in November 1988. According to reports, the ship sunk 700 miles off the coast of Nova Scotia after an explosion on board. The vessels cargo caught fire as it sank, dumping 43 million gallons of oil into the Atlantic Ocean. The oil spill covered an area of 4.8 km × 16 km, while the amount of oil that reached the shore was minimal. Moreover, all the 27 crew members onboard the Odyssey are presumed to have died in the incident.[218]

13.5.9.1.7 Gulf War Oil Spill[219]

The world's largest oil spill was not an accident. It was the result of a war. During the Gulf War in 1991, as the Iraqi forces withdrew from Kuwait, they opened pipelines and the valves of oil wells and set fire as a measure to block the forces of the United States from landing in the area. The fire that started after the opening of the first well in January 1991 lasted till the capping of the last well in the month of April that year. As a result, around 240 million gallons of oil were believed to have been discharged into the Persian Gulf, killing hundreds of fish and marine mammals.[220]

13.5.9.1.8 MT Haven

A very large crude tanker, MT Haven, carrying about 144,000 tons of crude oil, exploded off the coast of Genoa, Italy, in 1991. The tanker was unloading its

[217] Ibid.

[218] Mohit in Marine Environment (2021).

[219] The impact of the oil spill from the Gulf War and the resultant compensation were discussed in Sect. 10.4 of Chap. 10 of this book.

[220] Mohit in Marine Environment (2021).

230,000 tonnes of cargo to the Multedo floating platform at the time of the accident.[221] The explosion occurred when MT Haven was detached to allow the oil to be pumped into a central hold of the vessel from two side-holds after the transfer of 80,000 tonnes. Immediately after the explosion, the vessel sank, killing six people on board. In addition, 45 million gallons of oil were discharged into the Mediterranean waters, and the impact of the oil spill was seen for as many as 12 years following that.[222]

13.5.9.1.9 ABT Summer

On 28 May 1991, about 700 nautical miles from the coast of Angola, an oil tanker named ABT Summer witnessed an explosion on board and caught fire, expelling about 51 million gallons of oil into the sea. The oil slick resulting from the spill was measured around 80 square miles. The tanker burned for the next 3 days until it capsized, killing five of the 32 crew members aboard the vessel. No more information about this explosion is available since a major rescue operation did not immediately ensue, mainly because the oil spill occurred on the high seas. However, since the accident occurred on the high seas, most of the oil that leaked from the vessel is believed to have dispersed, minimising the impact on the marine environment.[223]

13.5.9.1.10 Exxon Valdez Oil Spill

One of the more widely known spills was the Exxon Valdez incident in Alaska. The ship ran aground and dumped a massive amount of oil into the ocean in March 1989. Despite efforts of scientists, managers and volunteers, over 400,000 seabirds, about 1000 sea otters and an immense number of fishes were killed.[224] In terms of the volume of oil discharged, the Exxon Valdez oil spill is the second largest in US waters after the Deepwater Horizon oil spill.

The accident occurred when the oil tanker Exxon Valdez ran aground on Prince William Sound's Bligh Reef in Alaska in March 1989. Out of the total capacity of 58 million gallons, 10.9 million gallons were moved into the Alaskan coastline after the accident. As a result, the ecosystem in the area was affected badly as it immediately killed over a lakh marine species, including around 250,000 seabirds, almost 2800 sea otters and 300 harbour seals, among others. Similarly, the Exxon Valdez oil spill affected the tourism and fishing industry in the region in the years to come.[225]

---

[221] Ibid.

[222] Ibid.

[223] Mohit in Marine Environment (2021).

[224] United Nations Environment Programme (2016).

[225] Mohit in Marine Environment (2021).

13.5.9.1.11 BP Deepwater Horizon Oil Spill Disaster

More than two decades after *Exxon Valdez,* an oil spill nearly 20 times bigger unfolded in the Gulf of Mexico. On 20 April 2010, the blowout of British Petroleum's (BP's) Macondo well and the sinking of the *Deepwater Horizon* mobile drilling platform resulted in the largest marine oil spill in history. For 16 agonising weeks, 210 million gallons of oil gushed from the deep ocean through the water column, into wetlands, and onto beaches.[226] The incident caused oil to spill from a seafloor oil gusher, leading to the explosion of the British Petroleum's (BP) oil rig, Deepwater Horizon, in its Macondo Prospect, off New Orleans in the United States of America (USA).[227]

The BP Deepwater Horizon accident killed 11 men working abroad on the rig and also resulted in an oil spill that continued for over 3 months it took to cap the well. An estimated 53,000 barrels were flowing into the Gulf of Mexico every day. The explosion caused extensive damage to the marine environment, including the ecosystem and property, resulting in economic loss to the affected region. According to the Centre for Biological Diversity, the oil spill killed over 82,000 birds; 25,900 marine mammals; 6000 sea turtles; and tens of thousands of fish, among others.[228]

The environmental cost of the BP Deepwater Horizon accident was enormous. Thousands of birds, mammals and sea turtles were plastered with leaked oil. There was speculation that the spike in cetacean strandings and deaths, which were recorded by the National Oceanic and Atmospheric Administration (NOAA) beginning in February 2010, was further exacerbated by the spill. The typical causes of such widespread fatalities, including morbillivirus and toxins from red tides, were ruled out, and there was an unusual incidence of Brucella infection in stranded dolphins, leading researchers to suspect that contaminants from the spill had made cetaceans more vulnerable to other environmental dangers.[229]

A December 2013 study of living dolphins in Barataria Bay, Louisiana, found that roughly half were extremely sick; many suffered from lung and adrenal disorders known to be linked to oil exposure. Some 1400 whales and dolphins had been found stranded by the end of 2015, a figure representing only a tiny percentage of the animals affected. Though the number of dead animals had begun to taper off, substantial decreases in dolphin fertility persisted. It was thought that the strandings represented the largest mortality event to occur in the Gulf of Mexico.[230]

Birds were particularly vulnerable to the oil's effects, and many perished from ingesting oil as they tried to clean themselves or because the substance interfered with their ability to regulate their body temperatures. The brown pelican, recently delisted as an endangered species, was among the species most affected. A 2014

---

[226] The Ocean Conservancy (2018).

[227] Eboh (2013).

[228] Eboh (2013).

[229] Pallardy (2021).

[230] Ibid.

study projected that perhaps 12% of the brown pelicans and more than 30% of the laughing gulls in the area hit by the spill had been wiped out. According to another 2014 study, up to 800,000 birds were thought to have died. Even individuals not directly contaminated by oil were affected. A 2012 study determined that white pelicans that had migrated from the gulf to Minnesota to breed were producing eggs that contained discernible amounts of compounds, which were traceable to the BP spill. Eggs containing traces of contaminants were found in Iowa and Illinois as well.[231]

Animals that were found alive in the wake of the spill were transported to rehabilitation centres and, after being cleaned and medically evaluated, were released into oil-free areas. Concerns about the offspring of sea turtles that nested on the gulf coasts of Alabama and Florida led wildlife officials to dig up thousands of eggs and hatch them in a warehouse for later release on the Atlantic coast. By late 2012, some 1700 turtles had been found dead. A long-term satellite tracking study released in May 2013 showed that the endangered Kemp's ridley sea turtle was likely severely affected as its preferred foraging territory was within the area damaged by the spill. It was estimated that up to 65,000 imperilled turtles died during 2010 alone, mostly as a result of oil contamination. It was also estimated that about 300,000 turtles, some of which were originally from breeding populations in other parts of the world, were in the region of the spill when it occurred, leading scientists to point out the global impacts of the disaster.[232]

When big oil spills hit the water, it has a devastating impact. The spill takes a toll on the marine ecosystem and people whose livelihoods are tied to the sea. Almost 30 years after the *Exxon Valdez* spill, there is still lingering oil on some beaches of Prince William Sound. Wildlife ranging from seabirds to killer whales still have not recovered from the spill. The commercial fishery for Pacific herring remains closed. The *Exxon Valdez* spill left deep wounds in Alaska that have yet to heal completely.[233]

In the Gulf of Mexico incident, scientists are still evaluating the long-term impacts of the *Deepwater Horizon* spill, but the immediate effects were awful. An area ten times the size of Rhode Island was closed to fishing, Gulf seafood lost market share, tourism tanked and coastal home property values fell. Residual oil in seafloor sediments poses a long-term threat to the Gulf ecosystem. The BP *Deepwater Horizon* disaster was rightfully labelled an injury to the entire northern Gulf ecosystem.[234]

What Then Must We Learn from the Past? The *Exxon Valdez* and *Deepwater Horizon* spills taught us that a big oil spill is all but impossible to clean up effectively. The mechanical recovery of spilt oil using booms and skimmers is

[231] Ibid.

[232] Pallardy (2021).

[233] The Ocean Conservancy (2018).

[234] Ibid.

woefully inefficient even under the best of conditions and will likely not work at all in icy Arctic waters or when it settles on the seafloor. Other forms of 'clean-up' involve burning the spilt oil, which generates huge plumes of thick black smoke, or using chemical dispersants, which can have their own adverse impacts on the marine ecosystem.[235]

13.5.9.2 Oil Spill Incidents in Nigeria and the Impact on the Marine Environment

There has been a series of oil spill incidents in Nigeria. Nigeria, a major oil producer, is not spared of the incident of oil spillage. In fact, hundreds of oil spills are reported in Nigeria every year, which are ruining the environment and putting human lives at risk. A new report from Amnesty International says spills in the Niger Delta are the result of pipeline corrosion, maintenance issues, equipment failure, sabotage and theft.[236] Other main sources of oil spill on the Niger Delta are vandalisation of the oil pipelines by the local inhabitants, ageing of the pipelines, oil blowouts from the flow stations, cleaning of oil tankers on the high seas and disposal of used oil into the drains by the roadside mechanics.[237]

According to Premium Times online Newspaper, Mohammad Abubakar, the Nigerian Minister of Environment, at that time, citing the National Oil Spill Detection Agency (NOSDRA) data, disclosed that the total number of oil spills recorded from 2015 to March 2021 is 4919, the number of oil spills cost by collation is 308, by the operational maintenance is 106, while sabotage is 3628 and yet to be determined 70, giving the total number of oil spills on the environment to 235,206 barrels of oil.[238]

The Minister,[239] while citing data from the Nigeria Natural Resources Charter, revealed that Nigeria lost approximately 4.75 trillion on oil activities in the 4 years between 2015 and 2018 and stated that 'several statistics have emphasised Nigeria as the most notorious country in the world for oil spills, loosing roughly 400,000 barrels per day'.[240]

In Nigeria's Niger Delta, the impact of environmental pollution arising from oil spill is so rampant that it had caused widespread socio-economic conflicts in the region, culminating in a recent trend tagged as the 'Niger Delta Militancy'. The Niger Delta region is an ecologically sensitive region that is rich in fisheries and other aquatic resources. However, oil production activities have in recent times

[235] The Ocean Conservancy (2018).

[236] The Christian Science Monitor (2013).

[237] Ibid.

[238] Premium Times (2021).

[239] Ibid.

[240] The second country is Mexico, which has reported only 5000 to 10,000 barrels per day, thus a difference of about 3900%.

reduced the yield of aquatic resources from these regions. The implication of this is the dislocation of the local people from their traditional occupation, which has led to violent resistance across the region.[241] Discussed below are some of the examples of oil spills in Nigeria and their devastating effects on the marine environment in the country.[242]

13.5.9.2.1 Funima 5 Blowout

In the Funima 5 blowout at Bonny, Nigeria, on 17 January 1980, over 400,000 barrels of crude oil were spilt. It caused the pollution of 23,390.9 km^2 of estuaries, lagoons, lakes, rivers, rivulets, creeks and other watercourses. It rendered 55 sources of drinking water unsafe for human consumption. The spills also affected 230,000 people, of which there were 180 deaths, and caused damage estimated at ₦554,494,658, out of which a total sum of ₦12.5 million was paid as compensation. These were in addition to the dislocation of social and economic activities in the Sangana area.[243]

13.5.9.2.2 Bonga Oil Spill

Another major incident of marine pollution in Nigeria arising from oil spills is the Shell Bonga oil spill. The spill emanated from a facility belonging to Shell Petroleum Development Company Ltd on 20 December 2011, during which 40,000 barrels of crude oil spilt into the Atlantic Ocean. The oil spill affected the fishers, whose source of livelihood is the ocean waters.[244] The announcement by the National Oil Spill Detection and Response Agency (NOSDRA) ordering the fishers out of the waters led to the suspension of their activities. Compliance with the stay-away directive by the NOSDRA from 22 December 2011 to 23 April 2012 caused hardship and loss of income for some 30,000 fishers across the five states of the Niger Delta.[245]

The communities alleged that harmful chemical dispersants, such as Slickgone NS, Corexit 9500 and 9527 and BioSolve, among others, used by Shell Nigeria Exploration and Production Company Limited to break and disperse the spilt crude oil on 20 December 2011 at Bonga field had spread to fishing areas, where they became the cause of diseases that were afterwards prevalent in the communities.[246]

[241] Premium Times (2021).

[242] There had been a series of not-too-large spills in the region as oil spills occur at every facet of the industry—from exploration and exploitation to refining and use.

[243] Shell Petroleum Development Company (1995), p. 6.

[244] United Nations General Assembly Human Rights Council (2014), A/HRC/26/NGO/100.

[245] Ibid.

[246] Ibid.

The common ailments affecting the communities included mental disorders; hypertension; eye irritations; nose, throat and skin lesions; vomiting and rectal bleeding; liver and kidney damage; short-term memory loss and confusion; respiratory problems; miscarriages; and blood in the urine.[247] Following this Bonga oil spill, the Federal Government of Nigeria, through NOSDRA, imposed a US$ 5 billion fine on Shell Petroleum Development Company.[248]

13.5.9.2.3 The Ogoni Oil Spill Clean-Up

The impact of the oil spill in Ogoniland requires special attention in terms of both magnitude and the international attention it has attracted. Ogoniland has a tragic history of pollution from oil spills and oil well fires. After decades of oil exploration and production in Ogoniland, with the attendant environmental dislocation, restiveness, litigation and disruption of oil production and people's life, the Nigerian government, in July 2006, invited the United Nations Environment Programme (UNEP) to conduct an independent assessment of the environment and the public health impacts of oil contamination in Ogoniland in the Niger Delta, as well as options for remediation. On 4 August 2011, UNEP submitted its report tagged *Environmental Assessment of Ogoniland Report.*[249]

The Report revealed the nature and extent of oil contamination in Ogoniland as it covered contaminated land, groundwater, surface water, sediment, vegetation, air pollution, public health, industry practices and institutional issues and represents the best available understanding of what had happened to the environment of Ogoniland and the corresponding implications for affected populations.[250]

On contaminated soil and groundwater, the Report found that the pollution of soil by petroleum hydrocarbons in Ogoniland is extensive in land areas, sediments and swampland. Most of the contamination is from crude oil, although contamination by refined products was found at three locations. 'At two-thirds of the contaminated land sites close to oil industry facilities which were assessed in detail, the soil contamination exceeds Nigerian national standards, as set out in the Environmental Guidelines and Standards for the Petroleum Industries in Nigeria (EGASPIN).'[251] 'The most serious case of groundwater contamination is at Nisisioken Ogale, in Eleme LGA, close to a Nigerian National Petroleum Company product pipeline

[247] United Nations General Assembly Human Rights Council (2014).

[248] Vanguard News Paper (2012).

[249] United Nations Environment Programme (2011).

[250] Ibid., 8.

[251] Ibid., 9.

where an 8 cm layer of refined oil was observed floating on the groundwater which serves the community wells.'[252]

A report on the impact of oil spills on vegetation showed that oil pollution, in many intertidal creeks, had left mangroves denuded of leaves and stems, leaving roots coated in a bitumen-like substance, sometimes 1 cm or more thick. Mangroves are spawning areas for fish and nurseries for juvenile fish, and the extensive pollution of these areas is impacting the fish life cycle. To this end, any crops in areas directly impacted by oil spills were damaged, and root crops, such as cassava, became unusable. When farming recommenced, plants generally showed signs of stress, and yields were reportedly lower than in non-impacted areas.[253] Without proper rehabilitation, former mangrove areas that have been converted to bare ground are being colonised by invasive species, such as *nipa* palm (which appears to be more resistant to heavy hydrocarbon pollution than native vegetation). Compounding the vegetation problem, when an oil spill occurs on land, fires often break out, killing vegetation and creating a crust over the land, making remediation or re-vegetation difficult.[254]

In terms of surface water, the UNEP investigation found that the surface water throughout the creeks contains hydrocarbons. Floating layers of oil vary from thick black oil to thin sheens. The highest reading of dissolved hydrocarbon in the water column, of 7420 μg/L, was detected at Ataba-Otokroma, bordering the Gokana and Andoni local government areas (LGAs).[255]

The Report[256] found that fish tend to leave polluted areas in search of cleaner water, and fishermen must therefore also move to less contaminated areas in search of fish. When encountered in known polluted areas, fishermen reported that they were going to fishing grounds further upstream or downstream. In this regard, the fishery sector suffered due to the destruction of fish habitat in the mangroves and the highly persistent contamination of many of the creeks, making them unsuitable for fishing. The result was that where a number of entrepreneurs had set up fish farms in or close to the creeks, their businesses had been ruined by an ever-present layer of floating oil.[257] Even the wetlands around Ogoniland were found to be highly degraded and facing disintegration.[258]

On the issue of the impact of the oil pollution on public health, the Report had it that the Ogoni community is exposed to petroleum hydrocarbons in outdoor air and drinking water, sometimes at elevated concentrations. They are also exposed through dermal contacts from contaminated soil, sediments and surface water.[259]

[252] United Nations Environment Programme (2011), p. 127.

[253] Ibid., 167.

[254] Ibid.

[255] Ibid., 169.

[256] Ibid., 175.

[257] United Nations Environment Programme (2011).

[258] Ibid.

[259] United Nations Environment Programme (2011), p. 183.

Hydrocarbon contamination was found in water taken from 28 wells at ten communities adjacent to contaminated sites. At seven wells, the samples were at least 1000 times higher than the Nigerian drinking water standard of 3 μg/L.[260]

Benzene was also detected in all air samples at concentrations ranging from 0.155 to 48.2 $\mu g/m^3$. Approximately 10% of detected benzene concentrations in Ogoniland were higher than the concentrations that the World Health Organization (WHO) and the United States Environmental Protection Agency (EPA) report as corresponding to 1 in 10,000 cancer risks. Many of the benzene concentrations detected in Ogoniland were similar to those measured elsewhere in the world, given the prevalence of fuel use and other sources of benzene. However, the findings showed that some benzene concentrations in Ogoniland were higher than those being measured in more economically developed regions, where benzene concentrations are declining because of efforts to reduce benzene exposure.[261]

13.6 Summary

The importance of the marine environment cannot be overemphasised. However, in recent years, an unrelenting siege has been unleashed on the marine environment through various forms of pollution that resulted from human activities. Preventing the pollution of the marine environment, especially stopping it before it starts, is so important. The reason is that preventing pollution is in the best interest of the environment, the ecosystems, marine-based economies and all people who live, work and earn their livelihood from marine living resources. To this end, there must be appropriate awareness of marine pollution and its impact on the marine ecosystem. Balanced information on the sources and harmful effects of marine pollution needs to become part of general public awareness through environmental education.

References

Adewale MB (2015) Harnessing economic growth through maritime sector. The Guardian Business, 25 August 2015. https://www.guardian.ng/business-services/harnessing-economic-growth-through-maritime-sector/. Accessed 27 July 2023

Ahnert A, Borowski C (2000) Environmental risk assessment of anthropogenic activity in the deep-sea. J Aquat Ecosyst Stress Recover 7(4):299–315. https://doi.org/10.1023/A:1009963912171

Akankali JA, Jamabo NA (2015) in Akankali JA, Elenwo EI, Sources of marine pollution on Nigerian coastal resources: an overview. Open J Mar Sci 5:226. http://www.scirp.org/journal/ojms. Accessed 25 July 2023

[260] Ibid.

[261] Ibid.

Akankali JA, Oronsaye JAO (2015) in Akankali JA, Elenwo EI, Sources of marine pollution on Nigerian coastal resources: an overview. Open J Mar Sci 5:226. http://www.scirp.org/journal/ojms. Accessed 25 July 2023

Arctic Network for the Support of the Indigenous Peoples of the Russian Arctic (2006) Indigenous peoples of the Russian North, Siberia and Far East: Nivkh. http://library.arcticportal.org/32/. Accessed 22 Mar 2023

Batrakova N et al (2014) Chemical and LLK, physical transformations of mercury in the ocean: a review. Ocean Sci 10:1047–1063

Boszke L et al (2002) Some aspects of speciation of mercury in a water environment. Environ Stud 11(4):285–298

Bryce E (2021) Twenty plastic-busting inventions to clean our rivers and seas, China Dialogue Ocean, 10 May 2021, https://chinadialogueocean.net/en/conservation/17153-twenty-plastic-busting-inventions-to-clean-our-rivers-and-seas/#:~:text, accessed 20 July 2023

Burkholder JM et al (2001) Bivalve shellfish aquaculture and eutrophication. In: Shumway SE (ed) Shellfish aquaculture and the environment. Wiley, New York

Clarkson TW, Magos L (2006) The toxicology of mercury and its chemical compounds. Crit Rev Toxicol 36(8):609

Dublin-Green, Hughes H (2015) in Akankali JA, Elenwo EI, Sources of marine pollution on Nigerian coastal resources: an overview. Open J Mar Sci 5:226. http://www.scirp.org/journal/ojms. Accessed 25 July 2023

Earle N (2005) in Jasny M et al, Sounding the depths: supertankers, sonar, and the rise of undersea noise. Natural Resources Defense Council Report, November 2005. https://www.nrdc.org. Accessed 15 May 2023

Eboh M (2013) US proposes $16bn settlement with BP over Gulf spill. http://www.vanguardngr.com/2013/02. Accessed 24 May 2023

Enger ED, Smith BF (2002) Environmental science, a study of interrelationships, 8th edn. McGraw Hill, Boston

Eureka Alert (2008). Addressing the nitrogen cascade. https://www.eurekalert.org/news-releases/584461. Accessed 27 July 2023

Farmer A (1998) Managing environmental pollution, 1st edn Routledge, London. ISBN: 9780415145152. https://www.routledge.com/Managing-Environmental-Pollution/Farmer/p/book/9780415145152. Accessed 20 July 2023

Food and Agricultural Organisation (FAO) (2015) FAO global capture production database, updated to 2013 – summary information. https://www.fao.org/3/i4883e/i4883e.pdf. Accessed 13 June 2023

G&O Maritime Group (2021) Gertsen and Olufsen bioreactors. https://bioreactors.gomaritimegroup.com/products/. Accessed 21 Mar 2023

Gerlach SA (2005) Marine pollution. Springer, Berlin

Goudie A (2005) The human impact on the natural environment, 6th edn. Blackwell, Oxford

Grigg RW, Kiwala RS (1970) Some ecological effects of discharged wastes on marine life. California Department of Fish and Game 56:145–155

Halfar J, Fujita RM (2007) Ecology: danger of deep-sea mining. Science 316(5827):987. https://doi.org/10.1126/science.1138289. PMID 17510349

Hamblin JD (2008) Poison in the well: radioactive waste in the oceans at the dawn of the nuclear age. Rutgers University, New York

Hawaii Newspaper (2005) Midway's Albatross population stable. The Honolulu Advertiser, 17 January 2005

Ike G (1991) The Nigerian oil industry from 1958. Starledger Communications, Lagos

IMO (2009) Second IMO greenhouse gas study. https://www.imo.org. Accessed 25 Mar 2023

Institute of Acoustics (2014) Ross on ocean underwater ambient noise. Institute of Acoustics Bulletin, St Albans, p 18

Intergovernmental Panel on Climate Change (IPCC) (2007) Observations: oceanic climate change and sea level. In: Climate change 2007: the physical science basis. Contribution of Working

Group I to the Fourth Assessment Report of the Intergovernmental Panel on Climate Change. www.ipccc.org/assessment report. Accessed 25 Mar 2023

International Maritime Organisation (IMO) (2008a) IMO targets greenhouse gas emissions. Petromedia Group, London, https://sustainableshipping.com/2008-06-17. Accessed 25 March 2023

International Maritime Organisation (IMO) (2008b) IMO Resolution MSC 255(84), Adoption of the Code of the International Standards and Recommended Practices for a Safety Investigation into a Marine Casualty or Marine Incident (Casualty Investigation Code) was adopted on 16 May 2008. http://www.cdn.imo.org. Accessed 28 May 2023

International Oil Pollution Compensation Funds (2022) Providing compensation for oil pollution damage resulting from spills of persistent oil from tankers 1971 and 1992 funds: summary of incidents up 2013. http://www.iopcfunds.org. Accessed 10 June 2023

Joint Group of Experts on the Scientific Aspects of Marine Pollution (1989) IMO/FAO/UNESCO/WMO/WHO/IAEA/UN/UNEP and World Health Organization, The atmospheric input of trace species to the world ocean, World Health Organisation. https://apps.who.int/iris/handle/10665/62877. Accessed 21 July 2023

Kirk JI et al (2012) Mercury in Arctic marine ecosystems: sources, pathways and exposure. Environ Resour 119:64–87

Lamborg CH et al (2014) A global ocean inventory of anthropogenic mercury based on water column measurements. Nature 512:65–68

Lindahl O et al (2005) Improving marine water quality by mussel farming: a profitable solution for Swedish Society. Ambio 34(2):131–138

Mangor K et al (2017) Shoreline management guidelines. DHI. https://www.dhigroup.com/marine-water/ebook-shoreline-management-guidelines. Accessed 22 June 2023

Marine Accident Investigation Branch (MAIB) (2019) Interim report on the investigation of the explosion and fire on board the chemical tanker Stolt Groenland on 28 September 2019, Ulsan. December. www.gov.uk/maib. Accessed 20 July 2023

Marine Insight Network (2021a) MV X-Press Pearl incident: container ship X-Press Pearl disaster: petition filed demanding compensation for fishermen. https://www.marineinsight.com/shipping-news/container-ship-x-press-pearl-disaster-petition-filed-demanding-compensation-for-fishermen/. Last updated 24 June 2021. Accessed 26 June 2023

Marine Insight Network (2021b) Singapore-bound container vessel catches fire in the Indian Ocean. https://www.marineinsight.com/shipping-news/singapore-bound-container-vessel-catches-fire-in-the-indian-ocean/. Last updated 25 June 2021. Accessed 26 June 2023

Mason RP et al (2012) Mercury biogeochemical cycling in the ocean and policy implications. Environ Resour 119:101–117

Meinesz A (2003) Deep sea invasion: the impact of invasive species PBS. NOVA: 12

Merchant Marine General Directorate Department of Maritime Casualty Investigations (2014) Report on the investigation of the collision of M.V. "CAPE MED" at Algeciras on the 30 May 2014. https://www.mitma.gob.es/recursos_mfom/amp_capemed_web.pdf. Accessed 19 July 2023

MI News Network (2021). Shipping News: MV Golden Ray shipwreck spills oil onto Georgia Beach, further delaying its removal. https://www.marineinsight.com/shipping-news/photos-mv-golden-ray-shipwreck-spills-oil-onto-georgia-beach-further-delaying-its-removal/? Last updated 5 Aug 2021. Accessed 7 Aug 2023

Milkov AV (2004) Global estimates of hydrate-bound gas in marine sediments: how much is really out there? Earth-Sci Rev 66(3–4):183–197

Mohit in Marine Environment (2021) 11 major oil spills of the maritime world. https://www.marineinsight.com/environment/11-major-oil-spills-of-the-maritime-world/. Last updated 3 Mar 2021. Accessed 14 May 2023

Monaco Declaration and Ocean Acidification (2008) A summary for policymakers from the second symposium on the ocean in a high-CO2 world. Intergovernmental Oceanographic Commission of UNESCO, International Geosphere-Biosphere Programme, Marine Environment

Laboratories (MEL) of the International Atomic Energy Agency, Scientific Committee on Oceanic Research
Moore C (2002) Great pacific garbage patch. News-Press, Santa-Barbara
Nathanson JA (2023) Pollution. Encyclopedia Britannica, 15 August 2023. https://www.britannica.com/science/pollution-environment. Accessed 18 Aug 2023
National Geographic Society (2023) Noise pollution. https://education.nationalgeographic.org/resource/noise-pollution/. Accessed 1 Aug 2023
National Oceanic and Atmospheric Administration (NOAA) (2023) What is the biggest source of pollution in the ocean? https://oceanservice.noaa.gov/facts/pollution.html. Updated 18 Jan 2023. Accessed 22 July 2023
National Research Council, Committee on Shipboard Wastes, Clean Ships, Clean Ports, Clean Oceans (1995) Controlling garbage and plastic wastes at sea. National Academy, New York, Tables 2–3, pp 38–39
Nigerian Environmental Study/Action Team (NEST) (1991) Nigeria's threatened environment, a national profile. NEST, Ibadan
Oskin B (2014) The deep ocean traps mercury, study finds. Live Science, 6 August 2014. http://www.livescience.com/47222-deep-ocean-traps-mercury-pollution.html. Accessed 22 July 2023
Pallardy R (2021) Deepwater horizon oil spill. https://www.britannica.com/event/Deepwater-Horizon-oil-spill/environmentalcosts. Last updated 3 Sept 2021. Accessed 3 Aug 2023
Panetta LE (2008) America's living oceans: charting a course for sea change. Pew Oceans Commission: 22
Peirce JJ et al (1998) Environmental pollution and control, 4th edn. Butterworth-Heinemann, Boston
Pimentel D et al (2005) Update on the environmental and economic costs associated with alien-invasive species in the United States. Ecol Econ 52(3):273–288. https://doi.org/10.1016/j.ecolecon. Accessed 25 Mar 2023
Podsadam J (2001) Lost sea cargo: beach bounty or junk? National Geographic. www.nationalgeographic.com. Accessed 21 July 2023
Premium Times (2021) Nigeria records 4,919 oil spills in 6 years, 4.5trn barrels stolen in 4 years. Premium Times, 16 July 2021. https://www.premiumtimesng.com/news/headlines/471901-nigeria-records-4919-oil-spills-in-6-years-4-5trn-barrels-stolen-in-4-years-minister.html. Accessed 10 Aug 2023
Prideaux G (2017) Technical support information to the CMS family guidelines on environmental impact assessments for marine noise-generating activities' convention on migratory species of wild animals, Bonn. https://www.un.org/depts/los/general_assembly/noise/noise_files/CMS_tsi.pdf. Accessed 22 June 2023
Qureshi A et al (2010) Photoreactions of mercury in surface ocean water: gross reaction kinetics and possible pathways. Environ Sci Technol 44(2):644–649
Ralph WT (2015) in Akankali JA, Elenwo EI, Sources of marine pollution on Nigerian coastal resources: an overview. Open J Mar Sci 5:226. http://www.scirp.org/journal/ojms. Accessed 25 July 2023
Raven JA et al (2005). Ocean acidification due to increasing atmospheric carbon dioxide. Policy document 12/05. The Royal Society, London, ISBN: 0 85403 617 2. https://www.royalsoc.ac.uk. Accessed 19 July 2023
Reilly SB et al (2009). "Eubalaena glacialis" IUCN red list of threatened species. Version 2009.1, International Union for Conservation of Nature. https://www.iucnredlist.org. Accessed 26 May 2023
Rios LM et al (2007) Persistent organic pollutants carried by synthetic polymers in the ocean environment. Mar Pollut Bull 54(8):1230–1237
Selin NE (2009) Global biogeochemical cycling of mercury: a review. Annu Rev Environ Resour 34:43–63
Shell Petroleum Development Company (1995) Nigeria brief: the environment. S P D C, Lagos

Sulton JC, Shun L (2015) in Akankali JA, Elenwo EI, Sources of marine pollution on Nigerian coastal resources: an overview. Open J Mar Sci 5:226. http://www.scirp.org/journal/ojms. Accessed 25 July 2023

The Christian Science Monitor (2013) What causes oil spill in Nigeria? https://www.csmonitor.com/Environment/Energy-Voices/2013/1111/What-s-causing-Nigeria-s-oil-spills. Accessed 10 Aug 2023

The Conversation (2015) Mercury pollution. https://theconversation.com/we-created-a-new-material-from-orange-peel-that-can-clean-up-mercury-pollution-49355. Accessed 15 May 2023

The Ocean Conservancy (2002) Cruise control. A report on how cruise ships affect the marine environment. 13 May 2002. http://www.cruiseresearch.org/Cruise%20Control.pdf. Accessed 15 July 2023

The Ocean Conservancy (2018) Exxon Valdez: 29 years later. https://oceanconservancy.org/blog/2018/03/22/exxon-valdez-29-years-later/. Accessed 19 May 2023

Thevenon F et al (eds) (2014) Plastic debris in the ocean: the characterization of marine plastics and their environmental impacts, situation analysis report. IUCN, Gland. ISBN: 978-2-8317-1696-1. https://doi.org/10.2305/IUCN.CH.2014.03.en. https://portals.iucn.org/library/sites/library/files/documents/2014-067.pdf. Accessed 22 July 2023

UNEP (2011) Environmental Assessment of Ogoniland Report. https://www.unep.org/explore-topics/disasters-conflicts/where-we-work/nigeria/environmental-assessment-ogoniland-report. Accessed 10 June 2023

UNEP (2013) Global mercury assessment: sources, emissions, releases and environmental transport. UNEP, Geneva

United Nations Environment Programme (UNEP) (2002) Global Mercury Assessment (Geneva, 2002). http://www.unep.org/gc/gc22/Document/UNEP-GC22-INF3.pdf. Accessed 22 July 2023

United Nations General Assembly Human Rights Council (2014) Twenty-sixth session Agenda item 3: promotion and protection of all human rights, civil, political, economic, social and cultural rights, including the right to development. A/HRC/26/NGO/100 26 May 2014. https://www.ecoi.net/en/file/local/1245905/1930_1403101174_g1404473.pdf. Accessed 10 Aug 2023

United States Department of Agriculture (USDA) National Invasive Species Information Centre (2020) Ballast water. http://www.invasivespeciesinfor.gov. Accessed 23 Mar 2023

United States Geological Survey (2010) Coral Mortality and African Dust. https://www.coastal.er.usgs.gov/african/dust. Accessed 25 May 2023

United Nations Environment Programme (2016) http://www.unep.org/dewa/giwa/publications/finalreport/. Accessed 23 May 2023

Vanderlaan SM, Taggart T (2007) Vessel collisions with whales: the probability of lethal injury based on vessel speed. Marine Mammal Science. https://www.nmfs.noaa.gov. Accessed 25 May 2023

Vanguard News Paper (2012) A commentary on the US$5 billion Fine imposed on Shell Nigeria exploration and production company by NOSDRA. Vanguard News Paper, 24 July 2012. vanguardngr.com/forum/topics/a-commentary-on-the-5-billion-imposed-on-snepco-by-nosdra. Accessed 10 Aug 2023

Walsh Medical Media (2023) Coastal region/coastal area. J Coast Zone Manag. https://www.walshmedicalmedia.com/scholarly/coastal-region-coastal-area-journals-articles-ppts-list-791.html. Accessed 27 July 2023

Wang X et al (2015) J Colloid Interface Sci 453:244–251

Ward-Geiger LI et al (2005) Characterization of ship traffic in right whale critical habitat. Coast Manag 33:263–278. https://doi.org/10.1080/08920750590951965. Accessed 21 May 2023

Washington State Department of Ecology (2008) Control of toxic chemicals in Puget sound, Phase 2: Development of simple numerical models. https://www.ecy.wa.gov/programs/wq/pstoxics/index.html. Accessed 20 July 2023

Watson T (2004) citing Blooming I, Ship pollution clouds USA's skies. USA Today. https://www.usatoday.com/news/nation/2004-08-30-ship-pollution_x.htm. Accessed 24 May 2023

Weiner JG et al (2006) Ecotoxicology of mercury, 2nd edn. CRC, Boca Raton
Weiss KR (2006) Plague of plastic chokes the seas. Los Angeles Times, 2 August 2006. https://www.latimes.com/world/la-me-ocean2aug02-story.html. Accessed 19 July 2023
Young E (2003) Copper decimates coral reef spawning. New Scientist, 18 November 2003. https://www.newsscientist.com. Accessed 20 July 2023
Zabbey N et al (2019) Nigerian coastal environments (Chapter 36). In: World seas: an environmental evaluation, vol 1: Europe, the Americas and West Africa, pp 835–854. https://www.sciencedirect.com/science/article/pii/B9780128050682000425. Accessed 20 July 2023

Chapter 14
Controlling Pollution and Damage to the Marine Environment

Abstract The marine environment encompasses the world's seas and oceans. Humans have benefited from the seas and oceans in a variety of ways. The maritime environment is one of the global commons and must be protected by the international community. Over the years, efforts for the protection of the marine environment have been made. Discussions in the chapter focus on the use of both international and domestic legal instruments established thereto to control and manage the pollution of the marine environment.

14.1 Prevention of Oil Discharges and Air Pollution from Ships

A number of international legal instruments have been put in place to combat the pollution of the marine environment, especially from ships. These include:

(1) The International Convention for the Prevention of Oil Pollution 1969
(2) The International Convention for the Prevention of Pollution from Ships 1973 as modified by the Protocol of 1978 (MARPOL 73/78)

14.1.1 International Convention for the Prevention of Oil Pollution (OILPOL) 1969

In 1954, under the auspices of the International Maritime Organization (IMO), a convention known as the International Convention for the Prevention of Pollution of the Sea by Oil was held on 12 May 1954 in London. The Convention came into force on 26 July 1958. This Convention laid the foundation for more defined conventions on the subject—to combat oil pollution and protect the marine environment.

In 1969, the International Convention Relating to Intervention on the High Sea in Cases of Oil Pollution Casualties was adopted. It empowered coastal states to take such measures on the high seas as may be necessary to prevent, mitigate or eliminate

E. Onyeabor, *Environmental Law*, https://doi.org/10.1007/978-3-031-68956-7_14

grave and imminent danger to their coastlines or related interests from pollution or the threat of pollution of the seas by oil. This Convention was adopted following the *Torrey Canyon* disaster on 18 March 1967, in which 120,000 tons of crude oil spilt off the coast of Britain, causing widespread damage to the British coastline and to marine life and eventually polluting the coast of France.[1]

The *Torrey Canyon* disaster led to the Brussels Conference of 1969 and the adoption of two new conventions.[2]

14.1.2 The International Convention for the Prevention of Pollution from Ships 1973 as Modified by the Protocol of 1978 (MARPOL 73/78)

The International Convention for the Prevention of Pollution from Ships 1973 as modified by the Protocol of 1978 is one of the most important international marine environmental conventions covering the prevention of pollution of the marine environment by ships from operational or accidental causes. It was developed by the International Maritime Organization with the objective of minimising the pollution of oceans and seas, including dumping and oil and air pollution.[3]

The original MARPOL was adopted on 2 November 1973 but did not come into force at the date of signing. The current MARPOL is a combination of MARPOL 1973 and the MARPOL Protocol of 1978,[4] hence MARPOL 73/78.[5] It entered into force on 2 October 1983. As of January 2018, 156 states are parties to the convention, being flag states of 99.42% of the world's shipping tonnage.[6] Under the Convention, all ships flagged under countries that are signatories to MARPOL are subject to its requirements, regardless of where they sail, and member nations are responsible for vessels registered on their national ship registry.[7]

[1] Other major oil spills that triggered international efforts at marine protection are the *Amoco Cadiz* in 1978, *Exxon Valdez* in 1989, *Erika* in 2001 and *Prestige* in 2003, among others.

[2] The 1969 Intervention Convention and the 1969 Civil Liability Convention (CLC); the latter has been the subject of three amending protocols, most recently by the 1992 Liability Protocol. With the coming into force of the 1992 Protocol, the 1969 CLC is now known as the International Convention on Civil Liability for Oil Pollution Damage 1992 (CLC 1992). These conventions were discussed in Chap. 15 under liability for damage to the marine environment.

[3] International Maritime Organization (IMO) (2021).

[4] This was adopted at the Conference on Tanker Safety and Pollution Prevention held in February 1978 in response to a spate of tanker accidents in 1976–1977.

[5] 73/78 short forms for the years 1973 and 1978.

[6] IMO (2021).

[7] Copeland (2008).

14.1.2.1 Provisions of MARPOL on Oil Pollution Discharges and Air Pollution

MARPOL is divided into 6 annexes and their appendix according to various categories of pollutants, each of which deals with the regulation of a particular group of ship emissions for controlling and eliminating marine pollution.[8] Of relevance to this segment of the discussions are Annexes I, II, III and VI.

MARPOL Annex I deals with regulations for the prevention of pollution by oil. It came into force on 2 October 1983[9] and comprises 11 chapters, which together contain 47 regulations for the prevention of pollution by oil. It regulates the control and prevention of any oil discharge from ships, intentionally or accidentally, or the discharge of oil into the ocean environment.

To achieve this objective, it incorporates the oil discharge criteria prescribed in the 1969 amendments to the 1954 International Convention for the Prevention of Pollution of the Sea by Oil (OILPOL). It specifies tanker design features that are intended to minimise oil discharge into the ocean during ship operations and in the case of accidents. It provides regulations with regard to the treatment of engine room bilge water (OWS) for all large commercial vessels and ballast and tank cleaning waste (ODME). It also introduces the concept of 'special sea areas (PPSE)', which are considered to be at risk of pollution by oil. The discharge of oil within them has been completely outlawed, with a few minimal exceptions.[10]

The first half of MARPOL Annex I deals with engine room waste. There are various generations of technologies and equipment that have been developed to prevent waste, such as oily water separators (OWS), oil content meters (OCM) and port reception facilities.[11] To this end, Chapter 3 deals with the requirements for machinery spaces for all ships and lists down the requirements under Regulations 12 to 17, so that the engine room and other machinery spaces are compliant with MARPOL Annex 1.[12]

The second part of MARPOL Annex I has more to do with cleaning cargo areas and tanks. Oil discharge monitoring equipment (ODME) is a very important technology mentioned in MARPOL Annex I that has greatly helped improve sanitation in these areas. The Oil Record Book is another integral part of MARPOL Annex I. The Oil Record Book helps crew members log and keep track of oily wastewater discharges, among other things.[13] Thus, Regulation 14[14] set the requirements for oil filtration equipment on board ships for discharging engine room bilges or ballast

[8] Raunek (2022).

[9] The Revised Annex I entered into force on 1 January 2007.

[10] IMO (2021).

[11] *Ibid.*

[12] Marine Insight (2022).

[13] MARPOL Annex 1, chapter 1.

[14] Ibid.

water from fuel oil (FO) tanks, followed by Regulation 15,[15] which restricts the discharge of treated bilges in special areas.

Regulation 16[16] explains the requirement of segregating oil and water ballast, which is carried in the fuel tank of the ship, while Regulation 17[17] lists down the need for a compliant oil record book for machinery space in oil tankers of 150 GT and above and other ships of 400 GT and above.

In addition, Chapter 8[18] deals with the prevention of pollution that may happen during cargo oil in between tankers at sea, also known as ship-to-ship transfer (STS). Regulation 40 provides the scope of application for this chapter, and Regulation 41 lists down the rules on safety and environmental protection during STS operations, followed by Regulation 42, which sets forth the notifications that need to be provided by the ship to the port state and all the other parties involved in the operation.

MARPOL Annex II regulates the control of pollution by noxious liquid substances in bulk, intentionally or accidentally. Annex II comprises ten chapters, which together contain 22 regulations and which came into force on 6 April 1987.[19] It details the discharge criteria for the elimination of pollution by noxious liquid substances carried in large quantities. It divides substances into and introduces detailed operational standards and measures. The discharge of pollutants is allowed only to reception facilities, with certain concentrations and conditions. No matter what, no discharge of residues containing pollutants is permitted within 12 nautical miles (22 km) of the nearest land. Stricter restrictions apply to 'special areas'.[20]

Annex II also covers the International Bulk Chemical (IBC) Code in conjunction with Chapter 7 of the International Convention for the Safety of Life at Sea 1974 (or 'SOLAS Convention').[21] Previously, chemical tankers constructed before 1 July 1986 must comply with the requirements of the Code for the Construction and Equipment of Ships Carrying Dangerous Chemicals in Bulk (or 'BCH Code'). The IBC Code provides an international standard for the safe carriage by sea of dangerous and noxious liquid chemicals in bulk. The Marine Environment Protection Committee (MEPC)[22] adopted, in 2019, IMO Resolution MEPC.318 (74) containing amendments to several chapters of the IBC Code, especially amendments to the International Code for the Construction and Equipment of Ships Carrying

[15] Ibid.

[16] MARPOL Annex 1, chapter 1.

[17] Ibid.

[18] Raunek (2022).

[19] Revised Annex II entered into force on 1 January 2007.

[20] Raunek (2022).

[21] This chapter deals with the prevention of pollution arising from an incident involving noxious liquid substances. SOLAS is discussed below (section 14.2.1).

[22] The functions of MEPC include the control and prevention of ship-source pollution covered by the MARPOL treaty, including oil, chemicals carried in bulk, sewage, garbage and emissions from ships, including air pollutants and greenhouse gas emissions.

Dangerous Chemicals in Bulk (Amendments to the IBC CODE Chapters 1, 15, 16, 17, 18, 19 and 21).[23] This followed concerns raised about the environmental impact of permissible discharges from tankers carrying noxious liquid substances (NLS). To this end, MEPC 74, in May 2019, adopted, by way of IMO Resolution MEPC.315 (74), amendments to MARPOL Annex II to strengthen the discharge requirements for cargo residues and tank washings from such vessels, which came into force on 1 January 2021.

In this respect, Regulation 8[24] details the need for different surveys for ships carrying noxious liquid substances in bulk, followed by the issuance and endorsement of the certificate under Regulation 9. The duration and validity of the certificate are provided in Regulation 10. Chapter 4[25] specifies the design, construction, arrangement and equipment for ships carrying noxious cargoes in bulk under Regulation 11, followed by Regulation 12, which provides the details for pumping, piping, unloading arrangement and slop tanks. Again, Regulations 14 and 15 provide the details for the procedure and arrangement manual and cargo record book, which need to be filled by the ships' officers.[26] While Chapter 7[27] deals with the prevention of pollution arising from an incident involving noxious liquid substances, Chapter 8[28] lists the requirements for the reception facilities to which the ship can dispose of the residues and mixture generated from noxious liquid substances.

MARPOL Annex III has regulations for the prevention of pollution by harmful substances carried at sea in packaged form. It came into force on 1 July 1992 and comprises two chapters containing 11 regulations.[29] The annex deals with those substances that are hazardous in nature and carried in packaged cargo. It contains general requirements for the standards on packing, marking, labelling, documentation, stowage, quantity subtraction, division and notification for preventing pollution by harmful substances. The annex is in line with the procedures detailed in the International Maritime Dangerous Goods (IMDG) Code, which has been expanded to include marine pollutants.[30]

MARPOL Annex VI deals explicitly with ways to prevent air pollution from ships. It has five chapters with 25 regulations and came into force on 19 May 2005. It introduces requirements to regulate air pollution emitted by ships, including the emission of ozone-depleting substances (ODS), nitrogen oxides (NOx), sulphur oxides (SOx), volatile organic compounds (VOCs) and shipboard incineration. To this end, Regulation 13[31] gives a brief about nitrogen oxides (NOx) with different

---

[23] IMO MEPC Resolutions (2019).

[24] Raunek (2022), MARPOL Annex II, chapter 3.

[25] MARPOL Annex II, chapter 4.

[26] Ibid.

[27] Ibid., Annex I1.

[28] Ibid.

[29] Ibid., Annex III.

[30] Ibid.

[31] MARPOL, Annex VI, chapter 3.

tiers (Tier I, II and III) in and outside emission control areas. Regulation 14 gives a brief about sulphur oxides (SOx) with the requirement for the quantity of sulphur in fuel oil as per the year, in and outside emission-controlled areas. The emissions of volatile organic compounds from oil tankers are taken into account in Regulation 15, providing the details to comply with the requirements.

To ensure compliance, Regulation 5 provides the need for different surveys for the vessel having the arrangement to prevent air pollution, while Regulation 6 follows this up by issuing and endorsing International Air Pollution Prevention (IOPP) certificates and International Energy Efficiency Certificates (IEEC). Regulation 7, on the other hand, provides the details for the issue or endorsement of certificates by another party, followed by the forms of certificates and statement of compliance related to fuel oil consumption reporting in Regulations 8 for both IOPP and IEEC.[32]

Annex VI also establishes requirements for reception facilities for wastes from exhaust gas cleaning systems, incinerators, fuel oil quality, offshore platforms and drilling rigs and for the establishment of SOx emission control areas (SECAs).[33]

MARPOL Annex VI has been amended. The amended Regulation 12 concerns the control and record keeping of ozone-depleting substances, while the amended Regulation 14 concerns mandatory fuel oil changeover procedures for vessels entering or leaving SECA areas and FO sulphur limits. The amendments came into force on 1 July 2010.[34] Regulation 13 of MARPOL Annex VI was also amended by IMO Resolution MEPC.271 (67).[35] This amendment requires records for operational compliance with NOx Tier III emission control areas and came into force on 1 September 2017.

On 1 January 2020, new emission standards were enforced for fuel oil used by ships, in a rule known as IMO 2020. The global sulphur limit (outside SECA's) dropped from an allowed 3.5% sulphur in marine fuels to 0.5%. This will significantly improve the air quality in many populated coastal and port areas, which will prevent over 100,000 early deaths each year and many more cases of asthma in these regions and cities.[36] Over 170 countries have signed on to the changes, including the United States.[37] This is expected to create massive changes for the shipping and oil industries, with major updates required of ships and for the increased production of lower sulphur fuel.[38]

The IMO has worked on ensuring the consistent implementation of the 0.5% sulphur limit in its Marine Environmental Protection Committee (MEPC) and its subcommittee on Pollution Prevention and Response (PPR). This has led to the development of several regulatory and practical measures (FONAR's, carriage ban,

[32] Raunek (2022); MARPOL, Annex VI, chapter 2.

[33] MARPOL, Annex VI, chapter 2.

[34] IMO MEPC (2008).

[35] IMO MEPC Resolutions (2019).

[36] Sofiev et al. (2018), pp. 1–12.

[37] Meredith (2019).

[38] Viens (2019).

ship implementation plan, etc.) to enable any non-compliance to be detected, for example during port state controls (PSCs).[39]

14.1.2.2 Implementation and Enforcement of MARPOL

In order for IMO standards to be binding, they must first be ratified by a total number of member countries whose combined gross tonnage represents at least 50% of the world's gross tonnage, a process that can be lengthy. A system of tacit acceptance has therefore been put in place, whereby if no objections are heard from a member state after a certain period has elapsed, it is assumed that they have assented to the treaty.[40]

All six annexes have been ratified by the requisite number of nations; the most recent is Annex VI, which took effect on 19 May 2005. The country where a ship is registered (flag state) is responsible for certifying the ship's compliance with MARPOL's pollution prevention standards. Each signatory nation is responsible for enacting domestic laws to implement the Convention and effectively pledges to comply with the Convention, annexes and related laws of other nations. In the United States, for example, the relevant implementation legislation is the Act to Prevent Pollution from Ships.[41]

Any violation of the MARPOL 73/78 Convention within the jurisdiction of any party to the Convention is punishable either under the law of that party or under the law of the flag state. In this respect, the term 'jurisdiction' in the Convention should be construed in the light of international law in force at the time the Convention is applied or interpreted. With the exception of very small vessels, ships engaged in international voyages must carry on board valid international certificates, which may be accepted at foreign ports as prima facie evidence that the ship complies with the requirements of the Convention.[42]

If, however, there are clear grounds for believing that the condition of the ship or its equipment does not correspond substantially with the particulars of the certificate or if the ship does not carry a valid certificate, the authority carrying out the inspection may detain the ship until it is satisfied that the ship can proceed to sea without presenting an unreasonable threat of harm to the marine environment.[43]

One of the difficulties in implementing MARPOL arises from the very international nature of maritime shipping. The country that the ship visits can conduct its own examination to verify a ship's compliance with international standards and can detain the ship if it finds significant non-compliance. When incidents occur outside such country's jurisdiction or jurisdiction cannot be determined, the country refers

---

[39] IMO MEPC Resolutions (2019).

[40] Raunek (2022).

[41] *Ibid.*

[42] Madden Marine (2015), p. 5.

[43] Ibid.

such cases to flag states, in accordance with MARPOL. A 2000 US GAO report documented that even when referrals have been made, the response rate from flag states has been poor.[44]

On 1 January 2015, maritime shipping levels became legally subject to new MARPOL directives because the sulphur emission controlled area (SECA) zone increased in size. This larger SECA zone now includes the North Sea, Scandinavia and parts of the English Channel and also all of the Republic of Ireland's international waters, culminating in all of Western Europe's subjection to the MARPOL directive.[45] This has proven controversial for shipping and ferry operators across Europe.[46]

Concerns have been raised about the environmental damage moving back to the roads by some of the larger ferry operators that ship substantial amounts of freight and passenger traffic via these routes affected by IMO standards. They claim that MARPOL will drive up ferry costs for the consumer and freight forwarding companies, pushing them back onto the European roadways as a financially more cost-effective measure compared to increased ferry costs, thereby defeating the object of reducing water pollution.[47]

Concerns have also been raised whether the emission regulation in MARPOL Annex VI, such as the 0.5% global sulphur limit, can be enforced on the high seas by non-flag states as some ships sail under a flag of convenience.[48] It is believed that the United Nations Convention on the Law of the Sea (UNCLOS) allows port states to assert jurisdiction over such violations of emission regulation (also of future regulations on greenhouse gases GHGs) when they occur on the high seas. Coastal states can assert jurisdiction over violations occurring within their waters, with certain exceptions pertaining to innocent passage and the right of transit passage. The special obligations of flag states and the broadened jurisdictions of coastal and port states to enforce MARPOL (including Annex VI) are found within the special provisions of part XII of UNCLOS.[49]

14.2 Control of Safety of Life at Sea

Another major concern of the international community in the maritime sector is the issue of the safety of vessels and crew at sea. A major international legal instrument to this effect is the International Convention for the Safety of Life at Sea 1974 (SOLAS Convention). The SOLAS Convention is an international maritime treaty

[44] US Government Accountability Office (2000), 20.
[45] This took effect on 1 January 2020.
[46] Madden Marine (2015).
[47] Machine (2014).
[48] Fanø (2019).
[49] Ibid.

that sets minimum safety standards for the construction, equipment and operation of merchant ships. The Convention requires signatory flag states to ensure that ships flagged by them comply with at least these standards.

14.2.1 International Convention on Safety of Life at Sea (SOLAS Convention)

14.2.1.1 History of the SOLAS Convention

The SOLAS Convention has had a chequered history. The first version of the SOLAS Treaty was passed in 1914 in response to the sinking of the *RMS Titanic*, which prescribed numbers of lifeboats and other emergency equipment, as well as safety procedures, including continuous radio watches.[50] The 1914 treaty never entered into force due to the outbreak of the First World War. Further versions were adopted in 1929 and 1948.[51] The 1960 Convention was adopted on 17 June 1960 and entered into force on 26 May 1965. It was the fourth SOLAS Convention and was the first major achievement of the International Maritime Organization (IMO). It represented a considerable step forward in modernising regulations and keeping up with technical developments in the shipping industry.[52]

In 1974, a completely new convention was adopted to allow SOLAS to be amended and implemented within a reasonable timescale, instead of the previous procedure to incorporate amendments, which proved to be very slow. Under SOLAS 1960, it could take several years for amendments to come into force since countries had to give notice of acceptance to the IMO, and there was a minimum threshold of countries and tonnage. Under SOLAS 1974, amendments enter into force via a tacit acceptance procedure—this allows an amendment to enter into force on a specified date, unless objections to an amendment are received from an agreed number of parties.[53]

The current version of SOLAS is the 1974 version, known as SOLAS 1974, which came into force on 25 May 1980, 12 months after its ratification by at least 25 countries with at least 50% of gross tonnage. As of November 2018, SOLAS 1974 had 164 contracting states, which flag about 99% of merchant ships around the world in terms of gross tonnage. As at March 2016, SOLAS 1974 had 162 contracting states, which flag about 99% of merchant ships around the world in terms of gross tonnage. As of 2015, the non-parties of SOLAS 1974 include Bolivia, Lebanon and Sri Lanka, all considered flag of convenience states. SOLAS,

---

[50] International Convention for the Safety at Sea (2009).

[51] International Convention for the Safety at Sea (1953).

[52] International Convention for the Safety at Sea (2009).

[53] IMO (2022).

in its successive forms, is generally regarded as the most important of all international treaties concerning the safety of merchant ships.[54]

SOLAS has been updated and amended on numerous occasions since then, though the Convention in force today is sometimes referred to as SOLAS 1974, as amended. In particular, amendments in 1988 based on the amendments of the International Radio Regulations in 1987 replaced the Morse code with the Global Maritime Distress Safety System (GMDSS) and came into force beginning 1 February 1992. Other amendments were made in May 2011.[55]

Another later amendment is the SOLAS Container Weight Verification Regulation VI/2 (2015).[56] This Regulation, implemented by the IMO Maritime Safety Committee (MSC), requires that the full weight of loaded containers must be obtained prior to being boarded on an ocean vessel. Communicating a weight value has called for the introduction of a new electronic data interchange (EDI) communication protocol called VGM (Verified Gross Mass) or VERMAS (Verification of Mass) and involves cooperation between ocean carriers, freight forwarders/non-vessel operating common carriers (NVOCCs), EDI providers as well as exporters. The Regulation states that exporters (shippers) are ultimately responsible for obtaining a verified container weight.[57] Originally scheduled for implementation on 1 July 2016,[58] the Regulation allows for flexibility and practical refinement according to the Maritime Safety Committee Memorandum #1548[59] of 1 October 2016.

14.2.1.2 Salient Provisions of SOLAS on the Protection of the Marine Environment

SOLAS 1974 comprises 14 chapters, and each chapter has its own set of regulations, which deal with safety precautions and safety procedures, starting from the construction of the ship to real emergencies like 'Abandon Ship'.[60] It therefore requires flag states to ensure that ships flagged by them comply with the minimum safety standards for the construction, equipment and operation of merchant ships. The treaty includes articles setting out general obligations, etc., followed by an annex divided into 12 chapters; two new chapters were added in 2016 and 2017.[61] Of these, Chapter 5 (often called 'SOLAS V') is the only one that applies to all vessels on the

[54] *Ibid.*

[55] Ibid.

[56] IMO (2015).

[57] Ibid.

[58] Maritime Safety Committee (MSC) (2014).

[59] IMO (2016).

[60] Marine Insight (2022).

[61] IMO (2020).

sea, including private yachts and small craft, for local trips, as well as to commercial vessels for international passage.[62]

In SOLAS Chapter I, General Provisions, the surveys and certification of all safety items, structures, machinery, etc. are included. This chapter is further subdivided into three parts: Part A, Part B and Part C.[63]

Part A contains five regulations, which explain the 'Application' of the chapter to different types of ships, along with the 'Definition' of the different terminologies used in the chapter. The regulation may not be applicable to all types of ships; hence, a separate section for 'Exceptions' and 'Exemptions' is also provided.[64]

Part B contains important regulations concerning surveys and certificates that seagoing ships need to have in order to be considered compliant with SOLAS. For this, 15 regulations are kept under Part B. Regulations 6 to 11 under Part B of SOLAS provide details of different survey requirement on different ships, equipment, machinery etc. clauses on how to do the repair and what kind of surveys to go through.[65]

SOLAS Chapter II-1 deals with the construction of a ship, including its subdivision, stability, machinery and electrical installations. The main focus of this chapter is the watertight integrity of the ship, including the passenger vessel. The seven parts of the chapter focus on the requirement for structural, machinery, electrical, stability and other criteria for a safe ship.[66]

Part A contains three regulations that explain the 'Application' of this chapter to ships, especially as regards keel laying. The regulations provide for the 'Definition' of the different terminologies used in the chapter.[67]

Part A-1 comprises regulations explaining the requirements for the structure of the ship, including protective coating, towing arrangements, deck equipment fittings, construction and drawings, etc. It also includes a regulation on how to provide access to different parts of the oil tanker and bulk carrier and discusses the structure access manual, which contains details on the ship's structure, including plans for a means of access. The method for the construction of a ship, which should comply with the regulation for protection against noise, is also included.[68]

Part B of this regulation explains the stability and watertight integrity requirement. Under Part B-1, the regulations (Regulations 5 to 8) define the necessary conditions for maintaining the intact stability of the cargo ship and passenger ship. It also includes the requirement to supply information to the master on the stability of the vessel, explaining how the stability factors are calculated in different conditions.[69]

---

[62] Ibid.

[63] Ibid.

[64] Ibid.

[65] Ibid.

[66] IMO (2020).

[67] Ibid.

[68] Ibid.

[69] Ibid.

Part B-2 comprises four regulations (Regulations 9 to 17), which take care of the watertight integrity of the ship (both passenger and cargo ships) by enlisting the constructional and testing requirements of watertight and other important bulkheads and the provision of the double bottom on ships other than tanker ships.[70]

While Part B-3 explains the requirement for the subdivision load-line assignment for passenger ships, Part B-4 comprises seven regulations (Regulations 19 to 25) that contain the requirements for stability management of cargo and passenger ships in areas of inspections, preventions, damage control drills and necessary information as they relate to the cargo and passenger ships in question.[71]

Part C focuses on the different machinery installations in the engine room, including the requirement for emergency installations in passenger ships (Regulations 26 to 39).[72]

Part D of this chapter (Regulations 40 to 45) focuses on the electrical installation requirement for cargo and passenger ships, including the emergency source and arrangements, along with electrical safety and hazards.[73]

Part E explicitly clarifies the requirement for unattended machinery space under Regulations 46 to 54, and Part F, in Regulation 55, provides details on the alternative design and arrangement of the ship's machinery and electrical system. It also explains the storage and distribution requirement for the low flash point fuel system. Part G with reference to regulations 56 and 57 explains the application and requirements when using low flash point fuels by ships.[74]

SOLAS Chapter II-2 focuses on fire protection, fire detection and fire extinction. This chapter is divided into seven parts, explaining the various requirements for the fire safety system installed on ships and elaborating on the means and measures for fire protection in accommodation and cargo spaces and engine rooms for passenger, cargo and tanker ships. Regulation 5, in particular, laid down the necessary steps to follow to curb the growth of fire in different spaces on the ship, which includes cutting any one side of the fire triangle, i.e., to control either the air supply, oil supply or heat source (using protection materials like insulation, linings, etc.) in potentially hazardous spaces.[75]

Part A of SOLAS Chapter II-2 contains Regulations 1 to 3, that apply more precisely to ships' construction date. The regulations further provides by way of defition the different terminologies used in the chapter. Part B specifies the requirement for the prevention of fire and explosion on cargo ships, including tankers. It has three regulations: Regulations 4 to 6. Regulation 4 provides details on how to prevent the ignition of a combustible source present on ships, including the

[70] Ibid.

[71] Ibid.

[72] Ibid.

[73] IMO (2020).

[74] Ibid.

[75] Ibid.

limitations and arrangements on the use of fuel and lube oils on board, and the prevention of fire in the cargo areas of tanker ships. Regulation 6 of this part focuses on the reduction of hazards to human life from products that release smoke and toxic gases (such as paint, varnish, etc.).[76]

Part C of SOLAS Chapter II-2 comprises five regulations (Regulations 7 to 11) and focuses on the requirement to suppress fire at the earliest, including the detection and control of smoke and flames, containment, ensuring the structural integrity of the space to prevent the spread of fire and the installation of firefighting systems and equipment to be used on ships' machinery and accommodation and cargo spaces.

Part G of SOLAS Chapter II-2 contains a special requirement for the operations carried out on tanker and bulk carrier ships, such as helicopter operations (Regulation 18), giving details on the different constructional, safety and firefighting arrangements. Regulation 19 provides safety measures for carrying dangerous goods in container, bulk, tanker or ro-ro ships. Regulation 20 focuses on ships that carry vehicles as cargo, along with passengers, explaining the prevention, detection and containment of fire on such ships. Regulations 21, 22 and 23 are passenger-centric, describing the requirement that a passenger ship should follow in the case of a fire incident on board a ship to save the passengers and the ship from a major accident.[77]

SOLAS Chapter III highlights the life-saving appliances and arrangements: all the life-saving appliances and their use in different situations according to ship type are described in this chapter. The chapter comprises three parts.

Part A contains five regulations that explain the 'Application' of this chapter to different types of ships, along with the 'Definition' of the different terminologies used in the chapter. Part B of SOLAS Chapter III comprises of 32 regulations and these regulations deal with the requirements on having life-saving appliances on passenger and cargo ships, including personal life-saving appliance such as lifejackets, lifebuoys, immersion suit etc.,[78] instructions on muster station, survival craft operation and manning, along with their embarkation arrangements explaining the different requirements,[79] location of survival craft in a cargo ship (other than free fall lifeboat).[80]

While Regulations 13 to 17 provide details on the stowage and necessary arrangements required for lifeboats, life rafts, the marine evacuation system, recovery boats on ships as well as man overboard operations, Regulation 19 deals with the various training and drill requirements for onboard crew.[81]

Regulation 20 applies to all the ships on operational readiness, maintenance and survey requirement of survival crafts and other life-saving appliances on board a

[76] Ibid.

[77] IMO (2020).

[78] Ibid., SOLAS, chapter III, Part B, regulation 7.

[79] Ibid., regulations 8–11.

[80] Ibid., regulation 12.

[81] Ibid.

ship. Regulations 21 to 30 provide for the additional requirement for passenger ships concerning survival crafts and all life-saving appliances on the passenger ships, including drills for passengers on board the ship and helicopter operation in a passenger ship (ro-ro passenger ships of 130 m in length should be provided with a helicopter landing area).[82]

SOLAS Chapter V deals with the safety of navigation. This chapter consists of a total of 35 regulations dealing with seagoing vessels of all sizes, from boats to very large crude carriers (VLCCs), and includes passage planning, navigation, distress signal, etc.[83]

While Regulations 4 and 5 list down different navigational and mineralogical service warnings, which are essential to navigating officers for a safe passage plan, Regulations 6 to 9 focus on services such as ice patrol services for safe navigation in the North Atlantic, search and rescue services (when receiving a distress alert from a ship), the use of life-saving signals and hydrographic services (for the compilation of hydrographic data and publication) by the contracting government.[84]

Regulations 31, 32, 33 and 34 contain a requirement for how the master of the ship should act in a dangerous situation by sending danger messages (while encountering any navigation situation dangerous to the contracting government using a message or an International Code of Signal). They also include the type of information that needs to be sent to the authorities.[85]

Furthermore, the Regulations also explain the obligation to provide/the procedures for providing assistance to a ship in danger and how to avoid a situation that can lead to danger. Regulation 35 strictly prohibits the use of distress signals for any other purpose than explained in the above regulations.[86]

While Regulation 10 contains the details for the requirement of a ship routeing system for safe and efficient navigation, Regulation 11 indicates the need for a reporting system, where the seagoing ship shall report to the concerned authorised body, to contribute towards maritime and environmental safety.[87]

Regulation 28 provides details on the records to be kept concerning all the navigational activities of the ship's navigation officer; Regulation 29 insists on the requirement that the ship's officer should be able to understand the different life-saving signals used in distress situations, while Regulation 30 lists down the operational limitations of passenger ships when it comes to safe navigation.[88]

SOLAS Chapter VI deals with the carriage of cargo and oil fuel. The chapter is divided into three parts—Part A, Part B and Part C—and focuses on the storage and securing of different types of cargoes and containers but does not include oil and gas

[82] SOLAS, chapter III, Part B, regulation 12.

[83] Ibid.

[84] IMO (2020).

[85] Ibid.

[86] Ibid.

[87] Ibid.

[88] Ibid.

cargoes. Part A contains Regulations 1 to 5. Regulation 1 explains the 'Application' of this chapter and also the 'Definition' of the different terminologies used in the chapter and the requirements for the carriage of solid cargoes other than grain.[89]

SOLAS Chapter VII deals with the carriage of dangerous goods. This chapter is divided into four parts—Part A, Part B, Part C and Part D—and defines the International Maritime Goods Code for the storage and transportation of dangerous goods. Part A provides information on the carriage of dangerous goods in packaged form under seven regulations. Regulation 7 is dedicated to the carriage of dangerous goods in solid bulk form, defining the terms used under this regulation, along with the application of the terms. Regulation 7 further explains the documentation and stowage processes involved with the segregation requirement for the carriage of dangerous goods in a solid bulk form. The reporting of the incident and other conditions related to the dangerous goods carried in solid bulk form is also provided.[90]

SOLAS Chapter VIII focuses on nuclear ships providing for the code of safety for nuclear-propelled ships. This chapter consists of 12 regulations explaining the application, exemptions, approvals and requirements for reactor installations; safety against radiation; safety assessment; the operating manual; surveys and certifications; the controlling authority; the steps to follow in the case of any causality due to radiation; etc.[91]

SOLAS Chapter IX focuses on management for the safe operation of ships. It covers the International Safety Management (ISM) Code for shipowners and operators, while SOLAS Chapter X focuses on safety measures for high-speed craft, explaining the safety requirements.

SOLAS Chapter XI is divided into two sections. Chapter XI-1, which deals with special measures to enhance maritime safety, including special and enhanced surveys for safe operation.[92]

Chapter XI-2 focuses on maritime security measures, which all parties involved in maritime trade, i.e. ships, ports, shipowners, contracting governments and authorities, need to follow. "This SOLAS chapter consists of 13 regulations, and Regulations 1 and 2 explain the 'Definition' of the different terminologies used in the chapter as well as present the details on the 'Application' of this chapter." Regulation 3 focuses on the contracting governments, highlighting their obligation towards maritime security. Regulation 4 lists down the requirement on the part of companies and ships to comply with the International Ship and Port Facility Security (ISPS) Code, followed by Regulation 5, which deals with the specific responsibility of companies towards maritime security.[93]

---

[89] IMO (2020).

[90] Ibid.

[91] Ibid.

[92] Ibid.

[93] IMO (2020).

SOLAS Chapter XII deals with additional safety measures for bulk carriers: the chapter includes safety requirements for above 150-metre-length bulk carriers. It consists of 14 regulations. In Regulation 4, the damage stability requirements for bulk carriers are explained.[94]

Apart from the above SOLAS 12 chapters, two new chapters were added in recent years. The first is SOLAS Chapter XII, which concerns the verification of compliance: this chapter was adopted on 22 May 2014, which requires all contracting parties to undergo periodic audits by the approved organisation, following audit standards for the verification of compliance with and the implementation of the present Convention. The chapter consists of Regulation 1 to Regulation 3, providing for the 'Definition' of the different terminologies used in the chapter and the details on the 'Application' of the chapter, followed by the verification system for contracting governments.[95]

The second is SOLAS Chapter XIV, titled Safety Measures for Ships Operating in Polar Waters. As the name suggests, SOLAS Chapter XIV deals with ships that intend to operate within the Arctic and Antarctic areas and need to carry a Polar Ship Certificate. This Code entered into force on 1 January 2017 and explains, for the shipowners and ship managers, the steps to be taken to have their ships in compliance with the different categories. This is one of the latest chapters introduced in 2017 in the SOLAS Convention. It comprises four regulations, starting from Regulations 1 and 2, which provide for the definitions of the terminologies used in the chapter and the application of the Code. Regulation 3 explains the requirements for ships to which this chapter applies, followed by Regulation 4, which suggests the terms for the alternative design and arrangement of vessels sailing in the Arctic and Antarctic areas.[96]

It should be noted that all chapters of SOLAS cover a general basic minimum criterion that applies to seagoing ships, regardless of their location and nationality. It is possible that the materials or appliances available in one country are not available for ships in another country. An 'Equivalent' section is also provided to deal with such a situation.[97]

On the whole, the SOLAS Convention can be said to have contributed to the prevention of oil pollution incidents as it details a number of minimum standards for the construction, equipment and operation of ships with a view to maintaining their safety. The SOLAS Convention also includes the International Safety Management (ISM) Code and the International Ship and Port Facilities Security (ISPS) Code. The broader principle behind the SOLAS Convention is that the safer the ship is, the less likely it is that an accident will occur, and as a consequence, the potential for polluting the marine environment is lowered.

[94] Ibid.

[95] Ibid.

[96] Ibid.

[97] Ibid.

14.3 Provisions for Oil Pollution Emergency Plans

Maritime disasters have also demonstrated the need for states to be prepared for and equipped to respond to incidents of oil pollution. Quicker response times and more efficient salvage and clean-up operations have the benefit of lessening the potential pollution damage and, in some cases, the resulting costs. Based on these considerations, the international community has adopted the following legal instruments for this purpose:

(1) The International Convention Relating to the Intervention on the High Seas in Cases of Oil Pollution Casualties 1969
(2) The International Convention on Oil Pollution Preparedness, Response and Co-operation (OPRC) 1990

14.3.1 International Convention Relating to the Intervention on the High Seas in Cases of Oil Pollution Casualties (Intervention Convention) 1969

This Convention was signed on 29 November 1969 in Brussels in 1969 and came into force on 6 May 1975.[98] The Intervention Convention 1969 provides vital powers to coastal states in the face of grave and imminent threats of oil pollution arising from shipping incidents. It affirms the right of states to take preventive measures to avoid pollution damage that would otherwise result from maritime casualties occurring outside their territorial waters. Thus, under Article I (1),

> Parties to the present Convention may take such measures on the high seas as may be necessary to prevent, mitigate or eliminate grave and imminent danger to their coastline or related interests from pollution or threat of pollution of the sea by oil, following upon a maritime casualty or acts related to such a casualty, which may reasonably be expected to result in major harmful consequences.

It should be noted that the Intervention Convention 1969 applied only to oil. However, with the passage of time, it became obvious that other substances may likely cause pollution casualties. To this end, a Protocol to the Intervention Convention 1969 became necessary. On 2 November 1973, the Protocol Relating to Intervention on the High Seas in Cases of Marine Pollution by Substances Other Than Oil (Protocol 1973) was adopted. It came into force on 20 March 1983.[99]

The Protocol 1973 extended the regime of the Intervention Convention 1969 to cover substances other than oil. According to the Protocol, 'substances other than oil' shall be:

---

[98] United Nations Treaties Series (1969), OPRC 1990.

[99] United Nations Treaties Series (1973), OPRC 1990.

(a) those substances enumerated in a list which shall be established by an appropriate body designated by the Organization[100] and which shall be annexed to the present Protocol, and
(b) those other substances which are liable to create hazards to human health, to harm living resources and marine life, to damage amenities or to interfere with other legitimate uses of the sea.[101] Such substances are list in an Annex to the Protocol, although the regime also applies to other substances with similar characteristics to those listed.

14.3.2 International Convention on Oil Pollution Preparedness, Response and Co-operation (OPRC) 1990[102]

OPRC 1990 is meant to deal with general pollution incidents and expressly covers oil pollution from offshore oil rigs. The importance of the Convention is that it regulates marine pollution caused by accidental oil spills. The main objective of the Convention is to support and facilitate international cooperation with mutual assistance to knowledge-based activities. It was developed to prepare for and respond to major oil spills and urges states parties to the Convention to develop adequate capability concerning the whole scope of dealing with oil pollution incidents to protect their marine-related environment.[103]

OPRC 1990 was signed in London on 30 November 1990 and came into force on 13 May 1995. As at November 2018, there were 112 members, and Nigeria ratified it on 25 May 1993. In 2000, a Protocol to the Convention relating to hazardous and noxious substances was added. The main thrust is on waste and hazardous substances based on its objective: to strengthen the legal framework for the control of environmental pollution by oil, in general, and marine pollution by oil, in particular.[104]

Article 2 of OPRC defines, *inter alia*, an oil pollution incident, an offshore unit, a seaport and oil handling facilities. Parties agree to ensure that all ships flying their flags have made oil pollution emergency plans on the basis of the conditions

---

[100] The organisation is defined as the Inter-Governmental Maritime Consultative Organization. See Intervention Convention 1969, art. I(5).

[101] Protocol 1973, art. I(2)(a)(b).

[102] In 1978, the Amoco Cadiz spilt 220,000 tonnes of crude oil near the Brittany coastline, and in 1989, the Exxon Valdez spilt 40,000 tonnes into Prince William Sound, Alaska. The IMO, as a result of these major and disastrous spills, decided to convene 'an international convention on oil pollution preparedness and response which would provide the framework for international cooperation for combating major oil pollution incident'.

The conference convened in London adopted the OPRC on 30 November 1990.

[103] United Nations Treaties Series (1990), OPRC 1990.

[104] United Nations Treaties Series (1990), OPRC 1990.

prescribed in the Convention[105] and to report all incidents of oil discharge.[106] The party receiving such report is to take appropriate control action and pass the information to all states whose interests are likely to be affected.[107]

The Convention contains provisions for collaborative initiatives, in research and development and in technical operations, in the search by the parties for appropriate controls to oil pollution incidents.[108] In this respect, the Global Initiative for West, Central and Southern Africa (GI WACAF) Project was launched in 2006. GI WACAF is a collaboration between the International Maritime Organization (IMO) and the International Petroleum Industry Environmental Conservation Association (IPIECA), the global oil and gas industry association for advancing environmental and social performance, to enhance the capacity of partner countries to prepare for and respond to marine oil spills. The mission is to strengthen the capability for preparedness and response to oil spills in 22 West, Central and Southern African countries in accordance with the provisions set out in the International Convention on Oil Pollution Preparedness, Response and Cooperation (OPRC) 1990.[109]

To achieve its mission, the GI WACAF Project organises and delivers workshops, seminars and exercises that aim to communicate good practices in all aspects of spill preparedness and response, drawing on expertise and experience from within governments, industries and other organisations working in this specialised field.[110] The Project's activities are supported and facilitated by its network of dedicated government and industry focal points. Promoting cooperation among all relevant government agencies, oil industry business units and stakeholders nationally, regionally and internationally is a major objective of the Project. GI WACAF is supported and funded by the IMO and seven oil company members of IPIECA, namely BP, Chevron, ExxonMobil, Eni, Shell, Total and Woodside.[111]

In 2019, GI WACAF held 11 collaborative activities organised in nine countries: five national activities in Liberia, Benin, the Democratic Republic of the Congo (DRC), Nigeria and South Africa; two national exercises in Côte d'Ivoire and Senegal; one trans-boundary exercise in Angola and Namibia; one sub-regional workshop in Côte d'Ivoire; and one regional conference in South Africa.[112]

A national workshop on oil spill liability and compensation was organised in Lagos, Nigeria, from 10 (Tuesday) to 12 (Thursday) September 2019. The event was co-hosted by two national agencies with responsibilities in oil spill preparedness and response—the National Oil Spill Detection and Response Agency (NOSDRA) and

---

[105] OPRC (1990), art 3.

[106] Ibid., art 4.

[107] Ibid., arts. 5, 6 and 7.

[108] Ibid., arts. 8, 9 and 10.

[109] Global Initiative for West, Central and Southern Africa (GI WACAF) (2019).

[110] Ibid.

[111] GI WACAF (2019).

[112] Ibid.

the Nigerian Maritime Administration and Safety Agency (NIMASA)—and brought together around 100 participants.[113]

The main objective of the workshop was to present and provide training to relevant national authorities on the scope and implementation of International Maritime Organization (IMO) conventions[114] related to liability and compensation in the case of an oil spill from a ship through case studies and tabletop exercises. International experts from International Tanker Owners Pollution Federation Limited (ITOPF) and the International Oil Pollution Compensation Funds (IOPC Funds) facilitated the exercise.[115]

In 2000, the Protocol on Preparedness, Response and Co-operation to Pollution Incidents by Hazardous and Noxious Substances (OPRC-HNS) further developed the principles of the OPRC by providing a basis for international cooperation in combating major incidents or threats of marine pollution with a specific focus on hazardous and noxious substances.[116]

The impact of the conventions discussed above has been tremendous in helping to secure the marine environment from pollution. Thus, while maritime transport in general and seaborne oil trade in particular have steadily grown over the years, the number of oil spills from tankers has decreased significantly over the past years. Moreover, both the number and the size of large spills, that is, spills with the potential to cause major economic loss and damage to the marine environment, have also dropped significantly over the same period of time. The reduction in oil spills from tankers can be buttressed by the following facts.[117]

According to the International Tanker Owners Pollution Federation Limited (ITOPF),[118] the average number of major oil spills per year in the 1970s was over 25, which dropped to approximately nine in the 1980s and eight in the 1990s, to just over three in the most recent decade. This clearly illustrates a decreasing trend too, with much fewer severe oil spills occurring from 2010 than during the previous decades, this despite the fact that both seaborne trade in oil and the cargo-carrying capacity of oil tankers have grown steadily since the 1970s.

The important reduction in large oil spill incidents over time may, to a considerable extent, be attributed to the development of a robust international regulatory framework to combat ship-source oil pollution, which, in turn, has been made in response to a number of major oil pollution incidents.[119]

---

[113] Ibid.

[114] Such as the International Convention for the Prevention of Oil Pollution 1969, the International Convention for the Prevention of Pollution from Ships 1973 as modified by the Protocol of 1978 (MARPOL 73/78), the International Convention for the Safety of Life at Sea (SOLAS) 1974, the International Convention on Oil Pollution Preparedness, Response and Cooperation 1990 (OPRC 1990).

[115] GI WACAF (2019).

[116] United Nations Environment Programme (UNEP) (2005).

[117] International Tanker Owners Pollution Federation Limited (2014).

[118] Ibid.

[119] Ibid.

Again, in line with the number of large tanker oil spills significantly falling over the years, regulatory measures for pollution prevention,[120] preparedness and control[121] and the improvement of ship design and safety standards[122] have significantly contributed to a steady reduction in both the size and the number of major oil pollution incidents, illustrating the important role of regulation as a tool to implement public policy objectives.[123]

In addition, the relevant international regulatory framework for liability and compensation has, over the past years, been further developed and refined, ensuring that victims of oil pollution incidents are adequately compensated for their losses.[124]

14.4 Control of Marine Litter

14.4.1 Introduction

Marine litter, sometimes referred to as marine debris, is defined as 'any persistent, manufactured, or processed solid material that is discarded, disposed of or abandoned in the marine and coastal environment'.[125] This definition includes items originating from land or sea-based sources. The major land-based sources of marine litter include waste from landfills sited near coastal areas, storm water run-off, ineffective sewage treatment, industrial outfalls, littering, ship-breaking yards and natural disasters and storms.[126] Sea-based waste is often the result of dumping from vessels at sea, fishing, shipping and lost or abandoned fishing gear.[127]

The full magnitude of marine litter is difficult to determine. While it is commonly estimated, for example, that 80% of marine litter comes from land-based sources, this figure may not account for all litter entering the marine environment.[128] The prevalence of marine litter is caused by many different factors, including changing production patterns, poor waste management and gaps in the regulation of waste materials.

The amount and composition of marine litter can vary between regions due to differences in waste management and in economic activities such as tourism, fisheries and shipping. It also varies by location due, in part, to currents that can

---

[120] OILPOL, MARPOL 73/78.

[121] OPRC (1990).

[122] SOLAS (1974).

[123] International Tanker Owners Pollution Federation Limited (2014).

[124] Compensation for pollution damage to the marine environment was discussed in Chap. 15.

[125] UNEP (2009).

[126] UNEP (2009).

[127] National Research Council of the National Academies (2005).

[128] Jambeck et al. (2015), pp. 768–771.

carry marine litter to accumulation sites.[129] Data from the 2014 International Coastal Cleanup Day, coordinated by the Ocean Conservancy, found that the most commonly collected items from beaches included cigarette butts, food wrappers, plastic bottles, bottle caps, straws and stirrers, plastic bags, glass bottles, beverage cans and plastic cups and plates.[130]

A 2014 study of litter on South Korean beaches from 2008 to 2009 found that fisheries and marine aquaculture accounted for approximately 35% of marine litter, household items made up 20% and beach recreation items made up 12%.[131]

Marine litter is not just on the sea's surface and on the beaches: a study of European waters found litter at depths ranging from 35 to 4500 metres, with plastic bags, glass bottles and derelict fishing gear being the most prevalent.[132] Plastics are estimated to make up as much as 95% of the marine litter found on coastlines, the sea surface and the ocean floor.[133] An estimated 4.8 to 12.7 million metric tonnes of plastic entered the ocean from land-based sources in 2010, and about another 8 metric tonnes have entered the oceans each year since then.[134]

Microplastics also present a significant problem for marine litter management. They can be found, for example, in personal care and industrial products (primary microplastics); they can also come from larger pieces of plastic that have degraded (secondary microplastics). Microplastics pose a significant problem as they can pass through wastewater filters with ease, making it impossible to recover them once in the ocean. Microplastics range in size but are commonly defined as plastic particles of less than 5 mm.[135]

Marine litter negatively impacts the environment, economy and public health. Marine life can become tangled in abandoned nets and fishing gear, leading to death and injury.[136] Several studies[137] have found that ingested microplastics can potentially disrupt cellular processes and degrade tissue as well as concentrate toxins across the food chain, leading to a bio-magnification effect.[138] Marine litter can also lead to economic losses due to the cost of coastal clean-up and lost tourism revenue.

The Asia-Pacific region is reported to lose US$1.265 billion annually due to damage to its fishing, shipping and marine tourism industries caused by marine litter.[139] Marine litter presents a serious non-point pollution problem to Scotland,

---

[129] UNEP (2005).

[130] The Ocean Conservancy (2015).

[131] Hong et al. (2014), pp. 27–34.

[132] Pham et al. (2014).

[133] Galgani et al. (2015), pp. 29–56.

[134] Jambeck et al. (2015), pp. 768–771.

[135] Joint Group of Experts on the Scientific Aspects of Marine Environmental Protection (GESAMP) (2015).

[136] The Ocean Conservancy (2015).

[137] Rochman et al. (2013), pp. 169–171.

[138] Wright et al. (2013), pp. 483–492.

[139] Asian-Pacific Economic Cooperation (APEC) (2009).

costing the state at least £16.8 million or US$24.3 million annually (when calculating consumptive uses, non-consumptive uses and indirect uses of Scottish coasts and waters).[140]

Arising from the above, marine litter poses serious environmental, health and economic threats to oceans and coastal ecosystems. It also presents a unique legal and regulatory challenge for many nation states as it can originate from diverse land-based and sea-based sources both within and outside a state. While the full magnitude of the problem can be difficult to ascertain, some estimates suggest that an average of 8 million tons of plastic waste entered the ocean in 2010, and this figure has been projected to increase.[141]

The prevalence of marine litter is the result of many different factors, including changing production and consumption patterns, inadequate waste management and gaps in the regulation of waste materials. The diverse sources require a comprehensive response. Accordingly, countries frequently utilise a variety of laws and policies to prevent, manage and reduce the proliferation of marine litter. Many of these approaches are part of the general frameworks to reduce the generation and spread of solid waste, rather than being part of frameworks specifically designed to address marine litter.[142]

14.4.2 Relevant International Legal Instruments Governing Marine Litter

Relevant international law governing marine litter can roughly be categorised as multilateral environmental agreements (MEAs) and principles of international law and customary international law.

14.4.2.1 Multilateral Environmental Agreements (MEAs)

Three MEAs are particularly relevant to discussions on the legal control of marine litter:

(i) The United Nations Convention on the Law of the Sea (UNCLOS) 1982
(ii) The International Convention for the Prevention of Pollution from Ships (MARPOL) 1973/1978
(iii) The Convention on the Prevention of Marine Pollution by Dumping of Wastes and Other Matter (London Convention) 1972

---

[140] Potts and Hastings (2011).
[141] UNEP (2016).
[142] UNEP (2005).

14.4.2.1.1 United Nations Convention on the Law of the Sea (UNCLOS) 1982

UNCLOS came into force in 1994, and 167 states are party to it.[143] The Convention provides a broad legal framework for ocean-related issues, placing a general obligation on states to protect and preserve the marine environment.

For instance, under Article 207, member states are enjoined to address land-based sources of marine pollution. To this end, 'States shall adopt laws and regulations to prevent, reduce and control pollution of the marine environment from land-based sources, including rivers, estuaries, pipelines and outfall structures, taking into account internationally agreed rules, standards and recommended practices and procedures'[144] and 'shall take other measures as may be necessary to prevent, reduce and control such pollution'.[145] Again, under Article 208(1), 'Coastal States shall adopt laws and regulations to prevent, reduce and control pollution of the marine environment arising from or in connection with seabed activities subject to their jurisdiction and from artificial islands, installations and structures under their jurisdiction'.

There are also provisions for the control of pollution from ships under UNCLOS 1982. Under Article 211(1),

> States, acting through the competent international organization or general diplomatic conference, shall establish international rules and standards to prevent, reduce and control pollution of the marine environment from vessels and promote the adoption, in the same manner, wherever appropriate, of routeing systems designed to minimize the threat of accidents which might cause pollution of the marine environment, including the coastline, and pollution damage to the related interests of coastal States. Such rules and standards shall, in the same manner, be re-examined from time to time as necessary.

To this end, states shall adopt laws and regulations for the prevention, reduction and control of pollution of the marine environment from vessels flying their flag or of their registry. Such laws and regulations shall at least have the same effect as that of generally accepted international rules and standards established through the competent international organisation or general diplomatic conference.[146]

There are also provisions for the control of pollution activities in the area,[147] pollution from or through the atmosphere[148] and seabed activities.[149] States shall also adopt laws and regulations to prevent, reduce and control pollution of the

[143] United Nations Convention on the Law of the Sea (UNCLOS) 1982.

[144] Ibid., art. 207(1).

[145] Ibid., art. 207(2).

[146] UNCLOS (1982), art. 211(2).

[147] Ibid., art. 209.

[148] Ibid., art. 212.

[149] Ibid., art. 208.

marine environment by dumping.[150] In all cases 'States shall take other measures as may be necessary to prevent, reduce and control such pollution'.[151]

The Convention further enjoins coastal states to cooperate with other states on marine issues and work to address marine issues beyond national jurisdiction.[152]

14.4.2.1.2 International Convention for the Prevention of Pollution from Ships (MARPOL), 1973/1978

MARPOL has a number of provisions for the control of litter from ships, namely Annexes IV and V. MARPOL Annex IV focuses on the prevention of sewage pollution from ships. It has seven chapters, comprising 18 regulations, and came into force on 27 September 2003. Chapter 3[153] provides the need to have equipment for and control of sewage discharge from the ship. Discharge regulations, according to MARPOL Annex IV, apply to ships of 400 GT and above and ships of less than 400 GT that are certified to carry more than 15 persons.[154]

Chapter 3 also provides details for the sewage system requirement of ships. The mandatory equipment, according to Regulations 9 and 10, includes:

(i) Sewage treatment plant of a type approved by the Administration in compliance with IMO criteria,
(ii) Comminuting and disinfecting system approved by the Administration fitted with facilities for the temporary storage of sewage when the ship is less than 3 nm from the nearest land, or
(iii) Holding tank of a capacity to the satisfaction of the administration, having regard to the operation of the ship, the number on persons on board, and provided with a means to indicate visually the amount of its contents.
(iv) The flanges for discharge connections must have the dimensions specified in Regulation 10.

Under Regulation 11 paragraph 1, the discharge of sewage into the sea is prohibited, except when the certain requirements specified therein are met.

MARPOL Annex V, which came into force on 31 December 1988, deals with the prevention of pollution by garbage from ships, especially garbage produced on board ships. The annex specifies the distances from land in which materials may be disposed of and subdivides different types of garbage and marine debris. The requirements are much stricter in a number of 'special areas', but perhaps the most

[150] Ibid., art. 210.
[151] Ibid., arts. 209(2) and 212(2).
[152] Ibid., art. 242.
[153] MARPOL, Annex IV.
[154] MARPOL, Annex IV, regulation 2.

prominent portion of the annex is the complete ban on the dumping of plastics into the ocean.[155]

Regulation 3 lists down the details of the general prohibition on the discharge of garbage at sea, followed by Regulation 4 for the discharge of garbage outside special areas. Regulation 5, on the other hand, specifies the special requirements for the discharge of garbage from fixed and floating platforms, while the requirement for the discharge of garbage in the special area is given under Regulation 6. To facilitate this, Regulation 10 deals with the need for a garbage management plan (GMP), including record books and placards.[156]

In July 2011, IMO adopted extensive amendments to Annex V, which entered into force on 1 January 2013. The revised Annex V prohibits the discharge of all garbage into the sea, except as provided otherwise, under specific circumstances.[157]

14.4.2.2 Convention on the Prevention of Marine Pollution by Dumping of Wastes and Other Matter (London Convention) 1972 and the London Protocol 1996

The Convention on the Prevention of Marine Pollution by Dumping of Wastes and Other Matter 1972 (London Convention 1972) and the London Protocol 1996 are sets of global conventions to protect the marine environment from human activities. The London Convention came into force in 1975, currently with 87 states as parties to it, while the Protocol entered into force on 24 March 2006, currently with 53 parties.[158] The objective of the London Convention and London Protocol is to promote the effective control of all sources of marine pollution. The contracting parties shall take effective measures to prevent pollution of the marine environment caused by dumping at sea.[159]

The purpose of the London Convention is to control all sources of marine pollution and prevent pollution of the sea through the regulation of dumping into the sea of waste materials. A so-called black- and grey-list approach is applied for wastes, which can be considered for disposal at sea according to the hazard they present to the environment. For the blacklist items, dumping is prohibited. The dumping of grey-listed materials requires a special permit from a designated national authority under strict control and provided certain conditions are met. All other materials or substances can be dumped after a general permit has been issued.[160]

---

[155] IMO (2018).

[156] MARPOL, Annex V, chapter I.

[157] Madden Marine (2015), p. 19.

[158] IMO (2010).

[159] London Convention (1972), arts. I and II, and the London Protocol (1996), art. 2.

[160] Ibid.

This purpose, though similar to that of the Convention, is more restrictive as the application of a 'precautionary approach' is included as a general obligation.[161] Also, under the London Protocol, a 'reverse list' approach is adopted, which implies that all types of dumping are prohibited unless explicitly permitted.[162] Moreover, the incineration of wastes at sea is prohibited,[163] and the export of wastes for the purpose of dumping or incineration at sea is also prohibited.[164] And extended compliance procedures[165] and technical assistance provisions have been included.[166]

Again, the London Protocol 1996 revised the London Convention 1972 and expanded the scope of the act of dumping. In this regard, though the London Convention 1972 allowed some acts of dumping, where it prohibited all dumping from ships except for materials listed on the so-called reverse list,[167] which by implication allows the dumping of plastics, the London Protocol 1996 does not include plastics on the reverse list; thus, the dumping of plastics is prohibited.[168]

There are no compliance mechanisms under the London Convention 1972; however, with the entry into force of the London Protocol on 26 March 2006, a set of Compliance Procedures and Mechanisms pursuant to Article 11 of the London Protocol 2006 was adopted in November 2007 and subsequently revised in 2017.[169]

The objective of the Compliance Procedures and Mechanisms under the London Protocol 2006 is to assess and promote compliance with the London Protocol with a view to allowing for the full and open exchange of information, in a constructive manner. The Meeting of Contracting Parties retains overall responsibility for compliance matters.[170]

For purposes of responsibility of parties and liability thereto, the London Protocol 2006 further provides that in accordance with the principles of international law regarding state responsibility for damage to the environment of other states or to any other area of the environment, the contracting parties undertake to develop procedures regarding liability arising from the dumping or incineration at sea of wastes or other matter.[171] To this end, 'Parties shall take into account the approach that the polluter should, in principle, bear the cost of pollution'. Thus, 'each Contracting Party shall endeavour to promote practices whereby those it has authorized to engage in dumping or incineration at sea bear the cost of meeting the pollution prevention

---

161 London Protocol (1996), art. 3(1).

162 Ibid., art. 4.

163 Ibid., art. 5.

164 Ibid., art. 6.

165 Ibid., art. 11.

166 Ibid., art. 13.

167 London Convention (1972), art. III (1)(a).

168 London Protocol (1996), art. 1(4)(1).

169 IMO (2010).

170 Ibid.

171 London Protocol (1996), art. 15.

and control requirements for the authorized activities, having due regard to the public interest'.[172]

14.4.2.3 Principles of International Law and Rules of Customary International Law[173]

Principles of international law and rules of customary international law are additional sources of international law. Rules of customary international law bind all states, except for those that persistently object. The key principles and rules relevant to marine litter are the following.

14.4.2.3.1 Prevention of Environmental Harm (The No Harm Rule)[174]

This principle calls for states to prevent pollution and minimise damage. Both principle 21 of the Stockholm Declaration 1972[175] and principle 2 of the Rio Declaration on Environment and Development (Rio Declaration) 1992[176] provide that states have the responsibility to ensure that activities under their jurisdiction or control do not cause damage to the environment of other states or areas beyond national jurisdiction. This principle is also reflected throughout UNCLOS,[177] including Article 194, requiring states to take 'all measures ... that are necessary to prevent, reduce and control pollution of the marine environment from any source ...'.[178] The International Court of Justice (ICJ) recognised this principle as a norm of customary international law in a number of decisions.[179]

[172] Ibid., art. 3(2).

[173] Some of the principles were discussed in Chap. 4 of this book.

[174] Discussed in section 4.2 of Chap. 4 of this book.

[175] Stockholm Declaration (1972).

[176] Rio Declaration on Environment and Development (1992).

[177] UNCLOS (1982).

[178] Other UNCLOS (1982) articles addressing the prevention of harm include arts. 195, 196, 199, 201–203, 207–217, 220, 222, 228, 230 and 234.

[179] Corfu Channel (*United Kingdom v Albania*), Merits, 1949 I.C.J. 4, 22 (April 9); Legality of the Threat or Use of Nuclear Weapons, Advisory Opinion, 1996 I.C.J. 226, paras. 29–30 (July 8); Gabcikovo-Nagymaros Project (*Hungary v Slovakia*), 1997 ICJ, 7, para. 53 (Sept. 25); Concerning Pulp Mills on the River Uruguay (*Argentina v Uruguay*), 2010, ICJ, para. 193 (Apr. 20). See also Trail Smelter Arbitration (*United States v Canada*), 3 R.I.A.A. 1905-81 (1941); In the Arbitration Regarding the Iron Rhine Railway (*Belgium v Netherland*), 23 R.I.A.A. 35 (Perm.Ct. Arb. 2005).

14.4.2.3.2 Precautionary Principle[180]

The precautionary principle encourages legislators and regulators to enact laws, regulations and policies that will help prevent environmental harm even in the absence of scientific certainty. Principle 15 of the Rio Declaration 1992 articulated the principle, and a 2011 advisory opinion of the International Tribunal on the Law of the Sea (ITLOS) addressing deep-seabed mining indicated that there is a trend towards making the precautionary approach part of customary international law, but it did not explicitly rule on its customary status.[181]

14.4.2.3.3 Polluter-Pays Principle[182]

The polluter-pays principle seeks to minimise, control, prevent, remediate and, at times, punish behaviours or activities that cause environmental damage. Principle 16 of the Rio Declaration 1992[183] calls upon national authorities to take the approach of making polluters bear the cost of environmental pollution. According to Thornton and Beckwith,[184] the premise upon which the principle is based is its allocation of economic obligations in relation to environmentally damaging activities, particularly in relation to liability, the use of economic instruments and the application of rules relating to competition and subsidy. The principle therefore imposes liability on a person who pollutes the environment to compensate for the damage caused and return the environment to its original state regardless of the intent.[185]

14.4.2.3.4 Principle of Cooperation[186]

While principle 24 of the Stockholm Declaration 1972 reflects a general political commitment to international cooperation in matters concerning the protection of the environment, principle 27 of the Rio Declaration 1992[187] states rather more succinctly the importance of multilateral and bilateral cooperation to 'effectively control, prevent, reduce and eliminate adverse environmental effects resulting in all spheres, in such a way that due account is taken of the sovereignty and interests of all States'.

---

[180] Discussed in section 4.6 of Chap. 4 of this book.

[181] Responsibilities and Obligations of States Sponsoring Persons and Entities with Respect to Activities in the Area (Advisory Opinion) ITLOS Case No. 17, February 1, 2011, para. 135.

[182] Discussed in section 4.7 of Chap. 4 of this book.

[183] Rio Declaration (1992).

[184] Thornton and Beckwith (2014), p. 14.

[185] S S Rana and Co (2017).

[186] Discussed in section 4.4 of Chap. 4 of this book.

[187] Rio Declaration (1992).

In the *MOX Plant* case,[188] ITLOS held that the duty to cooperate is 'a fundamental principle in the prevention of pollution of the marine environment under … the Convention on the Law of the Sea and general international law'.[189] Further binding status of the principle in international law was confirmed in the decisions of the International Court of Justice (ICJ) in the *Lac Lanoux* arbitration,[190] the *Pulp Mills* case[191] and the *Nuclear Test* cases.[192]

14.4.2.3.5 Environmental Impact Assessment

Principle 17 of the 1992 Rio Declaration calls for environmental impact assessments (EIAs) to be undertaken for 'proposed activities that are likely to have a significant adverse impact on the environment and are subject to a decision of a competent national authority'. Article 206 of UNCLOS[193] has a similar requirement for the assessment of potential activities when those activities may have significant effects on the marine environment. The need for impact assessment is also highlighted in Agenda 21 chapter 15.5(k).[194] In its *Pulp Mills* case,[195] the International Court of Justice held that there is a 'requirement under general international law' for states to undertake an EIA where there is a risk of significant adverse impact on a shared resource.[196] These reflect the view that environmental impact assessments could, in certain circumstances, be required as a matter of customary international law.

14.4.2.3.6 Principle of Sustainable Development[197]

Under the Rio Declaration 1992,[198] the principle of sustainable development requires that 'the right to development must be fulfilled so as to equitably meet developmental and environmental needs of present and future generations'.[199] Thus, 'in order to achieve sustainable development, environmental protection shall

188 *Ireland v United Kingdom ITLOS Documents*, 25 October 2001.

189 The *MOX Plant* case (*Ireland v. United Kingdom*) (Provisional Measures), ITLOS Case No. 10, Order of December 3, 2001, para.82.

190 *France v Spain* (1957) 12 RIAA 281; 24 I.L.R. 101, Arbitral Tribunal, November 16, 1957.

191 Concerning Pulp Mills on the River Uruguay (*Argentina v Uruguay*), 2010 ICJ.

192 *Australia v France* (1974) ICJ Reports 253 at 389.

193 UNCLOS (1982).

194 AGENDA 21 (1992).

195 Concerning Pulp Mills on the River Uruguay (*Argentina v Uruguay*), 2010, ICJ, para. 204 (Apr. 20).

196 Ibid.

197 Discussed in section 4.5 of Chap. 4 of this book.

198 Rio Declaration (1992).

199 Ibid., principle 3.

constitute an integral part of the development process and cannot be considered in isolation from it'.[200] Based on these provisions, it is suggested that for waste disposal, this means that marine litter issues should be taken into account, along with other environmental concerns (emissions, leachate, habitat degradation) and social concerns (land use, health risks), as well as economic costs.[201]

Besides multilateral environmental agreements (MEAs) and principles of international law, discussed above, there are some declarations and guidelines and other efforts reached by the international community that may be applied in the control of marine litter,[202] for instance the Global Programme of Action (GPA) for the Protection of the Marine Environment from Land-Based Activities.

The GPA was hosted by the United Nations Environment Programme (UNEP). It was created as a unique global intergovernmental mechanism that advises national and regional authorities on how to prevent and reduce marine degradation from land-based pollution and activities.[203] The GPA was adopted by 108 governments and the European Commission at an intergovernmental conference convened in Washington, D.C., USA, in 1995.[204]

The parties set, as their common goal, sustained and effective action to deal with all land-based impacts upon the marine environment, specifically those resulting from sewage, persistent organic pollutants, radioactive substances, heavy metals, oils (hydrocarbons), nutrients, sediment mobilisation, litter and physical alteration and destruction of habitat.[205]

However, after the Manila Declaration of 2012, the GPA focused its resources on addressing three priority source categories, namely marine litter, nutrient management and wastewater through global voluntary multi-stakeholder partnerships of governments, intergovernmental agencies, academia, the private sector and civil society.[206]

The implementation of the GPA is primarily the task of governments in close partnership with all stakeholders, including international and public organisations, local communities, non-governmental organisations and the private sector. The GPA, together with its partners and through the three global partnerships on marine litter, nutrient and wastewater management, is facilitating and assisting governments in their tasks.[207]

---

[200] Rio Declaration (1992), principle 4.

[201] UNEP (2005).

[202] These often referred to as soft law instruments are often persuasive in nature but may inspire and inform national legislation.

[203] UNEP (2018).

[204] Since 1995, GPA has held four intergovernmental review meetings (IGR): in Montreal, Canada, in 2001; in Beijing, China, in October 2006; in Manila, Philippines, in January 2012; and in Bali, Indonesia, in October 2018.

[205] UNEP (2018).

[206] Ibid.

[207] UNEP (2018).

The Principles from the Food and Agricultural Organization (FAO) of the United Nations is another of such guidelines. To promote long-term conservation and sustainable use of fishery resources, following a call from the International Conference on Responsible Fishing (1992) to strengthen the international legal framework for more effective conservation, management and sustainable exploitation and production of living aquatic resources, the 1995 FAO Conference, with more than 170 states, adopted the FAO Code of Conduct for Responsible Fisheries.[208]

The Code sets out principles and international standards of behaviour for responsible practices with a view to ensuring the effective conservation, management and development of living aquatic resources with due respect for the ecosystem and biodiversity. The Code recognises the nutritional, economic, social, environmental and cultural importance of fisheries and the interests of all stakeholders of fishing and aquaculture industries. The Code takes into account the biological characteristics of the resources and their environment and the interests of consumers and other users.[209]

To this end, section 7.2.2 of the Code states that management measures must be undertaken to minimise the impact of pollution and lost or abandoned gear on fish and non-fish species; section 8.3.2 asserts that port states should also have the responsibility to prevent pollution, for example providing adequate disposal systems; and section 8.9.1 states that harbours should have the same responsibilities as ports.[210]

A variety of instruments have been established within the framework of the Code to assist fishers, industries and governments in taking the necessary practical steps to implement the various facets of the Code, providing the broad framework within which FAO implements its programme of work in fisheries and aquaculture. These instruments include four international plans of action (IPOAs)—which are voluntary instruments that apply to all states and entities and to all fisheries on issues relating to seabirds (IPOA-seabirds), sharks (IPOA-sharks), fishing capacity (IPOA-capacity) and illegal, unreported and unregulated (IUU) fishing (IPOA-IUU)—and two strategies, which are also voluntary instruments that apply to all states and entities aimed at improving the knowledge and understanding of capture fisheries and aquaculture.[211]

Another of such guidelines is the one from the United Nations Conference on Sustainable Development (also known as 'Rio+20') in 2012. At the United Nations Conference on Sustainable Development (also known as 'Rio+20'), a series of measures to improve sustainable development was identified. Of relevance to the discussions on marine litter are the provisions of paragraph 163 of the *Future We Want*.[212] The Conference noted with concern that the health of oceans and marine

[208] Food and Agricultural Organization of the United Nations (FAO) (1995).

[209] Ibid.

[210] Ibid.

[211] FAO (1996).

[212] United Nations Organization (2010).

biodiversity is negatively affected by marine pollution, including marine debris, especially plastic, persistent organic pollutants, heavy metals and nitrogen-based compounds, from a number of marine and land-based sources, including shipping and land run-off.[213]

As a result, the international community is committed to taking action to reduce the incidence and impacts of such pollution on marine ecosystems, including through the effective implementation of relevant conventions adopted in the framework of the International Maritime Organization and the follow-up of relevant initiatives, such as the Global Programme of Action for the Protection of the Marine Environment from Land-Based Activities, as well as the adoption of coordinated strategies to this end. This is with the intention of achieving significant reductions in marine debris to prevent harm to the coastal and marine environment by 2025.[214]

On 21 October 2015, the United Nations General Assembly (UNGA) adopted Resolution 70/1 and endorsed the 2030 Agenda for Sustainable Development and the Sustainable Development Goals (SDGs). Goal 14 seeks to conserve and sustainably use the oceans, seas and marine resources for sustainable development and explicitly addresses marine debris.[215]

Again, on 23 December 2015, UNGA adopted Resolution 70/235 on Oceans and the Law of the Sea.[216] In the Resolution, UNGA noted with concern that the health of oceans and marine biodiversity are negatively affected by marine pollution, including marine debris, especially plastic, persistent organic pollutants, heavy metals and nitrogen-based compounds, from a number of marine and land-based sources, including shipping and land run-off, and that states committed to take action to reduce the incidence and impacts of such pollution on marine ecosystems, including through the effective implementation of relevant conventions adopted in the framework of the International Maritime Organization and the follow-up of relevant initiatives, such as the Global Programme of Action for the Protection of the Marine Environment from Land-Based Activities, as well as the adoption of coordinated strategies to this end, and that they further committed to take action, by 2025, based on collected scientific data, to achieve significant reductions in marine debris to prevent harm to the coastal and marine environment.[217]

It further noted with concern that the health of the oceans and marine biodiversity are negatively affected by marine debris, especially plastic, from land-based and marine sources and invites states to implement Resolution 1/6 on marine plastic debris and microplastics, adopted by the United Nations Environment Assembly of the United Nations Environment Programme at its first session, held in Nairobi from 23 to 27 June 2014.[218]

---

[213] Ibid.

[214] Ibid.

[215] United Nations General Assembly (UNGA) (2015), Resolution 70/1.

[216] Ibid.

[217] UNGA (2015), Resolution 70/235, para. 170.

[218] Ibid., para. 188.

It then urges states to integrate the issue of marine debris into national and, as appropriate, regional strategies dealing with waste management, especially in the coastal zone, ports and maritime industries, including recycling, reuse, reduction and disposal; to consider developing an integrated waste management infrastructure; and to encourage the development of appropriate economic incentives with the aim of reducing marine debris.[219]

Addressing this issue includes the development of cost-recovery systems that provide an incentive to use port reception facilities and discourage ships from discharging marine debris at sea as well as support for measures to prevent, reduce and control pollution from any source, including land-based sources, such as community-based coastal and waterway clean-up and monitoring activities. Thus, states are encouraged to cooperate regionally and sub-regionally to identify potential sources and coastal and oceanic locations where marine debris aggregates and to develop and implement joint prevention and recovery programmes for marine debris, as well as to raise awareness of the issue of marine debris and the need to consider environmentally sound options for its removal.[220]

To this end, the Resolution encourages states that have not yet done so to become parties to the 1997 Protocol (Annex VI—Regulations for the Prevention of Air Pollution from Ships) to the International Convention for the Prevention of Pollution from Ships 1973, as modified by the Protocol of 1978 relating thereto, as amended,[221] the 1996 Protocol to the Convention on the Prevention of Marine Pollution by Dumping of Wastes and Other Matter 1972 (the London Protocol)[222]

The application of these legal instruments can include the provisions of mandates, procedures and standards to prevent, reduce and manage marine litter. Although policies and laws are needed not only to address the removal of litter but more importantly to govern the production, use, and disposal of products, in addition, a circular economy approach[223] can reduce the quantity of waste by stopping it at its source. By designing products that are durable, reparable, recoverable and recyclable at the end of their productive use, circular economy approaches can prevent the generation of waste in the first place and, thereby, the entry of marine litter into the environment.[224]

---

[219] Ibid., para. 193.

[220] Ibid.

[221] UNGA (2015), Resolution 70/235, para. 195.

[222] Ibid., para. 196.

[223] A circular economy is restorative and regenerative by design. This means materials constantly flow around a 'closed loop' system, rather than being used once and then discarded. In the case of plastic, this means simultaneously keeping the value of plastics in the economy, without leakage into the natural environment.

[224] UNEP (2009).

In addition to the enforcement of the provisions of the legal instruments discussed above and the adoption of a circular economy approach, managing marine litter may also be achieved following these recommendations by UNEP:[225]

1. States that elect to adopt a comprehensive, holistic approach to marine litter management may:

    (a) Adopt legislation providing an overarching framework for preventing, reducing, and otherwise managing marine litter. This legislation should consider the relationship between the marine litter legislation and other relevant laws (for example, on waste management), and particularly whether the new overarching legislation supplements or replaces the existing laws. It should also provide for periodic review of the enacted legislation and its implementation.
    (b) Establish an inter-agency mechanism for coordinating among the diverse sectors with a role in addressing marine litter. This inter-agency coordination should address the development, implementation, and review of the marine litter legislation and implementing regulations. It should also engage key stakeholders from the private sector and civil society.

2. States that adopt a more piecemeal approach to marine litter may:

    (a) Develop and implement laws to ban or diminish the production of single-use trash items and other waste that is commonly found in marine litter. Single-use plastics, such as bottles, cups, and bags, are often found on beaches and are pervasive in the marine environment. Therefore, many countries and sub-national governments have banned certain types of single-use items (especially plastic bags).
    (b) Regulate non-recoverable items, such as plastic microbeads in personal care and cosmetics products. These are impossible to remove from an aquatic environment. By preventing their introduction into the marine environment, States can eliminate a source of marine plastic pollution.
    (c) Develop and implement legislation to prevent the waste, once created, from entering the marine environment. Preventing waste from entering the marine environment is a key approach, as once it has entered the marine environment, it is difficult or impossible to remove. Therefore establishing programs and practices, such as covered landfills near aquatic bodies, may help minimize waste. Approaches such as the circular economy model of economic development can be used to reduce the creation of items that easily become marine litter.
    (d) Support marine litter cleanup efforts. Through policy measures and government programmes, States can support regional and local marine debris monitoring and cleanup programmes, engage in education and awareness-raising initiatives, and extend producer responsibility.

[225] Ibid.

14.5 Protecting the Marine Environment and the Marine Living Resources: The United Nations Convention on the Law of the Sea

The United Nations Convention on the Law of the Sea, also called the Law of the Sea Convention or the Law of the Sea Treaty (UNCLOS 1982), is an international agreement that establishes a legal framework for all marine and maritime activities. It was signed on 10 December 1982 and came into force on 16 November 1994.[226] It has provisions for the protection of marine living resources, and as of June 2016, 167 countries and the European Union are parties.

UNCLOS 1982 sets up a comprehensive framework for the establishment of global rules on the protection of the marine environment and marine living resources, including detailed and important institutional arrangements and provisions on environmental impact assessment, technology transfer, dispute settlement and liability.

UNCLOS 1982 aims at establishing a legal order for the seas and oceans, which will facilitate international communication and therefore promote the peaceful uses of the seas and oceans, the equitable and efficient utilisation of their resources, the conservation of their living resources and the study, protection and preservation of the marine environment. To this end, the Convention requires states to pursue two main environmental objectives:

(a) To prevent, reduce and control marine pollution, and
(b) To conserve and manage marine living resources[227]

To achieve these objectives, the Convention established rules on information, scientific research, the monitoring of environmental assessment, enforcement and liability. More specifically, the Convention declares that states have the sovereign right to exploit their natural resources pursuant to their environmental policies and in accordance with their duty to protect and preserve the marine environment.[228]

This duty to protect and preserve the environment connotes states using measures that are necessary to prevent, reduce and control pollution of the marine environment from any source using the best practicable means at their disposal and in accordance with their capabilities. But in doing this, states must take into account internationally agreed rules, standards and recommended practices and procedures, characteristic regional features and the need to minimise, to the fullest extent possible, the release of toxic, harmful or noxious substances, especially those that are persistent, into the marine environment.[229] Thus, states are therefore directed to:

---

[226] UNCLOS (1982).

[227] UNCLOS (1982), preamble.

[228] Ibid., art. 193.

[229] Ibid., art. 207(1), (4) and (5).

> Take all measures necessary to ensure that activities under their jurisdiction or control are conducted as not to cause damage by pollution to other states and their environment, and that pollution arising from incidents or activities under their jurisdiction or control does not spread beyond the areas where they exercise sovereign rights in accordance with the Convention.[230]

To avoid multiple interpretations, the UNCLOS 1982 sets out to define what amounts to pollution. According to the Convention, pollution is:

> the introduction by man directly or indirectly, of substances or energy into the marine environment, including estuaries, which results or is likely to result in such deleterious effects as harm to living resources and marine life, hazards to human health, hindrance to marine activities, including fishing and other legitimate use of the sea; impairment of quality for uses of seawater and reduction of amenities.[231]

The Convention provides a number of far-reaching enforcement mechanisms. Generally, the flag state will be responsible for ensuring that vessels flying its flag or of its registry comply with applicable international pollution rules and standards and with laws and regulations adopted in accordance with UNCLOS 1982 and for the effective enforcement of such measures, irrespective of where the violation occurs.[232] Under Article 219,[233] a port state must take measures to prevent vessels from sailing where they have ascertained that the vessel is in violation of applicable international rules and standards relating to seaworthiness, which may threaten the marine environment.

Therefore, where there are grounds to believe that there is a substantial discharge causing or threatening significant pollution of the marine environment, the coastal state has the right to investigate and institute proceedings against vessels navigating in its territorial sea, to obtain information from vessels navigating in its exclusive economic zone (EEZ) and to undertake inspections of vessels in the zone. Such coastal state may also institute proceedings, with sanctions, including detention against vessels in its territorial sea or EEZ if there is clear evidence that a violation of applicable international rules and standards has occurred which results in a discharge causing major damage or threat of major damage to the coastline or related economic zone.[234]

A port state may also investigate and institute proceedings in respect of a vessel voluntarily within its port or at an offshore terminal for harmful discharges from that vessel outside the internal waters, territorial sea or EEZ in violation of international rules and standards or of its laws and regulations adopted in accordance with this Convention or applicable international rules and standards for environmental protection.[235]

---

[230] Ibid., art. 194 (2).

[231] UNCLOS (1982), art. 1(4).

[232] Ibid., art. 217 (1).

[233] UNCLOS (1982).

[234] Ibid., art. 216.

[235] Ibid., arts 218(1) and 220.

A wide range of procedures for dispute settlement is provided under the Convention. Part XV addresses compulsory dispute settlement and allows states at the time of signature, ratification or accession, or at any time thereafter, to designate any of the following dispute settlement procedures. These include the International Tribunal for the Law of the Sea (ITLOS), established in accordance with Annex VI of UNCLOS; the International Court of Justice (ICJ), an arbitral tribunal constituted in accordance with Annex VII of UNCLOS; and the special arbitral tribunal under Annex VII of UNCLOS.[236]

Failure to designate any of these dispute resolution mechanisms means that a state has powers to designate arbitration in accordance with Annex VII of UNCLOS 1982.[237] Areas of dispute to be referred for dispute settlement under UNCLOS 1982 include:

(i) Disputes arising in the exercise by a coastal state of its sovereign rights or jurisdiction under UNCLOS when it is alleged that there has been a violation of certain UNCLOS provisions, including internationally lawful uses of the EEZ, or specified international rules or standards for the protection and preservation of the marine environment.
(ii) Fishery disputes: where this occurs, it will be subject to the compulsory procedure, except for disputes over the sovereign right of a coastal state regarding living resources within the EEZ.
(iii) Other potential areas of dispute, like boundary delimitation, military activities and functions under the Security Council and exploration and exploitation of the international seabed and ocean floor.[238]

In respect of liability for damages, UNCLOS 1982 contains two rules. Under Article 139(1), which applies to the seabed, ocean floor and subsoil beyond the limits of national jurisdiction (referred to as the Area), states parties and international organisations have the responsibility to ensure that activities carried out by them or their nationals or those effectively controlled by them or their nationals in the Area comply with the UNCLOS 1982 rules on the Area. Failure to do so attracts liability on the party that caused the damage. Article 139(2)[239] provides, *inter alia*,

> That contractor shall have responsibility or liability for any damage arising out of wrongful acts in the conduct of operation in the Area, and that the authority shall have responsibility or liability for damage arising out of wrongful acts in the exercise of its powers and functions, in every case liability shall be for the actual amount of damage.

Where this is the case, a state party may argue, as a defence, that it has taken all necessary and appropriate measures to secure effective compliance under the relevant provisions of UNCLOS 1982.

[236] UNCLOS (1982), art. 287(1).

[237] Ibid., art. 287(3).

[238] Ibid., art. 297.

[239] UNCLOS (1982).

The second arm of liability shall arise where a state fails in its responsibility to fulfil the provisions of UNCLOS 1982 regarding its international obligations concerning the protection and preservation of the marine environment. Such state shall be liable in accordance with international law.[240] This provision was tested in the *Southern Bluefin Tuna*[241] case in 1999. In that case, Australia and New Zealand initiated arbitration proceedings, in July 1999, under Part XV of Annex VII of UNCLOS 1982, alleging that Japan had breached its obligation under Articles 64 and 116–119 of UNCLOS 1982 in relation to the conservation and management of southern bluefin tuna stock through the implementation of a unilateral experimental fishing programme.

14.6 Legal Regime for the Conservation of Wetlands

A wetland is a place in which the land is covered by saltwater, freshwater or somewhere in between, either seasonally or permanently. It functions as its own distinct ecosystem. Wetlands can be recognised from other types of land or bodies of water, primarily by the vegetation that has adapted to wet soil.[242] Wetland is thus a separate habitat that is constantly or periodically flooded or saturated by water. Flooding causes oxygen-free processes to prevail, particularly in soils.

Water saturation (hydrology) largely determines how the soil develops and the types of plant and animal communities living in and on the soil. Wetlands may support both aquatic and terrestrial species. The prolonged presence of water creates conditions that favour the growth of specially adapted plants (hydrophytes) and promotes the development of characteristic wetland (hydric) soils. Wetlands vary widely because of regional and local differences in soils, topography, climate, hydrology, water chemistry, vegetation and other factors, including human disturbance. Indeed, wetlands are found in the tundra and the tropics and on every continent, except Antarctica. Two general categories of wetlands are recognised: coastal or tidal wetlands and inland or non-tidal wetlands.[243]

The importance of wetlands lies in the fact that without wetlands, cities have to spend more money to treat water, floods are more devastating to nearby communities, storm surges from hurricanes can penetrate farther inland, animals are displaced or die out and food supplies are disrupted, along with livelihoods. It is for these reasons that it is important to conserve wetlands. There are a number of legal instruments for the conservation of wetlands. These include the following.

[240] UNCLOS (1982), art. 235.

[241] *Australia and New Zealand v Japan* 39 ILM 1359 (2000).

[242] World Wildlife Organisation (2023).

[243] United States Environmental Protection Agency (EPA) (2023).

14.6.1 *Wetlands of International Importance Especially for Waterfowl Habitat (Ramsar Convention) 1971*

The Convention on Wetlands of International Importance Especially for Waterfowl Habitat (Ramsar Convention) 1971[244] is a major international legal instrument for the conservation of wetlands. The Ramsar Convention was the first global agreement to address the conservation of a particular habitat or ecosystem.[245] The Convention was held on 2 February 1971 at Ramsar (Iran). It entered into force on 21 December 1975 and, as of January 2016, had 169 contracting parties, or member states, in all parts of the world. Though the central Ramsar message is the need for the sustainable use of all wetlands, the 'flagship' of the Convention is the List of Wetlands of International Importance (the 'Ramsar List'). Presently, the parties have designated for this list more than 2220 wetlands for special protection as 'Ramsar Sites', covering 214 million hectares (2.14 million km^2), larger than the surface area of Mexico.[246]

Wetlands include areas of marsh, fen, peatland or water, whether natural or artificial, permanent or temporary, with water that is static or flowing, fresh, brackish or salt, including areas of marine water the depth of which at low tide does not exceed 6 m.[247] Recent estimates suggest that globally, there remain between 5.3 and 5.7 million km^2 of wetlands. They serve a variety of functions, including flood and erosion control, water purification and shoreline stabilisation. Major threats to wetlands include pollution, hunting, human settlement, agriculture, siltation and diversion of water supplies.[248]

According to the Convention, without prejudice to their sovereign rights, each contracting party must designate suitable wetlands within its territory for inclusion in the List of Wetlands of International Importance, taking account of their international significance in terms of ecology, botany, zoology, immunology or hydrology.[249] The Convention requires each contracting party to designate upon signature or ratification or accession at least one wetland and, thereafter, the addition of further wetlands or the extension of listed wetlands.[250]

Each party's basic commitments include formulating and implementing policies in wetland conservation and its wise use, establishing nature reserves, endeavouring

---

[244] Convention on Wetlands of International Importance Especially as Waterfowl Habitat (Ramsar Convention) as amended by the Protocol of 3 December 1982 and the Amendments of 28 May 1987, https://www.ramsar.org/sites/default/files/documents/library/current_convention_text_e.pdf, accessed 11 December 2019.

[245] This Convention targets the protection of the wetlands, not necessarily the ocean but part of the marine environment.

[246] Ramsar Convention Secretariat (2016).

[247] Ibid., art. 1(1).

[248] Sands (2000), p. 389.

[249] Ramsar Convention (1971), arts. 2(1) and 3.

[250] Ibid., arts. 2(4) and 5.

to increase waterfowl population and ensuring that it is informed of any actual or likely change in the ecological character of any of its listed wetlands, which information is to be passed on to the convention secretariat.[251] The Convention also encourages the research exchange of data, the training of personnel as well as consultation between parties about implementing their obligations as are provided under Article 4(3) and (5). To improve implementation, particularly by developing countries, the conference of the parties organised since 1975 established the Wetland Conservation Fund in 1990.

14.6.2 National Environmental Standards and Regulations Enforcement Agency (Establishment) (NESREA) Act 2007[252]

At the national level, Nigeria had put in place some Regulations guiding the use and protection of both the wetlands and the coastal and marine area. These Regulations were made pursuant to the combined effects of sections 26(1) and 34(c) of the National Environmental Standards and Regulations Enforcement Agency (Establishment) (NESREA) Act 2007. Section 26(1) of the NESREA Act provides that 'the Agency[253] may make regulations, guidelines and standards for the protection and enhancement of the quality of land resources, natural watershed, coastal zone,[254] dams and reservoirs including prevention of flood and erosion'. Section 34(c) of the same Act on the other hand provides that 'the Minister[255] shall make regulations generally for the purposes of carrying out or giving full effect to the functions of the Agency under the Act'. The following Regulations were made:

(a) National Environmental (Wetlands, River Banks and Lake Shores) Regulations 2009
(b) National Environmental (Coastal and Marine Area Protection) Regulations 2011

[251] Ibid., arts 4(1) (4) and 5.

[252] Government Notice No. 61, Act No. 25 2007, Federal Republic of Nigeria Official Gazette No. 92, Vol. 97, 31 July 2007.

[253] The National Environmental Standards and Regulations Enforcement Agency established under the NESREA Act (2007), s. 1.

[254] For emphasis.

[255] Minister in charge of environmental matters; see NESREA Act (2007), s. 37.

14.6.2.1 The National Environmental (Wetlands, River Banks and Lake Shores) Regulations 2009

These Regulations[256] provide for the management of Nigeria's wetlands.[257] Wetlands are defined as areas permanently or seasonally flooded by water where plants and animals have become adapted and include swamps, areas of marsh, banks of rivers, vegetation, areas impeded drainage or blackish salt.[258] Wetlands are complex ecosystems that provide spawning and nursery grounds for saltwater and freshwater fish, habitat for more than half of the migratory birds, and plants, both exotic and commonplace. In addition to providing plant and animal habitat, wetlands play a crucial role in flood control and water filtration.

The National Environmental (Wetlands, River Banks and Lake Shores) Regulations 2009 have two sets of objectives. The first set pertains to objectives in respect of wetlands and wetland resources. The objectives are to provide for the conservation and wise use of wetlands and their resources in Nigeria,[259] ensure water catchment conservation and flood control,[260] ensure the sustainable use of wetlands for ecological and tourism purposes for the common good of all citizens,[261] ensure that wetlands are protected as habitats for species of fauna and flora[262] and minimise and control pollution.[263]

The second set of objectives relates to riverbanks and lake shores. These objectives are set to facilitate the sustainable utilisation and conservation of resources on riverbanks and lake shores for the benefit of the people and the community living in the area,[264] promote the integration of the sustainable use of resources in rivers and lakes into the local and national management of natural resources for socio-economic development,[265] enhance research and research-related activities[266] and prevent the silting of rivers and lakes and control pollution or degrading activities.[267]

In order to carry out its objectives, the Regulations provide that the Agency shall, in collaboration with relevant agencies, state and local governments, communities

---

[256] National Environmental (Wetlands, River Banks and Lake Shores) Regulations (2009), Government Notice No. 279, S.I. No. 26. Federal Republic of Nigeria Official Gazette No. 58 Vol. 96, 2 October 2009.

[257] Also known as swampy land: a marsh, swamp, or other area of land where the soil near the surface is saturated or covered with water, especially one that forms a habitat for wildlife.

[258] National Environmental (Wetlands, River Banks and Lake Shores) Regulations (2009), regulation 33.

[259] Ibid., regulation 2(a).

[260] Ibid., regulation 2(b).

[261] Ibid., regulation 2(c).

[262] Ibid., regulation 2(d).

[263] Ibid., regulation 2(e).

[264] Ibid., regulation 16(a).

[265] Ibid., regulation 16(b).

[266] Ibid., regulation 16(c).

[267] Ibid., regulation 16(d).

and other stakeholders, compile an inventory of all wetlands to determine the purposes of their conservation status based on the parameters as specified in the First Schedule,[268] periodically inspect the wetlands to determine the necessity for a revision or correction of the inventory on wetlands,[269] register changes in the boundaries of wetlands on maps in the inventory and make any other necessary changes in the inventory to reflect the actual situation on ground.[270] In conducting an inventory on wetlands, the state government shall consult with the local government with a view to involving the public in determining whether a wetland should be included in the list of wetlands of local or national or international importance.[271]

Another means of protecting the wetlands is by declaring an area as a protected wetland.[272] This declaration may be initiated by the Agency on the recommendation of the local government.[273] When this is the case, the Agency shall inform the local and state governments in writing, cause an environmental impact assessment (EIA) to be carried out by the EIA Department of the Federal Ministry of Environment, ensure that the views of the people inhabiting the areas contiguous to the wetland are taken into account by convening a meeting of the local inhabitants and ensure the preparation and submission of a report containing the above findings to the Agency.[274]

Where a local government initiates the declaration, it shall inform the Agency and state governments in writing, cause an environmental impact assessment (EIA) to be carried out by the EIA Department of the Federal Ministry of Environment, ensure that the views of the people inhabiting the areas contiguous to the wetland are taken into account by convening a meeting of the local inhabitants and ensure the preparation and submission of a report containing the above findings to the Agency. In addition, the local government shall provide the appropriate financial support to the inhabitants of the area for carrying out these tasks.[275]

Under the Regulations, a person commits an offence if he reclaims or drains a wetland; erects, constructs, places, alters, extends, removes or demolishes any structure that is fixed in, under or over a wetland; disturbs a wetland by drilling or tunnelling in a manner that has or is likely to have an adverse effect on a wetland; deposits in, on or under any wetland a substance in a manner that has or is likely to have an adverse effect on a wetland; destroys, damages or disturbs any wetland in a manner that has or is likely to have an adverse effect on any plant or animal or its habitat; introduces any exotic plant or animal in a wetland; removes soil from or

[268] National Environmental (Wetlands, River Banks and Lake Shores) Regulations (2009), regulation 4(1).

[269] Ibid., regulation 4(2).

[270] Ibid., regulation 4(3).

[271] Ibid., regulation 4(4).

[272] Ibid., regulation 7.

[273] Ibid., regulation 7(1).

[274] Ibid., regulation 7(2)(a)(d).

[275] Ibid., regulation 7(3).

burns any wetlands resource in a wetland; carries out any unauthorised activity in a protected wetland; carries out activities provided for in Regulation 20 without a permit; fails, neglects or refuses to protect a lake shore or riverbank from environmental degradation in accordance with these Regulations; and contravenes any of the provisions of these Regulations.[276]

The penalties are as follows: 'Any person found guilty of an offence under these Regulations is liable on conviction to imprisonment of not less than three months or to a fine not exceeding ₦500,000 or both.[277] In addition to the penalty provided, a person found guilty shall be required to carry out remediation work.'[278]

14.6.2.2 National Environmental (Coastal and Marine Area Protection) Regulations 2011

With reference to all users of coastal and marine areas in Nigeria, the objectives of the Regulations[279] in this respect are to:

(a) provide regulatory framework capable of preserving the natural ecological conditions of the estuarine system, the barrier islands system and the beaches so as to safeguard and perpetuate their natural productivity and their biological, economic and aesthetic values;
(b) provide regulatory framework for the application of preventive, precautionary and anticipatory approaches so as to avoid degradation of the marine environment, as well as to reduce the risk of long-term or irreversible effects on the coastal and marine environment;
(c) ensure the protection of the coastal and marine environment for sustainable development;
(d) ensure that land-based and industrial sources of marine and coastal pollution such as sewage, nutrients, synthetic compounds, litters, metals, other hydrocarbons; pollution associated with human activities, such as agriculture, forestry, urban development, tourism are controlled for the sustainable management of the coastal and marine environment;
(e) ensure that the development, use or preservation of resources of the coastal area proceeds in a manner consistent with the capability of the land and water for development, use, or preservation based on ecological considerations;
(f) ensure the sustainable use of resources, preservation and conservation of our coastal resources on behalf of the people of Nigeria;

[276] National Environmental (Wetlands, River Banks and Lake Shores) Regulations (2009), regulation 30 (a)–(k).

[277] Ibid., regulation 31(1).

[278] Ibid., regulation 31(2).

[279] National Environmental (Coastal and Marine Area Protection) Regulations (2011), Government Notice No. 132, S.I. No. 18. Federal Republic of Nigeria Official Gazette No.45 Vol. 98, 13 May 2011.

(g) provide national regulatory guidelines for enforcing compliance imperative for the domestication of international conventions, protocols, agreements and treaties relating to the coastal and marine environment to which Nigeria is signatory

(h) prohibit hazardous waste in coastal and marine areas, including:

   (i) sustainable protection, preservation and conservation of the coastal and marine area resources and other natural resources including but not limited to water use, scenic vistas, fish and wildlife; and management of transitional or intensely developed areas and areas especially suited to intensive use for development,
   (ii) the economic development of coastal areas, including but not limited to construction, location and design of industries, Port facilities, commercial establishments and other development,
   (iii) recreation and tourist facilities and parklands,
   (iv) transportation and circulation patterns for the coastal areas, major thoroughfares, transportation routes, navigation channels and harbours and other public utilities and facilities,
   (v) preservation and enhancement of historic, cultural, and scientific aspects of the coastal areas,
   (vi) protection of present common-law and statutory public right in the lands and waters of the coastal areas,
   (vii) prevent, minimise and ultimately eliminate the transfer of harmful aquatic organisms and pathogens through the control and management of ship's ballast water and sediment,
   (viii) any other purposes deemed necessary or appropriate to effectuate the (policies of these Regulations ; and
   (ix) Imposition of penalties on violators of the Coastal and Marine Areas Protection Regulations.[280]

To achieve these objectives, the Regulations provide for an inventory of the coastal and marine areas[281] and a classification of the coastal regulation zone,[282] set out prohibited areas[283] and provide regulation for permissible activities[284] and guidelines for regulated areas.[285] Further guidelines in respect of development

[280] National Environmental (Coastal and Marine Area Protection) Regulations (2011), regulation 2.
[281] Ibid., regulation 4.
[282] Ibid., regulation 5.
[283] Ibid., regulation 6.
[284] Ibid., regulation 7.
[285] Ibid., regulation 9.

activities on the coastal and marine areas were also set out in the Regulations,[286] as well as procedures for ballast water control,[287] under Regulation 11.

Violations of any of the provisions of these Regulations amount to an offence under Regulation 20. Penalties are also provided under the same regulation. Where the offence is committed by an individual, he shall, on conviction, be liable to a fine not exceeding ₦1,000,000 or imprisonment not exceeding 2 years or both fine and imprisonment and, in addition, to a fine of ₦10,000 for each day the offence subsists.[288] In the case of a body corporate, it shall, on conviction, be liable to a fine not exceeding ₦5,000,000 and, in addition, to a fine of ₦50,000 for each day the offence subsists.[289] In addition to the above penalties, the offender shall be required to carry our remediation work.[290]

14.7 National Laws for Pollution Control and the Protection of the Marine Environment

Nigeria, being a coastal state, has put in place a number of laws for pollution control and the protection of the marine environment. Some of these laws are:

(1) Oil in Navigable Waters Act (ONWA) 1968
(2) Merchant Shipping Act 2007
(3) National Oil Spill Detection and Response Agency (NOSDRA) Act 2006
(4) Nigerian Maritime Administration and Safety Agency (NIMASA) Act 2007

14.7.1 Oil in Navigable Waters Act (ONWA) 1968[291]

Oil in Navigable Waters Act (ONWA) 1968 is an Act to implement the terms of the International Convention for the Prevention of Pollution of the Sea by Oil 1954 to 1962 and to make provisions for such prevention in the navigable waters

[286] National Environmental (Coastal and Marine Area Protection) Regulations (2011), regulation 10.

[287] This relates to water pumped into the bottom of a ship to ensure its stability. See National Environmental (Coastal and Marine Area Protection) Regulations (2011), regulation 21.

[288] National Environmental (Coastal and Marine Area Protection) Regulations (2011), regulation 20(1).

[289] Ibid., regulation 20(2).

[290] Ibid., regulation 20(3).

[291] Cap O 6 Laws of the Federation of Nigeria (LFN) 2004.

of Nigeria.[292] The Act came into effect on 22 April 1968 as an Act to control and prohibit oil spillage in the navigable waterways of Nigeria.

Section 1(1) of the Act makes it an offence for a Nigerian ship[293] to discharge oil or any mixture containing not less than 100 parts of oil into prohibited sea areas.[294] This section applies to crude oil, fuel and lubricating oil and to heavy diesel oil. This offence can be committed by the owner or master of the ship from which the discharge occurred.

The Act, also by virtue of section 3(1)–(2), prohibits the discharge of oil into the sea from any vessels or from any place on land or from any apparatus used for transferring oil within the seaward limits of the territorial waters of Nigeria and all other waters (including inland waters) that are within those limits and are navigable by seagoing ships. If there is any such discharge, the owner or master of the vessel or the occupier of the land or the person in charge of such apparatus used for transferring oil shall be guilty of an offence.

Under section 5(5),[295] it is an offence for the master of a Nigerian- or foreign-owned ship to fail to install equipment considered suitable for the reduction or prevention of oil discharges. The equipment concerned is as may be specified by the Federal Ministry of Transport or his assignee.

Furthermore, it is an offence in the event of the failure of the master of a Nigerian ship exceeding gross tonnage of 80 tons to keep a log or record of oil discharges, oil spills and ballasting activities. And it is also an offence in case of the failure of a Nigerian or foreign ship to keep a record of any transfer of oil to and from its ships.[296] The making of fraudulent entries in connection with the offences is also an offence.[297] It is also the duty of the harbour authority to provide facilities in harbour for the disposal of oil residues. The failure to do this is an offence.[298]

Section 10 of ONWA 1968 imposes a duty on the owner or master of a ship or the occupier of the place on land from where oil or mixture containing oil is discharged into the waters of a Nigerian harbour in any of the named circumstances to report

---

[292]The provisions of the Act also apply to 'subsequent Convention'. 'Subsequent Convention' means any convention subsequent to the Conventions of 1954 to 1962, being a convention relating to the aforesaid Convention and accepted by the Federal Government of Nigeria (see ONWA 1968 (n 291), s. 1(4)).

[293]A Nigerian ship includes (i) government ships registered in Nigeria and (ii) government ships not so registered which are held for purposes of the federal military government or of the government of a state in Nigeria as they are considered other ships that are registered in Nigeria as Nigerian ships. See ONWA 1968 (n 291), s. 16(2).

[294]Prohibited sea areas are listed in the Schedule to ONWA. They include all sea areas within 50 miles (80 km) from land and outside the territorial waters of Nigeria and other geographically defined zones of the world.

[295]ONWA (1968).

[296]Ibid., s. 7(1), (3)(b).

[297]Ibid., s. 7(5)(b).

[298]Ibid., s. 8(8).

such and disclose the cause and source of the discharge to the master in charge of the affected harbour. Failure to do so is punishable by a fine.

14.7.2 Merchant Shipping Act 2007[299]

The Act was enacted as Act No. 27 of 2007 and came into force on 28 May 2008. Although the Act was enacted to provide for merchant shipping and for related matters, it has some provisions for the protection of the marine environment. Major provisions for the control of marine pollution can be found in some parts of the Act, particularly Parts XII,[300] XIV,[301] XV,[302] XVI,[303] XVII,[304] XIX,[305] XX[306] and XXIII.[307]

Under Part XII, the following international conventions, protocols and their amendments relating to maritime safety shall apply: the International Convention for the Safety of Life at Sea (SOLAS) 1974,[308] Protocol Relating to the International Convention for the Safety of Life at Sea 1988 and Annexes I to V thereto,[309] the International Convention on Maritime Search and Rescue (SAR) 1979,[310] the International Convention on Salvage 1989,[311] the International Ship and Ports Facility Security (ISPS) Code[312] and the International Convention for Safe Containers 1972.[313]

Furthermore, the Minister[314] may make such regulations as he deems necessary or expedient for the purpose of carrying out the provisions of Part XII of the Act. This is in respect of the construction of ships and ships' equipment, including the provision of life-saving and firefighter appliances;[315] radio communications in

[299] Enacted as Act No. 27 of 2007.
[300] Safety of Life at Sea.
[301] Radio Rules.
[302] Safety Provisions for Miscellaneous Vessels.
[303] Safety of Navigation (Especially on Prevention of Collisions).
[304] Unseaworthy Ships.
[305] Carriage of Bulk Cargoes.
[306] Dangerous Goods.
[307] Prevention of Pollution from Ships.
[308] Merchant Shipping Act (2007), s. 216(a).
[309] Ibid., s. 216(b).
[310] Ibid.
[311] Ibid., s. 216(i).
[312] Ibid., s. 216(k).
[313] Ibid., s. 216(l).
[314] Minister in charge of transportation.
[315] Merchant Shipping Act (2007), s. 217(2)(c).

ships;[316] the safety of navigation;[317] the carriage of grain by ships;[318] the carriage of dangerous goods by ships; the safety of navigation;[319] the design, construction, survey and marking of nuclear ships;[320] the management and safe operations of ships;[321] the construction, survey and marking of high-speed craft;[322] and special measures to enhance the memorandum on port state control.[323]

It should be noted that any person who fails to comply with and does or attempts to do any act contrary to the provisions of any safety regulations made under section 217 of the Act commits an offence and is liable on conviction to a fine not less than ₦300,000.[324]

14.7.3 National Oil Spill Detection and Response Agency (Establishment, Etc.) (Amendment) (NOSDRA) Act 2008[325]

The National Oil Spill Detection and Response Agency (NOSDRA)[326] is one of the two national agencies with responsibilities for oil spill preparedness and response.[327] It was established in 2006 as an institutional framework to coordinate the implementation of the National Oil Spill Contingency Plan (NOSCP) for Nigeria in accordance with the International Convention on Oil Pollution Preparedness, Response and Cooperation (OPRC) 1990, to which Nigeria is a signatory. Since its establishment, the Agency has been ensuring compliance with environmental legislation in the Nigerian petroleum sector.

The Agency embarks on joint investigation visits, ensures the remediation of impacted sites and monitors oil spill drill exercises and facility inspections. The Act enjoins the Agency to establish a National Control and Response Centre.[328] In line

[316] Ibid., s. 217(2)(d).

[317] Ibid., s. 217(2)(e).

[318] Ibid., s. 217(2)(f).

[319] Ibid., s. 217(2)(g).

[320] Ibid., s. 217(2)(i).

[321] Ibid., s. 217(2)(j).

[322] Merchant Shipping Act (2007), s. 217(2)(k).

[323] Ibid., s. 217(2)(l).

[324] Ibid., s. 218.

[325] Enacted as Act No. 15, 2006.

[326] The National Oil Spill Detection and Response Agency (NOSDRA) was established by the National Oil Spill Detection and Response Agency (Establishment, Etc.) (Amendment) Act, 2006.

[327] The second agency is the Nigerian Maritime Administration and Safety Agency (NIMASA), established by the Nigerian Maritime Administration and Safety Agency (NIMASA) Act 2007, Act No. 17 2007.

[328] NOSDRA Act (2006), s.18.

with this, the Agency has set up zonal offices in Port Harcourt, Warri and Uyo—all in the Niger Delta region, where much of the oil exploration and production in Nigeria is carried out; there are also zonal offices in Lagos, Kaduna, Kogi, Gombe and Akure. NOSDRA is currently liaising with relevant stakeholders in the Nigerian oil and gas industry to improve the practical methods of environmental management to cope with the dynamics of the petroleum sector.

According to the Act,[329] the objectives of the Agency shall be to monitor and regulate Tiers 1 and 2 oil spills as well as coordinate, implement and review the National Oil Spill Contingency Plan for Nigeria as follows:

(a) establish a viable national operational organization that ensures a safe, timely, effective and appropriate response to all oil pollution as well as hazardous and noxious substances in the petroleum sector;
(b) identify high-risk areas as well as priority areas for protection and clean up;
(c) establish the mechanism to monitor and assist or where expedient direct the response, including the capability to mobilize the necessary resources to save lives, protect threatened environment, and clean up to the best practical extent of the impacted sites;
(d) maximize the effective use of the available facilities and resources of corporate bodies, their international connections and oil spill co-operatives, that is Clean Nigeria Associates (CNA) in implementing appropriate spill response;
(e) ensure funding and appropriate and sufficient pre-positioned pollution combating equipment and materials, as well as functional communication network system required for effective response to major oil pollution;
(f) provide a programme of activation, training and drill exercises to ensure readiness to oil pollution preparedness and response and the management and operational personnel;
(g) co-operate and provide advisory services, technical support and equipment for purposes of responding to major oil pollution incident in the West African sub-region upon request by any neighbouring country, particularly where a part of the Nigerian territory may be threatened;
(h) provide support for research and development (R&D) in the local development of methods, materials and equipment for oil spill detection and response;
(i) co-operate with the International Maritime Organization and other national, regional and international organizations in the promotion and exchange of results of research and development programme relating to the enhancement of the state-of-the art of the oil pollution preparedness and response, including technologies, techniques for surveillance, containment, recovery, disposal and clean up to the best practical extent;
(j) establish agreements with neighbouring countries regarding the rapid movement of equipment, personnel and supplies into and out of the countries for emergency oil spill response activities;

[329] National Oil Spill Detection and Response Agency (Establishment, Etc.) (Amendment) Act, 2006.

(k) determine and preposition vital combat equipment at most strategic areas for rapid response;
(l) establish procedures by which the Nigeria Customs Service and the Nigerian Immigration Service shall ensure rapid importation of extra support response equipment and personnel;
(m) develop and implement an appropriate audit system for the entire plan;
(n) carry out such other activities as are necessary or expedient for the full discharge of its functions and the execution of the Plan under the Act.[330]

In addition, the Agency shall:

(a) be responsible for surveillance and ensure compliance with all existing environmental legislation in the petroleum sector including those relating to prevention, detection and general management of oil spills, oily wastes and gas flare;
(b) enforce compliance with the provisions of international agreements, protocols, conventions and treaties relating to oil and gas and oil spill response management and such other related agreements as may from time to time come into force;
(c) receive reports of oil spillages and co-ordinate oil spill response activities throughout Nigeria;
(d) co-ordinate the implementation of the Plan as may be formulated, from time to time, by the Federal Government;
(e) co-ordinate the implementation of the Plan for the removal of hazardous and noxious substances as may be issued by the Federal Government;
(f) ensure that all oil industry operators in Nigeria subscribe to and be bonafide members of Clean Nigeria Associates (CNA) or any other similar association by whatever name called; and
(g) perform such other functions as may be required to achieve the aims and objectives of the Agency under this Act or any plan as may be formulated by the Federal Government pursuant to this Act.[331]

Furthermore, the Agency shall, under the provisions of section 7 of the Act,

(a) ensure the co-ordination and implementation of the Plan within Nigeria including within 200 nautical miles from the baseline for which the breath of the territorial waters of Nigeria is measured;
(b) undertake surveillance, reporting, alerting and other response activities as they relate to oil spillages;
(c) encourage regional co-operation among member States of West African sub-region and in the Gulf of Guinea for combating oil spillage and pollution in our contiguous waters;

[330] National Oil Spill Detection and Response Agency (Establishment, Etc.) (Amendment) Act, 2006, s. 5.
[331] NOSDRA Act (2006), s. 6(1).

(d) strengthen the national capacity and regional action to prevent, control, combat and mitigate marine pollution;
(e) promote technical co-operation between Nigeria and member States of the West Africa sub-region.

As a way of expeditious tackling of oil spills, an oil spiller is to report an oil spill to the Agency[332] in writing, by fax or through electronic mail not later than 24 h after the occurrence of an oil spill, in default of which the failure to report shall attract a penalty in the sum of ₦2,000,000 for each day of failure to report the occurrence.[333] The failure to clean up the impacted site, to all practical extent, including the action plan for remediation, within 2 weeks of the occurrence of the spill, in accordance with the polluter-pays principle, shall constitute an offence, and on conviction, the oil spiller shall be liable to a fine not exceeding ₦5,000,000 or to imprisonment for a term not exceeding 2 years or to both such fine and imprisonment.[334]

It should be noted that the notice required shall be deemed to have been made if it is delivered at the nearest zonal or field office of the Agency closer to the impacted site or the National Control and Response Centre within the time stipulated under the Act.[335]

14.7.4 *Nigerian Maritime Administration and Safety Agency (NIMASA) Act 2007*[336]

The NIMASA Act[337] establishes the National Maritime Administration and Safety Agency (NIMASA). Under section 1(1) of the NIMASA Act 2007, the objective of the Agency shall be to:

(i) promote the development of indigenous commercial shipping in international and coastal shipping trade; and
(ii) regulate and promote maritime safety, security, marine pollution and maritime labour.

The scope of application of the Act includes ships, small ships and craft registered in Nigeria, and it extends to ships, small ships and craft flying a foreign flag in the exclusive economic zone, territorial and inland seas, inland waterways and the ports

[332] NOSDRA Act (2006).
[333] Ibid., s. 6(2).
[334] Ibid., s. 6(3).
[335] NOSDRA (2006), s. 6(4).
[336] Enacted as Act No. 17 2007.
[337] NIMASA Act (2007), s. 1(2)(a).

of the Federal Republic of Nigeria.[338] But the application of the Act does not extend to warships and military patrol ships.[339]

The functions and duties of the Agency, among other things, are to regulate the safety of shipping as regards the construction of ships and navigation,[340] provide search and rescue services,[341] control and prevent marine pollution,[342] receive and remove wrecks,[343] provide a national maritime search and rescue service,[344] provide maritime security[345] and establish the procedure for the implementation of the conventions of the International Maritime Organization and the International Maritime Labour Organisation and other international conventions to which the Federal Republic of Nigeria is a party on Maritime Safety and Security, Maritime Labour, Commercial Shipping and for the implementation codes, resolutions and circulars arising therefrom.[346]

To this end, the areas of focus of NIMASA include effective maritime safety administration, maritime labour regulation, marine pollution prevention and control, search and rescue, cabotage enforcement, shipping development and ship registration, training and certification of seafarers and maritime capacity development, using modern tools that guarantee efficiency and effectiveness, develop indigenous capacity and eliminate all hindrances to effective marine protection.[347]

In order to carry out the above functions, the Agency shall, pursuant to section 22(2) of the NIMASA Act 2007, (a) inspect ships for the purposes of maritime safety, maritime security, maritime labour and the prevention of maritime pollution and (b) make enquiries as to shipwrecks or other casualties affecting ship, or as to charges of incompetence or misconduct on the part of seafarers in relation to such casualties.

Under section 44(1) of the NIMASA Act 2007, the Agency may make such regulations with the approval of the Minister and not inconsistent with this Act for such provisions as it considered appropriate in relation to: (a) the dumping of ship and shore generated waste in Nigerian waters; and (b) removal of wrecks which constitute navigation risks and which is a threat to the marine environment.

But in making such regulations, the Agency shall take into account the need to give effect to provisions that are contained in any international convention agreement that Nigeria is a party.[348] Any person who contravenes a requirement under the

---

[338] NIMASA Act (2007), s. 2(1).

[339] Ibid., s. 2(2).

[340] Ibid., s. 22(1)(e).

[341] Ibid., s. 22(1)(f).

[342] Ibid., s. 22(1)(i).

[343] Ibid., s. 22(1)(n).

[344] Ibid., s. 22(1)(o).

[345] Ibid., s. 22(1)(p).

[346] Ibid., s. 22(1)(q).

[347] Kyanet (2021).

[348] NIMASA Act (2007), s. 44(2).

regulations shall be guilty of an offence and is liable, (a) on summary conviction, to a fine not exceeding the amount as may be determined by the Agency or, (b) on conviction on indictment, to imprisonment for a term not exceeding 2 years or to a fine not exceeding the amount as may be determined by the Agency or to both statutory maximum.[349]

To further protect the marine environment, the Act prohibits all ships to which the Act applies from (a) carrying harmful substances in packaged form, except in accordance with this part, or (b) jettisoning harmful substances in packaged form.[350] To this end, a person shall not ship or offer for shipment from any Nigerian port harmful substances in packaged form except in accordance with this part.[351] However, where such shipment is carried out, all documents relating to the carriage of harmful substances by sea where such substances are named, the correct technical name of each such substance shall be used.[352]

Thus, the shipping documents supplied by the shipper shall include or be accompanied by a signed certificate or declaration that the shipment offered for carriage is properly packaged and marked, labelled or placarded as appropriate and in proper condition for carriage to minimise any hazard to the marine environment.[353] In this regard, each ship carrying harmful substances shall have (a) a special list or manifest setting forth the harmful substances on board and the location thereof and (b) a detailed stowage plan setting out the location of all harmful substances on board in lieu of the special list or manifest referred to in paragraph (a) of this subsection; (c) copies of the documents referred to in this subsection shall also be retained on shore by the owner of the ship or his representative until the harmful substances are unloaded, and a copy of one of these documents shall be made available to the office of the Director General before departure.[354]

Finally, the Agency shall make regulations prescribing (a) detailed requirements on packing, marking, labelling, documentation, stowage, quantity limitations and exceptions for preventing or minimising pollution of the marine environment, in conformity with the IMDG Code; (b) the terms and conditions under which ships to which this Act applies may carry or persons may ship or offer for shipment harmful substances in packaged form; (c) measures to be taken to regulate the washing of leakages overboard based on the physical, chemical and biological properties of harmful substances; and (d) inspections to be made by the Agency of all ships to which this Act applies to ensure compliance.[355]

---

[349] Ibid., s. 44(3).

[350] Ibid., s. 45(1).

[351] Ibid., s. 45(2).

[352] Ibid., s. 45(3).

[353] Ibid., s. 45(4).

[354] Ibid., s. 45(5).

[355] NIMASA Act (2007), s. 45(6).

From all indications, NIMASA is committed to the enthronement of global best practices in the provision of maritime services in Nigeria. According to Kyanet,[356] 'with the coming into effect of IMO 2020,[357] we assure you as an Agency that the country's shipping community will be galvanised to ensure availability, supply, and, in fact, self-sufficiency in 0.5% sulphur content fuels in line with the IMO standard'.

The IMO 2020 rule limits the sulphur in the fuel oil used on board ships operating outside designated emission control areas to 0.50% m/m, a significant reduction from the previous limit of 3.5%. Within specifically designated emission control areas, the limits were already stricter (0.10%). This new limit was made compulsory following an amendment to Annex VI of the International Convention for the Prevention of Pollution from Ships (MARPOL).[358] The new sulphur-oxide-emission-cutting regulations mandate a maximum sulphur content of 0.5% in marine fuels globally. The change is driven by the need to reduce air pollution generated in the shipping industry by reducing the sulphur content of fuels that ships use.[359]

14.8 Summary

As a result of the insidious effects of marine pollutants such as shipping accidents and oil spillage and, more recently, plastic pollutants, legal regimes have been put in place at both international and national levels to control and manage pollution of the marine environment.

Over the years, the international community, realising the importance of the marine environment to humanity, has put a number of MEAs to control plastic pollution of the marine environment. Four MEAs are particularly relevant to the discussions on the legal regime for the control of plastic pollution in the marine environment of Nigeria.

First is the International Convention for the Prevention of Pollution from Ships 1973 as modified by the Protocol of 1978 (MARPOL 73/78). MARPOL 73/78 entered into force on 2 October 1983. The main purpose is the prevention of pollution of the marine environment by ships from operational or accidental causes. This is reflected in its objective, which is to minimise pollution of the oceans and seas, including dumping and oil and air pollution. Under the Convention, all ships flagged under countries that are signatories to MARPOL are subject to its requirements, regardless of where they sail, and member nations are responsible for vessels registered on their national ship registry. MARPOL 73/78 is divided into annexes

---

[356] Kyanet (2021).

[357] The regulation came into force on 1 January 2020, marking a significant milestone in the efforts to improve air quality, preserve the environment and protect human health.

[358] This Convention had been ratified by Nigeria via MARPOL (Ratification and Enforcement) Act No. 15, 2007.

[359] Kyanet (2021).

(six in all) according to various categories of pollutants, each of which deals with the regulation of a particular category of ship emissions.

Addressing the safety of vessels and crew at sea, the International Convention on Safety of Life at Sea (SOLAS) 1974 came into force on 25 May 1980. The Convention had been amended a number of times: in 1988, in May 2011 and in 2015. The SOLAS Convention is an international maritime treaty that sets minimum safety standards in the construction, equipment and operation of merchant ships. The Convention requires signatory flag states to ensure that ships flagged by them comply with at least these standards.

Maritime disasters have also demonstrated the need for states to be prepared for and be equipped to respond to incidents of oil pollution. Quicker response times and more efficient salvage and clean-up operations have the benefit of lessening the potential pollution damage and, in some cases, the resulting costs. Based on these considerations, the international community adopted the following legal instruments for this purpose: the International Convention Relating to the Intervention on the High Seas in Cases of Oil Pollution Casualties 1969 and the International Convention on Oil Pollution Preparedness, Response and Co-operation (OPRC) 1990.

The International Convention on Oil Pollution Preparedness, Response and Co-operation (OPRC) 1990 is one of the international legal instruments that are meant to deal with general pollution incidents. It was developed in preparation for and in response to major oil spills and urges states parties to the Convention to develop adequate capability to deal with oil pollution incidents to protect their marine-related environment. The Convention was signed in London on 30 November 1990 and came into force on 13 May 1995. In 2000, a Protocol to the Convention relating to hazardous and noxious substances (OPRC-HNS) was added. The OPRC-HNS further developed the principles of the OPRC by providing a basis for international cooperation in combating major incidents or threats of marine pollution, with a specific focus on hazardous and noxious substances.

The impact of the conventions discussed above has been tremendous in helping secure the marine environment from pollution. Thus, while maritime transport in general and seaborne oil trade in particular have steadily grown over the years, the number of oil spills from tankers has decreased significantly over the past years. Moreover, both the number and the size of large spills, that is, spills with the potential to cause major economic loss and damage to the marine environment, have also dropped significantly over the same period of time. This may be attributed to the regulatory measures for pollution prevention, preparedness and control and to the improvement in ship design and safety standards, which illustrates the important role of regulation as a tool to implement public policy objectives.

As shipping incidents are being contained, a new surge in marine pollution reared up: the issue of marine plastic. Like pollution from ships, the international community also set regulatory and policy measures to contain it. Relevant international law governing marine litter can roughly be categorised as multilateral environmental agreements (MEAs) and principles of international law and customary international law, such as the ‘no harm rule’, principle of cooperation, precautionary principle, polluter-pays principle and principle of sustainable development, among others.

Some of the applicable MEAs include the United Nations Convention on the Law of the Sea (UNCLOS) 1982, MARPOL 1973/1978 as well as the Convention on the Prevention of Marine Pollution by Dumping of Wastes and Other Matter (London Convention) 1972 and the London Protocol 1996. The London Convention, in particular, controls all sources of marine pollution and prevents pollution of the sea through the regulation of dumping into the sea of waste materials.

Besides multilateral environmental agreements (MEAs) and principles of international law, there are some declarations and guidelines and other efforts reached by the international community that may be applied to the control of marine litter. There is also some national legislation put in place to safeguard the sea and ocean from marine litter.

References

Asian-Pacific Economic Cooperation (APEC) Marine Resource Conservation Working Group (2009) Understanding the economic benefits and costs of controlling marine debris in the APEC region. http://www.nowpap.org/data/ML%20ref/2009. Accessed 10 June 2023

Copeland C (2008) Cruise Ship Pollution: Background, Laws and Regulations, and Key Issues. CRS Report for Congress, July 2008, http://www.earth-forum.com. Accessed 13 May 2023

Fanø JJ (2019) Enforcing international maritime legislation on air pollution through UNCLOS. Hart, Oxford

FAO (1996) Instruments under the Code http://www.fao.org/fishery/code/instruments/en. Accessed 14 July 2023

Food and Agricultural Organisation of the United Nations (FAO) (1995) Code of Conduct for Responsible Fisheries FAO, Rome, ISBN 92-5-103834

Galgani F et al (2015) Global distribution, composition, and abundance of marine litter. In: Bergmann M et al (eds) Marine anthropogenic Litter 29–56. Springer, Cham

Global Initiative for West, Central and Southern Africa (GI WACAF) (2019) Annual Report 2019. http://www.giwacaf.net. Accessed 20 June 2023

Hong S et al (2014) Quantities, composition, and sources of beach debris in Korea from the results of nationwide monitoring. Mar Pollut Bull 84:27–34

IMO (2015) IMO Requirement for Container weight verification, https://www.ensignfreight.com/media/documents/c18/a164/f213, Verification.pdf. Accessed 30 May 2023

IMO (2016) IMO MSC.1/Circular 1548 Updating SOLAS Regulation V12 Clauses. http://www.imo.org. Accessed 30 May 2023

IMO (2018) Simplified overview of the discharge provisions of the revised MARPOL Annex V which entered into force on 1 March 2018, https://wwwcdn.imo.org/localresources/en/OurWork/Environment/Documents/Simplified. Accessed 30 June 2023

IMO (2020) SOLAS: Consolidated Edition https://wwwcdn.imo.org/localresources/en/publications/Documents/Flyers/Flyers/IG110E.pdf. Accessed 25 June 2023

IMO (2021) Status of IMO Treaties. https://wwwcdn.imo.org/localresources/en/About/Conventions/StatusOfConventions/Status/pdf. Accessed 30 June 2023

IMO (2022) SOLAS 1974: Brief History-List of amendments to date and where to find them, www.imo.org, Accessed 30 May 2023

IMO MEPC (2008) Index of MEPC Resolutions and Guidelines related to MARPOL Annex VI. https://www.imo.org/en/OurWork/Environment/Pages/Index-of-MEPC-Resolutions-and-Guidelines-related-to-MARPOL-Annex-VI.aspx. Accessed 13 May 2023

IMO MEPC Resolutions (2019) Resolution MEPC.318(74) Amendments to the International Code for the Construction and Equipment of Ships Carrying Dangerous Chemicals In Bulk (Amendments to IBC CODE Chapters 1, 15, 16, 17, 18, 19 and 21) adopted on 17 May 2019 https://wwwcdn.imo.org/localresources/en/KnowledgeCentre/IndexofIMOResolutions/MEPCDocuments/MEPC.318(74).pdf. Accessed 1 Aug 2023

International Conference on Safety of Life at Sea (1953) Text of the Convention for the Safety of Life at Sea 10 June 1948. Her Majesty's Stationery Office, London https://www.imo.org/knowledgecentre/referencesandarchieves/historyofsolas/documents/solas1948uktreatyseries/pdf. Accessed 30 May 2023

(2009) Text of the Convention for the Safety of Life at Sea (1913-1914) H.M. Stationery Off. In: International Conference on Safety of Life at Sea. Harrison and Sons, London. https://www.archieves.org/details/textofconvention00inte. Accessed 30 May 2023

International Maritime Organisation (IMO) (2010). https://www.imo.org/en/OurWork/Environment/Pages/London-Convention-Protocol.aspx. Accessed 13 May 2023

International Tanker Owners Pollution Federation Limited (2014) Trends in Oil Spills from Tanker Ships 1995-2004, 23 May 2014. http://www.itopf.org. Accessed 15 June 2023

Jambeck JR et al (2015) Plastic waste inputs from land into the ocean. Science 347(6223):768–771

Joint Group of Experts on the Scientific Aspects of Marine Environmental Protection (GESAMP) (2015) (IMO/FAO/UNESCO-IOC/UNIDO/WMO/IAEA/UN/UNEP/UNDP: Joint Group of Experts on the Scientific Aspects of Marine Environmental Protection. "Sources, fate and effects of microplastics in the marine environment: A global assessment." #90.Rep. Stud. GESAMP, 2015 http://www.gesamp.org/data/gesamp/files/media/Publications/Reports_and_studies_90/gallery_2230/object_2500_large.pdf. Accessed 8 June 2023

Kyanet P (2021) Head, Corporate Communications, NIMASA, April 14, 2021. http://nimasa.gov.ng. Accessed 18 June 2023

Machine W (2014) What is MARPOL and its impact to freight market, Freight Link 28 October 2014. http://www.freightlink.co.uk. Accessed 14 March 2020

Madden Marine (2015) International Convention for the Prevention of Pollution from Ships (MARPOL 73/78) PRACTICAL GUIDE 2015, 54, https://maddenmaritime.files.wordpress.com/2015/08/marpol-practical-guide.pdf. Accessed 15 June 2023

Marine Insight (2022) MARPOL (The International Convention for Prevention of Marine Pollution for Ships): The Ultimate Guide, https://www.marineinsight.com/category/maritime-law, 4 June 2022. Accessed 4 May 2023

Maritime Safety Committee (MSC (2014) 94th Summary Session of SOLAS Container weight Requirement. http://www.worldshipping.org/indusrty-issues/safety. Accessed 30 May 2023

Meredith S (2019) The biggest change in oil market history is less than six months away, CNBC. https://www.cnbc.com/2019/07/15. Accessed 13 May 2023

National Research Council of the National Academies (2005) Tackling Marine Debris in the 21st century. National Academies, Washington, D.C http://www.nap.edu/catalog.php?record_id=12486, Accessed 10 June 2023

OPRC (1990) United Nations Treaties Series: International Convention on Oil Pollution Preparedness. Response and Co-operation 1891:1–32194

Pham CK et al (2014) Marine litter distribution and density in European seas, from the shelves to deep basins. PLoS One 9(4). https://doi.org/10.1371/journal.pone.00958390

Potts T, Hastings E (2011) Marine litter issues, impacts and actions. The Scottish Government, http://www.gov.scot/Resource/0040/00402421.2011pdf. Accessed 8 June 2023

Ramsar Convention Secretariat (2016) An Introduction to the Convention on Wetlands, 2016, Ramsar Convention Secretariat, Gland, Switzerland https://www.ramsar.org/sites/default/files/documents/library/handbook1_5ed_introductiontoconvention_e.pdf. Accessed 11 June 203

Raunek K (2022) MARPOL (The International Convention for Prevention of Marine Pollution For Ships): The Ultimate Guide. https://www.marineinsight.com/maritime-law/marpol-convention-shipping/#:~:text. Accessed 19 July 2023
Rochman CM et al (2013) Policy: classify plastic waste as hazardous. Nature 494:169–171
S S Rana and Co (2017) 'India: Polluter Pays Principle' November 10 2017 https://www.lexology.com/library/detail.aspx?g=c832a88c-7f8c-4628-bb96-c3e7d9189b2d. Accessed 28 June 2023
Sands P (2000) Principles of international environmental law Vol. 1 frameworks, standards and implementation. Manchester University, Manchester
Sofiev M et al (2018) Cleaner fuels for ships provide public health benefits with climate tradeoff. Nat Commun 9(1):1–12. https://doi.org/10.1038/s41467-017-02774-9. ISSN 2041-1723, www.nature.com/articles. Accessed 15 May 2023
SOLAS (1974) Text of the Convention for the Safety of Life at Sea, signed at London, January 20, 1914 [with Translation], London: His Majesty's Stationery Office by Harrison and Sons, 1914, https://www.archieves.org/details/textofconvention00inte, accessed 30 April 2023
The Ocean Conservancy (2015) International coastal cleanup 2015 report. http://www.oceanconservancy.org/our-work/international-coastal-cleanup/2015. Accessed 19 June 2023
Thornton J, Beckwith S (2014) Environmental law, 2nd edn. Sweet and Maxwell, London
U S Government Accountability Office Marine Pollution (2000) Progress made to reduce marine pollution by cruise ships, but important issues remain, (RCED-00-48, 28 February 2000, 20, https://www.gao.gov/new.items. Accessed 14 May 2023
UNEP (2005) Marine litter: An analytical overview. UNEP, Nairobi, Kenya. http://www.unep.org/regionalseas/marinelitter/publications/docs/anl_oview.pdf. Accessed 9 June 2023
UNEP (2009) Marine litter: A global challenge. UNEP, Nairobi, Kenya. http://www.unep.org/pdf/unep_marine_litter-a_global_challenge.pdf. Accessed 10 June 2023
UNEP (2016) Marine litter legislation: a toolkit for policy makers. UNEP, Nairobi, Kenya
UNEP (2018) Oceans and Seas. https://www.unep.org/explore-topics/oceans-seas/what-we-do/addressing-land-based-pollution/governing-global-programme. Accessed 10 July 2023
UNGA (2015) Oceans and the Law of the Sea, Resolution 70/235 of 23 December 2015. https://www.un.org/en/development/desa/population/migration/generalassembly/docs/globalcompact/A_RES_70_235.pdf. Accessed 10 July 2023
United Nations Environment Programme (UNEP) (2005) Register of International Treaties and Other Agreements in the Field of the Environment, UNEP/Env.Law/2005/3. UNEP Nairobi, Kenya. https://wedocs.unep.org/bitstream/handle/20.500.11822/8314/-Register. Accessed 20 May 2023
United Nations General Assembly (UNGA) (2015) Transforming our world: the 2030 Agenda for Sustainable Development, Resolution 70/1 of 25 September 2015, https://www.un.org/en/development/desa/population/migration/generalassembly/docs/globalcompact/A_RES_70_1_E.pdf. Accessed 10 July 2023
United Nations Organisation (2010) The Future We Want, Outcome document of the United Nations Conference on Sustainable Development, Rio de Janeiro Brazil, 20-22 June 2010, United Nations Organisation. https://sustainabledevelopment.un.org/content/documents/733FutureWeWant.pdf. Accessed 13 July 2023
United Nations Treaties Series (1969) International Convention relating to intervention on the high seas in cases of oil pollution casualties, 970 UNTS 211; 9 ILM 25 https://treaties.un.org/doc/Publication/UNTS/Volume%20970/volume-970-I-14049-English.pdf. Accessed 1 May 2023
United Nations Treaties Series (1973) Protocol Relating to Intervention on the High Seas in Cases of Pollution by Substances Other Than Oil, 131 UNTS 3; 13 ILM 605, https://treaties.un.org/doc/Publication/UNTS/Volume%20970/volume-970-I-14049-English.pdf. Accessed 1 May 2023
United Nations Treaties Series (1990) International Convention on Oil Pollution Preparedness, Response and Co-operation, Vol. 1891, 1-32194, OPRC 1990, https://treaties.un.org/doc/publication/unts/volume%201891/volume-1891-i-32194-english.pdf. Accessed 2 May 2023

United States Environmental Protection Agency (EPA) (2023) What is wetland, 4 May 2023, https://www.epa.gov/wetlands/what-wetland#:~:text=Wetlands. Accessed 25 May 2023.

Viens A (2019) The Big Shipping Shake-Up" Visual Capitalist, 12 June 2019 http://www.visualcapitalist.com. Accessed 18 May 2023

World Wildlife Organisation (2023) What is wetland and 8 other wetland fact, May 2023, https://www.worldwildlife.org/stories/what-is-a-wetland-and-8-other-wetland-facts#:~:text=, Accessed 25 May 2023.

Wright SL et al (2013) The physical impacts of microplastics on marine organisms: a review. Environ Pollut 178:483–492

Chapter 15
Liability and Compensation for Pollution Damage to the Marine Environment

Abstract Humans, in their quest for development, had laid, and have continued to lay, an unrestrained siege on the environment. This siege has dire consequences for man and his environment, causing environmental pollution. The major culprit to marine pollution comes from activities in the shipping industry. While pollution of the marine environment by persistent oils has fewer long-term effects than may be expected, its immediate impact on the marine environment, human life and marine resources is often very devastating. These devastating effects of some major tanker oil spills on the marine and coastal environment, as well as the resulting economic losses and significant clean-up costs, have led to much public attention on the issue of ship-source oil pollution from ships that carry oil as cargo. This has acted as a catalyst for the development of a considerable body of international legal instruments to prevent and respond to such incidents and to provide financial compensation in respect of losses resulting from an oil pollution incident involving tankers. This chapter discusses liability rules under ship-source persistent oil pollution, ship-source non-persistent oil pollution and liability rules for marine pollution damage under the United Nations Convention on the Law of the Sea. Claims and compensation for pollution damage under the International Oil Pollution Compensation (IOPC) Funds compensation regime and claims and compensation outside the IOPC Funds compensation regime as well as under voluntary agreements for compensating ship-sourced oil pollution damage are discussed.

15.1 Liability Rules Under Ship-Source Persistent Oil Pollution

15.1.1 Introduction

One of the major sources of marine pollution damage arises from ship-source oil pollution from ships that carry oil as cargo.[1]

---

[1] See discussions on the nature and impact of marine pollution in Chap. 13 of this book.

E. Onyeabor, *Environmental Law*, https://doi.org/10.1007/978-3-031-68956-7_15

Oil pollution from ships is particularly well regulated with a highly developed and robust international regulatory framework to deal with liability and compensation in the case of ship-source oil pollution from ships that carry oil as cargo. To this end, a number of liability schemes under various international conventions have been put in place for the purpose of establishing liability and compensation for the pollution of and damage to the marine environment. Such liability schemes include liability under ship-source persistent oil pollution, liability under ship-source non--persistent oil pollution and liability rules under the United Nations Convention on the Law of the Sea (UNCLOS). These are, in addition, two voluntary agreements that are now in force, namely the Small Tanker Oil Pollution Indemnification Agreement (STOPIA) and the Tanker Oil Pollution Indemnification Agreement (TOPIA).

The International Conventions for Liability and Compensation resulting from ship-source persistent oil pollution were developed under the auspices of the International Maritime Organization (IMO). The original conventions were the International Convention on Civil Liability for Oil Pollution Damage 1969 (or '1969 CLC') and the International Convention on the Establishment of an International Fund for Compensation for Oil Pollution Damage 1971 (or '1971 Fund Convention'). These conventions were amended in 1992 by two protocols to provide higher limits and an enhanced scope of application. The amended conventions, which entered into force on 30 May 1996, are known as the Civil Liability Convention 1992 (or '1992 CLC') and the Fund Convention 1992.[2] To this end, the legal framework for the international liability and compensation regime for oil pollution damage to the marine environment is currently based on:

(i) The International Convention on Civil Liability for Oil Pollution Damage 1992 (or '1992 Civil Liability Convention'/'1992 CLC')
(ii) The International Convention on the Establishment of an International Fund for Compensation for Oil Pollution Damage 1992 (or '1992 Fund Convention'), and
(iii) The Protocol of 2003 to the 1992 Fund Convention (or 'Supplementary Fund Protocol 2003').

These three instruments all apply to compensation for pollution damage caused by spills of persistent oil from tankers in the territory (including the territorial sea) and the exclusive economic zone (EEZ) or an equivalent area of a state party to the respective treaty instrument and are managed under the International Oil Pollution Compensation (IOPC) Funds.[3]

---

[2] International Maritime Organization (IMO) (2023), Report 2023/03/SDC-9-16.

[3] International Oil Pollution Compensation Funds (IOPC Funds) (2023), pp. 10–13.

15.1.2 International Convention on Civil Liability for Oil Pollution Damage (Civil Liability Convention) 1969 and 1992[4]

The Civil Liability Convention (CLC) 1969 was adopted in Brussels, Belgium, on 29 November 1969 following the accident involving the Liberian-registered ship *Torrey Canyon*, which ran aground in the Atlantic Ocean off the south-west coast of Britain on 18 March 1967. The ship had in its hull nearly 120,000 tons of crude oil. The escape of oil caused widespread damage to the British coastline and to marine life and eventually polluted the coast of France.[5]

The 1969 CLC entered into force in 1975 and established a first tier of compensation for oil spills from ships that carry oil as cargo. The 1969 CLC had been the subject of three amending protocols; the most recent was by the 1992 Civil Liability Convention Protocol (or '1992 CLC'), which entered into force on 30 May 1996.[6] Despite the entry into force of the 1992 CLC, the 1969 CLC remains active, but it offers lower limits of compensation than the 1992 CLC. As a result, IMO recommended that any state still a party to the Convention[7] should increase its protection by acceding to the 1992 CLC and denouncing the 1969 CLC as soon as possible.[8]

The CLC provides for the liability of a shipowner in respect of any oil pollution damage suffered in the territory or territorial sea of a contracting state. The scope of the applicability of the Civil Liability Convention was expanded under the 1992 CLC to include pollution damage caused:

(i) in the territory, including the territorial sea, of a Contracting State, and
(ii) in the exclusive economic zone of a Contracting State, established in accordance with international law, or, if a Contracting State has not established such a zone, in an area beyond and adjacent to the territorial sea of that State determined by that State in accordance with international law and extending not more than 200 nautical miles from the baselines from which the breadth of its territorial sea is measured.[9]

---

[4]Nigeria had domesticated this Convention in 2006 under the International Convention on the Establishment of an International Fund for Compensation for Oil Pollution Damage 1971, as amended (Ratification And Enforcement), Act (an Act to enable effect to be given in the Federal Republic of Nigeria to the International Convention on the Establishment of an International Fund for Compensation for Oil Pollution Damage 1971, as amended, and for related matters. The commencement date was 22 December 2006).

[5]International Maritime Organization (IMO) (2023), Report 2023/03/SDC-9-16.

[6]Ibid.

[7]Brazil, Equatorial Guinea, Kazakhstan, Libya, Sao Tomé and Principe as of 31 December 2023 are yet to renounce CLC 1969.

[8]IOPC Funds (2023), pp. 10–13.

[9]CLC (1992), art. II(a).

Liability under the 1992 CLC also applies to 'preventive measures, wherever taken, to prevent or minimize such damage'.[10] Preventive measure is defined as 'any reasonable measures taken by any person after an incident has occurred to prevent or minimize pollution damage'.[11]

Under the 1992 CLC, 'the owner of a ship at the time of an incident, or where the incident consists of a series of occurrences at the time of the first such occurrence, shall be liable for any pollution damage caused by oil which has escaped or been discharged from the ship as a result of the incident'.[12] This means that the liability is strict and that the owner of the ship that spills the oil shall be liable under the Convention, regardless of whether or not he was actually at fault. There are, however, some exceptions in the 1969 CLC.

These exceptions are provided under Article III.[13] For instance, 'no liability for pollution damage shall attach to the owner if he proves that the damage:

(a) resulted from an act of war, hostilities, civil war, insurrection or a natural phenomenon of an exceptional, inevitable and irresistible character,[14] or
(b) was wholly caused by an act or omission done with intent to cause damage by a third party,[15] or
(c) was wholly caused by the negligence or other wrongful act of any Government or other authority responsible for the maintenance of lights or other navigational aids in the exercise of that function'.[16]

Again, no liability shall arise 'if the owner proves that the pollution damage resulted wholly or partially either from an act or omission done with intent to cause damage by the person who suffered the damage or from the negligence of that person, the owner may be exonerated wholly or partially from his liability to such person'.[17] For all intents and purposes, for liability to arise, it must be established that there was pollution damage caused by the defendant. Pollution damage is defined in Article I(6)[18] as:

> Loss or damage caused outside the ship carrying oil by contamination resulting from the escape or discharge of oil from the ship, wherever such escape or discharge may occur, and includes the cost of preventive measures and further loss or damage caused by preventive measures.

---

[10] Ibid., art. II(b).

[11] Ibid., art. I(7).

[12] CLC (1992), art. III(1).

[13] CLC (1969).

[14] Ibid., art. III(2)(a).

[15] Ibid., art. III(2)(b).

[16] CLC (1992), art. III(2)(c).

[17] Ibid., art. III(3).

[18] Ibid.

Environmental damage may be gleaned from the above definition. This definition is reinstated by the 1992 CLC.[19] It defines pollution damage as:

(i) Loss or damage caused outside the ship by contamination, resulting from the escape or discharge of oil from the ship, wherever such escape or discharge may occur, provided that compensation for impairment of the environment other than loss of profit from such impairment shall be limited to costs of reasonable measures of reinstatement actually undertaken or to be undertaken;
(ii) The costs of preventative measures and further loss or damage caused by preventative measures.

The above definition under the 1992 CLC, which developed the definition provided under the 1969 CLC, implies that liability is intended to include compensation for the impairment of the environment.

However, no claim for compensation for pollution damage under the 1992 CLC or otherwise may be made against (a) the servants or agents of the owner or the members of the crew; (b) the pilot or any other person who, without being a member of the crew, performs services for the ship; (c) any charterer (how so ever described, including a bareboat charterer), manager or operator of the ship; (d) any person performing salvage operations with the consent of the owner or on the instructions of a competent public authority; (e) any person taking preventive measures; (f) all servants or agents of persons mentioned in sub-paragraphs (c), (d) and (e), unless the damage resulted from their personal act or omission, committed with the intent to cause such damage or recklessly and with knowledge that such damage would probably result.[20]

Under the 1969 CLC, the shipowner could limit liability to 2000 francs for each ton of the ship's net tonnage with an overall limit on the liability of 210 million francs but may not avail itself of the limit if the incident is the result of the owner's actual fault or privity.[21] The above-permitted limits were, however, increased to 3 million special drawing rights (SDRs)[22] for ships not exceeding 5000 units of tonnage and 420 SDRs for each additional unit of tonnage to a maximum of 59.7 million SDRs.[23]

However, for this to avail the shipowner, he must maintain insurance or other financial security to cover its liability and, to limit its liability, establish a fund for the total sum of liability with the court in which an action is brought.[24] Thus, under

---

[19] Ibid., art. I(6).

[20] CLC (1969), art. III(4).

[21] Ibid., art. V.

[22] A special draw right (SDR) is an accounting unit for International Monetary Fund (IMF) transactions with member countries. SDR is an asset, though not money in the classic sense because it cannot be used to buy things. The value of SDR is based on a basket of the world's five leading currencies: US dollar, euro, Chinese yuan, Japanese yen and British pound sterling. SDRs are allocated to IMF member countries in proportion to their relative share in the IMF.

[23] CLC (1992), art. VI(1).

[24] Ibid., art. VII(1).

Article V,[25] the owner of a ship shall be entitled to limit his liability under the Convention in respect of any one incident to an aggregate amount calculated as follows: (a) 4,510,000 units of account for a ship not exceeding 5000 units of tonnage and (b) for a ship with a tonnage in excess thereof, for each additional unit of tonnage, 631 units of account in addition to the amount mentioned in sub-paragraph (a), provided, however, that this aggregate amount shall not, in any event, exceed 89,770,000 units of account.

For the purpose of availing himself of the benefit of the limitation provided above, the owner shall constitute a fund for the total sum representing the limit of his liability with the court or other competent authority of any one of the contracting states in which an action is brought under Article IX or, if no action is brought, with any court or other competent authority in any one of the contracting states in which an action can be brought under Article IX. The fund can be constituted either by depositing the sum or by producing a bank guarantee or other guarantees, acceptable under the legislation of the contracting state where the fund is constituted and considered to be adequate by the court or other competent authority.[26]

It should be noted that the owner shall not be entitled to limit his liability under 1992 CLC if it is proved that the pollution damage resulted from his personal act or omission, committed with the intent to cause such damage or recklessly and with the knowledge that such damage would probably result.[27]

Where an incident has caused pollution damage in the territory, including the territorial sea or an area of one or more contracting states, or preventive measures have been taken to prevent or minimise pollution damage in such territory, including the territorial sea or area, actions for compensation may only be brought in the courts of any such contracting state or states. Reasonable notice of any such action shall be given to the defendant.[28] However, each contracting state shall ensure that its courts possess the necessary jurisdiction to entertain such actions for compensation.[29]

Any judgment given by such a court that is enforceable in the state of origin, where it is no longer subject to ordinary forms of review, shall be recognised in any contracting state, except (a) where the judgment was obtained by fraud or (b) where the defendant was not given reasonable notice and a fair opportunity to present his case.[30] Any judgment arising thereto shall be enforceable in each contracting state as soon as the formalities required in that state have been complied with. The formalities shall not permit the merits of the case to be reopened.[31]

---

[25] CLC (1992).

[26] CLC (1992), art. V(3).

[27] Ibid., art. V(2).

[28] Ibid., art. IX(1).

[29] Ibid., art. IX(2).

[30] Ibid., art. X(1).

[31] CLC (1992), art. X(2).

15.1.3 *International Convention on the Establishment of an International Fund for Oil Pollution Damage (Fund Convention) 1971 and 1992 Amendment*

The International Oil Pollution Compensation Fund, signed in 1971[32] (the '1971 Fund Convention' for brevity), is another international legal instrument that has provided for levels of liability in the event of pollution damage. The original 1971 Fund Convention was amended by the Fund Protocol 1992 (or '1992 Fund Convention') and the Supplementary Fund Protocol 2003 (or 'Supplementary Fund 2003').[33]

The 1992 Fund Convention was adopted under the auspices of an International Legal Conference on Marine Pollution Damage to provide additional compensation for victims of oil pollution and to transfer some of the economic consequences to the owners of the oil cargo, as well as the shipowner, subject to the original 1969 CLC, and was ratified on 27 September 1992. It came into force on 30 May 1996.[34] With the entry into force of the 1992 Protocol, the International Oil Pollution Compensation Fund 1992 (or '1992 Fund Convention') was established.[35]

The objective of the 1992 Fund Convention is to provide compensation for pollution damage, which is inadequately compensated by the 1992 CLC because no liability arises under the 1992 CLC or the owner cannot meet the obligations under that Convention or the liability exceeds the limit established by that Convention.[36]

To this end, the 1992 Fund Convention shall apply exclusively (a) to pollution damage caused (i) in the territory, including the territorial sea, of a contracting state and (ii) in the exclusive economic zone of a contracting state, established in accordance with international law or, if a contracting state has not established such a zone, in an area beyond and adjacent to the territorial sea of that state determined by that state in accordance with international law and extending not more than 200 nautical miles from the baselines from which the breadth of its territorial sea is measured and (b) to preventive measures, wherever taken, to prevent or minimise such damage.[37]

Under Article 4(2)(a) of the 1992 Fund Convention, a shipowner shall incur no obligation in certain situations, for instance, if:

---

[32] The Fund Convention 1971 represented the first time that linkage in an international legal instrument was explicitly made between the extent of a person's liability and compliance with obligations found in other treaties.

[33] International Oil Pollution Compensation Funds (IOPC Funds) (2018a).

[34] Ibid.

[35] Ibid.

[36] Fund Convention (1992), art. 2(1) (a).

[37] Fund Convention (1992), art. 3.

(i) it proves that the pollution damage resulted from an act of war, hostilities, civil war or insurrection or was caused by oil which has escaped or been discharged from a warship or other ship owned or operated by a State and used, at the time of the incident, only on Government non-commercial service; or
(ii) the claimant cannot prove that the damage resulted from an incident involving one or more ships (a case of contributory negligence).

The Fund provides a limit to compensation by polluters. For instance, the aggregate amount of compensation payable by the Fund in respect of any one incident shall not exceed 203,000,000 units of account,[38] and for pollution damage resulting from a natural phenomenon of an exceptional, inevitable and irresistible character, the amount shall not exceed 203,000,000 units of account.[39]

However, the maximum amount of compensation in respect of the above incidents shall be 300,740,000 units of account with respect to any incident occurring during any period when there are three parties to the 1992 Fund Convention in respect of which the combined relevant quantity of contributing oil received by persons in the territories of such parties, during the preceding calendar year, equalled or exceeded 600 million tons.[40] But the interest accrued on a fund, if any, shall not be taken into account for the computation of this maximum compensation payable by the Fund.[41] The amounts payable as maximum compensation shall be converted into national currency on the basis of the value of that currency by reference to the special drawing right (SDR) on the date of the decision of the assembly of the Fund as to the first date of the payment of compensation.[42]

Where the amount of established claims against the Fund exceeds the aggregate amount of compensation payable, the amount available shall be distributed in such a manner that the proportion between any established claim and the amount of compensation actually recovered by the claimant under this Convention shall be the same for all claimants.[43]

Rights to compensation shall be extinguished unless an action is brought thereunder or a notification has been made pursuant to Article 7(6)[44] within 3 years from the date when the damage occurred. However, in no case shall an action be brought after 6 years from the date of the incident that caused the damage.[45]

Any action against the Fund for compensation shall be brought only before a court competent under Article IX of the 1992 CLC in respect of actions against the owner who is or who would, but for the provisions of Article III(2) of the

[38] Ibid., art. 4(4)(a).
[39] Ibid., art. 4(4)(b).
[40] Ibid., art. 4(4)(c).
[41] Ibid., art. 4(4)(d).
[42] Ibid., art. 4(4)(e).
[43] Fund Convention (1992), art. 4(5).
[44] Fund Convention (1992).
[45] Ibid., art. 6.

Convention, have been liable for pollution damage caused by the relevant incident.[46] To this end, each contracting state shall ensure that its courts possess the necessary jurisdiction to entertain such actions against the Fund.[47]

However, where an action has been brought before a court against an owner under the 1992 CLC, that court has exclusive competence over any action against the Fund under Article 4 of the 1992 Fund Convention in respect of the same damage.[48] Where that court is in a state that is not a party to the 1992 Fund Convention, the claimant may bring the case before the court where the Fund is headquartered (London) or any court of a party to the 1992 Fund Convention competent under Article IX of the 1992 CLC.

Annual contributions to the 1992 Fund Convention are made, in respect of each party, by any person (including associated persons) who has received a total of more than 150,000 tons of contributing oil in the ports or terminals in the territory of that party contributing oil carried by sea and 'contributing oil'[49] first received in any installations situated in the territory of that party, which has first been carried by sea and discharged in a port or terminal of a non-party.[50] The assessment of each person's annual contribution, which may be needed to balance the budget, comprises a proportion of the total amount of contributions required by the Fund to fulfil its estimated annual expenditure. The 1992 Protocol's transitional provisions govern contributions and place a limit, for up to 5 years, on the contribution of any one party to a maximum of 27.5% of the total contributions to the Fund.

15.1.4 Protocol for Supplementary Fund on International Convention on the Establishment of an International Fund for Compensation for Oil Pollution Damage 2003 (Supplementary Fund 2003)

Affirming the importance of maintaining the viability of the international oil pollution liability and compensation system and noting that the maximum compensation afforded by the 1992 Fund Convention might be insufficient to meet compensation needs in certain circumstances in some contracting states to that Convention, the contracting states to the 1992 CLC and the 1992 Fund Convention considered it necessary as a matter of urgency to make available additional funds for compensation through the creation of a supplementary scheme to which states may accede if

---

[46] Ibid., art. 7(1).

[47] Ibid., art. 7(2).

[48] Ibid., art. 7(3).

[49] Contributing oil means crude oil and fuel oil. See Fund Convention (1992), art. 1(3) (a).

[50] Fund Convention (1992), arts. 10 and 12.

they so wish.[51] To this end, a Supplementary Fund Protocol was adopted in 2003 that entered into force in 2005. The Protocol establishes the International Oil Pollution Compensation Supplementary Fund 2003 (or 'Supplementary Fund 2003').[52] The Supplementary Fund provides a third tier of compensation on top of the amount available under the Fund Convention 1992 in states that are also parties to the Supplementary Fund Protocol.[53]

The Supplementary Fund 2003 seeks to ensure that victims of oil pollution damage are compensated in full for their loss or damage and should also alleviate the difficulties faced by victims in cases where there is a risk that the amount of compensation available under the 1992 CLC and the 1992 Fund Convention will be insufficient to pay established claims in full.[54]

The Supplementary Fund makes additional compensation available beyond the amount available under the 1992 CLC and the 1992 Fund Convention so that the total amount of compensation payable for any one incident for damage in a state that is a member of that Fund is 750 million SDR (US$1047 million), including the amount payable under the 1992 CLC and the 1992 Fund Convention. One important benefit of the Supplementary Fund is that, even in the most serious pollution incidents, there should rarely be any need to reduce compensation payments proportionately for pollution damage in states that are members of that Fund: it should be possible from the outset for claimants to receive 100% of their proven compensation claim.[55]

The Supplementary Fund shall, in each contracting state, be recognised as a legal person capable of, under the laws of that state, assuming rights and obligations and being a party in legal proceedings before the courts of that state. Each contracting state shall recognise the director of the Supplementary Fund as the legal representative of the Supplementary Fund.[56]

To this end, the Supplementary Fund 2003 shall pay compensation to any person suffering pollution damage if such person has been unable to obtain full and adequate compensation for an established claim for such damage under the terms of the 1992 Fund Convention because the total damage exceeds, or there is a risk that it will exceed, the applicable limit of compensation laid down in Article 4(4) of the 1992 Fund Convention in respect of any one incident.[57]

However, the aggregate amount of compensation payable by the Supplementary Fund under this article shall, in respect of any one incident, be limited so that the total sum of that amount, together with the amount of compensation actually paid under the 1992 CLC and the 1992 Fund Convention within the scope of application

---

[51] Supplementary Fund Protocol (2003), preamble, paras. (c) and (d).

[52] IOPC Funds (1992a).

[53] IOPC Funds (2023), pp. 10–13.

[54] Supplementary Fund (2003), para. (f).

[55] IOPC Funds (2019).

[56] Supplementary Fund (2003), art. 2(2).

[57] Ibid., art. 4(1).

of this Protocol, shall not exceed 750 million units of account.[58] But the above amount, that is, 750 million units of account, shall be converted into national currency on the basis of the value of that currency by reference to the special drawing right on the date determined by the assembly of the Fund Convention 1992 for conversion of the maximum amount payable under the 1992 CLC and the 1992 Fund Convention.[59]

Where the amount of established claims against the Supplementary Fund exceeds the aggregate amount of compensation payable, the amount available shall be distributed in such a manner that the proportion between any established claim and the amount of compensation actually recovered by the claimant under the Supplementary Fund Protocol shall be the same for all claimants.[60]

It should be noted that a claim made against the 1992 Fund Convention shall be regarded as a claim made by the same claimant against the Supplementary Fund 2003.[61] Thus, rights to compensation against the Supplementary Fund shall be extinguished only if they are extinguished against the 1992 Fund Convention under Article 6 of the Convention.[62] This is, however, subject to Article 15(2) and (3) of the Supplementary Fund 2003, where it is provided that:

> no compensation shall be paid by the Supplementary Fund for pollution damage in the territory, territorial sea or exclusive economic zone or area ... of a Contracting State in respect of a given incident or for preventive measures, wherever taken, to prevent or minimize such damage, until the obligations to communicate to the Director of the Supplementary Fund according to article 13(1)(i) of the Supplementary Fund have been complied with in respect of that Contracting State for all years prior to the occurrence of that incident. The Assembly shall determine in the Internal Regulations the circumstances under which a Contracting State shall be considered as having failed to comply with its obligations.[63]

Again, where compensation has been denied temporarily based on the above provisions, compensation shall be denied permanently in respect of that incident if the obligations to communicate to the director of the Supplementary Fund under Article 13(1)(i) have not been complied with within 1 year after the director of the Supplementary Fund has notified the contracting state of its failure to report.[64]

Annual contributions to the Supplementary Fund are made on the same basis as contributions to the 1992 Fund. However, the contribution system for the Supplementary Fund differs from that of the 1992 Fund in that, for the purpose of paying contributions, at least 1 million tonnes of contributing oil are deemed to have been received each year in each member state.[65]

---

[58] Ibid., art. 4(2)(a).

[59] Ibid., art. 4(2)(b).

[60] Ibid., art. 4(3).

[61] Ibid., art. 6(1).

[62] Ibid., art. 6(2).

[63] Supplementary Fund (2003), art. 15(2).

[64] Ibid., art. 15(3).

[65] Ibid., art. 10.

In 2022, 219 entities were liable to contribute to the 1992 Fund Convention, and 125 entities were also liable to contribute to the Supplementary Fund Protocol 2003. The member states participate in the IOPC Funds' meetings, deciding on compensation, policy matters and the management of the organisation.[66]

15.1.5 International Oil Pollution Compensation Funds (IOPC Funds)

The International Oil Pollution Compensation (IOPC) Funds are two intergovernmental organisations (the Fund Convention 1992 and the Supplementary Fund 2003) that provide financial compensation for oil pollution damage occurring in member states, resulting from spills of persistent oil from tankers.[67]

Although the IOPC Funds were established under the Conventions[68] and adopted under the auspices of the IMO, they are completely independent legal entities. Unlike IMO, the IOPC Funds are not agencies of the United Nations (UN) as they are not part of the UN system. They are intergovernmental organisations outside the UN but follow procedures that are similar to those of the UN. Only states can become members of the IOPC Funds. To become a member of the Fund, a state must accede to the CLC 1992 and to the Fund Convention 1992 by depositing a formal instrument of accession to the Secretary General of the IMO.[69]

The International Oil Pollution Compensation (IOPC) Funds manages the Fund and has legal personality under the laws of each party and is comprised of an assembly, in which all parties to the Convention are members. It has the overall responsibility for the administration of the Fund and for the proper execution of the Convention, and its functions include approving the settlement of claims, taking decisions in respect of distributions under Article 4(5) and provisional payments as well as electing the Executive Committee.[70]

Under Article 17,[71] there are 15 members of the Executive Committee, elected on the basis of equitable geographic distribution, including parties particularly exposed to the risks of oil pollution and having large tanker fleets, and approximately one-half of those parties in whose territory the largest quantities of oil were received.

---

[66] IOPC Funds (2023), pp. 10–13.

[67] IOPC Funds (2019), p. 6.

[68] International Convention on Civil Liability for Oil Pollution Damage (1969 1969) and 1992 CLC, International Convention on the Establishment of an International Fund for Oil Pollution Damage (1971 and 1992 Fund Convention) and the Protocol for Supplementary Fund on International Convention on the Establishment of an International Fund for Compensation for Oil Pollution Damage 2003 (Supplementary Fund 2003)

[69] International Maritime Organization (IMO) (2022).

[70] Fund Convention (1992), arts. 17 and 18.

[71] Fund Convention (1992).

Under Article 18,[72] the functions of the Executive Committee include approving the settlement of claims and giving instructions to the director.

With the coming into force of the 1992 CLC, the 1992 Fund Convention and the Supplementary Fund Convention 2003, three levels of liability party for purposes of compensation were established. The first or primary tier of compensation is the owner of the tanker from which oil is spilt, who is largely liable for the payment of compensation under the 1992 CLC, and the source of money is through insurance under the protection and indemnity (P&I) club. The amount payable as compensation is up to US$135 million, depending on the size of the ship. The second tier of compensation is the IOPC Funds under the 1992 Fund Convention. Compensation is up to US$306 million. The source of the fund is levies on oil receivers in the 1992 Fund member states. The third tier of compensation is on the Supplementary Fund based on the Supplementary Fund Protocol 2003. Compensation under this tier arises once the tanker owner's applicable limit of liability has been exceeded. Compensation is up to US$1 billion. The source of the fund is from levies on oil receivers in the Supplementary Fund member states.[73]

The IOPC Funds, in applying the provisions of the compensation regime on ship-source persistent oil pollution damage,[74] determines who can make a claim, to whom a claim should be submitted, how a claim should be presented, what information a claim should contain, the period within which a claim should be made, claim assessments and payments, how long it will take to assess and pay claims, the target time frame for assessing claims and the cause of action available to a claimant if such a claimant does not agree with the Fund's decision.[75] In other words, the IOPC Funds fast-tracks the whole gamut of processes and procedures in the assessment and payment of claims. The main categories of claims covered by the compensation regime are, namely:

(i) Claims for the costs of clean-up and preventive measures (determining the scope of compensation, the presentation of claims and claims for value added tax (VAT) by central governments)
(ii) Claims for property damage (determining the scope of compensation and the presentation of claims)
(iii) Claims for economic loss in the fishery, mariculture and fish-processing sectors (determining the scope of compensation and the presentation of claims)
(iv) Claims for economic loss in the tourism sector (determining the scope of compensation and the presentation of claims)
(v) Claims for the costs of measures to prevent pure economic loss (determining the scope of compensation and the presentation of claims)

[72] Ibid.

[73] International Petroleum Industry Environmental Conservation Association (IPIECA) and International Tanker Owners Pollution Federation Limited (ITOPF) (2007), p. 2.

[74] That is, the 1992 CLC, the Fund Convention and the Supplementary Fund Protocol 2003.

[75] IOPC Funds (2019), p. 3.

(vi) Claims for environmental damage and post-spill studies (determining the scope of compensation and the presentation of claims)[76]

In the case of claims for clean-up and preventive measures, compensation is payable for the cost of reasonable clean-up measures and other measures taken to prevent or minimise pollution damage in a state party, wherever these measures are taken. For example, if a response was undertaken on the high seas or within the territorial waters of a state that is not a party to the Conventions in order to prevent or reduce pollution damage within the territorial sea or EEZ of a state party, the cost of the response would, in principle, qualify for compensation. Expenses for preventive measures are recoverable even if no spill of oil occurs, provided that there is a grave and imminent threat of pollution damage. In addition, compensation is also payable under this head for reasonable costs associated with the capture, cleaning and rehabilitation of wildlife, in particular birds, mammals and reptiles.[77]

For property damage, compensation is payable for the reasonable costs of cleaning, repairing or replacing property that has been contaminated by oil. Compensation is also payable for consequential loss, such as loss of earnings suffered by the owners of property contaminated by oil as a result of a spill, for example the loss of income by fishermen as a result of their nets becoming oiled, preventing them from fishing until their nets are either cleaned or replaced.[78]

Besides consequential loss, compensation is also payable for pure economic loss, which may include the loss of earnings caused by oil pollution suffered by persons whose property has not been polluted. For example, a fisherman whose nets have not been contaminated may nevertheless be prevented from fishing because the area of the sea where he normally fishes is polluted and he cannot fish elsewhere. Similarly, an owner of a hotel or a restaurant located close to a contaminated public beach may suffer losses because the number of guests falls during the period of the pollution.[79]

Compensation may also be payable for the costs of reasonable measures, such as marketing campaigns, which are intended to prevent or reduce economic losses by countering the negative effects that can result from a major pollution incident.[80]

In the case of environmental damage, compensation is payable for the costs of reasonable reinstatement measures aimed at accelerating the natural recovery of environmental damage. Contributions may be made to the costs of post-spill studies, provided that they relate to damage that falls within the definition of pollution damage under the conventions, including studies to establish the nature and extent of environmental damage caused by an oil spill and to determine whether or not reinstatement measures are necessary and feasible.[81]

---

[76] Ibid.

[77] IOPC Funds (2019), p. 14.

[78] Ibid.

[79] Ibid.

[80] Ibid.

[81] Ibid, 15.

However, compensation is not paid in respect of claims for environmental damage based on an abstract quantification calculated in accordance with theoretical models. Nor is compensation paid for damages of a punitive nature on the basis of the degree of fault of the wrongdoer.[82]

For the efficient functioning of the compensation regime, the Assembly and the Executive Committee, the Fund's governing bodies,[83] have established the Fund's claim policy and have adopted criteria for the admissibility of claims, that is, when claims qualify for compensation. The following general criteria apply to all claims:

(i) Any expense, loss or damage must actually have been incurred.
(ii) Any expense must relate to measures that are considered reasonable and justifiable.
(iii) Any expense, loss or damage is compensated only if and to the extent that it can be considered as caused by contamination resulting from the spill.
(iv) There must be a reasonably close link of causation between the expense, loss or damage covered by the claim and the contamination caused by the spill.
(v) A claimant is entitled to compensation only if he or she has suffered a quantifiable economic loss.
(vi) A claimant has to prove the amount of his or her expense, loss or damage by producing appropriate documents or other evidence.[84]

To this end, a claim therefore qualifies for compensation only to the extent that the amount of the loss or damage is actually demonstrated. All elements of proof are considered, but sufficient evidence must be provided to give the shipowner, his insurer and the 1992 Fund the possibility of making their own judgment as to the amount of the expense, loss or damage actually suffered. The extent to which claimants are able to reduce their losses is taken into account.

On who can make a claim, it is provided under the various provisions of the compensation regime that anyone who has suffered pollution damage in a state that is a party to the conventions[85] may make a claim for compensation. If the damage is caused in a state that is only party to the 1992 CLC, claims can only be made against the shipowner and his insurer. Claims for damages in states that are parties to both the 1992 CLC and the 1992 Fund Convention, however, may be made against the shipowner and his insurer and the Fund under the 1992 Fund Convention.[86]

Claimants may be private individuals, partnerships, companies, private organisations or public bodies, including states or local authorities. If several claimants suffer similar damage, they may find it more convenient to submit coordinated claims, which will also facilitate the processing and assessment of the claims.[87]

---

[82] IOPC Funds (2019), p. 15.

[83] See the Fund Convention (1992), art. 17 (for membership) and art. 18 (for functions).

[84] IOPC Funds (2019), p. 15.

[85] That is, the 1992 CLC and the 1992 Fund Convention.

[86] IOPC Funds (2019), p. 18.

[87] Ibid., 19.

To whom should a claim be submitted? When an incident occurs, the 1992 Fund Convention cooperates closely with the shipowner's insurer, which will normally be one of the protection and indemnity associations (P&I clubs) that insure the third-party liabilities of shipowners, including liability for oil pollution damage. The P&I club concerned and the 1992 Fund Convention usually cooperate in the handling of claims, particularly when it is clear from the outset that compensation will be paid under both conventions. Since in most cases the Fund Convention 1992 only pays compensation once the shipowner/insurer has paid up to the limit applicable to the ship involved, claims should first be submitted to the shipowner or his P&I club. In practice, claims are often channelled through the office of the P&I club's correspondent closest to the incident location. Because of the close cooperation between the Fund and the insurer, claims, including supporting documentation, need only be sent to either the P&I club/correspondent or the Fund.[88]

Occasionally, when an incident gives rise to a large number of claims, the Fund Convention 1992 and the P&I club jointly set up a local claims office so that claims may be processed more easily. Claimants should then submit their claims to that local claims office.[89]

If claimants suffer damage in a state that is a party to the Supplementary Fund Protocol 2003, their claims will automatically be considered for compensation from the Supplementary Fund if the amount available from the shipowner/insurer and the Fund Convention 1992 is insufficient to pay full compensation for proven losses.[90]

All claims are referred to the 1992 Fund Convention and the shipowner's P&I club for decisions on whether or not they qualify for compensation and, if so, the amounts of compensation due to the claimants. Neither designated local correspondents nor local claims offices have the authority to make these decisions.[91] Each claim should contain the following basic information:

(i) The name and address of the claimant and of any representative
(ii) The identity of the ship involved in the incident
(iii) The date, place and specific details of the incident, if known to the claimant, unless this information is already available to the 1992 Fund
(iv) The type of pollution damage sustained
(v) The amount of compensation claimed[92]

The IOPC Funds endeavour to pay claims as promptly as possible and normally make provisional payments of compensation to mitigate undue financial hardship to victims of pollution incidents. However, for incidents involving larger claims or where a specific claim gives rise to a question of principle that has not previously been decided by the governing bodies, the director needs approval from the relevant

[88] Ibid., 18.
[89] Ibid.
[90] Ibid.
[91] IOPC Funds (2019), p. 19.
[92] Ibid., 20.

governing body of the Fund in question. In most cases, claims are settled out of court. However, in case it is not possible to reach an agreement on the assessment of the claim, the claimant has the right to bring his claim before a competent court in the state in which the damage occurred. However, since the international compensation regime was established in 1978, court actions by claimants have not proved necessary in the majority of incidents involving the 1992 Fund Convention and its predecessor.[93]

If the total amount of the established claims exceeds the total amount of compensation available, the 1992 Fund may have to restrict compensation payments to a percentage of the established losses to ensure that all claimants are given equal treatment. The level of payments will increase at a later stage if the uncertainty about the total amount of the established losses is reduced. In Supplementary Fund member states, in practically all cases, it should be possible from the outset to pay compensation for pollution damage at 100% of the amount of damage agreed between the Fund and the claimant.

15.2 Liability Under Ship-Source Non-persistent Oil Pollution

15.2.1 Introduction

Given the obvious potential for pollution associated with the carriage of vast quantities of oil as cargo, the tangible nature of pollution from persistent oil and the extensive damage and costs that often arise from such spills, it is not surprising that liability and compensation for oil pollution from tankers is well regulated. However, highly developed international legal frameworks, such as the 1969 CLC, 1992 CLC, 1971 Fund Convention and its amendment, the 1992 Fund Convention, including the Supplementary Fund Protocol 2003, are limited in their scope, covering only pollution damage arising from spills of persistent oil from tankers.

These conventions[94] did not provide compensation for bunker oil spills from ships other than those constructed or adapted for the carriage of oil as cargo and spills of other types of oil, such as non-persistent oil. The conventions do not also cover spills from other types of substances, such as chemicals, liquefied gases or noxious liquid substances. Since these types of substances also impact the marine environment in the event of spills, they were addressed, however, in two further international conventions that were also developed under the auspices of the International Maritime Organization (IMO):

[93] Ibid., 22.

[94] CLC (1969), CLC (1992), the 1971 Fund Convention and its amendment, the 1992 Fund Convention and the Supplementary Fund Protocol 2003.

(a) International Convention on Civil Liability for Bunker Oil Pollution Damage 2001 (or 'Bunker Oil Convention'/'BOPC 2001')
(b) International Convention on Liability and Compensation for Damage in Connection with the Carriage of Hazardous and Noxious Substances by Sea (or 'HNS Convention') 1996 as amended by its 2010 Protocol 74 (or 'HNS Convention 2010')

15.2.2 International Convention on Civil Liability for Bunker Oil Pollution Damage (the Bunker Oil Convention) 2001

The Bunker Oil Convention 2001 is another legal instrument through which liability may be established against oil pollution damage to the marine environment. Oil tankers are not the only vessels that cause oil pollution damage at sea. There have been numerous heavy fuel oil spills from non-tankers as a result of the escape or discharge of bunker oil from them. There have been incidents involving bulk carriers from which bunker oil escaped that caused significant damage to the environment and economic losses to third parties. Some of them, such as the *Kandalashka* in 1993, the *Borodinskye Polye* in 1993 and the *Cita*, which ran aground off the Isles of Scilly in 1997, caused extensive environmental damage and left large amounts of uncompensated losses to their victims.[95]

The problems associated with the cost and damage recovery following a bunker pollution incident had to do with one or more of the following reasons:

(i) Claimants needed to prove fault where a spill involved a persistent oil.
(ii) The vessel was flagged in another state, and it might have been difficult to enforce a judgement.
(iii) There was no automatic right to pursue a claim in the state where the spill occurred.
(iv) The legal costs of pursuing a claim could be prohibitive.
(v) The shipowner, usually a single-ship company owning a valueless ship, had no other assets (and was usually insolvent).
(vi) The registered shipowner had no insurance.
(vii) The vessel was insured, but the insurer, with an insolvent shipowner unable to pay, was sheltered behind the 'pay to paid' clause and/or any other policy coverage defences to avoid payment.[96]

In response to the above problems and with the desire to fill the gap in a uniform way at the international level, on 23 March 2001, the International Maritime Organization (IMO) in London adopted the International Convention on Civil

[95] Bachxevanis and Smith (2009), p. 2.

[96] Bachxevanis and Smith (2009), p. 2.

Liability for Bunker Oil Pollution Damage 2001 (or 'Bunker Oil Convention 2001').[97] It was developed as a preventive measure for the reduction and control of pollution to the marine environment as well as a mechanism providing compensation for the damage caused by bunker pollution. The Bunker Convention 2001 entered into force on 21 November 2008 following ratification, acceptance, approval or accession by at least 18 states, five of which have a combined gross tonnage in excess of 1 million.[98]

The Bunker Oil Convention 2001 is largely based on the 1992 CLC, which, under Article 3, makes shipowners strictly liable for fuel spills but also allows states to limit liability in accordance with national or international regimes, such as the amended Convention on Limitation of Liability for Maritime Claims 1976.[99] Article 7 of the Convention[100] requires owners of ships registered in states parties to maintain insurance or other financial security equal to the limitation provided in Article 6. The Bunker Oil Convention 2001 relies on the same approach to environmental damage as the 1992 CLC, limiting compensation for environmental damage to 'reasonable measures of reinstatement'.[101]

Liability under the Bunker Oil Convention is strict.[102] Article 3(1) of the Convention provides that the 'shipowner at the time of an incident shall be liable for pollution damage caused by any bunker oil on board or originating from the ship. . .'. There is no requirement of fault for the liability to arise; i.e., the 'Shipowner' is under strict liability for 'Pollution Damage' caused by anyone onboard the ship provided bunker oil was 'on board or originating from the ship'. The consequence of this is that when, for instance, a bulk carrier suffers fracture damage at one of its bunker tanks while berthed on the dock as a result of a collision with a harbour tug that is entirely caused by the tug, the bulk carrier will be liable for bunker pollution under the Bunker Convention, and the claimants can (and will) go against the bulk carrier despite the fact that the tug was 100% to blame.

Like the compensation regime on ship-source persistent oil pollution damage,[103] no liability for pollution damage shall attach to the shipowner if the shipowner proves that:

(a) The damage resulted from an act of war, hostilities, civil war, insurrection or a natural phenomenon of an exceptional, inevitable and irresistible character; or
(b) The damage was wholly caused by an act or omission done with the intent to cause damage by a third party; or

---

[97] IMO (2022).

[98] Bachxevanis and Smith (2009), p. 2.

[99] Bunker Oil Convention (2001), art. 6.

[100] Ibid.

[101] Ibid., art. 1(9)(a).

[102] The same applies to liability under the CLC (1992). See art. 3(1).

[103] That is, the 1992 CLC, the 1992 Fund Convention and the Supplementary Fund Protocol 2003).

(c) The damage was wholly caused by the negligence or other wrongful act of any government or other authority responsible for the maintenance of lights or other navigational aids in the exercise of that function.[104]

However, the Bunker Oil Convention 2001 is different from the compensation regime on ship-source persistent oil pollution damage[105] in the following respects: first, the Bunker Oil Convention 2001 has a different definition of 'oil'. While the 1992 CLC defines 'Oil' as 'any persistent hydrocarbon mineral oil such as crude oil, fuel oil, heavy diesel oil and lubricating oil, whether carried on board a ship as cargo or in the bunkers of such a ship', 'Bunker Oil' is defined under the Bunker Oil Convention 2001 as 'any hydrocarbon mineral oil, including lubricating oil, used or intended to be used for the operation or propulsion of the ship, and any residues of such oil'.[106] According to Bachxevanis and Smith,[107]

> this definition is again wide so as to include Higher fuel oil (HFO), Intermediate fuel oil (IFO) and lighter fuels such as marine diesel oil (MDO), marine gas oil (MGO) as well as lube oil, which in mariners common parlance are not bunkers, and engine room oily bilges, which usually are admixtures of water, bunker and lube oil. Solidified tank umpumpables, sludges or bunker that clings to a tank's wall would be probably covered under the term residues.

Unlike the compensation regime on ship-source persistent oil pollution damage, where the liability is channelled only to the registered owner of the ship, the shipowner under the Bunker Oil Convention 2001 is defined as 'the owner, including the registered owner, bareboat charterer, manager and operator of the ship'.[108] To this end, the Bunker Convention provides for joint and several liability. Article 3(2)[109] provides that 'where more than one person is liable in accordance with paragraph 1, their liability shall be joint and several'. The above provision, in essence, means that the damaged third party or state authorities can ignore litigation between the parties falling under the definition of a shipowner and recover in accordance with the best option available from the financially healthiest shipowner.

Furthermore, under Article 5,[110] 'when an incident involving two or more ships occurs and pollution damage results therefrom, the shipowners of all the ships concerned, unless exonerated under article 3, shall be jointly and severally liable for all such damage which is not reasonably separable'. The above provision refers to 'Pollution Damage' within the meaning of the Bunker Oil Convention 2001[111] caused by two or more ships and provides for joint and several liability when the

---

[104] Bunker Oil Convention (2001), art. 3(3)(4). See also CLC (1992), art. 3(2)–(4).

[105] That is, the 1992 CLC, the 1992 Fund Convention and the Supplementary Fund Protocol 2003.

[106] Bunker Oil Convention (2001), art. 1(7).

[107] Bachxevanis and Smith (2009), p. 2.

[108] Bunker Oil Convention (2001), art. 1(3).

[109] Bunker Oil Convention (2001).

[110] Ibid.

[111] Ibid., art. 1(9).

damage is not 'reasonably separable'. All the ships involved must be covered by the Bunker Oil Convention 2001.

Where, for instance, damage caused by one ship is covered by the Bunker Oil Convention 2001 while damage caused by the other is covered by another convention, for instance the 1992 CLC, Article 5 does not apply, and there is no joint and several liability even if the damage is not separable. In such a case, the claimant could presumably go against each ship separately, trying to quantify the damage suffered and showing the degree of fault. Such litigation may present difficulties, and if takes place in several jurisdictions, there may be peculiarities such as double recovery.

Another area of difference is the gross tonnage of cargo in terms of insurance. Article 7 of the Bunker Oil Convention 2001 provides for compulsory insurance or other financial security in much the same way as the 1992 CLC does. But this obligation is prescribed only for registered owners of ships greater than 1000 gross tonnage unlike under the Civil Liability Convention 1992, where the owner of a ship registered in a contracting state and carrying more than 2000 tons of oil in bulk as cargo shall be required to maintain insurance or other financial security.[112]

On the issue of jurisdiction, the Bunker Oil Convention 2001 provides that the courts of the state that suffered damage within its territory or exclusive economic zone (EEZ) have jurisdiction to hear any claim against the shipowner or the insurer or other guarantor.[113] However, reasonable notice of any action taken under the Bunker Oil Convention 2001 shall be given to each defendant.[114] Article 10 of the Bunker Oil Convention 2001 deals with the recognition and enforcement of judgments and provides as follows:

(1) Any judgement given by a Court with jurisdiction in accordance with article 9 which is enforceable in the State of origin where it is no longer subject to ordinary forms of review, shall be recognised in any State Party, except:
    (a) where the judgement was obtained by fraud; or
    (b) where the defendant was not given reasonable notice and a fair opportunity to present his or her case.

(2) A judgement recognised under paragraph 1 shall be enforceable in each State Party as soon as the formalities required in that State have been complied with. The formalities shall not permit the merits of the case to be re-opened.[115]

Final judgments from a state will be recognised and will be enforceable in all states parties irrespective of which limitation regime is applicable in the state where the enforcement is sought. It appears that, with the exceptions only mentioned in the above provision, no other reason, whether related to public policy or otherwise,

---

[112] CLC (1992), art. VII(1).

[113] Bunker Oil Convention (2001), art. 9(1).

[114] Ibid., art 9(2).

[115] Ibid., art. 10.

would allow a state party to fail to recognise a foreign judgment. This would probably be the case even if the party that suffered pollution damage was under a contract with the shipowner and the contract contained an exclusive jurisdiction clause. This clause would be unenforceable, and if enforced, the resulting judgment would be in breach of the Bunker Convention.[116]

15.2.3 International Convention on Liability and Compensation for Damage in Connection with the Carriage of Hazardous and Noxious Substances by Sea (HNS Convention)

The HNS Convention is an international convention created in 1996 to compensate for damages caused by the spillage of hazardous and noxious substances during maritime transportation. The Convention is officially known as the International Convention on Liability and Compensation for Damage in Connection with the Carriage of Hazardous and Noxious Substances by Sea, 1996.[117]

In May 1996, the International Maritime Organization held an international conference in London, where states adopted the HNS Convention. The Convention is based on the model of the International Convention on Civil Liability for Oil Pollution Damage 1992, which covers pollution damage caused by spills of crude oil from tankers.

In 2010, a second international conference adopted a protocol to the Convention, which came to be known as the HNS Convention 2010. The protocol was designed to overcome some implementation problems that had discouraged states from ratifying the original Convention.[118] To this end, the liability and compensation for damage in connection with the carriage of hazardous and noxious substances by sea regime are governed by the HNS Convention 2010. The 2010 HNS Convention had still not entered into force due to an insufficient number of ratifications. However, the 2010 HNS Convention will enter into force 18 months after the date on which:

(i) Container-carrying capacity has increased by around 1500% since 1968 and has almost doubled over the last decade.
(ii) Twelve states have ratified.
(iii) There are four contracting states with no less than 2 million units of gross tonnage each.

---

[116] Bachxevanis and Smith (2009), p. 18.
[117] HNS (2010).
[118] Ibid., 2.

(iv) The general account's contributing cargo volume is at least 40 million tonnes.[119]

Under Article 1(5) of the Convention,[120] hazardous and noxious substances (HNS) means:

(a) any substances, materials and articles carried on board a ship as cargo, referred to in (i) to (vii) below:

 (i) oils, carried in bulk, as defined in regulation 1 of Annex I to the International Convention for the Prevention of Pollution from Ships, 1973, as modified by the Protocol of 1978 relating thereto, as amended;
 (ii) noxious liquid substances, carried in bulk, as defined in regulation 1.10 of Annex II to the International Convention for the Prevention of Pollution from Ships, 1973, as modified by the Protocol of 1978 relating thereto, as amended, and those substances and mixtures provisionally categorized as falling in pollution category X, Y or Z in accordance with regulation 6.3 of the said Annex II;
 (iii) dangerous liquid substances carried in bulk listed in chapter 17 of the International Code for the Construction and Equipment of Ships Carrying Dangerous Chemicals in Bulk, as amended, and the dangerous products for which the preliminary suitable conditions for the carriage have been prescribed by the Administration and port administrations involved in accordance with paragraph 1.1.6 of the Code;
 (iv) dangerous, hazardous and harmful substances, materials and articles in packaged form covered by the International Maritime Dangerous Goods Code, as amended;
 (v) liquefied gases as listed in chapter 19 of the International Code for the Construction and Equipment of Ships Carrying Liquefied Gases in Bulk, as amended, and the products for which preliminary suitable conditions for the carriage have been prescribed by the Administration and port administrations involved in accordance with paragraph 1.1.6 of the Code;
 (vi) liquid substances carried in bulk with a flashpoint not exceeding 60 °C (measured by a closed-cup test);
 (vii) solid bulk materials possessing chemical hazards covered by the International Maritime Solid Bulk Cargoes Code, as amended, to the extent that these substances are also subject to the provisions of the International Maritime Dangerous Goods Code in effect in 1996, when carried in packaged form; and

(b) residues from the previous carriage in bulk of substances referred to in (a)(i) to (iii) and (v) to (vii)

---

[119] IOPC Funds (2023), pp. 30–31.

[120] HNS (2010).

The purpose of the HNS Convention is to provide adequate, prompt and effective compensation for loss or damage to persons, property and the environment arising from the carriage of hazardous and noxious substances by sea. The Convention covers both pollution damage and damage caused by other risks, e.g. fire and explosion.[121] Damage according to the HNS Convention 2010 means:

(a) loss of life or personal injury on board or outside the ship carrying the hazardous and noxious substances caused by those substances;
(b) loss of or damage to property outside the ship carrying the hazardous and noxious substances caused by those substances;
(c) loss or damage by contamination of the environment caused by the hazardous and noxious substances, provided that compensation for impairment of the environment other than loss of profit from such impairment shall be limited to costs of reasonable measures of reinstatement actually undertaken or to be undertaken; and
(d) the costs of preventive measures and further loss or damage caused by preventive measures.[122]

However, the 2010 HNS Convention does not cover damage caused during the transport of HNS to or from a ship. The cover starts from the time when the HNS enters the ship's equipment or passes its rail, on loading, and ends when the HNS ceases to be present in any part of the ship's equipment or passes its rail on discharge. Also, the HNS Convention does not apply to oil pollution damage from tankers, as defined in the International Convention on Civil Liability for Oil Pollution Damage, nor to loss or damage as covered by the Bunkers Convention. Loss or damage caused by radioactive materials is also excluded.[123] The 2010 HNS Convention applies exclusively:

(a) to any damage caused in the territory, including the territorial sea, of a State Party;
(b) to damage by contamination of the environment caused in the exclusive economic zone of a State Party, established in accordance with international law, or, if a State Party has not established such a zone, in an area beyond and adjacent to the territorial sea of that State determined by that State in accordance with international law and extending not more than 200 nautical miles from the baselines from which the breadth of its territorial sea is measured;
(c) to damage, other than damage by contamination of the environment, caused outside the territory, including the territorial sea, of any State, if this damage has been caused by a substance carried on board a ship registered in a State Party or, in the case of an unregistered ship, on board a ship entitled to fly the flag of a State Party; and

[121] HNS (2010), p. 2.
[122] HNS Convention (2010), art. 1(6)(a)–(d).
[123] HNS (2010).

(d) to preventive measures, wherever taken, to prevent or minimize such damage as referred to in (a), (b) and (c) above.[124]

Liability claims under the HNS Convention applies to claims, other than claims arising out of any contract for the carriage of goods and passengers, for damage arising from the carriage of hazardous and noxious substances by sea.[125] However, it is not reasonably possible to separate damage caused by hazardous and noxious substances from that caused by other factors; all such damage shall be deemed to be caused by hazardous and noxious substances except if, and to the extent that, the damage caused by other factors is damage of a type referred to in Article 4(3). These are:

(a) pollution damage as defined in the International Convention on Civil Liability for Oil Pollution Damage, 1969, as amended, whether or not compensation is payable in respect of it under that Convention; and
(b) damage caused by a radioactive material of class 7 either in the International Maritime Dangerous Goods Code, as amended, or in the International Maritime Solid Bulk Cargoes Code, as amended.

Under the HNS Convention 2010, the shipowner will be strictly liable for any damage caused by hazardous and noxious substances (HNS). In this case, the shipowner will be liable even without fault on the part of the ship or its crew.[126] In spite of the above provisions, there are instances under which no liability shall be incurred by the shipowner. This will arise if the owner proves that:

(a) the damage resulted from an act of war, hostilities, civil war, insurrection or a natural phenomenon of an exceptional, inevitable and irresistible character; or
(b) the damage was wholly caused by an act or omission done with the intent to cause damage by a third party; or
(c) the damage was wholly caused by the negligence or other wrongful act of any Government or other authority responsible for the maintenance of lights or other navigational aids in the exercise of that function; or
(d) the failure of the shipper or any other person to furnish information concerning the hazardous and noxious nature of the substances shipped either:

    (i) has caused the damage, wholly or partly; or
    (ii) has led the owner not to obtain insurance in accordance with article 12; provided that neither the owner nor its servants or agents knew or ought reasonably to have known of the hazardous and noxious nature of the substances shipped.[127] Liability may also be avoided by the ship owner if the owner proves that the damage resulted wholly or partly either from an act or omission done with intent to cause damage by the person who

---

[124] HNS Convention (2010), art. 3.

[125] HNS (2010), art. 4(1).

[126] HNS Convention (2010), art. 7(1).

[127] HNS Convention (2010), art. 7(2).

suffered the damage or from the negligence of that person, the owner may be exonerated wholly or partially from liability to such person.[128]

Whenever damage has resulted from an incident involving two or more ships, each of which is carrying hazardous and noxious substances, each owner, unless exonerated under Article 7, shall be liable for the damage. The owners shall be jointly and severally liable for all such damage which is not reasonably separable.[129] However, owners shall be entitled to the limits of liability applicable to each of them under Article 9.

Under Article 9(1) of the 2010 HNS Convention, the owner of a ship shall be entitled to limit liability in respect of any one incident to an aggregate amount calculated as follows:

(a) Where the damage has been caused by bulk HNS. Under the HNS Convention bulk HNS means any hazardous and noxious substances such as oils, carried in bulk, noxious liquid substances, carried in bulk, dangerous liquid substances carried in bulk listed in chapter 17 of the International Code for the Construction and Equipment of Ships Carrying Dangerous Chemicals in Bulk, as amended, and the dangerous products for which the preliminary suitable conditions for the carriage have been prescribed by the Administration and port administrations involved in accordance with paragraph 1.1.6 of the Code; liquefied gases as listed in chapter 19 of the International Code for the Construction and Equipment of Ships Carrying Liquefied Gases in Bulk, as amended, and the products for which preliminary suitable conditions for the carriage have been prescribed by the Administration and port administrations involved in accordance with paragraph 1.1.6 of the Code; liquid substances carried in bulk with a flashpoint not exceeding 60 °C (measured by a closed-cup test); solid bulk materials possessing chemical hazards covered by the International Maritime Solid Bulk Cargoes Code, as amended, to the extent that these substances are also subject to the provisions of the International Maritime Dangerous Goods Code in effect in 1996, when carried in packaged form; and residues from the previous carriage in bulk of substances referred therein.[130] The liability to which bulk HNS applies is in respect of:

   (i) 10 million units of account for a ship not exceeding 2000 units of tonnage; and
   (ii) for a ship with a tonnage in excess thereof, the following amount in addition to that mentioned in (i): for each unit of tonnage from 2001 to 50,000 units of tonnage, 1500 units of account; for each unit of tonnage in excess of 50,000 units of tonnage, 360 units of account; provided, however, that this

[128] Ibid., art. 7(3).

[129] Ibid., art. 8(1).

[130] HNS Convention (2010), art. 1(5).

aggregate amount shall not in any event exceed 100 million units of account.[131]

(b) Where the damage has been caused by packaged HNS,[132] or where the damage has been caused by both bulk HNS and packaged HNS, or where it is not possible to determine whether the damage originating from that ship has been caused by bulk HNS or by packaged HNS:

(i) 11.5 million units of account for a ship not exceeding 2,000 units of tonnage; and
(ii) for a ship with a tonnage in excess thereof, the following amount in addition to that mentioned in (i): for each unit of tonnage from 2,001 to 50,000 units of tonnage, 1,725 units of account; for each unit of tonnage in excess of 50,000 units of tonnage, 414 units of account; provided, however, that this aggregate amount shall not in any event exceed 115 million units of account.

The above provisions notwithstanding, the owner shall not be entitled to limit liability under this Convention if it is proved that the damage resulted from the personal act or omission of the owner, committed with the intent to cause such damage or recklessly and with the knowledge that such damage would probably result.[133]

The 2010 HNS Convention establishes a two-tier system for compensation in the event of accidents at sea involving hazardous and noxious substances. Tier 1 will be covered by the shipowner's compulsory insurance.[134] The shipowner will be able to limit his financial liability to an amount between 10 million and 100 million SDR (special drawing right is the International Monetary Fund's currency), which is approximately between 15 million United States dollar (US$) to US$150 million. The amount depends on the gross tonnage of the ship involved in the incident. If damage is caused by packaged HNS, the maximum liability for the shipowner is 115 million SDR, about US$175 million.[135]

In cases where the insurance is insufficient, a second tier of compensation will be paid from the HNS Fund. The second tier of compensation will be up to a maximum of 250 million SDR, about US$380 million. This includes any amount paid by the shipowner and his insurer. Companies that import hazardous and noxious substances in member states of the Convention will be required to contribute to this Fund.

---

[131] Ibid., art. 9(1).

[132] Packaged HNS means any dangerous, hazardous and harmful substances, materials and articles in packaged form covered by the International Maritime Dangerous Goods Code, as amended. HNS Convention (2010), art. 1(5).

[133] HNS Convention (2010), art. 9(2).

[134] In which the owner is obliged to maintain to cover his liabilities under art. 12. This insurance will normally be provided by protection and indemnity insurers.

[135] HNS (2010).

Contributions will be based on the amount of substances that companies receive each year.[136]

The 2010 HNS Convention contains provisions for the limitation of actions. First, rights to compensation under chapter II[137] shall be extinguished unless an action is brought thereunder within 3 years from the date when the person suffering the damage knew or ought to have reasonably known of the damage and of the identity of the owner.[138] Second, rights to compensation under chapter III[139] shall be extinguished unless an action is brought thereunder or a notification has been made pursuant to Article 39, paragraph 7, within 3 years from the date when the person suffering the damage knew or ought to have reasonably known of the damage.[140]

In no case, however, shall an action be brought later than 10 years from the date of the incident that caused the damage.[141] But where the incident consists of a series of occurrences, the 10-year period mentioned shall run from the date of the last of such occurrences.[142]

In terms of jurisdiction in respect of action against the owner, where an incident has caused damage in the territory, including the territorial sea, or in an area of one or more states parties or where preventive measures have been taken to prevent or minimise damage in such territory, including the territorial sea or in such area, actions for compensation may be brought against the owner or other persons providing financial security for the owner's liability only in the courts of any such states parties.[143]

Where an incident has caused damage exclusively outside of the territory, including the territorial sea, of any state and either the conditions for the application of this Convention set out in Article 3(c) have been fulfilled or preventive measures to prevent or minimise such damage have been taken, actions for compensation may be brought against the owner or other person providing financial security for the owner's liability only in the courts of:

(a) the State Party where the ship is registered or, in the case of an unregistered ship, the State Party whose flag the ship is entitled to fly; or
(b) the State Party where the owner has habitual residence or where the principal place of business of the owner is established; or

[136] Ibid.

[137] Dealing with liability generally under the HNS Convention (2010), arts. 7–12.

[138] HNS Convention (2010), art. 37(1).

[139] Dealing with compensation by the HNS Fund under the HNS Convention (2010), art. 13.

[140] HNS Convention (2010), art. 37(2).

[141] Ibid., art. 37(3).

[142] HNS Convention (2010), art. 37(4).

[143] Ibid., art. 38(1).

(c) the State Party where a fund has been constituted in accordance with article 9, paragraph 3.[144]

Article 13 of the 2010 HNS Convention provides for the establishment of the HNS Fund. The purpose of the HNS Fund is (a) to provide compensation for damage in connection with the carriage of hazardous and noxious substances by sea, to the extent that the protection afforded by chapter II is inadequate or not available, and (b) to give effect to the related tasks set out in Article 15, among other things, to consider claims made against the HNS Fund.[145]

Funds for the HNS Fund shall come by way of annual contributions,[146] to the general account,[147] to each separate account (levied only as required to make payments by the account in question),[148] from the initial contribution of member states[149] as well as from contributing cargo[150] received during the preceding calendar year or such other year as the Assembly may decide.[151]

The HNS Fund is divided into four accounts: general bulk solids and other HNS, oil, liquefied petroleum gas (LPG) and liquefied natural gas (LNG). Each separate account will meet claims attributable to the respective cargo and will be funded by the receivers of those cargoes in member states, which means that there will be no cross-subsidisation between accounts. The HNS Fund provides up to a total of SDR 250 million, irrespective of ship size.[152]

Annual contributions payable pursuant to the above[153] shall be determined by the Assembly.[154] In the end, the Assembly shall decide the total amount of annual contributions to be levied to the general account and to each separate account.[155]

---

[144] Ibid., art. 38(2).

[145] Ibid., art. 13(1).

[146] Ibid., art. 17.

[147] Ibid., art. 18.

[148] Ibid., art. 19.

[149] Ibid., art. 20.

[150] Contributing cargo means any bulk HNS that is carried by sea as cargo to a port or terminal in the territory of a state party and discharged in that state. Cargo in transit that is transferred directly, or through a port or terminal, from one ship to another, either wholly or in part, in the course of carriage from the port or terminal of original loading to the port or terminal of final destination shall be considered contributing cargo only in respect of receipt at the final destination. HNS Convention (2010), art. 1(10).

[151] HNS Convention (2010), art. 21(5).

[152] IOPC Funds (2023), pp. 30–31.

[153] As per the specific heads under the HNS Convention (2010), arts. 18, 19 and 21(5).

[154] HNS Convention (2010), art. 17(2).

[155] Ibid., art. 17(3).

The management of the HNS Fund is by an Assembly[156] and a secretariat[157] headed by the director. The Assembly shall consist of all states parties to the Convention.[158] Article 26 spells out the functions of the Assembly.

15.3 Liability Rules for Marine Pollution Damage Under the United Nations Convention on Law of the Sea (UNCLOS) 1982

The liability rules under the United Nations Convention on the Law of the Sea (UNCLOS), including the specific provisions in Part XI, appear to have two principal aims. The wording of Article 235, which is found in Part XII of UNCLOS,[159] captures these goals:

(1) States are responsible for the fulfilment of their international obligations concerning the protection and preservation of the marine environment. They shall be liable in accordance with international law.
(2) States shall ensure that recourse is available in accordance with their legal systems for prompt and adequate compensation or other relief in respect of damage caused by pollution of the marine environment by natural or juridical persons under their jurisdiction.
(3) With the objective of assuring prompt and adequate compensation in respect of all damage caused by pollution of the marine environment, States shall cooperate in the implementation of existing international law and the further development of international law relating to responsibility and liability for the assessment of and compensation for damage and the settlement of related disputes, as well as, where appropriate, development of criteria and procedures for payment of adequate compensation, such as compulsory insurance or compensation funds.

The first objective is to ensure prompt and adequate compensation to those persons or entities that have suffered damage because of pollution to the marine environment. This objective is the foundational purpose of any liability regime. Prompt and adequate compensation is consistent with the general requirements for restitution under the law of state responsibility[160] and is also reflected in principle 13 of the Rio Declaration.[161] Promptness requires that any procedures that are

[156] HNS Convention (2010), art. 24.
[157] Ibid., art. 29.
[158] Ibid., art. 25.
[159] United Nations Convention on the Law of the Sea (UNCLOS) 1982.
[160] International Law Commission (2001), Draft Articles, art. 36.
[161] Rio Declaration on Environment and Development (Rio Declaration) 1992, principle 13.

developed provide for efficient and accessible recourse for those persons or entities that have suffered damage.

The International Law Commission (ILC)[162] noted that given the often-protracted nature of compensation claims in domestic courts, consideration ought to be given to specialised procedures at the national or international level. The goal of adequacy speaks to the breadth of compensation and to the quantum of damages awarded. Article 22 of Annex III,[163] which speaks of the responsibility and liability of contractors and the International Seabed Authority (ISA) in connection with deep-seabed mining activities, explicitly addresses this point, noting: 'Liability in every case shall be for the actual amount of damage'.[164]

The second objective is to prevent and remediate harm to the environment. This objective is very clearly identified in paragraph 1, which links the protection of the marine environment with liability. Liability rules may provide a measure of deterrence by providing clear incentives for actors to meet their obligations. The harm prevention and remediation roles are affirmed in relation to deep-seabed mining in Article 145 of UNCLOS, which directs the ISA to protect the marine environment and provides the general framework for environmental protection in the Area as follows: necessary measures shall be taken in accordance with this Convention with respect to activities in the Area to ensure effective protection of the marine environment from harmful effects that may arise from such activities. To this end, the ISA shall adopt appropriate rules, regulations and procedures for, inter alia,[165]

(a) the prevention, reduction and control of pollution and other hazards to the marine environment, including the coastline, and of interference with the ecological balance of the marine environment, particular attention being paid to the need for protection from harmful effects of such activities as drilling, dredging, excavation, disposal of waste, construction and operation or maintenance of installations, pipelines and other devices related to such activities;
(b) the protection and conservation of the natural resources of the Area and the prevention of damage to the flora and fauna of the marine environment. The connection between liability and environmental goals is made explicitly by the Seabed Disputes Chamber (SDC) in its advisory opinion, where it links the availability (and quantification) of damage to the marine environment to restoration. In other words, the liability rules ought to operate so as to prevent harm, but where harm occurs, the compensation should be adequate to support reasonable restoration efforts. Identifying environmental protection as a key objective is consistent with the purposes of liability identified by the ILC in its work on allocation of environmental loss,[166] as well as the approach taken in

[162] ILC (2006), Draft Principles on Allocation of Loss, principles 3 and 4 at para.7.

[163] UNCLOS (1982).

[164] Centre for International Governance Innovation (2018).

[165] Centre for International Governance Innovation (2018).

[166] ILC (2006) Draft Principles on Allocation of Loss, principles 3 and 12.

numerous international civil liability regimes. The ILC identifies ancillary purposes that may be served by these two objectives, including the peaceful resolution of disputes, contributing to economic activities, and providing predictable, equitable, expeditious and cost-effective compensation.[167]

15.4 Claims and Compensation for Pollution Damage Under the International Oil Pollution Compensation Funds' Compensation Regime

15.4.1 Introduction

A number of claims for compensation arising from pollution damage had been made against the International Oil Pollution Compensation (IOPC) Funds. Since their establishment, the 1992 Fund and the preceding 1971 Fund, as at 31 December 2022, have been involved in over 150 incidents of varying sizes all over the world. Between 1978 and 31 December 2022, the IOPC Funds have paid some £752 million in compensation (£331 million of which was in respect of the 1971 Fund). However, as at 31 December 2022, there have been no incidents involving, or likely to involve, payment from the Supplementary Fund.[168] The IOPC Funds is currently dealing with claims and/or recourse actions in respect of 13 incidents.[169] Discussions on claims for compensation under the IOPC Funds were made in parts:

(1) Claims for compensation under the International Convention on Civil Liability for Oil Pollution Damage (1969 CLC) and the International Convention on the Establishment of an International Fund for Compensation for Oil Pollution Damage (1971 Fund)
(2) Claims for compensation under the Protocols to the International Convention on Civil Liability for Oil Pollution Damage (1992 CLC) and the International Convention on the Establishment of an International Fund for Compensation for Oil Pollution Damage (1992 Fund Convention) and the Supplementary Fund Protocol 2003.

[167] Centre for International Governance Innovation (2018).
[168] IOPC Funds (2023).
[169] Ibid.

15.4.2 Claims for Compensation Under Civil Liability Convention 1969 and Fund 1971

Prior to the coming into force of the Protocols of 1992 (1992 CLC),[170] establishing liability was based on whether the claim was on all fours with the definition of pollution damage under the 1969 CLC. Under this Convention, pollution damage is defined as a 'loss or damage caused outside the ship carrying oil by contamination resulting from the escape or discharge of oil from the ship, wherever such escape or discharge may occur, and includes the costs of preventive measures and further loss or damage caused by preventive measures'.[171] Damage here applies to 'pollution damage caused on the territory including the territorial sea of a Contracting State and to preventive measures taken to prevent or minimize such damage'.[172]

Although this definition expressly includes the costs of preventive measures taken to minimise damage, it does not refer explicitly to environmental damage and therefore does not recognise compensation for ecological damage.[173] Thus, the interpretation of pollution damage under 1969 CLC was left to national courts, which might allow claims for the notional costs of damage to the marine environment. A number of cases buttressed this point.

15.4.2.1 The *Antonio Gramsci* Incident

In the *Antonio Gramsci incident*,[174] a flag ship of the former Union of Soviet Socialist Republic (USSR), with 27,706 gross tonnage (GT), ran aground on 27 February 1979 at Ventspils, USSR, and spilt 5500 tonnes of oil, which affected the Swedish archipelago, the Aland Islands, Finland and the USSR coast.[175]

The incident raised the question of whether the definition of pollution damage under Article I(6) of the 1969 CLC and the 1971 Fund Convention included environmental damage or damage to natural resources, as claimed by the USSR and others. In response, the Fund Assembly stated that 'the assessment of compensation to be paid by the IOPC Funds is not to be made on the basis of an abstract quantification of damage calculated in accordance with theoretical models'.[176]

---

[170] Protocols to the International Convention on Civil Liability for Oil Pollution Damage (Civil Liability Convention 1969) and the International Convention on the Establishment of an International Fund for Compensation for Oil Pollution Damage (Fund Convention 1971).

[171] CLC (1969), art. I(6).

[172] Ibid., art. II.

[173] Birnie et al. (2009), p. 437.

[174] International Oil Pollution Compensation Funds (IOPC Funds) (1979).

[175] Ibid.

[176] International Oil Pollution Compensation Funds (*Fund Executive Committee*) (1980), FUND/A/ES 1/13, para. 11(a).

However, the International Oil Pollution Compensation Fund (1971 Fund) later agreed with the Swedish government on a settlement of Swedish claims amounting to about 112 million Swedish crowns. The sum of 93 million Swedish crowns was paid to Sweden, minus the Swedish share in the shipowner's limitation sum (about 4 million Swedish crowns), plus interest. The payment was made on 31 March 1981.[177]

15.4.2.2 The *Patmos* Incident

The second case under consideration is the *Patmos incident.*[178] The Patmos is a 51,627 gross tonnage Greek-registered tanker, which, as a result of a collision, spilt 700 tonnes of oil off the coast of Calabria, a Sicilian Port in Italy, on 21 March 1985. In the *Patmos incident,*[179] the Italian government claimed £9.2 million (later reduced to £2.3 million) for damage to the marine environment arising out of that spillage.[180]

The 1971 Fund addressed the claim by the Italian government and, in the absence of any documentation from the Italian government indicating the nature of the damage that had been caused or the basis on which the amount claimed had been calculated, rejected the claim.[181]

After the claim by the Italian government was rejected under the 1971 Funds, it had the recourse to her national legal system and then took the case[182] to Italian courts for redress. In 1986, the Court of First Instance rejected the government's claim for compensation for ecological damage to marine flora and fauna on the ground that the territorial sea was not crown or patrimonial property of the state but a *res communis omnium*, which could not be violated by private parties, and that even if it was, the state had not incurred any direct or indirect loss as a result of the oil spill since no disbursements for the cleaning of the coastline had been incurred, nor had any loss of profit occurred.[183]

The Italian government went on appeal. In 1989, the Italian Court of Appeal overruled the decision of the Court of First Instance. The Court of Appeal interpreted environmental damage to include 'everything which alters, causes deterioration in or destroys the environment in whole or in part'.[184] The court arrived at this definition

[177] IOPC Funds (1985).

[178] Ibid.

[179] *General Nation Maritime Transport Company and Others v Patmos Shipping Company and Others* (1999).

[180] Ibid.

[181] International Oil Pollution Compensation Funds (*Fund Executive Committee*) (1986), FUND/EXC. 16/8, para. 3.3.

[182] *General Nation Maritime Transport Company and Others v Patmos Shipping Company and Others* (1999).

[183] Ibid.

[184] International Oil Pollution Compensation Funds (*Fund Executive Committee*) (1991), FUND/EXC.30/2, para. 4.15.

by interpreting the provisions of the 1969 CLC[185] in reference to the International Convention Relating to Intervention on the High Seas in Cases of Oil Pollution Casualties (Intervention Convention 1969), which provides:

> Parties to the present Convention may take such measures on the high seas as may be necessary to prevent, mitigate or eliminate grave and imminent danger to their coastline or related interests from pollution or threat of pollution of the sea by oil, following upon a maritime casualty or acts related to such a casualty, which may reasonably be expected to result in major harmful consequences.[186]

In interpreting the above provisions of the Intervention Convention 1969, the Court of Appeal defines the threat to 'related interests', justifying intervention as including 'the conservation of living marine resources and of wildlife'. The court went on to hold that:

> The environment must be considered as a unitary asset, separate from those of which the environment is composed (territory, territorial waters, beaches, fish etc.) and it includes natural resources, health and landscape. The right to the environment belongs to the state, in its capacity as representative of the collectivities. The damage to the environment prejudices immaterial values, which cannot be assessed in monetary terms according to market prices, and consists of the reduced possibility of using the environment. The damage can be compensated on an equitable basis, which may be established by the Court on the grounds of an opinion of experts ... The definition of 'pollution damage' as laid down in Article 1(6) is wide enough to include damage to the environment of the kind described above.[187]

The Court of Appeal held that the traditional view of property damage was no longer valid and that the owner of the *Patmos*, the UK Club (an insurers' group) and the Fund 1971 were liable for the environmental damage claimed by the Italian government.[188] It appointed three experts to ascertain the existence, if any, of damage to the marine resources resulting from the oil spillage. In their March 1990 report, the experts found that, with the exception of damage to fishing activities, which they valued at approximately £465,000, there was a lack of data to evaluate the economic impact of the spillage on other activities and that a precise assessment of damage to such activities was impossible. The experts also determined that the court was the appropriate body to carry out the evaluation.[189]

In December 1993, the Court of Appeal awarded a final judgment of £827,000 for environmental damage. The court decided that the lack of data and the inability of the experts to determine a precise damage award for environmental harm were not reasons to refuse compensation. It found that the experts were wrong to calculate damages based only on market prices for fish. Because the environment and its natural resources were worth more to the community, the Court of Appeal

---

[185] CLC (1969), art. I(6).

[186] Intervention Convention (1969), art. 1.

[187] International Oil Pollution Compensation Funds (*Fund Executive Committee*) (1991), FUND/EXC.30/2 at 45.

[188] Ibid., at 59–60.

[189] Ibid.

determined damage according to principles of equity. The decision itself does not make clear exactly how the judge assessed and calculated the environmental damages beyond the £465,000 previously indicated by the panel of experts.[190]

15.4.2.3 The *Haven* Incident

Another case before the 1992 CLC was the *Haven incident.*[191] On 11 April 1991, the *Haven*, a Cypriot-registered tanker, 109,977 gross tonnage, caught fire and broke apart 7 miles from Genoa in Italy and released over 10,000 tonnes of oil, causing damage to the Italian and French coasts and necessitating extensive clean-up operations. The Italian government submitted a claim for damage to the marine environment, this time in the provisional amount of 100,000 million Italian lire (£47 million), a figure that the Region of Liguria requested should be doubled. One thousand two hundred Italian claimants, the French government, 22 French municipalities and two other public bodies also submitted claims.[192]

In the subsequent court proceedings at the Court of First Instance in Genoa, Italy, the question arose as to whether claims for damage to the marine environment could be pursued against the shipowners outside the conventions under the relevant Italian law if such damage was not admissible under the 1969 CLC and the 1971 Fund.[193]

In his report on this matter, the director of the 1971 Fund concluded that the 1969 CLC and the 1971 Fund were designed to provide compensation to victims of pollution damage, that claims which did not relate to such compensation fell outside the scope of the conventions and that claims relating to non-quantifiable elements of damage to the environment were of a punitive nature and were beyond the scope of the conventions.[194] The director took the view that the drafters of the 1971 Fund could not have intended that the Fund should pay damages of a punitive character calculated on the basis of the seriousness of the fault of the wrongdoer or the profit earned by the wrongdoer and that the result of including such damage would be unacceptable. On this basis, the director concluded that such claims could be pursued outside the conventions on the basis of national law.[195]

In rejecting the director's analysis during a session of the Executive Committee of the IOPC Fund, the Italian delegation maintained its view that the 1969 CLC and 1971 Fund did not exclude compensation for environmental damage which was non-quantifiable, that the state had a legal right to compensation for any damage to

[190] International Oil Pollution Compensation Funds (*Fund Executive Committee*) (1991), FUND/EXC.30/2.

[191] Ibid., paras. 31.1.13–31.1.18.

[192] Ibid.

[193] International Oil Pollution Compensation Funds (*Fund Executive Committee*) (1991), FUND/EXC.30/2.

[194] Ibid.

[195] Ibid.

the environment which had irreversible consequences or where the environment could not be reinstated and that Italian law envisaged the possibility of compensation for damage to the marine environment for quantifiable and non-quantifiable elements.[196] The director's point of view was supported by France, the United Kingdom, Japan and the observer delegation of the International Group of P&I Clubs (shipping insurance and freight companies).[197]

On 5 April 1996, the Court of First Instance in Genoa, Italy, ruled that 'pollution damage' in the 1969 CLC and 1971 Fund had a wide enough meaning to include natural resource and environmental damage. Since these damages could not be calculated according to commercial or economic valuations, the court awarded £13 million (40,000 million lire), about one-third of the clean-up cost, on the basis that the clean-up did not repair all the damage caused; the award essentially compensated the unremedied residual damage.[198]

The Fund 1971 appealed, and in response, Italy requested that the environmental damages be increased to £284 million (883,435 million lire). On 4 March 1999, the parties (Italy, the shipowner, the UK Mutual Steam Ship Assurance Association and the Fund 1971) withdrew all legal actions from Italian courts and signed an agreement.[199] The shipowner and the UK club made an *ex gratia* payment of £9.1 million (25,000 million lire), in addition to paying the amount indicated by the Court of First Instance to Italy, without admitting liability beyond the shipowner's limits under the 1969 CLC.[200]

15.4.2.4 The *Aegean Sea* Incident

The *Aegean Sea incident*[201] is another case handled under the Fund 1971. On 3 December 1992, the *Aegean Sea*, a 57, 801 gross tonnage (GT) Greek-registered ship, during heavy weather, ran aground while approaching La Coruña harbour in the northwest of Spain. The ship, which was carrying approximately 80,000 tonnes of crude oil, broke in two and burnt fiercely for about 24 hours. The forward section sank some 50 metres from the coast, though the stern section remained largely intact. The quantity of oil spilt was not known since most of the cargo was either dispersed in the sea or consumed by the fire on board the vessel, but it was estimated at some 73,500 tonnes. Several stretches of coastline east and north-east of La Coruña were contaminated, as well as the sheltered Ria de Ferrol. The oil remaining in the aft

[196] Ibid.

[197] Ibid.

[198] Ibid.

[199] International Oil Pollution Compensation Funds (*Fund Executive Committee*) (1991), FUND/EXC.30/2.

[200] Ibid.

[201] IOPC Funds (1992b).

section of the *Aegean Sea* was removed by salvors working from the shore. Extensive clean-up operations were carried out at sea and onshore.[202]

Claims totalling[203] 48,187 million pesetas (Pts) or €289.6 million (euro currency of the European Union) were submitted before the criminal and civil courts. Under the Civil Liability Convention 1969 and the Fund Convention 1971, the maximum amount of compensation payable in respect of the incident was 60 million SDR. When converted into pesetas (Pts) using the rate applied for the conversion of the shipowner's limitation, the maximum amount of compensation payable was Pts 9,513,473,400 or €57.2 million.[204]

In the ensuing civil proceedings, the Fund 1971 Administrative Council authorised the Fund director to conclude, on behalf of the Fund, an agreement with the Spanish state, the shipowner and the P&I Insurer United Kingdom Mutual Steamship Assurance Association (Bermuda) Limited (UK Club), a global solution to all outstanding issues in the *Aegean Sea* case termed global settlement.[205]

On 30 October 2002, an agreement was concluded between the Spanish government, the 1971 Fund, the shipowner and the UK Club, whereby the total amount due to the victims from the owner of the *Aegean Sea*, the UK Club and the 1971 Fund as a result of the distribution of liabilities determined by the Court of Appeal in La Coruña amounted to Pts 9000 million or €54 million.[206]

As a consequence of the agreement, the Spanish state undertook to compensate all the victims, who might obtain a final judgment in their favour by a Spanish court, which condemned the shipowner, the UK Club or the 1971 Fund to pay compensation as a result of the incident. The Fund 1971, in turn, also undertook to notify the Spanish state of any proceedings to which the Spanish state was not a party and not to accept the claims brought in the proceedings.[207] On 1 November 2002, pursuant to the agreement, the 1971 Fund paid €38,386,172, corresponding to Pts 6,386,921,613, to the Spanish government.[208]

In the claims before the court, in December 2005, the Court of First Instance issued a judgment ordering the Spanish government and the 1971 Fund to pay €363,746 to the claimants. The Spanish government and the 1971 Fund appealed against the judgment. The Court of Appeal returned the file to the Court of First Instance, ordering that the proceedings be restarted also against the pilot in order to correct an error by the Court of First Instance. The Court of First Instance gave time to the claimants to pursue their claim against the pilot, as decided by the Court of Appeal. However, the claimants decided not to continue with the claim against the

---

[202] Ibid.

[203] Spanish currency.

[204] IOPC Funds (2018c).

[205] International Oil Pollution Compensation Funds (*Fund Executive Committee*) (1991), FUND/EXC.30/2.

[206] Ibid.

[207] Ibid.

[208] Ibid.

pilot. The Court of First Instance ordered that the proceedings continue only against the 1971 Fund on the basis of a technical defence called the lack of *litis consortium*; i.e., the pilot was not a defendant in the proceedings, and therefore the vicarious liability of the state could not come into effect.[209]

In a judgment delivered in July 2012, the Court of First Instance decided to award the claimants the amount awarded in its prior decision in 2005 (€363,746), but since the claimants had not included the pilot/Spanish government in the proceedings, the 1971 Fund would only be liable in respect of 50% of the awarded amount (€181,873). In accordance with the global settlement agreement with the Spanish government, the 1971 Fund notified the Spanish government of the above judgment and lodged an appeal.[210]

In January 2013, at a meeting with the director, the Spanish government agreed not to object if the 1971 Fund tried to settle the claim with the remaining claimants. An initial discussion with the remaining claimants took place; however, no agreement was possible.[211]

In May 2013, the Court of Appeal (Audiencia Provincial) decided to hear the declarations of the experts acting on behalf of the parties. According to this decision, the experts appeared before the court in October 2013. In a judgment delivered in October 2013, and corrected in November 2013, the Court of Appeal reduced the amount awarded to the claimants to €163,439, plus interest and costs, of which the Fund 1971 would be liable for 50%. In February 2014, the court issued an order of enforcement for €243,377, which included the principal, interest and costs. In May 2014, in compliance with the global settlement agreement, the Spanish government paid the claimants €163,440, with the outstanding balance to be paid in due course.[212]

In June 2014, the 1971 Fund discontinued the defence of this case before the Spanish courts, and by October 2014, the director reported to the 1971 Fund Administrative Council that the case was closed in respect of the 1971 Fund, although one claim by a fish pond owner, totalling €799,921, is still pending in the civil proceedings.[213]

---

[209] Ibid.

[210] International Oil Pollution Compensation Funds (*Fund Executive Committee*) (1991), FUND/EXC.30/2.

[211] Ibid.

[212] Ibid.

[213] Ibid.

15.4.3 Claims for Compensation Under Civil Liability Convention 1992 (1992 CLC) and 1992 Fund Convention

15.4.3.1 Introduction

The *Aegean Sea incident* closed the chapter for compensation claims under the 1969 CLC and 1971 Fund. One of the major problems encountered in the pursuit of compensation claims for environmental damage under those conventions was the issue of defining pollution damage.

It will be recalled that these conventions,[214] in their definitions, restricted pollution damage to 'pollution damage caused on the territory including the territorial sea of a Contracting State and to preventive measures taken to prevent or minimize such damage'.[215] The Conventions, by making reference to 'pollution damage' only and without expliciy mention of 'environmental damage,' by implication, did not recognise compensation for ecological damage. This could be inferred, from the proceeding part, that payment of compensation for ecological damage was left to national courts which might allow claims for notional costs for damage to the marine environment.

However, there appears to be an improvement in this definition under the 1992 CLC, especially under Article 1(6), which makes it clear that compensation for the impairment of the environment is recoverable, though limited to 'the costs of reasonable measures of reinstatement actually undertaken or to be undertaken'. The new definition, according to Birnie et al.,[216] 'also allows recovery for loss of profit arising out of impairment of the environment, for example in the case of losses suffered by fishermen or hotel owners . . . and also includes pollution damage in the coastal state's EEZ, or in an area up to 200 miles from its territorial sea baselines'.

The IOPC Funds 1992 interpreted the phrase 'pollution damage' in the Conventions of 1992 (1992 CLC and 1992 Fund) to cover costs incurred in clean-up operations at sea and on the beach, preventive measures, additional costs and a proportion of the fixed costs incurred by public authorities in maintaining a pollution response capability, as well as economic loss suffered by persons who depend directly on earnings from coastal or sea related activities, including fishermen and hoteliers, and damage to property.[217] Claims for compensation arising from some incidents involving oil tankers resulting to oil pollution damage may buttress this assertion.

[214] CLC (1969) and the 1971 Fund.

[215] CLC (1969), art. II.

[216] Birnie et al. (2009), p. 437.

[217] Ibid.

15.4.3.2 The *Erika* Incident

On 12 December 1999, the Maltese-registered tanker Erika (19,666 GT) broke in two in the Bay of Biscay, some 60 nautical miles off the coast of Brittany, France. Some 400 kilometres of shoreline were affected by oil.[218]

The tanker was carrying a cargo of 31,000 tonnes of heavy fuel oil, of which some 19,800 tonnes were spilt at the time of the incident. The bow section sank in approximately 100 metres of water. The stern section sank to a depth of 130 metres approximately 10 nautical miles from the bow section. Some 6400 tonnes of cargo remained in the bow section and a further 4800 tonnes in the stern section.[219]

Although the removal of the bulk of the oil from shorelines was completed quite rapidly, considerable secondary cleaning was still required in many areas in 2000. Operations to remove residual contamination began in spring 2001. By the summer tourist season of 2001, almost all of the secondary cleaning had been completed, apart from a small number of difficult sites in Loire Atlantique and the islands of Morbihan. Clean-up efforts continued at these sites in the autumn, and most were completed by November 2001.[220]

More than 250,000 tonnes of oily waste were collected from shorelines and temporarily stockpiled. Total SA, the French oil company, engaged a contractor to deal with the disposal of the recovered waste, and the operation was completed in December 2003. The cost of the waste disposal was believed to have been some €46 million.[221]

The French government decided that the oil should be removed from the two sections of the wreck. The oil removal operations, which were funded by Total SA, were carried out by an international consortium during the period from June to September 2000. No significant quantities of oil escaped during the operations.[222]

At the time of the incident, France was a party to the 1992 CLC and 1992 Fund Convention. In accordance with the 1992 CLC, the *Erika* was insured for oil pollution liability with the Steamship Mutual Underwriting Association (Bermuda) Ltd (Steamship Mutual). At the request of the shipowner, the Commercial Court in Nantes issued an order on 14 March 2000 opening limitation proceedings. The court determined the limitation amount applicable to the *Erika* at 84,247,733 French francs (FFr), corresponding to €12,843,484, and declared that the shipowner had constituted the limitation fund by means of a letter of guarantee issued by the shipowner's liability insurer, Steamship Mutual.[223]

In 2002, the limitation fund was transferred from the Commercial Court in Nantes, France, to the Commercial Court in Rennes, also in France. In 2006, the

---

218 IOPC Funds (1999).

219 IOPC Funds (1999).

220 Ibid.

221 Ibid.

222 Ibid.

223 IOPC Funds (2018c), p. 3.

limitation fund was again transferred, this time to the Commercial Court in Saint-Brieuc, France. The maximum amount available for compensation under the 1992 CLC and the 1992 Fund Convention for the Erika incident was 135 million SDR, equal to FFr1 211,966,811 or €184,763,149. The level of payments by the 1992 Fund was initially limited to 50% of the amount of the loss or damage actually suffered by the respective claimants. The 1992 Fund Executive Committee decided in January 2001 to increase the level of payments from 50% to 60% and, in June 2001, to 80%. In April 2003, the level of payments was increased to 100%.[224]

Claims for compensation were made. Total SA and the French government undertook not to pursue claims against the IOPC Fund 1992 or against the limitation fund constituted by the shipowner or his insurer, relating to its costs arising from operations in respect of the wreck, the clean-up of shorelines and the disposal of oily waste and from a publicity campaign to restore the image of the Atlantic coast, if and to the extent the presentation of such claims would result in the total amount of all claims exceeding the maximum compensation available for this incident under the 1992 CLC, that is, 135 million SDR, equal to FFr1 211,966,811 or €184,763,149.[225]

The French government also undertook not to pursue claims for compensation against the IOPC Fund 1992 or the limitation fund established by the shipowner or his insurer if and to the extent that the presentation of such claims would result in the maximum amount available under the 1992 Conventions being exceeded. However, the French government's claims would rank before any claims by Total SA if funds were available after all other claims had been paid in full.[226]

On the basis of a report by an expert appointed by a magistrate in the Criminal Court of First Instance in Paris, criminal charges were brought in that court against the master of the *Erika*, the representative of the registered owner (Tevere Shipping), the president of the management company (Panship Management and Services Srl), the deputy manager of Centre Régional Opérationnel de Surveillance et de Sauvetage (CROSS), three officers of the French Navy who were responsible for controlling the traffic off the coast of Brittany, the classification society Registro Italiano Navale (RINA), one of RINA's managers, three companies of the Total Group (Total SA and two subsidiaries, Total Transport Corporation (TTC), voyage charterer of the *Erika*, and Total Petroleum Services Ltd, the agent of TTC) and some of its senior staff. A number of claimants, including the French government and several local authorities, joined the criminal proceedings as civil parties, claiming compensation totalling €400 million.[227]

The judgment by the Criminal Court of First Instance in Paris delivered in January 2008 found the following criminally liable for the offence of causing pollution:

---

224 IOPC Funds (2018c), p. 3.

225 Ibid.

226 Ibid.

227 Ibid.

(i) the representative of the shipowner (Tevere Shipping) and the president of the management company (Panship Management and Services Srl) guilty of lack of proper maintenance, leading to general corrosion of the ship and were sentenced to pay a fine of Euro(€)75,000 each;
(ii) the classification society (RINA) was found guilty of imprudence in renewing the Erika's classification certificate on the basis of an inspection that fell below the standards of the profession and was sentenced to pay a fine of Euro(€) 375,000; and
(iii) Total SA was found guilty of imprudence when carrying out its vetting operations prior to the chartering of the Erika and was sentenced to pay a fine of Euro(€)375,000.[228]

Regarding civil liabilities, the judgment held the four convicted parties[229] jointly and severally liable for the damage caused by the incident.[230]

The compensation awarded to the civil parties by the Criminal Court of First Instance was based on national law. The court held that the Conventions regime of 1992 (1992 CLC and 1992 Fund) did not deprive the civil parties of their right to obtain compensation for their damage in the Criminal Courts and, in the proceedings, awarded the claimants compensation for economic losses, damage to the image of several regions and municipalities, moral damages and damages to the environment.[231]

In this respect, the court recognised the right to compensation for damage to the environment for a local authority with special powers for the protection, management and conservation of a territory. The judgment also recognised the right of an environmental protection association to claim compensation, not only for the moral damage caused to the collective interests that were its purpose to defend but also for the damage to the environment that affected the collective interests which it had a statutory mission to safeguard. The Court assessed the total damages at the amount of €192.15 million.[232] Following the judgment, Total made voluntary payments to the majority of the civil parties, including the French government, for a total of €171.3 million.[233]

The four parties that were held criminally liable and some 70 civil parties appealed against the judgment. The Court of Appeal in Paris rendered its judgment in March 2010. In its decision, the Court of Appeal confirmed the judgment of the Criminal Court of First Instance, which held the four parties criminally liable for the offence of causing pollution. It also confirmed the fines imposed.

---

[228] IOPC Funds (2018c), p. 3.

[229] That is, Tevere Shipping, Panship Management and Services Srl, RINA and Total SA.

[230] IOPC Funds (2018c), p. 4.

[231] Ibid.

[232] Ibid.

[233] Ibid.

Regarding civil liabilities in the judgment of the Criminal Court of First Instance, the Court of Appeal ruled:

(i) The representative of the registered owner of the Erika was an 'agent of the owner', as defined by article III(4)(a)[234] and that, although, as such, he was theoretically entitled to benefit from the channelling provisions of the 1992 CLC, but had acted recklessly and with knowledge that damage would probably result, which deprived him of protection in the circumstances. The Court therefore confirmed the judgment of the Criminal Court of First Instance on the representative's civil liability;

(ii) The president of the management company (Panship) was the agent of a company who performs services for the ship as per the provisions of article III(4)(b) of 1992 CLC and as such was not protected by the channelling provisions of that Convention;

(iii) The classification society RINA, cannot be considered as a 'person who performs services for the ship,' as per the definition of article III(4)(b) of the 1992 CLC. Indeed the Court ruled that, in issuing statutory and safety certificates, the classification society had acted as an agent of the Maltese State (the Flag State). The Court also held that the classification society would have been entitled to take advantage of the immunity of jurisdiction, as would the Maltese State, but that in the circumstances it was deemed to have renounced such immunity by not having invoked it at an earlier stage in the proceedings; and

(iv) Total SA was 'de facto' charterer of the *Erika* and could therefore benefit from the channelling provision of article III(4)(c) of the 1992 CLC since the imprudence committed in its vetting of the *Erika* could not be considered as having been committed with the intent to cause such damage, or recklessly and with knowledge that such damage would probably result. The Court thus held that Total SA could benefit from the channelling provisions in the 1992 CLC and therefore did not have civil liability. The Court of Appeal also decided that the voluntary payments made by Total SA to the civil parties, including to the French Government following the judgment of the Criminal Court of First Instance were final payments which could not be recovered from the civil parties.[235]

Regarding reputation, image, moral and environmental damage, in its judgment, the Court of Appeal accepted not only material damages (clean-up, restoration measures and property damage) and economic losses but also moral damages resulting from the pollution, including the loss of enjoyment, damage to reputation and brand image and moral damage arising from damage to the natural heritage. The Court of Appeal's judgment confirmed the compensation rights for moral damages awarded by the Criminal Court of First Instance to a number of local authorities and, in addition, accepted claims for moral damages from other civil parties. The Court of

[234] CLC (1992).

[235] IOPC Funds (2018c), p. 5.

Appeal accepted the right to compensation for pure environmental damage, that is, damage to non-marketable environmental resources that constitute a legitimate collective interest. The Court of Appeal considered that it was sufficient that the pollution touched the territory of a local authority for these authorities to be able to claim for the direct or indirect damage caused to them by the pollution.

The Court of Appeal awarded compensation for pure environmental damage to the local authorities and environmental associations. The damages awarded by the courts include the following: material damage (€163.91million) by the Criminal Court of First Instance and (€165.4 million) by the Criminal Court of Appeal; moral damage (the loss of enjoyment, damage to reputation and brand image, moral damage arising from damage to the natural heritage) (€26.92 million) by the Criminal Court of First Instance and (€34.1 million) by the Criminal Court of Appeal; and pure environmental damage (€1.32 million) by the Criminal Court of First Instance and (€4.3 million) by the Criminal Court of Appeal. The total compensation awarded by the Criminal Court of First Instance was €192.15 million and by the Criminal Court of Appeal, €203.8 million.[236]

Taking into account the amounts paid in compensation by Total SA following the judgment of the Criminal Court of First Instance, the balance to be compensated by the representative of the shipowner (Tevere Shipping), the president of the management company (Panship Management and Services Srl) and the classification society (RINA) was €32.5 million.

However, some 50 parties, including the representative of Tevere Shipping, Panship Management and Services, RINA and Total SA, appealed to the French Supreme Court (Court of Cassation). On 25 September 2012, the Criminal Section of the Court of Cassation rendered its judgment and decided, *inter alia*, on the following:

(i) On issue of Jurisdiction the Court of Cassation decided that French courts had jurisdiction to determine both criminal and civil liabilities arising from the *Erika incident* even though the sinking of the vessel had taken place in the Exclusive Economic Zone (EEZ) of France and not within its territory and/or territorial waters. The Court, based on a number of dispositions of the United Nations Convention on the Law of the Sea, justified France exercising its jurisdiction to impose sanctions on those responsible for an oil spill from a foreign flagged vessel in the EEZ of France causing serious damage in its territorial sea and to its coastline.[237]

(ii) The Court of Cassation confirmed the decision by the Criminal Court of First Instance and by the Court of Appeal that the parties[238] were criminally liable for the offence of causing pollution.

---

[236] Ibid., 6.

[237] IOPC Funds (2018c), p. 5.

[238] The representative of the shipowner (Tevere Shipping), the president of the management company (Panship Management and Services Srl), the classification society (RINA) and Total SA.

(iii) Regarding civil liabilities, the Court of Cassation decided that under article IX (2) of the 1992 CLC, it was entitled to exercise jurisdiction in respect of actions for compensation.
(iv) The further held that RINA and Total SA were covered by the channelling provisions of the 1992 CLC,[239] but could not rely on this protection since the damage resulted from their personal acts or omissions, committed with the intent to cause such damage, or recklessly and with knowledge that such damage would probably result.
(v) In relation to Total SA, the Court quashed the decision by the Court of Appeal and decided that, since the damage had resulted from Total SA's recklessness, it could not rely on the protection awarded by the 1992 CLC.
(vi) On the issue of decision of the Court of Appeal on material, moral and pure environmental damages, the Court of Cassation confirmed the decision by the Court of Appeal upheld the amount awarded.

On the whole, as at 31 December 2008, 7131 claims for compensation had been submitted for a total of €389.9 million (£377 million). By that date, 99.7% of the claims had been assessed. Some 1016 claims, totalling €31.8 million (£30.7 million), had been rejected. Payments of compensation had been made in respect of 5938 claims for a total of €129.7 million (£95.1 million), out of which Steamship Mutual had paid €12.8 million (£9.4 million) and the IOPC Fund 1992, €116.9 million (£85.7 million).[240]

15.4.3.3 The *Prestige* Incident

On 13 November 2002, the Bahamas-registered tanker *Prestige*, a 42,820 GT, carrying 76,972 tonnes of heavy fuel oil, began listing and leaking oil some 30 kilometres off Cabo Finisterre, Galicia, Spain. On 19 November, while under tow away from the coast, the vessel broke in two and sank some 260 kilometres west of Vigo, Spain. The bow section sank to a depth of 3500 metres and the stern section to a depth of 3830 metres. The break-up and sinking released an estimated 63,200 tonnes of cargo. Over the following weeks, oil continued to leak from the wreck at a declining rate. It was subsequently estimated that approximately 13,700 tonnes of cargo remained in the wreck.[241]

Due to the highly persistent nature of the *Prestige*'s cargo, released oil drifted for an extended period of time with winds and currents and travelled great distances. The west coast of Galicia was heavily contaminated, and oil eventually moved into the Bay of Biscay, affecting the north coast of Spain and France. Traces of oil were

[239] CLC (1992), art. III(4).
[240] IOPC Funds (1985).
[241] IOPC Funds (2002).

detected in the United Kingdom (the Channel Islands, the Isle of Wight and Kent).[242]

At the time of the incident, Spain, France and Portugal were parties to the 1992 CLC and the 1992 Fund Convention. The *Prestige* was insured for oil pollution liability with the London P&I Club. The limitation amount applicable to the *Prestige* under the 1992 CLC is approximately SDR 18.9 million or €22,777,986.[243] On 28 May 2003, the shipowner deposited this amount with the Criminal Court in Corcubión, Spain, for the purpose of constituting the limitation fund required under the 1992 CLC. The maximum amount of compensation under the 1992 CLC and the 1992 Fund Convention is SDR 135 million, which corresponds to €171,520,703.[244] Claims for compensation were made by various countries: Spain France and Portugal.

The claims-handling office in La Coruña, Spain, received 845 claims totalling €1037 million. These included 15 claims from the Spanish government totalling €984.8 million. The claims by the Spanish government relate to costs incurred in respect of at-sea and onshore clean-up operations; the removal of oil from the wreck; compensation payments made in relation to the spill on the basis of national legislation (royal decrees); tax relief for businesses affected by the spill; administration costs; costs relating to publicity campaigns; costs incurred by local authorities and paid by the state; costs incurred by 67 towns that had been paid by the state; costs incurred by the regions of Galicia, Asturias, Cantabria and the Basque Country; and costs incurred in respect of the treatment of the oily residues.[245]

Provisional payments totalling €565,310 were made in respect of 176 of the assessed claims, mainly at 30% of the assessed amount. Compensation payments made by the Spanish government to the claimants had been deducted when calculating the provisional payments. Some claims were either rejected or could not be assessed due to a lack of documentation and the lack of response to the repeated requests from the IOPC Fund 1992. In respect of claims submitted by individual claimants, provisional payments totalling €101,625 were made at 30% of the assessed amount, taking into account the aid received, in respect of those court claims that had not been submitted to the claims-handling office.

The claims-handling office in France received 482 claims totalling €109.7 million. This includes the claims by the French government totalling €67.5 million in relation to the costs incurred for clean-up and preventive measures. In addition, 232 claimants, including the French government, brought legal actions against the shipowner, the London P&I Club and the 1992 Funds in 16 courts in France,

---

[242] Ibid.

[243] Under CLC (1992), art. V, the SDR amounts for the shipowner's liability limit shall be converted into national currency on the basis of the value of that currency by reference to the SDR on the date of the constitution of the fund. The rate of exchange on 7 February 2003 was €1 = SDR 0.78707700.

[244] IOPC Funds (2002).

[245] IOPC Funds (2002).

requesting compensation totalling some €111 million, including the amount of €67.7 million claimed by the government.[246]

The claims were assessed at €61.2 million, and provisional payments totalling €5.8 million were made at 30% of the assessed amounts. Some claims were either rejected or could not be assessed due to a lack of documentation and the lack of response to the repeated requests by the 1992 Fund. The claim by the French government was reassessed at €42.2 million. The French government did not agree with that assessment and decided to maintain its claim in court against the IOPC Fund 1992 and other parties.

The Portuguese government submitted a claim totalling €4.3 million in respect of the costs incurred for clean-up and preventive measures. The claim was finally assessed at €2.2 million, and the 1992 Fund made payment of €328,488 corresponding to 15% of the final assessment.[247]

The claims dragged on up to the Supreme Court. In the case of Spain, the IOPC Fund 1992 assessed the losses suffered by the Spanish state at €300 million, but the Supreme Court awarded €803 million. In the case of France, the Fund's assessment of the claim by the French government totalled €42.2 million, whereas the Supreme Court awarded €67.5 million. The court issued an order with a distribution list, and during the course of 2020, the Spanish court made payments totalling €51,537,619 to the claimants in the Spanish legal proceedings.

One notable departure from the claims under the conventions was that the Supreme Court, in its judgment, awarded €554.10 million for pure environmental damages and moral damages based on 30% of the losses awarded. Although the IOPC Fund 1992 is not liable for these two types of damages, as Article I (6) of the 1992 CLC does not recognise them and they are not confirmed by the court, the IOPC Fund 1992 director nonetheless expressed satisfaction that the court had applied the conventions in this point.[248]

Another notable take from the legal proceedings occasioned by the *Prestige incident* in the criminal procedure that took place in Spain is that the Spanish Supreme Court, deciding on the matter, held:

(i) the master of the *Prestige* was criminally liable, with civil liability
(ii) the shipowner had civil liability and was not entitled to limit its liability
(iii) the insurer, the London P&I Club, had civil liability up to the limit of its policy of USD 1000 million.
(iv) the 1992 Fund had civil liability within the limit provided under the 1992 Fund Convention.
(v) The Spanish Court awarded a total of EUR 1439.08 million to claimants, including the Spanish and French governments.[249]

[246] Ibid.

[247] IOPC Funds (2002).

[248] Ibid.

[249] IOPC (2023), pp. 30–31.

It should be noted that as at 31 December 2022, a number of legal proceedings in Spain are continuing. As at this date, claims for compensation amounted to some €1.151 million. This figure far exceeded the amount available under the 1992 CLC and the 1992 Fund Convention. But in order to ensure the equal treatment of claimants, a decision was taken to limit payments to 15% of the established losses. This was the lowest figure the 1992 Fund has had to establish to date, and the incident provided a major push towards the adoption of the Supplementary Fund Protocol in 2003 to ensure that sufficient compensation is available in future major incidents. Thus, the high amounts claimed in compensation, which were well above the amount available under the 1992 Fund Convention, highlighted to states the risk and potential financial impact of such incidents. This accelerated the entry into force of the Supplementary Fund Protocol, increasing the compensation available under the international liability and compensation regime.[250]

15.4.3.4 The *Volgoneft 139* Incident

On 11 November 2007, the Russian-registered tanker Volgoneft 139 (3463 GT, built in 1978) broke in two in the Strait of Kerch linking the Sea of Azov and the Black Sea between the Russian Federation and Ukraine. The tanker was at anchor when it was caught in a severe storm and heavy seas. After the vessel had broken in two, the stern section remained afloat, and using the casualty's own engines, the master managed to beach it on a nearby sandbank. The crew were then rescued and taken to the Port of Kavkaz (Russian Federation). The fore section remained afloat at anchor for a while and then sank.[251]

The tanker was loaded with 4077 tonnes of heavy fuel oil (HFO). Between 1200 and 2000 tonnes of fuel oil were spilt initially. A month after the incident, the fore section was temporarily raised, and 1200 tonnes of a mixture of fuel oil and water were recovered from tanks 1 and 2. Three other cargo vessels loaded with sulphur (Volnogorsk, Nakhichevan and Kovel) also sank in the same area within 2 hours of the incident. The impact affected some 250 kilometres of shoreline, both in the Russian Federation and in Ukraine, which are understood to have been affected by the oil. Heavy bird casualties, numbering in excess of 30,000 were reported.[252]

The Russian Federation is a party to the 1992 Fund,[253] while Ukraine was not at the time of the incident. In November and December 2007, the IOPC Funds Secretariat contacted the Russian Embassy in London and the Ministry of Transport in Moscow, offering the Russian authorities the help of the 1992 Fund in dealing with the incident.[254]

---

[250] IOPC (2023), pp. 30–31.

[251] IOPC Funds (2007a).

[252] Ibid., 1.

[253] CLC (1992).

[254] IOPC Funds (2007a), p. 2.

There were two proceedings in the Volgoneft 139 incident: limitation proceedings and civil proceedings. The limitation proceedings were based on the minimum limit of liability under the 1992 Fund. The Volgoneft 139 was owned by JSC Volgotanker. In March 2008, JSC Volgotanker was declared bankrupt by the Commercial Court in Moscow. The Volgoneft 139 was insured by Ingosstrakh (Russian Federation) for SDR 3 million, i.e. the minimum limit of liability under the 1992 CLC prior to November 2003. The minimum limit under the 1992 CLC after November 2003, however, is SDR 4.51 million. There was therefore an 'insurance gap' of some SDR 1.51 million. In February 2008, the Arbitration Court of Saint Petersburg and Leningrad Region issued a ruling declaring that the limitation fund had been constituted by means of a letter of guarantee for SDR 3 million (RUB[255] 116.3 million).[256] All the claimants in the limitation proceedings included the IOPC Funds as a defendant. Therefore, the IOPC Funds had been involved as a defendant in the limitation proceedings from the beginning.[257]

In a judgment delivered in November 2014, the Arbitration Court of Saint Petersburg and Leningrad Region decided that the difference between the limitation fund of SDR 3 million deposited in court by the shipowner's insurer and the amount of the shipowner's liability limit, which would correspond under the 1992 CLC to SDR 4.51 million, should be allocated between all claimants. The court decided therefore that the 'insurance gap' of SDR 1.51 million should be deducted pro rata from the amount previously awarded to all claimants. The shipowner appealed against the judgment, but the appeal was rejected by the Court of Appeal. The November 2014 judgment by the Arbitration Court of Saint Petersburg and Leningrad Region therefore became final.[258]

Under the civil proceedings, there were claims by Rosprirodnadzor, a Russian federal agency, for the protection of the environment. It submitted a claim for environmental damage for some 6048.6 million Russian roubles (RUB). This claim was based on the quantity of oil spilt multiplied by the number of roubles per ton ('Metodika').[259]

The IOPC Funds Secretariat informed the Russian authorities that the claim was based on an abstract quantification of damages calculated in accordance with a theoretical model and that this was in contravention of Article I(6) of the 1992 CLC and therefore not admissible for compensation.[260] However, the Secretariat was prepared to examine the activities undertaken by Rosprirodnadzor to combat oil pollution and to restore the environment to determine if and to what extent they

---

[255] Russian currency—the rouble (RUB).

[256] IOPC Funds (2007a), p. 3.

[257] Ibid.

[258] Ibid., 7.

[259] Ibid., 4.

[260] Ibid., 5.

qualified for compensation under the 1992 CLC based on the provisions of the 1992 Fund Convention.[261]

In September 2010, the Arbitration Court of Saint Petersburg and Leningrad Region rendered a judgment rejecting the 'Metodika' claim. In its judgment, the court noted that, under Article (I)6 of the 1992 CLC, compensation for damage to the environment, other than the loss of benefit caused by such damage, should be limited to expenses for reasonable reinstatement measures, as well as expenses for preventive measures and the subsequent damage caused by such measures. The court also noted that the expenses included in the other claims arising from the incident covered any preventive and reinstatement measures actually taken as a result of the incident. Rosprirodnadzor did not appeal, and the judgment therefore became final.[262]

In the claims against Ingosstrakh, the shipowner's insurer, it submitted a defence in court arguing that the incident was wholly caused by a natural phenomenon of an exceptional, inevitable and irresistible character (force majeure) and that therefore no liability should be attached to the owner of the Volgoneft 139 under Article (III)(2)(a) of the 1992 CLC.[263]

The IOPC Fund 1992 appointed a team of experts to examine the weather conditions in the area and the circumstances at the time of the incident to determine the validity of the shipowner's defence. In summary, the conclusions of the experts were as follows:

(i) The storm of 11 November 2007 was not exceptional since there are records of similar and comparable storms being experienced in the region four times in the past 20 years.
(ii) It was not inevitable that the Volgoneft 139 would be caught in the storm. There were timely forecasts of the storm, and conditions were accurately predicted, so there had been sufficient opportunities to avoid the vessel being exposed to the storm in the way it had been.
(iii) The storm of 11 November 2007 was irresistible in so far as the Volgoneft 139 was concerned, as the conditions associated with the storm were in excess of the vessel's design criteria.[264]

In September 2010, the Arbitration Court of Saint Petersburg and Leningrad Region decided that the shipowner and its insurer had not provided evidence that the oil spill resulted from an act of God, which was exceptional and unavoidable. The court concluded that the master, having had all the necessary storm warnings, had not taken all necessary measures to avoid the incident and that therefore the incident was not unavoidable for the vessel. The court also concluded that the storm was not exceptional since there was data on comparable storms in the area. In its judgment, the court decided that the spill did not result from a natural phenomenon of an

[261] IOPC Funds (2007a), p. 5.

[262] Ibid.

[263] Ibid.

[264] Ibid.

exceptional or inevitable character and that the shipowner and its insurer were therefore liable for the pollution damage caused by the spill. Ingosstrakh did not appeal, and the judgment therefore became final. It should be noted that if the defence of Ingosstrakh were to be accepted by the court, the shipowner and its insurer would be exonerated from liability, and the 1992 Fund would have been compelled under Article 4(1)(a) of the 1992 Fund Convention to pay the compensation to the victims of the spill from the outset.

In the final analysis, the total amount awarded against the shipowner/Ingosstrakh and the IOPC Fund 1992 in the June 2012 judgment, including costs, together with the amount settled out of court for the shipowner's claim, was RUB[265] 512.3 million, of which the insurer was liable for RUB 116.5 million and the 1992 Fund was liable for RUB 395.8 million. Following the November 2014 judgment, this amount was reduced to RUB 453.7 million, of which the insurer must pay RUB 116.5 million and the IOPC Fund 1992 was liable for RUB 337.2 million.[266]

The 2012 judgment ordered the shipowner to pay the claimants up to the amount of the liability limitation fund constituted by the ruling of the Arbitration Court of February 2008 in the amount of RUB 116,280,000 and ruled that the judgment be executed on account of the means of the liability limitation fund. However, since the judgment only directly orders the shipowner to pay and the shipowner is bankrupt, Ingosstrakhis denied payment, arguing that it is not strictly required to pay and that doing so would be illegal. The court rejected requests by some claimants for the court to change the wording of the judgment or clarify how the judgment could be executed against Ingosstrakh.[267]

One of the claimants, the Salvage Company, brought a separate action against Ingosstrakh, claiming, under the guarantee issued by Ingosstrakh, the amount of compensation awarded by the 2012 judgment to the claimant from the shipowner. The claimant was successful in obtaining a final judgment against Ingosstrakh, and the claimant obtained an enforcement certificate against Ingosstrakh. After some inquiries, in August 2018, Ingosstrakh informed the IOPC Funds that it had paid to this claimant the amounts owed by the shipowner/Ingosstrakh to this claimant.[268] In its final report, the IOPC Funds stated as follows:

> It is possible that the claimants, except for the Salvage Company who was paid after bringing a separate action directly against Ingosstrakh, will never receive the compensation owed to them under the 1992 CLC as awarded by the Court. However, since the 1992 Fund has paid the amounts the Fund owed to the claimants in accordance with the final judgment of the Arbitration Court of Saint Petersburg and Leningrad Region, and all other issues arising from this case have been solved, this incident was closed in October 2018.[269]

[265] Rub (rouble Russian currency).

[266] IOPC Funds (2007a), p. 3.

[267] Ibid., 8.

[268] IOPC Funds (2007a), p. 8.

[269] Ibid.

15.4.3.5 The *Hebei Spirit* Incident

Another example of compensation claims under the Funds is the *Hebei Spirit incident.* On 7 December 2007, the Hong Kong registered tanker *Hebei Spirit* (146,848 GT) was struck by the crane barge *Samsung N°1* while at anchor about 5 nautical miles off Taean on the west coast of the Republic of Korea. The crane barge was being towed by two tugs (*Samsung N°5* and *Samho T3*) when the tow line broke. Weather conditions were poor, and it was reported that the crane barge had drifted into the tanker, puncturing three of its port cargo tanks.[270]

The *Hebei Spirit* was laden with about 209,000 tonnes of four different crude oils. Due to inclement weather conditions, repairs of the punctured tanks took 4 days to complete. In the meantime, the crew of the *Hebei Spirit* tried to limit the quantity of cargo spilt through holes in the damaged tanks by making it list and transferring cargo between tanks. However, as the tanker was almost fully laden, the possibilities for such actions were limited. As a result of the collision, a total of 10,900 tonnes of oil (a mix of Iranian heavy, Upper Zakum and Kuwait Export) escaped into the sea.[271]

The *Hebei Spirit* was owned by the *Hebei Spirit* Shipping Company Limited. The P&I insurer of the ship was China Shipowners Mutual Insurance Association (China P&I Club/Assuranceföreningen Skuld (Gjensidig) (Skuld Club)) and managed by V-Ships Limited. The crane barge and the two tugs were owned and/or operated by Samsung Corporation and its subsidiary Samsung Heavy Industries Co., Ltd (SHI), which belongs to the Samsung Group, the Republic of Korea's largest industrial conglomerate.[272]

The Republic of Korea is a party to the Funds of 1992[273] but, at the time of the spill, had not ratified the Supplementary Fund Protocol 2003. The tonnage of the *Hebei Spirit* (146,848 GT) was in excess of 140,000 GT. The limitation amount applicable, therefore, is the maximum under the Civil Liability Convention 1992, namely SDR 89.77 million. The total amount available for compensation under the Funds of 1992 is SDR 203 million. The conversion of SDR 203 million into Korean won (KRW)[274] was made on the basis of the value of that currency against the SDR on the date of the adoption of the Executive Committee's Record of Decisions during its 40th session on 13 March 2008; the rate of SDR 1 is equivalent to KRW 1,584.330, giving a total amount available for compensation of KRW 321,618,990,000. But IOPC Funds experts noted that the total amount of losses arising as a result of the *Hebei Spirit incident* was likely to exceed the amount available under the Funds of 1992. Based on this, the IOPC Fund 1992 Executive

---

[270] Ibid.

[271] Ibid.

[272] IOPC Funds (2007a), p. 8.

[273] CLC (1992).

[274] South Korean currency.

Committee decided that payments should, for the time being, be limited to 60% of the established losses.[275]

The IOPC Fund 1992 and the Skuld Club opened a claims-handling office (*Hebei Spirit*) Centre in Seoul to assist claimants in the presentation of their claims for compensation and appointed a team of Korean and international surveyors to monitor the clean-up operations and investigate the potential impact of pollution on fisheries, mariculture and tourism activities.[276]

Some 127,483 claims, totalling KRW 4227 billion, were submitted to the limitation proceedings, and the Limitation Court appointed a court administrator to deal with them. As a matter of Korean law and practice, no further claims could be registered, nor can changes be made to the amounts claimed after 27 August 2012. The IOPC Fund 1992 and the Skuld Club had previously received 128,406 claims. The difference between the number of claims submitted to the Limitation Court, the Skuld Club and IOPC Fund 1992 was due to the fact that a number of claims were submitted in groups.[277]

The Skuld Club paid KRW 186.8 billion in compensation. The IOPC Fund 1992 made payments totalling KRW 134.8 billion to the Government of the Republic of Korea in compensation, of which KRW 67.3 billion was in subrogation at a level of payment of 60% of the established losses; KRW 40 billion was an advance payment to the Government of the Republic of Korea, and a further KRW 27.5 billion was paid as a balancing payment after the signing of a bilateral agreement with the government.[278]

In the end, the courts rendered decisions in respect of 127,483 claims, and a total of KRW 432.9 billion (£299 million) was awarded to the claimants. The amount available for compensation in respect of the *Hebei Spirit incident* (KRW 321.6 billion) was not sufficient to pay all claims in full. The Government of the Republic of Korea, therefore, stepped in by standing last in the queue for its claims and by paying all other claims in full. It then recovered from the IOPC Fund 1992 the amounts so paid at 60% of the established losses.[279]

All legal proceedings related to the incident were finalised in September 2019. In July 2020, the IOPC Fund 1992 made a payment to the Skuld Club for an outstanding balance of KRW 3.4 billion (£2.3 million) relating to the overpayment of compensation by the Skuld Club. The Skuld Club was, by this, reimbursed in full.[280]

In February 2021, the Limitation Court of the other vessels involved in the collision, owned by Samsung Heavy Industries Co., Ltd (SHI), issued a decision on the distribution of the SHI limitation fund and granted the 1992 Fund KRW 3,271,486,069 (£2.2 million). That amount was paid to the 1992 Fund in June 2021

[275] IOPC Funds (2007b).

[276] Ibid.

[277] IOPC Funds (2020a).

[278] IOPC Funds (2020a).

[279] Ibid.

[280] Ibid.

and reimbursed to the contributors when the Hebei Spirit Major Claims Fund was closed in 2023. Since all the outstanding claims arising from the Hebei Spirit incident had been settled and all the legal actions had been finalised, this incident was declared closed at the October 2022 meeting of the IOPC Funds' governing bodies.[281]

Since all the outstanding claims arising from the Hebei Spirit incident had been settled and all the legal actions had been finalised, this incident was declared closed at the October 2022 meeting of the IOPC Funds' governing bodies.[282]

According to IOPC Funds,[283] the *Hebei Spirit incident* is the largest incident handled by the IOPC Funds to date in terms of both the amounts claimed and the wide range of claim types submitted, and its successful conclusion was greatly aided by the excellent cooperation of the Funds, the insurer, and the Korean government. The three emphasised what led to the many successes obtained in the *Hebei Spirit incident* at the June 2022 conference, which could identify any areas for improvement for future spills. The highlights include the following:

(i) The involvement of governments in the management of an incident and the establishment of regular channels of communication throughout the incident between the government and state institutions involved in the incident, such as the national courts, is extremely important.
(ii) Engagement with the public and potential claimants from the outset of the incident, and for some time afterwards, is essential in order to educate the claimants on the claims handling process and to manage expectations.
(iii) This incident also brought to the fore a number of issues that had started to emerge from previous incidents, and a series of policies were implemented by the Funds even before the end of the incident:
(iv) The publication of a guidance document for Member States which provides a set of measures that governments could undertake to facilitate the handling of claims as well as to alleviate economic hardship caused to the victims of future spills;
(v) The development of a process which allows for more flexibility in the way large numbers of claims by small-scale businesses can be assessed by the Funds' Secretariat in future incidents;
(vi) The publication of a guidance document for Member States on what to consider when imposing fisheries restrictions following an oil spill to minimise the economic impact of such restrictions;
(vii) The translation of claim forms and Claims Manual in the language of the country of the incident, even when that is not one of the Funds' official language.[284]

---

[281] IOPC Funds (2023), pp. 32–33.

[282] Ibid.

[283] Ibid.

[284] IOPC Funds (2023), pp. 32–33.

15.5 Claims for Compensation Under Two Compensation Regimes

At times, an incident may involve the application of the provisions of divergent provisions of liability conventions for compensation claims from pollution damage. For instance, an incident may involve the application of the 1992 CLC and the 1992 Fund Convention,[285] on one hand, and the International Convention on Civil Liability for Bunker Oil Pollution Damage 2001 (or 'Bunkers Convention 2001'),[286] on the other hand, for claims for compensation. One such situation arose in the Bow Jubail incident.

On 23 June 2018, the oil and chemical tanker m.t.v. *Bow Jubail* (23 196 GT), owned by National Chemical Carriers Ltd (NCC), a flag ship of Norway, collided with a jetty owned by LBC Tank Terminals in Rotterdam, Kingdom of the Netherlands, while on its way to its assigned berth for loading. The ship ruptured its hull, causing a spill of about 217 tons of heavy fuel oil (HFO) from the vessel into the harbour, subsequently spreading throughout the Rotterdam port area. The spilt HFO had not been carried as cargo but concerned the vessel's own bunkers. The HFO spill led to damage in many forms. Other vessels in port became heavily polluted, necessitating cleaning operations and leading to extra port costs and loss of time while on hire, loss of hire, etc. The water, port facilities and shores became severely contaminated. Wildlife, in particular hundreds of protected birds, fell victim to the oil pollution, among which more than 500 swans.[287]

The issue for determination was whether the 1992 CLC, the 1992 Fund Convention and the Supplementary Fund Protocol 2003 or the Bunkers Convention 2001 would apply to the incident.

At the time of the incident, the *Bow Jubail* was in ballast.[288] The oil spilt was bunker oil.[289] The question was whether there were any residues of previous cargoes on board. The burden of proof that there were no residues on board lies with the shipowner. If the shipowner cannot prove that the *Bow Jubail* had no residues of oil in bulk on board, the 1992 CLC would apply. In that case, and since the total pollution damage is likely to exceed the limit that would apply to the ship under the 1992 CLC, both the 1992 Fund Convention and the Supplementary Fund Protocol 2003 could apply to the incident.[290]

The ship was insured with Gard P&I (Bermuda) Ltd, which is a member of the International Group of P&I Associations. The limitation amount applicable to the *Bow Jubail* if the Civil Liability Convention 1992 were to apply would be SDR

[285] These apply to liability arising from spills caused by persistent oil.

[286] Which applies to liability for spills caused by bunker oil.

[287] Zelfde (2020).

[288] Ballast means heavy material, such as gravel, sand, or iron, placed in the bilge of a ship to ensure its stability.

[289] To which the Bunkers Convention 2001 may apply.

[290] IOPC Funds (2020b).

15,991,676, but the owner of the *Bow Jubail* is a party to the Small Tanker Oil Pollution Indemnification Agreement (STOPIA) 2006 (as amended in 2017), whereby the shipowner would indemnify, on a voluntary basis, the IOPC Fund 1992 up to SDR 20 million.[291]

However, if the shipowner is successful in proving that there were no such residues on board, the incident would fall under the Bunkers Convention 2001, and therefore, the limitation amount under the Convention on Limitation of Liability for Maritime Claims 1976, as modified by the 1996 Protocol (or 'LLMC 76/96'), would apply. The liability limit applicable to the *Bow Jubail* under the Bunkers Convention 2001 would be SDR 14,312,384.[292]

By March 2021, the shipowner had received some 150 claims. Although the claims had not yet been quantified, there is some indication that the claimed amount may be over EUR 80 million.[293]

The shipowner applied for leave to limit its liability before the Rotterdam District Court in accordance with the LLMC Convention 76/96. Under the LLMC Convention, 'the following claims whatever the basis of liability may be, shall be subject to limitation of liability':[294]

(a) claims in respect of loss of life or personal injury or loss of or damage to property (including damage to harbour works, basins and waterways and aids to navigation), occurring on board or in direct connexion with the operation of the ship or with salvage operations, and consequential loss resulting therefrom;
(b) claims in respect of loss resulting from delay in the carriage by sea of cargo, passengers or their luggage;
(c) claims in respect of other loss resulting from infringement of rights other than contractual rights, occurring in direct connexion with the operation of the ship or salvage operations.[295]

However, this rule is subject to some exceptions under Articles 3 and 4. Under Article 3 of the LLMC Convention 76/96, the rules shall not apply to:

(a) claims for salvage, including, if applicable, any claim for special compensation under Article 14 of the International Convention on Salvage 1989, as amended, or contribution in general average
(b) claims for oil pollution damage within the meaning of the International Convention on Civil Liability for Oil Pollution Damage, dated 29 November 1969 or of any amendment or Protocol thereto is in force.

---

[291] Ibid.

[292] IOPC Funds (2020b).

[293] Ibid.

[294] LLMC 79/96, art. 2(1).

[295] Ibid., art. 2(1)(a)–(c).

Under Article 4,[296] 'a person liable shall not be entitled to limit his liability if it is proved that the loss resulted from his personal act or omission, committed with the intent to cause such loss, or recklessly and with knowledge that such loss would probably result'.

The shipowner therefore argued that the incident was covered under Article 1(8) of the Bunkers Convention 2001, which defines 'incident' to mean 'any occurrence or series of occurrences having the same origin, which causes pollution damage or creates a grave and imminent threat of causing such damage'. Accordingly, the shipowner requested to establish a limitation fund in the form of a guarantee issued by the shipowner's insurer, Gard P&I (Bermuda) Ltd.[297]

In response to a court request, the shipowner submitted a technical report concluding that no oil cargoes and/or their residues, persistent or non-persistent, remained on board the vessel prior to and at the time of the incident. At a hearing that took place on 28 September 2018, the shipowner argued that although it may be assumed that on the voyage prior to the incident, from Houston to Rotterdam via Antwerp, the *Bow Jubail* carried 'oil', as referred to in the 1992 CLC, the tanks were clean of oil cargo residues at the time of the incident, and therefore, the Bunkers Convention 2001 should apply to the incident.[298]

According to the information provided by the shipowner, the cargo tanks had been washed, and the resulting slops (tank washings mixed with cargo residues) had been discharged into reception facilities in accordance with the International Convention for the Prevention of Pollution from Ships (MARPOL). It is reported that the tanks had been given a second wash (a so-called commercial wash), as required by contractual specifications, to avoid the contamination of products to be carried on the next voyage and that the washings from the second wash had been discharged at sea. Furthermore, a third wash had then been carried out as some white spots had been found on heating coils in two of the tanks, and the washings from this third wash were still on board at the time of the incident. Given the circumstances, the shipowner has maintained that no oil cargoes and/or residues, persistent or non-persistent, remained on board the vessel at the time of the incident.[299]

However, the majority of the claimants present at the hearing argued that the evidence that had been presented to the court did not prove that the vessel was free of oil cargo residues and that, as a result, it was not the Bunkers Convention 2001 but instead the 1992 CLC, with the additional 1992 Fund Convention and the Supplementary Fund Protocol 2003, that should be governing the incident and the compensation.[300] The shipowner, however, argued that the facts of the case should

[296] LLMC 76/96.

[297] IOPC Funds (2020b), p. 3.

[298] Ibid.

[299] Ibid.

[300] Ibid.

dictate which convention and which limits should apply, not simply the desire of the claimants to apply the convention that is more beneficial to them.[301]

The court issued its decision in November 2018, holding that the shipowner had not sufficiently substantiated that the tanks of the *Bow Jubail* did not contain residues of persistent oil carried in bulk at the time of the incident, as provided in Article I(1) of the 1992 CLC. Article I(1) of the 1992 CLC defines a 'ship' as:

> any sea-going vessel and seaborne craft of any type whatsoever constructed or adapted for the carriage of oil in bulk as cargo, provided that a ship capable of carrying oil and other cargoes shall be regarded as a ship only when it is actually carrying oil in bulk as cargo and during any voyage following such carriage **unless it is proved that it has no residues of such carriage of oil in bulk aboard**.[302]

The court decided to leave the incompleteness of the documents and the lack of clarity with respect to the presence of residues in the sense of the 1992 CLC for the account of the shipowner and decided not to grant the shipowner an opportunity to complete their standpoint that the tanks were clean of oil cargo residues. The court assumed that the *Bow Jubail* qualified as a ship, as defined in the 1992 CLC, and decided not to grant the shipowner leave to limit its liability under the Bunkers Convention 2001.[303]

The shipowner appealed to the Court of Appeal in The Hague. In its appeal, the shipowner argued the following:

(i) All cargo that may qualify as oil in the meaning of the 1992 CLC 1992 had been discharged in Antwerp and Rotterdam. The key issue in the appeal was the proviso of the definition of ship in the 1992 CLC: were there any residues of the carriage of oil in bulk on board at the time of the incident? The shipowner's position is that the vessel does not qualify as a 'ship' under the Civil Liability Convention 1992 since there were no residues of persistent oil in bulk aboard.

(ii) A vessel can be a CLC vessel at one stage and a non-CLC vessel at another stage during its lifespan. Cleaning the vessel after the discharge of a cargo of persistent oil in bulk to 'oil free' means that the vessel no longer qualifies as a ship as defined in Article I(1) of the 1992 CLC.

(iii) The vessel's tanks were cleaned in order to be 'oil free' in accordance with the regulations of the MARPOL, and thus under these regulations, the vessel was no longer carrying oil or oil mixture on board. In addition, the vessel also had its tanks cleaned with a so-called 'commercial wash' in order to make the vessel fit to carry new cargo. This means that the vessel no longer was a ship in the sense of the 1992 CLC and therefore, the Bunkers Convention 2001 applied. Being 'oil free' according to MARPOL, which is documented in the Oil Record Book, is also free of residues as defined in Article I(1) of the 1992 CLC.

---

[301] That is, the 1992 CLC (1992), with the additional 1992 Fund Convention and the Supplementary Fund Protocol 2003.

[302] IOPC Funds (2020b), p. 3. Emphasis added.

[303] IOPC Funds (2020b), p. 3.

(iv) A vessel actually carrying cargo other than persistent oil has never been regarded as a 'ship' under the Civil Liability Convention 1992 and consequently, a bunker spill from such a vessel has never yet been considered to be governed by that Convention. Only bunker spills from tankers in ballast before cleaning have been considered potentially subject to the 1992 CLC.[304]

The Court of Appeal in The Hague delivered its judgment on 27 October 2020, confirming the decision of the Rotterdam District Court and holding that the shipowner had not sufficiently substantiated that the tanks of the *Bow Jubail* did not contain residues of persistent oil carried in bulk at the time of the incident, as provided for in Article I(1) of the 1992 CLC. The judgment stated that, accordingly, in the Court of Appeal's view, the Bunkers Convention 2001 did not apply, and the limitation of the shipowner's liability was governed by the 1992 CLC, not the LLMC 76/96.[305]

The Court of Appeal also noted in its judgment that there was no generally accepted standard procedure to determine when a ship that could serve as both an oil tanker under the 1992 CLC and a chemical tanker under the Bunkers Convention 2001 ceased to be a ship under the 1992 CLC. In the court's view, consideration should be given by the parties to the 1992 Fund Convention in the creation of a standard procedure.[306]

The shipowner appealed the judgment (filed for cassation) to the Supreme Court of the Netherlands on various grounds, the primary one being the unreasonable burden of proof imposed on the shipowner.

The IOPC Fund 1992, in December 2020, applied to join the shipowner in the appeal proceedings in the Supreme Court in order to request clarification from the Court on the question of the legal test to decide whether there were residues on board the *Bow Jubail*. It also requested the court to rule, first, that it may intervene as a party or, alternatively, that it may be admitted as an interested party in the proceedings and, in the further alternative, that it may intervene as a party on the shipowner's behalf (joinder) in the appeal in cassation. Several claimants have submitted allegations to the Fund's application.[307]

It should be noted that the interest of the IOPC Fund 1992 is purely a financial interest. The reason for this is that if the courts in the Netherlands rule that the 1992 CLC and the 1992 Fund Convention apply, the IOPC Fund 1992 would be required to pay compensation. However, if the shipowner is successful in its appeal to the Supreme Court, the Bunkers Convention 2001 would apply, and the IOPC Fund 1992 would not be involved in this case.[308] On 31 March 2023, a judgement was issued by the Supreme Court of the Netherlands in relation to the Bow Jubail

[304] IOPC Funds (2020b), p. 3.

[305] IOPC Funds (2021).

[306] IOPC Funds (2020b), p. 5.

[307] IOPC Funds (2021), p. 19.

[308] IOPC Funds (2020b), p. 5. Note that claims under the Bow Jubail incident are ongoing.

incident, in which it was confirmed that the International Convention on Civil Liability for Bunker Oil Pollution Damage, 2001 (Bunkers Convention 2001) did not apply to this incident and that the Bow Jubail therefore qualified as a'ship' as defined under the 1992 CLC. It is anticipated that the total pollution damage will exceed the limit applicable to the ship under the 1992 CLC, in which case the 1992 Fund Convention will apply to this incident.[309] STOPIA 2006 will apply to this case, and the 1992 Fund will be indemnified by the shipowner up to a limit of SDR 20 million. The Director has stated that this case might have implications for the definition of a ship under the 1992 CLC or a ship under the Bunkers Convention 2001.[310] In May 2023, the 1992 Fund Executive Committee authorised the Director to make payments in respect of this incident. At the first hearing of the Rotterdam Limitation Court in September 2023, some of the claimants argued that the guarantee to be provided by the shipowner's P&I Club should also include legal interest accruing between the date of the incident and the date of the setting up the limitation fund. In October 2023, the Rotterdam District Court rejected the shipowner's application to limit its liability to the amount of the 1992 CLC.[311] In December 2023, the shipowner submitted a new application to the Rotterdam District Court to limit its liability under the 1992 CLC to an amount that included interest counting from the start of the day after the incident up to the start of the day following which the fund would be constituted.[312]

15.6 Claims for Compensation if the Ship from Which the Oil Is Released Cannot Be Identified (the Incident in Israel)

At times the ship from which the persistent oil is released may not be identified. The question that may arise is what becomes of the damage caused by the polluting incident and whether any claim may be established under the Funds (1992 Fund Convention and/or Supplementary Fund 2003). The incident in Israel in February 2021 tends to answer the above questions.

In February 2021, the Government of Israel contacted the 1992 Fund, requesting assistance with a mystery spill, which resulted in tar balls being washed up along the Israeli coastline. The Israeli Ministry of Environment organised a full response to the spill, and an investigation was undertaken to identify the source.[313]

Analyses of samples collected from the polluted site confirmed that they were of crude oil which had originated from a single source. As there were no offshore

[309] IOPC Funds (2024), pp 26–27.

[310] Ibid

[311] Ibid

[312] Ibid

[313] IOPC Funds (2023), pp. 26–27.

platforms or pipelines in the area, experts concluded that the only possible source was a tanker carrying crude oil. Following its investigation, the Government of Israel identified only one tanker that it considered likely to be responsible for the spill. However, there was insufficient proof to establish that it was that specific tanker that had caused the pollution.[314]

The 1992 Fund Convention applies to spills of persistent oil even if the ship from which the oil is released cannot be identified, provided it is shown that the oil originated from a ship as defined in the 1992 Civil Liability Convention (CLC). With this in mind, the Executive Committee decided, in July 2021, that the 1992 Civil Liability and Fund Conventions would apply to this incident and authorised the director to make compensation payments for admissible claims. As at 31 December 2022, 33 claims had been submitted for the amount of ILS[315] 16.1 million (£3.08 million). Of these, two claims had been approved at a total of ILS 105,000 (£24,000) and 22 claims had been rejected. Estimates of the cost of the response to the oil spill are in the region of ILS 55 million (£12.5 million), and further claims for the cost of the response are expected. Additional claims for economic losses are also expected.[316]

15.7 Effect of Non-compliance with the Compensation Regimes' Requirements and Procedures: The *JS Amazing* Incident

15.7.1 Introduction

The procedure for claims for compensation arising from pollution damage is strict. The claimant has to comply with the existing requirements under the compensation regime and follow the procedure for claims for compensation, non-compliance with which may cause such claims to fail. A case in point is the *JS Amazing incident*.

15.7.1.1 The Incident and Impact

On 5 June 2009, the Nigerian-registered tanker *JS Amazing* received orders to proceed to the refinery loading berth II, owned by the Nigerian National Petroleum

[314] Ibid, 26–27.

[315] Israeli Shekel (Israeli currency).

[316] IOPC Funds (2023), pp. 26–27.

Corporation (NNPC),[317] to load 5000 tonnes of low pour fuel oil (LPFO). The loading of the cargo commenced on 5 June 2009, but shortly after midnight, an oil leak was noted from the vessel's hull. In the early hours of 6 June, shortly after loading was suspended, the vessel listed approximately 45° to port. Oil continued to spill from the casualty and spilt approximately 1000 tonnes of LPFO into the Warri River, Delta State, Nigeria.[318]

The next day, a diver's inspection revealed that the port side of the vessel's hull had been punctured by two iron pipes from the wreck of a submerged mooring dolphin under the hull of the vessel. It is understood that the tanker stopped leaking oil on 11 June 2009 when the two iron pipes were cut from the mooring dolphin wreck and the casualty was stabilised.[319]

According to a Pipelines and Product Marketing Company (PPMC) internal memorandum, the quantity of oil on board the *JS Amazing* before the incident totalled 3338.6 tonnes. After the incident, 2303.8 tonnes were pumped from the vessel. Accordingly, it is believed that some 1000 tonnes of oil leaked into the Warri River in the days following the incident.[320]

15.7.1.2 Preliminary Investigations and Actions at Remediation

Within days of the spill, the National Oil Spill Detection and Response Agency (NOSDRA)[321] was notified that some 12 communities had been impacted by the spill. This was contrary to the provisions of the NOSDRA Act 2006, which requires an oil spiller to report an oil spill to the Agency (that is, NOSDRA),[322] in writing, by fax or by electronic mail, not later than 24 hours after the occurrence of the oil spill, the default of which shall attract a penalty in the sum of ₦2000,000 for each day of failure to report the occurrence.[323]

Shortly thereafter, NOSDRA conducted a joint visit with Pipelines and Products Marketing Company (PPMC) to assess the impact of the spill on the environment and upon the communities affected. NOSDRA and PPMC visited 232 communities between July and September 2009 and listed the inventory of each community.[324]

[317] As it then was, now the Nigerian National Petroleum Corporation Limited, pursuant to the Petroleum Act 2021, Act No. 26 2021, s. 53.

[318] IOPC Funds (2009).

[319] Ibid.

[320] IOPC Funds (2009).

[321] NOSDRA was established by the NOSDRA Act 2006, Act No. 15 2006. This Act was discussed in Sect. 14.7.3 of Chap. 14 of this book.

[322] NOSDRA Act 2006.

[323] Ibid., s. 6(2).

[324] IOPC Funds (2009).

15.7.1.3 Damage Assessment and Valuation

NOSDRA, by virtue of its mandate under the NOSDRA Act 2006, the provisions of sections 6(1)(c) that enjoins it to 'receive reports of oil spillages and co-ordinate oil spill response activities throughout Nigeria,'[325] and section 7(b) that empowers it to 'undertake surveillance, reporting, alerting and other response activities as they relate to oil spillages,'[326] conducted a post-spill socio-economic impact assessment study of the incident.

The fieldwork was carried out between 15 July and 15 August 2009 (approximately 6–10 weeks after the incident) and consisted of samples taken from soil, surface water and sediment. In addition, top and bottom soil samples, surface water and sediments were taken from fishponds at various locations.[327]

The study listed 100 communities affected by the LPFO spill from the *JS Amazing*. The study stated that all water samples contained heavy metals in traces but that these were far below the Department of Petroleum Resources' (DPR's) intervention levels and noted that many of the heavily impacted sites were within 7.5 km of the site of the spill.[328]

The study concluded that the soil samples collected showed no significant increase in heavy metal concentrations as they were all below established DPR intervention levels but that there were 'heavily impacted' bottom sediments found around the PPMC loading jetty where the spill occurred and at three other areas/fishponds where the petroleum hydrocarbon concentrations exceeded the DPR intervention levels. The study also listed two other categories, namely 'moderately impacted' and 'low impacted' areas, which appear to have been categorised on the basis of the sedimentation readings obtained by the field study.[329]

The report also stated that there was a presence of petroleum hydrocarbons at all the sites within the study area. It is suggested that this could indicate a pre-existing presence of hydrocarbons, prior to the spill from the JS Amazing.[330]

A few days after the incident, NOSDRA and PPMC visited the impacted sites. As an interim measure, NOSDRA requested PPMC to take immediate steps to clean up and remediate the impacted areas. By December 2009, PPMC had not complied with NOSDRA's request for clean-up, as a result of which NOSDRA fined PPMC the sum of ₦1 million.[331] In September 2010, PPMC had still not paid this, and in December 2009 (15 months after the spill), NOSDRA commenced legal proceedings against PPMC for failing to clean up and remediate the impacted areas and for failing

[325] NOSDRA Act 2006, s. 6(1)(c).

[326] Ibid., s. 7(b).

[327] IOPC Funds (2009).

[328] IOPC Funds (2009).

[329] Ibid.

[330] Ibid.

[331] NGN (Nigerian currency, the naira).

to pay the fine.[332] The proceedings concluded in May 2012 when the judge decided that:

(i) PPMC was in breach of legislation when it failed to clean up the area impacted by the JS Amazing spill;
(ii) PPMC should pay the fine of NGN 1 million to NOSDRA; and
(iii) PPMC should immediately clean up and remediate the impacted sites as directed.[333]

The fine of ₦1 million is, in the first place, contrary to the provisions of section 6(3) of the NOSDRA Act, which provides that

> failure to clean up the impacted site, to all practical extent including action plan for remediation **within two weeks of the occurrence of the spill**[334] in accordance with the polluter pays principle shall constitute an offence and on conviction the oil spiller shall be liable to a fine not exceeding ₦5,000,000 or to imprisonment for a term not exceeding 2 years or to both such fine and imprisonment.

However, as a result of pressure from a number of committee groups established following the incident, PPMC, in 2010, paid to a number of communities the total sum of ₦30 million. In July 2011, PPMC appointed a valuer to conduct an assessment of damages in conjunction with an NNPC committee established to handle the assessment and payment of compensation. The results of the assessment and the details of any additional compensation paid by PPMC were not known.[335]

In March 2012, the Nigerian Federal Ministry of Transport established a Marine Board of Inquiry to carry out an investigation into the cause of the spill. The conclusions of the Marine Board of Inquiry were as follows:

(a) The Marine Board of Inquiry noted that the vessel was improperly moored with insufficient mooring lines and that as the tide flowed, it pushed the stern of the vessel approximately ten metres away from the jetty. As a consequence, the bow was pushed into the jetty where the vessel struck the underwater wreck of the mooring dolphin. It also appears that as tidal conditions changed, no crew members tended the mooring lines.
(b) The Marine Board of Inquiry report highlighted that the vessel was undermanned because:

    (i) there was no officer of the watch;
    (ii) the chief engineer was not certified competent to be the chief engineer; and
    (iii) there was no second engineer, which was unusual for a vessel of that size.

(c) The Marine Board of Inquiry report also highlighted that:

---

[332] IOPC Funds (2009).
[333] Ibid.
[334] Emphasis added.
[335] IOPC Funds (2009), p. 3.

(i) the master of the JS Amazing was not certified to take command of a vessel of such gross tonnage and did not possess an advanced tanker certificate endorsement which was necessary for a vessel such as the JS Amazing;
(ii) the master had no knowledge of the certificates the vessel was required to carry, the requirement to comply with the provisions of the International Safety Management Code, the relevant nautical publications the vessel was required to carry and the emergency procedures to follow after an incident; and
(iii) the master had no knowledge of the provisions of the Civil Liability Convention 1992 or the need to forward the certificate of insurance (blue card) from the insurer to the Nigerian Maritime Administration and Safety Agency (NIMASA)[336] for issuance of the CLC certificate.

(d) In addition, the master testified at the Inquiry that he could not locate the majority of the relevant certificates which were required under Nigerian and international law.[337]

15.7.1.4 Claims for Compensation and Applicability of the Conventions

Nigeria is a party to both the Civil Liability Convention 1992 and the Fund Convention 1992. The limit of liability of the owner of the *JS Amazing* under the Civil Liability Convention 1992 is estimated to be 4.51 million SDR.[338]

Analysis of the claims submitted showed that five sets of legal proceedings were commenced as follows:

(i) NOSDRA against PPMC
(ii) Some communities against the shipowner
(iii) The shipowner for the recovery of damage to the ship
(iv) Two hundred forty-eight communities for compensation; and
(v) Claimants to arrest the JS Amazing[339]

Only the legal proceedings commenced by 248 communities for compensation (item iv) involved claims against the IOPC Fund 1992. This arose from the report of a firm of estate surveyors and valuers commissioned by NOSDRA in July 2009 to conduct a damage assessment report on behalf of 245 communities allegedly affected by the incident. The report concluded that the losses suffered and the damage to the property, interests and rights of the communities as a result of the spill amounted to ₦2241 million.[340]

[336] Another agency for the protection of the Nigerian marine environment established under the NIMASA Act 2007, Act No. 17 2007. The Act was discussed in Sect. 14.7.4 of Chap. 14 of this book.

[337] IOPC Funds (2009), p. 4.

[338] Ibid., 3.

[339] Ibid., 6.

[340] Ibid., 5.

However, in May 2012, a claim for ₦30.5 billion was filed against the shipowner, the joint liquidators of the South of England P&I Club and the IOPC Fund 1992 by representatives of 248 communities allegedly affected by the spill. The claim was filed by 14 representatives on behalf of the 248 unnamed communities. Subsequently, some of the representatives submitted information on behalf of 189 communities to the IOPC Fund 1992 Secretariat for consideration.[341]

The information submitted was not complete and, in some instances, consisted only of individual photographs of claimants or copies of voter's cards, very few of which provided details of the claimants' occupations. In many other cases, the information comprising the claim simply consisted of a spreadsheet detailing each claim, but without any supporting evidence. Furthermore, no official government data had been provided to support the numbers of claimants alleged to be within the communities or generally within the Warri River area.[342]

The matter was commenced at the Federal High Court, Asaba,[343] in line with Article IX of the Civil Liability Convention 1992. In July 2012, the IOPC Fund 1992 applied to strike itself out as a defendant but sought leave to be an intervenor on the basis that primary liability for the first tier of compensation rested with the shipowner, but recognising that the IOPC Fund 1992 might be called upon to pay compensation in excess of the shipowner's limit of liability.[344]

In June 2013, the shipowner applied to have the proceedings by the claimants dismissed, arguing the lack of jurisdiction of the court and improper service of legal proceedings upon the defendants. In March 2014, the court granted the IOPC Funds' application to strike itself out as a defendant and to be replaced as an intervenor and ordered the claimants to amend their writ to include PPMC as a third party to the proceedings.

In March 2013, upon the claimants' application, the court ordered the arrest and detention of the *JS Amazing*, pending the provision of a bank guarantee to cover the claim, or the deposit of the sum of ₦30.5 billion into court.[345] In April 2014, the claimants filed a Notice of Discontinuance against the joint liquidators of the Club.[346]

In February 2015, the claimants applied for a further adjournment to serve the amended writ upon the defendants, and the matter was listed for a hearing in March 2015. However, the application was subsequently adjourned on two further occasions until October 2015.[347]

In April 2016, a hearing took place at which the claimant was ordered to amend its writ and regularise its process, and the matter was adjourned until May 2016. In

[341] IOPC Funds (2009), p. 5.

[342] Ibid.

[343] Though the suit was later transferred to the Federal High Court in Warri in February 2013.

[344] IOPC Funds (2009).

[345] Ibid.

[346] Ibid.

[347] Ibid.

May 2016, the court observed that the first defendant had a pending application dated June 2013 challenging the jurisdiction of the court. The court decided that the application must take precedence over other applications and set a date for the hearing of the first defendant's application.[348]

In December 2016, the claimants filed a notice of discontinuance at the Federal High Court in Warri, and the court dismissed the case. No reason was provided to the IOPC Funds' lawyers for the discontinuance of the action, and in the spring of 2017, the IOPC Fund 1992 received a copy of the notice of discontinuance.[349]

15.7.1.5 Response of the IOPC Funds with Respect to the Claims

Unfortunately, the IOPC Funds 1992 rejected the claims submitted by the claimants in the *JS Amazing incident*. Many factors contributed to this.

The IOPC Funds 1992 was not informed of the incident until May 2011. The incident was not widely reported outside of Nigeria, and preliminary investigations by the IOPC Funds 1992 failed to reveal a great deal of information regarding the spill from the *JS Amazing* or the identity of the shipowner.[350]

Although 248 communities submitted claims for ₦30.5 billion in court against the IOPC Funds 1992, the shipowner and the joint liquidators of the South of England P&I Club, information was only submitted to the IOPC Funds Secretariat on behalf of 189 communities. These 189 communities represented some 21,000 individual claimants whose claims totalled ₦18,015 million. The losses claimed were mainly for damage to fishing gear, loss of earnings from fishing, damage to economic trees and crops, general damage to communities, displacement and ecological damage, and damage to ancestral shrines. In some claims, damages were only estimated for losses to fishing interests (gear damage, loss of earnings or, in some cases, both); in other claims, general losses to the whole community had been claimed. The claimed losses of ₦850,000 per claimant represented, on average, a loss of 14 years' earnings on an average wage of ₦60,000 per year, as quoted in the post-spill impact assessment (PSIA) report conducted by NOSDRA following the incident.[351]

The number of claimants (more than 21,000) was far in excess of the data from the PSIA report, which suggested a total of approximately 3200 fishermen across the whole of the 245 communities purportedly affected by the spill from the *JS Amazing*. The overall average difference between the numbers of items in the claims and those reported in the NOSDRA JIV reports was at a ratio of 65:1. The IOPC Funds' experts considered this to be implausible and suggested that this showed a high degree of overestimation in a number of claims.[352]

[348] IOPC Funds (2009).

[349] Ibid., 2.

[350] Ibid.

[351] Ibid.

[352] IOPC Funds (2009), p. 8.

The IOPC Funds' experts had also stated that the number of fishing gear items was not feasible for the area of the river under consideration. For example, with reference to gill nets at an assumed length of 65 metres, the total length of nets would be in the region of 3200 km. Furthermore, as the river level was higher than normal at the time of the incident due to flood waters, it was unlikely that many gill nets would have been in use at the time of the incident due to high current speeds. Thus, the evidence submitted in support of the claims revealed a high degree of overestimation.[353]

The report of the socio-economic impact assessment study of the incident (PSIA) conducted by NOSDRA, carried out between 15 July and 15 August 2009, stated that there was a presence of petroleum hydrocarbons at all sites within the study area, suggesting that this could indicate a pre-existing presence of hydrocarbons prior to the spill from the *JS Amazing*. As a matter of fact, there was a large amount of unregulated oil refining occurring in the Niger Delta area, and there was a high likelihood that there was a degree of contamination from these operations as well as previous oil spills in the area. This raised additional difficulties for the Funds' experts when attempting to differentiate between the contamination that resulted from the *JS Amazing incident* and earlier contamination from previous spills. Thus, taking into account the background levels of pre-existing contamination in the area, there were great difficulties in ascertaining the level of damages suffered as a result of the *JS Amazing incident*.[354]

In addition, the shipowner took no steps to fully pay the first tier of compensation in accordance with the provisions of Article III(1) of the 1992 CLC. There was no evidence that the *JS Amazing* was insured in accordance with the provisions of Article VII of the 1992 CLC at the time of the incident.

The issue of insurance was compounded by the shipowner Equatorial Energy Ltd. When contacted by the IOPC Funds' Nigerian lawyers, the shipowner, who accepted that an oil spill took place in Ijala in June 2009, stated that they had resolved the problem but refused to divulge any information regarding either the actual steps they had taken or the identity of their insurers. Subsequently, the IOPC Funds 1992 Secretariat was informed that the *JS Amazing* was insured with the South of England P&I Club. Among the exhibits tendered to the Marine Board of Inquiry[355] were copies of a:

(i) Certificate of Entry from the South of England P&I Club for the 2008 policy year, and
(ii) Certificate (blue card) furnished as evidence of insurance pursuant to Article VII of the 1969 CLC and Article VII of the 1992 CLC for the period from July 2010 to January 2011, issued by the South of England P&I Club to NIMASA[356]

[353] Ibid.

[354] Ibid.

[355] Set up in March 2012 by the Federal Ministry of Transport.

[356] IOPC Funds (2009).

Evidence of insurance with the South of England P&I Club has been provided for the 2008 and 2010 policy years; however, no evidence of insurance has been provided for the 2009 policy year when the incident occurred. Under cross-examination at the Marine Board of Inquiry, the representative of the shipowner stated that the shipowners had paid the insurance cover annually to a broker since 2005 and that the vessel was insured at the time of the incident.[357]

Notwithstanding that no policy documents have been provided for the 2009 policy year, the Certificate of Entry for the 2008 policy year stated thus:

> This Certificate of Entry is only to provide cover for liability in respect of Cargo on board the Entered Ship in accordance with Rule 29A of the South of England Rules of the Association, when such cargo is homogenous liquids in bulk of a non-persistent nature.[358]

Accordingly, the tanker was not insured in the 2008 policy year to carry persistent mineral oils, as defined in Article I of the 1992 CLC.[359]

Among the documents tendered to the Marine Board of Inquiry was a Certificate of Class for Hull and Machinery Equipment issued by the International Naval Surveys Bureau in 2010, which stated that the vessel was not classed to carry heavy-grade oil. Accordingly, in 2010, the vessel was not designed to carry heavy-grade oils of the type covered by Article I of the 1992 CLC.[360]

As if the above ugly situation was not enough, the South of England P&I Club, in 2011, was liquidated by the Supreme Court of Bermuda, and it handed down an order that joint provisional liquidators be appointed to oversee the winding up of the Club. The IOPC Funds Secretariat contacted the joint liquidators to alert them of the existence of the incident and to enquire whether they had documentation that might assist in identifying the insurer at the time of the incident. The joint liquidators stated that they had not been provided with much information regarding the incident but that they had several conversations with the placing broker, who stated that the vessel was not insured with the South of England P&I Club at the time of the incident.[361]

In sum, the IOPC Funds Secretariat did not see any documentation that indicated that the vessel was insured for the 2009 policy year. It also appeared that it was not classed to carry heavy-grade oil in 2008 or 2010.

Again, due to the fact that the incident was caused by the hull of the tanker hitting the wreck of a submerged mooring dolphin, the existence and location of which were known to the authorities, the element of negligence can be raised.[362]

Having examined all of the information provided, the IOPC Funds 1992 rejected the claims in January and February 2014 on the basis that no sufficient evidence had

[357] Ibid.

[358] Ibid, 7.

[359] Making both the 1992 CLC and the 1992 Fund Convention inapplicable under their compensation regime.

[360] IOPC Funds (2009).

[361] IOPC Funds (2009).

[362] Ibid.

been submitted in their support. The IOPC Funds 1992 also stated that this lack of specific information did not permit it to positively assess the claims submitted; as a consequence, the claims submitted were rejected. The *JS Amazing incident* was closed in October 2017.

15.8 Claims and Compensation for Pollution Damage Outside the International Oil Pollution Compensation Funds' Compensation Regime

A number of claims for environmental pollution damage had been successfully concluded without recourse to the International Oil Pollution Compensation Funds' compensation regime. In such incidents, the government of the impacted state resorted to the use of domestic legislation to pursue such claims. A few examples may suffice.

15.8.1 Exxon Valdez Disaster 1989

One of such claims under discussion is the *Exxon Valdez disaster*. Exxon Valdez, an American oil tanker belonging to Exxon Corporation, went aground on a reef in Prince William Sound, Alaska, at night on 24 March 24 1989. The tanker leaked a total of 260,000 barrels of oil in 2 days. The tanker's remaining 1 million barrels of oil were removed from the hold of the damaged vessel and were transferred to other tankers operated by the Exxon Corporation.[363]

The oil slick eventually coated about 1770 kilometres (km), about 1100 miles, of the Alaska shoreline, including numerous islands in the south. Tens, possibly hundreds, of thousands of shore-nesting birds were killed by the slick, as were several thousand sea mammals, especially sea otters. The biggest economic concern was for Alaska's important salmon and herring fisheries. These were seriously affected in 1989.[364]

Exxon's exposure to liability for the grounding of the *Exxon Valdez* stems from the Clean Water Act (CWA) 1977, the Trans-Alaska Pipeline Authorization Act (TAPAA) 1973, general maritime law and Alaska state law.[365]

Under the CWA 1977, an owner of a vessel is liable for both clean-up costs that may be incurred by the federal government and for damage to natural resources under the trusteeship of the federal and state governments. Absent a successful defence, Exxon has approximately a US$14.3 million liability cap. If 'willful

---

[363] Mambra (2020).

[364] Ibid.

[365] Skinner and Reilly (1989), p. 34.

negligence or willful misconduct' can be proven, however, Exxon's liability under the CWA 1977 is unlimited. Without proof of wilful negligence or misconduct, section 311(f)(l) of the CWA 1977 limits Exxon's liability to US$150 per gross ton of the vessel (US$14.3 million). Each natural resource damage claim is prepared by the trustees: the Department of the Interior, the National Oceanic and Atmospheric Administration (NOAA) of the Department of Commerce, the Department of Agriculture and the state of Alaska.[366]

Section 311(k) of the CWA 1977 authorises the creation of a revolving fund to finance, among other things, the removal of oil and hazardous substances spilt from vessels, and as of 14 April 1989, US$13 million had been spent or obligated from this fund in connection with the use of those resources. To that date, Exxon had reimbursed a total of nearly $10 million under section 311(k) of the CWA 1977 Fund.[367]

The Trans-Alaska Pipeline Liability Fund (or 'TAP Fund'), on the other hand, was available to pay damage claims resulting from spills of oil that had been transported through the Trans-Alaska Pipeline and loaded on a vessel to be carried to another US port. The TAP Fund was created as part of the statute in which Congress authorised the construction and operation of the Trans-Alaska Pipeline in 1974. Money charged on each barrel of pipeline oil loaded on a vessel financed the fund.[368]

The Trans-Alaska Pipeline Authorization Act (TAPAA) covers all damages, including either public or private clean-up costs sustained by any person or entity. It also covers claims by Canadian residents. If total claims exceed US$100 million, each claim for TAPAA Funds is reduced proportionately. In such a case, the TAP Fund considers claims after the response is completed, and total claims are known. The TAP Fund is not designed to support ongoing response actions.[369]

When spills of oil from tankers carrying North Slope crude oil occur, the owner and operator designate a single contact person who coordinates with the TAP Fund for the resolution of claims arising from the spill. For spills exceeding a projected US $14 million in damages, the TAP Fund advertises the availability of the Fund and the person to whom claims should be directed. Exxon has designated a contact person to coordinate actions with the TAP Fund and is processing claims. The TAP Fund published an advertisement specifying that claims should be presented to Exxon. The advertisement set forth addresses and telephone numbers for the presentation of claims.[370]

As a result of the inadequacies in both the CWA 1977 and the TAPAA 1973, in 1991, the state of Alaska and the federal government came to an agreement with

[366] Ibid.

[367] Ibid.

[368] Skinner and Reilly (1989), p. 34.

[369] Ibid.

[370] Ibid.

Exxon and the Alaska Pipeline Service Company regarding damages caused by the *Exxon Valdez* oil spill. The settlement covered civil and criminal claims as well as restitution. Fines and restitution payments totalling more than US$1 billion were agreed upon, to be paid over a 10-year period.[371]

Based on the experience in addressing liability and compensation from the Exxon disaster, the National Response Team[372] recommended, among other things, that

> Congress should enact comprehensive oil spill liability and compensation provisions along the lines of the legislation proposed by the Administration. It should include implementation of the 1984 Protocols to the International Convention on Civil Liability for Oil Pollution Damage, 1969 and (2) the International Convention on the Establishment of an International Fund for Compensation for Oil Pollution Damage, 1971. Enactment of such legislation would make available means in all cases to address adequately oil tanker spills that could extensively damage our coast.

This recommendation gave rise to the enactment of the Comprehensive Oil Pollution Liability and Compensation Act of 1989, which established a domestic liability and compensation system for oil pollution from vessels and facilities and would implement the 1984 Protocols to the Civil Liability Convention 1969/1992 and Fund Conventions 1971/1992 concerning seagoing tanker-source oil pollution. The goal of this Act is to (1) strengthen the four existing oil pollution liability and compensation regimes under the Federal Water Pollution Control Act, the Trans-Alaska Pipeline Authorization Act, the Deepwater Port Act and the Outer Continental Shelf Lands Act to create a unified program; (2) establish a system financed by vessel and facility owners and the oil industry to compensate the US government, the states and Indian tribes for the removal and restoration costs associated with oil spills; and (3) provide greater protection from foreign tanker oil spills by implementing existing protocols and conventions.[373]

15.8.2 Deepwater Horizon Accident 2010

In the British Petroleum (BP) Gulf of Mexico oil spill in 2010, the USA made use of both international conventions on damage to the marine environment and its national laws[374] on environmental damage. The conventions, alongside US local legislation, were also applied in subsequent claims from 2011.

In the aftermath of the BP Deep Horizon accident, an assessment group was set up, and compensation was paid out of the fund to victims of the environmental damage—US$10 billion to businesses, individuals and local governments impacted

---

371 International Oil Pollution Compensation Funds (*Fund Executive Committee*) (1991), FUND/EXC.30/2.

372 Skinner and Reilly (1989), p. 35.

373 US Department of Energy Office of Scientific and Technical Information (OSTI) (1989).

374 Such as the Clean Water Act and the Natural Resources Damage Assessment Act.

by the spill and US$7.8 billion settlement to cover the bulk of the outstanding private claims for economic loss, property damage and medical problems.[375]

A formal civil and criminal investigation into the spill was initiated in June 2010 by the US Department of Justice (DOJ). In August 2010, Louisiana district court judge Carl Barbier was appointed to oversee the consolidated proceedings relating to the spill, which had prompted numerous lawsuits and precipitated a morass of complex legal entanglements, private and public. The DOJ sued BP, Transocean and Anadarko, a minority owner of the well, in the New Orleans civil court in December 2010 for violating the Clean Water Act and Oil Pollution Act.[376]

In early March 2012, BP agreed to settle claims made by the plaintiffs' steering committee, the consolidated representative body for many of the individual victims of the spill, for at least $7.8 billion. The monies were to be drawn from the compensation fund mandated by the Obama administration.[377] In addition to covering economic losses sustained in the wake of the spill, the settlement mandated the payment of medical claims (which had previously been denied by the fund) and provided for 21 years of further medical monitoring and care, allowing for the delayed onset of symptoms and illnesses. BP remained liable for substantial additional claims by local and state entities as well as by the federal government. An effort by the company to appeal the agreement, which received final approval in December 2012, was rejected by the US Supreme Court in December 2014.[378]

In November 2012, BP reached an agreement with the DOJ to plead guilty to 14 criminal charges, among them 11 counts of felony manslaughter, and violations of the Clean Water and Migratory Bird Treaty Acts. The agreement carried penalties and fines amounting to more than US$4.5 billion, of which nearly US$1.26 billion would go to a discretionary fund overseen by the DOJ, some US$2.4 billion to the National Fish and Wildlife Foundation (NFWF) and US$350 million to the National Academy of Sciences (NAS). BP also agreed to pay more than half a billion dollars (US$500 million) to the Securities and Exchange Commission for misleading its shareholders about the magnitude of the oil spill. The deal was approved in January 2013.[379]

Later in November 2012, the US Environmental Protection Agency (EPA) suspended BP from entering into any new federal contracts. That suspension, initially thought to be temporary, was reinforced in January 2013. In February, the EPA also issued a separate suspension to the BP subsidiary that had operated the well, the Dallas-based BP Exploration & Production Inc., citing a violation of the Clean Water Act. In August 2013, the company filed a suit against the EPA in the

---

[375] Eboh (2013).

[376] Pallardy (2021).

[377] At the time of the incident, BP was mandated by the Obama administration to make, and it did make, a deposit of US$20 billion, which was set aside for claims, clean-up and the compensation of victims.

[378] Pallardy (2021).

[379] Ibid.

Texas federal court, asking that the ban be lifted. It was not lifted until March 2014; the company successfully bid on 24 federal contracts later that month.[380]

In January 2013, Transocean agreed to a US$1 billion civil penalty under the Clean Water Act. Approximately, US$800 million of that amount was earmarked for restoration projects in the gulf, and the remainder was paid to the federal government. The company also pled guilty to criminal violations of the Clean Water Act, resulting in a US$400 million criminal penalty. Of that money, US$300 million was evenly divided between restoration projects administered by the NFWF and an offshore oil safety research endowment administered by the NAS. The remainder funded a liability trust to be drawn upon in the event of later spills. In May 2015, Transocean resolved claims made by the plaintiffs' steering committee for some US $211.7 million.[381]

The civil trial of BP, Halliburton and Transocean began in late February 2013 in New Orleans. The federal government, as well as individual states and entities, was among the plaintiffs. The trial was intended to determine liability under the Clean Water Act and Natural Resource Damage Assessments under the Oil Pollution Act, addressing charges not covered by previous settlement agreements. The proceedings were arranged in three phases.[382]

The first, which ended in April, was to assess the degrees to which the three companies were culpable. Of particular import was the distinction between 'gross negligence' and 'negligence'; the former designation would result in fines approximately four times higher than those assessed for the latter. The ruling on the first phase, announced in September 2014, found BP to be 67% culpable for the spill and thus grossly negligent. Transocean was held 30% liable and Halliburton 3% liable; both companies were deemed negligent.[383]

The second phase of the trial, which began in late September, was intended to establish the volume of oil released by the spill and whether the preparedness and damage-control efforts of the involved parties were adequate. It ended in late October. The ruling on the second phase, announced in January 2015, set the legal amount of oil for which the involved parties would be liable at 3.19 million barrels. BP had claimed that approximately 2.45 million barrels had leaked, while the US government contended that 4.19 million barrels had spewed into the gulf. In July 2015, in the wake of a rejected Supreme Court appeal regarding the maximum fines for the disaster, a tentative settlement was reached between BP, the federal government and the five states affected by the spill, with BP estimating that it would cost the company US$18.7 billion.[384]

The third phase, in which damages would be assessed, was determined in February 2015. A finalised settlement of US$20.8 billion was announced in October

[380] Ibid.

[381] Pallardy (2021).

[382] Ibid.

[383] Ibid.

[384] Ibid.

2015, bringing the third phase to a close. It was the largest financial penalty ever levelled by the US government against a single company. The settlement was formally approved in April 2016.[385]

In April 2012, the first criminal charges to come out of the disaster were filed against a former senior drilling engineer for BP. Kurt Mix, who had worked for BP until January 2012, was charged in a federal court with obstructing justice for deleting hundreds of text messages concerning the flow rate of oil despite having received legal notification to preserve the correspondence. Some of the messages were forensically recovered; one contained a flow rate estimate three times higher than what BP had publicly attested to at the time. He was convicted in December 2013.[386]

In November 2012, two senior officers on the Deepwater Horizon oil rig, Robert Kaluza and Donald Vidrine, were charged with manslaughter. David Rainey, the former vice president for exploration in the Gulf of Mexico, was charged with obstructing Congress and making false statements to law enforcement concerning the rate at which oil was leaking from the rig. The Supreme Court refused to hear a 2015 appeal by the latter official to dismiss the obstruction charge.[387]

In July 2013, Halliburton agreed to pay a US$200,000 penalty after pleading guilty to criminal charges that its employees had destroyed evidence related to the spill. It settled claims with the plaintiffs' steering committee for some US$1.1 billion in September 2014, and in November 2015, Anadarko was judged liable for some US$159.5 million in civil penalties for its role in the disaster.[388]

15.9 Voluntary Agreements for Compensation for Ship-Source Oil Pollution Damage

15.9.1 Introduction

Taking into account the past disproportionate financial burden on the oil industry in respect of small ships and recognising that the Supplementary Fund 2003 increases the financial exposure of oil receivers in some states, the International Group of P&I Clubs, with the support of shipowners, muted on the idea of voluntary agreements to alleviate the financial burden on the oil industry in respect of small ships. Thus, at the IOPC Fund 1992 Assembly's March 2005 session, the International Group of P&I Clubs[389] offered to increase, on a voluntary basis, the limitation amount for small

[385] Pallardy (2021).

[386] Ibid.

[387] Ibid.

[388] Ibid.

[389] P&I club is protection and indemnity insurance, or as is more commonly known, 'P&I' is the policy shipowner's purchase to protect him against liability claims from crew, passengers and third

tankers under the 1992 CLC by means of an agreement to be known as the Small Tanker Oil Pollution Indemnification Agreement (STOPIA).[390]

Again, at the Assembly's October 2005 session, the International Group of P&I Clubs made another proposal, whereby it would extend STOPIA to all states parties to the 1992 CLC, as well as establish a second agreement to be known as the Tanker Oil Pollution Indemnification Agreement (TOPIA), through which the Clubs would indemnify the Supplementary Fund 2003 in respect of 50% of the amounts paid in compensation by that Fund.[391]

The STOPIA and TOPIA were set up in 2006 to indemnify the 1992 Fund Convention and Supplementary Fund Protocol 2003, respectively, for compensation paid above the shipowner's limit of liability under the 1992 CLC, up to certain amounts. Though the 1992 Fund Convention and Supplementary Fund Protocol 2003 are not parties to these agreements, they nevertheless confer on the Funds legally enforceable rights to indemnification from the shipowner in states for which the 1992 Fund Convention or Supplementary Fund Protocol 2003 is in force.[392]

15.9.2 Small Tanker Oil Pollution Indemnification Agreement (STOPIA)

The STOPIA provisions apply to pollution damage in any state for which the 1992 Fund Convention is in force. It applies to owners of relevant tankers of 29,548 gross tonnage (GT) or less insured by one of the members of the International Group of P&I Clubs and re-insured through the Group's pooling arrangement. By this arrangement, STOPIA agrees to indemnify the 1992 Fund for the difference between the vessel's limit of liability under the 1992 CLC and SDR 20 million. This has the effect of increasing the minimum limit of liability for smaller tankers to SDR 20 million as compared to the minimum limit of SDR 4,500,000 applicable under the 1992 CLC.[393]

STOPIA 2006 contains a mechanism whereby the agreement may be adjusted to compensate prospectively if after the first 10 years of its operation (and after every subsequent 5 years) the proportion of claims paid by either shipowners or oil receivers under all three conventions (1992 CLC, the 1992 Fund Convention and the Supplementary Fund Protocol 2003) since 20 February 2006 is greater than 55%. If that proportion is greater than 60%, the agreements must be adjusted. STOPIA 2006 applies to all states parties to the Fund Convention 1992.[394]

---

parties. Liability claims include those such as collision, property damage, pollution, environmental damage and the removal of wrecks.

[390] IOPC Funds (1985), p. 42.

[391] Ibid.

[392] IOPC Funds (2021).

[393] The Steamship Mutual Underwriting Association Limited (2006).

[394] The Steamship Mutual Underwriting Association Limited (2006).

In respect of ships covered by STOPIA 2006, the 1992 Fund continues to be liable to compensate claimants if and to the extent that the total amount of admissible claims exceeds the limitation amount applicable to the ship in question under the 1992 CLC. If the incident involves a ship to which STOPIA 2006 applies, the IOPC Fund 1992 is entitled to indemnification by the shipowner of the difference between the shipowner's liability under the 1992 CLC and 20 million SDR or the total amount of the established claims, whichever is the lesser.[395]

The maximum amount of compensation payable by the 1992 Fund Convention for any one incident is SDR 203 million (about £214.5 million or US$312.7 million) in respect of incidents occurring on or after 1 November 2003. For incidents that took place before that date, the maximum amount payable is SDR 135 million (about £142.6 million or US$208 million). For each Fund, these amounts include the sum actually paid by the shipowner under the respective 1992 CLC. The Supplementary Fund Protocol 2003 made available a total amount of SDR 750 million (£792.4 million or US$1 155 million) in compensation for pollution damage in states that have become members of that Fund, including the amounts payable under the 1992 CLC and 1992 Fund Convention 1992.[396]

The first incident involving a vessel entered in STOPIA 2006 was the *Solar 1* spill, which occurred in the Philippines in 2006. In that incident, compensation payments made by the IOPC Fund 1992 in excess of *Solar 1*'s limitation amount under the 1992 CLC were reimbursed to the IOPC Fund 1992 within 2 weeks of being invoiced by the Fund. The second incident involving a vessel entered in STOPIA 2006 is the *Haekup Pacific*, which occurred off the southern coast of Republic of Korea in 2010.[397]

On 20 April 2010, the asphalt carrier *Haekup Pacific* collided with the *Zheng Hang*, a 1983-built bulk carrier of 35,838 GT, south of Yeosu, Republic of Korea. At the time of the collision, the *Haekup Pacific* was laden with 1135 tonnes of asphalt cargo loaded at Ulsan for Jeju Island, with 23.37 tonnes of intermediate fuel oil (IFO) and 13 tonnes of marine diesel oil (MDO) as bunkers. As a result of the collision with the *Zheng Hang,* the *Haekup Pacific* was heavily damaged on its aft port quarter and sank in waters approximately 90 metres deep on 21 April 2010, approximately 10 nautical miles off the coast of Baekdo Island, Republic of Korea.[398]

In April 2016, the shipowner/UK P&I Club took the precaution of filing a claim against the IOPC Fund 1992 to protect their rights in respect of the costs already incurred and their potential claim for the costs of the removal operations, before the expiry of the 6-year anniversary of the date of the incident that caused the damage. The claim, originally filed against the IOPC Fund 1992 in April 2016, amounted to US$ 46.9 million, plus interest, based on a shipowner's limit of liability of SDR 4.51 million.

[395] IOPC Funds (1985), p. 42.

[396] Ibid., 13.

[397] IOPC Funds (2018d).

[398] IOPC Funds (2010).

Subsequently, the shipowner/UK P&I Club amended the claim, to reflect the fact that the vessel fell under the provisions of STOPIA 2006, under which the insurer voluntarily agreed to increase its liability to SDR 20 million (US$28.14 million). Accordingly, following the amendment, the claim against the IOPC Fund 1992 amounted to US$ 25.13 million, while the IOPC Fund 1992 received service of the claim for US$ 46.9 million through diplomatic channels; as at December 2020, it had not been served with the amended claim form for US$25.13 million in accordance with the STOPIA 2006 arrangement.[399] In summary, indemnification was paid to the 1992 Fund under STOPIA in respect of the Solar 1 incident (Philippines, 2006) and the Trident Star incident (Malaysia, 2014). The Agreement also applies in respect of the Haekup Pacific (Republic of Korea, 2010), Bow Jubail (the Netherlands, 2016), and Princess Empress (the Philippines, 2023). As of December 2023, there have been no incidents involving the Supplementary Fund; thus, TOPIA has not been applied.[400]

STOPIA also applied to the *Trident Star incident*. The Trident Star incident occurred on 24 August 2016 when the ship overflowed, spilling an unconfirmed quantity of oil into the Tanjung Bin oil terminal, Port of Tanjung Pelepas, Johor, Malaysia, The oil spill from this incident drifted across the Pulai River, reaching a container terminal on the river's eastern bank (PTP container terminal) and contaminating several cargo vessels and tugs. Some of the container terminal's berths were closed for approximately 3 weeks. Claims for pollution damage arising from the incident exceeded the 1992 CLC limit of US$6.5 million applicable to the Trident Star. However, the amounts paid by the 1992 Fund have been recovered from the shipowner's insurer, the Shipowners' Club, under the Small Tanker Oil Pollution Indemnification Agreement (STOPIA) 2006.[401]

The last claims that remained outstanding, by five claimants belonging to a group of shipping companies totalling US$6.6 million, were assessed by the Shipowners' Club and the 1992 Fund at US$3.3 million, and these claims were settled in early 2022. All corresponding legal actions were subsequently withdrawn, and as such, the 1992 Fund Executive Committee noted at its March 2022 session that the incident could now be considered closed. At the time of the session, the delegation of Malaysia expressed its appreciation for the handling of the case.[402]

In the end, all claims were settled for some US$10.9 million, i.e. below the STOPIA limit of SDR 20 million, and therefore, the final compensation costs incurred by the 1992 Fund were nil.[403] The insurer has, therefore, been reimbursing the IOPC Fund 1992 for compensation payments made in respect of that incident. Since there have been no incidents involving the Supplementary Fund Protocol 2003, TOPIA has not been applied.[404]

---

[399] Ibid.

[400] IOPC Funds (2024), pp. 12–13.

[401] IOPC Funds (2023).

[402] IOPC Funds (2022).

[403] IOPC Funds (2023), pp. 34–35.

[404] IOPC Funds (2021), p. 10.

Since all the outstanding claims arising from the Trident Star incident were settled and all the legal actions had been finalised, this incident was declared closed at the March 2022 meeting of the IOPC Funds' governing bodies.

15.9.3 Tanker Oil Pollution Indemnification Agreement (TOPIA)

The TOPIA is similar to STOPIA 2006 but has two substantial differences. Firstly, under TOPIA, tanker owners undertake to indemnify the Supplementary Fund Protocol 2003 in respect of 50% of the amount of any claim falling on the Supplementary Fund.[405]

Secondly, TOPIA applies to all relevant tankers regardless of size. TOPIA contains identical review and adjustment provisions to those set out in STOPIA 2006 so that any imbalance in the proportion of claims borne by shipowners or oil receivers may be adjusted prospectively by amending TOPIA or STOPIA or both.[406]

TOPIA 2006 applies to all tankers entered in a P&I club that is a member of the International Group and re-insured through the pooling arrangements of the Group. In respect of incidents covered by TOPIA 2006, the Supplementary Fund Protocol 2003 will continue to be liable to compensate claimants as provided in the Supplementary Fund Protocol. If the incident involves a ship to which TOPIA 2006 applies, the Supplementary Fund is entitled to indemnification from the shipowner of 50% of the compensation payment it had made to claimants.[407]

Following the acceptance of both agreements by the IOPC Fund Assembly in February 2006, STOPIA 2006 and TOPIA took effect retrospectively from 20 February 2006, and 3 month's notice of termination of the original STOPIA was served on the IOPC Fund 1992 on that date. STOPIA 2006 and TOPIA are intended to have the effect, over time, of ensuring that the total cost of oil pollution claims falling within the Civil Liability Convention 1992, the Fund Convention 1992 and the Supplementary Fund Protocol 2003 is shared equally between shipowners and the oil receivers who contribute to the IOPC Fund 1992.[408]

In 2016, the agreements (STOPIA 2006 and TOPIA) were reviewed and amended based on the 10 years' experience of claims since the entry into force of the agreements. The new versions, STOPIA 2006 (as amended 2017) and TOPIA 2006 (as amended 2017), became effective on 20 February 2017.[409]

[405] The Steamship Mutual Underwriting Association Limited (2006).

[406] Ibid.

[407] Ibid.

[408] IOPC Funds (1979).

[409] Ibid.

15.10 Summary

The devastating effects of some major tanker oil spills on the marine and coastal environment, as well as the resulting economic losses and significant clean-up costs, have led to much public attention on the issue of ship-source oil pollution from ships that carry oil as cargo. This has acted as a catalyst for the development of a considerable body of international legal instruments to prevent and respond to such incidents and to provide financial compensation in respect of losses resulting from an oil pollution incident involving tankers.

The international liability and compensation regime for oil pollution damage to the marine environment is currently based on the International Convention on Civil Liability for Oil Pollution Damage 1992 (or '1992 Civil Liability Convention'/'1992 CLC'), the International Convention on the Establishment of an International Fund for Compensation for Oil Pollution Damage 1992 (or '1992 Fund Convention') and the Protocol of 2003 to the 1992 Fund Convention (or 'Supplementary Fund Protocol 2003'). These three instruments all apply to pollution damage caused by spills of persistent oil from tankers in the territory (including the territorial sea) and the exclusive economic zone (EEZ) or an equivalent area of a state party to the respective treaty instrument and are managed under the International Oil Pollution Compensation (IOPC) Funds.

For liability to arise under the 1992 CLC, it must be established that there was pollution damage caused by the defendant. Loss or damage to the marine environment caused outside the ship by contamination, resulting from the escape or discharge of oil from the ship, wherever such escape or discharge may occur, provided that compensation for impairment of the environment other than loss of profit from such impairment shall be limited to costs of reasonable measures of reinstatement actually undertaken or to be undertaken and the costs of preventative measures and further loss or damage caused by preventative measures.

However, no claim for compensation for pollution damage under the 1992 CLC or otherwise may be made against (a) the servants or agents of the owner or the members of the crew; (b) the pilot or any other person who, without being a member of the crew, performs services for the ship; (c) any charterer (how so ever described, including a bareboat charterer), manager or operator of the ship; (d) any person performing salvage operations with the consent of the owner or on the instructions of a competent public authority; (e) any person taking preventive measures; and (f) all servants or agents of persons mentioned in sub-paragraphs (c), (d) and (e), unless the damage resulted from their personal act or omission and was committed with the intent to cause such damage or recklessly and with knowledge that such damage would probably result.

Claims are made on the International Oil Pollution Compensation (IOPC) Funds, which manage the three compensatory regimes. Although the IOPC Funds were established under the conventions and adopted under the auspices of the IMO, they are completely independent legal entities. Unlike IMO, the IOPC Funds are not agencies of the United Nations (UN) as they are not part of the UN system.

The IOPC Funds, in applying the provisions of the three compensation regimes on ship-source persistent oil pollution damage, determine who can make a claim, to whom a claim should be submitted, how a claim should be presented, what information a claim should contain, the period within which a claim should be made, claim assessment and payment, how long it will take to assess and pay claims, the target time frame for assessing claims and the cause of action available to a claimant if such a claimant does not agree with the Fund's decision.

The main categories of claims covered by the compensation regime are, namely, claims for the costs of clean-up and preventive measures (determining the scope of compensation, the presentation of claims and claims for value-added tax (VAT) by central governments); claims for property damage (determining the scope of compensation and the presentation of claims); claims for economic loss in the fishery, mariculture and fish-processing sectors (determining the scope of compensation and the presentation of claims); claims for economic loss in the tourism sector (determining the scope of compensation and the presentation of claims); claims for costs of measures to prevent pure economic loss (determining the scope of compensation and the presentation of claims); and claims for environmental damage and post-spill studies (determining the scope of compensation and the presentation of claims).

It should be noted that a claim qualifies for compensation only to the extent that the amount of the loss or damage is actually demonstrated. All elements of proof are considered, but sufficient evidence must be provided to give the shipowner, his insurer and the 1992 Fund the possibility of making their own judgment as to the amount of the expense, loss or damage actually suffered. The extent to which claimants are able to reduce their losses is taken into account. Over the years, a number of claims have been made on both the 1971 Fund and the 1992 Fund Convention since 1978. As at 31 December 2023, a total of £766 million had been paid in compensation (£331 million of which was in respect of the 1971 Fund).

The 1969 CLC, the 1992 CLC, the 1971 Fund Convention and its amendment, the 1992 Fund Convention, including the Supplementary Fund Protocol 2003, are limited in their scope as they cover only pollution damage arising from spills of persistent oil from tankers. They did not provide compensation for spills of bunker oil from ships other than those constructed or adapted for the carriage of oil as cargo and spills of other types of oil, such as non-persistent oil. The conventions do not also cover spills from other types of substances, such as chemicals, liquefied gases or noxious liquid substances. Since these types of substances also impact the marine environment in the event of spills, they were addressed, however, in two further international conventions: the International Convention on Civil Liability for Bunker Oil Pollution Damage 2001 (or 'Bunker Oil Convention'/'BOPC 2001'), the International Convention on Liability and Compensation for Damage in Connection with the Carriage of Hazardous and Noxious Substances by Sea (or 'HNS Convention') 1996 as amended by its 2010 Protocol 74 (or 'HNS Convention 2010')

The International Convention on Civil Liability for Bunker Oil Pollution Damage (or 'Bunker Oil Convention 2001') was developed as a preventive measure for the reduction and control of pollution to the marine environment as well as a mechanism providing compensation for damages caused by bunker pollution. Though largely based on the 1992 CLC, liability under the Bunker Oil Convention is strict as there is no requirement of fault for the liability to arise. The consequence of this is that when, for instance, a bulk carrier suffers fracture damage at one of its bunker tanks while berthed on the dock as a result of a collision with a harbour tug, entirely caused by the tug, the bulk carrier will be liable for bunker pollution under the Bunker Convention, and the claimants can (and will) go against the bulk carrier, despite the fact that the tug was 100% to blame.

The purpose of the HNS Convention is to provide adequate, prompt and effective compensation for the loss or damage to persons, property and the environment arising from the carriage of hazardous and noxious substances by sea. The Convention covers both pollution damage and damage caused by other risks, e.g. fire and explosion. Damage according to the HNS Convention 2010 means the loss of life or personal injury on board or outside a ship carrying hazardous and noxious substances caused by those substances; the loss of or damage to property outside a ship carrying hazardous and noxious substances caused by those substances; loss or damage by the contamination of the environment caused by hazardous and noxious substances, provided that compensation for the impairment of the environment other than the loss of profit from such impairment shall be limited to the costs of reasonable measures of reinstatement actually undertaken or to be undertaken; and the costs of preventive measures and further loss or damage caused by preventive measures.

Generally, claims for damages under the HNS Convention applies to claims, other than claims arising out of any contract for the carriage of goods and passengers, for damage arising from the carriage of hazardous and noxious substances by sea. Under the HNS Convention 2010, the shipowner will be strictly liability for any damage caused by hazardous and noxious substances (HNS). In this case, the shipowner will be liable even without fault on the part of the ship or its crew, although there are some exceptions under Article 7(3).

However, the 2010 HNS Convention does not cover damages caused during the transport of HNS to or from a ship. Cover starts from the time when the HNS enters the ship's equipment or passes its rail, on loading, and the cover ends when the HNS ceases to be present in any part of the ship's equipment or passes its rail on discharge. Also, the HNS Convention does not apply to oil pollution damage from tankers, as defined in the International Convention on Civil Liability for Oil Pollution Damage, nor to loss or damage as covered by the Bunkers Convention. Loss or damage caused by radioactive materials is also excluded.

Taking into account the past disproportionate financial burden on the oil industry in respect of small ships and recognising that the Supplementary Fund 2003 increases the financial exposure of oil receivers in some states, the International Group of P&I Clubs, with the support of shipowners, muted on the idea of voluntary agreements to alleviate the financial burden on the oil industry in respect of small ships. In March 2005, the IOPC Fund 1992 Assembly and the International Group of P&I Clubs offered to increase, on a voluntary basis, the limitation amount for small tankers under the 1992 CLC by means of an agreement to be known as the Small Tanker Oil Pollution Indemnification Agreement (STOPIA). Again, at the

Assembly's October 2005 session, the International Group of P&I Clubs made another proposal, whereby it would extend STOPIA to all states parties to the 1992 CLC as well as establish a second agreement to be known as the Tanker Oil Pollution Indemnification Agreement (TOPIA), through which the Clubs would indemnify the Supplementary Fund 2003 in respect of 50% of the amounts paid in compensation by that Fund.

From the foregoing, it can be said that the liability and compensation regime on marine pollution involves liability under ship-source persistent oil pollution covered under the 1992 CLC, the 1971 Fund Convention, the 1992 Fund Convention and the Supplementary Protocol of 2003. In the case of liability for damages under ship-source non-persistent oil pollution are the Bunker Convention 2001 and the HNS 2010. In addition to these are the voluntary agreements under STOPIA and TOPIA. These regimes have helped control pollution of the marine environment.

References

Bachxevanis K, Smith R (2009) The Bunker Pollution Convention 2001, 2 https://www.reedsmith.com/-/media/files/perspectives/2009/09/the-bunker-pollution-convention-2001/files/the-bunker-pollution-convention-2001/fileattachment/the-bunker-pollution-convention-2001%2D%2Dk-bachxevani.pdf, 12 May 2023

Birnie P et al (2009) International law and the environment, 3rd edn. Oxford University, Oxford

Centre for International Governance Innovation (2018) "Legal Liability for Environmental Harm: Synthesis and Overview: Legal Working Group on Liability," Liability Issues for Deep Seabed Mining Series | Paper No. 1 — July 2018, www.cigionline.org. Accessed 12 May 2023

Eboh M (2013) US proposes $16bn settlement with BP over Gulf spill. http://www.vanguardngr.com/2013/02/us-proposes-16bn-settlemen-with-bp-over-gulf-spill/#sthash.nZGVBs1L,dpuf. Accessed 24 May 2023

Hazardous and Noxious Substances (HNS) (2010) An Overview of the International Convention on Liability and Compensation for Damage in connection with the Carriage of Hazardous and Noxious Substances By Sea, 2010 (The HNS Convention 2010). https://www.hnsconvention.org/wp-content/uploads/2019/04/HNS-Convention-Overview_e.pdf. Accessed 16 May 2023

HNS (2010) International Convention on Liability and Compensation for Damage in Connection with the Carriage of Hazardous and Noxious Substances by Sea 2010 (HNS Convention 2010), https://www.hnsconvention.org/wp-content/uploads/2019/05/2010-HNS-Convention-English.pdf. Accessed 16 May 2023 https://iopcfunds.org/wp-content/uploads/2018/06/Text-of-Conventions_e.pdf. Accessed 25 June 2023

ILC (2006) Draft principles on the allocation of loss in the case of transboundary harm arising out of hazardous activities, with commentaries, 58th Session, UN Doc A/61/10 (2006), ILC, Draft Principles on Allocation of Loss, principles 3 and 4 at para 7, http://legal.un.org/ilc/texts/instruments/english/commentaries/9_11_2011.pdf. Accessed 23 May 2023

IMO (2022) International Convention on the Establishment of an International Fund for Compensation for Oil Pollution Damage (FUND), https://www.imo.org/en/About/Conventions/Pages/International-Convention-on-the-Establishment-of-an-International-Fund-for-Compensation-for-Oil-Pollution-Damage-(FUND).aspx. Accessed 18 June 2023

IMO (2023) Report to the Maritime Safety Committee, Sub-Committee on Ship Design and Construction 9th Session (SDC 9/16) of 13 March 2023, https://iadc.org/wp-content/uploads/2023/03/SDC-9-16-Report-To-The-Maritime-Safety-Committee-Secretariat.pdf. Accessed 19 June 2023

International Law Commission (2001) Draft articles on Responsibility of States for Internationally Wrongful Acts," 53rd Session, UN Doc A/56/10 (2001), http://legal.un.org/ilc/texts/instruments/english/commentaries/9_11_2011.pdf. Accessed 23 May 2023

International Maritime Organization (2008) International Convention on Civil Liability for Bunker Oil Pollution Damage (BUNKER). https://www.imo.org/en/About/Conventions/Pages/International-Convention-on-Civil-Liability-for-Bunker-Oil-Pollution-Damage-(BUNKER).aspx. Accessed 12 May 2023 https://iadc.org/wp-content/uploads/2023/03/SDC-9-16-Report-To-The-Maritime-Safety-Committee-Secretariat.pdf. Accessed 25 June 2023

International Oil Pollution Compensation Funds *(Fund Executive Committee)* (1980) FUND/A/ES 1/13, 10 October 1980, htpp://www.iopcfund.org/99AR_English.htm. Accessed 19 June 2023

International Oil Pollution Compensation Funds (IOPC) (1979) Incidents Map, https://iopcfunds.org/incidents/incident-map/#3150-27-February-1979. Accessed 19 June 2023

International Oil Pollution Compensation Funds *Fund Executive Committee* (1986) FUND/EXC.16/8, 22 October 1986, http://www.iopcfund.org/99AR_English.htm. Accessed 19 July 2023

International Oil Pollution Compensation Funds *Fund Executive Committee* (1991) *Summary of the Court of Appeal,* FUND/EXC.30/2 16 December 1991, http://www.iopcfund.org/99AR_English.htm. Accessed 25 July 2023

International Petroleum Industry Environmental Conservation Association (IPIECA) and The International Tanker Owners Pollution Federation Limited (ITOPF) (2007) Oil Spill Compensation: A Guide to the International Conventions on Liability and Compensation for Oil Pollution Damage 2007, https://www.itopf.org/fileadmin/data/Documents/Company_Lit/IPEICAITOPFCompensation.pdf. Accessed 18 June 2023

IOPC Funds (1985) Incidents Map, https://iopcfunds.org/incidents/incident-map/#3172-21-March-1985. Accessed 19 July 2023

IOPC Funds (1992a) The 1992 Fund Convention, https://iopcfunds.org/about-us/legal-framework/1992-fund-convention-supplementary-fund-protocol/. Accessed 18 May 2023

IOPC Funds (1992b) Incident Map, https://iopcfunds.org/incidents/incident-map/#3208-03-December-1992. Accessed 29 May 2023

IOPC Funds (1999) Erika Incident, https://iopcfunds.org/incidents/incident-map/#3253-12-December-1999. Accessed 29 May 2023

IOPC Funds (2002) Incident Report: Prestige, https://iopcfunds.org/incidents/incident-map/#1916-13-November-2002. Accessed 30 May 2023

IOPC Funds (2007a) Volgoneft 139 Incident, 1, https://iopcfunds.org/incidents/incident-map/#6675-11-November-2007, updated 21 December 2018. Accessed 31 May 2023

IOPC Funds (2007b) Hebei Spirit Incident, https://iopcfunds.org/incidents/incident-map/#3276-07-December-2007, updated 31 December 2020. Accessed 31 May 2023

IOPC Funds (2009) JS Amazing Incident, https://iopcfunds.org/incidents/incident-map/#3279-06-June-2009. Accessed 3 June 2023

IOPC Funds (2010) Incident Map: *Haekup Pacific Incident,* https://iopcfunds.org/incidents/incident-map/#1915-20-April-2010, updated 30 December 2020. Accessed 2 May 2023

IOPC Funds (2018a) Liability and Compensation for Oil Pollution Damage Texts of the 1992 Civil Liability Convention, the 1992 Fund Convention and the Supplementary Fund Protocol, IOPC, 2018, https://iopcfunds.org/wp-content/uploads/2018/12/WEB-IOPC-Text-of-Conventions-ENGLISH.pdf. Accessed 18 May 2023

IOPC Funds (2018b) Internal Regulations of the International Oil Pollution Compensation Fund Established Under the 1992 Fund Convention Assembly at its 22nd extraordinary session, held from 30 April to 2 May 2018, https://www.iopcfunds.org/uploads/tx_iopcrulesandregs/InternalRegulations_1992Fund_APR18_e_01.pdf. Accessed 25 July 2023

IOPC Funds (2018c) Incident Report 2013, https://iopcfunds.org/wp-content/uploads/2018/12/incidents2013_e.pdf. Accessed 29 May 2023

IOPC Funds (2018d) Small Tanker Oil Pollution Indemnification Agreement (STOPIA) 2006 (as amended 2017) https://iopcfunds.org/wp-content/uploads/2018/03/STOPIA_2006_and_TOPIA_2006__as_amended_2017__e.pdf. Accessed 10 May 2023

IOPC Funds (2019) Claims Manual, 2019 Edition, IOPC Funds, 2019, 13, https://iopcfunds.org/wp-content/uploads/2018/12/2019-Claims-Manual_e-1.pdf. Accessed 18 June 2023

IOPC Funds (2020a) Information as presented at the December 2020 session of the 1992 Fund Executive Committee, https://iopcfunds.org/wp-content/uploads/2018/12/Judgments_relating_to_the_Hebei_Spirit_incident_01.pdf. Accessed 31 May 2023

IOPC Funds (2020b) Bow Jubail, 2, https://iopcfunds.org/wp-content/uploads/2019/04/archived-case-study-2020-bow-jubail__e.pdf, updated 31 December 2020. Accessed 1 June 2023

IOPC Funds (2021) Annual Report 2020, updated 1 April 2021, https://iopcfunds.org/wp-content/uploads/2021/03/Annual-Report-2020_e.pdf. Accessed 1 June 2023

IOPC Funds (2022) Settlement of final claims in the *Trident Star* incident, 27 April 2022 https://iopcfunds.org/news/settlement-of-final-claims-in-the-trident-star-incident/. Accessed 18 Aug 2023

IOPC Funds (2023) Annual Report 2022, https://iopcfunds.org/wp-content/uploads/2023/05/Annual-Report-2022_e-1.pdf. Accessed 10 Aug 2023

IOPC Funds (2024) Annual Report 2023, 26–27, https://iopcfunds.org/wp-content/uploads/2024/04/Annual-Report-2023_e.pdf. Accessed 21 November 2024

Mambra S (2020) The Complete Story of the Exxon Valdez Oil Spill. Last Updated on 19 December 2020, https://www.marineinsight.com/maritime-history/the-complete-story-of-the-exxon-valdez-oil-spill/. Accessed 18 May 2023

Pallardy R (2021) Deepwater Horizon oil spill. Updated 3 September 2021 https://www.britannica.com/event/Deepwater-Horizon-oil-spill/legalaction . Accessed 3 Aug 2023

Skinner SK, Reilly WK (1989) The EXXON VALDEZ Oil Spill: A Report to the President, The National Response Team, May 1989, 34, https://nrt.org/sites/2/files/Valdez%20spill%20RTP.pdf. Accessed 21 May 2023

Summary of Judgement of the Court of Appeal (1991) Doc. FUND/EXC.30/2, 29 November 1991, para 4.15, http://www.iopcfund.org/99AR_English.htm. Accessed 21 May October 2021

The Steamship Mutual Underwriting Association Limited (2006) Circular April 2006, https://www.steamshipmutual.com/Circulars-London/L.51.pdf. Accessed 10 May 2023

U S Department of Energy Office of Scientific and Technical Information (OSTI) (1989) H. R. 2325: Comprehensive Oil Pollution Liability and Compensation Act of 1989. Introduced in the House of Representatives, One Hundred First Congress, First Session, May 11, 1989 https://www.osti.gov/biblio/5237572-comprehensive-oil-pollution-liability-compensation-act-introduced-house-representatives-one-hundred-first-congress-first-session-may. Accessed 28 May 2023

Zelfde R (2020) The BOW JUBAIL – a case of providing too limited proof for the desired limited liability. https://caland.nl/wp-content/uploads/2020/11/The-BOW-JUBAIL-%E2%80%93-a-case-of-providing-too-limited-proof-for-the-desired-limited-liability.pdf. Accessed 1 June 2023

Part V
Regional Perspectives in Environmental Protection and Management

Chapter 16
Environmental Pollution Abatement and Control in Nigeria

Abstract From creation, man has enjoyed the environment and its resources in its unadulterated and unaltered state. Since the environment was just a creation of nature in the beginning and before creation, it was not legally protected. At creation, man was given dominion over the earth and its resources, and because man had not developed complicated environmental goals, the environment was never the focus of regulation, not even in the early post-creation era. As time went on, with the development of science and technology and the quest for development, man laid an unrelenting assault on the environment, necessitating the need for environmental protection laws. In this regard, the Nigerian government has, over the years, enacted several environmental laws in an effort to manage the environment for human survival as well as to conserve it for the use of future generations. This chapter discusses Nigeria's legislation on the environment, broadly categorised into framework legislation, sectoral legislation and incidental legislation.

16.1 Background

Nigeria is located in western Africa on the Gulf of Guinea and lies between latitudes 4° N and 14° N and longitudes 2^{O} E and 15° E. It has a total area of 923,768 km^2, out of which the land area is 910,769 km^2 and 13,000 km^2 is made up of water.[1] Its borders span 4047 km, and it shares borders with Benin (773 km), Niger (1497 km), Chad (87 km) and Cameroon 1690 km. Its coastline is at least 853 km^2.[2]

The terrain is made up of southern lowlands that merged into central hills and plateaux as well as mountains in the south-east and part of the north-east with plains in most northern parts. The highest point in Nigeria is the Chappal Waddi at 2419 m, which is located in Taraba State, near the border with Cameroon, on the edge of the

[1] Central Intelligent Agency (CIA) (2014).

[2] Ibid.

E. Onyeabor, *Environmental Law*, https://doi.org/10.1007/978-3-031-68956-7_16

Gashaka Gumti Forest Reserve and the Gashaka-Gumti National Park on the Mambilla Plateau.[3]

The main rivers are the Niger and the Benue, which converge and empty into the Niger Delta. This is one of the world's largest river deltas and is the location of a large area of Central African mangroves. The climate varies from equatorial climate in the south to tropical climate in the centre to arid climate in the north.[4]

The population density in Nigeria is 246 per sq km (636 people per sq ml), and the current population is 224,615,461 as of 26 August 2023, Saturday, based on the Worldometer elaboration of the latest United Nations data.[5] The population is estimated at 223,804,632 by mid-2023. With this population, Nigeria is ranked number 6 in the list of countries by population, which is equivalent to 2.78% of the total world population.[6]

The major environmental issues in Nigeria include soil degradation, rapid deforestation, urban air and water pollution, desertification, loss of arable land, rapid urbanisation, oil pollution and waste management, among others.[7]

16.2 Nigeria's Legislative Efforts in the Protection of the Environment

16.2.1 Introduction

In the beginning, there was the world, and in the world, there was man, and man enjoyed the world's environment, unabused and in its pristine form. The environment was a solitary property of nature during its genesis and pre-creation voidance and, hence, was not legally protected. Even in the immediate post-creation epoch, the environment was never the subject of legislation because man had been given sovereignty over the earth and its resources[8] and had no greed or sophisticated environmental ambitions.

Again, the universe, of which the environment was a geographical portion, was incapable of human possession at the time. While the precise moment when the environment became a topic of legal protection is unknown, it is certain that the beginning may be attributed to some authority and confidence in the advancement of global science and technology. As a result, rival world economies emerged in terms

[3] Free World Maps (2021).

[4] Ibid.

[5] United Nations, Department of Economic and Social Affairs, Population Division (2023).

[6] Ibid.

[7] Central Intelligent Agency (CIA) (2014).

[8] See Genesis 1,[28] where God said, 'Be fruitful and multiply, and fill the earth and subdue it, and have dominion over the fish of the sea and over the birds of the air and over every living thing that moves upon the earth'.

of states' deliberate sovereign, economic, political and social goals. Competition in the pursuit and exploitation of natural resources for economic wealth and political dominance has a negative impact on both natural and human environments. As a result, legislation was required to prevent environmental abuse in order to safeguard human life.

In this regard, governments must deal with the reduction of environmental pollution in accordance with their national laws and, occasionally, with international environmental treaties. The realisation that the environment is the most potent driver of national and global development and must be safeguarded against harm, destruction and annihilation and that there is a need to maintain a decent, healthy, disease-free and aesthetically pleasing environment led to the need for these laws. To achieve this goal of efficient environmental preservation and management, however, environmental regulation became necessary. As a result, several environmental pollution abatement laws have been passed to manage the environment for human survival as well as to safeguard it. These environmental pollution abatement laws primarily address water, oil and gas pollution; air quality and atmospheric protection; toxic and hazardous waste issues; noise regulation; and municipal waste disposal, among other things.

Over the years, the Nigerian government has passed pieces of environmental laws in order to not only protect the environment but also to manage it for human survival. This chapter discussed these environmental laws.[9] Nigerian environmental laws can broadly be categorised into framework legislation, sectoral legislation and incidental legislation.[10]

16.2.2 Framework Legislation

16.2.2.1 Introduction

Framework legislation includes those laws that were promulgated or enacted with overall environmental protection in mind. They target the protection of every aspect of the environment in Nigeria. They are comprehensive in nature in that their provisions target the protection of every segment of the environmental media.

Prior to 1988 Nigeria, no efforts were made at having laws that addressed the protection of the Nigerian environment in its entirety. There were therefore no adequate legal responses to the emerging grave problems of environmental abuse,

[9]The environmental laws discussed in this chapter are those laws promulgated during the military regime and retained as extant laws in Nigeria and those laws enacted by the National Assembly since the advent of the civil dispensation. However, the whole spectrum of legal framework for environmental protection in Nigeria includes the rules of common law tort and doctrines of equity (discussed in Sect. 2.2 of Chap. 2 of this book) and the various international environmental agreements to which Nigeria is a signatory.

[10]Using the United Nations Environment Programme (UNEP) (2007).

not only from the growing oil and gas sector but also from all segments of the Nigerian economy. Therefore, the environmental problems associated with economic and developmental activities were never given adequate national recognition. However, Nigerians woke up in the morning of June 1988 and found that an Italian, with some Nigerian collaborators, had dumped tonnes of toxic waste in the 'sleeping' port of Koko in the then Bendel State (now in Delta State). Efforts to prosecute the 'dead merchants' were abortive as there were no laws banning the importation, dumping or depositing of harmful wastes on the Nigerian environment.[11]

To forestall a reoccurrence of this ugly incident, it became necessary that there must be a change in our environmental protection attitude, especially environmental pollution abatement laws. In 1988, two pieces of legislation were promulgated in quick succession:

(i) Harmful Wastes (Special Criminal Provisions, etc.) Act (HWSCP Act) 1988 and
(ii) Federal Environmental Protection Agency (Establishment) Act 1988[12]

Subsequently, other environmental legislation followed:

(i) Environmental Impact Assessment Act 1992
(ii) Nigerian Urban and Regional Planning Act 1992
(iii) National Environmental Standards and Regulations Enforcement Agency (Establishment) Act 2007 and the Regulations made thereto
(iv) Climate Change Act 2021 (discussed in Chap. 7)

16.2.2.2 Harmful Waste (Special Criminal Provisions, Etc.) Act (HWSCP Act) 1988

The HWSCP Act was promulgated as Degree No. 42 of 1988.[13] It describes harmful waste under section 15 to include semi-solid, liquid or solid substances as well as 'any injurious, poisonous toxic or noxious substance ... which can subject any person to the risk of death, fatal injury or incurable impairment of physical and mental health...'.

The Act prohibits the carrying, depositing and dumping of harmful waste on any land, territorial waters and matters related thereto and therefore prohibits all activities relating to the purchase, sale, importation, transit, transportation, deposit and storage

[11] It was only through diplomatic means that the deadly cargo was eventually evacuated from Nigerian soil, but not after it had taken its first victim, Nana Sunday, the landlord where the cargo was dumped.

[12] Cap F10 LFN 2004. It should be noted that the Federal Environmental Protection Agency (Establishment) Act 1988 (FEPA Act) has been repealed by the National Environmental Standards and Regulations Enforcement Agency (Establishment) (NESREA) Act 2007, s. 36. This being the case, the FEPA Act not being an extant law in Nigeria, was not discussed in this book.

[13] Currently retained as Cap H1 LFN 2004.

of harmful wastes.[14] It is therefore an offence for any person who, without lawful authority, carries, deposits, dumps or causes to be carried, deposited or dumped or is in possession for the purpose of carrying, depositing or dumping any harmful waste on any land or in any territorial waters or contiguous zone or the exclusive economic zone of Nigeria or its inland waterways.[15] It is also an offence 'to transport, or cause to be transported or is in possession of transporting; imports, or causes to be imported or negotiates for the purposes of importing; or sell, offer for sale, buy or otherwise deal in any harmful waste'.[16]

Under the HWSCP Act, 'a person shall be deemed to deposit or dump harmful waste if he deposits or dumps the harmful waste ... in such circumstances, or for such period that he may be deemed to have abandoned it where it is deposited or dumped; or to have brought it to the place where it is so deposited or dumped for the purpose of its being disposed of or abandoned whether by him or any other person'.[17] An offence is committed under the Act if the person actually does the act or makes the omission that constitutes the crime or does or omits to do any act for the purpose of enabling or aiding another person to commit the crime or aids another person in committing the crime or counsels or procures any person to commit the crime, in which case he may himself be charged with committing the crime or with counselling or procuring the commission of the crime.[18]

Penalty on conviction includes life imprisonment and forfeiture of the vessel and the land on which harmful wastes were dumped.[19] Where the crime is committed by a body corporate and it is proved that it was committed with the consent or connivance of or is attributable to any neglect on the part of a director, manager, secretary or similar officer of the body corporate or any other person purporting to act in the capacity of a director, manager, secretary or similar officer, he, as well as the body corporate, shall be guilty of the crime and shall be liable to be proceeded against and punished accordingly.[20]

In addition to criminal liability, the HWSCP Act has provisions for civil liability.[21] Thus, where any damage arises as a result of the depositing or dumping of wastes, any person who deposited, dumped or imported the harmful waste shall be liable for damages.[22] Damage in this respect includes the death of or injury to any person (including any diseases or any impairment of the physical or mental

---

[14] HWSCP Act (1988), s. 1(1).

[15] Ibid., s. 1(2)(a).

[16] Ibid., s. 1(2)(b)–(d).

[17] HWSCP Act (1988), s. 1(3).

[18] Ibid, s. 2. See also the provisions of ss. 3–5 of the Act on crimes committed in prosecution of a common purpose, the mode of execution of the crime and accessories after the fact.

[19] HWSCP Act (1988), s. 6.

[20] Ibid., s. 7.

[21] Ibid., s. 12.

[22] Ibid., s. 12(1).

condition).[23] It should be noted that it is immaterial whether the offence was committed by an individual or a body corporate.[24]

An attempt to commit an offence under the HWSCP Act is punished in the same way as if a full offence had been committed.[25] Furthermore, immunity from prosecution conferred on certain persons by or under the Diplomatic Immunities and Privileges Act shall not extend to any crime committed under the Act by any of those persons.[26]

Again, any police officer may, without warrant, enter and search any land, building or carrier, including any aircraft, vehicle, container or other thing whatsoever, that he has reason to believe is related to the commission of a crime prohibited under the HWSCP Act. Such police officer may perform tests and take samples of substances found on the land, building or carrier relating to the commission of the crime. He may also arrest any person who he has reason to believe has committed a crime under the Act, as well as seize any item or substance that he has reason to believe has been used in the commission of a crime under the Act.[27]

The Minister in charge of works and housing, upon reasonable grounds, may seal an area or site believed to have been used, is being used or will or might be used, directly or indirectly, for the purpose of depositing or dumping any harmful waste. Any person who, knowingly and without a reasonable excuse, breaks a seal affixed on such an area or site or hinders or obstructs any operation or measure shall be guilty of an offence and, upon conviction, shall be liable to a fine of ₦50,000 or to imprisonment of not less than 5 years.[28]

Except in cases of a repeat of the Koko saga, a major area for the application of this Act should be in the oil industry. It is suggested that the Act be employed in prosecuting polluters in the oil industry.[29] For instance, crude oil, which is a major pollutant in the oil industry, is known to have toxic ingredients.[30] Such toxins contained therein have the characteristics of harmful waste as defined under the Act.

[23] Ibid., s. 12(2).

[24] Ibid., s. 7.

[25] Ibid., s. 8.

[26] HWSCP Act (1988), s. 9.

[27] Ibid., s. 10.

[28] Ibid., s. 11.

[29] The reason being that oil pollutants, because of their hazardous, harmful and toxic capabilities, may be brought under the harmful waste definition under the Act.

[30] Among the most troublesome are high molecular weight compounds, especially poly-cyclic aromatic hydrocarbons (PAHs), which include many known carcinogens, which can combine with common environmental materials to form other carcinogens.

16.2.2.3 Environmental Impact Assessment Act 1992

In discussing the Environmental Impact Assessment Act, the nature of environmental impact assessment was also discussed. This is to enable the reader to get acquainted with the scientific bases of and the rationale for an environmental impact assessment that gave rise to the enactment of the Environmental Impact Assessment Act.

16.2.2.3.1 Nature of Environmental Impact Assessment

Impact assessment originated from a desire for a profound change in both the philosophy and the methodology of resource and environmental management. It is a process used for predicting the environmental consequences of a proposed major development project and for planning appropriate measures to reduce adverse effects on human, social and physical environments.[31]

Impact assessment also 'means the process of identifying, predicting, evaluating and mitigating the biophysical, social and other relevant effects of development proposals prior to major decisions being taken and commitments made'.[32] According to Rostron,[33] environmental impact assessment (EIA) is regarded as 'a systematic procedure for considering the possible effects of any proposed development on the environment before a decision is made about whether the project should be given approval to proceed'.

Environmental impact assessment adopts the anticipate-and-prevent approach to environmental protection and is, therefore, implicit in the precautionary principle rather than the traditional, and often conventional, react-and-cure approach common with other legal approaches to environmental protection. The need for impact assessment is highlighted in Agenda 21. It provides that all countries:

> should assess the environmental suitability of infrastructure in human settlements,[34] should, as appropriate, ensure that relevant decisions are preceded by environmental impact assessments and also take into account the costs of any ecological consequences,[35] introduce appropriate environmental impact assessment procedures for proposed projects likely to have significant impacts upon biological diversity, providing for suitable information to be made widely available and for public participation, where appropriate, and encourage the assessment of the impacts of relevant policies and programmes on biological diversity.[36]

---

[31] Rostron (2001), p. 62.

[32] National Environmental (Textile, Wearing Apparel, Leather and Footwear Industry) Regulations 2009, regulation 56. See also National Environmental (Chemical, Pharmaceutical, Soap and Detergent Manufacturing Industries) Regulations 2009, regulation 54 (these Regulations made pursuant to the NESREA Act 2007 are discussed, post, in this chapter).

[33] Rostron (2001), p. 62.

[34] AGENDA 21 (1992), chapter 7.39.

[35] Ibid., chapter 7.41(b).

[36] Ibid., chapter 15.5(k).

Principle 17 of the Rio Declaration on Environment and Development (or 'Rio Declaration') 1992 reflects the view that environmental impact assessment, as a national instrument, 'shall be undertaken for proposed activities that are likely to have a significant adverse impact on the environment and are subject to a decision of a competent national authority'. To this end, 'States shall provide prior and timely notification and relevant information to potentially affected States on activities that may have a significant adverse trans-boundary environmental effect and shall consult with those States at an early stage and in good faith'.[37]

In order to achieve more rational management of resources and thus to improve the environment, states should adopt an integrated and coordinated approach to their development planning so as to ensure that development is compatible with the need to protect and improve the environment for the benefit of their population.[38]

Therefore, the rationale underlying environmental impact assessment is that 'rational planning constitutes an essential tool for reconciling any conflict between the needs of development and the need to protect and improve the environment'.[39] This is premised on the fact that EIA constitutes an essential tool for reconciling developmental and environmental needs and that planning (of which impact assessment represents) 'must be applied to human settlements and urbanization with a view to avoiding adverse effects on the environment and obtaining maximum social, economic and environmental benefits for all. . .'.[40] Furthermore, 'impact assessment is a central tool of the international law of prevention'.[41]

Based on the importance of environmental impact assessment as a veritable tool for environmental management and in compliance with major international instruments on the subject, the then Federal Military Government of Nigeria, in 1992, promulgated the Environmental Impact Assessment Decree No. 86 (hereinafter referred to as the 'EIA Act').[42]

16.2.2.3.2 Environmental Impact Assessment Act (EIA Act) 1992

The EIA Act is an Act to set out the general principles, procedures and methods to enable the prior consideration of environmental impact assessment on certain public or private projects. While section 1 sets out the objects of the EIA Act in environmental protection, section 2(1) restricts the taking off of certain projects, whether public or private, without an EIA.

---

[37] Rio Declaration (1992), principle 19.

[38] Stockholm Declaration on the Human Environment 1972 (Stockholm Declaration 1972), principle 13.

[39] Ibid., principle 14.

[40] Ibid., principle 15.

[41] Judge Szekely in the *MOX Plant* case (*Ireland v UK*) ITLOS Order of 3 December 2001.

[42] Enacted in 1992 as Decree No. 86, now retained as Cap E12 LFN 2004.

Section 2(2) therefore requires that environmental impact assessment of certain projects be carried out 'where the extent, nature or location of proposed project or activity is such that it is likely to significantly affect the environment'. Certain projects to which an EIA is mandatory (except if excluded under section 14 of the EIA Act) are stated in the Schedule to the Act.[43] The Schedule to the EIA Act contains 19 items to which an EIA is mandatory.[44]

The EIA Act prescribes the minimum content of an environmental impact statement (EIS).[45] Information provided in the EIS shall be examined impartially by the agency charged with environmental protection prior to any decision (whether in favour or adverse) to be made thereto.[46]

The agency referred to in the EIA Act 1992 was the Federal Environmental Protection Agency, established by the Federal Environmental Protection Agency (Establishment) (FEPA) Act 1988.[47] The FEPA Act has been repealed by section 37 of the National Environmental Standards Regulation and Enforcement Agency (Establishment) (NESREA) Act 2007.[48] A *lacuna* was left as a result.

However, in the case of *Helios Towers Nig. Ltd v NESREA and Kaduna State Environmental Protection Agency*,[49] the Court of Appeal (Kaduna Division), while interpreting the purport of section 61 of the EIA Act and citing several other laws, held that the National Environmental Standards Regulation and Enforcement Agency (NESREA), established under the National Environmental Standards Regulation and Enforcement Agency (Establishment) (NESREA) Act 2007,[50] should be regarded as the agency meant in section 61 of the EIA Act. Thus, the agency hereinafter referred to is the National Environmental Standards Regulation and Enforcement Agency (NESREA).

Once a standpoint is reached by the Agency based on the information provided in the EIS by a proponent, the EIA Act 1992 requires that the Agency give opportunity to government agencies, members of the public, experts in any relevant discipline

---

[43] EIA Act (1992), s. 12, makes EIA mandatory for projects specified in the Schedule to the EIA Act.

[44] There are 19 items in the Schedule. These are agricultural land development covering 500 hectares, airport construction with a 2500-metre runway, drainage and irrigation, fisheries (construction of a harbour, etc.), forestry conservation, housing in excess of 50 hectares, industrial development, infrastructural development, construction of ports, mining, petroleum development, power generation and transmission, quarries, railways, construction of mass transit projects, resort and recreational development, waste treatment and disposal, and water supply.

[45] EIA Act (1992), s. 4.

[46] Ibid., s. 6.

[47] Ibid., s. 61.

[48] Enacted in 2007 vide Government Notice No. 61, Act No. 25, 2007, Federal Republic of Nigeria Official Gazette No. 92, Vol. 94, 31 July 2007, and amended in 2018 vide Government Notice No. 106, Act No. 26 2018, Federal Republic of Nigeria Official Gazette No. 146, Vol. 105, 14 November 2018.

[49] Suit No. CA/K/123/2010 (unreported) delivered by the Court of Appeal (Kaduna Division) on 10 December 2014.

[50] NESREA Act (2007), s. 1.

and interested groups to make comments on the environmental impact activity of the proposed project.[51]

Furthermore, no decision shall be reached by the Agency[52] until the appropriate period given for the comment has elapsed.[53]

Again, after a decision has been reached by the Agency, its report, which shall be in writing stating the reasons for the decision and any provisions to prevent, reduce or mitigate damage to the environment from such activity, shall be made available to any interested person or group.[54] Therefore, in line with the current trend requiring public participation in decision-making in environmental protection, the EIA Act 1992, in sections 7, 9(2)–(4), 19(2), 21, 24, 36, 38 and 55, has ample provisions for public participation in decision-making in environmental protection matters. This is in consonance with international best practices.[55]

In fact, principle 10 of the Rio Declaration 1992[56] provides that environmental issues are best handled with the participation of all concerned citizens at the relevant level. At the national level, each individual shall have appropriate access to information concerning the environment that is held by public authorities, including information on hazardous materials and activities in their communities and the opportunity to participate in decision-making processes. It further provides that states shall facilitate and encourage public awareness of judicial and administrative proceedings, including redress and remedy. What this principle portends in the development of environmental law is the recognition of individual rights to participate in decision-making processes in environmental issues, to have access to information on environmental decisions held by public authorities and to have access to judicial and administrative remedies. It can therefore be said to aim at providing an effective means for the exercise of procedural rights in an environmental context.[57]

Notwithstanding these provisions, especially those of sections 7 and 9(3) of the Act, the Federal High Court of Nigeria, sitting in Port Harcourt, Nigeria, dismissed a suit[58] on the issue of non-compliance of the Agency (the then Federal Environmental Protection Agency (FEPA)) to the provisions of section 7 of the EIA Act 1992. The dismissal was on the basis of *locus standi*. Section 7 of the EIA Act 1992 requires the

---

[51] EIA Act (1992), s. 7.

[52] The agency so referred to is the National Environmental Protection Agency, established under the National Environmental Protection Agency (Establishment) Act 2007, s. 1.

[53] EIA Act (1992), s. 8.

[54] Ibid., s. 9.

[55] For instance, the Convention on Access to Information, Public Participation in Decision-Making and Access to Justice in Environmental Matters (Aarhus Convention)1998 and other legal instruments on the subject matter (public participation in decision-making) are discussed in Chap. 5 of this book.

[56] Rio Declaration (1992).

[57] Thornton and Beckwith (2004), p. 407.

[58] *Oronto Douglas v Shell Petroleum Development Company & 5 Ors*, Suit No. FHC/25C/573/93 (unreported), delivered by FHC PH on 17 February 1997.

Agency charged with environmental protection to adequately publicise any proposed EIA report to all interested persons before approval is given for the project to take off.

The EIA Act 1992 envisages a situation of disagreement between the Agency and a proponent.[59] To this end, provisions are made under the Act for the submission of disagreements to a review panel and/or for mediation, as the case may be. Where the decision is the subject of a review panel, section 16 sets out the factors to be considered by the panel. Such factors include the environmental effects of the project, its significance as well as the measures that are technically and economically feasible that would mitigate any significant and serious adverse environmental effects of the project. 'Environmental effect' means, in respect of a project, 'any change that the project may cause to the environment; as well as whether any such change occurs within or outside Nigeria, and includes any effect of any such change on health and socio-economic conditions'.[60]

For the effective participation of members of the public in environmental protection, after receiving a mandatory study report in respect of a project, the Agency is further enjoined to publish a public notice in the manner and way as required by section 24 of the EIA Act 1992. The comments arising thereto and the report in issue shall be forwarded to the Council.[61] The Council, in the event of any dispute, may refer the report for mediation provided for under sections 31–33 of the EIA Act 1992 or to a review panel pursuant to sections 35–37. Reference to a review panel will only arise where at any time after a project report has been referred to a mediation panel, the Council is of the opinion that mediation is not likely to produce a result that is satisfactory to all of the parties. Once this position is reached, the mediation is terminated and the project and report are referred to the review panel under section 35 of the EIA Act 1992.

All these provisions and processes are meant to make sure that before a project that may have a significant environmental effect is allowed to take off, it is subjected to a series of tests. This is in connection with the fact that all developmental projects are earthbound and that where no serious efforts are made to subject the project to rigorous tests to determine its level of environmental impact and the ways of mitigating such impact before the take-off of the proposed project, it will spell doom not only to the environment but also to man. To this end, the review panel, which is the final arbiter in the whole process, has the power to summon any person to appear as a witness to give evidence orally or in writing and to produce documents considered necessary to reach a just conclusion. This power to compel a witness to appear before it and give evidence or produce documents and other things, as the

---

[59] A person who is proposing a development project that is the subject of an environmental impact assessment.

[60] EIA Act (1992), s. 61.

[61] The Council is established under the NESREA Act (2007), s. 3.

case may be, is vested in the Federal High Court or a High Court of a state or Abuja.[62]

In the final analysis, once the review panel submits its report to the Agency, it shall make the report available to the public in any manner the Council considers appropriate and shall advise the public that the report is available.[63] Finally, pursuant to the provisions of section 39 of the Act, the Agency shall take any of the following decisions:

(a) the project is not likely to cause significant adverse environmental effect; or
(b) any such effect can be mitigated or justified in the circumstances.

However, where, in the opinion of the Agency, the project is likely to cause significant adverse environmental effects that cannot be mitigated and cannot be justified in the circumstances, the Agency takes no further action.[64] But where any environmental effect of the project can be mitigated or justified, the Agency shall design a follow-up programme that it considers appropriate for the project and arrange for the implementation of that programme. A certificate stating that an environmental assessment of a project has been completed shall then be finally issued to the proponent.[65]

Penalties are stipulated under the EIA Act 1992 for non-compliance with the provisions of the Act. Where the defaulter is an individual, a fine of ₦10,000 or 5 years imprisonment is imposed. And in the case of a firm or body corporate, the fine shall be between ₦50,000 and ₦1,000,000.[66]

16.2.2.3.3 Main Stages in the EIA Process

The EIA Act, under section 15, provides for various environmental assessment processes. One of these processes is screening. Screening is the first stage of the EIA process that results in a key EIA decision, namely to either conduct the assessment (based on the likely significant impacts) or not conduct it (in the anticipated absence of such impacts).[67] The reason for this is that a proposed project may not have been included in the items stated under the mandatory study list in the Schedule to the EIA Act for which an EIA is mandatory.[68]

However, such a proposed project may likely have a significant environmental impact. To determine whether or not the project requires an EIA, project proponents assess their project based on a set of criteria determined by a designated agency. The

[62] EIA Act (1992), s. 37(1) and (2).
[63] Ibid., s. 38.
[64] Ibid., s. 39(2).
[65] Ibid., s. 41.
[66] Ibid., s. 60.
[67] International Institute for Sustainable Development (2023).
[68] Pursuant to EIA Act (1992), s. 12.

criteria used in determining whether a proposed project may have a significant environmental impact include threshold, the size of projects and sensitivity of the environment. On the basis of these, the proposed project is subjected to screening.[69]

Screening is an inquiry into whether a development project is likely to have significant effects on the environment. The EIA Act, under section 18, enjoins the Agency to ensure that the screening of a project is conducted and a screening report prepared. Screening needs to follow specific procedures often described in the legislation so that all such proposed projects follow the same process. Under the provisions of section 18(2) of the Act, any available information may be used in conducting a screening exercise. The use of previously conducted screening results is permitted under section 20, as well as the declaration of a class screening report.[70] The key contributions of screening to a good EIA are as follows:

(i) Screening facilitates informed decision-making by providing a clear, well-structured, factual analysis of the effects and consequences of proposed actions.
(ii) Screening influences both project selection and policy design by screening out environmentally and/or socially unsound proposals, as well as modifying feasible actions.[71]

It is important that screening should be done as early as possible in the development of the proposal in order for the proponent and other stakeholders to be aware of possible EIA obligations. It is also important that screening be applied systematically and consistently so that the same decision would be reached if others did the screening.

Scoping is another aspect of the EIA process. The purpose of scoping is to focus on environmental impact issues to ensure that useful and relevant results will be obtained and to determine the parameters and boundaries of the assessment. The geographical area to be covered by the EIA may need to be much greater than just the local area in which the project is to be located.[72]

Scoping is the process of identifying the key environmental issues and is perhaps the most important step in an EIA. It occurs early on in the project cycle, at the same time as outline planning and pre-feasibility studies. Several groups, particularly decision-makers, the local population and the scientific community, have an interest in helping to deliberate the issues that should be considered, and scoping is designed to canvass their views.[73]

Scoping is important for two reasons: first, so that problems can be pinpointed early, allowing mitigating design changes to be made before expensive detailed work is carried out, and, second, to ensure that detailed prediction work is only carried out for important issues. It is not the purpose of an EIA to carry out

[69] EnviroNews Nigeria (2022a).
[70] EIA Act (1992), s. 19.
[71] International Institute for Sustainable Development (2023).
[72] EnviroNews Nigeria (2022a).
[73] International Institute for Sustainable Development (2023).

exhaustive studies on all environmental impacts for all projects. If key issues are identified and a full-scale EIA is considered necessary, then scoping should include terms of reference for these further studies.[74]

A major activity of scoping is to identify key interest groups, both governmental and non-governmental, and to establish good lines of communication. People who are affected by the project need to hear about it as soon as possible. Their knowledge and perspectives may have a major bearing on the focus of the EIA. Rapid rural appraisal techniques provide a means of assessing the needs and views of the affected population.[75]

The main EIA techniques used in scoping are baseline studies, checklists, matrices and network diagrams.[76] These techniques collect and present knowledge and information in a straightforward way so that logical decisions can be made about which impacts are most significant.[77]

After scoping, the next in the EIA process is the baseline study of the proposed project area: a baseline study is essential in order to be able to determine the level of impact expected and to enable the monitoring of impacts after the development has occurred. In some cases, baseline information will need to be gathered in the field, and in others, it will already be available and need only be collated. Where a project has a number of alternative sites, each of the sites should undergo a baseline study so that the relative severity of the impacts for each alternative can be assessed.[78]

The next stage involves impact identification, impact prediction and impact evaluation. Impact identification is a process designed to ensure that all potentially significant impacts are identified and taken into account in the EIA process; impact prediction, on the other hand, is a process designed to identify the magnitude of potential impacts and provides the basis for the assessment of significance; and, finally, impact evaluation is a process that helps assess the relative significance of an impact.[79]

The objective of prediction is to estimate the magnitude, extent and duration of the impact in comparison with the situation without that project/action. An environmental impact prediction should, at the minimum, perform the following: (i) determine the initial reference or baseline state (i.e. conditions/levels prior to the project), (ii) forecast the future state/conditions with and without the project and (iii) compare with environmental standards and guidelines, where appropriate.[80]

After establishing the range of impacts associated with a certain development, it is necessary to predict their magnitude. Here, baseline studies are used to establish

---

[74] Ibid.

[75] Ibid.

[76] A network diagram visually describes the linkages between pairs of environmental factors, providing some indication of how an ecosystem functions.

[77] International Institute for Sustainable Development (2023).

[78] EnviroNews Nigeria (2022a).

[79] Mwalyosi et al. (1999), pp. 284–285.

[80] Ibid., 284.

environmental condition levels prior to the project, forecasting methods to predict future conditions with and without the project and comparison with environmental standards and guidelines, where appropriate. Physico-chemical impacts like noise, air and water quality using quantitative modelling procedures are well established; other impacts, like socio-economic impacts, are more subjective.[81]

Impact magnitude relates to the severity of the impact, whether the impact is irreversible or reversible, and the potential rate of recovery from the impact. For instance, the magnitude of the impact is considered high if a major adverse impact cannot be mitigated. A major adverse impact would affect the potential subsistence/ recreational/commercial use of biophysical resources, with the result that the value of resources would be reduced far below the publicly acceptable level. Moderate to minor unmitigated impacts of a similar nature will result in resources being still usable but at some inconvenience to the public.[82]

The next stage is impact assessment. Impact assessment (IA) follows from prediction and involves an assessment of the relative significance of the impacts when compared with regulatory requirements. It is a structured process for considering the implications, for people and their environment, of proposed actions while there is still an opportunity to modify (or even, if appropriate, abandon) the proposals. It is applied at all levels of decision-making, from policies to specific projects.

The process involves the identification and characterisation of the most likely impacts of proposed actions (impact prediction/forecasting) and an assessment of the social significance of those impacts (impact evaluation). Impact assessment aims to:

(i) Provide information for decision-making that analyses the biophysical, social, economic and institutional consequences of proposed actions.
(ii) Promote transparency and the participation of the public in decision-making.
(iii) Identify procedures and methods for follow-up (monitoring and mitigation of adverse consequences) in policy, planning and project cycles.
(iv) Contribute to environmentally sound and sustainable development[83]—the significance of IA is a function not only of the magnitude of the predicted impact but also of the sensitivity of the receiving environment (which may also depend on the geographical scale being considered, the frequency or duration of the impact, etc.).[84]

Thus, the process of IA benefits proponents, stakeholders and local communities, as well as decision-makers. Although impact assessment has been criticised since its introduction for being a technocratic tool, based on rational decision-making models, contemporary guidelines and principles for IA practice tend to emphasise a participatory, inclusive approach, which recognises different types of knowledge,

---

[81] Ibid.

[82] Ibid.

[83] Fortuny (2022).

[84] EnviroNews Nigeria (2022a).

and the importance of representing the views of different groups in society, regardless of their economic and political status.

Environmental and social justice and distributional considerations are important guiding principles of impact assessment.[85] Ideally impact assessment shall be an integrated treatment of the likely impacts on any of the facets of the natural and human-modified environment, including people, communities and their well-being. To that end, different forms of IA have been developed to address specific challenges raised by the need to assess impacts within certain sectors of the environment: social IA, health IA, cultural IA, ecological IA, etc. All these forms of IA share the same basic principles, methodology and purpose but may differ in specific methods and techniques. The need to apply IA to strategic levels of decision-making (e.g. policies, legislation, plans and programmes) led to the development of strategic environmental assessment (SEA). SEA is generally understood as an impact assessment process that aims to mainstream environmental, social, economic and health issues and ensure the sustainability of strategic decisions.[86]

In recent years, IA has become strongly linked to sustainability concepts, and some would argue that sustainability is an integral part of all IA activities. For others, the integration of the environmental, social and economic dimensions of assessment justifies the adoption of a distinct term: sustainability assessment. On the other hand, it is possible to conduct impact assessments within other policy and value contexts without direct or indirect reference to sustainability thinking.[87]

On the whole, IA refers to the detailed evaluation of the environmental and social impacts of the planned project and identified alternatives, compared to the baseline conditions. This includes qualitative descriptions, such as measuring high, medium and low impacts, and quantitative descriptions, such as indicating the cubic metres of water withdrawn, sewage produced and pollutants released. This is done for the planned project as well as the identified alternatives, allowing for comparisons. Once the detailed assessment is complete, mitigation measures to reduce or avoid impacts are identified.[88]

Next in the process is mitigation. Mitigation involves taking measures to reduce or remove identified impacts and, if possible, remedy significant adverse effects through, for example,

(i) The control of solid and liquid wastes by recycling on-site
(ii) Minimal use of toxic substances to avoid impacts on local ecosystems
(iii) Sensitive design structures[89]

---

[85] Ibid.

[86] Fortuny (2022).

[87] Ibid.

[88] International Institute of Sustainable Development (2023).

[89] EnviroNews Nigeria (2022a).

Overall, mitigation measures are a response to findings from impact assessments; they need to cover all areas identified.[90] The key focus of mitigation actions should be on:

(i) Preventive measures that avoid the occurrence of impacts and thus avoid harm or even produce positive outcomes
(ii) Measures that focus on limiting the severity and duration of the impacts
(iii) Compensation mechanisms for those impacts that are unavoidable and cannot be reduced further[91]

Key impacts and potential mitigation actions often relate to land. Almost all development proposals involve the disturbance of the land surface. This is usually extensive for major linear projects (roads, pipelines), dams and reservoirs, and large-scale mining, agriculture, forestry and housing schemes. Environmental impacts of particular concern can include drainage of wetlands, conversion of natural areas or expansion into areas that are vulnerable to natural hazards.[92]

The next stage is the review of the EIA draft report. Once the proponent submits a draft EIA report, it shall be evaluated by the Agency[93] or the EIA Department of the Federal Ministry of Environment to establish the form of review. This may include in-house review, panel review or public review. For public review,[94] a public display and review of documents for a period of 21 working days are required. Venues for the display will include, among others, the local government authority (LGA), the state environmental protection authorities and the Federal Ministry of Environment Headquarters. The public shall be invited to participate in the review process through newspaper advertisements. The final EIA report must include all issues raised during the review process and the answers proffered to them by the proponent, including any amendments to the report of the EIA study.[95]

After the above stage, the EIA report is sent to the review committee for provisional approval. The review committee shall assess the report and decide whether the project could proceed, could go on with a few corrections, or should be totally repeated. If it meets the requirement to proceed, the Federal Ministry of Environment shall furnish the proponent with the reviewed report and provisional approval. The approval or disapproval of the EIA of the product by the Ministry shall be based on the recommendations of an independent panel of experts.

If the report passes the scrutiny of the independent panel of experts, final approval of the EIA report shall be submitted by the proponent to the Ministry. The EIA Department of the Federal Ministry of Environment shall ensure that all corrections have been implemented and that the report represents the position of the review

[90] International Institute of Sustainable Development (2023).

[91] Ibid.

[92] International Institute of Sustainable Development (2023).

[93] EIA Act (1992), s. 6.

[94] As required under the EIA Act (1992), s. 7.

[95] EIA Act (1992), s. 9.

committee. Once approval is granted, an EIA certificate and an environmental impact statement (EIS) are issued.

After the final approval is given to the proponent, it is still not the end. The Federal Ministry of Environment has to carry out impact mitigation monitoring (IMM) on the project in collaboration with the state Ministries of Environment and Local Governments to ensure the implementation of:

(i) The conditions for approval
(ii) Mitigation measures[96]
(iii) The environmental management plan (EMP)

16.2.2.4 Nigerian Urban and Regional Planning Act 1992 (NURPA 1992)[97]

Urban and regional planning involves the planning of the physical and social development of a city through the design of its layout and the provision of services and facilities. Before analysing the provisions of the Nigerian Urban and Regional Planning (NURP) Act, it will be pertinent to discuss the basis for planning.

16.2.2.4.1 Basis for Planning and Planning Process

The planning process is a veritable tool for land-use control, with the goal of better comprehending human activities and their operational environment and, as a result, being able to recognise dangers and possibilities more clearly than previously. Corrective action can be made if the system deviates from what was expected. Where areas of ignorance are identified as, perhaps, concealing areas of importance, exploratory work can be undertaken.

The planning process involves an interplay between a number of activities and steps, namely identification of the problem, formulation of general goals and definition of more specific and measurable objectives relating to the problem, identification of possible constraints or difficulties, projection of the future situation, formulation of alternative approaches to reach the desired end result, evaluation of the different solutions, interpretation of the findings and production of a comprehensive or master plan or development plan.[98]

A comprehensive plan provides the basis for policies and regulations affecting growth and establishes a framework for long-range planning.[99] In the same vein, 'the

[96]This is required during the construction and post-construction stages of the project.

[97]It was promulgated as Decree No. 86, 1992, currently retained as Cap N138 LFN 2004.

[98]Duxbury (1999), p. 90.

[99]Sections 2(a)(b), 3(2)(a)(b) and 4(a)–(d) of NURPA (1992) have provisions for all these.

development plan sets out the planning policies of local authorities and forms the basis for decisions on planning applications'.[100]

It also serves as the legal basis for land-use control. It is usually divided into six major components:[101]

(i) Issue identification—sets forth data and community opinions and discusses and analyses this information to determine the critical land-use issues and unique opportunities of the community
(ii) Public infrastructure—discusses the adequacy of existing public infrastructure, such as water supply, transportation, wastewater treatment facilities and solid waste disposal and examines the potential need for increased facilities
(iii) Public services—considers the adequacy of existing services, such as schools, emergency services and health care facilities and the potential need for increased services
(iv) Resource protection—discusses the adequacy of present efforts to preserve both the natural and man-made environment within the community and examines the need for increased protection of these resources
(v) Economic development—explains present economic development efforts, such as the promotion of tourism or light industry, and sets forth strategies for improving the community's economy; and
(vi) Implementation plan—establishes how the recommendations in each component of the plan will be implemented and coordinated with other plan components to achieve the goals of the comprehensive plan.

16.2.2.4.2 Legal Effects of a Comprehensive Plan

What then will be the legal effect of a comprehensive plan? The legal effects are threefold. First, all land-use regulations of a town or community must be consistent with the plan. Thus, any provision of a town's or community's municipal law concerning land use must be consistent with the goals, objectives and strategies set forth by the comprehensive plan. Second, where an agency of the local government, state or federal government chooses to undertake a capital project, the agency's plans must consider the goals, objectives and strategies of the comprehensive plan.

Other governmental agencies, such as state agencies, must consider the local comprehensive plan in shaping their capital projects within the locality. If, for example, the Ministry of Works plans to improve or build a road, bridge or highway in a town or community and the town or community has a formally adopted comprehensive plan, the ministry would be required to consider that plan and its transportation objectives before proceeding with the project. Without this requirement, government agencies could undermine the objectives of a town's or

[100] Rostron (2001), p. 40.
[101] Onyeabor (2016), p. 15.

community's comprehensive plan by undertaking capital projects that openly conflict with the community's comprehensive plan.

In the case of *AG Lagos State v AG Federation & 35 Ors*,[102] the Lagos State government instituted an action before the Supreme Court complaining that the agents of the Government of the Federation were developing land within Lagos that is not in conformity with the Lagos State master plan, asserting that this undermined the comprehensive plan of the state. The agents of the Government of the Federation, purportedly acting under the provisions of the Nigerian Urban and Regional Act, went ahead to develop land, though belonging to the Government of the Federation, in accordance with NURPA 1992, but in derogation of the Lagos State master plan. The court held in favour of Lagos State, holding that the NURPA 1992 in question shall not apply to Lagos State under the principle of federalism, to which Nigeria subscribes, and that any development of land within the state should be in conformity with the Lagos State's master plan.

Again, a comprehensive plan enables the planning authority to regulate land use for the purpose of protecting the public health, safety and general welfare of its citizens. It is the 'essence' of 'rational allocation of land use'.[103] It follows that any regulation by the planning authority that is not in conformity with the plan cannot stand if challenged by a land developer.

Even where a municipality has not adopted a comprehensive plan, land-use regulations must evidence a comprehensive planning rationale. In the absence of a comprehensive plan, if a land-use regulation is adopted without any comprehensive planning rationale, the regulation may be defeated for failure to meet the statutory requirement that all land-use regulations be in conformity with a comprehensive plan.

Thus, in the case of *Udell v Haas*,[104] the court was faced with a challenge to a land-use regulation where no formal comprehensive plan for the community had been adopted. In 1951, when the landowner bought the property, it was zoned Business 'A', allowing for retail, office and laboratory uses. Nine years later, the landowner's representative presented building plans to the village for business development. That same night, the planning board recommended that the zoning for the area where the landowner's property was located be 'changed from business to residential'. The local legislature, when it changed the zoning as recommended, did not articulate the comprehensive planning objectives to be achieved by the re-zoning. The court concluded that the 'vague desires of a segment of the public were not a proper reason to interfere with the landowner's right to use his property in a manner which for some twenty odd years was considered perfectly proper'.[105] If there is to be any justification for this interference with the landowner's use of his

[102] (2003) 35 WRN 1.

[103] *Udell v Haas* (1968) All ER, 290.

[104] Ibid., 290.

[105] *Udell v Haas* (1968), p. 290.

property, it must be found in the needs and goals of the community as articulated in a rational statement of land-use control policies, known as the 'comprehensive plan'.

The court examined 'all relevant evidence', including the zoning map and law, for evidence of comprehensive planning. The court also reviewed a 1958 zoning amendment entitled 'development policy' for the village. This amendment envisioned the village as a low-density, single-family community with commercial development limited to outlying areas. The court found that the landowner's parcel was located in areas such as these and that the previous zoning was in conformance with this development policy. The court reasoned that a 'comprehensive plan requires that the re-zoning should not conflict with the fundamental land use policies and development plans of the community' and invalidated the re-zoning.

To this end, all land-use regulations must be consistent with the comprehensive plan or evince comprehensive planning. Regulations and local laws are more likely to withstand challenges when they are supported by some rationale of this type that provides for the appropriate use of land in the public interest.

The decision in *Golden v Planning Board of Town of Ramapo*[106] recognised the ability of local governments to influence the pace of land development within their boundaries, provided that the goal was to control but not exclude development. In that case, several developers challenged the town's right to adopt a comprehensive plan and zoning law that worked to slow the subdivision of property, allowing it time to build and pay for supportive infrastructure, like water and sewer utilities, at a pace that the town could manage. 'The Town has utilized its comprehensive plan to implement its timing controls. Considered as a whole, it represents both in its inception and implementation a reasonable attempt to provide for the sequential, orderly development of land in conjunction with the needs of the community, as well as individual parcels of land.'[107]

In the final analysis, it should be noted that land-use regulations must not conflict with the goals, objectives and strategies set forth by the comprehensive plan. If regulations conflict with the comprehensive plan, they may be challenged by landowners as failing to meet the statutory requirement that regulations must conform to a comprehensive plan. A court may invalidate such regulations. In the case of *Osiecki v Town of Huntington*,[108] 'the Town maintained that it is not obliged to slavish servitude' to the comprehensive plan and that it was free, in 1989, to determine that the comprehensive plan should not be followed with regard to the property in question. The court determined that the town had failed to articulate a specific rationale for departing from its comprehensive plan in adopting a zoning amendment. The court held that the town's reasons for abandoning the comprehensive plan 'would invite the kind of *ad hoc* and arbitrary application of zoning power that the comprehensive planning requirement was designed to avoid'. The re-zoning

[106] 324 N.Y.S.2d 178 (1972).

[107] *Golden v Planning Board of Town of Ramapo* (1972), p. 178.

[108] 650 NY Cir 478 (1991).

of the plaintiff's parcel of land was void since it did not 'conform to the Town's comprehensive plan'.

From all that has been discussed so far, one thing is clear—the essence of planning law is to control development and therefore protect the environment. It is at this point that planning law imports elements of environmental protection, and the purpose of both aspects of law is fused. It was in this respect that NURPA 1992 was enacted for purposes of land-use control,[109] thereby creating a benign, friendly and aesthetically pleasing environment. In this respect, NURPA 1992 requires that all developmental activities that may have significant environmental impact shall not be commenced, except where such developer had obtained a planning permit.[110] In fact, what NURPA 1992 portends is that once an activity is considered development,[111] it shall not be commenced until a development permit is first had and obtained from the appropriate town planning authority.

16.2.2.5 National Environmental Standards and Regulations Enforcement Agency (Establishment) Act (NESREA Act) 2007

In 1999, when the Federal Ministry of Environment was established, it took over the environmental protection functions of the various federal government agencies and ministerial departments and units, including those of the Federal Environmental Protection Agency (FEPA). The FEPA Act, which established FEPA, continued to exist. In 2007, new legislation, the National Environmental Standards and Regulations Enforcement Agency (Establishment) (NESREA) Act,[112] was enacted. The Act, in section 36, repealed the Federal Environmental Agency Act and, under section 1, established the National Environmental Standards and Regulations Enforcement Agency (or 'the Agency'), which shall be the enforcement agency for environmental standards, regulations, rules, laws, policies and guidelines.[113]

The NESREA Act[114] provides for the establishment and composition of the NESREA Governing Council. The functions of the Agency are set out in section 7 (a)–(m).[115] Such functions include enforcing compliance with laws, guidelines, policies and standards on environmental matters and coordinating and liaising with stakeholders, within and outside Nigeria, on matters of environmental standards,

[109] NURPA (1992) as a legal instrument for land-use control and environmental protection was discussed in Chap. 8 of this book.

[110] NURPA (1992), s. 28.

[111] As defined under NURPA (1992), s. 91.

[112] NESREA Act (2007). The Act was amended in November 2018 by the National Environmental Standards and Regulations Enforcement Agency (Establishment) Amendment) Act (Amendment Act) 2018. See note 116 below.

[113] NESREA Act (2007), s. 1(2)(a).

[114] Ibid., s. 3.

[115] NESREA Act (2007).

regulations and enforcement. Meanwhile, the NESREA Amendment Act 2018 (or 'Amendment Act 2018')[116] amended section 7(c) of the NESREA Act 2007 by deleting 'enforcement of compliance with the provisions of international agreement, protocols, conventions and treaties on Oil and Gas' from the functions of NESREA.

Furthermore, the Agency[117] is empowered to submit, for approval by the Minister charged with the responsibility of environmental matters, proposals for the evolution and review of existing guidelines, regulations and standards on the environment. The areas covered include atmospheric protection, air quality, ozone-depleting substances, noise control, effluent limitations, water quality, waste management and environmental sanitation, erosion and flood control, coastal zone management, dams and reservoirs, watershed, deforestation and bush burning, other forms of pollution and sanitation, and the control of hazardous substances and removal control methods.[118] Section 8(q) of the NESREA Act 2007, which provides for the power of NESREA to charge fees for tests, investigations and other services performed by it, was amended. Under the Amendment Act 2018, section 8(q) was amended to include administrative fees as part of the fees that could be charged by the Agency.

To achieve its mandate, the Agency is empowered under the NESREA Act to make regulations and standards for water quality,[119] review effluent limitations for existing point sources and set up schedules for compliance,[120] make regulations for the purpose of protecting public health and promoting environmental sanitation[121] and make regulations, guidelines and standards for the protection and enhancement of the quality of land resources, natural watershed, coastal zone dams and reservoirs, including the prevention of flood and erosion.[122]

Acting under these mandates,[123] the Minister charged with the responsibility for environmental matters made 33 regulations between 2009 and 2014. These Regulations, in addition to the provisions of sections 20–27 of the parent legislation,[124] provide far-reaching mechanisms for the protection of the Nigerian environment in areas of air resources and water bodies through effluent limitations,[125] noise

[116]Government Notice No. 106, Act No. 26, 2018, Federal Republic of Nigeria Official Gazette No. 146, Vol. 105, 14 November 2018.

[117]National Environmental Standards and Regulations Enforcement Agency, established by the NESREA Act (2007), s. 1(1).

[118]NESREA Act (2007), s. 8 (k)(i)–(xiv).

[119]Ibid., s. 23(1) and (2).

[120]Ibid., s. 24(1) and (2).

[121]Ibid., s, 25(1).

[122]Ibid., s. 26(1) and (2).

[123]Ibid.

[124]NESREA Act (2007).

[125]See discussions in Sect. 7.5 of Chap. 7 of this book.

control,[126] the protection of the ozone layer[127] and the control of hazardous waste,[128] among others. These efforts are discussed next.

16.2.2.5.1 Setting Standards to Protect and Enhance the Quality of Nigeria's Air Resources

Under section 20(1) of the NESREA Act 2007, the Agency is mandated to make regulations setting standards to protect and enhance the quality of Nigeria's air resources so as to promote public health or welfare. Pursuant to the above, various emission standards have been set out for different sectors of the economy under the various Regulations.[129]

16.2.2.5.2 Protecting Water Bodies and Enhancing Water Quality Standards

Under section 23(1),[130] the Agency shall, in collaboration with other relevant agencies, make regulations for the purpose of protecting water bodies and public health or welfare and enhancing the quality of water. Pursuant to the above, NESREA sets out various effluent limitation standards for different industries and sectors of the economy. These effluent limitation standards for different industries and sectors of the economy are discussed under the following Regulations.[131]

16.2.2.5.2.1 National Environmental (Mining and Process of Coal, Ores and Industrial Minerals) Regulations 2009

In respect of the mining and processing of coal, ores and industrial minerals, regulation on effluent discharges is controlled by the National Environmental (Mining and Process of Coal, Ores and Industrial Minerals) Regulations 2009.[132]

[126] The Regulations setting standards to protect and enhance the quality of Nigeria's air resources and the control of air and noise pollution were discussed in Sects. 6.4.3.2 and 6.5 of Chap. 6 of this book.

[127] The National Environmental (Ozone Layer Protection) Regulations 2009 for the protection of the ozone layer was discussed in Sect. 6.3.3 of Chap. 6 of this book.

[128] This was discussed in Sect. 9.6.2 of Chap. 9 of this book.

[129] NESREA's standards to protect and enhance the quality of Nigeria's air resources and the protection and control of air pollution were discussed in Sect. 6.4.3.2 of Chap. 6 of this book.

[130] NESREA Act (2007), s. 20(4).

[131] The regulations for the purpose of protecting the water bodies are discussed in Sect. 7.5 of Chap. 7 of this book.

[132] Government Notice No. 284, S.I. No. 28. Federal Republic of Nigeria Official Gazette No. 63 Vol. 96, 12 October 2009.

Effluent is defined under regulation 47[133] as 'any liquid waste, discharge from mining facilities including mine water, tailings, acid leaching, acid mine drainage, fuels and lubricants'. Part 111 of the Regulations[134] sets out effluent limitation procedures for this industrial sector. Under the Regulations, no facility shall cause to be discharged any effluent into the natural water system and land without a permit from the Agency.[135] To this end, every facility that discharges effluent shall treat it to an acceptable limit.[136] Thus, no waste material beyond permissible limits is released from the premises at which the operation is being carried out.

Furthermore, all effluents are cleaned up and disposed of at an appropriate discharge point or waste treatment facility at the conclusion of each operation.[137] In line with the polluter-pays principle as one of the general principles and rules establishing standards in environmental protection, as reflected in treaties, national laws, binding acts of international organisations, state practices and soft law commitments, regulation 13 of the Regulations[138] provides that the collection, treatment, transportation and final disposal of wastes within specified standards and guidelines shall be the responsibility of the facility generating the waste. In addition, in the event of pollution resulting in an impact on the environment, whether socio-economically or health wise, the facility shall, as specified in Schedule 4 to these Regulations, be responsible for:

(a) the cost of clean-up;
(b) remediation;
(c) reclamation;
(d) compensation to all affected parties; and
(e) cost of damage assessment and control.[139]

The above liabilities notwithstanding, it shall be an offence, in addition to other offences, if a facility fails to comply and take reasonable measures to remove or treat and dispose of any effluent; fails to remediate the environment; does not comply with guidelines with respect to the handling, storing and transport of any effluent; releases effluent and sludge into the environment in excess of the permissible level; or fails to take reasonable measures to prevent, reduce or remedy the adverse effects

[133] National Environmental (Mining and Process of Coal, Ores and Industrial Minerals) Regulations (2009).

[134] Ibid.

[135] National Environmental (Mining and Process of Coal, Ores and Industrial Minerals) Regulations (2009), regulation 12.

[136] What constitutes an acceptable limit in the treatment of effluent is specified in the National Environmental (Mining and Process of Coal, Ores and Industrial Minerals) Regulations 2009, sch. 1.

[137] National Environmental (Mining and Process of Coal, Ores and Industrial Minerals) Regulations (2009), regulation 10(1) and (5).

[138] National Environmental (Mining and Process of Coal, Ores and Industrial Minerals) Regulations (2009).

[139] Ibid., regulation 13(2).

of effluent and sludge on the environment.[140] Any person who violates any of the provisions of regulation 28 of these Regulations[141] commits an offence and shall, on conviction, be liable to a fine of ₦100,000 or imprisonment for 2 years or both such fine and imprisonment. In addition, the offender shall be liable to an additional fine of ₦5000 for each day the offence subsists. Where the offender is a body corporate, the fine shall be ₦1,000,000 and an additional fine of ₦50,000 each day the offence subsists.[142]

It should be pointed out that the fine in the sum of ₦100,000 provided under regulation 29(1) of these Regulations[143] for individual offenders is below the sum provided in the parent statute. Under section 24(4) of the NESREA Act, the fine provided in respect of an individual offender is the sum of ₦200,000.

One wonders why there is this disparity as the Regulations[144] are subsidiary to the Act,[145] which is the parent statute. This is not supposed to be so because a subsidiary law shall not contradict the provisions of the parent law, from which the former takes its authority. This, in essence, shall be deemed *ultra vires* powers of the Minister of Environment to make regulations pursuant to the provisions of section 34 of the NESREA Act. This anomaly, as contained in regulation 29(1) of these Regulations, needs to be amended to fall in line with the provisions of section 24(4) of the NESREA Act 2007.

16.2.2.5.2.2 National Environmental (Textile, Wearing Apparel, Leather and Footwear Industry) Regulations 2009

For the textile, wearing apparel, leather and footwear industry, the National Environmental (Textile, Wearing Apparel, Leather and Footwear Industry) Regulations 2009[146] sets out the effluent limitation standards. In respect of this industry, effluent is defined as 'waste water treated or untreated; that flows out of a treatment plant, sewer, or industrial outfall resulting from the commercial or industrial use of water, generally to as waste discharged into surface waters'.[147]

Schedule 1 to the Regulations sets out effluent limitation standards for the industry in respect of various parameters, such as the appearance of wastewater, temperature, total suspended solids (TSS), chemical oxygen demand (COD),

---

[140] Ibid., regulation 28.

[141] National Environmental (Mining and Process of Coal, Ores and Industrial Minerals) Regulations (2009).

[142] Ibid., regulation 29.

[143] National Environmental (Mining and Process of Coal, Ores and Industrial Minerals) Regulations (2009).

[144] Ibid.

[145] NESREA Act (2007).

[146] Government Notice No. 287, S.I. No. 34. Federal Republic of Nigeria Official Gazette No. 66 Vol. 96, 16 October 2009.

[147] National Environmental (Textile, Wearing Apparel, Leather and Footwear Industry) Regulations (2009), regulation 56.

biological oxygen demand (BOD), metals, chlorine, phenol, dissolved oxygen, etc. Under regulation 15(2),[148] an effluent shall be deemed to be a pollutant if the concentration of any of these parameters exceeds the permissible limits as specified in column 2 of Schedule 1.[149] To this end, such facility shall not discharge the wastewater onto the land, into watercourses or into a water body unless the facility ensures that the parameters of the effluent do not exceed the permissible limits set out in Schedule 1.[150]

It shall therefore be an offence if a facility, *inter alia,* fails to take reasonable measures to remove or otherwise treat and dispose of any effluent to minimise adverse environmental impacts; releases effluent and sludge into the environment in excess of the permissible level; or fails to take reasonable measures to prevent, reduce or remedy the adverse effects of effluent, sludge and emissions released into the environment contrary to the standards prescribed by the Agency.[151] Any person who violates any of the provisions of regulation 47[152] commits an offence and shall, on conviction, be liable to a fine of ₦200,000 or imprisonment for 2 years or both such fine and imprisonment. In addition, the offender shall be liable to an additional fine of ₦5000 for each day the offence subsists. Where the offender is a body corporate, the fine shall be ₦1,000,000 and an additional fine of ₦50,000 each day the offence subsists.[153]

The Regulations[154] also have provisions for the polluter-pays principle. Regulation 5[155] provides that the collection, treatment, transportation and final disposal of wastes within specified standards and guidelines shall be the responsibility of the facility generating the waste.[156]

16.2.2.5.2.3 National Environmental (Chemical, Pharmaceutical, Soap and Detergent Manufacturing Industries) Regulations 2009

The control of effluent discharges in respect of chemical, pharmaceutical, soap and detergent manufacturing industries is controlled by the National Environmental

[148] National Environmental (Textile, Wearing Apparel, Leather and Footwear Industry) Regulations (2009).

[149] Ibid.

[150] National Environmental (Textile, Wearing Apparel, Leather and Footwear Industry) Regulations (2009).

[151] Ibid., regulation 47.

[152] National Environmental (Textile, Wearing Apparel, Leather and Footwear Industry) Regulations (2009).

[153] Ibid., regulation 51.

[154] National Environmental (Textile, Wearing Apparel, Leather and Footwear Industry) Regulations (2009).

[155] Ibid.

[156] The provisions are similar to the National Environmental (Mining and Process of Coal, Ores and Industrial Minerals) Regulations (2009), regulation 5, with regard to the subject matter (polluter-pays principle). The polluter-pays principle was discussed in section 4.7 of Chap. 4 of this book.

(Chemical, Pharmaceutical, Soap and Detergent Manufacturing Industries) Regulations 2009.[157] Effluent is defined[158] as 'waste water treated or untreated; that flows out of a treatment plant, sewer, or industrial outfall resulting from the commercial or industrial use of water, generally to as waste discharged into surface waters'.[159] National environmental standards in respect of effluent limitations for this industry are set out in Schedule I.[160] Thus, any effluent arising from this industry shall be deemed non-compliant and polluted if:

(a) the concentration of any of its parameters exceeds the permissible limits as specified in first column of Schedule 1 aforesaid.
(b) it does not comply with corresponding limit specified in the second or third column of Schedule 1 to these Regulations.
(c) it is discharged from a facility without treatment.[161]

Arising from the above, under regulation 17,[162] no facility shall discharge effluent onto land, into a watercourse or into a water body unless the facility ensures that the parameters of the effluent do not exceed the permissible limits specified in Schedule 1.[163] To this end, facilities that discharge effluent into the environment shall treat the effluent to a permissible level to ensure assimilation by the receiving medium. It is therefore an offence for any person to release effluent and sludge or to fail to report the release of effluent and sludge into the environment in excess of the permissible level in these Regulations.[164] An offence is also committed where any person fails to take reasonable measures to prevent, reduce or remedy the adverse effects of effluent, sludge and emissions into the environment.[165]

Any person who violates any of the provisions of regulation 50 of these Regulations commits an offence and shall, on conviction, be liable to a fine of ₦200,000 or imprisonment for 2 years or both such fine and imprisonment. In addition, the offender shall be liable to an additional fine of ₦5000 for each day the offence

[157] Government Notice No. 289, S.I. No. 36. Federal Republic of Nigeria Official Gazette No. 68 Vol. 96, 10 October 2009.

[158] National Environmental (Chemical, Pharmaceutical, Soap and Detergent Manufacturing Industries) Regulations (2009). Similar to the definition in the National Environmental (Mining and Process of Coal, Ores and Industrial Minerals) Regulations (2009), regulation 56.

[159] National Environmental (Chemical, Pharmaceutical, Soap and Detergent Manufacturing Industries) Regulations (2009), regulation 54.

[160] National Environmental (Chemical, Pharmaceutical, Soap and Detergent Manufacturing Industries) Regulations (2009).

[161] Ibid., regulation 16.

[162] National Environmental (Chemical, Pharmaceutical, Soap and Detergent Manufacturing Industries) Regulations (2009).

[163] Ibid.

[164] Ibid., regulation 50.

[165] National Environmental (Chemical, Pharmaceutical, Soap and Detergent Manufacturing Industries) Regulations (2009).

subsists. Where the offender is a body corporate, the fine shall be ₦1,000,000 and an additional fine of ₦50,000 each day the offence subsists.[166]

In addition to the above liabilities and in line with the polluter-pays principle, regulation 5 of the Regulations provides that the collection, treatment, transportation and final disposal of wastes within the specified standards and guidelines shall be the responsibility of the facility generating the waste.[167]

16.2.2.5.2.4 National Environmental (Food, Beverages and Tobacco Sector) Regulations 2009

For the food, beverage and tobacco sector, the National Environmental (Food, Beverages and Tobacco Sector) Regulations 2009[168] set out the effluent limitation. In respect of this industry, effluent is defined as 'waste water treated or untreated; that flows out of a treatment plant, sewer, or industrial outfall resulting from the commercial or industrial use of water, generally to as waste discharged into surface waters'.[169] National environmental standards in respect of effluent limitations for this industry are set out in Schedule 1 to these Regulations. To this end, any effluent arising from this industry shall be deemed non-compliant and polluted if:

(a) the concentration of any of its parameters exceeds the permissible limits as specified in first column of Schedule 1 aforesaid.
(b) it does not comply with corresponding limit specified in the second or third column of Schedule 1 to these Regulations.
(c) it is discharged from a facility without treatment.[170]

Based on the above, no facility shall discharge effluent onto land, into a water-course or into a water body unless the facility ensures that the parameters of the effluent do not exceed the permissible limits specified in Schedule 1 to these Regulations.[171] Therefore, facilities that discharge effluent into the environment shall treat the effluent to a permissible level to ensure assimilation by the receiving medium. It is therefore an offence for any person to release effluent and sludge or to fail to report the release of effluent and sludge into the environment in excess of the permissible level in these Regulations. An offence is also committed where any

---

[166] National Environmental (Chemical, Pharmaceutical, Soap and Detergent Manufacturing Industries) Regulations (2009), regulation 51.

[167] Other aspects of these provisions are similar to the National Environmental (Mining and Process of Coal, Ores and Industrial Minerals) Regulations (2009), regulation 5, with regard to the subject matter (polluter-pays principle).

[168] Government Notice No. 286, S.I. No. 33. Federal Republic of Nigeria Official Gazette No. 65 Vol. 96, 14 October 2009.

[169] National Environmental (Food, Beverages and Tobacco Sector) Regulations (2009), regulation 54.

[170] Ibid., regulation 15.

[171] Ibid., regulation 16.

person fails to take reasonable measures to prevent, reduce or remedy the adverse effect of effluent, sludge and emissions into the environment.[172]

Thus, any person who violates any of the provisions of regulation 48 of these Regulations commits an offence and shall, on conviction, be liable to a fine of ₦200,000 or imprisonment for 2 years or both such fine and imprisonment. In addition, the offender shall be liable to an additional fine of ₦5000 for each day the offence subsists. Where the offender is a body corporate, the fine shall be ₦1,000,000 and an additional fine of ₦50,000 each day the offence subsists.[173]

In line with the polluter-pays principle, regulation 5 of these Regulations provides that the collection, treatment, transportation and final disposal of wastes within the specified standards and guidelines shall be the responsibility of the facility generating the waste.[174]

In addition to the above-discussed specific provisions under the Regulations,[175] as they affect the different industrial sectors, every facility shall carry out effective treatment of effluent and sludge all the time that the plant or unit is operating, ensure environmentally sound management of sludge containing heavy metals or other toxins and dispose of the same in landfills or any designated disposal site approved by the Agency. Thus, wastes that contain toxic organics shall be subjected to thermal treatment to effectively destroy or remove 99.99% of toxic organics, and the resulting residuals shall be disposed of as set out under the Regulations.[176]

---

[172] National Environmental (Food, Beverages and Tobacco Sector) Regulations (2009), regulation 48.

[173] National Environmental (Food, Beverages and Tobacco Sector) Regulations (2009), regulation 49.

[174] Other aspects of these provisions are similar to the National Environmental (Mining and Process of Coal, Ores and Industrial Minerals) Regulations 2009, regulation 5, with regard to the subject matter (polluter-pays principle).

[175] National Environmental (Mining and Process of Coal, Ores and Industrial Minerals) Regulations (2009).

National Environmental (Textile, Wearing Apparel, Leather and Footwear Industry) Regulations (2009).

National Environmental (Chemical, Pharmaceutical, Soap and Detergent Manufacturing Industries) Regulations (2009) and National Environmental (Food, Beverages and Tobacco Sector) Regulations (2009).

[176] National Environmental (Textile, Wearing Apparel, Leather and Footwear Industry) Regulations (2009), regulation 17; National Environmental (Chemical, Pharmaceutical, Soap and Detergent Manufacturing Industries) Regulations (2009), regulation 18; and National Environmental (Food, Beverages and Tobacco Sector) Regulations (2009), regulation 17.

16.2.2.5.2.5 *National Environmental (Base Metal, Iron and Steel Manufacturing/Recycling Industries Sector) Regulations 2011*

The main thrust of the National Environmental (Base Metal, Iron and Steel Manufacturing/Recycling Industries Sector) Regulations 2011[177] is to prevent and minimise pollution from all operations and ancillary activities of the sector.[178] The Regulations require all facilities to provide pollution abatement equipment.[179] In order to minimise waste generation, the Regulations require operators of facilities to engage in best practices in waste minimisation by ensuring that pollution prevention programmes are directed towards the observance of the five Rs (reduce, repair, reuse, recycle and recover)[180] as well as the efficient practice of reduction and recycling of water.[181]

The Regulations[182] also provide for effluent limitation and[183] restrictions on the release of toxic effluent[184] and encourage engagement in effluent treatment[185] and the treatment of sludge before disposal.[186] In addition, the Regulations[187] provide for effluent levels for metal manufacturing industries[188] as well as effluent pollution abatement measures.[189]

Under the Regulations,[190] it shall be an offence where a facility contravenes permit conditions,[191] makes a false statement to the Agency,[192] fails to comply with abatement measures[193] and discharges effluent beyond the permissible level.[194]

[177] Government Notice No. 127, S.I. No. 14. Federal Republic of Nigeria Official Gazette No. 41 Vol. 98, 4 May 2011.

[178] National Environmental (Base Metal, Iron and Steel Manufacturing/Recycling Industries Sector) Regulations (2011), regulation 1.

[179] Ibid., regulation 5.

[180] National Environmental (Base Metal, Iron and Steel Manufacturing/Recycling Industries Sector) Regulations (2011), regulation 7(1).

[181] National Environmental (Base Metal, Iron and Steel Manufacturing/Recycling Industries Sector) Regulations (2011), regulation 7(2)(b).

[182] National Environmental (Base Metal, Iron and Steel Manufacturing/Recycling Industries Sector) Regulations (2011).

[183] Ibid., regulation 17.

[184] Ibid., regulation 18.

[185] Ibid., regulation 19.

[186] Ibid., regulation 20(1).

[187] National Environmental (Base Metal, Iron and Steel Manufacturing/Recycling Industries Sector) Regulations (2011).

[188] Ibid., sch I.

[189] Ibid., sch. VIII.

[190] National Environmental (Base Metal, Iron and Steel Manufacturing/Recycling Industries Sector) Regulations (2011).

[191] Ibid., regulation 50.

[192] Ibid., regulation 51.

[193] Ibid., regulation 52.

[194] Ibid., regulation 54.

Penalties are provided under regulation 56.[195] The Regulations also have provisions for the application of the polluter-pays principle.[196]

16.2.2.5.2.6 National Environmental (Domestic and Industrial Plastic Rubber and Foam Sector) Regulations 2011

The main thrust of the National Environmental (Domestic and Industrial Plastic Rubber and Foam Sector) Regulations 2011[197] is to prevent and minimise pollution to the Nigerian environment from all operations and ancillary activities of the domestic and industrial plastic rubber and foam sector.[198] The Regulations require all facilities to provide pollution abatement equipment.[199] In order to minimise waste generation, the Regulations require operators of facilities to engage in best practices in waste minimisation and ensure that pollution prevention programmes focus on reduction in the use of water and more efficient use of process chemicals.[200]

The Regulations[201] also provide for effluent limitations[202] as well as restrictions on the release of toxic effluent[203] and encourage engagement in effluent treatment[204] and the treatment of sludge before disposal.[205] In addition, the Regulations[206] provide for effluent limitation standards for plastic and rubber manufacturing industries,[207] effluent limitation standards for petroleum-based polymer industries,[208] pollution prevention and control techniques[209] as well as sludge disposal permissible limit.[210]

---

[195] The penalties are similar to those set out under the NESREA Act (2007), s. 24 (4).

[196] National Environmental (Base Metal, Iron and Steel Manufacturing/Recycling Industries Sector) Regulations (2011), regulation 6, similar to the provisions of the National Environmental (Mining and Process of Coal, Ores and Industrial Minerals) Regulations (2009), regulation 5.

[197] Government Notice No. 131, S.I. No. 17. Federal Republic of Nigeria Official Gazette No. 44 Vol. 98, 5 May 2011.

[198] National Environmental (Domestic and Industrial Plastic Rubber and Foam Sector) Regulations (2011), regulation 2.

[199] Ibid., regulation 5.

[200] Ibid., regulation 7(2)(b).

[201] National Environmental (Domestic and Industrial Plastic Rubber and Foam Sector) Regulations (2011).

[202] Ibid., regulation 17.

[203] Ibid., regulation 18.

[204] Ibid., regulation 19.

[205] Ibid., regulation 20(1).

[206] National Environmental (Domestic and Industrial Plastic Rubber and Foam Sector) Regulations (2011).

[207] Ibid., sch. 1.

[208] Ibid., sch. IV.

[209] Ibid., sch. VII.

[210] Ibid., sch. XIV.

Under the Regulations,[211] it shall be an offence where a facility contravenes permit conditions,[212] makes a false statement to the Agency,[213] uses banned chemicals,[214] fails to comply with abatement measures,[215] fails to maintain records of all discharges and file quarterly and annual reports of all discharges[216] and discharges effluent beyond the permissible level.[217] Penalties are provided under regulation 55. The Regulations also have provisions for the application of the polluter-pays principle.[218]

16.2.2.5.2.7 National Environmental (Non-Metallic Minerals Manufacturing Industries Sector) Regulations 2011

The National Environmental (Non-Metallic Minerals Manufacturing Industries Sector) Regulations 2011[219] is yet another set of regulations that have provisions for setting standards to protect and enhance water quality in Nigeria. The main thrust of the National Environmental (Non-Metallic Minerals Manufacturing Industries Sector) Regulations 2011 is to prevent and minimise pollution from all operations and ancillary activities of the non-metallic minerals manufacturing industries sector to the Nigerian environment.[220]

The Regulations[221] provide that every facility within the sector shall install pollution abatement equipment to enable such facility to engage in effective effluent and emission discharges so as to meet the prescribed effluent and emission discharge permissible limits.[222] Again, all facilities shall have a number of built-in pollution control features for the dry process precalciner.[223]

---

[211] National Environmental (Domestic and Industrial Plastic Rubber and Foam Sector) Regulations (2011).

[212] Ibid., regulation 49.

[213] Ibid., regulation 50.

[214] Ibid., regulation 51.

[215] Ibid., regulation 52.

[216] Ibid., regulation 53.

[217] Ibid., regulation 54.

[218] National Environmental (Domestic and Industrial Plastic Rubber and Foam Sector) Regulations (2011), regulation 6, similar to the provisions of the National Environmental (Mining and Process of Coal, Ores and Industrial Minerals) Regulations (2009), regulation 5.

[219] Government Notice No. 134, S.I. No. 21. Federal Republic of Nigeria Official Gazette No. 48 Vol. 98, 23 May 2011.

[220] National Environmental (Non-Metallic Minerals Manufacturing Industries Sector) Regulations (2011), regulation 1.

[221] National Environmental (Non-Metallic Minerals Manufacturing Industries Sector) Regulations (2011).

[222] Ibid., regulation 5.

[223] Ibid., regulation 8.

In order to minimise waste generation, the Regulations[224] require operators of facilities to engage in best practices in waste minimisation and ensure the creation of pollution prevention programmes, including the application of 5Rs.[225] Operators of such facilities are therefore enjoined to employ cleaner production processes and pollution prevention measures that would yield both economic and environmental benefits.[226]

The Regulations[227] also provide for effluent limitations[228] as well as restrictions on the release of toxic effluent[229] and encourage engagement in effluent treatment[230] and the treatment of sludge before disposal.[231] Other provisions for enhancing water quality standards in Nigeria include provisions on the maximum permissible effluent level for ceramics and tile manufacturing,[232] cement and lime manufacturing[233] and glass manufacturing[234] and sludge disposal permissible limits.[235]

Under the Regulations,[236] it shall be an offence where a facility contravenes permit conditions,[237] makes a false statement to the Agency,[238] fails to comply with abatement measures,[239] fails to maintain records of all discharges and file quarterly and annual reports of all discharges[240] and discharges effluent beyond the permissible level.[241] Penalties are provided under regulation 62.[242]

---

[224] National Environmental (Non-Metallic Minerals Manufacturing Industries Sector) Regulations (2011).

[225] Ibid., regulation 7(2).

[226] Ibid., regulation 7(3).

[227] National Environmental (Non-Metallic Minerals Manufacturing Industries Sector) Regulations (2011).

[228] Ibid., regulation 18.

[229] Ibid., regulation 19.

[230] Ibid., regulation 20.

[231] Ibid., regulation 21.

[232] Ibid., sch. I.

[233] National Environmental (Non-Metallic Minerals Manufacturing Industries Sector) Regulations (2011), sch. II.

[234] Ibid., sch. III.

[235] Ibid., sch. X.

[236] National Environmental (Non-Metallic Minerals Manufacturing Industries Sector) Regulations (2011).

[237] Ibid., regulation 57.

[238] Ibid., regulation 58.

[239] Ibid., regulation 59.

[240] Ibid., regulation 60.

[241] Ibid., regulation 61.

[242] National Environmental (Non-Metallic Minerals Manufacturing Industries Sector) Regulations (2011).

16.2.2.5.2.8 National Environmental (Pulp and Paper, Wood and Wood Products Sector) Regulations 2013

The National Environmental (Pulp and Paper, Wood and Wood Products Sector) Regulations 2013[243] is yet another set of regulations that have provisions for setting water quality standards and for the protection of Nigeria's water resources. The main thrust of the Regulations[244] is to prevent and minimise pollution from all operations and ancillary activities of the pulp and paper, wood and wood product sector.[245]

The Regulations[246] require all facilities to provide pollution abatement equipment.[247] In order to minimise waste generation, the Regulations require operators of facilities to engage in best practices in waste minimisation by ensuring that pollution prevention programmes are directed towards the use of the 5Rs[248] as well as engagement in pollution prevention programmes that shall focus on reduction in the use of water and more efficient use of process chemicals.[249]

The Regulations[250] also provide for effluent limitations[251] as well as restrictions on the release of toxic effluent[252] and encourage engagement in effluent treatment[253] and the treatment of sludge before disposal.[254] In addition, the Regulations[255] provide for effluent limitation standards[256] and sludge disposal.[257]

Under the Regulations,[258] it shall be an offence where a facility contravenes permit conditions,[259] makes a false statement to the Agency,[260] fails to comply with

---

[243] Government Notice No. 214, S.I. No. 34. Federal Republic of Nigeria Official Gazette No. 98 Vol. 100, 1 November 2013.

[244] National Environmental (Pulp and Paper, Wood and Wood Products Sector) Regulations (2013).

[245] Ibid., regulation 1.

[246] National Environmental (Pulp and Paper, Wood and Wood Products Sector) Regulations (2013).

[247] Ibid., regulation 6.

[248] Ibid., regulation 8(1). 5Rs as stated under this regulation means reduce, repair, reuse, recycle and recover.

[249] Ibid., regulation 8(3).

[250] National Environmental (Pulp and Paper, Wood and Wood Products Sector) Regulations (2013) (or 'Environmental Regulations 2013').

[251] Ibid., regulation 23.

[252] Ibid., regulation 24.

[253] Ibid., regulation 25.

[254] National Environmental (Pulp and Paper, Wood and Wood Products Sector) Regulations (2013), regulation 26.

[255] National Environmental (Pulp and Paper, Wood and Wood Products Sector) Regulations (2013).

[256] Ibid., sch. I.

[257] Ibid., sch. II.

[258] National Environmental (Pulp and Paper, Wood and Wood Products Sector) Regulations (2013).

[259] Ibid., regulation 55.

[260] Ibid., regulation 56.

abatement measures[261] and discharges effluent beyond the permissible level.[262] Operating without a permit is also an offence under the Regulations.[263] Penalties are provided under regulation 61.

16.2.2.5.2.9 National Environmental (Energy Sector) Regulations 2014

The National Environmental (Energy Sector) Regulations 2014[264] is yet another set of Regulations that have provisions for setting water quality standards and for the protection of Nigeria's water resources. The main purpose of the Regulations[265] is to prevent and minimise pollution and encourage energy efficiency in all operations and ancillary activities of the energy sector in achieving sustainable economic development in Nigeria.[266]

The Regulations[267] require all facilities to install anti-pollution abatement equipment,[268] prohibit the discharge of hazardous waste on water or land without prior treatment,[269] provide for effluent limitations[270] encourage the treatment of sludge before disposal[271] and place restrictions on the release of toxic effluent.[272]

Under the Regulations,[273] it shall be an offence where a facility contravenes the operator's conditions;[274] contravenes permit conditions;[275] makes a false statement to the Agency;[276] fails to comply with guidelines, standards[277] and abatement measures;[278] fails to maintain records of all discharges and file quarterly and annual

[261] Ibid., regulation 57.

[262] Ibid., regulation 59.

[263] Ibid., regulation 60.

[264] Government Notice No. 254, S.I. No. 63. Federal Republic of Nigeria Official Gazette No. 141, Vol. 102, 22 December 2014.

[265] National Environmental (Energy Sector) Regulations (2014).

[266] Ibid., regulation 1(1).

[267] National Environmental (Energy Sector) Regulations (2014).

[268] Ibid., regulation 8.

[269] National Environmental (Energy Sector) Regulations (2014), regulation 15.

[270] Ibid., regulation 13.

[271] Ibid., regulation 16.

[272] Ibid., regulation 14.

[273] National Environmental (Energy Sector) Regulations (2014).

[274] Ibid., regulation 44.

[275] Ibid., regulation 45.

[276] Ibid., regulation 46.

[277] Ibid., regulation 47.

[278] Ibid., regulation 48.

reports of all discharges;[279] or discharges effluent beyond the permissible level.[280] Penalties are provided under regulation 51.[281]

16.2.2.5.3 Control of Hazardous Substances in Nigeria

Discharging harmful quantities of any hazardous substance into the air or upon land and the waters of Nigeria or the adjoining shorelines is an offence under section 27 of the NESREA Act 2007.[282] A number of Regulations to this effect have been made by the Minister charged with environmental protection.[283]

16.2.2.5.4 Nigeria's Efforts at Biodiversity Conservation[284]

Biodiversity, according to regulation 25 of the National Environmental (Access to Genetic Resources and Benefit Sharing) Regulations 2009,[285] means 'the variability among living organisms from all sources of the ecosystems and the ecological complexes of which they are part of, this includes diversity within species, between species and the ecosystem'.

In the past years since the Rio De Janeiro Conference in 1992 and the ratification of the Convention on Biodiversity 1992, Nigeria has made rather bold efforts towards biodiversity conservation. These steps relate to the strengthening of policy, legislative and institutional frameworks and the implementation of intervention measures aimed at the conservation of biological diversity, the sustainable utilisation of its components and the equitable sharing of benefits.

On the policy level, Nigeria is committed to a national policy on the environment aimed at achieving development. In particular, the policy is to secure a quality environment that is adequate for good health and well-being, conserve and use the environment and natural resources for the benefit of present and future generations and restore, maintain and enhance the ecosystems and ecological processes for the conservation of biological diversity.[286] The policy[287] touches on areas such as

---

[279] Ibid., regulation 49.

[280] Ibid., regulation 50.

[281] National Environmental Regulations (2014).

[282] It is also an offence to do so under the HWSCP Act (1988), s. 1.

[283] These pieces of legislation are discussed in Sect. 9.6.2 of Chap. 9 of this book.

[284] Nigeria has made efforts at the protection of other environmental media using international instruments, but none is as elaborate as in the area of biodiversity, thus the necessity to analyse such efforts.

[285] Government Notice No. 283, S.I. 30. Federal Republic of Nigeria Official Gazette No. 62 Vol. 96, 9 October 2009.

[286] US Agency for International Development (USAID) (2002).

[287] National Policy on Environment. See Federal Republic of Nigeria (1999).

identifying implementation strategies on human population, culture, housing and human settlements. Strategies for biological diversity, natural resource conservation, land use and soil conservation, agriculture and water resources were given prominence.

The implementation strategies also cover such sections as wildlife, marine and coastal area resources, mining and mineral resources, industry, energy, oil and gas, construction, health, education, transport and communication systems, trade and tourism, science and technology, natural disasters and desertification, flood and erosion. Other aspects of the policy include sanitation and waste management; toxic, hazardous and radioactive substances; air pollution; the working environment; public participation; institutional arrangements; funding mechanisms; and monitoring and evaluation. Other policies directly relevant to biodiversity conservation are those on agriculture, integrated rural development, and forestry and water resources.[288]

Nigeria also has a number of legislative frameworks for the protection of the Nigerian environment in general and the protection of its biodiversity resources in particular. However, major legislation in this respect is the National Environmental (Access to Genetic Resources and Benefit Sharing) Regulations 2009.[289] The Regulations are divided into five parts, namely conservation monitoring,[290] access to genetic resources,[291] benefit sharing,[292] miscellaneous[293] and general.[294]

As part of the efforts to conserve and protect the biodiversity resources of Nigeria, the Regulations prohibit any person from engaging in any activity that has an adverse impact on any ecosystem and leads to the introduction of any exotic species[295] that may lead to the unsustainable use of natural resources without conducting an environmental impact assessment (EIA).[296] Any contravention of this requirement by any person amounts to an offence under regulation 2[297] and is punishable under regulation 23.[298] Under regulation 23, such a person is liable, on conviction, to a fine of not less than ₦1,000,000 but not exceeding ₦10,000,000 or to imprisonment for a term not exceeding 1 year or to both such fine and

[288] Federal Republic of Nigeria (1999).

[289] National Environmental (Access to Genetic Resources and Benefit Sharing) Regulations (2009).

[290] Ibid., part I.

[291] Ibid., part II.

[292] Ibid., part III.

[293] Ibid., part IV.

[294] Ibid., part V.

[295] Under the National Environmental (Access to Genetic Resources and Benefit Sharing) Regulations (2009), regulation 25, exotic species means any species of plants, animals or microorganisms whose natural range does not or did not in the past exist in a specific part or the whole of Nigeria.

[296] National Environmental (Access to Genetic Resources and Benefit Sharing) Regulations (2009), regulation 1.

[297] National Environmental (Access to Genetic Resources and Benefit Sharing) Regulations (2009).

[298] Ibid.

imprisonment and to an additional fine of ₦100,000 for every day the offence subsists.[299] Where the offence is committed by a body corporate, it shall, on conviction, be liable to a fine not less than ₦10,000,000 but not exceeding ₦100,000,000 and an additional fine of ₦1,000,000 for every day the offence subsists.[300]

Besides the EIA requirements as a means for conservation, the Regulations[301] require that the Agency,[302] in consultation with other relevant agencies, shall impose a ban or restriction or similar measures on the access and use of any threatened species in order to ensure its regeneration and sustainable use.[303] To this end, an inventory of biological diversity resources is to be maintained and updated[304] and the status of such species to be monitored.[305]

In addition, the Regulations provide for the control of access to genetic resources in Nigeria. Access to genetic resources in this context means obtaining, processing and using genetic resources conserved, whether derived products and where applicable intangible components for purposes of research, bio-prospecting, conservation, industrial application and commercial use.[306] Thus, any person who intends to access genetic resources in Nigeria shall apply to the Agency for an access permit.[307] The application shall be accompanied by evidence of prior informed consent (PIC),[308] as prescribed under the Regulations.[309] The Agency shall, within 60 days of receipt of such application, determine the application and communicate its decision to the applicant.[310] Furthermore, no person shall transfer any genetic

[299] Ibid., regulation 23(1).

[300] Ibid., regulation 23(2).

[301] National Environmental (Access to Genetic Resources and Benefit Sharing) Regulations (2009).

[302] NESREA.

[303] National Environmental (Access to Genetic Resources and Benefit Sharing) Regulations (2009), regulation 2(1).

[304] Ibid., regulation 3.

[305] Ibid., regulation 4.

[306] National Environmental (Access to Genetic Resources and Benefit Sharing) Regulations (2009), regulation 25.

[307] Prior informed consent (PIC) means consent given to the applicant for an access permit by the academic or research institute or relevant agency or concerned local community based on an access application containing a complete and accurate information on a person seeking access to a specified genetic resource or traditional knowledge. See the National Environmental (Access to Genetic Resources and Benefit Sharing) Regulations (2009), regulation 25.

[308] National Environmental (Access to Genetic Resources and Benefit Sharing) Regulations (2009), regulation 5.

[309] Ibid., regulation 6.

[310] Ibid., regulation 12.

resources outside Nigeria unless such person has executed a Material Transfer Agreement[311] (MTA).[312]

The Regulations[313] also provide for the benefit sharing of biodiversity resources. Benefit sharing connotes the sharing of benefits that accrue from the utilisation of genetic resources. To this end, the Agency shall ensure that the holder of the access permit facilitates the active involvement of Nigerian citizens and institutions in the execution of the activities under the access permit.[314] In addition, the Agency shall also ensure that the holder of the access permit shall, at all times, respect traditional and community rights over ownership and custody of genetic resources including the collective rights to benefit, accruing knowledge, innovation, discoveries, uses and practices acquired over time and for the conservation and sustainable use of the genetic resources.[315]

Taken together, Nigeria's priority action plan for biodiversity conservation is to:

(i) Decrease gas flaring: the private sector, with appropriate economic incentives, could capitalize on opportunities aimed especially at the energy and agricultural sectors.
(ii) Protect marine and coastal resources: Nigeria should proactively pursue a cohesive process with other sub-Saharan African countries to address the trans-boundary issues that threaten these resources.
(iii) Halt desertification: in the northern and central states, coordinated physical, biological, educational and political actions are needed to stop this threat.
(iv) Mitigate industrial and urban pollution: the health and quality of life of almost half of the nation's population are threatened by the decreasing quality of water, air and soil resources in urban areas.
(v) Reduce land-based sources of pollution of the marine environment: vegetative and fishery resources along Nigeria's 879 km of coastline are increasingly threatened by pollutants entering the country's air and watersheds.
(vi) Protect against the detrimental effects of exotic species: invasive species such as Nypa palm and water hyacinth are effectively undercutting economic activities and compromising the ecological systems associated with native species.
(vii) Stop gully erosion and provide shoreline protection: erosion is widespread throughout the country. Management of mine tailings, stream banks and floodplains, coastal shorelines and agricultural lands require immediate and more aggressive attention.

---

[311] Ibid., regulation 7.

[312] A material transfer agreement (MTA) is an agreement on access to genetic resources and benefit sharing negotiated between the holder of an access permit and a relevant agency or community. See the National Environmental (Access to Genetic Resources and Benefit Sharing) Regulations (2009), regulation 25.

[313] National Environmental (Access to Genetic Resources and Benefit Sharing) Regulations (2009).

[314] Ibid., regulation 18.

[315] Ibid., regulation 19.

(viii) Conserve biodiversity: sustainable resource management practices need to be more carefully adhered to in order to conserve and protect the nation's diminishing flora and fauna diversity.

(ix) Ensure food security: Nigeria's diminishing agricultural land base needs to be aggressively conserved, and programmes promoting biotechnology must be carefully scrutinized for potential negative impacts.

(x) Improve the management of protected areas and national parks: human encroachment should be prevented in Nigeria's protected areas, and these areas need to be managed cooperatively with local populations in order for them to yield their maximum benefit to the nation and the region.[316]

16.2.2.5.5 Other Aspects of Protection of the Environment Under the NESREA Act 2007

The NESREA Act empowers the Agency to make regulations, guidelines and standards for the protection and enhancement of the quality of land resources, natural watersheds, coastal zones, dams and reservoirs, including the prevention of flood and erosion.[317] A person who violates the provisions of the regulations made pursuant to the above provisions commits an offence and shall, on conviction, be liable to a fine not exceeding ₦200,000 or to imprisonment for a term not exceeding 1 year or to both such fine and imprisonment and an additional fine of ₦10,000 for every day the offence subsists.[318] Where the offence is committed by a body corporate, it shall, on conviction, be liable to a fine not exceeding ₦1,000,000 and an additional fine of ₦50,000 for every day the offence subsists.[319]

Pursuant to those powers vested on the Agency under section 26(1) and the powers vested on the Minister in charge of environmental matters under section 34, a number of regulations were made for the protection of wetlands, river banks and lake shores, watersheds, and mountainous, hilly and catchment areas; for soil erosion and flood control; for desertification control and drought mitigation; and for coastal and marine area protection. These Regulations include the:

(i) National Environmental (Watershed, Mountainous, Hilly and Catchment Areas) Regulations 2009

(ii) National Environmental (Wetlands, River Banks and Lake Shores) Regulations 2009[320]

(iii) National Environmental (Soil Erosion and Flood Control) Regulations 2011

---

[316] Adapted from the report submitted by the Hon. Minister of State of the Federal Ministry of Environment to USAID (2002).

[317] NESREA Act (2007), s. 26(1).

[318] NESREA Act (2007), s. 26(3).

[319] Ibid., s. 26(4).

[320] These Regulations were discussed under 'Conservation of Wetlands' in Sect. 14.6.2.1 of Chap. 14 of this book.

(iv) National Environmental (Desertification Control and Drought Mitigation) Regulations 2011, and
(v) National Environmental (Coastal and Marine Area Protection) Regulations 2011[321]

16.2.2.5.5.1 National Environmental (Watershed, Mountainous, Hilly and Catchment Areas) Regulations 2009

The National Environmental (Watershed, Mountainous, Hilly and Catchment Areas) Regulations 2009[322] enjoin every landowner or occupier, while utilising land in a watershed or mountainous, hilly or catchment area, shall observe and respect the carrying capacity of the land, carry out soil conservation measures, carry out measures for the protection of water catchment areas, use the best available environmentally friendly technologies to minimise significant risks and damage to ecological and landscape aspects and maintain adequate vegetation cover.[323] In addition, the Agency shall, with respect to watersheds and mountainous, hilly and catchment areas in a particular environment, control activities that are inconsistent with good land management practices, especially in areas prone to landslides, floods, drought, desertification, siltation, heavy sediment loads, falling rocks, fires and damage by wind.[324]

For effective management, the Agency, in conjunction with states and local governments, shall identify watersheds and mountainous, hilly and catchment areas within each state jurisdiction and indicate those that are at risk of degradation.[325] Under regulation 2(2), a watershed or a mountainous, hilly or catchment area is at risk of environmental degradation and exhibits any of the following characteristics: it is prone to point and non-point pollution, there are unsustainable intensive irrigation practices in the area, there is large-scale deforestation and over-cultivation at a rate faster than the regeneration of vegetation and nutrient replenishment, there is overgrazing, it is prone to soil erosion and flooding, landslides and mudslides have occurred in such an area, over-exploitation of water resources has occurred in such an area and any other land-use activity in such an area is likely to lead to environmental degradation.

As a way of preventing a watershed or mountainous, hilly or catchment area from being at risk of environmental degradation, any person desiring to graze livestock, establish a camping or other recreational facilities for tourist purposes, plant or

---

[321] These Regulations were discussed under 'Conservation of Wetlands' in section 14.6.2.2 of Chap. 14 of this book.

[322] Government Notice No. 280, S.I. No. 27. Federal Republic of Nigeria Official Gazette No. 59 Vol. 96, 5 October 2009.

[323] National Environmental (Watershed, Mountainous, Hilly and Catchment Areas) Regulations 2009), regulation 1(1).

[324] National Environmental (Watershed, Mountainous, Hilly and Catchment Areas) Regulations 2009), regulation 1(2).

[325] Ibid., regulation 2(1).

cultivate crops, carry out mining activities or carry out any development activity requiring an environmental impact assessment (EIA) in a watershed or mountainous, hilly or catchment area shall submit an application to the Agency. Such application shall be endorsed by the chairman of the local government area where the intended activity is to be performed.[326]

Again, the Agency, in collaboration with relevant federal, state and local government bodies, communities and other stakeholders, shall ensure that no individual, group of persons or corporation shall enter into any watershed or mountainous, hilly or catchment area for the following activities: logging, dredging, bush burning, disposal of any waste and any other land use that may cause land degradation in such area, such as agricultural practices, grazing and mining.[327] To this end, the Agency, in collaboration with the state, shall restrict grazing in such areas that are identified as threatened by environmental degradation.[328] Thus, a person shall not cause or permit any livestock belonging to him or under his control to graze on any watershed or mountainous, hilly or catchment area in respect of which there is in force an order made by the Agency prohibiting grazing.[329] In this regard, an offence is committed where such a person causes or permits any livestock belonging to him or under his control to graze on any such watershed or mountainous, hilly or catchment area.[330]

In addition, where a watershed or mountainous, hilly or catchment area is at risk of environmental degradation, the Agency, in collaboration with the state, local government council and other stakeholders may issue an order in writing to a person or persons holding interest in land in the affected area to plant trees and other vegetation as well as take appropriate measures to protect the area.[331]

Furthermore, every landowner, occupier or user whose land is situated in a watershed or mountainous, hilly or catchment area shall take measures to reduce water run-off through the gassing of medium and steep slopes; mulch and bund gardens on medium and steep slopes; practice agroforestry; prevent the burning of grass in areas of intensive agriculture or on steep slopes; prevent pollution of the river, streams, lakes or other water bodies; and prevent the use of harmful pesticides within designated watershed areas.[332] To this end, no person shall set fire to a forest (natural or man-made), grassland, watershed or mountainous, hilly and catchment area.[333]

---

[326] Ibid., regulation 4 (a)–(e).

[327] Ibid., regulation 5 (1) (a)–(e).

[328] National Environmental (Watershed, Mountainous, Hilly and Catchment Areas) Regulations 2009), regulation 9(1).

[329] National Environmental (Watershed, Mountainous, Hilly and Catchment Areas) Regulations 2009), regulation 9(4).

[330] Ibid., regulation 9(5).

[331] Ibid., regulation 8 (1).

[332] Ibid., regulation 5(5)(a)–(f).

[333] Ibid., regulation 6.

Any person who contravenes any of the provisions of these Regulations may have his permit revoked, if he is a permittee,[334] or shall be liable, upon conviction, to imprisonment of not more than 1 year or a fine of not more than ₦200,000 or both.[335] And in the case of afforestation and deforestation, the violator shall be liable, on conviction, to imprisonment for a term not exceeding six (6) months or a fine not less than ₦50,000 or both.[336] Where an offence is committed by a corporate body, it shall, on conviction, be liable to a fine not exceeding ₦1,000,000 and an additional fine of ₦50,000 for every day the offence subsists.[337]

16.2.2.5.5.2 National Environmental (Soil Erosion and Flood Control) Regulations 2011

The objectives of the National Environmental (Soil Erosion and Flood Control) Regulations 2011[338] touch on the following:

(i) the protection of human life and the environment;[339]
(ii) minimizing losses due to flood and erosion and their effects on vulnerable areas by regulating land disturbing activities[340] and
(iii) control accelerated soil erosion, flood and sediment deposition in water bodies and water courses in order to prevent pollution of these water resources.[341]

To achieve these objectives, the Regulations set out erosion control measures under Part II[342] and flood control mechanisms under Part III, comprising regulations 14–18.

Any violations of any of the provisions of these regulations amount to an offence under regulation 19. Penalties are also provided under the same regulation. Where the offence is committed by an individual, he shall, on conviction, be liable to a fine not exceeding ₦1,000,000 or imprisonment not exceeding 2 years or both fine and imprisonment and, in addition, a fine of ₦10,000 for each day the offence subsists.[343]

---

[334] Ibid., regulation 10(1)(a).

[335] Ibid., regulation 10(1)(b).

[336] Ibid., regulation 10(2).

[337] National Environmental (Watershed, Mountainous, Hilly and Catchment Areas) Regulations 2009), regulation 10(3).

[338] Government Notice No. 125, S.I. No. 12. Federal Republic of Nigeria Official Gazette No. 39 Vol. 98, 2 May 2011.

[339] National Environmental (Soil Erosion and Flood Control) Regulations (2011), regulation 2(1)(a).

[340] Ibid., regulation 2(1)(b).

[341] Ibid., regulation 2(1)(c).

[342] This part comprises regulations 10–13 (National Environmental (Soil Erosion and Flood Control) Regulations (2011)).

[343] National Environmental (Soil Erosion and Flood Control) Regulations (2011), regulation 19(1).

In the case of a body corporate, it shall, on conviction, be liable to a fine not exceeding ₦5,000,000 and, in addition, a fine of ₦50, 000 for each day the offence subsists.[344] In addition to the above penalties, the offender shall be responsible for the remediation of the damage to the environment and affected properties therein.[345]

16.2.2.5.5.3 The National Environmental (Desertification Control and Drought Mitigation) Regulations 2011

The National Environmental (Desertification Control and Drought Mitigation) Regulations 2011[346] set out, among other things, the following objective: to provide an effective and pragmatic regulatory framework for the sustainable use of all areas affected by desertification and the protection of vulnerable lands.[347]

To achieve this objective, provisions on desertification control were set out under Part II of the Regulations;[348] general provisions on drought mitigation under Part III, comprising regulations 11–13; and provisions on drought mitigation under Part IV, comprising regulations 14–20.

Any violations of any of the provisions of these regulations amount to an offence under regulation 21. Penalties are also provided under the same regulation. Where the offence is committed by an individual, he shall, on conviction, be liable to a fine not exceeding ₦1,000,000 or imprisonment not exceeding 2 years or both fine and imprisonment and, in addition, a fine of ₦10,000 for each day the offence subsists.[349] In the case of a body corporate, it shall, on conviction, be liable to a fine not exceeding ₦5,000,000 and, in addition, to a fine of ₦50,000 for each day the offence subsists.[350] In addition to the above penalties, the offender shall be responsible for the remediation of the damage to the environment and the affected properties therein.[351]

It has been observed that there are divergences between the penalties provided under the parent legislation[352] and the Regulations discussed above.[353]

---

[344] Ibid., regulation 19(2).

[345] Ibid., regulation 19(3).

[346] Government Notice No. 126, S.I. No. 13. Federal Republic of Nigeria Official Gazette No. 40 Vol. 98, 3 May 2011.

[347] National Environmental (Desertification Control and Drought Mitigation) Regulations (2011), regulation 2(a).

[348] This part comprises regulations 4–10 of the National Environmental (Desertification Control and Drought Mitigation) Regulations (2011).

[349] National Environmental (Desertification Control and Drought Mitigation) Regulations (2011), regulation 21(1).

[350] Ibid., regulation 21(2).

[351] Ibid., regulation 21(3).

[352] NESREA Act (2007).

[353] National Environmental (Watershed, Mountainous, Hilly and Catchment Areas) Regulations (2009), National Environmental (Soil Erosion and Flood Control) Regulations (2011) and National Environmental (Desertification Control and Drought Mitigation) Regulations (2011).

The NESREA Act 2017[354] empowers the Agency to make regulations, guidelines and standards for the protection and enhancement of the quality of land resources, natural watersheds, coastal zones, dams and reservoirs, including the prevention of flood and erosion.[355] Pursuant to the aforesaid powers vested on the Agency[356] and exercising the powers vested on the Minister in charge of environmental matters under section 34,[357] the Regulations[358] were made for the purposes above stated.[359] A person who violates the provisions of the Regulations made pursuant to the aforesaid powers vested on the Agency commits an offence and shall, on conviction, be liable, in the case of an individual, to a fine not exceeding ₦200,000 or to imprisonment for a term not exceeding 1 year or to both such fine and imprisonment and to an additional fine of ₦10,000 for every day the offence subsists.[360] In the case of a body corporate, it shall, on conviction, be liable to a fine not exceeding ₦1,000,000 and an additional fine of ₦50,000 for every day the offence subsists.[361]

However, the penalties provided in some of those Regulations[362] are at variance with those provided under section 26(3) and (4) of the NESREA Act 2007. For instance, penalties under the National Environmental (Soil Erosion and Flood Control) Regulations 2011,[363] in the case of an individual, are a fine not exceeding ₦1,000,000 or imprisonment not exceeding 2 years or both fine and imprisonment and, in addition, a fine of ₦10,000 for each day the offence subsists.[364] For a body corporate, the penalties are a fine not exceeding ₦5,000,000 and, in addition, a fine of ₦50,000 for each day the offence subsists.[365] In addition to the above penalties, the offender shall be responsible for the remediation of the damage to the environment and the affected properties therein.[366] In these Regulations, the terms of imprisonment are more than that provided under section 26(3) of the NESREA Act 2007,[367] and the fine is also higher than that provided under 26(3) of the NESREA Act 2007.[368]

---

[354] NESREA Act (2007).

[355] Ibid., s. 26(1).

[356] Ibid., s. 26(1).

[357] NESREA Act (2007).

[358] See note 353, pre.

[359] Under NESREA Act (2007), s. 26(1).

[360] NESREA Act (2007), s. 26(3).

[361] Ibid., s. 26(4).

[362] Ibid.

[363] National Environmental (Soil Erosion and Flood Control) Regulations (2011).

[364] Ibid., regulation 19(1).

[365] Ibid., regulation 19(2).

[366] Ibid., regulation 19(3).

[367] Here, imprisonment is for a term of 1 year, as against the 2 years provided under the Regulations.

[368] Here, the fine is ₦200,000 and ₦1,000,000 for individuals and body corporate, respectively, as against the fine of ₦1,000,000 and ₦5,000,000 for individuals and body corporate, respectively, provided under the Regulations.

The same scenario of disparity between the penalties under the NESREA Act 2007 and the penalties under the Regulations plays out in the case of the National Environmental (Desertification Control and Drought Mitigation) Regulations 2011.[369] Here, the penalties in the case of individuals are a fine not exceeding ₦1,000,000 or imprisonment not exceeding 2 years or both fine and imprisonment and, in addition, a fine of ₦10,000 for each day the offence subsists,[370] as against the penalty provided under section 26(3) of the NESREA Act 2007, which include a fine of ₦200,000 or 1-year imprisonment. In the case of a body corporate, the penalties are a fine not exceeding ₦5,000,000 and, in addition, a fine of ₦50,000 for each day the offence subsists,[371] as against ₦1,000,000 and an additional fine of ₦50,000 for every day the offence subsists.[372] The offender shall also be responsible for the remediation of the damage to the environment and the affected properties therein.[373]

Only the penalties under the National Environmental (Watershed, Mountainous, Hilly and Catchment Areas) Regulations 2009[374] are at par with the penalty under section 26(3) and (4) of the NESREA Act 2007, which includes imprisonment of not more than 1 year or a fine of not more than ₦200,000 or both.[375] For a corporate body, a fine not exceeding ₦1,000,000 and an additional fine of ₦ 50,000 for every day the offence subsists consist the penalty.[376]

The bottom line is that these disparities do not augur well for the effective enforcement of the provisions of the law for the protection of the environment. This is compounded by the fact that NESREA is saddled with the implementation of both the law and Regulations, and the issue of enforcement, especially of the penalties, should not be on a pick-or-choose basis. The penalties should be harmonised, and it is suggested that the penalties provided under these Regulations[377] replace those provided under the NESREA Act as these penalties meet the present realities in serving as a deterrent to would-be polluters.

---

369 National Environmental (Desertification Control and Drought Mitigation) Regulations (2011).

370 National Environmental (Desertification Control and Drought Mitigation) Regulations (2011), regulation 21(1).

371 National Environmental (Desertification Control and Drought Mitigation) Regulations (2011), regulation 21(2).

372 NESREA Act (2007), s. 26(4).

373 National Environmental (Desertification Control and Drought Mitigation) Regulations (2011), regulation 21(3).

374 National Environmental (Watershed, Mountainous, Hilly and Catchment Areas) Regulations 2009.

375 Ibid., regulation 10(1)(b).

376 Ibid., regulation 10(3).

377 National Environmental (Soil Erosion and Flood Control) Regulations (2011) and National Environmental (Desertification Control and Drought Mitigation) Regulations (2011).

16.2.2.6 Climate Change Act 2021

The Act provides a framework for the mainstreaming of climate change actions and a system for carbon budgeting and the establishment of the National Council on Climate Change.[378] This, it is hoped, will address the synergy between the various agencies of the government in mainstreaming climate change mitigation and adaptation into development planning.[379]

16.2.3 Sectoral Legislation

Sectoral legislation is another group of environmental legislation in Nigeria. These laws were enacted for the protection of a segment or sector of the environment, like land or water or the atmosphere. Major legislation within this category includes the:

(1) Oil in Navigable Waters Act 1968
(2) Oil Pipelines Act 1965
(3) National Oil Spill Detection and Response Agency (NOSDRA) Act 2006
(4) Nigerian Maritime Administration and Safety Agency (NIMASA) Act 2007
(5) Associated Gas Re-injection Act.[380]

16.2.3.1 Oil in Navigable Waters Act (ONWA) 1968

The Oil in Navigable Waters Act 1968[381] came into effect on 22 April 1968 as an Act to control and prohibit oil spillage in the navigable waterways of Nigeria. Section 1(1) of the Act[382] makes it an offence for a Nigerian ship[383] to discharge oil or any mixture containing not less than 100 parts of oil into prohibited sea areas.[384] This section applies to crude oil, fuel and lubricating oil and heavy diesel

---

[378] Climate Change Act 2021, explanatory memorandum.

[379] The Climate Change Act 2021 was discussed in detail in Sect. 6.4.3.3 of Chap. 6 of this book under domestic regulatory frameworks in combating air pollution.

[380] Cap A 26 LFN 2004. This Act has been in existence since 1979 but is not discussed as it has been repealed by the Petroleum Industry Act (2021), Act No. 6 2021, s. 310.

[381] Cap 06 LFN 2004.

[382] ONWA (1968).

[383] A Nigerian ship includes (i) government ships registered in Nigeria and (ii) government ships not so registered that are held for purposes of the Federal Military Government or of the government of a state in Nigeria as they apply to other ships that are registered in Nigeria as Nigerian ships. See ONWA (1968) s. 16(2).

[384] Prohibited sea areas are listed in the Schedule to ONWA. They include all sea areas within 50 miles (80 km) from land and outside the territorial waters of Nigeria and other geographically defined zones of the world.

oil. This offence can be committed by the owner or master of the ship from which the discharge occurred.

The Act,[385] by virtue of section 3(1), (2), also prohibits the discharge of oil into the sea from any vessels or from any place on land or from any apparatus used for transferring oil within the seaward limits of the territorial waters of Nigeria and all other waters (including inland waters) that are within those limits and are navigable by seagoing ships. If there is any such discharge, the owner or master of the vessel or the occupier of the land or the person in charge of such apparatus used for transferring oil shall be guilty of an offence. However, 'where a person is charged with an offence under sections 1 and 3 of this Act, it shall be a defence to prove that the oil or oil-mixture in question was discharged for the purpose of securing the safety of any vessel, or of preventing damage to any vessel or cargo, or of saving life'.[386]

It is also a defence to prove that the oil or mixture escaped in consequence of damage to the vessel or that the oil escaped by reason of leakage, which leakage was not due to any want of reasonable care.[387] By virtue of section 5(5),[388] it is an offence for the master of a Nigerian or foreign-owned ship to fail to install equipment considered suitable for the reduction or prevention of oil discharges. The equipment concerned is as may be specified by the Federal Ministry of Transport or his assignee.

Furthermore, it is an offence for the master of Nigerian ships exceeding gross tonnage of 80 tons to fail to keep a log or record of oil discharges, oil spills and ballasting activities. And it is also an offence in the case of the failure of a Nigerian or foreign ship to keep a record of the transfer of oil to and from its ships.[389] The making of fraudulent entries in connection with the foregoing offences is also an offence.[390] It is also the duty of the harbour authority to provide facilities in harbour for the disposal of oil residues. Failure to do this is an offence.[391]

Section 10 of ONWA 1968 imposes a duty on the owner or master of a ship or the occupier of the place on land from where oil or mixture containing oil is discharged into the waters of the Nigerian harbour under any of the named circumstances to report such and disclose the cause and source of the discharge to the master in charge of the affected harbour. Failure to do so is punishable by a fine.

A person found guilty of an offence under ONWA 1968 shall, on conviction by a High Court or on summary conviction by a court of inferior jurisdiction, be liable to a fine of £1,000.00.[392] And under section 13(1) of the Act, where a fine is imposed on a vessel or owner or master and such fine is not paid, the court, in order to enforce

385 ONWA (1968).

386 ONWA (1968), s. 4 (1).

387 Ibid., s. 4(2)(a) and (b).

388 ONWA (1968).

389 Ibid., s. 7(1)(3)(b).

390 Ibid., s. 7(5)(b).

391 Ibid., s. 8(8).

392 Ibid., s. 6.

payment, may direct that the unpaid amount be levied by distress or otherwise taken in execution by way of pounding and sale of the vessel and its tackle, furniture and apparel.

16.2.3.2 Oil Pipelines Act 1956

The Oil Pipelines Act (OPA) was enacted in 1956 as Act No. 31 and was amended by Act No. 24 of 1965. The commencement period was 4 October 1956,[393] and it contains very little regulation on the prevention of oil pollution in spite of the high probability of spills resulting from oil pipelines and ancillary installations. The closest provision that OPA 1956 has in regulating environmental degradation can be found in section 17(4).[394] It provides:

> Every license shall be subject to the provisions contained in this Act as in force at the date of its grant and to such regulations concerning public safety, the avoidance of interference with works of public utility in, over and under the land included in the license and the prevention of pollution of such land or any waters as may from time to time be in force.

Also, the duration of an oil pipeline licence, which is fixed for a term not exceeding 20 years,[395] may be in recognition of the fact that the nature of pipelines may make them less fit after the time limit due to corrosion and other wear and tear[396] arising from pressure and long usage. Section 11(5) of the Act[397] affords compensatory relief to persons who suffer damage as a result of the exercise of rights conferred on the licensee by the licensor. For instance, section 11(5)(a)[398] provides that any person whose land or interest in land is injuriously affected by the exercise of such rights is entitled to compensation if the injury has not been made good.

Under section 11(5)(b),[399] the licensee shall be liable to pay compensation for damage caused by any neglect on his part or his agents or servants for work executed under the licence. Most importantly, section 11(5) (c) of OPA 1958 confers compensatory rights on any person suffering damage as a result of any breakage of or leakage from an oil pipeline or ancillary installation if the damage was not occasioned by the injured persons' default or the malicious act of a third person.

Besides these provisions, OPA 1958 has no far-reaching provisions for the protection of the environment. This is notwithstanding the high incidents of oil spills resulting from the rupture of pipelines. Most of the time, oil spills from pipeline

---

[393] Currently retained as Cap 07 LFN 2004.

[394] OPA (1958).

[395] Ibid., s. 17(1). Licences granted prior to the commencement of the Act were granted for a term not exceeding 99 years and are valid for the period they were granted.

[396] Olisa (1997), p. 164.

[397] OPA (1958).

[398] Ibid.

[399] Ibid.

ruptures are attributed to the malicious act of a third party[400] not minding that some of these pipelines were laid since the beginning of oil exploration and exploitation in Nigeria. Thus, where sabotage is alleged, this should not absolve the oil pipeline licensee, in that where the defendant fails to take appropriate steps to guard against acts of trespassers and other third parties, equipment failure or natural events, the defence of the deliberate act of a third party or stranger shall not avail him.[401]

In this respect, all operators and owners of potentially dangerous substances or equipment that are capable of causing harm to humans or cause irreversible damage to property and the environment owe society an absolute and non-delegable duty to ensure that no harm results to anyone on account of his operations with the highest standards of safety. This is premised on the rule of strict and absolute liability.[402] Under this rule, 'if any person is engaged in an inherently dangerous or hazardous activity and if any harm is caused to any person due to any accident which occurred during carrying out such inherently dangerous and hazardous activity, then the person who is carrying out such activity will be held absolutely liable'.[403]

16.2.3.3 National Oil Spill Detection and Response Agency (Establishment, Etc.) Act, 2006 (NOSDRA) Act[404]

The National Oil Spill Detection and Response Agency (NOSDRA) Act,[405] in section 1(1), establishes the National Oil Spill Detection and Response Agency (NOSDRA) as one of the two national agencies with responsibilities in oil spill preparedness and response.[406] The National Oil Spill Detection and Response Agency (NOSDRA) was established in 2006 as an institutional framework to coordinate the implementation of the National Oil Spill Contingency Plan (NOSCP) for Nigeria in accordance with the International Convention on Oil Pollution Preparedness, Response and Cooperation (OPRC) 1990. The objectives

---

[400] This is often referred to as sabotage.

[401] On this argument, see the following cases: *National Rivers Authority v Wright Engineering Co. Ltd* [1994] 4 All ER, 281; *Shell Petroleum Development Co. Ltd v Graham Otoko and Ors* (1990) 6 NWLR (pt. 159) 693; and *Empress Cars (Arbertillery) Ltd v National Rivers Authority* [1998] Env LR, 369. The cases are discussed in Sect. 7.5.2 of Chap. 7 of this book.

[402] The concept of strict and absolute liability was discussed in section 3.9.3 of Chap. 3 of this book.

[403] Furtado (2019).

[404] Discussed in section 14.7.3 of Chap. 14 of this book.

[405] Act No. 15 2006 as amended by the National Oil Spill Detection and Response Agency (Establishment, Etc.) (Amendment) Act, 2008. The Act was discussed in Sect. 14.7.3 of Chap. 14 of this book.

[406] The second Agency is the Nigerian Maritime Administration and Safety Agency (NIMASA) established by the Nigerian Maritime Administration and Safety Agency (NIMASA) Act 2007, discussed in section 14.7.4 of Chap. 14 of this book.

of the Agency include: to monitor, regulate Tier 1 and oil spills as well as coordinate, implement and review the National Oil Spill Contingency Plan for Nigeria.[407]

16.2.3.4 Nigerian Maritime Administration and Safety Agency (NIMASA) Act 2007[408]

The National Maritime Administration and Safety Agency (NIMASA) Act 2007 established the National Maritime Administration and Safety Agency (NIMASA),[409] whose objective includes, among other things, 'to regulate and promote maritime safety, security, marine pollution…'.[410]

16.2.4 Incidental Legislation

Incidental legislation is a set of laws not enacted with environmental protection as the mischief they set to cure. However, some of the provisions of these laws[411] may be applied to the protection of the environment as part of the laws that make up Nigeria's legislation on environmental protection. The following laws that fall within this category are discussed:

(i) Criminal Code Act
(ii) Petroleum Act and Regulations 1969
(iii) Constitution of the Federal Republic of Nigeria 1999
(iv) Nigerian Minerals and Mining Act 2007
(v) Petroleum Industry Act 2021

---

[407] NOSDRA Act (2006), s. 5.

[408] Enacted as Act No. 17 2007. The Act was discussed in Sect. 14.7.4 of Chap. 14 of this book.

[409] NIMASA Act (2007), s. 1 (2)(a).

[410] Ibid., s. 1 (1).

[411] Such as the Agricultural (Control of Importation) Act, Animal Diseases (Control) Act, Bees (Impact Control and Management) Act, Civil Aviation Act, Constitution of the Federal Republic of Nigeria, Criminal Code, Endangered Species Act, Exclusive Economic Zone Act, Factories Act, Federal National Park Act, Hides and Skins Act, Hydrocarbon Oil Refineries Act, Land Use Act, Minerals and Mining Act, Niger-Delta Development Commission (NDDC) Act, Nuclear Safety and Radiation Protection Act, Pest Control of Production (Special Powers) Act, Petroleum Act, Petroleum Industry Act, Quarantine Act, River Basins Development Authority Act, Sea Fisheries Act, Territorial Waters Act and Water Resources Act.

16.2.4.1 Criminal Code Act

The Criminal Code Act, which was enacted in 1916,[412] has two relevant sections that can be applied to environmental protection. These are sections 245 and 247. Under section 245 of the Act,[413] 'any person who corrupts or fouls water of any spring, stream, well, reservoir so as to render it less fit for the purpose for which it is ordinary used, is guilty of a misdemeanour and is liable to imprisonment for six months'. Section 247,[414] on the other hand, proscribes noxious acts. Thus, any person who:

(i) vitiates the atmosphere in any place so as to make it noxious to the health of persons in general dwelling or carrying on business in the neighbourhood or passing along a public way; or
(ii) does any act which is, and which he knows or has reason to believe to be likely to spread the infection of any disease dangerous to life whether human or animal is guilty of a misdemeanour, and is liable to imprisonment for six months.

16.2.4.2 Petroleum Act 1969[415]

Of relevance to the subject matter on tacking is the provisions of section 9(1)(b)(iii) of the Act,[416] which empowers the Minister in charge of petroleum matters to make regulations for the protection of the environment from oil production operations. Pursuant to this power, a number of regulations were made by the Minister.

The first of its kind is the Petroleum Regulations, made in 1967. The Regulations seek to control oil production operations where such operations have the tendency to pollute water bodies. The relevant provisions of the Regulations on the issue of environmental protection are contained in regulation 13, which prohibits the discharge of petroleum into the waters of ports; regulation 63(3), which requires that the floor of an enclosed storage area be formed of concrete or other suitable materials to prevent the contamination of adjacent water supplies and watercourses of drainage systems in the event of a serious leakage; regulation 65, which prohibits the discharge of petroleum into any inlet or drain communication with a sewer; and regulation 67, which demands that all enclosed areas whose floors are made of concrete or non-porous materials be drained by pipe fitted with a valve actuated from the outside of the enclosure.

---

[412] This law has been amended on several occasions, and it is currently retained as C38 LFN 2004.

[413] Criminal Code.

[414] Criminal Code.

[415] Cap P 10 LFN 2004 and still an existing law in spite of the enactment of the Petroleum Industry Act 2021 (see the discussions on Petroleum Industry Act (2021) in section 16.2.4.5 of this chapter). By virtue of the Petroleum Industry Act 2021 s. 311(1), all Regulations made under the Petroleum Act 1969 are saved.

[416] Petroleum Act (1969).

The next in line is the Petroleum (Drilling and Production) Regulations 1969 as amended. Regulation 25 provides:

> the licensee or lessee shall adopt all practicable precautions . . . to prevent the pollution of inland water ways, rivers, water courses, the territorial water of Nigeria, of the high seas, by oil, mud or other fluids or substances which might contaminate the water, banks or shoreline or which might cause harm or destruction to fresh water or marine life, and where any such pollution occurs or has occurred, shall take prompt steps to control and, if possible, end it.

According to regulation 36,[417] 'the licensee or lessee . . . shall carry out all his operations in proper and workmanlike manner in accordance with these and other relevant regulations and method or practices accepted by the Head of the Petroleum Inspectorate as a good oil field practice . . . and shall take all steps practicable to:

(i) control the flow and to prevent the escape or avoid waste of petroleum discovered in or obtained from the relevant area;
(ii) prevent the escape into any water, well, spring, stream, river lake, reservoir, estuary or harbour, and
(iii) cause little damage as possible to the surface of relevant area and to the trees, crops, buildings, structures and other property thereon'.

While regulation 40[418] relates to the drainage of waste, brine, sludge or refuse so as to prevent land and water pollution, regulation 45[419] prescribes that the operator must, at the completion of his operations, leave the surface in a satisfactory condition from the point of view of land pollution.

Another in the series of Regulations made pursuant to section 9(1)(b)(iii) of the Petroleum Act is the Petroleum Refining Regulations 1974. The purpose of these Regulations is to control the refinery section of the oil industry, preventing it from polluting the environment with refinery wastes. Regulation 24(1)[420] provides stipulations as to the physical quality and capacity of permanently placed storage tanks for petroleum and petroleum products so as to contain leakages from any of the tanks. Under regulation 27 residues, sludges, rusts and similar matters from tanks are to be deposited at any such receptacle as are approved by the Head, Petroleum Inspectorate.

In addition, regulation 29 states that unprogrammed spillage of crude oil products or chemicals inside a refinery must be notified immediately to the Petroleum Inspectorate, to be followed within 7 days by a written report of the cause and nature of the spillage, the amount of spillage and the method of estimating it, the amount of spillage recovered and the precautionary measures taken since the spillage to prevent any hazard from arising in nature. The drainage and disposal of refinery

[417] Petroleum (Drilling and Production) Regulations (1969).

[418] Ibid.

[419] Ibid.

[420] Ibid.

effluent and drainage of water are to be undertaken in accordance with good refining practices.[421] Any contravention of these Regulations is an offence.

16.2.4.3 Constitution of the Federal Republic of Nigeria 1999, as Amended

The Constitution of the Federal Republic of Nigeria (CFRN) 1999, as amended,[422] provides some policy statements concerning the environment under Chap. 2, which deals with the Fundamental Objectives and Directive Principles of State Policy. The most relevant sections include the following:

Section 14 (2)(b)[423] provides as follows: 'It is hereby declared that security and welfare of the people shall be the primary purpose of government.' Section 16 (1) (a),[424] on the other hand, states that 'The State shall, within the context of the ideals and objectives for which provisions are made in this constitution, harness the resources of the nation and promote national prosperity and an efficient, a dynamic and self-reliant economy'.

Further, Section 17(2)(d)[425] stipulates that 'in furtherance of the social order, exploitation of human or natural resources in any form whatsoever for reasons, other than the good of the community, shall be prevented'. Finally, section 20[426] provides that 'the state shall protect and improve the environment and safeguard the water, air and land, forest and wildlife'.

However, the supposed gains of the above Constitutional provisions are rather weak as they are non-justiciable pursuant to section 6(6)(c).[427] This is because the declarations are contained in Chapter II of CFRN 1999 under the Fundamental Objectives and Directive Principles of State Policy. According to the Constitution Drafting Committee (CDC),

> By fundamental objectives we refer to the identification to the ultimate objectives of the Nation whilst Directive principles of state policy indicate the paths which lead to those objectives. Fundamental objectives are ideals towards which the Nation is expected to strive whilst Directive principles law down the policies which are expected to be pursued in the efforts to the Nation to realize the national ideals.[428]

A sad note, however, is that the Fundamental Objectives and Directive Principles of State Policy are not justiciable.[429] What this portends is that the non-attainment of

---

421 Petroleum Refining Regulations (1974), regulation 43.

422 Cap C23 LFN 2004.

423 CFRN (1999).

424 Ibid.

425 CFRN (1999).

426 Ibid.

427 Ibid.

428 Okere (1988), p. 74.

429 CFRN (1999), s. 6(6)(c).

environmental objectives and the failure of the state to protect and safeguard the environment cannot be questioned in any court. But it should be noted that the mere provision that these principles are not justiciable does not *per se* divest them of all legal values.[430] This is because what is not judicially enforceable cannot be preferred to what is justiciable.[431]

Although to protect and safeguard the environment is not judicially enforceable under the Constitution, this does not mean that where such failure impinges on the fundamental rights which are justiciable, that the court shall ignore this violation. This is because the 'Directive Principles . . . have to conform to and run as subsidiary to the Chapter on Fundamental Rights'.[432] It is therefore suggested that in order to give effect to the environmental objectives, the court should cloth them with the garb of fundamental rights and thus regard the failure to protect and safeguard the environment as a breach of the right to a clean environment.[433]

In addition, it is believed that for the effective conservation of natural resources, the provisions of sections 14(2)(b), 17(2)(d) and 20 of CFRN 1999 should be entrenched under Chapter 4 of the same CFRN 1999.[434] This position is predicated on the fact that for there to be effective management of our bio-resources, the government should play a prominent role, and where it fails, any citizen who suffers damage as a result of such failure may approach the courts to enforce non-compliance or non-provision of the enabling environment for bio-resource management, and indeed, overall environmental protection.

On the policy level, Nigeria is committed to a national policy on the environment aimed at achieving development. In particular, the National Policy on Environment (or 'the Policy')[435] is to secure a quality environment that is adequate for good health and well-being, conserve and use the environment and natural resources for the benefit of present and future generations and restore, maintain and enhance the ecosystems and ecological processes for the conservation of biological diversity.[436] The Policy[437] touches on areas such as identifying implementation strategies on human population, culture, housing and human settlements. Strategies for biological diversity, natural resource conservation, land use and soil conservation, agriculture and water resources were given prominence.

The implementation strategies also cover such sections as wildlife, marine and coastal area resources, mining and mineral resources, industry, energy, oil and gas, construction, health, education, transport and communication systems, trade and tourism, science and technology, natural disasters and desertification, flood and

---

[430] Okere (1988), p. 74.

[431] Ibid.

[432] Indian Supreme Court in *State of Madras v Champakan Dorairajin* (AIR) (1951) SC 226.

[433] *Madras v Champakan Dorairajin*, ibid.

[434] Chapter 4 of CFRN (1999), at ss. 33–44, contains provisions on fundamental human rights.

[435] Federal Republic of Nigeria (1999).

[436] USAID (2002).

[437] Federal Republic of Nigeria (1999).

erosion. Other aspects of the Policy include sanitation and waste management; toxic, hazardous and radioactive substances; air pollution; the working environment; public participation; institutional arrangements; funding mechanisms; and monitoring and evaluation. Other policies directly relevant to biodiversity conservation are those on agriculture, integrated rural development and forestry and water resources.[438]

16.2.4.4 Nigerian Minerals and Mining Act 2007

The Nigerian Minerals and Mining Act 2007 (Minerals and Mining Act 2007)[439] was passed into law on 16 March 2007 to repeal the Minerals and Mining Act, No. 34 of 1999.[440] The purpose of the Minerals and Mining Act 2007 is to regulate all aspects of the exploration and exploitation of solid minerals in Nigeria, as well as related purposes. It follows that the Act did not, *ab initio*, set out to regulate environmental protection. However, some sections of the Act have provisions for the protection of the environment.

For instance, section 123[441] prohibits the pollution of watercourses. Under the section, 'no person shall in the course of mining or exploration for minerals pollute or cause to be polluted any water or watercourse in the area within the mining lease or beyond that area'. Thus,

> every person who uses water in connection with mining operations whether for (a) generation of power for mining purpose; or (b) removal of mineral substance; or (c) concentration, milling or otherwise shall, whatever may be the nature ... make such provisions as shall ensure that the water so used does not contain injurious substances in quantities likely to prove detrimental to animal or vegetation life when the water leaves the mining area in which it has been so used.[442]

Also, 'no person shall make or permit any other person to make, without the permission of the Mines Inspectorate Department, any alterations in the water supply of any land so as to prejudicially affect the water supply enjoyed by any other person or land'.[443]

In addition, no lessee shall deposit a greater quantity of tailing[444] in any natural watercourse than that prescribed by regulations.[445] In furtherance of the measures to protect the environment, the Act[446] provides that every holder of a mineral title shall,

[438] Federal Republic of Nigeria (1999).
[439] Act No. 20 2007, Federal Republic of Nigeria Official Gazette Lagos.
[440] Cap M1 LFN 2004.
[441] Nigerian Minerals and Mining Act (2007).
[442] Ibid., s. 124.
[443] Nigerian Minerals and Mining Act (2007), s. 127.
[444] The waste left behind after ore had been extracted from the rock.
[445] Nigerian Minerals and Mining Act (2007), s. 126(1).
[446] Nigerian Minerals and Mining Act (2007).

as far as it is reasonably practicable, (a) minimise, manage and mitigate any environmental impact resulting from his and (b) rehabilitate and reclaim, where applicable, the land disturbed, excavated, explored, mined or covered with tailings arising from mining operations to its natural or predetermined state.[447] What this entails is that 'where land which is the subject of a Mining Lease has been exploited, the mined out areas shall be restored by the applicant under the condition of its grant. . . '.[448]

Again, under the Act,[449] every holder of an exploration licence, small-scale mining lease, mining lease, quarry lease and water-use permit shall, (a) prior to the commencement of mining operations or (b) upon an application for an extension of the term or (c) upon an application for the conversion of a mineral title, submit to the Mines Environmental Compliance Department (i) an environmental impact assessment statement approved by the Federal Ministry of the Environment in respect of the exploration or mining operations to be conducted within the Mineral Title Area and (ii) an environmental protection and rehabilitation programme. Such environmental protection and rehabilitation programme shall provide for (a) specific rehabilitation and reclamation actions, inspections and annual reports; (b) a reasonable estimate of the total cost of rehabilitation; (c) cost estimates for each specific rehabilitation and reclamation action; and (d) a timetable for the orderly and efficient rehabilitation and reclamation of the Mineral Title Area to a safe and environmentally sound condition suitable for future economic development or recreational use.[450] To this end, every holder of an exploration licence shall:

(i) Maintain and restore the land that is the subject of the licence to a safe state from any disturbance resulting from exploration activities, including, but not limited to, filling up any shafts, wells, holes or trenches made by the titleholder, and in compliance with applicable environmental laws and regulations[451]
(ii) Not abstract, divert or discharge water or effluent from any watercourse except in compliance with a water use permit and the Regulations[452]
(iii) Not explore in any forest reserve except with the approval of the Minister and in consultation with other relevant authorities and subject to such conditions as may be specified in the Regulations.[453]

[447] Ibid., s. 118.
[448] Ibid., s. 115.
[449] Ibid., s. 119.
[450] Ibid., s. 120.
[451] Nigerian Minerals and Mining Act (2007), s. 61(1)(d).
[452] Ibid., s. 61(1)(e).
[453] Ibid., s. 61(1)(f).

Furthermore, no person shall, in the course of exploration or mining, carry out operations, in or under any area held to be sacred, or permit the injury or destruction of any tree or other thing which is the object of veneration.[454]

The Act[455] further enjoins holders of a mining title to exercise their rights under the licence or lease having regard to the effect of mining operations on the environment and to take such steps as may be necessary to prevent pollution of the environment resulting from mining operations.

In the case of abandonment or permanent cessation of production within the title area, the mineral title holder shall (a) securely seal, fence or cover every mine shaft and adit; (b) make safe all tailings and water retention areas; and (c) demolish, fence or lock all potentially hazardous buildings, structures, plants and equipment.[456]

Under the Act, an offence is deemed to have been committed where a person conducts exploration or mines minerals or carries out quarrying operations otherwise than in accordance with the provisions of the Act.[457] Such a person shall, on conviction, have his licence revoked and, on conviction at first instance, be liable to a fine not less than ₦20,000,000 and imprisonment of not less 5 years, if the offence is a continuing one, whether or not it is the first offence; the person convicted shall, in addition, be liable to a fine of ₦20,000 in respect of each day during which the offence continues.[458]

In the end, a licensee or lessee shall pay compensation to the owner or occupier who suffers damage as a result of pollution of any source of water, used for domestic and other purposes, as a consequence of exploration or operations in any work connected with the property, for any such damage not otherwise made good.[459]

16.2.4.5 Petroleum Industry Act 2021

The Petroleum Industry Act (PIA) 2021[460] was enacted to provide for a legal, governance, regulatory and fiscal framework for the Nigerian petroleum industry; provide for the establishment and development of host communities; and deal with other related matters in the upstream, midstream and downstream sectors of the petroleum industry. For all intents and purposes, PIA 2021 did not set out to regulate environmental protection *per se*. However, some sections of the Act have provisions for the protection of the environment.

---

[454] Ibid., s. 98(1).

[455] Ibid., s. 111.

[456] Ibid., s. 159(6).

[457] Ibid., s.131(1)(a).

[458] Ibid., s. 133.

[459] Nigerian Minerals and Mining Act (2007), s. 125 (b).

[460] Act No. 6, 2021, Government Notice No. 134, Federal Republic of Nigeria Official Gazette Lagos. No. 42, Vol. 108, 27 August 2021.

For instance, under section 101(2) of PIA 2021, a person shall not, in the course of petroleum operations,

(a) injure or destroy a tree or object which is of commercial value or the object of veneration to the people resident within the license or lease area;
(b) damage or destroy any building or property; or
(c) disturb or damage the surface of the land or any other rights to any person who owns or is in lawful occupation of the surface area covered by the license or lease.

Again, under section 102(1) of PIA 2021, a licensee or lessee that engages in upstream and midstream petroleum operations shall, within (a) 1 year of the effective date or (b) 6 months after the grant of the applicable licence or lease, 'submit for approval an environmental management plan in respect of the projects which requires Environmental Impact Assessment to the Commission[461] or Authority,[462] as the case may be'. The environmental management plan shall be in accordance with extant Acts.[463]

To further protect the environment, 'chemicals shall not be utilized for upstream petroleum operations, except the Commission grants an applicable permit or approval'.[464] In addition to this, the storage, application, transportation and other petroleum operations of radioactive materials and other equipment generating ionising radiation in all aspects of the oil and gas operations shall be in compliance with the Nuclear Safety and Radiation Protection Act[465] and such other legislative provisions, as the case may be.[466]

PIA 2021, in section 310, repealed the Associated Gas Reinjection Act.[467] In place of the latter, the former set out provisions for the protection of the environment from problems associated with the flaring of gas. First, PIA 2021 imposes penalties on gas flaring, except as permitted under section 104(1)(a)–(c), that is to say, (a) in the case of emergency, (b) pursuant to an exemption granted by the Commission or (c) as an acceptable safety practice under established regulations. Failure to comply attracts penalties against the culprits.[468] Second, section 105 prohibits gas flaring or the venting of natural gas.[469] Contravention attracts a penalty upon the licensee or

[461] 'Commission' means Nigerian Upstream Petroleum Regulatory Commission established under the Petroleum Industry Act 2021, s. 4. See Petroleum Industry Act (PIA) 2021, s. 318.

[462] 'Authority' means Nigerian Midstream and Downstream Petroleum Regulatory Authority established under the PIA (2021), s. 29. See also PIA (2021), s. 318.

[463] PIA (2021), s. 102(2).

[464] Ibid., s. 102(7).

[465] Cap N 142 LFN 2004.

[466] PIA (2021), s. 225.

[467] Cap A 26 LFN 2004.

[468] See discussions on this in Sect. 11.2.2 generally, but particularly, see Sect. 11.2.2.5 of Chap. 11 of this book.

[469] Venting is a controlled release of unburned gases into the atmosphere, such as natural gas or other hydrocarbon vapours, water vapour or other gases. Venting may occur during several

lessee pursuant to the Flare Gas (Prevention of Waste Pollution) Regulations 2018.[470]

Other measures put in place by PIA 2021 include the provisions of section 106. Under this section, a licensee shall, prior to the commencement of petroleum production, install metering equipment conforming to the specifications prescribed for every facility from which natural gas may be flared or vented, as the Commission or Authority may prescribe in a regulation. However, section 107 of PIA 2021 provides an exemption. Under this section, the Commission or Authority may grant a permit to a licensee or lessee to allow gas flaring or the venting of natural gas for a specific period where it is required (a) for facility start-up or (b) for strategic operational reasons, including testing.

In all, PIA 2021 provides that notwithstanding any contrary provisions under the Act, a licensee or lessee producing natural gas shall, within 12 months of the effectivity date of the license or lease, submit a natural gas flare elimination or monetisation plan to the Commission, which shall be prepared in accordance with the regulations made by the Commission under PIA 2021.[471]

However, for including exemptions that allow gas flaring to continue and the use of gas flaring fines for more gas investments rather than hosting community development or environmental remediation, environmental groups criticised PIA 2021.[472]

To safeguard the health of Nigerians, PIA 2021 further provides that imported petroleum products shall conform to Afri-5 Specification (50 ppm sulphur) as per the Economic Commission of West African States (ECOWAS) Declaration of February 2020 on the adoption of Afri-Fuels Roadmap or as may be prescribed by regulations.[473]

The African Union Commission (AUC), in collaboration with the African Refiners and Distributors Association (ARA), hosted a 2-day workshop, from 10 to 11 December 2019 at Addis Ababa, Ethiopia, to validate 'The Benefits of Adopting AFRI Fuel Specifications Roadmap'. The goal of the AFRI-Fuel Roadmap was to ensure superior fuel quality and a significant emission reduction to achieve clean air in Africa.[474] This is premised on the fact that harmonised regional and continental fuel specifications are believed to make a positive and lasting impact on economies, air quality, health and the climate.

According to Obbguigwe,[475] a blueprint by ARA advocates common regional specifications and tax policies in order to promote trade and an efficient supply chain

---

processes, including well completion and well maintenance. Odours may be associated with venting.

[470] The Regulations are discussed below.

[471] PIA (2021), s. 108.

[472] EnviroNews Nigeria (2022b).

[473] PIA (2021), s. 317(11).

[474] Africa Union Directorate of Information and Commission (2021).

[475] Obbguigwe (2016).

across Africa. ARA's goal is to improve Africa's air quality, with the consequent improvements in public health, while recognising that:

(i) Air quality problems are localised, not universal.
(ii) Clean fuel demand can only be met by modernising refinery infrastructure or product imports.
(iii) Time is needed for the local economies and consumers to support the tightening of specifications and the consequent cost increase.
(iv) Refinery investment must be in line with car fleet modernisation and vehicle controls.

In furtherance of protecting the environment from incidents of gas flaring, in 2018, the Federal Government of Nigeria made the Flare Gas (Prevention of Waste and Pollution) Regulations 2018.[476] The Regulations were made by the President in his capacity as the Minister for Petroleum Resources pursuant to both section 9 of the Petroleum Act[477] and section 5 of the Associated Gas Reinjection Act. Like its 1985 predecessor, the present Regulations, though with the core objectives of reducing the environmental and social impacts that gas flaring has on the environment, protecting the environment, preventing the waste of natural resources and leveraging the social and economic benefits of flare capture,[478] still monetised the flaring of gas.[479] The Regulations revised the gas flaring fees previously being paid by producers or operators. The newly prescribed payments for gas flaring under the Regulations[480] are as follows:

(a) In the case of production of 10,000 barrels of oil and above (per day): $2 per thousand standard cubic feet (Mscf) of gas flared;
(b) In the case of production of less than 10,000 barrels of oil per day: $0.50 per Mscf of gas flared;
(c) Notwithstanding the prescribed payments for gas flaring, a Producer will be required to pay an additional sum of $2.50 per 28.317 Mscf of gas flared, within the OML or Marginal Field for each day that the Producer fails to.

16.3 Summary

Nigeria has, as far as possible, a long list of environmental laws. However, the application of these laws has not been generally successful in combating environmental problems. Their efforts have also failed in creating an environmentally

[476] Government Notice No. 59, S.I. No. 9. Federal Republic of Nigeria Official Gazette No. 88, Vol. 105, 9 July 2018.

[477] Cap P10 LFN 2004.

[478] Flare Gas (Prevention of Waste and Pollution) Regulations (2018), regulation 1.

[479] Even the Petroleum Industry Act (2021) in section 108 still monetised gas flaring.

[480] Flare Gas (Prevention of Waste and Pollution) Regulations (2018), regulation 13.

cleaner behaviour; technologies, products or green development; or an environment that is free from abuse and dislocation. In other words, the current legal mechanism has failed to provide an adequate push to limit activities that are environmentally damaging. Part of the reason for this is the obsolesce of some of the laws, with conflicting provisions in some cases. While some of the laws have a paucity of sanctions imposed for environmental crimes, others have flaws in the defences available, and some have ill-defined environmental terminologies, oftentimes ambiguous, and have overlapping, ill-defined and conflicting functions for some of the environmental enforcement agents.

Essentially, an environmental law should seek to prevent pollution and ecological degradation, promote conservation and secure ecologically sustainable development and the use of natural resources while promoting justifiable economic and social development and punishing deviant behaviour. It also seeks to create productive harmony between man and his environment by striking a balance between encouraging investment and growth and the need to protect the environment for present and future generations.

Furthermore, the existing environmental regulatory scheme is a complex and unyielding system of laws, regulations, standards and guidelines scattered all over the legal system and in various volumes of the laws of the Federation of Nigeria, leading to increasing conflict, confusion and gridlock.[481] In sum, the laws generally lack incentives for environmental protection compliance.

Under the existing conditions, what is required is a 'one-stop-shop' environmental law that is applicable, relevant and appropriate to current realities in international approaches to and acceptable practices in environmental protection, abatement and management. A 'one-stop-shop' environmental law will aid in environmental governance as all that will be required can be found in one volume.[482] This law is to be complimented by a handbook on environmental regulations, standards and guidelines.[483]

References

Africa Union Directorate of Information and Commission (2021). https://au.int/sites/default/files/pressreleases/37858-pr-press_release-_afri_fuel-rev.pdf. Accessed 21 June 2023

Central Intelligent Agency (CIA) (2014) The World Factbook, 28 January 2014, https://www.cia.gov/library/publications/the-world-factbook/geos/ni.html. Accessed 23 May 2023

[481] This is in addition to the avalanche of regulations, standards and guidelines contained in about 33 national environmental regulations made pursuant to the NESREA Act (2007).

[482] This has been done in respect of the petroleum industry, where the Petroleum Industry Act (2021) is a compendium for the industry.

[483] This should contain an edited version of the current 33 regulations made pursuant to the NESREA Act (2007) as volume 2 to Laws on Environmental Governance.

Duxbury RMC (1999) Telling and Duxbury's planning law and procedure, 11th edn. Butterworths, London

EnviroNews Nigeria (2022a) Environmental Impact Assessment Approach in Nigeria. https://environreview.com.ng/environmental-impact-assessment-approach-in-nigeria. Accessed 26 June 2023

EnviroNews Nigeria (2022b) Petroleum Industry Bill at variance with Nigeria's climate change pledges – Campaigners. https://www.environewsnigeria.com/petroleum-industry-bill-at-variance-with-nigerias-climate-change-pledges-campaigners/. Accessed 19 June 2023

Federal Republic of Nigeria (1999) National policy on environment. Government Press, Abuja

Fortuny (ed) (2022) Impact Assessment, Overview & History, International Association of Impact Assessment (iaia). https://www.iaia.org/. Accessed 7 May 2023

Free World Maps (2021) Nigeria Physical Map, 2005–2021 http://www.freeworldmaps.net/africa/nigeria/map.html. Accessed 24 May 2023

Furtado R (2019) Concept of Strict and Absolute Liability. 10 April 2019 https://blog.ipleaders.in/concept-strict-liability-absolute-liability/amp. Accessed 13 May 2023

International Institute for Sustainable Development (IISD) (2023)7 Steps EIA Learning On-Line Learning Platform. https://www.iisd.org/learning/eia/eia-7-steps/step-1-screening/. Accessed 26 June 2023

Mwalyosi R et al (1999) Orientation Course on Environmental Impact Assessment in Tanzania, "Impact Identification, Prediction and Evaluation," International Institute of Environment and Development, 277, jstor, http://www.jstor.com. Accessed 7 May 2023

Obbguigwe T (2016) Towards Low Sulphur Fuels-ECOWAS/ARA Roadmap, Accra, Ghana 31October 2016. https://wedocs.unep.org/bitstream/handle/20.500.11822/21479/. Accessed 21 June 2023

Okere BO (1988) "Fundamental Objectives and Directive Principles of State Policy under the Nigerian Constitution," (1979 – 1988). Nigeria Juridical Review, Faculty of Law University of Nigeria, Enugu Campus, 3:74

Olisa MM (1997) Nigeria petroleum law and practice, 2nd edn. Jonia Ventures Ltd, Lagos

Onyeabor EU (2016) Fundamentals of planning law in Nigeria. Lambert Academic, Saarbrucken, Germany. ISBN 978-3-659-95317-0, http://www.lap-publishing.com

Rostron J (2001) Environmental law for built environment. Cavendish, London

Thornton J, Beckwith S (2004) Environmental law, 2nd edn. Sweet and Maxwell, London

United Nations, Department of Economic and Social Affairs, Population Division (2023) World Population Projections, Updated on July 16, 2023 with the latest July 2023-July 2024, https://www.worldometers.info/world-population/nigeria-population/. Accessed 26 Aug 2023

United Nations Environment Programme (UNEP) (2007) Global Environmental Outlook Series. UNEP, London

US Agency for International Development (USAID) (2002) Nigeria Environmental Analysis Final Report. https://pdf.usaid.gov/pdf_docs/PNACP627.pdf. Accessed 16 May 2023

Chapter 17
Waste Management Perspectives in Some Selected African Regions

Abstract Managing waste generally, especially municipal solid waste (MSW), has been a reoccurring problem among nations. In recent past, plastic waste has become a worldwide issue in environmental management, next to climate-change-related issues. This is premised on the fact that the seas and oceans, which constitute the eventual natural sink for virtually all natural and anthropogenic activities on the globe, are now being polluted by wastes from plastic. What then are the sources of waste from plastic pollution? What are their effects on the environment and human health? What are the management strategies for managing and controlling such wastes? An attempt is made in this chapter to provide answers to these questions. Discussions in the chapter are based on some selected regions of Africa, such as the Western and Central African regions as well as the Eastern and Southern African regions. Emphases were based on countries such as Nigeria, Ghana and Senegal for the Western region, Angola and Democratic Republic of the Congo for the Central African region, Kenya for Eastern Africa and South Africa for the Southern African region.

17.1 Introduction

Plastic is currently at the top of the international trash management agenda. Recent Conferences of the Parties to the Basel and Stockholm Conventions meetings have expressed concerns about the effects of plastic waste, marine plastic litter and microplastics and have emphasised the significance of reducing consumption and ensuring the environmentally sound management of waste plastics.

According to the World Economic Forum,[1] the amount of waste generated by humanity represents a growing threat to our ecosystems and economies. The output of solid waste has grown from 25 gigatons (that is, 25 billion tons) in 1990 to 86 gigatons (that is, 86 billion tons) in 2020 and is projected to be 140 gigatons (that is, 140 billion tons) by 2050. This expansion exceeds population growth and is the

[1] World Economic Forum (2020).

E. Onyeabor, *Environmental Law*, https://doi.org/10.1007/978-3-031-68956-7_17

result of a disposable-goods system that combines short-term use and long-term environmental harm.[2] The most insidious of waste that fits into this description is waste from plastics.

Around the world, 1 million plastic bottles are purchased every minute, while up to 5 trillion plastic bags are used worldwide every year. In total, half of all plastics produced is designed for single-use purposes (used just once and then thrown away). Plastics, including microplastics, are now ubiquitous in our natural environment. They are becoming part of the earth's fossil record and a marker of the Anthropocene.[3]

From the 1950s to the 1970s, only a small amount of plastic was produced, and as a result, plastic waste was relatively manageable. However, between the 1970s and the 1990s, plastic waste generation more than tripled, reflecting a similar rise in plastic production. In the early 2000s, the amount of plastic waste we generated rose more in a single decade than it had in the previous 40 years. About 400 million tonnes of plastic waste is now produced every year, and if historic growth trends continue, the global production of primary plastic is forecasted to reach 1100 million tonnes by 2050.[4] Africa generates just about 16 million tonnes of plastic waste annually, which is only 6% of plastic waste generated globally. However, this 16 million tonnes of plastic waste constitutes only 13% of solid waste generated in Africa.[5] On a global scale, Africa is responsible for 5% of global plastic production and 4% of global plastic consumption but contributes to 24% of global emissions from mismanaged plastic waste.[6]

17.2 Nature of Plastic Waste

Pollution from plastic waste has been acknowledged as a major environmental problem. Several broad classes of plastics are used in packaging, including polyethylene (PE), polypropylene (PP), polystyrene (PS), polyethylene terephthalate (PET) and polyvinyl chloride (PVC).[7] Food wrappers, plastic bottles, plastic bottle caps, plastic grocery bags, plastic straws and stirrers are the common items. Packaging represents a large percentage of plastic consumption and consists of products that have a very short life span. Plastic waste can also be found in cigarette butts, whose filters contain tiny plastic fibres, which are the most common type of plastic waste found in the environment.[8]

---

[2] Ibid.

[3] United Nations Environment Programmes (UNEP) (2021a).

[4] Ibid.

[5] Munang (2022).

[6] UNEP (2018).

[7] National Oceanography Centre (2021).

[8] Ibid.

Another source of waste that impacts the environment, especially the marine environment, is marine debris.[9] Marine debris, also known as marine litter, is human-created waste that has deliberately or accidentally been released into the environment, which eventually ends up in a sea or ocean. According to the United Nations Environment Programme (UNEP),[10] marine litter or debris is 'any persistent, manufactured, or processed solid material that is discarded, disposed of or abandoned in the marine and coastal environment'. It should be noted that whatever is the source of marine litter, the full magnitude and impact of marine litter are difficult to determine. This is based on the fact that the amount and composition of marine litter can vary between regions due to differences in waste management and in economic activities, such as tourism, fisheries and shipping.[11]

The common types of marine litter include various plastic items like shopping bags and beverage bottles, along with cigarette butts, bottle caps, food wrappers and fishing gear. Plastic waste is particularly problematic as a pollutant because it is so long-lasting. Plastic items can take hundreds of years to decompose.[12]

Thus, part of marine litter includes microplastics. According to the Joint Group of Experts on the Scientific Aspects of Marine Environmental Protection (GESAMP),[13] microplastics range in size but are commonly defined as plastic particles of less than 5 mm. Microplastics can be found in personal care and industrial products. They can also come from larger pieces of plastic that have degraded. Microplastics pose a significant problem as they can pass through wastewater filters with ease, making it impossible to recover them once in the ocean.

In whatever form, a number of factors account for the prevalence of marine litter in the environment. These factors include (i) changing production and consumption patterns, (ii) inadequate waste management and (iii) gaps in the regulation of waste materials. Response to control and management requires a comprehensive approach. To this end, countries' utilisation of a variety of laws and policies to prevent, manage and reduce the proliferation of marine litter becomes an available choice. However, according to UNEP,[14] many of these approaches are part of general frameworks to reduce the generation and spread of solid waste, rather than being part of frameworks specifically designed to address marine litter.

What then is the nature of marine litter? In a research coordinated by the Ocean Conservancy[15] during the 2014 International Coastal Cleanup Day, it was found that the most commonly collected items from beaches included cigarette butts, food

[9]The countries discussed in this chapter (Nigeria, Ghana, Senegal, Angola, South Africa and Kenya) are all coastal states in Africa.

[10]UNEP (2009).

[11]UNEP (2015).

[12]Central Community College (2021).

[13]Joint Group of Experts on the Scientific Aspects of Marine Environmental Protection (GESAMP) (2015).

[14]UNEP (2015).

[15]The Ocean Conservancy (2015).

wrappers, plastic bottles, bottle caps, straws and stirrers, plastic bags, glass bottles, beverage cans and plastic cups and plates. Again, in 2014, a study of litter on South Korean beaches from 2008 to 2009 showed that fisheries and marine aquaculture accounted for approximately 35% of marine litter, household items made up 20% and beach recreation items made up 12%.[16]

It should be noted that marine litter is not just on the sea's surface and on beaches. In a study of European waters by Pharm et al.,[17] marine litter was found at depths ranging from 35 to 4500 metres, with plastic bags, glass bottles and derelict fishing gear being the most prevalent. In another study by Galgani et al.,[18] plastics were estimated to make up as much as 95% of marine litter found on coastlines, sea surface and the ocean floor. Again, Jambeck et al.[19] stated that an estimated 4.8 to 12.7 million metric tonnes of plastic entered the ocean from land-based sources in 2010, and approximately another 8 metric tonnes have entered the oceans each year since then.

In addition to the findings on the impact of plastics reported above, studies by Van Franeker[20] have shown that the composition of marine debris has changed from predominantly industrial to consumer-based plastics since the 1980s. To this end, Barnes[21] pointed out that plastic particles in the oceans are decreasing in average size with a subsequent increase in particle numbers due to continual fragmentation. This presents new issues as smaller organisms are able to ingest microplastics, and clean-up efforts are becoming more complicated and very expensive.

17.3 Plastic Waste Situation in the West African Region

The western region of Africa is made up of 15 countries that form the ECOWAS[22] regional block. Discussions on the plastic waste situation in this region were centred on Nigeria, Ghana and Senegal, selected on the basis that they are coastal states.

17.3.1 Plastic Waste Situation in Nigeria

Nigeria generates an estimated 32 million tonnes of solid waste yearly; one of the highest in Africa, from that figure, is plastic, which constitutes 2.5 million tonnes.

[16] Hong et al. (2014), pp. 27–34.
[17] Pham et al. (2014).
[18] Galgani et al. (2015), pp. 29–56.
[19] Jambeck et al. (2015), pp. 768–771.
[20] Van Franeker (2011), pp. 2609–2615.
[21] Barnes (2009), pp. 1985–1998.
[22] Economic Community of West African States.

Nigeria is among the top 20 nations that contribute 83% of the total volume of land-based plastic waste that ends up in the oceans. An estimate of over 200,000 metric tonnes of plastic waste from land-based sources in Nigeria is discharged into the Atlantic Ocean annually.[23] In the recent past, the demand for plastics in Nigeria has grown. About 70% of plastic raw materials used in Nigeria are imported (mainly from the Middle East, Europe and Asia), and only 30% are produced locally. In the years 2008 to 2015, imports of plastic raw materials increased annually by 7.2% from 464 kt to 754 kt, +62.5%. This makes Nigeria one of Africa's largest importers of plastics in primary forms.[24]

Over a 10-year period, the per capita consumption of plastics in Nigeria had grown by 5% annually from 4.0 kg in 2007 to 6.5 kg in 2017, and it is estimated to be 7.5 kg by 2020. Seasonal demand factors shortened product life cycle, fuelled by the growing utilisation of 'single-use' plastics (SUPs), and have increased the consumption patterns of plastic goods.[25]

A 2017 field survey on plastic waste generation in Nigeria revealed that the packaging industries contributed 63%, while the electrical and electronics contributed 8%, construction and demolition contributed 5%, agriculture 2% and non-packaging households and others contributed 18%. In that survey, it was estimated that about 1.5 million tonnes of plastic waste were generated in Nigeria every year. Of these, less than 30% are collected for recycling.[26]

In Nigeria, it is estimated that 63 million people do not have access to improved sources of drinking water as of 2013.[27] Given the inadequate public infrastructure to supply drinking water, the private sector started to produce plastic or nylon-packed sachet water, popularly known as 'pure water', in the late 1990s, and the business has grown as one of the leading industries in Nigeria. The sachet water has since diffused among the population as a source of potable drinking water, with 70% of Nigerians individually consuming an average of one bag of sachet water daily during the dry season.[28]

While sachet water is an important source of potable water, it is estimated that about 50–60 million used water sachet are thrown into the streets of Nigeria on a daily basis.[29] Another estimate shows that the total surface area of plastic wrappers discarded daily in Nigeria—nearly 1 million sq km—exceeds the area of the entire nation.[30] The environmental risks of sachet water disposal have become a serious

[23] United Nations Industrial Development Organization (UNIDO) (2021), p. 33.

[24] EnvironReview Nigeria (2021).

[25] Ibid.

[26] Ibid.

[27] World Health Organisation (WHO) (2019).

[28] United Nations Industrial Development Organization (UNIDO) (2021), p. 33.

[29] Edoga et al. (2008), pp. 642–646.

[30] Stoler (2017), p. 1206.

concern for reasons such as drainage obstruction/blockage, water pollution and air pollution (from burnt plastic sachet—a common practice in Nigeria).[31]

Thus, major sources of land-based plastic pollutants are sachet water and plastic shopping bags. The everyday use of plastic bags and other single-use plastic products, including takeaway food packs, straws, cups and spoons, among others, is widespread in Nigeria, but the packaging of drinking water in plastic sachet bags has become an increasingly important peculiar feature of the country. These plastic sachet bags (containing 500 mL) are used by the water industry to pack drinking water in Nigeria. Plastic sachet water bags are a ubiquitous sight and are widely accepted. Other sources include the use of polyethylene (cellophane) to wrap and sell different consumables.[32]

Nigeria is also home to three out of the top 20 plastic-polluting rivers globally, that is, the Cross, Imo and Kwa Ibo rivers. Studies have found microplastics in aquatic life due to pollution, especially due to the mismanagement of low-value plastics.[33]

17.3.2 Plastic Waste Situation in Ghana

Ghana has a population estimate of 34,121,985 inhabitants, of which 67% live in the urban areas. Ghana has an area of 227,540 km^2.[34] Like in many African countries, single-use plastics in Ghana have become a serious environmental pollution problem and an enduring menace. Plastic bags are indiscriminately used by vendors in cities and towns across Ghana, and it is common for drinking water to be sold in plastic sachets and food packed in single-use Styrofoam packaging. Almost 8.2 billion sachets of water are consumed in Ghana.[35]

According to Erinosho,[36] although exact data on total plastic production and importation is lacking, it is estimated that more than 3000 metric tons daily and 1 million tonnes yearly of plastic waste are generated. An estimated 86% of Ghana's waste plastic load is improperly disposed of, resulting in plastics clogging up stormwater drains, rivers and streams and ending up in the oceans. It is estimated that 250,000 metric tons of plastic waste are dumped from Ghana into the Atlantic Ocean.[37]

The impacts of plastics in the oceans have been well documented. In Ghana, plastics litter large swathes of the 500-kilometre coastline and impact marine spaces.

---

[31] Dumbili and Henderson (2020), pp. 569–583.

[32] Ibid.

[33] World Bank (2023).

[34] Worldometer (2023a).

[35] Stoler (2017).

[36] Erinosho (2023).

[37] World Bank (2020).

Estimates for Ghana's contribution to global marine debris range from approximately 92,000 to 260,000 metric tons every year or 1–3% of the global total. On the Ocean Health Index in 2019, Ghana's score was 59, and respect of Exclusive Economic Zones, it was ranked 188 out of 221.[38]

17.3.3 *Plastic Waste Situation in Senegal*

Similar to other West African countries, Senegal is a net importer of plastics. Senegal has an estimated population of 17,763,163 inhabitants, with 52% living in the urban areas. It occupies a total land area of 192,530 km^2.[39] In both 2018 and 2019, Senegal had no domestic resin production. Its conversion industry processed 47 kt of resin (22 kt of PE, 21 kt of PP, 4 kt of PET) in 2018 and 37 kt of resin (18 kt of PE, 11 kt PP and 9 kt of PET) in 2019. Senegal's largest plastic waste generation hotspot is in the capital city, Dakar, and it is ranked as the fifth-largest plastic generation location in West Africa. The generation rate for the Dakar hotspot is 75.32 kt per year over the hotspot area of 567 km^2.[40]

In Senegal, the average daily volume of urban solid waste is around 8,664.4 tonnes, consisting mainly of fine materials (around 50%), particularly sand. Municipal solid waste per capita is around 0.5 kg a day. In the Dakar region, waste generation is estimated to be 2,684.5 tonnes a day, or 979,842 tonnes a year.[41]

17.4 Plastic Waste Situation in Central African Region

A number of countries are found in the Central African region. However, for purposes of the discussions on land-based sources of plastic waste, Cameroon and Democratic Republic of the Congo (DRC) were selected. The Choice of Cameroon lies on the fact that it is a coastal State while that of DRC, though an in-land State is traversed by the Congo River and its tributaries that empty into the ocean

17.4.1 *Plastic Waste Situation in Cameroon*

Cameroon is a lower-middle-income country bordered by Nigeria, Chad, the Central African Republic, the Republic of the Congo, Gabon and Equatorial Guinea with an

[38] Miezah et al. (2015), pp. 15–27.

[39] Worldometer (2023b).

[40] United Nations (2019).

[41] German Agency for International Cooperation GmbH (2021).

area of 475,440 km^2.[42] Cameroon has an estimated population of about 28,647, 293, with 58% living in the urban area.[43]

In 2018 and 2019, Cameroon had no domestic resin production. Its conversion industry processed 34 kt of resin (9 kt polypropylene (PP), 10 kt PE (polyethylene), 15 kt PET (polyethylene terephthalate) in 2018 and 39 kt of resin (4 kt PP, 20 kt PE, 15 kt PET) in 2019.

Similar to other West African countries, Cameroon is a net importer of plastics. In 2019, 40 million kg of plastics were imported into the country, with PE, PP and PVC accounting for about 99% of the imports.[44] In comparison, 852,652 kg of scrap plastics were exported from Cameroon that same year.[45] Cameroon generates 0.77 kg of MSW (municipal solid waste) per capita per day, and this amounts to an overall daily MSW generation of 1.5 million kg.[46] However, about 81.4% of MSW generated is inadequately managed.[47] Plastic waste accounts for just below 6% of MSW arisings, with a daily generation rate of about 91,000 kg, of which 81% are inadequately managed;[48] 1820 kg/day of plastic waste leaks into the environment in Cameroon.[49]

17.4.2 Plastic Waste Situation in the Democratic Republic of the Congo (DRC)

Plastic pollution is a more-than-apparent reality in the Democratic Republic of the Congo (DRC). The DRC produces 48,154 kilos of plastic per day, 85% of which are poorly managed.[50] About 12 million inhabitants in Kinshasa, DRC's capital, produce 7000 tons of waste every day, or nearly 260 kilos per capita each year. Plastic bottles submerge the rivers of the Congo River, running through the city of Kinshasa.[51]

Plastic bottles, bottle caps, food packaging, plastic bags, lids and plastic straws are commonly used in Kinshasa and other cities in the DRC. This plastic waste is then dumped in garbage cans, gutters and streams, with adverse consequences to the ecology and human health. The human and the abiotic environments suffer massive damage due to this plastic pollution in the light and Congolese authorities' interest.

---

[42] World Bank Group (2021).

[43] Worldometer (2023c).

[44] United Nations (2019).

[45] Ibid.

[46] Jambeck et al. (2015), pp. 768–771.

[47] Ibid.

[48] Ibid.

[49] Ibid.

[50] United Nations Environment Programme (2018).

[51] Ibid.

In Kinshasa, the DRC capital, plastic waste accumulates and invades the waterways of the Congo River. They prevent water from entering the ground during massive flooding and clog the pipes. Pollution also poses health problems.[52]

In Kinshasa, plastic waste invades the Congo River's soils and waterways. Bottles, bags and miscellaneous packaging garbage accumulate, clog pipes and prevent water from entering the ground during massive flooding, sometimes resulting in some residents' death.[53] According to Jambeck et al.,[54] the DRC was reported to contribute 0.05% to global plastic waste in oceans.

17.5 Plastic Waste Situation Eastern African Region

Kenya was selected on the basis of being a coastal state, a hub in the East African Community.

17.5.1 Plastic Waste Situation in Kenya

Kenya is bordered to the north by Sudan and Ethiopia, to the east by Somalia, to the west by Uganda, to the south by Tanzania and to the southeast by the Indian Ocean. Much of the country, especially in the north and east, is arid or semi-arid. Kenya has a coastline on the Indian Ocean, which contains swamps of East African mangroves.[55] Inland are broad plains and numerous hills. Kenya has a population estimated at 55,100,586 inhabitants, with 46% living in urban areas.[56]

In Kenya, plastic constitutes an estimated 10–12% of solid waste, amounting to 966,000 tonnes per year. From these, plastic beverage bottles accounted for the largest share (13.26%) of all items collected from beaches in 2019, followed by plastic bottle caps (10.5%).[57]

[52] Bukasa et al. (2020), p. 184.

[53] Ibid, 185.

[54] Jambeck et al. (2015), pp. 768–771.

[55] Kenya Embassy (2023).

[56] Worldometer (2023e).

[57] United Nations Conference on Trade and Development (UNCTAD) (2022).

17.6 Plastic Waste Situation in the Southern African Region

Angola and the Republic of South Africa were selected for the discussion. Both are members of the Southern African Development Community (SADC) and were selected on the basis that they are coastal states.

17.6.1 Plastic Waste Situation in Angola

Angola is located on the west coast of Africa, with a geographical area of about 1,246,700 km^2, and bordered on the north by the Republic of the Congo, on the northeast by the Democratic Republic of the Congo, on the east by Zambia, on the south by Namibia and on the west by the Atlantic Ocean.[58] Angola has a population of about 36,684,202 inhabitants, of which 68% are in urban areas.[59]

According to a study carried out by the Ministry of Economy and Planning (MEP), the composition of municipal solid waste (MSW) in Luanda is 25% organic waste, 21% sand and earth, 16% paper and card, 15% plastic, 7% textiles, metals 7%, 7% glass and others 2%. Luanda produces an average of 2.5 million tonnes of garbage per year, 375,000 tonnes of which is plastic.[60]

17.6.2 Plastic Waste Situation in the Republic of South Africa

The Republic of South Africa has an estimated population of 60,414, 495 inhabitants, of which 69% live in the urban areas. South Africa occupies a total land space of 1,213,090 km^2.[61]

The Republic of South Africa generates 2.4 million tons of plastic waste every year, equivalent to 41 kg of plastic waste per citizen. The materials you throw away persist in nature long after they have been discarded. Only 14% of the 2.4 million tons of plastic thrown into bins is recycled.[62]

Almost all plastic that is consumed in South Africa is manufactured in the country from locally produced or imported primary or secondary plastic. According to IUCN, 70% of the plastic waste generated in South Africa is collected, of which 14% is recycled, 45% is disposed of in sanitary landfills or incineration facilities and the remaining 11% is disposed of in unsanitary landfills or dumpsites.[63]

---

[58] Knoema (2021).

[59] Worldometer (2023f).

[60] Bukasa et al. (2020), p. 185.

[61] Worldometer (2023g).

[62] World Wildlife Federation South Africa (2023).

[63] Naidu (2022).

17.7 Effects of Plastic Waste

The effects of plastic waste on humans and nature have long been identified by various authors. In 1969, Kenyon and Kridler[64] published a report on plastics entering the food chain. This report correlated with previous observations of plastic pollutants in the oceans. In 1971, Buchannan[65] reported that synthetic fibres were becoming increasingly obvious over the last decade in plankton hauls 0–100 m deep. In the same vein, plankton trawls conducted in the coastal waters of New England, USA, detected polystyrene spherules predicted to pollute ocean sediments due to their higher density compared to seawater.

Furthermore, the findings published by Carpenter[66] in 1972 indicated the ecological threats associated with plastic marine debris. In those findings, polystyrene spherules were discovered to contain polychlorinated biphenyl (PCB), which is now used in the production of plastic. It was also noted that, based on colour, spherules were selectively consumed by most of the fish species examined. Industrial plastic manufacturers were suggested as the source.

The above finding was supported in a 1974 report by Hays and Commons,[67] who investigated polystyrene spherules and other plastic particles found along the coast of Gull Island, New York. In a paper jointly published by Carpenter and Smith Jr[68] in early 1972 observed that plastics may be the source of PCBs found in marine creatures and that increases in plastic production and warned that poor waste disposal practices could exacerbate the problems. Confirming further the impact of plastics, DeLong et al.[69] reported as far back as 1973 that organo-chlorine pesticides and PCBs were associated with the premature pupping of California sea lions since 1968.

The shape, resilience and rate of degeneration of plastics vary. Plastics that are more durable take longer to dissolve, whereas throw-away plastics are those that have been combined with organic materials and degrade quickly.[70] Plastic waste will take tens if not hundreds of years to degrade, and over time, they will have a harmful impact on the environment, our health and our economy. When irresponsibly disposed of, SUPs make their way into the environment, where they block water channels, harm biodiversity, clog drains (causing flooding) and intensify soil degradation. When buried (such as in landfills), they leech dangerous chemicals, which pollute groundwater and soil. When burned (such as in open pits), they emit harmful

[64] Kenyon and Kridler (1969), pp. 339–343.

[65] Buchanan (1971), p. 23.

[66] Carpenter (1972), pp. 749–750.

[67] Hays and Commons (1974), pp. 44–46.

[68] Carpenter and Smith Jr (1972), pp. 1240–1241.

[69] DeLong et al. (1973), pp. 1168–1170.

[70] Dual (2022).

gases, which have been linked to various diseases such as asthma, cancer and heart disease.[71] The position is that the unregulated use of single-use plastics has severe consequences, including environmental pollution, health risks and economic losses.

In 2015, Jambeck et al.,[72] while highlighting the impact of marine plastic, discussed the challenges and emerging solutions to the land-based plastic waste issue in Africa. The work is an empirical policy paper that focuses on the quantitative analysis of problems of land-based plastic pollution in African countries. According to the authors,[73]

> the increasing trend in per capita consumption, urbanisation, and population growth is concerning when combined with a lack of sufficient infrastructure to manage the increased waste generation. Plastic waste presents not only an environmental issue for African countries but also a major socio-economic development challenge which impacts biodiversity, infrastructure, tourism and fisheries livelihoods. The lack of clean drinking water only exacerbates the problem, as in many city centers, even drinking water is packaged in single use sachets and plastic bags.

Generally speaking, plastic waste and marine litter negatively impact the lives of residents for several reasons: (i) increased flood risks from drainages and rivers that are clogged by plastic bags and debris; (ii) degradation of the marine ecosystem, contributing to the conversion and/or fragmentation of aquatic habitats (mangroves); (iii) negative economic impacts on a revenue base of countries, especially those that rely on the tourism, fishery and shipping sectors; (iv) health risks to the general public and particularly to informal waste pickers and scavengers resulting from the disposal of medical waste in dumpsites, drainages and rivers, which has been further compounded by the recent increase in COVID-19 patients.[74]

17.8 Management Strategies for Plastic Waste Management

Various approaches either have been put in place by various countries or are being considered in order to tackle the menace of plastic waste. Most of the approaches have been established through legislation

[71] UNEP (2023a).

[72] Jambeck et al. (2015), p. 257.

[73] Ibid.

[74] World Bank (2023).

17.8.1 *Legislative Approaches*

Some authors noted that common plastic-reduction instruments in Africa are legislative bans and, to a lesser extent, taxes.[75]

17.8.1.1 Legislative Approaches in the West African Region

17.8.1.1.1 Legislative Approaches in Nigeria

Nigeria's leading environmental protection measures are the National Environmental Standard Regulations and Enforcement (Establishment) Agency (NESREA) Act of 2007 and a few national environmental regulations for the following industries: food, beverages, tobacco, pharmaceuticals, soap and detergent, electrical and electronics, plastics and coastal and marine. Some of these regulations include requirements for the implementation of the Extended Producers Responsibility (EPR) Programme as a framework for creating a zero-waste society, including the mitigation of the environmental impact of packaging waste. A law prohibiting the use, production and importation of all plastic bags used for domestic and commercial packaging was approved in May 2019. However, the law has not yet come into effect because the President has not given his consent.

Additionally, there is the National Policy on Environment 1989, which was revised in 1999 and 2016 and which, in Chapter 5.1 of Policy Statement 7, secures and enforces a legislative ban on plastic bags and, in Chapter 7.8 of Policy Statement 12, restricts and/or taxes the use of polluting non-biodegradable consumer products, like plastic shopping bags.[76]

17.8.1.1.2 Legislative Approaches in Ghana

In Ghana, most national legal frameworks (approximately 59%) govern waste at the waste management stage of its life cycle. Most of the national legal framework on waste management is focused on addressing plastic waste (about 41%) through policies. Plastic bags, specifically, are governed by 12% of the legal framework through legislation.[77] A major law in this respect is the Customs and Excise (Duties and Other Taxes) Act (Act 512) 1996 (amended by Act 863 2013). The main aim of the Act is to tax plastic and all its derivatives.

At the time it was enacted in 1996, the Act dealt with environmental tax and imposed an ad valorem duty of 10% of the ex-factory price of plastic products. But with the amendment in 2013, the environmental excise tax on plastic and plastic

[75] Nwafor and Walker (2020).

[76] UNIDO (2021), p. 54.

[77] UNEP (2021b).

products was reviewed and 15% excise duty on polythene bags and other plastic packaging materials is now imposed. This obviously aims to limit the amount of plastic produced, as well as the plastic that is thrown away.

Ghana also has several policies in place to combat pollution from plastic waste. One such policy is the National Plastics Management Policy 2018, updated and adopted in 2021, and the Greater Accra Sustainable Sanitation and Livelihoods Improvement Project. The National Plastics Management Policy 2018, updated and adopted in 2021, aims to use the comprehensive management of plastics across their life cycle and value chain as a vehicle for sustainable development, enabling a shift towards a plastics circular economy. It also provides a comprehensive action strategy for multi-level engagement of stakeholders and the public. This policy shall guide the work of all governmental, statutory, industry, non-governmental and civic entities that are involved in, or that may seek to become involved in, the importation and exportation, manufacturing, use, management, recycling and disposal of plastics, particularly activities addressing adverse impacts posed by plastics on the environment and human health.[78]

From the foregoing, plastic waste regulation in Ghana is only partially addressed through the National Plastics Management Policy 2018, as amended. At present, there is no legislation or laws for plastic that are binding. Furthermore, there is no part of the legal framework that bans plastic bags, microbeads or other single-use plastics.

Notwithstanding the above scenario, Ghana shows the intention to commit to plastic reduction through its international participation in collaborations. Presently, Ghana is a participant in the Global Plastic Action Partnership (GPAP) and System Analysis Programme Development (SAP) of the World Economic Forum. In 2021, the country launched the National Plastic Action Partnership, which resulted in the publication of a blueprint for drastically reducing plastic pollution in Ghana.

17.8.1.1.3 Legislative Approaches in Senegal

Current legislation in Senegal for the control of plastic waste is the Act on the Prevention and Reduction of the Environmental Impact of Plastic Products, Act No. 2020-04, of 08 January 2020[79] This Law, also referred to as Anti-plastic Law No. 2020-04 of January 8, 2020, repealed Law No. 2015-09 of 04 May 2015.

The Law under Article 1 seeks to address the prevention and reduction of impacts on the environment and human health of plastic products and the ecological management of plastic waste and applies to plastic products, whether or not they are intended for one-time use. However, it does not apply to products that include one or

[78] Ibid.

[79] As was enacted in French: Loi relative à la prévention et la réduction de l'incidence sur l'environnement des produits plastiques, la loi n° 2020-04 du 08 Janvier 2020.

more plastic components if the product is designed so that the plastic components are not easily replaced by the consumer.[80]

The Law bans the production, import, stocking to sell, putting up for sale, selling, putting in place to be used and the use in any form of single-use or disposable plastics. This applies to beverage containers and lids, cutlery and plates, straws and beverage stir sticks and sachets used for selling water or other beverages.[81]

The ban also includes plastic bags out of their box, regardless of thickness or whether they have handles or not. However, this does not include plastic bags used at the point of sale to package food items. In any case, such bags used at the point of sale must be transparent and made from recyclable plastic materials, and the importation of these bags is subject to authorisation by the Minister of the Environment.[82]

For the efficient control of plastic waste, the Law creates a deposit-refund system for plastic bottles. In this respect, producers are to put in place collection points and be responsible for recovering the returned bottles in the following priorities: (1) reuse, (2) recycle or (3) all other recovering operations. In addition to reuse and recycling, allowable recovery operations include all other actions aimed at obtaining reusable materials or energy, for example through 'valorisation'.[83]

Another approach introduced under the Law is extended producer responsibility (EPR). It makes producers who put plastic products on the market responsible for the waste generated by these products. To meet this obligation, producers can set out individual programmes to collect and treat the waste generated from their products. The producers can also collectively create organisations sponsored by them that will take on this responsibility. To do this, the producers must demonstrate financial and technical capacity to get approval for an individual programme. However, such individual programmes must have the approval of the Minister of the Environment and must comply with the requirements issued by him.[84]

In order to prevent the production of plastic waste, producers must reduce at the source the quantity of waste that can result from their activities. They are implored to produce goods that are susceptible to being recycled or otherwise recovered in conditions that respect the environment. When it is technically and economically viable, producers must integrate recycled plastic into new products they put out for sale.[85] To this end, plastic products must have the name of the producer permanently marked on the product.[86] To discourage producing plastic products made from

[80] Act No.2020-04 of 08 January 2020, art. 2.

[81] Ibid., art. 4.

[82] Act No. 2020-04 of 08 January 2020, art. 5.

[83] Ibid., art. 8.

[84] Ibid., arts. 11 and 12.

[85] Ibid., arts. 15 and 16.

[86] Ibid., art. 17.

non-recyclable plastic, the Law provides for the imposition of taxes on such products.[87] A decree will list products to which the tax will apply (Article 22).

To further prevent and reduce the influx of plastic products into the country, the Law bans the importation of plastic waste under Article 19. Additionally, the Law bans the export of plastic waste unless the Minister of the Environment has approved it and there is ample evidence that the importing country has approved the import and has adequate treatment facilities.[88]

The contravention of any of the provisions of the Law amounts to an offence, and the offender shall be punished, depending on the nature of the offence, under Articles 25–39.

17.8.2 Legislative Approaches in the Central Africa Region

17.8.2.1 Legislative Approaches in Cameroon

Environmental Law 96/12, 1996, and Decree No. 2012/2809, 2012, are the primary laws governing environmental preservation in Cameroon. However, in 2014, the Cameroonian government passed Circular No. 0036/NC/CAB/MINEPDED Relating to Small Scale Violators of Joint Order No. 004/MINEPDED/MINCOMMERCE Relating to Among Others the Prohibition of Plastic Packages Inferior to 60 Microns, which outlawed the use of plastic bags smaller than 60 microns. The law forbids the use of plastic bags that are not biodegradable. The 'polluter pays' notion is also used in the National Strategy for Waste Management from 2007.

17.8.2.2 Legislative Approaches in DR Congo

To address the rising level of plastic waste pollution, the Democratic Republic of the Congo created the Politique Nationale d'Assainissement (PNA)[89] in 2013. Due to a lack of funding and infrastructure for waste treatment, this policy has not been put into effect.[90] In 2018, the government outlawed the production and sale of plastic goods, including bags and bottles, in an effort to reduce the negative effects of plastic trash pollution in Kinshasa. However, they can still be imported.

[87] Ibid., art. 22.

[88] Act No. 2020-04 of 08 January 2020, art. 20.

[89] National Sanitation Policy 2013.

[90] Bukasa et al. (2020), pp. 180–199.

17.8.3 Legislative Approaches in the Fast Africa Region

17.8.3.1 Legislative Approaches in Kenya

In 1999, Kenya enacted the Environmental Management and Co-ordination Act, an Act of Parliament to provide for the establishment of an appropriate legal and institutional framework for the management of the environment and for matters connected therewith and incidental thereto. The Act was amended in 2012, and nothing in it specifically mentioned plastic waste.

However, in 2017, the Kenyan Cabinet Secretary of Environment and Natural Resources[91] issued Notice No. 2356 of 2017 on Plastic Bags.[92] Under the Notice, 6 months after its coming into effect, a ban is placed on the use, manufacture and importation of all plastic bags utilised for commercial and household packaging defined as follows: (a) carrier bags (bags constructed with handles, and with or without gussets) and (b) flat bags (bags constructed without handles, and with or without gussets).[93] The idea is to ban the use, manufacture and importation of all plastic bags of the type specified in the Notice used for commercial and household packaging. In addition to the ban on single-use plastics in 2017, in 2020, single-use plastics were prohibited in protected areas, such as parks and forests.

This move, according to The Guardian,[94] was lauded as groundbreaking as the national environmental authority says 80% of the public has complied with the ban. Despite the acclaimed success of the ban, it has not been enough to eliminate the country's struggles with pollution as it did not include many other forms of plastic, including bottles, rubbish bags and takeaway containers. In this regard, despite the single-use bag ban in 2017, Nairobi and its waste collectors are still inundated with plastic.[95]

However, in 2019, the Plastic Action Plan 2019 was put in place. This plan is intended to be general in its consideration of plastics in all their forms and provides in-depth research into the Kenyan plastic sector. It incorporates the entire plastic value chain, spanning from imports of raw materials to manufacturing processes to the use and subsequent recycling of different plastic fractions.

Furthermore, there is no national legal framework that targets microbeads or single-use plastics besides plastic bags. Kenya does show the intention to manage plastic better through action plan development and membership in initiatives, such

---

[91] In the exercise of the powers conferred on the Cabinet Secretary for Environment and Natural Resources under sections 3 and 86 of the Environmental Management and Co-ordination Act 1999, as amended.

[92] Kenya Law, Gazette Notice No. 2356 of 14 March 2017.

[93] Ibid.

[94] The Guardian (2023).

[95] Ibid.

as #breakfreefromplastic, the Alliance to End Plastic Waste and the Commonwealth Clean Ocean Alliance.[96]

17.8.4 Legislative Approaches in the Sothern African Region

17.8.4.1 Legislative Approaches in Angola

Angola's environmental preservation efforts began in earnest in 1998, with the adoption of the Basic Environmental Law (LBA). It established the state's duty to protect the environment and uphold a National Environmental Management Plan, which eventually led to the promulgation of Presidential Decree No. 196/12 of 30 August 2012, which contains the Strategic Plan for the Management of Urban Waste (PESGRU). The National Waste Agency (ANR) was established in 2014, with the goal of implementing waste management policies and meeting environmental protection standards in the development of programmes for trash reduction, recycling, reuse and disposal.[97] The plastic ban policy was proposed in 2015, using a top-down method on a national level via a decree, which now appears to be under review and has yet to be implemented.[98]

17.8.4.2 Legislative Approaches in the Republic of South Africa

In 2003, the Minister of Environmental Affairs and Tourism, Republic of South Africa, issued the Plastic Carrier Bags and Plastic Flat Bags Regulations 2003. The Regulations were made under section 24(d) of the Environment Conservation Act 1989 (Act No. 73 of 1989).[99]

The Regulations prohibit the manufacture, trade or commercial distribution of domestically produced or imported plastic carrier bags and plastic flat bags, for use within the Republic of South Africa, other than those that comply with the Compulsory Specification for Plastic Carrier Bags and Flat Bags—VC 8087-2013.[100]

In addition, no person may manufacture, trade or commercially distribute domestically produced or imported plastic carrier bags and plastic flat bags, for use within the Republic of South Africa, unless they comply with the minimum post-consumer

[96] UNEP (2021b).

[97] Almeida (2017), pp. 27–29.

[98] Bezerra et al. (2021), p. 7.

[99] Government Notice R.625 in Government Gazette 24839 of 9 May 2003.

[100] Plastic Carrier Bags and Plastic Flat Bags Regulations, 2003 of South Africa as amended in 2021, sub-regulation 1.

recyclate content specifications.[101] The following are the specifications under the regulation:[102]

(a) Plastic carrier bags and plastic flat bags must be made from a minimum of 50% postconsumer recyclate from 1 January 2023;
(b) Plastic carrier bags and plastic flat bags must be made from a minimum of 75% postconsumer recyclate from 1 January 2025; and
(c) Plastic carrier bags and plastic flat bags must be made from 100% post-consumer recyclate from 01 January 2027.

Where a person is unable to comply with the requirements contained in regulation 2(3)(c), he may apply to the Minister for an exemption in terms of section 24M of the National Environmental Management Act 1998 (Act No. 107 of 1998), read with the National Exemption Regulations promulgated in terms of section 44(1)(a) and section 24M(3) of the Act.[103]

However, in 2021, regulation 3 of the Regulations was amended by virtue of the Amendment Regulations Regarding Plastic Carrier Bags and Plastic Flat Bags 2021.[104] Under this amendment, it is now an offence for any person who contravenes regulation 2 of the Regulations. Such a person shall be liable, on conviction, to a fine not exceeding R5 million or to imprisonment for a period not exceeding 5 years and, in the case of a second or subsequent conviction, to a fine not exceeding R10 million or to imprisonment for a period not exceeding 10 years or, in both instances, to both such fine and imprisonment and, in some cases, *to a fine not exceeding three times the commercial value of anything in respect of which the offence was committed.*

Commenting on the policies adopted by African countries in reducing SUPs, Issahaku Adam et al.[105] opined that the policies are mainly legislative with limited market-based approaches. The authors questioned tangible evidence of single-use plastic reduction. To them,

> the bans lack proper planning, coordination and implementation/enforcement as there was limited consultation when drafting the legislation, no national campaigns, and limited notification (less than one year) between ban announcement and subsequent implementation. There are no provisions for re-useable alternatives.

On the effectiveness of the legal frameworks, generally, Romer and Tamminen[106] stated that bans on the use of plastics encourage customers to switch to reusable bags. Charging, on the other hand, has a greater impact on overall reduction as this

---

[101] Plastic Carrier Bags and Plastic Flat Bags Regulations, 2003 of South Africa, as amended in 2021, sub-regulation 2.

[102] Under sub-regulation 3.

[103] Plastic Carrier Bags and Plastic Flat Bags Regulations, 2003 of South Africa, as amended in 2021, sub-regulation 4.

[104] Government Notice 317 of 2021.

[105] Adam et al. (2020) 103928.

[106] Romer and Tamminen (2014), pp. 237–275.

incentivises behavioural change and forces customers to make conscious decisions to purchase plastic bags. In the same vein, Taylor and Villas-Boas,[107] while analysing whether differences arose from plastic bag bans vs. fees, found that bans and fees both significantly reduce disposable plastic bag use and increase reusable and paper bag use and that bans were only more effective if stores offered inexpensive reusable bags and charged more for disposable paper bags.[108]

Aside from the aforementioned provisions in the Law, market-based instruments and consumer awareness approaches should be included as an integral part of the legislation as both approaches have been considered complementary tools within a broader policy package, and hybrid policies appear to be the most successful.[109] The overall intendment of the Law and policies should be to place emphasis on the prevention and reduction of the environmental impact of plastic products.

In order to give more force to the legislative approach, there is a need for comprehensive legislation among regional blocks. Such legislation should 'encompass control over various single-use products, along with consumer awareness campaigns and market-based instruments. This holistic approach, integrating a mix of regulatory and market-driven mechanisms, has demonstrated success in combating plastic waste pollution'.[110]

17.8.5 Other Strategies in Plastic Waste Management

Policies on plastic pollution appeared not to focus on recycling and other recovery methods but to a much greater extent on prevention and banning. As a result a non-legislative strategy such as recycling of plastic waste is being advocated in the control and management of marine plastic. Recycling is a major focus and a critical component of waste management everywhere.

In the 1970s, plastics came into wide use in the United States of America. Manufacturers recognised the disposal problem but did not try to solve it. Instead, they spent millions of US dollars on advertising the benefits of plastic and what it brings to modern life, diverting attention from problems of disposal. This campaign resulted in an increase in the public acceptance of plastic use from 30% to 60%. Rather than addressing the disposal problem associated with the use of plastic, they developed an extensive advertising programme to shift the sense of responsibility for disposal from the plastic/fossil fuel industry to the consumers. But soon after, people woke to the realities of a throw-away lifestyle, and pollution and waste became a concern.[111] The reason for this is simple: most plastics are not recycled, even those

[107] Taylor and Villas-Boas (2016), pp. 351–372.

[108] Ibid.

[109] Nwafor and Walker (2020), p. 10.

[110] Onyeabor and Uju Obuka (2024), p. 3.

[111] Glick (2021).

with a recycle symbol. Although it might be possible to recycle these materials, it simply is not economically feasible.[112]

Recycling most plastics usually is more expensive and energy intensive than creating new raw materials from fossil-fuel-based chemicals. As at 2021, about 91% of plastics produced have not been recycled but instead ended up in landfills or are simply dumped. It is a significant problem: plastics do not decompose; they just break apart.[113] Plastic trash has always been a concern, and for more than 50 years, fossil fuel companies have manipulated the public perception of the harms inflicted by plastic manufacture and disposal.[114] To this, Glick[115] queries:

> How is it, that after decades of manufacture and known problems with disposal, plastic products are widely used, with expanding manufacture and distribution? In local supermarkets we see plastic wrap and containers on every shelf, from plastic-covered paper products to 'clamshells' to deli containers to orange juice, even on fresh items that need no outer wrap. Plastic is hard to avoid, even when we try to do without it. After a single use the wrap is thrown away, or we recycle it. Or we think we do, because that's what the industry wants us to think.

Glick[116] concluded: 'Now, in response to obvious problems with recycling failures, fossil fuel companies are reviving their old tricks—trying to convince us that the fault is all ours, and again encouraging recycling, even though they know recycling plastics can never be successful.'

In the words of Simon,[117] 'the responsibility for plastics' impact lies with producers. The best choices for consumers, in order, are 'Refuse, Reduce, Reuse, Refill, Repair, Rot (compost), Recycle'. However, recycling is increasingly seen as an unsuitable solution to the growing volume of food waste produced by the world. According to Ranniger,[118] 'of all plastics the world has produced, only 9% of the nine billion tons has been recycled, most ends up in landfills, dumps, or in the environment'.

The problem of recycling lies in plastic waste generation. Approximately 8 billion tons of plastics have been produced since the 1950s, and more than 300 million tons are now made each year. Although recycling has been mainstream for decades and mechanical recycling works well for rigid plastics such as PET and mono-materials, 10% of all plastics ever made have actually been recycled, at best.[119] There are many factors contributing to this figure.

Some individuals and businesses still do not make efforts to separate plastic from other waste. Some plastic packaging—crisp packets for example—are multi-

[112] Ibid.

[113] Glick (2021).

[114] Ibid.

[115] Ibid.

[116] Glick (2021).

[117] Simon cited by Glick (2021).

[118] Ranniger (2021).

[119] Ibid.

laminates, that is, with other materials, such as paper or aluminium combined with plastic, which means it cannot be processed in the recycling system. Other forms of packaging, such as flexibles, are not economical to recycle. Plastic contaminated with food would not be recycled either. Only clean plastic makes it through the system.[120] Thus, the truth about recycling is much murkier. And just because a product features the recycle symbol means it is certain that it will be recycled, especially in the case of plastic.

One of the primary technological challenges faced by the recycling industry is the exorbitant energy cost of operating existing technologies for melting and re-forming plastic into new material. Currently, it is not profitable for the industry to melt recycled plastic, which in turn severely limits the range of products that can be produced and the overall volume of plastic that can pass through the recycling industry.[121]

From the foregoing, it means that recycling alone is not going to solve the plastic waste crisis because of the rate of our consumption and our use of plastic, past and present. As a result, other options are suggested. It will take a global effort to scale upstream and downstream solutions to combat plastic pollution. This may include reuse and improved waste collection, in addition to reducing our overall consumption levels. But shifting the spotlight towards reducing the production of plastic is critical to each of these efforts.

In addition, addressing the waste crisis will require more support for new forms of packaging, such as those made from compostable materials. This is so because a major scheme for reducing plastic production is replacing it with alternative, more sustainable materials. According to Moss et al.,[122] paper packaging can work. The reason is that it biodegrades significantly quicker than plastic and is easily recycled. But this option has its own environmental problem. For instance, trees grow too slowly to make this a truly sustainable option. They must be protected, and their use must be limited.

Paper also cannot offer the functionality of plastics required in our modern lives.[123] Food packaging is a case in point. We use plastic to preserve fresh produce because it acts as a barrier to elements that increase the speed of decomposition. It is the difficult-to-recycle plastic packaging that performs this purpose in most cases, which makes this a prime candidate for an alternative material.

On the whole, no one solution can be applied in solving plastic pollution. There should be an integration of both legislative and non-legislative strategies. However, there appears to be light in the murky waters of finding solutions to plastic pollution. According to Hart,[124] 'Earth's own response to plastic pollution may serve as inspiration for a solution: microbes that can break down the stuff. And the microbes

[120] Ibid.

[121] Enterprise Works Worldwide Programs & Strategy (2005).

[122] Moss et al. (2017), p. 58.

[123] Ibid.

[124] Hart (2021).

are already in hefty supply. Their population appears to be rising as plastic pollution in the ocean does.'

In his publication, Hart[125] stated that a team of scientists at Chalmers University in Sweden described how they came to the conclusion that plastic-eating microbes are growing in population size alongside marine plastic pollution. Incredibly, the team found a correlation between the number of microbes with plastic-degrading protein sequences and the amount of plastic pollution in their local environment. Thus, 'whether or not these plastic-degrading microbes could be useful for actively clearing out plastic pollution is still, of course, unclear. But the idea of degrading plastics with microbes seems to be catching on amongst researchers. There's certainly the scent of some biological solution to plastic pollution problem worth pursuing in the air,' Hart concluded.[126]

Although policies and laws are needed in order to address not only the removal of litter but more importantly the production, use and disposal of products, a circular economy approach, in addition, can reduce the quantity of waste by stopping it at its source. A circular economy is restorative and regenerative by design as products that are durable can be repaired, recovered and recycled at the end of their productive use. Thus, a circular economy helps prevent the generation of waste in the first place and, thereby, prevents the entry of plastic waste and litter into the environment. By these attributes, the circular economy simultaneously keeps the value of plastics in the economy, without leakage into the natural environment.[127] The good thing about this is that materials constantly flow around a 'closed loop' system, rather than being used once and then discarded.

17.9 Summary

Plastic is a material used daily by all industries. Its use has become pronounced due to its durability, low cost, lightweight and ease of production. Plastic is a material consisting of any wide range of synthetic or semi-synthetic organic compounds that are malleable and so can be moulded into solid objects. They have prevailed over traditional materials, such as wood, stone, horn and bone, leaves, leather, metal, glass and ceramic, in some products previously left to natural matter.

In major cities of Africa, plastic wastes are currently discarded in ways that are harmful and potentially hazardous to man and his environment. Million tonnes of plastic that litter the streets, clog up our rural and urban drains leading to flooding incidents, contaminate the soil affecting farmers and livestock's, and littering the oceans every year threatening biodiversity and human health, when openly burnt on

[125] Hart (2021).

[126] Ibid.

[127] World Economic Forum (2021).

dumpsites inadvertently releasing dioxins and furans thus increasing public health challenges and greenhouse gas emission.

Plastic pollution had, and still has, a number of impacts on the natural environment, human health and the economy of coastal cities. Marine litter poses serious environmental, health and economic threats to oceans and coastal ecosystems. It also presents a unique legal and regulatory challenge for many coastal states in Africa as plastic and marine litter can originate from diverse land-based and sea-based sources, both within and outside of a state.

The deleterious ecological consequences of plastics in the marine environment are well established. Drains, illegal dumps and beaches are choked with discarded bottles and plastic packaging, giving an unsightly spectacle. Marine organisms are injured or killed by ingestion and/or entanglement. The list of species that have been reported includes seabirds, marine mammals, fish and crustaceans. Death by drowning, suffocation, strangulation, starvation through reduced feeding efficiency, reproductive failure and injuries are caused by fishing gear, intact items and packaging, plastic fragments, plastic particles and microplastics.

Through human consumption of microplastic-contaminated food, microplastics could cause human health impacts, with potential effects mainly associated with the toxicity of the chemicals absorbed from the environment or additives used in the plastic materials themselves. Many chemicals found in plastics can have adverse effects on human health, including increased risk of infertility.

On the economy, the study found that marine litter can lead to economic losses due to the cost of coastal clean-up and lost tourism revenue. The economic and aesthetic impacts of marine plastic debris are also vast.

In spite of legislative provisions and other policies and action plans, the problem of plastic waste appears to be daunting. One observation on plastic waste generation is that waste management habits/behaviour facilitate the indiscriminate disposal of plastic waste, which in turn exacerbates plastic pollution. At times, the lack of awareness of the environmental and potential health risks of plastic pollution, poor resourcing of waste management and recycling infrastructure, an unskilled/inadequate waste collection workforce and untimely litter collection potentially exacerbate the scale of the problem. There is a need to change the political and social will in regulating single-use shopping bags through taxes/levies because a one-size-fits-all approach to plastic pollution should not be pursued. For instance, sachet water bags appear to be a greater source of plastic waste and should be tackled. In this regard, culturally specific strategies to reduce litter from sachet water bags must be developed.

To this end, policymakers should introduce interventions to encourage plastic sachet buybacks (buyback packs) from users. This measure would facilitate reuse as well as reduce the indiscriminate disposal of used plastic sachet bags. Refillable sachet water packaging, instead of the extant single-use sachets, should be encouraged. Media programmes and special education, focused on societal values and awareness/knowledge of the effect of the reckless disposal of sachet water bags, should be designed and implemented. Therefore, the government and other stakeholders should subsidise or fund the initiative. At the same time, it is paramount to note that any interventions or control should consider the health risks that could result from water shortage, which may emerge if plastic sachets were to become unavailable through aggressive control. In order to avoid creating unintended consequences that could have a deleterious effect on communities, there must be sustainable alternatives in place for these suggested regulations to succeed. To solve this problem, it is believed that refillable sachet water bags could be introduced.

In the long run, it is suggested that states integrate the issue of plastic waste abatement into national strategies dealing with waste management, including recycling, reuse, reduction and disposal. States should also consider developing an integrated waste management infrastructure and encourage the development of appropriate economic incentives with the aim of reducing plastic waste within the continent. In addressing this issue, the development of cost-recovery systems that provide an incentive that supports measures to prevent, reduce and control pollution from any source, including land-based sources, such as community-based coastal and waterway clean-up and monitoring activities, is recommended. This is based on one of the resolutions of the United Nations General Assembly Resolution,[128] which encourages cooperation among regional and sub-regional bodies in identifying potential sources and coastal and oceanic locations where marine debris aggregates and in developing and implementing joint prevention and recovery programmes for marine debris, as well as in raising awareness of the issue of marine debris and the need to consider environmentally sound options for its removal.

It should be noted that, at present, the legislative approach to combating plastic pollution in Africa is built around national laws. Legislation from the countries mentioned in this discussion centred on a defined government strategy to combat plastic pollution. This strategy is through either an outright ban on the use of plastic-based products or on its manufacture or importation or the imposition of taxes/levies. In the recent past, fines and/or terms of imprisonment have been added to the abatement and control mechanism.[129]

There is therefore the need for harmonised regional legislation. Harmonised regional legislation has been identified as a crucial step towards addressing the issue of plastic waste and litter. This is so because it ensures consistent enforcement across borders, facilitates a circular economy and enhances the voices of African countries in the ongoing negotiations towards a globally binding instrument against plastic pollution, which is under discussion at the UN.[130] The need for collaboration among stakeholders and the need for capacity building will help enhance awareness and understanding of plastic pollution issues and their social consequences.

It is important to note that change does not have to begin with legislation alone. It may begin in your home and in your purchasing patterns as there are many other plastic alternatives available, and rising consumer demand can transform the market

[128] United Nations General Assembly (UNGA) (2015), Resolution 70/235, para. 193.

[129] For instance, Kenya in 2017, Senegal in 2020 and the Republic of South Africa in 2021.

[130] UNEP (2023b).

for the manufacturing of plastic products. For example, instead of using plastic, use glass or metal alternatives for anything from water bottles to food storage containers or utilise a reusable water bottle to avoid sending 167 plastic bottles to the landfill; also, avoid using plastic wraps and switch to tinfoil or beeswax wraps. And instead of using plastic sponges, which are ineffective and easily ruined, use a bristle brush or steel wool. The message is to 'make the change for your health, wallet, and the environment'. In all these, environmental education is important, so that in the end, we reduce our 'plastic handprint'.

References

Adam I et al (2020) Policies to reduce single-use plastic marine pollution in West Africa. Marine Policy 116, 103928, https://www.sciencedirect.com/science/article/abs/pii/S0308597X19304865, Accessed 25 July 2023

Almeida A (2017) Problematic of Urban solid waste management in Angola: case study: province of Hufla Municipality of Lubango. University of New Lisbon. https://run.unl.pt/bitstream, Accessed 18 July 2023

Barnes DKA (2009) Accumulation and fragmentation of plastic debris in global environments. Philos Trans Royal Soc B Biol Sci 364(1526):1985–1998

Bezerra JC et al (2021) Single-use plastic bag policies in the Southern African development community. Environ Chall 3:100029. ISSN 2667-0100, https://doi.org/10.1016/j.envc.2021.100029. Accessed 7 July 2023

Buchanan JB (1971) Pollution by synthetic fibres. Mar Pollut Bull 2(2):23

Bukasa OT et al (2020) Influencing factors of plastic waste pollution reduction in Kinshasa. J Geosci Environ Protect 8:180–199. https://doi.org/10.4236/gep.2020.812011

Carpenter EJ (1972) Polystyrene spherules in coastal waters. Science 178(4062):749–750

Carpenter EJ, Smith KL Jr (1972) Plastics on the Sargasso Sea Surface. Science 175(4027): 1240–1241

Central Community College (2021) Marine Pollution. https://libguides.cccneb.edu/oceanpollution, Accessed 10 June 2023

DeLong RL et al (1973) Premature births in California sea lions: association with high organochlorine pollutant residue levels. Science 181(4105):1168–1170

Dual M (2022) Summary of Plastic Readings, SCRIBD https://www.scribd.com/document/596081174/Summary-of-Plastic-Readings. Accessed 7 July 2023

Dumbili EW, Henderson L (2020) "The Challenge of Plastic Pollution in Nigeria," chapter 22 in plastic waste and recycling: environmental impact, societal issues, prevention, and solutions, 1st edn. Elsevier, Amsterdam. https://doi.org/10.1016/B978-0-12-817880-5.00022-0. https://www.researchgate.net/publication/338805077_The_Challenge_of_Plastic_Pollution_in_Nigeria/link/5f22a75c458515b729f33f21/download, Accessed 23 July 2023

Edoga MO et al (2008) Achieving vision 20:2020 through waste produce candle. J Eng Appl Sci 3(8):642–646

Enterprise Works Worldwide Programs & Strategy (2005) Senegal Plastic Recycling Project. November 2003 — October 2005, http://www.enterpriseworks.org/prog_profile_plastic_sen.asp. Accessed 17 July 2023

EnvironReview Nigeria (2021) National policy on plastic waste management in Nigeria. EnvironReview, May 24, 2021 https://environreview.com.ng/national-policy-on-plastic-waste-management-in-nigeria/, Accessed 28 July 2023

Erinosho B (2023) Plastic pollution in Ghana United Nations environment programme's (UNEP's) law and environment assistance platform (UNEP-LEAP) https://leap.unep.org/countries/gh/

case-studies/ghana#:~:text=The%20Policy%20adopts%20a%20circular,while%20eliminating %20single%20use%20plastics. Accessed 7 July 2023
Galgani F et al (2015) Global distribution, composition, and abundance of marine litter. In: Bergmann M et al (eds) Marine anthropogenic litter. Springer International, Cham
German Agency for International Cooperation GmbH (2021) Sector brief senegal: solid waste management and recycling. Eschborn, Germany
Glick S (2021) Getting ready: will we ever get rid of plastic? https://www.seacoastonline.com/story/opinion/columns/2021/11/22/getting-ready-we-ever-get-rid-plastic/8688387002/, Accessed 28 July 2023
Hart M (2021) Ocean pollution is causing a rise in plastic-eating microbes. December 16 2021, https://nerdist.com/article/ocean-plastic-pollution-causing-rise-in-plastic-eating-microbes/, Accessed 18 Aug 2023
Hays H, Commons G (1974) Plastic particles found in tern pellets, on coastal beaches and at factory sites. Mar Pollut Bull 5(3):44–46
Hong S et al (2014) Quantities, composition, and sources of beach debris in Korea from the results of nationwide monitoring. Mar Pollut Bull 84:27–34, http://www.researchgate.net/publication/263391896_Quantities_composition_and_sources_of_beach_debris_in_Korea_from_the_results_of_nationwide_monitoring. Accessed 19 Aug 2023
Jambeck JR et al (2015) Plastic waste inputs from land into the ocean. Science 347 (6223):768–771. http://www.sciencemag.org/content/347/6223/768. Accessed 10 Aug 2023
Joint Group of Experts on the Scientific Aspects of Marine Environmental Protection (GESAMP) (2015) (IMO/FAO/UNESCO-IOC/UNIDO/WMO/IAEA/UN/UNEP/UNDP Joint Group of Experts on the Scientific Aspects of Marine Environmental Protection). "Sources, fate and effects of microplastics in the marine environment: A global assessment." #90.Rep. Stud. GESAMP, 2015 http://www.gesamp.org/data/gesamp/files/media/Publications/Reports_and_studies_90/gallery_2230/object_2500_large.pdf. Accessed 18 Aug 2023
Kenya Embassy (2023) About Kenya Geography, https://kenyaembassydc.org/aboutkenyageography/#:~:text=Kenya%20is%20bordered%20to%20the,is%20arid%20or%20semi%2Darid. Accessed 4 Aug 2023
Kenyon KW, Kridler E (1969) Laysan albatrosses swallow indigestible matter. The Auk 86(2): 339–343
Knoema (2021) Angola: Data and Statistics https://pt.knoema.com/atlas/Angola. Accessed 20 Aug 2023
Miezah K et al (2015) Municipal solid waste characterization and quantification as a measure towards effective waste management in Ghana. Waste Manage 45:15–27
Moss E et al (2017) Sea of opportunity: supply chain investment opportunities to address marine plastic pollution. Encourage Capital on behalf of Vulcan, Inc., New York
Munang R (2022) Fixing the plastic pollution problem: implications for Africa. https://www.linkedin.com/pulse/fixing-plastic-pollution-problem-dr-richard-munang, Accessed 17 July 2023
Naidu R (2022) South Africa is increasing plastic production but reducing recycled waste. Development Aid, 4 February 2022 https://www.developmentaid.org/news-stream/post/137299/south-africa-is-increasing-plastic-production-but-reducing-recycled-waste. Accessed 19 Aug 2023
National Oceanography Centre (2021) Sources, amounts and pathways of plastic entering the ocean. https://noc.ac.uk/files/documents/science/report-plastics-entering-the-global-ocean-noci-december-2021.pdf. Accessed 17 July 2023
National Plastic Action Partnership (2021) A roadmap for radical reduction of plastic pollution in Ghana, GPAP November 2021. https://www.wacaprogram.org/sites/waca/files/knowdoc/NPAP_Ghana_Action_Roadmap.pdf. Accessed 10 July 2023
Nwafor N, Walker TR (2020) Plastic bags prohibition bill: a developing story of crass legalism aiming to reduce plastic marine pollution in Nigeria. Mar Policy 120:104160, ISSN 0308-597X. https://doi.org/10.1016/j.marpol.2020.104160

Ocean Conservancy (2015) International coastal cleanup 2015 report. http://www.oceanconservancy.org/our-work/international-coastal-cleanup/2015. Accessed 19 Aug 2023

Onyeabor E, Uju Obuka U (2024) Building collaboration and synergy among regional blocs to reduce marine plastic waste pollution: a case for the Gulf of Guinea region, 198 January 2024. Mar Pollut Bull 115829. https://www.sciencedirect.com/science/article/pii/S0025326X2301264X

Pham CK et al (2014) Marine litter distribution and density in European seas, from the shelves to deep basins. PLoS ONE 9(4) https://doi.org/10.1371/journal.pone.0095839. Accessed 19 Aug 2023

Ranniger G (2021) How plastics damage our lives and the environment—and why recycling is not the answer. Environmental Health News. https://www.ehn.org/plastic-pollution-101-2646027569.htm. Accessed 26 July 2023

Romer J, Tamminen L (2014) Plastic bag reduction ordinances: New York City's proposed charge on all carryout bags as a model for U.S. cities. Tex Environ Law J (TELJ) 27:237–275

Schnurr REJ et al (2018) Reducing marine pollution from single-use plastics (SUPs): a review. Mar Pollut Bull 137:157–171, https://www.sciencedirect.com/science/article/pii/S0025326X18307033, Accessed 18 July 2023

Stoler J (2017) From curiosity to commodity: a review of evolution of sachet drinking water in West Africa: Sachet drinking water in West Africa. WIREs Water 2017:31206. https://doi.org/10.1002/wat2.1206

Taylor R, Villas-Boas S (2016) Bans vs. fees: disposable carryout bag policies and bag usage. Appl Econ Persp Policy 38(2):351–372

The Guardian (2023) After a plastic bag ban, Kenya takes another shot at its pollution problem. The Guardian, 30 May 2023, https://www.theguardian.com/global-development/2023/may/30/kenya-wrestles-with-its-plastic-pollution-problem#:~:text=Kenya%20banned%20single%2Duse%20plastic,such%20as%20parks%20and%20forests. Accessed 30 July 2023

UNEP (2009) Marine litter: a global challenge. Nairobi 2009 http://www.unep.org/pdf/unep_marine_litter-a_global_challenge.pdf. Accessed 10 Aug 2023

UNEP (2015) Marine litter: an analytical overview. Nairobi, 2005, http://www.unep.org/regionalseas/marinelitter/publications/docs/anl_oview.pdf. Accessed 10 Aug 2023

UNEP (2018) Mapping of global plastics value chain and plastics losses to the environment (with a particular focus on marine environment). UNEP, Nairobi, Kenya

UNEP (2021a) Drowning in plastics: Marine litter and plastic waste vital graphics. United Nations Environment Programme, Nairobi, Kenya. wedocs.unep.org/xmlui/bitstream/handle/20.500.11822/36964/VITGRAPH.pdf. Accessed 18 July 2023

UNEP (2021b) Africa Region Plastic Pollution and Marine litter Law and Policy. UNEP Law and Environment Assistant Platform (LEAP) Programme, https://leap.unep.org/countries/case-studies/africa-region-plastic-pollution-and-marine-litter-law-and-policy#:~:text. Accessed 17 July 2023

UNEP (2023a) State of Affairs: Policies, Regulations and Laws that Address the Harmful Effects of Single-Use Plastics in the East African Community, Project Book East Africa No,2, UNEP, Nairobi, Kenya

UNEP (2023b) East Africa Regional Workshop on Single Use Plastics (SUPs), East Africa Regional Workshop Report 2003. UNEP, Nairobi, Kenya

United Nations (2019) UN Comtrade database, https://comtradeplus.un.org/. Accessed 16 August 2023

United Nations Conference on Trade and Development (UNCTAD) (2022) Challenges and Opportunities in SUP Plastic substitutes; Insight from Kenya, UNCTAD, Geneva, https://unctad.org/system/files/non-official-document/tcsditcinf2022d3_fs2_en.pdf. Accessed 20 Aug 2023

United Nations Environment Programme (UNEP) (2005) Marine litter: An analytical overview. Nairobi, 2005, http://www.unep.org/regionalseas/marinelitter/publications/docs/anl_oview.pdf. Accessed 10 Aug 2023

United Nations General Assembly (UNGA) (2015) Oceans and the Law of the Sea, Resolution 70/235 of 23 December 2015. https://www.un.org/en/development/desa/population/migration/generalassembly/docs/globalcompact/A_RES_70_235.pdf. Accessed 10 July 2023

United Nations Industrial Development Organisation (UNIDO) (2021) Study on plastics value-chain in Nigeria, UNIDO Publications July 2021 https://www.unido.org/sites/default/files/files/2022-01/Plastic_value_chain_in_nigeria.pdf. Accessed 20 July 2023

Van Franeker JA (2011) Monitoring plastic ingestion by the northern fulmar Fulmarus glacialis in the North Sea. Environ Pollut 159(10):2609–2615

Wamba SF et al (2023) Assessing the potential of plastic waste management in the circular economy: a longitudinal case study in an emerging economy. Ann Operat Res. https://doi.org/10.1007/s10479-023-05386-3. Accessed 18 Aug 2023

World Bank (2020) Ghana - Country Environmental Analysis. https://www.worldbank.org/en/country/Ghana/overview#1. Accessed 19 Aug 2023

World Bank (2023) West Africa plastics circularity study: realising the circular economy potential for plastics in Nigeria. WACA Publications https://www.wacaprogram.org/sites/waca/files/knowdoc/13.%20Nigeria.pdf. Accessed 7 July 2023

World Bank Group (2021) "Cameroon-Overview," 2021. https://www.worldbank.org/en/country/Cameroon/overview#1, Accessed 19 Aug 2023

World Economic Forum (2020) Reusing 10% will stop almost half of plastic waste from entering the ocean. https://www.weforum.org/, Accessed 10 June 2023

World Economic Forum (2021) New Plastics Economy Rethinking the future of plastics. http://www3.weforum.org/docs/WEF_The_New_Plastics_Economy.pdf. Accessed 13 Aug 2023

World Health Organisation (WHO) (2019) UN-Water Global Analysis and Assessment of Sanitation and Drinking-Water. https://www.who.int/water_sanitation_health/monitoring/investments/nigeria-10-nov.pdf?ua=1. Accessed 19 July 2023

World Wildlife Federation South Africa (2023) My Plastic Smart journey. https://www.wwf.org.za/lifestyle_plastic_smart/#:~:text=SA%20generates%202.4%20million%20tons,of%20plastic%20waste%20per%20citizen.&text=The%20materials%20you%20throw%20away,after%20they%20have%20been%20discarded.&text=Only%2014%25%20of%20the%202.4,thrown%20into%20bins%20is%20recycled. Accessed 10 Aug 2023

Worldometer (2023a) United Nations, Department of Economic and Social Affairs, Population Division. World Population Prospects. https://www.worldometers.info/world-population/population-by-country/Ghana. Accessed 29 August 2023

Worldometer (2023b) United Nations, Department of Economic and Social Affairs, Population Division. World Population Prospects, https://www.worldometers.info/world-population/population-by-country/Senegal. Accessed 29 Aug 2023

Worldometer (2023c) United Nations, Department of Economic and Social Affairs, Population Division. World Population Prospects, https://www.worldometers.info/world-population/population-by-country/Cameroon. Accessed 29 Aug 2023

Worldometer (2023d) United Nations, Department of Economic and Social Affairs, Population Division. World Population Prospects. https://www.worldometers.info/world-population/population-by-country/Democratic Republic of Congo. Accessed 29 Aug 2023

Worldometer (2023e) United Nations, Department of Economic and Social Affairs, Population Division. World Population Prospects, https://www.worldometers.info/world-population/population-by-country/Kenya. Accessed 29 Aug 2023

Worldometer (2023f) United Nations, Department of Economic and Social Affairs, Population Division. World Population Prospects, https://www.worldometers.info/world-population/population-by-country/Angola, Accessed 29 Aug 2023

Worldometer (2023g) United Nations, Department of Economic and Social Affairs, Population Division. World Population Prospects, https://www.worldometers.info/world-population/population-by-country/Republic of South Africa, Accessed 29 Aug 2023

Xanthos D, Walker TR (2017) International policies to reduce plastic marine pollution from single-use plastics (plastic bags and microbeads): a review. Mar Pollut Bull 118:17–26. https://www.sciencedirect.com/science/article/pii/S0025326X17301650#bbb1000. Accessed 18 Aug 2023

MIX
Papier aus verantwortungsvollen Quellen
Paper from responsible sources
FSC® C105338

If you have any concerns about our products,
you can contact us on
ProductSafety@springernature.com

In case Publisher is established outside the EU,
the EU authorized representative is:
Springer Nature Customer Service Center GmbH
Europaplatz 3, 69115 Heidelberg, Germany

Printed by Libri Plureos GmbH
in Hamburg, Germany